The RIA Complete Analysis of the Revenue Reconciliation Act of 1993

With Code Sections as Amended and Committee Reports

To place an order for this or any other RIA publication, please call 1 800 562-0245 ext. 1.

For customer service regarding this or any other RIA publication, please call 1 800 431-9025.

To obtain the name and telephone number of your local account representative, please call 1 800 346-7377.

The RIA Complete Analysis of the Revenue Reconciliation Act of 1993

Prepared by **Research Institute of America**

James E. Cheeks (J.D., NY, IL Bar) *Senior Vice President and Publisher*
Thomas E. Delleart (M.B.A.) *Vice President and Publisher*
Robert Rywick (J.D. NY Bar) *Vice President, Editorial*

Professional Staff,
Englewood Cliffs, NJ

Jonathan E. Koschei
(J.D., NY Bar)
Editorial Director

Edward V. Titano
(J.D., NY Bar)
Managing Editor

Arthur Rosenberg
(J.D., NJ Bar)
Executive Editor

Jeffery E. Hollinger
(J.D., NY, NJ Bar)
Executive Editor

Melvin Orenstein
(LL.M., NY Bar)

Frederick L. Nakarai
(J.D., IN Bar)

John G. Clark
(LL.M., NY Bar)

Alan G. DeNee
(J.D., NY, NJ Bar)

Thomas J. McInerney
(LL.M., NY Bar)

Thomas J. Carroll
(J.D., NY, NJ Bar)

Stephen R. Tortorella
(LL.M., NY, CT Bar)

Martin A. Censor
(J.D., NY Bar)

John M. Melazzo
(J.D., NJ Bar)

Richard H. O'Donnell
(LL.M., NJ Bar)

Gregory J. Evanella
(J.D., NJ Bar)

Susan R. Bouchard
(J.D.)

Vidor A. Nosce
(LL.M., NY Bar)

Judith M. Richardson-Dunkley
(J.D., NY, NJ Bar)

Geoffrey I. Landau
(J.D., NY Bar)

Evelyn M. Manschal

Rebecca L. Taylor
(J.D., NJ, MN Bar)

Administrative Staff,
Englewood Cliffs, NJ

Ann Tusa
Patricia O'Reilly
Supervisors, Support Staff

Alison Aquino
Marilyn Darlington
Irma Fass
Beverly Genett
Mildred Genser
Patricia Labourdette
Denise Marshall
Mina Martin
David Minerley
Antoinette Nicoletti
Joseph Oliveri
Judith Pierson
Lisa Rosa
Susan Toleno

Indexing Department
David Thompson
Lillian O'Brien
Catherine Fisher
Tom Adewolu

Table of Contents

¶ 1. ’93 Revenue Reconciliation Act

This RIA Complete Analysis covers the tax law changes in the ’93 Revenue Reconciliation Act, Chapter 1 of Title XIII of the Omnibus Budget Reconciliation Act of ’93 (HR 2264), PL 103-66, signed into law August 10, ’93. All references to date of enactment in the following pages of RIA’s Complete Analysis are to that August 10, ’93 date. Dates measured from date of enactment are measured from August 10, ’93.

Act and Code cites, reprints. Most provisions of the ’93 Act directly amend the Internal Revenue Code. These provisions add, repeal, or change Code sections. The RIA’s Complete Analysis cites those code sections, and identifies the section of the ’93 Act that makes the addition or change.

New Code sections are cited: Code Sec. 197 as added by ’93 Act § 13261(a).

All other Code amendments, including new or repealed subsections, are cited: Code Sec. 168(j) as amended by ’93 § 13321(a).

The text of the ’93 Revenue Reconciliation Act can be found in the Conference Bill reprint sent to RIA Federal Tax Coordinator 2d, OnPoint™, and United States Tax Reporter subscribers. The text of Code Sections as added or amended by the ’93 Act are reproduced in this book starting at ¶ 2000.

Some provisions of the ’93 Act do not directly amend the Internal Revenue Code. Such a provision is cited in the RIA Complete Analysis in this form: ’93 Act § 13001(c). These ’93 Act provisions are reproduced in this book starting at ¶ 2500.

Source materials. The legislative materials in volved in constructing and explaining the ’93 Act are these:

- House Ways and Means Committee Bill and Report
- House-passed bill
- Senate Finance Committee Bill and Report
- Senate-passed bill
- House-Senate Conference Committee Bill and Committee Report

In this Analysis these materials are cited as follows:

Congressional Authority	*Cited as:*
House Ways and Means Report	H Rept
Senate Finance Committee Report	S Rept
House-Senate Conference Report	Conf Rept

¶ 2. Contents

Complete in-depth discussion of all provisions under the following general heading

¶ 100. Individuals: Tax Rates; Alternative Minimum Tax; Withholding; Estimated Tax

¶ 101. New tax rates of 36% and 39.6% ("surtax") added for individual taxpayers starting in '93

Under pre-'93 Act law, three graduated tax rates—15%, 28%, and 31%—were applied to an individual's taxable income to arrive at the individual's income tax liability. (FTC 2d/FIN ¶ A-1100; TG ¶ 501; USTR ¶ 140.8)

The '93 Act adds new 36% and 39.6% tax rates. For '93, the 36% rate applies to taxable income over the following thresholds:

Married couples filing jointly and surviving spouses	$140,000
Heads of household	$127,500
Single individuals	$115,000
Married individuals filing separate returns	$70,000

(Code Sec. 1(a), (b), (c), and (d) as amended by '93 Act § 13201(a))

The 39.6% rate applies to individuals with taxable income over $250,000 ($125,000 for married individuals filing separate returns). (Code Sec. 1(a), (b), (c), and (d) as amended by '93 Act § 13202(a)(1), (2), (3), and (4)) The 39.6% rate is described as a surtax in the title of Act § 13202 and in the committee report (H Rept p. 636), but not in the operative statutory language.

For the complete schedule of individual income tax rates for '93, see ¶ 102.

> ***observation:*** The 36% and 39.6% rate brackets impact a two-income married couple more than single individuals with comparable income, thus adding to the marriage penalty. For example, a single person with taxable income of $115,000 isn't subject to the 36% rate. But if two individuals with that income are married, $90,000 of their $230,000 joint income (taxable income above $140,000) is taxed at 36%.

Likewise, two singles, each with taxable income of $200,000, aren't subject to the 39.6% rate. But if married, $150,000 of their joint income ($400,000 − $250,000) is taxed at 39.6%.

> ***observation:*** The 36% and 39.6% rate brackets make some types of investments more attractive for high-income individuals. For example, investors might want tax-exempt bonds or investments designed to produce capital gains (which continue to be taxed at a maximum rate of 28%, see below). However, the Act also adds five new rules designed to bar the conversion of ordinary income into capital gain (see ¶ 109 *et seq.*). Qualified small business investments (see ¶ 702) would also be attractive. Gains on such investments would be effectively taxed at a top rate of 14%.

> ***observation:*** Unearned income of children under age 14 is generally taxed at their parents' marginal tax rate. A child 14 or older computes his tax using his own tax brackets. The higher rates may make family income-shifting more attractive. A parent being taxed at 39.6% would save about 25 cents on the dollar on income shifted to a child 14 or older whose tax rate is 15%.

> ***observation:*** The 36% and 39.6% rates, when combined with other pro-

FTC 2d References are to the Federal Tax Coordinator 2d
FIN References are to RIA's Analysis of Federal Taxes: Income
TG References are to the Tax Guide
USTR References are to the United States Tax Reporter

visions, some found in pre-'93 Act law and others added by the Act, can result in marginal rates higher than 36% and 39.6%.

For example, the exemption amount for personal and dependent exemptions ($2,350 for '93) is phased out for certain taxpayers with adjusted gross income above a specified level. (See FTC 2d/FIN ¶ A-3502; TG ¶ 1004; USTR ¶ 1514) The exemption is reduced by 2% for each $2,500 by which AGI exceeds $162,700 (married filing jointly), $108,450 (single), $135,600 (head of household), or $81,350 (married filing separately).

Each AGI multiple of $2,500 in the phaseout range increases '93 taxable income by $47 for each exemption claimed by a taxpayer. This means that, for a taxpayer subject to the 39.6% tax rate, every $2,500 multiple of AGI in the phaseout range increases his tax by $18.61 ($47 × 39.6%) per exemption. For a family of four, this translates to an additional $74.44. In other words, the phaseout adds $74.44 in tax per $2,500 of AGI, a rate of almost 3% that must be added to the 39.6% rate.

The phaseout range for married couples filing jointly extends to $285,200. Thus, married taxpayers with AGI of up to $285,200 and taxable income over $250,000 face a marginal rate above 39.6% as a result of the phaseout.

In addition, if an individual's AGI exceeds $108,450 ($54,225 for a married individual filing separately), otherwise allowable itemized deductions are reduced by the lesser of (a) 3% of AGI above $108,450, or (b) 80% of the amount of itemized deductions otherwise allowable. (See FTC 2d/FIN ¶ A-2704; TG ¶ 1074; USTR ¶ 684.01)

The 3% reduction has the effect of increasing the marginal tax rate of an affected 39.6% rate taxpayer by 1.188%, to 40.788%. This is in addition to any marginal rate increase produced by the phaseout of personal exemptions.

Also, the elimination of the cap on earnings subject to the Medicare tax (see ¶s 107 and 108) means that all earned income is subject to a tax of 1.45% (on employees) or 2.9% (for self-employeds) in addition to the income tax. This change applies to earnings received after '93.

observation: As a result of the Act, the top individual tax rates (36% and 39.6%) are higher than the top corporate tax rate (35%). For an analysis of how this rate difference may affect taxpayers' choice of business entity (C corporation v. S corporation or other flow-through entity), see ¶ 301.

observation: Some provisions of the Code require a determination of the highest rate of tax under Code Sec. 1 for purposes other than the imposition of tax. For example, the "high-taxed income" provisions provide special treatment for determining the foreign tax credit of a company that is subject to foreign taxes exceeding the highest U.S. tax rate. (See FTC 2d/FIN ¶ O-4086; TG ¶ 8437) Under the '93 Act, the highest rate of tax under Code Sec. 1 is 39.6%.

Capital gain rate stays at 28%. Net capital gain of individuals is taxed at a 28% maximum rate. (See FTC 2d/FIN ¶ I-6010; TG ¶ 4412; USTR ¶s 12,009, 12,274 *et seq.)* Because the surtax is not a 10% increase in total tax liability, net capital gain will continue to be taxed at a 28% maximum rate. (H Rept p. 636)

observation: This results in the largest difference between the highest tax rate on capital gains and ordinary income (28% versus 39.6%) since the Tax Reform Act of '86 was enacted.

Indexing. As under pre-'93 Act law, the tax rate bracket thresholds will be indexed each year for inflation. (See FTC 2d/FIN ¶ A-1103; TG ¶ 503; USTR ¶ 14.08) However, indexing of thresholds for the 36% and 39.6% brackets will apply to tax years beginning after Dec. 31, '94, at which time the 36% and 39.6% brackets will be adjusted for increases in the consumer price index since '93. (Code Sec. 1(f) as amended by '93 Act § 13201(b)(3))

> ***observation:*** The freeze on indexing until '95 applies only to the 36% rate and the 39.6% rate (see below). The current thresholds for the 28% and 31% rates will be adjusted in '94 under existing rules.

> ***observation:*** Retaining the '93 thresholds for '94 could cause "bracket creep" for some taxpayers whose '94 income increases above '93. For example, a single individual with '93 taxable income of $114,750 would have a top tax rate of 31%. If his '94 taxable income rose by an amount equal to the rate of inflation, he would have to pay 36% on the portion above $115,000.

For the election to pay the additional tax attributable to the rate increases in three annual installments, see ¶ 103. For new income tax rates on estates and trusts, see ¶ 902. For the increase in alternative minimum tax rates on noncorporate taxpayers, see ¶ 114. For the increase in the accumulated earnings tax rate, see ¶ 302. For the increase in the personal holding company tax rate, see ¶ 303.

☐ **Effective:** Tax years beginning after Dec. 31, '92. (§§ 13201(c), 13202(c)) The withholding tables for '93 will not be revised to reflect the changes in tax rates. (H Rept p. 636) Penalties for underpayment of estimated tax attributable to the changes in tax rates will be waived for any period before Apr. 16, '94. (§ 13001(d))

Code Sec. 15 requires a "straddle computation" when tax rates change during a taxpayer's tax year. (See FTC 2d/FIN ¶ A-1104 *et seq.;* TG ¶ 1063; USTR ¶ 154.02) However, the '93 Act provides that Code Sec. 15 does not apply to the changes in individual income tax rates. (§ 13001(c))

> ***observation:*** Thus, a fiscal-year individual will be taxed for the tax year beginning in '92 at the rates that apply to tax years beginning in '92 and for the tax year beginning in '93 at the rates set forth at ¶ 102.

For official explanation see Committee Reports ¶s 3028 and 3029.

¶ 102. Tax rate schedules for individuals

Here are the new individual income tax rates that apply for tax years beginning in '93. (Code Sec. 1(a), (b), (c), and (d) as amended by '93 Act §§ 13201(a) and 13202(a)(1), (2), (3), and (4))

For rates applicable to estates and trusts, see ¶ 902.

MARRIED INDIVIDUALS FILING JOINT RETURNS
AND SURVIVING SPOUSES

If taxable income is:	The tax is:
Not over $36,900 . . .	15% of taxable income
Over $36,900 but not over $89,150 . . .	$5,535, plus 28% of the excess over $36,900
Over $89,150 but not over $140,000 . . .	$20,165, plus 31% of the excess over $89,150

FTC 2d References are to the Federal Tax Coordinator 2d
FIN References are to RIA's Analysis of Federal Taxes: Income
TG References are to the Tax Guide
USTR References are to the United States Tax Reporter

Over $140,000 but not over $250,000 . . .	$35,928.50, plus 36% of the excess over $140,000
Over $250,000 . . .	$75,528.50, plus 39.6% of the excess over $250,000

HEADS OF HOUSEHOLD

If taxable income is:	The tax is:
Not over $29,600 . . .	15% of taxable income
Over $29,600 but not over $76,400 . . .	$4,440, plus 28% of the excess over $29,600
Over $76,400 but not over $127,500 . . .	$17,544, plus 31% of the excess over $76,400
Over $127,500 but not over $250,000 . . .	$33,385, plus 36% of the excess over $127,500
Over $250,000 . . .	$77,485, plus 39.6% of the excess over $250,000

UNMARRIED INDIVIDUALS (OTHER THAN SURVIVING SPOUSES AND HEADS OF HOUSEHOLD)

If taxable income is:	The tax is:
Not over $22,100 . . .	15% of taxable income
Over $22,100 but not over $53,500 . . .	$3,315, plus 28% of the excess over $22,100
Over $53,500 but not over $115,000 . . .	$12,107, plus 31% of the excess over $53,500
Over $115,000 but not over $250,000 . . .	$31,172, plus 36% of the excess over $115,000
Over $250,000 . . .	$79,772, plus 39.6% of the excess over $250,000

MARRIED INDIVIDUALS FILING SEPARATE RETURNS

If taxable income is:	The tax is:
Not over $18,450 . . .	15% of taxable income
Over $18,450 but not over $44,575 . . .	$2,767.50, plus 28% of the excess over $18,450
Over $44,575 but not over $70,000 . . .	$10,082.50, plus 31% of the excess over $44,575
Over $70,000 but not over $125,000 . . .	$17,964.25, plus 36% of the excess over $70,000
Over $125,000 . . .	$37,764.25, plus 39.6% of the excess over $125,000

☐ **Effective:** Tax years beginning after Dec. 31, '92. (§§ 13201(c), 13202(c)) See ¶ 101 for rules about withholding and straddle computations.

For official explanation see Committee Reports ¶s 3028 and 3029.

¶ 103. Taxpayers can elect to pay tax attributable to rate increases in three interest-free installments

Under pre-'93 Act law, individuals must pay the balance of tax shown to be due on their income tax returns at the time fixed for filing the return (without extensions). (FTC 2d/FIN ¶ S-5702; TG ¶ 1449; USTR ¶ 61,514)

The '93 Act allows individual taxpayers to elect to pay the additional '93 tax attributable to the new 36% and 39.6% tax rates (¶ 101) in three equal installments. ('93 Act § 13201(d)(1)) The first installment is due on the due date (without extensions) of the individual's tax return for the tax year that begins in calendar year '93. The second installment is due one year after that date, and the third installment is due two years after that date. (§ 13201(d)(2)) No interest is due on the installments. (§ 13201(d)(3)) The installment election does not apply to estates and trusts. (§ 13201(d)(7))

> ***observation:*** Thus, individuals can elect to pay the additional tax in three equal, interest-free installments due on Apr. 15 of '94, '95, and '96. In essence, this means a one-year, interest-free loan for one third of the additional tax and a similar two-year, interest-free loan for another third.

The amount eligible for the installment payment election is the excess of the individual's net liability under Chapter 1 of the Code, as shown on the individual's tax return, over the amount that would have been the individual's net liability but for the imposition of the 36% and 39.6% tax rates by the '93 Act. These amounts are computed after applying any credits (except the credits for wage withholding and special fuel uses) and before crediting any payment of estimated tax. (§ 13201(d)(4)) Amounts required to be shown on the return but not actually shown are ineligible for the installment payment election. (Conf Rept p. 573)

> ***illustration:*** X and Y, joint filers, have taxable income of $300,000 for '93. Under the tax rates that were to apply for '93 prior to the '93 Act, they would have a tax liability of $85,529. Under the Act, their tax liability is $95,329. Therefore, $9,800 of X and Y's tax liability is eligible for the installment payment election.

> ***observation:*** The extension applies only to additional tax due because of the increase in individual income tax rates, and not to any additional tax that may be due because of other provisions of the '93 Act, such as the increased alternative minimum tax rate.

The election must be made on the individual's return for the tax year that begins in '93 (§ 13201(d)(6)), which, in general, is due on April 15, '94. (Conf Rept p. 573)

IRS must immediately terminate the installment payment election, and the entire unpaid tax must be paid on notice and demand, if either (1) the taxpayer does not pay an installment by the required date, or (2) IRS believes that the collection of any amount under the installment payment election is in jeopardy. (§ 13201(d)(5))

> ***observation:*** Individuals with complex returns who are unable to file by Apr. 15, '94, may face a dilemma. The first installment payment is due on Apr. 15, '94, without extensions. The election must be made on the '93 return, which presumably can be filed with an extension. But if the return

FTC 2d References are to the Federal Tax Coordinator 2d
FIN References are to RIA's Analysis of Federal Taxes: Income
TG References are to the Tax Guide
USTR References are to the United States Tax Reporter

isn't completed by Apr. 15, the taxpayer won't know how much to pay as the first installment. Making a reasonable estimate may not suffice for purposes of the installment election since, if the amount paid turns out to be less than the required installment, the election will be terminated and the full amount of tax will be due.

observation: Taxpayers who qualify should make the installment payment election, since they will receive what amounts to an interest-free loan. On the other hand, there's no benefit to accelerating income into '93 merely to take advantage of the election. That's because the installment election doesn't apply to the portion of the tax that would have been due under pre-'93 Act tax rates. If income is accelerated into '93, that portion of the tax, plus one third of the additional tax, will be due a year early. Another third of the additional tax will be due on Apr. 15, '95, which is when the entire tax would have been due without the acceleration of income. Only with respect to one third of the additional tax will there be a one-year deferral, to Apr. 15, '96.

For example, say that a taxpayer can choose whether to take a $100,000 bonus in '93 or '94. Assume that he will be taxed at a marginal rate of 39.6% in either year and that his itemized deductions and personal exemptions will be fully phased out in both years. If he chooses to take the bonus in '93, $33,867 will be due on Apr. 15, '94, $2,867 on Apr. 15, '95, and $2,866 on Apr. 15, '96. If instead he takes the bonus in '94, the entire $39,600 will be due on Apr. 15, '95. Clearly, as far as the installment election goes, the taxpayer is better off without acceleration.

However, acceleration may make sense if the income is received much earlier than it otherwise would have. In that case, the gain from the early receipt of income may outweigh the loss from the early payment of tax.

Also, accelerating *earned income* into '93 may be advantageous because it avoids the uncapped Medicare tax, see ¶s 107 and 108. This isn't a matter of the time-value of money but of a tax that will never have to be paid.

Limitations period for collection. IRS must assess all taxes shown on a taxpayer's return and may collect unpaid taxes within ten years after the they were assessed. (See FTC 2d/FIN ¶s T-3618, V-5601; TG ¶s 9542, 9900; USTR ¶ 6201)

Because the installment payment election applies only to amounts actually shown on the individual's tax return, those amounts are considered assessed. Consequently, the 10-year statute of limitations on collection after assessment applies to the installment payments. (Conf Rept pp. 573-574)

☐ **Effective:** Tax years beginning after Dec. 31, '92. (§ 13201(c))
For official explanation see Committee Reports ¶ 3028.

¶ 104. Estimated tax penalties arising from '93 Act tax increases on individuals are waived

Individuals must pay a penalty on any underpayment of estimated tax. To avoid the underpayment of estimated tax penalty, individuals must pay 25% of a "required annual payment" of estimated tax by Apr. 15, June 15, Sept. 15, and Jan. 15 (for calendar year taxpayers). (FTC 2d/FIN ¶ S-5200 *et seq.;* TG ¶ 1406; USTR ¶ 66,544)

The '93 Act provides, however, that no estimated tax penalty will be imposed on individuals for any period before Apr. 16, '94 to the extent any underpayment is created or increased by any '93 Act provision. ('93 Act § 13001(d))

¶ 105. "Straddle computation" of tax for the year is not required because of changes made by the '93 Act tax rates for individuals

If the income tax rates for individuals change during a taxable year (except for changes effective on the first day of the year) a special computation must be made to take into account the different rates for the different parts of the year. Under this straddle computation, individuals must pay tax at the old and new rates in proportion to the number of days in the tax year which fall on either side of the effective date of the change. (FTC 2d/FIN ¶ A-1104 *et seq.;* TG ¶ 1063,; USTR ¶ 154 *et seq.)*

The '93 Act provides that no amendment made by the Act shall be considered a change in rates for purposes of the straddle computation rules except the increase in the corporate tax rates (see ¶ 301). ('93 Act § 13001(c))

¶ 106. Increase in Social Security benefits that are subject to tax

Under pre-'93 Act law, a taxpayer whose modified adjusted gross income (see FTC 2d/FIN ¶ J-1433; TG ¶ 5318; USTR ¶ 864.02) for the tax year plus 50% of the Social Security benefit, or of the Tier 1 Railroad Retirement benefit, received during the tax year exceeds a threshold amount (see below) must include in gross income the lesser of:

(1) one-half of the taxpayer's Social Security or Railroad Retirement Tier 1 benefit; or

(2) one-half of the excess of the sum of the modified adjusted gross income for that year plus one-half of the Social Security benefit or Railroad Retirement Tier 1 benefit received during that tax year over the threshold amount. (FTC 2d/FIN ¶ J-1431; TG ¶ 5316; USTR ¶ 864.04)

Under pre-'93 Act law, the threshold amount (called the "base amount") is $25,000 for single taxpayers and heads of households, $32,000 for taxpayers filing jointly and zero for married taxpayers filing separately. (See FTC/FIN ¶ J-1432; TG ¶ 5319; USTR ¶ 864.03)

Under the '93 Act, a second threshold is created at a level greater than the pre-'93 Act base amount (see above) creating a new tier at which the amount of social security benefits included in gross income is increased for certain higher income beneficiaries. (S Rept p. 260) This new threshold (called "the adjusted base amount") is $34,000 for single taxpayers and heads of households, $44,000 for taxpayers filing jointly and zero for married taxpayers filing separately. (Code Sec. 86(c)(2) as amended by '93 Act § 13215(b))

Taxpayers whose modified adjusted gross income for the tax year plus 50% of the Social Security benefit, or of the Tier 1 Railroad Retirement benefit, received during the tax year exceeds these increased applicable adjusted base amounts include in gross income the lesser of:

(1) 85% of the taxpayer's Social Security or Railroad Retirement Tier 1 benefit (Code Sec. 86(a)(2)(B) as amended by '93 Act § 13215(a)(1)); or

(2) the sum of:

(a) the smaller of

(i) the amount included under pre-'93 Act law; or

FTC 2d References are to the Federal Tax Coordinator 2d
FIN References are to RIA's Analysis of Federal Taxes: Income
TG References are to the Tax Guide
USTR References are to the United States Tax Reporter

(ii) an amount equal to one half of the difference between the adjusted base amount and the base amount ($4,5000 for single taxpayers and heads of households, and $6,000 for married taxpayers filing jointly), plus

(b) 85% of the excess of the taxpayer's modified adjusted gross income (see above) for the tax year plus 50 % of the Social Security benefit or of the Tier 1 Railroad Retirement benefit received during the tax year, over the applicable adjusted base amounts (Code Sec. 86(a)(2)(A))

For married taxpayers filing separate returns, gross income includes the lesser of 85% of the taxpayer's Social Security benefit or 85% of the taxpayer's modified adjusted gross income (see above) for the tax year plus 50% of the Social Security benefit or of the Tier 1 Railroad Retirement benefit received during the tax year. (S Rept p. 261)

illustration: H and W, a married couple filing a joint return, have modified adjusted gross income of $31,000. H has $4,000 of Social Security benefits, while W has none. The couple must include $500 of the benefits in gross income (unchanged from pre-'93 law), computed as follows:

(1) 50% of $4,000 .... $2,000

(2) $31,000 (modified adjusted gross income)

+2,000 (50% of Social Security benefit)

$33,000

−32,000 (applicable base amount)

$1,000 x 50% $500

(3) Lesser of (1) or (2) $500

illustration: If the couple in the above Illustration had $43,000 (rather than $31,000) of modified adjusted gross income, they would include $2,850 of the $4,000 Social Security benefit, computed as follows:

(1) 50% of $4,000 .... $2,000

(2) $43,000 (modified adjusted gross income)

+2,000 (50% of Social Security benefit)

$45,000

−32,000 (base amount)

$13,000 x 50% $6,500

(3) Lesser of (1) or (2) $2,000

(4) 50% of difference between adjusted base amount and base amount $6,000

(5) Lesser of (3) or (4)

(same as pre-'93 law computation) $2,000

(6) $43,000 (modified adjusted gross income)

+2,000 (50% of Social Security benefit)

$45,000

−44,000 (adjusted base amount)

$1,000 × 85% $850

(7) Total of (5) + (6) $2,850

(8) 85% of $4,000 .... $3,400

(9) Lesser of (7) or (8) $2,850

Illustration: H and W, a married couple who file jointly have $60,000 of modified adjusted gross income. In addition, H receives a Social Security benefit of $10,000 and W receives a Social Security benefit of $5,000. They include $12,750 of their combined $15,000 Social Security benefit in gross income, computed as follows:

(1) 50% of $15,000 .... $7,500

(2) $60,000 (modified adjusted gross income)
+7,500 (50% of Social Security benefit)
$67,500
−32,000 (base amount)
$35,500 × 50% $17,750

(3) Lesser of (1) or (2) $7,500

(4) 50% of difference between
adjusted base amount and base amount ... $6,000

(5) Lesser of (3) or (4)
(same as pre-'93 law computation) $6,000

(6) $60,000 (modified adjusted gross income)
+7,500 (50% of Social Security benefit)
$67,500
−44,000 (adjusted base amount)
$23,500 × 85% $19,975

(7) Total of (5) + (6) $25,975

(8) 85% of $15,000 .... $12,750

(9) Lesser of (7) or (8) $12,750

☐ **Effective:** For taxable years after Dec. 31, '93. ('93 Act § 13215(d))
For official explanation see Committee Reports ¶ 3042.

¶ 107. The limit on the amount of employee wages subject to the health insurance employment tax has been repealed

The Federal Insurance Contributions Act imposes social security taxes on the employee and the employer. These taxes are based on the amount of wages earned by the employee and received during the calendar year. Both the tax on the employees and the tax on the employers consist of two parts: a tax to provide old-age, survivor and disability insurance ("OASDI" portion), and a tax to provide Medicare hospital insurance ("HI" portion). For wages paid to covered employees in '93, the maximum amount of wages received by the employee during the calendar year that is subject to the HI tax is $135,000. (FTC 2d/FIN ¶ H-4769 *et seq.;* TG ¶ 3579.99)

The '93 Act repeals the dollar limit on wages subject to HI taxes. ('93 Act § 13207(a)(2))

☐ **Effective:** For '94 and later calendar years. (§ 13207(e))
For official explanation see Committee Reports ¶ 3034.

FTC 2d References are to the Federal Tax Coordinator 2d
FIN References are to RIA's Analysis of Federal Taxes: Income
TG References are to the Tax Guide
USTR References are to the United States Tax Reporter

¶ 108. The limit on the amount of self-employment income subject to the health insurance employment tax has been repealed

Under the Self-Employment Tax Act of '54 (SECA), an individual must pay social security tax on net earnings from self employment derived by the individual during the tax year. There is a maximum and a minimum limitation on the amount of self-employment income that is subject to the self-employment tax.

As in the case of employees (¶ 107), the social security tax on self-employed individuals is comprised of a tax to provide old-age survivor and disability insurance (OASDI portion) and a tax to provide Medicare hospital insurance (HI portion). For '93 the HI tax is applied to the first $135,000 of self-employment income. This amount of tax, however, is reduced to the extent that the individual had wages for which employment taxes were withheld during the tax year. (FTC 2d ¶ A-6030 *et seq.;* TG ¶ 1301 *et seq.;* USTR ¶ 14,024) The '93 Act, however, repeals the dollar limit on self employment income subject to HI taxes. (§ 13207(b)(2))

☐ **Effective:** For '94 and later calendar years. (§ 13207(e))
For official explanation see Committee Reports ¶ 3034.

¶ 109. Long-term capital gains excluded from calculation of investment income limit on deducting investment interest after '92

Noncorporate taxpayers may deduct investment interest only to the extent of their net investment income. Net investment income is defined as the excess of investment income over investment expenses. Pre-'93 Act law provided that, for this purpose, investment income included net gain on the disposition of investment property. (FTC 2d/FIN ¶ K-5315; TG ¶ 7199)

The '93 act increases the top income tax rate on individuals' ordinary income to 39.6%, while leaving the top rate imposed on net long-term capital gains at only 28% (see ¶ 101). Congress feels that it is inappropriate for a taxpayer who realizes long-term capital gain taxable at the lower rate to use that gain to deduct otherwise non-deductible investment interest against ordinary income. (H Rept p. 642)

The '93 Act provides that net capital gain on the disposition of investment property generally isn't included in investment income for purposes of computing the net investment income limitation on the deduction of investment interest. (H Rept p. 642)

> ***observation:*** "Net capital gain" is the excess of net long-term capital gain, i.e., the net gain (if any) on the sale or exchange of assets held for more than one year, over net short-term capital loss, i.e., the net loss (if any) on the sale or exchange of assets held for one year or less. Thus, the new rule doesn't affect the treatment of *net short term capital gain* in the calculation of net investment income.

However, a taxpayer may still include all or any part of his capital gain in investment income if he makes a special election. Any net capital gain that the taxpayer elects to so include in investment income must be excluded from capital gain that qualifies for the 28% ceiling on capital gain. (H Rept p. 642)

The '93 Act accomplishes this by:

. . . redefining investment income to consist of:

(1) gross income from property held for investment other than gain on the disposition of property held for investment, *plus*

(2) the excess of any (a) *net gain* attributable to the disposition of property held for investment over (b) any *net capital gain* determined by taking into account gains and losses from dispositions of property held for investment, *plus*

(3) so much of the taxpayer's *net capital gain* on the disposition of property held for investment (or, if less, his *net gain* on the disposition of property held for investment) as he elects to include in investment income. (Code Sec. 163(d)(4)(B) as amended by '93 Act § 13206(d)(1))

. . . providing that to the extent that a taxpayer elects to include net capital gain in his investment income, the amount of net capital gain qualifying for the 28% capital gain ceiling is reduced. (Code Sec 1(h) as amended by '93 Act § 13206(d)(2))

illustration: During '93, Bob Brown has a long-term gain of 50,000 on the sale of a parcel of land, a short-term gain of 25,000 on the sale of some stock in a corporation, and a short-term loss of 10,000 on the sale of some other corporate stock. All these properties had been held by Brown for investment purposes. He thus has net gain of 65,000 (50,000 plus 25,000 minus 10,000). This amount is includable in his investment income only to the extent that it exceeds his net capital gain, which amounts to 50,000 (net long-term capital gain of 50,000 over net short-term capital loss of zero.). Consequently, Brown may include only 15,000 in his investment income unless he makes the special election. Here, the election is available with respect to the entire amount of Brown's 50,000 long-term capital gain, since that amount is less than his 65,000 net gain attributable to the disposition of investment property.

illustration: Say that a taxpayer's only gains and losses from the disposition of investment property during the tax year were a 5,000 short-term gain and a 5,000 long-term loss. Here, since the taxpayer has no net gain from the disposition of investment property (the short-term gain and the long-term loss are netted against each other for this purpose), he may include no amount of gain in investment income even though he had a short-term capital gain.

observation: Under pre-'93 Act law, a popular year-end planning technique for taxpayers who expected to have excess investment interest was to sell appreciated investment property before the end of the tax year. This would generate gains includable in investment income that would help offset the otherwise nondeductible excess investment interest. This technique will still be usable for tax years beginning after '92 but only to the extent that the taxpayer sells assets that generate short-term gain.

observation: Investment interest not allowed as a deduction for a tax year because of the limitation is treated as interest paid or accrued in the following tax year and may eventually become deductible, either in the following tax year or in some later tax year. Consequently, in deciding whether or not to make the special election, taxpayers whose marginal rate exceeds 28% should make calculations comparing the relative tax cost of (1) postponing an interest deduction to a later year with (2) losing the benefit of the 28% capital gains tax ceiling. These calculations should take into account the time value of money, the length of the deferral and the taxpayer's tax brackets for the current year and for the year the deduction would likely be deferred to. Taxpayers whose marginal rate is 28% or lower in the current year should make the election, since they lose nothing by doing so.

FTC 2d References are to the Federal Tax Coordinator 2d
FIN References are to RIA's Analysis of Federal Taxes: Income
TG References are to the Tax Guide
USTR References are to the United States Tax Reporter

observation: Investment expenses, which are part of the calculation of net investment income (see above), are deductions other than interest that are directly connected with the production of investment income. (FTC 2d/FIN ¶ K-5317; TG ¶ 7197) Therefore, expenses directly connected with the production of net capital gain excluded from investment income under the new rules wouldn't be included in investment expenses.

☐ **Effective:** Tax years beginning after '92. (§ 13206(d)(3))
For official explanation see Committee Reports ¶ 3033.

¶ 110. Transactions involving partnership inventory generate ordinary income under broadened circumstances

Amounts received by a partner in exchange for his interest in a partnership are treated as ordinary income to the extent that they are attributable to "substantially appreciated inventory" (SAI). And, partnership distributions in which a partner receives SAI in exchange for all or part of his interest in other partnership property, or other partnership property in exchange for all or part of his interest in SAI, are treated as taxable sales and exchanges, rather than as nontaxable distributions. Gain on such deemed sales of SAI are treated as ordinary income. The tax treatment of property given up in exchange for SAI depends on the character of the property. (FTC 2d/FIN ¶ B-3900 *et seq.;* TG ¶ 1690 *et seq.;* USTR ¶ 7514.01)

Under pre-'93 Act law, a partnership's inventory was SAI if the value of the inventory exceeded *both* 120% of its adjusted basis and 10% of the value of all the partnership's property other than money. At any given time, either all of a partnership's inventory is SAI or none of it is. (FTC 2d/FIN ¶ B-3922; TG ¶ 1695; USTR ¶ 7514.02) "Inventory" for this purpose includes not only stock in trade or property held for sale to customers in the ordinary course of business, but also certain other types of property, such as property not treated as capital assets or Code Sec. 1231 property. (FTC 2d/FIN ¶ B-3921; TG ¶ 1694)

The '93 Act eliminates the requirement that the inventory's value exceed 10% of the value of all the partnership's assets other than money. (Code Sec. 751(d)(1) as amended by '93 Act § 13206(e)(1)) As a result, if a partnership's inventory is worth more than 120% of its adjusted basis, the inventory is SAI. (H Rept p. 643) The reason for this change is Congress's belief that the 10% exception created opportunities for the avoidance of the SAI rule through the manipulation of the partnership's gross assets. (H Rept p. 642)

Inventory acquired to avoid 120% limit is disregarded. Under pre-'93 Act law, the value of *all* partnership inventory items was taken into account in determining whether the partnership's inventory was SAI. (FTC 2d/FIN ¶ B-3922; TG ¶ 1695) Consequently, under pre-'93 Act law, the 120% limit could be avoided simply by acquiring a sufficient amount of additional, *nonappreciated* inventory. Congress felt a rule was needed to forestall this practice. (H Rept p. 642) As a result, the '93 Act provides that for purposes of calculating the 120% limit, certain inventory must be excluded. Inventory is excluded under this rule if a principal purpose for acquiring it was to avoid having the partnership's inventory treated as SAI. (Code Sec. 751(d)(1)(B) as amended by '93 Act § 13206(e)(1)(1))

observation: The pre-'93 Act rule discussed above—under which, at any given time, either all of a partnership's inventory is SAI or none of it is—is unchanged by the Act. Thus, inventory that is excluded from the 120% calculation as a result of the rule in the immediately preceding paragraph, will still be considered SAI if, as a result of that calculation, the partnership's inventory is SAI.

☐ **Effective:** Sales, exchanges and distributions after Apr. 30, '93. (§ 13206(e)(2))

> ***caution:*** Suppose that in Jan., '93, a partnership acquired a quantity of inventory, and that a principal purpose for doing so was to bring down the value of the partnership's inventory to 120% or less of its adjusted basis. This inventory acquisition was thus *before* Apr. 30, '93. However, since the new rules apply to sales, exchanges and distributions after that date, without regard to when the inventory was acquired, the inventory acquired in January would presumably be excluded in determining whether the partnership's inventory is SAI for purposes of a post-Apr. 30, '93 sale, exchange or distribution involving the partnership's inventory.

For official explanation see Committee Reports ¶ 3033.

¶ 111. Holders of stripped preferred stock required to accrue income

Original issue discount (OID) is the excess of the stated redemption price at maturity of a debt instrument over its issue price. (See FTC 2d/FIN ¶ J-3701; TG ¶ 5083) Holders of bonds that are issued with OID are required to accrue and include in their income a portion of the OID each year. (See FTC 2d/FIN ¶ J-3601; TG ¶ 5064) A stripped bond is a bond originally issued with interest coupons where there has been a separation in ownership between the bond and any of its coupons. A stripped bond is treated as a bond issued with OID equal to (1) the stated redemption price of the bond at maturity minus (2) the amount paid for it. (See FTC 2d/FIN ¶ J-3900 *et seq.;* TG ¶ 4520) Under pre-'93 Act law, stripped preferred stock, i.e., preferred stock that was stripped of some or all of its dividend rights, wasn't subject to the rules that apply to stripped bonds.

Congress expressed its belief that purchasers of stripped preferred stock may, in effect, have been purchasing at a discount the right to a fixed amount payable at a future date. It is conceived that taxpayers may have been doing this as a way of converting ordinary income into capital gains. In order to put a stop to this, the '93 Act provides that the rules that apply to stripped bonds also apply to stripped preferred stock. (H Rept p. 640)

The '93 Act provides that if any person purchases any stripped preferred stock (as defined below) after Apr. 30, '93, that person, while holding the stock, must include certain amounts in his gross income. The amounts that must be so included are the amounts that would have been includable if the preferred stock were a bond issued on the purchase date with OID equal to the excess of the stock's redemption price over its purchase price. These rules also apply to any person whose basis in stripped preferred stock is determined by reference to the basis of the stock in the hands of a post-Apr. 30, '93 purchaser. (Code Sec. 305(e)(1) as amended by '93 Act § 13206(c)(1))

> ***illustration:*** Smith purchases stripped stock on Oct. 1, '93. On Feb. 1, '94 he contributes the stock to a partnership in a tax-free transaction in which his basis for the stock carries over to the partnership. Following the transfer, the partnership must include in gross income amounts computed under the new rule based on the excess of the stock's redemption price at maturity over what Smith paid for it.

> ***observation:*** The calculation of income required to be recognized under the new rule, like the calculation of OID, requires the existence of a matu-

---

FTC 2d References are to the Federal Tax Coordinator 2d
FIN References are to RIA's Analysis of Federal Taxes: Income
TG References are to the Tax Guide
USTR References are to the United States Tax Reporter

rity date. No explanation is provided as to what the date of maturity is with respect to preferred stock subject to these new rules. Presumably, this is the earliest date at which the holder can demand that the shares be redeemed at the fixed redemption price. Where no such date exists, it is unclear how the above rules would apply.

"Purchase" defined. "Purchase" means any acquisition of stock where the basis of the stock isn't determined in whole or in part by reference to the adjusted basis of the stock in the hands of the person from whom it was acquired. (Code Sec. 305(e)(6))

observation: Thus, where stock is bought before May 1, '93 and then transferred after Apr. 30, '93 in a completely tax-free transaction with basis carryover (e.g., a partnership contribution), the new rules don't apply.

Basis adjustments. Appropriate adjustments to basis must be made for amounts included in income under the new rule. (Code Sec. 305(e)(2))

observation: What this means, presumably, is that the basis of stripped preferred stock is increased by amounts of income the holder is required to recognize under the new rule. Such an increase would reduce the amount of gain he must recognize on the ultimate sale or redemption of the stock.

Character of income recognized under new rule. Any amount included in gross income under the new rule is treated as ordinary income (Code Sec. 305(e)(4)) other than interest or dividends. (H Rept p. 641)

observation: Thus, for example, a corporate holder of stripped preferred stock presumably wouldn't be able to claim the dividends-received deduction (FTC 2d/FIN ¶ D-2200 *et seq.;* TG ¶ 5139) with respect to amounts included in its gross income under the new rule.

What is stripped preferred stock? Stripped preferred stock is stock:

. . . that is limited and preferred as to dividends,

. . . that doesn't participate in corporate growth to any significant degree,

. . . that has a fixed redemption price, and

. . . with respect to which there has been a separation in ownership between the stock and any dividend on the stock that hasn't yet become payable. (Code Sec. 305(e)(5))

How person who strips stock is treated. Special rules apply to a person who strips the rights to one or more dividends from any stock that satisfies the first three parts of the definition of stripped preferred stock (see preceding paragraph), but only if that person disposes of the rights after Apr. 30, '93. In that case, the stripper is treated as having bought the stripped preferred stock on the date that he disposed of the dividend right or rights, for a purchase price equal to his adjusted basis in the stripped preferred stock. (Code Sec. 305(e)(3))

observation: Code Sec. 305(e)(3) says that the purchase price of the stripped preferred stock is considered to be equal to the stripper's adjusted basis in the stock but doesn't say as of what date this adjusted basis is to be determined. Nor is there any indication as to what, if any, part of the stock's adjusted basis is to be allocated to the stripped dividend rights. However, rules applicable to holders of stripped bonds seem analogous. Under these rules, the purchase price of a bond is allocated between the stripped bond and the stripped coupons on the basis of their respective fair market values on the date they were purchased. (FTC 2d/FIN ¶ J-3907)

> **caution:** Note that the special rules for strippers of preferred stock don't require that the stock *actually* be purchased after Apr. 30, '93. For instance, if a taxpayer buys preferred stock in '91 and disposes of the dividend rights in May of '93, he is treated as if he bought the stripped stock after Apr. 30, '93, and the new rules apply.

Tax treatment of stripped dividend holders. Under pre-'93 Act law, Code Sec. 167(e) generally provides that no depreciation or amortization deduction may be claimed for any term interest in property for any period during which the remainder interest in the property is held by a related person. (FTC 2d/FIN ¶ L-7681.1; TG ¶ 5581) The '93 Act provides that this rule doesn't apply to holders of dividend rights that have been separated from stripped stock that is subject to the rules described above. (Code Sec. 167(e)(2) amended by '93 Act § 13206(e)(2))

> **observation:** Code Sec. 167(e) was enacted to knock out a common technique for deferring income tax. This technique involved the joint purchase, by two related people, of the term and remainder interests in a piece of property. Typically, a parent would purchase an income interest in the property (say the right to dividends from preferred stock), while at the same time, a child purchased a remainder interest in the property. The parent would reduce his taxable income by amortizing the cost of the term interest but, the remainderman didn't have to pay taxes on the annual accretions in wealth that he was enjoying. (FTC 2d/FIN ¶ L-7681.1) The amendment of Code Sec. 167(e) by the '93 Act reflects the fact that in the case of stripped preferred stock, the holder of the remainder is now in fact required to pay taxes on accrued income.

No implication intended as to other issues. Congress says that no implication is intended as to the tax treatment of stripped preferred stock with respect to any issues not directly addressed by these rules, including the availability of the dividends-received deduction to a holder of dividends stripped from the preferred stock, the allocation of basis by the creator of stripped preferred stock, or the proper characterization of a purported sale of stripped dividend rights. (H Rept p. 641)

☐ **Effective:** Apr. 30, '93. (§ 13206(c)(3))

For official explanation see Committee Reports ¶ 3033.

¶ 112. Exceptions to market discount bond rules repealed

Generally speaking, a market discount bond is one that has been acquired for a price that is less than the principal amount of the bond. (FTC 2d/FIN ¶ J-3950 *et seq.;* TG ¶ 5096; USTR ¶ 12,764.01) Market discount arises when the value of an obligation declines after issuance because, for example, of an increase in interest rates or a decline in the borrower's credit worthiness. (H Rept p. 639)

Pre-'93 Act law required, subject to certain exceptions, that gain on the disposition of a market discount bond be treated as ordinary income to the extent of any "accrued market discount." "Market discount" is generally the excess of a bond's stated redemption price at maturity over what the buyer paid for it. "Accrued market discount" is market discount multiplied by the number of days the taxpayer has held the bond and divided by the total number of days he would have held it if he held it to maturity. (FTC 2d/FIN ¶ J-3960; TG ¶ 5099; USTR ¶ 12,764.01)

FTC 2d References are to the Federal Tax Coordinator 2d
FIN References are to RIA's Analysis of Federal Taxes: Income
TG References are to the Tax Guide
USTR References are to the United States Tax Reporter

Pre-'93 Act law provided exceptions to the ordinary-income rule for tax exempt obligations and for bonds issued before July 19, '84. Thus, if these bonds were capital assets to a taxpayer, gain on their disposition was treated as capital gain. (FTC 2d/FIN ¶s J-3951 and J-3952; TG ¶s 5096 and 5097)

Congress expressed concern that taxpayers may be able to purchase market discount bonds as a way of converting into capital gain returns on investments that are in the nature of interest. (H Rept p. 640)

The '93 Act, while generally leaving the market discount rules intact, repeals the special exceptions for tax exempt obligations (§ 13206(b)(2)(A)(i)) and for bonds issued before July 19, '84. (§ 13206(b)(1)(A)) Thus, gain on the disposition of such bonds will generally be treated as ordinary income to the extent of accrued market discount and not as capital gain. (H Rept p. 640)

Changes to limits on deduction of interest incurred to carry market discount bonds, to reflect repeal of exceptions. Pre-'93 Act law (Code Sec. 1277) generally limited the deduction of interest incurred to carry market discount bonds to the excess of such interest over currently accrued market discount. (FTC 2d/FIN ¶ K-5340 *et seq.;* TG ¶ 7120; USTR ¶ 12,764.02) Interest disallowed under these rules (which don't apply to bonds *acquired* before July 19, '84) became available as a deduction in the year that the bond was disposed of. (FTC 2d/FIN ¶ K-5343; USTR ¶ 12,764.02) Pre-'93 Act law also provided a special rule, Code Sec. 1277(d), which treated as ordinary income any gain on the disposition of a bond *issued* before July 19, '84 to the extent of previously disallowed interest allowed in the year of disposition. (FTC 2d/FIN ¶ J-3951; TG ¶ 5069) The '93 Act generally leaves Code Sec. 1277 intact but repeals this special rule. (§ 13206(b)(1)(B))

> ***illustration:*** A bond *issued* before July 19, '84 is *acquired* by taxpayer after July 18, '84. Under the pre-'93 Act rules, the bond is *not* subject to the rule recharacterizing gain as ordinary income to the extent of accrued market discount. The bond is, however, subject to the rule limiting the deduction of interest incurred to carry it. Thus, under the old rules, capital gain on the disposition of such a bond is converted under Code Sec. 1277(d) to ordinary income to the extent of previously disallowed interest which becomes deductible in the year of disposition.

> ***observation:*** Under the new rules, Code Sec. 1277(d) is no longer necessary since gain on the disposition of the bond is recharacterized as ordinary income to the full extent of any accrued market discount. In other words, under the old rules, the amount of interest disallowed was limited to an amount not in excess of accrued market discount, which also became the amount of gain on disposition that was recharacterized as ordinary income. Under the new rules, all of the accrued market discount is converted to ordinary income, leaving nothing to be so converted under any other rule. (P:IF)Other changes. The '93 Act also provides that tax exempt bonds, though now treated as market discount bonds for purposes of the rule recharacterizing gain as ordinary income, are not subject to the Code Sec. 1277 rules limiting the deduction of interest incurred to carry market discount bonds, nor the rule allowing the deduction of previously disallowed interest in the year of disposition. (Code Sec. 1278(a)(1)(C) as amended by '93 Act § 13206(b)(2)(A))

As noted above, market discount is the excess of a bond's stated redemption price at maturity over what the buyer paid for it. In the case of a bond having an original issue discount (OID), the bond's stated redemption price is its "revised issue price." (OID is the excess of a bond's stated redemption price at maturity over its issue price, see FTC 2d/FIN ¶ J-3701; TG ¶ 5064; USTR ¶ 12,714.) The revised issue price of a bond having OID is the sum of its issue price increased by the total amount of OID includable in gross income for all the holders for periods before the bond was acquired by the taxpayer, determined without reduction for acquisition premiums paid by earlier holders. (FTC 2d/FIN ¶ J-3955; TG ¶ 5098; USTR ¶ 12,714) Tax-exempt bonds are exempt from the requirement that OID be currently included in the holder's gross income. (FTC 2d/FIN ¶ J-3657; TG ¶ 5063; USTR ¶ 12,714.01)

The '93 Act adds what the Conference Report calls a technical amendment to the definition of revised issue price to account for the accrual of tax-exempt original issue discount. (Conf Rept p. 577) Under this provision, with respect to a tax-exempt obligation, revised issue price means the bond's issue price increased by the aggregate amount of OID that has accrued during periods before the acquisition of the bond by the taxpayer, determined without reduction for acquisition premiums paid by earlier holders. (Code Sec. 1278(a)(4)(B) as amended by '93 Act § 13206(b)(2)(B)(ii))

> ***observation:*** As noted above, tax-exempt bonds are exempt from the requirement that OID be currently included in the gross income of the holder. Consequently, the '93 Act, in amending Code Sec. 1278(a)(4)(B), uses the language "accrued . . . during periods before the acquisition of the bond by the taxpayer," in contrast to "includable in the gross income of all holders for periods before the acquisition of the bond by the taxpayer." In other words, amounts of OID that have accrued with respect to a tax-exempt bond before the taxpayer acquires it are added to its issue price in determining revised issue price even though these amounts weren't includable in the previous holders' gross income. The effect of this rule is to increase the bond's revised issue price and thus the amount of any market discount.

Code Sec. 103 says that gross income generally doesn't include any interest on any state or local bond. (FTC 2d/FIN ¶ J-3060; TG ¶ 5291; USTR ¶ 1034) The '93 Act provides that market discount treated as ordinary income under the new rules isn't "interest" for purposes of Code Sec. 103. (Code Secs. 1276(a)(4) and 1278(b)(1) as amended by '93 Act § 13206(b)(2)(B))

☐ **Effective:** Obligations "purchased" (as defined in Code Sec. 1272(d)(1)) after Apr. 30, '93. (§ 12406(b)(3)) (Code Sec. 1272(d)(1) defines "purchase" as any acquisition of a debt instrument where the basis of the debt instrument isn't determined in whole or in part by reference to the basis of the instrument in the hands of the person from whom it was acquired. (FTC 2d/FIN ¶ J-3604) Thus, owners of bonds issued before July 19, '84 and owners of tax-exempt bonds aren't subject to these new rules with respect to instruments purchased before May 1, '93. (H Rept p. 640)

For official explanation see Committee Reports ¶ 3033.

¶ 113. Gain on transactions equivalent to loans treated as ordinary income

The '93 Act increases the top tax rate that individuals must pay on ordinary

FTC 2d References are to the Federal Tax Coordinator 2d
FIN References are to RIA's Analysis of Federal Taxes: Income
TG References are to the Tax Guide
USTR References are to the United States Tax Reporter

income to 39.6%, but leaves the top rate on net long term capital gain received by individuals at 28%, see ¶ 101.

According to the Senate Report, pre-'93 Act law leaves open the possibility that taxpayers may attempt to create capital gain by means of transactions whose economic substance is indistinguishable from loans, in terms of the return expected and the risks borne by the taxpayer. Because of the increased differential between the regular and capital gains rates, some taxpayers may enter into such transactions to avoid the higher rates on ordinary income. To keep this from happening (S Rept p. 233), the '93 Act imposes a new rule under which all or part of the gain on "conversion transactions" is treated as ordinary income. (Code Sec. 1258 added by '93 Act § 13206(a)(1))

Under a '93 Act provision that applies to all taxpayers—and not just to individuals—any gain that would otherwise be treated as capital gain, and which is recognized on the disposition or other termination of any position held as part of a "conversion transaction," is treated as ordinary income, but only to the extent that it doesn't exceed the "applicable imputed income amount." (Code Sec 1258(a)) No implication is intended as to when income from a "conversion transaction" is properly treated as capital gain under pre-'93 Act law. (S Rept p 233)

> ***observation:*** The top ordinary income and long-term capital gains rates for corporations have both been increased to 35% under the '93 Act. Nonetheless, despite the absence of any differential between the two rates, the new rule has been made applicable to corporations. The distinction between capital gains and ordinary income remains significant for corporations because such entities may deduct capital losses only to the extent of capital gains.

> ***observation:*** No definition is provided for the term "position," which is used in Code Sec. 1258(a) above in describing when and how much gain must be recharacterized under the new rule, as opposed to the term "property," which is used in Code Sec. 1258(c) (below) in defining what a "conversion transaction" is. Presumably, the term "position" is intended have a broad enough meaning to encompass "property" items, such as stock, and also certain positions taken by the taxpayer with respect to property such as a contract to sell stock. By contrast, for purposes of the tax straddle rules, "position" is defined as an interest, including a futures or forward contract or option, in personal property. (FTC 2d/FIN ¶ I-4305; TG ¶ 4155; USTR ¶ 10,924)

Also left undefined is the term "other termination." Presumably, the language "disposition or other termination" is meant to define in the broadest possible terms the events that may trigger the application of the new recharacterization rule, so as to include not only sales and exchanges, but also the worthlessness or abandonment of a position that forms part of a conversion transaction, and the expiration of rights with respect to such a position, such as the lapse of an option.

What is a "conversion transaction"? A conversion transaction generally consists of two or more positions taken with regard to the same or similar property. A conversion transaction is one in which the taxpayer is in the economic position of a lender. In other words, a taxpayer in a conversion transaction has an expectation of a return from the transaction which in substance is in the nature of interest, and he undertakes no significant risks other than those typical of a lender. (S Rept p. 234)

Specifically, a conversion transaction" is any one the following transactions if substantially all of the taxpayer's expected return from the transaction is attributable to the time value of the taxpayer's net investment in the transaction (Code Sec. 1258(c)):

. . . the holding of any property (whether or not actively traded), and the making of a contract to sell that property (or substantially identical property) at a price determined in accordance with the contract, but only if the property was acquired and the contract was made on a substantially contemporaneous basis. (Code Sec. 1258(c)(2)(A)) This rule encompasses transactions that consist of the acquisition of property by the taxpayer and a substantially contemporaneous agreement to sell the same or substantially identical property in the future. (S Rept p. 234)

. . . any "applicable straddle" (Code Sec. 1258(c)(2)(B)), i.e., any straddle within the meaning of Code Sec. 1092(c) except that stock is also treated as personal property in defining a straddle for purposes of this provision. (Code Sec. 1258(d)(1)) Code Sec. 1092(c) generally defines a straddle as offsetting positions with respect to personal property. (See FTC 2d/FIN ¶ I-4303; TG ¶ 4155; USTR ¶ 10,924)

. . . any other transaction that is marketed or sold as producing capital gains from a transaction if substantially all of the taxpayer's expected gain from the transaction is attributable to the time value of the taxpayer's net investment in the transaction. (Code Sec. 1258(c)(2)(C)) This category is limited to transactions marketed or sold on the basis that they have the economic characteristics of a loan and an interest-like return that will be taxed as capital gain. (S Rept p. 234)

. . . any other transaction specified in regs issued by IRS. (Code Sec. 1258(c)(2)(D))

Arrangements not *treated as conversion transactions.* The following is an example of an arrangement involving the simultaneous purchase of property and the making of a contract to sell the property that is *not* treated as a conversion transaction. This is because the taxpayer in the example takes a risk that isn't typical of a lender. The existence of a risk is apparently due to the fact that the transaction involves an option not substantially certain to be exercised. (S Rept p. 236)

> ***Illustration:*** On Jan. 1 of Year 1, X buys publicly-traded common stock for $100 and on the same day grants a call option on the same stock to Y for $106, exercisable at any time before Feb. 1 of Year 2, Y pays X a premium of $10 for the call. At the time the option is granted, there is no substantial certainty that it will be exercised. X's net investment in the transaction is $90 ($100 purchase price less $10 premium). X's gain on the transaction will be $16 if the option is exercised ($106 over X's $90 investment). This transaction is one in which X takes a risk not typical of a lender and is thus not a conversion transaction. (S Rept p. 236)

> ***observation:*** The risk element in the preceding Illustration apparently relates to the fact that the option held by Y may not be exercised. This uncertainty presumably exists because of the possibility that the stock's market price will remain below $106 during the option period, so that Y will allow the option to expire unexercised. If the option had been a put instead of a call—exercisable at *X's* choice, rather than Y's—the arrangement would presumably have been a conversion transaction.

Applicable imputed income amount. This is an amount equal to the excess of:

. . . the amount of interest which would have accrued on the taxpayer's "net investment in the conversion transaction" (as defined below) for the period ending on the date of the disposition or other termination, or, if earlier, the date on which the transaction ceased to fit the definition of "conversion transaction" (see below), computed at 120% of the "applicable rate," over

. . . the amount already treated as ordinary income under this conversion transaction rule with respect to any earlier disposition or other termination of a position held as part of the same transaction. (Code Sec. 1258(b))

"Applicable rate" means:

. . . if the transaction has a definite term, the applicable Federal rate determined under Code Sec. 1274(d), compounded semiannually, as if the "conversion transaction" were a debt instrument. (FTC 2d/FIN ¶ J-3742; TG ¶ 5074; USTR ¶ 12,714.04)

. . . if the term of the "conversion transaction" is indefinite, the Federal short-term rates in effect under Code Sec. 6621(b) for the period of the "conversion transaction," compounded daily. (FTC 2d/FIN ¶ T-8003; TG ¶ 9638; USTR ¶ 66,214) (Code Sec. 1258(d)(2))

IRS is to issue regs providing for appropriate reductions in applicable imputed income to reflect amounts capitalized under Code Sec. 263(g), ordinary income received or other circumstances. (Code Sec. 1258(b)) Code Sec. 263(g) generally requires the capitalization of interest and carrying charges incurred in connection with certain personal property straddles. (See FTC 2d/FIN ¶ L-5985; TG ¶ 6104; USTR ¶ 2634) IRS also has the authority, under Code Sec. 1274(d)(1)(D), to provide for the use of an applicable rate lower than the applicable federal rate in certain cases. (Conf Rept p. 575) Code Sec. 1274(d)(1)(D) (FTC 2d/FIN ¶ J-3520; USTR ¶ 2714.04) allows IRS to permit the use of a lower rate if the taxpayer establishes that the lower rate is based on the same principles as the applicable federal rate and that the lower rate is appropriate for the term of the debt instrument.

> ***Illustration:*** On Jan. 1 of Year 1, A buys 100 shares of stock for $100 and on the same day agrees to sell the stock to B on Jan. 1 of Year 3 for $115. This is a conversion transaction. On Jan. 1 of year 3, A delivers the stock to B in exchange for $115. A's gain is $15. Using the appropriate short-term interest rate for the two-year transaction, the applicable computed income amount is $12.36, which must be treated as ordinary income. (S Rept p. 235)

What is the taxpayer's "net investment" in a conversion transaction? In determining the taxpayer's net investment in any conversion transaction, the fair market value of any position that becomes part of the transaction (determined as of the time that the position becomes part of the transaction) is included. (Code Sec. 1258(d)(4)) However, the source of a taxpayer's funds generally isn't taken into account and the amount of gain that must be recharacterized is reduced by interest on borrowed funds that must be capitalized under Code Sec. 263(g). (S Rept p. 235)

> ***Illustration:*** The facts are the same as in the preceding Illustration, except that A borrows $^{9}0$ of the stock's purchase price from a bank. As a result, he is required under Code Sec. 263(g) (see above) to capitalize $10 of interest on that debt as part of the stock's cost. His net investment in the transaction remains $100, even though his basis is increased to $110 to reflect the $10 in interest he has been required to capitalize. However, when he sells the stock for $115, his gain is $5, of this, $2.36 is treated as ordinary income. This is

because the $12.36 amount that would otherwise have to be treated as ordinary income is reduced by the $10 in interest required to be capitalized under Code Sec. 263(g). (S Rept p. 235)

A taxpayer's net investment in a conversion transaction is generally reduced by any amount received as consideration for entering into any position that is part of the transaction. (S Rept p. 236)

Special rules for built-in loss property. "Built-in loss" means the loss (if any) which would have been realized if a position had been disposed of or otherwise terminated at its fair market value as of the time it became part of the conversion transaction. (Code Sec. 1258(d)(3)(B))

If any position with a built-in loss becomes part of a conversion transaction, then for purposes of applying the new rule for periods after the position becomes part of the conversion transaction, the position is taken into account at its fair market value as of the time it became part of the transaction. (Code Sec. 1258(d)(3)(A)(i)) However, on a disposition or other termination of the position in which gain or loss is recognized, the built-in loss is recognized and its character is determined without regard to the new rule. (Code Sec. 1258(d)(3)(A)(ii))

observation: What this means is that if the amount realized on the disposition or other termination of a position exceeds the position's fair market value on the date it became part of the conversion transaction, the amount of that excess is gain treated as ordinary income under the rule described above. At the same time, a loss, measured by the difference between basis and fair market value, is recognized. The character of that loss (capital or ordinary) is determined without regard to the recharacterization rule.

Illustration: Prior to Year 1, M bought stock for $150 and uses that stock as part of a conversion transaction entered into on Jan. 1 of Year 1. At the time of the transaction, the stock's value has declined to $100. The stock is treated as having a basis of $100 for purposes of recharacterizing gain as ordinary income. Thus, if M sells the stock for $115, he will have gain of $15, some or all of which may be recharacterized as ordinary income depending on the amount of applicable imputed income. At the same time he will have a $50 loss, whose character isn't affected by the recharacterization rule. (S Rept p. 235)

Amounts to be committed to conversion transaction in the future. Amounts that a taxpayer may be committed to provide in the future aren't treated a part of his investment in a conversion transaction until they are actually committed to the transaction and become unavailable to the taxpayer to invest in other ways. (S Rept p. 235)

Illustration: On Jan. 1 of Year 1, T enters into a long futures contract committing him to purchase a certain quantity of gold on Mar. 1 for $1,000. Also on Jan. 1, T enters into a short futures contract to sell the same quantity of gold on Apr. 1 for $1,006. Under these contracts, T isn't required to make any investment at the time he enters into them, but he does have to make a margin deposit (which may or may not bear interest) as security for his obligations under the contracts. T terminates both contracts on

Feb. 1 for a net profit of $2. No part of the $2 is subject to recharacterization since T has no investment in the transaction on which the $2 could be considered an interest-like return. (S Rept p. 236)

How recharacterized amounts are treated. Amounts recharacterized as ordinary income under the rule described above are generally treated as ordinary income (but not as interest) for all federal tax purposes. (S Rept p. 233)

Exempt organizations and regulated investment companies. Amounts recharacterized as ordinary income under the above rules continue to be treated as gain from the sale of property for purposes of the unrelated business income tax imposed on exempt organizations and the gross income requirement for regulated investment companies. (S Rept p. 233)

Special rules for options dealers and commodities traders. The rule recharacterizing capital gain as ordinary income doesn't apply to the transactions of:

. . . an options dealer in the normal course of his trade or business of dealing in options, or

. . . a commodities dealer in the normal course of his trade or business of trading in Code Sec. 1256 contracts. (Code Sec. 1256 contracts are regulated futures contracts, foreign currency contracts and certain other contracts subject to the mark-to-market rules, see FTC 2d/FIN ¶ I-4350; TG ¶ 4154; USTR ¶ 12,564). (Code Sec. 1258(c)(5)(A))

Transactions of options dealers and commodities traders subject to this special rule may include positions other than options or Code Sec. 1256 contracts. (S Rept p. 234)

A commodity trader is any person who is a member (or, except as otherwise provided in regs, who is entitled to trade as a member) of a domestic board of trade which is designated as a contract market by the Commodity Futures Trading Commission. (Code Sec. 1258(c)(5)(B)(ii))

The term "commodities trader" also includes:

. . . a member of a domestic board of trade who has member trading privileges only with respect to a portion of the contracts available for trading.

. . . except as otherwise provided in regs, a person entitled to trade as a member, such as a lessee of a membership or an entity that is (or is affiliated with) a beneficial owner of a membership if the entity is eligible for any preferential rates available to members with respect to transaction fees or margins imposed by the board of trade or for the clearing of trades on the board of trade.

. . . other persons eligible for member rates. (Conf Rept p. 575)

However, IRS may issue regs that prevent unwarranted expansion of the exception, by excluding from the definition of "commodities trader" a person who acquires some attributes of board of trade membership for the principal purpose of qualifying for the exception or whose margins or fees are substantially more than those associated with owned or leased memberships. (Conf Rept p. 575)

The term "options dealer" has the same meaning given that term by Code Sec. 1256(g)(6). (FTC 2d/FIN ¶ I-4359.3) Thus, an options dealer is any person registered with an appropriate national securities exchange as a market maker or a specialist in listed options and certain other persons determined by IRS to be performing similar functions.

Exception for options dealers and commodities traders not to apply to some limited partners and limited entrepreneurs. In certain cases, the exception for options dealers and traders doesn't apply to gain recognized by an entity that is allocable to a limited partner or to a limited entrepreneur. For this purpose, a limited entrepreneur is a person who has an interest in an enterprise other than as a limited partner and doesn't participate in the management of the enterprise. (Code Sec. 1258(c)(5)(C)) The recharacterization rule applies to gain allocable to a limited partner or limited entrepreneur (and the gain is thus subject to the new rule) if:

. . . substantially all the partner's (or entrepreneur's) expected return from the entity is attributable to the time value of the partner's (or the entrepreneur's) net investment in the entity (Code Sec. 1258(c)(5)(C)(i)), or

. . . the transaction (or interest in the entity) was marketed or sold as producing capital gains treatment from a transaction in which substantially all of the taxpayer's expected return is attributable to the time value of the taxpayer's investment. (Code Sec. 1258(c)(5)(C)(ii)), or

. . . the transaction (or the interest in the entity) is a transaction (or interest) specified in regs. (Code Sec. 1258(c)(5)(C)(iii))

> ***observation:*** The purpose of this special rule for limited partners and entrepreneur is to prevent taxpayers from acquiring a passive interest in an entity that is an options dealer or commodities trader in order to avoid the recharacterization rule.

☐ **Effective:** Conversion transactions entered into after Apr. 30, '93. (§ 13206(a)(3))
For official explanation see Committee Reports ¶ 3033.

¶ 114. Noncorporate taxpayers' alternative minimum tax rate and exemption amounts increased

An individual taxpayer is subject to an alternative minimum tax to the extent that the taxpayer's tentative minimum tax exceeds the taxpayer's regular tax liability. (See FTC 2d/FIN ¶ A-8101; TG ¶ 1351; USTR ¶ 554) Under pre-'93 Act law, a non-corporate taxpayer's tentative minimum tax equaled 24% of alternative minimum taxable income in excess of an exemption amount, less the alternative minimum tax foreign tax credit. (FTC 2d/FIN ¶ A-8101; TG ¶ 1351; USTR ¶ 554.01) Pre-'93 Act law provided a special application of this rule for nonresident aliens (FTC 2d/FIN ¶ A-8101.5; TG ¶ 1352; USTR ¶ 8974) The '93 Act raises the alternative minimum tax rate, makes the alternative minimum tax a two tiered tax rate structure, increases the exemption amounts, and restructures the rules for nonresident aliens.

Two-tier alternative minimum tax rate structure Congress believes that the progressivity of the individual tax system would be enhanced by creating a two-tier alternative minimum tax schedule for non-corporate taxpayers. (H Rept p. 635) Therefore, the '93 Act provides that, in the case of a non-corporate taxpayer other than a married individual filing a separate return, the tentative minimum tax for the tax year is equal to 26% of the "taxable excess" that doesn't exceed $175,000, plus 28% of the "taxable excess" that does exceed $175,000, reduced by the alternative

FTC 2d References are to the Federal Tax Coordinator 2d
FIN References are to RIA's Analysis of Federal Taxes: Income
TG References are to the Tax Guide
USTR References are to the United States Tax Reporter

minimum tax foreign tax credit for the tax year. (Code Sec. 55(b)(1)(A)(i) as amended by '93 Act § 13203(a)) In the case of a married individual filing a separate return, the tentative minimum tax for the tax year is equal to 26% of the "taxable excess" that doesn't exceed $87,500, plus 28% of the taxable excess that does exceed $87,500. The "taxable excess" is the excess of alternative minimum taxable income over the exemption amount. (Code Sec. 55(b)(1)(A)(iii)) Marital status for this purpose is determined under the rules for determining marital status for a tax year (See FTC 2d/FIN ¶ A-1601; TG ¶ 1430; USTR ¶ 77,034) (Code Sec. 55(b)(1)(A)(iii))

> ***observation:*** Although the AMT rate changes are effective for tax years beginning after Dec. 31, '92, the rules which allow taxpayers to elect to pay tax attributable to rate increases in three interest-free installments, see ¶ 103, don't apply to the AMT.

Increase in exemption amounts. Under pre-'93 Act law, the exemption amount was $40,000 for married taxpayers filing joint returns; $30,000 for unmarried taxpayers filing as single or head of household; and $20,000 for married taxpayers filing separate returns, estates and trusts. For all taxpayers, the exemption amount was phased out for taxpayers with alternative minimum taxable income above specified thresholds. (FTC 2d/FIN ¶ A-8101.1; TG ¶ 1353; USTR ¶ 554.01) And, married individuals filing separately had to add to alternative minimum taxable income the lesser of (a) 25% of the excess of alternative minimum taxable income over $155,000 or (b) $20,000. (FTC 2d/FIN ¶ A-8101.1; TG ¶ 1353; USTR ¶ 554.01)

The '93 Act provides that, in the case of married couples filing joint returns or surviving spouses, the exemption amount is $45,000; for unmarried individuals who aren't surviving spouses, the exemption amount is $33,750; for married individuals filing separate returns, estates and trusts, the exemption amount is $22,500. (Code Sec. 55(d)(1) as amended by '93 Act § 13203(b)) Married individuals filing separately must add to alternative minimum taxable income the lesser of (a) 25% of the excess of alternative minimum taxable income over $165,000 or (b) $22,500. (Code Sec. 55(d)(3) as amended by '93 Act § 13203(c)(1))

Nonresident aliens. Under pre-'93 Act law, the tentative minimum tax of a nonresident alien individual equalled the greater of (a) the tentative minimum tax as computed under the rules for resident individuals, or (b) the excess of 21% of the lesser of the nonresident alien's AMTI for the tax year, or net U.S. real property gain for the tax year, over the alternative minimum tax foreign tax credit. (FTC 2d/FIN ¶ A-8101.05; TG ¶ 1352; USTR ¶ 8974) Net U.S. real property gain is the excess of the aggregate gains for the tax year from dispositions of U.S. real property interests over the aggregate of the losses for the tax year from dispositions of those interests. (See FTC 2d/FIN ¶ A-8101.05; TG ¶ 8225 *et seq.;* USTR ¶ 8974)

The '93 Act provides that, in the case of a nonresident alien individual, the "taxable excess" used in computing tentative minimum tax can't be less than the lesser of the individual's alternative minimum taxable income for the tax year or the individual's net U.S. real property gain for the year. (Code Sec. 897(a)(2)(A) as amended by '93 Act § 13203(c)(2)(A))

☐ **Effective:** Tax years beginning after Dec. 31, $92. (§ 13203(d))
For official explanation see Committee Reports ¶ 3030.

¶ 115. Alternative minimum tax (AMT) preference repealed

Under pre-'93 Act law, in computing alternative minimum taxable income, the deduction for charitable contributions of capital gain property was disallowed to the extent that the fair market value of the property exceeded its adjusted basis. But, for contributions made in tax years beginning in '91 or made before July 1, '92 in a tax year beginning in '92, this rule didn't apply to contributions of tangible personal capital gain property. (FTC 2d/FIN ¶ A-8115; TG ¶ 1363; USTR ¶ 574) Generally, capital gain property was any capital asset which, if sold at is fair market value at the time of the contribution, would result in long-term capital gain. (See FTC 2d/FIN ¶ K-3698; TG ¶ 7368; USTR ¶ 1704.42)

The '93 Act eliminates the AMT preference for donated appreciated capital gain property. (Code Sec. 57(a) as amended by § 13171(a)) By permanently extending the above '91-'92 temporary rule, and expanding it to apply to gifts of all appreciated capital gain property, taxpayers will be allowed the same charitable contribution deduction for both regular tax and AMT purposes. Congress believes that this will provide an additional incentive for taxpayers to make charitable contributions of appreciated capital gain property. (H Rept p. 630)

☐ **Effective:** Contributions of capital gain property that isn't tangible personal property made after Dec. 31, '92; Contributions of all other capital gain property made after June 30, '92. (§ 13171(d))

For official explanation see Committee Reports ¶ 3025.

¶ 116. Deferred tax liability on outstanding installment obligations may be figured at capital gain rate

If an obligation that arose from an installment sale for more than $150,000 is outstanding at the end of the tax year, and the face amount of all such obligations that arose during the tax year and are outstanding at the end of the tax year exceeds $5,000,000, interest is due on the deferred tax attributable to the installment obligations. The amount of interest due equals the applicable percentage of the deferred tax liability with respect to the obligation multiplied by the interest rate on tax underpayments in effect for the last month of the tax year. The "applicable percentage" is the portion of the face amount of the obligations subject to the interest payments rules outstanding at the end of the year in excess of $5,000,000 divided by the total aggregate face amount of those obligations. (See FTC 2d/FIN ¶ G-6300 *et seq.;* TG ¶ 2900 *et seq.;* USTR ¶ 453A4)

Under pre-'93 Act law, the "deferred tax liability" with respect to an obligation was the amount of still-unrecognized gain on that obligation as of the end of the tax year multiplied by the top income tax rate in effect for that year under Code Sec. 1 (individuals) or Code Sec. 11 (corporations), whichever is appropriate. (FTC 2d/FIN ¶ G-6317; TG ¶ 2904; USTR ¶ 453A4)

The '93 Act provides that, with respect to so much of the gain that, when recognized, will be treated as long-term capital gain, the maximum rate under Code Sec. 1(h) or Code Sec. 1201 is used instead of the top income tax rate. (Code Sec. 453A(c)(3) as amended by '93 Act § 13201(b)(4))

> ***observation:*** The maximum capital gain rate under Code Sec. 1(h) is 28%. The maximum capital gain rate under Code Sec. 1201, as amended by the '93 Act, is 35% (see ¶ 301).

> ***observation:*** Thus, for individuals, the tax rate at which the "deferred tax liability" on the long-term capital gain portion is figured decreases from 31% to 28%. For corporations, the rate increases from 34% to 35%.

FTC 2d References are to the Federal Tax Coordinator 2d
FIN References are to RIA's Analysis of Federal Taxes: Income
TG References are to the Tax Guide
USTR References are to the United States Tax Reporter

☐ **Effective:** Tax years beginning after Dec. 31, '92. (§ 13201(c))
For official explanation see Committee Reports ¶ 3028.

¶ 117. Individual estimated tax: simple, 100%-of-prior-year's-tax safe harbor (110% for taxpayers with prior year AGI over $150,000) applies to post-'93 tax years

To avoid penalties for underpayment (see FTC 2d/FIN ¶ S-5200 *et seq.;* TG ¶ 1400 *et seq.;* USTR ¶ 66,544), individuals generally must make timely payments of estimated tax (see FTC 2d/FIN ¶ S-5202; TG ¶ 1404; USTR ¶ 66,544(c)) equal to at least:

. . . (a) 90% of the tax for the tax year (the year for which the estimated tax is being determined); or

. . . (b) 100% of the prior year's tax. (FTC 2d/FIN ¶ S-5203; TG ¶ 1406; USTR ¶ 66,544)

These estimated tax rules also apply to certain trusts and estates. (FTC 2d/FIN ¶ S-5301; TG ¶ 1743; USTR ¶ 66,544(h))

Under pre-'93 Act law, the 100%-of-last-year's-tax safe harbor was generally unavailable to taxpayers with (i) current year AGI exceeding $75,000 ($37,500 for married taxpayers filing separate returns), and (ii) current year modified AGI exceeding prior year AGI by more than $40,000 ($20,000 for married taxpayers filing separate returns). (FTC 2d/FIN ¶ S-5203.1 *et seq.;* TG ¶ 1406; USTR ¶ 66,544) This rule, as modified, also applied to trusts and estates. (FTC 2d/FIN ¶ S-5301 *et seq.;* TG ¶s 1411, 1743; USTR ¶ 66,544(h))

In such cases of the unavailability of the 100%-of-last-year's-tax safe harbor, the estimated tax payments had to be equal to at least:

(1) 90% of the tax for the tax year (same as (a), above), or

(2) the *greater* of 100% of the prior year's tax (same as (b), above), or 90% of the current year's tax with certain modifications (FTC 2d/FIN ¶ S-5203.1; TG ¶ 1406; USTR ¶ 66,544(e)(1)),

except for the first installment payment, which taxpayers could pay based on the general rule (options (a) and (b), above) (FTC 2d/FIN ¶ S-5203.8; TG ¶ 1406; USTR ¶ 66,544(e)(1)).

> ***observation:*** Taxpayers subject to this rule could be penalized to the extent that any of their second, third, or fourth quarter estimated tax payments were less than the required amount, determined without the protection of the 100%-of-last-year's-tax safe harbor. Yet, they had to make these payments based on possibly inadequate information collected before each installment due date.

The application of the pre-'93 Act rules (which limit the availability of the 100%-of-last-year's-tax safe harbor) was unduly cumbersome. (S Rept p. 653) Thus, the '93 Act repeals the pre-'93 Act rules limiting the availability of the safe harbor. Those rules were set forth in Code Sec. 6654(d)(1)(C), (D), (E), and (F). (§ 13214(a))

> ***observation:*** The repeal also applies to trusts and estates.

For individuals with adjusted gross income (AGI) shown on the prior year's tax return exceeding $150,000 (Code Sec. 6654(d)(1)(C)(i) as amended by '93 Act § 13214(a)), or $75,000 for married taxpayers (within the meaning of Code Sec. 7703 filing separate returns (Code Sec. 6654(d)(1)(C)(ii)), the '93 Act simplifies the estimated tax calculation by modifying the 100%-of-last-year's-tax safe harbor (H

Rept p. 258) to require payments of *110%* of the prior year's tax. (Code Sec. 6654(d)(1)(C)(i)) In the case of trusts and estates, AGI, for purposes of the $150,000 threshold, is determined under Code Sec. 67(e) (relating to the 2%-of-AGI floor on itemized deductions, see FTC 2d/FIN ¶s C-2202, C-7202 *et seq.;* TG ¶s 1778, 1787, 1801; USTR ¶ 674(d)). (Code Sec. 6654(d)(1)(C)(iii))

In other words, under the '93 Act an individual won't have an underpayment of estimated tax if he makes timely estimated payments at least equal to (A) 100% of the prior year's tax, for individuals with prior year AGI not exceeding $150,000 ($75,000 for married taxpayers filing separate returns) or (B) 90% of the tax for the tax year. (S Rept p. 653)

☐ **Effective:** Tax years beginning after Dec. 31, '93. (§ 13214(c)) Thus, these provisions apply to estimated tax payments applicable to tax years beginning after Dec. 31, '93. (S Rept p. 653)

For official explanation see Committee Reports ¶ 3041.

¶ 118. Withholding rate on supplemental wages increased to 28%

An employer can elect to withhold tax at a flat rate on supplemental wages such as bonuses, commissions, and overtime pay that are not paid concurrently with wages or that are paid concurrently but are separately stated. If the flat-rate method isn't elected, supplemental wages are added to regular wages for withholding purposes. (See FTC 2d/FIN ¶ H-4719 *et seq.;* TG ¶ 3516; USTR ¶ 34,024.13)

Under pre-'93 Act law, a 20% withholding rate applied to supplemental wages paid by employers electing the flat-rate method. (FTC 2d/FIN ¶ H-4723; TG ¶ 3516; USTR ¶ 34,024.13) The '93 Act increases this rate to 28%. ('93 Act § 13273) The 28% rate more closely approximates the ultimate tax liability for the supplemental wages. (H Rept p. 789)

☐ **Effective:** Payments made after Dec. 31, '93. (§ 13273)

For official explanation see Committee Reports ¶ 3068.

¶ 119. Earned income credit for low-income workers expanded, increased, and simplified for post-'93 years

A refundable "basic" EIC of up to $1,511 for '93 was provided under pre-'93 Act law for any eligible low-income worker (whether employee or self-employed) with two or more qualifying children. The maximum "basic" EIC for '93 for an eligible low-income worker with one qualifying child was $1,434. (FTC 2d/FIN ¶ A-4201 *et seq.;* TG ¶ 1240 *et seq.;* USTR ¶ 324 *et seq.)*

> ***observation:*** The "refundable" nature of the EIC means that the credit is not only available to offset tax liability, but it may also be collected from IRS to the extent it exceeds tax liability.

Under pre-'93 Act law, the refundable EIC consisted of the sum of these three components:

. . . The basic earned income credit. (FTC 2d/FIN ¶ A-4205; TG ¶ 1242; USTR ¶ 324.01)

FTC 2d References are to the Federal Tax Coordinator 2d
FIN References are to RIA's Analysis of Federal Taxes: Income
TG References are to the Tax Guide
USTR References are to the United States Tax Reporter

. . . The health insurance credit for workers who provided health insurance coverage for their qualifying children. (FTC 2d/FIN ¶ A-4208; TG ¶ 1244; USTR ¶ 324.01)

. . . The supplemental young child credit for workers with a qualifying child born during the tax year. (FTC 2d/FIN ¶ A-4212; TG ¶ 1243; USTR ¶ 324.01)

A taxpayer who claimed the supplemental young child credit couldn't treat that child as a qualifying individual in computing the dependent care credit. (See FTC 2d/FIN ¶ 4312; TG ¶ 1243)

Any amount taken as a health insurance credit reduced, dollar-for-dollar, the amount the taxpayer claimed (a) as itemized medical deductions. (See FTC 2d/FIN ¶ K-2002; TG ¶ 7250; USTR ¶ 324.01); and (b) as a business expense health insurance deduction. (See FTC 2d/FIN ¶ A-4211; TG ¶ 1244; USTR ¶ 324.01).

Each component of the EIC was computed by applying a different credit percentage to the same base amount that was adjusted annually for inflation. A single phaseout amount (also adjusted annually for inflation) limited the amount of each credit. (FTC 2d/FIN ¶ A-4202; TG ¶ 1242; USTR ¶ 324.01)

The '93 inflation adjusted base amount for each component credit of the EIC was ¶ 7,750; and the '93 inflation adjusted phaseout amount for each credit component was ¶ 12,200. Under the pre-'93 Act phaseout rule, each credit component was completely phased out for '93 (i.e., not available) when the worker's earned income or adjusted gross income reached $23,050. (H Rept p. 608)

Under pre-'93 Act law, the prescribed credits and phaseout percentages for each EIC component credit for tax years beginning in '93, '94 and thereafter were as follows: (See FTC 2d/FIN ¶ A-4205 *et seq.; TG ¶ 1242 et seq.;* USTR ¶ 324.01)

EIC Credit and Phaseout Percentages
(For Post-'92 Tax Years Under Pre-'93 Act Law)

Tax Year Beginning In	Eligible Individual (1 Qualif. Child) Credit %	Phaseout %	Eligible Individual (2 or More Qual. Ch.) Credit %	Phaseout %
. . . '93:				
(a) Basis EIC—	18.5%	13.21%	19.5%	13.93%
(b) Health Ins. credit—	6%	4.285%	6%	4.285%
(c) Young child credit—	5%	3.57%	5%	3.57%
TOTAL	29.5%	21.065%	30.5%	21.785%
. . . '94 and After:				
(a) Basic EIC—	23%	16.43%	25%	17.86%
(b) Health Ins. credit—	6%	4.285%	6%	4.285%
(c) Young child credit—	5%	3.57%	0%	3.57%
TOTAL	34%	24.285%	36%	25.715%

illustration: For '93, X (a calendar year, unmarried, taxpayer) had $15,200 in earned income and adjusted gross income. In '93, X had one child under one year of age and two three-year olds (twins) qualifying X for the EIC. X's '93 health insurance expense for X and the three children was $500. Under pre-'93 Act law, X was entitled to a refundable $1,710 EIC for '93 determined as follows:

. . . Total credit % X base amount (30.5% × $7,750):	$2,363.75
. . . Less: Phaseout limitation ($15,200−$12,200=$3,000; 21.785% × $3,000)	$ 653.55
. . . EIC for '93	$1,710.20

observation: The Code requires that the amount of each component of the EIC for which the taxpayer qualifies must be obtained from the appropriate EIC credit tables published annually by IRS. (See FTC 2d/FIN ¶ A-4202; TG ¶ 1240; USTR ¶ 324.06) This means that the above computation is not required and the allowable amount is based on whole dollars only.

Five substantive changes have been made to the EIC rules by the '93 Act. (Conf Rept pp. 536-537)

The '93 Act:

(1) extends coverage to low-income workers with no qualifying children, (Code Sec. 32(c)(1)(A)(ii) as amended by '93 Act § 13131(b)) and with earned income—or adjusted gross income—of under $9,000. (H Rept p. 610) For '94 and after, the maximum EIC under this new provision is $306. (H Rept p. 609) See ¶ 120.

(2) changes the credit percentages, base amounts, phaseout amounts, and phaseout percentages (see tables below) so as to result in an increased EIC credit. (Code Sec. 32(b))

For '94, the maximum EIC credit for an eligible worker with one eligible child is $2,038. It is $2,527 when there are two or more eligible children. (Conf Rept pp. 536-537))

The applicable credit and phaseout percentages for tax years beginning in '94, '95, and after (Code Sec. 32(b)(1)); and the applicable earned income and phaseout amounts for each of these years (Code Sec. 32(b)(2)) are as follows:

EIC Percentages and Computation Amounts for '94 and After

In the case of eligible individual with:	The Credit % is	The Phaseout % is	The Earned Income Amount is	The Phaseout Amount is
FOR '94				
1 qualifying child	26.3%	15.98%	$7,750	$11,000
2 or more qualifying children	30%	17.68%	$8,425	$11,000
No qualifying children	7.65%	7.65%	$4,000	$5,000
FOR '95				
1 qualifying child	34%	15.98%	$6,000	$11,000
2 or more qualifying child	36%	20.22%	$8,425	$11,000
No qualifying children	7.65%	7.65%	$4,000	$5,000
AFTER '95				
1 qualifying child	34%	15.98%	$6,000	$11,000
2 or more qualifying children	40%	21.06%	$8,424	$11,000
No qualifying children	7.65%	7.65%	$4,000	$5,000

illustration: For '94, a taxpayer having the same income and qualifying children as in the above illustration would be entitled to a $1,784.94 EIC

FTC 2d References are to the Federal Tax Coordinator 2d
FIN References are to RIA's Analysis of Federal Taxes: Income
TG References are to the Tax Guide
USTR References are to the United States Tax Reporter

computed as follows:

. . . Credit % × base amount (30% × $8,425)	$2,527.50
. . . Less: Phaseout limitation ($15,200 − $11,000 =$4,200; 17.68% of $4,200)	($742.56)
. . . '94 EIC allowed	$1,784.94

observation: As under pre-'93 Act law, presumably, IRS will require that the EIC amount for '94 and after (rounded to the nearest whole dollar) be obtained from IRS supplied tables so that taxpayers can avoid the above computation.

observation: The '93 Act continues unchanged the Code Sec. 32(c) rules for determining "qualifying child" for purposes of the EIC.

observation: Under the above rules, the EIC for '94 is completely phased out at the following earned income (or AGI) amounts, whichever is higher:

. . . $23,753 for an eligible individual with one qualifying child (15.98% of $12,753 in excess of the phaseout amount of $11,00);

. . . $25,293 for an eligible individual with two or more qualifying children (17.98% of $14,293 in excess of the phaseout amount of $11,000);

. . . $9,000 for an eligible individual with no qualifying children.

(3) Eliminates the health insurance component and the young child component of the EIC. (§ 13131(a))

observation: This is not a benefit reduction but a beneficial simplification of the EIC. This is because the retained "basic" EIC is higher than the three-pronged pre-'94 EIC. Moreover, under this simplification, an eligible worker no longer has to look into three IRS tables to determine total allowable EIC for '94 and after.

The elimination of the above two EIC components also provides the following related benefits to low-income taxpayers:

(a) Itemized medical expense deductions under Code Sec. 213 no longer are reduced by the eliminated health insurance credit component. (§ 13131(d)(3) deleting former Code Sec. 213(f))

(b) Business expense health insurance deductions by self-employeds and S shareholder-employees no longer are reduced by the eliminated health insurance credit component. (Code Sec. 162(l)(3) as amended by '93 Act § 13131(d)(2))

(c) The dependent care credit under Code Sec. 21 is no longer affected by the eliminated young child credit. (§ 13131(a))

(4) Earned income amounts and phaseout amounts for post-'94 years are adjusted annually for inflation under the consumer price index computation in Code Sec. 1(f)(3). The amount of the adjustment for a post-'94 year is the percentage by which the consumer price index for the preceding calendar year exceeds the consumer price index for calendar year '93. (Code Sec. 32(i)(1))

(5) Advance payments of the EIC after '93 are limited to 60% of the maximum credit available to a taxpayer with one qualifying child. (Code Sec. 3507(c)(2)(B)(i) as amended by '93 Act § 13131(d)(5)) This advance payment availability, however, must be pointed out by IRS to each low-income worker receiving a refund of the EIC. (Code Sec. 3507(f))

☐ **Effective:** Taxable years beginning after '93. (§ 13131(e))

For official explanation see Committee Reports ¶ 3011.

¶ 120. "Eligible individual" for earned income credit expanded to include taxpayers without qualifying children

As explained at ¶ 119, under pre-'93 Act law, a low-income worker without at least one qualifying child wasn't eligible for the EIC. The '93 Act law expands the definition of eligible individual to include a low-income worker who doesn't have a qualifying child for the tax year. (Code Sec. 32(c)(1)(A)(ii) as amended by '93 Act § 13131(b)) To qualify for the EIC, however, the individual must meet all of the following requirements:

. . . The individual's principal place of abode for more than half of the taxable year must be in the United States. (Code Sec. 32(c)(1)(A)(ii)(I))

> ***observation:*** The term "United States" is not defined. Presumably, the Code Sec. 7701(a)(9) definition of "United States" (i.e., the 50 States and the District of Columbia) would apply.

. . . The individual (or the individual's spouse, if married) must be 25 years of age or older (but not 65 years of age or older) before the end of the tax year. (Code Sec. 32(c)(1)(A)(ii)(II))

. . . The individual (or the individual's spouse, if married) must not qualify as a dependent on another taxpayer's return. (Code Sec. 32(c)(1)(A)(ii)(III))

A low-income worker meeting the above requirements is entitled to the EIC even though the worker has children who aren't qualifying children to that low-income worker. (H Rept p. 609)

> ***illustration:*** X is a 25-year old unmarried individual with two children (a two-year old, and a three-year old) both of whom are being cared for, and supported by, Y—X's mother. For '94, X has earned income and adjusted earned income (AGI) of $6,000 and otherwise meets all of the above requirements for an eligible individual with no qualifying children. For '94, Y, X's mother, has earned income (and AGI) of $11,500 and is an eligible individual with two or more qualifying children.
>
> The '94 EIC for X is $229.50 computed as follows:

(1) Base amount of $4,000 × 7.65% rate	$306.00
(2) Less: Phaseout amounts ($6,000 − $5,000 = $1,000; 7.65% × $1,000)	$76.50
(3) '94 EIC for X	$229.50

> The '94 EIC for Y is $2,439.10 computed as follows:

(1) Base amount of $8,425 × 30%	$2,527.50
(2) Less: Phaseout amount ($11,500 − $11,000 = $500; 17.68% × $500)	($88.40)
(3) '94 EIC for Y	$2,439.10

> ***observation:*** As under pre-'93 Act law, IRS tables for '94 (when issued) will compute the above EIC amounts to the nearest whole dollar. (See FTC 2d/FIN ¶ A-4206; TG ¶ 1241; USTR ¶ 324.06)

The EIC for an eligible individual with no qualifying children isn't available on an

FTC 2d References are to the Federal Tax Coordinator 2d
FIN References are to RIA's Analysis of Federal Taxes: Income
TG References are to the Tax Guide
USTR References are to the United States Tax Reporter

advance payment basis during the taxable year from the employer. (Code Sec. 3507(c)(2)(B) as amended by '93 Act § 13131(d)(5))

☐ **Effective:** Taxable years beginning after '93. (§ 13131(e))
For official explanation see Committee Reports ¶ 3011.

¶ 121. New involuntary conversion relief for principal residences damaged by a presidentially declared disasters

A property owner who receives insurance or other compensation for property involuntary converted ordinarily has taxable gain if the compensation received exceeds the adjusted basis of the converted property. But the owner may defer the tax on all or part of his involuntarily conversion gain by electing to replace the property within a certain period with property similar or related in service or use to the converted property. The taxpayer, upon making the election, recognizes gain only to the extent that the amount realized upon such conversion exceeds the cost of the replacement property. The replacement period begins with the date of the disposition of the converted property (or the earliest date of the threat or imminence of requisition or condemnation of the converted property, whichever is earlier) and generally ends two years after the close of the first taxable year in which any part of the gain upon conversion is realized. (FTC 2d/FIN ¶ I-3000 *et seq.;* TG ¶ 4232 *et seq.;* USTR ¶ 10,334 *et seq.)*

Under the '93 Act, if the taxpayer's principal residence, or any of its contents, is compulsorily or involuntarily converted because of a "Presidentially declared disaster" (defined below), any gain, resulting from the receipt of insurance proceeds for personal property that was part of the contents of the residence and was not scheduled property for insurance purposes, will not be recognized. Other insurance proceeds for the residence or its contents is treated as a common fund, i.e., the proceeds are treated as if received for a single item of property, and property which is similar or related in service or use to the converted residence (or its contents) is treated as property similar or related in service or use to the single item of property for purpose of the nonrecognition of gain rules involving involuntary conversions. (Code Sec. 1033(h)(1)(A) as amended by '93 Act § 13431(a)) Thus, nonrecognition of gain will result where the common pool of funds is used to purchase property similar to the converted residence or its contents.

> ***observation:*** Scheduled property is specifically insured property listed in the insurer's schedule.

The replacement period for the property involuntarily converted as a result of the presidentially declared disaster is extended to four years after the close of the first taxable year in which any part of the gain upon conversion is realized. (Code Sec. 1033(h)(1)(B) as added by '93 Act § 13431(a))

For these nonrecognition of gain rules to apply the taxpayer's residence must be located in a "presidentially declared disaster" area. To qualify as such an area, the President must have determined that the area warranted assistance by the federal government under the Disaster Relief and Emergency Assistance Act. (Code Sec. 1033(h)(2) as amended by '93 Act § 13431(a))

For purposes of the special rules allowing nonrecognition of gain for principal residences damaged by presidentially declared disasters, the taxpayer's principal residence need not be owned by him. (Code Sec. 1033(h)(3) as amended by '93 Act § 13431(a)) Renters would qualify for relief to the extent the rented residence would be their principal residence if they owned it. (Conf Rept p. 733)

The relief provisions of Code Sec. 1033(h) will benefit taxpayers in a number of areas throughout the country. Some of the biggest disasters have been in: Alameda County, California, (fire, Oct. 26-29, '91); counties in southern Florida, (hurricane Andrew, Aug. 23-25, '92; counties in Louisiana (hurricane Andrew, Aug. 25-30, '92); New York City and counties in southern New York (coastal storm, Dec. 10-14, '92); and some areas of Illinois, Iowa, Minnesota, Missouri, North Dakota, Wisconsin and Kansas (severe storms and flooding, summer of '93). For a complete list of disaster areas, see FTC 2d/FIN ¶ M-2001.

Casualties of personal use property are reported on Form 4684, Section A. The gains and losses from the different properties damaged by one casualty are netted together to determine if the taxpayer has a gain or loss from the casualty (FTC 2d/FIN ¶ M-1905; TG ¶ 6626)

> ***observation:*** IRS has informed RIA that Form 4684 is to be used to compute the net gain on the personal property where taxpayer's residence is involuntarily converted in presidentially declared disaster area.
>
> ***observation:*** Taxpayers who reported gain upon the receipt of insurance proceeds for unscheduled personal property should file refund claims for calendar years '91 thru '92.

☐ **Effective:** Applies to property compulsorily or involuntarily converted by presidentially declared disasters determined on or after Sept. 1, '91, and to taxable years ending on or after this date. (§ 13431(b))

For official explanation see Committee Reports ¶ 3077.

¶ 122. Presidential Election Campaign Fund checkoff increased to $3

Every individual (other than a nonresident alien) whose income tax liability for the tax year is $1 or more may designate that $1 be paid over to the Presidential Election Campaign Fund (the "Fund"). On joint returns with a tax liability of $2 or more, each spouse may designate that $1 be paid to the Fund. (FTC 2d/FIN ¶s S-5704, S-5705; TG ¶ 1462; USTR ¶ 60,964) The Fund is used to finance certain Presidential campaign expenses and convention costs. (S Rept p. 173)

The '93 Act increases the amount of the checkoff from $1 to $3 on returns with a tax liability of $3 or more. On joint returns with a tax liability of $6 or more, each spouse may designate that $3 be paid to the Fund. (Code Sec. 6096(a) as amended by '93 Act § 13441(a)) This increase will help to make up a projected shortfall in the Fund for the '96 election year. (S Rept p. 173)

☐ **Effective:** Tax returns required to be filed after Dec. 31, '93. (§ 13441(b))

For official explanation see Committee Reports ¶ 3078.

¶ 123. 6.2% FUTA tax rate is extended through calendar year '98; 6.0% FUTA tax rate will be imposed after '98

The Federal Unemployment Tax Act (FUTA) imposes a tax on employers based on wages they pay their employees for services that are considered covered employment. (FTC 2d/FIN ¶ H-4780; TG ¶ 3579.120; USTR ¶ 35,014.07) The FUTA tax is imposed at a fixed rate on a fixed dollar amount of wages paid to each employee. (FTC 2d/FIN ¶ H-4786; TG ¶ 3579.180; USTR ¶ 35,014.07)

Under pre-'93 Act law, the FUTA tax rate was 6.2% through calendar year '96, and 6.0% for calendar years after '96. (FTC 2d/FIN ¶ H-4786.1; TG ¶ 3579.181; USTR ¶ 35,014.07)

The '93 Act extends the imposition of the 6.2% FUTA tax rate through calendar year '98. (Code Sec. 3301(1) as amended by '93 Act § 13751(1)) The 6.0% FUTA tax rate will be imposed with respect to calendar years after '98. (Code Sec. 3301(2) as amended by '93 Act § 13751(2))

☐ **Effective:** Aug. 10, '93.

¶ 124. Report on advance determination of value of charitable gifts

IRS must report to the House Ways and Means Committee and the Senate Finance Committee, no later than one year after Aug. 10, '93, on developing a procedure for taxpayers to seek an agreement with IRS about the value of tangible personal property before donating that property to a qualified charity. The agreement would be binding if the time limits for donation and any other conditions in the agreement are satisfied.

The report will address setting threshold amounts of claimed value in order for taxpayers to seek an agreement, payment of fees by taxpayers, limiting use of the procedure to items of significant artistic or cultural value, and recommendations for legislative action needed to implement the procedure. (Conf Rept p. 562)

> ***observation:*** This report was mandated by § 14171(e) of the House-passed bill. Although the provision wasn't included in the '93 Act, the conference report states that IRS is still expected to submit the report.

¶ 200. Deductions

¶ 201. Moving expense deduction narrowed but deduction may be taken above-the-line

Distance requirement for moving expense deduction increased. An employee or self-employed person who moves his residence because of a new job or business can deduct certain moving and related expenses. (See FTC 2d/FIN ¶ L-3600 *et seq.;* TG ¶ 6325 *et seq.;* USTR ¶ 2174 *et seq.*) Under pre-'93 Act law, the distance from the old residence to the new place of work had to be at least 35 miles more than to the old place of work. (FTC 2d/FIN ¶ L-3616; TG ¶ 6327; USTR ¶ 2174.01)

The '93 Act increases the distance requirement from 35 to 50 miles. Thus, to qualify for the moving expense deduction, the distance from the old residence to the new place of work must be at least 50 miles more than to the old place of work. (Code Sec. 217(c)(1) as amended by '93 Act § 13213(b))

Definition of deductible moving expenses narrowed. Under pre-'93 Act law, deductible moving expenses included:

. . . costs of moving household goods and personal effects from the old to the new residence;

. . . traveling expenses (including meals and lodging) while moving;

. . . traveling expenses (including meals and lodging) while on pre-move househunting trips;

. . . costs of meals and lodging while occupying temporary quarters for up to 30 days (90 days in the case of foreign moves) in the general location of the new job; and

. . . certain expenses related to both the sale of or settlement of a lease on the old residence and purchase of or acquisition of a lease on a new residence in the general location of the new job ("qualified residence sale, purchase, or lease expenses"). (FTC 2d/FIN ¶ L-3623 *et seq.;* TG ¶ 6330 *et seq.;* USTR ¶ 2174)

The '93 Act narrows the definition of deductible moving expenses to include only the costs of (1) moving household goods and personal effects from the old residence to the new residence and (2) traveling (including lodging while en route) from the old to the new residence. Moving expenses do not include any expenses for meals. (Code Sec. 217(b)(1) as amended by '93 Act § 13213(a)(1))

Thus, the moving expense deduction is denied for the following items that were deductible under pre-'93 Act law:

. . . the cost of meals while moving from the old to the new residence;

. . . traveling expenses (including meals and lodging) while on pre-move househunting trips;

. . . the cost of meals and lodging while occupying temporary quarters in the location of the new job; and

. . . qualified residence sale, purchase, or lease expenses. (Conf Rept p. 592)

FTC 2d References are to the Federal Tax Coordinator 2d
FIN References are to RIA's Analysis of Federal Taxes: Income
TG References are to the Tax Guide
USTR References are to the United States Tax Reporter

observation: Although closing costs will no longer be a deductible moving expense, such costs will reduce any taxable gain on the sale of an old residence and increase the basis of a newly purchased residence.

Moving expense deduction allowed in computing adjusted gross income. Under pre-'93 Act law, the moving expense deduction was an itemized deduction. (FTC 2d/FIN 2d ¶ A-2701; TG ¶ 1072; USTR ¶ 2174)

The Act provides that moving expenses are deductible in computing adjusted gross income to the extent not paid or reimbursed by the employer. (Code Sec. 62(a)(15) as amended by '93 Act § 13213(c)(1)) Allowing an above-the-line deduction treats employees whose expenses are not paid for by their employer in a comparable manner to employees whose moving expenses are paid for by their employer (see below). (Conf Rept p. 592)

observation: Deducting moving expenses above-the-line means that the deduction can be claimed regardless of whether the taxpayer itemizes deductions. Also, the above-the-line deduction won't be subject to the reduction in itemized deductions that applies to certain high-income taxpayers. (See FTC 2d/FIN 2d ¶ A-2704 *et seq.;* TG ¶ 1074; USTR ¶ 684 *et seq.*) And by reducing adjusted gross income, the moving expense deduction will make it easier to claim other deductions that depend in part on adjusted gross income, such as the deductions for medical expenses and casualty losses, miscellaneous itemized deductions, and the deduction for contributions to an IRA.

Exclusion of employer-paid moving expenses. Under pre-'93 Act law, moving expenses that an employer paid or reimbursed, directly or indirectly, were included in the employee's gross income as compensation for services. (FTC 2d/FIN 2d ¶ L-3637; TG ¶ 3165; USTR ¶ 824)

The Act provides an exclusion from gross income for amounts received (directly or indirectly) by the taxpayer from an employer as a payment of or reimbursement for moving expenses that would have been deductible had the taxpayer paid them directly. But the expenses are not excludable if the taxpayer actually deducted the expenses in a prior year. (Code Sec. 132(a)(6) as amended by '93 Act § 13213(d)(1); Code Sec. 132(g) as amended by '93 Act § 13213(d)(2)) Since the reimbursed expenses are excluded from gross income under Code Sec. 132, they are also excluded from wages for employment tax purposes under Code Sec. 3121(a)(20). (Conf Rept p. 592)

Congress intends that employers treat moving expenses as excludable unless they have actual knowledge that an employee deducted the expenses in a prior year. The employer has no obligation to determine whether the individual deducted the expenses. (Conf Rept p. 592)

Congress intends that rules similar to the accountable plan rules of Code Sec. 62(c) will apply to reimbursed expenses. (Conf Rept p. 592)

observation: An "accountable plan" is a reimbursement or other expense allowance arrangement that (1) provides advances, allowances, or reimbursements only for deductible business expenses, (2) requires the employee to substantiate the expenses, and (3) requires the employee to return to the employer any amounts in excess of the substantiated expenses. Payments under an accountable plan don't have to be reported on the employee's Form W-2 or included in income by the employee. (See FTC 2d/FIN 2d ¶ A-2606; TG ¶ 1096; USTR ¶ 624.02)

recommendation: These changes to the moving expense deduction are effective for expenses incurred after Dec. 31, '93 (see below). Taxpayers who are planning a job-related move around year-end should consider whether it would be more advantageous to make the move in '93 or '94.

For example, if the move will qualify for deductions under the old 35-mile distance requirement but not under the new 50-mile requirement, the move should probably be made in '93.

Also, job-related moves should be accelerated into '93 in order to qualify for the broader range of deductions under pre-'93 Act law. As noted above, the cost of meals while moving from the old to the new residence, traveling expenses (including meals and lodging) while on pre-move househunting trips, the cost of meals and lodging while occupying temporary quarters in the location of the new job, and qualified residence sale, purchase, or lease expenses are all deductible in '93 but not in '94.

On the other hand, if you plan a job-related move but won't be able to benefit from the moving expense deduction because your standard deduction exceeds your itemized deductions, you will be better off making the move in '94, when the deduction will be taken above-the-line.

The same may be true if you will lose the benefit of *part* of your moving expense deduction if taken in '93. Say that a married couple has $4,500 of itemized deductions (other than moving expenses) for '93. Their '93 standard deduction is $6,200. They are planning a move from which they expect $2,000 of deductible expenses. They may be better off postponing the move until '94. That way, they can take the $6,200 standard deduction for '93 and deduct the $2,000 of moving expenses above-the-line in '94. But this strategy may be undercut by the fact that fewer types of moving expenses will be deductible in '94.

☐ **Effective:** Expenses incurred after Dec. 31, '93, except that the exclusion of employer reimbursements applies to reimbursements or other payments in respect of expenses incurred after Dec. 31, '93. (§ 13213(e))

observation: Note that the Act refers to "expenses incurred" after Dec. 31, '93. Thus, for example, expenses for pre-move househunting trips incurred in '93 may be deductible even if the actual move doesn't take place until '94.

For official explanation see Committee Reports ¶ 3040.

¶ 202. Health insurance premium deduction for self-employeds reinstated retroactively and extended through '93

Under pre-'93 Act law, for tax years that began before July 1, '92, a self-employed individual who was not a participant in a subsidized health plan maintained by an employer (and wasn't covered under a spouse's employer's plan), could have deducted 25% of the amount paid for medical care insurance for the individual, his spouse, and his dependents. No deduction was allowed for self-employed individuals to the extent that the deduction exceeded the individual's "earned income" (as defined in Code Sec. 401(c)). (FTC 2d/FIN ¶ L-3510; TG ¶ 6178; USTR ¶ 1624.403) For tax years beginning in '92, only amounts paid for insurance coverage before July 1, '92, counted in determining the amount deductible by the self-employed individual, and a formula was provided to determine the earned income limitation applicable for the first half of '92. (FTC 2d/FIN ¶ L-3511; TG ¶ 6178; USTR ¶ 1624.403)

FTC 2d References are to the Federal Tax Coordinator 2d
FIN References are to RIA's Analysis of Federal Taxes: Income
TG References are to the Tax Guide
USTR References are to the United States Tax Reporter

The '93 Act reinstates and extends the 25% medical care insurance premium deduction for self-employed individuals to tax years beginning before Jan. 1, '94, (Code Sec. 162(l)(6) as amended by '93 Act § 13174(a)(1)) and repeals (1) the denial of the deduction for amounts paid for insurance coverage after June 30, '92, and (2) the rule excluding earned income allocated to the second half of '92 from being taken into account for purposes of the earned income limitation on the deduction. (§ 13174(a)(2))) Thus, the Act extends the 25% self-employed individuals' health insurance deduction retroactively to July 1, '92. (H Rept p. 632)

> ***recommendation:*** Self-employed individuals who paid premiums for health insurance for himself, his spouse, and dependents after June 30, '92 and before '93, should file amended returns for '92 to claim a deduction for 25% of the amount paid in that period.

☐ **Effective:** Tax years ending after June 30, '92. (§ 13174(a)(3))

Month-by-month determination of whether a self-employed individual is eligible to participate in an employer's subsidized health plan. The 25% deduction for premiums for health insurance for a self-employed individual, his spouse, and dependents does not apply if the individual is eligible to participate in any subsidized health plan maintained by the individual's employer or his spouse's employer. Under pre-'93 Act law, if the self-employed individual was eligible for participation in an employer's subsidized health plan at all during the year, the deduction wasn't preserved for premiums paid for periods when there was no eligibility for employer-subsidized health benefits. (FTC 2d/FIN ¶ L-3510; TG ¶ 6178)

> ***observation:*** Thus, if the self-employed individual or his spouse were eligible to participate in an employer's subsidized health plan even for a short time during the year, this would have precluded taking the 25% deduction for any amounts paid for health insurance premiums during the year.

Under the '93 Act, the determination of whether a self-employed individual or his spouse is eligible for an employer's subsidized health plan is made for each calendar month. ('93 Act § 13174(b)(1))

> ***observation:*** Thus, if a self-employed individual or his spouse is eligible for an employer's subsidized health plan for one calendar month, the deduction is still available for premiums paid during the other months during the year.

☐ **Effective:** Taxable years beginning after '92. (§ 13174(b)(2))

For official explanation see Committee Reports ¶ 3027.

¶ 203. Limitation on itemized deductions made permanent

Itemized deductions are limited for individuals with adjusted gross income over an inflation-adjusted threshold. For '93, the threshold is $108,450 ($54,225 for a married person filing separately). For those individuals, itemized deductions (other than deductions for medical expenses, investment interest, nonbusiness casualty and theft losses, and gambling losses) are reduced by the lesser of (1) 3% of the excess over the threshold amount or (2) 80% of the amount of otherwise allowable itemized deductions. (See FTC 2d/FIN ¶ A-2704 *et seq.;* TG ¶ 1074; USTR ¶ 684.01)

Under pre-'93 Act law, the limitation on itemized deductions didn't apply to tax years beginning after '95. (FTC 2d/FIN ¶ A-2704; TG ¶ 1074; USTR ¶ 684.02) The '93 Act makes the limitation permanent. (Code Sec. 68 as amended by '93 Act § 13204)

☐ **Effective:** Aug. 10, '93.

For official explanation see Committee Reports ¶ 3031.

¶ 204. Phaseout of personal exemptions made permanent

The exemption amount for personal and dependent exemptions is phased out for certain high-income individuals. For '93, the phaseout begins at $162,700 of adjusted gross income (AGI) for joint return filers and surviving spouses, $135,600 for heads of household, $108,450 for single individuals, and $81,350 for married individuals filing separate returns. The personal exemption amount is reduced by 2% for each $2,500 (or fraction of that amount) by which the taxpayer's AGI exceeds the threshold amount. For married individuals filing separate returns, personal exemptions are reduced by 2% for each $1,250 (or fraction thereof) by which the taxpayer's AGI exceeds the threshold amount. (See FTC 2d/FIN ¶ A-3502; TG ¶ 1004; USTR ¶ 1514)

Under pre-'93 Act law, the phaseout didn't apply to tax years beginning after '96. (FTC 2d/FIN ¶ A-3502; TG ¶ 1004; USTR ¶ 1514) The '93 Act makes the phaseout of personal exemptions permanent. (Code Sec. 151(d)(3) as amended by '93 Act § 13205)

☐ **Effective:** Aug. 10, '93.

For official explanation see Committee Reports ¶ 3032.

FTC 2d References are to the Federal Tax Coordinator 2d
FIN References are to RIA's Analysis of Federal Taxes: Income
TG References are to the Tax Guide
USTR References are to the United States Tax Reporter

¶ 300. Business Provisions

¶ 301. Top corporate tax rate retroactively increased from 34% to 35%

Under the pre-'93 Act rate structure, a corporation is taxed at a 15% rate on the first $50,000 of taxable income, a 25% rate on taxable income that exceeds $50,000 but doesn't exceed $75,000, and a 34% rate on all taxable income that exceeds $75,000. (FTC 2d/FIN ¶ D-1003; TG ¶ 504; USTR ¶ 114.01) In addition, under pre-'93 Act law, a corporation that has taxable income in excess of $100,000 must increase its tax by the lesser of 5% of the excess or $11,750. The result was that corporations with income over $335,000 paid a flat 34% rate. (FTC 2d/FIN ¶ D-1004; TG ¶ 504; USTR ¶ 114.01)

The '93 Act leaves the 15% and 25% brackets unchanged, limits the 34% rate to taxable income that exceeds $75,000 but doesn't exceed $10,000,000 (Code Sec. 11(b)(1)(C) as amended by '93 Act § 13221(a)(2)) and adds a new 35% rate that applies to taxable income over $10,000,000. (Code Sec. 11(b)(1)(D))

The '93 Act leaves the 5%/$11,750 increase on taxable income over $100,000 unchanged, but adds a second increase for corporations with taxable income in excess of $15,000,000. The second increase is equal to the lesser of 3% of the taxable income in excess of $15,000,000 or $100,000. (Code Sec. 11(b)(1)) The second increase eliminates the benefit of the 34% rate in a manner similar to the way the benefit of the 15% and 25% tax rates is eliminated by the 5%/$11,750 increase. (H Rept p. 655)

Thus, after the '93 Act, corporations are subject to the following rates (the 5%/$11,750 and 3%/$100,000 increases are built into the Table):

Taxable income over	But not over	The tax is	Of the amount over
-0-	$50,000	15%	-0-
$50,000	75,000	$7,500 + 25%	$50,000
75,000	100,000	13,750 + 34%	75,000
100,000	335,000	22,250 + 39%	100,000
335,000	10,000,000	113,900 + 34%	335,000
10,000,000	15,000,000	3,400,000 + 35%	10,000,000
15,000,000	18,333,333	5,150,000 + 38%	15,000,000
18,333,333	——	6,416,667 + 35%	18,333,333

illustration: Here is a comparison of the corporate tax paid at various income levels before and after the '93 Act.:

Taxable income	Pre-'93 Act tax	'93 Act tax	Additional tax under '93 Act
$25,000	$3,750	$3,750	0
$50,000	$7,500	$7,500	0
$75,000	$13,750	$13,750	0
$100,000	$22,250	$22,250	0
$1,000,000	$340,000	$340,000	0
$5,000,000	$1,700,000	$1,700,000	0

FTC 2d References are to the Federal Tax Coordinator 2d
FIN References are to RIA's Analysis of Federal Taxes: Income
TG References are to the Tax Guide
USTR References are to the United States Tax Reporter

$10,000,000	$3,400,000	$3,400,000	0
$15,000,000	$5,100,000	$5,150,000	$50,000
$18,333,333	$6,233,333	$6,416,667	$183,334
$20,000,000	$6,800,000	$7,000,000	$200,000

The '93 Act also raises the tax rate on qualified personal service corporations from a flat 34% (FTC 2d/FIN ¶ D-1005; TG ¶ 504; USTR ¶ 114.02) to 35%. (Code Sec. 11(b)(2) as amended by '93 Act § 13221(b))

Alternative tax on net capital gains. Under pre-'93 Act law, a corporation that had a net capital gain and would ordinarily be subject to a tax rate over 34% (without regard to the 5%/$11,750 increase) was instead subject to an alternative tax equal to the regular tax on its taxable income minus its net capital gain plus a 34% tax on the net capital gain, if the alternative tax would result in a lower tax. Since corporations were not subject to a tax over 34% under pre-$93 Act law and the alternative tax did not result in a lower tax than the regular tax, the alternative tax did not apply. (FTC 2d/FIN ¶ I-6017; TG ¶ 4413)

The '93 Act changes the alternative tax so that a corporation that has a net capital gain and would be ordinarily be subject to a tax rate over 35% (without regard to the 3%/$100,000 increase) is subject to an alternative tax rate equal to the regular tax on its taxable income minus its net capital gain plus a 35% tax on the net capital gain, if the alternative tax rate would result in a lower tax. (Code Sec. 1201(a) as amended by '93 Act § 13221(c)(2))

> ***observation:*** Before the '93 Act, Code Sec. 1201 did not apply where the tax rate was higher than 34% because of the 5%/$11,750 increase. Because of changes to Code Sec. 11(b)(1), the reference is now to the 3%/$100,000 increase. Technically, the alternative tax should now apply where the tax rate is higher than 35% because of the 5%/$11,750 increase. However, this seems to be a technical error and that Congress did not intend to change the pre-'93 Act inapplicability of the alternative tax.

Basis adjustment for undistributed capital gains of regulated investment companies. The $93 Act decreases the basis adjustment for undistributed capital gains of regulated investment companies (FTC 2d/FIN ¶ E-6155; TG ¶ 7847; USTR ¶ 8524.02) from 66% to 65%. (Code Sec. 852(b)(3)(D)(iii) as amended by '93 Act § 13221(c)(1))

> ***observation:*** Under pre-'93 Act law, where a regulated investment company elects to pass through an undistributed capital gain to its shareholders, the shareholders are required to include the undistributed capital gain in income and the regulated investment company is required to pay tax on the undistributed capital gain. The shareholders receive a credit or refund for their proportionate shares of the tax paid by the regulated investment company and were allowed an increase in their bases in their stock equal to 66% (100% – the 34% tax imposed on the regulated investment company for which the shareholders received a credit) of the undistributed capital gain. The '93 Act reduction in the basis increase from 66% to 65% reflects the increase in the tax rate from 34% to 35%.

Withholding rate on gain realized on dispositions of U.S real property interests by domestic partnerships, trusts and estates. The '93 Act increases the withholding rate on the gain attributable to foreign persons, realized on dispositions of U.S real prop-

FTC 2d References are to the Federal Tax Coordinator 2d
FIN References are to RIA's Analysis of Federal Taxes: Income
TG References are to the Tax Guide
USTR References are to the United States Tax Reporter

erty interests by domestic partnerships, trusts and estates (FTC 2d/FIN ¶ O-11761; TG ¶ 8394; USTR ¶ 14,454), to 35%. (Code Sec. 1445(e)(1) as amended by '93 Act § 13221(c)(3)) However, the alternative 28% withholding rate provided for under Code Sec. 1445(e)(1) remains unchanged.

observation: The withholding rate continues to be imposed at the highest corporate tax rate in order to prevent foreign partners or beneficiaries from avoiding tax on partnership or trust income taxable in the U.S.

Withholding rate on gain realized by foreign corporations on distributions of U.S real property interests. The '93 Act increases the withholding rate on the gain realized on distributions of U.S real property interests by foreign corporations (FTC 2d/FIN ¶ O-11761; TG ¶ 8394; USTR ¶ 14,454) to 35%. (Code Sec. 1445(e)(2))

observation: The withholding rate continues to be imposed at the highest corporate tax rate in order to prevent foreign corporations from avoiding tax on gain realized on the distribution.

Corporate-individual rate differential and choice of entity.

observation: In contrast to the rate structure that existed under pre-'93 Act law, the top individual tax rates (see ¶ 101) are higher than the top corporate tax rates. Therefore, taxpayers who have chosen an S corporation, partnership, limited liability company or sole proprietorship form in which to do business because the income from the business was taxed at a lower rate if passed through to the owners than if subjected to corporate-level tax, should reconsider using a C corporation. However, in most cases the differential between individual and corporate tax rates won't offset the double tax incurred when dividends are paid by a C corporation or when the corporation is liquidated or its stock is redeemed. Among the factors to be considered in this regard are the extent to which profits will be reinvested in the business, the amount of earnings from the business which the owners need to have distributed to them or paid to them as compensation, and the owners' plans regarding eventual sale or liquidation of the business. (Of course, there are many other factors to consider in choosing the form of business entity as well, including differences in the treatment of certain fringe benefits between C corporations and other entities, the protection against unlimited liability afforded by the corporate form and the restrictions on an S corporation's number of shareholders and classes of stock.)

illustration: Individual T is the sole owner of Z Corp, an S corporation which has never been a C corporation. T is in the 39.6% marginal tax rate bracket, and, before the '93 Act, was in the 31% bracket. Z Corp's taxable income is a constant $350,000 each year. Under pre-'93 Act law, the federal tax on Z Corp's annual earnings was $108,500, since it was passed through to T and taxed at T's marginal rate of 31%. If Z Corp had been a C corporation, the corporate-level tax on its earnings would have been $119,000. So, $10,500 of federal tax was saved each year by Z Corp's having made an S election. After the '93 Act, while the tax on Z Corp's earnings if it becomes a C corporation remains $119,000, if its income as an S corporation continues to be passed through to T the tax will increase to $138,600, or $19,600 more than the corporate-level tax. However, whether Z Corp should convert from S corporation to C corporation status requires further analysis. For example, if all of Z Corp's after-tax earnings must be distributed to T, $139,524 ($350,000 − $119,000 − ($231,000 × 39.6%)) would be left after both the corporate-level and shareholder-level taxes if Z Corp were a C corporation, while $211,400 ($350,000 − $138,600) would be left if Z Corp were an S corporation. On the other hand, if Z Corp's earnings are invested in its business, $231,000 ($350,000 – $119,000) would be available for investment if Z Corp were a C corporation, while only $211,400 ($350,000 – $138,600) would be available if Z Corp were an S corporation.

Assume that Z Corp's after-tax earnings are invested in its business, that Z Corp remains an S corporation, and that it is liquidated in ten years. Assume that its fair market value at that time is $5 million, that it recognizes long-term capital gain on liquidation of $1.5 million (and no other income or expense items in the year of liquidation), that T's basis in the stock of Z Corp is $1 million, and that the tax law at that time is the same as current law. A tax of $1,120,000 ($4 million × 28%) is incurred on Z Corp's liquidation, leaving T with $3,880,000. (The corporate-level gain is passed through to T and taxed to T as long-term capital gain. That gain increases T's stock basis to $2.5 million. Thus, the total gain recognized on the liquidation is $4 million ($1.5 million + $2.5 million ($5 million – $2.5 million), all of which is taxed to T, and none of which is taxed to Z Corp.)

Now, assume that Z Corp converts to C corporation status and is liquidated after ten years. $19,600 more funds are available for investment in the business each year than if Z Corp had remained an S corporation. Assume, therefore, that Z Corp's fair market value in ten years is $5,300,000, or $300,000 more than if Z Corp had remained an S corporation, and that it recognizes long-term capital gain on liquidation of $1.7 million (rather than $1.5 million). Combined corporate-level and shareholder-level taxes of $1,620,160 are incurred on Z Corp's liquidation, computed as follows: Z Corp pays a tax of $578,000 ($1.7 million × 34%). This reduces T's liquidating distribution to $4,722,000 ($5,300,000 – $578,000). T's gain is therefore $3,722,000 ($4,722,000 – $1,000,000), resulting in a tax, at the 28% rate on long-term capital gains, of $1,042,160. Thus, $3,679,840 worth of cash and property remains for T after taxes if Z Corp becomes a C corporation. This is $200,160 less than the $3,880,000 which would have been left if Z Corp had stayed an S corporation, even though as a C corporation $300,000 of additional value has been added to Z Corp because its reinvested earnings have been taxed at a lower rate.

☐ **Effective:** For tax years beginning after Dec. 31, '92. However, the increases in the withholding rate on foreign persons is effective as of Aug. 10, '93. (§ 13221(d))

A fiscal year corporation must use a "blended rate" for its tax year that includes Jan 1, '93. This means that the tax is determined as a weighted average of the tax resulting from applying the '92 and the '93 rates, weighted by the number of days of the fiscal year in '92 and '93. (§ 13001(c); H Rept p. 655)

Penalties for underpayments of estimated tax are waived for underpayments of '93 taxes due to changes in tax rates, (see ¶ 301A). (H Rept p. 655)

Where a corporation filed an application for an extension of the time for filing corporate income tax for a tax year, the requirement that the taxpayer must remit the full amount of the tax, properly estimated (see FTC 2d/FIN ¶ S-5011; TG ¶ 2463; USTR ¶ 60,814.02) is determined on the basis of the law in effect on the date the application for the extension is filed. (Conf Rept p. 597)

FTC 2d References are to the Federal Tax Coordinator 2d
FIN References are to RIA's Analysis of Federal Taxes: Income
TG References are to the Tax Guide
USTR References are to the United States Tax Reporter

observation: This means that if a corporation's fiscal year that ended in '93 and filed an application for an extension before Aug. 10, '93, the corporation is not required to remit tax on the basis of the '93 Act rates.

For official explanation see Committee Reports ¶ 3043.

¶ 301A. Estimated tax penalties arising from '93 Act tax increases on corporations are waived

Corporations must pay a penalty for underpayment of estimated tax if they fail to pay estimated taxes equal to their "required annual payment." The payment of estimated tax is made in quarterly installments, each of which generally will be 25% of the "required annual payment." The failure to pay the installment, or an insufficient payment, will result in a penalty. However, no penalty is imposed if certain exceptions apply or a waiver is granted by IRS. (FTC 2d/FIN ¶ S-5400 *et seq.;* TG ¶ 2485 *et seq.*; USTR ¶ 66,554)

Under the '93 Act, however, no estimated tax penalty on corporations will be imposed for any period beginning before Mar. 16, '94 to the extent any underpayment is created or increased by any '93 Act provision. (§ 13001(d))

illustration: A calendar year corporation reports taxable income for '93 of $12,000,000, on which it pays a tax of $4,100,000. In Oct. '93 the corporation acquired the assets of a business, including intangible assets which the corporation could have amortized over periods significantly shorter than 15 years under pre-'93 Act law. However, the acquisition was subject to the '93 Act's 15-year amortization rules for certain intangibles (see ¶ 401). As a result, the corporation's '93 taxable income was $50,000 more than it would have been under pre'93 Act law. the corporation's '93 tax liability was not affected by any other provisions of the '93 Act, except the increase in the top marginal rate of tax on corporations (see ¶ 301). The corporation's '93 estimated tax payments through its fourth installment, due Dec. 15, '93, was $3,942,000. Because 97% of its '93 tax liability, its "required annual payment," is $3,977,000, the corporation has an estimated tax underpayment of $35,000 ($3,977,000 − $3,942,000). However, under the '93 Act rule discussed above, no estimated tax penalty will be imposed on the corporation on account of this underpayment. That's because he underpayment was created entirely by provisions of the '93 Act. But for (1) the increase in the top marginal rate and (2) the 15-year amortization of certain intangibles rules, the corporation's required annual payment wold have been $3,941,110 (97% of $4,063,000, which is what the corporation's tax liability wold have been under pre-'93 Act law ($11,950,000 × 34%)), and there would have been no underpayment of estimated tax.

¶ 302. Accumulated earnings tax rate increased to 39.6%

An annual penalty tax is imposed on certain corporations that accumulate earnings and profits to avoid income tax to shareholders. The tax is imposed on the corporation's "accumulated taxable income" for the year. (See FTC 2d/FIN ¶ D-2600 *et seq.;* TG ¶ 2130 *et seq.;* USTR ¶ 5314 *et seq.)*

Under pre-'93 Act law, the accumulated earnings tax was 28% of accumulated taxable income. (FTC 2d/FIN ¶ D-2601; TG ¶ 2162; USTR ¶ 5354) The '93 Act increases the tax rate to 39.6%. (Code Sec. 531 as amended by '93 Act §§ 13201(b)(1) and 13202(b))

observation: The new accumulated earnings tax rate conforms to the

39.6% maximum tax rate on individuals under the '93 Act, see ¶ 101. It is designed to eliminate the incentive for individuals to leave money in their corporations, since the retained income will be taxed at the highest individual rate.

observation: The accumulated earnings tax rate has traditionally been set at the highest individual tax rate. However, the '90 Act introduced the 31% bracket without a corresponding change to the accumulated earnings tax. The '93 Act restores the historical norm.

□ **Effective:** Tax years beginning after Dec. 31, '92. (§§ 13201(c), 13202(c)) Fiscal-year corporations do not make a "straddle computation" on account of the change in tax rate. (§ 13001(c))

For official explanation see Committee Reports ¶s 3028 and 3029.

¶ 303. Personal holding company tax rate increased to 39.6%

Under pre-'93 Act law, personal holding companies were subject to a flat 28% tax on undistributed personal holding company income, in addition to the regular corporate tax. (FTC 2d/FIN ¶ D-3202; TG ¶ 2171; 5409) The '93 Act increases the personal holding company tax rate to 39.6%. (Code Sec. 541 as amended by '93 Act §§ 13201(b)(2) and 13202(b))

observation: The new personal holding company tax rate conforms to the 39.6% maximum tax rate on individuals under the '93 Act, see ¶ 101. The personal holding company tax is designed to prevent individuals from escaping higher individual rates by retaining their income in a "corporate pocketbook." The increase in the personal holding company tax rate promotes that goal, since the retained income is taxed at the highest individual rate.

observation: The personal holding company tax rate has traditionally been set at the highest individual tax rate. However, the '90 Act introduced the 31% bracket without a corresponding change to the personal holding company tax. The '93 Act restores the historical norm.

□ **Effective:** Tax years beginning after Dec. 31, '92. (§§ 13201(c), 13202(c)) Fiscal-year corporations do not make a "straddle computation" on account of the change in tax rate. (§ 13001(c))

For official explanation see Committee Reports ¶s 3028 and 3029.

¶ 304. Deduction for allowable meal and entertainment expenses reduced from 80% to 50% of cost

Ordinary and necessary entertainment expenses generally are deductible if they are directly related to, or associated with, the active conduct of a trade or business or an individual's investment-related activities. (FTC 2d/FIN ¶ L-2100 *et seq.;* TG ¶ 6830 *et seq.;* USTR ¶ 2744.01) No deduction is allowed for any food or beverage expense if the expense is lavish or extravagant under the circumstances (see FTC 2d/FIN ¶ L-2134; TG ¶ 6835; USTR ¶ 2744.01), or if the taxpayer (or an employee) is not present when the meal is furnished (see FTC 2d/FIN ¶ L-2135; TG ¶ 6835; USTR ¶ 2744.01).

FTC 2d References are to the Federal Tax Coordinator 2d
FIN References are to RIA's Analysis of Federal Taxes: Income
TG References are to the Tax Guide
USTR References are to the United States Tax Reporter

Under pre-'93 Act law, the amount allowable as a deduction for expenses incurred for meals and entertainment was limited to 80% of the amount which would otherwise have been allowable as a deduction. (FTC 2d/FIN ¶ L-2136; TG ¶ 6833; USTR ¶ 2744.01) In determining the amount that is subject to the 80% limitation, taxes and tips are included. (See FTC 2d/FIN ¶ L-2136; USTR ¶ 2744.01)

The '93 Act reduces from 80% to 50% the amount allowable as a deduction for meal and entertainment expenses. (Code Sec. 274(n)(1) as amended by '93 Act § 13209(a))

> ***illustration:*** A taxpayer spends $200 to take a client out to dinner and a show. But for the 50% limitation, the entire $200 would be deductible. The amount actually allowable is $100.

> ***observation:*** The 50% limitation is applied to the amount otherwise allowable as a deduction—in other words, to food and beverage expenses that meet any applicable condition for deductibility. The limitation does not, for example, allow a deduction for any part of a lavish or extravagant meal, or one served while the taxpayer or an employee was not present.

> ***observation:*** In determining the amount that is subject to the 50% limitation, taxes and tips continue to be included.

> ***illustration:*** A business meal costs $200. Tax and tip come to $10 and $30, respectively. The amount deductible is $120 (i.e., 50% of $240).

> ***observation:*** The 50% limitation applies to all allowable meal deductions, not just those that are deductible as business expenses. For example, it applies to limit the deduction for meals associated with travel for medical reasons (see FTC 2d/FIN ¶ K-2213), and meals consumed while rendering charitable services away from home (see FTC 2d/FIN ¶ K-3623).

☐ **Effective:** Taxable years beginning after Dec. 31, '93. (§ 13209(c))

For official explanation see Committee Reports ¶ 3036.

¶ 305. Deduction barred for club dues after '93

Under pre-'93 Act law, if certain requirements were met (FTC 2d/FIN ¶ L-2155; TG ¶ 6865; USTR ¶s 1624.060, 2744.03), a deduction was permitted for club dues even though a significant element of personal enjoyment may have existed.

The '93 Act bars any deduction for amounts paid or incurred for membership in any club organized for business, pleasure, recreation or other social purpose. (Code Sec. 274(a)(3) as added by '93 Act § 13210(a))

This new rule applies to all types of clubs including business, social, athletic, luncheon and sporting clubs. Specific business expenses (meals for example) incurred at a club are deductible only to the extent that they otherwise satisfy the standards for deductibility. (S Rept p. 247)

No exception for employee recreational expenses. Under pre-'93 Act law, certain expenditures for recreational and social activities primarily for the benefit of employees (other than highly-compensated employees) were exempted from Code Sec 274(a) which disallows entertainment expenses that are not directly related to or associated with the active conduct of the taxpayer's business. (FTC 2d/FIN ¶ L-2126; USTR ¶ 2744.01) The '93 Act specifies that this exemption doesn't apply for purposes of new Code Sec. 274(a)(3). In other words, employee recreational expenditures are subject to the new rule generally barring the deduction of club dues. (Code Sec. 274(e)(4) as amended by '93 Act § 14210(b))

☐ **Effective:** Amounts paid or incurred after '93. (§ 13210(c))
For official explanation see Committee Reports ¶ 3037.

¶ 306. Deduction denied for travel expenses of taxpayer's spouse or dependents

Travel expenses incurred while away from home in pursuit of a trade or business are deductible to the extent that they are reasonable and necessary to the conduct of the taxpayer's business and are directly attributable to it. (FTC 2d/FIN ¶ L-1701; TG ¶ 6742; USTR ¶ 1624.114) Under pre-'93 Act law, travel expenses of a taxpayer's spouse were not deductible unless the spouse's presence on the business trip had a bona fide business purpose. The spouse's performance of some incidental service did not make the expenses deductible. The same rules applied to any other members of taxpayer's family who went on the trip. (FTC 2d/FIN ¶ L-1739; TG ¶ 6773; USTR ¶ 1624.119)

The '93 Act denies any deduction for travel expenses paid or incurred with respect to a spouse, dependent, or other individual accompanying the taxpayer (or an officer or employee of the taxpayer) on business travel unless (1) the spouse, etc., is an employee of the taxpayer, (2) the travel of the spouse, etc., is for a bona fide business purpose, *and* (3) the expenses would otherwise be deductible by the spouse, etc. The denial of the deduction does not apply to deductible moving expenses. (Code Sec. 274(m)(3) as amended by '93 Act § 13272(a))

> ***observation:*** Pre-'93 Act law, as stated in Rev Rul 63-44 (FTC 2d/FIN ¶ L-2105), didn't require that the spouse be an employee.

No inference is intended about the deductibility of these expenses under pre-'93 Act law. (H Rept p. 789)

☐ **Effective:** Amounts paid or incurred after Dec. 31, '93. (§ 13272(b))
For official explanation see Committee Reports ¶ 3067.

¶ 307. Denial of trade or business expense deduction for certain lobbying expenses

Under pre-'93 Act law, the taxpayer was allowed a deduction for certain expenses (including travel expenses, costs of preparing testimony and a portion of dues) paid in carrying on a trade or business if the expenses were in direct connection with: (1) appearances before, submitting statements to, or sending communications to Congress or any legislative body regarding legislation or proposed legislation of direct interest to the taxpayer, or (2) communications of information between taxpayer and an organization of which he was a member relating to legislation or proposed legislation of direct interest to the taxpayer and the organization. Expenses relating to the participation in or intervention in any political campaign or to attempts to influence the general public on legislative matters were not deductible. (FTC 2d/FIN ¶ L-2400 *et seq.;* TG ¶ 6285 *et seq.;* USTR ¶ 1624.395)

The '93 Act provides that no deduction is allowed as a trade or business expense for any amount paid or incurred in connection with influencing legislation. (Code Sec. 162(e)(1)(A) as amended by '93 Act § 13222(a))

> ***observation:*** The '93 Act effectively repeals the provisions under pre-'93

FTC 2d References are to the Federal Tax Coordinator 2d
FIN References are to RIA's Analysis of Federal Taxes: Income
TG References are to the Tax Guide
USTR References are to the United States Tax Reporter

Act law allowing for a deduction for expenses of appearing before legislative bodies, etc., and taxpayer/organization communication expenses, except for expenses incurred in connection with local legislation (discussed below).

Influencing legislation means any attempt to influence any legislation through communication with any member or employee of a legislative body, or with any government official or employee who may participate in the formulation of legislation. (Code Sec. 162(e)(4)(A))

Any communication compelled by subpoena or otherwise compelled by federal or state law is not an attempt to influence legislation or an official's action. (Conf Rept p. 607)

Legislation has the same meaning as under Code Sec. 4911(e)(2) (Code Sec. 162(e)(4)(B)) which defines legislation as including action relating to acts, bills, resolutions or similar items by Congress, any state legislature, any local council or similar governing body or by the public in a referendum, initiative, constitutional amendment or similar procedure. (See FTC 2d/FIN ¶ D-6503; TG ¶ 7915; USTR ¶ 49,114.01) A legislative body doesn't include executive, judicial or administrative bodies. (See FTC 2d/FIN ¶ D-6504.13; TG ¶ 7915) However, no deduction is allowed for expenses in connection with direct communication with covered executive branch officials (see below)

> ***observation:*** The '93 Act doesn't disallow deductions for costs of attempting to influence a regulatory or administrative agency with respect to its rules and regulations, since administrative regulations aren't legislation.

Exception for local legislation. The rule disallowing a deduction for amounts paid or incurred in connection with influencing legislation doesn't apply to any legislation of any local council or similar governing body. (Code Sec. 162(e)(2)(A)) In effect, the expenses of attempting to influence legislation of such bodies are deductible under rules identical to those of pre-'93 Act law. (Conf Rept p. 605) The deduction allowed for trade or business expenses under Code Sec. 162(a) includes all ordinary and necessary expenses (including but not limited to, traveling expenses and the cost of preparing testimony) paid or incurred during the tax year in carrying on any trade or business in direct connection with: (1) appearances before, submission of statements to, or sending communications to the committees or individual members of the council or body regarding legislation or proposed legislation of direct interest to the taxpayer or (2) communication of information between the taxpayer and an organization of which the taxpayer is a member relating to any legislation or proposed legislation which is of direct interest to the taxpayer and to the organization, and that portion of the dues paid or incurred with respect to any organization of which the taxpayer is a member which is attributable to the expenses of the activities described above carried on by the organization. (Code Sec. 162(e)(2)(B))

An Indian tribal government is treated in the same manner as a local council or similar governing body. (Code Sec. 162(e)(7)) Any legislative body of a political subdivision of a state (e.g., a county or city council) is considered a local council or similar governing body. (Conf Rept p. 605) For example, communications with and attempts to influence members of a local zoning board (acting in their capacity as members of that board, regardless of whether or not members are elected to their position) will not be affected by the provision denying a deduction for lobbying expenses. (H Rept p. 659)

The disallowance of a deduction for expenses incurred for participation in any political campaign or in connection with any attempt to influence the general public with respect to elections under pre-'93 Act law remains in effect under the '93 Act. (Code Sec. 162(e)(1)(B); Code Sec. 162(e)(1)(C)) Thus, expenditures for grass roots lobbying for local legislation or for participation in local elections are not deductible. (Conf Rept p. 605)

Direct communications with covered executive branch officials. No deduction is allowed for any amount paid or incurred in connection with any direct communication with a covered executive branch official in an attempt to influence the official actions or positions of the official. (Code Sec. 162(e)(1)(D))

Congress intends that direct communications include all written and oral communications with covered executive branch officials. A communication is a direct communication with a covered executive branch official if the official is the intended primary recipient of the communication, regardless of whether the communication is formally addressed to the official. (Conf Rept p. 605)

Covered executive branch officials are:

(1) the President (Code Sec. 162(e)(6)(A)),

(2) the Vice President (Code Sec. 162(e)(6)(B)),

(3) any officer or employee of the White House Office of the Executive Office of the President and the two most senior level officers of each of the other agencies in the Executive Office (Code Sec. 162(e)(6)(C)), and

(4) any individual serving in a position in level I of the Executive Schedule under 5 U.S. Code § 5312 (e.g., a Cabinet member) (Code Sec. 162(e)(6)(D)(i)),

(5) any other individual designated by the President as having Cabinet level status (Code Sec. 162(e)(6)(D)(ii)), and

(6) any immediate deputy of an individual described in (4) or (5). (Code Sec. 162(e)(6)(D)(iii))

For councils or other agencies within the Executive Office of the President where the President, Vice President or one or more Cabinet members serve as ranking members, the covered officers include the two most senior administrative officers (other than the ranking members) of the council or agency. (Conf Rept p. 605)

Activities in support of lobbying. Any amount paid or incurred for research for, or preparation, planning or coordination of any lobbying activity is treated as paid or incurred in connection with the activity. (Code Sec. 162(e)(5)(C))

IRS will provide guidance for distinguishing (1) attempts to influence legislation, from (2) mere monitoring of legislative activities where there is no attempt to influence the formulation or enactment of legislation. Where an individual or organization monitors legislation and later attempts to influence the formulation or enactment of the same (or similar) legislation, it is intended that the costs of the monitoring activities generally will be treated as a nondeductible expense. (H Rept p. 659) In addition, IRS will permit taxpayers to adopt reasonable methods for allocating expenses to lobbying (and related research and other background) activities in order to reduce taxpayer recordkeeping responsibilities. (Conf Rept p. 606)

In determining the expenses incurred in connection with any direct communication with a covered executive branch official in an attempt to influence the official actions or positions of the official, only the costs attributable to the direct communication itself are nondeductible. Thus, for example, if a taxpayer works for an extended period to influence the actions of non-covered executive branch officials and, at the end of the project, a covered executive branch official approves the final decision through a separate communication with the taxpayer (e.g., a briefing or review of the matter),

FTC 2d References are to the Federal Tax Coordinator 2d
FIN References are to RIA's Analysis of Federal Taxes: Income
TG References are to the Tax Guide
USTR References are to the United States Tax Reporter

only the direct costs of the communication with the covered official would be disallowed and not the costs of the work product from the earlier period. In contrast, if a taxpayer conducts research and analysis with a view toward directly communicating with a covered executive branch official, the costs of the research and analysis would be disallowed as attributable to the direct communication with the covered official. (Conf Rept pp. 606-607)

Application to dues. No deduction is allowed for the portion of dues or other similar amounts paid by the taxpayer to a tax-exempt organization if, and to the extent that: (a) those dues or other amounts are allocable to lobbying expenditures by the organization for which no deduction is allowed; and (b) the organization informs the taxpayer, under the reporting requirements discussed below, of the portion of dues or other amounts that are allocable to nondeductible lobbying expenditures. (Code Sec. 162(e)(3)) Amounts that are similar to dues include voluntary payments made by members and special assessments imposed by the recipient organization to conduct lobbying activities. This is similar to the treatment of special assessments for grassroots lobbying or campaign expenses under pre-$93 Act law (see FTC 2d/FIN ¶ L-2413; TG ¶ 6290; USTR ¶ 1624.395). (H Rept p. 659)

Anti-cascading rule. For any taxpayer engaged in the trade or business of conducting lobbying activities, the denial of a deduction does not apply to expenditures of the taxpayer in conducting those activities directly on behalf of another person, but does apply to payments by that other person to the taxpayer for conducting those activities. (Code Sec. 162(e)(5)(A)) The purpose of this provision is to ensure that, when multiple parties are involved, the general lobbying disallowance rule results in the denial of a deduction at only one level. The anti-cascading rule applies where there is a direct, one-on-one relationship between the taxpayer and the entity conducting the lobbying activity, such as a client or employee relationship. Thus, the anti-cascading rule will not apply to dues or other payments to taxable membership organizations which act to further the interests of all their members rather than the interests of any one particular member. (Conf Rept p. 610)

De minimis exception. The denial of a deduction for lobbying activities does not apply to any in-house expenditures for any tax year if the expenditures don't exceed $2,000. In determining whether a taxpayer exceeds the $2,000 limit, overhead costs otherwise allocable to activities of influencing legislation or direct communication with covered executive branch officials aren't taken into account. (Code Sec. 162(e)(5)(B)(i)) In-house expenditures means expenditures for influencing legislation or direct communication with covered executive branch officials other than (1) payments by the taxpayer to a person engaged in the trade or business of conducting lobbying activities for the conduct of those activities on behalf of the taxpayer or (2) dues or other similar amounts paid or incurred by the taxpayer which are allocable to lobbying activities. (Code Sec. 162(e)(5)(B)(ii)) Thus, payments made by a taxpayer to third party lobbyists and dues payments allocable to lobbying are subject to the disallowance rule, regardless of whether or not the taxpayer's in-house expenses are exempted under the de minimis rule. Also, the de minimis rule does not apply to expenses incurred for political activity or grass roots lobbying which continue to be disallowed in their entirety as under pre-'93 Act law. The de minimis rule is intended primarily to provide administrative convenience to taxpayers. Therefore, if during a tax year, a taxpayer incurs in-house expenditures in excess of $2,000, then the full amount of its lobbying expenses must be determined and that amount (including the first $2,000 of in-house expenditures) is subject to the disallowance rules. (Conf Rept p. 606)

Disallowance of charitable deduction. No deduction is allowed under Code Sec. 170 (relating to the charitable contributions deduction, see FTC 2d/FIN ¶ K-2800 *et* *seq.;* TG ¶ 7290 *et seq.;* USTR ¶ 1704 *et seq.)* for a contribution to a charity that conducts lobbying activities on matters of direct financial interest to the donor's trade or business, if a principal purpose of the contribution was to avoid federal income tax by securing a deduction for the lobbying activities under Code Sec. 170 which would be disallowed under Code Sec. 162(e) if the donor had conducted the activities directly. No deduction is allowed under Code Sec. 162(a) as a trade or business expense for any amount for which a deduction is disallowed under the above rule. (Code Sec. 170(f)(9) as amended by '93 Act § 13222(b)) This is an anti-avoidance rule designed to prevent donors from using charities as a conduit to conduct lobbying activities, whose cost would be nondeductible if conducted directly by the donor. The determination regarding a principal purpose of the contribution will be based on the facts and circumstances surrounding the contribution, including the existence of any formal or informal instructions relating to the charity's use of the contribution for lobbying efforts (including nonpartisan analysis), the temporal nexus between the making of the contribution and conduct of the lobbying activities, and any historical pattern of contributions by the donor to the charity. Rules under Code Secs. 501(c)(3) and 4911 regarding the impact of lobbying on a charity's tax-exempt status (see FTC 2d/FIN ¶ D-6400 *et seq.;* TG ¶ 7915 *et seq.;* USTR ¶ 5014.12) are not being altered. Thus, even if a contributor is subject to the anti-avoidance rule in a particular case because its payment to a charity is made with a principal purpose of funding lobbying, the charity's tax-exempt status will not be jeopardized if its activity qualifies as nonpartisan analysis or does not constitute substantial lobbying. (Conf Rept pp. 609-610)

Reporting requirements. Each tax-exempt organization (other than those discussed below) must include on its annual return information setting forth the total lobbying and political expenditures and the total amount of dues or other similar amounts paid to the organization to which the expenditures are allocable. (Code Sec. 6033(e)(1)(A)(i) as amended by '93 Act § 13222(c)) Lobbying expenditures are treated as paid out of dues or other similar amounts. If expenditures exceed the dues or other similar amounts for any tax year, the excess is treated as expenditures paid or incurred by the organization during the following tax year. (Code Sec. 6033(e)(1)(C))

> RIA ***observation:*** Lobbying expenditures are treated as paid only out of dues or other similar amounts even if the organization actually pays the lobbying expenditures from sources of income other than dues or similar amounts.

Except where an organization elects not to provide notice or establishes that the dues are not deductible (see below), an organization, at the time of assessment or payment of dues or other similar amounts, must provide notice to each person making the payment of a reasonable estimate of the portion of dues or other similar amounts to which the lobbying expenditures are allocable. (Code Sec. 6033(e)(1)(A)(ii)) Congress intends that the notice be provided in a conspicuous and easily recognizable format. Code Sec. 6113 and its regs (see FTC 2d/FIN ¶ D-4004 *et seq.;* TG ¶ 7975 *et seq.;* USTR ¶ 60,334) may be consulted for guidance regarding the appropriate format of the disclosure statement. (Conf Rept p. 608)

Exceptions to reporting requirements. The reporting requirements apply to any tax-exempt organization other than an organization described in Code Sec. 501(c)(3) (see FTC 2d/FIN ¶ D-4100 *et seq.;* TG ¶ 7910 *et seq.).* The reporting requirements don't apply to the in-house expenditures of an organization for a tax year if the

---

FTC 2d References are to the Federal Tax Coordinator 2d
FIN References are to RIA's Analysis of Federal Taxes: Income
TG References are to the Tax Guide
USTR References are to the United States Tax Reporter

expenditures don't exceed $2,000. In determining whether a taxpayer exceeds the $2,000 limit, overhead costs otherwise allocable to activities of influencing legislation and direct communication with covered executive branch officials aren't taken into account. (Code Sec. 6033(e)(1)(B))

An organization is also not subject to the reporting requirements if it establishes to the satisfaction of IRS that substantially all of the dues or other similar amounts paid to the organization are not deductible without regard to the denial of a deduction for lobbying expenses. (Code Sec. 6033(e)(3)) Congress intends that the waiver be available to any organization that receives 90% or more of its total dues and similar payments from persons not entitled to deduct those payments. Examples of those organizations include organizations that receive 90% or more of their dues monies from members that are tax-exempt charities or who are individuals not entitled to deduct the dues payments in determining taxable income because the payments are not ordinary and necessary business expenses. Another example would be a union that establishes to the satisfaction of IRS that 90% or more of its dues monies are paid by individuals who do not deduct the dues because of the operation of the two-percent floor on miscellaneous itemized deductions. Congress contemplates that waivers will be provided under IRS regs or other IRS procedure. (Conf Rept p. 609)

Proxy tax. If an organization elects not to provide the notices or fails to include in the notices the amount allocable to lobbying expenditures (determined on the basis of actual amounts rather than the reasonable estimates), then there is imposed on the organization for the tax year a tax at the highest corporate rate for the tax year on the aggregate amount not included in the notices because of an election not to provide notice or a failure to include. (Code Sec. 6033(e)(2)(A)) Thus, if an organization's actual lobbying and political expenditures for a tax year exceed the estimated allocable amount of the expenditures (either because of higher than anticipated lobbying expenses or lower than projected dues receipts), then the organization is required to pay a proxy tax on the excess amount. (Conf Rept p. 608) If the amount of lobbying expenditures exceeds the amount of dues or other similar payments for the tax year, the proxy tax is imposed on an amount equal to the dues or similar payments and any excess lobbying expenditures are carried forward to the next tax year. (Conf Rept pp. 608-609)

> RIA ***observation:*** Organizations are required to report the portion of dues or other similar amounts allocable to nondeductible lobbying expenses only on the basis of reasonable estimates, but the proxy tax is imposed if the reasonable estimates fall short.

> RIA ***Illustration:*** Organization X receives $100,000 in dues in Year 1. X spends $150,000 on lobbying and elects to pay the proxy tax rather than provide flow-through disclosure to members. The proxy tax for Year 1 would be imposed on $100,000 of lobbying expenditures. The remaining $50,000 of lobbying expenditures would be carried forward to the next year, during which X could comply with the disclosure requirements or elect to pay the proxy tax on that amount as well as any additional lobbying expenditures incurred during that year. (Conf Rept p. 609)

IRS may waive the tax for any tax year if the organization agrees to adjust its estimates for the following tax year to correct any failures. (Code Sec. 6033(e)(2)(B)) The tax imposed is treated as an income tax. (Code Sec. 6033(e)(2)(C)) Congress intends that IRS will prescribe regs governing the treatment of organizations that incur actual lobbying expenditures below the estimated amount. (Conf Rept p. 608)

Penalties. Any organization that underreports the total amount of its lobbying expenses in any tax year is required to pay the proxy tax on any undisclosed or unreported amount. This tax may be imposed regardless of whether the organization has elected disclosure of lobbying expenses to its members or payment of the proxy tax for the tax year. (Code Sec. 6033(e)(2)(A)) The proxy tax will be imposed in addition to interest charges and any other penalties which may apply—for example, the penalty for failure to file an annual return under Code Sec. 6652(c)(1)(A)(ii) (see FTC2d/FIN ¶ V-1906; TG ¶ 9790; USTR ¶ 66,524). (Conf Rept p. 609)

☐ **Effective:** For amounts paid or incurred after Dec. 31, '93. (§ 13222(e))
For official explanation see Committee Reports ¶ 3044.

¶ 308. Compensation deduction in excess of $1,000,000 disallowed for publicly-held companies

Under pre-'93 Act law, no dollar limit is imposed on the deduction by a publicly held corporation or any other taxpayer for compensation paid to an employee or independent contractor. Compensation, whether paid in cash or property, is fully deductible as long as the compensation is reasonable in amount and for services actually rendered. (See FTC 2d/FIN ¶ H-3700; USTR ¶ 1624.025)

The '93 Act bars a publicly held corporation's deduction for compensation paid to a "covered employee" in excess of $1 million per year if the compensation is "applicable employee remuneration." (Code Sec. 162(m) as amended by '93 Act § 13211(a))

> ***observation:*** Although the proposals do not impose any limitation on the amount of compensation that a privately-held company may deduct for any of its executives, the deduction would be subject to the "reasonable compensation" test under existing rules.

Publicly-held corporation defined. For purposes of this deduction limitation, a publicly held corporation is any corporation that has a class of common equity securities that are required to be registered under section 12 of the Securities Exchange Act of '34. (Code Sec. 162(m)(2))

In general the '34 Exchange Act requires a corporation to register its common equity securities under section 12 if: (a) the securities are listed on a national securities exchange, or (b) the corporation has $5 million or more of assets and 500 or more shareholders. However, a corporation will not be treated as publicly held, for purposes of this rule, if the registration of its equity securities is voluntary. For example, when a corporation that is not required to register its *equity* securities nevertheless registers these securities in order to take advantage of other procedures applicable to public offerings of *debt* securities then the corporation will not be considered a publicly held corporation for purposes of this rule. (S Rept p. 248)

Covered employee defined. For purposes of the $1 million per year compensation deduction limitation, the term "covered employee" refers to any employee who: (a) as of the close of the taxable year is the chief executive officer (CEO) of the corporation (or an individual acting as the corporation's CEO), or (b) is one of the corporation's four highest compensated officers (other than the CEO) for the tax year whose total compensation for the employee's tax year is required to be reported to shareholders under the '34 Exchange Act. (Code Sec. 162(m)(3))

FTC 2d References are to the Federal Tax Coordinator 2d
FIN References are to RIA's Analysis of Federal Taxes: Income
TG References are to the Tax Guide
USTR References are to the United States Tax Reporter

If the SEC's reporting rules apply to fewer than four company executives other than the CEO, then only those executives for whom reporting is required by the SEC are treated as covered employees under the rule limiting the compensation deduction to $1 million. (S Rept p. 249)

> ***observation:*** The compensation of corporate officers that has to be disclosed to shareholders under SEC rules is reported on proxy statements sent prior to the annual meeting of a corporation's shareholders.

Applicable employee remuneration defined. The term "applicable employee remuneration," for purposes of the $1 million per year compensation deduction limitation, applies to a covered employee's aggregate remuneration for services performed (either during the deduction year or during another tax year) which would be deductible in its entirety for the tax year if the $1 million limitation did not apply. The term does not include (Code Sec. 162(m)(4)(A)):

. . . commission payments (Code Sec. 163(m)(4)(B)),

. . . other performance-based compensation (Code Sec. 163(m)(4)(C)),

. . . remuneration paid under a written binding contract that was in effect on Feb. 17, '93 (Code Sec. 163(m)(4)(D)),

. . . qualified plan contributions for employees and certain excludable employee fringe benefits. (Code Sec. 162(m)(4)(E))

. . . The remuneration subject to the $1 million deduction limit includes all nonexempted remuneration paid for a covered employee's services in cash and the cash value of remuneration (e.g., benefits) not paid in cash. (S Rept p. 249)

> ***observation:*** Neither the statute nor the committee reports identify when to value non-cash remuneration. In situations where the non-cash remuneration is in the form of property (e.g., stock) that is used to compensate an executive for services rendered in a prior year there may be substantial differences between the value of the property at the time the services are rendered and when the property is actually transferred to the executive. Presumably, the general rule that compensatory property is valued at the time of payment would apply for purposes of the rule limiting the compensation deduction to $1 million.

If an individual to whom the compensation is payable is a covered employee for the tax year, the deduction limitation for that year applies to all compensation that is not specifically excluded from the limitation even if part of the compensation is for services that were rendered when the individual was not a covered employee. (S Rept p. 249)

Commission payments exempt from $1 million limit on compensation deduction. For purposes of the compensation deduction limitation rule, the term "applicable employee remuneration" does not include any remuneration that is payable on a commission basis but only if the commissions are payable solely on income that was generated directly by the individual performance of the employee to whom the commission is payable. (Code Sec. 162 (m)(4)(B)) For example, compensation that represents a percentage of sales made by an executive or a percentage of business income that is directly attributable to the executive will qualify as commission income that is exempt from treatment as applicable employee remuneration. The executive's use of support services, such as research or secretarial services, in generating the income on which the commissions are based will not disqualify the sales or business treatment as attributable directly to the executive's efforts. (S Rept p. 250)

Compensation paid to an executive that is based on performance standards that are broader than the executive's own efforts will not qualify as commissions that are exempt from the $1 million deduction limit. For example, compensation payable to an executive that represents a percentage of income generated by a business unit of the corporation would not be considered as commissions because it is not based on income that is directly attributable to the individual executive. (S Rept p. 250)

> ***observation:*** Compensation that fails to qualify as commissions because it is based on broad performance standards such those of the company or of a company division may qualify for exemption from the $1 million deduction limit as "performance-based" compensation, described below.

> ***observation:*** The advantage of having compensation characterized as a commission rather than as a "performance-based" payment is that various prerequisites have to be met in order to exempt a performance based payment from being taken into account for purposes of the $1 million deduction cap. These prerequisites include shareholder approval of the performance standards on which the executive's compensation is to be based. There are no such prerequisites for compensation paid on a commission basis.

Exemption of performance-based compensation from $1 million deduction limit. Performance-based compensation is excluded from the applicable employee remuneration that is subject to the $1 million compensation deduction limit but only if all of the following four requirements are met: (Code Sec. 162(m)(4)(C))

(1) *Payment solely on attainment of performance-goals.* Performance-based compensation must be payable solely on account of the attainment of one or more performance goals. (Code Sec. 162(m)(4)(C))

A performance goal may be defined broadly. For example, performance goals need not be applicable only to the individual executive but may consist of a performance standard that is applied to a business unit (e.g., a division or a line of business) or to the corporation as a whole. (S Rept p. 250) For example, performance standards can include increases in stock price, increases in market share, increases in sales, or increases in earnings per share. (S Rept p. 250)

Compensation (other than stock options or other stock appreciation rights) will not be treated as paid solely on account of the attainment of one or more performance goals unless it is paid to a particular executive pursuant to a preestablished objective formula or standard that precludes discretion. In general this means that a third party with knowledge of the relevant performance results could calculate the amount to be paid to the executive. Discretion does not exist merely because the outside directors have the authority to interpret a compensation plan, agreement, or contract in accordance with its terms. (Conf Rept p. 586)

For qualification of stock options and stock appreciation rights as performance-based compensation see discussion, below, of treatment of stock options, stock appreciation rights, and restricted stock as performance-based compensation.

(2) *Performance goals to be set by outside directors.* Performance goals must be established by a compensation committee consisting solely of two or more outside directors of the corporation. (Code Sec. 162(m)(4)(C)(i))

A director will be considered an outside director only if the director: (a) is not a

FTC 2d References are to the Federal Tax Coordinator 2d
FIN References are to RIA's Analysis of Federal Taxes: Income
TG References are to the Tax Guide
USTR References are to the United States Tax Reporter

current employee of the corporation or of related entities, (b) has not at any time been an officer of the corporation or of related entities, (c) is not receiving compensation for prior services as an employee of the corporation or of related entities, or (d) is not currently receiving compensation for services in any capacity other than as a director (e.g., is not receiving compensation for services as a consultant to the corporation). The receipt by a director of benefits under a tax-qualified pension plan will not be treated as receipt of compensation for prior services as an employee of the corporation or of related entities. (S Rept p. 251)

> ***observation:*** Under the Senate Report's definition, a director who is a retired employee of the corporation but was not one of its officers will be considered an outside director under the above rule if he receives benefits under a qualified plan but will not be considered an outside director if the benefits are received under a non-qualified plan.

(3) *Disclosure and shareholder approval of performance goals.* The performance goals and other material terms of the arrangement under which the performance-based compensation is to be paid must be: (a) disclosed to the shareholders, and (b) approved by a majority of the shareholders in a separate vote prior to the payment of the compensation. (Code Sec. 162(m)(4)(C)(ii))

The material terms of a performance-based compensation arrangement must be disclosed to the shareholders in a manner that permits a third party who is unfamiliar with the compensation arrangement to determine: (a) the maximum potential amount of compensation payable under the arrangement, or (b) the formula under which the performance-based compensation is payable. For example, disclosure to shareholders would be considered as adequate if the disclosure provided that an executive would receive X dollars of compensation when the corporation's return on equity exceeds a specified amount or upon the attainment of any one of a series of performance goals. But disclosure would not qualify as adequate if the shareholders were merely informed that the compensation committee could award the executive X dollars at its discretion. (H Rept p. 649)

All of the details or agreements of a performance-based compensation plan (or agreement) do not have to be disclosed in all cases. In developing standards as to whether disclosure of the terms of a plan or agreement is adequate, IRS is to take into consideration the SEC rules regarding disclosure and disclosure should be as specific as possible to the extent this would be consistent with SEC's disclosure rules. According to Congress, as a minimum, shareholders should be made aware of the general performance goals on which an executive's compensation is based and the maximum that could be paid to the executive if such performance goals were met. For example, it would not be adequate if the shareholders were merely informed that an executive would be awarded a specific dollar amount if he met "certain performance goals established by the compensation committee." (Conf Rept p. 588)

Compensation that is based on meeting performance goals that are not approved by shareholders will not qualify for the $1 million deduction limit that is available for performance-based compensation. (S Rept p. 250)

When performance-based compensation is payable under a plan, the shareholder approval requirement is satisfied if the shareholders approve the general terms of the plan, and the class of executives covered by the plan. Further shareholder approval of payments under the plan is not required after the plan has been approved. However, if there are material changes to the plan, then shareholder approval of these changes is required for the payments under the modified plan to qualify as performance-based payments that are exempt from the $1 million compensation deduction limit. (S Rept p. 252) *observation:* The requirement that shareholders approve performance goals could result in the disclosure of proprietary information that could place employers at a competitive disadvantage. Many corporations base their top executives' compensation on criteria that are confidential, especially for performance-based compensation. Much of the data on present levels of corporate activity and on plans for future corporate actions (to which performance-based executive compensation would be linked) is proprietary information that a company would not want revealed to its competitors in the process of obtaining shareholder approval for executives' performance goals. For example, a company would not want to disclose that one of the performance goals for its CEO would be the successful negotiation of a planned merger or that the performance goals for its top sales executive included a targeted increase in the company's market share.

For disclosure and shareholder approval requirements for stock options see discussion, below, of treatment of stock options, stock appreciation rights, and restricted stock as performance-based compensation.

(4) *Certification of performance goal attainment.* The compensation committee has to certify, prior to the payment of the performance-based compensation, that all of the performance goals and other material terms of the arrangement for payment of this compensation have been met. (Code Sec. 162(m)(4)(C)(iii))

If the executive is entitled to receive compensation based on performance goals despite the compensation committee's failure to certify the attainment of the performance goals then the compensation will not qualify for the exemption from the $1 million deduction limit that is available for performance-based compensation. (S Rept p. 250)

recommendation: Where possible, advance shareholder approval should be obtained for performance goals to be used with performance-based compensation offered to prospective executives. Otherwise, a company may be reluctant to offer significant performance-based compensation in its negotiations with the prospective executive if the deductibility of that compensation is dependent on subsequent shareholder approval.

For exemption from performance goal certification requirement for stock options and stock appreciation rights see discussion, below, of treatment of stock options, stock appreciation rights, and restricted stock as performance-based compensation.

Treatment of stock options, SARs, and restricted stock as performance-based compensation. Stock options and stock appreciation rights (SARs) will generally be treated as performance-based compensation if the requirements, described above, for establishment of performance goals by outside directors and for approval of these goals by shareholders are met. For this form of performance-based compensation the requirement for director certification that performance standards have been met does not have to be satisfied. Stock options and SARs qualify as performance-based compensation because the amount of compensation paid to the executive is based on an increase in the price of the corporation's stock. (S Rept p. 251)

The exemption for performance-based compensation will not apply to stock-based compensation that is dependent on factors other than corporate performance. For example, if a stock option that is granted to an executive has an exercise price that is less than the value, at the time of the option grant, of the stock subject to the option then the stock option will not meet the requirements for performance based compensation. This is because the executive would have a right to receive a compensatory benefit on the exercise of the option even if the stock price stays the same or decreases to a level that is higher than the executive's exercise price. (S Rept p. 251)

> ***illustration:*** If an executive is granted a 3 year stock option to purchase stock which has a market value, at option grant, of $15 per share and is exercisable with an option price of $10 per share and the executive exercises the option after the stock's market value declines to $13 per share this would still enable the executive to realize a 30% profit (stock worth $13 purchased for $10) despite the decline in the stock's value. Because the executive can benefit from the exercise of the option despite the decline in the price of the stock subject to the option, the compensation realized by the executive from the option exercise is not performance-based.

If an executive is otherwise protected against a decrease in the value of the stock subject to the option (e.g., if the option is automatically repriced by lowering the price at which stock subject to the option can be bought when there is a decline in the market value of the stock below the original price at which it could be acquired on option exercise) the compensatory benefit realized by the executive from option exercise will not qualify as performance-based compensation. (S Rept p. 251)

In the case of stock options, directors may retain discretion as to the exact number of options that are granted to an executive if the maximum number of options that the individual executive may receive during a specified period is predetermined. (Conf Rept p. 587)

Disclosure and shareholder approval requirements for stock options. When performance-based compensation is in the form of stock options granted to an executive, then disclosure is considered as adequate if the shareholders are informed of: (a) the maximum number of shares to be awarded to the executive, (b) the option price, (c) the option exercise period, and (d) any other conditions and restrictions to be placed on the stock subject to the option. (H Rept p. 649)

In the case of a stock option plan, the shareholders generally must approve the specific terms of the plan, the class of executives to which it applies, the option price, (or the formula under which the price is determined), and the maximum number of shares subject to the option that can be awarded under the plan to any executive. Further shareholder approval of payments under a plan or grants of options is not required after the plan has been approved. However, if there are material changes to the stock option plan, shareholder approval would have to be obtained again in order for the exception to apply to payments under the modified plan. (Conf Rept p. 588)

Treatment of restricted stock. Grants of restricted stock are not inherently performance-based compensation because the executive may receive compensation even if the price of the stock decreases or remains the same. (S Rept p. 251) Consequently, the restricted stock is treated the same as cash compensation and cannot qualify as performance-based compensation unless the granting or the vesting of the restricted stock is contingent on the attainment of a performance goal and otherwise satisfies the standards for performance-based compensation. (Conf Rept p. 587)

How disclosure and approval requirements apply when a privately held company goes public. The prospectus of a privately held company that becomes a publicly held company is subject to disclosure rules that are similar to the above disclosure rules for publicly held companies. If there has been disclosure that would satisfy the above rules, the purchasers of the company's stock will be aware of existing compensation arrangements. No further shareholder approval will be required of compensation arrangements that were in existence before the company became public unless there is a material modification of these arrangements. (S Rept p. 252)

Nondeductible parachute payments further reduce $1 million compensation deduction limit. The $1 million compensation deduction limit is reduced (but not below zero) by the amount, if any, that was paid to the executive but was not deductible under the Code Sec. 280G golden parachute rules. (Code Sec. 162(m)(4)(F))

> ***illustration:*** A publicly held corporation pays an executive $1.4 million total compensation (other than commissions or performance-based compensation) in '94. The $1.4 million includes a $400,000 nondeductible excess parachute payment. Only $600,000 ($1 million minus $400,000 excess parachute payment) of the $1 million paid to the executive would be deductible.

Other forms of compensation not taken into account for purposes of $1 million dollar limit on compensation deduction. The following forms of compensation are not taken into account in aggregating the compensation paid by a publicly held corporation that is subject to the $1 million deduction limit:

(1) Contributions made on behalf of an employee to any of the following tax-qualified retirement plan arrangements (including contributions to a qualified Code Sec. 401(k) cash or deferred arrangement and salary reduction contributions) as well as payments to an employee or beneficiary from these qualified retirement plans: (a) a qualified retirement plan trust that is tax-exempt under Code Sec. 401(a), (b) a qualified annuity plan described in Code Sec. 403(a), (c) a simplified employee pension plan as defined in Code Sec. 408(k)(1), (d) a qualified annuity contract described in Code Sec. 403(b). (Code Sec. 162(m)(4)(E)(i))

(2) Any benefit provided to, or on behalf of, an employee if it is reasonable to believe at the time that the benefit is provided that the employee will be able to exclude the benefit from his gross income. (Code Sec. 162(m)(4)(E)(ii)) Examples of these nontaxable benefits are employer-provided health benefits and miscellaneous fringe benefits excludable under Code Sec. 132. (S Rept p. 249)

> ***observation:*** Since only non-taxable fringe benefits are excludible from compensation taken into account for purposes of the $1 million compensation deduction limit, the value of taxable personal travel on employer-provided automobiles and aircraft would be aggregated with other taxable compensation.

Deduction year for which compensation limit is applied. The $1 million compensation deduction limitation applies to the tax year when the deduction for the remuneration would otherwise be taken. For example, in the case of a nonqualified stock option, the deduction is normally taken in the year the option is exercised, even though the option was granted for services performed in a prior year. However, if at the time the option is exercised the individual to whom the option was granted is no longer a covered employee then the deduction limitation would no longer apply. (S Rept p. 249)

> ***illustration:*** On Dec. 31, '93, executive Smith who as the controller of Zeno corporation is the seventh highest paid officer of the company becomes a participant in Zeno's stock option plan for key employees and is granted

FTC 2d References are to the Federal Tax Coordinator 2d
FIN References are to RIA's Analysis of Federal Taxes: Income
TG References are to the Tax Guide
USTR References are to the United States Tax Reporter

an option to purchase 20,000 shares of the company's stock for $100 per share, its fair market value at the option's grant. The stock options are granted to Smith for services rendered in '93. In '94 Smith is promoted to vice-president, his compensation is increased so that he is the fifth highest paid officer after the company's CEO and he exercises his option to buy 10,000 shares of Zeno stock which now has a value of $220 per share. In '95, Smith is promoted to senior vice-president/finance, his compensation is third highest after Zeno's CEO, and he exercises his remaining options to buy 10,000 shares of Zeno stock whose market value has dropped to $200 per share. Smith's compensatory benefit of $1.2 million from the '94 option exercise (stock with a value of $2.2 million purchased for $1 million option price) is not "applicable employee remuneration" because it is paid to Smith when he is neither the CEO nor among the next four most highly compensated employees of the company and consequently is not a covered employee for purposes of the $1 million compensation deduction limit. However, Smith's benefit of $1 million from the '95 option exercise (stock with a value of $2 million purchased for $1 million option price) is paid to Smith when he is the third highest paid officer of the company after the CEO. Consequently, this $1 million benefit is applicable employee remuneration that is, together with Smith's other '95 applicable employee remuneration, subject to the $1 million deduction limit. The fact that this $1 million benefit is attributable to services rendered by Smith when he was not a covered employee for purposes of the $1 million deduction limit does not exempt this remuneration from treatment as applicable employee remuneration.

☐ **Effective:** For amounts which would otherwise be deductible for tax years beginning after '93. (§ 13211(b))

caution: The effective date of this '93 Act provision may cause '93 performance-based bonuses that are payable and otherwise deductible in '94 to become nondeductible because corporations did not have the opportunity to seek shareholder approval of performance goals on which bonuses are based.

recommendation: Consideration should be given to accelerating payment into the '93 tax year of compensation that would otherwise be paid in the '94 tax year under a post-Feb. 17, '93 contract (see below) to avoid nondeductibility for '94 under the new rule.

Exception for remuneration paid under pre-Feb. 18, '93 contracts. Any remuneration that is payable under a written binding contract which was in effect on Feb. 17, '93 is not considered applicable employee remuneration that is subject to the $1 million deduction limit. This exception ceases to apply to amounts that are paid after a material modification to the terms of the contract. (Code Sec. 162(m)(4)(D))

Compensation paid under a plan (e.g. a deferred compensation plan for management employees of a corporation) will qualify for the pre-Feb. 18, '93 binding contract exception if the right to participate in the plan is part of a written binding contract with the covered employee that was in effect on Feb. 17, '93. (Conf Rept p. 588) Consequently, the exception will apply in the case of an employee who, though not a participant, was eligible to be a participant in a deferred compensation plan on Feb. 17, '93 under the circumstances illustrated below:

Illustration: A covered employee was hired by XYZ corporation on Jan. 17, '93. One of the terms of his written employment contract was that he was eligible to participate in the "XYZ Corporation Executive Deferred Compensation Plan." The plan provided for participation after 6 months of employment. Payments under the plan were not discretionary. The corporation did not have the right to materially amend the plan or to terminate the plan (except on a prospective basis before any services were performed for the employment period covered by the contract). If the other conditions required for the pre-Feb. 18, '93 binding contract exception are met (e.g., the plan itself is in writing), payments under the plan are grandfathered even though the employee was not actually a participant in the plan on Feb. 17, '93. (Conf Rept p. 589)

The fact that a plan was in existence on Feb. 17, '93, is not by itself sufficient to qualify for the binding written contract exception. (S Rept p. 252)

The binding written contract exception does not apply to contracts that are renewed after Feb. 17, '93. For purposes of this rule, any contract that was entered into before Feb. 18, '93 and was renewed after Feb. 17, '93 is treated as a new contract entered into on the day the renewal takes effect and therefore not eligible for the binding written contract exception. A contract that is terminable or cancelable unconditionally at will by either party to the contract without the consent of the other, or by both parties to the contract, is treated as a new contract that was entered into on the date that the termination or cancellation, if made, would be effective. However, a contract will not be treated as terminable or cancelable if it can be terminated or cancelled only by terminating the employment relationship of the covered employee. (S Rept p. 253)

caution: Amendments to pre-Feb. 18, '93 contracts should be carefully evaluated to determine whether the amendment could be interpreted as a renewal or replacement of the contract that would disqualify future payments under the contract from the exemption from the $1 million compensation deduction limit.

For official explanation see Committee Reports ¶ 3038.

¶ 309. Modification to alternative minimum tax depreciation rules

Under pre-'93 Act law, depreciation, for alternative minimum tax purposes, on most personal property to which the Modified Accelerated Cost Recovery System (MACRS) applies, was calculated using the 150% declining balance method (switching to straight line in the year necessary to maximize the deduction) over the property's class life. (FTC 2d/FIN ¶ A-8106; TG ¶ 1355; USTR ¶ 564.01) In addition, the alternative minimum taxable income of a corporation was increased by an amount equal to 75% of the amount by which adjusted current earnings of the corporation exceeded alternative minimum taxable income (as determined before this adjustment). (See FTC 2d/FIN ¶ A-8129; TG ¶ 1381; USTR ¶ 564.03) Generally, adjusted current earnings was alternative minimum taxable income with additional adjustments that corresponded to those made by corporations in computing their earnings and profits. (See FTC 2d/FIN ¶ A-8130; TG ¶ 1381; USTR ¶ 564.03) Under pre-'93 Act law, depreciation for purposes of adjusted current earnings was computed using the straight-line method over the class life of the property. (FTC 2d/FIN ¶ A-8130.4; TG ¶ 1381) Thus, under pre-'93 law, a corporation had to make two depreciation calculations for purposes of the alternative minimum tax—one

FTC 2d References are to the Federal Tax Coordinator 2d
FIN References are to RIA's Analysis of Federal Taxes: Income
TG References are to the Tax Guide
USTR References are to the United States Tax Reporter

using the 150% percent declining balance method over the class life and another using the straight-line method over the class life. (S Rept p. 187)

Congress believes that the two depreciation calculations required by the corporate alternative minimum tax is a source of considerable complexity. (S Rept p. 187)

Under the '93 Act, the adjusted current earnings depreciation adjustment is eliminated. (Code Sec. 56(g)(4)(A)(i) as amended by '93 Act § 13115(a))

☐ **Effective:** For property placed in service after '93, except that these provisions don't apply to MACRS property that is covered by one or more transitional rules of the '86 Tax Reform Act. (See FTC 2d/FIN ¶ L-7817; TG ¶ 5400; USTR ¶ 564.01) (§ 13115(b))

For official explanation see Committee Reports ¶ 3007.

¶ 309A. Modification of alternative minimum tax (AMT) adjusted current earnings rules

Modification of adjusted current earnings rules. Under pre-'93 Act law, the alternative minimum taxable income of a corporation was increased by 75% of the amount by which adjusted current earnings (ACE) exceeded alternative minimum taxable income (calculated before this adjustment). ACE was computed using rules similar to those that a corporation uses to determine its earnings and profits. (See FTC 2d/FIN ¶ A-8129; TG ¶ 1381)

The '93 Act provides that, notwithstanding the ACE adjustments that provide for (a) the inclusion in ACE of items included in earnings and profits (see FTC 2d/FIN ¶ A-8130.1; TG ¶ 1381) and (b) the disallowance for ACE purposes of items not deductible in computing earnings and profits (see FTC 2d/FIN ¶ A-8130.2; TG ¶ 1381), no adjustment related to the earnings and profits effects of any charitable contribution is to be made in computing ACE. (Code Sec. 56(g)(4)(J) as amended by '93 Act § 13171(b))

☐ **Effective:** Contributions of capital gain property that isn't tangible personal property made after Dec. 31, '92; Contributions of all other capital gain property made after June 30, '92. (§ 13171(d))

¶ 310. Deferred tax liability on outstanding installment obligations may be figured at capital gain rate

If an obligation that arose from an installment sale for more than $150,000 is outstanding at the end of the tax year, and the face amount of all such obligations that arose during the tax year and are outstanding at the end of the tax year exceeds $5,000,000, interest is due on the deferred tax attributable to the installment obligations. The amount of interest due equals the applicable percentage of the deferred tax liability with respect to the obligation multiplied by the interest rate on tax underpayments in effect for the last month of the tax year. The "applicable percentage" is the portion of the face amount of the obligations subject to the interest payments rules outstanding at the end of the year in excess of $5,000,000 divided by the total aggregate face amount of those obligations. (See FTC 2d/FIN ¶ G-6300 *et seq.;* TG ¶ 2900 *et seq.;* USTR ¶ 453A4))

Under pre-'93 Act law, the "deferred tax liability" with respect to an obligation was the amount of still-unrecognized gain on that obligation as of the end of the tax year multiplied by the top income tax rate in effect for that year under Code Sec. 1 (individuals) or Code Sec. 11 (corporations), whichever is appropriate. (FTC 2d/FIN ¶ G-6317; TG ¶ 2904; USTR ¶ 453A4)

The '93 Act provides that, with respect to so much of the gain that, when recognized, will be treated as long-term capital gain, the maximum rate under Code Sec. 1(h) or Code Sec. 1201 is used instead of the top income tax rate. (Code Sec. 453A(c)(3) as amended by '93 Act § 13201(b)(4))

> ***observation:*** The maximum capital gain rate under Code Sec. 1(h) is 28%. The maximum capital gain rate under Code Sec. 1201, as amended by the '93 Act, is 35% (see ¶ 301).

> ***observation:*** Thus, for individuals, the tax rate at which the "deferred tax liability" on the long-term capital gain portion is figured decreases from 31% to 28%. For corporations, the rate increases from 34% to 35%.

☐ **Effective:** Tax years beginning after Dec. 31, '92. (§ 13201(c))
For official explanation see Committee Reports ¶ 3028.

¶ 311. Repeal of stock-for-debt exception from debt cancellation income for bankrupt or insolvent taxpayers

In general, a corporation which satisfies a debt obligation by transferring its stock to a creditor recognizes income to the extent, if any, that the value of the stock transferred is less than the principal amount of the debt. (See FTC 2d/FIN ¶ J-7014; TG ¶ 5276; USTR ¶ 1084.04) This is consistent with the treatment where debt is satisfied by a payment of cash, or a transfer of other property, with a value less than the debt's principal amount. (See FTC 2d/FIN ¶ J-7200 *et seq.;* TG ¶ 5275; USTR ¶ 1084.04)

Under pre-'93 Act law, an exception to this rule applied where debt was satisfied by a transfer of the debtor's stock and (i) the debtor was in bankruptcy, or (ii) the debtor was insolvent. In the case of an insolvent but non-bankrupt taxpayer, the exception applied only to the extent of the insolvency. If this exception applied, then the difference between the value of the transferred stock and the principal amount of the debt was neither included in the debtor's income, nor applied to reduce the debtor's tax attributes, see ¶ 312. (FTC 2d/FIN ¶ J-7307; TG ¶ 5276; USTR ¶ 1084.04)

The '93 Act repeals the stock-for-debt exception for bankrupt or insolvent taxpayers (Code Sec. 108(e) as amended by '93 Act § 13226(a)(1)(A)), and provides that where a corporation transfers stock to a creditor in satisfaction of debt, the corporation is treated as having satisfied the debt with an amount of money equal to the fair market value of the stock. (Code Sec. 108(e)(8) as amended by '93 Act § 13226(a)(1)(B))

> ***observation:*** Because of this rule, the difference between the value of the stock transferred and the principal amount of the debt satisfied must be applied to reduce the tax attributes of a taxpayer who is either in a bankruptcy proceeding or is insolvent. In the case of a non-bankrupt but insolvent taxpayer, however, the reduction is applied only to the extent such taxpayer is insolvent.

> ***observation:*** The '93 Act does not change the rule that a taxpayer who is neither bankrupt nor insolvent must include the difference between the value of stock transferred and the principal amount of debt satisfied in income.

FTC 2d References are to the Federal Tax Coordinator 2d
FIN References are to RIA's Analysis of Federal Taxes: Income
TG References are to the Tax Guide
USTR References are to the United States Tax Reporter

The same rule also continues to apply to a taxpayer who is not bankrupt but is insolvent, to the extent that the difference exceeds the amount of the insolvency.

In repealing the stock-for-debt exception Congress intends no inference as to the treatment of cancellation of debt of a noncorporate entity in exchange for an ownership or equity interest. (Conf Rept p. 621)

Contributions of debt to the capital of a corporation. Under pre-'93 Act law, where a shareholder of a corporation contributed the corporation's own debt to the corporation, the corporation was treated as having satisfied the debt for an amount equal to the shareholder's basis in the debt. (FTC 2d/FIN ¶ J-7301; TG ¶ 5269; USTR ¶ 1084.04) The '93 Act provides that this rule will not apply to the extent provided in Regs. (Code Sec. 108(e)(6) as amended by '93 Act § 13226(a)(2)(B)) This grant of regulatory authority is intended to permit IRS to issue regs which will coordinate the treatment of contributions to capital with the repeal of the stock-for-debt exception. (Conf Rept p. 620)

☐ **Effective:** Stock transferred after Dec. 31, '94. (§ 13226(a)(3)(A)) However, the '93 Act amendments do not apply to stock transferred in satisfaction of debt in a Title 11 or similar case (see FTC 2d/FIN ¶ F-9202; USTR ¶ 3684) which was filed before Jan. 1, '94. (§ 13226(a)(3)(B))

> RIA ***recommendation:*** A corporation which is insolvent but not in bankruptcy and which anticipates that it will issue stock in exchange for a portion of its debt in a workout should seek to do so before the Jan. 1, '95 effective date of the repeal. If it appears that the terms of the workout cannot be negotiated by that time, consider filing for bankruptcy before Jan. 1, '94 in order to avoid the consequences of the repeal.

For official explanation see Committee Reports ¶ 3048.

¶ 312. Amendments to attribute reduction rules for debt cancellation income

In general, a taxpayer who is relieved of indebtedness without paying the full principal amount is required to include the difference in income. (See FTC 2d/FIN ¶ J-7000 *et seq.;* TG ¶ 5250 *et seq.;* USTR ¶s 614.14, 1084) A special exception applies (i) where debt is discharged in a bankruptcy case, (ii) to the extent a taxpayer is insolvent, or (iii) to discharges of qualified farm indebtedness. (See FTC 2d/FIN ¶ J-7400 *et seq.;* TG ¶ 5260 *et seq.;* USTR ¶ 1084) Where this exception applies, a taxpayer who is relieved of debt for less than its principal amount does not include the difference in income, but instead applies that amount to reduce certain specified tax attributes. Once those tax attributes are all reduced to zero, any additional amount by which debt has been discharged has no tax consequences.

Under pre-'93 Act law, the tax attributes which were required to be reduced on account of a discharge of indebtedness were (i) net operating losses, (ii) general business credit carryovers, (iii) capital losses and capital loss carryovers, (iv) the taxpayer's basis in depreciable and nondepreciable assets, and (v) foreign tax credit carryovers. These attributes were required to be reduced in the order specified, unless the taxpayer elected to apply the reduction first to his basis in depreciable property. (FTC 2d/FIN ¶ J-7404; TG ¶ 5265; USTR ¶ 1084.02)

The '93 Act adds two new tax attributes to the list of those that must be reduced on account of debt discharge income. After general business credit carryovers have been reduced, and before reducing capital losses and capital loss carryovers, a taxpayer is required to reduce his "minimum tax credit" for amounts of alternative minimum tax paid in earlier years (see FTC 2d/FIN ¶ A-8135; TG ¶ 1385; USTR ¶ 1084.02). (Code Sec. 108(b)(2)(C) as amended by '93 Act § 13226(b)(1)) After the basis of assets has been reduced, and before reducing foreign tax credit carryovers, a taxpayer is required to reduce the amount of any losses or credits which were disallowed under the passive loss limitation rules and which are therefore carried over (see FTC 2d/FIN ¶ M-4600 *et seq.;* TG ¶ 6660 *et seq.;* USTR ¶ 1084.02). (Code Sec. 108(b)(2)(F) as amended by '93 Act § 13226(b)(2))

In the case of minimum tax credits and passive activity credits, the amount of the reduction is $33^1/_3$ cents per dollar of debt cancellation. (Code Sec. 108(b)(3)(B) as amended by '93 Act § 13226(b)(3)(A))

> ***observation:*** This is consistent with the amount by which general business credits and foreign tax credits are reduced.

☐ **Effective:** taxable years beginning after Dec. 31, '93. (§ 13226(b)(4))

For official explanation see Committee Reports ¶ 3049.

¶ 313. Payments to retiring or deceased partners

Under pre-'93 Act law, the treatment of a payment by a partnership to a retiring or deceased partner depended on whether the payment was made in exchange for the partner's interest in partnership property. (FTC 2d/FIN ¶ B-4102; TG ¶ 1704; USTR ¶ 7364.01) A liquidating payment in exchange for the partner's interest in partnership property was treated as a partnership distribution to the partner, who recognized gain only to the extent that the amount of cash distributed exceeded the partner's basis. (FTC 2d/FIN ¶ B-4106; TG ¶ 1705; USTR ¶ 7364.02) The treatment of a liquidating payment not made in exchange for the partner's interest in partnership property depended on whether the payment was determined by reference to partnership income. If the payment was determined by reference to partnership income, the payment was treated as an allocation of partnership income, while if the payment was not determined by reference to partnership income, the payment was treated as a deductible guaranteed payment. Treating a payment as a guaranteed payment or as an allocation of partnership income was advantageous to the remaining partners, but was detrimental to the liquidating partner, since the payment was ordinary income, rather than capital gain. (FTC 2d/FIN ¶ B-4104; TG ¶ 1707; USTR ¶ 7364.03) Payments for unrealized receivables of the partnership were not treated as payments in exchange for the partner's interest in partnership property and payments in exchange for partnership goodwill were treated as payments in exchange for the partner's interest in partnership property only if the partnership agreement provided for payments to retiring partners in exchange for their interests in partnership goodwill. (FTC 2d/FIN ¶ B-4106; TG ¶ 1707; USTR ¶ 7364.02)

Under pre-'93 Act law, unrealized receivables included accounts receivable, unbilled amounts as well as a number of other items that are treated as ordinary income, such as various recapture items. (FTC 2d/FIN ¶ B-3914 *et seq.;* TG ¶ 1691 *et seq.;* USTR ¶ 7514.02)

Under the '93 Act, payments in exchange for unrealized receivables and goodwill are, except as described below, treated as made in exchange for partnership property. (Code Sec. 736(b)(3) as amended by '93 Act § 13262(a)) This ends the pre-'93 Act

FTC 2d References are to the Federal Tax Coordinator 2d
FIN References are to RIA's Analysis of Federal Taxes: Income
TG References are to the Tax Guide
USTR References are to the United States Tax Reporter

practice of setting the amount that is paid for goodwill (and not treated as in exchange for partnership property) at a level that would maximize the combined tax savings of the liquidating partner and the continuing partners. (H Rept p. 782)

> ***observation:*** Under pre-'93 Act law, in most cases the combined tax savings of the liquidating partner and the continuing partners were maximized by treating as much of the payment as possible as made for goodwill (and not treated as in exchange for partnership property), since the continuing partners' deduction reduced their taxes by an amount greater than the increase in the taxes of the liquidating partner resulting from treating the amount as ordinary income, rather than capital gain.

The '93 Act does not change the treatment of payments in exchange for unrealized receivables and goodwill made to a retiring or deceased general partner who is a general partner in a partnership in which capital is not a material income-producing factor. (Code Sec. 736(b)(3)) For this purpose, capital is not a material income-producing factor where substantially all the gross income of the business is derived from fees, commissions, or other compensation for personal services performed by an individual. Thus, a professional practice of a doctor, dentist, lawyer, architect, or accountant is not treated as a trade or business in which capital is a material income-producing factor, even though the practitioner has a substantial investment in professional equipment or in a physical plant constituting the professional office, so long as the capital investment is only incidental to the professional practice. (H Rept p. 783) The reason for the continuation of the pre-'93 rule in these situations is that service partnerships generally do not value goodwill in liquidating partners. (H Rept p. 782) The '93 Act also does not affect the deductibility of compensation paid to a retiring partner for past services. (H Rept p. 783)

The '93 Act also changes the definition of unrealized receivables for purposes of determining the treatment of payments to a retiring or deceased partner (but not for purposes of determining the treatment of sales of partnership interests and partnership distributions) to include only accounts receivable and unbilled amounts. (Code Sec. 751(c) as amended by '93 Act § 13262(b)(1)) This prevents a partnership from deferring income by taking a current deduction for payments made to a partner in exchange for his interest in ordinary income items that will result in income to the partnership in later taxable years. (H Rept p. 783)

> ***observation:*** Although amounts paid for the liquidating partner's share of the partnership's ordinary income items, other than accounts receivable and unbilled amounts, will not be currently deductible by the partnership, they will continue to be treated as ordinary income to the liquidating partner.

☐ **Effective:** For payments to partners retiring or dying after Jan. 4, '93. (§ 13262(c)(1)) However, the '93 Act rules don't apply to partners retiring after Jan. 4, '93 if a written contract to buy the partner's interest in the partnership was binding on Jan. 4, '93 and at all times thereafter until the purchase. (§ 13262(c)(2)) For this purpose, a written contract is binding only if the contract specifies the amount to be paid for the partnership interest and the timing of the payments under the contract. (H Rept p. 783)

> ***observation:*** Presumably, a buy-sell agreement with a formula price is not treated as a binding contract under this rule, unless the partners agreed before Jan. 5, '93 on the price under the formula and the timing of the payments to the liquidating partner.

For official explanation see Committee Reports ¶ 3065.

¶ 314. Securities dealers required to use mark-to-market rules for certain securities

Under pre-'93 Act law, a dealer in securities was allowed for tax purposes to value inventories of securities held for sale at (1) cost, (2) lower of cost or market value, or (3) market value. (FTC 2d/FIN ¶ G-5021; TG ¶ 2820; USTR ¶ 4714.67)

In determining income for financial accounting purposes, however, securities dealers value their inventories of securities at market value. (H Rept p. 661)

If the inventory of securities was valued at cost for tax purposes, unrealized gains and losses with respect to the securities were not taken into account. If the inventory of securities was valued at the lower of cost or market value, unrealized losses (but not unrealized gains) with respect to the securities were taken into account for tax purposes. If the inventory of securities was valued at market value, both unrealized gains and losses with respect to the securities were taken into account for tax purposes. (H Rept p. 661)

Congress believes that the market value method of valuing inventories of securities most clearly reflects the income of securities dealers, while the cost method and the lower of cost or market method generally understates the income of securities dealers. (H Rept p. 661)

Accordingly, the '93 Act generally requires securities dealers to mark their securities inventories to market for tax purposes, effective for tax years ending on or after Dec. 31, '93. (Code Sec. 475 as added by '93 Act 13223(a))

> ***observation:*** Thus, the new mark-to-market rules for securities dealers apply for calendar year '93.

Summary. The Act provides two mark-to-market rules for securities (defined below) held by a dealer in securities (see below). Under the first rule, any security that is inventory in the hands of the dealer must be included in inventory at its fair market value. Under the second rule, any security that is not inventory in the hands of the dealer and that is held at the close of any tax year is treated as sold by the dealer for its fair market value on the last business day of the tax year, and any gain or loss must be taken into account by the dealer in determining gross income for that year. (H Rept p. 661) Gain or loss taken into account under the second rule is generally treated as ordinary income or loss. (H Rept p. 662)

Hedges of securities that are subject to the mark-to-market rules are treated similarly to the hedged securities. Thus, such hedges are marked to market and any gain or loss with respect to the hedges is treated as ordinary gain or loss. (H Rept pp. 661 and 666)

The Act does not require the use of specific valuation methods for purposes of applying the mark-to-market rules. However, IRS will authorize the use of valuation methods that will alleviate unnecessary compliance burdens for taxpayers and clearly reflect income for tax purposes. (Conf Rept p. 616)

Exceptions to the mark-to-market rules apply in the case of securities held for investment and certain other securities. (Code Sec. 475(b)) See below.

Although the mark-to-market rules apply to tax years ending on or after Dec. 31, '93, the net amount of the adjustments to taxable income required as a result of the change in accounting method is generally taken into account ratably over a five-year period. (§ 13223(c)) See below.

FTC 2d References are to the Federal Tax Coordinator 2d
FIN References are to RIA's Analysis of Federal Taxes: Income
TG References are to the Tax Guide
USTR References are to the United States Tax Reporter

These mark-to-market rules do not apply for purposes of determining the holding period of any security. (H Rept p. 662)

Nor do they apply in determining whether gain or loss is recognized by any other taxpayer that may be a party to a contract with a dealer in securities. (H Rept p. 662)

These mark-to-market rules apply to securities held by a dealer notwithstanding any other Code provision relating to accounting methods for inventories. (Code Sec. 475(a))

Dealer in securities. For purposes of these mark-to-market rules, a dealer in securities is defined as a taxpayer who either (1) regularly purchases securities from or sells securities to customers in the ordinary course of a trade or business, (Code Sec. 475(c)(1)(A)) or (2) regularly offers to enter into, assume, offset, assign or otherwise terminate positions in securities with customers in the ordinary course of a trade or business. (Code Sec. 475(c)(1)(B))

What is a security? A security, for purposes of these mark-to-market rules, means the following:

(1) Any share of stock in a corporation. (Code Sec. 475(c)(2)(A))

(2) Any partnership or beneficial ownership interest in a widely held or publicly traded partnership or trust. (Code Sec. 475(c)(2)(B))

(3) Any note, bond, debenture, or other evidence of indebtedness. (Code Sec. 475(c)(2)(C))

(4) Any interest rate, currency, or equity notional principal contract. (Code Sec. 475(c)(2)(D)) But a security for this purpose doesn't include any other notional principal contract such as a notional principal contract that is based on the price of oil, wheat or any other commodity. (H Rept p. 662)

> RIA ***observation:*** A notional principal contract is generally a financial instrument that provides for payments based upon a specified index. (See FTC 2d/FIN ¶ O-10921; TG ¶ 8309; USTR ¶ 8634.05)

(5) Any evidence of an interest in, or a derivative financial instrument in, any security described in (1) through (4) above, or any currency, including any option, forward contract, short position, and any similar financial instrument in such a security or currency. (Code Sec. 475(c)(2)(E))

(6) Any position that (a) is not a security described in (1) through (5) above, (b) is a hedge with respect to such a security, and (c) is clearly identified in the dealer's records as being such a hedge. The position must be identified in the dealer's records as a hedge with respect to a security before the close of the day on which the position was acquired or entered into (or such other time as IRS may specify in regs). (Code Sec. 475(c)(2)(F)) For effect of improper identification of such a position, see below.

A security described in (5) above doesn't include any contract subject to the mark-to-market rules of Code Sec. 1256(a) (section 1256 contracts, see FTC 2d/FIN ¶ I-4350 *et seq.;* TG ¶ 4154; USTR ¶ 12,564) (Code Sec. 475(c)(2)), unless the contract is a hedge of a security to which Code Sec. 475 applies. (H Rept p. 662) If any such contract is a hedge of a security to which Code Sec. 475 applies, the character rule discussed below (rather than the character rule of Code Sec. 1256(a), see FTC 2d/FIN ¶ I-4352; TG ¶ 4154; USTR ¶ 12,564.01) applies to the contract. (H Rept p. 663)

For the definition of hedge, see below.

For specific exceptions to these mark-to-market rules in the case of certain securities, see below.

Hedge. A hedge for purposes of these mark-to-market rules is any position that reduces the dealer's risk of interest rate or price changes or currency fluctuations, including any position that is reasonably expected to become a hedge within 60 days after the acquisition of the position. (Code Sec. 475(c)(3))

Mark-to-market rule for security that is inventory. Any security that is inventory in the hands of the dealer must be included in inventory at its fair market value. (Code Sec. 475(a)(1))

Mark-to-market rule for security that is not inventory. In the case of any security that is not inventory in the hands of the dealer and that is held at the close of any tax year, the dealer must recognize gain or loss as if the security were sold for its fair market value on the last business day of that tax year, and any gain or loss must be taken into account for that tax year. (Code Sec. 475(a)(2)) The gain or loss is required to be taken into account by the dealer in computing gross income for that year. (H Rept p. 661)

For purposes of this rule, a security is treated as sold to a person that is not related to the dealer even if the security is itself a contract between the dealer and a related person. Thus, for example, Code Sec. 267 (relating to denial of deduction for losses on sales between related taxpayers, see FTC 2d/FIN ¶ I-2900 *et seq.;* TG ¶ 4100 *et seq.;* USTR ¶ 2674) and Code Sec. 707(b) (relating to disallowance of losses on sales with respect to controlled partnerships, see FTC 2d/FIN ¶ B-2016; TG ¶ 1643; USTR ¶ 7074.03) don't apply to any loss that must be taken into account under this rule. (H Rept p. 661)

The amount of any gain or loss subsequently realized must be properly adjusted for gain or loss taken into account under this rule. (Code Sec. 475(a)(2)) Thus, if gain or loss is taken into account under the rule with respect to a security that is not inventory, the amount of gain or loss subsequently realized as a result of a sale, exchange, or other disposition of the security, or as a result of the application of the mark-to-market rules, must be appropriately adjusted to reflect the gain or loss taken into account under this rule. (H Rept p. 661)

> ***observation:*** Presumably this means the basis of the security must be adjusted.

IRS is authorized to issue regs providing for the application of this mark-to-market rule at times other than the times specified above, (Code Sec. 475(a)(2)) for example, at times other than the close of a tax year or the last business day of a tax year. (H Rept p. 662)

For the character of the gain or loss, see below.

For disposition of securities before the close of the tax year, see below.

Character of gain or loss. Except as discussed below or in Code Sec. 1236(b) (dealing with losses on dealer's investment securities, see FTC 2d/FIN ¶ I-4265; TG ¶ 4503; USTR ¶ 12,364.01), any gain or loss taken into account with respect to a security under the mark-to-market rule for a security that isn't inventory (see above) is treated as ordinary income or loss. (Code Sec. 475(d)(3)(A)(i))

The above character rule doesn't apply to any gain or loss allocable to a period during which:

(1) the security is a hedge not subject to the mark-to-market rules, as described in (4) or (5) below under "Exceptions to mark-to-market rules for certain securities" (without regard to the identification requirement), (Code Sec. 475(d)(3)(B)(i)) or

FTC 2d References are to the Federal Tax Coordinator 2d
FIN References are to RIA's Analysis of Federal Taxes: Income
TG References are to the Tax Guide
USTR References are to the United States Tax Reporter

(2) the security is not held by the taxpayer in connection with its activities as a dealer in securities, (Code Sec. 475(d)(3)(B)(ii)) or

(3) the security is improperly identified (as explained below). (Code Sec. 475(d)(3)(B)(iii))

No inference is intended as to the character of any gain or loss recognized in tax years before the enactment of these mark-to-market rules or any gain or loss recognized with respect to any property to which this character rule does not apply. (H Rept p. 662)

Dispositions of securities before close of tax year. The character rule discussed above also applies in the case of dispositions of a security before the close of the tax year. Thus, the Act provides that if gain or loss is recognized with respect to a security before the close of the tax year, and the mark-to-market rule for a security that isn't inventory (see above) would have applied if the security were held as of the close of the tax year, the gain or loss is treated as ordinary income or loss. (Code Sec. 475(d)(3)(A)(ii))

Exceptions to mark-to-market rules for certain securities. Notwithstanding the definition of security (see above), (H Rept p. 663) the mark-to-market rules don't apply to the following securities:

(1) Any security held for investment. (Code Sec. 475(b)(1)(A)) To the extent provided in regs, however, this exception doesn't apply to any security described in (4) or (5) under "What is a security" (see above) that is held by a dealer in such securities. (Code Sec. 475(b)(4)) Thus, this exception doesn't apply to any notional principal contract or any derivative financial instrument held by a dealer in those securities. (H Rept p. 663)

(2) Any security that is a note, bond, debenture, or other evidence of indebtedness that is acquired (including originated) by the taxpayer in the ordinary course of the taxpayer's trade or business and that is not held for sale. (Code Sec. 475(b)(1)(B)(i))

(3) Any obligation to acquire a security described in (2) if the obligation is entered into in the ordinary course of the taxpayer's trade or business and is not held for sale. (Code Sec. 475(b)(1)(B)(ii))

(4) Any security that is a hedge (defined above) with respect to a security that is not subject to the mark-to-market rules. (Code Sec. 475(b)(1)(C)(i)) Thus, this exception applies to any security that is a hedge with respect to a security described in (1) through (3) above. (H Rept p. 663)

(5) Any security that is a hedge (defined above) with respect to a position, right to income, or a liability that is not a security in the hands of the taxpayer. (Code Sec. 475(b)(1)(C)(ii))

Debt issued by a taxpayer is not a security in the hands of that taxpayer for purposes of the mark-to-market rules. (H Rept p. 663)

To the extent provided in regs, the exceptions to the mark-to-market rules for certain hedges described in (4) and (5) above don't apply to any security held by a person in its capacity as a dealer in securities. (Code Sec. 475(b)(1)) Thus, regs may provide that the exceptions for hedges don't apply to securities that are entered into with customers in the ordinary course of a trade or business. (H Rept p. 663)

In addition, a dealer may not treat a security that is identified as a hedge or as an investment as also held in its capacity as dealer. Thus, securities identified as qualifying for one of the exceptions to the mark-to-market rules may not be accounted for using the lower of cost or market or other inventory method of accounting. (H Rept p. 663)

Whether or not a security or evidence of indebtedness must be marked-to-market under the applicable financial accounting rules is not dispositive for purposes of determining whether the security or evidence of indebtedness is treated as held for investment or as not held for sale under the above rules. (H Rept p. 663)

Identification required for exceptions to apply. A security isn't treated as qualifying for one of the exceptions to the mark-to-market rules listed above, unless the security is clearly identified in the dealer's records as being described in that exception. (Code Sec. 475(b)(2))

A security is treated as clearly identified in a dealer's records as being described in one of the exceptions listed above if all securities of the taxpayer that are not so described are clearly identified in the dealer's records as not being described in that exception. (H Rept p. 664)

> ***Illustration:*** In the ordinary course of its trade or business, a bank originates loans that are sold if the loans satisfy certain conditions. The bank determines whether a loan satisfies the conditions within 30 days after the loan is made. If a loan satisfies the conditions for sale, the bank records the loan in a separate account on the date that the determination is made. For purposes of the mark-to-market rules, the bank is a dealer in securities with respect to the loans that it holds for sale. In addition, by identifying these loans as held for sale, the bank is considered to have identified all other loans as not held for sale. Thus, the loans that are not held for sale are not subject to the mark-to-market rules. (H Rept. p. 664)

The identification rules with respect to hedges will be applied in such a manner as to minimize the imposition of additional accounting burdens on dealers in securities. For example, certain taxpayers engage in risk management strategies known as "global hedging." Under global hedging, the positions of one business unit of the taxpayer may be counter-balanced by positions of another separate business unit; any remaining net risk of the enterprise may then be hedged by entering into positions with unrelated third parties. Taxpayers engaging in global hedging often use accounting systems that clearly identify and treat the transactions entered into between the separate business units as if the transactions were entered into with unrelated third parties. Subject to IRS regs, such an accounting system generally will provide adequate evidence for purposes of determining whether, and to what extent, a hedge with a third party is (1) a hedge of a security that is subject to the mark-to-market rules or (2) a hedge of a position, right to income, or a liability that is not subject to a mark-to-market rule, for purposes of applying the mark-to-market rules and the special character rule to a hedge with a third party. (Conf Rept p. 615)

In order to satisfy the clear identification requirement, the security must be identified before the close of the day on which it was acquired, originated, or entered into (or such other time as IRS may specify in regs). (Code Sec. 475(b)(2))

IRS regs will permit a financial institution that is treated as a dealer under the mark-to-market rules and that originates evidences of indebtedness in the ordinary course of a trade or business to identify the evidences of indebtedness as held for investment based on the accounting practices of the institution, but in no event later than 30 days after the date that any such evidence of indebtedness is originated. Where appropriate, the regulations may provide similar identification rules for similar debt that is acquired, rather than originated, by a financial institution. (Conf Rept p. 615)

In addition, IRS regs will permit a dealer that enters into commitments to acquire mortgages to identify the commitments as being held for investment if the dealer acquires the mortgages and holds the mortgages as investments. This identification of commitments to acquire mortgages must occur within an appropriate period after the acquisition of the mortgages, but in no event later than 30 days after the date that the mortgages are acquired. (Conf Rept p. 615)

In the case of any security that is held on the date of enactment of the mark-to-market rules, the security must be identified as being described in one of the exceptions within a reasonable period after the date of enactment but in no event later than 30 days after the date of enactment. The date of enactment is Aug. 10, '93. (H Rept p. 667)

For the effect of changes in the capacity in which a security is held by the dealer, see below.

For the effect of improper identification, see below.

Changes in capacity in which security is held by dealer. In addition to clearly identifying a security as qualifying for one of the exceptions to the mark-to-market rules, a dealer must continue to hold the security in a capacity that qualifies the security for one of the exceptions listed above. (H Rept p. 664) If a security ceases to be described in one of the exceptions to the mark-to-market rules at any time after it was identified as such, as required under the rules above, the mark-to-market rules apply to any changes in value of the security occurring after the cessation. (Code Sec. 475(b)(3))

Any gain or loss that is attributable to the period that the security was not subject to the mark-to-market rules generally is to be taken into account at the time that the security is actually sold (rather than treated as sold by reason of the mark-to-market rules). (H Rept p. 664)

Different rules apply to a security that originally is held by the taxpayer in a capacity that subjects the security to the mark-to-market rules, but later becomes eligible for an exception to the mark-to-market rules. For example, if a security to which the mark-to-market rules apply is hedged (and thus the hedge is subject to the mark-to-market rules), and the security (but not the hedge) is sold before year end, then the "naked" hedge generally will be subject to the mark-to-market rules at year's end.

However, IRS has authority to issue regs that would allow the taxpayer to identify, on the date the security is sold, the "naked" hedge as a security to which one of the exceptions to the mark-to-market rules applies (assuming the "naked" hedge otherwise qualifies for the exception). In making this identification, the taxpayer must apply the mark-to-market rules to the "naked" hedge as of the date of the sale of the security, take any resulting gain or loss into account for the tax year of sale, and treat the "naked" hedge as a security to which the exceptions to the mark-to-market rules apply.

Whether or not the taxpayer is allowed under regs to make the identification described above (and whether or not the taxpayer makes the identification), any gain or loss attributable to the period after the date of sale of the security will not be subject to the special character rule (see above) if the hedge is not held by the taxpayer in its capacity as a dealer during that period. Thus, if the "naked" hedge is a capital asset in the hands of the taxpayer, any gain or loss recognized with respect to the "naked" hedge that is attributable to the period after the date of sale of the security will be capital gain or loss. (H Rept p. 664)

Improper identification. If a taxpayer either

(1) identifies a security as being described in one of the exceptions to the mark-to-market rules (as required in order for the exceptions to apply, see above) and the security is not so described, (Code Sec. 475(d)(2)(A)) or

(2) fails to identify a position that is a hedge with respect to a security, described in item (6) under "what is a security," see above, (without regard to the requirement for identification) at the time such identification is required, (Code Sec. 475(d)(2)(B)) then the mark-to-market rules apply to the security or position, except that any loss under these rules before the disposition of the security or position is recognized only to the extent of gain previously recognized under the these rules (and not previously taken into account under this improper identification rule) with respect to the security or position. (Code Sec. 475(d)(2))

The situation in (2) above exists if a dealer fails to identify a position that is not a security as a hedge of a security but the position is a hedge of a security. (H Rept p. 665)

Coordination with other rules. The following rules don't apply to securities that are subject to the above mark-to-market rules: (Code Sec. 475(d)(1))

(1) The uniform capitalization rules of Code Sec. 263A. (See FTC 2d/FIN ¶ G-5150 *et seq.*, TG ¶ 6080 *et seq.;* USTR ¶ 263A4)

(2) The capitalization rules of Code Sec. 263(g) for certain interest and carrying charges in the case of straddles. (See FTC 2d/FIN ¶ L-5985 *et seq.;* TG ¶ 6104; USTR ¶ 2634)

(3) The mark-to-market rules of Code Sec. 1256(a) for regulated futures contracts (section 1256 contracts). (See FTC 2d/FIN ¶ I-4350 *et seq.;* TG ¶ 4154 *et seq.;* USTR ¶ 12,564.01)

In addition, the wash sale rules of Code Sec. 1091 (see FTC 2d/FIN ¶ I-2700 *et seq.;* TG ¶ 4170 *et seq.;* USTR ¶ 10,914) do not apply to any loss recognized under the mark-to-market rule. Instead, the loss rules of Code Sec. 1092 for straddles (see FTC 2d/FIN ¶ I-4300 *et seq.;* TG ¶ 4150 *et seq.;* USTR ¶ 10,924) apply to the loss. (Code Sec. 475(d)(1)) Thus, a security subject to the mark-to-market rules is not treated as sold and reacquired for purposes of Code Sec. 1091. Code Sec. 1092 will apply to any loss recognized under the mark-to-market rules (but will have no effect if all the offsetting positions that make up the straddle are subject to the mark-to-market rules). (H Rept p. 665)

Furthermore, these mark-to-market rules don't apply to any section 988 transaction (generally, a foreign currency transaction, see FTC 2d/FIN ¶ G-6917 *et seq.;* TG ¶ 8346 *et seq.;* USTR ¶ 9884.02) that is part of a section 988 hedging transaction. The determination of whether a transaction is a section 988 transaction is made without regard to whether the transaction would otherwise be marked to market under these mark-to-market rules. (Code Sec. 988(d)(1) as amended by '93 Act § 13223(b)(1)) (FTC 2d/FIN ¶ G-6934; TG ¶ 8353; USTR ¶ 9884.02)

Regulations authorized. In addition to the regulations discussed above, IRS is authorized to issue such regulations as may be necessary or appropriate to carry out the purposes of the above mark-to-market rules for securities dealers. (Code Sec. 475(e)) This includes rules to:

. . . prevent the use of year-end transfers, related parties, or other arrangements to avoid the above mark-to-market rules. (Code Sec. 475(e)(1))

FTC 2d References are to the Federal Tax Coordinator 2d
FIN References are to RIA's Analysis of Federal Taxes: Income
TG References are to the Tax Guide
USTR References are to the United States Tax Reporter

For example, if an individual who is not subject to the mark-to-market rules contributes a security that has a built-in loss in the hands of the individual to a partnership that is subject to the mark-to-market rules, IRS regs may provide that any loss that arose prior to the contribution to the partnership may no be taken into account by the partnership under the mark-to-market rules and that the suspended loss may be taken into account when the security is sold. On the other hand, if, prior to year end, a partnership that is subject to the mark-to-market rules distributes a security with a built-in gain to a partner that is not subject to the rules, IRS regs may provide that the mark-to-market rules are to apply to the partnership with respect to the security as of the date of distribution. (Conf Rept p. 616)

. . . provide for application of these mark-to-market rules to any security that is a hedge that can't be identified with a specific security, position, right to income, or liability. (Code Sec. 475(e)(2))

Thus, IRS may issue regs that provide for the treatment of a hedge that reduce a dealer's risk of interest rate or price changes or currency fluctuations with respect to securities that are subject to the mark-to-market rules as well as with respect to securities, positions, rights to income, or liabilities that are not subject to the mark-to-market rules. The regs may allow taxpayers to treat any such hedge as not subject to the mark-to-market rules provided that such treatment is consistently followed from year to year. (H Rept p. 665)

. . . coordinate the mark-to-market rules with the original issue discount rules. (H Rept p. 665)

Change in accounting method. If a taxpayer is required by the above mark-to-market rules for securities dealers to change its accounting method for any tax year, the following rules apply: (§ 13223(c)(2))

(1) The change is treated as initiated by the taxpayer. (§ 13223(c)(2)(A))

(2) The change is treated as made with IRS consent. (§ 13223(c)(2)(B))

(3) Except in the case of a floor specialist or a market maker (see below), the net amount of adjustments required to be taken into account by the taxpayer under Code Sec. 481 (the section 481(a) adjustment) as a result of the change in accounting method (FTC 2d/FIN ¶ G-2250 *et seq.;* TG ¶ 2697 *et seq.;* USTR ¶ 4814) is taken into account ratably over the five-taxable year period beginning with the first tax year ending on or after Dec. 31, '93. (§ 13223(c)(2)(C))

The principles of section 8.03(1) and (2) of Rev Proc 92-20 (dealing with acceleration of the section 481(a) adjustment period in the case of certain reductions in inventory value and in cases where the taxpayer ceases to engage in the trade or business, see FTC 2d/FIN ¶ G-2275.31 *et seq.;* USTR ¶ 4814) apply to the section 481(a) adjustment. Section 8.03(1) of Rev Proc 92-20 (reduction in inventory value) will be applied by taking into account all securities of a dealer that are subject to the mark-to-market rules (including those securities that are not inventory in the hands of the dealer). In addition, net operating losses will be allowed to offset the section 481(a) adjustment, tax credit carryforwards will be allowed to offset any tax attributable to the section 481(a) adjustment, and, for purposes of determining liability for estimated taxes, the section 481(a) adjustment will be taken into account ratably throughout the tax year in question. (H Rept p. 666)

In determining the amount of the section 481(a) adjustment for tax years beginning before the date of enactment of the mark-to-market rules, the identification requirements are to be applied in a reasonable manner. It is anticipated that any security that was identified as being held for investment under Code Sec. 1236(a) (investment identification rules for securities dealers, see FTC 2d/FIN ¶ I-4259;

USTR ¶ 12,364) as of the last day of the tax year preceding the tax year of change is to be treated as held for investment for purposes of the mark-to-market rules. It is also anticipated than any other security that was held as of the last day of the tax year preceding the tax year of change is to be treated as properly identified if the dealer's records as of that date support identification. (H Rept p. 667)

Floor specialists and market makers. A special transitional rule applies for floor specialists and market makers. (§ 13223(c)(3))

If a taxpayer (or any predecessor) used the last-in first-out (LIFO) method of accounting for any qualified securities (defined below) for the five-taxable year period ending with its last tax year ending before Dec. 31, '93, and a portion of the net amount of the section 481(a) adjustment (see above) is attributable to the use of the LIFO method of accounting, then such portion of the adjustment is taken into account ratably over the 15-taxable year period beginning with the first tax year ending on or after Dec. 31, '93. (§ 13223(c)(3)(A))

A *qualified security* for this purpose means: (§ 13223(c)(3)(B))

(1) any security acquired by a floor specialist (defined in Code Sec. 1236(d)(2), see FTC 2d/FIN ¶ 4262; TG ¶ 4506; USTR ¶ 12,364.02) in connection with the specialist's duties as a specialist on an exchange, but only if the security is one in which the specialist is registered with the exchange, (§ 13223(c)(3)(B)(i)) or

(2) any security acquired by a taxpayer who is a market maker in connection with the taxpayer's duties as a market maker, but only if (a) the security is included on the National Association of Security Dealers Automated Quotation System (NASDAQ), (b) the taxpayer is registered as a market maker in the security with the National Association of Security Dealers, and (c) as of the last day of the tax year preceding the taxpayer's first tax year ending on or after Dec. 31, '93, the taxpayer (or any predecessor) has been actively and regularly engaged as a market maker in the security for the two-year period ending on such date (or, if shorter, the period beginning 61 days after the security was listed in NASDAQ and ending on such date). (§ 13223(c)(3)(B)(ii))

The portion of the section 481(a) adjustment that is attributable to the use of the LIFO inventory method of accounting for any qualified security is determined under the rules in Code Sec. 312(n)(4) (the rules for determining LIFO inventory adjustments to be made in computing a corporation's earnings and profits, see FTC 2d/FIN ¶ F-10212 *et seq.;* TG ¶ 2248; USTR ¶ 3124.07), without regard to the effective date of those rules. In addition, the portion of the section 481(a) adjustment that is eligible to be taken into account over the 15-year period for floor specialists and market makers may not exceed the taxpayer's overall section 481(a) adjustment for all securities under the mark-to-market rules. (S Rept p. 283)

☐ **Effective:** Tax years ending on or after Dec. 31, '93. (§ 13223(c)(1))
For official explanation see Committee Reports ¶ 3045.

¶ 315. Employers are allowed a tax credit for a portion of social security taxes paid on employee cash tip income

Under the '93 Act, food or beverage establishments are allowed a business tax credit for a portion of employer social security taxes paid with respect to their employees' cash tips. (Code Sec. 45B as added by '93 Act § 13443)

FTC 2d References are to the Federal Tax Coordinator 2d
FIN References are to RIA's Analysis of Federal Taxes: Income
TG References are to the Tax Guide
USTR References are to the United States Tax Reporter

The employer, however, may elect not to take the credit for the tax year. (Code Sec. 45B(d))

Amount of credit. The credit is equal to the "excess employer social security tax" paid or incurred by the employer during the tax year. (Code Sec. 45B(a)) The "excess employer social security tax" is the social security tax paid by the employer on tips received by the employee during the month, to the extent the tips:

(1) are considered to have been paid by the employer to the employee under Code Sec. 3121(q) (FTC 2d ¶ H-4765 *et seq.;* TG ¶ 3579.62) and

(2) are more than the amount by which the employee's wages (excluding tips), paid to the employee by the employer during the month, are less than the total amount payable, with respect to the employment, at the minimum wage rate applicable to the employee under the minimum wage provision—section 6(a)(1) of the Fair Labor Standards Act of 1938 (determined without regard to section 3(m) of the Act). (Code Sec. 45B(a); Code Sec. 45B(b)(1))

Tips taken into account. Only tips received at food and beverage establishments are taken into account in determining the amount of the credit. Thus, the employer must take into account only those tips received from customers in connection with providing food or beverages for consumption *on the premises of the establishment* and with respect to which the tipping of employees serving food or beverages by customers is customary. (Code Sec. 45B(b)(2))

This rule uses the same criteria as that used for reporting tips at large food and beverage establishments (FTC 2d/FIN ¶ S-3236; TG ¶ 9333; USTR ¶ 60,534), except that the number of employees (more than ten) is not taken into account. (Conf Rept. p. 736)

Double Benefit. To prevent double benefits, no deduction is allowed the employer for any amount used to compute the credit. (Code Sec. 45B(c))

Credit as part of general business credit. Various credits, such as the investment tax credit, targeted jobs credit, and the alcohol fuel credit, are combined into a "general business credit" in order to determine each credit's allowance limitation for the taxable year. (FTC 2d/FIN ¶ L-15200; TG ¶ 5701; USTR ¶ 384) The employer social security credit is part of the "general business credit." (Code Sec. 38(b)(11) as amended by '93 Act § 13443(b)(1))

Limitation on carrybacks. There is a three-year carryback and a 15-year carryforward for the current year unused business credits. (FTC 2d/FIN ¶ L-15209 *et seq.;* TG ¶ 5706; USTR ¶ 394) However, no portion of the unused business credit for a tax year which is attributable to the employer social security credit can be carried back to a tax year ending before Aug. 10, '93. (Code Sec. 39(b)(6) as amended by '93 Act § 13443(b)(2))

☐ **Effective:** For taxes paid after Dec. 31, '93. (§ 13443(d))

For official explanation see Committee Reports ¶ 3080.

¶ 316. Corporate estimated tax payments based on current year's tax permanently increased from 97% to 100% for tax years beginning after '93

Under pre-'93 Act law, a corporations generally was required to make estimated tax payments equal to the lesser of:

. . . (a) 97% of the tax shown on its return for the current year (91% for tax years beginning after '96); or

. . . (b) 100% of the tax for the prior year. (FTC 2d/FIN ¶ S-5404; TG ¶ 2490; USTR ¶ 66,554)

However, a "large corporation" (one with taxable income of $1,000,000 or more in any of its three immediately preceding years, see FTC 2d/FIN ¶ S-5412; TG ¶ 2491; USTR ¶ 66,554) can use the 100%-of-prior-year's-tax safe harbor only for its first quarter installment payment (see FTC 2d/FIN ¶ S-5408; TG ¶ 2491; USTR ¶ 66,554).

These estimated tax rules also apply to exempt organizations, for payment of unrelated business taxable income and, in the case of private foundations, for net investment income and other taxes. (See FTC 2d/FIN ¶s S-5601, S-5602; TG ¶ 2497; USTR ¶ 66,554)

Congress believes that corporations should remit more timely their current year tax liabilities. (H Rept p. 673) Therefore, under the '93 Act, a corporation that bases its estimated tax on its current year's tax must make estimated tax payments equal to 100% of the tax shown on its return for the current year (Code Sec. 6655(d)(1)(B)(i) as amended by '93 Act § 13225(a)(1)), for tax years beginning after Dec. 31, '93 (§ 13225(c)). The reversion to 91% after '96 is eliminated. (Code Sec. 6655(d)(1)(B)(i))

> **observation:** Thus, the 100% is permanent and won't revert to 91% after '96.

However, the '93 Act doesn't change the availability of the 100%-of-prior-year's-tax safe harbor for large or small corporations. (H Rept p. 673) (§ 13225(a)(2)(A)(i))

☐ **Effective:** For tax years beginning after Dec. 31, '93. (§ 13225(c))

For official explanation see Committee Reports ¶ 3047.

¶ 317. Additional annualization periods for estimated taxes for corporations (and exempt organizations)

A corporation is permitted to use an "annualized income" method in determining its required installment payment of estimated taxes. Under this method, a corporation must establish that the "annualized income installment" (see below) is less than the installment determined under the current or prior year methods. (See FTC 2d/FIN ¶ S-5414; TG ¶ 2493; USTR ¶ 66,554)

Under pre-'93 Act law, the annualized income method permits a corporation to compute its estimated tax installments as of (i) the first 3 months of the corporation's tax year for the installment due in the 4th month (the 1st installment), (ii) the first 3 or 5 months for the installment due in the 6th month (the 2nd installment), (iii) the first 6 or 8 months for the installment due in the 9th month (the 3rd installment), and (iv) the first 9 or 11 months for the installment due in the 12th month (the 4th installment). (FTC 2d/FIN ¶ S-5415; TG ¶ 2493; USTR ¶ 66,554)

Congress believes the calculation of annualized income should be rationalized and the annualization periods applied consistently. (H Rept p. 673)

The Act therefore strips out the "or 5 months," "or 8 months," and "or 11 months" from the pre-'93 Act rules described above (Code Sec. 6655(e)(2)(A)(i) as amended by '93 Act § 13225(b)(1)) (leaving just the 3-, 3-, 6-, and 9-month periods), but permits a corporation to instead elect one of two other sets of annualization

FTC 2d References are to the Federal Tax Coordinator 2d
FIN References are to RIA's Analysis of Federal Taxes: Income
TG References are to the Tax Guide
USTR References are to the United States Tax Reporter

periods. (Code Sec. 6655(e)(2)(C) as amended by '93 Act § 13225(b)(2)) Specifically, under the '93 Act, "annualized income" is determined based on:

. . . (A) the first 3 months of the corporation's tax year for the 1st and 2nd installments, the first 6 months for the 3rd installment, and the first 9 months for the 4th installment (Code Sec. 6655(e)(2)(A)(i)), or
if the corporation makes an election, applicable to the tax year for which the election is made (Code Sec. 6655(e)(2)(C)(iii) as amended by '93 Act § 13225(b)(2)), annualized income can be based on either

. . . (B) the first 2 months for the 1st installment, the first 4 months for the 2nd installment, the first 7 months for the 3rd installment, and the first 10 months for the 4th installment (Code Sec. 6655(e)(2)(C)(i)), or

. . . (C) the first 3 months for the 1st installment, the first 5 months for the 2nd installment, the first 8 months for the 3rd installment, and the first 11 months for the 4th installment. (Code Sec. 6655(e)(2)(C)(ii))

This election must be made annually in a manner prescribed by IRS (H Rept p. 674), by the due date for the 1st estimated tax installment. (Code Sec. 6655(e)(2)(C)(iii))

observation: The Act gives a corporation three sets of annualization periods, but requires the corporation to choose one of the two elective sets—to in effect pick one of the three sets available—by the due date for the 1st installment. Under pre-'93 Act law, a corporation had only two periods to choose from for the 2nd, 3rd, or 4th installments, but the corporation didn't have to decide by the 1st installment.

caution: A corporation that doesn't use the annualized income method for the 1st installment, and doesn't elect, will be limited to the periods in (A), above, if it uses the annualization method for later installments.

Here are the annualization periods before and after the Act:

	Pre-'93 Act	Tax Years Beginning after '93		
	(No Election)	(No Election)	(Must Elect)	(Must Elect)
1st installment	1st 3 months	1st 3	1st 2	1st 3
2nd installment	1st 3 or 5 months	1st 3	1st 4	1st 5
3rd installment	1st 6 or 8 months	1st 6	1st 7	1st 8
4th installment	1st 9 or 11 months	1st 9	1st 10	1st 11

100% (up from 97%) of annualized tax must be paid by the 4th quarter. The annualized income installment is the excess (if any) of:

(i) an amount equal to the applicable percentage (see below) of the current year's tax computed by placing on an annualized basis the taxable income, alternative minimum taxable income, and modified alternative minimum taxable income (used for environmental tax purposes under Code Sec. 59A(b)) for months (see below) in the tax year ending before the due date for the installment, *over*

(ii) the aggregate amount of any earlier required installments for the year.

Under pre-'93 Act law, the applicable percentages were (FTC 2d/FIN ¶ S-5415; TG ¶ 2493; USTR ¶ 66,554):

For tax years beginning:	Installment			
	1st	2nd	3rd	4th
Before '97	24.25	48.50	72.75	97
After '96	22.75	45.50	68.25	91

Under the '93 Act, the pre-'97 percentages are deleted (§ 13225(a)(2)(A)(i)), the drop-down to 91% after '96 is eliminated, and the applicable percentages are changed to: (Code Sec. 6655(e)(2)(B)(ii) as amended by '93 Act § 13225(a)(2)(B))

Installment			
1st	2nd	3rd	4th
25	50	75	100

Additional set of annualization periods for exempt organizations. Exempt organizations are subject to estimated tax rules that are similar to the corporate estimated tax rules. (See FTC 2d/FIN ¶s S-5601, S-5602; TG ¶ 2497; USTR ¶ 66,554) However, under pre-'93 Act law the exempt organizations had to modify the pre-Act annualization periods (described above) for regular corporations. For the 1st installment, instead of annualizing income of the first "3 months," the Code says to substitute "2 months." For the 2nd installment, instead of the first 3 or 5 months, substitute "'4 months' for '5 months.'" For the 3rd installment, instead of the first 6 or 8 months, substitute "'7 months' for '8 months.'" And for the 4th installment, instead of the first 9 or 11 months, substitute "'10 months' for '11 months.'" Thus, under pre-'93 Act law, exempt organizations computed estimated tax installments using the following annualization periods:

Installment	Months Annualized
1st	1st 2
2nd	1st 3 or 1st 4
3rd	1st 6 or 1st 7
4th	1st 9 or 1st 10

The Act doesn't change the pre-Act substitutions discussed above. The Act permits exempt organizations to also elect either of the same two groups of annualization periods that regular corporations can elect (see discussion above). (Code Sec. 6655(g)(3) as amended by '93 Act § 13225(b)(3))

> ***observation:*** Although, after the Act, the Code still requires the substitutions described above (unless an election is made), only the first substitution—2 months instead of 3 months—can still be made. It's not possible to substitute 4 months for 5 months, 7 months for 8 months, or 10 months for 11 months, because the Act stripped out the 5-, 8-, and 11-month alternatives (see discussion of the Act changes made to the regular corporation rules, above). Thus, it's not clear just which annualization periods are available to an exempt organization that doesn't elect one of the two sets of periods. The references to substitutions probably will require a future technical correction.

FTC 2d References are to the Federal Tax Coordinator 2d
FIN References are to RIA's Analysis of Federal Taxes: Income
TG References are to the Tax Guide
USTR References are to the United States Tax Reporter

☐ **Effective:** For tax years beginning after Dec. 31, '93. (§ 13225(c))

For official explanation see Committee Reports ¶ 3047.

¶ 318. Estimated tax payment percentage under adjusted seasonal installment method for corporations increased from 97% to 100% for tax years beginning after '93

For corporations (including exempt organizations) with seasonal income, the adjusted seasonal installment becomes the required one for payment of estimated taxes if it is less than the installment determined under the current year, the prior year, or the annualized income methods. The adjusted seasonal installment method is available if a corporation's "base period percentage" for any six consecutive months of the tax year equals or exceeds 70%. (See FTC 2d/FIN ¶ S-5420; TG ¶ 2494; USTR ¶ 66,554)

Under pre-'93 Act law, a corporation's adjusted seasonal installment is the excess of (a) 97% (91% for tax years beginning after '96) times an amount (determined below) over (b) the aggregate of all earlier required installments.

The amount in (a) is determined by (1) taking the taxable income for all months (during the tax year) before the month in which the installment is due (the filing month), (2) dividing the amount in (1), above, by the base period percentage (the average of taxable income as a percentage of annual taxable income for the corresponding months in each of the three earlier tax years) for all months in the tax year before the filing month, (3) determining the tax on the amount in (2), above, (4) multiplying that tax by the base period percentage for the filing month and all months before the filing month. (FTC 2d/FIN ¶ S-5422; TG ¶ 2493; USTR ¶ 66,554)

These estimated tax rules also apply to exempt organizations. (See FTC 2d/FIN ¶s S-5601, S-5602; TG ¶ 2497; USTR ¶ 66,554)

The '93 Act deletes the 97% (in (a), above) (13225(a)(2)(A)(i)) and increases the percentage to 100%. The drop-down to 91% is eliminated. (Code Sec. 6655(e)(3)(A) as amended by '93 Act § 13225(a)(2)(C))

☐ **Effective:** For tax years beginning after Dec. 31, '93. (§ 13225(c))

For official explanation see Committee Reports ¶ 3047.

¶ 319. Treatment of FSLIC financial assistance

The Federal Savings and Loan Insurance Corporation (FSLIC), which insured the deposits of its member savings and loan associations, entered into assistance agreements in which it agreed to provide loss protection to acquirers of troubled thrift institutions by compensating them for losses on "covered assets", such as nonperforming loans. These losses could occur on a sale of the assets or on a write down of the assets ordered by FSLIC. Under the Financial Institutions Reform, Recovery and Enforcement Act of '89 (FIRREA), FSLIC was abolished and the FSLIC Resolution Fund assumed all its assets and liabilities. Under pre-'93 Act law, various rules applied to FSLIC assistance. Until Jan. 1, '89, FSLIC assistance was generally not treated as income and did not reduce tax attributes. FSLIC assistance for acquisitions after Dec 31, '88, but before May 10, '89, was generally not included in income but caused a reduction in tax attributes. (H Rept p. 668) FSLIC assistance for acquisitions after May 9, '89, was generally included in income. (See FTC 2d/FIN ¶s E-3800.1, E-3801; TG ¶ 7797; USTR ¶ 5974)

Under the '93 Act:

(1) any FSLIC assistance (defined below) with respect to any loss of principal,

capital, or similar account on the disposition of any asset is treated as compensation for the loss for purposes of Code Sec. 165 (which doesn't allow for the deduction of compensated losses, see FTC 2d/FIN ¶ M-1303; TG ¶ 6481; USTR ¶ 1654.090) ('93 Act § 13224(a)(1)), and

(2) any FSLIC assistance with respect to any debt is taken into account for purposes of Code Secs. 166, 585 or 593 in determining whether, or to what extent, the debt is worthless and in determining the amount of any addition to any reserve for bad debts arising from the worthlessness or partial worthlessness. (§ 13224(a)(2))

FSLIC assistance means any assistance or right to assistance with respect to a domestic building and loan association (as defined in Code Sec. 7701(a)(19) (FTC 2d/FIN ¶ E-3504 *et seq.;* TG ¶ 7796; USTR ¶s 5934.01, 77,014.36), but without regard to the percentage of assets test under Code Sec. 7701(a)(19)(C) (FTC 2d/FIN ¶ E-3506; TG ¶ 7796; USTR ¶ 5934.36) under § 406(f) of the National Housing Act, § 21A of the Federal Home Loan Bank Act, or any similar provision of law. (§ 13224(b)) However, net worth assistance provided in an acquisition and calculated at the time of the acquisition without regard to losses on specific assets is not treated as FSLIC assistance. (H Rept p. 670)

The amount of FSLIC assistance is determined by reference to the gross amount of FSLIC assistance without taking into account any offsets that may reduce the net amount of the FSLIC assistance. (H Rept p. 670)

Under these rules, no deduction is allowed for a loss on a disposition of an asset to the extent an assistance agreement contemplates a right to receive FSLIC assistance for the loss. In addition, if a loan held by the taxpayer is an asset for which taxpayer is entitled to FSLIC assistance, the taxpayer cannot charge off the loan against its bad debt reserve (otherwise allowable under the rules described at FTC 2d/FIN ¶ E-3224; TG ¶ 7785; USTR ¶s 5854, 5934), cannot take the charge-off of the loan into account when calculating its bad debt reserve (otherwise allowable under the experience method, see FTC 2d/FIN ¶ E-3224; TG ¶ 7788; USTR ¶ 5854), and cannot deduct the amount of the loan under the specific charge-off method. (See FTC 2d/FIN ¶ E-3201; TG ¶ 7785; USTR ¶s 5854, 5934) (H Rept p. 670)

FSLIC assistance will not result in any adjusted current earnings adjustment for alternative minimum tax purposes (see FTC 2d/FIN ¶ A-8129 *et seq.;* TG ¶ 1381; USTR ¶ 564.03), since no loss or bad debt deduction is allowed for regular tax purposes. (H Rept p. 670) This rule applies even where taxpayers have received IRS determinations regarding the treatment of FSLIC assistance for earnings and profits purposes in the form of a ruling or closing agreement. (Conf Rept p. 618)

The Conference Report provides that for other earnings and profits purposes, IRS will treat FSLIC assistance in a manner that is consistent with the purposes of the above rules. (Conf Rept p. 618)

These rules remove the incentive for a taxpayer that receives FSLIC assistance to place a low value on its assets in order to both receive FSLIC assistance and take a deduction for the loss on the assets. (H Rept p. 669)

The '93 Act rules don't apply to any assistance subject to the amendments made by § 1401(a)(3) of FIRREA (generally, assistance for acquisitions after May 9, '89 that is included in income). (§ 13224(c)(2))

No inference is intended regarding the treatment of FSLIC assistance under pre-'93 Act law. (H Rept p. 670)

FTC 2d References are to the Federal Tax Coordinator 2d
FIN References are to RIA's Analysis of Federal Taxes: Income
TG References are to the Tax Guide
USTR References are to the United States Tax Reporter

☐ **Effective:** For taxable years ending after Mar. 4, '91, but only for FSLIC assistance credited after Mar. 3, '91. (§ 13224(c)(1)(A))

If FSLIC assistance is credited after Mar. 3, '91 for a loss taken into account in a tax year ending before Mar. 4, '91, the rules described above apply for purposes of determining any net operating loss carryovers for any tax years ending after Mar. 3 '91. (§ 13224(c)(1)(B))

FSLIC assistance is considered credited when the taxpayer sells the asset with FSLIC approval or when the taxpayer makes an approved debit entry to a Special Reserve Account maintained under the assistance agreement to reflect the disposition or write-down of the asset. (H Rept p. 671)

Under the '93 Act rule waiving estimated tax penalties for underpayments resulting from provisions of the '93 Act (see § 13001(d)), no estimated tax penalty (see FTC 2d/FIN ¶ S-5200 *et seq.;* TG ¶s 1400 *et seq.,* 2485 *et seq.;* USTR ¶s 66,544, 66,554) is imposed for any period before Mar. 16, '94 in the case of a corporation (Apr. 15, '94 in the case of an individual) for any underpayment resulting from the application of the rules described above. No inference is intended as to pre-'93 Act law, the effect of this provision under pre-'93 Act law, and the treatment of any provision to which this provision does not apply. (H Rept p. 672)

For official explanation see Committee Reports ¶ 3046.

¶ 320. Disallowance of deductions for amounts paid or incurred in connection with certain New York noncomplying group health plans

Under pre-'93 Act law, employers could generally deduct the full cost of health coverage provided to participants under a group health plan. (See FTC 2d/FIN ¶ H-4070 *et seq.;* TG ¶ 3180 *et seq.;* USTR ¶ 2644) Under New York state law, commercial insurers of inpatient hospital services, health maintenance organizations (HMOs), and Blue Cross and Blue Shield corporations are required to reimburse hospitals for inpatient hospital services at various rates set by the state of New York. In February of '93, a federal district court invalidated a number of New York statutes imposing inpatient hospital rate surcharges on the ground that they were preempted by ERISA, but ordered insurers of inpatient hospital services to comply with New York's rate-setting statutes pending a final determination of the case. (Conf Rept p. 734)

> ***observation:*** The district court case referred to in the Conference Report is *Travelers Ins. Co. v. Cuomo* (1993, DC NY) 813 F Supp 996.

Deduction disallowance rule. The '93 Act provides that no deduction is allowed to an employer for any amount paid or incurred in connection with a group health plan (defined below) if the plan doesn't reimburse for inpatient hospital care services provided in New York (except as discussed below for HMOs and for Blue Cross/ Blue Shield corporations) at the same rate as licensed commercial insurers (defined below) are required to reimburse hospitals for those services when the reimbursement isn't through a group health plan (Code Sec. 162(n)(1)(A) as amended by '93 Act § 13442(a))

> ***observation:*** If a group health plan sponsored by an employer has suspended payment of New York's hospital surcharges pending the outcome of the appeal in *Travelers* (see above), the employer may not deduct any payments to the plan.

> ***observation:*** The deduction disallowance rule applies where an employee of an out of state employer is treated in a New York hospital and the group

health plan covering that employee fails to pay the New York hospital surcharges. Thus, the employer may not deduct any payments, including payments made on behalf of other employees, to the group health plan.

Group health plan defined. A group health plan is a plan of, or contributed to by, an employer or employee organization (including a self-insured plan) to provide health care (directly or otherwise) to any employee, any former employee, the employer, or any other individual associated or formerly associated with the employer in a business relationship, or any member of their family. (Code Sec. 162(n)(3)) Amounts reimbursed through a voluntary employees' beneficiary association (VEBA) are considered to be provided under a group health plan. (Conf Rept p. 735)

Licensed commercial insurer defined. A licensed commercial insurer is a commercial insurer licensed to do business in New York and authorized to write accident and health insurance, and whose policies provide inpatient hospital coverage on an expense incurred basis. Blue Cross and Blue Shield isn't a licensed commercial insurer for this purpose. (Conf Rept p. 735)

Reimbursements from HMOs. No deduction is allowed to an employer for any amount paid or incurred in connection with a group health plan (see above) if the plan doesn't reimburse for inpatient hospital care services provided in New York, in the case of any reimbursement through a HMO, at the same rate as HMOs are required to reimburse hospitals for those services for individuals not covered by a group health plan (determined without regard to any government-supported individuals exempt from that rate). (Code Sec. 162(n)(1)(B))

Blue Cross/Blue Shield corporations and other nonprofit corporations. No deduction is allowed to an employer for any amount paid or incurred in connection with a group health plan (see above) if the plan doesn't reimburse for inpatient hospital care services provided in New York, in the case of any reimbursement through any corporation organized under Article 43 of the New York State Insurance Law, at the same rate as those corporations are required to reimburse hospitals for the services for individuals not covered by a group health plan. (Code Sec. 162(n)(1)(C)) This rule applies to coverage provided through Blue Cross and Blue Shield corporations. (Conf Rept p. 735)

observation: Article 43 of the New York State Insurance Law provides rules for non-profit medical and dental indemnity, or health and hospital service corporations.

State law exception. The deduction disallowance rules don't apply to any group health plan that is not required under New York laws (determined without regard to these rules or other provisions of federal law) to reimburse at the rates described above. (Code Sec. 162(n)(2)) Thus, self-insured plans aren't subject to the deduction disallowance rules with respect to the 11% surcharge imposed under New York's all-payer hospital reimbursement system on commercial insurers through Mar. 31, '93. Similarly, the deduction disallowance rule doesn't apply to self-insured plans that don't provide for reimbursement directly to hospitals on an expense incurred basis. The deduction denial also doesn't apply to payments by self-insured plans exempt from New York's all payer reimbursement system because of agreements in effect on May 1, '85. (Conf Rept p. 735)

ERISA preemption. No inference is intended as to whether any provision of the New York all-payer hospital reimbursement system is preempted by ERISA. (Conf Rept p. 736)

☐ **Effective:** For services provided after Feb. 2, '93 and on or before May 12, '95. (§ 13442(b))

For official explanation see Committee Reports ¶ 3079.

¶ 321. Changes to excise tax on nonconforming group health plans

An excise tax is imposed on an employer that contributes to a nonconforming group health plan. The tax equals 25% of the employer's expenses incurred during the calendar year for each group health plan to which the employer contributes.

A "nonconforming group health plan" is a group health plan or large group health plan that fails to comply with certain Social Security Act requirements related to the working aged, the disabled, and individuals with end-stage renal disease. (See FTC 2d/FIN ¶ H-4900 *et seq.;* TG ¶ 3386; USTR ¶ 50,004)

Under pre-'93 Act law, a "group health plan" was any plan of, or contributed to by, an employer to provide health care (directly or otherwise) to the employer's employees, former employees, or the families of employees or former employees. (FTC 2d/FIN ¶ H-4903; TG ¶ 3386) The '93 Act adds that the term "employer" includes a self-employed person and that the excise tax applies to a self-employed person who contributes to a nonconforming group health plan. (Code Sec. 5000(a) and 5000(b)(1) as amended by '93 Act § 13561(e)(2)(A))

Under pre-'93 Act law, a "large group health plan" was defined similarly to a group health plan, except that a large plan covered employees of at least one employer that normally employed at least 100 employees on a typical business day during the previous calendar year. (FTC 2d/FIN ¶ H-4904; TG ¶ 3386)

The '93 Act adds to the definition of "large group health plan" the following aggregation rules, which conform the excise tax provision to the related provisions of the Social Security Act:

(1) All employers treated as as single employer under Code Sec. 52(a) or (b), defining controlled groups of corporations, and partnerships, proprietorships, etc., under common control for purposes of the targeted jobs credit, (see FTC 2d/FIN ¶ L-17828; TG ¶ 5811; USTR ¶ 514), are treated as a single employer.

(2) All employees of the members of an affiliated service group, as defined in Code Sec. 414(m) (see FTC 2d/FIN ¶ H-7852; TG ¶ 3628; USTR ¶ 4144.03), are treated as employed by a single employer.

(3) Leased employees, as defined in Code Sec. 414(n)(2), are treated as employees of the person for whom they perform services to the extent they are so treated under Code Sec. 414(n) (see FTC 2d/FIN ¶ H-6272; TG ¶ 3630; USTR ¶ 4144.19). (Code Sec. 5000(b)(2) as amended by Act § 13561(d)(2))

☐ **Effective:** Aug. 10, '93, except that the aggregation rules are effective 90 days after Aug. 10, '93. (§ 13561(d)(3))

¶ 400. Intangibles

¶ 401. 15-Year amortization simplifies tax treatment of goodwill and other intangibles

Under pre-'93 Act law, the tax treatment of intangible assets has become a source of considerable controversy between taxpayers and IRS. Disputes have arisen at to (1) whether in the case of items such as customer lists an amortizable asset exists separately from nonamortizable goodwill and going concern value (2) in the case of an acquisition of a trade or business, the portion of the purchase price allocable to amortizable intangible assets, and (3) the proper method and period for recovering the cost of an amortizable intangible asset. (FTC 2d/FIN ¶ L-7750 *et seq.;* TG ¶ 5593 *et seq.;* USTR ¶ 1674.013)

These disputes were resolved only in part by the decision in April of '93 by the Supreme Court in *Newark Morning Ledger.* (FTC 2d/FIN ¶ L-7761; TG ¶ 5595; USTR ¶ 1675.014(85)) The Supreme Court held in that case that an intangible asset—subscriber lists—was amortizable when the taxpayer established a separate value (apart from nonamortizable goodwill and going concern value) and useful life for the asset. The Supreme Court so held despite the fact that the asset reflected the expectancy of continued patronage, which is itself an aspect of goodwill. However, the Supreme Court also said in *Newark Morning Ledger* that the taxpayer's burden of proof in such cases is substantial and that it "will often prove too great to bear."

According to the House Report, much of the controversy that arises under pre-'93 Act law with respect to acquired intangible assets can be eliminated by specifying a single method and period for recovering the cost of most acquired intangible assets and by treating acquired goodwill and going concern value as amortizable intangible assets. (H Rept p. 760)

As a result, effective for property acquired after Aug. 10, '93 (or, electively, after July 25, '91) ('93 Act § 13261(g)), the '93 Act generally requires the cost of most acquired intangible assets, including goodwill and going concern value, to be amortized ratably over a 15-year period. (Code Sec. 197 as added by '93 Act § 13261(a)) Congress recognizes that the useful lives of assets subject to new Code Sec. 197 will in fact be less than 15 years in some cases and longer than 15 years in others. (H Rept p. 760) IRS is urged to expedite the settlement of cases pending under pre-'93 Act law, see ¶ 437.

For official explanation see Committee Reports ¶ 3064.

¶ 402. Overview of new 15-year amortization rules

Under new Code Sec. 197, taxpayers are entitled to claim amortization deductions with respect to a broad range of intangible assets called "amortizable section 197 intangibles." The amount of any such deduction is determined by amortizing the adjusted basis (for purposes of determining gain) of an amortizable section 197 intangible ratably over a 15-year period beginning with the month in which the intangible is acquired. (Code Sec. 197(a)) At the same time, no change is being made in the tax treatment of self-created intangibles such as goodwill created through advertising. (H Rept p. 760)

Other than deductions permitted under the new 15-year amortization rules no

FTC 2d References are to the Federal Tax Coordinator 2d
FIN References are to RIA's Analysis of Federal Taxes: Income
TG References are to the Tax Guide
USTR References are to the United States Tax Reporter

other depreciation or amortization deduction is permitted with respect to any amortizable section 197 intangible. (Code Sec. 197(b))

An "amortizable section 197 intangible" is any section 197 intangible acquired after Aug. 10, '93 and held in connection with the conduct of a trade or business or a Code Sec. 212 activity for the production of income, etc. (Code Sec. 197(c)(1)) At the election of the taxpayer, assets acquired after July 25, '91, may also qualify as amortizable section 197 intangibles, or certain intangibles acquired *after* date of enactment may remain subject to pre-'93 Act law, see ¶ 434.

Subject to a number of important exceptions, Code Sec. 197 applies without regard to whether or not the intangible is acquired as part of a trade or business. Code Sec. 197 also applies to intangibles treated as acquired under a Code Sec. 338 election to treat the purchase of stock as an asset purchase. (H Rept p. 761)

Section 197 intangibles include:

. . . goodwill and going concern value. (¶ 404)

. . . workforce in place. (¶ 406)

. . . information base. (¶ 407)

. . . know-how. (¶ 409)

. . . customer-based intangibles. (¶ 413)

. . . supplier-based intangibles. (¶ 416)

. . . government licenses and permits. (¶ 419)

. . . franchises, trademarks and trade names. (¶ 420)

. . . insurance policy expirations. (¶ 408)

. . . bank deposit base. (¶ 415)

Section 197 intangibles also include any other item that is similar to workforce in place, information base, know-how, customer-based intangibles or supplier-based intangibles. (Code Sec. 197(d)(1)(C)(vi))

Assets treated as section 197 intangibles only if acquired in connection with the acquisition of a business. These consist of:

. . . covenants not to compete. (¶ 418)

. . . computer software. (¶ 410)

. . . films, sound recordings, video tapes and books. (¶ 411)

. . . copyrights and patents. (¶ 412)

. . . rights to receive tangible property or services. (¶ 417)

. . . interests in patents and copyrights. (¶ 412)

. . . mortgage servicing rights secured by residential real property. (¶ 414)

. . . contract rights good for less than 15 years or fixed in amount. (¶ 422)

Assets never treated as section 197 intangibles regardless of how acquired. These consist of:

. . . interests in corporations, partnerships, trusts and estates. (¶ 424)

. . . computer software that is readily available for purchase by the general public. (¶ 410)

. . . futures, foreign currency contracts and notional principal contracts. (¶ 424)

. . . land. (¶ 424)

. . . leases of tangible property. (¶ 423)

. . . debt instruments. (¶ 424)

. . . sports franchises. (¶ 420)

. . . tax-free transaction *(Indopco)* costs. (¶ 425)

. . . accounts receivable. (¶ 426)

Self-created intangibles. Amortizable section 197 intangibles generally don't include self-created intangibles. (¶ 427)

Losses generally disallowed on dispositions of section 197 intangibles. New Code Sec. 197 bars any loss deduction on the disposition, worthlessness or abandonment of a section 197 intangible if:

. . . any other section 197 intangible was acquired in the same transaction, and

. . . the taxpayer still retains any of the other section 197 intangibles so acquired. The amount of any loss barred under this rule is reallocated to the retained section 197 intangibles. (¶ 429)

> ***observation:*** This means that the cost of many section 197 intangibles must continue to be amortized over the prescribed 15-year period even if they become worthless for any reason or are abandoned before the end of the 15-year period.

Residual method used to allocate business purchase price to section 197 intangibles. Under pre-'93 Act law, the residual method requires that the purchase price of assets comprising an acquired business be allocated first to assets other than goodwill or going concern value, up to the fair market value of those other assets. Any excess of the purchase price over the value of the other assets is then allocated to goodwill and going concern value. (FTC 2d/FIN ¶ P-1400; TG ¶ 4644; USTR ¶ 10,604) The '93 Act retains these rules but requires that the excess be allocated to all section 197 assets rather than just to goodwill and going concern value. (¶ 430)

For official explanation see Committee Reports ¶ 3064.

¶ 403. Winners and losers under the '93 Act

The 15-year amortization period applies to all amortizable section 197 intangibles although some have useful lives shorter than 15 years while others have longer lives. Thus some intangibles are given shorter amortization periods than those provided under pre-'93 Act law (or, like goodwill, are for the first time made amortizable), while others are recoverable over longer periods than were allowed under pre-'93 Act law. In view of the fact that this new provision is considered to be a revenue

FTC 2d References are to the Federal Tax Coordinator 2d
FIN References are to RIA's Analysis of Federal Taxes: Income
TG References are to the Tax Guide
USTR References are to the United States Tax Reporter

gainer, there will be more losers than winners. However, the new rules also provide certainty and eliminate a lot of controversy. Where large amounts are at stake, as they typically are for section 197 intangibles, certainty makes many winners.

Taxpayers who purchase goodwill or going concern value (¶ 404), or renewable government permits and licenses (¶ 419) are benefitted by the new rules since these intangibles weren't amortizable under pre-'93 Act law. On the other hand, many intangibles acquired in connection with the acquisition of a business, such as movies (¶ 411), computer software (¶ 410), insurance policy expirations (¶ 408), bank deposit bases (¶ 415), and covenants not to compete (¶ 418), which have been held to be subject to pre-'93 Act recovery periods of less than 15 years, are subject to 15-year amortization under the new rules. (Movies and computer software *not* acquired in connection with the acquisition of a trade or business aren't subject to 15-year amortization.)

> ***recommendation:*** Taxpayers who wish to do so may elect to have the new rules apply to assets acquired after July 25, '91 (rather than after date of enactment). If this election is made, it applies to *all* property acquired after July 25, '91. (¶ 434) In deciding whether to make this election, a comparison should be made for all intangibles acquired after July 25, '91 and before date of enactment as to whether the old or new rules produce the best tax results.
>
> ***observation:*** The *seller* of a business should also take the new rules into account, since the price a buyer will pay for a business is to some extent affected by the tax treatment he expects to be accorded with respect to the purchased assets. The fact that the buyer of an asset can recover its cost through amortization deductions makes the asset worth more to him than if it were nonamortizable. Conversely, if the recovery period for an asset is made longer, its value to the buyer is reduced.

For official explanation see Committee Reports ¶ 3064.

¶ 404. Goodwill and going concern value

The pre-'93 Act law rule barring amortization for goodwill and going concern value (FTC 2d/FIN ¶ L-7750; TG ¶ 5593; USTR ¶ 1674.013) has produced an enormous amount of litigation. IRS has generally taken the position that any amount paid for intangibles in the acquisition of a business relates to nonamortizable goodwill or going concern value, while the taxpayer has attempted to show that amortizable intangibles such as customer lists have a value apart from goodwill or going concern value and a limited useful life.

New Code Sec. 197 eliminates this IRS-taxpayer conflict by providing that goodwill (Code Sec. 197(d)(1)(A)) and going concern value (Code Sec. 197(d)(1)(B)) are section 197 intangibles and are thus amortizable over the same 15-year period applicable to other section 197 intangibles.

For this purpose, goodwill is the value of a trade or business that is attributable to the expectancy of continued customer patronage, whether due to the name of a trade or business, the reputation of a trade or business, or any other factor.

Going concern value is the additional element of value of a trade or business that attaches to property by reason of its existence as an integral part of a going concern. Going concern value includes the value that is attributable to the ability of a trade or business to continue to function and generate income without interruption notwithstanding a change in ownership. Going concern value also includes the value that is attributable to the use or availability of an acquired trade or business (for example, the net earnings that otherwise would not be received during any period were the acquired trade or business not available or operational). (H Rept p. 762)

> ***observation:*** Self-created goodwill and going concern value generally aren't subject to 15-year amortization. (¶ 427)

For official explanation see Committee Reports ¶ 3064.

¶ 405. Professional practices

Under pre-'93 Act law, much of the cost of purchasing a professional practice may be held to be a nonamortizable asset in the nature of goodwill. (FTC 2d/FIN ¶ L-7755; USTR ¶ 10,604)

For instance, the Tax Court held in *Brooks* (FTC 2d/FIN ¶ L-5157; USTR ¶ 12,215.55(25)) that where a dentist sold his orthodontic practice for $240,000, $10,000 of that amount was paid for tangible assets and the rest for goodwill.

> ***observation:*** No explicit reference is made to professional practices in Code Sec. 197 or in the related committee reports. However, section 197 intangibles include goodwill and going concern value (¶ 404) and there is nothing to indicate that this new rule doesn't apply to the goodwill or going concern value inherent in a medical, dental or other professional practice.

Purchased patient and client lists are amortizable under the rules discussed at ¶ 407.

For official explanation see Committee Reports ¶ 3064.

¶ 406. Workforce in place

Taxpayers that have acquired an ongoing trade or business often allocate a portion of the purchase price to assets such as agency force, assembled workforce, or other similar workforce-based intangibles. These intangibles assets are generally said to represent the value of having a trained, experienced workforce in place as of the date of acquisition (as opposed to having to hire and train a workforce).

Under pre-'93 Act law, IRS took the position that any value associated with having a trained staff of employees in place represented the going concern value of an acquired business and, consequently, wasn't amortizable. This position of IRS has been upheld by the Tax Court in *Ithaca Industries.* (FTC 2d/FIN ¶ L-7756; USTR ¶ 1675.022(65))

Section 197 intangibles include workforce in place, including its composition, terms and conditions (contractual or otherwise) of its employment. (Code Sec. 197(d)(1)(C)(i)) For example, the portion of the purchase price of an acquired trade or business that is attributable to the existence of a highly-skilled workforce is amortized over the 15-year period. Similarly, the cost of acquiring an existing employment contract or a relationship with employees or consultants (including any "key employee" contract or relationship) as part of the acquisition of a trade or business is subject to 15-year amortization. (H Rept p. 762)

For official explanation see Committee Reports ¶ 3064.

¶ 407. Amortizable "information base" includes books and records, customer lists and other items

Section 197 intangibles include business books and records, operating systems,

---

FTC 2d References are to the Federal Tax Coordinator 2d
FIN References are to RIA's Analysis of Federal Taxes: Income
TG References are to the Tax Guide
USTR References are to the United States Tax Reporter

and any other information base including lists or other information with respect to current or prospective customers. (Code Sec. 197(d)(1)(c)(ii))

For example, the portion of the purchase price of an acquired trade or business that is attributable to the intangible value of technical manuals, training manuals or programs, data files, and accounting or inventory control systems is amortized over the 15-year period. The cost of acquiring customer lists, subscription lists, insurance expirations, patient or client files, or lists of newspaper, magazine, radio or television advertisers is also amortized over the 15-year period. (H Rept p. 763)

For official explanation see Committee Reports ¶ 3064.

¶ 408. Insurance policy expirations, "dailies," records, etc.

Among the assets acquired in the purchase of an insurance agency business are policy expirations and similar records, such as "dailies" (records of essential details of each policy including the renewal date) of health, accident, fire, casualty and similar insurance sold by the agency.

Under pre-'93 Act law, the depreciation or amortization of these items depends on whether the taxpayer establishes that the assets (1) have an ascertainable value separate and distinct from goodwill, and (2) have a limited useful life whose duration can be ascertained with reasonable accuracy. For example, in *Valler Insurance,* a district court found a 5-year life for fire, casualty, and automobile insurance expirations based on industry statistics and the taxpayer's own experience. (FTC 2d/FIN ¶ L-7763; TG ¶ 5595; USTR ¶ 1675.016(15))

Section 197 intangibles include business books and records, operating systems, and any other information base including lists or other information with respect to current or prospective customers. (Code Sec. 197(d)(1)(C)(ii))

This category of section 197 intangibles also includes insurance expirations. According to the House Report, insurance expirations are records maintained by insurance agents with respect to insurance customers. These records generally include information relating to the type of insurance, the amount of insurance, and the expiration date of the insurance. (H Rept p. 763)

> ***observation:*** The language of Code Sec. 197(d)(1)(C)(ii) seems broad enough also to include "dailies."

For official explanation see Committee Reports ¶ 3064.

¶ 409. Know-how

Section 197 intangibles include any patent, copyright, formula, process, design, pattern, know-how, format, or other similar item. (Code Sec. 197(d)(1)(C)(iii)) However, patents and copyrights are section 197 intangibles only if acquired in a transaction (or series or transactions) involving the acquisition of a trade or business or a substantial portion of a trade or business. (Code Sec. 197(e)(4)(C))

Also included in this category of section 197 intangibles, which the House Report uses the general term "know-how" to describe, are package designs. (H Rept p. 763)

For official explanation see Committee Reports ¶ 3064.

¶ 410. Computer software

Under pre-'93 Act law, the buyer of a computer software program generally treats it in one of two ways depending on how it was billed by the seller. If the charge for the computer software was included in the price of the computer hardware without a separate identification of the charge for software, then the buyer must treat the entire amount as the cost of the computer hardware to be depreciated over the useful life of the computer hardware. If the charge for the computer software is separately stated, it may be amortized over five years (or any shorter useful life the taxpayer can establish). (FTC 2d/FIN ¶ L-1612; USTR ¶ 1674.033)

With certain exceptions, computer software is treated as a section 197 intangible under the Code Sec. 197(d)(1)(C)(iii) "know-how" category. (H Rept p. 763) However, section 197 intangibles do *not* include computer software that:

. . . is readily available for purchase by the general public, subject to a nonexclusive license and hasn't been substantially modified, (Code Sec. 197(e)(3)(A)(i)), or

. . . wasn't acquired in a transaction (or a series of related transactions) that involves the acquisition of assets which constitute a trade or business or a substantial portion of a trade or business. (Code Sec. 197(e)(3)(A)(ii))

"Computer software" is any program that is designed to cause a computer to perform a desired function. (Code Sec. 197(e)(3)(B)) "Program" is any sequence of machine readable code. (H Rept p. 767)

The term "computer software" includes any incidental and ancillary rights with respect to computer software that (1) are necessary to effect the legal acquisition of the title to, and the ownership of, the computer softwear, and (2) are used only in connection with the software. (H Rept p. 767)

The term "computer software" does *not* include any data base or similar item unless the data base or item is in the public domain and is incidental to the operation of otherwise qualifying computer software. (Code Sec. 197(e)(3)(B)) This is true regardless of the form in which the data base or similar item is maintained or stored. A data base doesn't include a dictionary feature used to spell-check a word processing program. (H Rept p. 767)

> ***observation:*** A data base would appear to qualify as a section 197 intangible under the rules for information base at ¶ 407.

Depreciation. If a depreciation deduction is allowed with respect to any computer software that is not a section 197 intangible, the amount of the deduction is computed using the straight line method and a useful life of 36 months. (Code Sec. 167(f) as amended by '93 Act § 13261(b)(1))

The 36-month period begins with the month that the software is placed in service. The cost of any computer software that is taken into account as part of the cost of computer hardware under pre-'93 Act law should continue to be so treated. In addition, the cost of any software that is currently deductible under pre-'93 Act law is to continue to be taken into account in the same way. (H Rept p. 767)

The determination of whether assets constitute a business or a substantial part of a business is discussed at ¶ 428.

> ***recommendation:*** Where the main purpose of an acquisition is to obtain computer software, the taxpayer should consider buying just the software and not the seller's entire business. Where the software is purchased alone in a "free-standing" transaction, it is taken out of the section 197 intangible category and thus becomes subject to a 36-month (rather than a 15-year) writeoff.

For official explanation see Committee Reports ¶ 3064.

FTC 2d References are to the Federal Tax Coordinator 2d
FIN References are to RIA's Analysis of Federal Taxes: Income
TG References are to the Tax Guide
USTR References are to the United States Tax Reporter

¶ 411. Some interests in films, sound recordings, video tapes and books excluded

Interests in films, sound recordings, video tapes and other similar property are generally treated as section 197 intangibles under the Code Sec. 197(d)(1)(C)(iii) "know-how" category. (H Rept p. 763) However, Section 197 intangibles don't include any interest in a film, sound recording, video tape, book, or other similar property if the interest is not acquired in a transaction (or a series of related transactions) that involves the acquisition of assets which constitute a trade or business or a substantial portion of a trade or business. (Code Sec. 197(e)(4)(A)) Interests subject to this rule include interests held by licensees in a film, etc. (H Rept p. 768)

The determination of whether assets constitute a business or a substantial part of a business for purposes of this test is discussed at ¶ 428.

> ***observation:*** Pre-'93 Act law generally permits the depreciation of interests in films, video tapes, sound recordings and books under the straight line and income forecast methods. (FTC 2d/FIN ¶ L-9904; USTR ¶ 1674.001(6))

> ***recommendation:*** In planning the acquisition of a business whose major assets consist, say, of movies, consideration should be given to buying just the movies, rather than the entire business. If the movies are acquired in a "free-standing" transaction, the taxpayer will generally be able to recover their cost over a shorter period than 15 years.

For official explanation see Committee Reports ¶ 3064.

¶ 412. Copyrights and patents

Copyrights are generally good for the life of the author plus 50 years. However, under pre-'93 Act law, the cost of a purchased copyright may be amortized over a shorter useful life if one can be established. Similarly, patents, which generally have a legal life of 17 years, may be amortized over a shorter useful life. (FTC 2d/FIN ¶ L-7772; TG ¶ 5595; USTR ¶ 1674.025)

Code Sec. 197(d)(1)(C)(iii) specifies that copyrights and patents are generally treated as section 197 intangibles, subject to 15-year amortization. However, this treatment applies only if acquired in a transaction (or series of related transactions) involving the acquisition of a trade or business or a substantial portion of a trade or business. (Code Sec. 197(e)(4)(C))

Depreciation. If a depreciation deduction is allowable with respect to an interest in a patent or copyright and the interest isn't a section 197 intangible, the amount of the deduction is to be determined in accordance with regs to be issued by IRS. (Code Sec. 167(f)(2) as amended by '93 Act § 13261(b)(1))

These regs may provide that if the purchase price of a patent is payable on an annual basis as a fixed percentage of the revenue derived form the use of the patent, then the amount of the depreciation deduction allowed for any tax year with respect to the patent equals the amount of the royalty paid or incurred during that year. (H Rept p. 769)

For official explanation see Committee Reports ¶ 3064.

¶ 413. Customer-based intangibles

Section 197 intangibles include any customer-based intangible. (Code Sec. 197(d)(1)(C)(iv)) Customer based intangibles are the composition of market, market share, and any other value resulting from the future provision of goods or services out of relationships with customers (contractual or otherwise) in the ordinary course of business. (Code Sec. 197(d)(2)(A))

For example, the portion of the purchase price of an acquired trade or business that is attributable to the existence of customer base, circulation base, undeveloped market or market growth, insurance in force, investment management contracts, or other relationships with customers that involve the future provision of goods or services, is to be amortized over the 15-year period.

> ***observation:*** Under pre-'93 Act law customer based intangibles are generally amortizable only to the extent that the taxpayer can establish a separate value and useful life for them.

For official explanation see Committee Reports ¶ 3064.

¶ 414. Mortgage servicing contracts

Amortization deductions are permitted under pre-'93 Act law for mortgage servicing contracts. For example, the Tax Court, in *First Pennsylvania,* held that the right to service residential mortgage loans was amortizable over their average 8-year life expectancy. (FTC 2d/FIN ¶ L-7765; USTR ¶ 1675.014(5))

Section 197 intangibles subject to 15-year amortization don't include any right to service indebtedness secured by residential real property unless the right is acquired in a transaction (or series of related transactions) involving the acquisition of assets (other than rights to service debt secured by residential realty) constituting a trade or business or a substantial part of a trade or business. (Code Sec. 197(e)(7))

A special rule applies to rights to service debt secured by residential realty where the rights are excluded from Code Sec. 197 status under the rules described in the preceding paragraph. Any depreciation deduction available with respect to such excluded rights is to be computed based on the straight line method and a useful life of 108 months. (Code Sec. 167(f) as amended by '93 Act § 13261(b)(1))

Stripped coupons. Mortgage servicing rights aren't depreciable to the extent that the rights are treated as stripped coupons under Code Sec. 1286, see FTC 2d/FIN ¶s J-3914, J-3917; USTR ¶ 12,864. (Conf Rept p. 694)

For official explanation see Committee Reports ¶ 3064.

¶ 415. Bank deposit base

Section 197 intangibles include, as a customer-based intangible, the deposit base and any similar asset of a financial institution. (Code Sec. 197(d)(2)(B)) Thus, the portion of the purchase price of an acquired financial institution that is attributable to checking accounts, savings accounts, escrow accounts or similar items is amortizable over the 15-year period. (H Rept p. 763)

For official explanation see Committee Reports ¶ 3064.

¶ 416. Supplier-based intangibles

A taxpayer that acquires the assets of a business will often acquire rights under contracts that were made by the seller of the business with third parties. For example, the buyer may step into the shoes of the seller with respect to a supply contract that grants the buyer more favorable terms than the buyer could obtain on its own with respect to the subject matter of the contract. Under pre-'93 Act law, the portion of the purchase price of an acquired business assigned to a favorable contract may be amortized if the buyer establishes that (1) the contract has a limited useful life, the duration of which can be established with reasonable accuracy, and (2) the contract has an ascertainable value that is separate and distinct from goodwill.

For example, the Tax Court held in *Ithaca Industries* (FTC 2d/FIN ¶ L-7776; USTR ¶ 1675.022(65)) that the cost of acquiring contracts that allowed the taxpayer to purchase raw materials (yarn) at a price below market could be amortized over the useful lives of the contracts. On the other hand, taxpayers have frequently found it impossible to establish limited useful lives for contracts on account of renewal options.

Section 197 intangibles include any supplier-based intangible. (Code Sec. 197(d)(1)(C)(v)) Supplier-based intangibles are the value resulting from the future acquisitions of goods or services out of relationships (contractual or otherwise) in the ordinary course of business with suppliers of goods or services to be used or sold by the taxpayer. (Code Sec. 197(d)(3)) For example, the portion of the purchase price of an acquired business attributable to a favorable relationship with persons that provide distribution services (for example, favorable shelf or display space at a retail outlet), the existence of a favorable credit rating, or the existence of favorable supply contracts, is generally to be amortized over the 15-year period. (H Rept p. 764)

However, special rules apply with respect to:

. . . contractual rights to receive tangible property or services (see ¶ 417), which are section 197 intangibles only if acquired in a transaction involving the acquisition of a business.

. . . rights that (1) aren't acquired in connection with the acquisition of a business and (2) have a fixed duration of less than 15 years *or* are fixed in amount and subject to recovery under the unit of production method (see ¶ 422).

For official explanation see Committee Reports ¶ 3064.

¶ 417. When right to receive tangible property or services excluded from section 197 intangibles

Section 197 intangibles don't include any right to receive tangible property or services under a contract (or any right to receive tangible property or services granted by a governmental unit or an agency or instrumentality thereof) unless the right is acquired in a transaction (or a series of related transactions) that involves the acquisition of assets which constitute a trade or business or a substantial portion of a trade or business. (Code Sec. 197(e)(4)(B))

The determination of whether assets constitute a business or a substantial part of a business is discussed at ¶ 428.

If a depreciation deduction is allowable with respect to a right to receive tangible property or services that isn't a section 197 intangible, the amount of the deduction is to be determined in accordance with regs to be issued by IRS. (Code Sec. 167(f)(2) amended by '93 Act § 13261(b)(1))

These regs may provide, in the case of a right to receive tangible property or services in substantially equal amounts over a fixed period, that the cost of acquiring the right will be deducted ratably over the fixed period. In the case of a right to receive a fixed amount of tangible property or services over an unspecified period, the regs may provide that the cost of acquiring the right will be taken into account under a method that allows a deduction based on the amount of property or services received during a tax year compared to the total amount of property or services to be received.

The regs may also require the taxpayer "under appropriate circumstances" to amortize the cost of acquiring a renewable right over a period including all renewal options exercisable by the taxpayer at less than fair market value. (H Rept p. 768)

> ***Illustration:*** Jones acquires a favorable contract to receive a specified amount of raw materials monthly for three years. The right isn't acquired along with the assets of a business or any part of a business and thus isn't a section 197 intangible. IRS could require Jones to deduct the cost of acquiring the contract ratably over the three year period. Suppose instead that Jones acquired the right to receive a specified amount of raw materials over an unspecified period. Here IRS could require Jones to deduct the cost of the contract by multiplying that cost by a fraction consisting of raw materials received during the tax year over the total to be received (H Rept p. 768)

> RIA ***observation:*** Since contracts treated as section 197 intangibles (i.e., contracts that *are* acquired in a transaction that involves the acquisition of a business, see ¶ 416) are subject to 15-year amortization without regard to their actual duration, the existence of renewal options is irrelevant as to them.

For official explanation see Committee Reports ¶ 3064.

¶ 418. Covenants not to compete

Under pre-'93 Act law, whether a covenant not to compete is amortizable, and if so, over what period, has been held by the courts to be dependent on a number of factors. Was there a business purpose for covenant? What amount can be properly allocated to it? Can it be separated from goodwill? Was the purpose of the agreement to protect the business from competition or to protect the value of purchased assets? These and other questions as to the amortization of covenants not to compete have generated numerous disputes between IRS and taxpayers.

Under pre-'93 Act law, where an amortizable contract not to compete is found to exist, the cost of the contract must normally be amortized over the life of the contract. For instance, in *Warsaw Photographic Associates,* the Tax Court held that where a contract not to compete bound the other party for six years, the cost of the contract was amortizable over the six-year period. (FTC 2d/FIN ¶ L-7759; USTR ¶ 1675.015(25))

The term "section 197 intangible" includes any covenant not to compete (or other arrangement to the extent that the arrangement has substantially the same effect as a covenant not to compete) made in connection with the direct or indirect acquisition of an interest in a trade or business. (Code Sec. 197(d)(1)(E)) For this purpose, an interest in a trade or business includes not only the assets of a trade or business, but also stock in a corporation or partnership that is so engaged. (H Rept p. 764)

Any amount that is paid or incurred under a covenant not to compete made in connection with the acquisition of an interest in a trade or business is chargeable to capital account (Code Sec. 197(f)(3)) and must be amortized over the 15-year period. In addition, any amount that is paid or incurred under a covenant not to compete after the tax year in which the covenant was made would be amortized over the remaining months in the 15-year amortization period determined as of the beginning of the month in which the amount is paid or incurred. (H Rept p. 764)

An arrangement that requires the former owner of an interest in a trade or business to continue to perform services (or to provide property or the use of property) that benefits the trade or business is considered to have substantially the same effect as a covenant not to compete to the extent that the amount paid to the former owner exceeds reasonable compensation for the services actually rendered (or for the property or use of property actually provided). As under pre-'93 Act law, to the extent that the amount paid or incurred under a covenant not to compete represents additional consideration for the acquisition of stock the amount isn't taken into account under this Code Sec. 197 but, instead, is included as part of the acquirer's basis in the stock. (H Rept p. 765)

When covenant not to compete may be treated as disposed of or worthless. A covenant not to compete may in no event be treated as having been disposed of or as having become worthless before there has been a disposition of the entire interest in the trade or business that the covenant was made in connection with the acquisition of. (Code Sec. 197(f)(1)(B)) All persons treated as a single taxpayer under Code Sec. 41(f) (i.e., members of the same controlled group of corporations or commonly controlled trades and businesses) are treated as a single taxpayer for purposes of this special rule. (Code Sec. 197(f)(1)(C))

In the case of an indirect acquisition of a trade or business (e.g., through the acquisition of stock that isn't treated as an asset acquisition), a covenant not to compete made in connection with the indirect acquisition can't be written off any faster than on a straight-line basis over 15 years (even if the covenant earlier expires or becomes worthless) unless the trade or business indirectly acquired is also disposed of or becomes worthless. (Conf Rept p. 694)

For official explanation see Committee Reports ¶ 3064.

¶ 419. Licenses, permits and rights granted by governmental units

Under pre-'93 Act law, taxpayers generally haven't been allowed depreciation or amortization deductions with respect to renewable rights that are granted by a governmental entity because a useful life for the rights isn't determinable with reasonable accuracy. For example, in *Nachman* (FTC 2d/FIN ¶ L-7776; TG ¶ 5595; USTR ¶ 1675.018(10)), the Fifth Circuit denied depreciation deductions with respect to the premium paid for a retail liquor license that was valid for only 5 months after the date of acquisition. The court held that the useful life of the liquor license was likely to continue indefinitely because it was the established practice in issuing renewal licenses to favor the holders of existing licenses over other applicants.

Government licenses and permits subject to 15-year amortization. Section 197 intangibles include, subject to certain exceptions, any license, permit, or other right granted by a governmental unit or any agency or instrumentality thereof. (Code Sec. 197(d)(1)(D)) This rule applies even if the right is granted for an indefinite period or the right is reasonably expected to be renewed for an indefinite period.

Thus, the capitalized cost of acquiring from any person a liquor license, a taxi-cab medallion or license, an airport landing or takeoff right (sometimes called a slot), a regulated airline route, or a television or a radio broadcasting license is amortizable over the 15-year period.

The issuance or renewal of a license, etc., is considered an acquisition for this purpose. (H Rept p. 764)

Four exceptions. The following four exceptions apply to the rules described above:

(1) Any right to receive tangible property or services from a governmental unit isn't treated as a section 197 intangible unless the right is acquired in a transaction involving the acquisition of a business, see ¶ 417.

(2) Certain other government rights not acquired in connection with the acquisition of a business aren't treated as section 197 intangibles if the right has a duration of less than 15 years or is fixed as to amount, e.g., an emission allowance granted under the Clean Air Act, see ¶ 422.

(3) Interests in land granted by a governmental unit, see ¶ 424.

(4) Leases of tangible property, see ¶ 423.

Renewals treated as acquisitions. Any renewal of a license, permit or other right granted by a governmental unit, agency or instrumentality is treated as an acquisition, but only to the extent of costs incurred in connection with the renewal. (Code Sec. 197(f)(4)(B))

For official explanation see Committee Reports ¶ 3064.

¶ 420. Franchises, trademarks and trade names

Under pre-'93 Act law, Code Sec. 1253 prescribes several rules for deducting the cost of franchises (not including professional sports franchises), trademarks and trade names. Payments that are contingent on the productivity, use or disposition of a franchise, trademark or trade name and that meet certain other requirements are currently deductible as business expenses under Code Sec. 1253(d)(1).

If the transferor of a franchise, trademark or trade name retains certain powers or rights, and the principal sum paid the transferor doesn't exceed $100,000, noncontingent payments made to discharge the principal sum may generally be amortized over the lesser of 10 years or the term of the agreement.

Noncontingent payments in excess of $100,000 may be amortized over the useful life of the franchise, etc., if a useful life can be established. Alternatively, the purchaser of a franchise, trademark or trade name may elect under Code Sec. 1253 to amortize its cost over a 25-year period. (FTC 2d/FIN ¶ I-5250; TG ¶ 4532; USTR ¶ 12,534.01)

Outside of Code Sec. 1253, it is usually difficult under pre-'93 Act law to claim amortization deductions for franchises, trademarks and trade names because of the difficulty involved in showing that these assets have a limited useful life.

For example, in *Dunn* (FTC 2d/FIN ¶ L-7776; USTR ¶ 1675.018(25)) the Tenth Circuit held that various payments made in connection with a "Dairy Queen" franchise were not amortizable because the taxpayer failed to establish a useful life for the franchise agreement.

Section 197 intangibles include any franchise, trademark or trade name (Code Sec. 197(d)(1)(F)) other than a sports franchise. (Code Sec. 197(e)(6)) For this purpose, "franchise" continues to be defined, as under pre-'93 Act law, to include any agreement that gives one of the parties to the agreement the right to distribute, sell, or provide goods, services, or facilities, within a specified area. (Code Sec. 197(f)(4)(A))

Any renewal of a franchise, trademark or trade name is treated as the acquisition of a franchise, trademark or trade name. However, this rule only applies to costs incurred in connection with the renewal. (Code Sec. 197(f)(4)(B)) In other words, only the costs incurred in connection with the renewal are amortized over the 15-year period that begins with the month that the franchise, trademark, or trade name is renewed. Any costs incurred in connection with the issuance (or an earlier re-

FTC 2d References are to the Federal Tax Coordinator 2d
FIN References are to RIA's Analysis of Federal Taxes: Income
TG References are to the Tax Guide
USTR References are to the United States Tax Reporter

newal) of the franchise, trademark, or trade name continue to be taken into account over the remaining portion of the 15-year amortization period that began at the time of the issuance (or earlier renewal). (H Rept p. 765)

Payments for franchises, etc., that are contingent on productivity, use or disposition of the property as described in Code Sec. 1253(d)(1) continue to be currently deductible under the same rules prescribed under pre-'93 Act law by Code Sec. 1253(d)(1). (Code Sec. 197(f)(4)(C)) Other provisions permitting the amortization of amounts paid for franchises, trademarks and trade names under Code Sec. 1253 have been repealed. (Code Sec. 1253(d) as amended by '93 Act § 13261(c)) This repeal is subject to the same effective dates that generally apply to all of the changes made by § 13261(c), see ¶ 434. As a result of the repeal, any amount, whether fixed or contingent, that is paid or incurred on account of the transfer of a franchise, trademark, or trade name (other than amounts that are contingent on productivity, use or disposition of the property and which are currently deductible under Code Sec. 1253(d)(1)) must be capitalized and amortized over the 15-year period. (H Rept p. 765)

Professional sports franchises. Section 197 intangibles don't include a franchise to engage in professional baseball, basketball, football, or other professional sport, or any item acquired in connection with such a franchise. (Code Sec. 197(e)(6))

Consequently, the cost of acquiring a professional sports franchise and related assets (including any goodwill, going concern value, or other section 197 intangibles) is allocated among the assets acquired as provided under pre-'93 Act law and taken into account under pre-'93 Act law. For example, the amount that could be allocated to player contracts on the purchase of a sports franchise continues to be subject to the limits of Code Sec. 1056. (FTC 2d/FIN ¶ P-1309; TG ¶ 4668; USTR ¶ 10,564) (Player contracts are generally depreciable over the player's useful life under pre-'93 Act law.) (H Rept p. 770)

Broadcast licenses. Under pre-'93 Act law, the Fourth Circuit and the Tax Court, in *Jefferson Pilot,* held that an FCC broadcast license was a "franchise" governed by Code Sec 1253. (FTC 2d/FIN ¶ I-5261; USTR ¶ 1235.01(10)) Under the new rules, radio and television broadcast licenses are section 197 intangibles under the category of licenses and permits granted by governments, see ¶ 419.

For official explanation see Committee Reports ¶ 3064.

¶ 421. Assumption reinsurance transactions

Insurance companies are required to capitalize and amortize their "specified policy acquisition expenses" for any tax year. Amortization is required with respect to contracts which the company issues and, with certain modifications, those which the company reinsures.

Under Code Sec. 848, the amortization is generally done on a straight-line basis over a period of 120 months beginning with the first month in the second half of the taxable year in which the expenses are incurred. (FTC 2d/FIN ¶ E-5102; USTR ¶ 8484)

Under new Code Sec. 197, in the case of any amortizable section 197 intangible resulting from an assumption reinsurance transaction, the amount taken into account as the adjusted basis of the intangible is the excess of:

. . . the amount paid or incurred by the acquirer over

. . . the amount required to be capitalized under Code Sec. 848.

Code Sec. 197(b), which generally bars depreciation or amortization deductions for section 197 intangibles under any other provision, doesn't apply to any amount required to be capitalized under Code Sec. 848. (Code Sec. 197(f)(5)) Consequently, the amount required to be capitalized under Code Sec. 848 is amortized under the rules specified in that provision. (H Rept p. 775)

For official explanation see Committee Reports ¶ 3064.

¶ 422. Contract rights good for less than 15 years or fixed in amount aren't section 197 intangibles if regs say so

A special rule is provided for contract rights and government grants not acquired in connection with the acquisition of a business. Such rights are treated as not being section 197 intangibles to the extent provided in regs, but only if the right in question:

. . . has a fixed duration of less than 15 years, or

. . . is fixed in amount and, without regard to Code Sec. 197, would be recoverable under a method similar to the unit of production method.

These rules apply to any right under a contract (or granted by a governmental unit or an agency or instrumentality thereof) if the right wasn't acquired in a transaction (or series of related transactions) involving the acquisition of assets constituting a trade, business or substantial portion thereof). (Code Sec. 197(e)(4)(D))

These rules apply to an emission allowance granted to a public utility under Title IV of the Clean Air Act Amendments of 1990. This is a right that is limited in amount because each allowance grants a right to a fixed amount of emissions. (H Rept p. 770)

The mere fact that a taxpayer will have the opportunity to renew a contract or other right on the same terms as are available to others, in a competitive auction or similar process designed to reflect fair market value and in which the taxpayer isn't contractually advantaged, won't be taken into account in determining the duration of the right or whether it is for a fixed amount. However, the competitive bidding must actually produce a fair market value price comparable to the price that would obtain if the rights were purchased from a third party in an arm's-length transaction. Moreover, regs are to take into account all the facts and circumstances, including any facts indicating an actual practice of renewals or expectancy of renewals. (H Rept p. 771)

> ***Illustration:*** Goliath Corporation acquires a license from Tradescraft, Inc., to use know-how developed by Tradescraft. The license is for five years, can't be renewed except on terms that are fully available to Goliath's competitors, and the price paid by Goliath will reflect the arm's-length price that a third party would pay Goliath for the license immediately after renewal. The license wouldn't be treated as a section 197 intangible under the regs IRS is expected to issue. (H Rept p. 771)

The regs may also prescribe rules governing the extent to which renewal options and similar items will be taken into account in determining whether rights are fixed in duration or amount. The regs may also prescribe the appropriate method of amortizing rights not treated as section 197 intangibles. (H Rept p. 771)

Depreciation. If a depreciation deduction is allowable with respect to an intangible

FTC 2d References are to the Federal Tax Coordinator 2d
FIN References are to RIA's Analysis of Federal Taxes: Income
TG References are to the Tax Guide
USTR References are to the United States Tax Reporter

excluded from section 197 status under these rules, that depreciation deduction must be computed in accordance with regs to be issued by IRS. (Code Sec. 167(f)(2) as amended by '93 Act § 13261(b)(1))

For official explanation see Committee Reports ¶ 3064.

¶ 423. Leases of land and other tangible personal property

Section 197 intangibles don't include any interest as a lessor or lessee under an existing lease of tangible property (Code Sec. 197(e)(5)(A)), whether real or personal, and including sublessors and sublessees. (H Rept p. 769)

> ***observation:*** This is true regardless of whether the lease is acquired in the acquisition of a business or in a "free-standing" purchase, or whether the lessor is a governmental unit.

Lessor's basis where interest as lessor acquired in purchase of leased property. While excluding these leases from the definition of section 197 intangibles, the '93 Act provides that the cost of acquiring an interest as a lessor, where the interest is acquired in connection with the acquisition of the leased property, is added to the basis of the property. (Code Sec. 167(c) as amended by '93 Act § 13261(b)(2))

> ***Illustration:*** Taxpayer acquires a shopping center that is leased to tenants operating retail stores. Under the '93 Act, the portion of the purchase price of the shopping center that is attributable to the favorable attributes of the leases is to be taken into account as a part of the basis of the shopping center and in determining depreciation deductions with respect to the shopping center. (H Rept p. 769)

> ***observation:*** Back in '84, an Ohio district court reached the conclusion described in the preceding paragraph in regard to the purchase of a shopping center in *American Controlled Industries.* (FTC 2d/FIN ¶ L-7712; USTR ¶ 1675.023)

Determining lessee's lease amortization. The cost of acquiring an interest as a lessee under an existing lease of tangible property is taken into account under present law, e.g., Code Sec. 178 and Reg § 1.162-11(a). Code Sec. 178 generally requires that renewal options be reflected in the leasehold amortization period if less than 75% of the lease cost applies to the original term of the lease remaining on the acquisition date. (H Rept p. 769) Reg § 1.162-11(a) (FTC 2d/FIN ¶ L-4901; TG ¶ 6411; USTR ¶ 1622.11) generally provides that the cost of acquiring a lease must be amortized over the term of the lease.

Subleases treated as leases. For purposes of Code Sec. 197, a sublease is treated in the same manner as a lease of the underlying property involved. (Code Sec. 197(f)(6)) Thus section 197 intangibles don't include any interest as a sublessee or sublessor of tangible property, whether real or personal. (H Rept p. 769)

Allocation where lease acquired along with other intangibles. In the case of any interest as a lessee of tangible property, the portion of the total purchase price that is allocable to the lease can't exceed the excess of (1) the present value of the fair market value rent for the use of the property for the lease term, over (2) the present value of the rent reasonably expected to be paid. The present value of the fair market value rent for the use of the property for the lease term is never to exceed the fair market value of the tangible property on date of acquisition. The rent's present value is presumed to be less than the value of the property if the duration of the lease is less than the property's economic useful life. (H Rept p. 769)

Airport gates. The lease of a gate at an airport for the purpose of loading and unloading passengers and cargo is a lease of tangible property for this purpose. "It is anticipated that such treatment will serve as guidance to the Internal Revenue Service and taxpayers in resolving existing disputes." (H Rept p. 769)

For official explanation see Committee Reports ¶ 3064.

¶ 424. Interests in land, corporations, partnerships, trusts, financial contracts and indebtedness excluded

Section 197 intangibles don't include the assets listed below regardless of whether acquired in a transaction involving the acquisition of a business, or purchased as a single, "free-standing" asset.

Land. Section 197 intangibles don't include any interest in land. (Code Sec. 197(e)(2)) Thus, the cost of acquiring an interest in land would continue to be taken into account under pre-'93 Act law. For this purpose, an interest in land includes a fee interest, life estate, remainder, easement, mineral rights, timber rights, grazing rights, riparian rights, air rights, zoning variances and other similar rights with respect to land. An interest in land doesn't include an airport landing or takeoff right, a regulated airline route, or a franchise to provide cable television services.

The costs of acquiring licenses, permits, and other rights relating to improvements to land, such as building construction or use permits, continue to be taken into account in the same manner as the cost of the underlying improvement, in accordance with pre-'93 Act law. (H Rept p. 767)

> ***observation:*** Under pre-'93 Act law, various rules applied, and continue to apply, to the interests in land listed above. (FTC 2d/FIN ¶ L-7711 *et seq.;* USTR ¶ 1674.006) For instance, no depreciation is permitted for land apart from added improvements that themselves constitute depreciable assets; an easement for a pipeline may be depreciated over the useful life of the pipeline; mineral and timber rights are subject to depletion; grazing rights are nonamortizable.

Financial contracts. Section 197 intangibles don't include any interest under an existing futures contract, foreign currency contract, notional principal contract or other similar financial contract. (Code Sec. 197(e)(1)(B)) Excluded contracts also include interest rate swaps. The exclusion applies regardless of whether the contract is regularly traded on an established market. However, any interest under a credit card servicing contract or an assumption reinsurance contract (see ¶ 421) isn't excluded under this special rule. (H Rept p. 766)

Corporations, partnerships, trusts and estates. Section 197 intangibles don't include any interest in a corporation, partnership, trust or estate. (Code Sec. 197(e)(1)(A)) Thus, 15-year amortization doesn't apply to the cost of acquiring stock, partnership interests or interests in trusts and estates, regardless of whether such interests are regularly traded on an established market. (H Rept p. 766) However, a temporal interest in property, outright or in trust, can't be used to convert a section 197 intangible into property more rapidly amortizable. (H Rept p. 766)

> ***observation:*** Presumably, a "temporal interest" means a term interest such as one for a specified number of years or a life estate. Under pre-'93 Act law, Code Sec. 167(e) already provides that no depreciation deduction is available for any term interest in property while the remainder is held by a related person. (FTC 2d/FIN ¶ L-7681.1; TG ¶ 5418; USTR ¶ 1674.117)

FTC 2d References are to the Federal Tax Coordinator 2d
FIN References are to RIA's Analysis of Federal Taxes: Income
TG References are to the Tax Guide
USTR References are to the United States Tax Reporter

Indebtedness. Section 197 intangibles don't include any interest in any existing indebtedness (Code Sec. 197(e)(5)(B)), other than the deposit base or similar asset of a financial institution. (Code Sec. 197(d)(2)(B), see ¶ 415) For example, the value of assuming an existing indebtedness with a below-market interest rate is taken into account under pre-'93 Act law. (H Rept p. 770)

The premium paid for the right to receive an above-market rate of interest may be taken into account under Code Sec. 171 (FTC 2d/FIN ¶ K-5610; TG ¶ 7230; USTR ¶ 1714 *et seq.),* which generally permits the amount of the premium to be amortized on a yield-to-maturity basis over the remaining term of the debt instrument. (H Rept p. 770)

For official explanation see Committee Reports ¶ 3064.

¶ 425. Tax-free transaction *(Indopco)* costs

Section 197 intangibles don't include any fees for professional services or "transaction costs" incurred by parties to a transaction with respect to which any part of the gain or loss isn't recognized under the rules in Code Secs. 351 through 368 that govern corporate organizations and reorganizations. (Code Sec. 197(e)(8))

This provision blocks the possible argument that the new 15-year amortization rules apply to amounts that may be required to be capitalized under pre-'93 Act law but that don't relate to any asset with a readily identifiable useful life.

An example of such amounts were the costs dealt with by the Supreme Court in *Indopco.* In that case the Court held that a target corporation acquired in a friendly takeover had to capitalize investment banking and other acquisition-related expenses. (FTC 2d/FIN ¶ L-5602; USTR ¶ 1624.010)

This exception is provided solely to clarify that Code Sec. 197 doesn't provide 15-year amortization for any such amounts as those involved in *Indopco.* No inference is intended:

. . . that such amounts would (if it weren't for this exception) be properly characterized as eligible for 15-year amortization.

. . . that any amounts not specified in this exception should be so treated.

. . . as to the proper treatment of professional fees or transaction costs under other circumstances. (H Rept p. 770)

observation: No definition is provided for the term "transaction costs."

For official explanation see Committee Reports ¶ 3064.

¶ 426. Accounts receivable

It will often be the case that a portion of the purchase price of an acquired trade or business is attributable to accounts receivable or other similar rights to income for goods or services provided to customers of the acquired trade or business before its acquisition. The tax treatment of such receivables isn't affected by Code Sec. 197. Thus pre-'93 Act law continues to apply with the result that the portion of the purchase price of an acquired trade or business that is attributable to accounts receivable is allocated among them and is taken into account as payment is received on each receivable or at the time that a receivable becomes worthless. (H Rept p. 763)

For official explanation see Committee Reports ¶ 3064.

¶ 427. Self-created intangibles generally excluded from new rules

Under pre-'93 Act law, some costs that are paid or incurred to create, maintain, or enhance the value of intangible assets may be deducted as ordinary and necessary business expenses for the year that the costs are paid or incurred. For example, advertising expenses generally may be deducted for the year that the expenses are paid or incurred even though the advertising often results in income in future taxable years. (FTC 2d/FIN ¶ L-2301; TG ¶ 6145; USTR ¶ 1624.355) Similarly, immediate deduction is allowed for research and experimental costs that contribute to the creation of intangibles. (FTC 2d/FIN ¶ L-2601; TG ¶ 6250; USTR ¶ 1744) And costs incurred to train employees generally may be deducted for the year that the costs are paid or incurred even though the training results in a more knowledgeable or valuable workforce. (FTC 2d/FIN ¶ H-3603; TG ¶ 3130; USTR ¶ 2635.18(50)) Thus, while taxpayers must capitalize the costs of acquiring intangible assets from another person (such as the costs of acquiring a customer list or goodwill), they may currently deduct the costs incurred to develop or maintain these assets.

Code Sec. 197 leaves these rules intact by generally exempting self-created intangibles from the new 15-year amortization rules.

Thus, amortizable section 197 intangibles don't include any intangible created by the taxpayer other than:

. . . intangibles described in Code Sec. 197(d)(1)(D), (E) or (F), i.e., certain licenses and permits granted by a governmental unit (see ¶ 419), covenants not to compete made in connection with the acquisition of an interest in a trade or business (¶ 418), and franchises, trademarks and trade names (see ¶ 420), and

. . . intangibles created in connection with a transaction (or a series of related transactions) that involves the acquisition of assets which constitute a trade or business or a substantial portion thereof. (Code Sec. 197(c)(2))

Thus, for example, the capitalized costs incurred in connection with the development or registration of a trademark or trade name are amortized over the 15-year period. (H Rept p. 772)

> ***observation:*** No explanation or example is provided as to what is meant by "created in connection with . . . the acquisition of assets which constitute a trade or business."

An intangible owned by a taxpayer is considered to have been created by the taxpayer if the intangible is produced by another person under a contract with the taxpayer made before the production of the intangible. (H Rept p. 771) For example, a technological process or other know-how that is developed specifically for a taxpayer under an arrangement with another person under which the taxpayer retains all rights to the process or know-how is considered created by the taxpayer.

The exception for "self-created" intangibles doesn't apply to making (or renewing) a contract for the use of a section 197 intangible. Thus, the exception doesn't apply to the capitalized costs incurred by a licensee in connection with making (or renewing) a contract for the use of know-how or other section 197 intangible. These capitalized costs must be amortized over the 15-year period. (H Rept p. 772)

For official explanation see Committee Reports ¶ 3064.

¶ 428. When is intangible asset acquired as part of a business

A number of intangible assets aren't treated as section 197 intangibles unless

FTC 2d References are to the Federal Tax Coordinator 2d
FIN References are to RIA's Analysis of Federal Taxes: Income
TG References are to the Tax Guide
USTR References are to the United States Tax Reporter

acquired in a transaction (or series of related transactions) that involves the acquisition of assets which constitute a trade or business or a substantial portion of a trade or business, as noted in ¶ 412 *et seq.*

IRS is expected to issue regs requiring any intangible property that would otherwise be excluded to be treated as section 197 intangible where the acquisition of the property is, in and of itself, the acquisition of an asset which constitutes a trade or business or a substantial portion of a trade or business. (H Rept p. 766)

The determination of whether acquired assets constitute a substantial portion of a trade or business is to be based on all of the facts and circumstances, including the nature and the amount of the assets acquired as well as the nature and the amount of the assets retained by the transferor. It is not intended, however, that the value of the assets acquired relative to the value of the assets retained by the transferor is to be determinative of whether the acquired assets constitute a substantial portion of a trade or business.

A group of assets constitute a trade or business if the assets are of such a character that goodwill or going concern value could under any circumstances attach to them. In addition, the acquisition of a franchise, trademark or trade name constitutes the acquisition of a trade or business or a substantial portion of a trade or business. (H Rept p. 766)

For official explanation see Committee Reports ¶ 3064.

¶ 429. Loss deduction on disposition of section 197 intangible barred in some cases

No loss deduction is permitted on the disposition of an amortizable section 197 intangible if the taxpayer retains one or more other such intangibles acquired in the same transaction or series of related transactions along with the intangible disposed of. (Code Sec. 197(f)(1)(A)) For this purpose, the abandonment of an intangible or any event that renders it worthless is a disposition. (H Rept p. 772)

On the disposition of an intangible subject to this rule barring the deduction of any loss, the bases of the other intangibles acquired in the same transaction or series of related transactions is increased by the amount of the loss barred. (Code Sec. 197(f)(1)(A)(ii))

The basis of each retained section 197 intangible acquired in the same transaction or series of related transactions is increased by the product of (1) the amount of the loss not recognized solely by reason of this rule, and (2) a fraction consisting of the basis of the intangible over the total bases of all such retained section 197 intangibles. (H Rept p. 773)

All persons treated as a single taxpayer under Code Sec. 41(f)(1) (i.e., members of the same controlled group of corporations and commonly controlled trades and businesses) are treated as a single taxpayer for purposes of this special rule. (Code Sec. 197(f)(1)(C)) Thus, a loss isn't recognized by a corporation upon the disposition of a section 197 intangible if after the disposition a member of the same controlled group retains other section 197 intangibles that were acquired in the same transaction or series of related transactions as the intangible disposed of. IRS is expected to issue regs for taking into account the amount of any loss not recognized (for example, by allowing the corporation that disposed of the section 197 intangible to amortize the loss over the remaining portion of the 15-year amortization period). (H Rept p. 773)

These special rules don't apply to a section 197 intangible that is separately acquired (i.e., a section 197 intangible that is acquired other than in a transaction or a series of related transactions that involve the acquisition of other section 197 intangibles). Consequently, a loss may be recognized upon the disposition of a separately acquired section 197 intangible. In no event, however, is the termination or worthlessness of a portion of a section 197 intangible considered the disposition of a separately acquired section 197 intangible. For example, the termination of one or more customers from an acquired customer list or the worthlessness of some information from an acquired data base isn't considered the disposition of a separately acquired section 197 intangible. (H Rept p. 772)

illustration: In May of '94, Chutney Corporation, in a single-asset transaction, buys for $10,000 a 2,000-item customer list from a competitor that is going out of business and selling off its remaining assets to other, unrelated taxpayers. In August of the same year, Chutney buys for $400,000 all the operating assets of another business. These assets consist of land and building, equipment, furniture and fixtures, know-how and goodwill. Because the land and building, equipment, and furniture and fixtures have a fair market value of $300,000, $100,000 of the purchase price is allocated under the residual method (see ¶ 430) to section 197 assets consisting of know-how and goodwill. By the end of '96, 200 of the 2,000 customers on the purchased list have stopped doing business with Chutney. Also, the purchased know-how has been rendered obsolete by technological change and written off by Chutney. Nonetheless, Chutney can claim no loss deduction for either the customer list or the know-how and must continue to amortize the entire amount paid for section 197 intangibles in '93 ($110,000) over the remainder of the 15-year amortization periods that apply to them.

observation: Suppose that the section 197 intangibles acquired by a taxpayer in the purchase or a trade or business include goodwill or going concern value. The taxpayer can't claim any loss deduction on the disposition or worthlessness of any of the other section 197 intangibles so long as the goodwill or going concern value continues to exist.

observation: Code Sec. 197(f)(1) only bars the recognition of losses. Any gain on the disposition of a section 197 intangible must be recognized regardless of what other intangibles the taxpayer retains. To compute the amount of this gain, a separate basis must be computed for the intangible disposed of at a gain. Yet other than the reallocation rules described above (and a special rule for certain leasehold interests, see ¶ 423), the new rules make no provision for allocating the purchase price of a business among section 197 intangibles in order to determine separate bases for them.

For official explanation see Committee Reports ¶ 3064.

¶ 430. Purchase price of business allocated to section 197 intangibles under residual method

Under pre-'93 Act law, the purchase price of a business must generally be allocated under a so-called "residual method" prescribed in IRS regs. This method requires that all assets of an acquired trade or business be divided into the following four classes: (1) Class I assets, which include cash and cash equivalents; (2) Class II assets, which include certificates of deposit, U.S. government securities, readily marketable stock or securities, and foreign currency; (3) Class III assets, which include

FTC 2d References are to the Federal Tax Coordinator 2d
FIN References are to RIA's Analysis of Federal Taxes: Income
TG References are to the Tax Guide
USTR References are to the United States Tax Reporter

all assets other than those included in Class I, II, or IV (generally all furniture, fixtures, land, buildings, equipment, other tangible property, accounts receivable, covenants not to compete, and intangible assets other than goodwill and going concern value); and (4) Class IV assets, which include intangible assets in the nature of goodwill or going concern value. The purchase price of an acquired trade or business (reduced by the amount of the assets included in Class I) is allocated to the assets in Class II and Class III based on their value. To the extent that the purchase price exceeds the value of the assets included in Class, I, II and III, the excess is allocated to nonamortizable goodwill and going concern value. (FTC 2d/FIN ¶ P-1401; TG ¶ 2388; USTR ¶ 10,604)

Thus, under pre-'93 Act law, allocations to intangibles other than goodwill and going concern value continue to give rise to disputes as to (1) their existence, (2) their value and (3) their useful lives.

The '93 Act resolves all three of these issues by recasting the way in which the residual method is to be applied. This is to be accomplished by IRS regs that (1) reflect the fact that goodwill and going concern value are amortizable, and (2) treat all amortizable section 197 intangibles as Class IV assets subject to 15-year amortization. (H Rept p. 776)

> ***observation:*** The residual method generally applies not only to the outright purchase of a business but also where a Code Sec. 338 election is made to treat a stock purchase as an asset purchase. (FTC 2d/FIN ¶ F-3601; TG ¶ 2375; USTR ¶ 3384) The residual method also applies both to buyers, for purposes of determining the basis of the acquired assets, and to sellers, for purposes of determining their gain on each of the separate assets sold.

> ***illustration:*** Phil buys from Sam, for a total consideration of $500,000, assets that constitute a trade or business. These assets include equipment, furniture and fixtures, a building and land, marketable securities and accounts receivable (Class II and III assets) with a total fair market value of $450,000. The assets purchased by Phil also include, in addition to goodwill, a customer list (Class III asset under current law) which he claims is worth $40,000 and amortizable over a 5-year period. As a result, under the residual method as applied under pre-'93 Act law, Phil allocates only $10,000 of the purchase price to nonamortizable Class IV goodwill. Under the residual method as recast in accordance with the new law, both the customer list and goodwill are treated as Class IV assets ("section 197 intangibles") and the purchase price in excess of $450,000 is allocated to them. This excess amount, $50,000, is amortizable over the 15-year period.

> ***observation:*** The new law generally provides no rules (see ¶s 423 and 429 for limited exceptions) for allocating the amount attributed to section 197 intangibles among the particular intangibles that comprise that class.

Code Sec. 1060 information reporting and partnership rules amended. Under pre-'93 Act law, Code Sec. 1060(b) authorized IRS to require the transferor and transferee in certain asset acquisitions to furnish information as to the amount of any purchase price that is allocable to goodwill or going concern value. Asset acquisitions subject to this rule are transfers of assets that constitute a trade or business and with respect to which the transferee's basis is wholly determined by reference to the consideration paid for the assets. (FTC 2d/FIN ¶ P-1419; USTR ¶ 10,604)

The '93 Act amends Code Sec. 1060(b) to provide that the reporting requirement applies to section 197 intangibles rather than to goodwill or going concern value. (Code Sec. 1060(b)(1) as amended by '93 Act § 13261(e)(2))

Under pre-'93 Act law, Code Sec. 1060(d) provided that if a distribution of partnership property or a transfer of a partnership interest is made, the residual method applies, but only for purposes of determining the value of goodwill or going concern value (or similar items) in applying the Code Sec. 755 basis allocation rules. If Code Sec. 755 applies, the transaction is subject to the information reporting requirements imposed by Code Sec. 1060(b), see above. (FTC 2d/FIN ¶ B-4026; USTR ¶ 7554)

The '93 Act amends Code Sec. 1060(d) to provide that the residual method applies with respect to section 197 intangibles rather than to goodwill or going concern value (or similar items). (Code Sec. 1060(d)(1) as amended by '93 Act § 13261(e)(2))

IRS is to issue regs requiring taxpayers to furnish such additional information as may be necessary or appropriate to carry out the provisions of these new rules, including the amount of purchase price that is allocable to intangible assets that aren't amortizable section 197 intangibles. (H Rept p. 777)

> ***illustration:*** Sandbird Corporation, on Jan. 1, '94, buys all the assets of a sole proprietorship business for $1,000,000. These assets consist of land and buildings, equipment, furniture and fixtures, know-how, computer software, and goodwill. The fair market value, as of the date of acquisition, of the land and buildings, equipment, furniture and fixtures is $700,000. As a result, under the residual method as amended by the '93 Act, the remaining $300,000 of the purchase price ($1,000,000 – $700,000) must be allocated to section 197 intangibles (know-how, software and goodwill). By the end of '96, due to technological change, the know-how has been written off as obsolete. In '98, the software is also written off as obsolete. However, under the rules described in ¶ 429, no loss deduction is allowed under Code Sec. 197 for either writeoff since Sandbird still retains goodwill acquired in the same transaction with the know-how and software. As a result, the entire $300,000 continues to be amortized over the 15-year period beginning Jan. 1, '94 and ending Dec. 31, 2008.

> ***illustration:*** On Jan. 1, '93, Sandbird Corporation buys 100% of the stock in Zoom, Inc. for $900,000. Zoom holds the same assets, with the same fair market values, described in preceding illustration and also has $100,000 in liabilities. Sandbird makes a Code Sec. 338 election. Under this election, an amount called the "adjusted grossed-up basis" of the target corporation (Zoom) is allocated to target's assets. (FTC 2d/FIN ¶ F-3600; TG ¶ 2375; USTR ¶ 3384.09) Generally speaking, "adjusted grossed-up basis" is an amount determined by reference to what the acquiring corporation pays for target's stock, increased by target's liabilities and subject to certain other adjustments. Here Zoom's "adjusted grossed-up basis" is $1,000,000 ($900,000 + $100,000). Under the residual method, as amended by the '93 Act, $700,000 of that amount is allocated to land and buildings, equipment, furniture and fixtures. The remaining $300,000 is allocated to the section 197 intangibles (know-how, software and goodwill).

> ***observation:*** The taxpayer in *Newark Morning Ledger* (see ¶ 401) had to prove a separate value and useful life for subscriber lists acquired in the purchase of other newspaper publishers. Under Code Sec. 197 the purchase

price of a newspaper business is allocated first to assets other than section 197 intangibles up the fair market value of those assets. The excess, if any, is then allocated to the subscriber lists together with any other section 197 intangibles acquired as part of the same newspaper business and is deductible over the 15-year period. In other words, the taxpayer neither has to prove a value for the lists apart from goodwill nor does any useful life have to be established for the lists.

For official explanation see Committee Reports ¶ 3064.

¶ 431. Nonrecognition transactions

In the case of any section 197 intangible transferred in certain nonrecognition transfers, the transferee is treated as if he were the transferor for purposes of applying the new rules. This rule applies to so much of the basis of the transferred property in the transferee's hands that doesn't exceed the basis of the property in the hands of the transferor.

Nonrecognition transactions subject to this rule consist of:

. . . Code Sec. 332 subsidiary liquidations,

. . . Code Sec. 351 incorporation transfers,

. . . Code Sec. 361 reorganization transfers,

. . . Code Sec. 721 partnership contributions,

. . . Code Sec. 731 partnership distributions

. . . Code Sec. 1031 like-kind exchanges,

. . . Code Sec. 1033 involuntary conversions, and

. . . any transaction between members of an affiliated group during any tax year for which a consolidated return is filed. (Code Sec. 197(f)(2))

The termination of a partnership under Code Sec. 708(b)(1)(B) is a transaction to which this special rule applies. (H Rept p. 773)

> ***Illustration:*** Albert owns an amortizable section 197 intangible that he has amortized under section 197 for 4 full years and which has a remaining unamortized basis of $300,000. Albert exchanges the asset and $100,000 for a like-kind amortizable section 197 intangible in a transaction to which Code Sec. 1031 applies. Under the new rules, $300,000 of the basis of the acquired amortizable section 197 intangible is amortized over the 11 years remaining in the original 15-year amortization period for the transferred asset and the other $100,000 of basis is amortized over the 15-year period commencing with the month the new intangible was acquired. (H Rept p. 773)

No inference is intended by the preceding illustration as to whether any asset treated as a section 197 intangible under the new rules is eligible for like kind exchange treatment. (H Rept p. 773)

> ***observation:*** Neither Code Sec. 197 nor the House Report spells out exactly what all the consequences of this rule are intended to be. Presumably, the transferee would in all respects stand in the shoes of the transferor in regard to the transfered intangible, including the status of the asset as an

amortizable section 197 intangible, the date from which the 15-year amortization period is measured (i.e., from the beginning of the transferor's month of acquisition) and remaining amortizable basis (i.e., adjusted basis of the intangible in the hands of the transferor).

For official explanation see Committee Reports ¶ 3064.

¶ 432. Sales of partnership interests; payments in liquidation of deceased and retiring partners

The House Report includes several examples relating to the sale of partnership interests which are said to be "consistent" with the rules for nonrecognition transactions at ¶ 431. (H Rept p. 774) Also included is an example of how the new rules apply in regard to payments made in liquidation of a deceased or retiring partner's interest.

Illustration: Tom, Dick and Harry each contribute $700 for equal shares in partnership P, which on Jan. 1, '94, acquires as its sole asset an amortizable section 197 intangible for $2,100. On Jan. 1, '98, the sole asset of P is the intangible acquired in '94, the intangible has a remaining unamortized basis of $1,500 and Tom, Dick and Harry each has a $500 basis for his partnership interest. At this time, George buys Tom's interest in P for $800. If there is no Code Sec. 754 basis-step-up election (FTC 2d/FIN ¶ B-4027; TG ¶ 1584; USTR ¶ 7544) in effect for '97, there is no change in the basis or amortization of the intangible and George merely steps into the shoes of Tom with respect to the intangible. George's share of the basis in the intangible is $500, which is amortized over the 11 years remaining in the amortization period for the intangible. (H Rept p. 774)

Illustration: Same facts except that a Code Sec. 754 basis-step-up election is in effect for '98. In this situation, George is treated as having an $800 basis for his share of P's intangible. Under section 197, George's share of income and loss is determined as if P owns two intangible assets. George is treated as having a basis of $500 in one asset, which continues to be amortized over the 11 remaining years of the original 15-year life. With respect to the other asset, George is treated as having a basis of $300 (the amount of step-up obtained by George under the election) which is amortized over a 15-year period starting with January of '98. Dick and Harry each continue to share equally in a $1,000 basis in the intangible and amortize that amount over the remaining 11-year life. (H Rept p. 774)

Illustration: Same facts except that George buys the interests of both Tom and Dick for $1,600. Under Code Sec. 708(b), which treats a partnership as terminated if more than 50% is sold within a 12-month period, the transaction is treated as if P were liquidated with Harry and George each receiving their pro rata share of P's assets which they then immediately contribute to a new partnership. The distributions in liquidation are governed by Code Sec. 731 and thus constitute one of the nonrecognition transactions listed at ¶ 431. Harry's interest in the intangible is treated as having a $500

FTC 2d References are to the Federal Tax Coordinator 2d
FIN References are to RIA's Analysis of Federal Taxes: Income
TG References are to the Tax Guide
USTR References are to the United States Tax Reporter

> basis, with a remaining amortization period of 11 years. George is treated as having an interest in two assets: one with a basis of $1,000 and a remaining amortization period of 11 years, and the other with a basis of $600 and a new amortization period of 15 years. (H Rept p. 774)

Payments made in liquidation of deceased and retiring partners' interests. The '93 Act changes the treatment of payments made in liquidation of the interest of a retiring or deceased partner in exchange for goodwill, see ¶ 313. Except in the case of payments made on the retirement or death of a general partner of a partnership for which capital isn't a material income-producing factor, e.g., a law or accounting firm, such payments aren't treated as distributions of partnership income. Thus, they aren't deductible by the partnership. However, if the partnership makes a basis-step-up election under Code Sec. 754, the result will generally be a stepped-up basis in the hands of the partnership for the retiring or deceased partner's share of partnership goodwill and an amortization deduction for the increase in basis under Code Sec. 197. (H Rept p. 775)

> ***Illustration:*** Same facts as in the three preceding illustrations except that on Jan. 1, '98, Tom retires from the partnership in exchange for a payment from the partnership of $800, all of which is in exchange for Tom's interest in the intangible asset owned by P. If a Code Sec. 754 election is in effect for '98, P is treated as having two amortizable section 197 intangibles: one with a basis of $1,500 and a remaining life of 11 years, and the other with a basis of $300 and a new life of 15 years. (H Rept p. 775)

For official explanation see Committee Reports ¶ 3064.

¶ 433. Other special rules

IRS to issue regs. IRS is authorized to issue regs appropriate to carry out the purposes of the new law, including regs to prevent avoidance through related persons or otherwise. (Code Sec. 197(g)) IRS is also expected to issue regs clarifying what property constitutes section 197 intangibles. (H Rept p. 777)

Section 197 intangibles treated as depreciable assets for recapture and other purposes. Amortizable section 197 intangibles are treated as depreciable property under Code Sec. 167. (Code Sec. 197(f)(7)) Thus, an amortizable section 197 intangible isn't a capital asset under Code Sec. 1221 but if held for more than one year generally qualifies as a Code Sec. 1231 asset subject to the capital-gain, ordinary-loss rule. Similarly, such an asset is subject to recapture under Code Sec. 1245, and Code Sec. 1239 applies to bar capital gain treatment on a sale to a related person. (H Rept p. 775)

Amounts "properly taken into account" in determining cost of nonsection 197 property. The new rules don't apply to "any increment in value" if, under pre-'93 Act law, the increment is properly taken into account in determining the cost of property that isn't a section 197 intangible. (Code Sec. 197(f)(8)) For example, no part of the cost of acquiring real property held for the production of rental income (for example, an office building, apartment building or shopping center) is taken into account under Code Sec. 197 (i.e., no good-will, going concern value or any other section 197 intangible arises in connection with the acquisition of the property). Instead, the entire cost of acquiring it is included in the basis of the real property and is recovered under pre-'93 Act law. (H Rept p. 776)

Determination of basis. The basis of a section 197 intangible acquired from another person is generally determined under pre-'93 Act rules that apply to tangible property acquired from another person. Thus, if a portion of the cost of acquiring an amortizable section 197 intangible is contingent, the adjusted basis of the intangible is increased as of the beginning of the month that the contingent amount is paid or incurred. This additional amount is amortized ratably over the remaining months in the 15-year amortization period that applies to the intangible as of the beginning of the month that the contingent amount is paid or incurred. (H Rept p. 772)

Short tax years. The amount of any deduction allowed under Code Sec. 197 is determined by amortizing the adjusted basis of an amortizable section 197 intangible ratably over the 15-year period that begins with the month in which the intangible was acquired. (Code Sec. 197(a)) In the case of a short tax year, the amortization deduction is based on the number of months in the short tax year. (H Rept p. 761)

> ***Illustration:*** Vector acquires a section 197 intangible on Jan. 14, '94, during a tax year that begins on Jan. 1, '94 and ends on Oct. 31, '94. Vector pays $180,000 for the intangible, which means that Vector is entitled to an amortization deduction of $1,000 for each month in its tax year (15 × 12 = 180; $180,000 ÷ 180 = $1,000). As a result, Vector is entitled to a deduction of $10,000 for its short tax year that ends on Oct. 31, '94 (10 months × $1,000).

Certain inferences not to be drawn from enactment of Code Sec. 197. No inference is intended as to whether a depreciation or amortization deduction is allowed under pre-'93 Act law with respect to any intangible property that is either included in, or excluded from, the definition of section 197 intangibles. Also, no inference is intended as to whether an asset is to be considered tangible or intangible property for any other purpose of the Code. (H Rept p. 761)

Code Sec. 197 deductions apportioned between estates, trusts and beneficiaries. Amortization deductions with respect to section 197 intangibles owned by estates and trusts are apportioned between those entities and their beneficiaries in the same way as amortization deductions with respect to certain pollution control facilities are apportioned under pre-'93 Act law (Code Sec. 642(f) as amended by '93 Act § 13261(f)(2)), i.e., in the same way as depreciation and depletion. (FTC 2d/FIN ¶ C-2222; TG ¶ 1786; USTR ¶ 6424.06)

For official explanation see Committee Reports ¶ 3064.

¶ 434. Effective date

These new rules generally apply to property acquired after Aug. 10, '93. However, taxpayers may elect to apply current law to property acquired after that date under a binding written contract in effect on Aug. 10, '93. Under a second election, a taxpayer may elect to apply the new rules to all property acquired after July 25, '91. ('93 Act § 13261(g))

Retroactive election to have new rules apply to property acquired after July 25, '91. Taxpayers may elect to have the new rules apply to property acquired after July 25, '91. (§ 13261(g)(2)) If the election is made, it applies to *all* property acquired after that date. (H Rept p. 778) The election, if made, also applies to all property acquired after July 25, '91 by any taxpayer that is under common control with the electing

FTC 2d References are to the Federal Tax Coordinator 2d
FIN References are to RIA's Analysis of Federal Taxes: Income
TG References are to the Tax Guide
USTR References are to the United States Tax Reporter

taxpayer (as defined in Code Sec. 41(f)(1)) if this common control exists at any time after Aug. 2, '93 and on or before the date that the election is made. (§ 13261(g)(2)(B)(ii)) The Code Sec. 41(f)(1) rules governing controlled groups of corporations and commonly controlled trades and business are discussed at FTC 2d/FIN ¶ L-15316 *et seq.;* TG ¶ 5832; USTR ¶ 414.03)

The election is to be made when and as prescribed by IRS and may be revoked only with IRS consent. (§ 13261(g)(2)(B)) According to the House Report, IRS is expected to require that the election be made on a timely filed return for the tax year that includes the date of enactment. (H Rept p. 778)

Retroactive elections by affiliated groups filing consolidated returns. Any property acquired after July 25, '91 by a member of an affiliated group filing a consolidated return at the time of the acquisition is treated as property acquired by the affiliated group for purposes of any group election.

An election by an affiliated group filing a consolidated return doesn't force the acquirer of a former group member to make the election, even if the acquirer would normally continue the treatment of the former member's assets (for instance, an acquirer in a transaction that doesn't affect the inside basis of the assets of the former group member).

Similarly, a failure by the former group to make the retroactive election doesn't effect the ability of a former group member (or a new acquirer that is related to that member on the date of the election) to make an election that affects the post-July 25, '91 intangible asset acquisitions of the former group member (including intangible asset acquisitions made while it was a member of the former group.) (Conf Rept p. 695)

> ***Illustration:*** Polk Corporation is the parent of an affiliated group that files a consolidated return. One of Polk's subsidiaries included in the group is Sourwood, Inc. The Polk group files its consolidated return on the calendar year basis. Sourwood acquires some intangible assets on Aug. 1, '91. Sourwood's stock is sold to Xerxes Corporation on Dec. 31, '92 in a transaction in which Sourwood's adjusted basis in its assets isn't changed. Xerxes is also the parent of an affiliated group filing a joint return that now includes Sourwood. If the Xerxes group makes the retroactive election, this won't require the Polk group to also make the election. If the Polk group makes the retroactive election, the election will affect the amortization deductions allowed on the Polk group's '91 and '92 consolidated returns with respect to the assets acquired by Sourwood on Aug. 1, '91. However, the Xerxes group isn't required to also make the election. (Conf Rept p. 695)

IRS is to provide rules as to appropriate adjustments, if any, to be made where property acquired after July 25, '91 has been transferred from one group to another in a transaction that doesn't involve a change in asset basis and one or both groups independently make a retroactive election that affects the property's amortization. These rules might apply, for example, where a corporation that belongs to group that files a consolidated return (1) buys property after July 25, '91, and (2) before Aug. 2, '93 becomes a member of another group in a transaction that doesn't affect the basis of the corporation's assets. (Conf Rept p. 695)

Elective binding contract exception. A taxpayer may elect to have pre-'93 Act law apply to property acquired after date of enactment, rather than the new 15-year amortization rules, if the acquisition is made under a written binding contract in effect on the date of enactment and all times thereafter to the date of acquisition. This election can't be made if the taxpayer has elected to apply the new rules to property acquired after July 25, '91. (§ 13261(g)(3)(A))

This election is to be made when and as prescribed by IRS and may be revoked only with IRS consent. If this election is made, it applies to all property acquired under the contract with respect to which the election is made. (§ 13261(g)(3)(B)) According to the House Report, IRS is expected to require that the election be made on a timely filed return for the tax year that includes date of enactment. (H Rept p. 779)

For anti-churning rules, see ¶ 435.

For official explanation see Committee Reports ¶ 3064.

¶ 435. Anti-churning rules

Special rules are provided to keep taxpayers from converting existing goodwill, going concern value, or any other intangible for which a depreciation or amortization deduction isn't allowable under pre-'93 Act law into amortizable section 197 intangibles. (H Rept p. 779)

Thus, amortizable section 197 intangibles don't include goodwill, going concern value or any other section 197 intangible for which a depreciation or amortization deduction isn't allowed under pre-'93 Act law and which the taxpayer acquires after Aug. 10, '93 if:

. . . the taxpayer or a related person held or used the intangible at any time during the period that begins on July 25, '91, and that ends on Aug. 10, '93, *or*

. . . the taxpayer acquired the intangible from a person that held it at any time during the period that begins on July 25, '91, and that ends on Aug. 10, '93 and, as part of the transaction, the user of the intangible does not change, *or*

. . . the taxpayer grants the right to use the intangible to a person (or a person related to such person) that held or used the intangible at any time during the period that begins on July 25, '91, and that ends on Aug. 10, '93.

Whether the user of property changes as part of a transaction is to be determined in accordance with regs to be issued by IRS. For purposes of the anti-churning rules, deductions allowable under Code Sec. 1253(d), which prescribes the tax treatment of amounts paid for franchises, trademarks and trade names, are treated as amortization deductions. (Code Sec. 197(f)(9)(A))

Property acquired from a decedent. The anti-churning rules don't apply to the acquisition of property by a taxpayer if the basis of the property in the hands of the taxpayer is determined under the Code Sec. 1014(a) rules governing the basis of property acquired from a decedent. (Code Sec. 197(f)(9)(D))

What is a related person? For purposes of the anti-churning rules, a person is a "related person" with respect to the taxpayer if:

. . . there exists between the two of them one of the relationships specified in Code Sec. 267(b) or Code Sec. 707(b)(1), substituting 20% for 50%, *or*

. . . the two of them are engaged in trades or businesses under common control within the meaning of Code Secs. 41(f)(1)(A) and (B). (Code Sec. 197(f)(9)(C)(i))

A person is treated as a "related person" if the relationship exists immediately before or immediately after the acquisition of the intangible involved. (Code Sec. 197(f)(9)(C)(ii))

The relationships described in Code Sec. 267(b) include, among others, those that exist between family members, between an individual and his more-than-50% owned corporation, and two corporations that belong to the same more-than-50% controlled group. (FTC 2d/FIN ¶ G-2657; TG ¶ 4101; USTR ¶ 2674) However, for purposes of the anti-churning rules, 20% is substituted for 50%. (Code Sec. 197(f)(9)(C)(i)) Thus, for example, an individual and his more-than-20% owned corporation would be related persons. The relationships described in Code Sec. 707(b)(1) are between partnerships and their more-than-50% owners, and between partnerships each of which is more than 50% owned by the same persons. Here again, under Code Sec. 197(f)(9)(C)(i), 20% is substituted for 50% for purposes of the anti-churning rules. (FTC 2d/FIN ¶ B-2016; TG ¶ 1643) The Code Sec. 41(f)(1) rules governing controlled groups of corporations and commonly controlled trades and businesses are discussed at FTC 2d/FIN ¶ L-15316 *et seq.;* TG ¶ 5832; USTR ¶ 414.03)

Rules similar to Code Sec. 168 anti-churning rules to apply. Rules similar to the anti-churning rules under Code Sec. 168 are to apply in determining whether persons are related. In this regard, the House Report refers to Prop Reg § 1.168-4. (FTC 2d/FIN ¶ L-8230 *et seq.;* USTR ¶ 1688.408) For example, a corporation, partnership or trust that owned or used property at any time during the period that begins on July 25, '91 and ends on date of enactment, and that is no longer in existence, is considered to be in existence for purposes of determining whether the corporation, etc., is related to the taxpayer that acquired the property.

In the case of a transaction to which Code Sec. 338 applies, the corporation that is treated as selling its assets won't be considered related to the corporation that is treated as the purchaser of the assets if at least 80% of the stock of the corporation that is treated as the seller is acquired by purchase after July 25, '91. (H Rept p. 780)

Anti-churning rules don't apply to some less-than-50% relationships. If the anti-churning rules wouldn't apply to an intangible but for the rule treating 50% as 20% in defining a related person (see above), the anti-churning rules may be subject to a special limitation. The special limitation applies if the person from whom the intangible was acquired elects (1) to recognize gain on the intangible and (2) to pay a tax on that gain. That tax, when added to any other federal income tax imposed on that gain, must equal the gain multiplied by the highest rate of income tax applicable to the person from whom the intangible was acquired. If the special limitation applies, the anti-churning rules apply to the intangible only to the extent that the taxpayer's adjusted basis in the intangible exceeds the gain that the person from whom the intangible was acquired has elected to recognize. (Code Sec. 197(f)(9)(B))

Anti-abuse rules. Amortizable section 197 intangibles don't include any intangible acquired in a transaction one of the principal purposes of which is to avoid the requirement that the intangible be acquired after Aug. 10, '93, or to avoid the anti-churning rules. (Code Sec. 197(f)(9)(F))

Special rules for partnerships. Some special rules apply in determining whether the anti-churning rules apply with respect to any increase in the basis of partnership property under:

. . . Code Sec. 732 (basis of property distributed by a partnership to a partner),

. . . Code Sec. 734 (optional adjustment to basis of undistributed partnership property where Code Sec. 754 election in effect), or

. . . Code Sec. 743 (optional adjustment to basis of partnership property with respect to transferee partner where Code Sec. 754 election in effect).

In such cases, determinations under the anti-churning rules are made at the partner level and each partner is treated as having owned and used his proportionate share of the partnership's assets. (Code Sec. 197(f)(9)(E))

Thus, for example, the anti-churning rules don't apply to any increase in the basis of partnership property that occurs on the acquisition of an interest in a partnership that has made a Code Sec. 754 election if the person acquiring the interest isn't related to the person selling the interest. (H Rept p. 779)

Nonrecognition transactions. In the case of intangibles transferred in certain nonrecognition transfers, the transferee is treated as if he were the transferor for purposes of applying Code Sec. 197, see ¶ 431. Consequently, if the transferor of any section 197 property isn't allowed an amortization deduction with respect to that property under the anti-churning rules, then the transferee is also not allowed an amortization deduction under those rules to the extent of the adjusted basis of the transferee that doesn't exceed the transferor's adjusted basis. (H Rept p. 780)

Effect of anti-churning rules on taxpayers who elect to apply 15-year amortization to property acquired after July 25, '91. Taxpayers may elect to have the new 15-year amortization rules apply to property acquired after July 25, '91 (instead of after date of enactment) see ¶ 434. Where this election is made, the anti-churning rules apply to property acquired after July 25, '91. (§ 13261(g)(2)(A)(ii)) Also, in applying the anti-churning rules to any property acquired by the taxpayer on or before Aug. 10, '93, only holding or use of the property on July 25, '91 is taken into account. (§ 13261(g)(2)(A)(iii))

In other words, if an electing taxpayer acquires goodwill, etc., after July 25, '91, no amortization deduction is allowable if:

. . . the taxpayer or a related person held or used the intangible on July 25, '91, or

. . . the taxpayer acquired the intangible from a person who held it on July 25, '91 and, as part of the transaction, the user of the intangible doesn't change, or

. . . the taxpayer grants the right to use the intangible to a person (or a person related to that person) that held or used the intangible on July 25, '91. (H Rept p. 778)

For official explanation see Committee Reports ¶ 3064.

¶ 436. IRS urged to expedite settlement of pre-'93 Act cases

According to the Conference Report, IRS is urged "in the strongest possible terms to expedite the settlement of cases under [pre-'93 Act law]." In considering settlements and establishing procedures for handling existing controversies in an expedient and balanced manner, IRS is strongly encouraged to take into account the principles of Code Sec. 197 so as to produce consistent results for similarly situated taxpayers. However, no inference is intended that any deduction should be allowed in these cases for assets that aren't amortizable under pre-'93 Act law. (Conf Rept p. 696)

For official explanation see Committee Reports ¶ 3064.

¶ 437. Treasury to report on backlog and the effect of new rules

Treasury is to submit annual reports to the Ways and Means and Finance

Committees on the volume of pending disputes in audit and litigation involving the amortization of intangibles and the progress made in resolving disputes. These reports are also to address the effects of the new rules on the volume and nature of disputes regarding the amortization of intangibles. The first such report is to be made no later than Dec. 31, '94.

The Treasury is also to conduct a continuing study of the implementation and effects of the new rules, including effects on merger and acquisition activities (including hostile takeovers and leveraged buyouts). The study is to address effects of the new rules on the pricing of acquisitions and on the reported values of different types of intangibles (including goodwill). The initial results of this study are to be reported as expeditiously as possible and no later than Dec. 31, '94. Additional annual reports are to be provided annually thereafter. (Conf Rept p. 696)

For official explanation see Committee Reports ¶ 3064.

¶ 500. Real Estate Provisions

¶ 501. Taxpayer in real estate business may offset losses and credits from some rental real estate activities against nonpassive income after '93

Losses and credits generated by passive activities can't be used to offset other, non-passive income a taxpayer may receive, such as salaries, professional fees, interest and dividends, or income from an actively conducted trade or business. (FTC 2d/FIN ¶ M-4600; TG ¶ 6660; USTR ¶ 4694) Generally speaking, a passive activity is a trade or business in which the taxpayer doesn't materially participate. However, under pre-'93 Act law, rental activities are treated as passive without regard to material participation. This is true regardless of how intensively or extensively the taxpayer may have participated in other nonrental real estate activities. (FTC 2d/FIN ¶ M-5100; TG ¶ 6665; USTR ¶ 4694, 4694.03, 4694.60) For instance if, under pre-'93 Act law, a taxpayer has $500,000 in net income from a real estate brokerage business in which he works full-time and a $50,000 rental real estate loss, he can't offset the loss against his income from the brokerage business or from any other nonpassive source. However, if an individual taxpayer satisfies an active participation test, he may be able to offset up to $25,000 in nonpassive income with losses and credits from rental real estate activities. (FTC 2d/FIN ¶ M-5110; TG ¶ 6683; USTR ¶ 4694.60)

Some taxpayers' rental real estate activities not treated as passive activities. The '93 Act carves out an exception to the rule that provides that all rental activities are treated as passive activities. With respect to qualifying taxpayers, for any tax year in which they qualify, that rule doesn't apply to any rental real estate activity owned by them. (Code Sec. 469(c)(7) as amended by '93 Act § 13143(a))

> ***observation:*** The effect of this change is that the rental real estate activities of a qualifying taxpayer are subject to the same general rule that applies to non-rental activities. In other words, they will generally be treated as passive activities unless the taxpayer materially participates in them. If material participation is shown, the rental activity is nonpassive and any losses or credits generated by it may be used to offset the taxpayer's other, non-passive income.

Who qualifies for the new tax break. Subject to a special rule for closely held C corporations, a taxpayer qualifies for this new tax break, for a particular tax year, if:

. . . more than half the personal services performed by the taxpayer in trades or businesses during that year are performed in real property trades or businesses in which the taxpayer materially participates. (Code Sec. 469(c)(7)(B)(i)), and

. . . the taxpayer performs more than 750 hours of services during the tax year in real property trades or businesses in which the taxpayer materially participates (Code Sec. 469(c)(7)(B)(ii))

> ***observation:*** The House Report (H Rept p. 614) and the Conference Report (Conf Rept p 547) speak only of individuals and closely held C corporations in discussing the operation of this new rule, and make no refer-

FTC 2d References are to the Federal Tax Coordinator 2d
FIN References are to RIA's Analysis of Federal Taxes: Income
TG References are to the Tax Guide
USTR References are to the United States Tax Reporter

> ence to other kinds of taxpayers that are subject to the passive activity limitations such as estates, trusts and personal service corporations. (FTC 2d/FIN ¶ M-4700 *et seq.;* TG ¶ 6668) However, there is nothing in the language of new Code Sec. 469(c)(7) itself that explicitly excludes estates, trusts and personal service corporations from the benefit of the new rule.

Material participation has the same meaning under the new rules as it had under pre-'93 Act law. (H Rept p. 614)

How closely held C corporations qualify. In the case of a closely-held C corporation (generally speaking, a corporation more than 50% owned by five or fewer individuals during the last half of its tax year, see FTC 2d/FIN ¶ M-4706; TG ¶ 6668; USTR ¶ 4694), a special rule applies. Such a corporation qualifies for the new tax break for a particular tax year if more than 50% of its gross receipts for that tax year are derived from real property trades or businesses in which the corporation materially participates. (Code Sec. 469(c)(7)(D)(i)) Under pre-'93 Act rules that aren't affected by the '93 Act, a C corporation materially participates if shareholders owning more than 50% of the corporation's stock materially participate. (See FTC 2d/FIN ¶ M-5006; TG ¶ 6681; USTR ¶ 4694.04)

Real property trade or business defined. A real property trade or business is any real property development, redevelopment, construction, reconstruction, acquisition, conversion, rental, operation, management, leasing or brokerage trade or business. (Code Sec. 469(c)(7)(C))

> ***observation:*** The new rules discussed above impose no limit on the amount of rental real estate losses that may be freed up by these new rules. Thus, such losses aren't limited to the taxpayer's net income from real estate activities nor are they limited to the amount of his net taxable income before the deduction of the rental real estate losses. Where the losses exceed the taxpayer's other income they may become part of his net operating loss for the tax year and be carried back or forward to earlier or later tax years. (FTC 2d/FIN ¶ M-4118; USTR ¶ 4694.40 *et seq.*)

Joint returns. In the case of a joint return, the more-than-half and more-than-750-hours requirements are met if and only if either spouse separately satisfies them. For purposes of this rule, activities in which a spouse materially participates are determined under the Code Sec. 469(h) rules (FTC 2d/FIN ¶ M-4900; TG ¶ 6681; USTR ¶ 4694.06) that generally apply in determining the existence of material participation. (Code Sec. 469(c)(7)(B))

Thus, one of the spouses must separately satisfy both the requirements (i.e., both the more-than-half requirement and the more-than-750-hours requirement) without regard to services performed by the other spouse. However, in determining material participation, no change has been made in the Code Sec. 469(h)(5) rule under which the participation of the taxpayer's spouse is taken into account in determining whether the taxpayer has met the material participation standard. (Conf Rept p. 547)

As a result, a husband and wife who file a joint return meet the more-than-half requirement if one of the spouses performs more than half of his services in a real estate trade or business in which either spouse materially participates.

A couple won't fail the eligibility requirements just because less than half their business services, taken together, are performed in real estate trades or businesses in which either of them materially participates as long as one of the spouses so qualifies (i.e., one of them performs more than 50% of his services in a business in which one of them materially participates). (H Rept p. 614)

Election to aggregate rental real estate activities. This new tax break is generally applied as if each interest of the qualifying taxpayer in rental real estate were a separate activity. However, a taxpayer may elect to treat all such activities as a single activity. (Code Sec. 469(c)(7)(A))

> ***observation:*** As noted above, material participation is determined under the same standards that applied under pre-'93 Act law. Thus, material participation in a rental real estate activity exists if the owner participates more than 500 hours during the year or does substantially all the work done in connection with the activity or meets certain other standards. Electing to treat all of a taxpayer's rental real estate activities as a single activity may in certain cases make it easier to meet the material participation requirement by allowing the taxpayer to aggregate all of his participation in all such activities to satisfy say, the more-than-500-hours-a-year test.

> ***observation:*** Code Sec. 469(c)(7)(A) doesn't say whether this is a one-time only election binding for future tax years or if it may be made on a year-by-year basis

Personal services performed as an employee. For purposes of determining whether a taxpayer performs more than half his personal services in real property trades or businesses, services performed as an employee in such trades or businesses are disregarded unless the employee is a more-than-5% owner of the employer. A taxpayer is a more-than-5% owner if he:

. . . owns (taking into account the Code Sec. 318 constructive ownership rules) more than 5% of a corporation's outstanding stock or stock with more than 5% of the combined voting power of all the corporation's stock, or

. . . owns more than 5% of the capital or profits of a noncorporate taxpayer. (Code Sec. 469(c)(7)(D)(ii))

> ***illustration:*** Jeff Thompson is a full time real estate broker employed by a corporation in which he owns a 50% interest. He devotes about 2,000 hours a year to this employment. He has no other employment or profession except the ownership of an apartment building which generates a $100,000 loss during '94. Jeff devotes 600 hours of his time to the management of the building in '94, thus meeting the material participation standard. Since he has performed more than half of his personal services in real property trades or businesses in which he materially participates, and has also met the more-than-750-hours test, he is entitled to deduct the $100,000 loss against whatever nonpassive income he may have, say his salary and commissions as a broker or any interest or dividends he may have received.

> ***observation:*** The rule generally barring consideration of services performed as an employee only applies to services performed in real property trades or businesses and not to such services performed in other

activities. As a result, services performed by a taxpayer as, for example, an executive in an insurance company, would be taken into account in determining whether the taxpayer has performed more than half his services in real property trades or businesses.

Material participation by limited partner. Under pre-'93 Act law, an interest as a limited partner isn't treated as one in which the owner materially participates except to the extent provided in regs. (FTC 2d/FIN ¶ M-5003; TG ¶ 6681; USTR ¶ 4694.06) The '93 Act specifies that the new rules shouldn't be construed as affecting the determination of whether a taxpayer materially participates with respect to a limited partnership interest. (Code Sec. 469(c)(7)(A)) The House Report adds that the election permitting a taxpayer to aggregate his rental real estate activities (see above) for purposes of determining whether such activities are treated as nonpassive under the new law isn't intended to alter pre-'93 Act law with respect to material participation through partnership interests. (H Rept p. 614)

observation: Under IRS regs, a limited partner satisfies the material participation test if he participates more than 500 hours a year in the activity or if he met the test in any five of the preceding ten tax years. (FTC 2d/FIN ¶ M-5004; TG ¶ 6681; USTR ¶ 4694.06) These rules aren't changed by the aggregation election. What this means, apparently, is that the material participation test can't be satisfied with respect to a limited partnership interest by aggregating it with other rental realty interests interests in which, on an aggregate basis, the taxpayer participates more than 500 hours.

Suspended losses from nonqualifying years. Qualification for this special tax break is determined on a year-by-year basis. Thus losses from the same apartment building or other rental real estate may generate deductible nonpassive losses in some years and nondeductible passive losses in others.

New Code Sec. 469(c)(7) makes no specific provision for this kind of situation. But according to the House Report, suspended losses from any rental real property activity that is treated as not passive by reason of the new rules are treated as losses from a former passive activity. Thus, according to the House Report, such suspended losses are limited to income from the activity, and are not allowed to offset other income. When the taxpayer disposes of his entire interest in the activity in a fully taxable transaction with an unrelated party, any remaining suspended losses will be allowed in full. (H Rept p. 615)

Losses allowed under new rule disregarded in phasing out $25,000 deduction for active participation rental real estate. Under pre-'93 Act law, up to $25,000 of an individual taxpayer's rental real estate losses (or the deduction equivalent in credits) can be offset against nonpassive income if an active participation test is met. The $25,000 offset is generally reduced by 50% of the taxpayer's adjusted gross income (AGI), as modified specially for this purpose, in excess of $100,000. (FTC 2d/FIN ¶ M-5110; TG ¶ 6683; USTR ¶ 4694.60) These rules are generally unaffected by the '93 Act. However, the '93 Act does provide an additional modification to AGI for this purpose. Thus AGI for purposes of phasing out the $25,000 deduction isn't reduced by any loss allowable under the new rule for rental real estate losses. (Code Sec. 469(i)(3)(E)(iv) as amended by '93 Act § 13143(b)(2))

illustration: A taxpayer has adjusted gross income of $150,000 before the deduction of a $50,000 rental real estate loss he is entitled to under new Code Sec. 469(c)(7). That loss isn't taken into account in determining how the phase-out rules apply. Therefore, he is entitled to no deduction for losses from active participation rental real estate (50% of the excess of $150,000 over $100,000 is $25,000, and the deduction is thus entirely eliminated).

☐ **Effective:** Tax years beginning after Dec. 31, '93. (§ 13143(c))

> ***observation:*** As noted above, a particular property may generate nondeductible passive losses in certain years because of the owner's failure to meet the qualification requirements in those years. According to the House Report, these losses are to be treated as losses from a former passive activity and are only deductible against income from the activity. Presumably, this rule would apply to suspended losses incurred in tax years that began before '94.

For official explanation see Committee Reports ¶ 3014.

¶ 502. Depreciation period for nonresidential realty lengthened to 39 years from 31.5 years

Under pre-'93 Act law, nonresidential real property was depreciable under the modified accelerated cost recovery system ("MACRS") over a depreciation period of 31.5 years. (FTC 2d/FIN ¶s L-7811, L-7930; TG ¶ 5439; USTR ¶ 1684.02)

The '93 Act lengthens the depreciation period to 39 years. (Code Sec. 168(c)(1) as amended by '93 Act § 13151(a))

> ***observation:*** This lengthening of the depreciation period from 31.5 years to 39 years means that, except for the first and last year of the depreciation period, the depreciation rate is reduced to 2.5641% (i.e., 100 ÷ 39) per year from 3.1746%.

Under pre-'93 Act law, the depreciation period for nonresidential real property for alternative minimum tax purposes was 40 years. (FTC 2d/FIN ¶ A-8106; TG ¶ 1355; USTR ¶ 1684.03) The '93 Act does not change this period. (H Rept p. 626)

☐ **Effective:** Except as provided below, for property placed in service on or after May 13, '93. (§ 13151(b)(1))

The 31.5-year depreciation period of pre-'93 Act law continues to apply to property placed in service by taxpayer before Jan. 1, '94 if:

(1) the taxpayer or a qualified person entered into a binding written contract to buy or construct the property before May 13, '93 or

(2) the construction of the property by or for the taxpayer or a qualified person began before May 13, '93.

"Qualified person," means any person who transfers his rights in the contract or in the property itself to the taxpayer before the property is placed in service. (§ 13151(b)(2))

For official explanation see Committee Reports ¶ 3022.

¶ 503. Exclusion of income from discharge of qualified real property business indebtedness from gross income

The discharge of a taxpayer's indebtedness results in gross income to the taxpayer unless an exemption is available. (See FTC 2d/FIN ¶ J-7000 *et seq.;* TG ¶ 5250 *et seq.;* USTR ¶ 1084) The '93 Act adds a new exemption for qualified real property business indebtedness (defined below) of taxpayers other than C corporations. Under this exception, the discharge of qualified real property business indebtedness of taxpayers other than C corporations does not result in gross income. (Code Sec.

FTC 2d References are to the Federal Tax Coordinator 2d
FIN References are to RIA's Analysis of Federal Taxes: Income
TG References are to the Tax Guide
USTR References are to the United States Tax Reporter

108(a)(1)(D) as amended by '93 Act § 13150(a)) Instead, the amount excluded from gross income is applied to reduce the basis of the taxpayer's depreciable property. (Code Sec. 108(c)(1)(A) as amended by '93 Act § 13150(b))

The amount that may be excluded under this rule is limited to the excess (if any) of (1) the outstanding principal amount of the qualified real property business indebtedness over (2) the result of (a) the fair market value of the real property in connection with which the qualified real property business indebtedness was incurred or assumed and which secures the qualified real property business indebtedness minus (b) the outstanding principal amount of any other qualified real property business indebtedness secured by the property at that time. (Code Sec. 108(c)(2)(A)) In addition, the amount excluded may not exceed the aggregate adjusted basis of depreciable real property held by the taxpayer immediately before the discharge, determined after any reductions in basis under Code Sec. 108(b) (reduction in tax attributes resulting from the discharge of indebtedness of taxpayers in Title 11 (bankruptcy) or insolvent taxpayers, see FTC 2d/FIN ¶ J-7404; TG ¶ 5262; USTR ¶ 1084.02) and Code Sec. 108(g) (reduction in tax attributes resulting from the discharge of qualified farm indebtedness, see FTC 2d/FIN ¶ J-7405; TG ¶ 5264; USTR ¶ 1084.01). For this purpose, depreciable real property acquired by the taxpayer in contemplation of the discharge is not taken into account. (Code Sec. 108(c)(2)(B))

The taxpayer must make an election to treat an indebtedness as qualified real property business indebtedness. (Code Sec. 108(c)(3)(C)) The election must be made on the taxpayer's return for the taxable year in which the discharge occurs or at any other time permitted in IRS regulations. (Code Sec. 108(d)(9) as amended by '93 Act § 13150(c)(5))

> ***illustration:*** Individual J owns a building that is used in a trade or business. The building is worth $150,000 and is subject to a first mortgage securing J's debt of $110,000 and a second mortgage securing J's debt of $90,000. J agrees with the second mortgagee to reduce the second mortgage debt to $30,000, resulting in a $60,000 discharge of indebtedness. Under the above rule, assuming that J has sufficient basis in business real property to absorb the reduction, J may elect to exclude $50,000 of the discharge of indebtedness from gross income. That is because the principal amount of the discharged debt immediately before the discharge exceeds the fair market value of the property minus the first mortgage debt by $50,000 ($90,000 − ($150,000 − $110,000) = $50,000). The remaining $10,000 of discharge is included in gross income. (H Rept p. 623)

> ***observation:*** Many taxpayers are currently holding real estate that has declined in value and is, consequently, worth less than the debt secured by the real estate. Under pre-'93 Act law, the taxpayers were unwilling to dispose of the property or to restructure the debt because the disposition or restructuring would cause them to recognize gross income. This provision allows these taxpayers to dispose of the property or to restructure the debt without recognizing income currently, at the cost of being subject to the basis reduction discussed below.

Where a discharge of indebtedness would be excluded from income under both the Title 11 or insolvency exception and the qualified real property business indebtedness exception, only the Title 11 or insolvency exception applies. (Code Secs. 108(a)(2)(A) and (B) as amended by '93 Act §§ 13150(c)(1) and (2))

Qualified real property business indebtedness. Qualified real property business indebtedness is indebtedness that was incurred or assumed by the taxpayer in connection with real property used in a trade or business and that is secured by the real property. (Code Sec. 108(c)(3)(A) as amended by '93 Act § 13150(b)) In addition, for debt incurred or assumed after Dec. 31, '92, the indebtedness must be qualified acquisition indebtedness (Code Sec. 108(c)(3)(B)), i.e., indebtedness incurred or assumed to acquire, construct, reconstruct, or substantially improve the property. (Code Sec. 108(c)(4)) An indebtedness that is incurred to refinance pre-'93 indebtedness or qualified acquisition indebtedness qualifies as qualified real property business indebtedness, but only to the extent that it doesn't exceed the amount of the indebtedness being refinanced. Qualified farm indebtedness (see FTC 2d/FIN ¶ J-7406; TG ¶ 5264; USTR ¶ 1084.01) does not qualify as qualified real property business indebtedness. (Code Sec. 108(c)(3))

Application to partnerships and S corporations. The determination whether partnership debt is qualified real property business indebtedness is made at the partnership level. (Code Sec. 108(d)(6) as amended by '93 Act § 13150(c)(3)) Thus, the amount of the exclusion and whether the debt was incurred in a trade or business is made at the partnership level. (H Rept p. 624) However, the election to treat partnership debt as qualified real property business indebtedness is made at the partner level. (Code Sec. 703(b)(1) as amended by '93 Act § 13150(c)(9))

The qualified real property business indebtedness exception is applied to S corporations at the corporation level. (Code Sec. 108(d)(7)(A) as amended by '93 Act § 13150(c)(3)) Thus, the election, the exclusion from income, and the basis reduction are made at the S corporation level. (H Rept p. 625)

The rule treating an S corporation loss or deduction that is disallowed for the taxable year of the discharge of indebtedness under the basis limitation (see FTC 2d/FIN ¶ D-1712; TG ¶ 2076; USTR ¶ 1084.03) as a net operating loss for the taxable year (see FTC 2d/FIN ¶ J-7410; TG ¶ 2078) does not apply where the qualified real property business indebtedness exception applies. (Code Sec. 108(d)(7)(B) as amended by '93 Act § 13150(c)(4))

The reduction in basis as a result of the debt cancellation (described below) applies only to the basis of the property of the S corporation and does not result in a reduction in the basis of the S corporation shareholders in their stock. However, the basis reduction will result in lower depreciation and higher income at the S corporation level. Thus, the exclusion causes the shareholders' income to be deferred. (H Rept p. 625)

Reducing basis of depreciable property. The reduction in the basis of the taxpayer's property is made under the rules of Code Sec. 1017 (Code Sec. 1017(a)(2) as amended by '93 Act § 13150(c)(6)) and only the basis of depreciable real property may be reduced. (Code Sec. 1017(b)(3) as amended by '93 Act § 13150(c)(7)) For this purpose, only depreciable real property held by the taxpayer (see FTC 2d/FIN ¶ P-3010; TG ¶ 5266; USTR ¶ 1084.02) and partnership interests treated as depreciable property (see FTC 2d/FIN ¶ P-3013; TG ¶ 5266; USTR ¶ 1084.03) are treated as depreciable real property. (Code Sec. 1017(b)(3)(F)(i) as amended by '93 Act § 13150(c)(8)) The election to treat real property held as inventory as depreciable property (see FTC 2d/FIN ¶ P-3011; TG ¶ 5266; USTR ¶ 1084.02) does not apply. (Code Sec. 1017(b)(3)(F)(ii))

Where partnership interests are treated as depreciable property, the partner must reduce his basis in the partnership interest and the partnership must reduce its basis in its depreciable property. (See FTC 2d/FIN ¶ P-3013; TG ¶ 5266; USTR ¶ 1084.03) The reduction in the partner's basis in the partnership interest is in addition to the normal reduction in basis that is caused by the deemed cash distribution to the partner (see FTC 2d/FIN ¶ B-1605; TG ¶ 1682; USTR ¶ 1084.03) of an amount equal to the partner's share of the reduction in the partnership's debt. (H Rept p. 624)

FTC 2d References are to the Federal Tax Coordinator 2d
FIN References are to RIA's Analysis of Federal Taxes: Income
TG References are to the Tax Guide
USTR References are to the United States Tax Reporter

Where the basis of depreciable real property is reduced under this rule and the property is later disposed of, then for purposes of calculating the amount of recapture under Code Sec. 1250 (see FTC 2d/FIN ¶ I-6804; TG ¶ 5689):

(1) the reduction is treated as depreciation subject to recapture,

and

(2) the determination of what would have been the depreciation under the straight line method is made as if there were no reduction.

Thus the amount of basis reduction that is recaptured as ordinary income is reduced whenever the taxpayer's depreciation deductions are reduced because of the basis reduction. (H Rept p. 625)

The basis reduction is generally made at the beginning of the taxable year following the discharge. However, if the taxpayer disposes of the real property (in the transaction giving rise to the discharge or otherwise) before the beginning of the next taxable year, the reduction in basis is made immediately before the disposition of the property. (Code Sec. 1017(b)(3)(F)(iii) as amended by '93 Act § 13150(c)(8))

Regulations. IRS is directed to issue any regulations necessary to carry out the provisions of the qualified real property business indebtedness exclusion rule, including regulations preventing abuse of the exclusion through cross-collaterization or other means. (Code Sec. 108(c)(5) as amended by '93 Act § 13150(b))

☐ **Effective:** For discharges of indebtedness after '92, in taxable years ending after '92. (§ 13150(d))

For official explanation see Committee Reports ¶ 3021.

¶ 504. Restrictions relaxed on debt-financed acquisitions of real estate by pension funds and other exempt organizations: acquisitions from financial institutions encouraged; more seller-financing permitted; 25% leasebacks allowed

A pension fund or other tax-exempt organization is subject to the tax on unrelated business income (UBI) on income earned from investments acquired with acquisition indebtedness. (See FTC 2d/FIN ¶s D-6801, D-7101; TG ¶s 7897, 8013; USTR ¶ 5144) However, the indebtedness that a qualified organization (qualified pension and other retirement trusts, educational organizations and their affiliated support organizations, and Code Sec. 501(c)(25) title-holding organizations) incurs to acquire or improve any real property is not treated as acquisition indebtedness if among other restrictions, the organization avoids certain price and payment terms, doesn't use the seller for financing, and doesn't lease the property to the seller or certain others. (FTC 2d/FIN ¶ D-7141 *et seq.;* TG ¶ 8019; USTR ¶ 5144)

The '93 Act includes provisions to facilitate real estate investing by pension funds and other qualified organizations by modifying the debt-financed income rules to permit qualified organizations to make debt-financed investments in real property on commercially reasonable terms in circumstances with no potential for abuse. (H Rept p. 616)

Fixed price and participating loan restrictions eased for foreclosure or other property acquired from financial institutions. To comply with the real estate investment restrictions under pre-'93 Act law, the acquisition or improvement price has to be a fixed amount determined as of the date of acquisition or completion of the improvement. (FTC 2d/FIN ¶ D-7142; TG ¶ 8019; USTR ¶ 5144) Also, the amount of the indebtedness, any amount payable with respect to the indebtedness, and the time for making a payment of such an amount, can't be wholly or partly dependent on any revenue, income, or profits derived from the real property. (FTC 2d/FIN ¶ D-7143; TG ¶ 8019; USTR ¶ 5144)

Under the '93 Act, except as otherwise to be provided by regs, the undetermined acquisition price and contingent indebtedness restrictions don't apply to a qualifying sale by a financial institution (defined below), with respect to financing provided by the institution for the sale. (Code Sec. 514(c)(9)(H)(i) as amended by '93 Act § 13144(a))

To be a "qualifying sale":

(1) A qualified organization must acquire property from a financial institution (Code Sec. 514(c)(9)(H)(ii)(I));

(2) The property must be *either*—

. . . (a) foreclosure property (Code Sec. 514(c)(9)(H)(iii)), defined as any real property acquired by the financial institution as the result of having bid on the property at foreclosure, or by operation of an agreement or process of law, after default (or after default was imminent) on indebtedness secured by the property. (Code Sec. 514(c)(9)(H)(v)); *or*

. . . (b) real property acquired by the qualified organization from a financial institution that is in conservatorship or receivership or from the conservator or receiver of such an institution (Code Sec. 514(c)(9)(H)(iii)(I)), and held by the institution when it entered into conservatorship or receivership (Code Sec. 514(c)(9)(H)(iii)(II));

(3) Any gain recognized by the financial institution with respect to the property must be ordinary income (Code Sec. 514(c)(9)(H)(ii)(I));

(4) The stated principal amount of the financing provided by the financial institution must not exceed the amount of the institution's outstanding indebtedness (including accrued but unpaid interest) with respect to the property immediately before the acquisition by the financial institution (in the case of the foreclosure property in (2)(a), above) (Code Sec. 514(c)(9)(H)(ii)(II))—that is, at the time of default or foreclosure (H Rept p. 617)—or immediately before the acquisition by the qualified organization (in the case of the real property in (2)(b), above) (Code Sec. 514(c)(9)(H)(ii)(II)); and

(5) The present value of the maximum amount payable under the financing that is determined by reference to the revenue, income, or profits derived by the property can't exceed 30% of the amount of the total purchase price of the property, including the contingent payments. For this purpose, the present value is determined as of the time of sale by using the applicable federal rate determined under Code Sec. 1274(d) (Code Sec. 514(c)(9)(H)(ii)(III)) (i.e., the normal short-term, mid-term, or long-term rate, depending on the term of the debt, see FTC 2d/FIN ¶ J-3742 *et seq.;* TG ¶ 5074 *et seq.;* USTR ¶ 12,714 *et seq.).*

For purposes of this property foreclosure rule, a "financial institution" is:

(a) a financial institution described in Code Sec. 581 or 591(a) (Code Sec. 514(c)(9)(H)(iv)(I)) (i.e., banks or trust companies, or mutual savings banks);

(b) any other direct or indirect corporate subsidiary of an institution in (a), above, which is subject to supervision or examination by a federal or state agency that regulates such institutions as a result of such affiliation (Code Sec. 514(c)(9)(H)(iv)(II));

FTC 2d References are to the Federal Tax Coordinator 2d
FIN References are to RIA's Analysis of Federal Taxes: Income
TG References are to the Tax Guide
USTR References are to the United States Tax Reporter

(c) any person acting as a conservator or receiver of an entity in (a) or (b), above, or a government agency or corporation succeeding to such person's rights or interest. (Code Sec. 514(c)(9)(H)(iv)(III))

Seller-financing permitted if on commercially reasonable terms. Under pre-'93 Act law, if the seller (or certain disqualified persons, in the case of qualified retirement trusts, or other persons related to the seller) provided the retirement trusts or other exempt organization with financing in connection with the acquisition or improvement of the real property, acquisition indebtedness resulted. (FTC 2d/FIN ¶ D-7146; TG ¶ 8019; USTR ¶ 5144)

Under the '93 Act, except as otherwise to be provided by regs, such seller-financing is permitted if the financing is on commercially reasonable terms (Code Sec. 514(c)(9)(G)(ii)), independent of the sale and other transactions. IRS may issue regs for determining commercially reasonable financing terms. (H Rept p. 616)

The '93 Act provision permitting commercially reasonable seller-financing doesn't modify the fixed acquisition price and participating loan (contingent indebtedness) restrictions (see above). Thus, income from real property acquired with seller-financing where the timing or amount of payment depends on revenue, income, or profits from the real property generally will continue to be treated as income from debt-financed property unless another exception applies. (H Rept p. 616)

Leasebacks covering no more than 25% of leasable space permitted. Under pre-'93 Act law, a qualified organization has acquisition indebtedness if, at any time after acquiring real property, it leases the property to the seller or to certain persons related to the seller. (FTC 2d/FIN ¶ D-7144; TG ¶ 8019; USTR ¶ 5144) (Also, in the case of qualified retirement trusts, such leases are subject to the prohibited transaction rules under Code Sec. 4975. (See FTC 2d/FIN ¶s H-14018, H-14019; TG ¶ 3763)

The '93 Act provides an exception to the leaseback restriction. Except as otherwise to be provided by regs, a lease covering no more than 25% of the leasable floor space in a building (or complex of buildings) is disregarded if the lease is on commercially reasonable terms (Code Sec. 514(c)(9)(G)(i)), independent of the sale and other transactions. (H Rept p. 616) Thus, limited (up to 25%) leasebacks of debt-financed real property to the seller (or related persons) are permitted. (H Rept p. 616) (However, in the case of a qualified retirement trust, such leasebacks remain subject to the prohibited transaction rules under Code Sec. 4975. (H Rept p. 616))

> **caution:** Because of the severe penalties under the prohibited transaction rules, a leaseback to a disqualified person would need to comply with an exemption from those rules. (See FTC 2d/FIN ¶ H-14028; TG ¶ 3763; USTR ¶ 49,754)

Disqualified person leases covering no more than 25% of leasable space permitted. Under pre-'93 Act law, a qualified retirement trust has acquisition indebtedness if it acquires real property from certain disqualified person, or leases the property at any time after acquiring it to those disqualified persons. (FTC 2d/FIN ¶ D-7145; TG ¶ 8019; USTR ¶ 49,754) (Also, such acquisitions from, or leases to, disqualified persons are subject to the excise tax on prohibited transactions. (See FTC 2d/FIN ¶s H-14018, H-14019; TG ¶ 3763; USTR ¶s 49,404, 49,754))

The '93 Act provides an exception to the disqualified person lease restriction. Except as otherwise to be provided by regs, a lease covering no more than 25% of the leasable floor space in a building (or complex of buildings) is disregarded if the lease is on commercially reasonable terms (Code Sec. 514(c)(9)(G)(i)), independent of the sale and other transactions. (H Rept p. 616) Thus, limited (up to 25%) leasebacks of debt-financed real property to the disqualified persons are permitted.

(H Rept p. 616) (However, such leasebacks remain subject to the excise tax on prohibited transactions. (H Rept p. 616))

> ***observation:*** The Act doesn't change the rule that prohibits acquisitions by a qualified trust from a disqualified person. Under the Act only leases to a disqualified person, covering no more than 25% of leasable space, are disregarded.

Mortgages are not real property. Under pre-'93 Act law, real property, for purposes of the above rules excluding certain indebtedness to acquire or improve real property from treatment as acquisition indebtedness, does not include an interest in a mortgage. (FTC 2d/FIN ¶ D-7141; TG ¶ 8019; USTR ¶ 5144) Under pre-'93 Act law, this rule was set forth in the Code in the subparagraph—Code Sec. 514(c)(9)(B)—that described the exceptions to (i.e., the restrictions on) the general exclusion rule, even though the interest-in-a-mortgage rule, by its terms, applied generally.

The '93 Act moves the rule that prevents an interest in a mortgage from being treated as real property from Code Sec. 514(c)(9)(B) to Code Sec. 514(c)(9)(A), which states the general rule excluding certain indebtedness to acquire or improve real property. (Code Sec. 514(c)(9)(A) as amended by '93 Act § 13144(b))

> ***observation:*** It appears that no substantive change is intended by moving the rule that prevents an interest in a mortgage from being treated as real property. This rule, before and after the '93 Act change, states that it applies "[f]or purposes of this paragraph," which should be interpreted in either instance as a reference to all of Paragraph (9) of Subsection (c) of Section 514.

☐ **Effective:** Acquisitions after Dec. 31, '93. (§ 13144(c)(1))

25% of leasable space rule. In addition to any leases to which the 25%-of-leasable-space rule applies under the above general effective date, the 25%-of-leasable-space rule applies to leases entered into after Dec. 31, '93. (§ 13144(c)(2))

For official explanation see Committee Reports ¶ 3015.

¶ 505. Loan commitment fees and gains and losses from real estate option premiums and deposits excluded from UBTI after '93

Tax-exempt organizations are taxed on unrelated business taxable income (UBTI), which is income (less allowable deductions) from any regularly carried on trade or business that isn't substantially related to the organization's exempt purposes. (See FTC 2d/FIN ¶s D-6800 *et seq.*, D-6900 *et seq.;* TG ¶ 7990 *et seq.;* USTR ¶ 5124) In computing UBTI, passive (investment) income is excluded. (FTC 2d/FIN ¶ D-6901 *et seq.;* TG ¶s 8005, 8006; USTR ¶ 5124)

Loan commitment fees excluded from UBTI after '93. Pre-'93 Act law was unclear on whether loan commitment fees are UBTI. (H Rept p. 620)

> ***observation:*** Loan commitment fees are often received by a qualified pension fund or other exempt organization in connection with investments in real estate mortgage loans, which has raised the issue of whether the fees were excluded from UBTI as a form of passive income. Although interest earned by exempt organizations from mortgage loans are excluded from

FTC 2d References are to the Federal Tax Coordinator 2d
FIN References are to RIA's Analysis of Federal Taxes: Income
TG References are to the Tax Guide
USTR References are to the United States Tax Reporter

UBTI, IRS has ruled that fees charged for certain services performed in conjunction with such loans weren't excluded from UBTI. (see FTC 2d/FIN ¶ D-6901; TG ¶ 8005)

The '93 Act reflects a belief that taxing loan commitment fees is inconsistent with the tax-free treatment accorded to exempt organizations' income from investment activities. (H Rept p. 620)

Thus, under the '93 Act, amounts received after '93 (§ 13148(c)) as consideration for entering into agreements to make loans, and all directly connected deductions, are excluded from UBTI. (Code Sec. 512(b)(1) as amended by '93 Act § 13148(a)) For this purpose, such amounts ("loan commitment fees") are nonrefundable charges made by a lender to reserve a sum of money with fixed terms for a specified period of time. Loan commitment fees compensate the lender for potential lost opportunities and the risk in committing to make the loan, including exposure to interest rate changes. (H Rept p. 620)

Real estate options and deposits received after '93 excluded from UBTI. Under pre-'93 Act law, one type of income specifically excluded from UBTI is *gain* on the lapse or termination of options to buy or sell *securities,* if the options are written by the exempt organization in connection with its investment activities. (FTC 2d/FIN ¶ D-6905; TG ¶ 8006; USTR ¶ 5124) Pre-'93 Act law was unclear on whether premiums from unexercised options on *real estate* were UBTI. (H Rept p. 620) Also, pre-'93 Act law didn't provide for excluding all *losses* on an exempt organization's options. (FTC 2d/FIN ¶ D-6905; TG ¶ 8006; USTR ¶ 5124)

The '93 Act reflects a belief that gains and losses from options are to be treated consistently for UBTI purposes, and that taxing premiums from unexercised options on real estate is inconsistent with the tax-free treatment accorded to exempt organizations' income from investment activities. (H Rept p. 620)

Thus, the '93 Act expands the exclusion to cover real estate, certain forfeitures of real estate deposits, and losses (from both real property and securities). The '93 Act also eliminates the requirement that the options must be *written by* the exempt organization in connection with its investment activities. (H Rept p. 620)

Thus, under the '93 Act, with respect to amounts received after '93 (§ 13148(c)), the following are excluded from UBTI:

. . . (a) gains and losses recognized by an exempt organization, in connection with its investment activities, from the lapse or termination of options to buy or sell securities or real property (Code Sec. 512(b)(5) as amended by '93 Act § 13148(b)), whether or not the options are written by the exempt organization (H Rept p. 620); and

. . . (b) gains and losses from the forfeiture of good-faith deposits (that are consistent with established business practice) for the purchase, sale, or lease of real property in connection with the exempt organization's investment activities. (Code Sec. 512(b)(5))

☐ **Effective:** Amounts received after Dec. 31, '93. (§ 13148(c))

> ***observation:*** Since the '93 Act change applies to amounts received after '93, the new provision will apply to an amount accrued before it is received after '93.

For official explanation see Committee Reports ¶ 3019.

¶ 506. New look-thru rule treats beneficiaries of pension trusts, not the trusts, as holders of REIT stock (to avoid floor on number of investors)

Pension funds and other qualified retirement trusts (referred to as qualified trusts, see definition below) are taxed on unrelated business taxable income (UBTI), which is income (less allowable deductions) from any regularly carried on trade or business that isn't substantially related to the organization's exempt purposes. (See FTC 2d/FIN ¶s D-6800 *et seq.*, D-6900 *et seq.;* TG ¶ 7990 *et seq.;* USTR ¶ 5124) In computing UBTI, dividends and other passive (investment) income are excluded (see FTC 2d/FIN ¶ D-6901 *et seq.;* TG ¶s 8005, 8006; USTR ¶ 5124), unless the income is from debt-financed property (see FTC 2d/FIN ¶ D-7100 *et seq.;* TG ¶ 8012 *et seq.;* USTR ¶ 5144). For debt-financed property, income and deductions are taken into account in proportion to the average acquisition indebtedness divided by the average adjusted basis (see FTC 2d/FIN ¶ D-7100 *et seq.;* TG ¶ 8012 *et seq.;* USTR ¶ 5144).

Dividends paid by a REIT (H Rept p. 621) out of earnings and profits, including distributions to qualified trusts, are considered dividends. Thus, such dividends aren't subject to tax on UBTI (except if the REIT stock is debt-financed). (See FTC 2d/FIN ¶ D-6902; TG ¶ 8005; USTR ¶ 5144) However, to qualify as a REIT, the entity must not be closely held. (FTC 2d/FIN ¶ E-6511; TG ¶ 7856; USTR ¶ 8564.01) Under the closely held rule (which is also used in determining whether a corporation is a personal holding company), a REIT must meet a stock-ownership requirement. Under that requirement, a REIT is disqualified if at any time during the last half of its tax year more than 50% in value of its outstanding shares (or certificates of beneficial interest) is held directly or indirectly by, or for, five or fewer individuals. (See FTC 2d/FIN ¶ D-3401; TG ¶ 2172; USTR ¶ 8564.01)

Pre-'93 Act law treated a qualified trust as a single individual under this rule, for purposes of determining whether a corporation is a personal holding company (see FTC 2d/FIN ¶ D-3405; TG ¶ 2172; USTR ¶ 5424 *et seq.)* and therefore for purposes of the REIT qualification rule. (H Rept p. 621).

The '93 Act modifies the stock-ownership test. The Act provides that, in determining whether the stock-ownership test is met for purposes of qualification as a REIT, any stock held by a qualified trust (except for certain related trusts, see below) is treated as held directly by the trust's beneficiaries in proportion to their actuarial interests in the trust, and not as held by the trust. (Code Sec. 856(h)(3)(A)(i) as amended by '93 Act § 13149(a))

> ***observation:*** Thus, for purposes of qualification as a REIT, qualified trusts aren't treated as single individuals in determining whether the stock-ownership test is met.

> ***illustration:*** Five qualified trusts each own 11% of the value of A's stock and each trust has two beneficiaries with actuarial interests of 92% and 8% in the trust. Assume A otherwise qualifies as a REIT. Counting the beneficiaries instead of the trusts, the five 92% beneficiaries are each considered to hold 10.12% (92% × 11%), for a total of 50.6% (10.12% × 5). Thus, five or fewer individuals (in this case five) are considered to hold more than 50% of the value of A's outstanding shares. A fails to satisfy the stock-ownership test.

> ***illustration:*** Assume in the illustration above that each of the ten beneficiaries of the five trusts has equal actuarial interests in the trust, and that all the remaining stock of A is considered to be held by individuals each with no more than a fraction of one percent of the value of A's outstanding

shares. Counting the beneficiaries instead of the trusts, any group of five beneficiaries would be considered to hold an aggregate of 27.5% (11% × 50% × 5)—which is not more than 50%—of the value of A's outstanding shares. Thus, A meets the REIT stock-ownership test. (However, the trusts may be subject to tax on UBTI because they each hold more than 10% of the interests in a pension-held REIT, see below.)

observation: An individual may be a beneficiary of more than one qualified trust that holds an interest in a particular REIT. In such a situation, because of the look-thru rule treating stock held by a qualified trust as held directly by the trust's beneficiaries, the individual's actuarial interests in the trusts would presumably be aggregated in calculating the beneficiary's percentage of the value of the REIT's outstanding shares to determine whether the stock-ownership test is met.

observation: A beneficiary normally doesn't have an actuarial interest in a defined contribution plans; a beneficiary's interest is determined by reference to his account balance.

observation: Under another REIT qualification requirement, beneficial ownership must be held by 100 or more persons. A pension trust is treated as one person for purposes of this rule (FTC 2d/FIN ¶ D-6510). The '93 Act *doesn't* change the trust-equals-one-person rule for this purpose.

The '93 Act provision is intended to encourage increased pension fund investments in real estate investment trusts (REITs). (H Rept p. 621)

observation: Although supplemental unemployment compensation benefits trusts, portions of trusts permanently set aside for charitable purposes, and private foundations (but not other exempt charitable trusts, such as public charities) are also treated as single individuals (see FTC 2d/FIN ¶ D-3405; TG ¶ 2172; USTR ¶ 8564.01), the '93 Act modification treating qualified trusts as individuals doesn't extend to these other entities.

Qualified trust defined. Under these rules, a qualified trust is any trust described in Code Sec. 401(a) and exempt under Code Sec. 501(a) (Code Sec. 856(h)(3)(E)) (that is, pension, profit-sharing, and other employee retirement trusts, see FTC 2d/FIN ¶ H-5100 *et seq.;* TG ¶ 3850 *et seq.;* USTR ¶ 8564.01).

Exception for related qualified trusts. The modified '93 Act rule providing that a qualified trust isn't treated as an individual for purposes of REIT qualification (see above) doesn't apply if:

. . . (1) one or more disqualified persons—as defined in Code Sec. 4975(e)(2) (for purpose of prohibited transaction rules for qualified employee benefit plans, see FTC 2d/FIN ¶ H-14000 *et seq.;* TG ¶ 3760 *et seq.;* USTR ¶ 49,754), without regard to Code Sec. 4975(e)(2)(B) (service providers to qualified plans) and Code Sec. 4975(e)(2)(I) (10% partners or joint venturers of certain disqualified persons)—together hold 5% or more of the interests in the REIT as determined by value; and

. . . (2) the REIT has accumulated earnings and profits attributable to any period for which it didn't qualify as a REIT. (Code Sec. 856(h)(3)(A)(ii))

Pension trusts owning more than 10% of a REIT may be subject to tax on UBTI. Under the '93 Act, if a qualified trust holds at any time during its tax year more than 10% of the interests in a pension-held REIT (defined below), determined by value, part of the REIT dividends to the trust (see below) is treated as income from an unrelated trade or business (Code Sec. 856(h)(3)(C)) (and is thus subject to the UBTI tax).

A pension-held REIT is a REIT that is predominantly held by qualified trusts, and wouldn't have qualified as a REIT without Code Sec. 856(h)(3) (that is, the '93 Act modification). (Code Sec. 856(h)(3)(D)(i))

A REIT is predominantly held by qualified trusts if either:

. . . at least one qualified trust holds more than 25% of the value of the interests in the REIT, or (Code Sec. 856(h)(3)(D)(ii)(I))

. . . one or more qualified trusts, each owning more than 10% of such interests (determined by value), together hold more than 50% of such interests (by value). (Code Sec. 856(h)(3)(D)(ii)(II))

When the UBTI tax applies, the amount subject to the tax is the aggregate of dividends paid (or treated as paid) by the REIT to the qualified trust, for the REIT's tax year with or within which the qualified trust's tax year ends (the REIT year), times (Code Sec. 856(h)(3)(C) as amended by '93 Act § 13149(a))—

. . . (a) gross REIT income, less related direct expenses, for the REIT year, from unrelated trades or businesses (determined as if the REIT were a qualified trust), divided by (Code Sec. 856(h)(3)(C)(i))

. . . (b) gross REIT income, less related direct expenses, for the REIT year. (Code Sec. 856(h)(3)(C)(ii))

However, Code Sec. 856(h)(3)(C) (the rule subjecting qualified trusts owning more than 10% of a REIT to the tax on UBTI) doesn't apply if the ratio of (a) to (b) above is less than 5%. (Code Sec. 856(h)(3)(C))

Although pension fund investments in REITs are being encouraged by the '93 Act provision treating qualified trusts as individuals, the above provision subjecting qualified trusts owning more than 10% of a REIT to the tax on UBTI is designed to prevent circumvention of the tax on UBTI. (H Rept p. 621)

REITs as personal holding companies. Under the '93 Act, if an entity qualifies as a REIT for a tax year by reason of Code Sec. 856(h)(3)(A) (the rule providing for look-thru treatment of qualified trusts for purposes of REIT qualification, see above), the entity isn't treated as a personal holding company for that tax year for purposes of the personal holding company rules. (Code Sec. 856(h)(3)(B) as amended by '93 Act § 13149(a))

☐ **Effective:** Tax years beginning after Dec. 31, '93. (§ 13149(b))

For official explanation see Committee Reports ¶ 3020.

¶ 507. Gains from real property acquired from troubled financial institutions by pension funds and other exempt organizations excluded from UBTI

Qualified pension funds and other tax-exempt organizations are taxed on their unrelated business taxable income (UBTI), which is income (less allowable deductions) from any regularly carried on trade or business that isn't substantially related to the organization's exempt purposes. (See FTC 2d/FIN ¶s D-6800 *et seq.,* D-6900 *et seq.;* TG ¶ 7990 *et seq.;* USTR ¶ 5124) Gains and losses from the sale, exchange, or other disposition of property are generally excluded from UBTI. However, gains and losses from the sale, etc., of property held primarily for sale to customers in the ordinary course of a trade or business aren't excluded from UBTI (this is the "dealer UBTI rule"). (FTC 2d/FIN ¶ D-6905; TG ¶ 8006; USTR ¶ 5124) The dealer UBTI rule discourages investing by pension funds and other exempt organizations in properties bundled together by troubled financial institutions. (H Rept p. 619)

The '93 Act creates an exception to the dealer UBTI rule intended to make it easier for pension funds and other exempt organizations to invest in bundled packages of desirable and less desirable properties offered by troubled financial institutions. The exception also is intended to allow such organizations to pass on some of the burden of an orderly liquidation of the properties. (H Rept p. 619)

The '93 Act exception excludes from UBTI all gains or losses from the sale, exchange, or other disposition of real property (Code Sec. 512(b)(16)(A) as amended by '93 Act § 13147(a)) that is acquired from:

. . . (i) a financial institution described in Code Secs. 581 (banks or trust companies, see FTC 2d/FIN ¶ E-3002; TG ¶ 7771; USTR ¶ 5814 *et seq.)* or 591(a) (mutual savings banks, see FTC 2d/FIN ¶ E-3307; TG ¶ 7801; USTR ¶ 5914) that is in conservatorship or receivership (Code Sec. 512(b)(16)(A)(i)(I)); or

. . . (ii) the conservator or receiver of such an institution; or

. . . (iii) any government agency or corporation succeeding to the rights of the conservator or receiver. (Code Sec. 512(b)(16)(A)(i)(II))

To be eligible for the exclusion, the real property must be:

. . . held by the financial institution at the time the institution entered conservatorship or receivership (Code Sec. 512(b)(16)(B)(i)); or

. . . foreclosure property (as defined by Code Sec. 514(c)(9)(H)(v), as added by the Act, see ¶ 504) that secured indebtedness held by the institution at the time the institution entered conservatorship or receivership. (Code Sec. 512(b)(16)(B)(ii))

"Real property," for purposes of this exception, includes an interest in a mortgage. (Code Sec. 512(b)(16)(B))

The exclusion is limited to real property designated by the exempt organization, within the 9-month period beginning on the date of acquisition, as property held for sale. No more than one-half (as determined by value on the acquisition date) of the properties acquired in a single transaction may be so designated (Code Sec. 512(b)(16)(A)(ii)), that is, as disposal property. (H Rept p. 619) The properties must be sold, exchanged, or otherwise disposed of before the later of:

. . . (a) the date which is 30 months after the acquisition date (Code Sec. 512(b)(16)(A)(iii)(I)); or

. . . (b) a date specified by IRS to assure an orderly liquidation of the property by persons described in (i), (ii), or (iii), above. (Code Sec. 512(b)(16)(A)(iii)(II)) Thus, IRS may extend the disposition period if necessary. (H Rept p. 619)

The exclusion *isn't* available for properties that are improved or developed while held by the exempt organization, if the aggregate expenditures on improvement and development activities included in the real property's basis exceeds 20% of the net selling price of the property. (Code Sec. 512(b)(16)(A)(iv))

☐ **Effective:** Property acquired after Dec. 31, '93. (§ 13147(b))
For official explanation see Committee Reports ¶ 3018.

¶ 508. Repeal of automatic treatment of pension fund income from publicly traded partnerships as UBTI

In the case of a regular partnership, a qualified pension fund (or other tax-exempt organization) that is a general or limited partner reports as unrelated business taxable income (UBTI) the exempt organization's share in the partnership gross income which, with respect to the exempt organization, is income from an unrelated trade or business. In determining UBTI, otherwise applicable adjustments are made. Thus, for example, passive investment income is excluded. This means that taxability depends on the type of partnership activity that generated the income, determined as if the income were earned directly by the exempt organization. (The taxable gross income is reduced by the exempt organization's share in the partnership deductions directly connected with the income.) (See FTC 2d/FIN ¶ D-6908; TG¶ 8009; USTR ¶ 5124)

However, in the case of a publicly traded partnership (which is defined in Code Sec. 469(k)(2), see FTC 2d/FIN ¶ M-4710; TG ¶ 6669; USTR ¶ 69,485), under pre-'93 Act law an exempt organization's share of the gross income (reduced by deductions) was automatically treated as being from an unrelated trade or business. Thus, such income (including passive investment income) was taxable to a tax-exempt partner regardless of the type of partnership activity that generated the income. (FTC 2d/FIN ¶ D-6909; TG¶ 8009; USTR ¶ 5124) This pre-'93 Act rule effectively prevented pension fund and other exempt organization investments in publicly traded partnerships. (H Rept p. 617)

The '93 Act repeals the above rule, which automatically subjected income from investments by qualified pension funds and other tax-exempt investors in publicly traded partnerships to tax on UBTI. (Code Sec. 514(c) as amended by '93 Act § 13145(a)(1)) Thus, for UBTI purposes, investments by qualified pension funds and other tax-exempt investors in publicly traded partnerships will be treated the same as investments in other partnerships. (H Rept p. 617)

☐ **Effective:** Partnership years beginning after Dec. 31, '93. (§ 13145(b))
For official explanation see Committee Reports ¶ 3016.

¶ 509. Tax-exempt title-holding companies allowed incidental UBTI up to 10% of gross income without losing exemption

Exemption is granted under Code Sec. 501(c)(25) to any corporation or trust with up to 35 qualifying shareholders or beneficiaries (pension plans, governmental bodies, charitable organizations, and other Code Sec. 501(c)(25) title-holding companies qualify, whether or not related), if the exclusive purpose of the corporation or trust is investing in real estate. The exemption under Code Sec. 501(c)(25) in effect enables the shareholders or beneficiaries to pool real estate investment funds. (See FTC 2d/FIN ¶s D-5803, D-5804; TG ¶ 7901; USTR ¶ 5014.04) In addition, corporations organized exclusively for holding title to property and turning over the income to a single tax-exempt organization (or more than one if they are related) are tax-exempt under Code Sec. 501(c)(2). (See FTC 2d/FIN ¶ D-5801; TG ¶ 7964; USTR ¶ 5014.04)

Under pre-'93 Act law, IRS took the position that even a small amount of unrelated business taxable income (UBTI) disqualified an organization from being an exempt title-holding company (under Code Sec. 501(c)(25) or (2)). A title-holding company's rental income from shopping centers, office buildings, and apartment buildings generally isn't UBTI, but UBTI could result from laundry machines

FTC 2d References are to the Federal Tax Coordinator 2d
FIN References are to RIA's Analysis of Federal Taxes: Income
TG References are to the Tax Guide
USTR References are to the United States Tax Reporter

provided to tenants, vending machines in shopping centers, and similar sources. (H Rept p. 618)

The '93 Act includes provisions to prevent loss of exempt status by a title-holding company (under Code Sec. 501(c)(25) or (2)) merely because it receives small amounts of UBTI that are incidentally derived from holding real property. Under the '93 Act, although incidental unrelated income doesn't jeopardize the title-holding company's exemption (see below), it is subject to tax as UBTI. (H Rept p. 618)

Code Sec. 501(c)(25) title-holding companies. The '93 Act provides a *de minimis* rule, allowing a Code Sec. 501(c)(25) title-holding company to receive otherwise disqualifying income (Code Sec. 501(c)(25)(G)(ii) as amended by '93 Act § 13146(a))—that is, UBTI (H Rept p. 618)—of up to 10% of its gross income for the tax year without being treated as failing to be described in Code Sec. 501(c)(25). (Code Sec. 501(c)(25)(G)(ii)) Under the *de minimis* rule, such otherwise disqualifying income must be *incidentally* derived from holding real property. (Code Sec. 501(c)(25)(G)(i)) For example, income from vending machines or parking qualifies under the *de minimis* rule, while income from manufacturing and other activity not incidental to holding real property doesn't qualify. (H Rept p. 618)

Also, the '93 Act provides that otherwise disqualifying income that is incidentally derived from holding real property and exceeds the 10% limitation, doesn't result in loss of a title-holding company's exemption under Code Sec. 501(c)(25) if the company establishes to IRS's satisfaction that the excess income was received inadvertently and that reasonable steps are being taken to correct the circumstances giving rise to the income. (Code Sec. 501(c)(25)(G)(ii))

Code Sec. 501(c)(2) title-holding companies. Rules similar to those above will apply under the '93 Act to a title-holding company exempt under Code Sec. 501(c)(2). (Code Sec. 501(c)(2) as amended by '93 Act § 13146(b))

Thus, under a *de minimis* rule, Code Sec. 501(c)(2) title-holding companies are allowed to receive otherwise disqualifying income—that is, UBTI—of up to 10% of its gross income for the tax year without jeopardizing its exemption under Code Sec. 501(c)(2). Under this rule, such otherwise disqualifying income must be incidentally derived from holding real property. For example, income from vending machines or parking qualifies while income from manufacturing and other activity not incidental to holding real property doesn't qualify. (H Rept p. 618)

Also, otherwise disqualifying income that is incidentally derived from holding real property and exceeds the 10% limitation, doesn't result in loss of a title-holding company's exemption under Code Sec. 501(c)(2) if the company establishes to IRS's satisfaction that the excess income was received inadvertently and that reasonable steps are being taken to correct the circumstances giving rise to the income. (H Rept p. 619)

☐ **Effective:** Tax years beginning after Dec. 31, '93. (§ 13146(c))

For official explanation see Committee Reports ¶ 3017.

¶ 600. Empowerment Zones and Other Targeted Areas

¶ 601. Empowerment zones and enterprise communities

Under pre-'93 Act law, the Code does not contain general rules that target specific geographic areas for special tax incentives, although certain economically distressed areas are targeted for limited purposes such as the low-income housing credit (which has been permanently extended, see ¶ 705).

The '93 Act provides for the designation of certain distressed urban and rural areas as empowerment zones and enterprise communities. Special tax incentives are available for both empowerment zones and enterprise communities.

The Act provides for nine empowerment zones and 95 enterprise communities to be designated in '94 and '95 from among areas nominated for designation by states and local governments. Designations will remain in effect generally for ten years. To be eligible for designation an area must meet certain criteria regarding population and size and have a condition of "pervasive poverty, unemployment, and general distress." The area must satisfy specified poverty thresholds. The application for designation must include a strategic plan that describes the proposed development plans for the area and identifies baselines, methods, and benchmarks for measuring the success of the strategic plan, see ¶ 602.

The following tax incentives are provided for empowerment zones:

. . . Increased Code Sec. 179 expensing election. The expensing election is increased to $37,500 for qualified zone property of an enterprise zone business. Qualified zone property is in general depreciable tangible personal property purchased by the taxpayer after designation of an empowerment zone and used substantially in the zone. An enterprise zone business is in general a corporation, partnership, or proprietorship actively conducting a qualified business in an empowerment zone. In addition, at least 35% of its employees must live in the zone, and certain other requirements must be met, see ¶ 603.

. . . Empowerment zone employment credit. Employers are allowed a credit equal to 20% of the first $15,000 of qualified wages paid annually to each employee who lives and works in an empowerment zone, and who is employed by the employer for at least 90 days. The credit is allowed regardless of whether the employer meets the definition of an enterprise zone business, see ¶ 604. The credit may offset 25% of alternative minimum tax liability, see ¶ 605.

The '93 Act also creates a new category of tax-exempt facility private activity bonds—qualified enterprise zone facility bonds—for use in both empowerment zones and enterprise communities. These bonds generally are bonds 95% or more of whose net proceeds are used to finance an enterprise zone facility. An enterprise zone facility is qualified zone property the principal user of which is an enterprise zone business, and functionally related and subordinate land. But for tax-exempt financing purposes, the definitions of qualified zone property and enterprise zone business are broadened to include property and businesses in both empowerment zones and enterprise communities. These bonds are subject to the state private activity bond volume limitations.

The above tax incentives will be available during the period that the designation remains in effect. (H Rept p. 801)

The Act requires IRS to issue regulations that may be necessary or appropriate to carry out the purposes of these provisions, including regulations:

. . . limiting the benefit of these provisions in circumstances where the benefits, in combination with benefits provided under other federal programs, would result in an activity being 100% or more subsidized by the federal government, (Code Sec. 1397D(1) as added by '93 Act § 13301(a)) and

. . . preventing abuse of these provisions. (Code Sec. 1397D(2))

For addition of the items required to be taken into account under the empowerment zone provisions to the list of tax attributes that are inherited by a transferee corporation in tax-free reorganizations and subsidiary liquidations, see ¶ 607.

☐ **Effective:** Aug. 10, '93 (§ 13303)
For official explanation see Committee Reports ¶ 3069.

¶ 602. Designation of empowerment zones and enterprise communities

The '93 Act provides for the designation of certain distressed urban and rural areas as empowerment zones and enterprise communities. Special tax incentives are available for both empowerment zones and enterprise communities. An increased Code Sec. 179 expensing election is allowed for certain depreciable business property used by an enterprise zone business in an empowerment zone. (See ¶ 603) Employers are allowed a credit equal to the 20% of the first $15,000 of qualified wages paid annually to each employee who lives and works in an empowerment zone. (See ¶ 604) In addition, the Act creates a new category of tax-exempt facility bonds that can be used to finance facilities used by an enterprise zone business in an empowerment zone or enterprise community. (See ¶ 606)

Under the Act, the appropriate Secretaries (defined below) may designate empowerment zones and enterprise communities from among areas nominated for designation. (Code Sec. 1391(a) as added by '93 Act § 13301(a)) An area nominated for designation (nominated area) is an area that is nominated by one or more local governments and the state or states in which the area is located, as explained below. (Code Sec. 1393(a)(6) as added by '93 Act § 13301(a))

A total of nine empowerment zones and 95 enterprise communities may be designated. (Code Sec. 1391(b)) See below.

Designations may be made only after '93 and before $96 (i.e., only during '94 and '95). (Code Sec. 1391(c)) Designations generally will remain in effect for 10 years. (H Rept p. 792) See below.

Empowerment zones. The appropriate Secretaries may designate a total of nine nominated areas as empowerment zones, subject to availability of eligible nominated areas. Of that total, not more than six may be in urban areas, and not more than three may be in rural areas. If six empowerment zones are designated in urban areas, at least one must be designated in an urban area the most populous city of which has a population of 500,000 or less, and at least one must be a nominated area that includes areas in two states and that has a population of 50,000 or less. Empowerment zones located in urban areas must be designated in such a manner that the aggregate population of all such zones does not exceed 750,000. (Code Sec. 1391(b)(2))

For the definition of rural area and urban area, see below.

Enterprise communities. The appropriate Secretaries may designate a total of 95 nominated areas as enterprise communities, subject to availability of eligible nominated areas. Of that total, not more than 65 may be in urban areas, and not more than 30 may be in rural areas. (Code Sec. 1391(b)(1))

For the definition of rural area and urban area, see below.

Indian reservations not eligible for designation. No empowerment zone or enterprise community may include any area within an Indian reservation. An Indian reservation is defined in Code Sec. 168(j)(6) (which defines Indian reservation for purposes of the new accelerated depreciation tax incentive provided by the '93 act for property on Indian reservations, see ¶ 610). (Code Sec. 1393(a)(4))

Definition of rural area and urban area. A rural area, for purposes of these rules, is defined as (a) any area that is outside of a metropolitan statistical area within the meaning of Code Sec. 143(k)(2)(B) (dealing with the tax exemption of certain qualified mortgage bonds, see FTC 2d/FIN ¶ J-3183; TG ¶ 5303), or (b) any area that is determined to be a rural area by the Secretary of Agriculture, after consultation with the Secretary of Commerce. (Code Sec. 1393(a)(2))

An urban area is defined as an area that is not a rural area. (Code Sec. 1393(a)(3))

Appropriate secretary. The appropriate Secretary, for purposes of the rules on designation of empowerment zones and enterprise communities, means the Secretary of Housing and Urban Development in the case of any nominated area that is located in an urban area, and the Secretary of Agriculture in the case of any nominated area that is located in a rural area. (Code Sec. 1393(a)(1))

Period designation remains in effect. Designations of nominated areas as empowerment zones or as enterprise communities remain in effect for the period beginning on the date of designation and ending on the earliest of (a) the close of the 10th calendar year beginning on or after the date of designation, (b) the termination date designated by the state and local governments in their nomination of the area, or (c) the date the appropriate Secretary revokes the designation. (Code Sec. 1391(d)(1))

Revocation of designation. The appropriate secretary may revoke the designation of an area as an empowerment zone or enterprise community if the Secretary determines that the local government or the state in which the area is located has modified the boundaries of the area, or is not substantially complying with, or fails to make progress in achieving the benchmarks identified in, the strategic plan (see below) submitted with the application for designation. (Code Sec. 1391(d)(2))

The Code doesn't provide a procedure for the revocation of an area's designation. However, it is intended that the relevant Secretary will promulgate rules regarding the revocation process. Under these rules a designation will be revoked only after a hearing on the record involving officials of the state and local governments. It is also intended that , if an area's zone or community designation is revoked, the Secretary will not designate another area as a zone or community in its place. (Conf Rept p. 712)

Requirements for designation. An area may not be designated as an empowerment zone or as an enterprise community unless all the following requirements are satisfied: (Code Sec. 1391(e))

(1) The area is nominated for designation by one or more local governments (defined below) and the state or states in which it is located. (Code Sec. 1391(e)(1))

observation: Neither the Code nor the committee reports explain how an area is "nominated" for designation. Presumably, this is done by submitting an "application for designation" as an empowerment zone or as an enterprise community, which is discussed below.

(2) The state or states and the local governments provide written assurances satisfactory to the Secretary that the strategic plan submitted with the application for designation of the area as an empowerment zone or enterprise community (see below) will be implemented. (Code Sec. 1391(e)(3)) In the case of an urban empowerment zone located in two states, the nominating states and local governments must provide written assurances satisfactory to the Secretary that the incentives afforded the zone on account of the designation will be distributed equitably between the two states. (Conf Rept p. 712)

(3) The state or states and the local governments have the authority to nominate the area for designation, and to provide the assurances described in (2) above. (Code Sec. 1391(e)(2))

(4) The state or states and the local governments certify that no part of the nominated area is already included in an empowerment zone or in an enterprise community or in an area otherwise nominated for designation. (Code Sec. 1391(e)(5))

(5) The Secretary determines that the information furnished is reasonably accurate. (Code Sec. 1391(e)(4))

If more than one state or local government nominates an area, these rules apply to all such governments. (Code Sec. 1393(a)(7))

Local government. Local government means (a) any county, city, town, township, parish, village, or other general purpose political subdivision of a state, and (b) any combination of political subdivisions recognized by the appropriate Secretary. (Code Sec. 1393(a)(5))

An area is treated as nominated by a state and a local government if it is nominated by an economic development corporation chartered by the state. (Code Sec . 1393(a)(8))

Application for designation. An area may not be designated as an empowerment zone or as an enterprise community unless the application for designation (1) demonstrates that the nominated area satisfies the eligibility criteria discussed below, (2) includes a strategic plan (see below) for accomplishing the purpose of the empowerment zone and enterprise community provisions, and (3) includes such other information as may be required by the appropriate Secretary. (Code Sec. 1391(f))

Eligibility criteria for nominated area. A nominated area is eligible for designation as an empowerment zone or as an enterprise community only if it meets the criteria listed below. (Code Sec. 1392(a) as added by '93 Act § 13301(a)) To be eligible, the nominated area must possess *all* of the following characteristics: (H Rept p. 792)

(1) Population limit. If the nominated area is an urban area, its maximum population must not exceed the lesser of (a) 200,000, or (b) the greater of 50,000 or 10% of the population of the most populous city located within the nominated area. (Code Sec. 1392(a)(1)(A)) If the nominated area is a rural area, its maximum population must not exceed 30,000. (Code Sec. 1392(a)(1)(B)) For a population limit on all designated empowerment zones located in urban areas, see the discussion of empowerment zones above.

Population is determined by the most recent decennial census data available. (Code Sec. 1393(a)(9))

(2) Distressed condition. The nominated area must be one of pervasive , poverty, unemployment, and general distress. General distress may be indicated by factors such as high crime rates, high vacancy rates, or designation of an area as a disaster area or high intensity drug trafficking area ("HIDTA") under the Anti-Drug Abuse Act of 1988; job loss (including manufacturing job loss); and economic distress due to closures of military bases or restrictions on timber harvesting. In addition, consideration should be given to communities along the U.S. border in which population has increased significantly, without a corresponding expansion of basic infrastructure, and in which a significant portion of the area's population reside in substandard housing. (Conf Rept p. 712)

(3) Size. If the nominated area is an urban area, it must not exceed 20 square miles. If the nominated area is a rural area, it must not exceed 1,000 square miles. (Code Sec. 1392(a)(3)(A))

(4) Boundary. The nominated area must either (a) have a continuous boundary, or (b) except in the case of a rural area located in more than one state, consist of not more than three noncontiguous parcels. (Code Sec. 1392(a)(3)(B))

(5) Location in more than one state. If the nominated area is an urban area, it must be located entirely within no more than two contiguous states. (Code Sec. 1392(a)(3)(C)(i)) If the nominated area is a rural area, it must be located entirely within no more than three contiguous states. (Code Sec. 1392(a)(3)(C)(ii))

(6) Central business district. The nominated area must not include any part of a central business district (as that term is used for purposes of the most recent Census of Retail Trade), unless the poverty rate (see below) for each population census tract in the district is at least 35% (at least 30% in the case of an enterprise community). (Code Sec. 1392(a)(3)(D))

(7) Poverty rate. The population census tracts within the nominated must satisfy the following poverty rate criteria: (Code Sec. 1392(a)(4))

. . . Each population census tract within the area must have a poverty rate of at least 20%, (Code Sec. 1392(a)(4)(A))

. . . At least 90% of the population census tracts within the area must have a poverty rate of at least 25%, (Code Sec. 1392(a)(4)(B)) and

. . . At least 50% of the population census tracts within the area must have a poverty rate of at least 35%. (Code Sec. 1392(a)(4)(C))

For rules as to determination of the poverty rate, see below.

For discretion of the appropriate secretary to adjust the poverty rate requirements for enterprise communities, see below.

Determining poverty rate. For purposes of determining the poverty rate criteria (see (7) above), the rules discussed below apply. (Code Sec. 1392(b))

If a population census tract within the nominated area has no population, the tract is treated as meeting the 20% and 25% poverty rate requirements, but it is treated as having a zero poverty rate for purpose of applying the 35% requirement. (Code Sec. 1392(b)(1)(A)) If a census tract within the area has a population of less than 2,000, it is treated as meeting the 20% and 25% requirements if more than 75% of the tract is zoned for commercial or industrial use. (Code Sec. 1392(b)(1)(B))

FTC 2d References are to the Federal Tax Coordinator 2d
FIN References are to RIA's Analysis of Federal Taxes: Income
TG References are to the Tax Guide
USTR References are to the United States Tax Reporter

A nominated area may not include a noncontiguous parcel unless the parcel separately meets the poverty rate criteria listed in (7) above (subject to the rules for tracts with no population or with small populations, and the rules below regarding adjustment of the poverty rate) . (Code Sec. 1392(b)(3)) Thus, if the nominated area consists of noncontiguous parcels, each parcel must separately satisfy the poverty rate criteria. (H Rept p. 793)

If an area is not tracted for population census tracts, the equivalent county divisions (as defined by the Bureau of the Census for purposes of defining poverty areas) are used to determine poverty rates. (Code Sec. 1392(b)(4)) In this case, the equivalent county divisions would be treated as census tracts. (H Rept p. 793)

Population and poverty rate are determined by the most recent decennial census data available. (Code Sec. 1393(a)(9))

Adjustment of poverty rate requirements for enterprise communities. In determining whether a nominated area is eligible for designation as an enterprise zone community, the appropriate Secretary may, if necessary to carry out the purposes of these rules, reduce one of the poverty rate criteria listed in (7) above (i.e., the 20% threshold, the 25% threshold, or the 35% threshold). The Secretary may reduce one of these thresholds by five percentage points for not more than 10% of the population census tracts (or, if fewer, five population census tracts) in the nominated area. (Code Sec. 1392(b)(2)) But if the Secretary elects to reduce the 35% threshold, then the Secretary may, instead of applying the preceding rule, reduce the 35% threshold by ten percentage points for three population census tracts. (Code Sec. 1392(b)(2))

The Secretary does not have discretion to reduce the poverty rate criteria for an area nominated to be an empowerment zone. (Conf Rept p. 712)

Nor does the Secretary have discretion to reduce the 35% poverty rate requirement for population census tracts located in a central business district that is part of an empowerment zone or the 30% poverty rate requirement for tracts located in a central business district that is part of an enterprise community. (H Rept p. 793) For the central business district criteria, see (6) above.

Strategic plan. In order for a nominated area to be eligible for designation, the nominating body (i.e., the local government or governments and the state or states in which the area is located) must submit a strategic plan for purposes of accomplishing the goals of the empowerment zone and enterprise community provisions. (H Rept p. 793) The strategic plan must be submitted with the application for designation (see above). (Code Sec. 1391(f)(2))

The required strategic plan must:

(1) describe the coordinated economic, human, community, and physical development plan and related activities proposed for the nominated area, (Code Sec. 1391(f)(2)(A))

(2) describe the process by which the affected community is a full partner in the process of developing and implementing the plan and the extent to which local institutions and organizations have contributed to the planning process, (Code Sec. 1391(f)(2)(B))

(3) identify the amount of state, local, and private resources that will be available in the nominated area and the private/public partnerships to be used, which may include participation by, and cooperation with, universities, medical centers, and other private and public entities, (Code Sec. 1391(f)(2)(C))

(4) identify the funding requested under any federal program in support of the proposed economic, human, community, and physical development and related activities, (Code Sec. 1391(f)(2)(D)) and

(5) identify baselines, methods, and benchmarks for measuring the success of carrying out the strategic plan, including the extent to which poor persons and families will be empowered to become economically self-sufficient. (Code Sec. 1391(f)(2)(E))

In addition, the required strategic plan must generally not include any action to assist any establishment in relocating from one area outside the nominated area to the nominated area. However, assistance for the expansion of an existing business entity through the establishment of a new branch, affiliate, or subsidiary is permitted if (a) the establishment of the new branch, affiliate, or subsidiary will not result in the a decrease in employment in the area of original location or in any other area where the existing business entity conducts business operations, and (b) there is no reason to believe that the new branch, affiliate, or subsidiary is being established with the intention of closing down the operations of the existing business entity in the area of its original location or in any other area where the existing business entity conducts business operation. (Code Sec. 1391(f)(2)(F))

Factors considered by Secretary in making designations. The appropriate Secretary will make designations of empowerment zones and enterprise communities from among the nominated areas eligible for designation on the basis the following factors:

. . . Effectiveness of the strategic plan submitted with the application for designation as an empowerment zone or enterprise community and the assurances made by the state or states and the local governments nominating the area that the plan will be implemented (see above), (Code Sec. 1392(c)(1)) and

. . . Criteria specified by the appropriate secretary. (Code Sec. 1392(c)(2))

☐ **Effective:** Aug. 10, '93. (§ 13304)
For official explanation see Committee Reports ¶ 3069.

¶ 603. Increased Code Sec. 179 expensing election for "qualified zone property" of an "enterprise zone business"

Under pre-'93 Act law, taxpayers (other than trusts, estates, and certain noncorporate lessors) can elect under Code Sec. 179 to expense up to $10,000 per year of the cost of certain recovery property purchased and placed in service in the tax year. Property qualifying for the Code Sec. 179 expensing election (Code Sec. 179 property) includes only tangible depreciable personal property used in the active conduct of the taxpayer's trade or business. The maximum $10,000 deduction is phased out, however, dollar for dollar by the amount of qualifying property placed in service during the tax year that exceeds $200,000. In addition, the expensing deduction is limited to the amount of the taxpayer's taxable income from any active trades or businesses. Members of a controlled group are treated as one taxpayer for purposes of these limitations. Also, the limitations apply at both the partnership (and S corporation) and partner (and shareholder) levels. The expensing deduction is recaptured if the qualified property isn't predominantly used in a trade or business. (FTC 2d/FIN ¶ L-7960 *et seq.;* TG ¶ 5490 *et seq.)*

The '93 Act increases the maximum amount allowed to be expensed under Code Sec. 179 by an enterprise zone business by $20,000 for Code Sec. 179 property that is also qualified zone property, and takes into account only one-half the cost of the qualified zone property in computing the phaseout. The Act also provides for recapture of the increased expensing deduction for qualified zone property. (Conf Rept p. 714)

Under another provision of the '93 Act, the maximum amount that can be expensed each year under Code Sec. 179 is increased to $17,500, see ¶ 701.

Maximum deduction. Under pre-'93 Act law, the cost of qualifying Code Sec. 179 property placed in service during the tax year that a taxpayer may elect to expense is limited to $10,000. (FTC 2d/FIN ¶ L-7967; TG ¶ 5493)

The '93 Act provides that in the case of an enterprise zone business (defined below), the limitation on the amount allowed to be expensed under Code Sec. 179 is increased by the lesser of (a) $20,000, or (b) the cost of Code Sec. 179 property that is qualified zone property (defined below) placed in service during the tax year. (Code Sec. 1397A(a)(1) as added by '93 Act § 13301(a))

> ***observation:*** Since the maximum allowable deduction per year under Code Sec. 179 is increased to $17,500 by another provision of the '93 Act (see ¶ 701), the above rule increases the maximum amount allowed to be expensed per year in the case of an enterprise zone business to $37,500 ($17,500 plus $20,000).

The types of property eligible for Code Sec. 179 expensing under this provision do not include real property. (Conf Rept p. 714)

> ***observation:*** Qualified zone property, as defined below, means, in general, depreciable tangible property (including buildings). However, since the increased expensing deduction for enterprise zone businesses applies only to qualified zone property that is also Code Sec. 179 property, the expensing deduction under this rule doesn't apply to real property.

> ***illustration:*** Taxpayer, an enterprise zone business, places $60,000 of Code Sec. 179 property that is also qualified zone property in service during the tax year. The taxpayer does not place any property in service outside the zone. The taxpayer is allowed to claim a Code Sec. 179 expensing deduction of $37,500 ($17,500 plus $20,000) for the year. If the taxpayer had placed only $5,000 of Code Sec. 179 property that is also qualified zone property in service during the year, the taxpayer's Code Sec. 179 expensing deduction for the year would be only $22,500 ($17,500 plus $5,000).

Phaseout of maximum deduction. Under pre-'93 Act law, the maximum amount allowed to be expensed under Code Sec. 179 is reduced (but not below zero) by the amount by which the cost of qualifying Code Sec. 179 property placed in service during the tax year exceeds $200,000. (FTC 2d/FIN ¶ L-7967; TG ¶ 5493)

The '93 Act provides that in the case of an enterprise zone business, the amount taken into account under this phaseout rule with respect to any Code Sec. 179 property that is qualified zone property is 50% of the cost of such property. (Code Sec. 1397A(a)(2)) Thus, under the '93 Act, the pre-'93 Act phaseout range is applied by taking into account only one-half of the cost of qualified zone property that is Code Sec. 179 property. In applying the phaseout under the '93 Act, the cost of Code Sec. 179 property that is not qualified zone property is not reduced. (Conf Rept p. 714)

> ***observation:*** It's not clear whether, in computing the reduced maximum deduction under the phaseout, the cost of Code Sec. 179 property that is qualified zone property is reduced by one-half before or after application of the $200,000 threshold.

> ***illustration:*** Taxpayer, an enterprise zone business, places $250,000 of Code Sec. 179 property that is qualified zone property in service during the tax year. The taxpayer does not place any property in service outside the zone.

(1) If the $250,000 of Code Sec. 179 property that is qualified zone property is reduced by one-half *before* application of the $200,000 threshold, then the maximum allowable deduction of $37,500 would not be reduced under the phaseout. The computation would be as follows:

(a) Cost of Code Sec. 179 property that is qualified zone property	$250,000
(b) 50% of (a)	$125,000

Since one-half the cost of the Code Sec. 179 property that is qualified zone property does not exceed $200,000, the maximum deduction would not be reduced.

(2) On the other hand, if the $250,000 of the Code Sec. 179 property that is qualified zone property is reduced *after* application of the $200,000 threshold, then the maximum deduction would be reduced to $12,500, computed as follows:

(a) Cost of Code Sec. 179 property that is qualified zone property	$250,000
(b) Threshold	$200,000
(c) (a) less (b)	$50,000
(d) 50% of (c)	$25,000
(e) Maximum deduction before phaseout	$37,500
(f) Reduced maximum deduction ((e) less (d))	$12,500

observation: An earlier version of this phaseout provision included in the House bill made it clear that the qualified zone property was reduced after application of the $200,000 threshold, as shown in (2) above. Computation of the reduced maximum deduction under the phaseout for Code Sec. 179 property that is qualified zone property will probably be made clear before the designation of any empowerment zones.

Qualified zone property. For purposes of the increased Code Sec. 179 expensing deduction for qualified zone property of an enterprise zone business, qualified zone property means depreciable tangible property (or property that would be depreciable but for Code Sec. 179), provided the property satisfies the following requirements:

(1) The property was acquired by the taxpayer by purchase after the date on which the designation of the empowerment zone took effect. Purchase for this purpose is defined in Code Sec. 179(d)(2) (which does not treat property as purchased if it is acquired from certain related persons or with a carryover basis, see FTC 2d/FIN ¶ L-7978; TG ¶ 5492). (Code Sec. 1397C(a)(1)(A) as added by '93 Act § 13301(a))

(2) The original use of the property in an empowerment zone commences with the taxpayer. (Code Sec. 1397C(a)(1)(B)) Used property may be considered qualified zone property so long as it has not previously been used in the empowerment zone. (H Rept p. 797)

(3) Substantially all of the use of the property is in an empowerment zone in the active conduct of a qualified business by the taxpayer in the zone. (Code Sec. 1397C(a)(1)(C))

observation: The rules for determining whether property is qualified zone property don't define "qualified business" for purposes of requirement (3) above. Presumably "qualified business" as used here has the same meaning as it does for purposes of determining whether a corporation, partnership, or proprietorship is an enterprise zone business, see below.

Requirements (1) and (2) above are considered satisfied, however, if the property is substantially renovated by the taxpayer. Property is considered substantially renovated by the taxpayer if during any 24-month period beginning after the date the zone designation took effect, additions to the taxpayer's basis of the property exceed the greater of (a) the taxpayer's adjusted basis at the beginning of the 24-month period, or (b) $5,000. (Code Sec. 1397C(a)(2))

If property is sold and leased back by the taxpayer within three months after the date it was originally placed in service, the property, for purposes of requirement (2) above, is treated as originally placed in service not earlier than the date the property is used under the leaseback. (Code Sec. 1397C(b))

Enterprise zone business. The increased Code Sec. 179 expensing deduction for qualified zone property is available only with respect to trade or business activities that satisfy the criteria for an "enterprise zone business." An enterprise zone business is, in general, a corporation, partnership, or proprietorship that meets certain requirements for the tax year. (H Rept p. 796)

Under the Act, an enterprise zone business for purposes of the increased expensing election means any qualified business entity (see below), and any qualified proprietorship (see below). (Code Sec. 1397B(a) as added by '93 Act § 13301(a))

Qualified business entity. A qualified business entity means any corporation or partnership if all of the following requirements are satisfied for the tax year: (Code Sec. 1397B(b))

(1) Every trade or business of the entity is the active conduct of a qualified business (defined below) within an empowerment zone. (Code Sec. 1397B(b)(1)) Thus, the sole trade or business of the corporation or partnership must be the active conduct of a qualified business in the zone. (H Rept p. 796)

(2) At least 80% of the entity's total gross income is derived from the active conduct of the qualified business. (Code Sec. 1397B(b)(2))

(3) Substantially all of the use of the entity's tangible property (whether owned or leased) is in an empowerment zone. (Code Sec. 1397B(b)(3))

(4) Substantially all of the entity's intangible property is used in, and exclusively related to, the active conduct of any such business. (Code Sec. 1397B(b)(4))

(5) Substantially all of the services performed for the entity by its employees are performed in an empowerment zone. (Code Sec. 1397B(b)(5))

(6) At least 35% of the entity's employees are residents of an empowerment zone. (Code Sec. 1397B(b)(6)) IRS will prescribe regs to determine the treatment of part-time employees for purposes of calculating whether 35% of the employees are residents of the empowerment zone. (H Rept p. 797)

(7) Less than 5% of the average of the aggregate unadjusted bases of the entity's property is attributable to collectibles not held primarily for sale to customers in the ordinary course of such business. Collectibles has the same meaning as in Code Sec. 408(m)(2) (dealing with investment by IRAs in collectibles such as works of art, antiques, etc., see FTC 2d/FIN ¶ H-12061; TG ¶ 3729). (Code Sec. 1397B(b)(7))

(8) Less than 5% of the average of the aggregate unadjusted bases of the entity's property is attributable to nonqualified financial property (defined below). (Code Sec. 1397B(b)(8))

Activities of legally separate (even if related) parties are not aggregated for purposes of determining whether an entity qualifies as an enterprise zone business. (H Rept p. 797)

Qualified proprietorship. A qualified proprietorship means any qualified business (defined below) carried on by an individual as a proprietorship if all of the following requirements are satisfied for the tax year: (Code Sec. 1397B(c))

(1) At least 80% of the total gross income of the individual from the qualified business is derived from the active conduct of the business in an empowerment zone. (Code Sec. 1397B(c)(1))

(2) Substantially all of the use of the tangible property of the individual in the business (whether owned or leased) is in an empowerment zone. (Code Sec. 1397B(c)(2))

(3) Substantially all of the intangible property of the business is used in, and exclusively related to, the active conduct of the business. (Code Sec. 1397B(c)(3))

(4) Substantially all of the services performed for the individual in the business by its employees are performed in an empowerment zone. (Code Sec. 1397B(c)(4))

(5) At least 35% of the employees are residents of an empowerment zone. (Code Sec. 1397B(c)(5)) IRS will issue regs to determine the treatment of part-time employees for purposes of calculating whether 35% of the employees are residents of the empowerment zone. (H Rept p. 797)

(6) Less than 5% of the average of the aggregate unadjusted bases of the individual's property that is used in the business is attributable to collectibles not held primarily for sale to customers in the ordinary course of the business. Collectibles has the same meaning as in Code Sec. 408(m)(2) (dealing with investment by IRAs in collectibles such as works of art, antiques, etc., see FTC 2d/FIN ¶ H-12061; TG ¶ 3729). (Code Sec. 1397B(c)(6))

(7) Less than 5% of the average of the aggregate unadjusted bases of the individual's property that is used in the business is attributable to nonqualified financial property (defined below). (Code Sec. 1397B(c)(7))

For purposes of determining whether requirements (4) and (5) above are satisfied, an employee includes the proprietor. (Code Sec. 1397B(c)) Thus, employee for this purpose includes a self-employed individual within the meaning of Code Sec. 401(c)(1) (which treats self-employed individuals as employees for purposes of qualifying for certain qualified employee plans, see FTC 2d/FIN ¶ H-9311; TG ¶ 3603).

Unlike the requirements for a qualified business entity (see above), the qualified business doesn't have to be the sole trade or business of a qualified proprietorship. (H Rept p. 796)

Qualified business. For purposes of determining whether a corporation, partnership, or proprietorship is an enterprise zone business, a qualified business means any trade or business, with the exceptions and qualifications discussed below. (Code Sec. 1397B(d)(1))

Rental of real property. The rental of real property located in an empowerment zone to others is a qualified business if and only if (1) the property is not residential rental property (as defined in Code Sec. 168(e)(2) for purposes of the accelerated depreciation rules, see FTC 2d/FIN ¶ L-7803; TG ¶ 5430 *et seq.),* and (2) at least 50% of the gross rental income from the property is from enterprise zone businesses. (Code Sec. 1397B(d)(2))

Rental of tangible personal property. The rental of tangible personal property to others is a qualified business if and only if substantially all of the rental of the property is by enterprise zone businesses or by residents of an empowerment zone. (Code Sec. 1397B(d)(3))

Excluded businesses. A qualified business does not include:

. . . Any trade or business consisting predominantly of the development or holding of intangibles for sale or license. (Code Sec. 1397B(d)(4))

. . . Any trade or business consisting of the operation of any facility described in Code Sec. 144(c)(6)(B) (which prohibits the use of tax-exempt qualified redevelopment bond proceeds for provision of certain facilities, see FTC 2d/FIN ¶ J-3227). (Code Sec. 1397B(d)(5)(A)) Thus, a qualified business doesn't include a trade or business consisting of the operation of a private or commercial golf course, country club, massage parlor, hot tub facility, suntan facility, racetrack or other facility used for gambling, or any store the principal business of which is the sale of alcoholic beverages for consumption off premises. (H Rept p. 797)

. . . Any trade or business the principal activity of which is farming, but only if, as of the close of the preceding tax year, the sum of (a) the aggregate unadjusted bases (or, if greater, the fair market value) of the assets owned by the taxpayer and used in such trade or business, and (b) the aggregate value of assets leased by the taxpayer and used in the trade or business, exceeds $500,000. (Code Sec. 1397B(d)(5)(B))

> ***observation:*** If the total value of farm assets is $500,000 or less, the farm could be considered a qualified business provided the other requirements are met.

Farming for purposes of this rule has the meaning given it by Code Sec. 2032A(e)(5)(A) or (B) (which defines farming purposes under the estate tax special use valuation rules, see FTC 2d ¶ R-5213). (Code Sec. 1397B(d)(5)(B))

For purposes of this rule barring treatment of certain farms as a qualified business, rules similar to the rules of Code Sec. 1397(b) for the empowerment zone employment credit (dealing with corporations, partnerships, or proprietorships under common control, discussed at ¶ 604) will apply. (Code Sec. 1397B(d)(5)(B))

Nonqualified financial property. For purposes of determining whether a corporation, partnership, or proprietorship meets the above requirements for an enterprise zone business, nonqualified financial property means debt, stock, partnership interests, options, futures contracts, forward contracts, warrants, notional principal contracts, annuities, and other similar property specified in regulations. But such property doesn't include reasonable amounts of working capital held in cash, cash equivalents, or debt instruments with a term of 18 months or less, or debt instruments described in Code Sec. 1221(4) (certain receivables acquired in the ordinary course of trade or business, see FTC 2d/FIN ¶ I-4122; TG ¶ 4333). (Code Sec. 1397(e))

Failure to meet requirements for enterprise zone business. IRS will issue regulations dealing with inadvertent failures of entities to be enterprise zone businesses. (Code Sec. 1397D(3) as added by '93 Act § 13301)

Other provisions applicable. In general, all other Code Sec. 179 expensing provisions apply to the increased expensing for enterprise zone businesses. Thus, all component members of a controlled group are treated as one taxpayer for purposes of the expensing allowance and the application of the phaseout. The limitations apply at both the partnership (and S corporation) and partner (and shareholder) levels. The increased expensing allowance is allowed for purposes of the alternative minimum tax (i.e., it is not treated as an adjustment for purposes of the alternative minimum tax). (Conf Rept p. 714)

Recapture. Under pre-'93 Act law, the expensing deduction is recaptured if the Code Sec. 179 property is not predominantly used in a trade or business. (FTC 2d/FIN ¶ L-7985; TG ¶ 5498)

The '93 Act provides that similar rules will apply if the qualified zone property ceases to be used in an empowerment zone by an enterprise zone business. (Code Sec. 1397A(b))

☐ **Effective:** Aug. 10, '93. (§ 13303)
For official explanation see Committee Reports ¶ 3069.

¶ 604. New empowerment zone employment credit

The '93 Act provides a new empowerment zone employment credit. This credit is part of the general business credit (see below).

In general, the new empowerment zone employment credit is available to all employers and is equal to 20% of the first $15,000 of qualified wages paid to each employee who is a resident of an empowerment zone and performs substantially all employment services within the zone in a trade or business of the employer. The credit will be phased out beginning in 2002. (Conf Rept p. 713)

The empowerment zone employment credit is available to an employer, regardless of whether the employer meets the definition of an enterprise zone business (which applies for purposes of the increased Code Sec. 179 expensing election rules, see ¶ 604). (H Rept p. 794)

For offset of the alternative minimum tax by the empowerment zone employment credit, see ¶ 605.

Amount of credit. The amount of an employer's empowerment zone employment credit for any tax year is the applicable percentage of the qualified zone wages (defined below) paid or incurred during the calendar year that ends with or within such tax year. (Code Sec. 1396(a) as added by '93 Act § 13301(a))

The applicable percentage is determined under the following table: (Code Sec. 1396(b))

Wages paid or incurred during calendar year	*Applicable Percentage*
'94 through 2001	20
2002	15
2003	10
2004	5

The credit will not be available after 2004. (Conf Rept p. 713)

Rules similar to the following rules applicable to the targeted jobs credit also apply for purposes of the empowerment zone employment credit: (Code Sec. 1397(c) as added by '93 Act § 13301(a))

. . . Denial of credit to tax-exempt organizations, under Code Sec. 52(c).

. . . Apportionment of the credit between an estate or trust and the beneficiaries, under Code Sec. 52(d). (See FTC 2d/FIN ¶ L-17830; TG ¶ 5812; USTR ¶ 514)

. . . Limitations on the amount of the credit for mutual savings banks, regulated investment companies, REITs, and certain cooperatives, under Code Sec. 52(e). (See FTC 2d/FIN ¶ L-17831; USTR ¶ 514)

> ***observation:*** The targeted jobs credit which was scheduled to expire on June 30, '92 has been extended through '94 by another provision of the '93 Act, see ¶ 717.

FTC 2d References are to the Federal Tax Coordinator 2d
FIN References are to RIA's Analysis of Federal Taxes: Income
TG References are to the Tax Guide
USTR References are to the United States Tax Reporter

Qualified zone wages. Qualified zone wages means any wages (as defined below) paid or incurred by an employer for services performed by an employee while the employee is a qualified zone employee (see below). (Code Sec. 1396(c)(1))

The amount of qualified zones wages taken into account for each qualified zone employee may not exceed $15,000 for a calendar year. (Code Sec. 1396(c)(2)) Thus, the maximum credit per qualified employee is $3,000 per year (i.e., 20% of $15,000 for calendar years '94 through 2001). (Conf Rept p. 713)

Wages paid to a qualified employee continue to be eligible for the credit if the employee earns more than $15,000, although only the first $15,000 of wages will be eligible for the credit. (Conf Rept p. 713)

The credit is available for a qualified employee, regardless of the number of other employees who work for the employer. (H Rept p. 794)

Qualified zone wages do not include wages taken into account in determining the employer's targeted jobs credit under Code Sec. 51. (Code Sec. 1396(c)(3)(A)) The $15,000 amount of qualified zone wages taken into account for each qualified employee for a calendar year must be reduced by the amount of wages paid or incurred during such year that are taken into account in determining the targeted jobs credit. (Code Sec. 1396(c)(3)(B))

Rules similar to the following rules for computing the targeted jobs credit also apply for purposes of computing the empowerment zone employment credit: (Code Sec. 1397(c))

. . . Treatment of wages paid by a successor employer as if the wages were paid by the predecessor employer, under Code Sec. 51(k)(1). (See FTC 2d/FIN ¶ L-17832; TG ¶ 5801)

. . . Denial of credit for remuneration paid by an employer to an employee performing services for another person, under Code Sec. 51(k)(2). (See FTC 2d/FIN ¶ L-17817; USTR ¶ 514)

Wages defined. Wages for purposes of the empowerment zone employment credit have the same meaning as when used in Code Sec. 51 for purposes of the targeted jobs credit (see FTC 2d/FIN ¶ L-17810; TG ¶ 5802; USTR ¶ 514). (Code Sec. 1397(a)(1)) Thus, wages include salary and wages as generally defined for purposes of the Federal Unemployment Tax Act (FUTA). (H Rept p. 794)

In addition, wages for purposes of the employment credit include amounts paid or incurred by an employer for educational assistance to an employee, provided (a) the amounts are excludable from the employee's gross income under Code Sec. 127 as educational assistance under a qualified educational assistance program (see FTC 2d/FIN ¶ H-2064 *et seq.;* TG ¶ 3152 *et seq.),* and (b) the amounts are paid or incurred to a person not related to the employer. (Code Sec. 1397(a)(2)(A)(i))

> ***observation:*** Although the exclusion from gross income under Code Sec. 127 for educational assistance benefits expired on July 1, '92, that exclusion has been extended through '94 by another provision of the '93 Act, see ¶ 802.

Persons are considered related for this purpose if they are related under Code Sec. 267(b) (which defines related persons for purposes of the rule disallowing deduction for losses between related taxpayers, see FTC 2d/FIN ¶ I-2904 *et seq.;* TG ¶ 4101; USTR ¶ 2674) or Code Sec. 707(b)(1) (which disallows deduction of losses involving controlled partnerships, see FTC 2d/FIN ¶ B-2016; TG ¶ 1643; USTR ¶ 7074.03), but in applying those Code sections for purposes of the empowerment zone employment credit, 10% is substituted for 50%. Persons are also considered related if they are engaged in trades or businesses under common control within the meaning of Code Sec. 52(a) and (b) (which treats employees of corporations, partnerships, or proprietorships under common control as employed by the same employer for purposes of the targeted jobs credit, see FTC 2d/FIN ¶ L-17828; TG ¶ 5811; USTR ¶ 514). (Code Sec. 1397(a)(2)(B))

In the case of an employee who is under age 19, wages for purposes of the employment credit also include amounts paid or incurred by an employer for any youth training program operated by the employer in conjunction with local educational officials. (Code Sec. 1397(a)(2)(A)(ii))

Qualified zone employee. With the exceptions listed below, a qualified zone employee with respect to any period means any employee if:

(1) substantially all of the services performed by the employee for the employer during that period are performed within an empowerment zone in a trade or business of the employer, (Code Sec. 1396(d)(1)(A)) and

(2) the principal place of abode of the employee while performing those services is within that empowerment zone. (Code Sec. 1396(d)(1)(B))

It is intended that employers undertake reasonable measures to verify an employee's residence within the zone, so that the employer will be able to substantiate any wage credit claimed. (H Rept p. 794)

It is also intended that employers take reasonable steps to notify all qualified zone employees of the availability to eligible individuals of receiving advanced payments of the earned income tax credit under Code Sec. 32 (see FTC 2d/FIN ¶ H-4800 *et seq.;* TG ¶ 1251; USTR ¶ 324 *et seq.*). (Conf Rept p. 713)

The empowerment zone employment credit is allowed with respect to part-time employees, if the employee satisfies the minimum 90-day employment rule for qualified zone employees (see below). (H Rept p. 795)

Individuals not eligible for consideration as qualified zone employee. A qualified zone employee does not include the following individuals: (Code Sec. 1396(d)(2))

. . . Any individual employed by the employer for less than 90 days. (Code Sec.1396(d)(2)(C)) For exceptions and special rules relating to termination of employment, see below.

. . . Certain individuals related to the employer, as described in Code Secs. 51(i)(1)(A), (B), or (C) (dealing with related individuals for whom no targeted jobs credit is allowed, see FTC 2d/FIN ¶ L-17816; TG ¶ 5806; USTR ¶ 514). (Code Sec. 1396(d)(2)(A)) Thus, wages aren't eligible for the credit if paid to certain relatives of the employer or, if the employer is a corporation or partnership, certain relatives of a person who owns more than 50% of the business. (H Rept p. 795) For disallowance by the '93 Act of the targeted jobs credit for relatives of a person who owns more than 50% of a business that is not a corporation, see ¶ 718.

. . . Any 5% owner, as defined in Code Sec. 416(i)(1)(B) (dealing with who is a "key employee" for purposes of determining whether an employee benefit plan is top heavy, see FTC 2d/FIN ¶ H-7919; TG ¶ 3608; USTR ¶ 4164.03). (Code Sec. 1396(d)(2)(B)) In general, this means that wages aren't eligible for the credit if paid to a person who owns more than 5% of the stock (or capital or profits interests) of the employer. (H Rept p. 795)

. . . Any individual employed at any facility described in Code Sec. 144(c)(6)(B) (which prohibits the use of tax-exempt qualified redevelopment bond proceeds for provision of certain facilities, see FTC 2d/FIN ¶ J-3227; USTR ¶ 1444.02). (Code Sec. 1396(d)(2)(D)) Thus, the wage credit isn't available for wages paid to an individual employed at a private or commercial golf course, country club, massage parlor, hot tub facility, suntan facility, racetrack or other facility used for gambling, or any store the principal business of which is the sale of alcoholic beverages for consumption off premises. (H Rept p. 795)

. . . Any individual employed in a trade or business, the principal activity of which is farming, but only if, as of the close of the tax year, the sum of (a) the aggregate unadjusted bases (or, if greater, the fair market value) of the assets owned by the employer and used in that trade or business, and (b) the aggregate value of assets leased by the employer for use in the trade or business (as determined under IRS regs), exceeds $500,000. (Code Sec. 1396(d)(2)(E))

> ***observation:*** If the total value of farm assets is $500,000 or less, wages paid to a farm employee would be eligible for the credit.

Farming for purposes of this rule has the meaning given it by Code Sec. 2032A(e)(5)(A) or (B) (which defines farming purposes under the estate tax special use valuation rules, see FTC 2d ¶ R-5213). (Code Sec. 1396(d)(2)(E)) Thus, farming under this rule includes (a) cultivating the soil or raising or harvesting any agricultural or horticultural commodity (including the raising, shearing, feeding, caring for, training, and management of animals) on a farm, or (b) handling, drying, packing, grading, or storing on a farm any agricultural or horticultural commodity in its unmanufactured state, but only if the owner, tenant or operator of the farm regularly produces more than half of the commodity so treated. (See FTC 2d ¶ R-5213)

> ***observation:*** The activities listed in (a) and (b) above are the activities specified in Code Sec. 2032A(e)(5)(A) and (B) under the definition of farming purposes for the estate tax special use valuation rules. However, the definition of farming purposes for the estate tax special use rules also includes planting, cultivating, caring for, or cutting of trees, or the preparation (other than milling) of trees for market. (See FTC 2d ¶ R-5213) These tree-related activities are specified in Code Sec. 2032A(e)(5)(C), and apparently are not treated as farming for purposes of Code Sec. 1396(d)(2)(E) above.

Termination of employment for purposes of minimum 90-day employment rule. An individual isn't considered a qualified zone employee if the individual is employed by the employer for less than 90 days, see above. This minimum 90-day employment rule doesn't apply to termination of employment if the individual becomes disabled before the close of the 90-day period, unless the disability is removed before that time and the taxpayer fails to offer reemployment to the individual. (Code Sec.1396(d)(3)(A)(i)) Nor does this rule apply to termination of employment if it is determined under the applicable state unemployment compensation law that the termination was due to the misconduct of the individual. (Code Sec. 1396(d)(3)(A)(ii))

Also, the employment relationship between the taxpayer and an employee isn't treated as terminated for purposes of this minimum 90-day employment rule by a transaction to which Code Sec. 381(a) (involving carryover of tax items in the case of the acquisition of the assets of one corporation by another corporation, see FTC 2d/FIN ¶ F-7000 *et seq.;* TG ¶ 2249.1; USTR ¶ 3814.01) applies, if the employee continues to be employed by the acquiring corporation. (Code Sec. 1396(d)(3)(B)(i)) Nor is the employment relationship terminated by reason of a mere change in the form of conducting the trade or business of the taxpayer, if the employee continues to be employed in the trade or business and the taxpayer retains a substantial interest in the trade or business. (Code Sec. 1396(d)(3)(B)(ii))

Controlled groups treated as single employer. To prevent avoidance of the $15,000 limit on qualified zone wages (see above), all employers of a controlled group of corporations (or partnerships or proprietorships under common control) are treated as a single employer. (Conf Rept p. 713) Thus, all employers that are treated as a single employer under Code Sec. 52(a) or (b) (which treats employees of certain employers as employed by the same employer for purposes of the targeted jobs credits, see FTC 2d/FIN ¶ L-17828; TG ¶ 5811; USTR ¶ 514) are also treated as a single employer for purposes of the empowerment zone employment credit. (Code Sec. 1397(b)(1))

If employers are treated as a single employer under this rule, the employment credit (if any) with respect to each employer is its pro rata share of wages giving rise to the credit. (Code Sec. 1397(b)(2))

Empowerment zone employment credit part of general business credit. Several business tax credits are combined into one general business credit for the purpose of applying uniform allowance rules (based on net tax liability limitations) for the tax year. (FTC 2d/FIN ¶ L-15100 *et seq.;* TG ¶ 5700 *et seq.;* USTR ¶ 384 *et seq.*)

The '93 Act adds the new empowerment zone employment credit under Code Sec. 1396(a) to the list of current year business credits that make up the general business credit. (Code Sec. 38(b)(9) as amended by '93 Act § 13302(a)(1))

In general, if part or all of the general business credit can't be used because of the tax liability limitations, the unused business credit can be carried back three years and carried forward 15 years. (FTC 2d/FIN ¶ L-15209 *et seq.;* TG ¶ 5706; USTR ¶ 384.04)

Under the '93 Act, no part of the unused business credit that is attributable to the empowerment zone employment credit under Code Sec. 1396 may be carried to any tax year ending before '94. (Code Sec. 39(d)(4) as amended by '93 Act § 13302(a)(2))

Employer's deduction for wages paid reduced by empowerment zone employment credit Under pre-'93 Act law, an employer's deduction for wages paid for a tax year is reduced by the targeted jobs credit for the year. (FTC 2d/FIN ¶ L-17806; TG ¶ TG-5809; USTR ¶ 514) The '93 Act provides that the employer's deduction for wages paid must also be reduced by the empowerment zone employment credit for the year. (Code Sec. 280C(a) as amended by '93 Act § 13302(b)(1))

> ***observation:*** This requires that the deduction for compensation be reduced by the amount of the empowerment zone employment credit, even if some part (or all) of the credit is "unusable" because it exceeds the allowable general business credit for the year.

Deduction of unused empowerment zone employment credit. As part of the general business credit, the empowerment zone employment credit may be carried back three years (with the exception noted above) and carried forward 15 years. (See FTC 2d/FIN ¶ L-15209 *et seq.;* TG ¶ 5706; USTR ¶ 384.04) A deduction is allowed for certain "qualified business credits" that remain unused at the expiration of the 15-year carryover period. (FTC 2d/FIN ¶ L-15212; TG ¶ 5708; USTR ¶ 394.02) The '93 Act adds the empowerment zone employment credit to the list of qualified business credits that may be deducted if unused. (Code Sec. 196(c) as amended by '93 Act § 13302(b)(2))

☐ **Effective:** Aug. 10, '93. (§ 13303)

For official explanation see Committee Reports ¶ 3069.

¶ 605. Empowerment zone employment credit may offset 25% of minimum tax

Under pre-'93 Act law, in general, the amount of the general business credit which a taxpayer could claim in any year was limited to the excess of the taxpayer's

FTC 2d References are to the Federal Tax Coordinator 2d
FIN References are to RIA's Analysis of Federal Taxes: Income
TG References are to the Tax Guide
USTR References are to the United States Tax Reporter

net income tax over the greater of (i) the tentative minimum tax, or (ii) 25% of so much of the taxpayer's net regular tax liability as exceeded $25,000. The effect of this limitation was that, in general, the general business credit could not offset a taxpayer's liability for the alternative minimum tax. (FTC 2d/FIN ¶ L-15202; TG ¶ 5703; USTR ¶ 384.02)

The '93 Act provides that the rules of Code Sec. 38 dealing with the general business credit (including the limitation discussed above) and the rules governing carrybacks and carryovers of unused tax credits shall apply separately to the "empowerment zone employment credit." (Code Sec. 38(c)(2)(A)(i) as amended by '93 Act § 13302(c)) The limitation on such credit is equal to the excess of the taxpayer's net income tax over the greater of (i) 75% of the tentative minimum tax, or (ii) 25% of so much of the taxpayer's net regular tax liability as exceeds $25,000. (Code Sec. 38(c)(2)(A)(ii)(I)) Such limitation is reduced by the amount of the general business credit other than that portion which is attributable to the empowerment zone employment credit. (Code Sec. 38(c)(2)(A)(ii)(II)) For purposes of the foregoing rules, "empowerment zone employment credit" means that portion of the general business credit which is attributable to the newly-enacted empowerment zone employment credit (see ¶ 604). (Code Sec. 38(c)(2)(B)) The effect of this provision is that the empowerment zone employment credit may be used to offset up to 25% of a taxpayer's alternative minimum tax liability. (H Rept p. 795)

illustration: Taxpayer X, before taking into account any credits, has regular income tax liability of $30,000 and tentative minimum tax of $45,000. Before taking into account the limitations on the general business credit, X has a general business credit (other than the empowerment zone employment credit) of $10,000 and has an empowerment zone employment credit of $8,000. X has no other tax credits.

X's general business credit (other than the empowerment zone employment credit) is limited to the excess of $45,000 (X's net income tax for the year) over the greater of (i) X's tentative minimum tax of $45,000, or (ii) $1,250, which is 25% of the excess of $30,000 (X's regular tax liability) over $25,000. Therefore, no general business credit can be claimed.

With respect to the empowerment zone employment credit, the limitation is separately computed. The limitation is equal to the excess of $45,000 (X's net income tax for the year) over the greater of (i) $33,750, which is 75% of X's tentative minimum tax of $45,000, or (ii) $1,250, which is 25% of the excess of X's regular tax liability of $30,000 over $25,000. Therefore, the limitation is $11,250 ($45,000 less $33,750), and so the entire empowerment zone employment credit of $8,000 can be claimed.

☐ **Effective:** Aug. 10, '93. (§ 13303)

For official explanation see Committee Reports ¶ 3069.

¶ 606. New tax-exempt enterprise zone facility bonds for empowerment zones and enterprise communities

Private activity bonds (i.e., state and local bonds whose proceeds are used for nongovernmental, private purposes) normally don't qualify for tax-exempt status. Tax-exempt status, however, is granted to private activity bonds that are "qualified bonds." Tax-exempt qualified bonds include exempt facility bonds (i.e., bonds whose proceeds are used to finance certain facilities, such as airports, sewage plants, etc.). (FTC 2d/FIN ¶ J-3152 *et seq.;* TG ¶ 5296 *et seq.;* USTR ¶ 1424 *et seq.)* The '93 Act creates a new category of tax-exempt facility bonds—enterprise zone facility bonds.

Enterprise zone facility bonds available for empowerment zones and enterprise communities. Qualified enterprise zone facility bonds, a new category of exempt facility private activity bonds created by the '93 Act, are available for use in areas designated as empowerment zones and enterprise communities (see ¶ 602). (Conf Rept p. 715) The Act provides that for purposes of the rules on tax-exempt state and local bonds, an exempt facility bond includes any bond that is part of an issue, 95% or more whose net proceeds (defined in Code Sec. 150(a)(3), see FTC 2d/FIN ¶ J-3062) are used to provide an enterprise zone facility (defined below). (Code Sec. 1394(a) as added by '93 Act § 13301(a))

These enterprise zone facility bonds may only be issued while an empowerment zone or enterprise community designation is in effect. (Conf Rept p. 715)

Except as discussed below, all tax-exempt bond rules relating to exempt facility bonds (including the restrictions on bank deductibility of interest allocable to tax-exempt bonds, see FTC 2d/FIN ¶ E-3111 *et seq.;* TG ¶ 7782; USTR ¶ 2654) apply to qualified enterprise zone facility bonds. (Conf Rept p. 716)

These bonds are fully subject to the state private activity "volume cap" limitations (which limit the amount of tax-exempt private activity bonds that a state may issue, see FTC 2d/FIN ¶ J-3231 *et seq.;* TG ¶ 5304; USTR ¶ 1464 *et seq.).* (Conf Rept p. 715)

Enterprise zone facility. An enterprise zone facility means qualified zone property (see below) the principal user of which is an enterprise zone business (see below), and any land that is functionally related and subordinate to the qualified zone property. (Code Sec. 1394(b)(1))

Qualified zone property for purposes of enterprise zone facility bond requirements. Qualified zone property has the same meaning for purposes of the enterprise zone facility bond requirements as in Code Sec. 1397C for purposes of the increased Code Sec. 179 expensing election for qualified zone property of an enterprise zone business (see ¶ 603), except that references to empowerment zones in Code Sec. 1397C are treated as including enterprise communities. (Code Sec. 1394(b)(2)) Thus, qualified zone property for tax-exempt financing purposes includes property that would qualify as qualified zone property for purposes of the increased expensing election except for the fact that it is located in an enterprise community rather than an empowerment zone. (Conf Rept p. 715)

Enterprise zone business for purposes of enterprise zone facility bond requirements. Enterprise zone business for purposes of the enterprise zone facility bond requirements has the same meaning as in Code Sec. 1397B for purposes of the increased Code Sec. 179 expensing election for qualified zone property of an enterprise zone business (see ¶ 603), with two exceptions. First, references to empowerment zones in Code Sec. 1397B are treated as including references to enterprise communities. (Code Sec. 1394(b)(3)(A)) Second, enterprise zone business for purposes of the enterprise zone facility bond requirements includes any trades or businesses that would qualify as an enterprise zone business (after taking into account the above modification concerning references to enterprise communities) if the trades or businesses were separately incorporated. (Code Sec. 1394(b)(3)(B)) For example, an establishment that is part of a national chain could qualify as an enterprise zone business for purposes of tax-exempt financing, provided that the establishment would satisfy the definition of an enterprise zone business if it were separately incorporated. (Conf Rept p. 715)

FTC 2d References are to the Federal Tax Coordinator 2d
FIN References are to RIA's Analysis of Federal Taxes: Income
TG References are to the Tax Guide
USTR References are to the United States Tax Reporter

Limitation on amount of the enterprise zone facility bonds. Tax-exempt status doesn't apply to any issue of enterprise zone facility bonds if the aggregate amount of outstanding enterprise zone facility bonds allocable to any person (taking into account such issue) exceeds:

. . . $3,000,000 for any one empowerment zone or enterprise community, (Code Sec. 1394(c)(1)(A)) or

. . . $20,000,000 for all empowerment zones and enterprise communities. (Code Sec. 1394(c)(1)(B))

Thus, the total face amount of all outstanding qualified enterprise zone bonds per qualified enterprise zone business may not exceed $3,000,000 for each zone or community. In addition, total outstanding qualified enterprise zone bond financing for each principal user of these bonds may not exceed $20,000,000 for all zones and communities. (Conf Rept p. 715)

The aggregate amount of outstanding enterprise zone facility bonds allocable to any person is determined under rules similar to the rules in Code Sec. 144(a)(10) (dealing with the limitation on beneficiaries of small issue bonds, see FTC 2d/FIN ¶ J-3218), taking into account only bonds to which tax-exempt status applies. (Code Sec. 1394(c)(2))

As with other exempt facility bonds, these bonds may be issued only to finance identified facilities. The $3,000,000 per enterprise zone business requirement, however, doesn't limit issuance of a single issue of bonds in excess of $3,000,000 for more than one identified facility, provided the $3,000,00 limit is satisfied for each zone business. Ease of marketing these exempt facility bonds may require common marketing of separate issues of bonds for discrete facilities if such issues are simultaneous or proximate in time. (H Rept p. 799)

Exemption from existing property limitations. Certain types of qualified bonds are subject to the existing property limitations of Code Sec. 147(d), which restrict financing the acquisition of existing property. (FTC 2d/FIN ¶ J-3252 *et seq.;* TG ¶ 5305) These limitations don't apply to qualified enterprise zone facility bonds. (Code Sec. 1394(d))

Exemption from land acquisition limitations. Certain types of qualified bonds are subject to land acquisition limitations under Code Sec. 147(c)(1)(A), which restrict financing of land (or an interest in land) with 25% or more of the net proceeds of a bond issue. (FTC 2d/FIN ¶ J-3249 *et seq.;* TG ¶ 5305; USTR ¶ 1474.01) These limitations don't apply to qualified enterprise zone facility bonds. (Code Sec. 1394(d))

Failure to continue as zone business or to use bond-financed property in zone. A change in use of property financed with certain tax-exempt qualified bonds to a use not qualifying for tax-exempt financing may result in loss of income tax deductions for interest. (FTC2d/FIN ¶ J-3151 *et seq.;* TG ¶ 5300 *et seq.;* USTR ¶ 1504.01) The '93 Act extends these change of use rules to qualified enterprise zone facility bonds. (H Rept p. 799)

The Act provides that no deduction is allowed for interest on any financing provided from qualified enterprise zone facility bonds with respect to any facility, to the extent that the interest accrues during the period beginning on the first day of the calendar year which includes the date on which:

(1) substantially all of the facility as to which the financing was provided ceases to be used in an empowerment zone or enterprise community, (Code Sec. 1394(e)(2)(i)) or

(2) the principal user of the facility ceases to be an enterprise zone business, as defined above. (Code Sec. 1394(e)(2)(ii))

The penalty is waived if a good faith rule is satisfied. (H Rept p. 799) Under this rule a bond issue that fails to meet one or more of the requirements under Code Sec. 1394(a) and Code Sec. 1394(b), (see above) for tax-exempt enterprise zone facility bonds is treated as meeting those requirements if the issuer and principal user in good faith attempted to meet the requirements, and any failure to meet the requirements is corrected within a reasonable period after the failure is first discovered. (Code Sec. 1394(e)(1))

These rules don't apply solely by reason of the termination or revocation of a designation as an empowerment zone or an enterprise community. (Code Sec. 1394(e)(3))

Nor do these rules apply to any cessation resulting from bankruptcy. (Code Sec. 1394(e)(4))

☐ **Effective:** Aug 10, '93. (§ 13303)
For official explanation see Committee Reports ¶ 3069.

¶ 607. Empowerment zone and enterprise community items carry over in tax-free reorganizations and liquidations

A corporation which acquires the assets of another corporation in certain tax-free reorganizations and liquidations of subsidiaries inherits certain tax attributes of the transferor or distributor corporation. (See FTC 2d/FIN ¶ F-7000 *et seq.;* TG ¶ 2406 *et seq.;* USTR ¶ 3814 *et seq.)*

The '93 Act expands the list of inherited tax attributes to include certain items related to the newly-enacted empowerment zone and enterprise community provisions. Under regs to be issued, the acquiring/transferee corporation in a reorganization or tax-free subsidiary liquidation shall take into account (to the extent proper to carry out the purposes of Code Sec. 381 (which provides for the carryover of tax attributes in such transactions) and subchapter U (which includes newly-enacted Code Sec. 1391-1397D, see ¶ 601 *et seq.),* the items required to be taken into account for purposes of subchapter U in respect of the transferor or distributor. (Code Sec. 381(c)(26) as amended by '93 Act § 13302(e))

> ***observation:*** The '93 Act does not specify the particular items to be inherited by a transferee corporation. Presumably, such items would include any carryover of the general business credit which is attributable to the empowerment zone employment credit, as well as the ability to deduct any portion of that credit which remains unused at the end of the carryover period.

☐ **Effective:** Aug. 10, '93. (§ 13303)
For official explanation see Committee Reports ¶ 3069.

¶ 608. Tax credit available for contributions to community development corporations

Several incentive tax credits (jobs credit, research credit, etc.) are combined into a single "general business credit" with uniform allowance rules based on a "net tax liability" limitation. (See FTC 2d/FIN ¶ L-15200 *et seq.;* TG ¶ 5700 *et seq.;* USTR

FTC 2d References are to the Federal Tax Coordinator 2d
FIN References are to RIA's Analysis of Federal Taxes: Income
TG References are to the Tax Guide
USTR References are to the United States Tax Reporter

¶ 384.01) This limitation generally means that the general business credit cannot be claimed by taxpayers who are subject to the alternative minimum tax. (See FTC 2d/ FIN ¶ L-15202; TG ¶ 5703; USTR ¶ 384.02)

Under pre-'93 Act law, no tax credit was available for contributions to community development corporations. (H Rept p. 801)

Under the '93 Act, the general business credit includes a credit for qualified contributions to community development corporations (CDCs). The credit equals five percent of the qualified contribution for each tax year during the ten-year period beginning with the tax year in which the contribution was made. (§ 13311(a), (b), (c)) Thus, the taxpayer may claim a total of 50 percent of the contribution during the 10-year credit period. (H Rept p. 801)

> ***illustration:*** In '94, X makes a $10,000 qualified contribution to a CDC. X can take a $500 tax credit for each of the ten years '94-'03, for a total credit of $5,000.

Qualified contributions. A "qualified contribution" is any transfer of cash that meets the following requirements:

(1) it is made to a CDC during the five-year period beginning on the date that it was selected as a CDC;

(2) the amount is available for use by the CDC for at least 10 years;

(3) the CDC is to use the contribution to provide qualified low-income assistance (defined below) within its operational area; and

(4) the CDC designates the contribution as eligible for the credit. (§ 13311(d)(1))

"Qualified low-income assistance" means assistance that (1) is designed to provide employment and business opportunities to low-income individuals who reside in the CDC's operational area and (2) is approved by the secretary of HUD. (§ 13311(f))

The requirement that the contribution be available for use by the CDC for at least 10 years (above) means that a qualified contribution may take the form of a 10-year loan or other long-term investment, the principal of which is to be returned to the taxpayer after the 10-year period. Such a contribution would be eligible for the credit even though it doesn't qualify for the charitable deduction. A taxpayer who makes a cash gift to a CDC that qualifies for the charitable deduction can claim both the deduction and the credit. (H Rept p. 801)

The total amount of contributions that a CDC may designate as eligible for the credit may not exceed $2 million. (§ 13311(d)(2))

Selection of CDCs. The Secretary of HUD may select up to 20 eligible corporations (below) as CDCs, at least eight of which must operate in rural areas (as defined under the rules for empowerment zones and enterprise communities (¶ 602). The selections must be made before July 1, '94. (§ 13311(e)(2))

In selecting CDCs, the Secretary of HUD must give priority to corporations with a demonstrated record of performance in administering community development programs that target at least 75 percent of the jobs emanating from their investment funds to low-income or unemployed individuals. (Conf Rept p. 717)

Eligible corporations. To be eligible for selection as a CDC, a corporation must be a Code Sec. 501(c)(3) tax-exempt organization (i.e., a religious, charitable, scientific, etc., organization) whose principal purposes include promoting employment and business opportunities for individuals who reside in the operational area. (§ 13311(e)(1)) In addition, its operational area must: (1) meet the size requirements that would apply if the area were designated as an empowerment zone or enterprise community; (2) have an unemployment rate not less than the national average; and

(c) have a median family income that does not exceed 80 percent of the median family income of residents within the jurisdiction of the local government. (§ 13311(e)(3))

Credit limitations. Because the credit is part of the general business credit, it is subject to the general business credit limitations. Therefore, it may not be claimed by taxpayers who are subject to the alternative minimum tax. (H Rept p. 802)

> ***observation:*** Presumably, the carryback and carryforward rules that apply to the general business credit (see FTC 2d/FIN ¶ L-15209 *et seq.;* TG ¶ 5706; USTR ¶ 394) likewise apply to the credit for qualified contributions to a CDC.

☐ **Effective:** Aug. 10, '93. (H Rept p. 801)

For official explanation see Committee Reports ¶ 3070.

¶ 609. New 20% credit for employing Indians on reservations after '93 and before year 2004

Pre-'93 Act law provided employers no special tax incentives for employing American Indians except where these individuals were hired as qualifying members of one of nine targeted (generally disadvantaged) groups for whom the employer was eligible for the targeted jobs credit (discussed at ¶ 717). (Conf Rept p. 718)

The '93 Act provides employers an incremental tax credit (referred to as the "Indian employment credit") for hiring certain American Indians who are "qualified employees" (described below). (Conf Rept p. 720)

The Indian employment credit is 20% of the excess, if any, of the sum of "qualified wages" and "qualified employee health insurance costs" (both terms explained below) paid or incurred during the taxable year, (Code Sec. 45A(a)(1) as added by '93 Act § 13322(b)) over the sum of these same costs paid or incurred in calendar year '93—determined as if the Indian employment credit were in effect in '93. (Code Sec. 45A(a)(2))

> ***illustration:*** In '94, X Corp, a calendar year taxpayer located on an Indian reservation employs 20 local, unemployed Indians, qualifying X Corp for the Indian employment credit. X Corp pays each employee wages at the rate of $15,000 per year. For '94, total qualified wages and health insurance costs for these employees were $300,000. If the credit had been available for '93, X Corp's qualified wages and health insurance costs for '93 would have been $200,000. Under these facts, X Corp's Indian employment credit for '94 is $20,000 computed as follows:

'94 qualified costs	$300,000
less: '93 qualified costs	200,000
	$100,000
Credit rate	x 20%
'94 Indian employment credit	$20,000

Summary of key Indian employment credit provisions. The principal features of the post-'93 Indian employment credit (as further explained below) are as follows:

. . . No more than $20,000 of "wages" per year per qualified employee hired after '93 is eligible for the 20% credit. This $20,000 amount is disqualified if it is determined at an annual rate in excess of $30,000 (as adjusted for inflation after '94),

FTC 2d References are to the Federal Tax Coordinator 2d
FIN References are to RIA's Analysis of Federal Taxes: Income
TG References are to the Tax Guide
USTR References are to the United States Tax Reporter

see "Wages and employee health insurance (H-I) costs qualifying for the credit," below.

. . . Employment must be substantially within an Indian reservation and the principal place of abode of the qualified employee must be on or near the reservation, see "Who is a qualified employee," below.

. . . no relative or dependent of the employer, or a 5% or more owner of the employer is a qualified employee, see "No credit for certain qualified employee," below.

. . . The credit is allowed with respect to full-time or part-time qualified employees provided employment is generally for more than one year, see "Duration-of-employment and recapture requirements," below.

. . . The credit is proportionately reduced for a short taxable year, see "Proportionate reduction rule for short taxable years," below.

. . . The credit is a component of the "current year business credit." The credit may not be carried back to a tax year ending before Aug. 10, '93; but a full deduction—as an expense—is allowed for any remaining unused credit after its carryback-carryover period expires, see "Unused credit's carryback and deduction limitations," below.

. . . The credit may not be used to reduce tentative minimum tax, see "Recapture effect on other credits or alternative minimum tax," below.

. . . The credit is scheduled to end for tax years beginning after Dec. 31, 2003. (Code Sec. 45A(f))

Wages and employee health insurance costs qualifying for the credit. Up to $20,000 per year of wages and health insurance (H-I) costs per qualified employee is eligible for the 20% credit for the taxable year. (Code Sec. 45A(b)(3)) This $20,000 amount is nevertheless disqualified if it is determined at an annual rate in excess of $30,000, (Code Sec. 45A(c)(2)) as adjusted for inflation for years beginning after '94. (Code Sec. 45A(c)(3))

Only wages paid or incurred by the employer, (Code Sec. 45A(b)(1)(A)) or any predecessor, (Code Sec. 45A(e)(3)) for services by a "qualified employee" are eligible for the credit. But if any portion of these wages are used to determine the targeted jobs credit, the wages paid to this employee for the tax year don't qualify for the Indian employment credit. (Code Sec. 45A(b)(1)(B))

> ***observation:*** This means that for a year that the targeted jobs credit is in effect (see ¶ 717) an employer must choose between the targeted jobs credit and the Indian employment credit with respect to qualifying wages of an employee who qualifies the employer for both credits. Apportionmnent of qualified wages between the two credits is apparently not permitted by the language of Code Sec. 45A(b)(1)(B), above.
>
> ***observation:*** The maximum Indian employment credit (i.e., 20% of $20,000 or $4,000) exceeds the maximum targeted jobs credit of $2,400 (i.e., 40% of $6,000).

"Wages," under the above rules, has the same meaning as under the targeted jobs credit rules. (Code Sec. 45A(e)(1))

Under the Indian employment credit rules, the phrase "qualified employee health insurance (H-I) costs" means (with one exception) any amount paid or incurred by the employer for H-I coverage of a "qualified employee." (Code Sec. 45A(b)(2)(A))

But, amounts paid for H-I coverage under salary reduction arrangements don't qualify under this rule. (Code Sec. 45A(b)(2)(B))

Income tax deductions for wages and H-I costs used to determine the Indian employment credit must be reduced by the full amount of the credit. (Code Sec. 280C(a) as amended by '93 Act § 13322(c)(1))

Who is a qualified employee? An individual is a qualified employee if all of the following conditions are met:

(1) The individual is an enrolled member of an Indian tribe or the spouse of an enrolled member of an Indian tribe. (Code Sec. 45A(c)(1)(A)) For this purpose, an Indian tribe is any Indian tribe, band, nation, pueblo, or other organized group or community, including any Alaska Native village, or regional or village corporation, as defined in, or established under, the Alaska Native Claims Settlement Act (43 U.S.C. 1601 *et seq.),* as in effect on Aug. 10, '93, which is recognized as eligible for the special programs and services provided by the United States to Indians because of their status as Indians. (Code Sec. 45A(c)(6); Code Sec. 45A(e)(4))

(2) The above employee performs substantially all of the services for the taxable year within an Indian reservation. (Code Sec. 45A(c)(1)(B))

Furthermore, more than 50% of the wages for the tax year paid or incurred by the employer to this employee must be for services performed in a trade or business of the employer. This "more than 50%" rule is applied to each employer who is a member of a controlled group; the rule of Code Sec. 45A(e)(2)—treating all employers who are members of a controlled group as a single employer—doesn't apply for this purpose. (Code Sec. 45A(c)(4))

The term "Indian reservation" is defined in the same way as under the depreciation rules of Code Sec. 168(j)(6), discussed at ¶ 610. (Code Sec. 45A(c)(7))

(3) The employee's principal place of abode while working for the employer is on or near the reservation in which the services are performed. (Code Sec. 45A(c)(1)(C))

(4) The employee began work for the employer on or after Jan. 1, '94. (Conf Rept p. 721)

(5) The total wages for the tax year for the above employee paid or incurred by the employer (whether or not for services within an Indian reservation) may not exceed $30,000 annual rate, per year (Code Sec. 45A(c)(2)) (adjusted for inflation for years beginning after '94). (Code Sec. 45A(c)(3))

> ***observation*** The above rule triggers disqualification when the wage-rate is in excess of $30,000 per year and not whether the employee receives more than $30,000 as wages for that year. In other words, an employee who is paid $3,000 per month (an annualized wage of $36,000) is not a qualified employee, even if the employee works for only six months and receives only $18,000 in wages.

No credit for certain qualified employees. An individual meeting all of the requirements listed above is not a qualified employee if he or she is:

(1) An employee who is a relative or dependent of the employer (determined under the existing targeted jobs credit rules of Code Sec. 51(i)(1)). (Code Sec. 45A(c)(5)(A))

> ***observation:*** Generally, under Code Sec. 51(i)(1) no Indian employment credit is generated by hiring an individual having any of the following relationships to the taxpayer-employer: son, daughter or descendant of either; stepson, stepdaughter; brother, sister, stepbrother or stepsister; father

or mother, or ancestor of either; stepfather, stepmother; son or daughter of brother or sister; brother or sister of father or mother; son-in-law, daughter-in-law, father-in-law, mother-in-law, brother-in-law, or sister-in-law. If the taxpayer is a corporation, a person standing in any of the above relationships to anyone who owns, directly or indirectly, more than 50% in value of its outstanding stock won't qualify. (See FTC 2d/FIN ¶ L-17818; TG ¶ 5806; USTR ¶ 2674)

(2) An employee who owns more than 5% of the stock, capital, or profit interest of the employer. (Code Sec. 45A(c)(5)(B))

(3) An employee whose services: (a) involve conducting class I, II, or III gaming activities as defined in section 4 of the Indian Regulatory Act; i.e., 25 U.S.C. 2703, (Code Sec. 45A(c)(5)(C)) as in effect on Aug. 10, '93; (Code Sec. 45A(e)(4)) or (b) are performed in a building housing the above gaming activities. (Code Sec. 45A(c)(5)(C))

Duration-of-employment and recapture requirements. Generally, no Indian employment credit is allowed for an otherwise qualified employee where the employer, with exceptions described below, terminates the employment before the day one year after the day on which employment began. (Code Sec. 45A(d)(1)(A)) Furthermore, Indian employment credits previously claimed with respect to that employee are recaptured—i.e., added to the tax due for the tax year of employment termination. (Code Sec. 45A(d)(1)(B))

observation: The above pitfalls are avoided by employing the qualified individual for a year and one day.

Where previously claimed credits that must be recaptured under the above rule are included in a carryback-carryover account, a proper adjustment of this account is required for the recaptured credit. (Code Sec. 45A(d)(2))

The above rules apply to termination of full-time and part-time qualified employees. (Conf Rept p. 722)

The disallowance and recapture rules described above don't apply where:

. . . the employee voluntarily terminates the employment; (Code Sec. 45A(d)(3)(A)(i)) or

. . . the employee is terminated because of the employee's misconduct; (Code Sec. 45A(d)(3)(A)(iii)) or

. . . the employee becomes disabled. But, if the disability ends before the close of the one-year period of employment, the employer must offer re-employment to the former employee for the disallowance or recapture rules not to apply. (Code Sec. 45A(d)(3)(A)(ii))

Changes in form of business—Effect on employment relationship. For purposes of the disallowance and recapture rules described above, the employment relationship is not treated as terminated where the employer is acquired by another corporation under the liquidation and reorganization rules of Code Sec. 381(a) and the qualified employee continues to be employed by the acquiring corporation. (Code Sec. 45A(d)(3)(B)(i)) The same is true where the employer undergoes a mere change in the form of conducting the trade or business and: (a) the qualified employee continues to be employed in that trade or business; (b) the pre-form-change employer retains a substantial interest in the post-form-change business. (Code Sec. 45A(d)(3)(B)(ii))

Recapture effect on other credits or alternative minimum tax. Where an employer's tax is increased because the Indian employment credit is recaptured, this increase in tax may not be used in determining any other income tax credit, (Code Sec. 45A(d)(4)(A)) and may not be used in determining the alternative minimum tax. (Code Sec. 45A(d)(4)(B)) This means that the Indian employment credit may not be used to reduce tentative minimum tax. (Conf Rept p. 722)

Businesses under common control as single employer. Members of a controlled group of corporations and businesses under common control are treated as a single employer in determining the Indian employment credit for the group. (Code Sec. 45A(e)(2)(A)) Members share in the credit in proportion to that member's qualified wages and H-I costs giving rise to the credit. (Code Sec. 45A(e)(2)(B))

Credit for loaned employees, successor employers, estates, trusts, cooperatives and other special taxpayers. The rules for the allowance of the Indian employment credit are similar to those under the targeted jobs credit when that credit is determined for qualified employees performing services for others under Code Sec. 51(k)(2) or for the special taxpayers listed below: (Code Sec. 45A(e)(3))

. . . Successor employers under Code Sec. 51(k)(1). Under this rule, (see FTC 2d/FIN ¶ L-17832; TG ¶ 5801; USTR ¶ 514) a successor employer is treated as if it were the predecessor employer in computing the Indian employment credit. (Code Sec. 45A(e)(3))

. . . Loaned employees under Code Sec. 51(k)(2). As in the case of the targeted jobs credit (see FTC 2d/FIN ¶ L-17817; TG ¶ 5801; USTR ¶ 514), an employer who allows a qualified employee to work for another person is entitled to the Indian employment credit for the loaned employee only if the payment received by the employer for the services of the qualified employee exceed the remuneration paid by the employer to the employee. (Code Sec. 45A(e)(3))

. . . Tax-exempt organizations under Code Sec. 52(c).

. . . Estates and trusts under Code Sec. 52(d).

. . . Cooperatives, banks, and regulated investment companies under Code Sec. 52(e). (Code Sec. 45A(e)(3))

> ***observation:*** The special rules of Code Sec. 52(c), (d), and (e) deny the targeted jobs credit to tax-exempt organizations; require a credit allocation between an estate or trust and its beneficiaries; and generally provide a reduced targeted jobs credit for farmers' and other cooperatives, banks, and regulated investment companies. (See FTC 2d/FIN ¶ L-17830 *et seq.;* TG ¶ 5812; USTR ¶ 514)

Proportionate reduction rule for short taxable years. In the case of a short taxable year, the full year's Indian employment credit is reduced by multiplying the credit by a fraction, the numerator of which is the number of days in the short taxable year and the denominator of which is 365. (Code Sec. 45A(e)(5))

> ***caution:*** Code Sec. 45A(e)(5), above, reduces the Indian employment credit as that credit is "determined under subsection (a)(2) . . ." This appears to be a drafting error. The entire "subsection (a)" was presumably intended since "subsection (a)(2) . . ." is only a part of the entire rule for determining the credit amount.

> ***observation:*** The language of the above rule in the Senate Finance bill and the Finance Committee's explanation of that rule makes it clear that

qualified wages and H-I costs for the short tax year are first annualized, then the credit rate is applied, and then prorated for the number of days in the short year by the above short year's fraction. Presumably, IRS will issue guidelines for the application of Code Sec. 45A(e)(5), above.

Unused credit's carryback and deduction limitations. The Indian employment credit, is a component of the general business credit. (Code Sec. 38(b)(10) as amended by $93 Act § 13322(a)) As one of several business tax credits subject to the allowance limitations of the general business credit under Code Sec. 38, the Indian employment credit may not be allowed in full in the year earned. Under the business credit carryback-carryover rules of Code Sec. 39, applicable to the general business credit (see FTC 2d/FIN ¶ L-15209 *et seq.;* TG ¶ 5706; USTR ¶ 394), no portion of the Indian employment credit that is included in the unused business credit amount for the tax year may be carried back to a tax year ending before Aug. 10, '93. (Code Sec. 39(d)(5) as amended by '93 Act § 13322(d))

A full deduction is allowed for any Indian employment credit remaining unused after the carryback-carryover period expires. (Code Sec. 196(c) as amended by '93 Act § 13322(c)(2))

☐ **Effective:** For wages paid or incurred after Dec. 13, '93, (§ 13322(f)) in tax years ending before year 2004. (Code Sec. 45A(f))

For official explanation see Committee Reports ¶ 3071A.

¶ 610. Shorter MACRS depreciation periods for Indian reservation property placed in service after '93 and before year 2004

The depreciation rules under pre-'93 Act law provided no special treatment for otherwise depreciable tangible property used in a trade or business located within an Indian reservation. Thus, this property was depreciable only to the extent allowed by depreciation Code Sec. 168, generally referred to as "MACRS." (See FTC 2d/FIN ¶ L-7401 *et seq.;* TG ¶ 5400 *et seq.;* USTR ¶ 1684)

The '93 Act shortens the applicable depreciation period under the general (i.e., accelerated) depreciation system of Code Sec. 168 for each class of MACRS property—except for 27.5-year residential rental property and 50-year railroad property—that is "qualified Indian reservation property" (described below). (Code Sec. 168(j) as amended by '93 Act § 13321(a))

The shortened (i.e., accelerated) depreciation periods for "qualified Indian reservation property" are as follows: (Code Sec. 168(j)(2))

In the case of:	*The applicable recovery period is:*
3-year property . . .	2 years
5-year property . . .	3 years
7-year property . . .	4 years
10-year property . . .	6 years
15-year property . . .	9 years
20-year property . . .	12 years
Nonresidential real property . . .	22 years

In determining alternative minimum taxable income under the Alternative Minimum Tax (AMT) rules of Code Sec. 55 (see FTC 2d/FIN ¶ A-8100 *et seq.;* TG ¶ 1350 *et seq.;* USTR ¶ 554 *et seq.)* The above shortened depreciation periods apply, and the depreciation adjustment rules of Code Sec. 56 do not apply. (Code Sec. 168(j)(3))

observation: As a result, depreciation with respect to qualified Indian reservation property is not a tax preference item for purposes of the AMT.

The above liberalized depreciation periods are scheduled to end for qualified property placed in service after Dec. 31, 2003. (Code Sec. 168(j)(8))

What is qualified Indian reservation property? This is MACRS property included in the table of shortened depreciation periods described above and used by the taxpayer predominantly in the active conduct of a trade or business within an Indian reservation. (Code Sec. 168(j)(4)(A)(i)) The rental of real property located within a reservation is treated as an active trade or business under this provision. (Code Sec. 168(j)(5))

> ***observation:*** Residential rental property in the 27.5-year class apparently gets no benefit under this rule since this new Code provision fails to provide a shortened depreciation period for this activity.

The term "Indian reservation" means, for purposes of the above rules, a reservation as defined in either of two non-Code statutes; namely:

(1) Section 3(d) of the '74 Indian Financing Act, 25 U.S.C. 1452(d), (Code Sec. 168(j)(6)(A)) as in effect on Aug. 10, '93, (Code Sec. 168(j)(7)) or

(2) Section 4(10) of the '78 Indian Child Welfare Act; 25 U.S.C. 1903(10), (Code Sec. 168(j)(6)(B)) as in effect on Aug. 10, '93. (Code Sec. 168(j)(7))

Qualified Indian reservation property does not include the following otherwise depreciable property:

(1) Property used or located outside the Indian reservation on a regular basis. (Code Sec. 168(j)(4)(A)(ii)) But, as explained below, certain infrastructure property does qualify even if it is located outside the Indian reservation.

(2) Property acquired directly or indirectly by the taxpayer from a person who is related to the taxpayer under the at-risk loss-deduction limitation rules of Code Sec. 456(b)(3)(C). (Code Sec. 168(j)(4)(A)(iii)).

> ***observation:*** A person is related to the taxpayer under the at-risk, loss-deduction limitation rules if:
>
> (a) the relationship is described in Code Sec. 267(b) (disallowing the deduction of accrued expenses payable to related cash basis taxpayer), or Code Sec. 707(b)(1) (disallowing losses on sales of property with respect to a controlled partnership), except that in applying these rules, a 10% ownership test is used instead of 50%; or
>
> (b) they are engaged in trades or business under common control as defined in Code Sec. 52(a) and (b) (dealing with the targeted jobs credit. (See FTC 2d/FIN ¶ M-4543; TG ¶ 2670 *et seq.;* USTR ¶ 4654)

(3) Property placed in service for purposes of conducting or housing class I, II, or III gaming activities as defined in section 4 of the Indian Regulatory Act i.e., 25 U.S.C. 2703, (Code Sec. 168(j)(4)(A)(iv)) as in effect on Aug. 10, '93. (Code Sec. 168(j)(7))

(4) Property depreciable only under the MACRS straight-line Alternative Depreciation System of Code Sec. 168(j). But property for which the taxpayer may elect the straight-line Alternative Depreciation System or listed property required to be depreciated under the straight-line Alternative Depreciation System because its business use falls to 50% or less for the tax year is not excluded from the definition of qualified Indian reservation property. (Code Sec. 168(j)(4)(B))

Off-reservation infrastructure property qualifying as Indian reservation property. Where infrastructure property (such as, roads, power lines, water systems, railroad spurs, communication facilities, etc.) is located outside an Indian reservation, it is

---

FTC 2d References are to the Federal Tax Coordinator 2d
FIN References are to RIA's Analysis of Federal Taxes: Income
TG References are to the Tax Guide
USTR References are to the United States Tax Reporter

nevertheless "qualified Indian reservation property" (as defined above) if its purpose is to connect with qualified infrastructure property located within the reservation, (Code Sec. 168(j)(4)(C)(i)) and meets all of the following conditions:

. . . It benefits the tribal infrastructure; (Code Sec. 168(j)(4)(C)(ii)(I))

. . . It is available to the general public; (Code Sec. 168(j)(4)(C)(ii)(II))

. . . It is placed in service in connection with the taxpayer's active conduct of a trade or business within an Indian reservation; (Code Sec. 168(j)(4)(C)(ii)(III)) and

. . . It is depreciable under MACRS. (Conf Rept p. 723)

☐ **Effective:** For property placed in service after Dec. 31, '93 (§ 13321(b)) and before Dec. 31, 2003. (Code Sec. 168(j)(8))

For official explanation see Committee Reports ¶ 3071.

¶ 700. Small Business and Other Investment Incentives

¶ 701. Expense-election amount increased to $17,500

Pre-'93 Act law allowed taxpayers—except estates trusts, and certain noncorporate lessors—to elect to deduct as an expense, rather than to depreciate, up to $10,000 of the cost of purchased new or used tangible personal property placed in service during the taxable year in an active trade or business of the taxpayer. Property used for the production of income not in a trade or business didn't qualify. (FTC 2d/FIN ¶ L-7960 *et seq.;* TG ¶ 5490 *et seq.;* USTR ¶ 1794 *et seq.)*

The '93 Act raises the ceiling for the annual expense-election amount from $10,000 to $17,500. (Code Sec. 179(b)(1) as amended by '93 Act § 13116(a))

☐ **Effective:** For tax years beginning after Dec. 31, '92 (§ 13116(b))
For official explanation see Committee Reports ¶ 3008.

¶ 702. 50% exclusion for gain from certain small business stock

In order to encourage the flow of capital to small businesses, many of which have difficulty attracting equity financing (H Rept p. 600), the '93 Act permits noncorporate taxpayers to exclude 50% of any gain realized on the sale or exchange of "qualified small business stock" ("QSBS") held for more than 5 years (Code Sec. 1202(a) as added by '93 Act § 13113(a)), subject to certain limitations and special rules discussed below.

For a special application of the this rule where the stock is owned by a pass-thru entity, see "Stock owned by pass-thru entities," below.

Dollar amount limitation on eligible gain. For each taxable year of the investor, with respect to each corporation in which he invests, the amount of gain eligible for the 50% exclusion may not exceed the following amounts: (Code Sec. 1202(b)(1))

(1) Except in the case of married individuals filing separate returns: the greater of (a) $10 million, less the amount of eligible gain (as defined below) taken into account under these rules by the taxpayer with respect to dispositions of stock issued by that corporation in an earlier year (Code Sec. 1202(b)(1)(A)), or (b) 10 times the taxpayer's adjusted basis in the stock of that corporation (Code Sec. 1202(b)(1)(B)), subject to the "Special stock basis rules" discussed below.

(2) In the case of married individuals filing separate returns: the same rule as above, except with $5 million substituted for $10 million. (Code Sec. 1202 (b)(3)(A))

The amount of gain that qualifies for the exclusion is allocated equally between spouses who file a joint return, for purposes of applying this limitation to later tax years. (Code Sec. 1202(b)(3)(B)) Marital status for purposes of this rule and the above rules is determined under the rules of Code Sec. 7703 (Code Sec. 1202(b)(3)(C)), i.e., the rules that apply for determining filing status. (See FTC 2d/FIN ¶ A-1600; TG ¶ 1118; USTR ¶ 77,034 *et seq.*)

"Eligible gain," for these purposes, is gain on the sale or exchange of QSBS held for more than 5 years. (Code Sec. 1202(b)(2))

Special stock basis rules. For purposes of the rule at (1)(b) above, the adjusted basis of the stock is determined:

FTC 2d References are to the Federal Tax Coordinator 2d
FIN References are to RIA's Analysis of Federal Taxes: Income
TG References are to the Tax Guide
USTR References are to the United States Tax Reporter

. . . without regard to any addition to its basis after the date on which the stock was originally issued (Code Sec. 1202(b)(1))

> ***observation:*** In order to understand the logic of this rule, it is necessary to know that stock that qualifies for the exclusion must generally have been acquired by the taxpayer at its original issue. See "Circumstances under which stock must be acquired," under "Qualified Small Business Stock," below.

and

. . . by valuing any contributed property at its fair market value on the date of the contribution. (Conf Rept p. 527)

> ***observation:*** It would appear that the above Conference Report rule means that where the calculation of an investor's basis in his stock involves a dollar amount associated with property contributed to the corporation, for purposes of the rule at (1)(b) above, that dollar amount would be the fair market value of the property on the date of the contribution.

> ***illustration:*** Contributions to corporations in exchange for its stock, that qualify under Code Sec. 351, result in the transferor receiving a basis in the stock that is calculated by using the *basis* , not the *fair market value* , of the property transferred. (See FTC 2d/FIN ¶ F-1801; TG ¶ 2326; USTR ¶ 3514 *et seq.*) However, for purposes of the rule at (1)(b) above, the basis of stock received in a Code Sec. 351 transaction is computed by taking into consideration the fair market value of the property he contributed.

Other rules. For a special application of the above rules where the stock is owned by a pass-thru entity, see "Stock owned by pass-thru entities," below. For other limitations on the amount of gain eligible for the exclusion, see "Other limitations on the gain eligible for exclusion," below.

Qualified small business stock. In order for stock held by a taxpayer to qualify as QSBS, the following requirements must be met.

Circumstances under which stock must be acquired. Except as provided below under "Certain tax-free and other transfers . . . " and "Rules that apply to stock acquired via options . . .," the stock must be acquired by the taxpayer at its original issue, either directly or through an underwriter. (Code Sec. 1202(c)(1)(B)) It must be acquired in exchange for money or other property (but not stock) (Code Sec. 1202(c)(1)(B)(i)), or as compensation for services provided to the issuing corporation, other than services performed as an underwriter of the stock. (Code Sec. 1202(c)(1)(B)(ii))

In order to prevent evasion of the requirement that the stock be newly issued (H Rept p. 600), the Act provides that stock is not QSBS if the issuing corporation either:

. . . directly or indirectly purchases any of its stock from the shareholder, or from a person related to the taxpayer, anytime during the period that begins two years before the issuance of the stock and ends two years after the issuance. For this purpose, a related party is one who is considered related either under Code Sec. 267(b) (see FTC 2d/FIN ¶ G-2657; TG ¶ 2651; USTR ¶ 2674) or under Code Sec. 707(b) (see FTC 2d/FIN ¶ B-2016; TG ¶ 1643; USTR ¶ 7074 *et seq.*) (Code Sec. 1202(c)(3)(A))

or

. . . during the two-year period that begins on the date one year before the issuance of the stock, made purchases of its own stock that in the aggregate were more than

5% of the value of its stock as of the beginning of that two-year period. For this purpose, the value of stock purchased is determined as of the date of that purchase. (Code Sec. 1202(c)(3)(A))

For purposes of these two anti-evasion rules, the corporation is considered to have purchased an amount of stock equal to the amount of stock, if any, that is treated as a redemption under the redemption-through-related-corporations rule of Code Sec. 304(a). (See FTC 2d/FIN ¶ F-11800 *et seq.;* TG ¶ 2341 *et seq.;* USTR ¶ 3044 *et seq.)* (Code Sec. 1202(c)(3)(B))

Types of corporations whose stock may be QSBS.

(1) *At the date of its issuance of the stock* (Code Sec. 1202(c)(1)(A)), the corporation must be a domestic C corporation. (Code Sec. 1202(d)(1))

(2) *During substantially all of the taxpayer's holding period of the stock,* the corporation must be a C corporation (Code Sec. 1202(c)(2)(A)) that is an "eligible corporation." (Code Sec. 1202(e)(1)(B)) An eligible corporation is a domestic corporation *other than:*

. . . a DISC or former DISC,

. . . a corporation with respect to which an election under Code Sec. 936 is in effect or that has a direct or indirect subsidiary with respect to which such an election is in effect. (The Code Sec. 936 election allows corporations a credit with respect to certain income derived from U.S. possessions; see FTC 2d/FIN ¶ O-1500 *et seq.;* TG ¶ 8135 *et seq.;* USTR ¶ 9314.06) (Code Sec. 1202(e)(4))

> ***observation:*** The term "direct or indirect subsidiary" isn't defined by the Act.

. . . a regulated investment company, a real estate investment trust, a REMIC or a cooperative. (Code Sec. 1202(e)(4))

> ***caution:*** It is reasonably common for start-up businesses to initially elect to be S corporations, principally so that they can pass through to their shareholders losses that they anticipate incurring in their early years of operation. However, the decision to make that election should be reexamined if the shareholders anticipate taking advantage of the 50% exclusion; if the S corporation results in the corporation not being a C corporation during "substantially all" of a given shareholder's holding period for the stock, the 50% election will not be available to that shareholder.

Unfortunately, Congress has not given any indication as to what will be considered "substantially all" of a shareholder's holding period, for this purpose.

(3) *At the date the stock is sold or exchanged,* the corporation must be a C corporation. (Code Sec. 1202(c)(1))

Active business requirement. During substantially all of the taxpayer's holding period for the stock, at least 80% of the value of the corporation's assets must be used by the corporation in the active conduct of one or more "qualified trades or businesses" ("QTOBs"). (Code Sec. 1202(e)(1)(A))

A QTOB is any trade or business *other than:*

. . . one involving the performance of services in the fields of health, law,

FTC 2d References are to the Federal Tax Coordinator 2d
FIN References are to RIA's Analysis of Federal Taxes: Income
TG References are to the Tax Guide
USTR References are to the United States Tax Reporter

engineering, architecture, accounting, actuarial science, performing arts, consulting, athletics, financial services, brokerage services; (Code Sec. 1202(e)(3)(A))

. . . one where the principal asset of the trade or business is the reputation or skill of one or more of its employees; (Code Sec. 1202(e)(3)(A))

> ***observation:*** Note that while the two immediately preceding phrases are both contained in Code Sec. 1202(e)(3)(A), the first is limited to service businesses, while the second is not so limited.

> ***observation:*** Other than in the preceding phrase, there is no instance in which either the Code or the regs use the term "principal asset" in the context of an intangible human quality like "reputation" or "skill." And, the Congressional Committee reports to the Act do not add any insight as to Congress's intent with respect to this language. Thus, it is quite unclear which trades or businesses will fail this test for treatment as a QTOB as a result of this language, or which more-specific characteristics of any given trade or business are indicative of it failing this test.

. . . any banking, insurance, financing, leasing, investing, or similar business (Code Sec. 1202(e)(3)(B)); any farming business, including the business of raising or harvesting trees (Code Sec. 1202(e)(3)(C)); any business involving the production or extraction of products of a character for which percentage depletion is allowable (see FTC 2d/FIN ¶s N-2300 *et seq.,* N-2400 *et seq.;* TG ¶ 7665 *et seq.);* USTR ¶ 6134 *et seq.,* 6134A *et seq.)* (Code Sec. 1202(e)(3)(D)); and any business of operating a hotel, motel, restaurant or similar business. (Code Sec. 1202(e)(3)(E))

The following are treated as used in the active conduct of a QTOB:

(1) Assets used in certain activities with respect to *future* QTOBs, without regard to whether the corporation has any gross income from these activities at the time this rule is applied. Those activities are (a) start-up activities described in Code Sec. 195(c)(1)(A) (see FTC 2d/FIN ¶ L-5009; TG ¶ 6193; USTR ¶ 1954 *et seq.*); (b) activities that result in the payment or incurrence of expenditures that qualify as research and experimental expenditures under the rules of Code Sec. 174 (see FTC 2d/FIN ¶ L-3101; TG ¶ 6254; USTR ¶ 1744 *et seq.*); and (c) activities with respect to in-house research expenses (see FTC 2d/FIN ¶ L-15411; TG ¶ 5836; USTR ¶ 414 *et seq.*). (Code Sec. 1202(e)(2))

(2) Assets held to meet the reasonably required working capital needs of a QTOB (Code Sec. 1202(e)(6)(A)) and assets held for investment that are reasonably expected to be used within two years to finance research and experimentation in a QTOB or to finance increases in working capital needs of a QTOB. (Code Sec. 1202(e)(6)(B)) But, after the corporation has been in existence for at least two years, no more than 50% of its assets may qualify as being used in the active conduct of a QTOB by reason of the rules in the immediately preceding sentence. (Code Sec. 1202(e)(6))

> ***observation:*** Reg § 1.537-2(b)(4) provides that earnings and profits accumulated "to provide necessary working capital" for a business are not subject to the accumulated earnings tax. (See FTC 2d/FIN ¶ D-2840; TG ¶ 2159; USTR ¶ 5374) And a formula has been developed under case law, the *Bardahl* formula, for calculating "necessary working capital." (See FTC 2d/FIN ¶ D-2840; TG ¶ 2160; USTR ¶ 5374) Although Congress has not indicated that these rules have application for purposes of computing "reasonably required working capital needs" for purposes of the above rule, and the language in the Act is not identical to that in the reg, it would appear that the reg, and other rules that have been developed to interpret the reg, including the *Bardahl* formula, would have application for purposes of computing "reasonably required working capital needs."

(3) The rights to computer software which produces active business computer software royalties (as defined in Code Sec. 543(d)(1), see FTC 2d/FIN ¶ D-3547 *et seq.;* TG ¶ 2194; USTR ¶ 5434.10). (Code Sec. 1202(e)(8))

> ***observation:*** As indicated above, the assets described at (1)-(3) above are *treated* as used in the active conduct of a QTOB. Of course, assets that are *actually* used in the active conduct of a QTOB are also treated as so used.

But, except as provided in the paragraph that begins "Notwithstanding" below (Code Sec. 1202(c)(2)(B)(i)), a corporation will be treated as failing to meet the active business requirement for any period during which:

. . . more than 10% of the value of its assets in excess of its liabilities consists of stock or securities in other corporations which are not subsidiaries of the corporation, other than working capital assets described at (2) above. (Code Sec. 1202(e)(5)(B)) and/or

. . . more than 10% of the total value of its assets consists of real property which is not used in the active conduct of a QTOB. For this purpose, the ownership of, dealing in, or renting of real property is not considered to be active conduct of a QTOB. (Code Sec. 1202(e)(7))

Where a corporation ("parent") owns more than 50% of the combined voting power of all classes of voting stock of another corporation ("sub"), or it owns more than 50% of the value of all the outstanding stock of the sub (Code Sec. 1202(e)(5)(C)), the parent is treated as owning its ratable share of the sub's assets and as conducting its ratable share of the sub's activities. (Code Sec. 1202(e)(5)A)) The parent's ratable share is based on the percentage of outstanding stock that it owns, determined on the basis of value. (Conf Rept p. 527)

Without regard to any of the above "Active business requirement" rules, a corporation will be treated as meeting the active business requirement for any period during which it is a specialized small business investment company ("SSBIC"). (Code Sec. 1202(c)(2)(B)(i)) For this purpose, an SSBIC is defined the same way that it is under new Code Sec. 1044 (see ¶ 704), except that it must also be an "eligible corporation," as that term is defined under "Types of corporations whose stock can be QSBS," above. (Code Sec. 1202(c)(2)(B)(ii))

Gross asset limitation. At all times during the period that begins with Aug. 10, '93 (Code Sec. 1202(d)(1)(A)) and ends immediately after the issuance of the stock, the corporation must have aggregate gross assets (as defined below) that do not exceed $50 million. For this purpose, amounts received in the issuance are taken into account. (Code Sec. 1202(d)(1)(B))

If a corporation satisfies this gross assets test as of the date of issuance but later exceeds the $50 million threshold, stock that otherwise constitutes QSBS does not lose that character solely because of that later event. (H Rept p. 602) But if a corporation or a predecessor corporation exceeds the $50 million threshold at any time after Aug. 10, '93, the corporation can never again issue QSBS. (H Rept p. 602; § 13113(e))

"Aggregate gross assets" means the sum of cash and the adjusted bases of other property held by the corporation. (Code Sec. 1202(d)(2)(A)) For this purpose, the adjusted basis of any property contributed to the corporation, and of any property whose basis is determined in whole or in part by reference to the adjusted basis of property so contributed, is determined by treating the basis of the contributed property immediately after the contribution as equal to its fair market value at that time. (Code Sec. 1202(d)(2)(B))

All corporations that are part of a "parent-subsidiary controlled group" are treated as one corporation for purposes of the gross assets test. (Code Sec. 1202(d)(3)(A)) For this purpose, the term "parent-subsidiary controlled group" has the same meaning as it does for purposes of the controlled group rules (see FTC 2d/FIN ¶ E-10701; TG ¶ 2441; USTR ¶ 15,634), except that (a) "more than 50%" is substituted for "at least 80%" in each place that the latter appears in those rules and (b) the rule under which life insurance companies are treated as members of separate controlled groups (see FTC 2d/FIN ¶ E-10720; TG ¶ 2441; USTR ¶ 15,634) doesn't apply. (Code Sec. 1202(d)(3)(B))

Reports to IRS and shareholders. The corporation that issued the stock must submit to IRS and to the corporation's shareholders any reports that IRS requires to carry out the purposes of any of the rules that pertain to the 50%-exclusion. (Code Sec. 1202(d)(1)(C))

Stock owned by pass-thru entities. Subject to the rule in the paragraph below that begins "However, the rules in the . . .":

(1) Gain from the disposition of stock by a partnership, S corporation, regulated investment company or common trust fund (a "pass-thru entity", Code Sec. 1202(g)(4)), that is included in the gross income (Code Sec. 1202(g)(1)) of a partner, shareholder or participant other than a C Corporation (H Rept p. 602) (a "participant") by reason of his holding an interest in the pass-thru entity, is eligible for the exclusion (Code Sec. 1202(g)(1)(A)) if the following requirements are met: (Code Sec. 1202(g)(1))

. . . the stock is QSBS in the hands of the entity, determined by treating the entity as an individual;

. . . the entity held the stock for more than 5 years; (Code Sec. 1202(g)(2)(A))

. . . the participant held the interest, with respect to which the gain is includible in his income, on the date on which the entity acquired the stock and at all times thereafter until the entity disposed of the stock. (Code Sec. 1202(g)(2)(B))

(2) Where each of the three requirements listed immediately above is met, the rules under "Dollar amount limitation on eligible gain", above, are applied to the participant in the following manner, with respect to the disposition of stock by the pass-thru entity: (a) the pass-thru gain is treated as gain from a disposition of stock in the corporation; and (b) for purposes of the 10-times-adjusted-basis rule (under "Dollar amount limitation on eligible gain," above), the participant's proportionate share of the pass-thru entity's adjusted basis in the stock is taken into account. (Code Sec. 1202(g)(1)(B))

> ***observation:*** The rule at (2)(b) above means that the participant's pro rata share of the entity's basis in the stock is treated as if it were the participant's basis in the stock.

However, the rules described at (1) and (2) immediately above don't apply to the extent that an amount determined under those rules exceeds the amount that would have been determined under those rules if they were applied by reference to the participant's interest in the entity on the date the entity acquired the stock. (Code Sec. 1202(g)(3))

> ***illustration:*** On Jan. 1, Year 1, individual I was a 25% partner in the P partnership. On that day, P purchased stock in Corporation C for $1 million.

On Jan. 1, Year 6, I is a 40% partner in P, and P sells all of its C stock, for $1.5 million. If the stock is QSBS, the amount of I's gain that is eligible for exclusion (before consideration of the dollar amount limitation), and the amount that is taken into consideration for purposes of the $10 million limitation is $125,000, i.e., 25% of P's $500,000 gain. The adjusted basis that is used for purposes of the 10-times-adjusted basis limitation is $250,000, i.e., 25% of P's $1 million basis.

Other limitations on the gain that is eligible for exclusion. In addition to the "Dollar amount limitation on eligible gain" discussed above, the following limitations apply to the amount of gain that is eligible for the exclusion:

Where taxpayer contributed property to the corporation. For purposes of all the rules in this article (§ 13113), (Code Sec. 1202(i))

(1) Where the taxpayer transferred property other than money or stock to the corporation in exchange for the corporation's stock, (a) the stock is treated as having been acquired by the taxpayer on the date of the exchange; (Code Sec. 1202(i)((1)(A)) and (b) the basis of the stock is treated as being no less than the fair market value of the property exchanged. (Code Sec. 1202(i)(1)(B))

(2) Where the taxpayer made a contribution to capital after the date on which QSBS was issued, for purposes of determining any resulting adjustment to the stock's adjusted basis, the basis of the contributed property is treated as being no less than its fair market value on the date of the contribution. (Code Sec. 1202(i)(2))

The effect of (1)(a) and (2) above is to limit the gain eligible for exclusion to gains that accrue after the property is transferred to the corporation. (H Rept p. 603)

Where taxpayer or a related party takes certain short positions in the stock. A taxpayer may not exclude gain from the sale of QSBS if he held an "offsetting short position" with respect to the stock anytime *before* the five-year holding period requirement is satisfied. And, in order for his gain on QSBS to be eligible for exclusion, in cases in which he acquires the offsetting short position *after* the five-year holding period is satisfied, the taxpayer must elect to treat the acquisition of the offsetting short position as a sale of the QSBS at its fair market value on the day of that acquisition. (Code Sec. 1202(j)(1))

A taxpayer has an offsetting short position with respect to any QSBS if he or a related party (as defined below) has either (Code Sec. 1202(j)(2)):

. . . made a short sale of property that is substantially identical to the QSBS. (Code Sec. 1202(j)(2)(A)) Writing a call option that the holder is more likely than not to exercise, or selling the stock for future delivery, qualify under this provision; (H Rept p. 603)

. . . acquired an option to sell substantially identical property at a fixed price; (Code Sec. 1202(j)(2)(B))
or

. . . to the extent provided in regulations, entered into any other transaction which substantially reduces the risk of loss from holding the QSBS. (Code Sec. 1202(j)(2)(C))

For this purpose, a related party is one who is considered related either under

Code Sec. 267(b) (See FTC 2d/FIN ¶ G-2657; TG ¶ 2651; USTR ¶ 2674) or under Code Sec. 707(b). (See FTC 2d/FIN ¶ B-2016; TG ¶ 1643; USTR ¶ 7074 *et seq.*) (Code Sec. 1202(j)(2))

Certain tax-free and other transfers subject to special rules. *Gifts and bequests.* If stock is transferred by gift (Code Sec. 1202(h)(2)(A)) or at death (Code Sec. 1202(h)(2)(B)), then, for purposes of all the rules in this article (§ 13113) (Code Sec. 1202(h)), the transferee is treated:

. . . as having acquired the stock in the same manner as the transferor (Code Sec. 1202(h)(1)(A)) and

. . . as having held the stock during any continuous period that immediately preceded the transfer and during which it was held by the transferor or treated as having been so held under any of the rules described under "Certain tax-free and other transfers . . . ." (Code Sec. 1202(h)(1)(B))

Transfers from partnerships to partners. The rules for gifts and bequests described above also apply to transfers from partnerships to partners, but only if requirements that are similar to those described at "Stock owned by pass-thru entities" above, except the 5-year holding period requirement described there, are met at the time of the transfer. (Code Sec. 1202(h)(2)(C)) Thus, at the time of the transfer, (a) the stock must have been QSBS in the hands of the partnership; and (b) the partner must have held the interest (with respect to which the gain is includible in his income) on the date on which the partnership acquired the stock and at all times thereafter until the partnership disposed of the stock. In addition, a partner may not treat stock distributed by a partnership as QSBS to the extent that his share of the stock distributed by the partnership exceeded his interest in the partnership at the time the partnership acquired the stock. (H Rept p. 602)

> ***observation:*** The provision contained in the immediately preceding sentence applies a rule that is similar to the rule of Code Sec. 1202(g)(3), which is discussed under "Stock owned by pass-thru entities," above.

Recapitalizations, name changes. Under pre-'93 Act law that was not changed by the Act, a loss with respect to an investment in "Section 1244 stock" is treated as an ordinary loss up to certain dollar limits. (See FTC 2d/FIN ¶ I-6200; TG ¶ 4301; USTR ¶ 12,444 *et seq.*) Just as is the case with respect to QSBS, in order to qualify as Section 1244 stock, (a) the corporation must meet certain size requirements at a particular point in time (see FTC 2d/FIN ¶ I-6219; TG ¶ 4306; USTR ¶ 12,444.04), (b) the stock must have been issued for money or property other than stock or securities, (see FTC 2d/FIN ¶ I-6212; TG ¶ 4305; USTR ¶ 12,444.03) and (c) the corporation is subject to an active business requirement that it must meet for a significant period of time before the sale or exchange. (See FTC 2d/FIN ¶ I-6225; TG ¶ 4307; USTR ¶ 12,444.03)

Code Sec. 1244(d)(2) provides that, to the extent prescribed in regs:

. . . If a shareholder owns stock in a corporation ("stock A"), his basis in that stock is determined in whole or in part by reference to his basis in other stock of that corporation, and that other stock meets the requirements described at (a) and (b) above, then stock A is also treated as meeting those requirements.

. . . If a shareholder owns stock ("stock A") that he received in an F reorganization (mere change of identity, name, or place of organization, see FTC 2d/FIN ¶ F-9100 *et seq.;* TG ¶ 2297; USTR ¶ 3684.06) in exchange for stock that meets the requirements described at (a) and (b) above, then stock A is treated as also meeting those tests.

. . . For purposes of (a) and (c) above, a successor corporation in an F reorganization is treated as the same corporation as its predecessor. (See FTC 2d/FIN ¶ I-6214 *et seq.;* TG ¶ 4306)

The '93 Act provides that rules similar to the rules of Code Sec. 1244(d)(2) apply for purposes of the 50% exclusion of gain on the sale of QSBS. (Code Sec. 1202(h)(3))

Incorporations and reorganizations involving non-QSBS. Where a taxpayer transfers QSBS to a corporation that he controls, in a Code Sec. 351 transaction (See FTC 2d/FIN ¶ F-1100 *et seq.;* TG ¶ 2250 *et seq.;* USTR ¶ 3514 *et seq.*), or transfers QSBS in a Code Sec. 368 reorganization (See FTC 2d/FIN ¶ F-4000 *et seq.;* TG ¶ 2275 *et seq.;* USTR ¶ 3684 *et seq.*), and he receives in exchange stock that does not qualify as QSBS, the stock received in exchange will nevertheless be treated as QSBS, subject to the following rule: (Code Sec. 1202(h)(4)(A)) If the transfer is made in a Code Sec. 351 transaction, then, immediately after the transaction, the corporation that issued the stock received in the exchange must directly or indirectly own stock representing control of the corporation that issued the original stock. For this purposes, "control" means ownership of stock possessing at least 80% of the total combined voting power and ownership of at least 80% of the total number of shares of all other classes of stock. (Code Sec. 1202(h)(4)(D))

The following special rules apply to stock treated as QSBS under this rule:

. . . The holding period of the original stock is added to that of the stock received. (Code Sec. 1202(h)(4)(A))

. . . Except as provided in the following sentence, gain eligible for the 50% exclusion is limited to the amount of gain that would have been recognized at the time of the transfer described above, had Code Sec. 351 or Code Sec. 368 not applied at that time. This rule doesn't apply if, at the time of the transfer, the corporation issuing the other stock meets the "Gross asset limitation" rules described above. (Code Sec. 1202(h)(4)(B))

. . . The stock will be continue to be treated as QSBS for purposes of the above rules if it is transferred by the taxpayer in later Code Sec. 351 or Code Sec. 368 transactions. But with respect to any such later transactions, the rules of the immediately preceding paragraph ("Except as provided . . .") are applied as of the time of the first transfer. (Code Sec. 1202(h)(4)(C))

Rules that apply to stock acquired via options, convertible debt or convertible stock. *Stock acquired via exercise of options or conversion of convertible debt.* Stock acquired through the exercise of options or warrants, or through the conversion of convertible debt, is treated as acquired at original issue. The determination of whether the gross assets test described above is met is made at the time of the exercise or conversion, and the holding period of the stock is treated as beginning at that time. (H Rept p. 603)

Stock acquired via conversion of convertible stock. If stock is acquired solely through the conversion of QSBS of the same corporation, the acquired stock is treated as QSBS, and the holding period of that stock includes the holding period of the convertible stock. (Code Sec. 1202(f)) The gross assets test described above is applied at the date the convertible stock is issued. (H Rept p. 603)

Other rules. Stock received in connection with the performance of services is treated as issued by the corporation and acquired by the taxpayer when it is included in the taxpayer's gross income under the Code Sec. 83 rules (see FTC 2d/FIN ¶ H-2515 *et seq.;* TG ¶ 3036 *et seq.;* USTR ¶ 834 *et seq.).* (H Rept p. 603)

Regulations. IRS is to prescribe regulations that are needed to carry out the purposes of the above rules, including regulations to prevent the avoidance of those purposes via split-ups, shell corporations, partnerships or otherwise. (Code Sec. 1202(k))

☐ **Effective:** Stock issued after Aug. 10, '93. (§ 13113(e))

For official explanation see Committee Reports ¶ 3005.

¶ 703. Other rules changed as a result of small business stock gain exclusion rules

The '93 Act made the following changes to various provisions of the Internal Revenue Code as a result of the creation of the new rules described in § 13113(a) that provide for an exclusion of 50% of the gain realized from the sale or exchange of qualified small business stock ("QSBS").

Capital gains and loss. The '93 Act provides that any gain that is excluded from gross income under the 50% exclusion rule is not taken into account in computing long-term capital gain, in applying the capital loss limitation (see FTC 2d/FIN ¶ I-6012 *et seq.;* TG ¶ 4418; USTR ¶ 12,114) or in computing the capital loss carry-over (see FTC 2d/FIN ¶ I-6022 *et seq.;* TG ¶ 4419 *et seq.;* USTR ¶ 12,124 *et seq.*) rules. And, the taxable portion of the gain is taxed at a maximum rate of 28%. (H Rept p. 603)

Investment interest. Investment interest is deductible only to the extent that it doesn't exceed net investment income. Net investment income is the excess of investment income over investment expenses. (See FTC 2d/FIN ¶ K-5310 *et seq.;* TG ¶ 7199; USTR ¶ 1634.053) The '93 Act provides that the amount treated as investment income for purposes of this investment interest limitation doesn't include any gain that is excluded under the 50% exclusion rule. (H Rept p. 604)

Alternative minimum tax provisions. The '93 Act provides that an amount equal to one-half the amount excluded from gross income under the 50% exclusion rule is an alternative minimum tax ("AMT") preference. (Code Sec. 57(a)(8) as amended by '93 Act § 13113(b)(1))

> RIA ***observation:*** Thus 1/4 (1/2 of 50%) of the total gain on the sale or exchange is an AMT preference.

All AMT preferences are either exclusion preferences or deferral preferences. (FTC 2d/FIN ¶ A-8135.1; TG ¶ 1385) Deferral preferences increase noncorporate taxpayers' minimum tax credit (a credit available to taxpayers in years after they incur an AMT), while exclusion preferences have no effect on that credit. (See FTC 2d/FIN ¶ A-8135; TG ¶ 1385)

The '93 Act provides that the preference described above, i.e., the preference caused by the 50% exclusion, is an exclusion preference. (Code Sec. 53(d)(1)(B)(ii)(II) as amended by '93 Act § 13113(b)(2))

Penalty for failure to file required reports. As discussed in "Reports to IRS and shareholders" under "Qualified small business stock" in ¶ 702, the corporation that issues the stock that qualifies for the 50% exclusion must make certain prescribed reports to IRS. Except as provided in the following two sentences, there is a $50 penalty for each report that the corporation fails to make with the required information or by the prescribed due date (determined after considering any extension of time for filing). If the failure is due to negligence or intentional disregard, the penalty is $100 per instance. If the report in question covers a period of two or more years, the two above penalties are computed by multiplying the penalty amounts by the number of years in the period. (Code Sec. 6652(k) as amended by '93 Act § 13113(c))

Net operating loss carryover modifications and "intervening year modifications."

Taxpayers who incur net operating losses ("NOLs") are allowed a deduction, the "net operating loss deduction," in tax years that either precede or follow the year(s) in which the taxpayer incurred the NOL(s); the amount of that deduction is based on the amount of the NOLs that are carried forward or carried back to the year in question. (See FTC 2d/FIN ¶ M-4001; TG ¶ 6725)

A NOL is computed by (a) starting with the taxpayer's taxable income in a year in which that taxable income is a negative amount, and (b) making prescribed "modifications" to that amount. (See FTC 2d/FIN ¶ M-4100; TG ¶ 6701) The '93 Act makes the following changes to these "modifications":

. . . It provides a new modification that provides that the 50% exclusion for gain on QSBS is not allowed in the calculation of a noncorporate taxpayer's NOL. (Code Sec. 172(d)(2)(B) as amended by '93 Act § 13113(d)(1)(A))

. . . Under pre-'93 Act law, there is a modification under which nonbusiness deductions of a noncorporate taxpayer aren't deductible to the extent they exceed nonbusiness income. (See FTC 2d/FIN ¶ M-4111; TG ¶ 6702) The '93 Act provides that the 50% exclusion is not considered a nonbusiness deduction for this purpose. (Code Sec. 172(d)(4)(B) as amended by '93 Act § 13113(d)(1)(B))

> ***observation:*** The change in this last paragraph is necessary in order not to eliminate the 50% exclusion twice in the calculation of NOL. The change in the paragraph before that one eliminates the 50% exclusion once; if the exclusion were also considered a nonbusiness deduction, it would be eliminated again by the rule that eliminates nonbusiness deductions to the extent they exceed nonbusiness income.

In addition, under pre-'93 Act law, if a net operating loss is not absorbed in the first year to which it is carried, the amount of loss carried to a second year must be reduced by the first carryover year's taxable income adjusted for certain "intervening year modifications." If the loss is carried to more than two years, modifications must be made to the taxable income of each of the years to which it is carried other than the last one (the "intervening years"). (See FTC 2d/FIN ¶ M-4200; TG ¶ 6721) The '93 Act provides a new intervening year modification: no 50% exclusion is allowed in any intervening year. (Code Sec. 172(b)(2)(A); Code Sec. 172(d)(2)(B) as amended by '93 Act § 13113(d)(1)(A))

Trusts and estates. *Charitable deductions of estates and complex trusts.* Under pre-'93 Act law, estates and complex trusts (as defined in See FTC 2d/FIN ¶ C-2601; TG ¶ 1810) may, with specified exceptions, deduct any amount of income which, as provided by their governing instruments, is paid for a charitable purpose. (FTC 2d/FIN ¶s C-2301, C-7301; TG ¶ 1789) The '93 Act provides an additional exception to this rule by providing that, to the extent that the amount otherwise deductible under that rule consists of gain that qualifies for the 50% exclusion, proper adjustment must be made for the 50% exclusion. (Code Sec. 642(c)(4) as amended by '93 Act § 13113(d)(2))

Distributable net income. Distributable net income (DNI) is the amount that is both (a) the upper limit on the amount that beneficiaries must include in their income with respect to distributions from estates and trusts and (b) the upper limit on the amount that estates and trusts may claim as a deduction for these distributions. DNI equals taxable income with certain modifications. (See FTC 2d/FIN ¶s C-2604, C-2605, C-8101; TG ¶ 1809)

FTC 2d References are to the Federal Tax Coordinator 2d
FIN References are to RIA's Analysis of Federal Taxes: Income
TG References are to the Tax Guide
USTR References are to the United States Tax Reporter

The '93 Act provides an additional modification: the 50% exclusion is added back when computing DNI. (Code Sec. 643(a)(3) as amended by '93 Act § 13113(d)(3))

Exclusion reduced if gain is income in respect of decedent. Where the qualified small business stock (as defined in ¶ 702) was sold or exchanged by a decedent before his death, but the gain on that transaction is recognized by his estate or heirs for income tax purposes as income in respect of a decedent (as defined in FTC 2d/FIN ¶ C-9500 *et seq.;* TG ¶ 1916), the 50% exclusion is computed by first reducing the gain (but not below zero) by the amount of the allowable deduction for estate tax attributable to that gain. (Code Sec. 691(c)(4) as amended by '93 Act § 13113(d)(4))

Nonresident aliens. The excess of certain capital gains over certain capital losses of nonresident aliens may be subject to a 30% U.S. tax. (See FTC 2d/FIN ¶ O-10238 *et seq.;* TG ¶ 8103) The '93 Act provides that when that provision comes into play, the nonresident computes his capital gains and losses without regard to the 50% exclusion. (Code Sec. 871(a)(2) as amended by '93 Act § 13113(d)(5))

☐ **Effective:** Stock issued after Aug. 10, '93. (§ 13113(e))

For official explanation see Committee Reports ¶ 3005.

¶ 704. Tax-free rollover of publicly traded securities gain into "specialized small business investment companies"

Under pre-'93 Act law, gain or loss generally is recognized on any sale, exchange or other disposition of property. (See FTC 2d/FIN ¶ I-1950; TG ¶ 4002; USTR ¶ 10,114)

The '93 Act provides that, subject to the limitations described below, taxpayers other than estates, trusts, partnerships and S corporations (Code Sec. 1044(c)(4) as added by '93 Act § 13114(a)) may elect to limit the amount of capital gain they recognize on the sale of publicly traded securities to the excess of the amount realized on the sale over: (Code Sec. 1044(a))

. . . the cost of any common stock or partnership interest in a "specialized small business investment company" (SSBIC) purchased by the taxpayer during the 60-day period that begins on the date of the sale,

reduced by (Code Sec. 1044(a)(1))

. . . any portion of that cost previously taken account under the above rule. (Code Sec. 1044(a)(2))

> ***observation:*** The above rule applies to *sales,* but not to *exchanges,* of publicly traded securities. Thus, a transfer of publicly traded securities for money or a promise to pay money will qualify, but a transfer of publicly traded securities for other property won't qualify.

Any gain not recognized under the above rule reduces the taxpayer's basis in any SSBIC investment made during the 60-day period; where the taxpayer makes more than one SSBIC investment during the 60-day period, the bases of those investments are reduced in the order they were acquired. (Code Sec. 1044(d))

> ***observation:*** As a result of the fact that the Act provides for an exclusion of gain and a corresponding reduction in the basis of the SSBIC investment, the effect of the Act is to "roll over" the gain.

However, basis in SSBIC common stock isn't reduced for purposes of calculating the gain eligible for the 50% exclusion for qualified small business stock discussed at ¶ 702. (Code Sec. 1044(d))

To the extent the proceeds from the sale of the publicly-traded securities exceed the cost of the SSBIC investment, gain must be recognized currently. (H Rept p. 604)

Limitations. *Individuals.* The amount of gain an individual whose filing status is not married-filing-jointly may exclude under this rule for any tax year is limited to the lesser of (a) $50,000 or (b) $500,000 reduced by gain excluded under this rule in all preceding years. (Code Sec. 1044(b)(1)) For individuals whose filing status is married-filing-jointly, the same rule applies, except that $25,000 is substituted for $50,000, and $250,000 is substituted for $500,000. (Code Sec. 1044(b)(3))

The amount of gain that qualifies for the exclusion is allocated equally between spouses who file a joint return, for purposes of applying the limitation to later tax years. (Code Sec. 1044(b)(3)(B)) Marital status for purposes of this rule and the above rules is determined under the rules of Code Sec. 7703 (Code Sec. 1044(b)(3)(C)), i.e., the rules that apply for determining filing status. (See FTC 2d/FIN ¶ A-1600; TG ¶ 1118)

Corporations. The amount of gain a corporation may exclude under the above rule for any tax year is limited to the lesser of (a) $250,000 or (b) $1,000,000 reduced by gain excluded under this rule in all preceding years. (Code Sec. 1044(b)(2)) For purposes of this rule, all corporations that are members of the same controlled group are treated as one corporation. The term "controlled group" has the same meaning for this purpose that it does for purposes of the targeted jobs credit (See FTC 2d/FIN ¶ L-17828; TG ¶ 5811). (Code Sec. 1044(b)(4)(A))

Any gain excluded under the above rule by a predecessor corporation is treated as having been excluded by the successor corporation. (Code Sec. 1044(b)(4)(B))

Definitions. *Publicly traded securities* are securities traded on an established market. (Code Sec. 1044(c)(1))

Purchase. The Act provides that the term "purchase" has the meaning given that term by Code Sec. 1043(b)(4). (Code Sec. 1044(c)(2)) Code Sec. 1043(b)(4) provides that a taxpayer is considered to have purchased property if that property's basis would be its cost to him, were it not for the rule that reduces the basis of U.S. obligations, etc. by unrecognized gains on the sale of property to comply with conflict-of-interest rules. (See FTC 2d/FIN ¶ I-3704 *et seq.;* TG ¶ 4245 *et seq.)*

> ***observation:*** It appears that Congress made a technical error in its definition of "purchase," i.e., that it meant to provide that a taxpayer is considered to have purchased property if that property's basis would be its cost to him, were it not for the (Code Sec. 1044(d)) basis reduction rules with respect to purchases of an SSBIC interest that are discussed above.

An SSBIC is any partnership or corporation licensed by the Small Business Administration under Sec. 301(d) of the Small Business Investment Act of '58 as in effect on May 13, '93. (Code Sec. 1044(c)(3)) That Sec. 301(d) authorizes the licensing of small business investment companies organized to invest in small business concerns in such a way as to facilitate ownership by persons whose participation in the free enterprise system has been hampered by social or economic disadvantages.

☐ **Effective:** Sales made on or after Aug. 10, '93. (§ 13114(d))

For official explanation see Committee Reports ¶ 3006.

¶ 705. Low-income housing credit made permanent with some modifications

The low-income housing credit is a business tax credit for investment in residential rental property that qualifies as low-income housing under certain statutory requirements. (See FTC 2d/FIN ¶ L-15700; TG ¶ 5860; USTR ¶ 424 *et seq.)* The amount of the low-income housing credit for any year in the credit period is computed by multiplying an applicable percentage times the qualified basis of each qualified low-income building. (See FTC 2d/FIN ¶ L-15702; TG ¶ 5860; USTR ¶ 424.02)

With the exception of certain high-cost areas (discussed in more detail in ¶ 711), the credit percentages (i.e., applicable percentages) are set so that over a ten-year period, credit amounts will have a present value equal to: (1) 70% of the qualified basis of new buildings which are not federally subsidized for the tax year; and (2) 30% of the qualified basis of existing buildings and of new buildings which are federally subsidized for the tax year. (See FTC 2d/FIN ¶ L-15714; TG ¶ 5862; USTR ¶ 424.02)

In two types of high-cost areas (i.e., a qualified census tract or difficult development area), the eligible basis of a new building or the eligible basis of the rehabilitation expenditures of an existing building undergoing substantial rehabilitation is considered to be 130% of the eligible basis for depreciation. That is: (1) the 70% credit for of the qualified basis of new buildings which are not federally subsidized for the tax year becomes 91%; and (2) the 30% credit for the qualified basis of existing buildings and of new buildings which are federally subsidized for the tax year becomes 39%. (See FTC 2d/FIN ¶ L-15908; USTR ¶ 424.02)

Permanent extension of the credit. Under pre-'93 Act law, the population component (i.e., $1.25 per state resident) of the state housing credit ceiling (i.e., the amount which may be allocated from a state housing credit agency to the owners of low-income buildings) was terminated on June 30, '92. In addition, under pre-'93 Act law, for buildings that were exempt from the state housing allocations because they were financed by tax-exempt bonds, the exemption from the state housing credit allocation rules terminated for any building placed in service after June 30, '92. For buildings in progress that were exempt from the state housing allocations because they were financed by tax-exempt bonds there were transitional rules. Thus, with limited exceptions, the low-income housing credit expired on June 30, '92. (FTC 2d/FIN ¶ L-15703; TG ¶s 5860, 5866)

Congress believes that the low-income housing credit is a useful incentive for increasing the stock of affordable housing available to low-income individuals. Further, making the low-income housing credit permanent will provide greater planning certainty needed for the efficient delivery of this federal subsidy. (H Rept p. 612)

The '93 Act eliminates the provisions which terminated the low-income housing credit as of June 30, '92. It does this by eliminating the provisions which: (1) terminated the low-income housing credit allocation of $1.25 per resident; (2) terminated the exemption from the allocation requirements for buildings financed with tax-exempt bonds; and (3) provided the transitional rule for certain bond-financed buildings in progress. (Code Sec. 42(o) as amended by '93 Act § 13142(a)(1)) Thus, the '93 Act permanently extends the low-income housing credit. (H Rept p. 612)

☐ **Effective:** Periods after June 30, '92. (§ 13142(a)(2))

Other modifications to the low-income housing credit.

(1) For requirement that the housing credit agency must consider the reasonableness of the developmental and operational costs of the project in making the determination of the amount necessary for the financial feasibility of the project, for purposes of determining the amount of the credit, see ¶ 706.

(2) For whether buildings receiving assistance under the Home Investment Partnership Act are treated as federally subsidized for purposes of the low-income housing credit if stricter income targeting requirements are satisfied, see ¶ 711.

(3) For whether a unit will fail to be treated as a low-income unit merely because it is occupied entirely by full-time students who are: (1) single parents and their children, if neither the parents nor the children are dependents of another individual, or (2) married and file a joint return, see ¶ 707.

(4) For a one-time election to apply liberalization of rules for deep rent skewed projects to credit allocations before '90, see ¶ 712.

(5) For an election to determine whether a low-income unit is rent-restricted based on the number of bedrooms for years before '90, see ¶ 712.

(6) For IRS waiver of recapture of the low-income housing credit in the case of any de minimis error in complying with the minimum set-aside requirements, on application by the building owner, see ¶ 708.

(7) For IRS waiver of annual recertification of tenant income for purposes of determining whether the project is a qualified low-income housing project eligible for the credit, if the entire building is occupied by low-income tenants, on application by the building owner, see ¶ 709.

(8) For requirement that the extended low-income housing commitment prohibit the refusal to lease to a holder of a voucher or certificate of eligibility under Section 8 of the United States Housing Act of '37 because of the status of the prospective tenant as a holder of that voucher or certificate, see ¶ 710.

(9) For discussion of the rule which allows the buyer and the seller to agree to use either the exact number of days or the mid-month convention to determine the division of the credit in the month of disposition, see ¶ 714.

For official explanation see Committee Reports ¶ 3013.

¶ 706. Low-income housing project feasibility linked to reasonable developmental and operational costs

The low-income housing credit may be claimed for any taxable year if, and to the extent that, the owner of a qualified low-income building receives a housing credit allocation from a state or local housing credit agency. (See FTC 2d/FIN ¶ L-16001; TG ¶ 5866; USTR ¶ 424.03) The housing credit dollar amount allocated to a project may not exceed the amount the housing credit agency determines is necessary for the financial feasibility of the project and its viability as a qualified low-income housing project throughout the credit period. (See FTC 2d/FIN ¶ L-16012; USTR ¶ 424.03) In making the determination of the amount necessary for the financial feasibility of the project, the housing credit agency must consider:

. . . the sources and uses of funds and the total financing planned for the project,

. . . any proceeds or receipts expected to be generated by reason of tax benefits, and

. . . the percentage of the housing credit dollar amount used for project costs other than the cost of intermediaries. (FTC 2d/FIN ¶ L-16012; USTR ¶ 424.03)

FTC 2d References are to the Federal Tax Coordinator 2d
FIN References are to RIA's Analysis of Federal Taxes: Income
TG References are to the Tax Guide
USTR References are to the United States Tax Reporter

The '93 Act provides that, in addition to the three factors discussed above, in making the determination of the amount necessary for the financial feasibility of the project, the housing credit agency must consider the reasonableness of the developmental and operational costs of the project. (Code Sec. 42(m)(2)(B)(iv) as amended by '93 Act § 13142(b)(1))

Reasons for a determination of unreasonableness might include, for example, costs not comparable to those expended to develop or operate similar projects in the locality, inefficient development practices, building design of a nature above what is necessary to provide basic, or safe housing for the intended population in the locality. Congress also intended that an allocating agency make a determination as to the appropriateness of amenities included in a project. Amenities, and the space attributable to those amenities, should be appropriate to the size and type of the resident population to be served. (S Rept p. 199)

This provision is not intended to create a national standard of reasonableness. Congress intended for allocating agencies to set standards of reasonableness reflecting the applicable facts and circumstances including the location of the projects and the uses for which the projects are built. (Conf Rept p. 545)

☐ **Effective:** Determinations under the low-income housing credit rules with respect to housing credit dollar amounts allocated from State housing credit ceilings after June 30, '92, (§ 13142(b)(6)(A)(i)) or buildings placed in service after June 30, '92, to the extent the state ceiling limits do not apply to any building because the buildings are financed by tax-exempt bonds, but only with respect to bonds issued after June 30, '92. (§ 13142(b)(6)(A)(ii))

For official explanation see Committee Reports ¶ 3013.

¶ 707. Units with certain full-time students may be low-income units

A unit in a building will not fail to qualify as a low-income unit for purposes of the low-income housing credit merely because the unit is occupied by an individual who is one of the following:

. . . a student and receiving assistance under title IV of the Social Security Act (i.e., Aid to Families with Dependent Children (AFDC)), or

. . . enrolled in a job training program receiving assistance under the Job Training Partnership Act or under other similar Federal, State, of local laws. (FTC 2d/FIN ¶ L-15811; TG ¶ 5863; USTR ¶ 424.04)

The '93 Act provides that, in addition to students receiving AFDC and individuals enrolled in the job training programs noted above, the existence of certain other students will not prevent the housing unit from being eligible for the low-income housing credit. A unit will not fail to be treated as a low-income unit merely because it is occupied entirely by full-time students if those students are:

(1) single parents and their children, but only if neither the parents nor the children are dependents (as defined in Code Sec. 152) of another individual, (Code Sec. 42(i)(3)(D)(ii)(I) as amended by '93 Act § 13142(b)(2))

or

(2) married and file a joint return. (Code Sec. 42(i)(3)(D)(ii)(II))

Thus, the '93 Act provides that a housing unit occupied entirely by full-time students may qualify for the low-income housing credit if the full-time students are single parents and their minor children, and none of the tenants is a dependent of a third party. In addition, the '93 Act codifies the present-law exception regarding married students filing joint returns (which continues to apply to all buildings placed in service since the enactment of the low-income housing tax credit). (S Rept p. 198)

☐ **Effective:** Determinations under the low-income housing credit rules with respect to housing credit dollar amounts allocated from State housing credit ceilings after June 30, '92, (§ 13142(b)(6)(A)(i)) or buildings placed in service after June 30, '92, to the extent the state ceiling limits do not apply to any building because the buildings are financed by tax-exempt bonds, but only with respect to bonds issued after June 30, '92. (§ 13142(b)(6)(A)(ii))

The present-law exception regarding married students filing joint returns continues to apply to all buildings placed in service since the enactment of the low-income housing tax credit. (S Rept p. 198)

For official explanation see Committee Reports ¶ 3013.

¶ 708. Waiver of de minimis errors in satisfying minimum set-aside (tenant occupancy) requirements

For purposes of the low-income housing credit, a taxpayer/building owner whose building fails to remain part of a qualified low-income project due to noncompliance with the minimum set-aside (i.e., tenant occupancy, see FTC 2d/FIN ¶ L-15804; TG ¶ 5861) requirement must recapture a portion of the credit for all earlier years. (See FTC 2d/FIN ¶ L-16051; TG ¶ 5868; USTR ¶ 424.02)

The '93 Act provides that on application by the taxpayer, IRS may waive any recapture of the low-income housing credit in the case of any de minimis error in complying with the minimum set-aside requirements. (Code Sec. 42(g)(8)(A) as amended by '93 Act § 13142(b)(3))

☐ **Effective:** Aug. 10, '93. (§ 13142(b)(6)(B))

For official explanation see Committee Reports ¶ 3013.

¶ 709. IRS may waive annual recertification of tenant income if entire project is occupied by low-income tenants

For purposes of the low-income housing credit, generally, the taxpayer/owner of a low-income housing project is required to annually recertify tenant incomes to meet the low-income tenant occupancy requirements, regardless of whether the building is entirely occupied by low-income tenants. (See FTC 2d/FIN ¶ S-3401; USTR ¶ 424.03)

The '93 Act provides that, on application by the taxpayer, IRS may waive any annual recertification of tenant income for purposes of determining whether the project is a qualified low-income housing project eligible for the credit, if the entire building is occupied by low-income tenants. (Code Sec. 42(g)(8)(B) as amended by '93 Act § 13142(b)(3))

Third-party verification. Third-party verification of a tenant's or prospective tenant's income from his combined assets is not necessary if: (1) the combined assets do not exceed $5000, and (2) the tenant or prospective tenant provides a signed, sworn statement to this effect to the building owner. (Conf Rept p. 544)

Treatment of Section 8 assistance. Congress did not intend to modify the treatment of individuals receiving Section 8 assistance. (Conf Rept p. 544)

FTC 2d References are to the Federal Tax Coordinator 2d
FIN References are to RIA's Analysis of Federal Taxes: Income
TG References are to the Tax Guide
USTR References are to the United States Tax Reporter

☐ **Effective:** Aug. 10, '93. (§ 13142(b)(6)(B))
For official explanation see Committee Reports ¶ 3013.

¶ 710. Discrimination against Section 8 tenants must be prohibited by the minimum long-term commitment to low-income housing requirement

No low-income housing credit is allowed for any building for the tax year unless an extended low-income housing commitment is in effect at the end of the year. An extended low-income housing commitment is any agreement between the taxpayer and the housing credit agency that includes the following provisions:

. . . An applicable fraction commitment;

. . . An allowance of rights to low-income tenants to enforce the applicable fraction commitment;

. . . A prohibition against disposition;

. . . A provision making the agreement binding on all successors of the taxpayer;

. . . A provision requiring the agreement to be recorded as a restrictive covenant with respect to the building under applicable state law. (FTC 2d/FIN ¶ L-15705; TG ¶ 5861)

Under pre-'93 Act law the low-income housing tax credit provisions did not include any specific provisions concerning the grounds for denial of admission to low-income housing projects, for termination of a tenancy, or for refusal to renew the lease of a tenant. (S Rept p. 197)

The '93 Act requires the extended low-income housing commitment to prohibit the refusal to lease to a holder of a voucher or certificate of eligibility under Section 8 of the United States Housing Act of '37 because of the status of the prospective tenant as a holder of that voucher or certificate. (Code Sec. 42(h)(6)(B)(iv) as amended by '93 Act § 13142(b)(4))

☐ **Effective:** Aug. 10, '93. (§ 13142(b)(6)(B))
For official explanation see Committee Reports ¶ 3013.

¶ 711. Certain buildings receiving assistance under the Home Investment Partnership Act are not treated as federally subsidized for purposes of the low-income housing credit

For purposes of determining the applicable percentages (30%/70% credit, discussed in ¶ 705), with certain exceptions, a new building is treated as federally subsidized for any tax year if, at any time during the year, or earlier tax year, there is outstanding any below market federal loan, the proceeds of which are or were used directly or indirectly for the building or its operation. For these purposes, a below market federal loan means any loan funded in whole or in part with federal funds if the interest rate payable on the loan is less than the applicable federal rate in effect under Code Sec. 1274(d)(1) as of the date on which the loan was made. (See FTC 2d/FIN ¶ L-15729)

The '93 Act provides that assistance provided under the Home Investment Partnerships Act (as in effect on Aug. 10, '93) with respect to any building is not treated as a below market federal loan if 40% or more of the residential units in the building are occupied by individuals whose income is 50% or less of the area median gross income. (Code Sec. 42(i)(2)(E)(i) as amended by '93 Act § 13142(b)(5)(i))

> ***observation:*** The Home Investment Partnership Act is Title II of the Cranston-Gonzalez National Affordable Housing Act of 1990 (PL 101-625). Those provisions were enacted to make assistance available in coordination with mortgage insurance, rental assistance and other housing assistance to expand the supply of housing available to low-income Americans.

Thus, a building will not be treated as Federally subsidized solely by reason of assistance under the National Affordable Housing Act of '90 if the stricter income targeting requirements are satisfied. (H Rept p. 612)

> ***observation:*** The stricter income targeting requirement means that if a 40-50 test (i.e., 40% or more of the residential units in the building must be occupied by individuals whose income is 50% or less of area gross median income) is satisfied, the assistance will not be treated as a below market federal loan. Unlike the normal 20-50 and 40-60 minimum set-aside tests (discussed in FTC 2d/FIN ¶ L-15804; TG ¶ 5681; USTR ¶ 424.04), the stricter income targeting requirement for buildings receiving assistance under the National Affordable Housing Act of '90 does not specifically require that the 40% or more of the residential units in the building must be rent restricted.

In the case of a building located in a city having 5 boroughs and a population in excess of 5,000,000 (i.e., New York City), the '93 Act also provides that the assistance provided under the Home Investment Partnerships Act (as in effect on Aug. 10, '93) with respect to any building is not treated as a below market federal loan if 25% or more of the residential units in the building are occupied by individuals whose income is 50% or less of the area median gross income. (Code Sec. 42(i)(2)(E)(ii))

Application to high-cost areas. The '93 Act provides that the increase in the credit percentage (i.e., to 91% and 39%) for qualified census tracts and difficult development areas (discussed in ¶ 705) does not apply to any building that receives assistance provided under the Home Investment Partnerships Act that is not treated as a below market federal loans because 40% or more of the residential units in the building are occupied by individuals whose income is 50% or less of the area median gross income. (Code Sec. 42(i)(2)(E)(i)) Thus, these projects are eligible for the 70% and 30% credits, but not for the 91% or 39% credits otherwise available in qualified census tracts and difficult development areas. (H Rept p. 612)

☐ **Effective:** Periods after Aug. 10, '93. (§ 13142(b)(6)(C))
For official explanation see Committee Reports ¶ 3013.

¶ 712. Election to determine whether a low-income unit is rent-restricted based on the number of bedrooms for years before '90—deadline: 180 days starting Aug. 10, '93

For purposes of determining whether the minimum set-aside (i.e., tenant occupancy, see FTC 2d/FIN ¶ L-15804; TG ¶ 5861; USTR ¶ 424.03) requirements have been satisfied, a residential unit is rent-restricted if the gross rent with respect

FTC 2d References are to the Federal Tax Coordinator 2d
FIN References are to RIA's Analysis of Federal Taxes: Income
TG References are to the Tax Guide
USTR References are to the United States Tax Reporter

to the unit does not exceed 30% of the imputed income limitation applicable to the unit. The gross rent limitation for low-income housing units is based on family size. (See FTC 2d/FIN ¶ L-15807; USTR ¶ 424.04)

Pre-'90 law for maximum rent. Under pre-'90 law a residential unit was rent-restricted if the gross rent for the unit did not exceed 30% of the income limitations under the set-aside requirements applicable to individuals occupying the unit adjusted for actual family size of the occupants. (Conf Rept (PL 101-239) p. 12)

Maximum rent post-'89. The gross rent limitation for low-income housing units is based on an imputed family size determined by the number of bedrooms in the unit. That is, the imputed income limitation applicable to a unit is the income limitation which would apply under the minimum set-aside rules to individuals occupying the unit if the number of individuals occupying the unit were as follows:

. . . in the case of a unit which does not have a separate bedroom—1 individual;

. . . in the case of a unit which has one or more separate bedrooms—1.5 individuals for each separate bedroom.

For projects financed with tax-exempt bonds described in Code Sec. 142(a)(7), the imputed income limitation applies instead of the otherwise applicable income limitations for purposes of determining whether a project satisfies the gross rent requirements for purposes of applying the requirements for the deep rent skewed projects election. (See FTC 2d/FIN ¶ L-15807)

Treatment of units occupied by individuals whose incomes rise above the minimum set-aside income limits—pre-'90 law. A tenant who qualified for a rent-restricted unit could continue to be considered to qualify even if his or her income grew to as much as 140% of the qualifying income limitation. When the income of a tenant in a qualified rent-restricted unit exceeded 140% of the qualifying income limitation, that unit ceased to be a qualified low-income unit and the rent restrictions under the low-income housing credit no longer applied. (Conf Rept (PL 101-239) p. 13)

Treatment of units occupied by individuals whose incomes rise above the minimum set-aside income limits—post '89 law. Except as provided below, despite an increase in the income of the occupants of a low-income unit above the minimum set-aside income limitations, the unit will continue to be treated as a low-income unit if the income of the occupants initially met the income limitation and that unit continues to be rent restricted. If, however, the income of the occupants of the unit increases above 140% of the income limitation, the rule that the unit will continue to be treated as a low-income unit will cease to apply if any residential rental unit (of a size comparable to, or smaller than that unit) in the building is occupied by a new resident whose income exceeds the income limitation. Another exception applies to deep rent-skewed projects. In the case of a deep rent skewed project, if the income of the occupants of the unit increases above 170% of the income limitation applicable under the minimum set-aside requirement for deep rent skewed projects, the rule which provides that the unit will not lose low-income unit status, will not apply if any low-income unit in the building is occupied by a new resident whose income exceeds 40% of the area median gross income. (See FTC 2d/FIN ¶ L-15809; USTR ¶ 424.04)

Election to apply '89 Act rules before '90. The '93 Act provides that in the case of a building to which the amendments made by Sec. 7108(e)(1) of the '89 Act (discussed above) did not apply, the taxpayer may elect to have those amendments apply to that building. (§ 13142(c)(1)) Thus, the '93 Act allows an election by the owner of a low-income building placed in service before '90 to use either apartment size (i.e., the current law standard) or family size (i.e., the pre-'89 Act standard) in determining maximum allowable rent. (S Rept p. 198)

> ***observation:*** It is not clear whether or not Congress intended to allow taxpayers to elect the post-'89 Act treatment with respect to units occupied by individuals whose incomes rise above the minimum set-aside income limits. The committee reports only discuss the election to use either apartment size or family size in determining maximum allowable rent. In addition, it is not clear whether any taxpayer would ever want to elect the post-'89 Act treatment for units occupied by individuals whose incomes rise above the minimum set-aside income limits. However, since this provision was included in section 7108(e)(1) of the '89 Act, the '93 Act gives taxpayers the right to elect the post-'89 Act treatment for units occupied by individuals whose incomes rise above the minimum set-aside income limits.

The election to have the post '89 amendments apply may be made only if the taxpayer has met the normal requirements for monitoring for noncompliance with the low-income housing credit rules and for notifying IRS of noncompliance (see FTC 2d/FIN ¶ L-16016). (§ 13142(c)(1))

In addition, the election to have the post '89 amendments apply will only apply to tenants first occupying any unit in the building after the date of the election. (§ 13142(c)(2))

The election may be made only during the 180 day period beginning on Aug. 10, '93 and, once made, will be irrevocable. (§ 13142(c)(4))

☐ **Effective:** The election may be made only during the 180 day period beginning on the date of enactment. The date of enactment is Aug. 10, '93. (§ 13142(c)(4))

For official explanation see Committee Reports ¶ 3013.

¶ 713. One-time election to apply liberalization of rules for deep rent skewed projects to credit allocations before '90—deadline: 180 days starting Aug. 10, '93

The Code provides a special deep-rent skewing set aside rule for projects that elect to satisfy a stricter set-aside (i.e., tenant occupancy) requirement and significantly restrict the rents on the low-income units relative to the other units in the building. (See FTC 2d/FIN ¶ L-15805)

Under pre-'90 law, gross rent for each low-income unit in a deep rent skewed project could not exceed one-third of the average gross rent with respect to units of comparable size which were not occupied by individuals who met the applicable income limit. This meant that the average rent charged to tenants in the residential rental units which weren't low-income units had to be at least 300% of the average rent charged to low-income tenants of comparable units.

For years after '89 the gross rent rule was liberalized—gross rent for each low-income unit in the project may not exceed one-half of the average gross rent with respect to units of comparable size which are not occupied by individuals who meet the applicable income limit. This means that the average rent charged to tenants in the residential rental units which aren't low-income units is at least 200% of the average rent charged to low-income tenants of comparable units. (See FTC 2d/FIN ¶ L-15805)

Election to apply 200% rent restriction instead of 300% rent restriction. The '93

FTC 2d References are to the Federal Tax Coordinator 2d
FIN References are to RIA's Analysis of Federal Taxes: Income
TG References are to the Tax Guide
USTR References are to the United States Tax Reporter

Act provides that in the case of a building to which the '89 Act amendment discussed above, did not apply, the taxpayer may elect to have the amendments apply to the building. (§ 13142(c)(1)) Thus, the '93 Act allows an election by the owner of a low-income building receiving a credit allocation before '90 to satisfy the 200% rent restriction rather than the 300% rent restriction. (S Rept p. 198)

The election to have the post-'89 amendments apply may be made only if the taxpayer has met the regular requirements for monitoring for noncompliance with the low-income housing credit rules and for notifying IRS of noncompliance (FTC 2d/FIN ¶ L-16016). (§ 13142(c)(1))

In addition, the election will apply only if rents of low-income tenants in the building do not increase as a result of the election. (§ 13142(c)(3)) The election would apply to both current and future tenants but would not allow rent increases on existing low-income tenants. (Conf Rept p. 544)

The election may be made only during the 180-day period beginning on Aug. 10, '93 and, once made, will be irrevocable. (§ 13142(c)(4))

☐ **Effective:** The election may be made only during the 180 day period beginning on the date of enactment. The date of enactment is Aug. 10, '93. (§ 13142(c)(4))

For official explanation see Committee Reports ¶ 3013.

¶ 714. Buyer and seller can allocate low-income housing credit based on exact number of days each held the property in the month of disposition

Under Code Sec. 42(f)(4), if a building (or an interest in a building) is disposed of during any year for which the low-income housing credit is allowable, the credit must be allocated between the parties on the basis of the number of days during the year the building (or interest) was held by each. (See FTC 2d/FIN ¶ L-15706) However, in Rev Rul 91-38 IRS said that the owner who has held the property for the longest period during the month in which a transfer occurred is considered to have held the property for the entire month and can claim the credit accordingly. In cases in which the transferor and transferee had held the property for the same amount of time during the month of the transfer, the transferor was considered to have held the property for the entire month and the transferee's ownership of the property was considered to have begun the first day of the following month. (FTC 2d/FIN ¶ L-15706) Congress says IRS issued guidance that required a mid-month averaging convention. (S Rept p. 197)

> ***observation:*** The term mid-month averaging convention presumably refers to the Rev Rul 91-38 rule discussed above.

Congress states that "The bill ['93 Act] provides that the buyer and seller may agree to use either the exact number of days or the mid-month convention to determine the division of the credit in the month of disposition." (S Rept p. 199)

☐ **Effective:** Aug.10, '93. (S Rept p. 199)

> ***observation:*** This language is not part of the bill or the '93 Act language. Congress apparently intended to make it clear that IRS could not take a position that taxpayers were prohibited from using the exact number of days standard provided in the Code. Since the language allowing the taxpayer to use the exact number of days already appears in Code Sec. 42(f)(4), there was no need to put language to that effect in the '93 Act.

For official explanation see Committee Reports ¶ 3013.

¶ 715. 20% incremental research credit reinstated retroactive to July 1, '92—and extended through June 30, '95

Under pre-'93 Act law, a taxpayer carrying on a trade or business—or a qualifying startup company, described below—was allowed a 20% research credit for:

(1) Qualified incremental research expenses paid or incurred in the tax year (but before July 1, '92); and

(2) Cash, qualified grants, or contributions paid in the tax year (but before July 1, '92) to universities for qualified research. (FTC 2d/FIN ¶ L-15300 *et seq.;* TG ¶ 5830 *et seq.;* USTR ¶ 414 *et seq.)*

To determine the incremental research credit described at (1) above, for a tax year ending before July 1, '92, the 20% credit rate was applied to the excess (if any) of qualified research expenses for that tax year over the "base amount," described below. (See FTC 2d/FIN ¶ L-15302; TG ¶ 5831; USTR ¶ 414.01) However, for a tax year straddling July 1, '92 (i.e., a tax year beginning before July 1, '92 and ending after that date, including calendar year '92), the "base amount" was proportionately reduced to an amount that bore the same ratio to the "base amount" for that year as the number of days in that year but before July 1, '92 bore to the total number of days in that year. (FTC 2d/FIN ¶ L-15312; TG ¶ 5838; USTR ¶ 414.01)

> ***observation:*** For a '92 calendar year taxpayer, the "base amount," described below, was reduced by 50% under the above rule.

The term "base amount" was the amount derived from multiplying; (a) the fixed-base percentage, described below; by (b) the average gross receipts of the taxpayer for the four tax years before the credit year. If the base amount determined under this computation was 50% or less than the qualified research expenses for the credit year, a "minimum base amount" was used in computing the credit. This minimum base amount was 50% of the qualified research expenses for the credit year. (See FTC 2d/FIN ¶ L-15312; TG ¶ 5838; USTR ¶ 414.01)

The "fixed-base percentage" for a taxpayer that wasn't a startup company was the percentage derived by dividing (a) the total qualified research expenses of the taxpayer for tax years beginning after '83 and before '89 (i.e., the "'84-'88 period") by (b) the total gross receipts of the taxpayer for the '84-'88 period—subject to a maximum of 16%. For startup companies, the assigned fixed-base percentage was 3%. (See FTC 2d/FIN ¶ L-15310; TG ¶ 5838; USTR ¶ 414.01)

A "startup company" under the research expense credit rules of Code Sec. 41(c)(3)(B), was defined as a taxpayer who didn't have both gross receipts and qualified research expenses during each of at least three tax years beginning after '83 and before '89. (FTC 2d/FIN ¶ L-15311; TG ¶ 5838; USTR ¶ 414.01)

> ***illustration:*** In '92, X Corp, a calendar-year taxpayer (not a startup company) had total qualifying research expenses of $500,000 qualifying for the 20% incremental research credit. Of this amount, $210,000 was paid or incurred before July 1, '92, and the balance of $290,000 was paid or incurred after June 30, '92 and before '93. For purposes of determining (a) average annual gross receipts, and (b) the fixed base percentage, X Corp's records show the following:
>
> | | |
> |---|---|
> | . . . Total qualified research expenses for the '84-'88 period | $390,000 |
> | . . . Total qualified gross receipts for the '84-'88 period | $4,200,000 |

FTC 2d References are to the Federal Tax Coordinator 2d
FIN References are to RIA's Analysis of Federal Taxes: Income
TG References are to the Tax Guide
USTR References are to the United States Tax Reporter

. . . Total qualified gross receipts
for the preceding 4-year
period ('88-'91): $9,200,000

(a)'92 average annual gross receipts was $2,300,000 computed by dividing total gross receipts for the '88-'91 period (here, $9,200,000) by 4;

(b)'92 fixed-base percentage was 9.29% computed by dividing the total research expenses for the '84-'88 period (here, $390,000) by the total gross receipts for the same period (here, $4,200,000).

Thus, the '92 "base amount" for X Corp (reduced by 50% for a '92 calendar year taxpayer under the "base amount proportionate reduction" rule described above) was $106,835 (i.e., 1/2 of 9.29% of $2,300,000) since the minimum base amount rule did not apply.

Under the pre-'93 Act law, therefore, X Corp's research expense credit was $20,633, computed as follows:

'92 qualified research expense (pre-July 1, '92)	$210,000
Less: base amount	(106,835)
Excess over base amount	$103,165
Credit rate	×20%
Pre-'93 Act Law Credit	$ 20,633

The '93 Act:

(1) retroactively reinstates the research expense credit as of July 1, '92, and extends it to qualified research expenses paid or incurred before July 1, '95. (Code Sec. 41(h)(1) as amended by '93 Act § 13111(a)(1)(A)) Thus, the research tax credit (including the university basic research credit) is extended for three years; that is, for qualified expenses paid or incurred during the period July 1, '92 through June 30, '95. (Conf Rept p. 8)

(2) Modifies the computation of the fixed-base percentage for startup companies, as explained at ¶ 716.

(3) Requires that the "base amount" for a tax year straddling July 1, '95 (i.e., a tax year beginning before July 1, '95 and ending after June 30, '95 be reduced by the ratio of the number of days in that year before July 1, '95 bears to the total number of days in that year. (Code Sec. 41(h)(2))

observation: Except for the above three changes, the '93 Act makes no changes to the existing rules for determining "eligible" research expenses for either the incremental research credit component or the university basic research credit component. It also makes no change to (a) the existing credit rate of 20%, or to (b) the component credit for university basic research payments.

illustration: Because of the '93 Act's retroactive reinstatement of the research credit, X Corp's base amount in the above illustration is $213,670 (i.e., 9.29% of $2,300,000). Thus, X Corp's research credit for '92 is $57,266, computed as follows:

Total '92 qualified research expenses	$500,000
Less: base amount	$213,670
Excess over base amount	$286,330
Credit rate	× 20%
'92 credit	$57,266

recommendation: The retroactive reinstatement of the research credit permitting otherwise qualified research expenses paid or incurred after June 30, '92 to qualify for the reinstated credit forces taxpayers with these post-June 30, '92 expenses to evaluate the feasibility of filing a refund claim for calendar year-, or fiscal year-'92.

☐ **Effective:** For tax years ending after June 30, '92. (§ 13111(c))
For official explanation see Committee Reports ¶ 3003.

¶ 716. Fixed-base percentage in research credit formula for startup companies modified for post-'93 years

As explained at ¶ 715, qualified research expenses in excess of a base amount (or a minimum base amount) qualify for the 20% research expense credit. Under pre-'93 Act law, the base amount for a startup company was 3% (the "fixed-base percentage") of that company's average amount of its gross receipts for the four preceding years. However, as in the case of non-startup companies, a minimum base amount equal to 50% of the qualified research expenses for the tax year was used in the credit computation if 50% of the qualified research expenses for the tax year was higher than the amount determined under the 3% rule. A startup company was defined as a taxpayer who didn't have both gross receipts and qualified research expenses during each of at least three tax years beginning after '83 and before '89—generally referred to as "the '84-'88 period." (FTC 2d ¶ L-15311; TG ¶ 5838; USTR ¶ 414.01)

illustration: In '88, Z Corp, a calendar year taxpayer, was incorporated for the purpose of developing new productivity equipment in the electronic and communication industries. In '92, Z Corp had total qualifying research expenses of $500,000 qualifying for the research credit. Of this amount, $210,000 was paid or incurred before July 1, '92 and the balance of $290,000 was paid or incurred after June 30, '92 but before '93. Z Corp's total qualified gross receipts for the '88-'91 period was $9,200,000.

Under these facts, Z Corp's:

(1)'92 average annual gross receipts was $2,300,000 computed by dividing total gross receipts for the $88-'91 period (here, $9,200,000) by 4;

(2)'92 fixed-base percentage was 3% since it is a startup company under the above rule;

(3)'92 base amount—reduced 50% for '92 calendar year taxpayers under the "proportionate reduction rule" discussed at ¶ 715, above—was $105,000; i.e., the higher of:

(a)$34,500 [3% of $2,300,000 divided by 2], or

(b)$105,000 ['92 qualified research expenses of $210,000 divided by 2],

Under the pre-'93 Act law, therefore, Z Corp's research expense credit was $21,000 computed as follows:

. . . '92 qualified expenses	$210,000
. . . Less: base amount	(105,000)
. . . Excess over base amount	$105,000
. . . Credit rate	× 20%
. . . Pre-'93 Act law credit	$21,000

The '93 Act modifies the computation of the fixed-base percentage for startup companies beginning with their sixth taxable year beginning after '93. (Code Sec. 41(c)(3)(B)(ii) as amended by '93 Act § 13112(a))

FTC 2d References are to the Federal Tax Coordinator 2d
FIN References are to RIA's Analysis of Federal Taxes: Income
TG References are to the Tax Guide
USTR References are to the United States Tax Reporter

Under the modified rule, a startup company (as defined under per-'93 Act law, above) continues to use the prescribed 3% fixed-base percentage for the base amount computation for each of its first five tax years beginning after Dec. 31, '93 in which the startup company has qualified research expenses. (Code Sec. 41(c)(3)(B)(ii)(I))

> ***observation:*** This rule appears to be over-board in that it prescribes methods for determining the fixed-base percentage for years when no research expenses credit is provided for by the '93 act. This is because both the House and Senate tax committees (before agreeing to only a three-year extension of the credit in Conference) had intended to make the credit permanent and this rule—adapted verbatim by the Conference Committee—prescribes computation methods for determining the fixed-base percentage, as described below, for the first ten tax years in which a startup company has qualified research expenses.

> ***observation:*** The phase "beginning after Dec. 31, '93" in the above rule forces startup companies that came into existence during the $84-88 period to continue using the prescribed 3% fixed-based percentage for their first five tax years beginning after '93. Apparently, use of the 3% rule for pre-'94 tax years don't count under the above five-year rule.

> ***observation:*** Z Corp in the above example would continue to use the higher of 3% or one-half of qualified expenses for its '94 through '98 tax years in computing its base amount during the '94-'98 period if the research expense credit becomes available for qualified expenses paid or incurred after June 30, '95.

For the next five tax years beginning after '93, however (e.g., from '99 through year 2003 for a pre-'94 calendar year startup company), the fixed-base percentage is no longer pre-set at 3%. Instead, it is a specified amount of the ratio or percentage—increased annually during this second five year period—determined by dividing qualified research expenses by gross receipts. (H Rept p. 599) The increasing fixed-base percentage for each tax year of the second five year period beginning after '93 for a startup company is determined as follows:

. . . *Sixth tax year:* One-sixth (1/6th) of the ratio (or percentage) of qualified research expenses to gross receipts for the taxpayer's fourth and fifth tax years. (Code Sec. 41(c)(3)(B)(ii)(II))

. . . *Seventh tax year:* One-third (1/3rd) of the ratio (or percentage) of qualified research expenses to gross receipts for the taxpayer's fifth and sixth tax years. (Code Sec. 41(c)(3)(B)(ii)(III))

. . . *Eighth tax year:* One-half (1/2) of the ratio (or percentage) of qualified research expenses to gross receipts for the taxpayer's fifth, sixth, and seventh tax years. (Code Sec. 41(c)(3)(B)(ii)(IV))

. . . *Ninth tax year:* Two-thirds (2/3rd) of the ration (or percentage) of qualified research expenses to gross receipts for the taxpayer's four preceding tax years. (Code Sec. 41(c)(3)(B)(ii)(V))

. . . *Tenth tax year:* Five-sixths (5/6th) of the ratio (or percentage) of qualified research expenses to gross receipts for the taxpayer's five preceding tax years. (Code Sec. 41(c)(3)(B)(ii)(VI))

For the eleventh and later tax years, a startup company's fixed-base percentage is its actual ratio (or percentage) of qualified research expenses to gross receipts for any five tax years selected by the taxpayer from its fifth through tenth tax years. (Code Sec. 41(c)(3)(B)(ii)(VII))

The fixed-base percentages computed under the above rules are rounded to the nearest 1/100th of 1%. (Code Sec. 41(c)(3)(D))

observation: The '93 Act's reinstatement of the research expense (as discussed at ¶ 715) means that Z Corp in the above illustration should consider filing a refund claim for its '92 increased research credit of $50,000 computed as follows:

Total '92 qualified expenses	$500,000
Less: Base amount (higher of 3% of $2,300,000 or 50% of $500,000	(250,000)
Excess over base amount	$250,000
Credit rate	× 20%
'92 Research expense credit	$50,000

☐ **Effective:** Taxable years beginning after '93. (§ 13112(c))
For official explanation see Committee Reports ¶ 3003.

¶ 717. Targeted jobs credit reinstated retroactive to July 1, '92—and extended through Dec. 31 '94

Business employers who hired before July 1, '92 certain individuals certified as members of nine "targeted" (generally disadvantaged) groups could elect a credit against income tax of 40% of first-year wages limited to $6,000 of qualifying wages per eligible employee. For qualified summer youth employees, however, the limit was $3,000 instead of $6,000 of qualified wages per employee, (FTC 2d/FIN ¶ L-17800 *et seq.;* TG ¶ 5800 *et seq.;* USTR ¶ 514)

These nine targeted groups included: (1) qualified summer youth employees; (2) economically disadvantaged youths; (3) youths participating in a cooperative education program; (4) eligible work incentive employees; (5) vocational rehabilitation referrals; (6) economically disadvantaged Vietnam-era veterans; (7) general assistance recipients; (8) supplemental security income (SSI) recipients; and (9) economically disadvantaged ex-convicts, (See FTC 2d/FIN ¶ L-17801; TG ¶ 5805; USTR ¶ 514)

The '93 Act retroactively reinstates the targeted jobs credit for the nine qualifying groups of pre-'93 Act law who begin—or began—work after June 30, '92. (§ 13102(a)) The reinstated credit for the nine qualifying groups is scheduled to end for qualified individuals beginning work after '94. (Code Sec. 51(c)(4) as amended by '93 Act § 13102(a))

recommendation: For the '92 calendar tax year and for tax years straddling June 30, '92, employers may want to identify qualifying wages paid for work performed after June 30, '92 by qualifying individuals. The above retroactive reinstatement may allow employers to qualify for the maximum credit allowable for each qualifying employee. Where this is the case, an amended return and refund claim may be required. (See FTC 2d/FIN ¶ T-6700 *et seq.;* TG ¶ 9605 *et seq.;* USTR ¶ 74,224)

illustration: For '92, X Corp, a calendar year taxpayer, hired the following three certified targeted group individuals subject to the ¶ 6,000 of qualified wage-credit limitation and paid each of them the following wages:

Period	Individual A	Individual B	Individual C
Jan. to Jun. '92	$6,000	$3,000	-0-
Jul. to Dec. '92	-0-	$3,000	$6,000
Total	$6,000	$6,000	$6,000

FTC 2d References are to the Federal Tax Coordinator 2d
FIN References are to RIA's Analysis of Federal Taxes: Income
TG References are to the Tax Guide
USTR References are to the United States Tax Reporter

On its timely-filed income tax return for '92, X Corp properly claimed and was allowed:

. . . $2,400 credit for individual A (i.e., 40% of $6,000);

. . . $1,200 credit for individual B (i.e., 40% of $3,000);

. . . Zero credit for individual C.

Under the retroactive reinstatement of the '93 Act Law, X Corp may file a refund claim for '92 and claim:

. . . an additional $1,200 credit for individual B;

. . . a $2,400 credit for individual C.

> ***observation:*** The '93 Act doesn't include a credit for certain participants (16-to-20 years of age) in approved school-to-work programs—a tenth group—as originally provided in the House Wages and Means Committee Bill.
>
> ***observation:*** It isn't clear how the retroactive reinstatement to July 1, '92 of the targeted jobs credit is applied to new qualified employees hired after June 30, '92 and before Aug. '93. The Committee Reports are silent as to how the employee-certification requirements of Code Sec. 51(d)(16)(A) (see FTC 2d/FIN ¶ L-17815; TG ¶ 5807)—which presumably were not followed for post-June 30, '92 new qualified employees since no targeted jobs credit was available for hiring them—would be applied if the employer is retroactively filing a refund claim for the applicable credit. Presumably, IRS will issue guidelines on the need (if any) of retroactive certification for new post-June 30, '92 qualified employees.

☐ **Effective:** For qualified individuals who begin work for the employer after June 30, '92. (§ 13102(b))

For official explanation see Committee Reports ¶ 3002.

¶ 718. Targeted jobs credit not available for wages paid to employees related to equity owners of noncorporate entities

The targeted jobs credit is not available for wages paid to employees who are related to the employer/taxpayer. Where the taxpayer is a corporation, the credit is not available for wages paid to employees who are related to any individual who owns, directly or indirectly (taking into account attribution rules), more than 50% (by value) of the corporation's stock. (FTC 2d/FIN ¶ L-17816; TG ¶ 5806; USTR ¶ 514)

The '93 Act extends this rule to cover employees who are related to certain equity owners of noncorporate entities. In the case of a taxpayer which is an entity other than a corporation, no targeted jobs credit is available for wages paid to an employee who is related to an individual who owns, directly or indirectly, more than 50% of the capital and profits interests in the entity. (Code Sec. 51(i)(1)(A) as amended by '93 Act § 13302(d))

> ***observation:*** The same rule applies to disallow the newly-enacted empowerment zone employment credit for wages paid to persons related to 50% owners of a business. (See ¶ 604)
>
> ***observation:*** The '93 Act provides that the same attribution rules (namely, those set forth in Code Sec. 267(c), see FTC 2d/FIN ¶ G-2661; TG ¶ 2653; USTR ¶ 2674) which apply in determining constructive ownership of corporate stock also apply in determining constructive

ownership of noncorporate equity interests. However, by its terms, Code Sec. 267(c) only refers to ownership of stock. Since the apparent intention in enacting the foregoing provision is to place corporate and noncorporate businesses in the same position, presumably attribution rules analogous to those of Code Sec. 267(c) will apply.

☐ **Effective:** Aug. 10, '93. (§ 13303)

¶ 719. Credit for clinical-testing expenses for "orphan drugs" reinstated retroactive to July 1, '92—and extended through Dec. 31, '94

The 50% credit for qualified human clinical testing expenses, generally performed in the U.S., to obtain FDA approval for the U.S. sale of drugs for rare diseases or conditions—the so called "orphan drugs"—ended for otherwise qualified expenses paid or incurred after June 20, '92. (FTC 2d/FIN ¶ L-15600; TG ¶ 5890; USTR ¶ 284)

The '93 Act allows the above credit for otherwise qualified clinical-testing expenses paid or incurred though Dec. 31, '94. (Code Sec. 28(e) as amended by '93 Act § 13111(b)) Thus, the orphan drug tax credit is retroactively extended for 30 months (i.e., for qualified expenses paid or incurred during the period July 1, '92 through Dec. 31, '94). (Conf Rept p. 534)

☐ **Effective:** Tax years ending after June 30, '92. (§ 13111(c))

For official explanation see Committee Reports ¶ 3004.

¶ 720. Authority to issue tax-exempt "small-issue" bonds permanently extended

Pre-'93 Act law provided that "small-issues" of state or local bonds issued before July 1, '92 were tax-exempt if at least 95% of the net proceeds of those bonds were used to finance: (1) manufacturing facilities for the production of tangible personal property; or (2) the acquisition of up to $250,000 per farmer of farmland or depreciable farm property by a first-time farmer who materially and substantially participated in the operation of that farm. (FTC 2d/FIN ¶s J-3208, J-3251; TG ¶s 5301, 5305; USTR ¶ 1444.01)

"Small-issue," for this purpose, meant bond issues having an aggregate authorized face amount, including certain outstanding prior issues, of $1 million or less ($10 million or less over a 6-year measuring period in certain cases) and issued under an allocation from the state private activity volume limitation. (See FTC 2d/FIN ¶ J-3212 *et seq.;* USTR ¶ 1444.01)

Reg § 1.103-8(a)(5) (as in effect before July 1, '93) generally required that qualified small-issue bonds be issued within one year after the entire facility being financed was first placed in service. (See FTC 2d/FIN ¶ J-3152; USTR ¶ 1444.01)

The '93 Act removes the July 1, '92 termination date noted above. Thus, state or local bonds issued after June 30, '92 may qualify as tax-exempt small issues if they satisfy the requirements noted above. (Code Sec. 144(a)(12)(B) as amended by '93 Act § 13122(a))

The '93 Act provides that if the one-year period specified in Reg § 1.103-8(a)(5) (as in effect before July 1, '93) or any successor regulation would (except for this provision) expire after June 30, '92, and before Jan. 1, '94, that one-year period would not expire before Jan. 1, '94. (§ 13122(c))

☐ **Effective:** For the permanent extension of the authority to issue tax-exempt small issue bonds, for bonds issued after June 30, '92, (§ 13122(b))

For the provision relating to Reg § 1.103-8(a)(5), Aug. 10, '93. (Conf Rept p. 533)

For official explanation see Committee Reports ¶ 3010.

¶ 721. Governmental authority to issue QMBs and MCCs is permanently extended

Under pre-'93 Act law, states and local governments subsidized—from the net proceeds of qualified, tax-exempt mortgage bonds ("QMBs") issued before July 1, '92—the purchase, rehabilitation, or improvement of single-family, owner-occupied residences of qualified low-income persons located within their respective jurisdictions. (FTC 2d/FIN ¶ J-3175 *et seq.;* TG ¶ 5303; USTR ¶ 1434)

Also, under pre-'93 Act law, instead of issuing QMBs, local jurisdictions could have elected, before July 1, '92, to partly or totally exchange their QMB authority for authority to issue mortgage credit certificates ("MCCs"). (FTC 2d/FIN ¶ J-3204 *et seq.;* TG ¶ 1203; USTR ¶ 254)

Under the MCC program, certificate holders would arrange financing for their residences through conventional sources without the subsidy from QMBs. In this case, the MCC-holders qualified for a nonrefundable tax credit for a specified percentage of interest paid on the qualified mortgage loan. The credit is limited to $2,000 if the specified percentage is more than 20%. (See FTC 2d/FIN ¶ A-4008 *et seq.;* TG ¶ 1203; USTR ¶ 254.02)

The '93 Act permanently extends the authority of states and local governments to issue QMBs. (Code Sec. 143(a)(1) as amended by '93 Act ¶ 13141(a)) Similarly, the '93 Act permanently extends the availability of the election to issue MCCs. (Code Sec. 25(h) as amended by '93 Act § 13141(b))

☐ **Effective:**

(1) The extension of the governmental authority to issue qualified mortgage bonds applies to QMBs issued after June 30, '92. (§ 13141(f)(1))

(2) The election to issue MCCs, instead of QMBs, applies to elections for periods after June 30, '92. (§ 13141(f)(2))

For official explanation see Committee Reports ¶ 3012.

¶ 722. Loans other than first mortgage loans on homes in high housing cost area generally not taken into account for QMB or MCC purposes

The '93 Act provides that the fact that an issuer of QMBs or MCCs also provides certain mortgage loans or grants other than first mortgage loans or grants to home buyers in conjunction with QMB- or MCC-financing will not prevent the availability of QMB- or MCC-assistance on the purchase of a residence. (Conf Rept p. 538)

The '93 Act provides that in the case of a residence which is located in a high housing cost area (see below), the interest of a governmental unit in that residence, by reason of financing provided under any qualified program (defined below), is not taken into account for purposes of the QMB or MCC programs, except to the following extent:

(1) The recapture "tax" (see below) still applies, and

(2) for purposes of the purchase price requirement (see below), the acquisition cost of a residence is reduced by the amount of financing provided under a qualified program. (Code Sec. 143(k)(10)(A) as amended by '93 Act § 13141(c))

Thus, any interest of a governmental unit in a QMB- or MCC-financed residence attributable to a qualifying subordinated mortgage loan will be disregarded for purposes of (1) the first-time homebuyer and owner-occupied residence requirements of the QMB and MCC programs; (2) the maximum purchase price limit for QMB- and MCC-financed residences; (3) the rules for determining who is the owner of a QMB- or MCC-financed residence; and (4) the rules for determining the effective rate of interest on QMB financed loans. (Conf Rept p. 538)

High housing cost area. If a residence for which financing is provided under a QMB issue is located in a high housing cost area, a higher income limitation, generally, 140% of applicable median family income, is substituted for the 115% income limitation for mortgages in areas not considered to be high housing cost areas. (See FTC 2d/FIN ¶ J-3185.1; USTR ¶ 1434.01) Lower percentages apply for mortgages with families of less than three individuals. (See FTC 2d/FIN J-3185.2; USTR ¶ 1434.01) A high housing cost area is any area for which the housing cost/income ratio is greater than 1.2. (See FTC 2d/FIN ¶ J-3185.3 *et seq.;* USTR ¶ 1434.01)

Recapture "tax." A recapture "tax" for the disposition year is imposed on a taxpayer who after '90 disposes of any interest in a residence whose purchase was financed, generally after '90, from the proceeds of QMBs or MCCs if the disposition occurs within nine years after the date the loan was provided. (See FTC 2d/FIN ¶ I-4900 *et seq.;* TG ¶s 4290, 5306; USTR ¶ 1434.02)

Purchase price requirement. A QMB issue meets the purchase price requirement if the acquisition cost of each residence for which owner-financing is provided isn't more than 90% of the average area purchase price applicable to the residence. Different percentages apply to targeted area residences. (See FTC 2d/FIN ¶s J-3183 *et seq.;* TG ¶ 5303; USTR ¶ 1434.04)

Qualified program. Under the '93 Act, for purposes of Code Sec. 143(k)(10)(A) (discussed above), the term "qualified program" means any governmental program providing mortgage loans (other than first mortgage loans) or grants:

(1) which restricts (for the nine-year recapture tax period beginning on the date the financing is provided) the resale of the residence to a purchaser qualifying under the requirements of Code Sec. 143 and to a price determined by an index that reflects less than the full amount of any appreciation in the residence's value, or

(2) which provides for deferred or reduced interest payments on that financing and grants the governmental unit a share in the appreciation of the residence but only if that financing is not provided directly or indirectly through the use of any tax-exempt private activity bond. (Code Sec. 143(k)(10)(B))

Qualifying subordinate mortgage loans or grants either must be accompanied by a "resale price control restriction" (see below) , (or in the case of loans must be, "shared appreciation loans," see below). (Conf Rept p. 538)

observation: Neither '93 Act § 13141(c) nor the related Committee

FTC 2d References are to the Federal Tax Coordinator 2d
FIN References are to RIA's Analysis of Federal Taxes: Income
TG References are to the Tax Guide
USTR References are to the United States Tax Reporter

Reports define "qualifying subordinate mortgage loan." Presumably it is a mortgage other than a first mortgage.

Resale price control restriction defined. A "resale price control restriction" is defined as a deed restriction, right of repurchase, or similar mechanism which (1) requires the owner to sell the unit to a purchaser qualifying for QMB or MCC financing and (2) limits the resale price to an amount not exceeding the initial purchase price plus an indexed amount that is less than the full appreciation on the residence. (Conf Rept p. 538)

Shared appreciation loan" defined. A "shared appreciation loan" is defined as a below-market rate or deferred interest loan which entitles the governmental lender to a share of any appreciation in value (attributable to the portion of the residence financed with the share appreciation loan) realized upon disposition of the residence as repayment for the subsidy provided by the loan. (Conf Rept p. 538)

It is intended that the special rules for these housing affordability programs will not apply to any subordination loans or grant if the governmental unit's interest under the loan or grant is structured so as to realize an amount in excess of the pro rata portion of the appreciation on the residence financed with the subordinated mortgage loan or grant (e.g., by allocating to the governmental unit an amount of gain on disposition greater than the proportionate amount of the total subsidy to the homebuyer that is provided by the subordinated mortgage loan). (Conf Rept pp. 538-9)

☐ **Effective:** For QMBs issued and MCCs provided on or after Aug. 10, '93. (§ 13141(f)(3))

For official explanation see Committee Reports ¶ 3012.

¶ 723. Certain land ownership by QMB- and MCC-financed homeowners exempted from first-time homebuyer and new mortgage requirements

Three-year requirement. Under pre-'93 Act law a qualified mortgage issue must meet the three-year requirement. Under this requirement at least 95% of the net proceeds of the issue must be used to finance the residences of mortgagors who had no present ownership interest in their principal residences (other than the residence for which financing is being provided) during the three-year period ending on the date the mortgage is executed. (See FTC 2d/FIN ¶ J-3182)

> ***observation:*** While the Conference Report (p. 539) refers to the statutory three-year requirement as the "first-time homebuyer" requirement, it would appear that a mortgagor could still qualify under the three-year requirement and not be a first-time homebuyer. For example, a mortgagor having previously owned a principal residence which he sold prior to the three-year period and who rented thereafter, would appear to meet the three-year requirement.

The '93 Act adds an exception to the three-year requirement for financing with respect to land possessed under a contract for deed (defined below) and the construction of any residence on that land. (Code Sec. 143(d)(2)(C) as amended by '93 Act § 13141(d)(1)(C))

New mortgage requirement. Under pre-'93 Act law, the proceeds of a qualified mortgage issue may not be used to acquire or replace existing mortgages (the "new mortgage requirement," see FTC 2d /FIN ¶ J-3197).

The '93 Act adds an exception for certain contract for deed (defined below) agreements to the new mortgage requirement. Under this exception the contract for deed will not be treated as an existing mortgage by a mortgagor (1) whose family income (defined below) is not more than 50% of applicable median family income (defined below) and (2) whose principal residence (within the meaning of the Code Sec. 1034 rules on rollover of gain on the sale of a principal residence) is located on that land. (Code Sec. 143(i)(1)(C)(i) as amended by '93 Act § 13141(d)(2))

Contract for deed defined. The '93 Act defines "contract for deed" as a seller-financed contract for the conveyance of land under which:

. . . legal title does not pass to the purchaser until the consideration under the contract is fully paid to the seller, and

. . . the seller's remedy for nonpayment is forfeiture rather than judicial or nonjudicial foreclosure. (Code Sec. 143(i)(1)(C)(ii) as amended by '93 Act § 13141(d)(2))

Family income defined. Family income of mortgagors is determined by IRS after taking into account the regulations under Section 8 of the Housing Act of '37 (or, if Section 8 is terminated, under the regulations in effect immediately before the termination). (See FTC 2d/FIN ¶ J-3185)

Applicable median family income defined. The applicable median family income with respect to a residence is the greater of:

. . . the area median gross income for the area in which the residence is located; or

. . . the statewide median gross income for the State in which the residence is located. (See FTC 2d/FIN ¶ J-3185; USTR ¶ 1434.01)

Acquisition cost. Under pre-'93 Act law, "acquisition cost," for purposes of the purchase price requirement for a qualified mortgage (see FTC 2d/FIN ¶ J-3183 *et seq.)* issue does not include the cost of land which has been owned by the mortgagor for at least two years before the date on which construction of the residence begins. (See FTC 2d/FIN ¶ J-3183)

The '93 Act includes as part of the acquisition cost for the purchase price requirement for a qualified mortgage, land possessed under a contract for deed by a mortgagor. (Code Sec. 143(k)(3)(B)(iii) as amended by '93 Act § 13141(d)(3))

☐ **Effective:** For loans originated and credit certificates provided after Aug. 10, '93. (§ 13141(f)(4))

For official explanation see Committee Reports ¶ 3012.

¶ 724. Exception to single-family residence requirement under QMB- and MCC-financing is expanded

Under pre-'93 Act law, all residences receiving QMB- or MCC-financing (see ¶ 721) must be single-family owner-occupied residences. (See FTC 2d/FIN ¶ J-3181) An exception, under pre-'93 Act law, provides that the terms "single-family" and "owner-occupied" include two-, three-, or four-family residences if (1) one unit is occupied by the owner of the units and (2) the units were first occupied as a residence at least five years before the mortgage is executed. (See FTC 2d/FIN ¶s J-3181, J-3202)

The '93 Act provides that the (five-year minimum occupancy) requirement in (2), above, will not apply to any two-family residence if the residence is a targeted area residence (see below) and the family income of the mortgagor is 140% or less of the applicable median family income (see below). (Code Sec. 143(k)(7) as amended by '93 Act § 13141(e))

Targeted area residence. A targeted area residence is located either (1) in an area in which at least 70% of the families have an income that is 80% or less of the statewide median family income ("qualified census tract") or (2) an "area of chronic economic distress." (See FTC 2d/FIN ¶ J-3194)

Applicable median family income is the greater of:

. . . the area median gross income for the area in which the residence is located; or

. . . the statewide median gross income for the state in which the residence is located. (See FTC 2d/FIN ¶ J-3185)

☐ **Effective:** For QMBs issued and MCCs provided on or after Aug. 10, '93. (§ 13141(f)(3))

For official explanation see Committee Reports ¶ 3012.

¶ 725. Qualified bonds to finance governmentally owned high-speed intercity rail facilities fully exempted from volume cap restrictions

Private activity bonds issued after Aug. 15, '86 normally do not qualify for tax-exempt status. (See FTC 2d/FIN ¶ J-3100 *et seq.;* TG ¶ 5296; USTR ¶s 1034, 1424.04) Tax-exempt status, however, is granted to private activity bonds that constitute "qualified bonds." (See FTC 2d/FIN ¶ J-3150 *et seq.;* TG ¶ 5297; USTR ¶ 1414) An exempt facility bond may qualify as a tax-exempt qualified bond. (See FTC 2d/FIN ¶ J-3152; TG ¶ 5297; USTR ¶ 1424) An exempt facility bond that is part of an issue, 95% or more of whose net proceeds are used to finance a high-speed intercity rail facility qualifies as an exempt facility bond. (See FTC 2d/FIN ¶ J-3173.1; TG ¶ 5297; USTR ¶ 1424.01)

Certain types of qualified bonds are subject to "volume caps"—that is, states and their subordinate bond issuing authorities may not issue more than a certain amount of these qualified bonds in any given calendar year. (See FTC 2d/FIN ¶ J-3231; TG ¶ 5304; USTR ¶ 1464)

Under pre-'93 Act law the volume cap restrictions do not apply with respect to 75% of any exempt facility bond issued to finance high-speed intercity rail facilities. (FTC 2d/FIN ¶ J-3232; USTR ¶ 1464.01)

> ***observation:*** Thus, under pre-'93 Act law, the volume cap restrictions do apply to only 25% of an exempt facility bond issued to finance high-speed intercity rail facilities.

The '93 Act provides that the volume cap restrictions do not apply to any portion of an exempt facility bond issued as part of an issue 95% or more of the net proceeds of which are to be used to provide high-speed intercity rail facilities if all of the property to be financed by the net proceeds of the issue is to be owned by a governmental unit. (Code Sec. 146(g)(4) as amended by '93 Act § 13121(a)) Bonds issued for privately-owned property would remain subject to the pre-'93 Act law requirement under which volume cap restrictions apply to 25% of an exempt facility bond issued to finance high-speed intercity rail facilities. (Conf Rept p. 532)

☐ **Effective:** For bonds issued after Dec. 31, '93. (§ 13121(b))

For official explanation see Committee Reports ¶ 3009.

¶ 726. Congress asks IRS to study AMT's effect on incentives for long-term investments

No deduction is allowed for miscellaneous itemized deductions in the computation of alternative minimum taxable (AMT) income. (See FTC 2d/FIN ¶ A-8119.4; TG ¶ 1372; USTR ¶ 554) Expenses for the production of income are miscellaneous itemized deductions. (See FTC 2d/FIN ¶ A-2709; TG ¶ 6015 *et seq.;* USTR ¶ 674)

Congress has stated that it feels that the AMT imposed on individual taxpayers may operate to disallow deductions that are associated with the production of income, including expenses associated with income derived through partnerships. (Conf Rept p. 528)

> ***observation:*** It appears that the language used by Congress, i.e., its statement that the AMT *may* operate to disallow these deductions, is somewhat imprecise. As explained above, those deductions *are* disallowed.

A provision was included in proposed legislation that was vetoed by President Bush in '92, to allow a certain amount of the distributive share of Sec. 212 expenses (expenses for the production of income, see FTC 2d/FIN ¶ L-1400 *et seq.;* TG ¶ 6016; USTR ¶ 2124 *et seq.*) of a partner in a partnership to be deductible for AMT purposes. Concern has been expressed in Congress that the present-law AMT treatment of Sec. 212 expenses might create a disincentive for the long-term investments that the 50% capital gain exclusion described in ¶ 702 is intended to foster.

Accordingly, Congress has urged IRS to study the question of whether the present-law AMT treatment of Sec. 212 expenses creates such a disincentive, and to provide the House Ways and Means Committee and the Senate Finance Committee with a report of this study, by Mar. 1, '94. The study should include IRS's views and recommendations as to whether legislation would be appropriate with respect to the AMT treatment of Sec. 212 expenses, along with a discussion of the merits and consequences of any such legislation. (Conf Rept p. 528)

For official explanation see Committee Reports ¶ 3005.

FTC 2d References are to the Federal Tax Coordinator 2d
FIN References are to RIA's Analysis of Federal Taxes: Income
TG References are to the Tax Guide
USTR References are to the United States Tax Reporter

¶ 800. Pensions and Employee Benefits

¶ 801. Maximum compensation considered for qualified retirement plans and certain welfare plans reduced to $150,000

Under pre-'93 Act law, the amount of an employee's annual compensation that may be taken into consideration by qualified retirement plans and simplified employee pensions is limited to $235,840 in '93. The amount was $200,000 in '89 and is indexed annually for inflation. A plan may not base contributions or benefits on compensation above this annual limit, and any amount over the limit is disregarded when applying certain nondiscrimination rules. (FTC 2d/FIN ¶ H-6965 *et seq.;* TG ¶ 3681; USTR ¶ 4014.18)

The '93 Act reduces the annual limit to $150,000 (Code Sec. 401(a)(17) as amended by '93 Act § 13212(a)(1)), to be adjusted for inflation after '94. (§ 13212(a)(2))

> ***illustration:*** A defined contribution plan calls for employer contributions equal to 10% of each employee's compensation. For an employee earning $200,000 the contribution is $15,000 (10% of $150,000 compensation considered).

> ***observation:*** A plan sponsor can maintain its pre-'93 Act level of contributions and benefits for affected employees by raising the level of contributions or benefits for all plan participants. For example, to maintain a $30,000 annual allocation for an individual earning over $150,000, a money purchase pension plan could be amended to raise its formula to 20% of compensation. Alternatively, the sponsor can use other forms of compensation, such as nonqualified deferred compensation plans, to provide a comparable compensation package to its highly paid employees.

> ***caution:*** An employer may provide deferred compensation to a "select group of management and highly compensated employees" through a "top-hat plan" that is exempt from ERISA's funding and participation requirements. However, the Code's definition of "highly compensated" does not apply for ERISA purposes, so employers can't be certain that a plan covering all highly compensated employees (or even all those earning over $150,000) will necessarily meet the "top-hat plan" exemption from ERISA.

Limits on employer deductions. Deductions for employer contributions to qualified plans are sometimes limited by law to a percentage of participants' compensation. For example, deductions for contributions to profit sharing and stock bonus plans are limited to 15% of participants' compensation, while deductions for employers who maintain both defined contribution and defined benefit plans are limited (in some instances) to 25% of participants' compensation. In applying these percentage limits, any employee's compensation above $235,840 (in '93) is disregarded. (FTC 2d/FIN ¶ H-10009; USTR ¶ 4044) The '93 Act reduces the annual limit to $150,000, to be adjusted for inflation after '94. (Code Sec. 404(l) as amended by '93 Act § 13212(c)(1))

> ***recommendation:*** A one-person profit sharing plan is limited to an annual contribution of $22,500 (15% of $150,000) under the '93 Act, instead of $30,000 (the Code Sec. 415(c) limit) under pre-'93 Act law. To continue the

full $30,000 contributions, consider installing a money purchase pension plan with a 5% contribution rate, and contribute $7,500 (5% of $150,000) to the money purchase plan and up to $22,500 to the profit sharing plan.

Compensation considered in nondiscrimination tests. The annual limit also applies when a plan is tested for nondiscrimination in the amount of contributions or benefits (See FTC 2d/FIN ¶ H-6700 *et seq.;* TG ¶ 3631 *et seq.;* USTR ¶ 4044), and when the actual deferral percentage test is applied to elective deferrals under a Code Sec. 401(k) plan (See FTC 2d/FIN ¶ H-9043.1A; TG ¶ 3596; USTR ¶ 4014.17 *et seq.*). The '93 Act reduces the amount of compensation that may be taken into account from $235,840 (in '93) to $150,000 (Code Sec. 401(a)(17)), to be adjusted for inflation after '94.

illustration: An employee earning $225,000 defers $7,500 into a 401(k) plan. The employee's deferral percentage is 5.00% ($7,500÷$150,000 compensation considered), instead of 3.33% ($7,500÷$225,000) under pre-'93 Act law.

observation: This increase in deferral percentages for highly compensated employees might require that more contributions be made by, or on behalf of, the non-highly compensated employees in order to satisfy the actual deferral percentage test. Alternatively, the test can be satisfied either by limiting the amount of deferrals by highly compensated employees or by returning deferrals to the highly compensated employees with the largest deferral percentages.

The reduction from $235,840 to $150,000 per year also applies to nondiscrimination testing for simplified employee pensions (Code Sec. 408(k)(3)(C) as amended by '93 Act § 13212(b)(1)), with adjustment for post-'94 inflation. (Code Sec. 408(k)(6)(D)(ii) as amended by '93 Act § 13212(b)(2))

VEBAs, SUB trusts, and group legal services trusts. Certain employee benefit trusts must meet nondiscrimination requirements to be tax exempt. These trusts include voluntary employee beneficiary associations (VEBAs) under Code Sec. 501(c)(9), supplemental unemployment compensation benefit trusts (SUB trusts) under Code Sec. 501(c)(17), and group legal services trusts under Code Sec. 501(c)(20). The nondiscrimination requirements limit the benefits received by highly compensated employees, when measured as a percentage of their compensation. In applying the nondiscrimination requirements, any employee's compensation over $235,840 (in '93) is disregarded. (FTC 2d/FIN ¶ D-4414; USTR ¶ 5054.01) The '93 Act reduces this limit to $150,000, to be adjusted for inflation after '94. (Code Sec. 505(b)(7) as amended by '93 Act § 13212(c)(1))

Inflation adjustments. The $150,000 limit will be increased in multiples of $10,000, by applying an inflation adjustment factor and rounding the result down to the next multiple of $10,000.

illustration: If inflation is 4% after '93, the $150,000 limit will be $150,000 in '95 (rounded down from $156,000), $160,000 in '96 (rounded down from $162,240), and $160,000 in '97 (rounded down from $168,730).

☐ **Effective:** Plan years beginning after '93 (§ 13212(d)(1). Benefits accrued before the effective date are grandfathered and not reduced. (H Rept p. 651)

FTC 2d References are to the Federal Tax Coordinator 2d
FIN References are to RIA's Analysis of Federal Taxes: Income
TG References are to the Tax Guide
USTR References are to the United States Tax Reporter

For plans maintained under pre-Aug. 10, '93 collective bargaining agreements, effective for plan years beginning after expiration (disregarding extensions) of the agreement or plan years after '96 if sooner. (§ 13212(d)(2)) State and local governments may amend their plans to apply the reduced limits only to new participants. (§ 13212(d)(3))

> ***observation:*** The effective date provision refers only to "benefits accruing" in plan years beginning after '93. Presumably, these changes also apply to contributions allocated and to deductions taken in plan years beginning after '93.
> *For official explanation see Commitee Reports ¶ 3039.*

¶ 802. Employer-provided educational assistance exclusion retroactively reinstated and extended through '94

Under pre-Act law, for tax years that began before July 1, '92, an employee's gross income didn't include up to $5,250 per year of employer-paid educational benefits paid under a qualified educational assistance program. For tax years beginning in '92, only amounts paid by the employer before July 1, '92 for qualified educational assistance were excludable. Post-June 30, '92 educational assistance was not treated as excludable for '92. Amounts that were not excludable from gross income as educational assistance benefits might have been excludable as working condition fringes (i.e., as deductible job-related expenses of the employee). (FTC 2d/FIN ¶ H-2064; TG ¶ 3222; USTR ¶ 1274)

The '93 Act reinstates the educational assistance program benefit exclusion, and extends it through Dec. 31, '94. (Code Sec. 127(d) as amended by '93 Act § 13101(a)(1)) The Act also repeals the denial of the exclusion for educational assistance payments made after June 30, '92. (§ 13101(a)(2))

> ***recommendation:*** Employers that are making educational assistance program payments and are withholding on these benefits even though they are not in excess of $5,250, should no longer withhold on these payments.

> ***observation:*** Unless procedures provided by IRS for the recoupment of taxes paid on educational assistance in the second half of '92 (see below) provide otherwise, an employee will have to file an amended return for '92 to get a refund of income tax paid on post-June 30, '92, pre-'93 educational assistance. (See FTC 2d/FIN ¶ T-5601; TG ¶ 9622; USTR ¶ 64,024)

Congress intends that IRS will use its existing authority to the fullest extent possible to alleviate any administrative problems that may result from the expiration and retroactive extension of the educational assistance exclusion. IRS is to provide the simplest way possible for employees to recoup taxes paid on excludable educational assistance provided in the last half of '92. (Conf Rept p. 518)

> ***observation:*** The educational assistance exclusion is scheduled to end for qualified employer-provided benefits paid by employers after '94. For the excludability of employer payments for job-related educational assistance payments made after '94 that qualify as working condition fringe benefit rules, see below.

> ***observation:*** Under the '93 Act, as under pre-'93 Act rules, the exclusion for qualified educational assistance program payments applies regardless of whether the educational assistance is job-related.

☐ **Effective:** Tax years ending after June 30, '92. (§ 13101(c)(1))

Clarification of the availability of the working condition fringe exclusion for educational assistance. Under pre-Act law, amounts which would have qualified for the exclusion from income as educational assistance but for (1) exceeding the dollar limitation (see FTC 2d/FIN ¶ H-2066; TG ¶ 3152; USTR ¶ 1324.05), or (2) the relationship of the expenses to sports, games, or hobbies, may nonetheless be excludable as working condition fringes. (See FTC 2d/FIN ¶ H-2064; TG ¶ 3152; USTR ¶ 1324.05)

> ***observation:*** However, amounts paid for education that would not have qualified as excludable educational assistance for other reasons, e.g., the payments were for meals, lodging, or transportation, or for certain tools or supplies which an employee could have kept after a course had ended, would not have been excludable as working condition fringes.

The '93 Act, retroactively to tax years beginning after '88, (§ 13101(c)(2)) provides that amounts paid, or expenses incurred, by the employer for education or training provided to an employee, which are not excludable from income as educational assistance, are excluded from income as long as the amounts qualify as working condition fringes. (Code Sec. 132(i)(8))

> ***observation:*** Thus, any educational expenses that don't qualify for the educational assistance exclusion, such as meals, lodging, transportation, tools, or supplies, may be excludable as working condition fringes if the requirements for the working condition fringe exclusion are met.

☐ **Effective:** Tax years beginning after '88. (§ 13101(c)(2))
For official explanation see Committee Reports ¶ 3001.

¶ 803. Group health plans must continue to cover the cost of pediatric vaccines

Employers must provide continuation ("COBRA") coverage under a group health plan to qualified beneficiaries who would otherwise lose their coverage for reasons such as death, termination, divorce, retirement, cessation of a child's dependency, or an employer's bankruptcy. An excise tax of $100 per day per beneficiary is imposed if a group health plan fails to meet the continuation coverage requirements. (See FTC 2d/FIN ¶ H-1250 *et seq.;* TG ¶ 3384 *et seq.;* USTR ¶ 4980B4) Under pre-'93 Act law, this tax did not apply to plans that reduced their coverage of pediatric vaccines.

The '93 Act imposes the COBRA excise tax on group health plans that reduce their coverage of the costs of pediatric vaccines below the level of coverage provided as of May 1, '93. (Code Sec. 4980B(f)(1) as amended by '93 Act § 13422(a))

☐ **Effective:** Plan years beginning after Aug. 10, '93. (§ 13422(b))
For official explanation see Committee Reports ¶ 3076.

FTC 2d References are to the Federal Tax Coordinator 2d
FIN References are to RIA's Analysis of Federal Taxes: Income
TG References are to the Tax Guide
USTR References are to the United States Tax Reporter

¶ 900. Estates, Gifts, and Trusts

¶ 901. Top estate and gift tax rates that applied before '93 are reinstated for post-'92 transfers

Under pre-'93 Act law, the top estate and gift tax rate for decedents dying, or gifts made, after '92 was 50%. This rate applied to taxable transfers over $2,500,000. (FTC 2d Tax Rates and Tables tab in Volume 3; ¶s Q-8004, R-7008; TG ¶s 510, 511).

Under the '93 Act, the estate and gift tax rate on taxable transfers over $2,500,000 but not over $3,000,000 is 53%. The estate and gift tax rate on taxable transfers over $3,000,000 is 55%. (Code Sec. 2001(c)(1) as amended by '93 Act § 13208(a))

> ***observation:*** The estate and gift tax rates imposed by the '93 Act on taxable transfers over $2,500,000 are the same rates that applied to taxable transfers over $2,500,000 for decedents dying, or gifts made, before '93. Thus, the '93 Act reinstates the pre-'93 estate and gift tax rate schedule.

The benefits of the graduated estate and gift tax rates and the unified credit are phased out for taxable transfers that exceed $10,000,000. Under pre-'93 Act law, this was done by increasing the tax computed under the rate table by an amount equal to 5% of so much of the amount subject to tax that's over $10,000,000 but not over $21,040,000 (except that $18,340,000 was substituted for $21,040,000 in the case of decedents dying, and gifts made, after '92). (FTC 2d ¶s Q-8008, R-7009; TG ¶ 510) The '93 Act changes the phase-out formula by deleting the requirement that $18,340,000 be substituted for $21,040,000 in computing the increased tax on post-'92 taxable transfers that exceed $10,000,000. (Code Sec. 2001(c))2))

> ***observation:*** Under the pre-'93 Act phase-out formula, if a post-'92 taxable transfer exceeded $18,340,000, a flat rate of 50% (the top rate imposed on post-'92 transfers under pre-'93 Act law) in effect would have applied to the entire transfer. Using ²1,040,000 in the phase-out formula has the effect of applying a flat rate of 55% (the top rate on post-'92 transfers under the '93 Act) to the entire transfer.

A generation-skipping transfer (GST) tax is imposed on certain transfers to beneficiaries who are more than one generation below the transferor's generation. The GST tax is computed by reference to the maximum estate tax rate in effect at the time of the transfer. (FTC 2d ¶ R-9566; TG ¶ 8960) Under pre-'93 Act law, the rate used in computing the GST tax on post-'92 transfers was therefore 50%. Under the '93 Act, the rate used in computing the GST tax on post-'92 transfers is 55%. (H Rept p. 644)

☐ **Effective:** Decedents dying, and gifts made, after '92. (§ 14208(c))

> ***observation:*** IRS issued a new Form 706 (the federal estate and GST tax return) in Feb. '93. The Instructions to the Feb. '93 revision of Form 706 say that the tax is figured under the rate schedule that applied to post-'92 transfers under pre-'93 Act law. Since the '93 Act specifically says that the changes in the top estate and gift tax rates apply to all transfers after '92, estates of decedents who died early in '93 can't take advantage of the lower rates that applied under pre-'93 Act law by filing an estate tax return on the Feb. '93 revision of Form 706.

For official explanation see Committee Reports ¶ 3035.

¶ 902. New estate and trust income tax rates starting in '93

Under pre-'93 Act law, the income tax rate brackets for estates and trusts for '93 were:

15% on taxable income not over $3,750;

28% on taxable income over $3,750 but not over $11,250;

31% on taxable income over $11,250. (FTC 2d ¶s C-1003, C-7002; TG ¶ 505; USTR ¶s 14.08, 6414.07)

The estate and trust income tax rates are indexed each year for inflation. (See FTC 2d ¶s C-1005, C-7004; TG ¶ 505; USTR ¶ 14.08) Net capital gain of estates and trusts is taxed at a maximum 28% rate. (See FTC 2d ¶s C-1003, C-7002; TG ¶ 4412; USTR ¶ 14.08)

The '93 Act revises the estate and trust income tax rate bracket amounts and adds a new 36% rate bracket. (Code Sec. 1(e) as amended by '93 Act § 13201(a)) The Act also imposes a 10% surtax, creating a marginal rate of 39.6%, on taxable income over $7,500. (Code Sec. 1(e) as amended by '93 Act § 13202(a)(5)) The surtax is not a 10% increase in total tax liability. Thus, net capital gain will still be taxed at a 28% maximum rate. (H Rept p. 636, under Section 13202)

For '93, the rate brackets are as follows:

15% on taxable income not over $1,500;

28% on taxable income over $1,500 but not over $3,500;

31% on taxable income over $3,500 but not over $5,500;

36% on taxable income over $5,500 but not over $7,500;

39.6% on taxable income over $7,500.

The revised rates are arranged so that the benefit for '93 of having estate and trust income taxed at graduated rates (rather than at 39.6% from the first dollar) is approximately equal to the benefit of the graduated rates that were to apply for '93 under pre-'93 Act law. (H Rept p. 635, under Section 13201)

> ***observation:*** The benefit of the graduated rates under pre-'93 Act law was $825; under current law it is $845.

Indexing. As under pre-'93 Act law, the tax rate bracket thresholds will be indexed for inflation. However, indexing of thresholds for the 36% and 39.6% brackets will apply to tax years beginning after Dec. 31, '94. The 36% and 39.6% brackets will be adjusted for increases in the consumer price index since '93. (Code Sec. 1(f)(7) as amended by '93 Act § 13201(b)(3)(B))

☐ **Effective:** Tax years beginning after Dec. 31, '92. (§§ 13201(c), 13202(c)) Penalties for underpayment of estimated tax attributable to the changes in tax rates will be waived for any period before Apr. 16, '94. (§ 13001(d))

Code Sec. 15 requires a "straddle computation" when tax rates change during a taxpayer's tax year. (See FTC 2d/FIN ¶ A-1104 *et seq.;* TG ¶ 1063; USTR ¶ 154 *et seq.*) However, the '93 Act provides that the Code Sec. 15 rules do not apply to these rate changes. (§ 13001(c))

observation: Thus, fiscal-year estates will not make a straddle computation. Trusts must use a calendar year. (See FTC 2d/FIN ¶ G-1401; TG ¶ 1746; USTR ¶ 6554)

For official explanation see Committee Reports ¶s 3028 and 3029.

¶ 903. Estimated tax penalties arising from '93 Act tax increases on individuals are waived

Some estates must pay a penalty on any underpayment of estimated tax. To avoid the underpayment of estimated tax penalty, estates and trusts must pay 25% of a "required annual payment" of estimated tax by Apr. 15, June 15, Sept. 15, and Jan. 15 (for calendar year taxpayers.). (FTC 2d/FIN ¶ S-5300 *et seq.;* TG ¶ 1406; USTR ¶ 66,544)

The '93 Act provides, however, that no estimated tax penalty will be imposed on estates and trusts for any period before Apr. 16, '94 to the extent any underpayment is created or increased by any '93 Act provision. (§ 13001(d))

¶ 904. "Straddle computation" of tax for the year is not required because of changes made by the '93 Act tax rates for estates and trusts

If the income tax rates for estates and trusts change during a taxable year (except for changes effective on the first day of the year) a special computation must be made to take into account the different rates for the different parts of the year. Under this straddle computation, estates and trusts must pay tax at the old and new rates in proportion to the number of days in the tax year which fall on either side of the effective date of the change. (FTC 2d/FIN ¶s C-1006, C-7005; USTR ¶ 154 *et seq.)*

The '93 Act provides that no amendment made by the Act shall be considered a change in rates for purposes of the straddle computation rules except the increase in the corporate tax rates (see ¶ 301). (§ 13001(c))

observation: This means, for example, that an estate with a fiscal year ending June 30 doesn't have to make a straddle computation for its tax year ending June 30, '93 to take into the increased rates on estates for tax years beginning after Dec. 31, '92, (see ¶ 102). However, a corporation with the same fiscal year would have to make the straddle computation if its income is high enough to make it subject to the 35% rate, (see ¶ 301).

¶ 1000. Excise Taxes

¶ 1001. Luxury tax on boats, aircraft, jewelry and furs repealed; tax on passenger vehicles liberalized

Pre-'93 Act law imposes upon the first retail sale of passenger vehicles (automobiles and certain trucks and vans), boats, aircraft, jewelry and furs a tax of 10% of the sales price of the item, to the extent that sales price exceeds a specified threshold amount—$30,000 for passenger vehicles, $100,000 for boats, $250,000 for aircraft, $10,000 for jewelry, and $10,000 for furs. That is, the 10% tax applies only to the difference between the applicable threshold amount and the sales price of the luxury item. The seller is liable for the tax which he collects from the buyer and pays over to IRS. (FTC 2d ¶ W-4500 *et seq.;* TG ¶ 9000 *et seq.;* USTR ¶ 40,014 *et seq.)*

Repeal of boat, aircraft, jewelry and fur tax. The '93 Act repeals the 10% tax on boats, aircraft, jewelry and furs (§ 13161; H Rept p. 627) for sales after Dec. 31, '92. (§ 13161(c); H Rept p. 627)

> ***observation:*** A seller, who has been required to make quarterly Form 720 excise tax returns, must file a final Form 720 (FTC 2d ¶ S-2506; TG ¶ 9261; USTR ¶ 60,114), if, by reason of this change in the law, the seller is no longer liable for, or liable for the collection of, any excise tax reported on Form 720.

$30,000 threshold for passenger vehicles indexed for inflation. Under the '93 Act, the $30,000 threshold for imposition of the luxury tax on passenger vehicles is adjusted for inflation. First, an amount must be determined (if any) by which (1) $30,000, increased by the cost-of-living adjustment for the calendar year, exceeds (2) the threshold dollar amount in effect for passenger vehicles for the calendar year. If the resulting excess amount is equal to or greater than $2,000, then the $30,000 threshold (as previously adjusted for inflation) for any subsequent calendar year must be increased by that excess amount, rounded to the next lowest multiple of $2,000. (Code Sec. 4001(e)(1) as amended by '93 Act § 13161(a)) The cost-of-living adjustment for any calendar year is determined based on the cost-of-living adjustment formula provided in Code Sec. 1(f)(3), as amended by '93 Act § 13201(b)(3)(A)(ii), modified to reflect inflation after calendar year '90. That is, the cost-of-living adjustment, for purposes of the luxury tax, for any calendar year is the percentage (if any) by which (a) the consumer price index (CPI) for the preceding calendar year, exceeds (b) the CPI for the calendar year '90. (Code Sec. 4001(e)(2))

Thus, the luxury tax threshold for passenger vehicles for any year will be computed by increasing $30,000 by the cumulative inflation since '90 with the result rounded down to the nearest increment of $2,000. Congress says that the applicable threshold for purchases in '93, on or after the effective date of this provision (i.e. sales on or after Aug. 10, '93, see below), will be $30,000 increased by the '91 and '92 inflation rates (8.49%), or $32,547, which when rounded down to the nearest $2,000 is a threshold of $32,000. (Conf Rept p. 558)

> ***observation:*** However, it is not clear, based on the actual wording of Code Sec. 4001(e), that indexing for inflation of the threshold can occur before '94. Code Sec. 4001(e) seems to provide that in order for there to be a '93 inflation adjustment, it must be computed in '92. Further, the

FTC 2d References are to the Federal Tax Coordinator 2d
FIN References are to RIA's Analysis of Federal Taxes: Income
TG References are to the Tax Guide
USTR References are to the United States Tax Reporter

computation of the adjustment considers only the previous year's (i.e. '91's) consumer price index. But the '91 adjustment alone would not bring the threshold amount to over $32,000. Thus, leaving the '93 threshold at '30,000. Capitol Hill sources have told RIA that a technical correction to address this problem is possible. However, an IRS spokesman has told RIA that the threshold for '93 will be $30,000.

recommendation: Auto dealers should continue collecting the luxury tax using the $30,000 threshold until there is further clarification.

Exemption for demonstration use. Under pre-'93 Act law, if an article is used before its first retail sale, the user is, generally, liable for tax as if the article were sold at retail by him (see FTC 2d ¶ W-4530; TG ¶ 9020; USTR ¶ 40,114). Use of a vehicle as a demonstrator for a potential customer while the customer is in the vehicle, however, is exempted from this rule. Therefore, luxury tax on vehicles used exclusively for that purpose is not due until the sale of the demonstration vehicle to the customer. However, personal use of a demonstrator vehicle by a dealer's sales staff does trigger the tax. (FTC 2d ¶ W-4504; TG ¶ 9001; USTR ¶ 40,114)

The '93 Act exempts from the use-treated-as-sale rule *any* use of a passenger vehicle as a demonstrator. (Code Sec. 4002(b)(3)) The tax, if any, on a demonstrator vehicle is to be assessed and paid on the sales price of the vehicle when it is sold. (H Rept p. 627)

observation: Thus, use of a demonstrator vehicle by sales staff for personal use will not trigger tax at the time of that use.

Exemption for equipment installed in passenger vehicle for use by disabled. Under pre-'93 Act law, luxury tax is imposed on the separate purchase and installation of component parts and accessories installed within six months of the date an article is placed in service. (FTC 2d ¶ W-4511 *et seq.;* TG ¶ 9008 *et seq.;* USTR ¶ 40,114) A limitation applies with respect to this tax (see below).

The '93 Act provides that tax isn't imposed, under the separate-parts-and-accessories purchase and installation rule, on the cost of a part or accessory installed to enable or assist an individual with a disability to operate the vehicle, or to enter or exit the vehicle, by compensating for the effect of the disability. (Code Sec. 4003(a)(3)(B)) The exemption does not apply to accessories commonly available from the manufacturer or dealer, such as power steering, power door locks, power seats, or power windows. (H Rept p. 627)

observation: Code Sec. 4003(c) (pre-'93 Act Code Sec. 4011(e)) provides that parts and accessories sold on, in connection with, or with the sale of any passenger vehicle are treated as part of the vehicle. This provision could be read to require the imposition of luxury tax where parts and accessories for use by disabled persons are installed on, before, or in connection with the sale of the vehicle at retail. It seems clear, however, that Congress does not intend that anomalous result.

The separate-parts-and-accessories purchase rule is an anti-abuse rule intended to prevent avoidance of luxury tax by the separate later purchase of major component parts that if purchased with, or as part of, the vehicle, would have been taxed. Further, since disabled persons require parts and accessories specific to their individual needs, this type of customizing is likely to be done separately from the purchase of the basic vehicle from the retail dealer. Thus, exempting purchase and installation of these items from tax under the separate-parts-and-accessories purchase rule, also suggests that Congress intends to bar imposition of any luxury tax on these items.

Limitation on tax imposed on separate purchase and installation of parts and

accessories. Under pre-'93 Act law, where tax is imposed on the separate purchase of parts and accessories and their installation, the amount of tax is subject to a limitation. The tax can not exceed 10% of the excess of (1) the sum of the price paid for (a) those parts and accessories and their installation, (b) all earlier installed parts and accessories and their installation, and (c) the article itself, over (2) the applicable threshold amount. (FTC 2d ¶ W-4511; TG ¶ 9008; USTR ¶ 40,114)

The '93 Act adds that in applying the limitation on the amount of tax imposed on the separate purchase and installation of parts and accessories, the price of any parts, accessories and installation exempted from tax under Code Sec. 4003(a) (e.g., parts or accessories installed for use by disabled individuals, see above) is not taken into account under (1) above. (Code Sec. 4003(a)(3))

> ***observation:*** This change seems simply to clarify how Congress has always intended the limitation to apply. That is, if the price paid for parts, accessories and installation already exempted from tax is added in computing the limitation, a full or partial tax on those parts, accessories and installation might result.

> ***illustration:*** X buys a car for $25,000 on Sept. 1, installs $3,000 in exempt parts and accessories (including installation) on Oct. 1, and installs $8,000 in taxable parts and accessories (including installation) on Nov. 1. Based on the limitation as clarified under the '93 Act, the tax due with respect to the $8,000 parts-and-accessories installation, assuming a $30,000 threshold, is $300 (10% of $3,000, the amount by which the sum of $8,000 plus $25,000, exceeds $30,000). However, if the $3,000 in parts and accessories were taken into account in computing the limitation, the tax would be $600 (10% of $6,000, the amount by which the sum of $8,000 plus $3,000 plus $25,000, exceeds $30,000).

Refunds and credits. The '93 Act changes create the opportunity for refunds (see "Effective dates" below) for tax that was paid on: sales in '93 of boats, aircraft, jewelry, and furs; use in '93 of demonstrator vehicles other than for test drives; and purchase and installation of parts and accessories for use by disabled persons in '91, '92, and '93.

Persons entitled to a refund may request it from the seller from whom the taxed item was purchased. The seller can then obtain a refund as provided under Code Sec. 6416 (the general retailers' and manufacturers' excise tax refund rules, see FTC 2d ¶s W-1415 *et seq.,* W-4541; TG ¶s 9028, 9144 *et seq.;* USTR ¶ 64,164. (H Rept p. 627)

> ***observation:*** The seller is the party entitled to refund under Code Sec. 6416 because it paid the tax to IRS. Further, with respect to the overpayments created by the '93 Act changes, the seller may not obtain a refund under Code Sec. 6416 unless it either shows that it actually repaid the tax to the "ultimate purchaser" or provides IRS with a written consent to allowance to the refund obtained from the ultimate purchaser. The refund claim is made on Form 843. As an alternative to a refund claim, the seller may claim a credit against excise tax on a later filed Form 720.

If refund or credit of any overpayment of tax resulting from the retroactive application of the exemption from tax for parts and accessories installed for use by disabled persons is prevented at any time before the close of the one-year period

FTC 2d References are to the Federal Tax Coordinator 2d
FIN References are to RIA's Analysis of Federal Taxes: Income
TG References are to the Tax Guide
USTR References are to the United States Tax Reporter

beginning on Aug. 10, '93 by operation of any law or rule of law (including res judicata, see FTC 2d/FIN ¶ U-1100 *et seq.;* USTR ¶ 74,337 *et seq.),* refund or credit of the overpayment (to the extent applicable to the exemption from tax) may, nevertheless, be made or allowed if the refund or credit claim is filed before the close of that one-year period. (§ 13162(c))

☐ **Effective:** For repeal of the boat, aircraft, jewelry and fur taxes—Jan. 1, '93 (§ 13161(c)), i.e., for sales after Dec. 31, '92. (H Rept p. 627)

For indexing for inflation of $30,000 threshold amount—on Aug. 10, '93. (§ 13161(c))

For expansion of demonstrator vehicle use exemption—Jan. 1, '93 (§ 13161(c)), i.e., for use after Dec. 31, '92. (H Rept p. 627)

For exemption of equipment installed for use by disabled—as if included in the legislation originally creating the luxury tax on passenger vehicles (§ 11221(a) of the Omnibus Budget Reconciliation Act of '90) (§ 14162(b)), i.e., for purchases after Dec. 31, '90 (H Rept p. 627), and as to the luxury tax Code provisions as modified by the '93 Act, Jan. 1, '93. (§ 14161(c))

For official explanation see Committee Reports ¶ 3023.

¶ 1002. Transportation fuel taxes increased

Under pre-'93 Act law, several separate taxes were imposed on transportation fuels: the Code Sec. 4081 tax on removal at the terminal of gasoline; the Code Sec. 4091 tax on producer/importer sales of diesel and aviation fuels; the Code Sec. 4041 tax on retail sales of diesel fuel used in noncommercial aviation (not taxed under Code Sec. 4091), aviation (jet) fuels (not taxed under Code Sec. 4091), special motor fuels, and gasoline used in noncommercial aviation; and the Code Sec. 4042 tax on retail sales of any liquid fuel used in commercial transportation on inland waterways. Reduced rates applied under some of these provisions for fuels used to produce qualified fuel-alcohol mixtures, fuel-alcohol mixtures themselves, fuels used in trains and certain qualified buses, and fuels used in commercial aviation. (FTC 2d ¶s W-1800 *et seq.,* W-1860 *et seq.,* W-4700 *et seq.,* W-4800 *et seq.;* TG ¶s 9052 *et seq.,* 9062, 9101 *et seq.,* 9108 *et seq.,* 9113 *et seq.)*

The '93 Act, increases the taxes on transportation fuels—in most cases by 4.3 cents a gallon. The increases are, generally, effective Oct. 1, '93. (§ 13241(g)) The 4.3 cents per gallon tax is imposed permanently. The tax increase on jet fuel and gasoline used in commercial aviation, however, first takes effect on Oct. 1, '95. In addition, the Code Sec. 4041 retail tax is modified to impose a tax on compressed natural gas. (Code Secs. 4041, 4042, 4081, and 4091 as amended by '93 Act §§ 13241 and 13242)

The '93 Act, in addition, effective Jan. 1, '94 (§ 13242(e)), replaces the Code Sec. 4091 tax on sales of diesel fuel by producers and importers with a tax under Code Sec. 4081 on the removal of diesel fuel at the terminal. After Dec. 31, '93, Code Sec. 4081 taxes gasoline and diesel fuel upon removal at the terminal, and Code Sec. 4091 taxes producer/importer sales of aviation fuel only. The Code Sec. 4041 retail taxes continue to apply. (See ¶ 1005) The '93 Act makes changes to both the pre-Jan. 1, '94 and post-Dec. 31, '93 versions of these Code sections.

> ***observation:*** With respect to most of the transportation fuels, the taxes are first increased under the applicable pre-Jan. 1, '94 Code provision, effective Oct. 1, '93, and then those new rates are included in the post-Dec. 31, '93 version of the Code provision.

Here's a rundown of the fuels affected by the Act:

Gasoline. Under pre-'93 Act law, Code Sec. 4081 taxed gasoline at a rate of 14.1 cents per gallon—the total of: (a) an 11.5 cents Highway Trust Fund (HTF) financing rate, (b) a 0.1 cent Leaking Underground Storage Tank Trust Fund (LUSTTF) financing rate, and (c) a 2.5 cents deficit reduction rate. (FTC 2d ¶ W-1801; TG ¶ 9101.1) The '93 Act raises this tax by 4.3 cents as follows. Under pre-Jan. 1, '94 Code Sec. 4081, the deficit reduction rate is increased to 6.8 cents per gallon. (Code Sec. 4081(a)(2)(B) as amended by '93 Act § 13241(a)) Under post-Dec. 31, '93 Code Sec. 4081, tax is imposed at the total of (a) an 18.3 cents per gallon tax rate (which replaces the HTF and deficit reduction rates) (Code Sec. 4081(a)(2)(A)(i) as amended by '93 Act § 13242(a)), and (b) the 0.1 cent per gallon LUSTTF tax rate. (Code Sec. 4081(a)(2)(B)) However, the tax decreases to 4.3 cents after Sept. 30, '99. (Code Sec. 4081(d)(1) as amended by '93 Act § 13242(a)) The LUSTTF rate terminates after Dec. 31, '95. (Code Sec. 4081(d)(2) as amended by '93 Act § 13242(a))

> ***observation:*** Thus, gasoline is taxed at 18.4 cents per gallon from Oct. 1, '93 through Dec. 31, '95, 18.3 cents per gallon from Jan. 1, '96 through Sept. 30, '99, and 4.3 cents per gallon thereafter.

Gasohols. Under pre-'93 Act law, Code Sec. 4081 taxed 10%, 7.7% and 5.7% ethanol, and nonethanol, gasohols (gasoline-alcohol mixtures) at reduced rates based on the gasoline tax rate (i.e., reduced HTF rates were substituted). For example, 10% ethanol gasohol was taxed at 8.7 cents per gallon—the total of a 6.1 cents HTF rate, the 0.1 cent LUSTTF rate and the 2.5 cents deficit reduction rate. (See FTC 2d ¶ W-1802.1; TG ¶ 9111) The '93 Act continues to apply reduced rates on these gasohols computed based on the gasoline tax rate. Thus, the 4.3 cents increase in the gasoline tax rate under pre-Jan 1, '94 (to the deficit reduction rate) and post-Dec,. 31, '93 Code Sec. 4081, as discussed above, results in a 4.3 cents increase in the "gasohol tax rates." (Pre-Jan. 1, '94 Code Sec. 4081(c) as amended by '93 Act § 13241(a); Post-Dec. 31, '93 Code Sec. 4081(c) as amended by '93 Act § 13242(a))

Specifically, post-Dec. 31, '93 Code Sec. 4081 provides that the "alcohol mixture rates" (on 10%, 7.7% and 5.7% ethanol and nonethanol gasohols) are based on the gasoline tax rate. For example, the rate for 10% ethanol gasohol is the excess of the gasoline tax rate (18.4 cents) over 5.4 cents per gallon (Code Sec. 4081(c)(4)(A)(i) as amended by '93 Act § 13242(a)). But in no event will any alcohol mixture rate be less than 4.3 cents per gallon. (Code Sec. 4081(c)(6) as amended by '93 Act § 13242(a))

> ***observation:*** Thus, for example, 10% ethanol gasohol is taxed at 13 cents per gallon, effective Oct. 1, '93. For the dates the gasoline tax decreases, and the LUSTTF tax terminates, see "Gasoline" above.

Gasoline used to produce gasoline-alcohol mixture. Under both pre- and post-'93 Act law, gasoline destined for use in producing a gasoline-alcohol mixture is taxed at reduced rates computed based on a fraction of the applicable gasohol tax rate imposed on the type of gasohol to be produced. For example, gasoline used to produce 10% ethanol gasohol is taxed at 10/9 of the rate imposed on 10% ethanol gasohol. Thus, the "gasohol production rates" increase because the gasohol tax rates increase (see above). (See FTC 2d ¶ W-1802; TG ¶ 9108) (Code Sec. 4081(c)(2)(B)(i)(I) as amended by '93 Act § 13242(a))

> ***observation:*** Thus, the tax on gasoline used to produce a 10% ethanol gasohol increases, effective Oct. 1, '93, to 14.44 cents per gallon (10/9 × 13.0 (the gasohol tax rate for 10% ethanol gasohol)).

Diesel fuel. Under pre-'93 Act law, Code Sec. 4091 sales by producer/importers of diesel fuel were taxed at 20.1 cents per gallon—the total of (a) a 17.5 cents HTF tax rate, (b) the 0.1 cent LUSTTF rate, and (c) a 2.5 cents diesel fuel deficit reduction rate. (FTC 2d ¶ W-1867; TG ¶ 9113) The '93 Act raises this tax by 4.3 cents as follows. Under pre-Jan. 1, '94 Code Sec. 4091, the deficit reduction rate is increased to 6.8 cents per gallon. (Code Sec. 4091(b)(4) as amended by '93 Act § 13241(b)(1)) Under post-Dec. 31, '93 Code Sec. 4081, the diesel fuel removal-at-terminal tax is the total of (a) a 24.3 cent tax rate (which replaces the HTF and diesel fuel deficit reduction rates) (Code Sec. 4081(a)(2)(A)(ii) as amended by '93 Act § 13242(a)), and (b) the 0.1 cent LUSTTF rate on diesel fuel upon removal at the terminal. (Code Sec. 4081(a)(2)(B)) However, the tax decreases to 4.3 cents after Sept. 30, '99. (Code Sec. 4081(d)(1)) The LUSTTF rate does not apply after Dec. 31, '95. (Code Sec. 4081(d)(2))

> ***observation:*** Thus, diesel fuel is taxed at 24.4 cents per gallon from Oct. 1, '93 through Dec. 31, '95, 24.3 cents per gallon from Jan. 1, '96 through Sept. 30, '99, and 4.3 cents per gallon thereafter.

Diesel fuel-alcohol mixtures, and diesel fuel used to produce those mixtures. Under both pre- and post-'93 Act law: (1) diesel fuel-10% ethanol and nonethanol alcohol mixtures are taxed at reduced rates computed based on the diesel fuel tax rate; and (2) diesel fuel destined for use in producing those mixtures is taxed at a rate equal to 10/9 of the diesel fuel-10% alcohol mixture rate for the mixture to be produced. For example, the tax on a diesel-fuel 10% ethanol alcohol mixture is 5.4 cents less than the regular diesel fuel tax, and the diesel fuel-alcohol production tax rate is 10/9 of that reduced rate. (See FTC 2d ¶ W-1868 *et seq.;* TG ¶ 9114 *et seq.;* Code Secs. 4081(c)(2)(B)(ii) and 4081(c)(5) as amended by '93 Act § 13242(a))

> ***observation:*** Thus, the tax on a diesel fuel-10% ethanol alcohol mixture is increased to 19 cents per gallon (the 24.4 cents diesel fuel rate −5.4 cents). And the tax on diesel fuel destined for use in producing a diesel fuel-10% ethanol alcohol mixture is increased to 21.11 cents per gallon (10/9 × 19).

Diesel fuel used in motorboats. The '93 Act, effective Jan. 1, '94, imposes a tax under Code Sec. 4081 on removal at the terminal of diesel fuel used in noncommercial motor boats, and under Code Sec. 4041 (if the Code Sec. 4081 tax isn't imposed) on retail sale of the fuel. (See ¶ 1007) See discussion above for rate of tax on diesel fuel under Code Sec. 4081.

Under the Code Sec. 4041 retail tax, diesel fuel is, generally, taxed at the Code Sec. 4081 rates. (Code Sec. 4041(a)(1)(C)(i) as amended by '93 Act § 13242(d)(3)) In addition, with respect to diesel fuel used in (noncommercial) motorboats: (1) effective during the period after Sept. 30, '99, and before Jan. 1, 2000, a tax rate of 24.3 cents per gallon applies, and (2) the 0.1 cent LUSTTF does not terminate before Jan. 1, 2000. (Code Sec. 4041(a)(1)(D) as amended by '93 Act § 13242(d)(3))

> ***observation:*** Thus, the tax on diesel fuel used in (noncommercial) motorboats is 24.4 cents per gallon under either Code Sec. 4081 or 4041, effective Jan. 1, '94. The Code Sec. 4081 tax decreases to 24.3 cents after Dec. 31, '95, and to 4.3 cents after Sept. 30, '99. However, the Code Sec. 4041 tax remains at 24.4 cents through Dec. 31, '99, and decreases to 4.3 cents thereafter.

Retail tax on diesel fuel. Under pre-'93 Act law, the Code Sec. 4041 retail tax on diesel fuel was imposed (if the Code Sec. 4091 tax wasn't imposed) at the same rates imposed under Code Sec. 4091 at the time of the retail sale or use. (FTC 2d ¶ W-4702; TG ¶ 9053) Under the '93 Act, the tax is imposed on retail sales of diesel fuel at the same rate imposed at the time of the retail sale or use under either the pre-Jan. 1, '94 Code Sec. 4091 producer/importers tax, or the post-Dec. 31, '93 Code Sec. 4081 removal-at-terminal tax, as applicable, except as provided below for fuels used in trains and certain buses. (Code Sec. 4041(a)(1)(C)(i) as amended by '93 Act § 13242(d)(3))

Diesel fuel used in trains. Under pre-'93 Act law, tax on diesel fuel used in trains was imposed under the Code Sec. 4091 producers/importers tax at a partially exempt (reduced) rate of 2.6 cents per gallon (the total of the 0.1 cent LUSTTF rate and the 2.5 cents diesel fuel deficit reduction rate) (see FTC 2d ¶ W-1890). Under pre-Jan. 1, '94 Code Sec. 4091, this partial exemption continues to apply, however, the increase in the diesel fuel deficit reduction rate to 6.8 cents a gallon (discussed above) results in an increased tax on this fuel. (Code Sec. 4093(c)(2) as amended by '93 Act § 13241(f)(3))

After Dec. 31, '93, diesel fuel used in trains is only taxed under Code Sec. 4041 on the retail sale of the fuel (see ¶ 1005). Under Code Sec. 4041, the tax on diesel fuel sold for use, or used in trains is (1) 6.8 cents per gallon after Sept. 30, $93, and before Oct. 1, '95; (2) 5.55 cents per gallon after Sept. 30, '95, and before Oct. 1, '99; and 4.3 cents per gallon after Sept. 30, '99. (Code Sec. 4041(a)(1)(C)(ii) as amended by '93 Act § 13242(d)((3)) The 0.1 LUSTTF rate is also imposed on this fuel. (Code Secs. 4041(a) and 4041(d) as amended by '93 Act §§ 13242(d)(3) and 13242(d)(9)) For termination of the LUSTTF rate, see above.

Diesel fuel used in certain buses. Under pre-'93 Act law, tax on diesel fuel used in certain nonscheduled intercity buses was imposed under the Code Sec. 4091 producers/importers tax at a reduced rate of 3.1 cents per gallon. This rate resulted from limiting the tax to the amount not refundable under Code Sec. 6427(b)(2)(A). (FTC 2d ¶ W-1901) The Code Sec. 4041 tax applied (where the Code Sec. 4091 tax wasn't imposed) at an equivalent rate to the Code Sec. 4091 tax rate. (FTC 2d ¶ W-4748) The '93 Act increases the pre-Jan. 1, '94, Code Sec. 4091 tax to 7.4 cents per gallon (Code Sec. 6427(b)(2)(A) as amended by '93 Act § 13241(f)(8))

After Dec. 31, '93, diesel fuel sold for use, or used in these buses is taxed only under Code Sec. 4041 on the retail sale of the fuel (see ¶ 1005). Under Code Sec. 4041, a 7.3 cent tax is imposed, which is reduced to a 4.3 cent tax after Sept 30, '99. (Code Sec. 4041(a)(1)(C)(ii) as amended by '93 Act § 13242(a)) The 0.1 LUSTTF rate is also imposed on this fuel. (Code Sec. 4041(d)(1)) For termination of the LUSTTF rate, see "Gasoline" above.

Aviation fuels. Under pre-'93 Act law, Code Sec. 4091 taxed producer/importers sales of aviation fuel used in noncommercial aviation at 17.6 cents per gallon—the total of (a) a 17.5 cents airport and airway trust fund (AATF) financing rate, and (b) the 0.1 cent LUSTTF rate. (FTC 2d ¶ W-1867; TG ¶ 9119) The '93 Act raises this tax 4.3 cents as follows. Under pre-Jan. 1, '94 Code Sec. 4091, a 4.3 cents per gallon aviation fuel deficit reduction rate is added. (Code Secs. 4091(b)(1)(A) and 4091(b)(6) as amended by '93 Act § 13241(b)(2)(B)) Under post-Dec. 31, '93, Code Sec. 4091, the producer/importers tax on aviation fuel used in noncommercial aviation is the total of a 21.8 cent tax rate (which replaces the AATF and aviation fuel deficit reduction rates) (Code Sec. 4091(b)(1) as amended by '93 Act § 13242(a)), and the 0.1 cent LUSTTF rate. (Code Sec. 4091(b)(2) as amended by '93 Act § 13242(a))

The 21.8 cent rate, however, decreases to 4.3 cents per gallon after Dec. 31, '95. (Code Sec. 4091(b)(3) as amended by '93 Act § 13242(a)) The LUSTTF tax terminates after Dec. 31, '95, see above.

> ***observation:*** Thus, aviation fuel used in noncommercial aviation is taxed at 21.9 cents per gallon from Oct. 1, '93 through Dec. 31, '95, and 4.3 cents per gallon thereafter.

Under pre-'93 Act law, Code Sec. 4091 imposed a 0.1 cent tax on aviation fuel used in commercial aviation. This rate resulted from exemption of the fuel from the AATF tax rate, i.e. only the 0.1 LUSTTF rate applied (see FTC 2d ¶ W-1890). Under the '93 Act, aviation fuel sold for use in commercial aviation (other than as supplies for vessels or aircraft within the meaning of Code Sec. 4221(d)(3) (see FTC 2d ¶ W-1222 *et seq.;* TG ¶ 9139) is taxed under Code Sec. 4091 at (1) the 0.1 cent LUSTTF tax, and (2) for fuel sold after Sept. 30, '95, a tax of 4.3 cents per gallon. (Code Sec. 4092(b) as amended by '93 Act § 13242(a)))

> ***observation:*** Thus, the tax on aviation fuel used in commercial aviation increases to 4.4 cents per gallon effective Oct. 1, '95. But the rate decreases to 4.3 cents per gallon after Dec. 31, '95 when the LUSTTF rate terminates.

Aviation fuel-alcohol mixtures, and aviation fuel used to produce those mixtures. Under pre- and post-'93 Act law: (1) aviation fuel-10% ethanol and nonethanol alcohol mixtures are taxed at reduced rates computed based on the aviation fuel rate; and (2) aviation fuel destined for use in producing those mixtures is taxed at a rate equal to 10/9 of the aviation fuel-10% alcohol mixture rate for the mixture to be produced. For example, the tax on an aviation-fuel 10% ethanol alcohol mixture is 13.4 cents less than the regular aviation fuel tax, and the aviation fuel-alcohol production tax rate is 10/9 of that reduced rate. (See FTC 2d ¶ W-1870 *et seq.;* TG ¶ 9121 *et seq.;* Code Secs. 4091(c)(1) and 4091(c)(2) as amended by '93 Act § 13242(a))

> ***observation:*** Thus, the tax on an aviation fuel-10% ethanol alcohol mixture is increased to 8.5 cents per gallon (21.9 cents per gallon - 13.4 cent). And the tax on aviation fuel destined for use in producing a aviation fuel-10% ethanol alcohol mixture is increased to 9.44 cents per gallon (10/9 × 8.5 cents per gallon (the 10% ethanol-aviation fuel mixture rate).
>
> Post-Dec. 31, '93, Code Sec. 4091 also provides that in no event will the aviation fuel-10% alcohol mixture rate be less than 4.3 cents per gallon. (Code Sec. 4091(c)(4) as amended by '93 Act § 13242(a))

Gasoline used in commercial aviation. Under pre-'93 Act law, the user of gasoline in commercial aviation was entitled to a refund of Code Sec. 4081 tax imposed on that gasoline, except for the 0.1 cent LUSTTF tax rate (see FTC 2d ¶ W-1836, TG ¶ 9107). The '93 Act provides, in addition, that 4.3 cents of the Code Sec. 4081 tax will not be refunded for gasoline purchased after Sept. 30, '95. (Code Sec. 6721(f) as amended by '93 Act § 13242(d)(23))

> ***observation:*** The result of this change is to increase the tax imposed on gasoline used in commercial aviation to 4.4 cents per gallon, effective Oct. 1, '95. The tax will decrease to 4.3 cents per gallon after Dec. 31, '95 when the LUSTTF tax terminates.

Retail taxes on aviation fuels. Under pre- and post-'93 Act, Code Sec. 4041, nongasoline aviation fuels used in noncommercial aviation are taxed at the same rates in effect under Code Sec. 4091 at the time of the retail sale or use. (See FTC 2d ¶ W-4715, TG ¶ 9052; pre-Jan. 1, '94 Code Sec. 4041(c)(1) as amended by '93 Act § 13241((b)(2)(B)(iii); post-Dec. 31, '93 Code Sec. 4041(c)(1) as amended by '93 Act

§ 13242(d)(6)) The Code Sec. 4041 tax, like the Code Sec. 4091 tax, decreases to 4.3 cents per gallon after Dec. 31, '95. (Code Sec. 4041(c)(5) as amended by '93 Act § 13242(d)(8))

Under pre- and post-'93 Act, Code Sec. 4041, gasoline used in noncommercial aviation is taxed at a rate of one cent per gallon. This tax is imposed in addition to the Code Sec. 4081 tax on the gasoline. (See FTC 2d ¶ W-4716; TG ¶ 9052; Code Sec. 4041(c)(3) as amended by '93 Act § 13241(b)(2)(A))

Special motor fuels. The Code Sec. 4041 retail tax on special motor fuels (e.g., benzol, benzene, naphtha, liquefied petroleum gas, casing head and natural gasoline) is imposed on sale for use, or use of, fuel as a motor vehicle or motorboat fuel at the tax rate in effect at the time of the retail sale or use of the fuel on gasoline under Code Sec. 4081. Thus, the increase in the gasoline tax rates results in an increase in the tax on special motor fuels. (See ¶ W-4703, TG ¶ 9054; Code Sec. 4041(a)(2) as amended by '93 Act § 13242(d)(4))

Partially exempt ethanol or methanol fuels. Under pre-'93 Act law, the Code Sec. 4041 retail tax on special motor fuels, and nongasoline aviation fuel used in noncommercial aviation, was imposed at reduced rates if the fuel was a partially exempt methanol or ethanol fuel. The tax on partially exempt ethanol or methanol, special motor fuel was 7.1 cents per gallon, computed as the total of (a) a 5.75 cents HTF rate, (b) a 1.25 cent deficit reduction rate, and (a) the 0.1 cent LUSTTF rate. The tax on partially exempt methanol or ethanol, nongasoline aviation fuel was imposed at the reduced rates under Code Sec. 4091 on aviation fuel-10% alcohol mixtures. (FTC 2d ¶ W-4730) The '93 Act, effective Oct. 1, '93 (§ 13241(g)), increases these partially exempt methanol and ethanol rates by 4.3 cents per gallon. (Pre-Jan. 1, '94, Code Sec. 4041(m)(1) as amended by '93 Act § 13241(c) and post-Dec. 31, '93, Code Sec. 4041(m)(1) as amended by '93 Act § 13242(d)(13)(A)(i)) Also see, "Aviation fuels" above. The total tax imposed on partially exempt methanol and ethanol motor fuels drops to 4.3 cents after Sept. 30, '99. (Code Sec. 4041(m)(1)(A)(ii) as amended by '93 Act § 13241(c))

> RIA ***observation:*** Thus, the tax on partially exempt methanol and ethanol motor fuels is 11.4 cents per gallon from Oct. 1, '93 through Dec. 31, '95, 11.3 cents per gallon from Jan. 1, '96 through Sept. 30, '99, and 4.3 cents per gallon thereafter.

Compressed natural gas. The '93 Act imposes, effective Oct. 1, '93 (§ 13241(g)), a new Code Sec. 4041 retail tax on compressed natural gas. The tax is imposed where compressed natural gas is (1) sold by any person to an owner, lessee or other operator of a motor vehicle or motorboat to be used as a fuel in the motor vehicle or motorboat, or (2) used by any person as a fuel in a motor vehicle or motorboat unless there was a taxable sale of the gas under (1) above. The tax is 48.54 cents per MCF (thousand cubic feet) (determined at standard temperature and pressure). (Code Sec. 4041(a)(3)(A) as amended by '93 Act § 13241(e)(1)) The tax does not apply to any sale for use, or use of, fuel in the school bus transportation of students and employees of schools, or in intracity passenger land transportation. (Code Sec. 4041(a)(3)(B) as amended by '93 Act § 13241(e)(3)(B)) The '93 Act exempts compressed natural gas from the LUSTTF tax. (Code Sec. 4041(d) as amended by '93 Act § 13241(e)(2))

Fuel used in commercial transportation on inland waterways. Under pre-'93 Act

FTC 2d References are to the Federal Tax Coordinator 2d
FIN References are to RIA's Analysis of Federal Taxes: Income
TG References are to the Tax Guide
USTR References are to the United States Tax Reporter

law, the tax on fuel used in '93 in commercial transportation on inland waterways is 17.1 cents per gallon, computed as the total of (a) a 17 cents tax rate (for '93) and (b) the 0.1 cent LUSTTF rate. The rate in (a) above increases for use in '94 to 19 cents, and for use after '94 to 20 cents. (FTC 2d ¶ W-4800 *et seq.;* TG ¶ 9062) The '93 Act, effective Oct. 1, '93 (§ 13241(g)), adds a 4.3 cent deficit reduction rate. (Code Sec. 4042(b)(1)(C) and Code Sec. 4042(b)(2)(C) as amended by '93 Act § 13241(d))

> ***observation:*** Thus, the tax on fuel used in commercial transportation on inland waterways is increased for fuel used for Oct. 1, '93 through Dec. 31, '93 to 21.4 cents per gallon.

☐ **Effective:** As discussed above.

For official explanation see Committee Reports ¶ 3059.

¶ 1003. Floor stock taxes are imposed on gasoline, diesel fuel, and aviation fuel held on Oct. 1, '93

Under the '93 Act, persons holding gasoline, diesel fuel, or aviation fuel on Oct. 1, '93, which is subject to an excise tax, must pay a 4.3 cents per gallon floor stock tax on or before Nov. 30, '93. IRS will issue rules governing the manner in which the floor stock taxes are to be paid. These fuels will be considered "held by a person" if the person has received title. It does not matter whether the person has received delivery. (§§ 13241(h)(1), (h)(2) and (h)(3)(A))

When floor tax not imposed. The floor stock tax will not apply to gasoline, diesel fuel, or aviation fuel held by any person exclusively for any use if a credit or refund of the tax is allowable for such use. Nor will the floor stock tax be imposed on gasoline or diesel fuel held in the tank of a motor vehicle or motorboat. (§§ 13241(h)(4) and (h)(5))

No floor stock tax is imposed on gasoline held on Oct. 1, '93 where the aggregate amount held by the person on such date is not more than 4,000 gallons. Nor is the floor stock tax imposed on diesel fuel and aviation fuel held on Oct. 1, '93 where the aggregate amount of diesel fuel is aviation fuel held by the person on such ate does not exceed 2,000 gallons. These exceptions to the floor stock tax will apply only if the holder of the fuel submits to IRS the necessary information supporting a right to exemption at the time and in the manner prescribed by IRS. In determining the amounts of fuel when applying this exception, fuel exempt from tax because of its use (see above) and fuel held in the tank of a motor vehicle or motorboat (see above) is not taken into account. (§§ 13241(h)(6)(A) and (B))

Controlled groups. For purposes of the above rules, all persons treated as a controlled group are treated as one person. A controlled group has the same meaning as it does for consolidated return purposes in Code Sec. 1563(a) (see FTC 2d/FIN ¶ E-10700), except that "more than 50 percent" is substituted for "at least 80 percent" each place it appears in the subsection. Under regulations to be presented by IRS, principles similar to the above will apply to a group of persons under common control where one or more of these persons is not a corporation. (§ 13241(h)(6)(C))

Definitions. The following terms are defined for purposes of the imposition of the floor tax:

Gasoline. This term includes, to the extent required in regulations, gasoline blend sticks and products commonly used as additives in gasoline (see Code Sec. 4082).

Diesel fuel. This term means any liquid (other than a taxable gasoline product) which is suitable for use as a fuel in a diesel-powered highway vehicle or a diesel-powered train (see Code Sec. 4092).

Aviation fuel. This term means any liquid (other than a taxable gasoline product) which is suitable for use as a fuel in an aircraft (see Code Sec. 4092). (§§ 13241(h)(B) through (D))

☐ **Effective:** Aug. 10, '93.

For official explanation see Committee Reports ¶ 3059.

¶ 1004. Floor stocks tax on commercial aviation fuel held on Oct. 1, '95

The '93 Act imposes a floor stocks tax on commercial aviation fuel subject to tax under Code Sec. 4091 (relating to the tax on sales by producers and importers, FTC 2d ¶ W-1867; TG ¶ 9119) before Oct. 1, '95. and which is held on that date by any person. (§ 13245(a)) The term "commercial aviation fuel" means aviation fuel (as defined in Code Sec. 4093) which is held on Oct. 1, '95, for sale or use in commercial aviation (as defined in Code Sec. 4092(b)). (§ 13245(c)(2))

Rate of tax. The floor stocks tax is 4.3 cents per gallon. (§ 13245(a))

> RIA ***observation:*** The floor stocks tax equals the difference between the pre-'93 Act tax rate on the sale of aviation fuels and the tax rate imposed on those sales as of Oct. 1, '95 as increased by the '93 Act.

Liability for the tax. A person holding aviation fuel on Oct. 1, '93 is liable for the floor stocks tax. (§ 13245(b)(1)) For this purpose, aviation fuel is considered as held by a person if title to the fuel has passed to that person (whether or not delivery to the person has been made). (§ 13245(c)(1))

Payment of floor stocks tax. The floor stocks tax must be paid in the manner prescribed by IRS (§ 13245(b)(2)) on or before Apr. 30, '96. (§ 13245(b)(3))

Exceptions.

Fuel held for an exempt use. The floor stocks tax doesn't apply to aviation fuel held by any person exclusively for any use for which a credit or refund of the entire tax imposed under Code Sec. 4091 is allowable for aviation fuel bought after Sept. 30, '95, for that use. (§ 13245(d))

Less than 2,000 gallons of fuel held. The floor stocks tax also doesn't apply to aviation fuel held on Oct. 1, '95, by any person if the aggregate amount of commercial aviation fuel held by that person doesn't exceed 2,000 gallons. This exception will only apply if the person submits to IRS (at the time and in the manner required by IRS) the information as IRS may require. (§ 13245(e)(1)) Fuel held by any person which is exempt from the floor stocks tax by reason of the exempt use of the fuel is not taken into account in determining whether a person holds 2,000 gallons of fuel. (§ 13245(e)(2))

All persons treated as a controlled group are treated as one person. (§ 13245(e)(3)(A)(i)) The term controlled group has the meaning given to that term in Code Sec. 1563(a) (relating to the definition of controlled group for purposes of the limitations on the tax benefits of the members of the group, see FTC 2d/FIN ¶ E-10700 *et seq.;* TG ¶ 2441; USTR ¶ 15,634); except that for this purpose the phrase "more than 50%" is substituted for the phrase "at least 80%" each place that it appears. (§ 13245(e)(3)(A)(ii)) Under regs to be issued by IRS, principles similar to the controlled group rules for corporations will apply to a group of persons under common control where one or more of those persons isn't a corporation. (§ 13245(e)(3)(B))

Law applicable to floor stocks tax. All provisions of law, including penalties, that apply to taxes imposed by Code Sec. 4091 are, to the extent applicable and not inconsistent with the floor stocks taxes discussed above, are applicable to the floor stocks taxes. Those provisions will apply to the same extent as if the floor stocks taxes were imposed by Code Sec. 4091. (§ 13245(f))

☐ **Effective:** Aug. 10, '93.

¶ 1005. Tax on removal of diesel fuel at terminal replaces tax on producers/importers sales of diesel fuel

Pre-'93 Act diesel fuel producers/importers tax. Under pre-'93 Act law, Code Sec. 4091 imposed an excise tax totaling 20.1 cents per gallon on sales by producers and importers of diesel fuel for highway transportation uses. (FTC 2d ¶ W-1867 *et seq.;* TG ¶ 9113) Reduced rates applied for sales of diesel fuel for use in certain intercity buses (3.1 cents per gallon), use in diesel-powered trains (2.6 cents per gallon), use in producing diesel fuel-10% alcohol mixtures, and for sales of diesel fuel-10% alcohol mixtures themselves. Where certain registration and other requirements were met, the following sales could be made without payment of the Code Sec. 4091 diesel fuel tax: (1) sales of heating oil; (2) sales by a producer to another producer; and (3) sales for nontaxable uses including (a) use other than as a fuel in a diesel-powered highway vehicle or diesel-powered train, (b) use in off-highway business use, (c) use on a farm for farming purposes, (d) exclusive use by a state or local government, (e) export, (f) exclusive use by a nonprofit educational organization, (g) use by certain aircraft museums, and (h) use in certain qualified school, intercity and local buses. (FTC 2d ¶s W-1868 *et seq.,* W-1888 *et seq.;* TG ¶s 9114 *et seq.,* 9123)

Exempt and reduced-rate users who bought diesel fuel after tax had been paid on the fuel could file a claim for a credit or refund. (FTC 2d ¶ W-1914 *et seq.;* TG ¶ 9125) Where the Code Sec. 4091 producers/importers tax wasn't imposed on fuel used in highway transportation, a retail tax—equal to the producers/importers tax—was imposed. (FTC 2d ¶ W-4702 *et seq.;* TG ¶ 9053 *et seq.).*

Wholesale distributors who elected to register as producers were treated as producers for purposes of the 4091 tax (see FTC 2d ¶ W-1862; TG ¶ 9122) Thus, in general, most diesel fuel tax was collected at the wholesale distributor level. (S Rept p. 381)

Pre-'93 Act gasoline, removal-at-terminal tax. Under pre-'93 Act law, Code Sec. 4081 imposed an excise tax totalling 14.1 cents per gallon (FTC 2d ¶ W-1801, TG ¶ 9101.1) on certain removals, entries into the U.S. and sales of gasoline (e.g., removal of gasoline at the terminal or refinery was a taxable event). The tax didn't apply to any entry or removal of gasoline transferred in bulk to a terminal if all the persons involved, including the terminal operator, were registered under Code Sec. 4101. (FTC 2d ¶ W-1803 *et seq.;* TG ¶ 9101)

Taxpayers who used gasoline for an exempt use, e.g., for farming or off-highway business use, could claim a credit or refund of the Code Sec. 4081 tax included in the price of the gasoline. (FTC 2d ¶ W-1828 *et seq.;* TG ¶ 9105)

> ***observation:*** Gasoline, unlike diesel fuel, may not be purchased tax-free by exempt users. Rather, the tax must be recovered by a claim for credit or refund.

'93 Act changes. The '93 Act modifies Code Sec. 4081 to make it applicable to diesel fuel and gasoline, thus advancing the point of collection of tax on diesel fuel to removal at the terminal, etc. Diesel fuel will no longer be taxed under Code Sec. 4091 (which continues to impose a tax on sales of aviation fuels by producers and importers). Purchases of diesel fuel for exempt uses continue to be permitted to be made tax-free subject to certain fuel dyeing and marking requirements. (Code Secs. 4081, 4082, 4083, 4091, 4092 and 4093 as amended by '93 Act § 13242(a))

The change to the point of collection of tax on diesel fuel reduces the number of times diesel fuel will change ownership before tax is imposed, and reduces the number of taxpayers. The intended purpose is to reduce evasion of tax on diesel fuel. However, Congress intends the change in the point of collection of diesel fuel tax to be accomplished in a manner that preserves the pre-'93 Act exemptions from diesel fuel tax and the ability of exempt users to buy diesel fuel (including heating oil) without payment of tax. (S Rept p. 382).

A retail tax on diesel fuel will continue in effect. It will apply where the Code Sec. 4081 removal-at-terminal tax hasn't been imposed on the fuel. (Code Sec. 4041(a)(1) as amended by '93 Act § 13242(d)(3))

> ***observation:*** The tax rates imposed on diesel fuel (as well as gasoline and other transportation fuels) are increased under the '93 Act. The 20.1 cent diesel fuel tax is increased, effective Oct. 1, '93, to 24.4 cents per gallon. For discussion of the rate increases, see ¶ 1002.

Imposition of tax—collection point changed. Specifically, under the '93 Act, Code Sec. 4081 is modified to apply to taxable fuels. (Code Sec. 4081(a)) "Taxable fuels" are defined as gasoline and diesel fuel. (Code Sec. 4083(a)(1)) "Diesel fuel" is defined as any liquid (other than gasoline) which is suitable for use as a fuel in a diesel-powered highway vehicle, a diesel-powered train, or a diesel-powered boat. (Code Sec. 4083(a)(3))

> ***observation:*** Under pre-'93 Act law, diesel fuel used in boats wasn't taxed. As explained below and at ¶ 1007, this tax on diesel fuel used in motorboats applies to diesel fuel used in noncommercial motorboats only.

The point of collection of the tax on diesel fuel (like gasoline) is its (1) removal from any refinery, (2) removal from any terminal, (3) entry into the U.S. for consumption, use, or warehousing, and (4) sale to any person who is not registered under Code Sec. 4101 unless there was an earlier taxable removal or entry. (Code Sec. 4081(a)(1)(A)) Thus, the tax on diesel fuel will, generally, be imposed when it is removed by truck from a registered terminal (so-called removal at the "terminal rack"). (S Rept, p. 383) No tax applies to any removal or entry transferred in bulk to a terminal or refinery if the person removing or entering the taxable fuel and the operator of the terminal or refinery are registered under Code Sec. 4101. (Code Sec. 4081(a)(1)(B)) Use of taxable fuel (other than in the production of gasoline, diesel fuel, or special fuels referred to in Code Sec. 4041) is considered a removal. (Code Sec. 4083(b))

Removal or subsequent sale by blender. Tax is also imposed on diesel fuel removed or sold by the blender of the fuel. (Code Sec. 4081(b)(1)) If tax is imposed on such a removal or sale, and the blender establishes the amount of that tax paid, a credit in the amount of the tax paid is allowed. (Code Sec. 4081(b)(2))

Liability for tax. Code Sec. 4081 doesn't specify who is generally liable for payment of tax. Regs issued under pre-'93 Act, Code Sec. 4081 (i.e., the gasoline tax) provide that the person liable for tax on gasoline removed from the terminal rack is the "position holder," which, in general, is the person that holds the inventory position with respect to the gasoline as reflected on the records of the terminal operator (see FTC 2d ¶ W-1806.1; TG ¶ 9101.2). In addition, the terminal operator may be jointly and severally liable for the tax if the position holder is not registered with IRS. Terminal operators are required to be registered and, as a condition of registration, may be required to post a bond in the sum IRS determines. (See FTC 2d ¶ W-1806.2; TG ¶ 9101.2.)

Regs to be issued with respect to post-'93 Act Code Sec. 4081 are expected to provide that a terminal operator will be jointly and severally liable for any unpaid tax if a position holder is not registered with IRS. In addition, the terminal operator may be held jointly and severally liable for any unpaid tax if the terminal operator fails to keep any required records or to make any required reports on the removal of dyed and undyed diesel fuel. (S Rept p. 384)

As under the pre-'93 Act law, certain additional persons are specifically made jointly and severally liable with the taxpayer for diesel fuel tax where there has been a willful failure to pay tax. (Code Sec. 4103 as amended by '93 Act § 13242(d)(1))

Exemptions from tax—fuel dyeing requirement added. The tax imposed under Code Sec. 4081 will not apply to diesel fuel which: (1) IRS determines is destined for a nontaxable use; (2) is indelibly dyed in accordance with regs to be prescribed by IRS; and (3) meets the marking requirements (if any) that IRS may prescribe. The regs are to allow an individual choice of dye color approved by IRS or chosen from any list of approved dye colors that IRS publishes. (Code Sec. 4082(a)) Thus, unlike gasoline, removal of diesel fuel destined for an exempt use (e.g., heating oil or off-highway farming purposes) will not be taxed as the fuel is removed from the terminal if the dyeing requirements above are satisfied. (S Rept p. 383)

"Nontaxable use" is defined as: (1) any use exempt from the retail fuels tax imposed by Code Sec. 4041(a)(1), other than by reason of the imposition of that tax; (2) any use in a train; and (3) any use described in Code Sec. 6427(b)(1) after application of Code Sec. 6427(b)(3) (i.e. use in school buses or certain scheduled, intercity or local buses.) (Code Sec. 4082(b))

> ***observation:*** The nontaxable uses described in (1) and (3) are the nontaxable uses listed at (a) through (h) in the description of pre-'93 Act law above.
>
> A specific exemption from Code Sec. 4081 tax for heating oil is not provided, although as noted above Congress intends that this exemption continue to apply under post-'93 Act law. Code Sec. 4041(a)(1), as amended by '93 Act § 13242(d)(3), continues to tax only diesel fuel sold to owners, lessees and operators of diesel-powered highway vehicles, trains, and motorboats, for use in those vehicles. Presumably, this is the authority for exempting heating oil from tax under both post-'93 Act Code Secs. 4041(a)(1) and 4081.
>
> ***observation:*** A specific category of use exempted from tax under Code Sec. 4041(a)(1) is off-highway business use. Under '93 Act § 13163 (see ¶ 1007), the applicable definition of "off-highway business use" is modified to include use in a motorboat used for certain commercial purposes, but not other motorboats. That is, only diesel fuel used in noncommercial motorboats is taxed.

IRS will prescribe regs as may be necessary to carry out the exemption provisions—including regs requiring the conspicuous labeling of retail diesel fuel pumps and other delivery facilities to assure that persons are aware of which fuel is available only for nontaxable uses. (Code Sec. 4082(c))

> *observation:* '93 Act § 13242(b) (see ¶ 1009) adds a civil penalty for sale for use, or use of, dyed fuel for a taxable use.

Retail tax applies to diesel fuel used in trains and certain buses. Sales of diesel fuel for use in a train or certain intercity buses are subject to the Code Sec. 4041 retail excise tax where no Code Sec. 4081 tax was imposed on the fuel. (Code Sec. 4041(a)(1)(A)(i)) Thus, although removal of diesel fuel that is destined for use by these intercity buses and trains will not be taxed as the fuel is removed from the terminal, tax will be imposed on the sale of the fuel at the time that the fuel is sold to these reduced-rate users. (S Rept p. 383)

Registration and recordkeeping. As under pre-'93 Act law, IRS is permitted to require appropriate registration of persons necessary to implement the diesel fuel tax, including diesel fuel producers and dye manufacturers. IRS is also authorized to require position holders, terminal operators, and other appropriate persons to keep records and to report the quantity of dyed and undyed fuel that is removed from a terminal or refinery. (Code Sec. 4101(a) as amended by '93 Act § 13242(d)(1); Code Sec. 4102 as amended by '93 Act § 13242(d)(2); S Rept p. 384)

> *observation:* The '93 Act details IRS administrative authority for enforcing compliance with the Code Sec. 4081 taxes and related penalties and provisions (see discussion at ¶ 1008).

Refund of tax. Under regs prescribed by IRS, if any person who paid Code Sec. 4081 tax on diesel fuel establishes to the satisfaction of IRS that a prior tax was paid (and not credited or refunded) with respect to that fuel, then an amount equal to the tax paid by that person will be allowed as a refund (without interest) to that person in the same manner as if it were an overpayment of tax imposed by Code Sec. 4081. (Code Sec. 4081(e))

In addition, as under pre-'93 Act law, most exempt or reduced-rate users that use tax-paid undyed diesel fuel are permitted a refund if the user establishes that a prior tax (under Code Sec. 4081 or 4041) was paid with respect to the diesel fuel and that the fuel has been used for an exempt or reduced-rate use. (Code Sec. 6427(l) as amended by '93 Act § 13241(d)(31); S Rept p. 384) That is, in cases of exempt use of tax-paid fuel (e.g., construction, mining, mineral extraction, timber, home heating fuel, non-profit educational organizations), the exempt user applies for the refund if tax-paid fuel is used. (Conf Rept, p. 664) However, the '93 Act adds a new rule that permits refunds for tax-paid fuel sold to farmers and state and local governments to be claimed by registered vendors, only (see ¶ 1010). In addition, the '93 Act modifies the rules for obtaining refunds or credits for diesel fuel used in diesel-powered trains (see §§ 13241(f)(9) and 13242(d))

☐ **Effective:** Jan. 1, '94 (§ 13242(e)), i.e., for diesel fuel removed from terminals after Dec. 31, '93. IRS is also authorized to require dyeing of bulk quantities of diesel fuel held beyond the terminal rack for nontaxable uses on Dec. 31, '93. (S Rept p. 385)

For official explanation see Committee Reports ¶ 3060.

¶ 1006. Floor stocks tax on diesel fuel held on Jan. 1, '94

The '93 Act imposes a floor stocks tax on diesel fuel held on Jan. 1, '94, if:

(1) no tax was imposed on the diesel fuel under Code Sec. 4041(a) (the retail excise tax on diesel fuel, see FTC ¶ W-4702; TG ¶ 9053) or Code Sec. 4091 as in effect on Dec. 31, '93 (the pre-'93 Act tax on sales of diesel fuel by producers or importers, see FTC ¶ W-1860 *et seq.;* TG ¶ 9113 *et seq.)* (§ 13243(a)(1)); and

(2) tax would have been imposed under Code Sec. 4081, as amended under the '93 Act (see ¶ 1005), on any prior removal, entry, or sale of the fuel had Code Sec. 4081 applied to diesel fuel for periods before Jan. 1, '94. (§ 13243(a)(2)) That is, the floor stocks tax is imposed on diesel fuel held for sale or in bulk quantities for business use on Jan. 1, '94. The tax applies only to fuel held beyond the terminal rack on Jan. 1, '94. (S Rept p. 385) For purposes of the floor stocks tax, "diesel fuel" is defined the same as it is under Code Sec. 4083(a) (see ¶ 1005). (§ 13243(d)(1))

> ***observation:*** Under '93 Act § 13242 (see ¶ 1005), the point of collection of tax on diesel fuel is moved from the sale by the producer or importer to removal from a terminal (i.e., at the rack) under, generally, the same rules as those applicable to gasoline tax. This change is made by modifying Code Sec. 4081 (the pre-'93 Act "gasoline tax" provisions) to apply to both gasoline and diesel fuel and by modifying Code Sec. 4091 to no longer apply to diesel fuel.

The rate of the floor stocks tax is the amount of tax which would be imposed under Code Sec. 4081 if there were a taxable sale of the fuel on Jan. 1, '94. (§ 13243(b))

> ***observation:*** Under the '93 Act, the total tax imposed on diesel fuel under Code Sec. 4081 is increased 4.3 cents per gallon to 24.4 cents per gallon (see ¶ 1002).

The person holding the diesel fuel on Jan. 1, '94 to which the floor stocks tax applies is liable for the tax. (§ 13243(c)(1))

The tax must be paid in the manner to be prescribed by IRS (§ 13243(c)(2)), on or before July 31, '94. (§ 13243(c)(3))

No floor stocks tax is imposed on fuel held by any person exclusively for any use to the extent a credit or refund of tax imposed under Code Sec. 4081 is allowable for that use (see ¶ 1005). (§ 13243(e)(1)) However, this exception to the floor stocks tax will not apply if the holder of the fuel fails to comply with any requirement imposed by IRS with respect to dyeing and marking the fuel. (§ 13243(e)(2))

All provisions of the law, including penalties, that apply to taxes imposed under Code Sec. 4081 (see FTC ¶ W-1800 *et seq.;* TG ¶ 9100 *et seq.;* ¶ 1005) are also, insofar as applicable and not inconsistent with the rules above, applicable to the floor stocks tax. For this purpose, the floor stocks tax is treated as if imposed under Code Sec. 4081. (§ 13243(f))

☐ **Effective:** As discussed above.

For official explanation see Committee Reports ¶ 3060.

¶ 1007. Excise tax imposed on diesel fuel used in noncommercial boats

Pre-'93 Act law imposes an excise tax of 20.1 cents per gallon on sales by producers and importers of diesel fuel for use in highway transportation. A tax of 2.6 cents per gallon is imposed on producer/importer sales of diesel fuel for use in trains. (FTC 2d ¶ W-1860 *et seq.;* TG ¶ 9113 *et seq.)* Specifically, the producers/importers tax is imposed on diesel fuel that is suitable for use in a diesel-powered highway vehicle or a diesel-powered train. (FTC 2d ¶ W-1861; TG ¶ 9118) But fuel used in an "off-highway business use" (a term defined by cross reference to Code Sec. 6421(e)(2), see FTC 2d ¶ W-1837; TG ¶ 9107) is exempt from tax (see FTC 2d ¶ W-1892; TG¶ 9123). Where the producers/importers tax isn't imposed on fuel used in highway transportation, a retail tax—equal to the producers/importers tax—is imposed. (FTC 2d ¶ W-4702 *et seq.;* TG ¶ 9053 *et seq.)* Under pre-'93 Act law, diesel fuel used in boats is not taxed. (S Rept p. 215)

The point of collection of tax on diesel fuel, effective Jan. 1, '94, is changed from sales by producers and importers to removal at the terminal rack. This diesel fuel removal-at-terminal tax is imposed under Code Sec. 4081. As of that date, diesel fuel is no longer taxed under the Code Sec. 4091 producers/importers tax. A retail tax, however, continues to apply after Dec. 31, '93, to diesel fuel that hasn't been taxed under the removal-at-terminal tax. The "off-highway business use" exemption applies under both the removal-at-terminal and retail tax. These taxes are imposed at a rate that is 4.3 cents higher than the pre-'93 Act producers/importers tax on diesel fuel. (See ¶s 1002, 1005)

Diesel fuel used in noncommercial boats taxed. Under the '93 Act, "diesel fuel" subject to the removal-at-terminal tax is defined as any liquid fuel (other than gasoline) which is suitable for use as a fuel in a diesel-powered highway vehicle, a diesel-powered train, or a diesel-powered boat. (Code Sec. 4083(a)(3) as amended by '93 Act § 13242(a)) The retail diesel fuel tax is also extended to apply to diesel fuel sold for use, or used before sale, as fuel in a diesel-powered boat. (Code Sec. 4041(a)(1) as amended by '93 Act § 13242(d)(3)) However, diesel fuel used in boats used for commercial purposes remains exempt from these taxes. The '93 Act accomplishes this result by providing that the term "off-highway business use" (i.e., a use that is exempt from tax) does not include any use of diesel fuel in a motorboat *except* for use in a boat in the active conduct of: (1) a trade or business of commercial fishing or transporting persons or property for compensation or hire; or (2) any other trade or business (Code Sec. 6421(e)(2)(B)(iii) as amended by '93 Act § 13163(b)), unless the boat is used predominantly in any activity which is of a type generally considered to constitute entertainment, amusement, or recreation (i.e., noncommercial use). (Code Sec. 6421(e)(2)(B)(iv))

> ***observation:*** That is, use of a boat as described in (1) or (2) (i.e. commercial use) is an off-highway business use—a nontaxable use for purposes of the diesel fuel taxes. But a tax of 24.4 cents will apply upon removal at the terminal rack, or sale (or use before sale) at retail, of diesel fuel for use in a diesel-powered motorboat in a noncommercial use—an other-than off-highway-business-use described at (1) or (2) above.

☐ **Effective:** Jan. 1, '94. (§ 13163(d); § 13242(e))
For official explanation see Committee Reports ¶ 3024.

¶ 1008. IRS authority to administer compliance with diesel and gasoline taxes clarified

The '93 Act, effective Jan. 1, '94, replaces the Code Sec. 4091 tax on sales of diesel fuel by producers and importers with a tax under Code Sec. 4081 on the removal of diesel fuel at the terminal. Thus, Code Sec. 4081 is modified to tax gasoline and diesel fuel upon removal at the terminal. Code Sec. 4041 also continues to impose a

FTC 2d References are to the Federal Tax Coordinator 2d
FIN References are to RIA's Analysis of Federal Taxes: Income
TG References are to the Tax Guide
USTR References are to the United States Tax Reporter

tax on the retail sale of diesel fuel that hasn't previously been taxed. (See ¶ 1005) Code Sec. 4041 also imposes retail taxes on special motor fuels, aviation fuels (see FTC 2d ¶ W-4700 *et seq.;* TG ¶ 9052 *et seq.)* and, as amended under '93 Act § 13421(e) (see ¶ 1002), compressed natural gas.

The '93 Act clarifies how IRS may enforce compliance with the post-'93 Act Code Sec. 4081 rules, Code Sec. 4041, and penalties and other related administrative rules. This authority is in addition to the authority otherwise granted under the Code. (Code Sec. 4083(c)(1) as amended by '93 Act § 13242(a)) Specifically, IRS may:

(1) enter any place at which taxable fuel is produced or is stored (or may be stored) for purposes of (a) examining the equipment used to determine the amount or composition of the fuel (Code Sec. 4083(c)(1)(A)(i)), and (b) taking and removing samples of the fuel (Code Sec. 4083(c)(1)(A)(ii)); and

(2) detain, for the purposes referred to in (1), any container which contains or may contain any taxable fuel. (Code Sec. 4083(c)(1)(B))

In addition, IRS may establish inspection sites for purposes of carrying out its authority under (2) above. (Code Sec. 4083(c)(2))

Thus, IRS has authority to physically inspect terminals, dyes and dyeing equipment and storage facilities, and downstream storage facilities, to stop, detain and inspect vehicles, and to establish vehicle inspection sites. (Conf Rept p. 664)

The penalty imposed under Code Sec. 7342 (for refusal to permit IRS agents entry or examination, see FTC 2d ¶ V-3206; TG ¶ 9870) will apply to any refusal to admit entry or other refusal to permit an action by IRS authorized under (1) or (2) above. Thus, the penalty would apply where a facility owner refused to permit IRS to preform its inspection duties. (Conf Rept p. 664) (Code Sec. 4083(c)(3)) However, the amount of the penalty is $1,000 for each refusal (rather than $500 as generally applicable under Code Sec. 7342). (Code Sec. 4083(c)(3))

☐ **Effective:** Jan. 1, '94. (§ 13242(e))
For official explanation see Committee Reports ¶ 3060.

¶ 1009. Civil penalty imposed for improper sale for use, or use of, dyed diesel fuel

The '93 Act effective Jan. 1, '94, replaces the Code Sec. 4091 tax on sales of diesel fuel by producers and importers with a tax under Code Sec. 4081 on the removal of diesel fuel at the terminal. However, Code Sec. 4082 (as amended by '93 Act § 13242(a)), exempts diesel fuel from the removal-at-terminal tax if the fuel is destined for a "nontaxable use," and fuel dyeing and marking requirements are met. (See ¶ 1005) The '93 Act adds a new penalty where dyed diesel fuel is sold for use, or used, in a taxable use. (Code Sec. 6714 as added by '93 Act § 13242(b)(1))

The penalty, which is to be paid in addition to tax due (if any), is imposed where:

(1) any dyed fuel is sold or held for sale by any person for any use which that person knows or has reason to know is not a nontaxable use of the fuel (Code Sec. 6714(a)(1));

(2) any dyed fuel is held for use or used by any person for a use other than a nontaxable use and that person knew, or had reason to know, that the fuel was so dyed (Code Sec. 6714(a)(2)); or

(3) any person willfully alters, or attempts to alter, the strength or composition of any dye or marking done pursuant to Code Sec. 4082 (see ¶ 1005) in any dyed fuel. (Code Sec. 6714(a)(3))

"Dyed fuel" for purposes of the penalty is defined as any dyed diesel fuel whether or not the fuel was dyed pursuant to Code Sec. 4082. (Code Sec. 6714(c)(1))

observation: The Clean Air Act also imposes a fuel dyeing requirement.

"Nontaxable use" for purposes of the penalty is defined the same way as under Code Sec. 4082(b) (see ¶ 1005). (Code Sec. 6714(c)(2))

The amount of the penalty for each act is the greater of (a) $1,000 (Code Sec. 6714(b)(1)(A)), or (b) $10 for each gallon of dyed fuel involved. (Code Sec. 6714(b)(1)(B)) However, in determining the penalty on any person this formula is modified in cases of multiple violations. The amount in (a) is increased by the product of $1,000 × the number of prior penalties (if any) imposed by Code Sec. 6714 on that person (or a related person or any predecessor of that person or related person). (Code Sec. 6714(b)(2))

If a penalty is imposed under the above rules on any business entity, each officer, employee, or agent of the entity who willfully participated in any act giving rise to the penalty is jointly and severally liable with the entity for the penalty. (Code Sec. 6714(d))

☐ **Effective:** Jan. 1, '94. (§ 13242(e))
For official explanation see Committee Reports ¶ 3060.

¶ 1010. Refunds for tax paid on diesel fuel sold to farmers and state and local governments may be claimed by registered vendors only

The '93 Act, effective Jan. 1, '94, replaces the Code Sec. 4091 tax on sales of diesel fuel by producers and importers with a tax under Code Sec. 4081 on the removal of diesel fuel at the terminal. A retail tax is imposed under Code Sec. 4041 on diesel fuel that hasn't previously been taxed under Code Sec. 4081. However, diesel fuel is exempted from the removal-at-terminal tax if the fuel is destined for a "nontaxable use"—which includes use on a farm for farming purposes and exclusive use by a state or local government—and certain fuel dyeing and other requirements are met. Fuel used for these nontaxable uses is also exempt from the retail tax. (See ¶ 1005)

As under pre-'93 Act law, most exempt or reduced-rate users that use tax-paid undyed diesel fuel are permitted a refund under Code Sec. 6427(l) if the user establishes that a prior tax (under Code Sec. 4081 or 4041) was paid with respect to the diesel fuel and that the fuel has been used for an exempt or reduced-rate use. (Code Sec. 6427(l) as amended by '93 Act § 13241(d)(31); S Rept p. 384) However, the '93 Act requires that registered vendors of diesel fuel to farmers and state and local governments apply for refunds for these exempt users if the vendors sell tax-paid fuel to these persons for use in an exempt use. (Code Sec. 6427(l)(5) as added by '93 Act § 13242(c)(1); Code Sec. 6427(i)(5) as added by '93 Act § 13242(c)(2); Conf Rept p. 664)

Specifically, Code Sec. 6427(l)(1) (i.e., the provision permitting users to claim refunds and credits for nontaxable use of diesel fuel) does not apply to diesel fuel used:

(1) on a farm for farming purposes (within the meaning of Code Sec. 6420(c), see FTC 2d ¶ W-1829 *et seq.;* TG ¶ 9106) (Code Sec. 6427(l)(5)(A)(i)), or

(2) by a state or local government. (Code Sec. 6427(l)(5)(A)(ii)

Rather, the amount that would have been paid under Code Sec. 6427(l)(1) with respect to the fuel, is to be paid to the ultimate vendor of the fuel (Code Sec. 6427(l)(5)(B)) if the ultimate vendor is (a) registered under Code Sec. 4101 (Code Sec. 6427(l)(5)(B)(i)), and (b) meets the requirements of Code Sec. 6416(a)(1)(A), (B), or (D). (Code Sec. 6427(l)(5)(B)(ii)) That is, the vendor must (i) show that it did not include the tax in the price, (ii) show that it repaid any tax to the ultimate purchaser, or (iii) file with IRS a written consent from the ultimate purchaser permitting allowance of the refund to the vendor (see FTC 2d ¶ W-1416 *et seq.;* TG ¶ 9146).

Expedited refund claim permitted. Claim for the registered vendor refund may be filed by any person with respect to fuel sold by that person for any period (1) for which $200 or more is payable under Code Sec. 6427(l)(5) (Code Sec. 6427(i)(5)(A)(i)), and (2) which is not less than one week. (Code Sec. 6427(i)(5)(A)(ii))

The claim must be filed on or before the last day of the first quarter following the earliest quarter included in the claim. (Code Sec. 6427(i)(5)(B))

Where IRS does not pay a proper claim for refund under this procedure within 20 days, IRS will pay interest on the refund. (S Rept p.385)

> RIA ***observation:*** There is no statutory authority for the interest payment provision stated in the Senate Report. For a similar interest payment provision with statutory authority, see ¶ 1011.

☐ **Effective:** Jan. 1, '94. (§ 13242(e))

For official explanation see Committee Reports ¶ 3060.

¶ 1011. Expedited refund procedure for claims relating to gasoline and diesel fuel used to produce qualified fuel-alcohol mixtures modified

The '93 Act, effective Jan. 1, '94, replaces the Code Sec. 4091 tax on sales of diesel fuel by producers and importers with a tax under Code Sec. 4081 on the removal of diesel fuel at the terminal. As under pre-'93 Act law, reduced rates apply for gasoline or diesel fuel used to produce a qualified alcohol-fuel mixture. (See ¶ 1005) Pre-'93 Act law provides an expedited procedure for claiming a refund (equal to the difference between the regular Code Sec. 4081 tax rate and the reduced, gasohol production tax rate) where Code Sec. 4081 tax was imposed on gasoline that was later used to produce gasohol (see FTC 2d ¶ W-1846 *et seq.;* TG ¶ 9109).

The '93 Act expands the expedited refund procedure to apply where the regular Code Sec. 4081 tax rate is imposed on diesel fuel that is later used to produce a qualified diesel-fuel alcohol mixture. (Code Sec. 6427(i)(3) as amended by '93 Act § 13242(d)(28))

Thus, a refund claim may be filed with respect to gasoline or diesel fuel used to produce a qualified alcohol mixture (as defined in Code Sec. 4081(c)(1)) for any period (1) for which $200 or more is payable under Code Sec. 6427(f) (which provides the rules for computing the amount of the refund, see FTC 2d ¶ W-1846; TG ¶ 9109) (§ 13242(d)(26)), and (2) which is not less than one week. (Code Sec. 6427(i)(3)(A))

Where IRS does not pay a claim made under this procedure within 20 days of the date the claim is filed, IRS must pay interest on the refund. (Code Sec. 6427(i)(3)(B))

The '93 Act also adds the requirement that the expedited refund claim be filed on or before the last day of the first quarter following the earliest quarter included in the claim. (Code Sec. 6427(i)(3)(C) as added by '93 Act § 13242(c)(2)(D))

☐ **Effective:** Jan. 1, '94. (§ 13242(e))

For official explanation see Committee Reports ¶ 3060.

¶ 1012. Exemption from excise tax for liquids used, or sold for use, on farms, made permanent

Except for the additional taxes to fund the leaking underground storage trust fund, no tax is imposed on liquids used, or sold for use, on a farm for farming purposes. This exemption was scheduled to expire after Sept. 30, '99. (FTC 2d ¶ W-4731; TG ¶ 9057) Under the '93 Act, the exemption is made permanent. (§ 13241(f)(1))

☐ **Effective:** Oct. 1, '93. (§ 13241(g))

For official explanation see Committee Reports ¶ 3059.

¶ 1013. Exemptions from excise tax of sales of fuels to state and local governments and schools are made permanent

Sales of fuels for the exclusive use of state and local governments and their political subdivisions are exempt from the fuels tax. And sales of fuels to a nonprofit educational organization for its exclusive use are also exempt. Except for certain additional taxes on fuels to fund the Leaking Underground Storage Tank Trust Fund, these exemptions were scheduled to expire after Sept. 30, '99. (FTC 2d ¶s W-4734, W-4736; TG ¶ 9057) Under the '93 Act, these exemptions are made permanent. (Code Sec. 4041(g) as amended by '93 Act § 13241(f)(2))

☐ **Effective:** Oct. 1, '93. (§ 13241(g))

For official explanation see Committee Reports ¶ 3059.

¶ 1014. Aviation fuel deficit reduction rate doesn't apply to aviation fuel used as supplies for vessels or aircraft

The Leaking Underground Storage Tank Trust Fund financing rate does not apply to aviation fuel sold for use, or used, as supplies for vessels or aircraft. (Code Sec. 4093(d)) Under the '93 Act, the aviation fuel deficit reduction rate also doesn't apply to aviation fuel sold for use, or used, for such purposes. (Code Sec. 4093(d) as amended by '93 Act § 13241(f)(4))

☐ **Effective:** Oct. 1, '93. (§ 13241(g))

For official explanation see Committee Reports ¶ 3059.

¶ 1015. New rules on exemption from excise taxes of fuels used in diesel-powered trains and commercial aviation

There is an exemption from the fuel tax for sales of fuels used for off-highway business and noncommercial aviation. This exemption doesn't apply—and therefore the fuel tax *does* apply—to any portion of the tax on fuel sold for use in a diesel-powered train that is attributable to the Leaking Underground Storage Tank Trust Fund (LUSTTF) financing rate and the diesel fuel deficit reduction rate. (FTC 2d ¶ W-1890; TG ¶ 9123) Under the '93 Act, the exemption will apply where the fuel is

---

FTC 2d References are to the Federal Tax Coordinator 2d
FIN References are to RIA's Analysis of Federal Taxes: Income
TG References are to the Tax Guide
USTR References are to the United States Tax Reporter

sold to a state or its political subdivision for its exclusive use. (Code Sec. 4093(c)(2)(A) as amended by '93 Act § 13241(f)(3))

There is also an exception to the exemption from tax on fuel used in an aircraft that is attributable to the LUSTTF financing rate. (FTC 2d ¶ W-1890; TG ¶ 9123) Under the Act, where fuel is sold for use in commercial aviation (other than certain supplies for vessels or aircraft) the exemption doesn't apply to the extent the fuel tax is attributable to the LUSTTF financing rate. The term "commercial aviation" means use of an aircraft other than in noncommercial aviation, i.e., use of an aircraft, other than use in a business of transporting persons or property for compensation or hire by air. (Code Sec. 4093(c)(2)(B) as amended by '93 Act § 13241(f)(3))

☐ **Effective:** Oct. 1, '93. (§ 13241(g))

¶ 1016. Credits and refunds of the farmer's gasoline tax have been made permanent

Except with respect to taxes imposed at the Leaking Underground Storage Tank Trust Fund financing rate, the farmers' gasoline tax credit and refund provisions were scheduled to expire with respect to gasoline purchased after Sept. 30, '99. (FTC 2d ¶ W-1829) Under the '93 Act, these credits and refunds are permanent. (§ 13241(f)(5))

☐ **Effective:** Oct. 1, '93. (§ 13241(g))

¶ 1017. Refund provisions for purchasers of gasoline who use gasoline for exempt purposes have been made permanent

A refund is allowed to a purchaser of gasoline who uses the gasoline for certain exempt purposes. Except with respect to taxes imposed at the Leaking Underground Storage Tank Trust Fund rate, the refund provisions were scheduled to expire for gasoline purchased on or after Oct. 1, '99. (FTC 2d ¶ W-1827; TG ¶ 9107) Under the '93 Act, these refund provisions have been made permanent. (§ 13241(f)(7))

☐ **Effective:** Oct. 1, '93. (§ 13241(g))

¶ 1018. Refund and credit rules for tax on fuels used in diesel-powered trains and commercial aviation modified

Under pre-'93 Act law, no refund or credit was allowed on the tax attributable to the Leaking Underground Storage Tank Trust Fund (LUSTTF) financing rate of 0.1 cents per gallon for fuel sold for use in a diesel-powered train or in any aircraft (except for certain supplies for vessels or aircraft). A refund or credit was also not allowed on the tax attributable to the diesel fuel deficit reduction rate of 2.5 cents a gallon for fuel used in a diesel-powered train. (FTC 2d ¶ W-1916) Under the '93 Act, a refund or credit is not allowed on the portion of the tax on fuel used in a diesel-powered train that is attributable to the LUSTTF financing rate and the diesel fuel deficit reduction rate. This no-refund rule does not apply where the fuel sold is used exclusively by a state or political subdivision. Where fuel is used in commercial aviation (other than certain supplies for vessels or aircraft) no refund or credit is allowed for the fuel tax which is attributable to the Leaking Underground Storage Tank Trust Fund financing rate. (Code Secs. 6247(l)(3) and (l)(4) as amended by '93 Act § 13241(f)(9))

☐ **Effective:** Oct. 1, '93. (§ 13241(g))

For official explanation see Committee Reports ¶ 3059.

¶ 1019. Credits and refunds available for tax on gasoline used as a fuel on a train with respect to tax imposed at a deficit reduction rate

Credits and refunds are available for tax on gasoline purchased for off-highway business use. (FTC 2d ¶ W-1836; TG ¶ 9107) Under the '93 Act, these credits and refunds will not apply for tax on gasoline used as a fuel on a train with respect to the tax imposed at the deficit reduction rate. (Code Sec. 6421(f)(3) as amended by '93 Act § 13241(f)(6))

☐ **Effective:** Oct. 1, '93. (§ 13241(g))

For official explanation see Committee Reports ¶ 3059.

¶ 1020. Manufacturers excise tax on certain vaccines reinstated and made permanent; floor stocks tax imposed

Pre-'93 Act law imposed an excise tax under Code Sec. 4131 on a manufacturer's sale of vaccines for: diphtheria, pertussis, and tetanus (DPT); diphtheria and tetanus (DT); measles, mumps and rubella (MMR); and polio. The tax—$4.56 for DPT, $0.06 for DT, $4.44 for MMR, and $0.29 for polio, per dose—was paid into the Vaccine Injury Compensation Trust Fund from which individuals who were injured (or who died) as a result of the administration of these vaccines after Sept. 30, '88, and before Oct. 1, '92 are compensated under the National Vaccine Injury Compensation Program, a Federal "no-fault" insurance program. The tax was scheduled to expire on the later of: (1) Dec. 31, '92; or (2) the date on which the Vaccine Trust Fund revenues exceeded projected liabilities with respect to compensable injuries from vaccines administered before Oct. 1, '92. The tax expired on Dec. 31, '92. (FTC 2d ¶ W-1950 *et seq.;* TG ¶ 9134 *et seq.;* USTR ¶ 41,314)

Tax reinstated and made permanent. Under the '93 Act, the Code Sec. 4131 vaccine excise tax is modified to provide that the vaccine excise tax applies for (1) the period after Dec. 31, '87, and before Jan. 1, '93 (Code Sec. 4131(c)(1) as amended by '93 Act § 13421(a)), and (2) during periods after Aug. 10, '93. (Code Sec. 4131(c)(2))

> ***observation:*** That is, the vaccine tax is reinstated and made permanent on Aug. 11, '93.

Further, compensation from the trust fund is no longer limited to injuries or death resulting from the administration of the vaccines before Oct. 1, '92. (Code Sec. 9510(c)(1) as amended by '93 Act § 13421(b))

Floor stocks tax imposed. Under the '93 Act, a floor stocks tax in the amount determined under Code Sec. 4131(b) (FTC 2d ¶ W-1953; TG ¶ 9134; USTR ¶ 41,314) is imposed on any taxable vaccine: (1) which was sold by the manufacturer, producer, or importer before Aug. 10, '93 (§ 13421(c)(1)(A)); (2) on which no tax was imposed under the Code Sec. 4131 vaccine excise tax (FTC 2d ¶ W-1953 *et seq.;* TG ¶ 9134 *et seq.;* USTR ¶ 41,314) (or, if tax was imposed, was credited or refunded) (§ 13421(c)(1)(B)); and (3) which is held on Aug. 10, '93 for sale or use. (§ 13421(c)(1)(C))

> ***observation:*** Thus, the floor stocks tax rates are the same as the Code Sec. 4131 vaccine excise tax rates—$4.56 for DPT, $0.06 for DT, $4.44 for MMR, and $0.29 for polio, per dose.

The person holding any taxable vaccine to which the floor stocks tax applies, is liable for the floor stocks tax. The tax is to be paid in the manner to be prescribed by IRS in regs. (§ 13421(c)(2)(A))

> ***observation:*** IRS in Ann 93-107 notes that there are no exceptions to this floor stocks tax. Thus, doctors, hospitals, federal, state and local governments, and other purchasers of vaccines will be subject to the floor stocks tax if they hold taxable vaccines in inventory on Aug. 10, '93 (and the other conditions for application of the tax apply). IRS directs any person holding a taxable vaccine on Aug. 10, '93 to make an inventory of the number of doses in stock.

The tax must be paid on or before the last day of the sixth month beginning after Aug. 10, '93. (§ 13421(c)(2)(B))

> ***observation:*** IRS confirms in Ann 93-107 that the due date for payment of the floor stocks tax is Feb. 28, '94. The tax is reported on Form 720. The filing due date for that return will be determined by regs.

The definitions that apply with respect to Code Sec. 4131 also apply for purposes of the floor stocks tax. (§ 13421(c)(3)) Further, all provisions of the law, including penalties, applicable with respect to Code Sec. 4131, to the extent applicable to and not inconsistent with the floor stocks tax, apply for purposes of the floor stocks tax, as if that tax was imposed by Code Sec. 4131. (§ 13421(c)(4))

☐ **Effective:** For application of Code Sec. 4131 tax, as discussed above.

For coverage under the National Vaccine Injury Compensation Program—vaccines administered on or after Oct. 1, '92. (H Rept p. 811)

For floor stocks tax—vaccines purchased after Dec. 31, '92, that are being held for sale or use on Aug. 10, '93. (H Rept p. 811)

For official explanation see Committee Reports ¶ 3076.

¶ 1100. International Tax Provisions

¶ 1101. Modification of rules regarding taxation of investment in U.S. property by CFCs

A "U.S. shareholder" (in general, a U.S. person who owns 10% or more, by vote, of the stock, see FTC 2d/FIN ¶ O-2603; TG ¶ 8242; USTR ¶ 9514.01) of a controlled foreign corporation (CFC) is required to include in income his pro rata share of the CFC's increase in earnings invested in U.S. property. Under pre-'93 Act law, the amount of earnings taxed under this provision was measured by comparing the CFC's investment in U.S. property as of the close of a taxable year to that amount as of the close of the prior taxable year, in each case limited to the amount that would have been taxable as a dividend had it been distributed at the close of the taxable year being measured. (FTC 2d/FIN ¶ O-2787; TG ¶ 8246; USTR ¶ 9564.01) The amount invested in U.S. property was measured by its actual adjusted basis, less liabilities to which it was subject. (FTC 2d/FIN ¶ O-2784; USTR ¶ 9564.01)

The '93 Act modifies the manner in which the amount taxable under this rule is calculated. Under the '93 Act, the amount taxable to a U.S. shareholder on account of a CFC's investment in U.S. property is the lesser of (1) the U.S. shareholder's pro rata share of the average amount of U.S. property held (directly or indirectly) by the CFC as of the close of each quarter of the taxable year (Code Sec. 956(a)(1)(A) as amended by '93 Act § 13232(a)), less that portion of the CFC's earnings and profits attributable to amounts included previously in that shareholder's gross income on account of investment in U.S. property (or which would have been so included except that it had already been included under another provision of the CFC rules) (Code Sec. 956(a)(1)(B)), or (2) that shareholder's pro rata share of the CFC's applicable earnings (see below). (Code Sec. 956(a)(2))

> ***observation:*** This method of calculation is consistent with the approach used under the newly-enacted excess passive assets rules. (See ¶ 1110)

> ***observation:*** The '93 Act does not change the definition of "U.S. property" from that which applied under pre-'93 Act law. (See FTC 2d/FIN ¶ O-2778 *et seq.;* TG ¶ 8246; USTR ¶ 9564.01)

Any amount otherwise includible in income on account of excess passive assets will not be includible if it has already been included in income. (Code Sec. 951(a)(1)(B) as amended by '93 Act § 13232(c)(1)) For a discussion of when an amount otherwise includible is deemed to have already been included in income, see ¶ 1111.

In determining the amount of U.S. property held by a CFC, property is measured by its adjusted basis as determined for purposes of computing earnings and profits, less any liability to which the property is subject. (Code Sec. 956(a) as amended by '93 Act § 13232(a))

> ***observation:*** The basis of depreciable property for purposes of computing earnings and profits (which is used for measuring a CFC's investment in U.S. property under the '93 Act) may differ from its basis for purposes of determining gain or loss on sale or other disposition. (See FTC 2d/FIN ¶ F-10300 *et seq.;* TG ¶ 2248; USTR ¶ 3124.04)

Short-term loans or other temporary arrangements will be disregarded in

FTC 2d References are to the Federal Tax Coordinator 2d
FIN References are to RIA's Analysis of Federal Taxes: Income
TG References are to the Tax Guide
USTR References are to the United States Tax Reporter

determining the amount of a CFC's investment in U.S. property as of the close of each quarter if a principal purpose of such loan or arrangement is to avoid taking assets into account. For this purpose, IRS's interpretation of pre-'93 Act law in Rev. Rul. 89-73, in which it ruled that a two-month interruption in a CFC's investment in a debt obligation would be disregarded (see FTC 2d/FIN ¶ O-2787; USTR ¶ 9564.01), continues to be relevant under the '93 Act.

The '93 Act is not intended to change the rule set forth in Notice 88-108 (see FTC 2d/FIN ¶ O-2779; USTR ¶ 9564.01), which provides that obligations collected within 30 days of issuance are excluded from the calculation of a CFC's investment in U.S. property, unless the CFC's holds such obligations for an aggregate period of 60 days or more during the year. (S Rept p. 336)

Applicable earnings. The amount of a CFC's applicable earnings is determined in the same manner as under the newly-enacted excess passive assets rules, see ¶ 1110, except that the rule excluding earnings and profits accumulated in taxable years beginning before Oct. 1, '93 is disregarded. (Code Sec. 956(b)(1) as amended by '93 Act § 13232(a)). Therefore, applicable earnings are equal to the CFC's current and accumulated earnings and profits, reduced by (1) distributions during the taxable year, and (2) amounts previously included in the U.S. shareholder's income by virtue of investments in U.S. property or investment in excess passive assets. (Code Sec. 956A(b) as added by '93 Act § 13231(b))

U.S. property acquired before a corporation became a CFC. In applying the rules described above, U.S. property that was acquired by a CFC before the first day on which it was treated as a CFC is not taken into account. (Code Sec. 956(b)(2)) For this purpose, tracing of specific items of property is required. (Conf Rept p. 642)

> ***observation:*** Taxpayers should be sure that their accounting systems permit such specific tracing.

The aggregate amount of property disregarded under this rule cannot exceed the portion of the CFC's accumulated earnings which were accumulated during periods before such first day. (Code Sec. 956(b)(2)) In determining the amount of accumulated earnings which are attributable to periods before a corporation became a CFC, all distributions and inclusions in income are treated as coming first from the most recent earnings of the corporation. Thus, accumulated earnings attributable to pre-CFC periods will not be reduced on account of distributions or inclusions in income until all earnings from later periods have been exhausted. (Conf Rept p. 643)

Decontrolled CFCs. If a foreign corporation ceases to be a CFC during a tax year, rules similar to those which apply under the newly-enacted excess passive assets provision (see ¶ 1110) are applicable. (Code Sec. 956(b)(3) as amended by '93 Act § 13232(a))

> ***observation:*** Under these rules as applied to investment in U.S. property, it appears that:
>
> (1) the determination of a U.S. shareholder's *pro rata* share will be made based on the stock owned (or deemed owned under attribution rules, see FTC 2d/FIN ¶ O-2615 *et seq.;* TG ¶ 8244; USTR ¶ 9584 *et seq.)* by that shareholder on the last day in the tax year on which the foreign corporation is a CFC,
>
> (2) the amount of the corporation's investment in U.S. property for that tax year will be determined by taking into account only quarters ending on or before that last day, and
>
> (3) the current earnings and profits used to determine applicable earnings is ~~that portion of current earnings and profits allocated on a *pro rata* basis to~~ that part of the year during which the corporation was a CFC.

Regulatory authority. IRS is directed to issue Regs to carry out the purposes of the rules described above, including Regs to prevent avoidance through reorganizations or otherwise. (Code Sec. 956(e)) Such Regs might prevent taxpayers from taking advantage of the differences between the rules governing investment in U.S. property and those which deal with excess passive assets. (Conf Rept p. 643)

> ***observation:*** Since the rules governing investment in U.S. property and those which deal with excess passive assets generally operate in a parallel manner, it is not clear just which differences concern the Conference Committee.

Study concerning investments in noncorporate obligations. U.S. property does not include certain obligations of unrelated U.S. corporations. (See FTC 2d/FIN ¶ O-2778; USTR ¶ 9564.01). The Conference Committee has requested that the Treasury Department conduct a study of whether a similar rule should be extended to investments in noncorporate obligations. (Conf Rept p. 643)

☐ **Effective:** Tax years of CFCs beginning after Sept. 30, '93, and taxable years of U.S. shareholders in which or with which such years end. (§ 13232(d))

For official explanation see Committee Reports ¶ 3052.

¶ 1102. Effect on foreign tax credit limitation of distribution of previously taxed CFC earnings

A U.S. shareholder of a controlled foreign corporation (CFC) who is required to include amounts in income before they are actually distributed by the CFC is generally entitled to a credit, subject to certain limitations, for foreign taxes paid by the CFC. (See FTC 2d/FIN ¶ O-4200 *et seq.;* TG ¶ 8425; USTR ¶ 9604). If such a shareholder later receives a distribution of earnings which were already taxed, a "direct" credit is also available for any additional foreign taxes (such as withholding taxes) which were imposed with respect to the distribution itself. In that case, the shareholder is, under certain circumstances, entitled to increase his foreign tax credit limitation in the year of the distribution. The increase in the limitation is available only where (i) the taxpayer elected to claim a credit (rather than a deduction) for any foreign taxes paid or accrued in the year the CFC earnings were taxed to him (unless he paid or accrued no creditable taxes in that year), (ii) the taxpayer elects to claim a credit (rather than a deduction) for foreign taxes paid or accrued in the year of the distribution, and (iii) foreign taxes are paid or accrued in the year of the distribution with respect to the distribution. (See FTC 2d/FIN ¶ O-4209; USTR ¶ 9604.02)

> ***observation:*** Evidently, the purpose of this rule is to avoid a situation where a U.S. shareholder who receives a distribution is unable to claim a credit for foreign tax paid with respect to the distribution itself (for example, withholding taxes imposed by the foreign government on outbound dividends) because the distribution itself is not subject to U.S. tax (even though the *earnings* of the CFC which gave rise to the distribution were subject to U.S. tax in an earlier year).

Under pre-'93 Act law, the amount of the increased limitation, measured separately for each CFC, each taxable year, and each foreign tax credit limitation category (S Rept p. 321), was equal to the excess of (i) the amount by which, in the year the distributed earnings were earned, the taxpayer's foreign tax credit limitation was increased on account of the inclusion of income under the CFC rules, over (ii) the amount of foreign taxes actually creditable in that earlier year on account of such inclusion in income. (FTC 2d/FIN ¶ O-4209)

The '93 Act simplifies the calculation of the increase in the foreign tax credit limitation by eliminating the requirement that the amount of the increase be determined separately for each year and each CFC. (S Rept p. 326) Under the '93 Act, the amount by which the foreign tax credit limitation is increased on account of one or more distributions of previously taxed earnings is equal to the lesser of (i) the amount of foreign income, war profits or excess profits taxes paid, deemed paid or accrued with respect to the distributions, or (ii) the amount of the taxpayer's excess limitation account (see below) as of the beginning of the taxable year. (Code Sec. 960(b)(1) as amended by '93 Act § 13233(b)(1))

Excess limitation account. An excess limitation account must be maintained for each taxpayer who (i) elected to claim a credit (rather than a deduction) for foreign taxes paid or accrued in any taxable year beginning after Sept. 30, '93, in which he was required to include in income any amounts under the CFC rules, or (ii) did not pay or accrue any income, war profits or excess profits taxes to any foreign country or U.S. possession in any such year. Initially, the balance of the excess limitation account will be zero. (Code Sec. 960(b)(2)(A)) Thereafter, for each year the excess limitation account will be *increased* by the excess of (i) the amount by which the taxpayer's foreign tax credit limitation for such year is increased on account of the total amount of the inclusions of income under the CFC rules (Code Sec. 960(b)(2)(B)(i)), over (ii) the amount of foreign taxes actually creditable in that earlier year on account of such inclusions in income (Code Sec. 960(b)(2)(B)(ii)). The excess limitation account will be *decreased* (i) to the extent amounts are applied to increase the taxpayer's foreign tax credit on account of distributions of previously taxed earnings (Code Sec. 960(b)(2)(C)), and (ii) to the extent there is an increase in the foreign tax credit allowable by reason of a carryback, if the increase would not have been allowable but for the inclusion in income of amounts under the CFC rules. (Code Sec. 960(b)(2)(B))

A separate excess limitation account must be maintained for each of the categories of income for which a separate foreign tax credit limitation applies (see FTC 2d/FIN ¶ O-4080 *et seq.;* TG ¶ 8426). (S Rept p. 337)

□ **Effective:** Taxable years beginning after Sept. 30, '93. (§ 13233(b)(2)) However, where an amount is distributed which is attributable to earnings previously included in income under the CFC rules for a taxable year beginning before Oct. 1, '93, the increase in the foreign tax credit limitation on account of the distribution is determined under pre-'93 Act law. (Code Sec. 960(b)(3) as amended by '93 Act § 13233(b)(1)) Distributions in taxable years beginning after Sept. 30, '93 will be treated as attributable first to taxable years beginning after such date, to the extent of such earnings. (S Rept p. 337)

For official explanation see Committee Reports ¶ 3052.

¶ 1103. Foreign tax credit; 50-50 allocation of R&D expenses to U.S. and to foreign source income; temporary extension of modified statutory provision

Credit is allowed for foreign tax paid on a U.S. taxpayer's foreign income, limited to the amount of U.S. tax to be paid on the foreign taxable income. The larger the amount of deductions allocated to foreign income, the lower the foreign taxes and the smaller the amount of foreign tax credit allowed. (See FTC 2d/FIN ¶ O-11000 *et seq.;* TG ¶ 8295; USTR ¶ 8614.29)

Under pre-'93 law, qualified research and experimental expenses made solely to meet legal requirements imposed by a government for the improvement or marketing of specific products or processes which can't reasonably be expected to yield gross income beyond *de minimis* amounts outside the government's jurisdiction are allocated only to that geographic source. Any other qualified research and experimental expenses are allocated as follows:

. . . 64% of expenses attributable to activities conducted in the U.S. are allocated and apportioned to U.S. source income, and

. . . 64% of expenses attributable to activities conducted outside the U.S. are allocated to foreign source income.

The remainder of the qualified research and experimental expenditures is apportioned on the basis of gross sales or gross income. If the taxpayer apportions on the basis of gross income, the amount apportioned to foreign source income must be at least 30% of the amount that would have been apportioned on the basis of gross sales. (FTC 2d/FIN ¶ O-11026; TG ¶ 8312; USTR ¶ 8614.29)

Reg § 1.861-8 (promulgated in '77) provides detailed rules for allocating and apportioning several categories of expenses, including deductible research and experimental expenditures (FTC 2d/FIN ¶ O-11021 *et seq.;* USTR ¶ 8614.29) (Conf Rept p. 644) However, since '81, Congress has enacted various temporary moratoria and statutory modifications to the reg. (S Rept p. 165-168) The most recent statutory provision, set out in Code Sec. 864(f), was applicable to tax years beginning after Aug. 1, '89 through the first six months of the first tax year beginning after Aug. 1, '91. In '92, IRS issued Rev Proc 92-56, announcing that taxpayers could continue to allocate research expenses under the statutory method during what would ordinarily be an 18-month transition period—that is, the last six months of the taxpayer's first tax year beginning after Aug. 1, '91 and the immediately succeeding tax year. (See FTC 2d/FIN ¶ O-11021) (Conf Rept p. 644)

In the 12 years since the first temporary moratorium was enacted, Congress, IRS, and representatives of affected industries have studied the effects of the research expense allocation rules on research activities and on the availability of the foreign tax credit. That examination has not resulted in an unambiguous recommendation on the appropriateness of allocating U.S.-based research expense to U.S. source income under either the 1977 reg or the moratoria.

At the same time, taxpayers have faced a prolonged period of uncertainty as to the research expense allocation rules that will apply in the future, making it more difficult for them to predict the after-tax costs of research in which they must engage over future periods. While Congress believes that the period of uncertainty with respect to future years' tax rules should end, it has chosen not to settle the rules permanently at this time. In the interim, the substantive rules temporarily applicable under Code Sec. 864(f) continue to apply for another year. (S Rept p. 350)

Temporary extension of statutory rules. The '93 Act repeals the limitation on the tax years to which Code Sec. 864(f) applies (Code Sec. 864(f)(5) before repeal by '93 Act § 13234(b)(1)) and temporarily adopts for one tax year the changes in allocation percentages and the added regulatory authority of Code Sec. 864(f) described below.

The statutory rules apply to the first tax year beginning on or before Aug. 1, '94 following the taxpayer's last tax year to which Rev Proc 92-56 applies, or would have applied had the taxpayer elected the benefits of that Rev Proc. (Conf Rept p. 645)

> ***observation:*** The extension of time for the application of the statutory rules under Rev Proc 92-56 applies whether or not the taxpayer actually elected the benefits of that Rev Proc.

Changes in portion of research expenses allocated to place of performance. Under the '93 Act, research and experimental expenses, other than those incurred to meet certain legal requirements, are allocated as follows:

. . . 50% of expenses attributable to activities conducted in the U.S. is allocated and apportioned to U.S. source income and deducted from that income to determine U.S. source taxable income (Code Sec. 864(f)(1)(B)(i) as amended by '93 Act § 13234(a)) and

. . . 50% of expenses attributable to activities conducted outside the U.S. is allocated and apportioned to foreign source income and deducted from that income to determine foreign source taxable income. (Code Sec. 864(f)(1)(B)(ii) as amended by '93 Act § 13234(a))

> ***observation:*** The changes in the portion of research and experimental expenses allocated to the place of performance do not go into effect until the taxpayer's first tax year beginning on or before Aug. 1, '94 following the last tax year to which Rev Proc 92-56 applies or would have applied if the taxpayer had elected to apply that Rev Proc.

Additional regulatory authority. The '93 Act authorizes IRS to prescribe regs to carry out the purposes of the rules for allocating research and experimental expenditures, including regs relating to the determination of whether any expenses are attributable to activities conducted in the U.S. or outside the U.S. and regs providing for appropriate adjustments in the case of cost-sharing arrangements and contract research (Code Sec. 864(f)(5) as amended by '93 Act § 13234(b)(1))

IRS is also authorized to prescribe regs providing for the source of gross income and the allocation and apportionment of deductions to take into account the adjustments regarding Code Sec. 936 possessions corporations that have elected either the cost-sharing or profit split method for determining the tax treatment of its intangible property income. (Code Sec. 864(f)(4)(D) as amended by '93 Act § 13234(b)(2))

☐ **Effective:** For taxpayer's first tax year beginning on or before Aug. 1, '94 and following taxpayer's last tax year to which Rev Proc 92-56 applies or would apply if the taxpayer elected the benefits of the Rev Proc. (Code Sec. 864(f)(6) as amended by '93 Act § 13234(b)(1))

For official explanation see Committee Reports ¶ 3053.

¶ 1104. Foreign tax credit: retroactive elimination of working capital exception for foreign oil and gas and shipping income

Foreign tax credit limitations are computed separately for eight specific categories of foreign source income, including passive income and shipping income, and one residual or general limitation category for all other types of income. (See FTC 2d/FIN ¶ O-4080 *et seq.;* USTR ¶ 9044.01)

Passive income includes income that typically is not subject to high levels of foreign tax. The separate limitation for passive income generally prevents crediting high foreign taxes on income in the general limitation category against the residual U.S. tax on passive income. (Conf Rept p. 646) Under pre-'93 Act law, Code Sec. 904(d) passive income included foreign personal holding company income, such as dividends and interest, but did not include shipping income or foreign oil and gas extraction income (FOGEI). (FTC 2d/FIN ¶ O-4082; TG ¶ 8437; USTR ¶ 9044.01)

The separate foreign tax credit limitation for passive income was enacted in '86 and replaced the earlier separate limitation category for passive interest income. Under the pre-'87 law, the passive interest separate limitation category excluded certain types of interest on working capital. No general working capital exception exists under the passive income definition in Code Sec. 904(d) established in '86.

As a result of the interaction of the Code and IRS regs originally developed before '87 under other Code provisions, the working capital exception has been retained for the oil and gas and shipping industries. (H Rept p. 714) However, taxpayers who are not engaged in oil and gas or shipping operations include interest income on working capital in the separate foreign tax credit limitation category for passive income. Congress believes that the foreign tax credit rules should operate fairly and uniformly to all taxpayers. Thus, it changed the treatment of passive income earned by taxpayers with oil and gas and shipping operations to conform to the treatment of similar income earned by other taxpayers. (H Rept p. 714-5)

The '93 Act places certain passive income related to oil and gas and shipping operations in the passive category for foreign tax credit limitation purposes. (H Rept p. 715)

Exclusion of FOGEI from the passive income separate limitation category deleted. The '93 Act modifies the definition of passive income for purposes of applying the foreign tax credit limitations to separate categories of income by deleting the exclusion for FOGEI. (Code Sec. 904(d)(2)(A)(iii) as amended by '93 Act § 13235(a)(2)) Thus, if a taxpayer has gross income that falls within the definition of passive income under the separate income category rules, and also satisfies the definition of FOGEI, the income is treated as passive income in determining the taxpayer's foreign tax credit. (H Rept p. 715)

Changes to the definition of FORI that affect the passive income limitation category. For purposes of the separate foreign tax credit limitation categories, passive income is any income which would be subpart F foreign personal holding income under Code Sec. 954(c). (See FTC 2d/FIN ¶ O-4082; USTR ¶ 9044.01)

> ***observation:*** Thus, passive income includes dividends, interest, royalties, rents, annuities, and income from certain property transactions.

The '93 Act provides that, for purposes of the subpart F rules defining foreign base company income, foreign oil-related income (FORI) does not include any foreign personal holding company income as defined in Code Sec. 954(c). (Code Sec. 954(g)(1) as amended by '93 Act § 13235(a)(3)(A)) In addition, the provision that foreign base company oil-related income is not considered foreign personal holding company income for purposes of the foreign base company income rules under subpart F is deleted. (Code Sec. 954(b)(8) as amended by '93 Act § 13235(a)(3)(B))

Thus, foreign base company oil-related income that qualifies as foreign personal holding company income is treated as foreign personal holding company income. As such, the income generally would be passive income for foreign tax credit purposes. (H Rept p. 715)

FTC 2d References are to the Federal Tax Coordinator 2d
FIN References are to RIA's Analysis of Federal Taxes: Income
TG References are to the Tax Guide
USTR References are to the United States Tax Reporter

observation: Since the definition of foreign base-company oil-related income in Code Sec. 954(g)(1) was modified by the '93 Act to exclude foreign personal holding company income, such as dividends and interest, and since the definition of FORI in Code Sec. 907(c)(2) was also modified to exclude interest and dividends as defined the foreign personal holding company rules (see below), the amendment to Code Sec. 954(b)(8) would not seem to have much practical effect.

Dividend and interest income excluded from the definition of shipping income. For foreign tax credit purposes, passive income does not include shipping income, defined as foreign base company shipping income under the subpart F rules of Code Sec. 954(f). (See FTC 2d/FIN ¶s O-4082; O-4110; USTR ¶ 9044.01) However, under regs developed under pre-'86 law, shipping income under the subpart F rules of Code Sec. 954(f) included incidental income derived in the course of the active conduct of foreign base company shipping operations. (H Rept p. 713)

observation: Incidental income from the active conduct shipping operations would include interest and dividend income from the temporary investment of working capital.

The '93 Act provides that foreign base company shipping income does not include any dividend or interest income which is foreign personal holding company income (FTC 2d/FIN ¶ O-2721 *et seq.;* USTR ¶ 9544.04). (Code Sec. 954(f) as amended by '93 Act § 13235(b)) Thus, for foreign tax purposes, the interest and dividends on the temporary investment of working capital would fall in the passive income category rather than the shipping income category. (H Rept p. 715)

However, dividends and interest received from a foreign corporation for which taxes are deemed paid under Code Sec. 902 rules (relating to the deemed paid credit where domestic corporation owns 10% or more of the voting stock of a foreign corporation, see FTC 2d/FIN ¶ O-4160 *et seq.;* USTR ¶ 9024 *et seq.)* are, to the extent attributable to foreign base company shipping income, still included in the definition of foreign base shipping income for purposes of determining subpart F income. (Code Sec. 954(f))

Dividends and interest excluded from FOGEI and FORI. The '93 Act also excludes certain passive income related to FOGEI and FORI from the computation of the FOGEI and FORI foreign tax credit limitations. (H Rept p. 715)

FOGEI, as well as FORI, is subject to a special limitation on the amount of foreign taxes that is creditable under the foreign tax credit rules. (See FTC 2d/FIN ¶ O-4290 *et seq.;* TG ¶ 8411; USTR ¶ 9074 *et seq.)* Under this special limitation, amounts claimed as taxes paid on FOGEI of a U.S. corporation qualify as creditable taxes only to the extent they do not exceed the product of the highest marginal U.S. tax rate on corporations multiplied by FOGEI. A similar special limit may apply to FORI where that type of income is subject to a materially greater level of tax by a foreign jurisdiction than non-oil and gas income would be. Under this limitation, a portion of the foreign taxes on FORI may be deductible, but not creditable. (H Rept p. 714) In general, these limitations are intended to prevent crediting high foreign taxes on FOGEI and FORI against the residual U.S. tax on other types of lower-taxed foreign source income. (H Rept p. 715) Under regs developed under pre-'86 law, both FOGEI and FORI were defined to include interest on working capital (FTC 2d/FIN ¶s O-4295, O-4302; USTR ¶ 9074.03). (H Rept p. 714)

Under '93 Act law, the FOGEI does not include any dividend or interest income which is passive income as defined in Code Sec. 904(d)(2)(A) for purposes of the foreign tax credit separate limitation category. (Code Sec. 907(c)(1) as amended by '93 Act § 13235(a)(1)(A)) Since, the '93 Act treats interest income, including interest on working capital related to foreign oil and gas extraction activities, as passive income, then interest income is not considered FOGEI for purposes of computing the special limitation for foreign taxes paid on FOGEI. (H Rept p. 716)

In addition, under '93 Act law, FORI does not include any dividend or interest income which is passive income as defined in Code Sec. 904(d)(2)(A) for purposes of the foreign tax credit separate limitation category. (Code Sec. 907(c)(2) as amended by '93 Act § 13235(a)(1)(B)) As a result, gross interest income on working capital related to activities that generate FORI would not be treated as FORI for purposes of computing the special limitation for foreign taxes paid on FORI. (H Rept p. 716)

Congress intends that dividends and interest received from a foreign corporation for which taxes are deemed paid under Code Sec. 902 rules (relating to the deemed paid credit where a domestic corporation owns 10% or more of the voting stock of a foreign corporation, see FTC 2d/FIN ¶ O-4160 *et seq.;* USTR ¶ 9024 *et seq.)* are classified as FOGEI or FORI, respectively, to the extent attributable to FOGEI or FORI. (Conf Rept p. 648)

☐ **Effective:** Tax years beginning after Dec. 31, '92. (§ 13235(c)) Where there is a post-effective date corporate distribution of income earned by the payor in a pre-effective date tax year, the determination of whether the pre-effective date income was shipping income will be made under the laws defining shipping income in effect when the income was earned. (Conf Rept p. 648)

For official explanation see Committee Reports ¶ 3054.

¶ 1105. Accuracy-related penalty for Code Sec. 482 adjustments

Under pre-'93 Act law, the 20% accuracy related penalty applied to understatements of tax attributable to substantial valuation misstatements on income tax returns where either (1) the price for any property or services subject to a Code Sec. 482 adjustment (relating to transactions between parties under common ownership or control, see FTC 2d/FIN ¶ G-4000 *et seq.* ; TG ¶ 2770 *et seq.;* USTR ¶ 4824) was 200% or more (or 50% or less) of the correct amount or (2) the amount of the Code Sec. 482 adjustment was $10,000,000 or more. (FTC 2d/FIN ¶ V-2201; TG ¶ 9770; USTR ¶ 66,624) The 20% penalty was increased to 40% for "gross valuation misstatements" where either (1) the price for any property or services subject to adjustment was 400% or more (or 25% or less) of the correct amount or (2) the amount of the adjustment was $20,000,000 or more. (FTC 2d/FIN ¶ V-2203; TG ¶ 9770; USTR ¶ 66,624) An adjustment was excluded for purposes of determining whether the $10,000,000 threshold was met if the adjustment resulted from a redetermination of a price where the taxpayer had reasonable cause for the price used and the taxpayer acted in good faith. (FTC 2d/FIN ¶ V-2207; USTR ¶ 66,624) Also, any portion of the net increase in taxable income that is attributable to transactions between two foreign corporations was excluded for purposes of the threshold requirement, unless, in the case of any of the corporations, the treatment of the transaction affected the determination of U.S. source income or income effectively connected with a U.S. trade or business. (See FTC 2d/FIN ¶ V-2207; USTR ¶ 66,624)

The '93 Act changes the $10,000,000 threshold for the 20% penalty to the lesser of $5,0000,000 or 10% of the taxpayer's gross receipts. Accordingly, under the '93 Act a taxpayer is subject to the 20% penalty if either (1) the price for any property

FTC 2d References are to the Federal Tax Coordinator 2d
FIN References are to RIA's Analysis of Federal Taxes: Income
TG References are to the Tax Guide
USTR References are to the United States Tax Reporter

or services subject to adjustment was 200% or more (or 50% or less) of the correct amount or (2) the amount of the adjustment was equal to or greater than the lesser of $5,0000,000 or 10% of the taxpayer's gross receipts. (Code Sec. 6662(e)(1)(B) as amended by '93 Act § 13236(a)) The reduction in the threshold amount reflects Congress's view that the threat of penalties discourages valuation misstatements. (H Rept p. 719) The pre-'93 Act $20,000,000 threshold for the 40% penalty is also changed to the lesser of $20,000,000 or 20% of the taxpayer's gross receipts. (Code Sec. 6662(h)(2)(A)(iii) as amended by '93 Act § 13236(d))

The '93 Act also eliminates the reasonable cause/good faith exception from the penalty, adds two new exceptions, and retains the foreign corporation exception. Thus, if the threshold is met, the penalty applies unless the taxpayer falls into the foreign corporation exception or one of the new exceptions described below. (Code Sec. 6662(e)(3)(B) as amended by '93 Act § 13236(b); Code Sec. 6662(e)(3)(D) as amended by '93 Act § 13236(c))

The first new exception applies only if the taxpayer uses a pricing method set forth in IRS regulations. Under this safe harbor, for purposes of the threshold requirement, any portion of the net increase in taxable income that is attributable to the redetermination of a price is excluded if (1) it is established that the taxpayer determined the price in accordance with a specific pricing method set forth in the IRS regulations under Code Sec. 482 and that the use of the method was reasonable (Code Sec. 6662(e)(3)(B)(i)(I) as amended by '93 Act § 13236(b)), (2) the taxpayer has documentation (which was in existence as of the time of filing the return) that sets forth the determination of the price in accordance with the specific pricing method and which establishes that the use of the method was reasonable (Code Sec. 6662(e)(3)(B)(i)(II)), and (3) the taxpayer provides the documentation to IRS within 30 days of a request for the documentation. (Code Sec. 6662(e)(3)(B)(i)(III))

The House Ways and Means Committee gives, as examples of specific pricing methods set forth in IRS regulations, the following methods in Temporary Regulations for sales of tangible personal property: the comparable uncontrolled price method, the resale price method, the cost plus method, and the comparable profits method. (See FTC 2d/FIN ¶ G-4402; TG ¶ 2785; USTR ¶ 4824) Any other method does not qualify for the safe harbor. Where IRS regulations do not specify a method for a given transaction, such as transactions involving services, this safe harbor is not available. (H Rept p. 721)

The requirement that the use of a specific method be reasonable means that the taxpayer must observe any procedural requirements for the use of a method and make any required adjustments. In addition, where more than one method is potentially applicable, the method applied must be chosen under appropriate criteria under the "best method" rule. (See FTC 2d/FIN ¶ G-4403; TG ¶ 2774.2; USTR ¶ 4824) (H Rept p. 721)

Also, where the taxpayer becomes aware before filing its tax return that a particular method more likely than not will not result in a clear reflection of income, the use of the method is not reasonable. (H Rept pp. 722-723)

The use of a transfer pricing method must be determined on the basis of the information available. In some cases, only information from prior years is available at the time the tax return is filed. The use of prior years' information is reasonable, unless more recent information becomes available before the tax return is filed. (H Rept p. 723)

The second new exception applies where the taxpayer does not use a pricing method set forth in IRS regulations. Under this safe harbor, for purposes of the threshold requirement, any portion of the net increase in taxable income that is attributable to the redetermination of a price is excluded if (1) the taxpayer establishes that none of the specific pricing methods set forth in IRS regulations was likely to result in a price that would clearly reflect income, the taxpayer used another pricing method to determine the transfer price, and the taxpayer's method was likely to result in a price that would clearly reflect income (Code Sec. 6662(e)(3)(B)(ii)(I)), (2) the taxpayer has documentation (which was in existence as of the time of filing the return) that sets forth the determination of the price in accordance with the method used and establishes that the requirements under (1) were satisfied (Code Sec. 6662(e)(3)(B)(ii)(II)), and (3) the taxpayer provides the documentation to IRS within 30 days of a request for the documentation. (Code Sec. 6662(e)(3)(B)(ii)(III))

In establishing that no specified method was likely to result in a price that would clearly reflect income and that an unspecified method was likely to result in a price that would clearly reflect income, the taxpayer must set out good and sufficient reasons for these conclusions. For example, a reason why a particular method was not likely to result in a price that would clearly reflect income may be that data relating to comparable uncontrolled transactions is unavailable. A reason why a particular unspecified method was likely to result in a price that would clearly reflect income, may be that the method took into consideration the significant factors that unrelated parties engaged in arm's length transactions would have considered and gave appropriate weight to these factors. (H Rept p. 722)

A taxpayer may also establish that a method was likely to result in a price that would clearly reflect income by establishing that IRS entered into an advance pricing method with the taxpayer based on the method, that the taxpayer applied the agreed upon method reasonably and consistently with its prior application, and that the facts and circumstances surrounding the use of the method had not changed. (H Rept p. 722)

For transactions such as the provision of services, where there are no IRS regulations setting forth acceptable pricing methods, the taxpayer must only establish that the transaction is of a type for which no methods are specified in the Code Sec. 483 regs. (Conf Rept p. 650) It is not necessary to establish that none of the specified pricing methods was likely to result in a price that would clearly reflect income. (H Rept p. 722)

Where the taxpayer falls into one of the safe harbors, the accuracy related penalty does not apply, although IRS is not precluded from making a Code Sec. 482 adjustment. (H Rept p. 720)

☐ **Effective:** For taxable years beginning after Dec. 31, '93. (§ 13236(e))
For official explanation see Committee Reports ¶ 3055.

¶ 1106. Denial of portfolio interest exemption for contingent interest

A nonresident alien individual or foreign corporation is subject to a 30% withholding tax on U.S. source interest that is not effectively connected with a U.S. trade or business. However, portfolio interest is exempted from the 30% withholding tax. Portfolio interest includes interest paid on obligations that satisfy certain registration requirements and that is not received by a 10% owner of the issuer. For corporate recipients, portfolio interest does not include interest received by a bank in the ordinary course of business or interest received by a controlled foreign

FTC 2d References are to the Federal Tax Coordinator 2d
FIN References are to RIA's Analysis of Federal Taxes: Income
TG References are to the Tax Guide
USTR References are to the United States Tax Reporter

corporation from a related person. (See FTC 2d/FIN ¶s O-10204, O-10404; TG ¶ 8378; USTR ¶ 8714.02)

Under pre-'93 Act law, the portfolio interest exemption applied to contingent interest. Thus, even where contingent interest on an instrument issued by a U.S. real property holding corporation caused gain on the sale of the instrument to be subject to tax under the Foreign Investment in Real Property Tax Act (Code Sec. 897, see FTC 2d/FIN ¶ O-10756; TG ¶ 8227; USTR ¶ 8974), the interest was not taxed if it qualified as portfolio interest. The characterization of contingent interest as portfolio interest allowed foreign investors to receive equity participation rights in the U.S. without being subject to tax. (H Rept p. 724)

The '93 Act provides that, for purposes of the portfolio interest exemption for nonresident alien individuals, portfolio interest does not include any contingent interest that is determined by reference to:

. . . any receipts, sales or other cash flow of the debtor or a related person;

. . . any income or profits of the debtor or a related person;

. . . any change in value of any property of the debtor or a related person;

. . . any dividend, partnership distributions, or similar payment made by the debtor or a related person; or

. . . any other contingent interest identified in IRS regulations, where denial of the portfolio interest exemption is necessary or appropriate to prevent avoidance of Federal income tax. (Code Sec. 871(h)(4)(A) as amended by '93 Act § 13237(a)(1))

Contingent interest that is not treated as portfolio interest for purposes of the portfolio interest exemption for nonresident alien individuals is also not treated as portfolio interest for purposes of the portfolio interest exemption for foreign corporations. (Code Sec. 881(c)(4) as amended by '93 Act § 13237(a)(2))

Where an instrument includes a minimum noncontingent interest rate, only the excess of the contingent amount over the minimum is treated as contingent interest. For instance, where the interest rate is stated as the greater of (1) 6% or (2) 10% of gross profits, only the gross-profits-based interest in excess of the minimum fixed interest of 6% is contingent interest. (Conf Rept p. 653)

Contingent interest is also not treated as portfolio interest for purposes of the rule that treats instruments that would qualify as obligations with portfolio interest (without regard to the requirement that the payor receive a statement that the beneficial owner of the instrument is not a U.S. person) as not having a U.S. situs, which are thus excluded from the gross estate of a nonresident alien. (See FTC 2d/FIN ¶ R-8019; TG ¶ 8798) Where a portion of the interest is contingent, then an appropriate portion (as determined under IRS regs) of the value (as determined for tax purposes) of the instrument is treated as having a U.S. situs. (Code Sec. 2105(b) as amended by '93 Act § 13237(b)) Until IRS rules provide guidance on how to determine the appropriate portion situated in the U.S., taxpayers may use any reasonable method for making this determination. (Conf Rept p. 653-654)

The term "related person" is defined as a person who is related to the debtor under Code Sec. 267(b) (disallowing losses between related persons, see FTC 2d/FIN ¶ G-2657; TG ¶ 4101; USTR ¶ 2674) or under Code Sec. 707(b)(1) (disallowing losses between partners and partnerships, see FTC 2d/FIN ¶ B-2016; TG ¶ 1643; USTR ¶ 7074.03) or a person who is a party to any arrangement undertaken for the purpose of avoiding the rules preventing contingent interest from being treated as portfolio interest. (Code Sec. 871(h)(4)(B) as amended by '93 Act § 13237(a)(1))

Contingent interest does not include:

. . . any amount of interest solely because the timing of any interest or principal payment is subject to a contingency. (Code Sec. 871(h)(4)(C)(i)) Thus, a debt instrument that provides for fixed interest at a market rate, but that allows the borrower to defer payments before the maturity date if its cash flow is insufficient, and does not eliminate the borrower's liability for the deferred amount or the interest on the deferred amount, is not treated as having contingent interest. (H Rept p. 725);

. . . any amount of interest solely because the interest is paid with respect to nonrecourse or limited recourse debt. (Code Sec. 871(h)(4)(C)(ii)) Thus, a limited recourse instrument that pays fixed interest at a market rate and is secured by the receivables of the borrower is not treated as having contingent interest. (H Rept p. 726);

. . . any amount of interest all or substantially all of which is determined by reference to any other amount of interest that is not contingent interest (under the rules described above) or by reference to the principal amount of debt on which the interest is not contingent interest. (Code Sec. 871(h)(4)(C)(iii));

. . . any amount of interest solely because the debtor or a related person enters into a hedging transaction to reduce the risk of interest rate or currency fluctuations with respect to the interest. (Code Sec. 871(h)(4)(C)(iv)) Thus, interest based on a commodity index is not treated as contingent merely because the debtor hedges its interest rate risk by buying an offsetting commodities position that produces a cash flow offsetting the interest payments. Similarly, interest paid by reference to a stock market index is not treated as contingent merely because an affiliate of the debtor holds stock. (H Rept p. 727);

. . . any amount of interest determined by reference to (1) changes in the value of property (including stock) that is actively traded (as defined under the Code Sec. 1092 straddle rules, see FTC 2d/FIN ¶ I-4307; TG ¶ 4155; USTR ¶ 6924), other than property described in Code Sec. 897(c)(1) (a U.S. real property interest, see FTC 2d/FIN ¶ O-10746; TG ¶ 8227; USTR ¶ 8974) or Code Sec. 897(g) (a partnership, trust, or estate holding U.S. real property interests, see FTC 2d/FIN ¶ O-10734; TG ¶ 8231; USTR ¶ 8974); (2) changes in the yield on property described in (1), other than a debt instrument that pays contingent interest or stock or other property that represents a beneficial interest in the debtor or a related person; or (3) changes in any index of the value of property described in (1) or the yield on property described in (2). (Code Sec. 871(h)(4)(C)(v)); and

. . . any other type of interest identified in IRS regs. (Code Sec. 871(h)(4)(C)(vi))

The exclusions described above from the definition of contingent interest may not be used to inappropriately avoid contingent interest treatment. For instance, a nonrecourse debt instrument that provides for interest in excess of a market rate, but allows all or part of the interest to be deferred if the debtor's cash flow is insufficient, can be used to structure what is in substance interest based on the debtor's cash flow. Thus, if it is expected that under such an instrument a portion of the interest will be deferred and ultimately will never be paid, the instrument is treated as having contingent interest. (H Rept p. 727)

A regular interest in a REMIC (see FTC 2d/FIN ¶ E-6904; TG ¶ 7884; USTR ¶ 860A4.01) that pays interest at a market rate is not treated as having contingent interest because the period for which it will remain outstanding depends on the extent that the mortgages held by the REMIC are prepaid and on other contingencies related to the income or expenses of the REMIC. Also, an interest in a REMIC that pays interest on the basis of a percentage of the noncontingent interest earned by the REMIC is not treated as having contingent interest. This rule applies even where the interest is not fixed. For instance, where a REMIC pays interest based on the excess of the interest received by the REMIC over the principal amount of the mortgages it holds multiplied by a variable rate based on LIBOR (the London Inter-Bank Offered Rate) subject to a cap, the fact that the interest paid varies inversely with LIBOR does not cause the interest to be treated as contingent interest. (H Rept p. 726)

IRS may issue regs to supplement the statutory description of contingent interest where a denial of portfolio interest is necessary or appropriate to prevent tax avoidance. IRS may also issue regs exempting any type of interest from being treated as contingent interest. (H Rept p. 727)

Where interest is not treated as portfolio interest because it is contingent, the person who would normally be required to withhold tax under Code Sec. 1441 (relating to payments to nonresident aliens, see FTC 2d/FIN ¶ O-11710; TG ¶ 8378; USTR ¶ 14,414.04) or under Code Sec. 1442 (relating to payments to foreign corporations, see FTC 2d/FIN ¶ O-11704; TG ¶ 8378; USTR ¶ 14,414) is not required to withhold unless the person knows or has reason to know that the interest is not portfolio interest because it is contingent interest. (Code Sec. 1441(c)(9) as amended by '93 Act § 13237(c)(4); Code Sec. 1442(a) as amended by '93 Act § 13237(b)(5))

☐ **Effective:** For interest received after Dec. 31, '93. The rule treating an instrument with contingent interest as situated, in whole or part, in the U.S. applies to estates of decedents dying after Dec. 31, '93. (§ 13237(b))

However, the above rules do not apply to any interest paid or accrued with respect to any indebtedness with a fixed term that was issued before Apr. 8, '93 or that was issued after Apr. 7, '93 under a written binding contract in effect on Apr. 7, '93 and at all time afterwards until the debt is issued. (Code Sec. 871(h)(4)(D) as amended by '93 Act § 13237(a)(1))

For official explanation see Committee Reports ¶ 3056.

¶ 1107. Earnings stripping disallowance broadened to cover guaranteed debt

Payment of deductible interest by a corporation to a related person on whom there is no U.S. tax on the corresponding income is generally referred to as earnings stripping. Since the recipient of the income doesn't have to pay tax on the income, persons with a shared economic interests are able to avoid a certain amount of tax. To prevent earnings stripping, a corporation's interest deduction for "disqualified interest" is denied to the extent the corporation's net interest expense exceeds 50% of its adjusted taxable income in any year that the corporation has a debt to equity ratio greater than 1.5 to 1. (See FTC 2d/FIN ¶ K-5360 *et seq.;* TG ¶ 7189 *et seq.;* USTR ¶ 1634.058)

> ***observation:*** Earnings stripping commonly occurs when a foreign parent, not taxable in the U.S., loans money to its U.S. sub, which deducts the interest paid on the debt owed to the parent. Since the foreign parent doesn't pay U.S. income tax, the U.S. can't tax the interest income that corresponds to the interest deduction of the U.S. taxpayer.

Where a group of related corporations earns income that is at least in part subject to U.S. tax, Congress believes that it is important to preserve for U.S. taxing jurisdiction, an appropriate share of the net income of the group. The earnings stripping provision is designed to deny deductions for interest expenses that are disqualified under the criteria specified. Where the deductions are for interest paid to tax-exempt related parties, net income is shifted from the payor to the related party. Congress is concerned about situations in which a U.S. corporation is able to borrow from an unrelated party on the basis of the credit of a tax exempt related party who guarantees the debt. Although the interest on guaranteed debt is paid to an unrelated lender, the debt is seen as a substitute for a direct related party loan to the extent that money is fungible. (H Rept p. 682) Thus, the amount of U.S. tax paid with respect to the U.S. operations of a related group depends on whether the creditor lends to the parent, which in turn lends to the sub, or whether the creditor lends directly to the sub. In either case, loans from unrelated creditors may be viewed as supporting the income-producing activities of the group as a whole. (H Rept p. 685)

Disqualified interest defined. Under pre-'93 Act law, disqualified interest was any interest paid or accrued directly or indirectly to a related person if no U.S. income tax is imposed on that interest. (FTC 2d/FIN ¶ K-5363; TG ¶ 7189; USTR ¶ 1634.058) Although granted broad authority to issue regs to prevent the avoidance of the earnings stripping limitations, IRS hasn't issued either proposed or final regs applying the earnings stripping rules to third-party debt guaranteed by a party related to the debtor or to so-called back-to-back loans (see FTC 2d/FIN ¶ K-5383; USTR ¶ 1634.058). However, legislative history when the earnings stripping rules were enacted in '89 indicates that unrelated party interest payments should not be disallowed if the guarantee is given in the ordinary course of business. Further, the history indicates that regs applying the earnings stripping rules to third-party debt guaranteed by a person related to the debtor should not apply to debt outstanding before notice of the rule. (H Rept p. 681)

Accordingly, the '93 Act provides that disqualified interest is any interest—

(a) paid or accrued directly or indirectly to a related person if no U.S. income tax is imposed on that interest and (Code Sec. 163(j)(3)(A) as amended by '93 Act § 13228(a))

(b) paid or accrued on any indebtedness to a person who is not a related person, if there is a disqualified guarantee of that debt and a gross basis tax is not imposed on that interest. (Code Secs. 163(j)(3)(B)(i) and (j)(3)(B)(ii) as amended by '93 Act § 13228(a))

Disqualified guarantee defined. A disqualified guarantee is any guarantee by a related person which is an organization exempt from U.S. income tax or a foreign person. (Code Sec. 163(j)(6)(D)(i) as amended by '93 Act § 13228(b))

A disqualified guarantee does not include a guarantee (see below), in any circumstances identified by regs, where the interest on the indebtedness would have been subject to a net basis tax if the interest had been paid to the guarantor. (Code Sec. 163(j)(6)(D)(ii)(I)) Congress anticipates that IRS will exercise its authority to treat a foreign guarantor like a taxable U.S. person where the foreign person conducts a U.S. business and IRS is satisfied that income on a hypothetical loan by the foreign person to the debtor (similar to the third-party guaranteed loan) would have been effectively connected with the conduct of that U.S. business, and thus subject to U.S.

FTC 2d References are to the Federal Tax Coordinator 2d
FIN References are to RIA's Analysis of Federal Taxes: Income
TG References are to the Tax Guide
USTR References are to the United States Tax Reporter

tax after application of any relevant treaty. Congress intends that IRS have broad discretion to limit the scope of this exception to cases where it is fully satisfied that taxpayers are prevented from engaging in tax avoidance schemes, such as establishing an insubstantial U.S. business for purposes of qualifying for the exception. (H Rept p. 686)

A disqualified guarantee also does not include a guarantee if the debtor owns a controlling interest in the guarantor. (Code Sec. 163(j)(6)(D)(ii)(II)) Except as provided in regs, a controlling interest, for this purpose, means direct or indirect ownership of at least 80% of the total voting power and value of all classes of stock of a corporation, or 80% of the profit and capital interests in any other entity. The rules for determining the constructive ownership of stock at Code Sec. 267(c)(1) and Code Sec. 267(c)(5) (see FTC 2d/FIN ¶s I-2909, 2910; TG ¶ 2653; USTR ¶ 2674) apply to corporations as well as to interests in other entities. (Code Sec. 163(j)(6)(D)(ii))

Except as provided in regs, a guarantee includes any arrangement under which a person (directly or indirectly through an entity or otherwise) assures, on a conditional or unconditional basis, the payment of another person's obligation under any indebtedness. (Code Sec. 163(j)(6)(D)(iii))

Guarantees include arrangements that are not legally enforceable obligations. Congress intends that a guarantee be interpreted broadly enough to include any form of credit support, including a commitment to make a capital contribution to the debtor or otherwise maintain its financial viability. It would also include an arrangement reflected in a "comfort letter," regardless of whether that arrangement is a legally enforceable obligation. If a guarantee is contingent upon the occurrence of an event, the rule for defining a guarantee would apply as if the event had occurred. (H Rept p. 686)

Congress is also concerned that taxpayers not avoid the purposes of the earnings stripping rules through conduit arrangements, including transactions in which the conduit is a U.S. taxpayer, and through certain types of guarantees that can be used to achieve results similar to back-to-back loans. Applying the earnings stripping rules to all guaranteed debt avoids these difficulties. (H Rept p. 684)

Gross basis tax. A gross basis tax is any U.S. income tax which is determined by reference to the gross amount of any item of income without reduction for any allowable deduction. (Code Sec. 163(j)(6)(E)(i)) The 30% statutory tax on interest paid to a foreign person (see FTC 2d/FIN ¶s O-10200 *et seq.*, O-10400 *et seq.;* TG ¶s 8099, 8191; USTR ¶s 8714.02, 8814.02) is a gross basis tax for this purpose. (H Rept p. 685)

If a treaty reduces the statutory gross basis tax on any interest paid by the taxpayer, without eliminating it, a ratable portion of the interest paid to a foreign person that would have been subject to the 30% statutory tax is treated as having no gross basis tax imposed on it. (See FTC 2d/FIN ¶ K-5368; TG ¶ 7192; USTR ¶ 1634.058) Thus, if the treaty-reduced rate were 15%, then half of the interest would be treated as subject to the full 30% gross basis tax and the other half would be treated as subject to no gross basis tax. (H Rept p. 685) Under pre-'93 Act law, the rule for the reduction of the tax on part of the interest applied to interest paid by the taxpayer to a related person. (Code Sec. 163(j)(5)(B) before amend by '93 Act § 13228(c)(1)) The '93 Act applies this rule to disqualified guarantees by deleting the limitation that the interest be paid to a related person. (§ 13228(c)(1))

Net basis tax defined. A net basis tax is any U.S. income tax which is not a gross basis tax. (Code Sec. 163(j)(6)(E)(ii)).

Treaty conflict. Congress does not believe that the impact of the rules on foreign-owned entities conflicts with U.S. tax treaties. While Congress understands that the impact of these rules may fall heavily on foreign-based multinational companies, the rules generally apply to guarantees provided by all tax-exempt U.S. persons and tax-exempt foreign persons. For example, the rules don't distinguish between payments to U.S. residents and payments to residents of other countries. In either case, deductions are denied on the basis of the presence or absence of a disqualifying guarantee. Furthermore, the earnings stripping rules deny deductions only in cases believed to satisfy an objective standard of "thin capitalization." Disallowance in these cases may be consistent with treaties regardless of whether the disallowance applies only to thinly capitalized foreign-owned companies. (H Rept p. 687)

☐ **Effective:** For interest paid or accrued in taxable years ending after Dec. 31, '93. (§ 13228(d))

Interest on pre-July 10, '89 debt no longer escapes earnings stripping disallowance. Under pre-'93 Act law, disqualified interest did not apply to interest on debt with a fixed term that was issued on or before July 10, '89 (FTC 2d/FIN ¶ K-5363; TG ¶ 7189; USTR ¶ 1634.058). However, under the '93 Act, interest may be treated as disqualified interest regardless of when the obligation on which the interest is paid was issued. (H Rept p. 685)

For official explanation see Committee Reports ¶ 3051.

¶ 1108. Limitation of same-country dividend exclusion from foreign personal holding company income

A "U.S. shareholder" (in general, a U.S. person who owns 10% or more, by vote, of the stock, see FTC 2d/FIN ¶ O-2603; TG ¶ 8242; USTR ¶ 9514.01) of a controlled foreign corporation (CFC) is required to include in income certain amounts, including his pro rata share of the CFC's foreign personal holding company income (FPHCI). (See FTC 2d/FIN ¶ O-2820 *et seq.;* TG ¶ 8240 *et seq.;* USTR ¶ 9514.01) In general, FPHCI includes dividends received by the CFC (see FTC 2d/FIN ¶ O-2658; TG ¶ 8247; USTR ¶ 9544.02); however, pre-'93 Act law provided an exclusion from FPHCI for dividends received from certain corporations which (i) were related to the CFC, (ii) were organized under the laws of the same country as the CFC, and (iii) had a substantial part of their business assets located in that country. (FTC 2d/FIN ¶ O-2663; TG ¶ 8247; USTR ¶ 9544.02)

The '93 Act provides that the same-country dividend exclusion does not apply to dividends attributable to earnings and profits accumulated during any period during which the recipient CFC did not own the stock with respect to which the dividends are paid. Ownership of stock of the payor corporation may be either direct or indirect through one or more subsidiaries each of which (i) is related to the CFC, (ii) is organized under the laws of the same country as the CFC, and (iii) has a substantial part of its business assets located in that country. (Code Sec. 954(c)(3)(C) as amended by '93 Act § 13233(a)(1))

> ***observation:*** The '93 Act does not define the extent of ownership which is required for a corporation to be considered a "subsidiary" of another corporation. However, in order for a corporation to be "related" to another corporation, there must generally be ownership of more than 50% (by vote or value) of the other corporation's stock (see FTC 2d/FIN ¶ O-2657; USTR ¶ 9544.02)

observation: The '93 Act provides no explicit rules for determining when distributed earnings and profits are deemed to have been accumulated. Presumably, this determination will be made under the general rule that any distribution is deemed to have been made first out of current year earnings and profits, and then out of the most recently accumulated earnings and profits.

observation: The '93 Act does not affect the availability of the same-country exclusion for interest (see FTC 2d/FIN ¶ O-2663; TG ¶ 8247; USTR ¶ 9544.02), and therefore provides an added incentive to structure an investment in a related corporation as debt rather than equity.

caution: Read literally, the '93 Act limits the same-country dividend exclusion to dividends paid out of earnings and profits accumulated at a time when the particular entity which receives the dividends was the owner (directly or indirectly) of the particular shares of stock with respect to which the dividends are paid. Evidently, the exclusion is not available where, between the time earnings and profits are accumulated and the time they are distributed, (i) the recipient corporation has undergone a change of identity in a tax-free reorganization, (ii) the payor corporation has undergone a change of identity in a tax-free reorganization, or (iii) the payor corporation has undergone a recapitalization in which the particular shares of stock owned by the recipient CFC are exchanged for other shares.

☐ **Effective:** Tax years of CFCs beginning after Sept. 30, '93, and taxable years of U.S. shareholders in which or with which such years end. (§ 13233(a)(2))

For official explanation see Committee Reports ¶ 3052.

¶ 1109. IRS authorized to issue regs dealing with conduit arrangements

The tax treatment of a transaction may depend on the identity of the parties to the transaction. (H Rept p. 727) Under the Code, interest payments by U.S. persons to related foreign persons may be subject to 30% gross-basis withholding tax. However, under many treaties, interest payments by U.S. persons to related foreign persons who are residents in a treaty country are subject to little or no U.S. gross-basis tax. On the other hand, if the related recipient of interest payments is resident in a country where there is no U.S. income tax treaty in force, the 30% gross-basis tax would be imposed. (See FTC 2d/FIN ¶s O-10200 *et seq.;* O-10400 *et seq.;* USTR ¶ 8714.02) (H Rept p. 728)

illustration: Foreign corporation P is a resident of country A, which does not have a tax treaty with the U.S. P has a wholly-owned subsidiary, Sub 1, which is a U.S. corporation. P has another wholly-owned subsidiary, Sub 2, which is a finance and holding company in Country B. Country B has a tax treaty with the U.S. under which interest from U.S. persons paid to related Country B persons is exempt from withholding. Country B also has a favorable tax treaty with Country A. Interest on a direct loan from P to Sub 1 would be taxable. However, P could loan money to Sub 2 in Country B, which could in turn loan money to Sub 1 in the U.S. Interest payments from Sub 1 to Sub 2 would be exempt from withholding under the Country B income tax treaty with the U.S. Payments from Sub 2 in Country B to P in Country A would be subject to favorable terms under the tax treaty between Country A and Country B.

Courts have stated that the incidence of taxation depends upon the substance of a transaction as a whole. In certain cases, courts have recharacterized transactions in order to impose tax consistent with this principle. For example, where three parties have engaged in a chain of transactions, the courts have at times ignored the "middle" party as a mere "conduit," and imposed tax as if a single transaction had been carried out between the parties at the ends of the chain. (Conf Rept p. 654)

Congress noted with approval IRS rulings on facts similar to those described in the above illustration which ignored the conduit entities and recharacterized the transactions as direct payments from the U.S. subsidiary to the foreign parent. (H Rept p. 729) In Rev Rul 84-152 and Rev Rul 84-153, loans in which a foreign parent loaned money to a foreign subsidiary, which in turn loaned money to a U.S. subsidiary, where the intermediary foreign subsidiary did not have complete dominion and control over the interest payments, were recharacterized as interest payments by the U.S. subsidiary directly to the foreign parent. Thus, the treaty benefits that otherwise applied to the U.S. subsidiary's interest payments to the intermediary subsidiary were lost. (See FTC 2d ¶ O-30009) In Rev Rul 87-89, there was a similar result when an unrelated financial intermediary was interposed between two related parties as lender to one and borrower from the other, where the intermediary would not have made the loan on the same terms without the corresponding borrowing. (See FTC 2d/FIN ¶ O-2875) Congress also cited an additional case and other IRS rulings that contained similar facts and similar conclusions. (Conf Rept p. 654-5)

> ***observation:*** Loan arrangements in which one member of a related group makes a loan to an unrelated party which, in turn, makes a corresponding loan to another member of the related group are referred to generally as back-to-back loans, see FTC 2d/FIN ¶ K-5383.

Congress wants to bolster IRS's ability to prevent unwarranted avoidance of tax through multiple-party financial engineering and to provide a mechanism for issuing additional guidance to taxpayers. (H Rept p. 729) Thus, the '93 Act authorizes IRS to prescribe regs recharacterizing any multiple-party financing transaction as a transaction directly among any two or more of the parties, wherever IRS finds that recharacterization is appropriate to prevent tax avoidance. (Code Sec. 7701(l) as amended by '93 Act § 14238)

Congress intends that this provision apply not only to back-to-back loan transactions as described above, but also to other financing transactions. For example, it would be within the scope of the provision for IRS to issue regs dealing with multiple-party transactions involving debt guarantees or equity investments. (Conf Rept p. 655)

> ***observation:*** Restricting back-to-back loans and similar multiple-party financial transactions is also the purpose of the earnings stripping provisions, see ¶ 1107.

Congress does not intend that IRS be bound by the standards on which the above described rulings were based in developing the regs. If IRS finds it necessary or appropriate, it may adopt other standards in order to properly recharacterize a financing transaction.

> ***observation:*** It appears that Congress does not intend that IRS be limited to "lack of dominion and control" as the standard for ignoring an intermediary entity and recharacterizing multiple-party financing transactions.

Congress noted that the passage of this legislation is not intended to cast negative inference on positions taken by IRS under present law. (H Rept p. 729)

> **observation:** Although the examples and discussion in the Committee Reports relate to foreign taxpayers, the statutory authorization is broad enough to apply to domestic transactions.

☐ **Effective:** Aug. 10, '93. (H Rept p. 729)
For official explanation see Committee Reports ¶ 3057.

¶ 1110. Extension of controlled foreign corporation rules to earnings invested in excess passive assets

A "U.S. shareholder" (as defined) of a controlled foreign corporation (CFC) is required to include in income his *pro rata* share of (1) the CFC's Subpart F income, and (2) the CFC's increase in earnings invested in U.S. property. (See FTC 2d/FIN ¶ O-2820 *et seq.;* TG ¶ 8240 *et seq.;* USTR ¶ 9514.01)

The '93 Act provides that a U.S. shareholder will also be required to include in income (Code Sec. 951(a)(1)(C) as amended by '93 Act § 13231(a)) an amount equal to the lesser of (1) the U.S. shareholder's *pro rata* share of the CFC's excess passive assets (see below) for that tax year (Code Sec. 956A(a)(1)(A) as added by '93 Act § 13231(b)) less that portion of the CFC's earnings and profits attributable to amounts included previously in that shareholder's gross income on account of excess passive assets (or which would have been so included except for the fact that they had already been included in the shareholder's income under another provision of the CFC rules) (Code Sec. 956A(a)(1)(B)), or (2) that shareholder's pro rata share of the CFC's applicable earnings (see below), determined after including in the shareholder's income his pro rata share of the CFC's increase in earnings invested in U.S. property. (Code Sec. 956A(a)(2))

Any amount otherwise includible in income on account of excess passive assets will not be includible if it has already been included in income. (Code Sec. 951(a)(1)(C)) For a discussion of when an amount otherwise includible is deemed to have already been included in income, see ¶ 1111.

> **observation:** Under pre-'93 Act law, if a CFC had income which was not Subpart F income, U.S. shareholders could defer taxation on those earnings as long as they were reinvested abroad. The '93 Act limits this possibility of deferral where more than 25% of a CFC's total assets are invested in passive assets.

Excess passive assets. The amount of a CFC's excess passive assets for a taxable year is the excess of (1) the average amount of such corporation's passive assets at the close of each quarter of such year (Code Sec. 956A(c)(1)(A)), over (2) 25% of the CFC's average total assets as of the end of each such quarter (Code Sec. 956A(c)(1)(B)). In making this determination, assets are measured by their adjusted basis as determined for purposes of computing earnings and profits. (Code Sec. 956A(c)(1))

> **observation:** The basis of depreciable property for purposes of computing earnings and profits can differ from its basis for purposes of determining gain or loss on sale or other disposition. (See FTC 2d/FIN ¶ F-10300 *et seq.;* TG ¶ 2248; USTR ¶ 3124.04)

> **observation:** Because the computation of excess passive assets is made according to basis, a CFC which owns passive assets with a basis in excess of fair market value may wish to consider disposing of those assets in a tax-

able transaction to recognize a loss, and reinvesting the proceeds in other assets, thereby reducing the basis of the CFC's passive assets.

Short-term loans or other temporary arrangements will be disregarded in determining whether a CFC has excess passive assets if a principal purpose of such loan or arrangement is to avoid taking passive assets into account. (S Rept p. 329)

Passive assets are any assets which produce, or which are held for the production of, passive income. (Code Sec. 956A(c)(2)(A)) However, passive assets do not include any U.S. property. (Code Sec. 956A(c)(2)(B)) *Passive income* is defined under the rules which apply to passive foreign investment companies (PFICs). (See FTC 2d/ FIN ¶ O-2001; TG ¶ 8322: USTR ¶ 12,914 *et seq.)*

Aggregation rules. In determining whether a CFC has excess passive assets, all CFCs which are members of the same "CFC group" are treated as though they were a single CFC. (Code Sec. 956A(d)(1)(A)) The amount of excess passive assets as determined for the group is then allocated among the member CFCs in proportion to their relative amounts of applicable earnings. (Code Sec. 956A(d)(1)(B)) In applying the excess passive assets test to a CFC group, intercompany stock and debt is disregarded. (Conf Rept p. 639)

> ***observation:*** The Conference Committee states that the rule which disregards intercompany stock or debt "generally" applies, but does not indicate where the general rule would not apply.

> ***observation:*** Intercompany distributions can affect the amount of applicable earnings of each member of a CFC group, and hence the portion of the group's excess passive assets which will be allocated to each member. The use of distributions as a planning technique should therefore be considered.

A "CFC group" is one or more chains of CFCs connected through stock ownership with a top tier corporation which is a CFC (Code Sec. 956A(d)(2)), if (1) the top tier corporation directly owns more than 50% (by vote or value) of the stock of at least one other CFC (Code Sec. 956A(d)(2)(A)), and (2) more than 50% (by vote or value) of the stock of each CFC other than the top tier corporation is owned, directly or indirectly, by one or more other members of the group. (Code Sec. 956A(d)(2)(B))

> ***illustration:*** Corporations F, G, H and I are all CFCs. F owns 75% of the stock of G and 60% of the stock of H. G and H each own 50% of the stock of I. F, G, H and I together are a CFC group.

> ***illustration:*** Corporations J, K, L and M are all CFCs. J owns 50% of the stock of K. K owns 75% of the stock of M and 60% of the stock of L. L owns 25% of the stock of M. Because J does not own more than 50% of the stock of any other corporation in the group, it is not a top tier corporation; since its stock, in turn, is not owned by other members of the group, it is not a member of the group at all. However, K, L and M together are a CFC group, with K as the top tier corporation.

Look-through rule. In determining whether a CFC has excess passive assets, the "look-through" rules applicable to the determination of whether a corporation is a PFIC apply. (Code Sec. 956A(c)(3)(A)) Under these rules, in general, a corporation which owns at least 25% (by value) of the stock of another corporation is treated as though it directly held its proportionate share of that other corporation's assets, and received its proportionate share of that other corporation's income. (See FTC 2d/ FIN ¶ O-2002; TG ¶ 8321; USTR ¶ 12,914.01 *et seq.)* However, the look-through rules do not apply within a CFC group (see above), because under the aggregation rules stock of one member of such a group which is owned by another member is disregarded. (Conf Rept p. 639)

> ***illustration:*** Corporations N, O and P are all CFCs. N owns 75% of the stock of O, which in turn owns 30% of the stock of P. Because N and O are a CFC group, they are treated as a single corporation under the aggregation rule. In determining the amount of passive assets of the N-O "single" corporation, that corporation is deemed to own 30% of P's assets under the look-through rule.

> ***observation:*** Under the aggregation rule, all of the assets of the corporations which are members of a CFC group are combined, even if there is less than 100% stock ownership. Under the look-through rule, by contrast, an upper-tier corporation is deemed to own only its proportionate share of a lower-tier corporation's assets.

Currency conversions. In applying the aggregation and look-through rules, all assets and earnings must ordinarily be converted into U.S. dollars. Until Regs are issued taxpayers may use any reasonable method in making this conversion, as long as the method is consistently applied. It is expected that Regs, when issued, will authorize conversion using the spot exchange rate on the date of measurement, and may also authorize taxpayers, as an alternative, to use the historical U.S.-dollar cost of foreign-currency-denominated assets. (Conf Rept p. 640)

> ***observation:*** Depending on fluctuations in exchange rates between the time an asset was acquired by a CFC and the time its basis is being measured for purposes of the excess passive assets test, one method or the other could be more favorable to a taxpayer.

Leasing and intangible asset rules. The determination of whether a CFC has excess passive assets also takes into account the rules, added by § 13231(d)(4), under which (1) certain property leased for a term of 12 months or more is treated as though it were owned by the lessee (Code Sec. 956A(c)(3)(B) as added by '93 Act § 13231(b)), and (2) adjustments to the basis of a corporation's assets are made to reflect certain research expenditures and costs of licensed intangibles. (Code Sec. 956A(c)(3)(C))

Applicable earnings. A CFC's applicable earnings are equal to the sum of (1) its earnings and profits for the current taxable year (Code Sec. 956A(b)(2)), and (2) its earnings and profits accumulated in taxable years beginning after Sept. 30, $93 (Code Sec. 956A(b)(1)), reduced by (3) distributions during the taxable year, and (4) amounts which were accumulated in taxable years beginning after Sept. 30, '93 and previously included in the U.S. shareholder's income by virtue of investments in U.S. property or investment in excess passive assets. (Code Sec. 956A(b))

> ***Illustration:*** Domestic corporation D owns all of the stock of foreign corporation F, which is not, and has never been, a PFIC. F holds an average of $100 of assets, of which $35 are passive, and holds no U.S. property. At the close of Year 1, F has earnings and profits of $25, none of which is Subpart F income or has otherwise previously been included in the income of a U.S. shareholder under the CFC rules. Under the rules added by the '93 Act, F has excess passive assets of $10. The amount includible in the income of D is

$10 (the lesser of the $10 of excess passive assets or the $25 of accumulated earnings). Thereafter, $10 of F's earnings will be treated as previously taxed. F's accumulated earnings of $25 are unchanged by D's inclusion in income of $10 under the excess passive assets rules. (S Rept p. 331)

Decontrolled CFCs. If a foreign corporation ceases to be a CFC during a tax year:

(1) the determination of a U.S. shareholder's pro rata share will be made based on the stock owned (or deemed owned under attribution rules, see FTC 2d/FIN ¶ O-2615 *et seq.;* TG ¶ 8244; USTR ¶ 9584 *et seq.)* by that shareholder on the last day in the tax year on which the foreign corporation is a CFC (Code Sec. 956A(e)(1)),

(2) the amount of the corporation's excess passive assets for that tax year will be determined by taking into account only quarters ending on or before that last day (Code Sec. 956A(e)(2)), and

(3) the current earnings and profits used to determine applicable earnings is that portion of current earnings and profits allocated on a pro rata basis to that part of the year during which the corporation was a CFC. (Code Sec. 956A(e)(3))

Regulatory authority. IRS is directed to issue such Regs as may be necessary to carry out the purposes of Code Sec. 956A, including Regs to prevent avoidance through reorganizations or otherwise. (Code Sec. 956A(f)) It is intended that such Regs will provide rules under which two or more CFC's which are related but which are not treated as a single CFC under the aggregation rules (see above) may nevertheless be treated as though they were a single corporation where a principal purpose for using multiple corporations is to avoid inclusion of income under the excess passive assets rules. Those Regs may apply presumptions of a tax avoidance purpose which are analogous to those provided in Temp Regs under the anti-avoidance provisions of the foreign base company income and insurance provisions of the CFC rules, see FTC 2d/FIN ¶ O-2741; USTR ¶ 9544 *et seq.* (S Rept pp. 334-5)

☐ **Effective:** Tax years of CFCs beginning after Sept. 30, '93, and taxable years of U.S. shareholders in which or with which such CFC taxable years end. (§ 13231(e))

For official explanation see Committee Reports ¶ 3052.

¶ 1111. Modification of rules governing exclusion of previously taxed CFC income from U.S. shareholder's gross income

Under pre-'93 Act law, earnings and profits of a controlled foreign corporation (CFC) that were already included in a U.S. shareholder's gross income were not included again in that shareholder's gross income when those earnings were actually distributed or invested in U.S. property. Earnings actually distributed were treated as coming first from amounts that were previously taxed as investments in U.S. property, next as amounts that were previously taxed as subpart F income, and last as from other earnings. (FTC 2d/FIN ¶ O-2836; USTR ¶ 9594 *et seq.)*

The '93 Act extends the rule that previously taxed earnings and profits of a CFC are not taxed again to cover amounts which would otherwise be included in a U.S. shareholder's gross income under the newly-enacted excess passive assets provision (see ¶ 1110). (Code Sec. 959(a)(3) as amended by '93 Act § 13231(c)(1))

The '93 Act also modifies the ordering rules which govern the determination of when earnings and profits will be deemed to have been previously taxed.

FTC 2d References are to the Federal Tax Coordinator 2d
FIN References are to RIA's Analysis of Federal Taxes: Income
TG References are to the Tax Guide
USTR References are to the United States Tax Reporter

Distributions. Where there is an actual distribution by a CFC, the distribution is deemed to be first out of the aggregate amount of earnings and profits which were already taxed under either the investment in U.S. property rules (see ¶ 1101) or the excess passive assets rules (see ¶ 1110). Where a distribution occurs which is insufficient to exhaust the CFC's earnings and profits which were previously taxed under the investment in U.S. property rules and the excess passive assets rules, the distribution is allocated between the two classes of earnings in proportion to the relative amounts of earnings and profits of each such class. (Code Sec. 959(a) as amended by '93 Act § 13231(c)(2)(A); Code Sec. 959(c)(1) as amended by '93 Act § 13231(c)(2)(C)) As under pre-'93 Act law, distributions in excess of the amounts previously taxed under the foregoing rule are deemed to be next out of earnings and profits which were already taxed as Subpart F income, and finally, out of other earnings and profits. (See FTC 2d/FIN ¶ O-2836; USTR ¶ 9594)

Amounts includible in income under the investment in U.S. property or excess passive assets rules. Where a CFC has earnings which are (or, but for the ordering rules, would be) includible in a U.S. shareholder's income under the investment in U.S. property rules, such earnings are treated as attributable, first, to amounts already included in income as Subpart F income, and then to other earnings and profits. (Code Sec. 959(a); Code Sec. 959(f)(1)(A)) Where a CFC has earnings which are (or, but for the ordering rules, would be) includible in a U.S. shareholder's income under the excess passive assets rules, such earnings are treated as attributable, first, to amounts already included in income as Subpart F income (but only to the extent such earnings were accumulated in taxable years beginning after Sept. 30, '93), and then to other earnings and profits. (Code Sec. 959(a); Code Sec. 959(f)(1)(B)) In applying these rules, however, actual distributions are taken into account before amounts includible (or that would, but for the ordering rules, be includible) under the investment in U.S. property or excess passive assets rules. (Code Sec. 959(f)(2))

> ***Illustration:*** *Year 1.* Domestic corporation D owns all the stock of foreign corporation F, which is not (and has never been) a passive foreign investment company (PFIC). F holds an average of $100 of assets of which $35 are passive, and has no U.S. property. F has accumulated earnings and profits of $25 at the close of year 1, none of which is subpart F income or has otherwise previously been included in the income of a U.S. shareholder under the CFC rules. Under the excess passive assets rules (see ¶ 1110), D is required to include $10 of F's earnings and profits in income for Year 1.

Year 2. In Year 2, F still has average total assets of $100, but now $40 (rather than $35) of these assets are passive. F earns $5 of subpart F income, and makes no actual distributions. As a result of the Subpart F income, F has accumulated earnings and profits of $30 at the close of Year 2. The Subpart F income of $5 is included in D's Year 2 income.

Under the excess passive assets rules, the amount potentially includible in D's income is $5 (the lesser of (i) $5, which is the difference between the $15 of excess passive assets in year 2 and the $10 of previous inclusions of earnings invested in excess passive assets, or (ii) $20, which is the difference between the $30 of accumulated earnings and the $10 of previous inclusions of excess passive assets). Under the ordering rules, however, the potential income inclusion of $5 is deemed to come first from amounts already taxed as Subpart F income. Since there is $5 of earnings already included as Subpart F income, the entire amount of D's potential income on account of F's investment in excess passive assets is treated as previously taxed, and so is not again includible. Thereafter, the $5 of earnings that would have been included in income under the excess passive assets rules but for the previously taxed subpart F income is treated as earnings previously taxed as investments in excess passive assets rather than as earnings previously taxed as subpart F income. Therefore, at the end of Year 2, the total amount of earnings treated as having been already taxed under the investment in U.S. property or excess passive assets rules is $15 ($10 from Year 1 plus $5 from Year 2). F's accumulated earnings of $30 are unaffected by the income inclusions.

Year 3. As in Year 2, F has an average of $40 of passive assets and $100 of total assets. F earns $5 of subpart F income, earns $10 of other income, and makes an actual distribution of $20 to D. F thus has accumulated earnings and profits of $45 at year end, before taking the current-year distribution into account.

F's Year 3 Subpart F income of $5 is included in D's income. The actual distribution of $20 is accounted for next. The distribution of earnings is treated as attributable first to the $15 of earnings and profits which were previously taxed under the investment in U.S. property or excess passive assets rules, and next to amounts previously taxed as Subpart F income ($5, in this case all from Year 3). Thus, the distribution of $20 is treated as fully attributable to previously taxed earnings, and is therefore not subject to tax again as a result of being distributed. Since the amount of the distribution fully exhausted F's previously taxed earnings, thereafter no portion of F's earnings is treated as previously taxed.

Last, the income inclusion (if any) on account of excess passive assets is determined. The amount includible under these rules is $15 (the lesser of (i) $15 (which is the amount of excess passive assets, unreduced because no portion of F's earnings is treated as previously taxed), or (ii) $25 (the amount of accumulated earnings after the distribution, unreduced because no portion of F's retained earnings is treated as previously taxed). The amount included in D's income for Year 3 is therefore $15, again unreduced because no portion of F's retained earnings is treated as previously taxed. D has a total income inclusion under the CFC rules of $20 for Year 3: $5 on account of F's Subpart F income, plus $15 on account of excess passive assets. As of the end of Year 3, F has $15 of earnings previously taxed as investments in excess passive assets, and has accumulated earnings and profits of $25. (S Rept pp. 331-333)

Coordination with PFIC inclusions. If a passive foreign investment company (PFIC) is a "qualified electing fund," then, in general, any U.S. person who owns stock in the PFIC must include in income his pro rata share of the PFIC's earnings and profits. (See FTC 2d/FIN ¶ O-2022; TG ¶ 8327; USTR ¶ 12,914.01) If a corporation is both a CFC and a PFIC, any amounts included in a shareholder's income under the CFC rules are not included again under the PFIC rules. (See FTC 2d/FIN ¶ O-2016; USTR ¶ 9514.03) Under pre-'93 Act law, where amounts which were already included in income under the PFIC rules were distributed, they were not taxed as dividends; however, in order to take advantage of this rule a taxpayer had to establish that a distribution was actually out of previously taxed earnings. (FTC 2d/FIN ¶ O-2022; USTR ¶ 12,914.04)

The '93 Act provides that, where a corporation is both a CFC and a PFIC, any amounts which were included in a U.S. shareholder's income as a result of the PFIC being a qualified electing fund are treated, for purposes of applying the ordering rules discussed above, as though they were included as Subpart F income under the CFC rules. (Code Sec. 1293(c)(3) as amended by '93 Act § 13231(c)(3))

observation: This eliminates the need to trace the source of a distribution in order to establish that it is attributable to previously taxed earnings.

observation: The new rule is limited to "U.S. shareholders," which, in general, means U.S. persons who own at least 10% (by vote) of the stock of a CFC. (See FTC 2d/FIN ¶ O-2603; TG ¶ 8242; USTR ¶ 9514.01) In the case of a qualified electing fund which is not also a CFC, and in the case of U.S. persons who are not U.S. shareholders of a CFC, the pre-'93 Act rule which required a taxpayer to establish the source of a distribution continues to apply.

☐ **Effective:** Tax years of CFCs beginning after Sept. 30, '93, and taxable years of U.S. shareholders in which or with which such CFC taxable years end. (§ 13231(e))

For official explanation see Committee Reports ¶ 3052.

¶ 1112. Measurement of assets for purposes of PFIC definition

If a foreign corporation is a passive foreign investment company (PFIC), U.S. persons who own stock in the PFIC are subject to special rules which may eliminate or reduce the potential benefit of tax deferral on income earned by the PFIC. (See FTC 2d/FIN ¶ O-2000 *et seq.;* TG ¶ 8320 *et seq.;* USTR ¶ 12,914) In general, a PFIC is any foreign corporation if either (i) 75% or more of its gross income is passive income (the "income test"), or (ii) 50% of its assets produce, or are held for the production of, passive income (the "assets test"). Under pre-'93 Act law, the assets test was applied by looking to the *value* of a foreign corporation's assets, unless the corporation elected to apply the test according to its assets' adjusted bases. (FTC 2d/FIN ¶ O-2001; TG ¶ 8321; USTR ¶ 12,914.01)

Under the '93 Act, where a corporation is a controlled foreign corporation (CFC), the use of adjusted basis (as determined for purposes of computing earnings and profits), rather than value, is made mandatory in applying the assets test for determining PFIC status. In the case of a corporation which is not a CFC, the pre-'93 Act law rule is retained—that is, the assets test continues to apply by looking to value unless the corporation elects to have it apply by looking to basis. (Code Sec. 1296(a) as amended by '93 Act § 13231(d)(1))

observation: This rule is consistent with the measurement of passive assets under the newly-enacted excess passive assets provisions which apply to CFCs. (See ¶ 1110)

observation: The basis of depreciable property for purposes of computing earnings and profits may differ from its basis for purposes of determining gain or loss on sale or other disposition. (See FTC 2d/FIN ¶ F-10300 *et seq.;* TG ¶ 2248)

observation: In order to avoid classification as a PFIC by virtue of the assets test, a CFC which owns passive assets with a basis in excess of fair market value may wish to consider disposing of those assets in a taxable transaction to recognize a loss, and reinvesting the proceeds in other assets, thereby reducing the basis of the CFC's passive assets.

The legislative history of the above provision indicates that the '93 Act rule requiring that CFCs measure their assets according to adjusted basis is only applicable for purposes of determining the tax treatment of "U.S. shareholders" (generally, U.S. persons who own at least 10% of the voting power of a CFC). (S Rept p. 338)

observation: The language of the '93 Act itself does not contain any such restriction.

Research and intangibles expenditures. The '93 Act provides for a special adjustment to the basis of a corporation's total assets for purposes of applying the PFIC definition to corporations which are CFCs. The adjusted basis of a CFC's assets is increased by the amount of research or experimental expenditures (see FTC 2d/FIN ¶ L-3101; TG ¶ 6254; USTR ¶ 1744 *et seq.)* paid or incurred by the corporation during the taxable year and the preceding two taxable years (other than research or experimental expenditures for which the CFC is reimbursed by another party). (Code Sec. 1297(e)(1) as amended by '93 Act § 13231(d)(4)) In addition, where a CFC is a licensee of intangible property which it uses in the active conduct of a trade or business, the adjusted basis of the CFC's total assets is increased by an amount equal to 300% of the payments made during the taxable year by the CFC for the use of such property. (Code Sec. 1297(e)(2)(A)) The adjustment for payments for the use of intangible property does not apply, however, to (i) payments to a foreign person who is related to the CFC, see FTC 2d/FIN ¶ O-2657 (Code Sec. 1297(e)(2)(B)(i)), or (ii) any payments under a license if a principal purpose of entering into the license was to avoid the PFIC provisions or the newly-enacted excess passive assets provisions. (Code Sec. 1297(e)(2)(B)(ii))

> ***observation:*** Although less than entirely clear, it appears that the effect of a basis adjustment for research expenditures or intangibles licensing costs is to increase a corporation's basis in its total assets, without affecting its basis in its passive assets. Accordingly, such an adjustment makes it less likely that the assets test for PFIC status will be satisfied.

The Conference Committee has requested that the Treasury Department prepare a study as to whether a similar rule should be enacted which would permit a basis adjustment for marketing expenditures. (Conf Rept p. 642)

☐ **Effective:** Tax years of foreign corporations beginning after Sept. 30, '93, and taxable years of U.S. shareholders in which or with which such years end. (§ 13231(e))

For official explanation see Committee Reports ¶ 3052.

¶ 1113. CFC income inclusions treated as distributions under PFIC rules

If a foreign corporation is a passive foreign investment company (PFIC), U.S. persons who own stock in the PFIC are subject to special rules which may eliminate or reduce the potential benefit of tax deferral on income earned by the PFIC. (See FTC 2d/FIN ¶ O-2000 *et seq.;* TG ¶ 8320 *et seq.;* USTR ¶ 12,914) In general, a U.S. person who receives an "excess distribution" with respect to stock of a PFIC is required to pay an interest charge with respect to that portion of the excess distribution which is deemed to be attributable to earlier years. In addition, that portion is taxed at the highest tax rate in effect during those earlier years. (See FTC 2d/FIN ¶ O-2007 *et seq.;* TG ¶ 8324; USTR ¶ 12,914.02) A distribution is an excess distribution to the extent it exceeds 125% of the average amount distributed during the preceding three years. (See FTC 2d/FIN ¶ O-2008; TG ¶ 8325; USTR ¶ 12,914.02)

The '93 Act adds a new provision applicable to cases where a corporation is both a controlled foreign corporation (CFC) and a PFIC. Under the new provision, amounts which must be included in the income of a U.S. shareholder of a CFC on account of the investment in U.S. property rules (see ¶ 1101) or the newly-enacted excess passive assets rules (see ¶ 1101) are treated as though they were actual distributions for purposes of the PFIC rules. (Code Sec. 1297(b)(9) as amended by '93 Act § 13231(d)(2))

> ***observation:*** Since amounts included in a U.S. shareholder's income under the CFC rules are taxable to the U.S. shareholder in any event, the primary significance of the new provision is to subject those amounts to a possible interest charge, as well as possibly a higher rate of tax, under the excess distribution provisions.

> ***observation:*** Because the determination of whether a distribution (including a deemed distribution under the CFC rules) is an excess distribution is made by comparing it to distributions made during the prior three years, the timing of transactions which would give rise to deemed distributions can be critical. The effect of this provision should be carefully considered when making investment decisions for a corporation which is both a CFC and a PFIC.

☐ **Effective:** Tax years of foreign corporations beginning after Sept. 30, '93, and taxable years of U.S. shareholders in which or with which such years end. (§ 13231(e))

For official explanation see Committee Reports ¶ 3052.

¶ 1114. Exclusion of certain income of securities dealers from passive income for purposes of PFIC definition

In general, a foreign corporation is a passive foreign investment company (PFIC) if either (i) 75% or more of its gross income is passive income, or (ii) 50% of its assets produce, or are held for the production of, passive income. For this purpose, certain income earned in the active conduct of a banking business or an insurance business is excluded from the definition of "passive income." (See FTC 2d/FIN ¶ O-2001; TG ¶ 8322; USTR¶ 12,914.01)

The '93 Act adds a new exclusion from passive income for income derived in the active conduct of a securities business by a corporation which (i) is registered as a securities broker or dealer under Sec. 15(a) of the Securities Exchange Act of '34, or (ii) is registered as a Government securities broker or dealer under Sec. 15C(a) of the Securities Exchange Act of '34. In addition, IRS may issue regs extending the exclusion to income derived in the active conduct of a securities business by persons not so registered. (Code Sec. 1296(b)(3)(A) as amended by '93 Act § 13231(d)(3))

Exclusion only applies to U.S. shareholders of CFCs. The exclusion for income from the active conduct of a securities business only applies to corporations which are controlled foreign corporations (CFCs). (Code Sec. 1296(b)(3)(A)) In addition, the exclusion only applies for purposes of determining the tax treatment of persons who are U.S. shareholders, as defined under the CFC rules. (Code Sec. 1296(b)(3)(C))

> ***observation:*** Under the CFC rules, the term "U.S. shareholder" is limited to U.S. persons who own at least 10% of the voting power of a CFC (see FTC 2d/FIN ¶ O-2603; TG ¶ 8242; USTR ¶ 9514.01). Therefore, it is possible that a CFC could be treated as a PFIC for purposes of determining the tax treatment of U.S. persons who own less than 10% of its stock, yet not be treated as a PFIC by virtue of the exclusion for securities business income in determining the treatment of 10% shareholders.

Active conduct of a securities business. IRS is to issue Regs which will provide guidance as to what is the active conduct of a securities business, and which will distinguish between *bona fide* active business activities (which are entitled to the exclusion) and investment vehicles (which are not entitled to the exclusion). Such Regs may take into account various activities which could indicate the existence of an active business, including buying and selling inventory securities (including stock, debt instruments, commodities and derivative financial products), arranging purchases and sales of securities on behalf of unrelated persons, arranging hedging or foreign exchange transactions for, or entering into such transactions with, unrelated customers, underwriting issues of securities, lending inventory securities to unrelated persons, servicing mortgages, investment banking, providing investment and financial advice, providing trust or custodial services, providing margin financing for customers, and similar activities. The fact that a CFC is subject to regulatory requirements applicable to securities dealers in the jurisdiction where it conducts its principal business might also be a factor indicating that the CFC is engaged in the active conduct of a securities business.

Existing areas of the law which IRS might consider as possible analogies for formulating Regs in this area are (i) the rules defining a "regular dealer" for purposes of the exclusion of certain gains and losses from foreign personal holding company income (see FTC 2d/FIN ¶ O-2675; USTR ¶ 9544.02); (ii) the rules which exclude income from the active conduct of a banking business from passive income for PFIC purposes (see FTC 2d/FIN ¶ O-2001; TG ¶ 8322; USTR ¶ 12,914.01); and (iii) the rules governing the separate foreign tax credit limitation applicable to financial services income (see FTC 2d/FIN ¶ O-4104 *et seq.;* USTR ¶ 9044.01). (S Rept p. 339)

A single corporation which is engaged in both banking and securities activities could, under Regs to be issued, exclude the income from both of those activities from passive income. (Conf Rept p. 641)

> ***observation:*** The Conference Committee indicated that Regs permitting a single corporation to claim exclusions for both banking and securities income would apply in "appropriate circumstances." Presumably, it is left for IRS to define what circumstances are appropriate for this treatment.

The Conference Committee has requested that the Treasury Department study whether the treatment of income from financing and credit services businesses, for which there is no comparable exclusion, should be amended. (Conf Rept p. 641)

Income from related persons. Where a foreign corporation receives dividends, interest, rents or royalties from a related person, such amounts are not treated as passive income to the extent allocable (under Regs to be issued) to income of the related person which is not passive. (See FTC 2d/FIN ¶ O-2001; TG ¶ 8322; USTR ¶ 12,914.01) Under the '93 Act, the exclusion for income derived from the active conduct of a securities business applies in determining whether income of a related person is passive. (Code Sec. 1296(b)(3)(B)

☐ **Effective:** Tax years of foreign corporations beginning after Sept. 30, '93, and taxable years of U.S. shareholders in which or with which such years end. (§ 13231(e))

For official explanation see Committee Reports ¶ 3052.

¶ 1115. Treatment of leased property for purposes of PFIC definition

In general, a foreign corporation is a passive foreign investment company (PFIC)

FTC 2d References are to the Federal Tax Coordinator 2d
FIN References are to RIA's Analysis of Federal Taxes: Income
TG References are to the Tax Guide
USTR References are to the United States Tax Reporter

if either (i) 75% or more of its gross income is passive income, or (ii) 50% of its assets produce, or are held for the production of, passive income. (FTC 2d/FIN ¶ O-2001; TG ¶ 8321; USTR ¶ 12,914.01)

The '93 Act provides a new rule under which, for purposes of determining whether this test is satisfied, tangible personal property leased by a foreign corporation for a term of at least twelve months is treated as though it were owned by the corporation. (Code Sec. 1297(d)(1) as amended by '93 Act § 13231(d)(4))

> ***observation:*** The rule which treats leased property as though it were owned does not apply to real property or to intangible assets. Where a foreign corporation enters into a lease which covers both realty and personalty, the impact of this rule should be considered in allocating the lease payments between the two types of property.

Where property is considered to be owned under this rule, its adjusted basis (which is taken into account in applying the PFIC definition for controlled foreign corporations and for other corporations which so elect, see ¶ 1112) is deemed to be the unamortized portion (determined under Regs to be issued) of the present value of the lease payments. (Code Sec. 1297(d)(2)(A)) Under Regs to be issued, the present value of the lease payments is determined as of the beginning of the lease term (Code Sec. 1297(d)(2)(B)(i)), using a discount rate equal to the applicable Federal rate (AFR) (see FTC 2d/FIN ¶ J-3742 *et seq.;* TG ¶ 5074 *et seq.;* USTR ¶ 12,714.04) for debt instruments with a term equal to that of the lease. (Code Sec. 1297(d)(2)(B)(ii)(I)) However, for this purpose, the rule which looks to the lowest AFR in effect within three months before there is a binding contract in determining the issue price of an actual debt instrument (see FTC 2d/FIN ¶ J-3743; TG ¶ 5074; USTR ¶ 12,714.03) does not apply. (Code Sec. 1297(d)(2)(B)(ii)(II))

> ***observation:*** It appears, therefore, that the AFR which will be used is that in effect on the date the lease term begins.

In determining the AFR used to determine the present value of lease payments, options to renew or extend the lease term are not taken into account. (Code Sec. 1297(d)(2)(B)(ii)(II))

> ***observation:*** The '93 Act does not, however, make clear whether options to renew or extend a lease will be considered in determining whether it has a term of 12 months or more and is therefore subject to the deemed ownership rule in the first place. Presumably, Regs will address this issue.

Exceptions. The rule which treats leased property as though it were owned by the lessee does not apply (i) if the lessor is a related person, within the meaning of the CFC rules, see FTC 2d/FIN ¶ O-2657; USTR ¶ 9544.03 (Code Sec. 1297(d)(3)(A)), or (ii) a principal purpose of leasing the property is to avoid the PFIC provisions or the newly-enacted excess passive assets provisions (see ¶ 1110). (Code Sec. 1297(d)(3)(B) as amended by '93 Act § 13231(d)(4))

☐ **Effective:** Tax years of foreign corporations beginning after Sept. 30, '93, and taxable years of U.S. shareholders in which or with which such years end. (§ 13231(e))

For official explanation see Committee Reports ¶ 3052.

¶ 1116. Limitation on Code Sec. 936 credit

Under pre-'93 Act law, a domestic corporation that had a substantial portion of its business in a U.S. possession, including Puerto Rico and the Virgin Islands, could elect under Code Sec. 936 to claim a tax credit equal to the U.S. tax on the sum of its: (1) income from the active conduct of a possession trade or business, including income from the disposition of substantially all of the assets used in that trade or business, and (2) qualified possession source investment income (QPSII). The credit equalled the U.S. tax on that income regardless of the amount of tax paid to the government of the possession. (FTC 2d/FIN ¶ O-1500 *et seq.;* TG ¶ 8138; USTR ¶ 9314.06) No other credit or deduction was allowed for any tax paid to a foreign country or U.S. possession on income taken into account in determining the Code Sec. 936 tax credit. (FTC 2d/FIN ¶ O-1514; TG ¶ 8141; USTR ¶ 9314.06) Under the '93 Act, the tax credit otherwise available to a possession corporation on income that is attributable to its active possession trade or business (including the sale of substantially all the assets used in that trade or business) is subject to one of two limitations: a limitation based on the possession corporation's activities in the possession (the economic-activity limitation), or a limitation based on a percentage of the pre-'93 Act credit (the percentage limitation). The economic-activity limitation will apply unless the taxpayer elects to use the percentage limitation. The '93 Act also allows certain possession taxes to be deducted, and it defines a possession corporation as a domestic corporation for which the Code Sec. 936 election is in effect. ('93 Act § 13227)

Economic-activity limitation. Under the economic-activity limitation, a possession corporation's Code Sec. 936 credit on its active possession business income for a tax year is limited to the sum of the following amounts for that year:

(1) 60% of the possession corporation's total qualified possession wages (Code Sec. 936(a)(4)(A)(i)(I) as amended by '93 Act § 13227(a)(2)),

(2) 60% of the possession corporation's allocable employee fringe benefit expenses (Code Sec. 936(a)(4)(A)(i)(II)),

(3) 15% of the depreciation allowance for short-life qualified tangible property (Code Sec. 936(a)(4)(A)(ii)(I)),

(4) 40% of the depreciation allowance for medium-life qualified tangible property (Code Sec. 936(a)(4)(A)(ii)(II)), and

(5) 65% of the depreciation allowance for long-life qualified tangible property. (Code Sec. 936(a)(4)(A)(ii)(III))

A possession corporation that hasn't elected to use the profit split method to allocate income from intangible property (see FTC 2d/FIN ¶ O-1561; TG ¶ 8138; USTR ¶ 9314.06), may increase the economic-activity limitation by the amount of qualified possession income taxes for the year that are allocable to nonsheltered income. (Code Sec. 936(a)(4)(A)(iii))

A possession corporation that uses the profit split method is allowed to deduct a certain amount of possession income taxes for that year in determining its U.S. income tax liability. (Code Sec. 936(i)(3)(B) as amended by '93 Act § 13227(b))

Qualified possession wages. Qualified possession wages are wages paid or incurred by a possession corporation during a tax year: (a) in connection with the active conduct of a trade or business in a U.S. possession; and (b) to an employee for services performed in that possession, but only if the services are performed while the employee's principal place of employment is in that possession. (Code Sec. 936(i)(1)(A)) The wages, however, that are taken into account during a tax year for an individual employee are limited to 85% of the maximum wages subject to the old-age, survivors, and disability insurance portion of Social Security. (Code Sec. 936(i)(1)(B)(i)) For '93, that amount is $57,600. (S Rept p. 302)

FTC 2d References are to the Federal Tax Coordinator 2d
FIN References are to RIA's Analysis of Federal Taxes: Income
TG References are to the Tax Guide
USTR References are to the United States Tax Reporter

If the employee isn't a full-time employee of the possession corporation for the entire tax year or the employee's principal place of employment with the possession corporation isn't in the possession for the entire tax year, IRS will make an appropriate reduction in the wage limitation. (Code Sec. 936(i)(1)(B)(ii)) It is assumed that the limitation will be prorated to take into account the fact that the employee didn't work for the possession corporation on a full-time basis or didn't work for the corporation for the entire tax year.

> ***observation:*** If the wage limitation is reduced, the amount of qualified possession wages will be a smaller amount, resulting in a reduced Code Sec. 936 credit.

Qualified possession wages don't include wages paid to employees assigned by the employer to provide services for another person, unless the employer's principal trade or business is to provide employees on a temporary basis in return for compensation. However, if an affiliated group elects to treat all possession corporations as one corporation (as described below), all possession corporations will be treated as one employer for this purpose. (Code Sec. 936(i)(1)(C))

For these purposes, the term "wages" means wages as defined at Code Sec. 3306(b) (definition of wages for Federal Unemployment Tax Act (FUTA) purposes, see FTC 2d/FIN ¶ H-4784.1; TG ¶ 3579.161; USTR ¶ 31,114), but without any dollar limitation and including all U.S. possessions in the term "U.S." (Code Sec. 936(i)(1)(D)(i)) However, if the employees perform agricultural or railway labor as defined at Code Sec. 51(h)(1) (regarding the targeted jobs credit, see FTC 2d/FIN ¶ L-17812; TG ¶ 5808; USTR ¶ 514), the definition of wages for Code Sec. 936 purposes is the same as that used for the targeted jobs credit under Code Sec. 51(h)(2). (Code Sec. 936(i)(1)(D)(ii))

Allocable employee fringe benefit expenses. A possession corporation's allocable employee fringe benefit expenses for a tax year equal the total amount of employee fringe benefit expenses multiplied by a fraction. The fraction consists of the possession corporation's total qualified possession wages for that tax year divided by the corporation's total wages paid or incurred for that year. In no event, however, may allocable employee fringe benefit expenses exceed 15% of the possession corporation's qualified possession wages for the year. (Code Sec. 936(i)(2)(A))

For these purposes, employee fringe benefit expenses equal the total amount deductible by the possession corporation in the tax year for:

(1) employer contributions to stock bonus, pension, profit-sharing, or annuity plans (Code Sec. 936(i)(2)(B)(i)),

(2) employer-provided health or accident plan coverage for employees (Code Sec. 936(i)(2)(B)(ii)), and

(3) the cost of life or disability insurance provided to employees. (Code Sec. 936(i)(2)(B)(iii))

However, any amount treated as wages for Code Sec. 936 purposes won't be treated as an employee fringe benefit expense. (Code Sec. 936(i)(2)(B))

> ***Illustration (1):*** Possession corporation P doesn't elect to use the percentage limitation, and it doesn't use the profit-split method for computing its income. P pays cash wages of $18,000, of which $15,000 are qualified possession wages. In addition, P makes pension, accident, health and life insurance payments of $3,000 for its employees for the tax year. Because P's qualified wages are $15,000, $2,500 of fringe benefit expenses (15/18 × $3,000) are potentially includible in the credit-limitation base. However,

allocable fringe benefit expenses are limited to 15% of qualified possession wages, which in this case equals $2,250 (15% of $15,000). Thus, the total of qualified possession wages and allocable employee fringe benefit expenses is $17,250 ($15,000 + $2,250), and the compensation component of the credit-limitation base is $10,350 (60% of $17,250). (S Rept p. 305)

Depreciation rules. The term "depreciation allowance" means the depreciation deduction allowed under Code Sec. 167 to the possession corporation. (Code Sec. 936(i)(4)(A))

Qualified tangible property is tangible property used by a possession corporation in the active conduct of a trade or business in a U.S. possession. (Code Sec. 936(i)(4)(B)(i))

Short-life qualified tangible property is qualified tangible property which is 3-year or 5-year property under Code Sec. 168 (see FTC 2d/FIN ¶s L-7804, L-7806; TG ¶s 5433, 5434; USTR ¶ 1684.01). (Code Sec. 936(i)(4)(B)(ii))

Medium-life qualified tangible property is qualified tangible property which is 7-year or 10-year property under Code Sec. 168 (see FTC 2d/FIN ¶s L-7807, L-7808; TG ¶s 5435, 5436; USTR ¶ 1684.01). (Code Sec. 936(i)(4)(B)(iii))

Long-life qualified tangible property is qualified tangible property subject to Code Sec. 168 which isn't short or medium-life qualified tangible property (see FTC 2d/FIN ¶ 7809 *et seq.;* TG ¶ 5437 *et seq.;* USTR ¶ 1684.01). (Code Sec. 936(i)(4)(B)(iv))

If qualified tangible property is subject to Code Sec. 168 as in effect on the day before enactment of the Tax Reform Act of '86, the above references to Code Sec. 168 will be treated as referring to that Code section as then in effect. (Code Sec. 936(i)(4)(B)(v))

observation: The Tax Reform Act of '86 was enacted on Oct. 22, '86. Thus, the above depreciation rules will apply to property subject to ACRS as well as to MACRS, see FTC 2d/FIN ¶ L-8170 *et seq.;* TG ¶ 5530 *et seq.;* USTR ¶ 1688.400 *et seq.*

Qualified possession income taxes allocable to nonsheltered income. The qualified possession income taxes allocable to nonsheltered income for a tax year equals the possession income taxes for that year, but not exceeding 9% of taxable income (Code Sec. 936(i)(3)(A)(ii)), multiplied by a fraction. The fraction consists of the possession corporation's increased U.S. tax liability resulting from the economic-activity limitation (computed without taking into account the qualified possession income taxes allocable to nonsheltered income) and divided by the possession corporation's U.S. tax liability determined without the Code Sec. 936 credit. (Code Sec. 936(i)(3)(A)(i))

illustration (2): Possession corporation P doesn't elect to use the percentage limitation, and it doesn't use the profit-split method for computing its income. P pays cash wages of $18,000, of which $15,000 are qualified possession wages. In addition, P makes pension, accident, health and life insurance payments of $3,000 for its employees for the tax year. P is entitled to $5,000 in depreciation deductions for short-life qualified tangible property, $2,000 for long-life qualified tangible property, and it pays $6,000 in possession income taxes.

FTC 2d References are to the Federal Tax Coordinator 2d
FIN References are to RIA's Analysis of Federal Taxes: Income
TG References are to the Tax Guide
USTR References are to the United States Tax Reporter

P has $100,000 of taxable income for the year, computed under the pre-'93 Act rules for determining its taxable income (i.e., taking into account compensation and depreciation deductions otherwise allowed by the Code, but not allowing a deduction for possession income taxes). P's $100,000 of taxable income consists of $90,000 of active business income, $5,000 of QPSII, and $5,000 of other taxable income. Without taking into account the limitation imposed by the '93 Act (and assuming a 35% tax rate), P's Code Sec. 936 credit would be $33,250 (35% of $95,000), and it would have a U.S. tax liability of $1,750 (($100,000 × 35%) – $33,250).

P's Code Sec. 936 credit on QPSII remains at $1,750 (35% of $5,000). However, the remaining $31,500 of the otherwise allowable credit is subject to the economic-activity limitation. As explained in *Illustration (1),* the compensation component of P's credit-limitation base is $10,350. The depreciation component of the credit-limitation base is $2,050 (15% of the $5,000 depreciation on short-life property plus 65% of the $2,000 depreciation on long-life property). Thus, the sum of the depreciation and compensation components of P's credit-limitation base is $12,400.

The $6,000 of possession income taxes paid by P represents 6% of taxable income. Thus, none of those taxes are disqualified from the credit-limitation base as a result of the provision that limits possession income taxes to 9% of taxable income. The portion of the $6,000 that is allocated to nonsheltered income is determined by comparing the increase in tax attributable to the compensation and depreciation components of the credit-limitation to the tax that the corporation would pay in the absence of the Code Sec. 936 credit. The amount of qualified possession taxes allocable to nonsheltered income is determined as follows. Absent the credit-limitation, P's U.S. tax liability would be $1,750. With the credit-limitation (but computed without considering the possession income tax component of the limitation), P's Code Sec. 936 credit on active business income would be $12,400 (35% of $90,000 $31,500, but the credit is limited to the credit-limitation base of $12,400). P's tentative Code Sec. 936 credit would be $14,150 ($12,400 + $1,750 credit on QPSII). P's tentative U.S. tax liability would be $20,850 (($100,000 × 35%) – $14,150). Thus, P's tentative increased U.S. tax liability would be $19,100 ($20,850 – $1,750). The qualified possession taxes allocable to nonsheltered income would be $3,274 ($6,000 × $19,100 ÷ $35,000). P's total credit-limitation base for Code Sec. 936 purposes would be $15,674 ($12,400 + $3,274), and its total Code Sec. 936 credit would be $17,424 ($15,674 + $1,750 QPSII credit). Thus, P's actual U.S. tax liability would be $17,576 ((35% × $100,000) – $17,424).

Deductibility of possession income taxes. A possession corporation that uses the economic-activity limitation to compute its Code Sec. 936 credit and which also uses the profit split method to allocate income from intangible property in a tax year (see FTC 2d/FIN ¶ O-1561; TG ¶ 8138; USTR ¶ 9314.06) is allowed to deduct a certain amount of possession income taxes for that year in determining its U.S. income tax liability. The amount allowed as a deduction equals the possession income taxes for that tax year multiplied by a fraction. The fraction consists of the possession corporation's increased U.S. tax liability resulting from the economic-activity limitation divided by the possession corporation's U.S. tax liability determined without the Code Sec. 936 credit. However, no deduction for possession income taxes is allowed in computing the Code Sec. 936 credit or in determining the amount of possession income taxes that may be deducted. (Code Sec. 936(i)(3)(B)(i))

> ***observation:*** The calculations required under this provision are similar to the ones required to determine possession taxes allocable to nonsheltered income, see Illustration (2).

Possession income taxes. For purposes of determining: (1) qualified possession income taxes allocable to nonsheltered income and (2) the deduction for possession income taxes by a possession corporation using profit split, the term "possession income taxes" means taxes of a U.S. possession which, under Code Sec. 936(c), are not treated as income, war profits, or excess profits taxes paid or accrued to a U.S. possession. (Code Sec. 936(i)(3)(C))

Election to compute Code Sec. 936 credit on consolidated basis. An affiliated group may elect to treat all foreign and possession corporations which would be members of that group, except for the fact that they are foreign or possession corporations, as one corporation for purposes of determining the Code Sec. 936 credit as computed under the economic-activity limitation. IRS will prescribe how the credit determined under this election will be allocated among the possession corporations. (Code Sec. 936(i)(5)(A)) The election will apply to the tax year for which made and all later tax years unless revoked with IRS's consent. (Code Sec. 936(i)(5)(B))

Percentage limitation. If a possession corporation elects to use the percentage limitation, the economic-activity limitation won't apply. (Code Sec. 936(a)(4)(B)(i)(I) as amended by '93 Act § 13227(a)(2)) Instead, the corporation is entitled to the applicable percentage of the Code Sec. 936 credit otherwise allowable on its active possession business income. (Code Sec. 936(a)(4)(B)(i)(II)) The applicable percentage is determined as follows:

Tax year beginning in:	Applicable percentage:
1994	60
1995	55
1996	50
1997	45
1998 and thereafter	40

(Code Sec. 936(a)(4)(B)(ii))

> ***Illustration (3):*** Possession corporation P has a Code Sec. 936 credit on business income for '98 of $1,000,000. The percentage limitation would reduce that credit to $400,000. (S Rept p. 307)

A possession corporation that elects to use the percentage limitation may deduct possession income taxes that are allocable to taxable income that is subject to U.S. tax because of the disallowed Code Sec. 936 credit. (Code Sec. 936(a)(4)(B)(i)) For these purposes, taxable income is determined before taking into account any deduction for possession taxes. (S Rept p. 307)

> ***Illustration (4):*** In a tax year beginning after '97, possession corporation P elects to use the percentage limitation. P has active business income from its possession-based operations of $900,000 and QPSII of $100,000. The U.S. tax on those amounts before the Code Sec. 936 credit (assuming a 35% tax rate) is $315,000 and

$35,000 respectively. P incurs possession income taxes of $50,000 for that year. P's Code Sec. 936 credit for the year would be limited to $161,000 (i.e., a full credit against tax on QPSII and a 40% credit against tax on active business income). In this case, the U.S. tax on $540,000 of P's taxable income ($900,000 × 60%) isn't offset by the Code Sec. 936 credit because of the limitation. As a result, $27,000 of P's possession income tax may be deducted ($50,000 × $540,000 ÷ $1,000,000 = $27,000). This reduces P's taxable income to $973,000. Thus, P's U.S. tax liability before the Code Sec. 936 credit is $340,550 ($973,000 × 35%), and P's U.S. tax liability after the Code Sec. 936 credit is $179,550 ($340,550 – $161,000). (S Rept p. 307)

Affiliated groups. The percentage limitation applies only if all possession corporations that are members of an affiliated group make the election. If the election isn't in effect for a possession corporation for a tax year in which that corporation is a group member, the elections for all other possession corporations that are group members are revoked for that year and all later years. (Code Sec. 936(a)(4)(B)(iii)(III))

For these purposes, Code Sec. 1504(b) (which provides that tax-exempt corporations, insurance companies, foreign corporations, possession corporations, regulated investment companies, real estate investment trusts, and DISCs may not be group members) doesn't apply. In addition, the constructive ownership rules of Code Sec. 1563(e) do apply to determine if a corporation is a group member. IRS may prescribe regulations to prevent avoidance of these rules through deconsolidation or otherwise. (Code Sec. 936(a)(4)(B)(iii)(III))

Election. The election to use the percentage limitation may be made only for a corporation's first tax year beginning after Dec. 31, '93, in which it is a possession corporation. (Code Sec. 936(a)(4)(B)(iii)(I)) Once made, the election remains in effect for all later tax year unless revoked. (Code Sec. 936(a)(4)(B)(iii)(II))

☐ **Effective:** Taxable years beginning after Dec. 31, '93. (§ 13227(f))
For official explanation see Committee Reports ¶ 3050.

¶ 1117. Coordination of Code Sec. 904 with Code Sec. 936

Pre-'93 Act law provided that in computing the foreign tax credit limitation under Code Sec. 904, a corporation's taxable income used to determine the limitation excluded any income taken into account in determining the Code Sec. 936 credit. (See FTC 2d/FIN ¶ O-4253; TG ¶ 8141; USTR ¶ 9314.06)

Because of changes made to Code Sec. 936 by the '93 Act, the Act contains a conforming amendment to Code Sec. 904. The amendment clarifies that in computing a corporation's foreign tax credit limitation, taxable income excludes any income considered in computing the Code Sec. 936 credit before the Code Sec. 936 credit is reduced by any limitation. (Code Sec. 904(b)(4) as amended by '93 Act § 13227(d))

observation: This means that taxable income is excluded from the foreign tax credit limitation calculation even if U.S. tax is paid on that income because of the Code Sec. 936 credit limitation.

☐ **Effective:** Taxable years beginning after Dec. 31, '93. (§ 13227(f))
For official explanation see Committee Reports ¶ 2050.

¶ 1118. Alternative minimum tax treatment for dividends from a possession corporation

Pre-'93 Act law provided that when making the adjusted current earnings (ACE) modifications to a U.S. corporation's alternative minimum taxable income, no deduction was allowed for dividends received from a corporation to the extent that those dividends were attributable to income of the paying corporation which was exempt from U.S. tax under Code Sec. 936. (FTC 2d/FIN ¶ A-8130.2; TG ¶ 1381; USTR ¶ 564.03) As a result, the ACE of the recipient increased. (S Rept p. 298) For purposes of determining the alternative minimum foreign tax credit, dividends paid to an affiliated U.S. corporation by a possession corporation (i.e., a domestic corporation for which a Code Sec. 936 election was in effect) were treated as foreign source income subject to the separate foreign tax credit limitation for passive income. (FTC 2d/FIN ¶s O-10923, O-4082; TG ¶s 8298, 8437) Also, in computing the alternative minimum foreign tax credit, 75% of any withholding or income tax paid to a possession with respect to dividends received from a possession corporation was treated as a creditable tax. (FTC 2d/FIN ¶ A-8130.2B)

The '93 Act provides that the restriction on deducting dividends received from a corporation that are attributable to income that is exempt from U.S. tax under Code Sec. 936 applies after taking into account the limitation on the Code Sec. 936 credit. (Code Sec. 56(g)(4)(C)(ii)(I) as amended by '93 Act § 13227(c)(1))

> ***observation:*** Thus, dividends attributable to income that is subject to U.S. tax because of the Code Sec. 936 credit-limitation may be deducted in determining ACE.

In computing the alternative minimum foreign tax credit, dividends from a possession corporation are treated as a separate foreign tax credit limitation category. (Code Sec. 56(g)(4)(C)(iii)(IV) as amended by '93 Act § 13227(c)(2))

The '93 Act clarifies that the credit for 75% of the withholding or income tax paid to a possession with respect to dividends received from a possession corporation refers to that portion of the dividend for which the dividends received deduction is disallowed after taking into account the Code Sec. 936 credit-limitation. (Code Sec. 56(g)(4)(C)(iii)(V))

☐ **Effective:** Taxable years beginning after Dec. 31, '93. (§ 13227(f))
For official explanation see Committee Reports ¶ 3050.

¶ 1119. Export of unprocessed timber—FSCs, DISCs, source rules, and elimination of deferral

FSCs. A portion of the foreign trade income of a foreign sales corporation (FSC) may be excluded from federal income tax. (See FTC 2d/FIN ¶ O-1612; TG ¶ 8148; USTR ¶ 9214.04) If the income earned by the FSC is determined under special administrative pricing rules, then where there are corporate FSC shareholders, the exempt foreign trade income is 15/23 of the foreign trade income derived from the transaction. (See FTC 2d/FIN ¶ O-1653; TG ¶ 8149; USTR ¶ 9214.02) At the same time, a U.S. corporate shareholder is allowed a 100% dividends-received deduction for dividends from the FSC out of earnings and profits attributable to foreign trade income. Thus, there is no corporate-level tax imposed on a portion of the FSC's income from exports. (See FTC 2d/FIN ¶ O-1600; TG ¶ 8146; USTR ¶ 9214.13)

Foreign trade income is defined as the gross income of a FSC attributable to foreign trading gross receipts. Foreign trade income includes both the profits earned by the FSC itself from exports, and commissions earned by exports and commissions earned by the FSC from products or services exported by others.(See FTC 2d/FIN ¶ O-1660.1; TG ¶ 8150; USTR ¶ 9214.02) In general, foreign trading gross receipts

FTC 2d References are to the Federal Tax Coordinator 2d
FIN References are to RIA's Analysis of Federal Taxes: Income
TG References are to the Tax Guide
USTR References are to the United States Tax Reporter

means the gross receipts of a FSC attributable to the export of certain goods and services. Except for certain receipts not included in foreign trading gross receipts, foreign trading gross receipts means the gross receipts of any FSC that are attributable to, among other things, a sale of export property. (See FTC 2d/FIN ¶ O-1670.1; TG ¶ 8151; USTR ¶ 9214.06)

Export property is property:

. . . in the hands of any person (whether or not a FSC);

. . . manufactured, produced, grown or extracted in the U.S. by a person other than a FSC;

. . . held primarily for sale, lease, or rental, in the ordinary course of a trade or business by, or to a FSC for direct use, consumption, or disposition outside the U.S.; and

. . . not more than 50% of the fair market value of which is attributable to articles imported into the U.S. (See FTC 2d/FIN ¶ O-1673; TG ¶ 8163; USTR ¶ 9214.14)

Export property does not include:

. . . property leased or rented by a FSC for use by any member of a controlled group of corporations of which that FSC is a member;

. . . patents, inventions, models, designs, formulas or processes whether or not patented, copyrights (other than films, tapes, records or similar reproductions, for commercial or home use), good will, trademarks, trade brands, franchises, or other like property;

. . . oil or gas; or

. . . products whose export is prohibited or curtailed to effectuate the policy set forth in paragraph 2(c) of section 3 of the Export Administration Act of '79 (relating to the protection of the domestic economy). (FTC 2d/FIN ¶ O-1673; TG ¶ 8163; USTR ¶ 9214.14)

Congress was concerned about features of the Code that may tend to accelerate the removal of old-growth forests, and it understood that the export of raw logs may in effect cause American milling jobs to be exported overseas. (S Rept p. 376)

The '93 Act provides that, in addition to the items discussed above, export property does not include any unprocessed timber which is a soft wood. (Code Sec. 927(a)(2)(E) as amended by '93 Act § 13239(a)) For these purposes, the term unprocessed timber means any log, cant or similar form of timber. (Code Sec. 927(a)(2)(E))

> ***observation:*** Thus, income from exporting unprocessed timber will not be foreign trade income of a FSC which may be excluded from federal income tax.

DISCs. An Interest Charge Domestic International Sales Corporation (IC-DISC) can defer income attributable to $10 million or less of qualified export receipts, but the IC-DISC's shareholders are subject to an interest charge based on the amount of tax otherwise due on the deferred income, computed as if the income were distributed. (See FTC 2d/FIN ¶ O-1710; TG ¶ 8169; USTR ¶ 9914) The amount of the interest to be paid by the shareholder (his DISC-related deferred tax liability) is based on the tax otherwise due on the deferred income, computed as if it were distributed. (See FTC 2d/FIN ¶ O-1701; TG 8171; USTR ¶ 9914) A shareholder of an IC-DISC is treated as having a distribution taxable as a dividend with respect to his stock in an amount that is equal to his pro rata share of the taxable income of the DISC attributable to qualified export receipts of the DISC for the year that exceed $10 million. (See FTC 2d/FIN ¶ O-1705; TG ¶ 8172; USTR ¶ 9914)

To qualify as a DISC, at least 95% of the corporation's gross receipts for the tax year must consist of qualified export receipts. (See FTC 2d/FIN ¶ O-1736; USTR ¶ 9924) Qualified export receipts include not only receipts from the sale or lease of export property, but also include investment income such as interest on producer's loans to parents and others, dividends from foreign subs, interest on export asset obligations, etc. (See FTC 2d/FIN ¶ O-1762; TG ¶ 8477; USTR ¶ 9934.01)

Export property is property:

(a) manufactured, produced, grown or extracted in the U.S. by a person other than a DISC;

(b) held primarily for sale, lease or rental, in the ordinary course of trade or business, by, or to, a DISC, for direct use, consumption, or disposition outside the U.S.; and

(c) not more than 50% of the fair market value of which is attributable to articles imported into the U.S. (See FTC 2d/FIN ¶ O-1776; USTR ¶ 9934.01)

Export property does not include:

. . . property leased or rented by a DISC for use by any member of a controlled group which includes the DISC; (FTC 2d/FIN ¶ O-1785; USTR ¶ 9934.01)

. . . patents, inventions, models, designs, formulas, or processes, whether or not patented, copyrights (other than films, tapes, records, or similar reproductions, for commercial or home use), good will, trademarks, trade brands, franchises, or other like property; (FTC 2d/FIN ¶ O-1781; USTR ¶ 9934.01)

. . . depletable property; (FTC 2d/FIN ¶ O-1782; USTR ¶ 9934.01) or

. . . products subject to the export limitations under Sec. 7(a) of the Export Administration Act of '79 to effectuate the policy set forth in relating to the protection of the domestic economy in Sec. 3 paragraph (2)(C) of the Act.(FTC 2d/FIN ¶ O-1783; USTR ¶ 9934.01)

The '93 Act provides that, in addition to the items discussed above, the term export property does not include any unprocessed timber which is a softwood. (Code Sec. 993(c)(2)(E)) The term unprocessed timber means any log, cant, or similar form of timber. (Code Sec. 993(c)(2))

> RIA ***observation:*** Thus, this new rule makes it more difficult for a corporation to qualify as a DISC and will make shareholders unable to defer income from unprocessed timber, because the income from unprocessed timber will not be qualified export receipts.

Source rules. Certain tax rules depend on the source of income. Thus, it may be necessary to determine whether income is from sources within or outside of the U.S. for purposes of, among other things, the foreign tax credit.(See FTC 2d/FIN ¶ O-10901; TG ¶ 8295; USTR ¶ 8614) Income from the sale, exchange or other disposition of personal property is generally sourced at the seller's residence. However, in the case of income derived from the sale of inventory property, the residence

FTC 2d References are to the Federal Tax Coordinator 2d
FIN References are to RIA's Analysis of Federal Taxes: Income
TG References are to the Tax Guide
USTR References are to the United States Tax Reporter

sourcing rule discussed above does not apply. (See FTC 2d/FIN ¶ O-10946; TG ¶ 8303; USTR ¶ 8614.25) Instead, the following source rules apply:

(1) Gains, profits, and income derived from the purchase of inventory property outside the U.S. and its sale or exchange within the U.S. are treated as income from sources within the U.S. (See FTC 2d/FIN ¶ O-10954; TG ¶ 8306; USTR ¶ 8614.25)

(2) Gains, profits, and income from the purchase of inventory property within the U.S. and its sale or exchange outside the U.S. are treated as income from sources outside the U.S. (See FTC 2d/FIN ¶ O-10954; TG ¶ 8306; USTR ¶ 8614.25)

(3) Gains, profits and income derived from the purchase of inventory property produced by the taxpayer within and sold or exchanged outside the U.S., or produced (in whole or in part) by the taxpayer outside and sold or exchanged within the U.S. are treated as derived partly from sources within and partly from sources outside the U.S. (See FTC 2d/FIN ¶ O-10959; TG ¶ 8308; USTR ¶ 8634.02)

If an independent factory or production price (IFP) exists, it must be used to determine the division between domestic and foreign sources of income from sales outside the U.S. of inventory produced (in whole or in part) in the U.S. (See FTC 2d/FIN ¶ O-10960; USTR ¶ 8634.02) Where an independent factory or production price has not been established, a complex method of allocation is prescribed for computing income from sources within the U.S. That method (the 50/50 method) apportions one half of the taxable income in accordance with the respective values of the taxpayer's property in the U.S. and the foreign country. The second half of taxable income is apportioned in accordance with the respective gross sales of the taxpayer in the U.S. and the foreign country. (See FTC 2d/FIN ¶ O-10965; USTR ¶ 8634.02)

The '93 Act provides that despite the rules described above, any income from the sale of any unprocessed timber which is a softwood and was cut from an area in the U.S. is sourced in the U.S. and the rules discussed in (2) and (3) above do not apply to this income. (Code Sec. 865(b)) For purposes of this rule, the term unprocessed timber means any log, cant, or similar form of timber. (Code Sec. 865(b))

observation: Since income from the sale of unprocessed timber is U.S. sourced it will not be eligible for the foreign tax credit.

CFCs. The U.S. shareholders of a controlled foreign corporation (CFC) are taxed on their pro rata share of certain undistributed income of the CFC—its subpart F income. The subpart F income that is taxed to the U.S. shareholders for a tax year includes amounts earned by the CFC and amounts it invests in U.S. property, as well as previously excludible amounts that are withdrawn during the current year from the investment that allowed for exclusion in that year. (See FTC 2d/FIN ¶ O-2630; TG ¶ 8240; USTR ¶ 9524.01) Subpart F income consists of several types of income including foreign base company income (FBCI). (See FTC 2d/FIN ¶ O-2631; TG ¶ 8247; USTR ¶ 9524.01) Among other amounts, FBCI includes foreign base company sales income (FBCSI). (See FTC 2d/FIN ¶ O-2648; USTR ¶ 9544.01)

A special reduction is allowed in the amount of the subpart F income taxed to U.S. shareholders of a CFC which qualifies as an Export Trade Corporation (ETC). The subpart F income of an ETC is reduced by the amount of its export trade income which is also FBCI for that year. (See FTC 2d/FIN ¶ O-2768; TG ¶ 8258; USTR ¶ 9704.01) A U.S. shareholder of a CFC that was an ETC for any tax year, and that reduced the amount of subpart F income it derived in that year to account for its export trade investment, must include in a later tax year, his pro rata share of the CFC's decrease in those investments over that year. (See FTC 2d/FIN ¶ O-2767; TG ¶ 8258; USTR ¶ 9704.01) No CFC may qualify as an ETC unless it qualified as an ETC for any taxable year beginning before Oct. 31, '71. (See FTC 2d/FIN ¶ O-2769; TG ¶ 8258; USTR ¶ 9704)

The '93 Act provides that for purposes of determining foreign base company income (FBCI), foreign base company sales income (FBCSI) includes any income (whether in the form of profits, commissions, fees or otherwise) derived in connection with:

. . . the sale of any unprocessed timber (as defined for purposes of the source rules discussed above), (Code Sec. 954(d)(4)(A)), or

. . . the milling of any unprocessed timber outside the U.S. (Code Sec. 954(d)(4)(B))

Subpart G (i.e., the rules for export trade corporations) does not apply to any amount treated as subpart F (CFC) income by reason of this rule. (Code Sec. 954(d)(4)) Thus, any income treated as subpart F income that is earned by an export trade corporation is not subject to reduction by the export trade income of the corporation. (S Rept p. 377)

☐ **Effective:** Sales, exchanges or other dispositions after Aug 10, '93. (§ 13239(e))

For official explanation see Committee Reports ¶ 3058.

FTC 2d References are to the Federal Tax Coordinator 2d
FIN References are to RIA's Analysis of Federal Taxes: Income
TG References are to the Tax Guide
USTR References are to the United States Tax Reporter

¶ 1200. Tax Administration and Compliance

¶ 1201. Substantiation required for charitable donations of $250 or more

A deduction is available for charitable contributions to qualified organizations. (See FTC 2d/FIN ¶ K-2800 *et seq.;* TG ¶ 7290 *et seq.;* USTR ¶ 1704i) Under pre-'93 Act law, a taxpayer making a charitable contribution of cash had to keep a cancelled check; a receipt or letter from the charity showing the amount and date of the contribution and the name of the donee; or other reliable written records with that information. For noncash contributions, a receipt had to be kept showing the name of the donee, the date and location of the contribution, and a description of the property. (FTC 2d/FIN ¶ K-3900 *et seq.;* TG ¶ 7390 *et seq.;* USTR ¶ 1704.40i)

Taxpayers don't have to provide specific information on their tax return regarding cash contributions. However, taxpayers must provide certain information on Form 8283 if the amount of the claimed deduction for all noncash contributions exceeds $500. If the claimed deduction for a noncash gift exceeds $5,000 per item or group of similar items, the taxpayer must obtain a qualified appraisal and must attach to his return a Form 8323 signed by a qualified appraiser, which serves as the appraisal summary. In addition, an authorized representative of the donee charity must sign the Form 8323, acknowledging receipt of the gift and providing certain other information. (FTC 2d/FIN ¶s K-3936, K-3960; TG ¶ 7396; USTR ¶ 1704.50)

The '93 Act denies a deduction for charitable contributions of $250 or more (cash or noncash) unless the taxpayer substantiates the contribution by a written acknowledgment from the donee organization. (Code Sec. 170(f)(8)(A) as amended by '93 Act § 13172(a)) Taxpayers may not rely solely on a cancelled check to substantiate a cash contribution of $250 or more. (S Rept p. 222)

> ***observation:*** If the substantiation requirement isn't met, the deduction will be denied even there is other reliable evidence of the contribution (e.g., testimony).

> ***observation:*** For contributions of less than $250, the pre-'93 Act rules (above) continue to apply.

This provision doesn't place an information-reporting duty on charities. Where an acknowledgment is required, it is the taxpayer's responsibility to obtain one from the charity and keep it in his records. (S Rept p. 222)

> ***recommendation:*** Taxpayers making one-time contributions of $250 or more should request the substantiation at the time of the contribution. Although most charitable organizations will probably furnish the written substantiation as a matter of routine after the end of the year, early tax season filers may have to delay filing if they haven't yet received the substantiation.

Computation of $250 threshold. Separate payments are generally treated as separate contributions and aren't aggregated for purposes of the $250 threshold. Where contributions are paid by withholding from wages, the deduction from each paycheck is a separate payment. However, it is expected that IRS will issue anti-abuse rules to prevent avoidance of the substantiation requirement by writing several checks on the same date. (S Rept pp. 221-222)

illustration: Once every three months Smith sends a $200 donation to his church. He would not need written substantiation from the church for his total contribution of $800.

illustration: On Dec. 31, Brown writes 20 checks, each for $240, to his university alumni fund. Although each contribution is less than $250, the anti-abuse rule would presumably require written substantiation for what, in reality, is a $4,800 contribution.

observation: Where the anti-abuse rules do not apply, taxpayers can avoid the substantiation requirement by dividing larger contributions into payments of less than $250.

Content of acknowledgment. The acknowledgment must include the following information:

(1) the amount of cash and a description (but not the value) of any property other than cash contributed;

(2) whether the donee organization provided any goods or services in consideration, in whole or in part, for the contribution; and

(3) a description and good-faith estimate of the value of those goods or services or, if the goods or services consist entirely of intangible religious benefits, a statement to that effect. (Code Sec. 170(f)(8)(B) as amended by '93 Act § 13172(a))

An "intangible religious benefit" is one that is provided by an charity organized exclusively for religious purposes and that is generally not sold in a commercial transaction outside the donative context. (Code Sec. 170(f)(8)(B) as amended by '93 Act § 13172(a)) An example is admission to a religious ceremony. Tuition for education leading to a recognized degree, travel services, and consumer goods are not intangible religious benefits. But de minimis tangible benefits (such as wine) that are incidental to a religious ceremony may generally be disregarded. (S Rept p. 223)

The acknowledgment need not contain the taxpayer's social security number or taxpayer identification number. (S Rept p. 222)

observation: Although the charity need not value the gift, where an item or group of similar items exceeds $5,000, the donor must obtain a qualified appraisal and submit an appraisal summary as under pre-'93 Act law (above).

Form of acknowledgment. No particular form is prescribed for the acknowledgment. It may be a letter, postcard, or computer-generated form. The organization may prepare a separate acknowledgment for each contribution or may give donors periodic (e.g., annual) acknowledgments that set forth the required information for each contribution of $250 or more during the period. (S Rept p. 222)

Due date of acknowledgment. The taxpayer must obtain the acknowledgment on or before the date on which he files his return for the tax year of the contribution or, if earlier, the due date (including extensions) of the return. (Code Sec. 170(f)(8)(C) as amended by '93 Act § 13172(a))

observation: Presumably, the taxpayer has the burden of proving that the acknowledgment was obtained by the due date. Therefore, taxpayers should make sure that the acknowledgment is dated and should retain any postmarks or other evidence of the date of receipt.

Where charity files return with IRS. If a charity files a return with IRS, under regs to be issued, reporting information sufficient to substantiate the amount of a deductible contribution, the taxpayer need not substantiate that contribution. (Code Sec. 170(f)(8)(D) as amended by '93 Act § 13172(a))

> ***observation:*** Filing such a return is optional with the charity, since the provision imposes no information-reporting duty (see above).

IRS regulatory authority. IRS has authority to issue all necessary or appropriate regs, including regs that waive some or all the substantiation requirements in appropriate cases. (Code Sec. 170(f)(8)(E) as amended by '93 Act § 13172(a)) Congress intends that the authority to waive requirements be used to clarify the treatment of contributions made through payroll deductions. (Conf Rept p. 567)

Sanctions on charity for providing false acknowledgment. A charitable organization that knowingly provides a false written acknowledgment to a donor will be subject to the Code Sec. 6701 penalty for aiding and abetting an understatement of tax liability (see FTC 2d/FIN ¶ V-2350 *et seq.;* TG ¶ 9828; USTR ¶ 67,014). (S Rept p. 222)

IRS announcement. Congress expects IRS to expeditiously issue a notice or other announcement providing guidance with respect to the substantiation requirement. It is expected that the guidance will urge charities to assist taxpayers in meeting the requirement. (S Rept p. 224)

☐ **Effective:** Contributions made after Dec. 31, '93. (§ 13172(b))
For official explanation see Committee Reports ¶ 3026.

¶ 1202. Disclosure requirement imposed for quid pro quo charitable contributions

A payment to a charity in exchange for which the payor receives an economic benefit is deductible only to the extent that the payment exceeds the value of the benefit. (See FTC 2d/FIN ¶ K-3086; TG ¶ 7314; USTR ¶ 1704.38) Under Rev Procs 90-12 and 92-49, certain small items and token benefits, such as key chains or mugs, received in exchange for a contribution are deemed to have insubstantial value, so that the full amount of the contribution is deductible. (See FTC 2d/FIN ¶ K-3101; TG ¶ 7316; USTR ¶ 1704.38)

IRS has asked charities to determine the fair market value of benefits offered for contributions and to state, in the solicitation and tickets, receipts, or other documents issued in connection with the contribution, how much is deductible and how much is not. (See FTC 2d/FIN ¶ K-3100; TG ¶ 7315; USTR ¶ 1704.38) However, under pre-'93 Act law, charities were not required to disclose to contributors whether a payment to the charity was a deductible contribution or whether all or part of the payment was consideration for goods or services furnished to the payor.

The '93 Act requires a charitable organization that receives a quid pro quo contribution (defined below) in excess of $75 to provide a written statement, in connection with soliciting or receiving the contribution, that (1) informs the donor that the amount of the contribution that is deductible for federal income tax purposes is limited to the excess of the amount of any money (and the value of any property other than money) contributed by the donor over the value of the goods or services provided by the organization and (2) provides the donor with a good-faith estimate of the value of those goods or services. These requirements do not apply to Code Sec. 170(c)(1) organizations (states, their political subdivisions, the United States, and the District of Columbia). (Code Sec. 6115(a) as added by '93 Act § 13173(a))

A "quid pro quo contribution" is a payment made partly as a gift and partly in consideration for goods or services provided to the donor. But the term does not include any payment made to an organization, organized exclusively for religious purposes, in return for which the taxpayer receives solely an intangible religious benefit that generally is not sold in a commercial transaction outside the donative context. (Code Sec. 6115(b) as added by '93 Act § 13272(a))

An example of an intangible religious benefit is admission to a religious ceremony. Tuition for education leading to a recognized degree, travel services, and consumer goods are not intangible religious benefits. But de minimis tangible benefits (such as wine) that are incidental to a religious ceremony may generally be disregarded. (S Rept p. 223)

When disclosure requirement applies. The disclosure requirement applies to all quid pro quo contributions where the donor makes a payment of more than $75. Thus, if a charity receives a $100 contribution in exchange for which the donor receives a dinner valued at $40, the charity must inform the donor in writing that only $60 is deductible as a charitable contribution. (S Rept pp. 223-224)

However, the disclosure requirement does not apply if the donor receives only de minimis, token goods or services, such as those that are deemed to be of insubstantial value under Rev Procs 90-12 and 92-49 (see above). Also, the disclosure requirement does not apply to transactions that have no gift element, such as sales of goods by a museum gift shop. (S Rept p. 224)

Aggregation of payments. For purposes of the $75 threshold, separate payments made at different times of the year with respect to separate fundraising events generally will not be aggregated. However, it is intended that IRS will issue anti-abuse rules to prevent avoidance of the quid pro quo disclosure requirement by writing several checks for the same transaction. (Conf Rept p. 566)

How disclosure is made. The disclosure must be made in a manner that is reasonably likely to come the donor's attention. For example, disclosing the required information in small print within a larger document might not meet the requirement. (S Rept p. 223)

IRS announcement. Congress expects IRS to expeditiously issue a notice or other announcement providing guidance with respect to the disclosure requirement. (S Rept p. 224)

Penalty for noncompliance with disclosure requirement. A penalty of $10 per contribution, capped at $5,000 per fundraising event or mailing, may be imposed on charities that fail to make the required disclosure, unless it is shown that the failure was due to reasonable cause. (Code Sec. 6714 as added by '93 Act § 13173(b)) The penalty applies if the charity fails to make a disclosure in connection with a quid pro quo contribution or makes an incomplete or inaccurate disclosure. For example, the penalty will apply if a charity makes an estimate of the value of goods and services provided to a donor that was not determined in good faith. (S Rept p. 224)

☐ **Effective:** Contributions made after Dec. 31, '93. (§ 13173(d))

For official explanation see Committee Reports ¶ 3026.

¶ 1203. "Reasonable basis" replaces "not frivolous" standard in applying accuracy-related penalty

A 20% accuracy-related penalty applies to any underpayment of tax that is attrib-

FTC 2d References are to the Federal Tax Coordinator 2d
FIN References are to RIA's Analysis of Federal Taxes: Income
TG References are to the Tax Guide
USTR References are to the United States Tax Reporter

utable to, among other things, negligence or disregard of rules and regs or a substantial understatement of income tax. (See FTC 2d/FIN ¶s V-2100 *et seq.*, V-2150 *et seq.;* TG ¶s 9766 *et seq.*, 9774 *et seq.;* USTR ¶ 66,624) Under pre-'93 Act law, a taxpayer could avoid the accuracy-related penalty for negligence, disregard of rules and regs, and substantial understatement if the position taken on the tax return wasn't frivolous and was adequately disclosed. A position wasn't "frivolous" if it wasn't "patently improper." (FTC 2d/FIN ¶s V-2107, V-2167; TG ¶s 9766, 9774; USTR ¶ 66,624)

The '93 Act replaces the "not frivolous" standard with a "reasonable basis" standard. (Code Sec. 6662(d)(2)(B)(ii) as amended by '93 Act § 13251(a)) Thus, under the '93 Act, taxpayers can avoid the penalties for substantial understatement and disregard of rules and regs by adequate disclosure only if the position has at least a reasonable basis. Disclosure isn't necessary to avoid the negligence penalty because, under Reg § 1.6662-3(b)(1), a taxpayer isn't considered negligent with respect to a return position that has a reasonable basis. (S Rept p. 391)

"Reasonable basis" is a relatively high standard of tax reporting and is significantly higher than the "not patently improper" standard that applied prior to the '93 Act. The "reasonable basis" standard isn't satisfied by a return position that is merely arguable or merely a colorable claim. (S Rept p. 390)

> ***observation:*** Under pre-'93 Act law, the substantial understatement penalty could be avoided if the position was adequately disclosed and wasn't frivolous *or* if there was "substantial authority" for the tax treatment of the item. The "reasonable basis" standard, while imposing a higher standard than "not patently improper," presumably calls for something less than a showing of "substantial authority" or a "realistic possibility" of being sustained.

□ **Effective:** Returns due (without regard to extensions) after Dec. 31, '93. (§ 13251(b))

For official explanation see Committee Reports ¶ 3062.

¶ 1204. Information returns for discharges of indebtedness

Under pre-'93 Act law, lenders were not required to file information returns with respect to discharged debt. Only Federal agencies were required to report forgiven debt amounts exceeding $600 to IRS on Form 1099-G, except where prohibited by law. The Federal Deposit Insurance Corporation (FDIC) and the Resolution Trust Corporation (RTC) did not file reports regarding forgiveness of indebtedness because of concerns that such reporting might violate the Right to Financial Privacy Act of 1978 (RFPA). (S Rept p. 394)

Under the '93 Act, an applicable financial entity (defined below) that discharges (in whole or in part) the indebtedness of any person during any calendar year is required to file a return setting forth:

(1) the name, address, and taxpayer identification number (TIN) of each person whose indebtedness was discharged during the calendar year,

(2) the date of the discharge and the amount of the indebtedness discharged, and

(3) any other information that IRS may require. (Code Sec. 6050P(a) as added by '93 Act § 13252(a))

This return must be filed regardless of whether the debtor is subject to tax on the discharge. The applicable financial entity is not required to determine whether the debtor may exclude the discharge from income. (S Rept p. 395)

The above reporting rule does not apply with respect to discharges of less than $600. (Code Sec. 6050P(b))

An applicable financial entity that is required to make a return must also provide each person whose name must be set forth in the return a written statement showing:

(1) the name and address of the entity that must make the return; and

(2) the information that must be shown on the return with respect to the person.

The written statement must be provided before Jan. 31 of the year following the calendar year for which the return must be made. (Code Sec. 6050P(d))

An "applicable financial entity" is:

. . . any financial institution described in Code Sec. 581 (see FTC 2d/FIN ¶ E-3002; TG ¶ 7771; USTR ¶ 5814) or Code Sec. 591(a) (see FTC 2d/FIN ¶ E-3307; TG ¶ 7801; USTR ¶ 5914) and any credit union (see FTC 2d/FIN ¶ D-4900 *et seq.;* TG ¶ 7864; USTR ¶ 5014.23);

. . . any other corporation that is a direct or indirect subsidiary of a financial institution or credit union described above and that, because of its affiliation with the above institution, is subject to supervision or examination by a Federal or state agency that regulates financial institutions or credit unions; and

. . . the FDIC, the RTC, the National Credit Union Administration, and any of their successors or subunits and any other Federal executive agency (defined by reference to the Code Sec. 6050M rules requiring reporting of contracts by Federal agencies, see FTC 2d/FIN ¶ S-3621; TG ¶ 9350; USTR ¶ 6050M4.01). (Code Sec. 6050P(c)(1))

Thus, federal agencies that were required to report forgiveness of indebtedness before the '93 Act are also subject to the reporting rules, with the result that all federal agencies are subject to uniform rules. (Conf Rept p. 672)

Where a governmental unit is required to file a return, the return must be made by the officer or employee appropriately designated for the purpose of making the return. (Code Sec. 6050P(c)(2))

The failure to file the above return subjects the taxpayer to the normal penalty for failure to file an information return (see FTC 2d/FIN ¶ V-1800 *et seq.;* TG ¶ 9785; USTR ¶ 67,214 *et seq.)* and the failure to provide persons with the above written statement subjects the taxpayer to the normal penalty for failure to provide payee statements (see FTC 2d/FIN ¶ V-1815 *et seq.;* TG ¶ 9791; USTR ¶s 67,224, 67,244). (Code Sec. 6724(d)(1)(B)(viii) as amended by '93 Act § 13252(b)(1); Code Sec. 6724(d)(2)(P))

☐ **Effective:** For discharges of indebtedness after Dec. 31, '93. (§ 13252(d)(1)) However, for governmental entities that are applicable financial entities, these rules are effective for discharges of indebtedness after Aug. 10, '93. (§ 13252(d)(2))

For official explanation see Committee Reports ¶ 3063.

¶ 1205. Interest-free period for tax refunds expanded

IRS pays no interest on a refund arising from an income tax return if the refund is issued by the 45th day after the later of the due date of the return (without

FTC 2d References are to the Federal Tax Coordinator 2d
FIN References are to RIA's Analysis of Federal Taxes: Income
TG References are to the Tax Guide
USTR References are to the United States Tax Reporter

extensions) or the date the return is filed. (See FTC 2d/FIN ¶ T-8024; TG ¶ 9636; USTR ¶ 66,114) Under pre-'93 Act law, there was no interest-free processing period for refunds of taxes other than income tax or for refunds arising from an amended return or refund claim. (H Rept p. 787)

The '93 Act provides that no interest will be paid on a refund arising from any original tax return, including employment, excise, estate, and gift tax returns, if the refund is issued by the 45th day after the later of the due date of the return (without extensions) or the date when the return was filed. (Code Sec. 6611(e)(1) as amended by '93 Act § 13271(a))

In the case of an amended return or refund claim, the '93 Act provides that if the refund is issued by the 45th day after the date the amended return or refund claim was filed, no interest is paid for that period of up to 45 days. (Code Sec. 6611(e)(2) as amended by '93 Act § 13271(a)) However, interest is paid for the period from the due date of the return to the date the amended return or refund claim was filed. If IRS doesn't issue the refund by the 45th day, interest will be paid (as under pre-'93 Act law) for the period from the due date of the return (if timely filed) to the date the refund is paid. (H Rept pp. 787-8)

Under the '93 Act, if IRS initiates an adjustment that results in a refund or credit of an overpayment, interest on the overpayment is computed by subtracting 45 days from the number of days that interest would otherwise be allowed. (Code Sec. 6611(e)(3) as amended by '93 Act § 13271(a)) This rule applies to both computational adjustments and audit adjustments. (H Rept p. 788)

☐ **Effective:** The rule about original tax returns applies to returns due after Dec. 31, '93, without regard to extensions. (§ 13271(b)(1)) The rule about amended returns and refund claims applies to claims filed after Dec. 31, '94, regardless of the taxable period to which the refund relates. (§ 13271(b)(2)) The rule about IRS-initiated adjustments applies to refunds paid after Dec. 31, '94, regardless of the taxable period to which the refund relates. (§ 13271(b)(3))

For official explanation see Committee Reports ¶ 3066.

¶ 1206. Rules on disclosures relating to Medicare secondary-payer situations extended

As a health-care provider, Medicare is a secondary payer for certain individuals who are covered by third-party payers, such as employer health plans. Thus, for example, where an employer health plan pays part of an individual's medical bill, Medicare is liable, as a secondary payer, for the balance.

To assist in the administration of these secondary-payer rules, IRS must, on written request from the Social Security Administration (SSA), disclose to SSA certain information about the marital status of Medicare beneficiaries identified by SSA. Also, SSA must, on written request from the Health Care Financing Administration (HCFA), disclose to HCFA certain information about Medicare beneficiaries. (See FTC 2d/FIN ¶ S-6354; USTR ¶ 61,034.01)

Under pre-'93 Act law, the rules on disclosure of taxpayer information by IRS didn't apply to requests made after Sept. 30, '95, or to requests made before Sept. 30, '95 for information relating to '94 or later years. The rules on disclosure of taxpayer information by SSA didn't apply to requests made after Sept. 30, '95, or to requests made before Sept. 30, '95 for information relating to '95 or later years. (FTC 2d/FIN ¶ S-6354; USTR ¶ 61,034.01 *et seq.*)

The '93 Act extends these expiration dates. Under the Act, the rules on disclosure of information by IRS do not apply to requests made after Sept. 30, '98, or to requests made before Sept. 30 '98 for information relating to '97 or later years. The rules on disclosure of information by SSA do not apply to any request made after Sept. 30, '98, or to any request made before Sept. 30 '98 for information relating to '98 or later years. (Code Sec. 6103(l)(12)(F) as amended by '93 Act § 13561(a)(2)(C))

Under pre-'93 Act law, a "group health plan" for purposes of the disclosure provision included both a "group health plan" as defined by Code Sec. 5000(b)(1) and a "large group health plan" as defined by Code Sec. 5000(b)(2). (FTC 2d/FIN ¶ S-6354; USTR ¶ 50,004) The '93 Act changes the definition of "group health plan" to include only group health plans under Code Sec. 5000(b)(1) and not large group health plans under Code Sec. 5000(b)(2). (Code Sec. 6103(l)(12)(E)(ii) as amended by '93 Act § 13561(e)(2)(B))

☐ **Effective:** Aug. 10, '93.

¶ 1207. Availability and use of death information from states by federal agencies

Under pre-'93 Act law, IRS could disclose tax returns and return information to state tax agencies solely for the purpose of the administration of state tax laws. (FTC 2d/FIN ¶ S-6324; USTR ¶ 61,034.07) In addition, the Secretary of Health and Human Services could enter into voluntary contracts with the states for the purpose of obtaining death certificates and other related information. The Secretary could redisclose this information to other federal, state, and local agencies for certain specified purposes, subject to the safeguards as the Secretary determines are necessary to prevent any unauthorized redisclosure. However, because these contracts with the states were entirely voluntary, the states were able, at their discretion, to include contract provisions preventing the Secretary from redisclosing this information to other federal, state, and local agencies. (Conf Rept p. 737)

The '93 Act modifies the IRS disclosure rule by providing that IRS may not disclose returns or return information to any state agency, body, or commission (or any legal representative of the state) in connection with the administration of any state tax laws during any period during which a contract meeting the requirements discussed below isn't in effect between the state and the Secretary of Health and Human Services. (Code Sec. 6103(d)(4)(A) as amended by '93 Act § 13444(a))

Contractual requirements. A contract meets the requirements of the disclosure rule discussed above if: (Code Sec. 6103(d)(4)(B))

. . . the contract requires the state to furnish the Secretary of Health and Human Services information concerning individuals with respect to whom death certificates (or equivalent documents maintained by the state or any subdivision of the state) have been officially filed with it, and (Code Sec. 6103(d)(4)(B)(i))

. . . the contract doesn't include any restriction on the use of information obtained by the Secretary under the contract, except that the contract may provide that the information is only to be used by the Secretary (or any other federal agency) for purposes of ensuring that federal benefits or other payments aren't erroneously paid to deceased individuals. (Code Sec. 6103(d)(4)(B)(ii))

Any information obtained by the Secretary of Health and Human Services under the

FTC 2d References are to the Federal Tax Coordinator 2d
FIN References are to RIA's Analysis of Federal Taxes: Income
TG References are to the Tax Guide
USTR References are to the United States Tax Reporter

contract must be exempt from disclosure under 5 USC 552 (Freedom of Information Act) and 5 USC 552a (Privacy Act). (Code Sec. 6103(d)(4)(B))

Exception for states not having a contract with the Secretary of Health and Human Services on July 1, '93. The disclosure rule discussed above doesn't apply to any state which on July 1, '93, wasn't, under a contract, furnishing the Secretary of Health and Human Services information concerning individuals with respect to whom death certificates (or equivalent documents maintained by the state or any subdivision of the state) have been officially filed with it. (Code Sec. 6103(d)(4)(C))

☐ **Effective:** One year after date of enactment. (§ 13444(b)(1)) The date of enactment is Aug. 10, '93. The effective date is extended to two years after the date of enactment in the case of any state if it is established to IRS's satisfaction that (§ 13444(b)(2)):

. . . under the law of the state as in effect on Aug. 10, '93, it is impossible for the state to enter into an agreement meeting the contractual requirements discussed above (§ 13444(b)(2)(A)), and

. . . it is likely that the state will enter into that agreement during the extension period. (§ 13444(b)(2)(B))

Congress intends that IRS's authority to grant an extension of the effective date will ensure that those states that have not yet entered into a contract with the federal government allowing for government-wide dissemination of death information have up to two years to resolve, through their state legislatures, any legal impediment to the timely signing of a contract meeting the requirements. (Conf Rept p. 738)

For official explanation see Committee Reports ¶ 3081.

¶ 1208. Department of Education given access to certain tax information to implement direct student loan program

Tax returns and return information are confidential and may not be disclosed by government employees except as authorized by statute. (See FTC 2d/FIN ¶ S-6200 *et seq.;* TG ¶ 1468; USTR ¶ 61,034)

Under pre-'93 Act law, IRS could disclose to the Department of Education the mailing address of taxpayers who had defaulted on a loan made under part B or E of Title IV of the Higher Education Act of '65 or under Section 3(a)(1) of the Migration and Refugee Assistance Act of '62. The Department of Education could in turn make this information available to its agents and to the holders of such loans (and their agents) for the purpose of locating the taxpayers and collecting the loan. (FTC 2d/FIN ¶ S-6348; USTR ¶ 61,034.06)

In order to implement a new federal direct student loan program that allows loans to be repaid on an income-contingent basis, the '93 Act gives the Department of Education access to certain additional tax information. Under the Act, IRS may disclose to officers and employees of the Department of Education, on written request, return information about a taxpayer who has received an applicable student loan (defined below) and whose loan repayments are based in whole or part upon his income. The information that may be disclosed includes the taxpayer's name, address, taxpayer identification number, filing status, and adjusted gross income. (Code Sec. 6103(l)(13)(A) as amended by '93 Act § 13402(a))

The Department of Education may use the information thus disclosed only for purposes of, and to the extent necessary in, establishing the income-contingent repayment amount for a student loan. (Code Sec. 6103(l)(13)(B))

An "applicable student loan" is (1) a loan made under Part D of Title IV of the

Higher Education Act of '65 (the new federal direct student loan program) or (2) a loan made under Part B or E of the Higher Education Act of '65 that is in default and has been assigned to the Department of Education. (Code Sec. 6103(l)(13)(C))

The authority to disclose tax information to the Department of Education under this provision doesn't apply to requests for information made after Sept. 30, '98. (Code Sec. 6103(l)(13)(D))

The '93 Act also expands the Department of Education's existing authority to obtain mailing addresses from IRS (see above). The Department of Education may now obtain the address of any taxpayer who owes an overpayment (i.e., has received more than the proper amount) on a Federal Pell Grant or who has defaulted on a loan made under part D of Title IV of the Higher Education Act of '65. As under pre-'93 Act law, the information may be used only to locate the taxpayer and collect the overpayment or loan. (Code Sec. 6103(m)(4) as amended by '93 Act § 13402(b)) This authority is permanent. (H Rept p. 805)

Study of IRS collection of student loans. Congress directs the Treasury Department, in consultation with the Department of Education, to study the feasibility of a system of student loan repayment through wage withholding or other means involving IRS. The study is to examine (1) whether IRS could implement such a system with its current resources and without impairing its ability to collect taxes, (2) the impact of increased disclosure of tax information and increased IRS involvement in nontax collection activities on voluntary taxpayer compliance, (3) IRS's ability to enforce collection of student loans using an alternate system of dispute resolution, penalties, and collection devices, (4) the effect of separating loan collection from other loan servicing functions, and (5) the anticipated effect on the management of federal student loan collections and on repayment of such loans. If the study concludes that IRS collection is feasible, the Treasury Department and the Department of Education should develop a plan to implement the collection system. The feasibility study, any plan that is developed, and any legislative recommendations should be submitted to Congress within six months of the Aug. 10, '93. (Conf Rept p. 728)

☐ **Effective:** Aug. 10, '93. (§ 13402(c))

For official explanation see Committee Reports ¶ 3073.

¶ 1209. Department of Housing and Urban Development given access to tax information

Tax returns and tax information are confidential and may not be disclosed by government employees except as authorized by statute. (See FTC 2d/FIN ¶ S-6200 *et seq.;* TG ¶ 1468; USTR ¶ 61,034)

The Social Security Administration must, on written request, disclose tax information about net earnings from self-employment, wages, and retirement income to federal, state, or local agencies administering the programs listed in Code Sec. 6103(l)(7). Likewise, IRS must, on written request, disclose tax information about unearned income to those same agencies. The disclosure may be made only for purposes of, and to the extent necessary in, determining eligibility for and the correct amount of benefits under the program. (FTC 2d/FIN ¶ S-6353; USTR ¶ 61,034.06)

No tax information may be disclosed to an agency listed in Code Sec. 6103(l)(7)

FTC 2d References are to the Federal Tax Coordinator 2d
FIN References are to RIA's Analysis of Federal Taxes: Income
TG References are to the Tax Guide
USTR References are to the United States Tax Reporter

unless the agency establishes procedures satisfactory to IRS for safeguarding the information it receives. (FTC 2d/FIN ¶ S-6405; USTR ¶ 61,034.02) Unauthorized disclosure of information obtained under Code Sec. 6103(l)(7) is a felony punishable by a fine of up to $5,000 or imprisonment for up to five years, or both. (FTC 2d/FIN ¶ V-3305; TG ¶ 9678) An action for civil damages may also be brought for unauthorized disclosure. (FTC 2d/FIN ¶ S-6500 *et seq.;* USTR ¶ 61,034)

Under pre-'93 Act law, the list of agencies to which tax information had to be disclosed under Code Sec. 6103(l)(7) didn't include the Department of Housing and Urban Development (HUD). The '93 Act requires the Social Security Administration and IRS to disclose the tax information described above to HUD with respect to housing assistance programs administered by HUD that involve initial and periodic review of an applicant's or participant's income. The information may only be disclosed on written request from HUD and only for use by HUD employees in verifying the eligibility of applicants for and participants in the programs and their correct amount of benefits. (Code Sec. 6103(l)(7)(D)(ix) as amended by '93 Act § 13403(a)(3))

The inclusion of HUD in the list of agencies in Code Sec. 6103(l)(7) extends the pre-'93 Act restrictions on unauthorized disclosure to HUD and its employees. HUD employees may not redisclose tax information to state or local housing agencies, public housing authorities, or any other third party. However, they may inform those parties that a discrepancy exists between the information provided by the applicant or participant and information from other sources. (S Rept p. 166)

The authority to disclose tax information to HUD expires after Sept. 30, '98. (Code Sec. 6103(l)(7)(D) as amended by '93 Act § 13403(a)(4))

Study. Congress intends that the Treasury Department, in consultation with HUD, will conduct a study to determine (1) whether the tax information disclosed to HUD is being used effectively, (2) whether HUD is complying with the Code's safeguards against unauthorized disclosure of the information, and (3) the impact on the privacy rights of applicants and participants in HUD housing programs. The study must be submitted to the tax-writing committees before Jan. 1, '98. (Conf Rept p. 729)

☐ **Effective:** Aug. 10, '93. (§ 13403(c))

For official explanation see Committee Reports ¶ 3074.

¶ 1210. Authority to disclose tax information to Department of Veterans Affairs extended until Sept. 30, '98

Tax returns and return information are confidential and may not be disclosed by government employees except as authorized by statute. (See FTC 2d/FIN ¶ S-6200 *et seq.;* TG ¶ 1468; USTR ¶ 61,034)

Under one such exception, IRS and the Social Security Administration must disclose to the Department of Veterans Affairs (DVA) certain tax information and self-employment tax information necessary to determine eligibility for and the amount of benefits under certain needs-based pension and other programs. Under pre-'93 Act law, this disclosure provision was scheduled to expire on Sept. 30, '97. (FTC 2d/FIN ¶ S-6353; USTR ¶ 61,034.06)

The '93 Act extends the authority to disclose return information to the DVA for one year, through Sept. 30, '98. (Code Sec. 6103(l)(7)(D)(viii) as amended by '93 Act § 13401(a) The extension will provide time to assess the impact of the disclosure on taxpayers' voluntary compliance with the tax laws. (H Rept p. 803)

☐ **Effective:** Aug. 10, '93. (§ 13401(b))

For official explanation see Committee Reports ¶ 3072.

Next page is 401.

[¶ 2000] New Law

This section reproduces new law enacted by Chapter 1 of Title XIII of the Omnibus Budget Reconciliation Act of 1993 (P.L. 103-66). Code sections appear as amended, added or repealed starting at ¶ 2001. They are in Code section order. New matter is shown in *italics.* Deleted matter and effective dates are shown in footnotes.

Act sections that do not amend Code sections start at ¶ 2500.

Cross references at the end of each Code section refer to both the paragraph in the Analysis section where the law change is explained, and the paragraph in the Committee Report section of this book.

[¶ 2001] Code Sec. 1. Tax imposed.

[1]***(a) Married individuals filing joint returns and surviving spouses.*** *There is hereby imposed on the taxable income of—*

(1) every married individual (as defined in section 7703) who makes a single return jointly with his spouse under section 6013, and

(2) every surviving spouse (as defined in section 2(a)),

a tax determined in accordance with the following table:

If taxable income is:	The tax is:
Not over $36,900	15% of taxable income.
Over $36,900 but not over $89,150	$5,535, plus 28% of the excess over $36,900.
Over $89,150 but not over $140,000.	$20,165, plus 31% of the excess over $89,150.
Over $140,000 but not over $250,000.	$35,928.50, plus 36% of the excess over $140,000.
Over $250,000	$75,528.50, plus 39.6% of the excess over $250,000.

[2]***(b) Heads of households.*** *There is hereby imposed on the taxable income of every head of a household (as defined in section 2(b)) a tax determined in accordance with the following table:*

If taxable income is:	The tax is:
Not over $29,600	15% of taxable income.
Over $29,600 but not over $76,400	$4,440, plus 28% of the excess over $29,600.
Over $76,400 but not over $127,500	$17,544, plus 31% of the excess over $76,400.
Over $127,500 but not over $250,000.	$33,385, plus 36% of the excess over $127,500.
Over $250,000	$77,485, plus 39.6% of the excess over $250,000.

[Footnote Code Sec. 1] Matter in *italics* in Code Sec. 1(a)-(e) added by section 13201(a) of P.L. 103-66 which struck out:

1. "(a) Married individuals filing joint returns and surviving spouses.

"There is hereby imposed on the taxable income of—

"(1) every married individual (as defined in section 7703) who makes a single return jointly with his spouse under section 6013, and

"(2) every surviving spouse (as defined in section 2(a)), a tax determined in accordance with the following table:

If taxable income is:	The tax is:
Not over $32,450	15% of taxable income.
Over $32,450 but not over $78,400	$4,867.50, plus 28% of the excess over $32,450.
Over $78,400	$17,733.50, plus 31% of the excess over $78,400.

2. "(b) Heads of households.

"There is hereby imposed on the taxable income of every head of a household (as defined in section 2(b)) a tax determined in accordance with the following table:

If taxable income is:	The tax is:
Not over $26,050	15% of taxable income.
Over $26,050 but not over $67,200	$3,907.50, plus 28% of the excess over $26,500.
Over $67,200	$15,429.50, plus 31% of the excess over $67,200.

[3]*(c) **Unmarried individuals (other than surviving spouses and heads of households).** There is hereby imposed on the taxable income of every individual (other than a surviving spouse as defined in section 2(a) or the head of a household as defined in section 2(b)) who is not a married individual (as defined in section 7703) a tax determined in accordance with the following table:*

If taxable income is:	The tax is:
Not over $22,100	15% of taxable income.
Over $22,100 but not over $53,500	$3,315, plus 28% of the excess over $22,100.
Over $53,500 but not over $115,000	$12,107, plus 31% of the excess over $53,500.
Over $115,000 but not over $250,000	$31,172, plus 36% of the excess over $115,000.
Over $250,000	$79,772, plus 39.6% of the excess over $250,000.

[4]*(d) **Married individuals filing separate returns.** There is hereby imposed on the taxable income of every married individual (as defined in section 7703) who does not make a single return jointly with his spouse under section 6013, a tax determined in accordance with the following table:*

If taxable income is:	The tax is:
Not over $18,450	15% of taxable income.
Over $18,450 but not over $44,575	$2,767.50, plus 28% of the excess over $18,450.
Over $44,575 but not over $70,000	$10,082.50, plus 31% of the excess over $44,575.
Over $70,000 but not over $125,000	$17,964.25, plus 36% of the excess over $70,000.
Over $125,000	$37,764.25, plus 39.6% of the excess over $125,000.

[5]*(e) **Estates and trusts.** There is hereby imposed on the taxable income of—*

(1) every estate, and

[Footnote Code Sec. 1 continued]

3. "(c) Unmarried individuals (other than surviving spouses and heads of households).

"There is hereby imposed on the taxable income of every individual (other than a surviving spouse as defined in section 2(a) or the head of a household as defined in section 2(b)) who is not a married individual (as defined in section 7703) a tax determined in accordance with the following table:

If taxable income is:	The tax is:
Not over $19,450	15% of taxable income.
Over $19,450 but not over $47,050	$2,917.50, plus 28% of the excess over $19,450.
Over $47,050	$10,645.50, plus 31% of the excess over $47,050.

4. "(d) Married individuals filing separate returns.

"There is hereby imposed on the taxable income of every married individual (as defined in section 7703) who does not make a single return jointly with his spouse under section 6013, a tax determined in accordance with the following table:

If taxable income is:	The tax is:
Not over $16,225	15% of taxable income.
Over $16,225 but not over $39,200	$2,433.75, plus 28% of the excess over $16,225.
Over $39,200	$8,866.75, plus 31% of the excess over $39,200.

5. "(e) Estates and trusts.

"There is hereby imposed on the taxable income of—

"(1) every estate, and

"(2) every trust,

"taxable under this subsection a tax determined in accordance with the following table:

If taxable income is:	The tax is:
Not over $3,300	15% of taxable income.
Over $3,300 but not over $9,900	$495, plus 28% of the excess over $3,300.
Over $9,900	$2,343, plus 31% of the excess over $9,900."

Effective Date (Sec. 13201(c) of P.L. 103-66) effective for tax. yrs. begin. after 12/31/92.

Matter in *italics* in Code Sec. 1(a)-(e) [as amended by Sec. 13201(A) above] added by section 13202(a)(1)-(5) of P.L. 103-66 which struck out:

"Over $140,000	$35,928.50, plus 36% of the excess over $140,000."
"Over $127,500	$33,385, plus 36% of the excess over $127,500."
"Over $115,000	$31,172, plus 36% of the excess over $115,000."

(2) every trust,
taxable under this subsection a tax determined in accordance with the following table:

If taxable income is:	The tax is:
Not over $1,500	15% of taxable income.
Over $1,500 but not over $3,500	$225, plus 28% of the excess over $1,500.
Over $3,500 but not over $5,500	$785, plus 31% of the excess over $3,500.
Over $5,500 but not over $7,500	$1,405, plus 36% of the excess over $5,500.
Over $7,500	$2,125, plus 39.6% of the excess over $7,500.

(f) Adjustments in tax tables so that inflation will not result in tax increases.

(1) In general. Not later than December 15 of [6]*1993*, and each subsequent calendar year, the Secretary shall prescribe tables which shall apply in lieu of the tables contained in subsections (a), (b), (c), (d), and (e) with respect to taxable years beginning in the succeeding calendar year.

* * * * * * * * * * * *

(3) Cost-of-living adjustment. For purposes of paragraph (2), the cost-of-living adjustment for any calendar year is the percentage (if any) by which—

(A) the CPI for the preceding calendar year, exceeds

(B) the CPI for the calendar year [7]*1992*

* * * * * * * * * * * *

(7) Special rule for certain brackets.

(A) Calendar year 1994. In prescribing the tables under paragraph (1) which apply with respect to taxable years beginning in calendar year 1994, the Secretary shall make no adjustment to the dollar amounts at which the 36 percent rate bracket begins or at which the 39.6 percent rate begins under any table contained in subsection (a), (b), (c), (d), or (e).

(B) Later calendar years. In prescribing tables under paragraph (1) which apply with respect to taxable years beginning in a calendar year after 1994, the cost-of-living adjustment used in making adjustments to the dollar amounts referred to in subparagraph (A) shall be determined under paragraph (3) by substituting "1993" for "1992".

* * * * * * * * * * * *

(h) Maximum capital gains rate. If a taxpayer has a net capital gain for any taxable year, then the tax imposed by this section shall not exceed the sum of—

(1) a tax computed at the rates and in the same manner as if this subsection had not been enacted on the greater of—

(A) taxable income reduced by the amount of the net capital gain, or

(B) the amount of taxable income taxed at a rate below 28 percent, plus

(2) a tax of 28 percent of the amount of taxable income in excess of the amount determined under paragraph (1).

For purposes of the preceding sentence, the net capital gain for any taxable year shall be reduced (but not below zero) by the amount which the taxpayer elects to take into account as investment income for the taxable year under section 163(d)(4)(B)(iii).

[For explanation, see ¶ 101, ¶ 102 and ¶ 902, for text of Committee Report, see ¶ 3028, and ¶ 3029]

[Footnote Code Sec. 1 continued]

"Over $70,000	$17,964.25, plus 36% of the excess over $70,000."
"Over $5,500	$1,405, plus 36% of the excess over $5,500."

Effective Date (Sec. 13202(c) of P.L. 103-66) effective for tax. yrs. begin. after 12/31/92.

Matter in *italics* in Code Sec. 1(f)(1), (3)(B) and (7) added by sections 13201(b)(3)(A)(i), (ii), and (3)(B) of P.L. 103-66 which struck out:

6. "1990"
7. "1989"

Effective Date (Sec. 13201(c) of P.L. 103-66) effective for tax. yrs. begin. after 12/31/92.

[¶ 2002] **Code Sec. 11. Tax imposed.**

* * * * * * * * * * * * *

(b) Amount of tax.

(1) In general. The amount of the tax imposed by subsection (a) shall be the sum of—

(A) 15 percent of so much of the taxable income as does not exceed $50,000,

(B) 25 percent of so much of the taxable income as exceeds $50,000 but does not exceed $75,000, [1]

[2]*(C) 34 percent of so much of the taxable income as exceeds $75,000 but does not exceed $10,000,000, and*

(D) 35 percent of so much of the taxable income as exceeds $10,000,000.

In the case of a corporation which has taxable income in excess of $100,000 for any taxable year, the amount of tax determined under the preceding sentence for such taxable year shall be increased by the lesser of (i) 5 percent of such excess, or (ii) $11,750. *In the case of a corporation which has taxable income in excess of $15,000,000, the amount of the tax determined under the foregoing provisions of this paragraph shall be increased by an additional amount equal to the lesser of (i) 3 percent of such excess, or (ii) $100,000.*

(2) Certain personal service corporations not eligible for graduated rates. Notwithstanding paragraph (1), the amount of the tax imposed by subsection (a) on the taxable income of a qualified personal service corporation (as defined in section 448(d)(2)) shall be equal to [3]*35 percent* of the taxable income.

* * * * * * * * * * * * *

[For explanation, see ¶ 301, for text of Committee Report, see ¶ 3043]

[¶ 2003] **Code Sec. 25. Interest on certain home mortgages.**

* * * * * * * * * * * * *

[1]***(h)* Regulations; contracts.**

(1) Regulations. The Secretary shall prescribe such regulations as may be necessary to carry out the purposes of this section, including regulations which may require recipients of mortgage credit certificates to pay a reasonable processing fee to defray the expenses incurred in administering the program.

(2) Contracts. The Secretary is authorized to enter into contracts with any person to provide services in connection with the administration of this section.

[2]***(i)* Recapture of portion of federal subsidy from use of mortgage credit certificates.** For provisions increasing the tax imposed by this chapter to recapture a portion of the Federal subsidy from the use of mortgage credit certificates, see section 143(m).

[For explanation, see ¶ 721, for text of Committee Report, see ¶ 3012]

[Footnote Code Sec. 11] Matter in *italics* in Code Sec. 11(b)(1), (b)(1)(B)-(D), (b)(2) added by sections 13221(a)(1)-(3) and (b) of P.L. 103-66 which struck out:

1. "and"
2. "(C) 34 percent of so much of the taxable income as exceeds $75,000."
3. "34 percent"

Effective Date (Sec. 13221(d) of P.L. 103-66) effective for tax. yrs. begin. on or after 1/31/93.

[Footnote Code Sec. 25] Matter in *italics* in Code Sec. 25(h)-(i) added by section 13141(b) of P.L. 103-66 which struck out:

1. "(h) Termination. No election may be made under subsection (c)(2)(A)(ii) for any period after June 30, 1992."
2. "(h)"

Effective Date (Sec. 13141(f)(2) of P.L. 103-66) effective for elections for periods after 6/30/92.

[¶ 2004] Code Sec. 28. Clinical testing expenses for certain drugs for rare diseases or conditions.

* * * * * * * * * * * *

(b) Qualified clinical testing expenses. For purposes of this section—

(1) Qualified clinical testing expenses.

* * * * * * * * * * * *

(D) Special rule. For purposes of this paragraph, section 41 shall be deemed to remain in effect for periods after [1] *June 30, 1995.*

* * * * * * * * * * * *

(e) Termination. This section shall not apply to any amount paid or incurred after [2] *December 31, 1994.*

[For explanation, see ¶ 719, for text of Committee Report, see ¶ 3004]

[¶ 2005] Code Sec. 32. Earned income.

* * * * * * * * * * * *

[1]***(a) Allowance of credit.***

(1) In general. *In the case of an eligible individual, there shall be allowed as a credit against the tax imposed by this subtitle for the taxable year an amount equal to the credit percentage of so much of the taxpayer's earned income for the taxable year as does not exceed the earned income amount.*

[Footnote Code Sec. 28] Matter in *italics* in Code Sec. 28(b)(1)(D) and (e) added by sections 13111(a)(2) and (b) of P.L. 103-66 which struck out:

1. "June 30, 1992"
2. "June 30, 1992"

Effective Date (Sec. 13111(c) of P.L. 103-66) effective for tax. yrs. end. after 6/30/92.

[Footnote Code Sec. 32] Matter in *italics* in Code Sec. 32(a), (b), (c)(1)(A), (c)(3)(D)(ii) and (iii), and (i)(1) and (2) added by sections 13131(a), (b), (c)(1), (c)(2) and (d)(1)(A)-(C) of P.L. 103-66, which struck out:

1. "(a) Allowance of credit.

In the case of an eligible individual, there shall be allowed as a credit against the tax imposed by this subtitle for the taxable year an amount equal to the sum of—

"(1) the basic earned income credit, and

"(2) the health insurance credit.

"(b) Computation of credit.

For purposes of this section—

"(1) Basic earned income credit.

"(A) In general. The term 'basic earned income credit' means an amount equal to the credit percentage of so much of the taxpayer's earned income for the taxable year as does not exceed $5,714.

"(B) Limitation. The amount of the basic earned income credit allowable to a taxpayer for any taxable year shall not exceed the excess (if any) of—

"(i) the credit percentage of $5,714, over

"(ii) the phaseout percentage of so much of the adjusted gross income (or, if greater the earned income) of the taxpayer for the taxable year as exceeds $9,000.

"(C) Percentages. For purposes of this paragraph—

"(i) In general. Except as provided in clause (ii), the percentages shall be determined as follows:

In the case of an eligible individual with:	The credit percentage is:	The phaseout percentage is:
1 qualifying child	23	16.43
2 or more qualifying children	25	17.86

"(ii) Transition percentages.

"(I) For taxable years beginning in 1991, the percentages are:

*(2) **Limitation.** The amount of the credit allowable to a taxpayer under paragraph (1) for any taxable year shall not exceed the excess (if any) of—*

(A) the credit percentage of the earned income amount, over

(B) the phaseout percentage of so much of the adjusted gross income (or, if greater, the earned income) of the taxpayer for the taxable year as exceeds the phaseout amount.

*(b) **Percentages and amounts.** For purposes of subsection (a)—*

*(1) **Percentages.** The credit percentage and the phaseout percentage shall be determined as follows:*

(A) In general. In the case of taxable year beginning after 1995:

In the case of an eligible individual with:	The credit percentage is:	The phaseout percentage is:
1 qualifying child	34	15.98
2 or more qualifying children	40	21.06
No qualifying children	7.65	7.65

(B) Transitional percentages for 1995. In the case of taxable years beginning in 1995:

[Footnote Code Sec. 32 continued]

In the case of an eligible individual with:	The credit percentage is:	The phaseout percentage is:
1 qualifying child	16.7	11.93
2 or more qualifying children	17.3	12.36

"(II) For taxable years beginning in 1992, the percentages are:

In the case of an eligible individual with:	The credit percentage is:	The phaseout percentage is:
1 qualifying child	17.6	12.57
2 or more qualifying children	18.4	13.14

"(III) For taxable years beginning in 1993, the percentages are:

In the case of an eligible individual with:	The credit percentage is:	The phaseout percentage is:
1 qualifying child	18.5	13.21
2 or more qualifying children	19.5	13.93

"(D) Supplemental young child credit. In the case of a taxpayer with a qualifying child who has not attained age 1 as of the close of the calendar year in which or with which the taxable year of the taxpayer ends—

"(i) the credit percentage shall be increased by 5 percentage points, and

"(ii) the phaseout percentage shall be increased by 3.57 percentage points.

If the taxpayer elects to take a child into account under this subparagraph, such child shall not be treated as a qualifying individual under section 21.

"(2) Health insurance credit.

"(A) In general. The term 'health insurance credit' means an amount determined in the same manner as the basic earned income credit except that—

"(i) the credit percentage shall be equal to 6 percent, and

"(ii) the phaseout percentage shall be equal to 4.285 percent.

"(B) Limitation based on health insurance costs. The amount of the health insurance credit determined under subparagraph (A) for any taxable year shall not exceed the amounts paid by the taxpayer during the taxable year for insurance coverage—

"(i) which constitutes medical care (within the meaning of section 213(d)(1)(C)), and

"(ii) which includes at least 1 qualifying child.

For purposes of this subparagraph, the rules of section 213(d)(6) shall apply.

"(C) Subsidized expenses. A taxpayer may not take into account under subparagraph (B) any amount to the extent that—

"(i) such amount is paid, reimbursed, or subsidized by the Federal Government, a State or local government, or any agency or instrumentality thereof; and

"(ii) the payment, reimbursement, or subsidy of such amount is not includible in the gross income of the recipient."

In the case of an eligible individual with:	The credit percentage is:	The phaseout percentage is:
1 qualifying child	34	15.98
2 or more qualifying children	36	20.22
No qualifying children	7.65	7.65

(C) Transitional percentages for 1994. In the case of a taxable year beginning in 1994:

In the case of an eligible individual with:	The credit percentage is:	The phaseout percentage is:
1 qualifying child	26.3	15.98
2 or more qualifying children	30	17.68
No qualifying children	7.65	7.65

(2) Amounts. *The earned income amount and the phaseout amount shall be determined as follows:*

(A) In general. In the case of taxable years beginning after 1994:

In the case of an eligible individual with:	The earned income amount is:	The phaseout percentage is:
1 qualifying child	$6,000	$11,000
2 or more qualifying children	$8,425	$11,000
No qualifying children	$4,000	$ 5,000

(B) Transitional amounts. In the case of a taxable year beginning in 1994:

In the case of an eligible individual with:	The earned income amount is:	The phaseout amount is:
1 qualifying child	$7,750	$11,000
2 or more qualifying children	$8,425	$11,000
No qualifying children	$4,000	$ 5,000

(c) Definitions and special rules. For purposes of this section—

(1) Eligible individual.

* * * * * * * * * * * * *

[2]*(A) In general. The term "eligible individual' means—*

(i) any individual who has a qualifying child for the taxable year, or

(ii) any other individual who does not have a qualifying child for the taxable year, if—

(I) such individual's principal place of abode is in the United States for more than one-half of such taxable year,

(II) such individual (or, if the individual is married, either the individual or the individual's spouse) has attained age 25 but not attained age 65 before the close of the taxable year, and

(III) such individual is not a dependent for whom a deduction is allowable under section 151 to another taxpayer for any taxable year beginning in the same calendar year as such taxable year.

For purposes of the preceding sentence, marital status shall be determined under section 7703.

* * * * * * * * * * * * *

(3) Qualifying child.

* * * * * * * * * * * * *

[Footnote Code Sec. 32 continued]

2. "(A) In general. The term 'eligible individual' means any individual who has a qualifying child for the taxable year."

[3]*(ii)* Other methods. The Secretary may prescribe other methods for providing the information described in [4] *clause (i).* [5]

* * * * * * * * * * * * *

(i) Inflation adjustments.

[6]***(1) In general.*** *In the case of any taxable year beginning after 1994, each dollar amount contained in subsection (b)(2)(A) shall be increased by an amount equal to—*

(A) such dollar amount, multiplied by

(B) the cost-of-living adjustment determined under section 1(f)(3), for the calendar year in which the taxable year begins, by substituting "calendar year 1993" for "calendar year 1992."

[7]***(2)* Rounding.** If any dollar amount after being increased under paragraph (1) is not a multiple of $10, such dollar amount shall be rounded to the nearest multiple of $10 (or, if such dollar amount is a multiple of $5, such dollar amount shall be increased to the next higher multiple of $10).

* * * * * * * * * * * * *

[For text of Committee Reports, see ¶ 3011]

[¶ 2006] Code Sec. 38. General business credit.

* * * * * * * * * * * * *

(b) Current year business credit. For purposes of this subpart, the amount of the current year business credit is the sum of the following credits determined for the taxable year:

(1) the investment credit determined under section 46,

(2) the targeted jobs credit determined under section 51(a),

(3) the alcohol fuels credit determined under section 40(a),

(4) the research credit determined under section 41(a),

(5) the low-income housing credit determined under section 42(a),

(6) the enhanced oil recovery credit under section 43(a),

(7) in the case of an eligible small business (as defined in section 44(b)), the disabled access credit determined under section 44(a), [1]

(8) the renewable electricity production credit under section 45(a),[2]

[Footnote Code Sec. 32 continued]

3. "(ii) Insurance policy number. In the case of any taxpayer with respect to which the health insurance credit is allowed under subsection (a)(2), the Secretary may require a taxpayer to include an insurance policy number or other adequate evidence of insurance in addition to any information required to be included in clause (i)."

4. "clause "(i), (ii) or (iii)"

5. "(c)(3)(D)(iii)"

6. "(1) In general. In the case of any taxable year beginning after the applicable calendar year, each dollar amount referred to in paragraph (2)(B) shall be increased by an amount equal to—

"(A) such dollar amount, multiplied by

"(B) the cost-of-living adjustment determined under section 1(f)(3), for the calendar year in which the taxable year begins, by substituting 'calendar year 1984' for 'calendar year 1989' in subparagraph (B) thereof.

"(2) Definitions, etc. For purposes of paragraph (1)—

"(A) Applicable calendar year. The term 'applicable calendar year' means—

"(i) 1986 in the case of the dollar amounts referred to in clause (i) of subparagraph (B), and

"(ii) 1987 in the case of the dollar amount referred to in clause (ii) of subparagraph (B).

"(B) Dollar amounts. The dollar amounts referred to in this subparagraph are—

"(i) the $5,714 dollar amounts contained in subsection (b)(1), and

"(ii) the $9,000 amount contained in subsection (b)(1)(B)(ii)."

7. "(i)(3)"

Effective Date (Sec. 13131(e), P.L. 103-66) effective for tax. yrs. begin. after 12/31/93.

[Footnote Code Sec. 38] In Code Sec. 38(b)(7), section 13302(a)(1) of P.L. 103-66, struck out:

1. "plus"

Effective Date (Sec. 13303, P.L. 103-66) effective 8/10/93.

In Code Sec. 38(b)(8), section 13322(a) of P.L. 103-66 struck out:

2. "plus" [sic and]

which was added by section 13302(a)(1) of P.L. 103-66 (see above for effective date).

(9) the empowerment zone employment credit determined under section 1396(a), [3]

(10) the Indian employment credit as determined under section 45A [4]*, plus*

(11) the employer social security credit determined under section 45B(a).

(c) Limitation based on amount of tax.

* * * * * * * * * * * *

(2) Empowerment zone credit may offset 25 percent of minimum tax.

(A) In general. In the case of the empowerment zone employment credit credit—

(i) this section and section 39 shall be applied separately with respect to such credit, and

(ii) for purposes of applying paragraph (1) to such credit—

(I) 75 percent of the tentative minimum tax shall be substituted for the tentative minimum tax under subparagraph (A) thereof, and

(II) the limitation under paragraph (1) (as modified by subclause (I)) shall be reduced by the credit allowed under subsection (a) for the taxable year (other than the empowerment zone credit).

(B) Empowerment zone employment credit. For purposes of this paragraph, the term "empowerment zone employment credit" means the portion of the credit under subsection (a) which is attributable to the credit determined under section 1396 (relating to empowerment zone employment credit).

[5]*(3)* Special rules.

(A) Married individuals. In the case of a husband or wife who files a separate return, the amount specified under subparagraph (B) of paragraph (1) shall be $12,500 in lieu of $25,000. This subparagraph shall not apply if the spouse of the taxpayer has no business credit carryforward or carryback to, and has no current year business credit for, the taxable year of such spouse which ends within or with the taxpayer's taxable year.

(B) Controlled groups. In the case of a controlled group, the $25,000 amount specified under subparagraph (B) of paragraph (1) shall be reduced for each component member of such group by apportioning $25,000 among the component members of such group in such manner as the Secretary shall by regulations prescribe. For purposes of the preceding sentence, the term "controlled group" has the meaning given to such term by section 1563(a).

(C) Limitations with respect to certain persons. In the case of a person described in subparagraph (A) or (B) of section 46(e)(1) (as in effect on the day before the date of the enactment of the Revenue Reconciliation Act of 1990), the $25,000 amount specified under subparagraph (B) of paragraph (1) shall equal such person's ratable share (as determined under section 46(e)(2) (as so in effect)) of such amount.

(D) Estates and trusts. In the case of an estate or trust, the $25,000 amount specified under subparagraph (B) of paragraph (1) shall be reduced to an amount which bears the same ratio to $25,000 as the portion of the income of the estate or trust which is not allocated to beneficiaries bears to the total income of the estate or trust.

* * * * * * * * * * * *

[For explanation, see ¶ 315, ¶ 604,¶ 605 and ¶ 609, for Committee Report, see ¶ 3070]

[Footnote Code Sec. 38 continued]

Effective Date (Sec. 13322(f), P.L. 103-66) effective for wages paid or incurred after 12/31/93.

Matter in *italics* in Code Sec. 38(b)(9)-(11) added by section 13443(b)(1), P.L. 103-66, which struck out:

3. "plus"

which was added by section 13322(a) of P.L. 103-66 (see above for effective date).

4. "."

Effective Date (Sec. 13443(d), P.L. 103-66) effective for taxes paid after 12/31/93.

Matter in *italics* in Code Sec. 38(c)(2) and (c)(3) added by section 13302(c)(1), P.L. 103-66, which struck out:

2. "(2)"

Effective Date (Sec. 13303, P.L. 103-66) effective 8/10/93.

[¶ 2007] **Code Sec. 39. Carryback and carryforward of unused credits.**

* * * * * * * * * * * * *

(d) Transitional rules.

* * * * * * * * * * * * *

(4) Empowerment zone employment credit. *No portion of the unused business credit which is attributable to the credit determined under section 1396 (relating to empowerment zone employment credit) may be carried to any taxable year ending before January 1, 1994.*

* * * * * * * * * * * * *

(5) No carryback of section 45 credit before enactment. *No portion of the unused business credit for any taxable year which is attributable to the Indian employment credit determined under section 45A may be carried to a taxable year ending before the date of the enactment of section 45A.*

* * * * * * * * * * * * *

(6) No carryback of section 45 credit before enactment.
No portion of the unused business credit for any taxable year which is attributable to the employer social security credit determined under section 45B may be carried back to a taxable year ending before the date of the enactment of section 45B.
[For explanation, see ¶ 315, ¶ 604 and ¶ 609]

[¶ 2008] **Code Sec. 41. Credit for increasing research activities.**

* * * * * * * * * * * * *

(c) Base amount.

* * * * * * * * * * * * *

(3) Fixed-base percentage.

* * * * * * * * * * * * *

(B) Start-up companies.

* * * * * * * * * * * * *

[1]*(ii) Fixed-base percentage. In a case to which this subparagraph applies, the fixed-base percentage is—*

(I) 3 percent for each of the taxpayer's 1st 5 taxable years beginning after December 31, 1993, for which the taxpayer has qualified research expenses,

(II) in the case of the taxpayer's 6th such taxable year, ⅙ of the percentage which the aggregate qualified research expenses of the taxpayer for the 4th and 5th such taxable years is of the aggregate gross receipts of the taxpayer for such years,

(III) in the case of the taxpayer's 7th such taxable year, ⅓ of the percentage which the aggregate qualified research expenses of the taxpayer for the 5th and 6th such taxable years is of the aggregate gross receipts of the taxpayer for such years,

---

[Footnote Code Sec. 39] Matter in *italics* in Code Sec. 39(d)(4) added by section 13302(a)(2) of P.L. 103-66.
Effective Date (Sec. 13303 of P.L. 103-66) effective 8/10/93.
Matter in *italics* in Code Sec. 39(d)(5) added by section 13322(d) of P.L. 103-66.
Effective Date (Sec. 13322(f) of P.L. 103-66) effective for wages paid or incurred after 12/31/93.
Matter in *italics* in Code Sec. 39(d)(6) added by section 13443(b)(2) of P.L. 103-66.
Effective Date (Sec. 13443(d) of P.L. 103-66) effective for taxes paid or incurred after 12/31/93.
[Footnote Code Sec. 41] Matter in *italics* in Code Sec. 41(c)(3)(B)(ii), (3)(B)(iii), and (3)(D) added by section 13112(a), P.L. 103-66, which struck out:
1. "(ii) Fixed-base percentage. In a case to which this subparagraph applies, the fixed-base percentage is 3 percent."

(IV) in the case of the taxpayer's 8th such taxable year, ½ of the percentage which the aggregate qualified research expenses of the taxpayer for the 5th, 6th, and 7th such taxable years is of the aggregate gross receipts of the taxpayer for such years,

(V) in the case of the taxpayer's 9th such taxable year, ⅔ of the percentage which the aggregate qualified research expenses of the taxpayer for the 5th, 6th, 7th, and 8th such taxable years is of the aggregate gross receipts of the taxpayer for such years,

(VI) in the case of the taxpayer's 10th such taxable year, ⅚ of the percentage which the aggregate qualified research expenses of the taxpayer for the 5th, 6th, 7th, 8th, and 9th such taxable years is of the aggregate gross receipts of the taxpayer for such years, and

(VII) for taxable years thereafter, the percentage which the aggregate qualified research expenses for any 5 taxable years selected by the taxpayer from among the 5th through the 10th such taxable years is of the aggregate gross receipts of the taxpayer for such selected years.

(iii) Treatment of de minimis amounts of gross receipts and qualified research expenses. The Secretary may prescribe regulations providing that de minimis amounts of gross receipts and qualified research expenses shall be disregarded under [2]*clauses (i) and (ii).*

* * * * * * * * * * * * *

(D) Rounding. The percentages determined under [3] *subparagraphs (A) and (B)(ii)* shall be rounded to the nearest 1/100th of 1 percent.

* * * * * * * * * * * * *

(e) Credit allowable with respect to certain payments to qualified organizations for basic research. For purposes of this section—

* * * * * * * * * * * * *

(5) Maintenance-of-effort amount. For purposes of this subsection—

* * * * * * * * * * * * *

(C) Cost-of-living adjustment defined.

(i) In general. The cost-of-living adjustment for any calendar year is the cost-of-living adjustment for such calendar year determined under section 1(f)(3), by substituting "calendar year 1987" for "calendar year [4]*1992* " in subparagraph (B) thereof.

(ii) Special rule where base period ends in a calendar year other than 1983 or 1984. If the base period of any taxpayer does not end in 1983 or 1984, section 1(f)(3)(B) shall, for purposes of this paragraph, be applied by substituting the calendar year in which such base period ends for [4]*1992.* Such substitution shall be in lieu of the substitution under clause (i).

* * * * * * * * * * * * *

(h) Termination.

(1) In general. This section shall not apply to any amount paid or incurred after [5]*June 30, 1995.*

(2) Computation of base amount. In the case of any taxable year which begins before [6]*July 1, 1995,* and ends after [5] *June 30, 1995.* the base amount with respect to such taxable year shall be the amount which bears the same ratio to the base amount for such year (deter-

[Footnote Code Sec. 41 continued]

2. "clause (i)"
3. "subparagraph (A)"

Effective Date (Sec. 13112(c), P.L. 103-66) effective for tax. yrs. begin. after 12/31/93.

Matter in *italics* in Code Sec. 41(e)(5)(C) added by section 13201(b)(3)(C), P.L. 103-66, which struck out:

4. "1989"

Effective Date (Sec. 13201(c), P.L. 103-66) effective for tax. yrs. begin. after 12/31/92.

Matter in *italics* in Code Sec. 41(h) added by sections 13111(a)(1)(A) and (B), P.L. 103-66, which struck out:

5. "June 30, 1992"
6. "July 1, 1992"

Effective Date (Sec. 13111(c), P.L. 103-66) effective for tax. yrs. end. after 6/30/92.

mined without regard to this paragraph) as the number of days in such taxable year before [6] *July 1, 1995,* bears to the total number of days in such taxable year.
[For explanation, see ¶ 715 and ¶ 716, for text of Committee Report, see ¶ 3003]

[¶ 2009] **Code Sec. 42. Low-income housing credit.**

* * * * * * * * * * * * *

(g) Qualified low-income housing project. For purposes of this section—

* * * * * * * * * * * * *

(8) Waiver of certain de minimis errors and recertifications. *On application by the taxpayer, the Secretary may waive—*

(A) any recapture under subsection (j) in the case of any de minimis error in complying with paragraph (1), or

(B) any annual recertification of tenant income for purposes of this subsection, if the entire building is occupied by low-income tenants.

(h) Limitation on aggregate credit allowable with respect to projects located in a state.

* * * * * * * * * * * * *

(6) Buildings eligible for credit only if minimum long-term commitment to low-income housing.

* * * * * * * * * * * * *

(B) Extended low-income housing commitment. For purposes of this paragraph, the term "extended low-income housing commitment" means any agreement between the taxpayer and the housing credit agency—

(i) which requires that the applicable fraction (as defined in subsection (c)(1)) for the building for each taxable year in the extended use period will not be less than the applicable fraction specified in such agreement and which prohibits the actions described in subclauses (I) and (II) of subparagraph (E)(ii),

(ii) which allows individuals who meet the income limitation applicable to the building under subsection (g) (whether prospective, present, or former occupants of the building) the right to enforce in any State court the requirement and prohibitions of clause (i),

(iii) which prohibits the disposition to any person of any portion of the building to which such agreement applies unless all of the building to which such agreement applies is disposed of to such person,

(iv) which prohibits the refusal to lease to a holder of a voucher or certificate of eligibility under section 8 of the United States Housing Act of 1937 because of the status of the prospective tenant as such a holder,

[1]*(v)* which is binding on all successors of the taxpayer, and

[2]*(vi)* which, with respect to the property, is recorded pursuant to State law as a restrictive covenant.

* * * * * * * * * * * * *

(i) Definitions and special rules. For purposes of this section—

* * * * * * * * * * * * *

(2) Determination of whether building is federally subsidized.

* * * * * * * * * * * * *

(E) Buildings receiving home assistance.

[Footnote Code Sec. 42] Matter in *italics* in Code Sec. 42(h)(6)(B)(iv)-(vi) added by section 13142(b)(4), P.L. 103-66, which struck out:
1. "(iv)"
2. "(v)"
Effective Date (Sec. 13142(b)(6)(B), P.L. 103-66) effective 8/10/93.

(i) In general. Assistance provided under the HOME Investment Partnerships Act (as in effect on the date of the enactment of this subparagraph) with respect to any building shall not be taken into account under subparagraph (D) if 40 percent or more of the residential units in the building are occupied by individuals whose income is 50 percent or less of area median gross income. Subsection (d)(5)(C) shall not apply to any building to which the preceding sentence applies.

(ii) Special rule for certain high-cost housing areas. In the case of a building located in a city described in section 142(d)(6), clause (i) shall be applied by substituting "25 percent" for "40 percent".

(3) Low-income unit.

* * * * * * * * * * * * *

[3]*(D) Certain students not to disqualify unit. A unit shall not fail to be treated as a low-income unit merely because it is occupied—*

(i) by an individual who is—

(I) a student and receiving assistance under title IV of the Social Security Act, or

(II) enrolled in a job training program receiving assistance under the Job Training Partnership Act or under other similar Federal, State, or local laws, or

(ii) entirely by full-time students if such students are—

(I) single parents and their children and such parents and children are not dependents (as defined in section 152) of another individual, or

(II) married and file a joint return.

(m) Responsibilities of housing credit agencies.

* * * * * * * * * * * * *

(2) Credit allocated to building not to exceed amount necessary to assure project feasibility.

* * * * * * * * * * * * *

(B) Agency evaluation. In making the determination under subparagraph (A), the housing credit agency shall consider—

(i) the sources and uses of funds and the total financing planned for the project,

(ii) any proceeds or receipts expected to be generated by reason of tax benefits, [4]

[4](iii) the percentage of the housing credit dollar amount used for project costs other than the cost of intermediaries [5], *and*

(iv) the reasonableness of the developmental and operational costs of the project.

[Footnote Code Sec. 42 continued]

Matter in *italics* in Code Sec. 42(i)(3)(D) added by section 13142(b)(2), P.L. 103-66, which struck out:

3. "(D) Certain students not to disqualify unit. A unit shall not fail to be treated as a low-income unit merely because it is occupied by an individual who is—

"(i) a student and receiving assistance under title IV of the Social Security Act, or

"(ii) enrolled in a job training program receiving assistance under the Job Training Partnership Act or under other similar Federal, State, or local laws."

Effective Date (Sec. 13142(b)(6)(C), P.L. 103-66) effective for periods after 8/10/93.

Matter in *italics* in Code Sec. 42(i)(2)(E), and (m)(2)(B)(ii)-(iv) added by sections 13142(b)(1)(A)-(C), and (b)(5), P.L. 103-66, which struck out:

4. "and"

5. "."

Effective Date (Sec. 13142(b)(6)(A), P.L. 103-66) effective as provided in Sec. 13142(b)(6)(A) of this Act, which read as follows:

"(A) In general. —Except as provided in subparagraphs (B) and (C), the amendments made by this subsection shall apply to—

"(i) determinations under section 42 of the Internal Revenue Code of 1986 with respect to housing credit dollar amounts allocated from State housing credit ceilings after June 30, 1992, or

"(ii) buildings placed in service after June 30, 1992, to the extent paragraph (1) of section 42(h) of such Code does not apply to any building by reason of paragraph (4) thereof, but only with respect to bonds issued after such date.

"(B) Waiver authority and prohibited discrimination. —The amendments made by paragraphs (3) and (4) shall take effect on the date of the enactment of this Act.

"(C) Home assistance. The amendment made by paragraph (2) shall apply to periods after the date of the enactment of this Act."

Clause (iii) shall not be applied so as to impede the development of projects in hard-to-develop areas. Such a determination shall not be construed to be a representation or warranty as to the feasibility or viability of the project.

* * * * * * * * * * * *

[6]**(o) Repealed.**

[For explanation, see ¶ 705, ¶ 706, ¶ 707, ¶ 708, ¶ 709, ¶ 710 and ¶ 711]

[¶ 2010] Code Sec. 45A. Indian employment credit.

(a) Amount of credit. For purposes of section 38, the amount of the Indian employment credit determined under this section with respect to any employer for any taxable year is an amount equal to 20 percent of the excess (if any) of—

(1) the sum of—

(A) the qualified wages paid or incurred during such taxable year, plus

(B) qualified employee health insurance costs paid or incurred during such taxable year, over

(2) the sum of the qualified wages and qualified employee health insurance costs (determined as if this section were in effect) which were paid or incurred by the employer (or any predecessor) during calendar year 1993.

(b) Qualified wages; qualified employee health insurance costs. For purposes of this section—

(1) Qualified wages.

(A) In general. The term "qualified wages" means any wages paid or incurred by an employer for services performed by an employee while such employee is a qualified employee.

(B) Coordination with targeted jobs credit. The term "qualified wages" shall not include wages attributable to service rendered during the 1-year period beginning with the day the individual begins work for the employer if any portion of such wages is taken into account in determining the credit under section 51.

(2) Qualified employee health insurance costs.

(A) In general. The term "qualified employee health insurance costs" means any amount paid or incurred by an employer for health insurance to the extent such amount is attributable to coverage provided to any employee while such employee is a qualified employee.

(B) Exception for amounts paid under salary reduction arrangements. No amount paid or incurred for health insurance pursuant to a salary reduction arrangement shall be taken into account under subparagraph (A).

(3) Limitation. The aggregate amount of qualified wages and qualified employee health insurance costs taken into account with respect to any employee for any taxable year (and for the base period under subsection (a)(2)) shall not exceed $20,000.

[Footnote Code Sec. 42 continued]

Code Sec. 42(o) repealed by section 13142(a)(1), P.L. 103-66, which struck out:

6. "(o) Termination.

"(1) **In general.** Except as provided in paragraph (2)—

"(A) clause (i) of subsection (h)(3)(C) shall not apply to any amount allocated after June 30, 1992, and

"(B) subsection (h)(4) shall not apply to any building placed in service after June 30, 1992.

"(2) **Exception for bond-financed buildings in progress.** For purposes of paragraph (1)(B), a building shall be treated as placed in service before July 1, 1992 if—

"(A) the bonds with respect to such building are issued before July 1, 1992,

"(B) the taxpayer's basis in the project (of which the building is a part) as of June 30, 1992, is more than 10 percent of the taxpayer's reasonably expected basis in such project as of June 30, 1994, and

"(C) such building is placed in service before July 1, 1994."

Effective Date (Sec. 13142(a)(2), P.L. 103-66) effective for for periods end. after 6/30/92.

[Footnote Code Sec. 45A] Code Sec. 45A was added by section 13322(b) of P.L. 103-66.

Effective Date (Sec. 13322(f) of P.L. 103-66) effective for wages paid or incurred after 12/31/93.

(c) **Qualified employee.** For purposes of this section—

(1) **In general.** Except as otherwise provided in this subsection, the term "qualified employee" means, with respect to any period, any employee of an employer if—

(A) the employee is an enrolled member of an Indian tribe or the spouse of an enrolled member of an Indian tribe,

(B) substantially all of the services performed during such period by such employee for such employer are performed within an Indian reservation, and

(C) the principal place of abode of such employee while performing such services is on or near the reservation in which the services are performed.

(2) **Individuals receiving wages in excess of $30,000 not eligible.** An employee shall not be treated as a qualified employee for any taxable year of the employer if the total amount of the wages paid or incurred by such employer to such employee during such taxable year (whether or not for services within an Indian reservation) exceeds the amount determined at an annual rate of $30,000.

(3) **Inflation adjustment.** The Secretary shall adjust the $30,000 amount under paragraph (2) for years beginning after 1994 at the same time and in the same manner as under section 415(d).

(4) **Employment must be trade or business employment.** An employee shall be treated as a qualified employee for any taxable year of the employer only if more than 50 percent of the wages paid or incurred by the employer to such employee during such taxable year are for services performed in a trade or business of the employer. Any determination as to whether the preceding sentence applies with respect to any employee for any taxable year shall be made without regard to subsection (e)(2).

(5) **Certain employees not eligible.** The term "qualified employee" shall not include—

(A) any individual described in subparagraph (A), (B), or (C) of section 51(i)(1),

(B) any 5-percent owner (as defined in section 416(i)(1)(B)), and

(C) any individual if the services performed by such individual for the employer involve the conduct of class I, II, or III gaming as defined in section 4 of the Indian Gaming Regulatory Act (25 U.S.C. 2703), or are performed in a building housing such gaming activity.

(6) **Indian tribe defined.** The term "Indian tribe" means any Indian tribe, band, nation, pueblo, or other organized group or community, including any Alaska Native village or regional or village corporation, as defined in, or established pursuant to, the Alaska Native Claims Settlement Act (43 U.S.C. 1601 et seq.) which is recognized as eligible for the special programs and services provided by the United States to Indians because of their status as Indians.

(7) **Indian reservation defined.** The term "Indian reservation" has the meaning given such term by section 168(j)(6).

(d) **Early termination of employment by employer.**

(1) **In general.** If the employment of any employee is terminated by the taxpayer before the day 1 year after the day on which such employee began work for the employer—

(A) no wages (or qualified employee health insurance costs) with respect to such employee shall be taken into account under subsection (a) for the taxable year in which such employment is terminated, and

(B) the tax under this chapter for the taxable year in which such employment is terminated shall be increased by the aggregate credits (if any) allowed under section 38(a) for prior taxable years by reason of wages (or qualified employee health insurance costs) taken into account with respect to such employee.

(2) **Carrybacks and carryovers adjusted.** In the case of any termination of employment to which paragraph (1) applies, the carrybacks and carryovers under section 39 shall be properly adjusted.

(3) **Subsection not to apply in certain cases.**

(A) In general. Paragraph (1) shall not apply to—

(i) a termination of employment of an employee who voluntarily leaves the employment of the taxpayer,

(ii) a termination of employment of an individual who before the close of the period referred to in paragraph (1) becomes disabled to perform the services of such employment unless such disability is removed before the close of such period and the taxpayer fails to offer reemployment to such individual, or

(iii) a termination of employment of an individual if it is determined under the applicable State unemployment compensation law that the termination was due to the misconduct of such individual.

(B) Changes in form of business. For purposes of paragraph (1), the employment relationship between the taxpayer and an employee shall not be treated as terminated—

(i) by a transaction to which section 381(a) applies if the employee continues to be employed by the acquiring corporation, or

(ii) by reason of a mere change in the form of conducting the trade or business of the taxpayer if the employee continues to be employed in such trade or business and the taxpayer retains a substantial interest in such trade or business.

(4) Special rule. Any increase in a tax under paragraph (1) shall not be treated as a tax imposed by this chapter for purposes of—

(A) determining the amount of any credit allowable under this chapter, and

(B) determining the amount of the tax imposed by section 55.

(e) Other definitions and special rules. For purposes of this section—

(1) Wages. The term "wages" has the same meaning given to such term in section 51.

(2) Controlled groups.

(A) All employers treated as a single employer under section (a) or (b) of section 52 shall be treated as a single employer for purposes of this section.

(B) The credit (if any) determined under this section with respect to each such employer shall be its proportionate share of the wages and qualified employee health insurance costs giving rise to such credit.

(3) Certain other rules made applicable. Rules similar to the rules of section 51(k) and subsections (c), (d), and (e) of section 52 shall apply.

(4) Coordination with nonrevenue laws. Any reference in this section to a provision not contained in this title shall be treated for purposes of this section as a reference to such provision as in effect on the date of the enactment of this paragraph.

(5) Special rule for short taxable years. For any taxable year having less than 12 months, the amount determined under subsection (a)(2) shall be multiplied by a fraction, the numerator of which is the number of days in the taxable year and the denominator of which is 365.

(f) Termination. This section shall not apply to taxable years beginning after December 31, 2003.

[For explanation, see ¶ 607 and ¶ 609, for text of Committee Report, see ¶ 3071A]

[¶ 2011] Code Sec. 45B. Credit for portion of employer social security taxes paid with respect to employee cash tips.

(a) General rule. For purposes of section 38, the employer social security credit determined under this section for the taxable year is an amount equal to the excess employer social security tax paid or incurred by the taxpayer during the taxable year.

(b) Excess employer social security tax. For purposes of this section—

(1) In general. The term "excess employer social security tax" means any tax paid by an employer under section 3111 with respect to tips received by an employee during any month, to the extent such tips—

(A) are deemed to have been paid by the employer to the employee pursuant to section 3121(q), and

---

[Footnote Code Sec. 45B] Code Sec. 45B was added by section 13443(a) of P.L. 103-66.
Effective Date (Sec. 13443(d) of P.L. 103-66) effective for taxes paid after 12/31/93.

(B) exceed the amount by which the wages (excluding tips) paid by the employer to the employee during such month are less than the total amount which would be payable (with respect to such employment) at the minimum wage rate applicable to such individual under section 6(a)(1) of the Fair Labor Standards Act of 1938 (determined without regard to section 3(m) of such Act).

(2) Only tips received at food and beverage establishments taken into account. In applying paragraph (1), there shall be taken into account only tips received from customers in connection with the provision of food or beverages for consumption on the premises of an establishment with respect to which the tipping of employees serving food or beverages by customers is customary.

(c) Denial of double benefit. No deduction shall be allowed under this chapter for any amount taken into account in determining the credit under this section.

(d) Election not to claim credit. This section shall not apply to a taxpayer for any taxable year if such taxpayer elects to have this section not apply for such taxable year.
[For explanation, see

[¶ 2012] **Code Sec. 51. Amount of credit.**

* * * * * * * * * * * * *

(c) Wages defined. For purposes of this subpart—

* * * * * * * * * * * * *

(4) Termination. The term "wages" shall not include any amount paid or incurred to an individual who begins work for the employer after [1]*December 31, 1994.*

* * * * * * * * * * * * *

(i) Certain individuals ineligible.

(1) Related individuals. No wages shall be taken into account under subsection (a) with respect to an individual who—

(A) bears any of the relationships described in paragraphs (1) through (8) of section 152(a) to the taxpayer, or, if the taxpayer is a corporation, to an individual who owns, directly or indirectly, more than 50 percent in value of the outstanding stock of the corporation , *or, if the taxpayer is an entity other than a corporation, to any individual who owns, directly or indirectly, more than 50 percent of the capital and profits interests in the entity* (determined with the application of section 267(c)),

(B) if the taxpayer is an estate or trust, is a grantor, beneficiary, or fiduciary of the estate or trust, or is an individual who bears any of the relationships described in paragraphs (1) through (8) of section 152(a) to a grantor, beneficiary, or fiduciary of the estate or trust, or

(C) is a dependent (described in section 152(a)(9)) of the taxpayer, or, if the taxpayer is a corporation, of an individual described in subparagraph (A), or, if the taxpayer is an estate or trust, of a grantor, beneficiary, or fiduciary of the estate or trust.
[For explanation, see ¶ 717, ¶ 718, for text of Committee Report, see ¶ 3002]

[Footnote Code Sec. 51] Matter in *italics* in Code Sec. 51(c)(4) added by section 13102(a) of P.L. 103-66 which struck out:
1. "June 30, 1992"
Effective Date (Sec. 13102(b) of P.L. 103-66) effective for individuals who begin work for the employer after 6/30/92.
Matter in *italics* in Code Sec. 51(i)(1)(A) added by section 13302(d) of P.L. 103-66.
Effective Date (Sec. 13303 of P.L. 103-66) effective 8/10/93.

[¶ 2013] Code Sec. 53. Credit for prior year minimum tax liability.

* * * * * * * * * * * *

(d) Definitions. For purposes of this section—

(1) Net minimum tax.

(A) In general. The term "net minimum tax" means the tax imposed by section 55.

(B) Credit not allowed for exclusion preferences.

* * * * * * * * * * * *

(ii) Specified items. The following are specified in this clause—

(I) the adjustments provided for in subsection (b)(1) of section 56, and

(II) the items of tax preference described in paragraphs (1), [1]*(5) and (7)* of section 57(a).

* * * * * * * * * * * *

[For explanation, see ¶ 703]

[¶ 2014] Code Sec. 55. Alternative minimum tax imposed.

* * * * * * * * * * * *

(b) Tentative minimum tax. For purposes of this part—

[1]***(1) Amount of tentative tax.***

(A) Noncorporate taxpayers.

(i) In general. In the case of a taxpayer other than a corporation, the tentative minimum tax for the taxable year is the sum of—

(I) 26 percent of so much of the taxable excess as does not exceed $175,000, plus

(II) 28 percent of so much of the taxable excess as exceeds $175,000.

The amount determined under the preceding sentence shall be reduced by the alternative minimum tax foreign tax credit for the taxable year.

(ii) Taxable excess. For purposes of clause (i), the term "taxable excess" means so much of the alternative minimum taxable income for the taxable year as exceeds the exemption amount.

(iii) Married individual filing separate return. In the case of a married individual filing a separate return, clause (i) shall be applied by substituting "$87,500" for "$175,000" each place it appears. For purposes of the preceding sentence, marital status shall be determined under section 7703.

(B) Corporations. In the case of a corporation, the tentative minimum tax for the taxable year is—

[Footnote Code Sec. 53] Matter in *italics* in Code Sec. 53(d)(1)(B)(ii)(II) added by section 13171(c) of P.L. 103-66 which struck out:

1. "(5), (6) and (8)"

Effective Date (Sec. 13171(d) of P.L. 103-66) effective for contributions made after 6/30/92, except in the case of any contribution of capital gain property which is not tangible personal property, such amendments shall apply only if the contribution is made after 12/31/92.

Code Sec. 53(d)(1)(B)(ii)(II) was previously amended by section 13113(b)(2) of P.L. 103-66 which struck out "and (6)" and inserted "(6) and (8)"

Effective Date (Sec. 13113(e) of P.L. 103-66) effective for stock issued after 8/10/93.

[Footnote Code Sec. 55] Matter in *italics* in Code Sec. 55(b)(1), (d)(1)(A)-(C) and (d)(3) added by sections 13203(a), (b)(1)-(3) and (c)(1) of P.L. 103-66 which struck out:

1. "(1) In general. The tentative minimum tax for the taxable year is—

"(A) 20 percent (24 percent in the case of a taxpayer other than a corporation) of so much of the alternative minimum taxable income for the taxable year as exceeds the exemption amount, reduced by

"(B) the alternative minimum tax foreign tax credit for the taxable year."

(i) 20 percent of so much of the alternative minimum taxable income for the taxable year as exceeds the exemption amount, reduced by

(ii) the alternative minimum tax foreign tax credit for the taxable year.

* * * * * * * * * * * * *

(d) Exemption amount. For purposes of this section—

(1) Exemption amount for taxpayers other than corporations. In the case of a taxpayer other than a corporation, the term "exemption amount" means—

(A) [2]*$45,000* in the case of—

(i) a joint return, or

(ii) a surviving spouse,

(B) [3]*$33,750* in the case of an individual who—

(i) is not a married individual, and

(ii) is not a surviving spouse, and

(C) [4]*$22,500* in the case of—

(i) a married individual who files a separate return, or

(ii) an estate or trust.

For purposes of this paragraph, the term "surviving spouse" has the meaning given to such term by section 2(a), and marital status shall be determined under section 7703.

* * * * * * * * * * * * *

(3) Phase-out of exemption amount. The exemption amount of any taxpayer shall be reduced (but not below zero) by an amount equal to 25 percent of the amount by which the alternative minimum taxable income of the taxpayer exceeds—

(A) $150,000 in the case of a taxpayer described in paragraph (1)(A) or (2),

(B) $112,500 in the case of a taxpayer described in paragraph (1)(B), and

(C) $75,000 in the case of a taxpayer described in paragraph (1)(C).

In the case of a taxpayer described in paragraph (1)(C)(i), alternative minimum taxable income shall be increased by the lesser of (i) 25 percent of the excess of alternative minimum taxable income (determined without regard to this sentence) over [5]*$165,000, or (ii) $22,500.*

[For explanation, see ¶ 114, for text of Committee Report, see ¶ 3030][For explanation, see ¶ 114, for text of Committee Report, see ¶ 3030]

[¶ 2015] Code Sec. 56. Adjustments in computing alternative minimum taxable income.

* * * * * * * * * * * * *

(g) Adjustments based on adjusted current earnings.

* * * * * * * * * * * * *

(4) Adjustments. In determining adjusted current earnings, the following adjustments shall apply:

(A) Depreciation.

* * * * * * * * * * * * *

(i) Property placed in service after 1989. The depreciation deduction with respect to any property placed in service in a taxable year beginning after 1989 shall be determined under the alternative system of section 168(g). *The preceding sentence shall not apply to*

[Footnote Code Sec. 55 continued]

2. "$40,000"
3. "$30,000"
4. "$20,000"
5. "$155,000 or (ii) $20,000"

Effective Date (Sec. 13203(d) of P.L. 103-66) effective for tax. yrs. begin. after 12/31/92.

[Footnote Code Sec. 56] Matter in *italics* in Code Sec. 56(g)(4)(A)(i) added by section 13115(a), P.L. 103-66.

Effective Date (Sec. 13115(b), P.L. 103-66) effective for property placed in service after 12/31/93, except as provided in Sec. 13115(b)(2) of this Act, which reads as follows:

any property placed in service after December 31, 1993, and the depreciation deduction with respect to such property shall be determined under the rules of subsection (a)(1)(A).

* * * * * * * * * * * * *

(C) Disallowance of items not deductible in computing earnings and profits.

* * * * * * * * * * * * *

(ii) Special rule for certain dividends.

* * * * * * * * * * * * *

(I) In general. Clause (i) shall not apply to any deduction allowable under section 243 or 245 for any dividend which is a 100-percent dividend or which is received from a 20-percent owned corporation (as defined in section 243(c)(2)), but only to the extent such dividend is attributable to income of the paying corporation which is subject to tax under this chapter (determined after the application of [1]*sections 936 (including subsections (a)(4) and (i) thereof) and 921* .

(II) 100-percent dividend. For purposes of the subclause (I), the term "100 percent dividend" means any dividend if the percentage used for purposes of determining the amount allowable as a deduction under section 243 or 245 with respect to such dividend is 100 percent.

(iii) Treatment of taxes on dividends from 936 corporations.

* * * * * * * * * * * * *

(IV) Separate application of foreign tax credit limitations. In determining the alternative minimum foreign tax credit, section 904(d) shall be applied as if dividends from a corporation eligible for the credit provided by section 936 were a separate category of income referred to in a subparagraph of section 904(d)(1).

(V) Coordination with limitation on 936 credit. Any reference in this clause to a dividend received from a corporation eligible for the credit provided by section 936 shall be treated as a reference to the portion of any such dividend for which the dividends received deduction is disallowed under clause (i) after the application of clause (ii)(I).

* * * * * * * * * * * * *

(J) Treatment of charitable contributions. Notwithstanding subparagraphs (B) and (C), no adjustment related to the earnings and profits effects of any charitable contribution shall be made in computing adjusted current earnings.

* * * * * * * * * * * * *

[For explanation, see ¶ 309, ¶ 321, and ¶ 1118, for text of Committee Report, see ¶ 3007, ¶ 3025 and ¶ 3050]

[Footnote Code Sec. 56 continued]

. "(2) Coordination with transitional rules. The amendments made by this section shall not apply to any property to which paragraph (1) of section 56(a) of the Internal Revenue Code of 1986 does not apply by reason of subparagraph (C)(i) thereof."

Matter in *italics* in Code Sec. 56(g)(4)(C)(ii)(I), (g)(4)(C)(iii)(IV) and (V) added by sections 13227(c)(1) and (2), P.L. 103-66, which struck out:

1. "sections 936 and 921"

Effective Date (Sec. 13227(f), P.L. 103-66) effective for tax. yrs. begin. after 12/31/93.

Matter in *italics* in Code Sec. 56(g)(4)(j) added by section 13171(b), P.L. 103-66.

Effective Date (Sec. 13171(d), P.L. 103-66) effective for contributions made after 6/30/92, except that in the case of any contribution of capital gain property which is not tangible personal property, such amendments shall apply only if the contribution is made after 12/31/92.

[¶ 2016] Code Sec. 57. Items of tax preference.

* * * * * * * * * * * * *

(a) General rule. For purposes of this part, the items of tax preference determined under this section are—

* * * * * * * * * * * * *

[1]*(6)* Accelerated depreciation or amortization on certain property placed in service before January 1, 1987. The amounts which would be treated as items of tax preference with respect to the taxpayer under paragraphs (2), (3), (4), and (12) of this subsection (as in effect on the day before the date of the enactment of the Tax Reform Act of 1986). The preceding sentence shall not apply to any property to which section 56(a)(1) or (5) applies.

[2]***(7) Exclusion for gains on sale of certain small business stock.*** *An amount equal to one-half of the amount excluded from gross income for the taxable year under section 1202.*

(b) Straight line recovery of intangibles defined. For purposes of paragraph (2) of subsection (a)—

(1) In general. The term "straight line recovery of intangibles", when used with respect to intangible drilling and development costs for any well, means (except in the case of an election under paragraph (2)) ratable amortization of such costs over the 120-month period beginning with the month in which production from such well begins.

(2) Election. If the taxpayer elects with respect to the intangible drilling and development costs for any well, the term "straight line recovery of intangibles" means any method which would be permitted for purposes of determining cost depletion with respect to such well and which is selected by the taxpayer for purposes of subsection (a)(2).

[For explanation, see ¶ 115 and ¶ 703, for text of Committee Report, see ¶ 3025]

[¶ 2017] Code Sec. 62. Adjusted gross income defined.

(a) General rule. For purposes of this subtitle, the term "adjusted gross income" means, in the case of an individual, gross income minus the following deductions:

* * * * * * * * * * * * *

(15) Moving expenses.
The deduction allowed by section 217.

* * * * * * * * * * * * *

[Footnote Code Sec. 57] Matter in *italics* in Code Sec. 57(a)(6) and (a)(7) added by section 13171(a), P.L. 103-66, which struck out:

1. " (6) Appreciated property charitable deduction.

"(A) In general. The amount by which the deduction allowable under section 170 or 642(c) would be reduced if all capital gain property were taken into account at its adjusted basis.

"(B) Capital gain property. For purposes of subparagraph (A), the term 'capital gain property' has the meaning given to such term by section 170(b)(1)(C)(iv). Such term shall not include any property to which an election under section 170(b)(1)(C)(iii) applies. In the case of any taxable year beginning in 1991, such term shall not include any tangible personal property. In the case of a contribution made before July 1, 1992, in a taxable year beginning in 1992, such term shall not include any tangible personal property."

"(7)"

2. "(8)"

Effective Date (Sec. 13171(d), P.L. 103-66) effective for contributions made after 6/30/92, except that in the case of any contribution of capital gain property which is not tangible personal property, such amendments shall apply only if the contribution is made after 12/31/92.

Code Sec. 57(a)(8) was added by section 13113(b)(1) of P.L. 103-66 which was redesignated as Code Sec. 57(a)(7) by section 13171(a) of P.L. 103-66.

Effective Date (Sec. 13113(e) of P.L. 103-66) effective for stock issued after 8/10/93.

[Footnote Code Sec. 62] Matter in *italics* in Code Sec. 62(a)(15) was added by section 13213(c)(1) of P.L. 103-66.

Effective Date (Sec. 13213(e) of P.L. 103-66) effective for expenses incurred after 12/31/93.

[For explanation, see ¶ 201]

[¶ 2018] Code Sec. 63. Taxable income defined.

* * * * * * * * * * * * *

(c) Standard deduction. For purposes of this subtitle—

* * * * * * * * * * * * *

(4) Adjustments for inflation. In the case of any taxable year beginning in a calendar year after 1988, each dollar amount contained in paragraph (2) or (5)(A) or subsection (f) shall be increased by an amount equal to—

(A) such dollar amount, multiplied by

(B) the cost-of-living adjustment determined under section 1(f)(3) for the calendar year in which the taxable year begins, by substituting "calendar year 1987" for "calendar year [1]*1992*" in subparagraph (B) thereof.

[¶ 2019] Code Sec. 67. 2-percent floor on miscellaneous itemized deductions.

* * * * * * * * * * * * *

(b) Miscellaneous itemized deductions. For purposes of this section, the term "miscellaneous itemized deductions" means the itemized deductions other than—

* * * * * * * * * * * * *

[1]*(6)* any deduction allowable for impairment-related work expenses,

[2]*(7)* the deduction under section 691(c) (relating to deduction for estate tax in case of income in respect of the decedent),

[3]*(8)* any deduction allowable in connection with personal property used in a short sale,

[4]*(9)* the deduction under section 1341 (relating to computation of tax where taxpayer restores substantial amount held under claim of right),

[5]*(10)* the deduction under section 72(b)(3) (relating to deduction where annuity payments cease before investment recovered),

[6]*(11)* the deduction under section 171 (relating to deduction for amortizable bond premium), and

[7]*(12)* the deduction under section 216 (relating to deductions in connection with cooperative housing corporations). [8]

[Footnote Code Sec. 63] Matter in *italics* in Code Sec. 63(c)(4)(B) added by section 13201(b)(3)(D) of P.L. 103-66 which struck out:

1. "1989"

Effective Date (Sec. 13201(c) of P.L. 103-66) effective for tax. yrs. begin. after 12/31/92.

[Footnote Code Sec. 67] Matter in *italics* in Code Sec. 67(b)(6)-(12) added by section 13213(c)(2) of P.L. 103-66 which struck out:

1. "(6) the deduction under section 217 (relating to moving expenses),"
2. "(7)"
3. "(8)"
4. "(9)"
5. "(10)"
6. "(11)"
7. "(12)"
8. "(13)"

Effective Date (Sec. 13213(e) of P.L. 103-66) effective for expenses incurred after 12/31/93.

[¶ 2020] Code Sec. 68. Overall limitation on itemized deductions.

* * * * * * * * * * * * *

(b) Applicable amount.

* * * * * * * * * * * * *

(2) Inflation adjustments. In the case of any taxable year beginning in a calendar year after 1991, each dollar amount contained in paragraph (1) shall be increased by an amount equal to—

(A) such dollar amount, multiplied by

(B) the cost-of-living adjustment determined under section 1(f)(3) for the calendar year in which the taxable year begins, by substituting "calendar year 1990" for "calendar year [1]*1992* " in subparagraph (B) thereof.

* * * * * * * * * * * * *

[2]***(f) Repealed.***

[For explanation, see ¶ 203, for text of Committee Reports, see ¶ 3031]

[¶ 2021] Code Sec. 82. Reimbursement for expenses of moving.

[1] *Except as provided in section 132(a)(6), there shall* be included in gross income (as compensation for services) any amount received or accrued, directly or indirectly, by an individual as a payment for or reimbursement of expenses of moving from one residence to another residence which is attributable to employment or self-employment.

[¶ 2022] Code Sec. 86. Social security and tier 1 railroad retirement benefits.

(a) In general.

(1) In general.[1] *Except as provided in paragraph (2), gross* **income for the taxable year of any taxpayer described in subsection (b) (notwithstanding section 207 of the Social Security Act) includes social security benefits in an amount equal to the lesser of—**

(A) one-half of the social security benefits received during the taxable year, or

[3]*(B)* one-half of the excess described in subsection (b)(1).

(2) Additional amount. *In the case of a taxpayer with respect to whom the amount determined under subsection (b)(1)(A) exceeds the adjusted base amount, the amount included in gross income under this section shall be equal to the lesser of—*

[Footnote Code Sec. 68] Matter in *italics* in Code Sec. 68(b)(2)(B) added by section 13201(b)(3)(E) of P.L. 103-66 which struck out:

1. "1989"

Effective Date (Sec. 13201(c) of P.L. 103-66) effective for tax. yrs. begin. after 12/31/92.

Code Sec. 68(f) added by section 13204 of P.L. 103-66 which struck out:

2. "(f) **Termination.**

This section shall not apply to any taxable year beginning after December 31, 1995."

Effective Date effective 8/10/93.

[Footnote Code Sec. 82] Matter in *italics* in Code Sec. 82 added by section 13213(d)(3)(A) of P.L. 103-66 which struck out:

1. "There shall"

Effective Date (Sec. 13213(e) of P.L. 103-66) effective for reimbursements or other payments in respect of expenses incurred after 12/31/93.

[Footnote Code Sec. 86] Matter in *italics* in Code Sec. 86(a)(1), (a)(1)(A), (a)(1)(B) and (c) added by sections 13215(a)(1), (a)(2)(A), (B) and (b) of P.L. 103-66 which struck out:

1. "Gross"
2. "(a)(1)"
3. "(a)(2)"

(A) the sum of—

(i) 85 percent of such excess, plus

(ii) the lesser of the amount determined under paragraph (1) or an amount equal to one-half of the difference between the adjusted base amount and the base amount of the taxpayer, or

(B) 85 percent of the social security benefits received during the taxable year.

* * * * * * * * * * * *

[4]***(c) Base amount and adjusted base amount.*** *For purposes of this section—*

(1) Base amount. *The term "base amount" means—*

(A) except as otherwise provided in this paragraph, $25,000,

(B) $32,000 in the case of a joint return, and

(C) zero in the case of a taxpayer who—

(i) is married as of the close of the taxable year (within the meaning of section 7703) but does not file a joint return for such year, and

(ii) does not live apart from his spouse at all times during the taxable year.

(2) Adjusted base amount. *The term "adjusted base amount" means—*

(A) except as otherwise provided in this paragraph, $34,000,

(B) $44,000 in the case of a joint return, and

(C) zero in the case of a taxpayer described in paragraph (1)(C).

* * * * * * * * * * * *

[For explanation, see ¶ 106, for text of Committee Report, see ¶ 3042]

[¶ 2023] Code Sec. 108. Income from discharge of indebtedness.

(a) Exclusion from gross income.

(1) In general. Gross income does not include any amount which (but for this subsection) would be includible in gross income by reason of the discharge (in whole or in part) of indebtedness of the taxpayer if—

(A) the discharge occurs in a title 11 case,

(B) the discharge occurs when the taxpayer is insolvent

[1](C) the indebtedness discharged is qualified farm indebtedness [2], *or*

(D) in the case of a taxpayer other than a C corporation, the indebtedness discharged is qualified real property business indebtedness.

(2) Coordination of exclusions.

(A) Title 11 exclusion takes precedence. Subparagraphs (B) [3], *(C), and (D)* of paragraph (1) shall not apply to a discharge which occurs in a title 11 case.

[4]*(B) Insolvency exclusion takes precedence over qualified farm exclusion and qualified real property business exclusion. Subparagraphs (C) and (D) of paragraph (1) shall not apply to a discharge to the extent the taxpayer is insolvent.*

4. "(c) Base amount. For purposes of this section, the term 'base amount' means—

"(1) except as otherwise provided in this subsection, $25,000,

"(2) $32,000, in the case of a joint return, and

"(3) zero, in the case of a taxpayer who—

"(A) is married at the close of the taxable year (within the meaning of section 7703) but does not file a joint return for such year, and

"(B) does not live apart from his spouse at all times during the taxable year."

Effective Date (Sec. 13215(d) of P.L. 103-66) effective for tax. yrs. begin. after 12/31/93.

[Footnote Code Sec. 108] Matter in *italics* in Code Sec. (a)(1)(B)-(D), (a)(2)(A), and (a)(2)(B) added by sections 13150(a), (c)(1) and (c)(2) of P.L. 103-66 which struck out:

1. "or"
2. "."
3. "and (C)"
4. "(B) Insolvency exclusion takes precedence over qualified farm exclusion. Subparagraph (C) of paragraph (1) shall not apply to a discharge to the extent the taxpayer is insolvent."

* * * * * * * * * * * * *

(b) Reduction of tax attributes.

* * * * * * * * * * * * *

(2) Tax attributes affected; order of reduction. Except as provided in paragraph (5), the reduction referred to in paragraph (1) shall be made in the following tax attributes in the following order:

(A) NOL. Any net operating loss for the taxable year of the discharge, and any net operating loss carryover to such taxable year.

(B) General business credit. Any carryover to or from the taxable year of a discharge of an amount for purposes for determining the amount allowable as a credit under section 38 (relating to general business credit).

[5]*(C) Minimum tax credit. The amount of the minimum tax credit available under section 53(b) as of the beginning of the taxable year immediately following the taxable year of the discharge.*

(D) Capital loss carryovers. Any net capital loss for the taxable year of the discharge, and any capital loss carryover to such taxable year under section 1212.

[6]*(E)* Basis reduction.

(i) In general. The basis of the property of the taxpayer.

(ii) Cross reference. For provisions for making the reduction described in clause (i), see section 1017.

[7]*(F) Passive activity loss and credit carryovers. Any passive activity loss or credit carryover of the taxpayer under section 469(b) from the taxable year of the discharge.*

(G) Foreign tax credit carryovers. Any carryover to or from the taxable year of the discharge for purposes of determining the amount of the credit allowable under section 27.

(3) Amount of reduction.

* * * * * * * * * * * * *

[8]*(B) Credit carryover reduction. The reductions described in subparagraphs (B), (C), and (G) shall be 33 ⅓ cents for each dollar excluded by subsection (a). The reduction described in subparagraph (F) in any passive activity credit carryover shall be 33 ⅓ cents for each dollar excluded by subsection (a).*

(4) Ordering rules.

* * * * * * * * * * * * *

(B) Reductions under subparagraph (A) or [9]*(D)* of paragraph (2). The reductions described in subparagraph (A) or [9]*(D)* of paragraph (2) (as the case may be) shall be made first in the loss for the taxable year of the discharge and then in the carryovers to such taxable year in the order of the taxable years from which each such carryover arose.

(C) Reductions under subparagraphs (B) and [10]*(G)* of paragraph (2). The reductions described in subparagraphs (B) and [10]*(G)* of paragraph (2) shall be made in the order in which carryovers are taken into account under this chapter for the taxable year of the discharge.

* * * * * * * * * * * * *

[Footnote Code Sec. 108 continued]

Effective Date (Sec. 13150(d) of P.L. 103-66) effective for discharges after 12/31/92, in tax. yrs. end. after 12/31/92.

Matter in *italics* in Code Sec. (b)(2)(C)-(G), (b)(3)(B), and (b)(3)(F)-(G) added by sections 13226(b)(1)-(3)(C) of P.L. 103-66 which struck out:

5. "(D)"
6. "(D)"
7. "(E)"
8. "(B) Credit carryover reduction. The reductions described in subparagraphs (B) and (E) of paragraph (2) shall be 33 ⅓ cents for each dollar excluded by subsection (a)."
9. "(C)"
10. "(E)"

Effective Date (Sec. 13226(b)(4) of P.L. 103-66) effective for discharges of indebtedness in tax. yrs. begin. after 12/31/93.

*(c) **Treatment of discharge of qualified real property business indebtedness.***

*(1) **Basis reduction.***

(A) In general. The amount excluded from gross income under subparagraph (D) of subsection (a)(1) shall be applied to reduce the basis of the depreciable real property of the taxpayer.

(B) Cross reference. For provisions making the reduction described in subparagraph (A), see section 1017.

*(2) **Limitations.***

(A) Indebtedness in excess of value. The amount excluded under subparagraph (D) of subsection (a)(1) with respect to any qualified real property business indebtedness shall not exceed the excess (if any) of—

(i) the outstanding principal amount of such indebtedness (immediately before the discharge), over

(ii) the fair market value of the real property described in paragraph (3)(A) (as of such time), reduced by the outstanding principal amount of any other qualified real property business indebtedness secured by such property (as of such time).

(B) Overall limitation. The amount excluded under subparagraph (D) of subsection (a)(1) shall not exceed the aggregate adjusted bases of depreciable real property (determined after any reductions under subsections (b) and (g)) held by the taxpayer immediately before the discharge (other than depreciable real property acquired in contemplation of such discharge).

*(3) **Qualified real property business indebtedness.** The term "qualified real property business indebtedness" means indebtedness which—*

(A) was incurred or assumed by the taxpayer in connection with real property used in a trade or business and is secured by such real property,

(B) was incurred or assumed before January 1, 1993, or if incurred or assumed on or after such date, is qualified acquisition indebtedness, and

(C) with respect to which such taxpayer makes an election to have this paragraph apply. Such term shall not include qualified farm indebtedness. Indebtedness under subparagraph (B) shall include indebtedness resulting from the refinancing of indebtedness under subparagraph (B) (or this sentence), but only to the extent it does not exceed the amount of the indebtedness being refinanced.

*(4) **Qualified acquisition indebtedness.** For purposes of paragraph (3)(B), the term "qualified acquisition indebtedness" means, with respect to any real property described in paragraph (3)(A), indebtedness incurred or assumed to acquire, construct, reconstruct, or substantially improve such property.*

*(5) **Regulations.** The Secretary shall issue such regulations as are necessary to carry out this subsection, including regulations preventing the abuse of this subsection through cross-collateralization or other means.*

(d) Meaning of terms; special rules relating to [11]*certain provisions.*

* * * * * * * * * * * *

(6)[12]**Certain provisions to be applied at partner level.** In the case of a partnership, [13]*subsections (a), (b), (c) and (g)* shall be applied at the partner level.

(7) Special rules for S corporation.

(A) [14]*Certain provisions* to be applied at corporate level. In the case of an S corporation, [15]*subsections (a), (b), (c), and (g)* shall be applied at the corporate level.

[Footnote Code Sec. 108 continued]

Matter in *italics* in Code Sec. 108(c), (d), (d)(6)-(7)(B), and (d)(9)(A) added by sections 13150(b), (c)(3)(A)-(C), and (c)(4)-(5) of P.L. 103-66 which struck out:

11. "subsections (a), (b), and (g)"
12. "Subsections (a), (b), and (g)"
13. "subsections (a), (b), and (g)"
14. "Subsections (a), (b), and (g)"
15. "subsections (a), (b), and (g)"

Effective Date (Sec. 13150(d) of P.L. 103-66) effective for discharges after 12/31/92, in tax. yrs. end. after 12/31/92.

(B) Reduction in carryover of disallowed losses and deductions. In the case of an S corporation, for purposes of subparagraph (A) of subsection (b)(2), any loss or deduction which is disallowed for the taxable year of the discharge under section 1366(d)(1) shall be treated as a net operating loss for such taxable year. *The preceding sentence shall not apply to any discharge to the extent that subsection (a)(1)(D) applies to such discharge.*

* * * * * * * * * * * * *

(9) Time for making election, etc.

(A) Time. An election under paragraph (5) of subsection (b) *or under paragraph (3)(B) of subsection (c)* shall be made on the taxpayer's return for the taxable year in which the discharge occurs or at such other time as may be permitted in regulations prescribed by the Secretary.

* * * * * * * * * * * * *

(e) General rules for discharge of indebtedness (including discharges not in title 11 cases or insolvency). For purposes of this title—

* * * * * * * * * * * * *

(6) Indebtedness contributed to capital. [16] *Except as provided in regulations, for* purposes of determining income of the debtor from discharge of indebtedness, if a debtor corporation acquires its indebtedness from a shareholder as a contribution to capital—

* * * * * * * * * * * * *

[17]***(8) Indebtedness satisfied by corporation's stock.*** *For purposes of determining income of a debtor from discharge of indebtedness, if a debtor corporation transfers stock to a creditor in satisfaction of its indebtedness, such corporation shall be treated as having satisfied the indebtedness with an amount of money equal to the fair market value of the stock.*

* * * * * * * * * * * * *

[18]*(10)* Indebtedness satisfied by issuance of debt instrument.

(A) In general. For purposes of determining income of a debtor from discharge of indebtedness, if a debtor issues a debt instrument in satisfaction of indebtedness, such debtor

[Footnote Code Sec. 108 continued]

Matter in *italics* in Code Sec. 108(e)(6), (8), and (10) added by sections 13226(a)(1)(A)-(B) and (a)(2)(B) of P.L. 103-66 which struck out:

16. "For"

17. "(8) Stock for debt exception not to apply in de minimis cases. For purposes of determining income of the debtor from discharge of indebtedness, the stock for debt exception shall not apply—

"(A) to the issuance of nominal or token shares, or

"(B) with respect to an unsecured creditor, where the ratio of the value of the stock received by such unsecured creditor to the amount of his indebtedness cancelled or exchanged for stock in the workout is less than 50 percent of a similar ratio computed for all unsecured creditors participating in the workout.

Any stock which is disqualified stock (as defined in paragraph (10)(B)(ii)) shall not be treated as stock for purposes of this paragraph."

18. "(10) Indebtedness satisfied by corporation's stock.

"(A) In general. For purposes of determining income of a debtor from discharge of indebtedness, if a debtor corporation transfers stock to a creditor in satisfaction of its indebtedness, such corporation shall be treated as having satisfied the indebtedness with an amount of money equal to the fair market value of the stock.

"(B) Exception for certain stock in title 11 cases and insolvent debtors.

"(i) In general. Subparagraph (A) shall not apply to any transfer of stock of the debtor (other than disqualified stock)—

"(I) by a debtor in a title 11 case, or

"(II) by any other debtor but only to the extent such debtor is insolvent.

"(ii) Disqualified stock. For purposes of clause (i), the term 'disqualified stock' means any stock with a stated redemption price if—

"(I) such stock has a fixed redemption date,

"(II) the issuer of such stock has the right to redeem such stock at one or more times, or

"(III) the holder of such stock has the right to require its redemption at one or more times."

Effective Date (Sec. 13226(a)(3) of P.L. 103-66) effective for stock transferred after 12/31/94, in satisfaction of any indebtedness, except as provided in Sec. 13226(a)(3)(B) of this Act, which reads as follows:

"(B) Exception for title 11 cases.—The amendments made by this subsection shall not apply to stock transferred in satisfaction of any indebtedness if such transfer is in a title 11 or similar case (as defined in section 368(a)(3)(A) of the Internal Revenue Code of 1986) which was filed on or before December 31, 1993."

shall be treated as having satisfied the indebtedness with an amount of money equal to the issue price of such debt instrument.

(B) Issue price. For purposes of subparagraph (A), the issue price of any debt instrument shall be determined under sections 1273 and 1274. For purposes of the preceding sentence, section 1273(b)(4) shall be applied by reducing the stated redemption price of any instrument by the portion of such stated redemption price which is treated as interest for purposes of this chapter.

* * * * * * * * * * * * *

(g) Special rules for discharge of qualified farm indebtedness.

* * * * * * * * * * * * *

(3) Amount excluded cannot exceed sum of tax attributes and business and investment assets.

* * * * * * * * * * * * *

(B) Adjusted tax attributes. For purposes of subparagraph (A), the term "adjusted tax attributes" means the sum of the tax attributes described in [19]*subparagraphs (A), (B), (C), (D), (F), and (G)* of subsection (b)(2) determined by taking into account $3 for each $1 of the attributes described in [20]*subparagraphs (B), (C), and (G)* of subsection (b)(2)*and the attribute described in subparagraph (F) of subsection (b)(2) to the extent attributable to any passive activity credit carryover* .

* * * * * * * * * * * * *

[For explanation, see ¶ 312, for text of Committee Reports, see ¶s 3021, 3048, and 3049

[¶ 2024] Code Sec. 127. Educational assistance programs.

* * * * * * * * * * * * *

[1]**(d) Termination.** This section shall not apply to taxable years beginning after December 31, 1994.

* * * * * * * * * * * * *

[For explanation, see ¶ 802 for text of Committee Report, see ¶ 3001]

[¶ 2025] Code Sec. 132. Certain fringe benefits.

(a) Exclusion from gross income. Gross income shall not include any fringe benefit which qualifies as a—

* * * * * * * * * * * * *

(4) de minimis fringe,[1]

(5) qualified transportation fringe [2], *or*

Matter in *italics* in Code Sec. 108(g)(3)(B) added by sections 13226(b)(3)(D)(i)-(iii) of P.L. Sec. 103-66 which struck out:

19. "subparagraphs (A), (B), (C), and (E)"
20. subparagraphs (B) and (E)"

Effective Date (Sec. 13226(b)(4) of P.L. 103-66) effective for discharges of indebtedness in tax. yrs. begin. after 12/31/93.

[Footnote Code Sec. 127] Matter in *italics* in Code Sec. 127 and 127(d) added by sections 13101(a)(1) and (2) of P.L. 103-66 which struck out:

1. "(d) **Termination.**

This section shall not apply to taxable years beginning after June 30, 1992."

[Footnote Code Sec. 132] Matter in *italics* in Code Sec. 132(a)(4) through (6) added by section 13213(d)(1) of P.L. 103-66 which struck out:

1. "or"
2. the period at the end of para. (a)(5)

(6) qualified moving expense reimbursement.

* * * * * * * * * * * * *

(f) Qualified transportation fringe.

* * * * * * * * * * * * *

(6) Inflation adjustment. In the case of any taxable year beginning in a calendar year after 1993, the dollar amounts contained in paragraph (2)(A) and (B) shall be increased by an amount equal to—

(A) such dollar amount, multiplied by

(B) the cost-of-living adjustment determined under section 1(f)(3) for the calendar year in which the taxable year begins [3].

If any increase determined under the preceding sentence is not a multiple of $5, such increase shall be rounded to the next lowest multiple of $5.

* * * * * * * * * * * * *

[4]***(g) Qualified moving expense reimbursement.*** *For purposes of this section, the term "qualified moving expense reimbursement" means any amount received (directly or indirectly) by an individual from an employer as a payment for (or a reimbursement of) expenses which would be deductible as moving expenses under section 217 if directly paid or incurred by the individual. Such term shall not include any payment for (or reimbursement of) an expense actually deducted by the individual in a prior taxable year.*

(h) **Certain individuals treated as employees for purposes of subsections (a)(1) and (2).** For purposes of paragraphs (1) and (2) of subsection (a)—

(1) Retired and disabled employees and surviving spouse of employee treated as employee. With respect to a line of business of an employer, the term "employee" includes—

(A) any individual who was formerly employed by such employer in such line of business and who separated from service with such employer in such line of business by reason of retirement or disability, and

(B) any widow or widower of any individual who died while employed by such employer in such line of business or while an employee within the meaning of subparagraph (A).

(2) Spouses and dependent children.

(A) In general. Any use by the spouse or a dependent child of the employee shall be treated as use by the employee.

(B) Dependent child. For purposes of subparagraph (A), the term "dependent child" means any child (as defined in section 151(c)(3) of the employee—

(i) who is a dependent of the employee, or

(ii) both of whose parents are deceased and who has not attained age 25.

For purposes of the preceding sentence, any child to whom section 152(e) applies shall be treated as the dependent of both parents.

(3) Special rule for parents in the case of air transportation. Any use of air transportation by a parent of an employee (determined without regard to paragraph (1)(B)) shall be treated as use by the employee.

[5]***(i)*** **Reciprocal agreements.** For purposes of paragraph (1) of subsection (a), any service provided by an employer to an employee of another employer shall be treated as provided by the employer of such employee if—

(1) such service is provided pursuant to a written agreement between such employers, and

---

[Footnote Code Sec. 132 continued]

Effective Date (Sec. 13213(d)(1) of P.L. 103-66) effective for reimbursements or other payments in respect of expenses incurred after 12/31/93.

Matter in *italics* in Code Sec. 132(f)(6)(B) added by section 13201(b)(3)(F) of P.L. 103-66 which struck out:

3. ", determined by substituting 'calendar year 1992' for 'calendar year 1989' in subparagraph (B) thereof."

Effective Date (Sec. 13201(b)(3)(F) of P.L. 103-66) effective for tax. yrs. begin. after 12/31/92.

Matter in *italics* in Code Sec. 132(g) through (j)(4)(B)(iii) added by section 13213(d)(2) and (3)(B) of P.L. 103-66 which struck out:

4. "(g)"
5. "(h)"

(2) neither of such employers incurs any substantial additional costs (including foregone revenue) in providing such service or pursuant to such agreement.

[6]***(j)*** **Special rules.**

* * * * * * * * * * * * *

(4) On-premises gyms and other athletic facilities.

(A) In general. Gross income shall not include the value of any on-premises athletic facility provided by an employer to his employees.

(B) On-premises athletic facility. For purposes of this paragraph, the term "on-premises athletic facility" means any gym or other athletic facility—

(i) which is located on the premises of the employer,

(ii) which is operated by the employer, and

(iii) substantially all the use of which is by employees of the employer, their spouses, and their dependent children (within the meaning of [7]*subsection (h)*).

* * * * * * * * * * * * *

[8]***(8) Application of section to otherwise taxable educational or training benefits.*** *Amounts paid or expenses incurred by the employer for education or training provided to the employee which are not excludable from gross income under section 127 shall be excluded from gross income under this section if (and only if) such amounts or expenses are a working condition fringe.*

[9]***(k)*** **Customers not to include employees.** For purposes of this section (other than subsection (c)(2)), the term "customers" shall only include customers who are not employees.

[10]***(l)*** **Section not to apply to fringe benefits expressly provided for elsewhere.** This section (other than [11]*subsections (e) and (g)*) shall not apply to any fringe benefits of a type the tax treatment of which is expressly provided for in any other section of this chapter.

[12]***(m)*** **Regulations.** The Secretary shall prescribe such regulations as may be necessary or appropriate to carry out the purposes of this section.

[For text of Committee Reports, see ¶ 3001]

[¶ 2026] Code Sec. 143. Mortgage revenue bonds: qualified mortgage bond and qualified veterans' mortgage bond.

(a) Qualified mortgage bond.

[1]***(1) Qualified mortgage bond defined.*** *For purposes of this title, the term "qualified mortgage bond" means a bond which is issued as part of a qualified mortgage issue.*

---

6. "(i)"
7. "subsection (f)"

Effective Date (Sec. 13213(d)(2) of P.L. 103-66) effective for reimbursements or other payments in respect of expenses incurred after 12/31/93.

Matter in *italics* in Code Sec. 132(j)(8) [as redesignated by 13213(d)(2) of P.L. 103-66] added by section 13101(1)(b) of P.L. 103-66 which struck out:

8. "(8) **Application of section to otherwise taxable employer-provided educational assistance.** Amounts which would be excludible from gross income under section 127 but for subsection (a)(2) thereof or the last sentence of subsection (c)(1) thereof shall be excluded from gross income under this section if (and only if) such amounts are a working condition fringe."

Effective Date (Sec. 13101(b) of P.L. 103-66) effective for tax. yrs. begin. after 12/31/88.

Matter in *italics* in Code Sec. 132(k) and (l) added by section 13213(d)(2) of P.L. 103-66 which struck out:

9. "(j)"
10. "(k)"
11. "subsection (e)"
12. "(l)"

Effective Date (Sec. 13213(d)(2) and (3)(C) of P.L. 103-66) effective for reimbursements or other payments in respect of expenses incurred after 12/31/93.

[Footnote Code Sec. 143] Matter in *italics* in Code Sec. 143(a)(1) added by section 13141(a), P.L. 103-66, which struck out:

1. "(1) Qualified mortgage bond defined.

* * * * * * * * * * * * *

(d) 3-year requirement.

* * * * * * * * * * * * *

(2) Exceptions. For purposes of paragraph (1), the proceeds of an issue which are used to provide—

(A) financing with respect to targeted area residences, [2]

(B) qualified home improvement loans and qualified rehabilitation loans, *and*

(C) financing with respect to land described in subsection (i)(1)(C) and the construction of any residence thereon,

shall be treated as used as described in paragraph (1).

* * * * * * * * * * * * *

(i) Other requirements.

(1) Mortgages must be new mortgages.

* * * * * * * * * * * * *

(C) Exception for certain contract for deed agreements.

(i) In general. In the case of land possessed under a contract for deed by a mortgagor—

(I) whose principal residence (within the meaning of section 1034) is located on such land, and

(II) whose family income (as defined in subsection (f)(2)) is not more than 50 percent of applicable median family income (as defined in subsection (f)(4)),

the contract for deed shall not be treated as an existing mortgage for purposes of subparagraph (A).

(ii) Contract for deed defined. For purposes of this subparagraph, the term "contract for deed" means a seller-financed contract for the conveyance of land under which—

(I) legal title does not pass to the purchaser until the consideration under the contract is fully paid to the seller, and

(II) the seller's remedy for nonpayment is forfeiture rather than judicial or nonjudicial foreclosure.

* * * * * * * * * * * * *

(k) Other definitions and special rules. For purposes of this section—

* * * * * * * * * * * * *

(3) Acquisition cost.

* * * * * * * * * * * * *

(B) Exceptions. The term "acquisition cost" does not include—

(i) usual and reasonable settlement or financing costs,

(ii) the value of services performed by the mortgagor or members of his family in completing the residence, and

(iii) the cost of land*(other than land described in subsection (i)(1)(C)(i))* which has been owned by the mortgagor for at least 2 years before the date on which construction of the residence begins.

* * * * * * * * * * * * *

[Footnote Code Sec. 143 continued]

"(A) In general. For purposes of this title, the term 'qualified mortgage bond' means a bond which is issued as part of a qualified mortgage issue.

"(B) Termination on June 30, 1992. No bond issued after June 30, 1992, may be treated as a qualified mortgage bond." **Effective Date** (Sec. 13141(f)(1), P.L. 103-66) effective for bonds issued after 6/30/92.

Matter in *italics* in Code Sec. 143(d)(2)(A)-(C), (i)(1)(C), and (k)(3)(B)(iii) added by sections 13141(d)(1)(A)-(C), (d)(2), and (d)(3), P.L. 103-66, which struck out:

2. "and"

Effective Date (Sec. 13141(f)(4), P.L. 103-66) effective for loans originated and credit certificates provided after 8/10/93.

(7) Single-family and owner-occupied residences include certain residences with 2 to 4 units. Except for purposes of subsection (h)(2), the terms "single-family" and "owner-occupied", when used with respect to residences, include 2, 3, or 4 family residences—

(A) one unit of which is occupied by the owner of the units, and

(B) which were first occupied at least 5 years before the mortgage is executed.

Subparagraph (B) shall not apply to any 2-family residence if the residence is a targeted area residence and the family income of the mortgagor meets the requirement of subsection (f)(3)(B).

* * * * * * * * * * * * *

(10) Treatment of resale price control and subsidy lien programs.

(A) In general. In the case of a residence which is located in a high housing cost area (as defined in section 143(f)(5)), the interest of a governmental unit in such residence by reason of financing provided under any qualified program shall not be taken into account under this section (other than subsection (m)), and the acquisition cost of the residence which is taken into account under subsection (e) shall be such cost reduced by the amount of such financing.

(B) Qualified program. For purposes of subparagraph (A), the term "qualified program" means any governmental program providing mortgage loans (other than 1st mortgage loans) or grants—

(i) which restricts (throughout the 9-year period beginning on the date the financing is provided) the resale of the residence to a purchaser qualifying under this section and to a price determined by an index that reflects less than the full amount of any appreciation in the residence's value, or

(ii) which provides for deferred or reduced interest payments on such financing and grants the governmental unit a share in the appreciation of the residence,

but only if such financing is not provided directly or indirectly through the use of any tax-exempt private activity bond.

* * * * * * * * * * * * *

[For explanation, see ¶s 721, 722, 723 and 724, for text of Committee Reports, see ¶ 3012]

[¶ 2027] **Code Sec. 144. Qualified small issue bond; qualified student loan bond; qualified redevelopment bond.**

* * * * * * * * * * * * *

(12) Termination dates.

* * * * * * * * * * * * *

[1]*(B) Bonds issued to finance manufacturing facilities and farm property. Subparagraph (A) shall not apply to any bond issued as part of an issue 95 percent or more of the net proceeds of which are to be used to provide—*

(i) any manufacturing facility, or

(ii) any land or property in accordance with section 147(c)(2).

Matter in *italics* in Code Sec. 143(k)(7), and (k)(10) added by sections 13141(c) and (e), P.L. 103-66.

Effective Date (Sec. 13141(f)(3), P.L. 103-66) effective for qualified mortgage bonds issued and mortgage credit certificates provided on or after 8/10/93.

[Footnote Code Sec. 144] Matter in *italics* in Code Sec. 144(a)(12)(B) added by section 13122(a) of P.L. 103-66 which struck out:

1. "(B) Bonds issued to finance manufacturing facilities and farm property. In the case of any bond issued as part of an issue 95 percent or more of the net proceeds of which are to be used to provide—

"(i) any manufacturing facility, or

"(ii) any land or property in accordance with section 147(c)(2),

subparagraph (A) shall be applied by substituting 'June 30, 1992' for 'December 31, 1986'."

Effective Date (Sec. 13122(b) of P.L. 103-66) effective for bonds issued after 6/30/92.

* * * * * * * * * * * * *

[For explanation, see ¶ 720, for text of Committee Report, see ¶ 3010]

[¶ 2028] Code Sec. 146. Volume cap.

* * * * * * * * * * * * *

(g) Exception for certain bonds. Only for purposes of this section, the term "private activity bond" shall not include—

(1) any qualified veterans' mortgage bond,

(2) any qualified 501(c)(3) bond,

(3) any exempt facility bond issued as part of an issue described in paragraph (1), (2), or (12) of section 142(a) (relating to airports, docks and wharves, and environmental enhancements of hydroelectric generating facilities), and

(4) 75 percent of any exempt facility bond issued as part of an issue described in paragraph (11) of section 142(a) (relating to high-speed intercity rail facilities).

Paragaraph (4) shall be applied without regard to "75 percent of" if all of the property to be financed by the net proceeds of the issue is to be owned by a governmental unit (within the meaning of section 142(b)(1)).

* * * * * * * * * * * * *

[For explanation, see ¶ 725, for text of Committee Report, see ¶ 3009]

[¶ 2029] Code Sec. 151. Allowance of deductions for personal exemptions.

* * * * * * * * * * * * *

(d) Exemption amount. For purposes of this section—

* * * * * * * * * * * * *

(3) Phaseout.

[1]*(E) Repealed.*

(4) Inflation adjustments.

(A) Adjustment to basic amount of exemption. In the case of any taxable year beginning in a calendar year after 1989, the dollar amount contained in paragraph (1) shall be increased by an amount equal to—

(i) such dollar amount, multiplied by

(ii) the cost-of-living adjustment determined under section 1(f)(3) for the calendar year in which the taxable year begins, by substituting "calendar year 1988" for "calendar year [2]*1992"* in subparagraph (B) thereof.

(B) Adjustment to threshold amounts for years after 1991. In the case of any taxable year beginning in a calendar year after 1991, each dollar amount contained in paragraph (3)(C) shall be increased by an amount equal to—

(i) such dollar amount, multiplied by

[Footnote Code Sec. 146] Matter in *italics* in Code Sec. 146(g)(4), added by section 13121(a) of P.L. 103-66.

Effective Date (Sec. 13121(b) of P.L. 103-66) effective for bonds issued after 12/31/93.

[Footnote Code Sec. 151] Matter in *italics* in Code Sec. 151(d)(3)(E) added by section 13205 of P.L. 103-66 which struck out:

1. "(E) Termination. This paragraph shall not apply to any taxable year beginning after December 31, 1996."

Effective Date effective 8/10/93.

Matter in *italics* in Code Sec. 151(d)(4)(A)(ii) and (B)(ii) added by secion 13201(b)(3)(G) of P.L. 103-66 which struck out:

2. "1989"

(ii) the cost-of-living adjustment determined under section 1(f)(3) for the calendar year in which the taxable year begins, by substituting "calendar year 1990" for "calendar year [3]*1992"* in subparagraph (B) thereof.

[For explanation, see ¶ 204, for text of Committee Reports, see ¶ 3032]

[¶ 2030] Code Sec. 162. Trade or business expenses.

* * * * * * * * * * * *

[1](e) Denial of deduction for certain lobbying and political expenditures.

(1) In general. *No deduction shall be allowed under subsection (a) for any amount paid or incurred in connection with—*

(A) influencing legislation,

(B) participation in, or intervention in, any political campaign on behalf of (or in opposition to) any candidate for public office,

(C) any attempt to influence the general public, or segments thereof, with respect to elections, legislative matters, or referendums, or

(D) any direct communication with a covered executive branch official in an attempt to influence the official actions or positions of such official.

(2) Exception for local legislation. *In the case of any legislation of any local council or similar governing body—*

(A) paragraph (1)(A) shall not apply, and

(B) the deduction allowed by subsection (a) shall include all ordinary and necessary expenses (including, but not limited to, traveling expenses described in subsection (a)(2) and the cost of preparing testimony) paid or incurred during the taxable year in carrying on any trade or business—

(i) in direct connection with appearances before, submission of statements to, or sending communications to the committees, or individual members, of such council or body with respect to legislation or proposed legislation of direct interest to the taxpayer, or

(ii) in direct connection with communication of information between the taxpayer and an organization of which the taxpayer is a member with respect to any such legislation or proposed legislation which is of direct interest to the taxpayer and to such organization,

3. "1989"

Effective Date (Sec. 13201(c) of P.L. 103-66 effective for tax. yrs. begin. after 12/31/92.

[Footnote Code Sec. 162] Matter in *italics* in code Sec. 162(e) added by section 13222(a) of P.L. 103-66 which struck out:

1. "(e) Appearances, etc., with respect to legislation.

"(1) In general. The deduction allowed by subsection (a) shall include all the ordinary and necessary expenses (including, but not limited to, traveling expenses described in subsection (a)(2) and the cost of preparing testimony) paid or incurred during the taxable year in carrying on any trade or business—

"(A) in direct connection with appearances before, submission of statements to, or sending communications to, the committees, or individual members, of Congress or of any legislative body of a State, a possession of the United States, or a political subdivision of any of the foregoing with respect to legislation or proposed legislation of direct interest to the taxpayer, or

"(B) in direct connection with communication of information between the taxpayer and an organization of which he is a member with respect to legislation or proposed legislation of direct interest to the taxpayer and to such organization,

"and that portion of the dues so paid or incurred with respect to any organization of which the taxpayer is a member which is attributable to the expenses of the activities described in subparagraphs (A) and (B) carried on by such organization.

"(2) Limitation. The provisions of paragraph (1) shall not be construed as allowing the deduction of any amount paid or incurred (whether by way of contribution, gift, or otherwise)— "(A) for participation in, or intervention in, any political campaign on behalf of any candidate for public office, or

"(B) in connection with any attempt to influence the general public, or segments, thereof, with respect to legislative matters, elections, or referendums."

Effective Date (Sec. 13222(e) of P.L. 103-66) effective for amounts paid or incurred after 12/31/93.

and that portion of the dues so paid or incurred with respect to any organization of which the taxpayer is a member which is attributable to the expenses of the activities described in clauses (i) and (ii) carried on by such organization.

(3) Application to dues of tax-exempt organizations. *No deduction shall be allowed under subsection (a) for the portion of dues or other similar amounts paid by the taxpayer to an organization which is exempt from tax under this subtitle which the organization notifies the taxpayer under section 6033(e)(1)(A)(ii) is allocable to expenditures to which paragraph (1) applies.*

(4) Influencing legislation. *For purposes of this subsection—*

(A) In general. The term "influencing legislation" means any attempt to influence any legislation through communication with any member or employee of a legislative body, or with any government official or employee who may participate in the formulation of legislation.

(B) Legislation. The term "legislation" has the meaning given such term by section 4911(e)(2).

(5) Other special rules.

(A) Exception for certain taxpayers. In the case of any taxpayer engaged in the trade or business of conducting activities described in paragraph (1), paragraph (1) shall not apply to expenditures of the taxpayer in conducting such activities directly on behalf of another person (but shall apply to payments by such other person to the taxpayer for conducting such activities).

(B) De minimis exception.

(i) In general. Paragraph (1) shall not apply to any in-house expenditures for any taxable year if such expenditures do not exceed $2,000. In determining whether a taxpayer exceeds the $2,000 limit under this clause, there shall not be taken into account overhead costs otherwise allocable to activities described in paragraphs (1)(A) and (D).

(ii) In-house expenditures. For purposes of clause (i), the term "in-house expenditures" means expenditures described in paragraphs (1)(A) and (D) other than—

(I) payments by the taxpayer to a person engaged in the trade or business of conducting activities described in paragraph (1) for the conduct of such activities on behalf of the taxpayer, or

(II) dues or other similar amounts paid or incurred by the taxpayer which are allocable to activities described in paragraph (1).

(C) Expenses incurred in connection with lobbying and political activities. Any amount paid or incurred for research for, or preparation, planning, or coordination of, any activity described in paragraph (1) shall be treated as paid or incurred in connection with such activity.

(6) Covered executive branch official. *For purposes of this subsection, the term "covered executive branch official" means—*

(A) the President,

(B) the Vice President,

(C) any officer or employee of the White House Office of the Executive Office of the President, and the 2 most senior level officers of each of the other agencies in such Executive Office, and

(D) (i) any individual serving in a position in level I of the Executive Schedule under section 5312 of title 5, United States Code, (ii) any other individual designated by the President as having Cabinet level status, and (iii) any immediate deputy of an individual described in clause (i) or (ii).

(7) Special rule for Indian tribal governments. *For purposes of this subsection, an Indian tribal government shall be treated in the same manner as a local council or similar governing body.*

(8) Cross reference. *For reporting requirements and alternative taxes related to this subsection, see section 6033(e).*

* * * * * * * * * * * * *

(l) Special rules for health insurance costs of self-employed individuals.

* * * * * * * * * * * * *

(2) Limitations.

* * * * * * * * * * * * *

[2]*(B) Other coverage. Paragraph (1) shall not apply to any taxpayer for any calendar month for which the taxpayer is eligible to participate in any subsidized health plan maintained by any employer of the taxpayer or of the spouse of the taxpayer.*

* * * * * * * * * * * * *

[3]***(3) Coordination with medical deduction.*** *Any amount paid by a taxpayer for insurance to which paragraph (1) applies shall not be taken into account in computing the amount allowable to the taxpayer as a deduction under section 213(a).*

* * * * * * * * * * * * *

(6) Termination. This subsection shall not apply to any taxable year beginning after [4]*December 31, 1993.*

(m) Certain excessive employee remuneration.

(1) In general. *In the case of any publicly held corporation, no deduction shall be allowed under this chapter for applicable employee remuneration with respect to any covered employee to the extent that the amount of such remuneration for the taxable year with respect to such employee exceeds $1,000,000.*

(2) Publicly held corporation. *For purposes of this subsection, the term "publicly held corporation" means any corporation issuing any class of common equity securities required to be registered under section 12 of the Securities Exchange Act of 1934.*

(3) Covered employee. *For purposes of this subsection, the term "covered employee" means any employee of the taxpayer if—*

(A) as of the close of the taxable year, such employee is the chief executive officer of the taxpayer or an individual acting in such a capacity, or

(B) the total compensation of such employee for the taxable year is required to be reported to shareholders under the Securities Exchange Act of 1934 by reason of such employee being among the 4 highest compensated officers for the taxable year (other than the chief executive officer).

(4) Applicable employee remuneration. *For purposes of this subsection—*

(A) In general. Except as otherwise provided in this paragraph, the term "applicable employee remuneration" means, with respect to any covered employee for any taxable year, the aggregate amount allowable as a deduction under this chapter for such taxable year (determined without regard to this subsection) for remuneration for services performed by such employee (whether or not during the taxable year).

(B) Exception for remuneration payable on commission basis. The term "applicable employee remuneration" shall not include any remuneration payable on a commission basis solely on account of income generated directly by the individual performance of the individual to whom such remuneration is payable.

[Footnote Code Sec. 162 continued]

Matter in *italics* in code Sec. 162(l)(2)(B) added by section 13174(b)(1) of P.L. 103-66 which struck out:

2. "(B) Other coverage. Paragraph (1) shall not apply to any taxpayer who is eligible to participate in any subsidized health plan maintained by any employer of the taxpayer or of the spouse of the taxpayer."

Effective Date (Sec. 13174(b)(2) of P.L. 103-66) effective for tax. yrs. begin. after 12/31/92.

Matter in *italics* in Code Sec. 162(l)(3) added by section 13131(d)(2) of P.L. 103-66 which struck out:

3. "(3) Coordination with medical deduction, etc.

"(A) Medical deduction. Any amount paid by a taxpayer for insurance to which paragraph (1) applies shall not be taken into account in computing the amount allowable to the taxpayer as a deduction under section 213(a).

"(B) Health insurance credit. The amount otherwise taken into account under paragraph (1) as paid for insurance which constitutes medical care shall be reduced by the amount (if any) of the health insurance credit allowable to the taxpayer for the taxable year under section 32."

Effective Date (Sec. 13131(e) of P.L. 103-66) effective for tax. yrs. begin. after 12/31/93.

Matter in *italics* in Code Sec. 162(l)(6) added by section 13174(a)(1) of P.L. 103-66 which struck out:

4. "June 30, 1992"

Effective Date (Sec. 13174(a)(3) of P.L. 103-66) effective for tax. yrs. end. after 6/30/92.

(C) Other performance-based compensation. The term "applicable employee remuneration" shall not include any remuneration payable solely on account of the attainment of one or more performance goals, but only if—

(i) the performance goals are determined by a compensation committee of the board of directors of the taxpayer which is comprised solely of 2 or more outside directors,

(ii) the material terms under which the remuneration is to be paid, including the performance goals, are disclosed to shareholders and approved by a majority of the vote in a separate shareholder vote before the payment of such remuneration, and

(iii) before any payment of such remuneration, the compensation committee referred to in clause (i) certifies that the performance goals and any other material terms were in fact satisfied.

(D) Exception for existing binding contracts. The term "applicable employee remuneration" shall not include any remuneration payable under a written binding contract which was in effect on February 17, 1993, and which was not modified thereafter in any material respect before such remuneration is paid.

(E) Remuneration. For purposes of this paragraph, the term "remuneration" includes any remuneration (including benefits) in any medium other than cash, but shall not include—

(i) any payment referred to in so much of section 3121(a)(5) as precedes subparagraph (E) thereof, and

(ii) any benefit provided to or on behalf of an employee if at the time such benefit is provided it is reasonable to believe that the employee will be able to exclude such benefit from gross income under this chapter.

For purposes of clause (i), section 3121(a)(5) shall be applied without regard to section 3121(v)(1).

(F) Coordination with disallowed golden parachute payments. The dollar limitation contained in paragraph (1) shall be reduced (but not below zero) by the amount (if any) which would have been included in the applicable employee remuneration of the covered employee for the taxable year but for being disallowed under section 280G.

[5]***(n) Special rule for certain group health plans.***

(1) In general. *No deduction shall be allowed under this chapter to an employer for any amount paid or incurred in connection with a group health plan if the plan does not reimburse for inpatient hospital care services provided in the State of New York—*

(A) except as provided in subparagraphs (B) and (C), at the same rate as licensed commercial insurers are required to reimburse hospitals for such services when such reimbursement is not through such a plan,

(B) in the case of any reimbursement through a health maintenance organization, at the same rate as health maintenance organizations are required to reimburse hospitals for such services for individuals not covered by such a plan (determined without regard to any government-supported individuals exempt from such rate), or

(C) in the case of any reimbursement through any corporation organized under Article 43 of the New York State Insurance Law, at the same rate as any such corporation is required to reimburse hospitals for such services for individuals not covered by such a plan.

(2) State law exception. *Paragraph (1) shall not apply to any group health plan which is not required under the laws of the State of New York (determined without regard to this subsection or other provisions of Federal law) to reimburse at the rates provided in paragraph (1).*

(3) Group health plan. *For purposes of this subsection, the term "group health plan" means a plan of, or contributed to by, an employer or employee organization (including a self-insured plan) to provide health care (directly or otherwise) to any employee, any former employee, the employer, or any other individual associated or formerly associated with the employer in a business relationship, or any member of their family.*

[Footnote Code Sec. 162 continued]

Matter in *italics* in Code Sec. 162(m)-(n) added by Sec. 13211(a) which struck out:

5. "(n)"

Effective Date (Sec. 13211(b) of P.L. 103-66) effective for amounts which would otherwise be deductible for tax. yrs. begin. on or after 1/1/94.

[6]*(o)* **Cross reference.**

(1) For special rule relating to expenses in connection with subdividing real property for sale, see section 1237.

(2) For special rule relating to the treatment of payments by a transferee of a franchise, trademark, or trade name, see section 1253.

(3) For special rules relating to—

(A) funded welfare benefit plans, see section 419, and

(B) deferred compensation and other deferred benefits, see section 404.

[For explanation, see ¶ 307, for text of Committee Reports, see ¶s 3001, 3027, 3038, 3044, and 3079]

[¶ 2031] Code Sec. 163. Interest.

* * * * * * * * * * * *

(d) Limitation on investment interest.

* * * * * * * * * * * *

(4) Net investment income. For purposes of this subsection—

* * * * * * * * * * * *

[1]*(B) Investment income. The term "investment income" means the sum of—*

(i) gross income from property held for investment (other than any gain taken into account under clause (ii)(I)),

(ii) the excess (if any) of—

(I) the net gain attributable to the disposition of property held for investment, over

(II) the net capital gain determined by only taking into account gains and losses from dispositions of property held for investment, plus

(iii) so much of the net capital gain referred to in clause (ii)(II) (or, if lesser, the net gain referred to in clause (ii)(I)) as the taxpayer elects to take into account under this clause.

* * * * * * * * * * * *

(j) Limitation [2]*of deduction for interest on certain indebtedness.*

* * * * * * * * * * * *

[3]***(3) Disqualified interest.*** *For purposes of this subsection, the term "disqualified interest" means—*

Matter in *italics* in Code Sec. 162(n)-(o) was added by section 13442(a) of P.L. 103-66 which struck out:

6. "(n)"

Effective Date (Sec. 13442(b) of P.L. 103-66) effective for services provided after 2/2/93, and on or before 5/12/95.

[Footnote Code Sec. 163] Matter in *italics* in Code Sec. 163(d)(4)(B) added by section 13206(d)(1), P.L. 103-66, which struck out:

1. "(B) Investment income. The term 'investment income' means the sum of—

"(i) gross income (other than gain taken into account under clause (ii)) from property held for investment, and

"(ii) any net gain attributable to the disposition of property held for investment."

Effective Date (Sec. 13206(d)(3), P.L. 103-66) effective for tax. yrs. begin. after 12/31/92.

Matter in *italics* in Code Sec. 163(j), (j)(3), (j)(5)(B), (j)(6)(D) and (j)(6)(E) added by sections 13228(a), (b), (c)(1) and (c)(2), P.L. 103-66, which struck out:

2. "(j) Limitation on deduction for certain interest paid by corporation to related person."

3. "(3) Disqualified interest. For purposes of this subsection—

"(A) In general. Except as provided in subparagraph (B), the term 'disqualified interest' means any interest paid or accrued by the taxpayer (directly or indirectly) to a related person if no tax is imposed by this subtitle with respect to such interest.

"(B) Exception for certain existing indebtedness. The term 'disqualified interest' does not include any interest paid or accrued under indebtedness with a fixed term—

"(i) which was issued on or before July 10, 1989, or

"(ii) which was issued after such date pursuant to a written binding contract in effect on such date and all times thereafter before such indebtedness was issued."

(A) any interest paid or accrued by the taxpayer (directly or indirectly) to a related person if no tax is imposed by this subtitle with respect to such interest, and

(B) any interest paid or accrued by the taxpayer with respect to any indebtedness to a person who is not a related person if—

(i) there is a disqualified guarantee of such indebtedness, and

(ii) no gross basis tax is imposed by this subtitle with respect to such interest.

* * * * * * * * * * * * *

(5) Special rules for determining whether interest is subject to tax.

* * * * * * * * * * * * *

(B) Interest treated as tax-exempt to extent of treaty reduction. If any treaty between the United States and any foreign country reduces the rate of tax imposed by this subtitle on any interest paid or accrued by the taxpayer [4], such interest shall be treated as interest on which no tax is imposed by this subtitle to the extent of the same proportion of such interest as—

(i) the rate of tax imposed without regard to such treaty, reduced by the rate of tax imposed under the treaty, bears to

(ii) the rate of tax imposed without regard to the treaty.

(6) Other definitions and special rules. For purposes of this subsection—

* * * * * * * * * * * * *

(D) Disqualified guarantee.

(i) In general. Except as provided in clause (ii), the term "disqualified guarantee" means any guarantee by a related person which is—

(I) an organization exempt from taxation under this subtitle, or

(II) a foreign person.

(ii) Exceptions. The term "disqualified guarantee" shall not include a guarantee—

(I) in any circumstances identified by the Secretary by regulation, where the interest on the indebtedness would have been subject to a net basis tax if the interest had been paid to the guarantor, or

(II) if the taxpayer owns a controlling interest in the guarantor.

For purposes of subclause (II), except as provided in regulations, the term "a controlling interest" means direct or indirect ownership of at least 80 percent of the total voting power and value of all classes of stock of a corporation, or 80 percent of the profit and capital interests in any other entity. For purposes of the preceding sentence, the rules of paragraphs (1) and (5) of section 267(c) shall apply; except that such rules shall also apply to interest in entities other than corporations.

(iii) Guarantee. Except as provided in regulations, the term "guarantee" includes any arrangement under which a person (directly or indirectly through an entity or otherwise) assures, on a conditional or unconditional basis, the payment of another person's obligation under any indebtedness.

(E) Gross basis and net basis taxation.

(i) Gross basis tax. The term "gross basis tax" means any tax imposed by this subtitle which is determined by reference to the gross amount of any item of income without any reduction for any deduction allowed by this subtitle.

(ii) Net basis tax. The term "net basis tax" means any tax imposed by this subtitle which is a [sic] not a gross basis tax.

* * * * * * * * * * * * *

[For explanation, see ¶s 109, 308, and 1107, for text of Commitee Reports, see ¶ 3051]

[Footnote Code Sec. 163 continued]

4. "to a related person"

Effective Date (Sec. 13228(d), P.L. 103-66) effective for interest paid or accrued in tax. yrs. begin. after 12/31/93.

[¶ 2032] Code Sec. 167. Depreciation.

* * * * * * * * * * * * *

[1]*(c)* ***Basis for depreciation.***

(1) In general. *The basis on which exhaustion, wear and tear, and obsolescence are to be allowed in respect of any property shall be the adjusted basis provided in section 1011, for the purpose of determining the gain on the sale or other disposition of such property.*

(2) Special rule for property subject to lease. *If any property is acquired subject to a lease—*

(A) no portion of the adjusted basis shall be allocated to the leasehold interest, and

(B) the entire adjusted basis shall be taken into account in determining the depreciation deduction (if any) with respect to the property subject to the lease.

* * * * * * * * * * * * *

(e) Certain term interests not depreciable.

* * * * * * * * * * * * *

[2]***(2) Coordination with other provisions.***

(A) Section 273. This subsection shall not apply to any term interest to which section 273 applies.

(B) Section 305(e). This subsection shall not apply to the holder of the dividend rights which were separated from any stripped preferred stock to which section 305(e)(1) applies.

* * * * * * * * * * * * *

[Footnote Code Sec. 167] Matter in *italics* in Code Sec. 167(c) added by section 13261(b)(2), P.L. 103-66, which struck out:

1. "(c) Basis for depreciation.

"The basis on which exhaustion, wear and tear, and obsolescence are to be allowed in respect of any property shall be the adjusted basis provided in section 1011 for the purpose of determining the gain on the sale or other disposition of such property."

Effective Date (Sec. 13261(g), P.L. 103-66) effective for property acquired after 8/10/93, except as provided in Sec. 13261(g)(2) and (3) of this Act, which reads as follows:

"(2) Election to have amendments apply to property acquired after July 25, 1991.—

"(A) In general.— If an election under this paragraph applies to the taxpayer—

"(i) the amendments made by this section shall apply to property acquired by the taxpayer after July 25, 1991,

"(ii) subsection (c)(1)(A) of section 197 of the Internal Revenue Code of 1986 (as added by this section) (and so much of subsection (f)(9)(A) of such section 197 as precedes clause (i) thereof) shall be applied with respect to the taxpayer by treating July 25, 1991, as the date of the enactment of such section, and

"(iii) in applying subsection (f)(9) of such section, with respect to any property acquired by the taxpayer on or before the date of the enactment of this Act, only holding or use on July 25, 1991, shall be taken into account.

"(B) Election.—An election under this paragraph shall be made at such time and in such manner as the Secretary of the Treasury or his delegate may prescribe. Such an election by any taxpayer, once made—

"(i) may be revoked only with the consent of the Secretary, and

"(ii) shall apply to the taxpayer making such election and any other taxpayer under common control with the taxpayer (within the meaning of subparagraphs (A) and (B) of section 41(f)(1) of such Code) at any time after August 2, 1993, and on or before the date on which such election is made.

"(3) Elective binding contract exception.—

"(A) In general.—The amendments made by this section shall not apply to any acquisition of property by the taxpayer if—

"(i) such acquisition is pursuant to a written binding contract in effect on the date of the enactment of this Act and at all times thereafter before such acquisition,

"(ii) an election under paragraph (2) does not apply to the taxpayer, and

"(iii) the taxpayer makes an election under this paragraph with respect to such contract.

"(B) Election.— An election under this paragraph shallbe made at such time and in such manner as the Secretary of the Treasury or his delegate shall prescribe. Such an election, once made—

"(i) may be revoked only with the consent of the Secretary, and

"(ii) shall apply to all property acquired pursuant to the contract with respect to which such election was made."

Matter in *italics* in Code Sec. 167(e)(2) added by section 13206(c)(2), P.L. 103-66, which struck out:

2. "(2) Coordination with section 273. This subsection shall not apply to any term interest to which section 273 applies."

Effective Date (Sec. 13206(c)(3), P.L. 103-66) effective 4/30/93.

(f) Treatment of certain property excluded from section 197.

(1) Computer software.

(A) In general. If a depreciation deduction is allowable under subsection (a) with respect to any computer software, such deduction shall be computed by using the straight line method and a useful life of 36 months.

(B) Computer software. For purposes of this section, the term "computer software" has the meaning given to such term by section 197(e)(3)(B); except that such term shall not include any such software which is an amortizable section 197 intangible.

(2) Certain interests or rights acquired separately. *If a depreciation deduction is allowable under subsection (a) with respect to any property described in subparagraph (B), (C), or (D) of section 197(e)(4), such deduction shall be computed in accordance with regulations prescribed by the Secretary.*

(3) Mortgage servicing rights. *If a depreciation deduction is allowable under subsection (a) with respect to any right described in section 197(e)(7), such deduction shall be computed by using the straight line method and a useful life of 108 months.*

[3]***(g) Cross references.***

(1) For additional rule applicable to depreciation of improvements in the case of mines, oil and gas wells, other natural deposits, and timber, see section 611.

(2) For amortization of goodwill and certain other intangibles, see section 197.

[For explanation, see ¶ 111, for text of Committee Reports, see ¶ 3064]

[¶ 2033] Code Sec. 168. Accelerated cost recovery system.

* * * * * * * * * * * * *

(c) Applicable recovery period. For purposes of this section—

(1) In general. Except as provided in paragraph (2), the applicable recovery period shall be determined in accordance with the following table:

In the case of:	The applicable recovery period is:
3-year property	3 years
5-year property	5 years
7-year property	7 years
10-year property	10 years
15-year property	15 years
20-year property	20 years
Residential rental property	27.5 years
[1]*Nonresidential real property*	*39 years*
Any railroad grading or tunnel bore	50 years

* * * * * * * * * * * * *

Matter in *italics* in Code Sec. 167(f) and (g), added by sections 13261(b)(1) and (f)(1), P.L. 103-66, which struck out:

4. "(f)"

"(g) Depreciation of improvements in the case of mines, etc.

"For additional rule applicable to depreciation of improvements in the case of mines, oil and gas wells, other natural deposits, and timber, see section 611."

Effective Date (Sec. 13261(g), P.L. 103-66) effective—See above.

[Footnote Code Sec. 168] Matter in *italics* in Code Sec. 168(c)(1) added by section 13151(a) of P.L. 103-66 which struck out:

1. "Nonresidential real property . . . . 31.5 years"

Effective Date (Sec. 13151(b) of P.L. 103-66) effective for property placed in service by the taxpayer on or after May 13, 1993, except as provided in Sec. 13151(b)(2) of this Act, which reads as follows:

"(2) Exception.—The amendments made by this section shall not apply to property placed in service by the taxpayer before January 1, 1994, if—

"(A) the taxpayer or a qualified person entered into a binding written contract to purchase or construct such property before May 13, 1993, or

"(B) the construction of such property was commenced by or for the taxpayer or a qualified person before May 13, 1993.

(j) Property on Indian reservations.

(1) In general. *For purposes of subsection (a), the applicable recovery period for qualified Indian reservation property shall be determined in accordance with the table contained in paragraph (2) in lieu of the table contained in subsection (c).*

(2) Applicable recovery period for Indian reservation roperty. *For purposes of paragraph (1)—*

In the case of:	The applicable recovery period is:
3-year property	2 years
5-year property	3 years
7-year property	4 years
10-year property	6 years
15-year property	9 years
20-year property	12 years
Nonresidential real property	22 years

(3) Deduction allowed in computing minimum tax. *For purposes of determining alternative minimum taxable income under section 55, the deduction under subsection (a) for property to which paragraph (1) applies shall be determined under this section without regard to any adjustment under section 56.*

(4) Qualified Indian reservation property defined. *For purposes of this subsection—*

(A) In general. The term "qualified Indian reservation property" means property which is property described in the table in paragraph (2) and which is—

(i) used by the taxpayer predominantly in the active conduct of a trade or business within an Indian reservation,

(ii) not used or located outside the Indian reservation on a regular basis,

(iii) not acquired (directly or indirectly) by the taxpayer from a person who is related to the taxpayer (within the meaning of section 465(b)(3)(C)), and

(iv) not property (or any portion thereof) placed in service for purposes of conducting or housing class I, II, or III gaming (as defined in section 4 of the Indian Regulatory Act (25 U.S.C. 2703)).

(B) Exception for alternative depreciation property. The term "qualified Indian reservation property" does not include any property to which the alternative depreciation system under subsection (g) applies, determined—

(i) without regard to subsection (g)(7) (relating to election to use alternative depreciation system), and

(ii) after the application of section 280F(b) (relating to listed property with limited business use).

(C) Special rule for reservation infrastructure investment.

(i) In general. Subparagraph (A)(ii) shall not apply to qualified infrastructure property located outside of the Indian reservation if the purpose of such property is to connect with qualified infrastructure property located within the Indian reservation.

(ii) Qualified infrastructure property. For purposes of this subparagraph, the term "qualified infrastructure property" means qualified Indian reservation property (determined without regard to subparagraph (A)(ii)) which—

(I) benefits the tribal infrastructure,

(II) is available to the general public, and

(III) is placed in service in connection with the taxpayer's active conduct of a trade or business within an Indian reservation.

[Footnote Code Sec. 168 continued]

"For purposes of this paragraph, the term 'qualified person' means any person who transfers his rights in such a contract or such property to the taxpayer but only if the property is not placed in service by such person before such rights are transferred to the taxpayer."

Matter in *italics* in Code Sec. 168(j) was added by section 13321(a) of P.L. 103-66.

Effective Date (Sec. 13321(b) of P.L.103-66) effective for property placed in service after 12/31/93.

Such term includes, but is not limited to, roads, power lines, water systems, railroad spurs, and communications facilities.

(5) Real estate rentals. *For purposes of this subsection, the rental to others of real property located within an Indian reservation shall be treated as the active conduct of a trade or business within an Indian reservation.*

(6) Indian reservation defined. *For purposes of this subsection, the term "Indian reservation" means a reservation, as defined in—*

(A) section 3(d) of the Indian Financing Act of 1974 (25 U.S.C. 1452(d)), or

(B) section 4(10) of the Indian Child Welfare Act of 1978 (25 U.S.C. 1903(10)).

(7) Coordination with nonrevenue laws. *Any reference in this subsection to a provision not contained in this title shall be treated for purposes of this subsection as a reference to such provision as in effect on the date of the enactment of this paragraph.*

(8) Termination. *This subsection shall not apply to property placed in service after December 31, 2003.*

[For explanation, see ¶ 502 and ¶ 610, for Committee Reports, see ¶ 3022 and ¶ 3064.]

[¶ 2034] Code Sec. 170. Charitable, etc., contributions and gifts.

* * * * * * * * * * * * *

(f) Disallowance of deduction in certain cases and special rules.

* * * * * * * * * * * * *

(8) Substantiation requirement for certain contributions.

(A) General rule. No deduction shall be allowed under subsection (a) for any contribution of $250 or more unless the taxpayer substantiates the contribution by a contemporaneous written acknowledgment of the contribution by the donee organization that meets the requirements of subparagraph (B).

(B) Content of acknowledgement. An acknowledgement meets the requirements of this subparagraph if it includes the following information:

(i) The amount of cash and a description (but not value) of any property other than cash contributed.

(ii) Whether the donee organization provided any goods or services in consideration, in whole or in part, for any property described in clause (i).

(iii) A description and good faith estimate of the value of any goods or services referred to in clause (ii) or, if such goods or services consist solely of intangible religious benefits, a statement to that effect.

For purposes of this subparagraph, the term "intangible religious benefit" means any intangible religious benefit which is provided by an organization organized exclusively for religious purposes and which generally is not sold in a commercial transaction outside the donative context.

(C) Contemporaneous. For purposes of subparagraph (A), an acknowledgment shall be considered to be contemporaneous if the taxpayer obtains the acknowledgment on or before the earlier of—

(i) the date on which the taxpayer files a return for the taxable year in which the contribution was made, or

(ii) the due date (including extensions) for filing such return.

(D) Substantiation not required for contributions reported by the donee organization. Subparagraph (A) shall not apply to a contribution if the donee organization files a return, on such form and in accordance with such regulations as the Secretary may prescribe, which includes the information described in subparagraph (B) with respect to the contribution.

[Footnote Code Sec. 170] Matter in *italics* in Code Sec. 170(f)(8) was added by section 13172(a) of P.L. 103-66
Effective Date (Sec. 13172(b) of P.L. 103-66) effective for contributions made on or after 1/1/94.

(E) Regulations. The Secretary shall prescribe such regulations as may be necessary or appropriate to carry out the purposes of this paragraph, including regulations that may provide that some or all of the requirements of this paragraph do not apply in appropriate cases.

(9) Denial of deduction where contribution for lobbying activities. *No deduction shall be allowed under this section for a contribution to an organization which conducts activities to which section 162(e)(1) applies on matters of direct financial interest to the donor's trade or business, if a principal purpose of the contribution was to avoid Federal income tax by securing a deduction for such activities under this section which would be disallowed by reason of section 162(e) if the donor had conducted such activities directly. No deduction shall be allowed under section 162(a) for any amount for which a deduction is disallowed under the preceding sentence.*

* * * * * * * * * * * * *

[For explanation, see ¶ 307 and ¶ 1201, for text of Committee Report, see ¶ 3026 and ¶ 3044]

[¶ 2035] **Code Sec. 172. Net operating loss deduction.**

* * * * * * * * * * * * *

(d) Modifications. The modifications referred to in this section are as follows:

* * * * * * * * * * * * *

[1]***(2) Capital gains and losses of taxpayers other than corporations.*** *In the case of a taxpayer other than a corporation—*

(A) the amount deductible on account of losses from sales or exchanges of capital assets shall not exceed the amount includable on account of gains from sales or exchanges of capital assets; and

(B) the exclusion provided by section 1202 shall not be allowed.

* * * * * * * * * * * * *

(4) Nonbusiness deductions of taxpayers other than corporations. In the case of a taxpayer other than a corporation, the deductions allowable by this chapter which are not attributable to a taxpayer's trade or business shall be allowed only to the extent of the amount of the gross income not derived from such trade or business. For purposes of the preceding sentence—

(A) any gain or loss from the sale or other disposition of—

(i) property, used in the trade or business, of a character which is subject to the allowance for depreciation provided in section 167, or

(ii) real property used in the trade or business,

shall be treated as attributable to the trade or business;

(B) the modifications specified in paragraphs (1), *(2)(B),* and (3) shall be taken into account;

* * * * * * * * * * * * *

[For explanation, see ¶ 703]

Matter in *italics* in Code Sec. 170(f)(9) was added by section 13222(b) of P.L. 103-66

Effective Date (Sec. 13222(e) of P.L. 103-66) effective for amounts paid or incurred after 12/31/93.

[Footnote Code Sec. 172] Matter in *italics* in Code Sec. 172(d)(2) and (4)(B) added by sections 13113(d)(1)(A) and (B) of P.L. 103-66 which struck out:

1. "(2) Capital gains and losses of taxpayers other than corporations.

"In the case of a taxpayer other than a corporation, the amount deductible on account of losses from sales or exchanges of capital assets shall not exceed the amount includible on account of gains from sales or exchanges of capital assets."

Effective Date (Sec. 13113(e) of P.L. 103-66) effective for stock issued after 8/10/93.

[¶ 2036] Code Sec. 179. Election to expense certain depreciable business assets.

* * * * * * * * * * * *

(b) Limitations.

(1) Dollar limitation. The aggregate cost which may be taken into account under subsection (a) for any taxable year shall not exceed [1]*$17,500.*

* * * * * * * * * * * *

[For explanation, see ¶ 701, for text of Committee Reports, see ¶ 3008]

[¶ 2037] Code Sec. 196. Deduction for certain unused business credits.

* * * * * * * * * * * *

(c) Qualified business credits. For purposes of this section, the term "qualified business credits" means—

(1) the investment credit determined under section 46 (but only to the extent attributable to property the basis of which is reduced by section 50(c)),

(2) the targeted jobs credit determined under section 51(a),

(3) the alcohol fuels credit determined under section 40(a),

(4) the research credit determined under section 41(a) (other than such credit determined under section 280C(c)(3)) for taxable years beginning after December 31, 1988, [1]

(5) the enhanced oil recovery credit determined under section 43(a), [2]

(6) the empowerment zone employment credit determined under section 1396(a) [3]*, and*

(7) the Indian employment credit determined under section 45A(a).

[For explanation, see ¶ 609]

[¶ 2038] Code Sec. 197. Amortization of goodwill and certain other intangibles.

(a) General rule. A taxpayer shall be entitled to an amortization deduction with respect to any amortizable section 197 intangible. The amount of such deduction shall be determined by

[Footnote Code Sec. 179] Matter in *italics* in Code Sec. 179(b)(1) added by section 13116(a) of P.L. 103-66 which struck out:

1. "$10,000"

Effective Date (Sec. 13116(b) of P.L. 103-66) effective for tax. yrs. begin. after 12/31/92.

[Footnote Code Sec. 196] Matter in *italics* in Code Sec. 196(c)(4)-(6) added by section 13302(b)(2) of P.L. 103-66, which struck out:

1. "and"

Effective Date (Sec. 13303 of P.L. 103-66) effective 8/10/93.

Matter in *italics* in Code Sec. 196(c)(5)-(7) added by section 13322(c)(2) of P.L. 103-66 which struck out:

2. "and"
3. "."

Effective Date (Sec. 13322(f) of P.L. 103-66) effective for wages paid or incurred after 12/31/93.

[Footnote Code Sec. 197] Code Sec. 197 was added by section 13261(a) of P.L. 103-66

Effective Date (Sec. 13261(g) of P.L. 103-66) effective for property acquired after 8/10/93, except as provided in Sec. 13261(g)(2) and (3) of this Act, which reads as follows:

"(2) Election to have amendments apply to property acquired after July 25, 1991.

"(A) In general. If an election under this paragraph applies to the taxpayer—

"(i) the amendments made by this section shall apply to property acquired by the taxpayer after July 25, 1991,

"(ii) subsection (c)(1)(A) of section 197 of the Internal Revenue Code of 1986 (as added by this section) (and so much of subsection (f)(9)(A) of such section 197 as precedes clause (i) thereof) shall be applied with respect to the taxpayer by treating July 25, 1991, as the date of the enactment of such section, and

"(iii) in applying subsection (f)(9) of such section, with respect to any property acquired by the taxpayer on or before the date of the enactment of this Act, only holding or use on July 25, 1991, shall be taken into account.

amortizing the adjusted basis (for purposes of determining gain) of such intangible ratably over the 15-year period beginning with the month in which such intangible was acquired.

(b) No other depreciation or amortization deduction allowable. Except as provided in subsection (a), no depreciation or amortization deduction shall be allowable with respect to any amortizable section 197 intangible.

(c) Amortizable section 197 intangible. For purposes of this section—

(1) In general. Except as otherwise provided in this section, the term "amortizable section 197 intangible" means any section 197 intangible—

(A) which is acquired by the taxpayer after the date of the enactment of this section, and

(B) which is held in connection with the conduct of a trade or business or an activity described in section 212.

(2) Exclusion of self-created intangibles, etc. The term "amortizable section 197 intangible" shall not include any section 197 intangible—

(A) which is not described in subparagraph (D), (E), or (F) of subsection (d)(1), and

(B) which is created by the taxpayer.

This paragraph shall not apply if the intangible is created in connection with a transaction (or series of related transactions) involving the acquisition of assets constituting a trade or business or substantial portion thereof.

(3) Anti-churning rules. For exclusion of intangibles acquired in certain transactions, see subsection (f)(9).

(d) Section 197 intangible. For purposes of this section—

(1) In general. Except as otherwise provided in this section, the term "section 197 intangible" means—

(A) goodwill,

(B) going concern value,

(C) any of the following intangible items:

(i) workforce in place including its composition and terms and conditions (contractual or otherwise) of its employment,

(ii) business books and records, operating systems, or any other information base (including lists or other information with respect to current or prospective customers),

(iii) any patent, copyright, formula, process, design, pattern, knowhow, format, or other similar item,

(iv) any customer-based intangible,

(v) any supplier-based intangible, and

(vi) any other similar item,

(D) any license, permit, or other right granted by a governmental unit or an agency or instrumentality thereof,

(E) any covenant not to compete (or other arrangement to the extent such arrangement has substantially the same effect as a covenant not to compete) entered into in connection

---

[Footnote Code Sec. 196 continued]

"(B) Election. An election under this paragraph shall be made at such time and in such manner as the Secretary of the Treasury or his delegate may prescribe. Such an election by any taxpayer, once made—

"(i) may be revoked only with the consent of the Secretary, and

"(ii) shall apply to the taxpayer making such election and any other taxpayer under common control with the taxpayer (within the meaning of subparagraphs (A) and (B) of section 41(f)(1) of such Code) at any time after August 2, 1993, and on or before the date on which such election is made.

"(3) Elective binding contract exception.

"(A) In general. The amendments made by this section shall not apply to any acquisition of property by the taxpayer if—

"(i) such acquisition is pursuant to a written binding contract in effect on the date of the enactment of this Act and at all times thereafter before such acquisition,

"(ii) an election under paragraph (2) does not apply to the taxpayer, and

"(iii) the taxpayer makes an election under this paragraph with respect to such contract.

"(B) Election. An election under this paragraph shall be made at such time and in such manner as the Secretary of the Treasury or his delegate shall prescribe. Such an election, once made—

"(i) may be revoked only with the consent of the Secretary, and

"(ii) shall apply to all property acquired pursuant to the contract with respect to which such election was made."

with an acquisition (directly or indirectly) of an interest in a trade or business or substantial portion thereof, and

(F) any franchise, trademark, or trade name.

(2) Customer-based intangible.

(A) In general. The term "customer-based intangible" means—

(i) composition of market,

(ii) market share, and

(iii) any other value resulting from future provision of goods or services pursuant to relationships (contractual or otherwise) in the ordinary course of business with customers.

(B) Special rule for financial institutions. In the case of a financial institution, the term "customer-based intangible" includes deposit base and similar items.

(3) Supplier-based intangible. The term "supplier-based intangible" means any value resulting from future acquisitions of goods or services pursuant to relationships (contractual or otherwise) in the ordinary course of business with suppliers of goods or services to be used or sold by the taxpayer.

(e) Exceptions. For purposes of this section, the term "section 197 intangible" shall not include any of the following:

(1) Financial interests. Any interest—

(A) in a corporation, partnership, trust, or estate, or

(B) under an existing futures contract, foreign currency contract, notional principal contract, or other similar financial contract.

(2) Land. Any interest in land.

(3) Computer software.

(A) In general. Any—

(i) computer software which is readily available for purchase by the general public, is subject to a nonexclusive license, and has not been substantially modified, and

(ii) other computer software which is not acquired in a transaction (or series of related transactions) involving the acquisition of assets constituting a trade or business or substantial portion thereof.

(B) Computer software defined. For purposes of subparagraph (A), the term "computer software" means any program designed to cause a computer to perform a desired function. Such term shall not include any data base or similar item unless the data base or item is in the public domain and is incidental to the operation of otherwise qualifying computer software.

(4) Certain interests or rights acquired separately. Any of the following not acquired in a transaction (or series of related transactions) involving the acquisition of assets constituting a trade business or substantial portion thereof:

(A) Any interest in a film, sound recording, video tape, book, or similar property.

(B) Any right to receive tangible property or services under a contract or granted by a governmental unit or agency or instrumentality thereof.

(C) Any interest in a patent or copyright.

(D) To the extent provided in regulations, any right under a contract (or granted by a governmental unit or an agency or instrumentality thereof) if such right—

(i) has a fixed duration of less than 15 years, or

(ii) is fixed as to amount and, without regard to this section, would be recoverable under a method similar to the unit-of-production method.

(5) Interests under leases and debt instruments. Any interest under—

(A) an existing lease of tangible property, or

(B) except as provided in subsection (d)(2)(B), any existing indebtedness.

(6) Treatment of sports franchises. A franchise to engage in professional football, basketball, baseball, or other professional sport, and any item acquired in connection with such a franchise.

(7) Mortgage servicing. Any right to service indebtedness which is secured by residential real property unless such right is acquired in a transaction (or series of related transactions) involving the acquisition of assets (other than rights described in this paragraph) constituting a trade or business or substantial portion thereof.

(8) Certain transaction costs. Any fees for professional services, and any transaction costs, incurred by parties to a transaction with respect to which any portion of the gain or loss is not recognized under part III of subchapter C.

(f) Special rules.

(1) Treatment of certain dispositions, etc.

(A) In general. If there is a disposition of any amortizable section 197 intangible acquired in a transaction or series of related transactions (or any such intangible becomes worthless) and one or more other amortizable section 197 intangibles acquired in such transaction or series of related transactions are retained—

(i) no loss shall be recognized by reason of such disposition (or such worthlessness), and

(ii) appropriate adjustments to the adjusted bases of such retained intangibles shall be made for any loss not recognized under clause (i).

(B) Special rule for covenants not to compete. In the case of any section 197 intangible which is a covenant not to compete (or other arrangement) described in subsection (d)(1)(E), in no event shall such covenant or other arrangement be treated as disposed of (or becoming worthless) before the disposition of the entire interest described in such subsection in connection with which such covenant (or other arrangement) was entered into.

(C) Special rule. All persons treated as a single taxpayer under section 41(f)(1) shall be so treated for purposes of this paragraph.

(2) Treatment of certain transfers.

(A) In general. In the case of any section 197 intangible transferred in a transaction described in subparagraph (B), the transferee shall be treated as the transferor for purposes of applying this section with respect to so much of the adjusted basis in the hands of the transferee as does not exceed the adjusted basis in the hands of the transferor.

(B) Transactions covered. The transactions described in this subparagraph are—

(i) any transaction described in section 332, 351, 361, 721, 731, 1031, or 1033, and

(ii) any transaction between members of the same affiliated group during any taxable year for which a consolidated return is made by such group.

(3) Treatment of amounts paid pursuant to covenants not to compete, etc. Any amount paid or incurred pursuant to a covenant or arrangement referred to in subsection (d)(1)(E) shall be treated as an amount chargeable to capital account.

(4) Treatment of franchises, etc.

(A) Franchise. The term "franchise" has the meaning given to such term by section 1253(b)(1).

(B) Treatment of renewals. Any renewal of a franchise, trademark, or trade name (or of a license, a permit, or other right referred to in subsection (d)(1)(D)) shall be treated as an acquisition. The preceding sentence shall only apply with respect to costs incurred in connection with such renewal.

(C) Certain amounts not taken into account. Any amount to which section 1253(d)(1) applies shall not be taken into account under this section.

(5) Treatment of certain reinsurance transactions. In the case of any amortizable section 197 intangible resulting from an assumption reinsurance transaction, the amount taken into account as the adjusted basis of such intangible under this section shall be the excess of—

(A) the amount paid or incurred by the acquirer under the assumption reinsurance transaction, over

(B) the amount required to be capitalized under section 848 in connection with such transaction.

Subsection (b) shall not apply to any amount required to be capitalized under section 848.

(6) Treatment of certain subleases. For purposes of this section, a sublease shall be treated in the same manner as a lease of the underlying property involved.

(7) Treatment as depreciable. For purposes of this chapter, any amortizable section 197 intangible shall be treated as property which is of a character subject to the allowance for depreciation provided in section 167.

(8) Treatment of certain increments in value. This section shall not apply to any increment in value if, without regard to this section, such increment is properly taken into account in determining the cost of property which is not a section 197 intangible.

(9) Anti-churning rules. For purposes of this section —

(A) In general. The term "amortizable section 197 intangible" shall not include any section 197 intangible which is described in subparagraph (A) or (B) of subsection (d)(1) (or for which depreciation or amortization would not have been allowable but for this section) and which is acquired by the taxpayer after the date of the enactment of this section, if—

(i) the intangible was held or used at any time on or after July 25, 1991, and on or before such date of enactment by the taxpayer or a related person,

(ii) the intangible was acquired from a person who held such intangible at any time on or after July 25, 1991, and on or before such date of enactment, and, as part of the transaction, the user of such intangible does not change, or

(iii) the taxpayer grants the right to use such intangible to a person (or a person related to such person) who held or used such intangible at any time on or after July 25, 1991, and on or before such date of enactment.

For purposes of this subparagraph, the determination of whether the user of property changes as part of a transaction shall be determined in accordance with regulations prescribed by the Secretary. For purposes of this subparagraph, deductions allowable under section 1253(d) shall be treated as deductions allowable for amortization.

(B) Exception where gain recognized. If—

(i) subparagraph (A) would not apply to an intangible acquired by the taxpayer but for the last sentence of subparagraph (C)(i), and

(ii) the person from whom the taxpayer acquired the intangible elects, notwithstanding any other provision of this title—

(I) to recognize gain on the disposition of the intangible, and

(II) to pay a tax on such gain which, when added to any other income tax on such gain under this title, equals such gain multiplied by the highest rate of income tax applicable to such person under this title,

then subparagraph (A) shall apply to the intangible only to the extent that the taxpayer's adjusted basis in the intangible exceeds the gain recognized under clause (ii)(I).

(C) Related person defined. For purposes of this paragraph—

(i) Related person. A person (hereinafter in this paragraph referred to as the "related person") is related to any person if—

(I) the related person bears a relationship to such person specified in section 267(b) or section 707(b)(1), or

(II) the related person and such person are engaged in trades or businesses under common control (within the meaning of subparagraphs (A) and (B) of section 41(f)(1)).

For purposes of subclause (I), in applying section 267(b) or 707(b)(1), "20 percent" shall be substituted for "50 percent".

(ii) Time for making determination. A person shall be treated as related to another person if such relationship exists immediately before or immediately after the acquisition of the intangible involved.

(D) Acquisitions by reason of death. Subparagraph (A) shall not apply to the acquisition of any property by the taxpayer if the basis of the property in the hands of the taxpayer is determined under section 1014(a).

(E) Special rule for partnerships. With respect to any increase in the basis of partnership property under section 732, 734, or 743, determinations under this paragraph shall be made at the partner level and each partner shall be treated as having owned and used such partner's proportionate share of the partnership assets.

(F) Anti-abuse rules. The term "amortizable section 197 intangible" does not include any section 197 intangible acquired in a transaction, one of the principal purposes of which is to avoid the requirement of subsection (c)(1) that the intangible be acquired after the date of the enactment of this section or to avoid the provisions of subparagraph (A).

(g) **Regulations.** The Secretary shall prescribe such regulations as may be appropriate to carry out the purposes of this section, including such regulations as may be appropriate to prevent avoidance of the purposes of this section through related persons or otherwise.
[For explanation, see ¶s 402, 404, 406, 407, 408, 409, 413, 415, 416, 418, 419, 420, and 424, for text of Committee Reports, see ¶ 3064]

[¶ 2039] Code Sec. 213. Medical, dental, etc., expenses.

* * * * * * * * * * * *

[1](f) Repealed

[For text of Committee Report, see ¶ 3011]

[¶ 2040] Code Sec. 217. Moving expenses.

* * * * * * * * * * * *

[1](b) Definition of moving expenses.

(1) In general. For purposes of this section, the term "moving expenses" means only the reasonable expenses—

[Footnote Code Sec. 213] Matter in *italics* in Code Sec. 213(f) added by Sec. 13131(d)(3) of P.L. 103-66 which struck out:

1. "(f) Coordination with health insurance credit under section 32.

"The amount otherwise taken into account under subsection (a) as expenses paid for medical care shall be reduced by the amount (if any) of the health insurance credit allowable to the taxpayer for the taxable year under section 32."

Effective Date (Sec. 13131(e) of P.L. 103-66) effective for tax. yrs. begin. after 12/31/93.

[Footnote Code Sec. 217] Matter in *italics* in Code Sec. 217(b), (c)(1), (f), (g)(3)(A) and (B) and (h)(1)-(3) added by sections 13213(a)(1), (a)(2)(A)-(D) and (b) of P.L. 103-66 which struck out:

1. "(b) Definition of moving expenses.

"(1) In general. For purposes of this section, the term 'moving expenses' means only the reasonable expenses—

"(A) of moving household goods and personal effects from the former residence to the new residence,

"(B) of traveling (including meals and lodging) from the former residence to the new place of residence,

"(C) of traveling (including meals and lodging), after obtaining employment, from the former residence to the general location of the new principal place of work and return, for the principal purpose of searching for a new residence,

"(D) of meals and lodging while occupying temporary quarters in the general location of the new principal place of work during any period of 30 consecutive days after obtaining employment, or

"(E) constituting qualified residence sale, purchase, or lease expenses.

"(2) Qualified residence sale, etc., expenses. For purposes of paragraph (1)(E), the term 'qualified residence sale, purchase, or lease expenses' means only reasonable expenses incident to—

"(A) the sale or exchange by the taxpayer or his spouse of the taxpayer's former residence (not including expenses for work performed on such residence in order to assist in its sale) which (but for this subsection and subsection (e)) would be taken into account in determining the amount realized on the sale or exchange,

"(B) the purchase by the taxpayer or his spouse of a new residence in the general location of the new principal place of work which (but for this subsection and subsection (e)) would be taken into account in determining—

"(i) the adjusted basis of the new residence, or

"(ii) the cost of a loan (but not including any amounts which represent payments or prepayments of interest),

"(C) the settlement of an unexpired lease held by the taxpayer or his spouse on property used by the taxpayer as his former residence, or

"(D) the acquisition of a lease by the taxpayer or his spouse on property used by the taxpayer as his new residence in the general location of the new principal place of work (not including amounts which are payments or prepayments of rent).

"(3) Limitations.

"(A) Dollar limits. The aggregate amount allowable as a deduction under subsection (a) in connection with a commencement of work which is attributable to expenses described in subparagraph (C) or (D) of paragraph (1) shall not exceed $1,500. The aggregate amount allowable as a deduction under subsection (a) which is attributable to qualified residence sale,

(A) of moving household goods and personal effects from the former residence to the new residence, and

(B) of traveling (including lodging) from the former residence to the new place of residence. Such term shall not include any expenses for meals.

(2) *Individuals other than taxpayer. In the case of any individual other than the taxpayer, expenses referred to in paragraph (1) shall be taken into account only if such individual has both the former residence and the new residence as his principal place of abode and is a member of the taxpayer's household.*

(c) Conditions for allowance. No deduction shall be allowed under this section unless—

(1) the taxpayer's new principal place of work—

(A) is at least [2]*50 miles* farther from his former residence than was his former principal place of work, or

(B) if he had no former principal place of work, is at least [3]*50 miles* from his former residence, and

* * * * * * * * * * * * *

[4]**(e) Repealed.**

[5]***(f) Self-employed individual.*** *For purposes of this section, the term "self-employed individual" means an individual who performs personal services—*

(1) *as the owner of the entire interest in an unincorporated trade or business, or*

(2) *as a partner in a partnership carrying on a trade or business.*

(g) Rules for members of the Armed Forces of the United States. In the case of a member of the Armed Forces of the United States on active duty who moves pursuant to a military order and incident to a permanent change of station—

(1) the limitations under subsection (c) shall not apply;

(2) any moving and storage expenses which are furnished in kind (or for which reimbursement or an allowance is provided, but only to the extent of the expenses paid or incurred) to such member, his spouse, or his dependents, shall not be includible in gross income, and no reporting with respect to such expenses shall be required by the Secretary of Defense or the Secretary of Transportation, as the case may be; and

(3) if moving and storage expenses are furnished in kind (or if reimbursement or an allowance for such expenses is provided) to such member's spouse and his dependents with regard to moving to a location other than the one to which such member moves (or from a location

[Footnote Code Sec. 217 continued]

purchase, or lease expenses shall not exceed $3,000, reduced by the aggregate amount so allowable which is attributable to expenses described in subparagraph (C) or (D) of paragraph (1).

"(B) Husband and wife. If a husband and wife both commence work at a new principal place of work within the same general location, subparagraph (A) shall be applied as if there was only one commencement of work. In the case of a husband and wife filing separate returns, subparagraph (A) shall be applied by substituting '$750' for '$1,500', and by substituting '$1,500' for '$3,000'.

"(C) Individuals other than taxpayer. In the case of any individual other than the taxpayer, expenses referred to in subparagraphs (A) through (D) of paragraph (1) shall be taken into account only if such individual has both the former residence and the new residence as his principal place of abode and is a member of the taxpayer's household."

2. "35 miles"

3. "35 miles"

4. "(e) **Denial of double benefit.**

The amount realized on the sale of the residence described in subparagraph (A) of subsection (b)(2) shall not be decreased by the amount of any expenses described in such subparagraph which are allowed as a deduction under subsection (a), and the basis of a residence described in subparagraph (B) of subsection (b)(2) shall not be increased by the amount of any expenses described in such subparagraph which are allowed as a deduction under subsection (a). This subsection shall not apply to any expenses with respect to which an amount is included in gross income under subsection (d)(3)."

5. "(f) **Rules for self-employed individuals.**

"(1) **Definition.** For purposes of this section, the term 'self-employed individual' means an individual who performs personal services—

"(A) as the owner of the entire interest in an unincorporated trade or business, or

"(B) as a partner in a partnership carrying on a trade or business.

"(2) **Rule for application of subsections (b)(1)(C) and (D).** For purposes of subparagraphs (C) and (D) of subsection (b)(1), an individual who commences work at a new principal place of work as a self-employed individual shall be treated as having obtained employment when he has made substantial arrangements to commence such work."

other than the one from which such member moves), this section shall apply with respect to the moving expenses of his spouse and dependents—

(A) as if his spouse commenced work as an employee at a new principal place of work at such location; *and*

[6]*(B)* without regard to the limitations under subsection (c). [7]

(h) Special rules for foreign moves.

[8]***(1)* Allowance of certain storage fees.** In the case of a foreign move, for purposes of this section, the moving expenses described in subsection (b)(1)(A) include the reasonable expenses—

(A) of moving household goods and personal effects to and from storage, and

(B) of storing such goods and effects for part or all of the period during which the new place of work continues to be the taxpayer's principal place of work.

[9]***(2)*** Foreign move. For purposes of this subsection, the term "foreign move" means the commencement of work by the taxpayer at a new principal place of work located outside the United States.

[10]***(3)*** United States defined. For purposes of this subsection and subsection (i), the term "United States" includes the possessions of the United States. [11]

* * * * * * * * * * * * *

[For explanation, see ¶ 201, for text of Committee Report, see ¶ 3040]

[¶ 2041] Code Sec. 274. Disallowance of certain entertainment, etc., expenses.

* * * * * * * * * * * * *

(a) Entertainment, amusement, or recreation.

* * * * * * * * * * * * *

(3) Denial of deduction for club dues.

Notwithstanding the preceding provisions of this subsection, no deduction shall be allowed under this chapter for amounts paid or incurred for membership in any club organized for business, pleasure, recreation, or other social purpose.

* * * * * * * * * * * * *

(e) Specific exceptions to application of subsection (a). Subsection (a) shall not apply to—

* * * * * * * * * * * * *

(4) Recreational, etc., expenses for employees. Expenses for recreational, social, or similar activities (including facilities therefor) primarily for the benefit of employees (other than employees who are highly compensated employees (within the meaning of section 414(q))). For purposes of this paragraph, an individual owning less than a 10-percent interest in the tax-

6. "(B) for purposes of subsection (b)(3), as if such place of work was within the same general location as the member's new principal place of work, and"
7. "(C)"
8. "(h) **Special rules for foreign moves.**
"(1) **Increase in limitations.** In the case of a foreign move—
"(A) subsection (b)(1)(D) shall be applied by substituting '90 consecutive days' for '30 consecutive days',
"(B) subsection (b)(3)(A) shall be applied by substituting '$4,500' for '$1,500' and by substituting '$6,000' for '$3,000', and
"(C) subsection (b)(3)(B) shall be applied as if the last sentence of such subsection read as follows: 'In the case of a husband and wife filing separate returns, subparagraph (A) shall be applied by substituting "$2,250" for "$4,500", and by substituting "$3,000" for "$6,000"."
9. "(2)"
10. "(3)"
11. "(4)"

Effective Date (Sec. 13213(e) of P.L. 103-66) effective for expenses incurred after 12/31/93.

[Footnote Code Sec. 274] Matter in *italics* in Code Sec. 274(a)(3) and (e)(4) added by sections 13210(a) and (b) of P.L 103-66.

Effective Date (Secs. 13210(c) of P.L. 103-66) effective for amounts paid or incurred after 12/31/93.

payer's trade or business shall not be considered a shareholder or other owner, and for such purposes an individual shall be treated as owning any interest owned by a member of his family (within the meaning of section 267(c)(4)). *This paragraph shall not apply for purposes of subsection (a)(3).*

* * * * * * * * * * * * *

(m) Additional limitations on travel expenses.

* * * * * * * * * * * * *

(3) Travel expenses of spouse, dependent, or others.
No deduction shall be allowed under this chapter (other than section 217) for travel expenses paid or incurred with respect to a spouse, dependent, or other individual accompanying the taxpayer (or an officer or employee of the taxpayer) on business travel, unless—

(A) the spouse, dependent, or other individual is an employee of the taxpayer,

(B) the travel of the spouse, dependent, or other individual is for a bona fide business purpose, and

(C) such expenses would otherwise be deductible by the spouse, dependent, or other individual.

* * * * * * * * * * * * *

(n) Only [1]*50* percent of meal and entertainment expenses allowed as deduction.

(1) In general. The amount allowable as a deduction under this chapter for—

(A) any expense for food or beverages, and

(B) any item with respect to an activity which is of a type generally considered to constitute entertainment, amusement, or recreation, or with respect to a facility used in connection with such activity,

shall not exceed [2]*50 percent* of the amount of such expense or item which would (but for this paragraph) be allowable as a deduction under this chapter.

* * * * * * * * * * * * *

[For explanation, see ¶ 304, ¶ 305, and ¶ 306, for Committee Reports, see ¶ 3036, ¶ 3037, and ¶ 3067.]

[¶ 2042] Code Sec. 280C. Certain expenses for which credits are allowable.

(a) Rule for [1]*employment credits* . No deduction shall be allowed for that portion of the wages or salaries paid or incurred for the taxable year which is equal to [2]*the sum of the credits determined for the taxable year under sections [3]45A, 51(a) and* and [sic]1396(a). In the case of a corporation which is a member of a controlled group of corporations (within the meaning of section 52(a)) or a trade or business which is treated as being under common control with other trades or businesses (within the meaning of section 52(b)), this subsection shall be applied under rules prescribed by the Secretary similar to the rules applicable under subsections (a) and (b) of section 52.

Matter in *italics* in Code Sec. 274(m)(3) added by section 13272(a) of P.L. 103-66.

Effective Date (Sec. 13272(b) of P.L. 103-66) effective for amounts paid or incurred after 12/31/93.

Matter in *italics* in Code Sec. 274(n) and (n)(1) added by section 13209(a) and (b) of P.L. 103-66 which struck out:

1. "80 percent"
2. "80"

Effective Date (Secs. 13209(c) of P.L. 103-66) effective for tax. yrs. begin. after 12/31/93.

[Footnote Code Sec. 280C] Matter in *italics* in Code Sec. 280C(a) added by sections 13302(b)(1)(A) and (B) of P.L. 103-66 which struck out:

1. "targeted jobs credit"
2. "the amount of the credit determined for the taxable year under section 51(a)"

Effective Date (Section 13303 of P.L. 103-66) effective 8/10/93.

Matter in *italics* in Code Sec. 280C(a) added by section 13322(c)(1) amended by section 13302(b)(1)(A) of P.L. 103-66 above] which struck out:

3. "51(a)"

Effective Date (Section 13322(f) of P.L. 103-66) effective for wages paid or incurred after 12/31/93.

* * * * * * * * * * * * *

[For explanation, see ¶s 604, 609]

[¶ 2043] Code Sec. 305. Distributions of stock and stock rights.

* * * * * * * * * * * * *

(e) Treatment of purchaser of stripped preferred stock.

(1) In general. *If any person purchases after April 30, 1993, any stripped preferred stock, then such person, while holding such stock, shall include in gross income amounts equal to the amounts which would have been so includible if such stripped preferred stock were a bond issued on the purchase date and having original issue discount equal to the excess, if any, of—*

(A) the redemption price for such stock, over

(B) the price at which such person purchased such stock.

The preceding sentence shall also apply in the case of any person whose basis in such stock is determined by reference to the basis in the hands of such purchaser.

(2) Basis adjustments. *Appropriate adjustments to basis shall be made for amounts includible in gross income under paragraph (1).*

(3) Tax treatment of person stripping stock. *If any person strips the rights to 1 or more dividends from any stock described in paragraph (5)(B) and after April 30, 1993, disposes of such dividend rights, for purposes of paragraph (1), such person shall be treated as having purchased the stripped preferred stock on the date of such disposition for a purchase price equal to such person's adjusted basis in such stripped preferred stock.*

(4) Amounts treated as ordinary income. *Any amount included in gross income under paragraph (1) shall be treated as ordinary income.*

(5) Stripped preferred stock. *For purposes of this subsection—*

(A) In general. The term "stripped preferred stock" means any stock described in subparagraph (B) if there has been a separation in ownership between such stock and any dividend on such stock which has not become payable.

(B) Description of stock. Stock is described in this subsection if such stock—

(i) is limited and preferred as to dividends and does not participate in corporate growth to any significant extent, and

(ii) has a fixed redemption price.

(6) Purchase. *For purposes of this subsection, the term "purchase" means—*

(A) any acquisition of stock, where

(B) the basis of such stock is not determined in whole or in part by the reference to the adjusted basis of such stock in the hands of the person from whom acquired.

[1]*(f)* Cross references. For special rules—

(1) Relating to the receipt of stock and stock rights in corporate organizations and reorganizations, see part III (sec. 351 and following).

(2) In the case of a distribution which results in a gift, see section 2501 and following.

(3) In the case of a distribution which has the effect of the payment of compensation, see section 61(a)(1).

[For text of Committee Reports, see ¶ 3033]

[Footnote Code Sec. 305] Matter in *italics* in Code Sec. 305(e) and (f) added by section 13206(c)(1) of P.L. 103-66 which struck out:
1. "(e)"

Effective Date (Sec. 13206(c)(3) of P.L. 103-66) effective 4/30/93.

[¶ 2044] Code Sec. 381. Carryovers in certain corporate acquisitions.

* * * * * * * * * * * * *

(c) Items of the distributor or transferor corporation. The items referred to in subsection (a) are:

(26) Enterprise zone provisions.

The acquiring corporation shall take into account (to the extent proper to carry out the purposes of this section and subchapter U, and under such regulations as may be prescribed by the Secretary) the items required to be taken into account for purposes of subchapter U in respect of the distributor or transferor corporation.

[For explanation, see ¶ 607.]

[¶ 2045] Code Sec. 382. Limitation on net operating loss carryforwards and certain built-in losses following ownership change.

* * * * * * * * * * * * *

(l) Certain additional operating rules. For purposes of this section—

* * * * * * * * * * * * *

(5) Title 11 or similar case.

* * * * * * * * * * * * *

[1]*(C) Coordination with section 108. In applying section 108(e)(8) to any case to which subparagraph (A) applies, there shall not be taken into account any indebtedness for interest described in subparagraph (B).*

* * * * * * * * * * * * *

[¶ 2046] Code Sec. 401. Qualified pension, profit-sharing, and stock bonus plans.

(a) Requirements for qualification. A trust created or organized in the United States and forming part of a stock bonus, pension, or profit-sharing plan of an employer for the exclusive benefit of his employees or their beneficiaries shall constitute a qualified trust under this section—

* * * * * * * * * * * * *

[Footnote Code Sec. 381] Matter in *italics* in Code Sec. 381(c)(26), added by section 13302(e), P.L. 103-66.
Effective Date (Sec. 13303, P.L. 103-66) effective 8/10/93.

[Footnote Code Sec. 382] Matter in *italics* in Code Sec. 382(l)(5)(C) added by section 13226(a)(2)(A) of P.L. 103-66 which struck out:

1. "(C) Reduction of tax attributes where discharge of indebtedness.

"(i) In general. In any case to which subparagraph (A) applies, 50 percent of the amount which, but for the application of section 108(e)(10)(B), would have been applied to reduce tax attributes under section 108(b) shall be so applied.

"(ii) Clarification with subparagraph (B). In applying clause (i), there shall not be taken into account any indebtedness for interest described in subparagraph (B)."

Effective Date (Sec. 13226(a)(3) of P.L. 103-66) effective for stock transferred after 12/31/94, in satisfaction of any indebtedness, except as provided in Sec. 13226(a)(3)(B) of this Act, which read as follows:

"(B) Exception for title 11 cases. The amendments made by this subsection shall not apply to stock transferred in satisfaction of any indebtedness if such transfer is in a title 11 or similar case (as defined in section 368(a)(3)(A) of the Internal Revenue Code of 1986) which was filed on or before December 31, 1993."

(17) [1]*Compensation limit.*

(A) In general. A trust shall not constitute a qualified trust under this section unless, under the plan of which such trust is a part, the annual compensation of each employee taken into account under the plan for any year does not exceed [2]*$150,000.* [3] In determining the compensation of an employee, the rules of section 414(q)(6) shall apply, except that in applying such rules, the term "family" shall include only the spouse of the employee and any lineal descendants of the employee who have not attained age 19 before the close of the year.

(B) Cost-of-living adjustment.

(i) In general. If, for any calendar year after 1994, the excess (if any) of—

(I) $150,000, increased by the cost-of-living adjustment for the calendar year, over

(II) the dollar amount in effect under subparagraph (A) for taxable years beginning in the calendar year, is equal to or greater than $10,000, then the $150,000 amount under subparagraph (A) (as previously adjusted under this subparagraph) for any taxable year beginning in any subsequent calendar year shall be increased by the amount of such excess, rounded to the next lowest multiple of $10,000.

(III) Cost of living adjustment. The cost-of-living adjustment for any calendar year shall be the adjustment made under section 415(d) for such calendar year, except that the base period for purposes of section 415(d)(1)(A) shall be the calendar quarter beginning October 1, 1993.

* * * * * * * * * * * * *

[For explanation, see ¶ 801, for text of Committee Reports, see ¶ 3039]

[Footnote Code Sec. 401] Matter in *italics* in Code Sec. 401(a)(17), and (a)(17)(B) added by sections 13212(a)(1)(A)-(C), and (a)(2), P.L. 103-66, which struck out:

1. "A trust"
2. "$200,000"
3. "The Secretary shall adjust the $200,000 amount at the same time and in the same manner as under section 415(d)."

Effective Date (Sec. 13212(d), P.L. 103-66) effective for benefits accruing in plan yrs. begin. after 12/31/93, except as provided in Sec. 13212(d)(2) and (3) of this Act, which reads as follows:

"(2) Collectively bargained plans. — In the case of a plan maintained pursuant to 1 or more collective bargaining agreements between employee representatives and 1 or more employers ratified before the date of the enactment of this Act, the amendments made by this section shall not apply to contributions or benefits pursuant to such agreements for plan years beginning before the earlier of—

"(A) the latest of—

"(i) January 1, 1994

"(ii) the date on which the last of such collective bargaining agreements terminates (without regard to any extension, amendment, or modification of such agreements on or after such date of enactment), or

"(iii) in the case of a plan maintained pursuant to collective bargaining under the Railway Labor Act, the date of execution of an extension or replacement of the last of such collective bargaining agreements in effect on such date of enactment, or

"(B) January 1, 1997.

"(3) Transition rule for state and local plans. —

"(A) In general. — In the case of an eligible participant in a governmental plan (within the meaning of section 414(d) of the Internal Revenue Code of 1986), the dollar limitation under section 401(a)(17) of such Code shall not apply to the extent the amount of compensation which is allowed to be taken into account under the plan would be reduced below the amount which was allowed to be taken into account under the plan as in effect on July 1, 1993.

"(B) Eligible participant. — For purposes of subparagraph (A), an eligible participant is an individual who first became a participant in the plan during a plan year beginning before the 1st plan year beginning after the earlier of —

"(i) the plan year in which the plan is amended to reflect the amendments made by this section, or

"(ii) December 31, 1995.

"(C) Plan must be amended to incorporate limits. — This paragraph shall not apply to any eligible participant of a plan unless the plan is amended so that the plan incorporates by reference the dollar limitation under section 401(a)(17) of the Internal Revenue Code of 1986, effective with respect to noneligible participants for plan years beginning after December 31, 1995 (or earlier if the plan amendment so provides)."

[¶ 2047] Code Sec. 404. Deduction for contributions of an employer to an employees' trust or annuity plan and compensation under a deferred-payment plan.

* * * * * * * * * * * * *

(l) Limitation on amount of annual compensation taken into account. For purposes of applying the limitations of this section, the amount of annual compensation of each employee taken into account under the plan for any year shall not exceed [1]*$150,000.* [2]*The Secretary shall adjust the $150,000 amount at the same time, and by the same amount, as any adjustment under section 401(a)(17)(B).* For purposes of clause (i), (ii), or (iii) of subsection (a)(1)(A), and in computing the full funding limitation, any adjustment under the preceding sentence shall not be taken into account for any year before the year for which such adjustment first takes effect. In determining the compensation of an employee, the rules of section 414(q)(6) shall apply, except that in applying such rules, the term "family" shall include only the spouse of the employee and any lineal descendants of the employee who have not attained age 19 before the close of the year.

[For explanation, see ¶ 801, for text of Committee Report, see ¶ 3039]

[¶ 2048] Code Sec. 408. Individual retirement accounts.

* * * * * * * * * * * * *

(k) Simplified employee pension defined.

* * * * * * * * * * * * *

(3) Contributions may not discriminate in favor of the highly compensated, etc.

* * * * * * * * * * * * *

[Footnote Code Sec. 404] Matter in *italics* in Code Sec. 404(l) added by sections 13212(c)(1)(A) and (B) of P.L. 103-66 which struck out:

1. "$200,000"
2. "The Secretary shall adjust the $200,000 amount at the same time and in the same manner as under section 415(d)."

Effective Date (Sec. 13212(d) of P.L. 103-66) effective for benefits accruing in plan yrs. begin. after 12/31/93, except as provided in Sec. 13212(d)(2) and (3) of this Act, which reads as follows:

"(2) Collectively bargained plans.—In the case of a plan maintained pursuant to 1 or more collective bargaining agreements between employee representatives and 1 or more employers ratified before the date of the enactment of this Act, the amendments made by this section shall not apply to contributions or benefits pursuant to such agreements for plan years beginning before the earlier of—

"(A) the latest of—

"(i) January 1, 1994

"(ii) the date on which the last of such collective bargaining agreements terminates (without regard to any extension, amendment, or modification of such agreements on or after such date of enactment), or

"(iii) in the case of a plan maintained pursuant to collective bargaining under the Railway Labor Act, the date of execution of an extension or replacement of the last of such collective bargaining agreements in effect on such date of enactment, or

"(B) January 1, 1997.

"(3) Transition rule for state and local plans.—

"(A) In general.—In the case of an eligible participant in a governmental plan (within the meaning of section 414(d) of the Internal Revenue Code of 1986), the dollar limitation under section 401(a)(17) of such Code shall not apply to the extent the amount of compensation which is allowed to be taken into account under the plan would be reduced below the amount which was allowed to be taken into account under the plan as in effect on July 1, 1993.

"(B) Eligible participant.—For purposes of subparagraph (A), an eligible participant is an individual who first became a participant in the plan during a plan year beginning before the 1st plan year beginning after the earlier of—

"(i) the plan year in which the plan is amended to reflect the amendments made by this section, or

"(ii) December 31, 1995.

"(C) Plan must be amended to incorporate limits.—This paragraph shall not apply to any eligible participant of a plan unless the plan is amended so that the plan incorporates by reference the dollar limitation under section 401(a)(17) of the Internal Revenue Code of 1986, effective with respect to noneligible participants for plan years beginning after December 31, 1995 (or earlier if the plan amendment so provides)."

(C) Contributions must bear uniform relationship to total compensation. For purposes of subparagraph (A), and except as provided in subparagraph (D), employer contributions to simplified employee pensions (other than contributions under an arrangement described in paragraph (6)) shall be considered discriminatory unless contributions thereto bear a uniform relationship to the compensation (not in excess of the first [1]*$150,000)* of each employee maintaining a simplified employee pension.

* * * * * * * * * * * * *

(6) Employee may elect salary reduction arrangement.

* * * * * * * * * * * * *

(D) Deferral percentage. For purposes of this paragraph, the deferral percentage for an employee for a year shall be the ratio of—

(i) the amount of elective employer contributions actually paid over to the simplified employee pension on behalf of the employee for the year, to

(ii) the employee's compensation (not in excess of the first [2]*$150,000)* for the year.

* * * * * * * * * * * * *

[3]***(8) Cost-of-living adjustment.*** *The Secretary shall adjust the $300 amount in paragraph (2)(C) at the same time and in the same manner as under section 415(d) and shall adjust the $150,000 amount in paragraphs (3)(C) and (6)(D)(ii) at the same time, and by the same amount, as any adjustment under section 401(a)(17)(B).*

* * * * * * * * * * * * *

[For explanation, see ¶ 801, for Committee Reports, see ¶ 3039.]

[¶ 2049] Code Sec. 453A. Special rules for nondealers.

* * * * * * * * * * * * *

(c) Interest on deferred tax liability.

* * * * * * * * * * * * *

(3) Deferred tax liability. For purposes of this section, the term "deferred tax liability" means, with respect to any taxable year, the product of—

(A) the amount of gain with respect to an obligation which has not been recognized as of the close of such taxable year, multiplied by

(B) the maximum rate of tax in effect under section 1 or 11, whichever is appropriate, for such taxable year.

For purposes of applying the preceding sentence with respect to so much of the gain which, when recognized, will be treated as long-term capital gain, the maximum rate on net capital gain under section 1(h) or 1201 (whichever is appropriate) shall be taken into account.

* * * * * * * * * * * * *

[For explanation, see ¶ 116 and ¶ 310.]

[Footnote Code Sec. 408] Matter in *italics* in Code Sec. 408(k)(3)(C), (k)(6)(D)(ii), and (k)(8) added by sections 13212(b)(1) and (b)(2), P.L. 103-66, which struck out:

1. "$200,000"
2. "$200,000"
3. "(8) **Cost-of-living adjustment.** The Secretary shall adjust the $300 amount in paragraph (2)(C) and the $200,000 amount in paragraphs (3)(C) and (6)(D)(ii) at the same time and in the same manner as under section 415(d), except that in the case of years beginning after 1988, the $200,000 amount (as so adjusted) shall not exceed the amount in effect under section 401(a)(17)."

Effective Date (Sec. 13212(d), P.L. 103-66) effective for benefits accruing in plan yrs. begin. after 12/31/93.

[Footnote Code Sec. 453A] Matter in *italics* in Code Sec. 453A(c)(3) was added by section 13201(b)(4) of P.L. 103-66

Effective Date (Sec. 13201(c) of P.L. 103-66) effective for tax. yrs. begin. after 12/31/92.

[¶ 2050] **Code Sec. 469. Passive activity losses and credits limited.**

* * * * * * * * * * * * *

(c) Passive activity defined. For purposes of this section—

* * * * * * * * * * * * *

(2) Passive activity includes any rental activity. [1]*Except as provided in paragraph (7), the* term "passive activity" includes any rental activity.

* * * * * * * * * * * * *

(7) Special rules for taxpayers in real property business.

(A) In general. If this paragraph applies to any taxpayer for a taxable year—

(i) paragraph (2) shall not apply to any rental real estate activity of such taxpayer for such taxable year, and

(ii) this section shall be applied as if each interest of the taxpayer in rental real estate were a separate activity.

Notwithstanding clause (ii), a taxpayer may elect to treat all interests in rental real estate as one activity. Nothing in the preceding provisions of this subparagraph shall be construed as affecting the determination of whether the taxpayer materially participates with respect to any interest in a limited partnership as a limited partner.

(B) Taxpayers to whom paragraph applies. This paragraph shall apply to a taxpayer for a taxable year if—

(i) more than one-half of the personal services performed in trades or businesses by the taxpayer during such taxable year are performed in real property trades or businesses in which the taxpayer materially participates, and

(ii) such taxpayer performs more than 750 hours of services during the taxable year in real property trades or businesses in which the taxpayer materially participates.

In the case of a joint return, the requirements of the preceding sentence are satisfied if and only if either spouse separately satisfies such requirements. For purposes of the preceding sentence, activities in which a spouse materially participates shall be determined under subsection (h).

(C) Real property trade or business. For purposes of this paragraph, the term "real property trade or business" means any real property development, redevelopment, construction, reconstruction, acquisition, conversion, rental, operation, management, leasing, or brokerage trade or business.

(D) Special rules for subparagraph (B).

(i) Closely held C Corporations. In the case of a closely held C corporation, the requirements of subparagraph (B) shall be treated as met for any taxable year if more than 50 percent of the gross receipts of such corporation for such taxable year are derived from real property trades or businesses in which the corporation materially participates.

(ii) Personal services as an employee. For purposes of subparagraph (B), personal services performed as an employee shall not be treated as performed in real property trades or businesses. The preceding sentence shall not apply if such employee is a 5-percent owner (as defined in section 416(i)(1)(B)) in the employer.

* * * * * * * * * * * * *

(i) $25,000 offset for rental real estate activities.

* * * * * * * * * * * * *

[Footnote Code Sec. 469] Matter in *italics* in Code Sec. 469(c)(2), (c)(7), and (i)(3)(E)(iv) added by sections 13143(a)-(b)(2) of P.L. 103-66 which struck out:

1. "The"

Effective Date (Sec. 13143(c) of P.L. 103-66) effective for tax. yrs. begin. after 12/31/93.

(3) Phase-out of exemption.

* * * * * * * * * * * * *

(E) Adjusted gross income. For purposes of this paragraph, adjusted gross income shall be determined without regard to—

(i) any amount includible in gross income under section 86,

(ii) the amount excludable from gross income under section 135,

(iii) any amount allowable as a deduction under section 219, and

(iv) any passive activity loss*or any loss allowable by reason of subsection (c)(7).*

* * * * * * * * * * * * *

For explanation, see ¶ 501, for text of Committee Report, see ¶ 3014]

[¶ 2051] Code Sec. 475. Mark to market accounting method for dealers in securities.

(a) General rule. Notwithstanding any other provision of this subpart, the following rules shall apply to securities held by a dealer in securities:

(1) Any security which is inventory in the hands of the dealer shall be included in inventory at its fair market value.

(2) In the case of any security which is not inventory in the hands of the dealer and which is held at the close of any taxable year—

(A) the dealer shall recognize gain or loss as if such security were sold for its fair market value on the last business day of such taxable year, and

(B) any gain or loss shall be taken into account for such taxable year.

Proper adjustment shall be made in the amount of any gain or loss subsequently realized for gain or loss taken into account under the preceding sentence. The Secretary may provide by regulations for the application of this paragraph at times other than the times provided in this paragraph.

(b) Exceptions.

(1) In general. Subsection (a) shall not apply to—

(A) any security held for investment,

[Footnote Code Sec. 475] Code Sec. 475 was added by section 13223(a) of P.L. 103-66.

Effective Date (Sec. 13223(c) of P.L. 103-66) effective for tax. yrs. ending on or after 12/31/93. For special rules, see Sec. 13223(c)(2) and (c)(3) of this Act, which reads as follows:

"(2) Change in method of accounting.—In the case of any taxpayer required by this section to change its method of accounting for any taxable year—

"(A) such change shall be treated as initiated by the taxpayer,

"(B) such change shall be treated as made with the consent of the Secretary, and

"(C) except as provided in paragraph (3), the net amount of the adjustments required to be taken into account by the taxpayer under section 481 of the Internal Revenue Code of 1986 shall be taken into account ratably over the 5-taxable year period beginning with the first taxable year ending on or after December 31, 1993.

"(3) Special rule for floor specialists and market makers.—

"(A) In general—If—

"(i) a taxpayer (or any predecessor) used the last-in first-out (LIFO) method of accounting with respect to any qualified securities for the 5-taxable year period ending with its last taxable year ending before December 31, 1993, and

"(ii) any portion of the net amount described in paragraph (2)(C) is attributable to the use of such method of accounting, then paragraph (2)(C) shall be applied by taking such portion into account ratably over the 15-taxable year period beginning with the first taxable year ending on or after December 31, 1993.

"(B) Qualified security.—For purposes of this paragraph, the term 'qualified security' means any security acquired—

"(i) by a floor specialist (as defined in section 1236(d)(2) of the Internal Revenue Code of 1986) in connection with the specialist's duties as a specialist on an exchange, but only if the security is one in which the specialist is registered with the exchange, or

"(ii) by a taxpayer who is a market maker in connection with the taxpayer's duties as a market maker, but only if—

"(I) the security is included on the National Association of Security Dealers Automated Quotation System,

"(II) the taxpayer is registered as a market maker in such security with the National Association of Security Dealers, and

"(III) as of the last day of the taxable year preceding the taxpayer's first taxable year ending on or after December 31, 1993, the taxpayer (or any predecessor) has been actively and regularly engaged as a market maker in such security for the 2-year period ending on such date (or, if shorter, the period beginning 61 days after the security was listed in such quotation system and ending on such date)."

(B) (i) any security described in subsection (c)(2)(C) which is acquired (including originated) by the taxpayer in the ordinary course of a trade or business of the taxpayer and which is not held for sale, and (ii) any obligation to acquire a security described in clause (i) if such obligation is entered into in the ordinary course of such trade or business and is not held for sale, and

(C) any security which is a hedge with respect to—

(i) a security to which subsection (a) does not apply, or

(ii) a position, right to income, or a liability which is not a security in the hands of the taxpayer.

To the extent provided in regulations, subparagraph (C) shall not apply to any security held by a person in its capacity as a dealer in securities.

(2) Identification required. A security shall not be treated as described in subparagraph (A), (B), or (C) of paragraph (1), as the case may be, unless such security is clearly identified in the dealer's records as being described in such subparagraph before the close of the day on which it was acquired, originated, or entered into (or such other time as the Secretary may by regulations prescribe).

(3) Securities subsequently not exempt. If a security ceases to be described in paragraph (1) at any time after it was identified as such under paragraph (2), subsection (a) shall apply to any changes in value of the security occurring after the cessation.

(4) Special rule for property held for investment. To the extent provided in regulations, subparagraph (A) of paragraph (1) shall not apply to any security described in subparagraph (D) or (E) of subsection (c)(2) which is held by a dealer in such securities.

(c) Definitions. For purposes of this section—

(1) Dealer in securities defined. The term "dealer in securities" means a taxpayer who—

(A) regularly purchases securities from or sells securities to customers in the ordinary course of a trade or business; or

(B) regularly offers to enter into, assume, offset, assign or otherwise terminate positions in securities with customers in the ordinary course of a trade or business.

(2) Security defined. The term "security" means any—

(A) share of stock in a corporation;

(B) partnership or beneficial ownership interest in a widely held or publicly traded partnership or trust;

(C) note, bond, debenture, or other evidence of indebtedness;

(D) interest rate, currency, or equity notional principal contract;

(E) evidence of an interest in, or a derivative financial instrument in, any security described in subparagraph (A), (B), (C), or (D), or any currency, including any option, forward contract, short position, and any similar financial instrument in such a security or currency; and

(F) position which—

(i) is not a security described in subparagraph (A), (B), (C), (D), or (E),

(ii) is a hedge with respect to such a security, and

(iii) is clearly identified in the dealer's records as being described in this subparagraph before the close of the day on which it was acquired or entered into (or such other time as the Secretary may by regulations prescribe).

Subparagraph (E) shall not include any contract to which section 1256(a) applies.

(3) Hedge. The term "hedge" means any position which reduces the dealer's risk of interest rate or price changes or currency fluctuations, including any position which is reasonably expected to become a hedge within 60 days after the acquisition of the position.

(d) Special rules. For purposes of this section—

(1) Coordination with certain rules. The rules of sections 263(g), 263A, and 1256(a) shall not apply to securities to which subsection (a) applies, and section 1091 shall not apply (and section 1092 shall apply) to any loss recognized under subsection (a).

(2) Improper identification. If a taxpayer—

(A) identifies any security under subsection (b)(2) as being described in subsection (b)(1) and such security is not so described, or

(B) fails under subsection (c)(2)(F)(iii) to identify any position which is described in subsection (c)(2)(F) (without regard to clause (iii) thereof) at the time such identification is required,

the provisions of subsection (a) shall apply to such security or position, except that any loss under this section prior to the disposition of the security or position shall be recognized only to the extent of gain previously recognized under this section (and not previously taken into account under this paragraph) with respect to such security or position.

(3) Character of gain or loss.

(A) In general. Except as provided in subparagraph (B) or section 1236(b)—

(i) In general. Any gain or loss with respect to a security under subsection (a)(2) shall be treated as ordinary income or loss.

(ii) Special rule for dispositions. If—

(I) gain or loss is recognized with respect to a security before the close of the taxable year, and

(II) subsection (a)(2) would have applied if the security were held as of the close of the taxable year,

such gain or loss shall be treated as ordinary income or loss.

(B) Exception. Subparagraph (A) shall not apply to any gain or loss which is allocable to a period during which—

(i) the security is described in subsection (b)(1)(C) (without regard to subsection (b)(2)),

(ii) the security is held by a person other than in connection with its activities as a dealer in securities, or

(iii) the security is improperly identified (within the meaning of subparagraph (A) or (B) of paragraph (2)).

(e) Regulatory authority. The Secretary shall prescribe such regulations as may be necessary or appropriate to carry out the purposes of this section, including rules—

(1) to prevent the use of year-end transfers, related parties, or other arrangements to avoid the provisions of this section, and

(2) to provide for the application of this section to any security which is a hedge which cannot be identified with a specific security, position, right to income, or liability.

[For explanation, see ¶ 314, for text of Committee Report, see ¶ 3045]

[¶ 2052] Code Sec. 501. Exemption from tax on corporations, certain trusts, etc.

* * * * * * * * * * * * *

(c) List of exempt organizations. The following organizations are referred to in subsection (a):

* * * * * * * * * * * * *

(2) Corporations organized for the exclusive purpose of holding title to property, collecting income therefrom, and turning over the entire amount thereof, less expenses, to an organization which itself is exempt under this section. *Rules similar to the rules of subparagraph (G) of paragraph (25) shall apply for purposes of this paragraph.*

* * * * * * * * * * * * *

(25) (A) Any corporation or trust which—

(i) has no more than 35 shareholders or beneficiaries,

(ii) has only 1 class of stock or beneficial interest, and

(iii) is organized for the exclusive purposes of—

[Footnote Code Sec. 501] Matter in *italics* in Code Sec. 501(c)(2) and (c)(25)(G) was added by sections 13146(a) and (b) of P.L. 103-66

Effective Date (Sec. 13146(c) of P.L. 103-66) effective for tax. yrs. begin. on or after 1/1/94.

(I) acquiring real property and holding title to, and collecting income from, such property, and

(II) remitting the entire amount of income from such property (less expenses) to 1 or more organizations described in subparagraph (C) which are shareholders of such corporation or beneficiaries of such trust.

For purposes of clause (iii), the term "real property" shall not include any interest as a tenant in common (or similar interest) and shall not include any indirect interest.

* * * * * * * * * * * *

(G)

(i) An organization shall not be treated as failing to be described in this paragraph merely by reason of the receipt of any otherwise disqualifying income which is incidentally derived from the holding of real property.

(ii) Clause (i) shall not apply if the amount of gross income described in such clause exceeds 10 percent of the organization's gross income for the taxable year unless the organization establishes to the satisfaction of the Secretary that the receipt of gross income described in clause (i) in excess of such limitation was inadvertent and reasonable steps are being taken to correct the circumstances giving rise to such income.

[For explanation, see ¶ 509, for text of Committee Report, see ¶ 3017]

[¶ 2053] Code Sec. 505. Additional requirements for organizations described in paragraph (9), (17), or (20) of section 501(c).

* * * * * * * * * * * *

(b) Nondiscrimination requirements.

* * * * * * * * * * * *

(7) [1]Compensation limit. A plan shall not be treated as meeting the requirements of this subsection unless under the plan the annual compensation of each employee taken into account for any year does not exceed [2]*$150,000.* [3] *The Secretary shall adjust the $150,000 amount at the same time, and by the same amount, as any adjustment under section*

[Footnote Code Sec. 505] Matter in *italics* in Code Sec. 505(b)(7) added by sections 13212(c)(1)(A), (B), and (c)(2) of P.L. 103-66 which struck out:

1. "$200,000"
2. "$200,000"
3. "The Secretary shall adjust the $200,000 amount at the same time and in the same manner as under section 415(d)."

Effective Date (Sec. 13212(d) of P.L. 103-66) effective for benefits accruing in plan yrs. begin. after 12/31/93, except as provided by Sec. 13212(d)(2) and (3) of this Act, which reads as follows:

"(2) Collectively bargained plans.—In the case of a plan maintained pursuant to 1 or more collective bargaining agreements between employee representatives and 1 or more employers ratified before the date of the enactment of this Act, the amendments made by this section shall not apply to contributions or benefits pursuant to such agreements for plan years beginning before the earlier of—

"(A) the latest of—

"(i) January 1, 1994

"(ii) the date on which the last of such collective bargaining agreements terminates (without regard to any extension, amendment, or modification of such agreements on or after such date of enactment [8/10/93]), or

"(iii) in the case of a plan maintained pursuant to collective bargaining under the Railway Labor Act, the date of execution of an extension or replacement of the last of such collective bargaining agreements in effect on such date of enactment, or

"(B) January 1, 1997.

"(3) Transition rule for state and local plans.—

"(A) In general.—In the case of an eligible participant in a governmental plan (within the meaning of section 414(d) of the Internal Revenue Code of 1986), the dollar limitation under section 401(a)(17) of such Code shall not apply to the extent the amount of compensation which is allowed to be taken into account under the plan would be reduced below the amount which was allowed to be taken into account under the plan as in effect on July 1, 1993.

"(B) Eligible participant.—For purposes of subparagraph (A), an eligible participant is an individual who first became a participant in the plan during a plan year beginning before the 1st plan year beginning after the earlier of—

"(i) the plan year in which the plan is amended to reflect the amendments made by this section, or

"(ii) December 31, 1995.

401(a)(17)(B). This paragraph shall not apply in determining whether the requirements of section 79(d) are met.

[For explanation, see ¶ 801 for text of Committee Reports, see ¶ 3039

[¶ 2054] Code Sec. 512. Unrelated business taxable income.

* * * * * * * * * * * *

(b) Modifications. The modifications referred to in subsection (a) are the following:

(1) There shall be excluded all dividends, interest, payments with respect to securities loans (as defined in section 512(a)(5)), *amounts received or accrued as consideration for entering into agreements to make loans,* and annuities, and all deductions directly connected with such income.

* * * * * * * * * * * *

(5) There shall be excluded all gains or losses from the sale, exchange, or other disposition of property other than—

(A) stock in trade or other property of a kind which would properly be includible in inventory if on hand at the close of the taxable year, or

(B) property held primarily for sale to customers in the ordinary course of the trade or business.

There shall also be excluded [1]*all gains or losses recognized, in connection with the organization's investment activities, from* the lapse or termination of options [2]to buy or sell securities (as defined in section 1236(c))*or real property and all gains or losses from the forfeiture of good-faith deposits (that are consistent with established business practice) for the purchase, sale, or lease of real property in connection with the organization's investment activities* . This paragraph shall not apply with respect to the cutting of timber which is considered, on the application of section 631, as a sale or exchange of such timber.

* * * * * * * * * * * *

(16) *(A) Notwithstanding paragraph (5)(B), there shall be excluded all gains or losses from the sale, exchange, or other disposition of any real property described in subparagraph (B) if—*

(i) such property was acquired by the organization from—

(I) a financial institution described in section 581 or 591(a) which is in conservatorship or receivership, or

(II) the conservator or receiver of such an institution (or any government agency or corporation succeeding to the rights or interests of the conservator or receiver),

(ii) such property is designated by the organization within the 9-month period beginning on the date of its acquisition as property held for sale, except that not more than one-half (by value determined as of such date) of property acquired in a single transaction may be so designated,

(iii) such sale, exchange, or disposition occurs before the later of—

(I) the date which is 30 months after the date of the acquisition of such property, or

---

"(C) Plan must be amended to incorporate limits.—This paragraph shall not apply to any eligible participant of a plan unless the plan is amended so that the plan incorporates by reference the dollar limitation under section 401(a)(17) of the Internal Revenue Code of 1986, effective with respect to noneligible participants for plan years beginning after December 31, 1995 (or earlier if the plan amendment so provides)."

[Footnote Code Sec. 512] Matter in *italics* in Code Sec. (b)(1) and (5) added by sections 13148(a)-(b)(3) of P.L. 103-66 which struck out:

1. "all gains on"
2. ", written organization in connection with its investment activities,"

Effective Date (Sec. 13148(c) of P.L. 103-66) effective for amounts received on or after 1/1/94.

Matter in *italics* in Code Sec. 512(b)(16) was added by section 13147(a) of P.L. 103-66

Effective Date (Sec. 13147(b) of P.L. 103-66) effective for property acquired on or after 1/1/94.

(II) the date specified by the Secretary in order to assure an orderly disposition of property held by persons described in subparagraph (A), and

(iv) while such property was held by the organization, the aggregate expenditures on improvements and development activities included in the basis of the property are (or were) not in excess of 20 percent of the net selling price of such property.

(B) Property is described in this subparagraph if it is real property which—

(i) was held by the financial institution at the time it entered into conservatorship or receivership, or

(ii) was foreclosure property (as defined in section 514(c)(9)(H)(v)) which secured indebtedness held by the financial institution at such time.

For purposes of this subparagraph, real property includes an interest in a mortgage.

(c) Special rules for partnerships.

* * * * * * * * * * * * *

[3]*(4)* Special rule where partnership year is different from organization's year. If the taxable year of the organization is different from that of the partnership, the amounts to be included or deducted in computing the unrelated business taxable income under [4]*paragraph (1)* shall be based upon the income and deductions of the partnership for any taxable year of the partnership ending within or with the taxable year of the organization.

[For explanation, see ¶ 505 and ¶ 507, for text of Committee Report, see ¶ 3016, ¶ 3018 and ¶ 3019]

[¶ 2055] **Code Sec. 513. Unrelated trade or business.**

* * * * * * * * * * * * *

(h) Certain distributions of low cost articles without obligation to purchase and exchanges and rentals of member lists.

* * * * * * * * * * * * *

(2) Low cost article defined. For purposes of this subsection—

* * * * * * * * * * * * *

(C) Indexation of $5 amount. In the case of any taxable year beginning in a calendar year after 1987, the $5 amount in subparagraph (A) shall be increased by an amount equal to—

(i) $5, multiplied by

(ii) the cost-of-living adjustment determined under section 1(f)(3) for the calendar year in which the taxable year begins, by substituting "calendar year 1987" for "calendar year [1]*1992* " in subparagraph (B) thereof.

* * * * * * * * * * * * *

[For explanation, see ¶ 504, ¶ 508, for text of Committee Report, see ¶ 3015]

Matter in *italics* in Code Sec. 512(c)(2) added by sections 13145(a)(1)-(3) of P.L. 103-66 which struck out:

3. "(2) Special rule for publicly traded partnerships. Notwithstanding any other provision of this section—

"(A) any organization's share (whether or not distributed) of the gross income of a publicly traded partnership (as defined in section 469(k)(2)) shall be treated as gross income derived from an unrelated trade or business, and

"(B) such organization's share of the partnership deductions shall be allowed in computing unrelated business taxable income."

4. "paragraph (1) or (2)"

Effective Date (Sec. 13145(b) of P.L. 103-66) effective for partnership yrs. begin. on or after 1/1/94.

[Footnote Code Sec. 513] Matter in *italics* in Code Sec. 513(h)(2)(C)(ii) added by section 13201(b)(3)(H) of P.L. 103-66 which struck out:

1. "1989"

Effective Date (Sec. 13201(c) of P.L. 103-66) effective for tax. yrs. begin. after 12/31/92.

[¶ 2056] Code Sec. 514. Unrelated debt-financed income.

* * * * * * * * * * * *

(c) Acquisition indebtedness.

* * * * * * * * * * * *

(9) Real property acquired by a qualified organization.

(A) In general. Except as provided in subparagraph (B), the term "acquisition indebtedness" does not, for purposes of this section, include indebtedness incurred by a qualified organization in acquiring or improving any real property. *For purposes of this paragraph, an interest in a mortgage shall in no event be treated as real property.*

(B) Exceptions. The provisions of subparagraph (A) shall not apply in any case in which—

(i) the price for the acquisition or improvement is not a fixed amount determined as of the date of the acquisition or the completion of the improvement;

(ii) the amount of any indebtedness or any other amount payable with respect to such indebtedness, or the time for making any payment of any such amount, is dependent, in whole or in part, upon any revenue, income, or profits derived from such real property;

(iii) the real property is at any time after the acquisition leased by the qualified organization to the person selling such property to such organization or to any person who bears a relationship described in section 267(b) or 707(b) to such person;

(iv) the real property is acquired by a qualified trust from, or is at any time after the acquisition leased by such trust to, any person who—

(I) bears a relationship which is described in subparagraph (C), (E), or (G) of section 4975(e)(2) to any plan with respect to which such trust was formed, or

(II) bears a relationship which is described in subparagraph (F) or (H) of section 4975(e)(2) to any person described in subclause (I);

(v) any person described in clause (iii) or (iv) provides the qualified organization with financing in connection with the acquisition or improvement; or

(vi) the real property is held by a partnership unless the partnership meets the requirements of clauses (i) through (v) and unless—

(I) all of the partners of the partnership are qualified organizations,

(II) each allocation to a partner of the partnership which is a qualified organization is a qualified allocation (within the meaning of section 168(h)(6)), or

(III) such partnership meets the requirements of subparagraph (E).

For purposes of subclause (I) of clause (vi), an organization shall not be treated as a qualified organization if any income of such organization is unrelated business taxable income. [1]

* * * * * * * * * * * *

(G) Special rules for purposes of the exceptions. Except as otherwise provided by regulations—

(i) Small leases disregarded. For purposes of clauses (iii) and (iv) of subparagraph (B), a lease to a person described in such clause (iii) or (iv) shall be disregarded if no more than 25 percent of the leasable floor space in a building (or complex of buildings) is covered by the lease and if the lease is on commercially reasonable terms.

[Footnote Code Sec. 514] Matter in *italics* in Code Sec. 514(c)(9)(A), (B), (G), and (H) added by sections 13144(a)-(b)(2) of P.L. 103-66 which struck out:

1. "For purposes of this paragraph, an interest in a mortgage shall in no event be treated as real property."

Effective Date (Sec. 131449(c) of P.L. 103-66) effective for acquisitions on or after 1/1/94. Sec. 13144(c)(2) of this Act provides:

"(2) Small leases. The provisions of section 514(c)(9)(G)(i) of the Internal Revenue Code of 1986 shall, in addition to any leases to which the provisions apply by reason of paragraph (1), apply to leases entered into on or after January 1, 1994."

(ii) Commercially reasonable financing. Clause (v) of subparagraph (B) shall not apply if the financing is on commercially reasonable terms.

(H) Qualifying sales by financial institutions.

(i) In general. In the case of a qualifying sale by a financial institution, except as provided in regulations, clauses (i) and (ii) of subparagraph (B) shall not apply with respect to financing provided by such institution for such sale.

(ii) Qualifying sale. For purposes of this clause, there is a qualifying sale by a financial institution if—

(I) a qualified organization acquires property described in clause (iii) from a financial institution and any gain recognized by the financial institution with respect to the property is ordinary income,

(II) the stated principal amount of the financing provided by the financial institution does not exceed the amount of the outstanding indebtedness (including accrued but unpaid interest) of the financial institution with respect to the property described in clause (iii) immediately before the acquisition referred to in clause (iii) or (v), whichever is applicable, and

(III) the present value (determined as of the time of the sale and by using the applicable Federal rate determined under section 1274(d)) of the maximum amount payable pursuant to the financing that is determined by reference to the revenue, income, or profits derived from the property cannot exceed 30 percent of the total purchase price of the property (including the contingent payments).

(iii) Property to which subparagraph applies. Property is described in this clause if such property is foreclosure property, or is real property which—

(I) was acquired by the qualified organization from a financial institution which is in conservatorship or receivership, or from the conservator or receiver of such an institution, and

(II) was held by the financial institution at the time it entered into conservatorship or receivership.

(iv) Financial institution. For purposes of this subparagraph, the term "financial institution" means—

(I) any financial institution described in section 581 or 591(a),

(II) any other corporation which is a direct or indirect subsidiary of an institution referred to in subclause (I) but only if, by virtue of being affiliated with such institution, such other corporation is subject to supervision and examination by a Federal or State agency which regulates institutions referred to in subclause (I), and

(III) any person acting as a conservator or receiver of an entity referred to in subclause (I) or (II) (or any government agency or corporation succeeding to the rights or interest of such person).

(v) Foreclosure property. For purposes of this subparagraph, the term "foreclosure property" means any real property acquired by the financial institution as the result of having bid on such property at foreclosure, or by operation of an agreement or process of law, after there was a default (or a default was imminent) on indebtedness which such property secured.

* * * * * * * * * * * * *

[¶2057] Code Sec. 531. Imposition of accumulated earnings tax.

In addition to other taxes imposed by this chapter, there is hereby imposed for each taxable year on the accumulated taxable income (as defined in section 535) of each corporation described in section 532, an accumulated earnings tax equal to [1]*39.6 percent* of the accumulated taxable income.

[Footnote Code Sec. 531] Matter in *italics* in Code Sec. 531 added by section 13202(b) of P.L. 103-66 which struck out:

[For explanation, see ¶ 302]

[¶ 2058] Code Sec. 541. Imposition of personal holding company tax.
In addition to other taxes imposed by this chapter, there is hereby imposed for each taxable year on the undistributed personal holding company income (as defined in section 545) of every personal holding company (as defined in section 542) a personal holding company tax equal to [1]*39.6 percent*of the undistributed personal holding company income.
[For explanation, see ¶ 303]

[¶ 2059] Code Sec. 642. Special rules for credits and deductions.

* * * * * * * * * * * *

(c) Deduction for amounts paid or permanently set aside for a charitable purpose.

* * * * * * * * * * * *

[1]***(4) Adjustments.*** *To the extent that the amount otherwise allowable as a deduction under this subsection consists of gain described in section 1202(a), proper adjustment shall be made for any exclusion allowable to the estate or trust under section 1202. In the case of a trust, the deduction allowed by this subsection shall be subject to section 681 (relating to unrelated business income).*

* * * * * * * * * * * *

(f) Amortization deductions. The benefit of the deductions for amortization provided by [2] *sections 169 and 197* , shall be allowed to estates and trusts in the same manner as in the case

1. "36 percent"
Effective Date (Sec. 13202 of P.L. 103-66) effective for tax. yrs. begin. after 12/31/92.
Code Sec. 541 was previously amended by section 13201(b)(2) of P.L. 103-66, which struck out "28 percent" and inserted "36 percent"
Effective Date (Sec. 13201(c) of P.L. 103-66) effective for tax. yrs. begin. after 12/31/92.
[Footnote Code Sec. 541] Matter in *italics* in Code Sec. 541 added by section 13202(b) of P.L. 103-66 which struck out:
1. "36 percent"
Effective Date (Sec. 13202(c) of P.L. 103-66) effective for tax. yrs. begin. after 12/31/92.
Code Sec. 541 was previously amended by section 13201(b)(2) of P.L. 103-66, which struck out "28 percent" and inserted "36 percent"
Effective Date (Sec. 13201(c) of P.L. 103-66) effective for tax. yrs. begin. after 12/31/92.
[Footnote Code Sec. 642] Matter in *italics* in Code Sec. 642(c)(4) added by section 13113(d)(2) of P.L. 103-66 which struck out:
1. "(4) Coordination with section 681. In the case of a trust, the deduction allowed by this subsection shall be subject to section 681 (relating to unrelated business income)."
Effective Date (Sec. 13113(e) of P.L. 103-66) effective for stock issued after 8/10/93.
Matter in *italics* in code Sec. 642(f) added by section 13261(f)(2) of P.L. 103-66 which struck out:
2. "section 169"
Effective Date (Sec. 13261(g) of P.L. 103-66) effective for property acquired after 8/10/93, except as provided in Sec. 14261(g)(2) and (3) which reads as follows:
"(2) Election to have amendments apply to property acquired after July 25, 1991.
"(A) In general. If an election under this paragraph applies to the taxpayer—
"(i) the amendments made by this section shall apply to property acquired by the taxpayer after July 25, 1991,
"(ii) subsection (c)(1)(A) of section 197 of the Internal Revenue Code of 1986 (as added by this section) (and so much of subsection (f)(9)(A) of such section 197 as precedes clause (i) thereof) shall be applied with respect to the taxpayer by treating July 25, 1991, as the date of the enactment of such section, and
"(iii) in applying subsection (f)(9) of such section, with respect to any property acquired by the taxpayer on or before the date of the enactment of this Act, only holding or use on July 25, 1991, shall be taken into account.
"(B) Election. An election under this paragraph shall be made at such time and in such manner as the Secretary of the Treasury or his delegate may prescribe. Such an election by any taxpayer, once made—
"(i) may be revoked only with the consent of the Secretary, and
"(ii) shall apply to the taxpayer making such election and any other taxpayer under common control with the taxpayer (within the meaning of subparagraphs (A) and (B) of section 41(f)(1) of such Code) at any time after August 2, 1993, and on or before the date on which such election is made.

of an individual. The allowable deduction shall be apportioned between the income beneficiaries and the fiduciary under regulations prescribed by the Secretary.

* * * * * * * * * * * * *

[For explanation, see ¶s 433, 703]

[¶ 2060] Code Sec. 643. Definitions applicable to subparts A, B, C, and D.

(a) Distributable net income. For purposes of this part, the term "distributable net income" means, with respect to any taxable year, the taxable income of the estate or trust computed with the following modifications—

* * * * * * * * * * * * *

(3) Capital gains and losses. Gains from the sale or exchange of capital assets shall be excluded to the extent that such gains are allocated to corpus and are not (A) paid, credited, or required to be distributed to any beneficiary during the taxable year, or (B) paid, permanently set aside, or to be used for the purposes specified in section 642(c). Losses from the sale or exchange of capital assets shall be excluded, except to the extent such losses are taken into account in determining the amount of gains from the sale or exchange of capital assets which are paid, credited, or required to be distributed to any beneficiary during the taxable year. *The exclusion under section 1202 shall not be taken into account.*

* * * * * * * * * * * * *

[For explanation, see ¶ 703.]

[¶ 2061] Code Sec. 691. Recipients of income in respect of decedents.

* * * * * * * * * * * * *

(c) Deduction for estate tax.

* * * * * * * * * * * * *

(4) Coordination with capital gain provisions. For purposes of sections 1(h), [1] *1201, 1202, and 1211,* the amount of any gain taken into account with respect to any item described in subsection (a)(1) shall be reduced (but not below zero) by the amount of the deduction allowable under paragraph (1) of this subsection with respect to such item.

[For explanation, see ¶ 703.]

"(3) Elective binding contract exception.

"(A) In general. The amendments made by this section shall not apply to any acquisition of property by the taxpayer if—

"(i) such acquisition is pursuant to a written binding contract in effect on the date of the enactment of this Act and at all times thereafter before such acquisition,

"(ii) an election under paragraph (2) does not apply to the taxpayer, and

"(iii) the taxpayer makes an election under this paragraph with respect to such contract.

"(B) Election. An election under this paragraph shall be made at such time and in such manner as the Secretary of the Treasury or his delegate shall prescribe. Such an election, once made—

"(i) may be revoked only with the consent of the Secretary, and

"(ii) shall apply to all property acquired pursuant to the contract with respect to which such election was made."

[Footnote Code Sec. 643] Matter in *italics* in Code Sec. 643(a)(3) was added by section 13113(d)(3) of P.L. 103-66

Effective Date (Sec. 13113(e) of P.L. 103-66) effective for stock issued after 8/10/93.

[Footnote Code Sec. 691] Matter in *italics* in Code Sec. 591(c)(4) added by section 13113(d)(4) of P.L. 103-66 which struck out:

1. "1201, and 1211"

Effective Date (Sec. 13113(e) of P.L. 103-66) effective for stock issued after 8/10/93.

[¶ 2062] Code Sec. 703. Partnership computations.

* * * * * * * * * * * * *

(b) Elections of the partnership. Any election affecting the computation of taxable income derived from a partnership shall be made by the partnership, except that any election under—

(1) [1]*subsection (b)(5) or (c)(3)* of section 108 (relating to income from discharge of indebtedness),

[For explanation, see ¶ 503, for Committee Reports, see ¶ 3021.]

[¶ 2063] Code Sec. 736. Payments to a retiring partner or a deceased partner's successor in interest.

* * * * * * * * * * * * *

(b) Payments for interest in partnership.

* * * * * * * * * * * * *

(3) Limitation on application of paragraph (2). *Paragraph (2) shall apply only if—*

(A) capital is not a material income-producing factor for the partnership, and

(B) the retiring or deceased partner was a general partner in the partnership.

[1]***(c) Repealed.***

[For explanation, see ¶ 313, for Committee Reports, see ¶ 3065.]

[¶ 2064] Code Sec. 751. Unrealized receivables and inventory items.

* * * * * * * * * * * * *

(c) Unrealized receivables. For purposes of this subchapter, the term "unrealized receivables" includes, to the extent not previously includible in income under the method of accounting used by the partnership, any rights (contractual or otherwise) to payment for—

(1) goods delivered, or to be delivered, to the extent the proceeds therefrom would be treated as amounts received from the sale or exchange of property other than a capital asset, or

(2) services rendered, or to be rendered.

For purposes of this section and [1], *sections 731 and 741 (but not for purposes of section 736)*, such term also includes mining property (as defined in section 617(f)(2)), stock in a DISC (as described in section 992(a)), section 1245 property (as defined in section 1245(a)(3)), stock in certain foreign corporations (as described in section 1248), section 1250 property (as

[Footnote Code Sec. 703] Matter in *italics* in Code Sec. 703(b)(1) added by section 13150(c)(9) of P.L. 103-66 which struck out:

1. "subsection (b)(5)"

Effective Date (Sec. 13150(d) of P.L. 103-66) effective for discharges after 12/31/92, in tax. yrs. end. after 12/31/92.

[Footnote Code Sec. 736] Matter in *italics* in Code Sec. 736(b)(3) and (c) added by sections 13262(a) and (b)(2)(B) of P.L. 103-66 which struck out:

1. "(c) Cross reference. For limitation on the tax attributable to certain gain connected with section 1248 stock, see section 751(e)."

Effective Date (Sec. 13262(c) of P.L. 103-66) effective for partners retiring or dying on or after 1/5/93, except as provided in Sec. 13262(c)(2) of this Act which reads as follows:

"(2) Binding contract exception. The amendments made by this section shall not apply to any partner retiring on or after January 5, 1993, if a written contract to purchase such partner's interest in the partnership was binding on January 4, 1993, and at all times thereafter before such purchase."

[Footnote Code Sec. 751] Matter in *italics* in Code Sec. 751(c) added by sections 13262(b)(1)(A) and (B) of P.L. 103-66 which struck out:

1. "sections 731, 736, and 741"

defined in section 1250(c)), farm land (as defined in section 1252(a)), franchises, trademarks, or trade names (referred to in section 1253(a)), and an oil, gas, or geothermal property (described in section 1254) but only to the extent of the amount which would be treated as gain to which section 617(d)(1), 995(c), 1245(a), 1248(a), 1250(a), 1252(a), 1253(a) or 1254(a) would apply if (at the time of the transaction described in this section or [2] *section 731 or 741* , as the case may be) such property had been sold by the partnership at its fair market value. For purposes of this section and [1], *sections 731 and 741 (but not for purposes of section 736)* , such term also includes any market discount bond (as defined in section 1278) and any short-term obligation (as defined in section 1283) but only to the extent of the amount which would be treated as ordinary income if (at the time of the transaction described in this section or [2]*section 731 or 741* , as the case may be) such property had been sold by the partnership.

(d) Inventory items which have appreciated substantially in value.

[3]***(1) Substantial appreciation.***

(A) In general. Inventory items of the partnership shall be considered to have appreciated substantially in value if their fair market value exceeds 120 percent of the adjusted basis to the partnership of such property.

(B) Certain property excluded. For purposes of subparagraph (A), there shall be excluded any inventory property if a principal purpose for acquiring such property was to avoid the provisions of this section relating to inventory items.

* * * * * * * * * * * * *

(e) Limitation on tax attributable to deemed sales of section 1248 stock. For purposes of applying this section and [4]*sections 731 and 741* to any amount resulting from the reference to section 1248(a) in the second sentence of subsection (c), in the case of an individual, the tax attributable to such amount shall be limited in the manner provided by subsection (b) of section 1248 (relating to gain from certain sales or exchanges of stock in certain foreign corporation). [For explanation, see ¶ 110 and ¶ 313]

[¶ 2065] Code Sec. 848. Capitalization of certain policy acquisition expenses.

* * * * * * * * * * * * *

(g) Treatment of certain ceding commissions. Nothing in any provision of law (other than [1]*this section or section 197*) shall require the capitalization of any ceding commission incurred

---

2. "section 731, 736, or 741"

Effective Date (Sec. 13262(c) of P.L. 103-66) effective in the case of partners retiring or dying on or after 1/5/93, except as provided in Sec. 13262(c)(2) of this Act, which reads as follows:

"(2) Binding contract exception. The amendments made by this section shall not apply to any partner retiring on or after January 5, 1993, if a written contract to purchase such partner's interest in the partnership was binding on January 4, 1993, and at all times thereafter before such purchase."

Matter in *italics* in code Sec. 751(d)(1) added by Code Sec. 13206(e)(1) of P.L. 103-66 which struck out:

3. "(1) Substantial appreciation. Inventory items of the partnership shall be considered to have appreciated substantially in value if their fair market value exceeds—

"(A) 120 percent of the adjusted basis to the partnership of such property, and

"(B) 10 percent of the fair market value of all partnership property, other than money."

Effective Date (Sec. 13206(e)(2) of P.L. 103-66) effective for sales, exchanges, and distributions after 4/30/93.

Matter in *italics* in Code sec. 751(e) added by section 13262(b)(2)(A) of P.L. 103-66 which struck out:

4. "sections 731, 736, and 741"

Effective Date (Sec. 13262(c) of P.L. 103-66) effective in the case of partners retiring or dying on or after 1/5/93, except as provided in Sec. 13262(c)(2) of this Act, which reads as follows:

"(2) Binding contract exception. The amendments made by this section shall not apply to any partner retiring on or after January 5, 1993, if a written contract to purchase such partner's interest in the partnership was binding on January 4, 1993, and at all times thereafter before such purchase."

[Footnote Code Sec. 848] Matter in *italics* in Code Sec. 848(g) added by section 13261(d), P.L. 103-66, which struck out:

1. "this section"

Effective Date (Sec. 13261(g), P.L. 103-66) effective for property acquired after 8/10/93, except as provided in Sec. 13261(g)(2) and (3) of this Act, which reads as follows:

"(2) Election to have amendments apply to property acquired after July 25, 1991.

on or after September 30, 1990, under any contract which reinsures a specified insurance contract.

* * * * * * * * * * * * * *

[¶ 2066] **Code Sec. 852. Taxation of regulated investment companies and their shareholders.**

* * * * * * * * * * * * * *

(b) Method of taxation of companies and shareholders.

* * * * * * * * * * * * * *

(3) Capital gains.

* * * * * * * * * * * * * *

(D) Treatment by shareholders of undistributed capital gains.

* * * * * * * * * * * * * *

(iii) The adjusted basis of such shares in the hands of the shareholder shall be increased, with respect to the amounts required by this subparagraph to be included in computing his long-term capital gains, by [1] *65 percent* of so much of such amounts as equals the amount subject to tax in accordance with section 1201(a).

* * * * * * * * * * * * * *

[For explanation, see ¶ 301, for text of Committee Reports, see ¶ 3043]

[¶ 2067] **Code Sec. 856. Definition of real estate investment trust.**

* * * * * * * * * * * * * *

(h) Closely held determinations.

* * * * * * * * * * * * * *

"(A) In general. If an election under this paragraph applies to the taxpayer—

"(i) the amendments made by this section shall apply to property acquired by the taxpayer after July 25, 1991,

"(ii) subsection (c)(1)(A) of section 197 of the Internal Revenue Code of 1986 (as added by this section) (and so much of subsection (f)(9)(A) of such section 197 as precedes clause (i) thereof) shall be applied with respect to the taxpayer by treating July 25, 1991, as the date of the enactment of such section, and

"(iii) in applying subsection (f)(9) of such section, with respect to any property acquired by the taxpayer on or before the date of the enactment of this Act, only holding or use on July 25, 1991, shall be taken into account.

"(B) Election. An election under this paragraph shall be made at such time and in such manner as the Secretary of the Treasury or his delegate may prescribe. Such an election by any taxpayer, once made—

"(i) may be revoked only with the consent of the Secretary, and

"(ii) shall apply to the taxpayer making such election and any other taxpayer under common control with the taxpayer (within the meaning of subparagraphs (A) and (B) of section 41(f)(1) of such Code) at any time after August 2,1993, and on or before the date on which such election is made.

"(3) Elective binding contract exception.

"(A) In general. The amendments made by this section shall not apply to any acquisition of property by the taxpayer if—

"(i) such acquisition is pursuant to a written binding contract in effect on the date of the enactment of this Act and at all times thereafter before such acquisition,

"(ii) an election under paragraph (2) does not apply to the taxpayer, and

"(iii) the taxpayer makes an election under this paragraph with respect to such contract.

"(B) Election. An election under this paragraph shall be made at such time and in such manner as the Secretary of the Treasury or his delegate shall prescribe. Such an election, once made—

"(i) may be revoked only with the consent of the Secretary, and

"(ii) shall apply to all property, acquired pursuant to the contract with respect to which such election was made."

[Footnote Code Sec. 852] Matter in *italics* in Code Sec. 852(b)(3)(D)(iii) added by section 13221(c)(1), P.L. 103-66, which struck out:

1. "66 percent"

Effective Date (Sec. 13221(d), P.L. 103-66) effective for tax. yrs. begin. on or after 1/1/93.

(3) Treatment of trusts described in section 401(a).

(A) Look-thru treatment.

(i) In general. Except as provided in clause (ii), in determining whether the stock ownership requirement of section 542(a)(2) is met for purposes of paragraph (1)(A), any stock held by a qualified trust shall be treated as held directly by its beneficiaries in proportion to their actuarial interests in such trust and shall not be treated as held by such trust.

(ii) Certain related trusts not eligible. Clause (i) shall not apply to any qualified trust if one or more disqualified persons (as defined in section 4975(e)(2), without regard to subparagraphs (B) and (I) thereof) with respect to such qualified trust hold in the aggregate 5 percent or more in value of the interests in the real estate investment trust and such real estate investment trust has accumulated earnings and profits attributable to any period for which it did not qualify as a real estate investment trust.

(B) Coordination with personal holding company rules. If any entity qualifies as a real estate investment trust for any taxable year by reason of subparagraph (A), such entity shall not be treated as a personal holding company for such taxable year for purposes of part II of subchapter G of this chapter.

(C) Treatment for purposes of unrelated business tax. If any qualified trust holds more than 10 percent (by value) of the interests in any pension-held REIT at any time during a taxable year, the trust shall be treated as having for such taxable year gross income from an unrelated trade or business in an amount which bears the same ratio to the aggregate dividends paid (or treated as paid) by the REIT to the trust for the taxable year of the REIT with or within which the taxable year of the trust ends (the "REIT year") as—

(i) the gross income (less direct expenses related thereto) of the REIT for the REIT year from unrelated trades or businesses (determined as if the REIT were a qualified trust), bears to

(ii) the gross income (less direct expenses related thereto) of the REIT for the REIT year.

This subparagraph shall apply only if the ratio determined under the preceding sentence is at least 5 percent.

(D) Pension-held REIT. The purposes of subparagraph (C)—

(i) In general. A real estate investment trust is a pension-held REIT if such trust would not have qualified as a real estate investment trust but for the provisions of this paragraph and if such trust is predominantly held by qualified trusts.

(ii) Predominantly held. For purposes of clause (i), a real estate investment trust is predominantly held by qualified trusts if—

(I) at least 1 qualified trust holds more than 25 percent (by value) of the interests in such real estate investment trust, or

(II) 1 or more qualified trusts (each of whom own more than 10 percent by value of the interests in such real estate investment trust) hold in the aggregate more than 50 percent (by value) of the interests in such real estate investment trust.

(E) Qualified trust. For purposes of this paragraph, the term "qualified trust" means any trust described in section 401(a) and exempt from tax under section 501(a).

* * * * * * * * * * * * *

[For explanation, see ¶ 506, for text of Committee Report, see ¶ 3058]

[Footnote Code Sec. 856] Matter in *italics* in Code Sec. 856(h)(3) added by section 13149(a) of P.L. 103-66.
Effective Date (Sec. 13149(b), P.L. 103-66) effective for tax. yrs. begin. after 12/31/93.

[¶ 2068] Code Sec. 864. Definitions and special rules.

* * * * * * * * * * * * *

(f) Allocation of research and experimental expenditures.

(1) In general. For purposes of sections 861(b), 862(b), and 863(b), qualified research and experimental expenditures shall be allocated and apportioned as follows:

* * * * * * * * * * * * *

(B) In the case of any qualified research and experimental expenditures (not allocated under subparagraph (A)) to the extent—

(i) that such expenditures are attributable to activities conducted in the United States, [1]*50 percent* of such expenditures shall be allocated and apportioned to income from sources within the United States and deducted from such income in determining the amount of taxable income from sources within the United States, and

(ii) that such expenditures are attributable to activities conducted outside the United States, [1]*50 percent* of such expenditures shall be allocated and apportioned to income from sources outside the United States and deducted from such income in determining the amount of taxable income from sources outside the United States.

* * * * * * * * * * * * *

(4) Affiliated group.

* * * * * * * * * * * * *

(D) The Secretary may prescribe such regulations as may be necessary to carry out the purposes of this paragraph, including regulations providing for the source of gross income and the allocation and apportionment of deductions to take into account the adjustments required by [2]*subparagraph (B) or (C).*

* * * * * * * * * * * * *

[3]***(5) Regulations.*** *The Secretary shall prescribe such regulations as may be appropriate to carry out the purposes of this subsection, including regulations relating to the determination of whether any expenses are attributable to activities conducted in the United States or outside the United States and regulations providing such adjustments to the provisions of this subsection as may be appropriate in the case of cost-sharing arrangements and contract research.*

(6) Applicability. *This subsection shall apply to the taxpayer's first taxable year (beginning on or before August 1, 1994) following the taxpayer's last taxable year to which Revenue Procedure 92-56 applies or would apply if the taxpayer elected the benefits of such Revenue Procedure.*

[For explanation, see ¶ 1103, for text of Committee Reports, see ¶ 3053]

[Footnote Code Sec. 864] Matter in *italics* in Code Sec. 864(f)(1)(B), (4)(D), (5) and (6) added by sections 13234(a), (b)(1) and (b)(2) which struck out:

1. "64 percent"
2. "subparagraph (C)"
3. "(5) Years to which rule applies.

"(A) In general. This subsection shall apply to the taxpayer's first 3 taxable years beginning after August 1, 1989, and on or before August 1, 1992.

"(B) Reduction. Notwithstanding subparagraph (A), in the case of the taxpayer's first taxable year beginning after August 1, 1991, this subsection shall only apply to qualified research and experimental expenditures incurred during the first 6 months of such taxable year."

Effective Date effective 8/10/93.

[¶ 2069] Code Sec. 865. Source rules for personal property sales.

* * * * * * * * * * * * *

(b) Exception for inventory property. In the case of income derived from the sale of inventory property—

(1) this section shall not apply, and

(2) such income shall be sourced under the rules of sections 861(a)(6), 862(a)(6), and 863(b).

Notwithstanding the preceding sentence, any income from the sale of any unprocessed timber which is a softwood and was cut from an area in the United States shall be sourced in the United States and the rules of sections 862(a)(6) and 863(b) shall not apply to any such income. For purposes of the preceding sentence, the term "unprocessed timber" means any log, cant, or similar form of timber.

* * * * * * * * * * * * *

[For explanation, see ¶ 1119]

[¶ 2070] Code Sec. 871. Tax on nonresident alien individuals.

(a) Income not connected with United States business—30 percent tax.

* * * * * * * * * * * * *

(2) Capital gains of aliens present in the United States 183 days or more. In the case of a nonresident alien individual present in the United States for a period or periods aggregating 183 days or more during the taxable year, there is hereby imposed for such year a tax of 30 percent of the amount by which his gains, derived from sources within the United States, from the sale or exchange at any time during such year of capital assets exceed his losses, allocable to sources within the United States, from the sale or exchange at any time during such year of capital assets. For purposes of this paragraph, gains and losses shall be taken into account only if, and to the extent that, they would be recognized and taken into account if such gains and losses were effectively connected with the conduct of a trade or business within the United States, except that *such gains and losses shall be determined without regard to section 1202 and* such losses shall be determined without the benefits of the capital loss carryover provided in section 1212. Any gain or loss which is taken into account in determining the tax under paragraph (1) or subsection (b) shall not be taken into account in determining the tax under this paragraph. For purposes of the 183-day requirement of this paragraph, a nonresident alien individual not engaged in trade or business within the United States who has not established a taxable year for any prior period shall be treated as having a taxable year which is the calendar year.

* * * * * * * * * * * * *

(h) Repeal of tax on interest of nonresident alien individuals received from certain portfolio debt investments.

* * * * * * * * * * * * *

(2) Portfolio interest. For purposes of this subsection, the term "portfolio interest" means any interest (including original issue discount) which would be subject to tax under subsection (a) but for this subsection and which is described in any of the following subparagraphs:

* * * * * * * * * * * * *

(B) Certain registered obligations. Interest which is paid on an obligation—

[Footnote Code Sec. 865] Matter in *italics* in Code Sec. 865(b) added by section 13239(c), P.L. 103-66.
Effective Date (Sec. 13239(e), P.L. 103-66) effective for sales, exchanges, or other dispositions after 8/10/93.

(i) which is in registered form, and

(ii) with respect to which the United States person who would otherwise be required to deduct and withhold tax from such interest under section 1441(a) receives a statement (which meets the requirements of [1]*paragraph (5)*) that the beneficial owner of the obligation is not a United States person.

* * * * * * * * * * * * *

(4) Portfolio interest not to include certain contingent interest. *For purposes of this subsection—*

(A) In general. Except as otherwise provided in this paragraph, the term "portfolio interest" shall not include—

(i) any interest if the amount of such interest is determined by reference to—

(I) any receipts, sales or other cash flow of the debtor or a related person,

(II) any income or profits of the debtor or a related person,

(III) any change in value of any property of the debtor or a related person, or

(IV) any dividend, partnership distributions, or similar payments made by the debtor or a related person, or

(ii) any other type of contingent interest that is identified by the Secretary by regulation, where a denial of the portfolio interest exemption is necessary or appropriate to prevent avoidance of Federal income tax.

(B) Related person. The term "related person" means any person who is related to the debtor within the meaning of section 267(b) or 707(b)(1), or who is a party to any arrangement undertaken for a purpose of avoiding the application of this paragraph.

(C) Exceptions. Subparagraph (A)(i) shall not apply to—

(i) any amount of interest solely by reason of the fact that the timing of any interest or principal payment is subject to a contingency,

(ii) any amount of interest solely by reason of the fact that the interest is paid with respect to nonrecourse or limited recourse indebtedness,

(iii) any amount of interest all or substantially all of which is determined by reference to any other amount of interest not described in subparagraph (A) (or by reference to the principal amount of indebtedness on which such other interest is paid),

(iv) any amount of interest solely by reason of the fact that the debtor or a related person enters into a hedging transaction to reduce the risk of interest rate or currency fluctuations with respect to such interest,

(v) any amount of interest determined by reference to—

(I) changes in the value of property (including stock) that is actively traded (within the meaning of section 1092(d)) other than property described in section 897(c)(1) or (g),

(II) the yield on property described in subclause (I), other than a debt instrument that pays interest described in subparagraph (A), or stock or other property that represents a beneficial interest in the debtor or a related person, or

(III) changes in any index of the value of property described in subclause (I) or of the yield on property described in subclause (II), and

(vi) any other type of interest identified by the Secretary by regulation.

(D) Exception for certain existing indebtedness. Subparagraph (A) shall not apply to any interest paid or accrued with respect to any indebtedness with a fixed term—

(i) which was issued on or before April 7, 1993, or

(ii) which was issued after such date pursuant to a written binding contract in effect on such date and at all times thereafter before such indebtedness was issued.

[2]*(5)* Certain statements. A statement with respect to any obligation meets the requirements of this paragraph if such statement is made by—

[Footnote Code Sec. 871] Matter in *italics* in Code Sec. 871(a)(2), (h)(2)(B)(ii), and (h)(4)-(7) added by sections 13113(d)(5), 13237(a)(1) and (c)(1), P.L. 103-66, which struck out:

1. "paragraph (4)"
2. "(4)"

(A) the beneficial owner of such obligation, or

(B) a securities clearing organization, a bank, or other financial institution that holds customers' securities in the ordinary course of its trade or business.

The preceding sentence shall not apply to any statement with respect to payment of interest on any obligation by any person if, at least one month before such payment, the Secretary has published a determination that any statement from such person (or any class including such person) does not meet the requirements of this paragraph.

[3]*(6)* Secretary may provide subsection not to apply in cases of inadequate information exchange.

(A) In general. If the Secretary determines that the exchange of information between the United States and a foreign country is inadequate to prevent evasion of the United States income tax by United States persons, the Secretary may provide in writing (and publish a statement) that the provisions of this subsection shall not apply to payments of interest to any person within such foreign country (or payments addressed to, or for the account of, persons within such foreign country) during the period—

(i) beginning on the date specified by the Secretary, and

(ii) ending on the date that the Secretary determines that the exchange of information between the United States and the foreign country is adequate to prevent the evasion of United States income tax by United States persons.

(B) Exception for certain obligations. Subparagraph (A) shall not apply to the payment of interest on any obligation which is issued on or before the date of the publication of the Secretary's determination under such subparagraph.

[4]*(7)* Registered form. For purposes of this subsection, the term "registered form" has the same meaning given such term by section 163(f).

[For explanation, see ¶ 703 and ¶ 1106, for text of Committee Report, see ¶ 3056]

[¶ 2071] Code Sec. 881. Tax on income of foreign corporations not connected with United States business.

* * * * * * * * * * * * *

(c) Repeal of tax on interest of foreign corporations received from certain portfolio debt investments.

* * * * * * * * * * * * *

(2) Portfolio interest. For purposes of this subsection, the term "portfolio interest" means any interest (including original issue discount) which would be subject to tax under subsection (a) but for this subsection and which is described in any of the following subparagraphs:

(A) Certain obligations which are not registered. Interest which is paid on any obligation which is described in section 871(h)(2)(A).

(B) Certain registered obligations. Interest which is paid on an obligation—

(i) which is in registered form, and

* * * * * * * * * * * * *

(ii) with respect to which the person who would otherwise be required to deduct and withhold tax from such interest under section 1442(a) receives a statement which meets the requirements of [1]*section 871(h)(5)* that the beneficial owner of the obligation is not a United States person.

* * * * * * * * * * * * *

3. "(5)"
4. "(6)"

Effective Date (Sec. 13237(d), P.L. 103-66) effective for interest received after 12/31/93.

[Footnote Code Sec. 881] Matter in *italics* in Code Sec. 881(c)(2)(B)(ii), (c)(4)-(7) added by sections 13237(a)(2), (c)(2) and (c)(3), P.L. 103-66, which struck out:

1. "section 871(h)(4)"

(4) Portfolio interest not to include certain contingent interest. *For purposes of this subsection, the term "portfolio interest" shall not include any interest which is treated as not being portfolio interest under the rules of section 871(h)(4).*

[2]*(5)* Special rules for controlled foreign corporations.

(A) In general. In the case of any portfolio interest received by a controlled foreign corporation, the following provisions shall not apply:

(i) Subparagraph (A) of section 954(b)(3) (relating to exception where foreign base company income is less than 5 percent or $1,000,000).

(ii) Paragraph (4) of section 954(b) (relating to exception for certain income subject to high foreign taxes).

(iii) Clause (i) of section 954(c)(3)(A) (relating to certain income received from related persons).

(B) Controlled foreign corporation. For purposes of this subsection, the term "controlled foreign corporation" has the meaning given to such term by section 957(a).

[3]*(6)* Secretary may cease application of this subsection. Under rules similar to the rules of [4]*section 871(h)(6),* the Secretary may provide that this subsection shall not apply to payments of interest described in [5]*section 871(h)(6).*

[6]*(7)* Registered form. For purposes of this subsection, the term "registered form" has the meaning given such term by section 163(f).

* * * * * * * * * * * *

For explanation see ¶ 1106 for text of Committee Reports, see ¶ 3056

[¶ 2072] Code Sec. 897. Disposition of investment in United States real property.

(a) General rule.

* * * * * * * * * * * *

(2) [1]*Minimum tax on nonresident alien individuals.*

(A) In general. In the case of any nonresident alien individual, [2]*the taxable excess for purposes of section 55(b)(1)(A) shall not be less than* the lesser of—

(i) the individual's alternative minimum taxable income (as defined in section 55(b)(2)) for the taxable year, or

(ii) the individual's net United States real property gain for the taxable year.

* * * * * * * * * * * *

[For explanation, see ¶ 114]

[¶ 2073] Code Sec. 904. Limitation on credit.

* * * * * * * * * * * *

(b) Taxable income for purpose of computing limitation.

* * * * * * * * * * * *

---

2. "(4)"
3. "(5)"
4. "section 871(h)(5)"
5. "section 871(h)(5)"
6. "(6)"

Effective Date (Sec. 13237(d), P.L. 103-66) effective for interest received after 12/31/93.

[Footnote Code Sec. 897] Matter in *italics* in Code Sec. 897(a)(2) and (a)(2)(A) added by sections 13202(c)(2)(A) and (B) of P.L. 103-66 which struck out:

1. "21-percent"
2. "the amount determined under section 55(b)(1)(A) shall not be less than 21 percent of"

Effective Date (Sec. 13203(d) of P.L. 103-66) effective for tax. yrs. begin. after 12/31/92.

(4) Coordination with section 936. For purposes of subsection (a), in the case of a corporation, the taxable income shall not include any portion thereof taken into account for purposes of the credit (if any) allowed by section 936 *(without regard to subsections (a)(4) and (i) thereof).*

* * * * * * * * * * * * *

(d) Separate application of section with respect to certain categories of income.

* * * * * * * * * * * * *

(2) Definitions and special rules. For purposes of this subsection—

(A) Passive income.

(i) In general. Except as otherwise provided in this subparagraph, the term "passive income" means any income received or accrued by any person which is of a kind which would be foreign personal holding company income (as defined in section 954(c)).

(ii) Certain amounts included. Except as provided in clause (iii), the term "passive income" includes any amount includible in gross income under section 551 or, except as provided in subparagraph (E)(iii) or paragraph (3)(I), section 1293 (relating to certain passive foreign investment companies).

(iii) Exceptions. The term "passive income" shall not include—

(I) any income described in a subparagraph of paragraph (1) other than subparagraph (A),

(II) any export financing interest, *and*

(III) any high-taxed income [1]. [2]

(iv) Clarification of application of section 864(d)(6). In determining whether any income is of a kind which would be foreign personal holding company income, the rules of section 864(d)(6) shall apply only in the case of income of a controlled foreign corporation.

* * * * * * * * * * * * *

[For explanation, see ¶ 1104 and ¶ 1117, for text of Committee Report, see ¶ 3054]

[¶ 2074] Code Sec. 907. Special rules in case of foreign oil and gas income.

* * * * * * * * * * * * *

(c) Foreign income definitions and special rules. For purposes of this section—

(1) Foreign oil and gas extraction income. The term "foreign oil and gas extraction income" means the taxable income derived from sources without the United States and its possessions from—

(A) the extraction (by the taxpayer or any other person) of minerals from oil or gas wells, or

(B) the sale or exchange of assets used by the taxpayer in the trade or business described in subparagraph (A).

Such term does not include any dividend or interest income which is passive income (as defined in section 904(d)(2)(A)).

(2) Foreign oil related income. The term "foreign oil related income" means the taxable income derived from sources outside the United States and its possessions from—

[Footnote Code Sec. 904] Matter in *italics* in Code Sec. 904(b)(4), (d)(2)(A)(iii)(II) and (III) added by sections 13227(d) and 13235(a)(2), P.L. 103-66, which struck out:

1. ", and"
2. "(IV) any foreign oil and gas extraction income (as defined in section 907(c))."

Effective Date (Sec. 13235(c), P.L. 103-66) effective for tax. yrs. begin. after 12/31/92.

[Footnote Code Sec. 907] Matter in *italics* in Code Sec. 907(c)(1) and (2) added by sections 13235(a)(1)(A) and (B), P.L. 103-66.

Effective Date (Sec. 13235(c), P.L. 103-66) effective for tax. yrs. begin. after 12/31/92.

(A) the processing of minerals extracted (by the taxpayer or by any other person) from oil or gas wells into their primary products,

(B) the transportation of such minerals or primary products,

(C) the distribution or sale of such minerals or primary products,

(D) the disposition of assets used by the taxpayer in the trade or business described in subparagraph (A), (B), or (C), or

(E) the performance of any other related service.

Such term does not include any dividend or interest income which is passive income (as defined in section 904(d)(2)(A)).

[For explanation, see ¶ 1104, for text of Committee Report, see ¶ 3054]

[¶ 2075] Code Sec. 927. Other definitions and special rules.

(a) Export property. For purposes of this subpart—

* * * * * * * * * * * * *

(2) Excluded property. The term "export property" shall not include—

* * * * * * * * * * * * *

(C) oil or gas (or any primary product thereof), [1]

(D) products the export of which is prohibited or curtailed to effectuate the policy set forth in paragraph (2)(C) of section 3 of the Export Administration Act of 1979 (relating to the protection of the domestic economy) [2], *or*

(E) any unprocessed timber which is a softwood.

For purposes of subparagraph (E), the term "unprocessed timber" means any log, cant, or similar form of timber.

[For explanation, see ¶ 1119 for text of Committee Report, see

---

[¶ 2076] Code Sec. 936. Puerto Rico and possession tax credit.

* * * * * * * * * * * * *

(a) Allowance of credit.

* * * * * * * * * * * * *

(1) In general. Except [1]*as otherwise provided in this section,* if a domestic corporation elects the application of this section and if the conditions of both subparagraph (A) and subparagraph (B) of paragraph (2) are satisfied, there shall be allowed as a credit against the tax imposed by this chapter an amount equal to the portion of the tax which is attributable to the sum of—

(A) the taxable income, from sources without the United States, from —

(i) the active conduct of a trade or business within a possession of the United States, or

(ii) the sale or exchange of substantially all of the assets used by the taxpayer in the active conduct of such trade or business, and

(B) the qualified possession source investment income.

[Footnote Code Sec. 927] Matter in *italics* in Code Sec. 927(a)(2)(C)-(E) added by section 13239(a) of P.L. 103-66, which struck out:

1. "or"
2. "."

Effective Date (Sec. 13239(e) of P.L. 103-66)effective for sales, exchanges, or other dispositions after 8/10/93.

[Footnote Code Sec. 936] Matter in *italics* in Code Sec. 936(a)(1), (a)(4) and (i) added by sections 13227(a)(1), (a)(2) and (b) of P.L. 103-66 which struck out:

1. "as provided in paragraph (3)"

Effective Date (Sec. 13227(f) of P.L. 103-66) effective for tax. yrs. begin. after 12/31/93.

* * * * * * * * * * * * *

(4) Limitations on credit for active business income.

(A) In general. The amount of the credit determined under paragraph (1) for any taxable year with respect to income referred to in subparagraph (A) thereof shall not exceed the sum of the following amounts:

(i) 60 percent of the sum of—

(I) the aggregate amount of the possession corporation's qualified possession wages for such taxable year, plus

(II) the allocable employee fringe benefit expenses of the possession corporation for the taxable year.

(ii) The sum of—

(I) 15 percent of the deprecation allowances for the taxable year with respect to short-life qualified tangible property,

(II) 40 percent of the depreciation allowances for the taxable year with respect to medium-life qualified tangible property, and

(III) 65 percent of the depreciation allowances for the taxable year with respect to long-life qualified tangible property.

(iii) If the possession corporation does not have an election to use the method described in subsection (h)(5)(C)(ii) (relating to profit split) in effect for the taxable year, the amount of the qualified possession income taxes for the taxable year allocable to nonsheltered income.

(B) Election to take reduced credit.

(i) In general. If an election under this subparagraph applies to a possession corporation for any taxable year—

(I) subparagraph (A), and the provisions of subsection (i), shall not apply to such possession corporation for such taxable year, and

(II) the credit determined under paragraph (1) for such taxable year with respect to income referred to in subparagraph (A) thereof shall be the applicable percentage of the credit which would otherwise have been determined under such paragraph with respect to such income.

Notwithstanding subclause (I), a possession corporation to which an election under this subparagraph applies shall be entitled to the benefits of subsection (i)(3)(B) for taxes allocable (on a pro rata basis) to taxable income the tax on which is not offset by reason of this subparagraph.

(ii) Applicable percentage. The term "applicable percentage" means the percentage determined in accordance with the following table:

In the case of taxable years beginning in:	The percentage is:
1994	60
1995	55
1996	50
1997	45
1998 and thereafter	40

(iii) Election.

(I) In general. An election under this subparagraph by any possession corporation may be made only for the corporation's first taxable year beginning after December 31, 1993, for which it is a possession corporation.

(II) Period of election. An election under this subparagraph shall apply to the taxable year for which made and all subsequent taxable years unless revoked.

(III) Affiliated groups. If, for any taxable year, an election is not in effect for any possession corporation which is a member of an affiliated group, any election under this subparagraph for any other member of such group is revoked for such taxable year and all subsequent taxable years. For purposes of this subclause, members of an affiliated group shall be determined without regard to the exceptions contained in section 1504(b) and as if the constructive ownership rules of section 1563(e) applied for pur-

poses of section 1504(a). The Secretary may prescribe regulations to prevent the avoidance of this subclause through deconsolidation or otherwise.

(C) Cross reference. For definitions and special rules applicable to this paragraph, see subsection (i).

* * * * * * * * * * * *

(i) Definitions and special rules relating to limitations of subsection (a)(4).

(1) Qualified possession wages. *For purposes of this section—*

(A) In general. The term "qualified possession wages" means wages paid or incurred by the possession corporation during the taxable year in connection with the active conduct of a trade or business within a possession of the United States to any employee for services performed in such possession, but only if such services are performed while the principal place of employment of such employee is within such possession.

(B) Limitation on amount of wages taken into account.

(i) In general. The amount of wages which may be taken into account under subparagraph (A) with respect to any employee for any taxable year shall not exceed 85 percent of the contribution and benefit base determined under section 230 of the Social Security Act for the calendar year in which such taxable year begins.

(ii) Treatment of part-time employees, etc. If—

(I) any employee is not employed by the possession corporation on a substantially full-time basis at all times during the taxable year, or

(II) the principal place of employment of any employee with the possession corporation is not within a possession at all times during the taxable year,

the limitation applicable under clause (i) with respect to such employee shall be the appropriate portion (as determined by the Secretary) of the limitation which would otherwise be in effect under clause (i).

(C) Treatment of certain employees. The term "qualified possession wages" shall not include any wages paid to employees who are assigned by the employer to perform services for another person, unless the principal trade or business of the employer is to make employees available for temporary periods to other persons in return for compensation. All possession corporations treated as 1 corporation under paragraph (5) shall be treated as 1 employer for purposes of the preceding sentence.

(D) Wages.

(i) In general. Except as provided in clause (ii), the term "wages" has the meaning given to such term by subsection (b) of section 3306 (determined without regard to any dollar limitation contained in such section). For purposes of the preceding sentence, such subsection (b) shall be applied as if the term "United States" included all possessions of the United States.

(ii) Special rule for agricultural labor and railway labor. In any case to which subparagraph (A) or (B) of paragraph (1) of section 51(h) applies, the term "wages" has the meaning given to such term by section 51(h)(2).

(2) QPSII assets. *For purposes of this section—*

(A) In general. The QPSII assets of a possession corporation for any taxable year is the average of the amounts of the possession corporation's qualified investment assets as of the close of each quarter of such taxable year.

(B) Qualified investment assets. The term "qualified investment assets" means the aggregate adjusted bases of the assets which are held by the possession corporation and the income from which qualifies as qualified possession source investment income. For purposes of the preceding sentence, the adjusted basis of any asset shall be its adjusted basis as determined for purposes of computing earnings and profits.

(3) Qualified tangible business investment. *For purposes of this section—*

(A) In general. The qualified tangible business investment of any possession corporation for any taxable year is the average of the amounts of the possession corporation's qualified possession investments as of the close of each quarter of such taxable year.

(B) Qualified possession investments. The term "qualified possession investments" means the aggregate adjusted bases of tangible property used by the possession corporation in a possession of the United States in the active conduct of a trade or business within such possession. For purposes of the preceding sentence, the adjusted basis of any property shall be its adjusted basis as determined for purposes of computing earnings and profits.

(4) Relocated businesses.

(A) In general. In determining—

(i) the possession corporation's qualified possession wages for any taxable year, and

(ii) the possession corporation's qualified tangible business investment for such taxable year,

there shall be excluded all wages and all qualified possession investments which are allocable to a disqualified relocated business.

(B) Disqualified relocated business. For purposes of subparagraph (A), the term "disqualified relocated business" means any trade or business commenced by the possession corporation after May 13, 1993, or any addition after such date to an existing trade or business of such possession corporation unless—

(i) the possession corporation certifies that the commencement of such trade or business or such addition will not result in a decrease in employment at an existing business operation located in the United States, and

(ii) there is no reason to believe that such commencement or addition was done with the intention of closing down operations of an existing business located in the United States.

(5) Election to compute credit on consolidated basis.

(A) In general. Any affiliated group may elect to treat all possession corporations which would be members of such group but for section 1504(b)(4) as 1 corporation for purposes of this section. The credit determined under this section with respect to such 1 corporation shall be allocated among such possession corporations in such manner as the Secretary may prescribe.

(B) Election. An election under subparagraph (A) shall apply to the taxable year for which made and all succeeding taxable years unless revoked with the consent of the Secretary.

***(6) Treatment of certain taxes.** Notwithstanding subsection (c), if—*

(A) the credit determined under subsection (a)(1) for any taxable year is limited under subsection (a)(4), and

(B) the possession corporation has paid or accrued any taxes of a possession of the United States for such taxable year which are treated as not being income, war profits, or excess profits taxes paid or accrued to a possession of the United States by reason of subsection (c),

such possession corporation shall be allowed a deduction for such taxable year equal to the portion of such taxes which are allocable (on a pro rata basis) to taxable income of the possession corporation the tax on which is not offset by reason of the limitations of subsection (a)(4). In determining the credit under subsection (a) and in applying the preceding sentence, taxable income shall be determined without regard to the preceding sentence.

***(7) Possession corporation.** The term "possession corporation" means a domestic corporation for which the election provided in subsection (a) is in effect.*

***(8) Transitional rule.** If any possession corporation elects the benefits of this paragraph for any taxable year beginning in 1994 or 1995—*

(A) subsection (a)(4) shall not apply to such taxable year, and

(B) the credit determined under subsection (a)(1) for such taxable year shall be the following percentage of the credit which would otherwise have been determined under such subsection:

(i) 80 percent in the case of a taxable year beginning in 1994.

(ii) 60 percent in the case of a taxable year beginning in 1995.

A possession corporation which elects the benefits of this paragraph shall be entitled to the benefits of paragraph (6) for taxes allocable to taxable income the tax on which is not offset by reason of this paragraph.

[For explanation, see ¶ 1116, for Committee Reports, see ¶ 3050.]

[¶ 2077] Code Sec. 951. Amounts included in gross income of United States shareholders.

(a) Amounts included.

(1) In general. If a foreign corporation is a controlled foreign corporation for an uninterrupted period of 30 days or more during any taxable year, every person who is a United States shareholder (as defined in subsection (b)) of such corporation and who owns (within the meaning of section 958(a)) stock in such corporation on the last day, in such year, on which such corporation is a controlled foreign corporation shall include in his gross income, for his taxable year in which or with which such taxable year of the corporation ends—

(A) the sum of—

(i) his pro rata share (determined under paragraph (2)) of the corporation's subpart F income for such year,

(ii) his pro rata share (determined under section 955(a)(3) as in effect before the enactment of the Tax Reduction Act of 1975) of the corporation's previously excluded subpart F income withdrawn from investment in less developed countries for such year, and

(iii) his pro rata share (determined under section 955(a)(3)) of the corporation's previously excluded subpart F income withdrawn from foreign base company shipping operations for such year; [1]

[2]*(B) the amount determined under section 956 with respect to such shareholder for such year (but only to the extent not excluded from gross income under section 959(a)(2)); and 14231(a)*

(C) the amount determined under section 956A with respect to such shareholder for such year (but only to the extent not excluded from gross income under section 959(a)(3)).

* * * * * * * * * * * * *

[3]**(4) Repealed.**

[For explanation, see ¶ 1101 and ¶ 1110, for text of Committee Report, see ¶ 3052]

[¶ 2078] Code Sec. 954. Foreign base company income.

* * * * * * * * * * * * *

(b) Exclusions and special rules.

* * * * * * * * * * * * *

[Footnote Code Sec. 951] Matter in *italics* Code Sec. 951(a)(1)(A)-(C) added by Sec. 13231(a) which struck out:
1. "and"

Effective Date (Sec. 13231(e) of P.L. 103-66) effective for tax. yrs. of foreign corporations begin. after 9/30/93, and to tax. yrs. of U.S. shareholders in which or with which such tax. yrs. of foreign corporations end.

Matter in *italics* in Code Sec. 951(a)(1)(B) added by section 13232(c)(1) and (2) which struck out:

2. "(B) his pro rata share (determined under section 956(a)(2)) of the corporation's increase in earnings invested in United States property for such year (but only to the extent not excluded from gross income under section 959(a)(2)); and"

3. "(4) Limitation on pro rata share of investment in United States property. For purposes of paragraph (1)(B), the pro rata share of any United States shareholder in the increase of the earnings of a controlled foreign corporation invested in United States property shall not exceed an amount (A) which bears the same ratio to his pro rata share of such increase (as determined under section 956(a)(2)) for the taxable year, as (B) the part of such year during which the corporation is a controlled foreign corporation bears to the entire year."

Effective Date (Sec. 13232(d) of P.L. 103-66) effective for tax. yrs. of controlled foreign corporations begin. after 9/30/93, and to tax. yrs. of U.S. shareholders in which or with which such tax. yrs. of controlled foreign corporations end.

(8) Foreign base company oil related income not treated as another kind of base company income. Income of a corporation which is foreign base company oil related income shall not be considered foreign base company income of such corporation under paragraph [1](2), or (3) of subsection (a).

(c) Foreign personal holding company income.

* * * * * * * * * * * * *

(3) Certain income received from related persons.

* * * * * * * * * * * * *

(C) Exception for certain dividends. Subparagraph (A)(i) shall not apply to any dividend with respect to any stock which is attributable to earnings and profits of the distributing corporation accumulated during any period during which the person receiving such dividend did not hold such stock either directly, or indirectly through a chain of one or more subsidiaries each of which meets the requirements of subparagraph (A)(i).

(d) Foreign base company sales income.

* * * * * * * * * * * * *

(4) Special rule for certain timber products. *For purposes of subsection (a)(2), the term "foreign base company sales income" includes any income (whether in the form of profits, commissions, fees, or otherwise) derived in connection with—*

(A) the sale of any unprocessed timber referred to in section 865(b), or

(B) the milling of any such timber outside the United States.

Subpart G shall not apply to any amount treated as subpart F income by reason of this paragraph.

* * * * * * * * * * * * *

(f) Foreign base company shipping income. For purposes of subsection (a)(4), the term "foreign base company shipping income" means income derived from, or in connection with, the use (or hiring or leasing for use) of any aircraft or vessel in foreign commerce, or from, or in connection with, the performance of services directly related to the use of any such aircraft, or vessel, or from the sale, exchange, or other disposition of any such aircraft or vessel. Such term includes, but is not limited to—

(1) dividends and interest received from a foreign corporation in respect of which taxes are deemed paid under section 902, and gain from the sale, exchange, or other disposition of stock or obligations of such a foreign corporation to the extent that such dividends, interest, and gains are attributable to foreign base company shipping income, and

(2) that portion of the distributive share of the income of a partnership attributable to foreign base company shipping income.

Such term includes any income derived from a space or ocean activity (as defined in section 863(d)(2)). *Except as provided in paragraph (1), such term shall not include any dividend or interest income which is foreign personal holding company income (as defined in subsection (c)).*

(g) Foreign base company oil related income. For purposes of this section—

(1) In general. Except as otherwise provided in this subsection, the term "foreign base company oil related income" means foreign oil related income (within the meaning of

---

[Footnote Code Sec. 954] Matter in *italics* in Code Sec. 954(b)(8) added by section 13235(a)(3)(B) of P.L. 103-66 which struck out:

1. "(1),"

Effective Date (Sec. 13235(c) of P.L. 103-66) effective for tax. yrs. begin. after 12/31/92.

Matter in *italics* in Code Sec. 954(c)(3)(C) was added by section 13233(a)(1) of P.L. 103-66.

Effective Date (Sec. 13233(a)(2) of P.L. 103-66) effective for tax. yrs of controlled foreign corporations begin. after 9/30/93, and for tax. yrs. of U.S. shareholders in which or with which such tax. yrs. of controlled foreign corporpations end.

Matter in *italics* in Code Sec. 954(d)(4) was added by section 13239(d) of P.L. 103-66.

Effective Date (Sec. 13239(e) of P.L. 103-66) effective for sales, exchanges, or other dispositions after 8/10/93.

Matter in *italics* in Code Sec. 954(f) and (g)(1) was added by sections 13235(a)(3)(A) and (b) of P.L. 103-66.

Effective Date (Sec. 13235(c) of P.L. 103-66) effective for tax. yrs. begin. after 12/31/92.

paragraphs (2) and (3) of section 907(c)) other than income derived from a source within a foreign country in connection with—

(A) oil or gas which was extracted from an oil or gas well located in such foreign country, or

(B) oil, gas, or a primary product of oil or gas which is sold by the foreign corporation or a related person for use or consumption within such country or is loaded in such country on a vessel or aircraft as fuel for such vessel or aircraft.

Such term shall not include any foreign personal holding company income (as defined in subsection (c)).

* * * * * * * * * * * * *

[For explanation, see ¶ 1104, ¶ 1108 and ¶ 1119, for text of Committee Report, see ¶ 3052, ¶ 3054 and ¶ 3058]

[¶ 2079] Code Sec. 956. Investment of earnings in United States property.

[1]***(a) General rule.*** *In the case of any controlled foreign corporation, the amount determined under this section with respect to any United States shareholder for any taxable year is the lesser of—*

(1) the excess (if any) of—

(A) such shareholder's pro rata share of the average of the amounts of United States property held (directly or indirectly) by the controlled foreign corporation as of the close of each quarter of such taxable year, over

(B) the amount of earnings and profits described in section 959(c)(1)(A) with respect to such shareholder, or

(2) such shareholder's pro rata share of the applicable earnings of such controlled foreign corporation.

The amount taken into account under paragraph (1) with respect to any property shall be its adjusted basis as determined for purposes of computing earnings and profits, reduced by any liability to which the property is subject.

[2]***(b) Special rules.***

(1) Applicable earnings. *For purposes of this section, the term "applicable earnings" has the meaning given to such term by section 956A(b), except that the provisions of such section excluding earnings and profits accumulated in taxable years beginning before October 1, 1993, shall be disregarded.*

(2) Special rule for U.S. property acquired before corporation is a controlled foreign corporation. *In applying subsection (a) to any taxable year, there shall be disregarded any*

[Footnote Code Sec. 956] Matter in *italics* in Code Sec. 956(a)-(e) added by sections 13232(a)(1), (a)(2), and (b), P.L. 103-66, which struck out:

1. "(a) **General rules.**

For purposes of this subpart—

"(1) **Amount of investment.** The amount of earnings of a controlled foreign corporation invested in United States property at the close of any taxable year is the aggregate amount of such property held, directly or indirectly, by the controlled foreign corporation at the close of the taxable year, to the extent such amount would have constituted a dividend (determined after the application of section 955(a)) if it had been distributed.

"(2) **Pro rata share of increase for year.** In the case of any United States shareholder, the pro rata share of the increase for any taxable year in the earnings of a controlled foreign corporation invested in United States property is the amount determined by subtracting his pro rata share of—

"(A) the amount determined under paragraph (1) for the close of the preceding taxable year, reduced by amounts paid during such preceding taxable year to which section 959(c)(1) applies, from

"(B) the amount determined under paragraph (1) for the close of the taxable year.

The determinations under subparagraphs (A) and (B) shall be made on the basis of stock owned (within the meaning of section 958(a)) by such United States shareholder on the last day during the taxable year on which the foreign corporation is a controlled foreign corporation.

"(3) **Amount attributable to property.** The amount taken into account under paragraph (1) or (2) with respect to any property shall be its adjusted basis, reduced by any liability to which the property is subject."

2. "(b)"

item of United States property which was acquired by the controlled foreign corporation before the first day on which such corporation was treated as a controlled foreign corporation. The aggregate amount of property disregarded under the preceding sentence shall not exceed the portion of the applicable earnings of such controlled foreign corporation which were accumulated during periods before such first day.

(3) Special rule where corporation ceases to be controlled foreign corporation. *Rules similar to the rules of section 956A(e) shall apply for purposes of this section.*

[3]***(c)* United States property defined.**

(1) In general. For purposes of subsection (a), the term "United States property" means any property acquired after December 31, 1962, which is—

(A) tangible property located in the United States;

(B) stock of a domestic corporation;

(C) an obligation of a United States person; or

(D) any right to the use in the United States of—

(i) a patent or copyright,

(ii) an invention, model, or design (whether or not patented),

(iii) a secret formula or process, or

(iv) any other similar property right,

which is acquired or developed by the controlled foreign corporation for use in the United States.

(2) Exceptions. For purposes of subsection (a), the term "United States property" does not include—

(A) obligations of the United States, money, or deposits with persons carrying on the banking business;

(B) property located in the United States which is purchased in the United States for export to, or use in, foreign countries;

(C) any obligation of a United States person arising in connection with the sale or processing of property if the amount of such obligation outstanding at no time during the taxable year exceeds the amount which would be ordinary and necessary to carry on the trade or business of both the other party to the sale or processing transaction and the United States person had the sale or processing transaction been made between unrelated persons;

(D) any aircraft, railroad rolling stock, vessel, motor vehicle, or container used in the transportation of persons or property in foreign commerce and used predominantly outside the United States;

(E) an amount of assets of an insurance company equivalent to the unearned premiums or reserves ordinary and necessary for the proper conduct of its insurance business attributable to contracts which are not contracts described in section 953(a)(1);

(F) the stock or obligations of a domestic corporation which is neither a United States shareholder (as defined in section 951(b)) of the controlled foreign corporation, nor a domestic corporation, 25 percent or more of the total combined voting power of which, immediately after the acquisition of any stock in such domestic corporation by the controlled foreign corporation, is owned, or is considered as being owned, by such United States shareholders in the aggregate;

(G) any movable property (other than a vessel or aircraft) which is used for the purpose of exploring for, developing, removing, or transporting resources from ocean waters or under such waters when used on the Continental Shelf of the United States;

(H) an amount of assets of the controlled foreign corporation equal to the earnings and profits accumulated after December 31, 1962, and excluded from subpart F income under section 952(b); and

[Footnote Code Sec. 956 continued]

3. "(c)"

Effective Date (Sec. 13232(d), P.L. 103-66) effective for tax. yrs. of controlled foreign corporations begin. after 9/30/93, and for tax. yrs. of U.S. shareholders in which or with which such tax. yrs. of controlled foreign corporations end.

(I) to the extent provided in regulations prescribed by the Secretary, property which is otherwise United States property which is held by a FSC and which is related to the export activities of such FSC.

(3) Certain trade or service receivables acquired from related United States persons.

(A) In general. Notwithstanding paragraph (2) (other than subparagraph (H) thereof), the term "United States property" includes any trade or service receivable if—

(i) such trade or service receivable is acquired (directly or indirectly) from a related person who is a United States person, and

(ii) the obligor under such receivable is a United States person.

(B) Definitions. For purposes of this paragraph, the term "trade or service receivable" and "related person" have the respective meanings given to such terms by section 864(d).

(d) Pledges and guarantees. For purposes of subsection (a), a controlled foreign corporation shall, under regulations prescribed by the Secretary, be considered as holding an obligation of a United States person if such controlled foreign corporation is a pledgor or guarantor of such obligation.

(e) Regulations. *The Secretary shall prescribe such regulations as may be necessary to carry out the purposes of this section, including regulations to prevent the avoidance of the provisions of this section through reorganizations or otherwise.*

[For explanation, see ¶ 1101 and ¶ 1110, for text of Committee Report, see ¶ 3052]

[¶ 2080] Code Sec. 956A. Earnings invested in excess passive assets.

(a) General rule. In the case of any controlled foreign corporation, the amount determined under this section with respect to any United States shareholder for any taxable year is the lesser of—

(1) the excess (if any) of—

(A) such shareholder's pro rata share of the amount of the controlled foreign corporation's excess passive assets for such taxable year, over

(B) the amount of earnings and profits described in section 959(c)(1)(B) with respect to such shareholder, or

(2) such shareholder's pro rata share of the applicable earnings of such controlled foreign corporation determined after the application of section 951(a)(1)(B).

(b) Applicable earnings. For purposes of this section, the term "applicable earnings" means, with respect to any controlled foreign corporation, the sum of—

(1) the amount referred to in section 316(a)(1) to the extent such amount was accumulated in taxable years beginning after September 30, 1993, and

(2) the amount referred to in section 316(a)(2),

but reduced by distributions made during the taxable year and reduced by the earnings and profits described in section 959(c)(1) to the extent that the earnings and profits so described were accumulated in taxable years beginning after September 30, 1993.

(c) Excess passive assets. For purposes of this section—

(1) In general. The excess passive assets of any controlled foreign corporation for any taxable year is the excess (if any) of—

(A) the average of the amounts of passive assets held by such corporation as of the close of each quarter of such taxable year, over

(B) 25 percent of the average of the amounts of total assets held by such corporation as of the close of each quarter of such taxable year.

For purposes of the preceding sentence, the amount taken into account with respect to any asset shall be its adjusted basis as determined for purposes of computing earnings and profits.

[Footnote Code Sec. 956A] Code Sec. 956A was added by section 13231(b) of P.L. 103-66

Effective Date (Sec. 13231(e) of P.L. 103-66) effective for tax. yrs. of foreign corporations begin. after 9/30/93, and for tax. yrs. of U.S. shareholders in which or with which such tax. yrs. of foreign corporations end.

(2) Passive asset.

(A) In general. Except as otherwise provided in this section, the term "passive asset" means any asset held by the controlled foreign corporation which produces passive income (as defined in section 1296(b)) or is held for the production of such income.

(B) Coordination with section 956. The term "passive asset" shall not include any United States property (as defined in section 956).

(3) Certain rules to apply. For purposes of this subsection, the rules of the following provisions shall apply:

(A) Section 1296(c) (relating to look-thru rules).

(B) Section 1297(d) (relating to leasing rules).

(C) Section 1297(e) (relating to intangible property).

(d) Treatment of certain groups of controlled foreign corporations.

(1) In general. For purposes of applying subsection (c)—

(A) all controlled foreign corporations which are members of the same CFC group shall be treated as 1 controlled foreign corporation, and

(B) the amount of the excess passive assets determined with respect to such 1 corporation shall be allocated among the controlled foreign corporations which are members of such group in proportion to their respective amounts of applicable earnings.

(2) CFC group. For purposes of paragraph (1), the term "CFC group" means 1 or more chains of controlled foreign corporations connected through stock ownership with a top tier corporation which is a controlled foreign corporation, but only if—

(A) the top tier corporation owns directly more than 50 percent (by vote or value) of the stock of at least 1 of the other controlled foreign corporations, and

(B) more than 50 percent (by vote or value) of the stock of each of the controlled foreign corporations (other than the top tier corporation) is owned (directly or indirectly) by one or more other members of the group.

(e) Special rule where corporation ceases to be controlled foreign corporation during taxable year. If any foreign corporation ceases to be a controlled foreign corporation during any taxable year—

(1) the determination of any United States shareholder's pro rata share shall be made on the basis of stock owned (within the meaning of section 958(a)) by such shareholder on the last day during the taxable year on which the foreign corporation is a controlled foreign corporation, and

(2) the amount of such corporation's excess passive assets for such taxable year shall be determined by only taking into account quarters ending on or before such last day, and

(3) in determining applicable earnings, the amount taken into account by reason of being described in paragraph (2) of section 316(a) shall be the portion of the amount so described which is allocable (on a pro rata basis) to the part of such year during which the corporation is a controlled foreign corporation.

(f) Regulations. The Secretary shall prescribe such regulations as may be necessary to carry out the purposes of this section, including regulations to prevent the avoidance of the provisions of this section through reorganizations or otherwise.

[For explanation, see ¶ 1101 and ¶ 1110, for text of Committee Report, see ¶ 3052]

[¶ 2081] Code Sec. 959. Exclusion from gross income of previously taxed earnings and profits.

(a) Exclusion from gross income of United States persons. For purposes of this chapter, the [1]*earnings and profits* of a foreign corporation attributable to amounts which are, or have

---

[Footnote Code Sec. 959] Matter in *italics* in Code Sec. 959(a), (a)(1)-(a)(3), (b), (c)(1) and (c)(2), and (f) added by sections 13231(c)(1), (c)(2)(A)-(C), (c)(4)(A) and (c)(4)(B), P.L. 103-66, which struck out:

1. "earnings and profits for a taxable year"

been, included in the gross income of a United States shareholder under section 951(a) shall not, when—

(1) such amounts are distributed to, [2]

(2) such amounts would, but for this subsection, be included under section 951(a)(1)(B) in the gross income of, *or*

(3) such amounts would, but for this subsection, be included under section 951(a)(1)(C) in the gross income of,

such shareholder (or any other United States person who acquires from any person any portion of the interest of such United States shareholder in such foreign corporation, but only to the extent of such portion, and subject to such proof of the identity of such interest as the Secretary may by regulations prescribe) directly or indirectly through a chain of ownership described under section 958(a), be again included in the gross income of such United States shareholder (or of such other United States person). *The rules of subsection (c) shall apply for purposes of paragraph (1) of this subsection and the rules of subsection (f) shall apply for purposes of paragraphs (2) and (3) of this subsection.*

(b) Exclusion from gross income of certain foreign subsidiaries. For purposes of section 951(a), the [3]*earnings and profits* of a controlled foreign corporation attributable to amounts which are, or have been, included in the gross income of a United States shareholder under section 951(a), shall not, when distributed through a chain of ownership described under section 958(a), be also included in the gross income of another controlled foreign corporation in such chain for purposes of the application of section 951(a) to such other controlled foreign corporation with respect to such United States shareholder (or to any other United States shareholder who acquires from any person any portion of the interest of such United States shareholder in the controlled foreign corporation, but only to the extent of such portion, and subject to such proof of identity of such interest as the Secretary may prescribe by regulations).

(c) Allocation of distributions. For purposes of subsections (a) and (b), section 316(a) shall be applied by applying paragraph (2) thereof, and then paragraph (1) thereof—

[4]*(1) first to the aggregate of—*

(A) earnings and profits attributable to amounts included in gross income under section 951(a)(1)(B) (or which would have been included except for subsection (a)(2) of this section), and

(B) earnings and profits attributable to amounts included in gross income under section 951(a)(1)(C) (or which would have been included except for subsection (a)(3) of this section),

with any distribution being allocated between earnings and profits described in subparagraph (A) and earnings and profits described in subparagraph (B) proportionately on the basis of the respective amounts of such earnings and profits,

[5]*(2) then to earnings and profits attributable to amounts included in gross income under section 951(a)(1)(A) (but reduced by amounts not included under subparagraph (B) or (C) of section 951(a)(1) because of the exclusions in paragraphs (2) and (3) of subsection (a) of this section), and*

(3) then to other earnings and profits.

* * * * * * * * * * * * *

2. "or"
3. "earnings and profits for a taxable year"
4. "(1) first to earnings and profits attributable to amounts included in gross income under section 951(a)(1)(B) (or which would have been included except for subsection (a)(2) of this section),"
5. "(2) then to earnings and profits attributable to amounts included in gross income under section 951(a)(1)(A) (but reduced by amounts not included under section 951(a)(1)(B) because of the exclusion in subsection (a)(2) of this section), and"

Effective Date (Sec. 13231(e), P.L. 103-66) effective for tax. yrs. of foreign corporations begin. after 9/30/93, and for tax. yrs. of U.S. shareholders in which or with which such tax. yrs. of foreign corporations end.

(f) Allocation rules for certain inclusions.

(1) In general. *For purposes of this section—*

(A) amounts that would be included under subparagraph (B) of section 951(a)(1) (determined without regard to this section) shall be treated as attributable first to earnings described in subsection (c)(2), and then to earnings described in subsection (c)(3), and

(B) amounts that would be included under subparagraph (C) of section 951(a)(1) (determined without regard to this section) shall be treated as attributable first to earnings described in subsection (c)(2) to the extent the earnings so described were accumulated in taxable years beginning after September 30, 1993, and then to earnings described in subsection (c)(3).

(2) Treatment of distributions. *In applying this section, actual distributions shall be taken into account before amounts that would be included under subparagraphs (B) and (C) of section 951(a)(1) (determined without regard to this section).*

[For explanation, see ¶ 1111, for text of Committee Report, see ¶ 3052]

[¶ 2082] Code Sec. 960. Special rules for foreign tax credit.

* * * * * * * * * * * *

(b) Special rules for foreign tax credit in year of receipt of previously taxed earnings and profits.

[1]***(1) Increase in section 904 limitation.*** *In the case of any taxpayer who—*

(A) either (i) chose to have the benefits of subpart A of this part for a taxable year beginning after September 30, 1993, in which he was required under section 951(a) to include any amount in his gross income, or (ii) did not pay or accrue for such taxable year any income, war profits, or excess profits taxes to any foreign country or to any possession of the United States,

(B) chooses to have the benefits of subpart A of this part for any taxable year in which he receives 1 or more distributions or amounts which are excludable from gross income under section 959(a) and which are attributable to amounts included in his gross income for taxable years referred to in subparagraph (A), and

---

[Footnote Code Sec. 960] Matter in *italics* in Code Sec. 960(b)(1) through (5) added by sections 13233(b)(1)(A) and (B) which struck out:

1. "(1) **Increase in section 904 limitation.** In the case of any taxpayer who—

"(A) either (i) chose to have the benefits of subpart A of this part for a taxable year in which he was required under section 951(a) to include in his gross income an amount in respect of a controlled foreign corporation, or (ii) did not pay or accrue for such taxable year any income, war profits, or excess profits taxes to any foreign country or to any possession of the United States, and

"(B) chooses to have the benefits of subpart A of this part for the taxable year in which he receives a distribution or amount which is excluded from gross income under section 959(a) and which is attributable to earnings and profits of the controlled foreign corporation which was included in his gross income for the taxable year referred to in subparagraph (A), and

"(C) for the taxable year in which such distribution or amount is received, pays, or is deemed to have paid, or accrues income, war profits, or excess profits taxes to a foreign country or to any possession of the United States with respect to such distribution or amount,

the limitation under section 904 for the taxable year in which such distribution or amount is received shall be increased as provided in paragraph (2), but such increase shall not exceed the amount of such taxes paid, or deemed paid, or accrued with respect to such distribution or amount.

"(2) **Amount of increase.** The amount of increase of the limitation under section 904(a) for the taxable year in which the distribution or amount referred to in paragraph (1)(B) is received shall be an amount equal to—

"(A) the amount by which the limitation under section 904(a) for the taxable year referred to in paragraph (1)(A) was increased by reason of the inclusion in gross income under section 951(a) of the amount in respect of the controlled foreign corporation, reduced by

"(B) the amount of any income, war profits, and excess profits taxes paid, or deemed paid, or accrued to any foreign country or possession of the United States which were allowable as a credit under section 901 for the taxable year referred to in paragraph (1)(A) and which would not have been allowable but for the inclusion in gross income of the amount described in subparagraph (A)."

(C) for the taxable year in which such distributions or amounts are received, pays, or is deemed to have paid, or accrues income, war profits, or excess profits taxes to a foreign country or to any possession of the United States with respect to such distributions or amounts,

the limitation under section 904 for the taxable year in which such distributions or amounts are received shall be increased by the lesser of the amount of such taxes paid, or deemed paid, or accrued with respect to such distributions or amounts or the amount in the excess limitation account as of the beginning of such taxable year.

(2) Excess limitation account.

(A) Establishment of account. Each taxpayer meeting the requirements of paragraph (1)(A) shall establish an excess limitation account. The opening balance of such account shall be zero.

(B) Increases in account. For each taxable year beginning after September 30, 1993, the taxpayer shall increase the amount in the excess limitation account by the excess (if any) of—

(i) the amount by which the limitation under section 904(a) for such taxable year was increased by reason of the total amount of the inclusions in gross income under section 951(a) for such taxable year, over

(ii) the amount of any income, war profits, and excess profits taxes paid, or deemed paid, or accrued to any foreign country or possession of the United States which were allowable as a credit under section 901 for such taxable year and which would not have been allowable but for the inclusions in gross income described in clause (i).

Proper reductions in the amount added to the account under the preceding sentence for any taxable year shall be made for any increase in the credit allowable under section 901 for such taxable year by reason of a carryback if such increase would not have been allowable but for the inclusions in gross income described in clause (i).

(C) Decreases in account. For each taxable year beginning after September 30, 1993, for which the limitation under section 904 was increased under paragraph (1), the taxpayer shall reduce the amount in the excess limitation account by the amount of such increase.

(3) Distributions of income previously taxed in years beginning before October 1, 1993. *If the taxpayer receives a distribution or amount in a taxable year beginning after September 30, 1993, which is excluded from gross income under section 959(a) and is attributable to any amount included in gross income under section 951(a) for a taxable year beginning before October 1, 1993, the limitation under section 904 for the taxable year in which such amount or distribution is received shall be increased by the amount determined under this subsection as in effect on the day before the date of the enactment of the Revenue Reconciliation Act of 1993.*

[2]***(4)*** **Cases in which taxes not to be allowed as deduction.** In the case of any taxpayer who—

(A) chose to have the benefits of subpart A of this part for a taxable year in which he was required under section 951(a) to include in his gross income an amount in respect of a controlled foreign corporation, and

(B) does not choose to have the benefits of subpart A of this part for the taxable year in which he receives a distribution or amount which is excluded from gross income under section 959(a) and which is attributable to earnings and profits of the controlled foreign corporation which was included in his gross income for the taxable year referred to in subparagraph (A),

no deduction shall be allowed under section 164 for the taxable year in which such distribution or amount is received for any income, war profits, or excess profits taxes paid or accrued to any foreign country or to any possession of the United States on or with respect to such distribution or amount.

[Footnote Code Sec. 960 continued]

2. "(3)"

[3]*(5)* Insufficient taxable income. If an increase in the limitation under this subsection exceeds the tax imposed by this chapter for such year, the amount of such excess shall be deemed an overpayment of tax for such year.
[For explanation see ¶ 1102, for text of Committee Reports, see ¶ 3052]

[¶ 2083] Code Sec. 988. Treatment of certain foreign currency transactions.

* * * * * * * * * * * *

(d) Treatment of 988 hedging transactions.

(1) In general. To the extent provided in regulations, if any section 988 transaction is part of a 988 hedging transaction, all transactions which are part of such 988 hedging transaction shall be integrated and treated as a single transaction or otherwise treated consistently for purposes of this subtitle. For purposes of the preceding sentence, the determination of whether any transaction is a section 988 transaction shall be determined without regard to whether such transaction would otherwise be marked-to-market under [1]*section 475 or 1256* and such term shall not include any transaction with respect to which an election is made under subsection (a)(1)(B). Sections [2]*475, 1092, and 1256* shall not apply to a transaction covered by this subsection.
[For explanation, see ¶ 314]

---

3. "(4)"

Effective Date (Sec. 13233(b)(2) of P.L. 103-66) effective for tax. yrs. begin. after 9/30/93.

[Footnote Code Sec. 988] Matter in *italics* in Code Sec. 988(d)(1) added by sections 13223(b)(1)(A) and (B) of P.L. 103-66 which struck out:

1. "section 1256"
2. "section 1092 and 1256"

Effective Date (Sec. 13223(c) of P.L. 103-66) effective for tax. yrs. end. on or after 12/31/93. Sec. 13223(c)(2) and (3) of this Act provides:

"(2) Change in method of accounting. In the case of any taxpayer required by this section to change its method of accounting for any taxable year—

"(A) such change shall be treated as initiated by the taxpayer,

"(B) such change shall be treated as made with the consent of the Secretary, and

"(C) except as provided in paragraph (3), the net amount of the adjustments required to be taken into account by the taxpayer under section 481 of the Internal Revenue Code of 1986 shall be taken into account ratably over the 5-taxable year period beginning with the first taxable year ending on or after December 31, 1993.

"(3) Special rule for floor specialists and market makers.

"(A) In general. If—

"(i) a taxpayer (or any predecessor) used the last-in first-out (LIFO) method of accounting with respect to any qualified securities for the 5-taxble year period ending with its last taxable year ending before December 31, 1993, and

"(ii) any portion of the net amount described in paragraph (2)(C) is attributable to the use of such method of accounting, then paragraph (2)(C) shall be applied by taking such portion into account ratably over the 15-taxable year period beginning with the first taxable year ending on or after December 31, 1993.

"(B) Qualified security. For purposes of this paragraph, the term 'qualified security' means any security acquired—

"(i) by a floor specialist (as defined in section 1236(d)(2) of the Internal Revenue Code of 1986) in connection with the specialist's duties as a specialist on an exchange, but only if the security is one in which the specialist is registered with the exchange, or

"(ii) by a taxpayer who is a market maker in connection with the taxpayer's duties as a market maker, but only if—

"(I) the security is included on the National Association of Security Dealers Automated Quotation System,

"(II) the taxpayer is registered as a market maker in such security with the National Association of Security Dealers, and

"(III) as of the last day of the taxable year preceding the taxpayer's first taxable year ending on or after December 31, 1993, the taxpayer (or any predecessor) has been actively and regularly engaged as a market maker in such security for the 2-year period ending on such date (or, if shorter, the period beginning 61 days after the security was listed in such quotation system and ending on such date)."

[¶ 2084] Code Sec. 989. Other definitions and special rules.

* * * * * * * * * * * *

(b) Appropriate exchange rate. Except as provided in regulations, for purposes of this subpart, the term "appropriate exchange rate" means—

(1) in the case of an actual distribution of earnings and profits, the spot rate on the date such distribution is included in income,

(2) in the case of an actual or deemed sale or exchange of stock in a foreign corporation treated as a dividend under section 1248, the spot rate on the date the deemed dividend is included in income,

(3) in the case of any amounts included in income under section 951(a)(1)(A), 551(a), or 1293(a), the weighted average exchange rate for the taxable year of the foreign corporation, or

(4) in the case of any other qualified business unit of a taxpayer, the weighted average exchange rate for the taxable year of such qualified business unit.

For purposes of the preceding sentence, any amount included in income under [1]*subparagraph (B) or (C) of section 951(a)(1)* shall be treated as an actual distribution made on the last day of the taxable year for which such amount was so included.

[¶ 2085] Code Sec. 993. Definitions.

* * * * * * * * * * * *

(c) Export property.

* * * * * * * * * * * *

(2) Excluded property. For purposes of this part, the term "export property" does not include—

(A) property leased or rented by a DISC for use by any member of a controlled group (as defined in subsection (a)(3)) which includes the DISC,

(B) patents, inventions, models, designs, formulas, or processes, whether or not patented, copyrights (other than films, tapes, records, or similar reproductions, for commercial or home use), good will, trademarks, trade brands, franchises, or other like property,

(C) products of a character with respect to which a deduction for depletion is allowable (including oil, gas, coal, or uranium products) under section 613 or 613A, [1]

(D) products the export of which is prohibited or curtailed under section 7(a) of the Export Administration Act of 1979 to effectuate the policy set forth in paragraph (2)(C) of section 3 of such Act (relating to the protection of the domestic economy) [2], *or*

(E) any unprocessed timber which is a softwood.

Subparagraph (C) shall not apply to any commodity or product at least 50 percent of the fair market value of which is attributable to manufacturing or processing, except that subparagraph (C) shall apply to any primary product from oil, gas, coal, or uranium. For purposes of the preceding sentence, the term "processing" does not include extracting or han-

[Footnote Code Sec. 989] Matter in *italics* in Code Sec. 989(b) added by section 13231(c)(4)(C) of P.L. 103-66 which struck out:

1. "section 951(a)(1)(B)"

Effective Date (Sec. 13231(e) of P.L. 103-66) effective for tax. yrs. of foreign corporations begin. after 9/30/93, and for tax. yrs. of U.S. shareholders in which or with which such tax. yrs. of foreign corporations end.

[Footnote Code Sec. 993] Matter in *italics* in Code Sec. 933(c)(2), (c)(2)(C)-(E) added by section 13239(b)(1) and (b)(2), P.L. 103-66, which struck out:

1. "or"
2. "."

Effective Date (Sec. 13239(e) of P.L. 103-66) effective for sales, exchanges, or other dispositions after 8/10/93.

dling, packing, packaging, grading, storing, or transporting. *For purposes of subparagraph (E), the term "unprocessed timber" means any log, cant, or similar form of timber.*

* * * * * * * * * * * * *

[For explanation, see ¶ 1119, for text of Committee Report, see ¶ 3058]

[¶ 2086] Code Sec. 1001. Determination of amount of and recognition of gain or loss.

* * * * * * * * * * * * *

[1]***(f) Repealed.***

[¶ 2087] Code Sec. 1016. Adjustments to basis.

(a) General rule. Proper adjustment in respect of the property shall in all cases be made—

* * * * * * * * * * * * *

[1]*(19)* to the extent provided in section 50(c), in the case of expenditures with respect to which a credit has been allowed under section 38;

[2]*(20)* for amounts allowed as deductions under section 59(e) (relating to optional 10-year writeoff of certain tax preferences);

[3]*(21)* to the extent provided in section 1059 (relating to reduction in basis for extraordinary dividends);

[4]*(22)* in the case of qualified replacement property the acquisition of which resulted under section 1042 in the nonrecognition of any part of the gain realized on the sale or exchange of any property, to the extent provided in section 1042(d),

---

[Footnote Code Sec. 1001] Code Sec. 1001(f) repealed by section 13213(a)(2)(E) of P.L. 103-66 which struck out:

1. "(f) **Cross reference.**

For treatment of certain expenses incident to the sale of a residence which were deducted as moving expenses by the taxpayer or his spouse under section 217(a), see section 217(e)."

Effective Date (Sec. 13213(e) of P.L. 103-66) effective for expenses incurred after 12/31/93.

[Footnote Code Sec. 1016] Matter in Code Sec. (a)(19)-(23) added by section 13261(f)(3) of P.L. 103-66 which struck out:

1. "(19) for amounts allowed as deductions for payments made on account of transfers of franchises, trademarks, or trade names under section 1253(d)(2);" "(20)"
2. "(21)"
3. "(22)"
4. "(23)"

[5]*(23)* in the case of property the acquisition of which resulted under [6]*section 1043 or 1044* in the nonrecognition of any part of the gain realized on the sale of other property, to the extent provided in [7]*section 1043(c) or section 1044(d), as the case may be* ,

[8]*(24)* to the extent provided in section 179A(e)(6)(A), and

[9]*(25)* to the extent provided in section 30(d)(1).

[Footnote Code Sec. 1016 continued]

5. "(24)"

Effective Date (Sec. 13261(g) of P.L. 103-66) effective for property acquired after 8/10/93, except as provided in Sec. 13261(g)(2) and (3) of this Act which reads as follows:

"(2) Election to have amendments apply to property acquired after July 25, 1991.

"(A) In general. If an election under this paragraph applies to the taxpayer—

"(i) the amendments made by this section shall apply to property acquired by the taxpayer after July 25, 1991,

"(ii) subsection (c)(1)(A) of section 197 of the Internal Revenue Code of 1986 (as added by this section) (and so much of subsection (f)(9)(A) of such section 197 as precedes clause (i) thereof) shall be applied with respect to the taxpayer by treating July 25, 1991, as the date of the enactment of such section, and

"(iii) in applying subsection (f)(9) of such section, with respect to any property acquired by the taxpayer on or before the date of the enactment of this Act, only holding or use on July 25, 1991, shall be taken into account.

"(B) Election. An election under this paragraph shall be made at such time and in such manner as the Secretary of the Treasury or his delegate may prescribe. Such an election by any taxpayer, once made—

"(i) may be revoked only with the consent of the Secretary, and

"(ii) shall apply to the taxpayer making such election and any other taxpayer under common control with the taxpayer (within the meaning of subparagraphs (A) and (B) of section 41(f)(1) of such Code) at any time after August 2, 1993, and on or before the date on which such election is made.

"(3) Elective binding contract exception.

"(A) In general. The amendments made by this section shall not apply to any acquisition of property by the taxpayer if—

"(i) such acquisition is pursuant to a written binding contract in effect on the date of the enactment of this Act and at all times thereafter before such acquisition,

"(ii) an election under paragraph (2) does not apply to the taxpayer, and

"(iii) the taxpayer makes an election under this paragraph with respect to such contract.

"(B) Election. An election under this paragraph shall be made at such time and in such manner as the Secretary of the Treasury or his delegate shall prescribe. Such an election, once made—

"(i) may be revoked only with the consent of the Secretary, and

"(ii) shall apply to all property, acquired pursuant to the contract with respect to which such election was made."

Matter in Code Sec. 1016(a)(23) added by sections 13114(b)(1)-(2) of P.L. 103-66 which struck out:

6. "section 1043"

7. "section 1043(c)"

Effective Date (Sec. 13114(d) of P.L. 103-66) effective for sales on and after 8/10/93, in tax. yrs. end. on and after 8/10/93.

Matter in *italics* in Code Sec. 1016(a)(24) and (25) added by section 13261(f)(3) of P.L. 103-66 which struck out:

8. "(25)"

9. "(26)"

Effective Date (Sec. 13261(g) of P.L. 103-66) effective for property acquired after 8/10/93, except as provided in Sec. 13261(g)(2) and (3) of this Act which reads as follows:

"(2) Election to have amendments apply to property acquired after July 25, 1991.

"(A) In general. If an election under this paragraph applies to the taxpayer—

"(i) the amendments made by this section shall apply to property acquired by the taxpayer after July 25, 1991,

"(ii) subsection (c)(1)(A) of section 197 of the Internal Revenue Code of 1986 (as added by this section) (and so much of subsection (f)(9)(A) of such section 197 as precedes clause (i) thereof) shall be applied with respect to the taxpayer by treating July 25, 1991, as the date of the enactment of such section, and

"(iii) in applying subsection (f)(9) of such section, with respect to any property acquired by the taxpayer on or before the date of the enactment of this Act, only holding or use on July 25, 1991, shall be taken into account.

"(B) Election. An election under this paragraph shall be made at such time and in such manner as the Secretary of the Treasury or his delegate may prescribe. Such an election by any taxpayer, once made—

"(i) may be revoked only with the consent of the Secretary, and

"(ii) shall apply to the taxpayer making such election and any other taxpayer under common control with the taxpayer (within the meaning of subparagraphs (A) and (B) of section 41(f)(1) of such Code) at any time after August 2, 1993, and on or before the date on which such election is made.

"(3) Elective binding contract exception.

"(A) In general. The amendments made by this section shall not apply to any acquisition of property by the taxpayer if—

"(i) such acquisition is pursuant to a written binding contract in effect on the date of the enactment of this Act and at all times thereafter before such acquisition,

"(ii) an election under paragraph (2) does not apply to the taxpayer, and

"(iii) the taxpayer makes an election under this paragraph with respect to such contract.

"(B) Election. An election under this paragraph shall be made at such time and in such manner as the Secretary of the Treasury or his delegate shall prescribe. Such an election, once made—

"(i) may be revoked only with the consent of the Secretary, and

"(ii) shall apply to all property, acquired pursuant to the contract with respect to which such election was made."

* * * * * * * * * * * * *

[10]***(e) Cross reference.*** *For treatment of separate mineral interests as one property, see section 614.*

[¶ 2088] Code Sec. 1017. Discharge of indebtedness.

(a) General rule. If—

(1) an amount is excluded from gross income under subsection (a) of section 108 (relating to discharge of indebtedness), and

(2) under subsection (b)(2)(D) [1], *(b)(5), or (c)(1)* of section 108, any portion of such amount is to be applied to reduce basis,

then such portion shall be applied in reduction of the basis of any property held by the taxpayer at the beginning of the taxable year following the taxable year in which the discharge occurs.

(b) Amount and properties determined under regulations.

* * * * * * * * * * * * *

(3) Certain reductions may only be made in the basis of depreciable property.

(A) In general. Any amount which under subsection (b)(5) *or (c)(1)* of section 108 is to be applied to reduce basis shall be applied only to reduce the basis of depreciable property held by the taxpayer.

* * * * * * * * * * * * *

(F) Special rules for qualified real property business indebtedness. In the case of any amount which under section 108(c)(1) is to be applied to reduce basis—

(i) depreciable property shall only include depreciable real property for purposes of subparagraphs (A) and (C),

(ii) subparagraph (E) shall not apply, and

(iii) in the case of property taken into account under section 108(c)(2)(B), the reduction with respect to such property shall be made as of the time immediately before disposition if earlier than the time under subsection (a).

* * * * * * * * * * * * *

[For explanation, see ¶ 503, for text of Committee Report, see ¶ 3021]

[¶ 2089] Code Sec. 1033. Involuntary conversions.

* * * * * * * * * * * * *

(h) Special rules for principal residences damaged by Presidentially declared disasters.

(1) In general. *If the taxpayer's principal residence or any of its contents is compulsorily or involuntarily converted as a result of a Presidentially declared disaster—*

(A) Treatment of insurance proceeds.

Matter in *italics* in Code Sec. 1016(e) added by 13213(a)(2)(F) of P.L. 103-66 which struck out:

10. "(e) Cross references.

"(1) For treatment of certain expenses incident to the purchase of a residence which were deducted as moving expenses by the taxpayer or his spouse under section 217(a), see section 217(e).

"(2) For treatment of separate mineral interests as one property, see section 614."

Effective Date (Sec. 13213(e) of P.L. 103-66) effective for expenses incurred after 12/31/93.

[Footnote Code Sec. 1017] Matter in *italics* in Code Sec. 1017(a)(2), (b)(3)(A), and (b)(3)(F) added by sections 13150(c)(6)-(8) of P.L. 103-66 which struck out:

1. "or (b)(5)"

Effective Date (Sec. 13150(d) of P.L. 103-66) effective for discharges after 12/31/92, in tax. yrs. end. after 12/31/92.

(i) Exclusion for unscheduled personal property. No gain shall be recognized by reason of the receipt of any insurance proceeds for personal property which was part of such contents and which was not scheduled property for purposes of such insurance.

(ii) Other proceeds treated as common fund. In the case of any insurance proceeds (not described in clause (i)) for such residence or contents—

(I) such proceeds shall be treated as received for the conversion of a single item of property, and

(II) any property which is similar or related in service or use to the residence so converted (or contents thereof) shall be treated for purposes of subsection (a)(2) as property similar or related in service or use to such single item of property.

(B) Extension of replacement period. Subsection (a)(2)(B) shall be applied with respect to any property so converted by substituting "4 years" for "2 years".

(2) Presidentially declared disaster. *For purposes of this subsection, the term "Presidentially declared disaster" means any disaster which, with respect to the area in which the residence is located, resulted in a subsequent determination by the President that such area warrants assistance by the Federal Government under the Disaster Relief and Emergency Assistance Act.*

(3) Principal residence. *For purposes of this subsection, the term "principal residence" has the same meaning as when used in section 1034, except that such term shall include a residence not treated as a principal residence solely because the taxpayer does not own the residence.*

[1]*(i)* Cross references.

(1) For determination of the period for which the taxpayer has held property involuntarily converted, see section 1223.

(2) For treatment of gains from involuntary conversions as capital gains in certain cases, see section 1231(a).

(3) For one-time exclusion from gross income of gain from involuntary conversion of principal residence by individual who has attained age 55, see section 121.

[For explanation, see ¶ 121, for Commmittee Reports see ¶ 3077]

[¶ 2090] Code Sec. 1044. Rollover of publicly traded securities gain into specialized small business investment companies.

(a) Nonrecognition of gain. In the case of the sale of any publicly traded securities with respect to which the taxpayer elects the application of this section, gain from such sale shall be recognized only to the extent that the amount realized on such sale exceeds—

(1) the cost of any common stock or partnership interest in a specialized small business investment company purchased by the taxpayer during the 60-day period beginning on the date of such sale, reduced by

(2) any portion of such cost previously taken into account under this section.

This section shall not apply to any gain which is treated as ordinary income for purposes of this subtitle.

(b) Limitations.

(1) Limitation on individuals. In the case of an individual, the amount of gain which may be excluded under subsection (a) for any taxable year shall not exceed the lesser of—

(A) $50,000, or

[Footnote Code Sec. 1033] Matter in *italics* in Code Sec. 1033(h)-(i) added by section 13431(a) of P.L. 103-66 which struck out:

1. "(h)"

Effective Date (Sec. 13431(b) of P.L. 103-66) effective for property compulsorily or involuntarily converted as a result of disasters for which the determination referred to in Code Sec. 1033(h)(2) (as added by this section) is made on or after 9/1/91, and for tax. yrs. end. on or after such date.

[Footnote Code Sec. 1044] Code Sec. 1044 was added by section 13114(a) of P.L. 103-66

Effective Date (Sec. 13114(d) of P.L. 103-66) effective for sales on and after 8/10/93, in tax yrs. end. 8/10/93.

(B) $500,000, reduced by the amount of gain excluded under subsection (a) for all preceding taxable years.

(2) Limitation on C corporations. In the case of a C corporation, the amount of gain which may be excluded under subsection (a) for any taxable year shall not exceed the lesser of—

(A) $250,000, or

(B) $1,000,000, reduced by the amount of gain excluded under subsection (a) for all preceding taxable years.

(3) Special rules for married individuals. For purposes of this subsection—

(A) Separate returns. In the case of a separate return by a married individual, paragraph (1) shall be applied by substituting "$25,000" for "$50,000" and "$250,000" for "$500,000".

(B) Allocation of gain. In the case of any joint return, the amount of gain excluded under subsection (a) for any taxable year shall be allocated equally between the spouses for purposes of applying this subsection to subsequent taxable years.

(C) Marital status. For purposes of this subsection, marital status shall be determined under section 7703.

(4) Special rules for C corporation. For purposes of this subsection—

(A) all corporations which are members of the same controlled group of corporations (within the meaning of section 52(a)) shall be treated as 1 taxpayer, and

(B) any gain excluded under subsection (a) by a predecessor of any C corporation shall be treated as having been excluded by such C corporation.

(c) Definitions and special rules. For purposes of this section—

(1) Publicly traded securities. The term "publicly traded securities" means securities which are traded on an established securities market.

(2) Purchase. The term "purchase" has the meaning given such term by section 1043(b)(4).

(3) Specialized small business investment company. The term "specialized small business investment company" means any partnership or corporation which is licensed by the Small Business Administration under section 301(d) of the Small Business Investment Act of 1958 (as in effect on May 13, 1993).

(4) Certain entities not eligible. This section shall not apply to any estate, trust, partnership, or S corporation.

(d) Basis adjustments. If gain from any sale is not recognized by reason of subsection (a), such gain shall be applied to reduce (in the order acquired) the basis for determining gain or loss of any common stock or partnership interest in any specialized small business investment company which is purchased by the taxpayer during the 60-day period described in subsection (a). This subsection shall not apply for purposes of section 1202.

[For explanation, see ¶ 704, for Committee Reports, see ¶ 3006.]

[¶ 2091] Code Sec. 1060. Special allocation rules for certain asset acquisitions.

* * * * * * * * * * * * *

(b) Information required to be furnished to Secretary. Under regulations, the transferor and transferee in an applicable asset acquisition shall, at such times and in such manner as may be provided in such regulations, furnish to the Secretary the following information:

(1) The amount of the consideration received for the assets which is allocated to [1]*section 197 intangibles.*

* * * * * * * * * * * * *

[Footnote Code Sec. 1060] Matter in *italics* in Code Sec. 13261(b)(1) and (d)(1) added by sections 13261(e)(1) and (2) of P.L. 103-66 which struck out:

1. "goodwill or going concern value"

(d) Treatment of certain partnership transactions. In the case of a distribution of partnership property or a transfer of an interest in a partnership—

(1) the rules of subsection (a) shall apply but only for purposes of determining the value of [2]*section 197 intangibles* for purposes of applying section 755, and

* * * * * * * * * * * * *

[For explanation, see ¶ 430]

[¶ 2092] Code Sec. 1201. Alternative tax for corporations.

(a) General rule. If for any taxable year a corporation has a net capital gain and any rate of tax imposed by section 11, 511, or 831(a) or (b) (whichever is applicable) exceeds [2]*35 percent* (determined without regard to the last sentence of section 11(b)(1)), then, in lieu of any such tax, there is hereby imposed a tax (if such tax is less than the tax imposed by such sections) which shall consist of the sum of—

(1) a tax computed on the taxable income reduced by the amount of the net capital gain, at the rates and in the manner as if this subsection had not been enacted, plus

(2) a tax of [2]*35 percent* of the net capital gain.

[For explanation, see ¶ 301 for text of Committee, ee ¶ 3043]

[¶ 2093] Code Sec. 1202. 50-percent exclusion for gain from certain small business stock.

(a) 50-percent exclusion. In the case of a taxpayer other than a corporation, gross income shall not include 50 percent of any gain from the sale or exchange of qualified small business stock held for more than 5 years.

---

2. "goodwill or going concern value (or similar items)"

Effective Date (Sec. 13261(g) of P.L. 103-66) effective for property acquired after 8/10/93, except as provided in Sec. 13261(g)(2) and (3) of this Act which reads as follows:

"(2) Election to have amendments apply to property acquired after July 25, 1991.

"(A) In general. If an election under this paragraph applies to the taxpayer—

"(i) the amendments made by this section shall apply to property acquired by the taxpayer after July 25, 1991,

"(ii) subsection (c)(1)(A) of section 197 of the Internal Revenue Code of 1986 (as added by this section) (and so much of subsection (f)(9)(A) of such section 197 as precedes clause (i) thereof) shall be applied with respect to the taxpayer by treating July 25, 1991, as the date of the enactment of such section, and

"(iii) in applying subsection (f)(9) of such section, with respect to any property acquired by the taxpayer on or before the date of the enactment of this Act, only holding or use on July 25, 1991, shall be taken into account.

"(B) Election. An election under this paragraph shall be made at such time and in such manner as the Secretary of the Treasury or his delegate may prescribe. Such an election by any taxpayer, once made—

"(i) may be revoked only with the consent of the Secretary, and

"(ii) shall apply to the taxpayer making such election and any other taxpayer under common control with the taxpayer (within the meaning of subparagraphs (A) and (B) of section 41(f)(1) of such Code) at any time after August 2, 1993, and on or before the date on which such election is made.

"(3) Elective binding contract exception.

"(A) In general. The amendments made by this section shall not apply to any acquisition of property by the taxpayer if—

"(i) such acquisition is pursuant to a written binding contract in effect on the date of the enactment of this Act and at all times thereafter before such acquisition,

"(ii) an election under paragraph (2) does not apply to the taxpayer, and

"(iii) the taxpayer makes an election under this paragraph with respect to such contract.

"(B) Election. An election under this paragraph shall be made at such time and in such manner as the Secretary of the Treasury or his delegate shall prescribe. Such an election, once made—

"(i) may be revoked only with the consent of the Secretary, and

"(ii) shall apply to all property, acquired pursuant to the contract with respect to which such election was made."

[Footnote Code Sec. 1202] Code Sec. 1202 added by section 13113(a) of P.L. 103-66.

Effective Date (Sec. 13113(e) of P.L. 103-66) effective for stock issued after 8/10/93.

(b) Per-issuer limitation on taxpayer's eligible gain.

(1) In general. If the taxpayer has eligible gain for the taxable year from 1 or more dispositions of stock issued by any corporation, the aggregate amount of such gain from dispositions of stock issued by such corporation which may be taken into account under subsection (a) for the taxable year shall not exceed the greater of—

(A) $10,000,000 reduced by the aggregate amount of eligible gain taken into account under subsection (a) for prior taxable years and attributable to dispositions of stock issued by such corporation, or

(B) 10 times the aggregate adjusted bases of qualified small business stock issued by such corporation and disposed of by the taxpayer during the taxable year.

For purposes of subparagraph (B), the adjusted basis of any stock shall be determined without regard to any addition to basis after the date on which such stock was originally issued.

(2) Eligible gain. For purposes of this subsection, the term "eligible gain" means any gain from the sale or exchange of qualified small business stock held for more than 5 years.

(3) Treatment of married individuals.

(A) Separate returns. In the case of a separate return by a married individual, paragraph (1)(A) shall be applied by substituting "$5,000,000" for "$10,000,000".

(B) Allocation of exclusion. In the case of any joint return, the amount of gain taken into account under subsection (a) shall be allocated equally between the spouses for purposes of applying this subsection to subsequent taxable years.

(C) Marital status. For purposes of this subsection, marital status shall be determined under section 7703.

(c) Qualified small business stock. For purposes of this section—

(1) In general. Except as otherwise provided in this section, the term "qualified small business stock" means any stock in a C corporation which is originally issued after the date of the enactment of the Revenue Reconciliation Act of 1993, if—

(A) as of the date of issuance, such corporation is a qualified small business, and

(B) except as provided in subsections (f) and (h), such stock is acquired by the taxpayer at its original issue (directly or through an underwriter)—

(i) in exchange for money or other property (not including stock), or

(ii) as compensation for services provided to such corporation (other than services performed as an underwriter of such stock).

(2) Active business requirement; etc.

(A) In general. Stock in a corporation shall not be treated as qualified small business stock unless, during substantially all of the taxpayer's holding period for such stock, such corporation meets the active business requirements of subsection (e) and such corporation is a C corporation.

(B) Special rule for certain small business investment companies.

(i) Waiver of active business requirement. Notwithstanding any provision of subsection (e), a corporation shall be treated as meeting the active business requirements of such subsection for any period during which such corporation qualifies as a specialized small business investment company.

(ii) Specialized small business investment company. For purposes of clause (i), the term "specialized small business investment company" means any eligible corporation (as defined in subsection (e)(4)) which is licensed to operate under section 301(d) of the Small Business Investment Act of 1958 (as in effect on May 13, 1993).

(3) Certain purchases by corporation of its own stock.

(A) Redemptions from taxpayer or related person. Stock acquired by the taxpayer shall not be treated as qualified small business stock if, at any time during the 4-year period beginning on the date 2 years before the issuance of such stock, the corporation issuing such stock purchased (directly or indirectly) any of its stock from the taxpayer or from a person related (within the meaning of section 267(b) or 707(b)) to the taxpayer.

(B) Significant redemptions. Stock issued by a corporation shall not be treated as qualified business stock if, during the 2-year period beginning on the date 1 year before the issuance of such stock, such corporation made 1 or more purchases of its stock with an aggregate value (as of the time of the respective purchases) exceeding 5 percent of the aggregate value of all of its stock as of the beginning of such 2-year period.

(C) Treatment of certain transactions. If any transaction is treated under section 304(a) as a distribution in redemption of the stock of any corporation, for purposes of subparagraphs (A) and (B), such corporation shall be treated as purchasing an amount of its stock equal to the amount treated as such a distribution under section 304(a).

(d) Qualified small business. For purposes of this section—

(1) In general. The term "qualified small business" means any domestic corporation which is a C corporation if—

(A) the aggregate gross assets of such corporation (or any predecessor thereof) at all times on or after the date of the enactment of the Revenue Reconciliation Act of 1993, and before the issuance did not exceed $50,000,000,

(B) the aggregate gross assets of such corporation immediately after the issuance (determined by taking into account amounts received in the issuance) does not exceed $50,000,000, and

(C) such corporation agrees to submit such reports to the Secretary and to shareholders as the Secretary may require to carry out the purposes of this section.

(2) Aggregate gross assets.

(A) In general. For purposes of paragraph (1), the term "aggregate gross assets" means the amount of cash and the aggregate adjusted bases of other property held by the corporation.

(B) Treatment of contributed property. For purposes of subparagraph (A), the adjusted basis of any property contributed to the corporation (or other property with a basis determined in whole or in part by reference to the adjusted basis of property so contributed) shall be determined as if the basis of the property contributed to the corporation (immediately after such contribution) were equal to its fair market value as of the time of such contribution.

(3) Aggregation rules.

(A) In general. All corporations which are members of the same parent-subsidiary controlled group shall be treated as 1 corporation for purposes of this subsection.

(B) Parent-subsidiary controlled group. For purposes of subparagraph (A), the term "parent-subsidiary controlled group" means any controlled group of corporations as defined in section 1563(a)(1), except that—

(i) "more than 50 percent" shall be substituted for "at least 80 percent" each place it appears in section 1563(a)(1), and

(ii) section 1563(a)(4) shall not apply.

(e) Active business requirement.

(1) In general. For purposes of subsection (c)(2), the requirements of this subsection are met by a corporation for any period if during such period—

(A) at least 80 percent (by value) of the assets of such corporation are used by such corporation in the active conduct of 1 or more qualified trades or businesses, and

(B) such corporation is an eligible corporation.

(2) Special rule for certain activities. For purposes of paragraph (1), if, in connection with any future qualified trade or business, a corporation is engaged in—

(A) start-up activities described in section 195(c)(1)(A),

(B) activities resulting in the payment or incurring of expenditures which may be treated as research and experimental expenditures under section 174, or

(C) activities with respect to in-house research expenses described in section 41(b)(4),

assets used in such activities shall be treated as used in the active conduct of a qualified trade or business. Any determination under this paragraph shall be made without regard to whether a corporation has any gross income from such activities at the time of the determination.

(3) Qualified trade or business. For purposes of this subsection, the term "qualified trade or business" means any trade or business other than—

(A) any trade or business involving the performance of services in the fields of health, law, engineering, architecture, accounting, actuarial science, performing arts, consulting, athletics, financial services, brokerage services, or any other trade or business where the principal asset of such trade or business is the reputation or skill of 1 or more of its employees,

(B) any banking, insurance, financing, leasing, investing, or similar business,

(C) any farming business (including the business of raising or harvesting trees),

(D) any business involving the production or extraction of products of a character with respect to which a deduction is allowable under section 613 or 613A, and

(E) any business of operating a hotel, motel, restaurant, or similar business.

(4) Eligible corporation. For purposes of this subsection, the term "eligible corporation" means any domestic corporation; except that such term shall not include—

(A) a DISC or former DISC,

(B) a corporation with respect to which an election under section 936 is in effect or which has a direct or indirect subsidiary with respect to which such an election is in effect,

(C) a regulated investment company, real estate investment trust, or REMIC, and

(D) a cooperative.

(5) Stock in other corporations.

(A) Look-thru in case of subsidiaries. For purposes of this subsection, stock and debt in any subsidiary corporation shall be disregarded and the parent corporation shall be deemed to own its ratable share of the subsidiary's assets, and to conduct its ratable share of the subsidiary's activities.

(B) Portfolio stock or securities. A corporation shall be treated as failing to meet the requirements of paragraph (1) for any period during which more than 10 percent of the value of its assets (in excess of liabilities) consists of stock or securities in other corporations which are not subsidiaries of such corporation (other than assets described in paragraph (6)).

(C) Subsidiary. For purposes of this paragraph, a corporation shall be considered a subsidiary if the parent owns more than 50 percent of the combined voting power of all classes of stock entitled to vote, or more than 50 percent in value of all outstanding stock, of such corporation.

(6) Working capital. For purposes of paragraph (1)(A), any assets which—

(A) are held as a part of the reasonably required working capital needs of a qualified trade or business of the corporation, or

(B) are held for investment and are reasonably expected to be used within 2 years to finance research and experimentation in a qualified trade or business or increases in working capital needs of a qualified trade or business,

shall be treated as used in the active conduct of a qualified trade or business. For periods after the corporation has been in existence for at least 2 years, in no event may more than 50 percent of the assets of the corporation qualify as used in the active conduct of a qualified trade or business by reason of this paragraph.

(7) Maximum real estate holdings. A corporation shall not be treated as meeting the requirements of paragraph (1) for any period during which more than 10 percent of the total value of its assets consists of real property which is not used in the active conduct of a qualified trade or business. For purposes of the preceding sentence, the ownership of, dealing in, or renting of real property shall not be treated as the active conduct of a qualified trade or business.

(8) Computer software royalties. For purposes of paragraph (1), rights to computer software which produces active business computer software royalties (within the meaning of section 543(d)(1)) shall be treated as an asset used in the active conduct of a trade or business.

(f) Stock acquired on conversion of other stock. If any stock in a corporation is acquired solely through the conversion of other stock in such corporation which is qualified small business stock in the hands of the taxpayer—

(1) the stock so acquired shall be treated as qualified small business stock in the hands of the taxpayer, and

(2) the stock so acquired shall be treated as having been held during the period during which the converted stock was held.

(g) Treatment of pass-thru entities.

(1) In general. If any amount included in gross income by reason of holding an interest in a pass-thru entity meets the requirements of paragraph (2)—

(A) such amount shall be treated as gain described in subsection (a), and

(B) for purposes of applying subsection (b), such amount shall be treated as gain from a disposition of stock in the corporation issuing the stock disposed of by the pass-thru entity and the taxpayer's proportionate share of the adjusted basis of the pass-thru entity in such stock shall be taken into account.

(2) Requirements. An amount meets the requirements of this paragraph if—

(A) such amount is attributable to gain on the sale or exchange by the pass-thru entity of stock which is qualified small business stock in the hands of such entity (determined by treating such entity as an individual) and which was held by such entity for more than 5 years, and

(B) such amount is includible in the gross income of the taxpayer by reason of the holding of an interest in such entity which was held by the taxpayer on the date on which such pass-thru entity acquired such stock and at all times thereafter before the disposition of such stock by such pass-thru entity.

(3) Limitation based on interest originally held by taxpayer. Paragraph (1) shall not apply to any amount to the extent such amount exceeds the amount to which paragraph (1) would have applied if such amount were determined by reference to the interest the taxpayer held in the pass-thru entity on the date the qualified small business stock was acquired.

(4) Pass-thru entity. For purposes of this subsection, the term "pass-thru entity" means—

(A) any partnership,

(B) any S corporation,

(C) any regulated investment company, and

(D) any common trust fund.

(h) Certain tax-free and other transfers. For purposes of this section—

(1) In general. In the case of a transfer described in paragraph (2), the transferee shall be treated as—

(A) having acquired such stock in the same manner as the transferor, and

(B) having held such stock during any continuous period immediately preceding the transfer during which it was held (or treated as held under this subsection) by the transferor.

(2) Description of transfers. A transfer is described in this subsection if such transfer is—

(A) by gift,

(B) at death, or

(C) from a partnership to a partner of stock with respect to which requirements similar to the requirements of subsection (g) are met at the time of the transfer (without regard to the 5-year holding period requirement).

(3) Certain rules made applicable. Rules similar to the rules of section 1244(d)(2) shall apply for purposes of this section.

(4) Incorporations and reorganizations involving nonqualified stock.

(A) In general. In the case of a transaction described in section 351 or a reorganization described in section 368, if qualified small business stock is exchanged for other stock which would not qualify as qualified small business stock but for this subparagraph, such other stock shall be treated as qualified small business stock acquired on the date on which the exchanged stock was acquired.

(B) Limitation. This section shall apply to gain from the sale or exchange of stock treated as qualified small business stock by reason of subparagraph (A) only to the extent of the gain which would have been recognized at the time of the transfer described in subparagraph (A) if section 351 or 368 had not applied at such time. The preceding sentence shall not apply if the stock which is treated as qualified small business stock by reason of subparagraph (A) is issued by a corporation which (as of the time of the transfer described in subparagraph (A)) is a qualified small business.

(C) Successive application. For purposes of this paragraph, stock treated as qualified small business stock under subparagraph (A) shall be so treated for subsequent transactions or reorganizations, except that the limitation of subparagraph (B) shall be applied as of the time of the first transfer to which subparagraph (A) applied (determined after the application of the second sentence of subparagraph (B)).

(D) Control test. In the case of a transaction described in section 351, this paragraph shall apply only if, immediately after the transaction, the corporation issuing the stock owns directly or indirectly stock representing control (within the meaning of section 368(c)) of the corporation whose stock was exchanged.

(i) Basis rules. For purposes of this section—

(1) Stock exchanged for property. In the case where the taxpayer transfers property (other than money or stock) to a corporation in exchange for stock in such corporation—

(A) such stock shall be treated as having been acquired by the taxpayer on the date of such exchange, and

(B) the basis of such stock in the hands of the taxpayer shall in no event be less than the fair market value of the property exchanged.

(2) Treatment of contributions to capital. If the adjusted basis of any qualified small business stock is adjusted by reason of any contribution to capital after the date on which such stock was originally issued, in determining the amount of the adjustment by reason of such contribution, the basis of the contributed property shall in no event be treated as less than its fair market value on the date of the contribution.

(j) Treatment of certain short positions.

(1) In general. If the taxpayer has an offsetting short position with respect to any qualified small business stock, subsection (a) shall not apply to any gain from the sale or exchange of such stock unless—

(A) such stock was held by the taxpayer for more than 5 years as of the first day on which there was such a short position, and

(B) the taxpayer elects to recognize gain as if such stock were sold on such first day for its fair market value.

(2) Offsetting short position. For purposes of paragraph (1), the taxpayer shall be treated as having an offsetting short position with respect to any qualified small business stock if—

(A) the taxpayer has made a short sale of substantially identical property,

(B) the taxpayer has acquired an option to sell substantially identical property at a fixed price, or

(C) to the extent provided in regulations, the taxpayer has entered into any other transaction which substantially reduces the risk of loss from holding such qualified small business stock.

For purposes of the preceding sentence, any reference to the taxpayer shall be treated as including a reference to any person who is related (within the meaning of section 267(b) or 707(b)) to the taxpayer.

(k) Regulations. The Secretary shall prescribe such regulations as may be appropriate to carry out the purposes of this section, including regulations to prevent the avoidance of the purposes of this section through split-ups, shell corporations, partnerships, or otherwise.

[For explanation, see ¶ 702, for text of Committee Report, see ¶ 3005]

[¶ 2094] Code Sec. 1245. Gain from dispositions of certain depreciable property.

(a) General rule.

* * * * * * * * * * * * *

(2) Recomputed basis. For purposes of this section—

* * * * * * * * * * * * *

(C) Certain deductions treated as amortization. Any deduction allowable under section 179, 190, [1]*or 193* shall be treated as if it were a deduction allowable for amortization.

(3) Section 1245 property. For purposes of this section, the term "section 1245 property" means any property which is or has been property of a character subject to the allowance for depreciation provided in section 167 (or subject to the allowance of amortization provided in [2]) and is either—

(A) personal property,

(B) other property (not including a building or its structural components) but only if such other property is tangible and has an adjusted basis in which there are reflected adjustments described in paragraph (2) for a period in which such property (or other property)—

(i) was used as an integral part of manufacturing, production, or extraction or of furnishing transportation, communications, electrical energy, gas, water, or sewage disposal services,

(ii) constituted a research facility used in connection with any of the activities referred to in clause (i), or

(iii) constituted a facility used in connection with any of the activities referred to in clause (i) for the bulk storage of fungible commodities (including commodities in a liquid or gaseous state),

(C) so much of any real property (other than any property described in subparagraph (B)) which has an adjusted basis in which there are reflected adjustments for amortization under section 169, 179, 185, 188 (as in effect before its repeal by the Revenue Reconciliation Act of 1990), 190, 193, or 194[,]

(D) a single purpose agricultural or horticultural structure (as defined in section 168(i)(13)),

(E) a storage facility (not including a building or its structural components) used in connection with the distribution of petroleum or any primary product of petroleum, or

(F) any railroad grading or tunnel bore (as defined in section 168(e)(4)).

[Footnote Code Sec. 1245] Matter in *italics* in Code Sec. (a)(2)(C) and (a)(3) added by sections 13261(f)(4) and (5) of P.L. 103-66 which struck out:

1. "193, 253(d)(2) or (3)"
2. "section 185 or 1253(d)(2) or (3)"

Effective Date (Sec. 13261(g) of P.L. 103-66) effective for property acquired after 8/10/93, except as provided in Sec. 14261(g)(2) and (3) of this Act, which reads as follows:

"(2) Election to have amendments apply to property acquired after July 25, 1991.

"(A) In general. If an election under this paragraph applies to the taxpayer—

"(i) the amendments made by this section shall apply to property acquired by the taxpayer after July 25, 1991,

"(ii) subsection (c)(1)(A) of section 197 of the Internal Revenue Code of 1986 (as added by this section) (and so much of subsection (f)(9)(A) of such section 197 as precedes clause (i) thereof) shall be applied with respect to the taxpayer by treating July 25, 1991, as the date of the enactment of such section, and

"(iii) in applying subsection (f)(9) of such section, with respect to any property acquired by the taxpayer on or before the date of the enactment of this Act, only holding or use on July 25, 1991, shall be taken into account.

"(B) Election. An election under this paragraph shall be made at such time and in such manner as the Secretary of the Treasury or his delegate may prescribe. Such an election by any taxpayer, once made—

"(i) may be revoked only with the consent of the Secretary, and

"(ii) shall apply to the taxpayer making such election and any other taxpayer under common control with the taxpayer (within the meaning of subparagraphs (A) and (B) of section 41(f)(1) of such Code) at any time after August 2, 1993, and on or before the date on which such election is made.

"(3) Elective binding contract exception.

"(A) In general. The amendments made by this section shall not apply to any acquisition of property by the taxpayer if—

"(i) such acquisition is pursuant to a written binding contract in effect on the date of the enactment of this Act and at all times thereafter before such acquisition,

"(ii) an election under paragraph (2) does not apply to the taxpayer, and

"(iii) the taxpayer makes an election under this paragraph with respect to such contract.

"(B) Election. An election under this paragraph shall be made at such time and in such manner as the Secretary of the Treasury or his delegate shall prescribe. Such an election, once made—

"(i) may be revoked only with the consent of the Secretary, and

"(ii) shall apply to all property, acquired pursuant to the contract with respect to which such election was made."

[¶ 2095] Code Sec. 1253. Transfers of franchises, trademarks, and trade names.

* * * * * * * * * * * *

(d) Treatment of payments by transferee.

* * * * * * * * * * * *

[1]*(2) **Other payments.** Any amount paid or incurred on account of a transfer, sale, or other disposition of a franchise, trademark, or trade name to which paragraph (1) does not apply shall be treated as an amount chargeable to capital account.*

[Footnote Code Sec. 1253] Matter in *italics* in Code Sec. 1253(d)(2) and (d)(3) added by section 13261(c), P.L. 103-66, which struck out:

1. "(2) Certain payments in discharge of principal sums.

"(A) In general. If a transfer of a franchise, trademark, or trade name is not (by reason of the application of subsection (a)) treated as a sale or exchange of a capital asset, any payment not described in paragraph (1) which is made in discharge of a principal sum agreed upon in the transfer agreement shall be allowed as a deduction—

"(i) in the case of a single payment made in discharge of such principal sum, ratably over the taxable years in the period beginning with the taxable year in which the payment is made and ending with the ninth succeeding taxable year or ending with the last taxable year beginning in the period of the transfer agreement, whichever period is shorter;

"(ii) in the case of a payment which is one of a series of approximately equal payments made in discharge of such principal sum, which are payable over—

"(I) the period of the transfer agreement, or

"(II) a period of more than 10 taxable years, whether ending before or after the end of the period of the transfer agreement,

in the taxable year in which the payment is made; and

"(iii) in the case of any other payment, in the taxable year or years specified in regulations prescribed by the Secretary, consistently with the preceding provisions of this paragraph.

"(B) $100,000 limitation on deductibility of principal sum. Subparagraph (A) shall not apply if the principal sum referred to in such subparagraph exceeds $100,000. For purposes of the preceding sentence, all payments which are part of the same transaction (or a series of related transactions) shall be taken into account as payments with respect to each such transaction.

"(3) Other payments.

"(A) In general. Any amount paid or incurred on account of a transfer, sale, or other disposition of a franchise, trademark, or trade name to which paragraph (1) or (2) does not apply shall be treated as an amount chargeable to capital account.

"(B) Election to recover amounts over 25 years.

"(i) In general. If the taxpayer elects the application of this subparagraph, an amount chargeable to capital account—

"(I) to which paragraph (1) would apply but for subparagraph (B)(ii) thereof, or

"(II) to which paragraph (2) would apply but for subparagraph (B) thereof,

shall be allowed as a deduction ratably over the 25-year period beginning with the taxable year in which the transfer occurs.

"(ii) Consistent treatment. An election under clause (i) shall apply to all amounts which are part of the same transaction (or a series of related transactions).

"(4) Renewals, etc. For purposes of determining the term of a transfer agreement under this section or any period of amortization under this subtitle for any payment described in this section, there shall be taken into account all renewal options (and any other period for which the parties reasonably expect the agreement to be renewed).

"(5) Certain rules made applicable. Rules similar to the rules of section 168(i)(7) shall apply for purposes of this subsection."

Effective Date (Sec. 13261(g), P.L. 103-66) effective for property acquired after 8/10/93, except as provided in Sec. 13261(g)(2) and (3) of this Act which reads as follows:

"(2) Election to have amendments apply to property acquired after July 25, 1991.

"(A) In general. If an election under this paragraph applies to the taxpayer—

"(i) the amendments made by this section shall apply to property acquired by the taxpayer after July 25, 1991,

"(ii) subsection (c)(1)(A) of section 197 of the Internal Revenue Code of 1986 (as added by this section) (and so much of subsection (f)(9)(A) of such section 197 as precedes clause (i) thereof) shall be applied with respect to the taxpayer by treating July 25, 1991, as the date of the enactment.of such section, and

"(iii) in applying subsection (f)(9) of such section, with respect to any property acquired by the taxpayer on or before the date of the enactment of this Act, only holding or use on July 25, 1991, shall be taken into account.

"(B) Election. An election under this paragraph shall be made at such time and in such manner as the Secretary of the Treasury or his delegate may prescribe. Such an election by any taxpayer, once made—

"(i) may be revoked only with the consent of the Secretary, and

"(ii) shall apply to the taxpayer making such election and any other taxpayer under common control with the taxpayer (within the meaning of subparagraphs (A) and (B) of section 41(f)(1) of such Code) at any time after August 2, 1993, and on or before the date on which such election is made.

"(3) Elective binding contract exception.

"(A) In general. The amendments made by this section shall not apply to any acquisition of property by the taxpayer if—

*(3) **Renewals, etc.** For purposes of determining the term of a transfer agreement under this section, there shall be taken into account all renewal options (and any other period for which the parties reasonably expect the agreement to be renewed).*

* * * * * * * * * * * *

[For explanation, see ¶ 113

[¶ 2096] Code Sec. 1258. Recharacterization of gain from certain financial transactions.

(a) General rule. In the case of any gain—

(1) which (but for this section) would be treated as gain from the sale or exchange of a capital asset, and

(2) which is recognized on the disposition or other termination of any position which was held as part of a conversion transaction,

such gain (to the extent such gain does not exceed the applicable imputed income amount) shall be treated as ordinary income.

(b) Applicable imputed income amount. For purposes of subsection (a), the term "applicable imputed income amount" means, with respect to any disposition or other termination referred to in subsection (a), an amount equal to—

(1) the amount of interest which would have accrued on the taxpayer's net investment in the conversion transaction for the period ending on the date of such disposition or other termination (or, if earlier, the date on which the requirements of subsection (c) ceased to be satisfied) at a rate equal to 120 percent of the applicable rate, reduced by

(2) the amount treated as ordinary income under subsection (a) with respect to any prior disposition or other termination of a position which was held as a part of such transaction.

The Secretary shall by regulations provide for such reductions in the applicable imputed income amount as may be appropriate by reason of amounts capitalized under section 263(g), ordinary income received, or otherwise.

(c) Conversion transaction. For purposes of this section, the term "conversion transaction" means any transaction—

(1) substantially all of the taxpayer's expected return from which is attributable to the time value of the taxpayer's net investment in such transaction, and

(2) which is—

(A) the holding of any property (whether or not actively traded), and the entering into a contract to sell such property (or substantially identical property) at a price determined in accordance with such contract, but only if such property was acquired and such contract was entered into on a substantially contemporaneous basis,

(B) an applicable straddle,

(C) any other transaction which is marketed or sold as producing capital gains from a transaction described in paragraph (1), or

(D) any other transaction specified in regulations prescribed by the Secretary.

(d) Definitions and special rules. For purposes of this section—

(1) Applicable straddle. The term "applicable straddle" means any straddle (within the meaning of section 1092(c)); except that the term "personal property" shall include stock.

[Footnote Code Sec. 1253 continued]

"(i) such acquisition is pursuant to a written binding contract in effect on the date of the enactment of this Act and at all times thereafter before such acquisition,

"(ii) an election under paragraph (2) does not apply to the taxpayer, and

"(iii) the taxpayer makes an election under this paragraph with respect to such contract.

"(B) Election. An election under this paragraph shall be made at such time and in such manner as the Secretary of the Treasury or his delegate shall prescribe. Such an election, once made—

"(i) may be revoked only with the consent of the Secretary, and

"(ii) shall apply to all property, acquired pursuant to the contract with respect to which such election was made."

[Footnote Code Sec. 1258] Code Sec. 1258 was added by section 13206(a)(1) of P.L. 103-66

Effective Date (Sec. 13206(a)(3) of P.L. 103-66) effective for conversion transactions entered into after 4/30/93.

(2) Applicable rate. The term "applicable rate" means—

(A) the applicable Federal rate determined under section 1274(d) (compounded semiannually) as if the conversion transaction were a debt instrument, or

(B) if the term of the conversion transaction is indefinite, the Federal short-term rates in effect under section 6621(b) during the period of the conversion transaction (compounded daily).

(3) Treatment of built-in losses.

(A) In general. If any position with a built-in loss becomes part of a conversion transaction—

(i) for purposes of applying this subtitle to such position for periods after such position becomes part of such transaction, such position shall be taken into account at its fair market value as of the time it became part of such transaction, except that

(ii) upon the disposition or other termination of such position in a transaction in which gain or loss is recognized, such built-in loss shall be recognized and shall have a character determined without regard to this section.

(B) Built-in loss. For purposes of subparagraph (A), the term "built-in loss" means the loss (if any) which would have been realized if the position had been disposed of or otherwise terminated at its fair value as of the time such position became part of the conversion transaction.

(4) Position taken into account at fair market value. In determining the taxpayer's net investment in any conversion transaction, there shall be included the fair market value of any position which becomes part of such transaction (determined as of the time such position became part of such transaction).

(5) Special rule for options dealers and commodities traders.

(A) In general. Subsection (a) shall not apply to transactions—

(i) of an options dealer in the normal course of the dealer's trade or business of dealing in options, or

(ii) of a commodities trader in the normal course of the trader's trade or business of trading section 1256 contracts.

(B) Definitions. For purposes of this paragraph—

(i) Options dealer. The term "options dealer" has the meaning given such term by section 1256(g)(8).

(ii) Commodities trader. The term "commodities trader" means any person who is a member (or, except as otherwise provided in regulations, is entitled to trade as a member) of a domestic board of trade which is designated as a contract market by the Commodity Futures Trading Commission.

(C) Limited partners and limited entrepreneurs. In the cse of any gain from a transaction recognized by an entity which is allocable to a limited partner or limited entrepreneur (within the meaning of section 464(e)(2)), subparagraph (A) shall not apply if—

(i) substantially all of the limited partner's (or limited entrepreneur's) expected return from the entity is attributable to the time value of the partner's (or entrepreneur's) net investment in such entity,

(ii) the transaction (or the interest in the entity) was marketed or sold as producing capital gains treatment from a transaction described in subsection (c)(1), or

(iii) the transaction (or the interest in the entity) is a transaction (or interest) specified in regulations prescribed by the Secretary.

[For explanation, see ¶ 113, for text of Committee Report, see ¶ 3033]

[¶ 2097] Code Sec. 1276. Disposition gain representing accrued market discount treated as ordinary income.

(a) Ordinary income.

* * * * * * * * * * * *

(4) Gain treated as interest for certain purposes. Except for purposes of [1]*sections 103, 871(a),* 881, 1441, 1442, and 6049 (and such other provisions as may be specified in regulations), any amount treated as ordinary income under paragraph (1) or (3) shall be treated as interest for purposes of this title.

* * * * * * * * * * * *

[2]***(e) Repealed.***

[For explanation, see ¶ 112, for Committee Reports, see ¶ 3033.]

[¶ 2098] Code Sec. 1277. Deferral of interest deduction allocable to accrued market discount.

* * * * * * * * * * * *

[1]***(d) Repealed.***

[For text of Committee Report, see ¶ 3033]

[¶ 2099] Code Sec. 1278. Definitions and special rules.

(a) In general. For purposes of this part—

(1) Market discount bond.

* * * * * * * * * * * *

(B) Exceptions. The term "market discount bond" shall not include—

(i) Short-term obligations. Any obligation with a fixed maturity date not exceeding 1 year from the date of issue.

[1]*(ii)* United States savings bonds. Any United States savings bond.

[2]*(iii)* Installment obligations. Any installment obligation to which section 453B applies.

(C) Section 1277 not applicable to tax-exempt obligations. For purposes of section 1277, the term "market discount bond" shall not include any tax-exempt obligation (as defined in section 1275(a)(3)).

[3]*(D)* Treatment of bonds acquired at original issue.

(i) In general. Except as otherwise provided in this subparagraph or in regulations, the term "market discount bond" shall not include any bond acquired by the taxpayer at its original issue.

[Footnote Code Sec. 1276] Matter in *italics* in Code Sec. 1276(a)(4) and (e) was added by sections 13206(b)(1)(A) and (b)(2)(B)(i) of P.L. 103-66 which struck out:

1. "sections 871(a)"
2. "(e) Section not to apply to market discount bonds issued on or before date of enactment of section.

This section shall not apply to any market discount bond issued on or before July 18, 1984."

Effective Date (Sec. 14206(b)(3) of P.L. 103-66) effective 4/30/93

[Footnote Code Sec. 1277] Code Sec. 1277(d) was repealed by section 13201(b)(1)(B) of P.L. 103-66 which struck out:

1. "(d) Special rule for gain recognized on disposition of market discount bonds issued on or before date of enactment of section.

"In the case of a market discount bond issued on or before July 18, 1984, any gain recognized by the taxpayer on any disposition of such bond shall be treated as ordinary income to the extent the amount of such gain does not exceed the amount allowable with respect to such bond under subsection (b)(2) for the taxable year in which such bond is disposed of."

Effective Date (Sec. 13206(b)(3) of P.L. 103-66) effective for obligations purchased (within the meaning of Code Sec. 1272(d)(1)) after 4/30/93.

[Footnote Code Sec. 1278] Matter in *italics* in Code Sec. 1278(a)(1)(B)(ii)-(iii)-(a)(1)(d), (a)(4)(B), and (b)(1) added by sections 13206(b)(2)(A)(i)-(B)(ii) of P.L. 103-66 which struck out:

1. "(ii) Tax-exempt obligations. Any tax-exempt obligation (as defined in section 1275(a)(3)).
2. "(iv)"
3. "(C)"

(ii) Treatment of bonds acquired for less than issue price. Clause (i) shall not apply to any bond if—

(I) the basis of the taxpayer in such bond is determined under section 1012, and

(II) such basis is less than the issue price of such bond determined under subpart A of this part.

(iii) Bonds acquired in certain reorganizations. Clause (i) shall not apply to any bond issued pursuant to a plan of reorganization (within the meaning of section 368(a)(1)) in exchange for another bond having market discount. Solely for purposes of section 1276, the preceding sentence shall not apply if such other bond was issued on or before July 18, 1984 (the date of the enactment of section 1276) and if the bond issued pursuant to such plan of reorganization has the same term and the same interest rate as such other bond had.

(iv) Treatment of certain transferred basis property. For purposes of clause (i), if the adjusted basis of any bond in the hands of the taxpayer is determined by reference to the adjusted basis of such bond in the hands of a person who acquired such bond at its original issue, such bond shall be treated as acquired by the taxpayer at its original issue.

* * * * * * * * * * * * *

(4) Revised issue price. The term "revised issue price" means the sum of—

* * * * * * * * * * * * *

(B) the aggregate amount of the original issue discount includible in the gross income of all holders for periods before the acquisition of the bond by the taxpayer (determined without regard to section 1272(a)(7) or (b)(4))*or, in the case of a tax-exempt obligation, the aggregate amount of the original issue discount which accrued in the manner provided by section 1272(a) (determined without regard to paragraph (7) thereof) during periods before the acquisition of the bond by the taxpayer* .

* * * * * * * * * * * * *

(b) Election to include market discount currently.

(1) In general. If the taxpayer makes an election under this subsection—

(A) sections 1276 and 1277 shall not apply, and

(B) market discount on any market discount bond shall be included in the gross income of the taxpayer for the taxable years to which it is attributable (as determined under the rules of subsection (b) of section 1276).

Except for purposes of [4]*sections 103, 871(a)* , 881, 1441, 1442, and 6049 (and such other provisions as may be specified in regulations), any amount included in gross income under subparagraph (B) shall be treated as interest for purposes of this title.

[For explanation, see ¶ 112, for Committee Reports, see ¶ 3033.]

[¶ 2100] Code Sec. 1293. Current taxation of income from qualified electing funds.

* * * * * * * * * * * * *

(c) Previously taxed amounts distributed tax free. If the taxpayer establishes to the satisfaction of the Secretary that any amount distributed by a passive foreign investment company is paid out of earnings and profits of the company which were included under subsection (a) in the income of any United States person, such amount shall be treated, for purposes of this chapter, as a distribution which is not a dividend; except that such distribution shall immediately reduce earnings and profits. *If the passive foreign investment company is a controlled foreign corpora-*

[Footnote Code Sec. 1278 continued]

4. "sections 871(a)"

Effective Date (Sec. 13206(b)(3) of P.L. 103-66) effective for obligations purchased (within the meaning of Code Sec. 1272(d)(1)) after 4/30/93.

[Footnote Code Sec. 1293] Matter in *italics* in Code Sec. 1239(c) added by section 13231(c)(3) of P.L. 103-66.

Effective Date (Sec. 13231(e) of P.L. 103-66) effective for tax. yrs. of foreign corporations begin. after 9/30/93, and for tax. yrs. of U.S. shareholders in which or with which such tax. yrs. of foreign corporations end.

tion (as defined in section 957(a)), the preceding sentence shall not apply to any United States shareholder (as defined in section 951(b)) in such corporation, and, in applying section 959 to any such shareholder, any inclusion under this section shall be treated as an inclusion under section 951(a)(1)(A).

* * * * * * * * * * * * *

[For explanation, see ¶ 1111, for text of Committee Report, see ¶ 3052]

[¶ 2101] Code Sec. 1296. Passive foreign investment company.

* * * * * * * * * * * * *

(a) In general. For purposes of this part, except as otherwise provided in this subpart, the term "passive foreign investment company" means any foreign corporation if—

(1) 75 percent or more of the gross income of such corporation for the taxable year is passive income, or

(2) the average percentage of assets (by value) held by such corporation during the taxable year which produce passive income or which are held for the production of passive income is at least 50 percent. [1] *In the case of a controlled foreign corporation (or any other foreign corporation if such corporation so elects), the determination under paragraph (2) shall be based on the adjusted bases (as determined for purposes of computing earnings and profits) of its assets in lieu of their value. Such an election, once made, may be revoked only with the consent of the Secretary.*

(b) Passive income. For purposes of this section—

* * * * * * * * * * * * *

(3) Treatment of certain dealers in securities.

(A) In general. In the case of any foreign corporation which is a controlled foreign corporation (as defined in section 957(a)), the term "passive income" does not include any income derived in the active conduct of a securities business by such corporation if such corporation is registered as a securities broker or dealer under section 15(a) of the Securities Exchange Act of 1934 or is registered as a Government securities broker or dealer under section 15C(a) of such Act. To the extent provided in regulations, such term shall not include any income derived in the active conduct of a securities business by a controlled foreign corporation which is not so registered.

(B) Application of look-thru rules. For purposes of paragraph (2)(C), rules similar to the rules of subparagraph (A) of this paragraph shall apply in determining whether any income of a related person (whether or not a corporation) is passive income.

(C) Limitation. The preceding provisions of this paragraph shall only apply in the case of persons who are United States shareholders (as defined in section 951(b)) in the controlled foreign corporation.

* * * * * * * * * * * * *

[For explanation, see ¶ 1112 and ¶ 1114, for Committee Reports, see ¶ 3052.]

[Footnote Code Sec. 1296] Matter in *italics* in Code Sec. 1296(a) and (b)(3) added by sections 13231(d)(1) and (3) of P.L. 103-66 which struck out:

1. "A foreign corporation may elect to have the determination under paragraph (2) based on the adjusted bases of its assets in lieu of their value. Such an election, once made, may be revoked only with the consent of the Secretary."

Effective Date (Sec. 13231(e) of P.L. 103-66) effective for tax. yrs. of foreign corporations begin. after 9/30/93, and for tax. yrs. of U.S. shareholders in which or with which such tax. yrs. of foreign corporations end.

[¶ 2102] Code Sec. 1297. Special rules.

* * * * * * * * * * * *

(b) Other special rules. For purposes of this part—

* * * * * * * * * * * *

(9) Treatment of certain subpart F inclusions. *Any amount included in gross income under subparagraph (B) or (C) of section 951(a)(1) shall be treated as a distribution received with respect to the stock.*

* * * * * * * * * * * *

(d) Treatment of certain leased property. *For purposes of this part—*

(1) In general. *Any tangible personal property with respect to which a foreign corporation is the lessee under a lease with a term of at least 12 months shall be treated as an asset actually held by such corporation.*

(2) Determination of adjusted basis.

(A) In general. The adjusted basis of any asset to which paragraph (1) applies shall be the unamortized portion (as determined under regulations prescribed by he Secretary) of the present value of the payments under the lease for the use of such property.

(B) Present value. For purposes of subparagraph (A), the present value of payments described in subparagraph (A) shall be determined in the manner provided in regulations prescribed by the Secretary—

(i) as of the beginning of the lease term, and

(ii) except as provided in such regulations, by using a discount rate equal to the applicable Federal rate determined under section 1274(d)—

(I) by substituting the lease term for the term of the debt instrument, and

(II) without regard to paragraph (2) or (3) thereof.

(3) Exceptions. *This subsection shall not apply in any case where—*

(A) the lessor is a related person (as defined in section 954(d)(3)) with respect to the foreign corporation, or

(B) a principal purpose of leasing the property was to avoid the provisions of this part or section 956A.

(e) Special rules for certain intangibles.

(1) Research expenditures. *The adjusted basis of the total assets of a controlled foreign corporation shall be increased by the research or experimental expenditures (within the meaning of section 174) paid or incurred by such foreign corporation during the taxable year and the preceding 2 taxable years. Any expenditure otherwise taken into account under the preceding sentence shall be reduced by the amount of any reimbursement received by the controlled foreign corporation with respect to such expenditure.*

(2) Certain licensed intangibles.

(A) In general. In the case of any intangible property (as defined in section 936(h)(3)(B)) with respect to which a controlled foreign corporation is a licensee and which is used by such foreign corporation in the active conduct of a trade or business, the adjusted basis of the total assets of such foreign corporation shall be increased by an amount equal to 300 percent of the payments made during the taxable year by such foreign corporation for the use of such intangible property.

(B) Exceptions. Subparagraph (A) shall not apply to—

[Footnote Code Sec. 1297] Matter in *italics* in Code Sec. 1297(b)(9) and (d) through (f) added by sections 13231(d)(2) and (4) of P.L. 103-66 which struck out:

1. "(d)"

Effective Date (Secs. 13231(d)(2) and (4) of P.L. 103-66) effective for tax. yrs. of foreign corporations begin. after 9/30/93, and to tax. yr. of U.S. shareholders in which or with which such tax. yrs. of foreign corporations end.

(i) any payments to a foreign person if such foreign person is a related person (as defined in section 954(d)(3)) with respect to the controlled foreign corporation, and

(ii) any payments under a license if a principal purpose of entering into such license was to avoid the provisions of this part or section 956A.

***(3) Controlled foreign corporation.** For purposes of this subsection, the term "controlled foreign corporation" has the meaning given such term by section 957(a).*

(2) Regulations. The Secretary shall prescribe such regulations as may be necessary or appropriate to carry out the purposes of this part.

[For explanation, see ¶s 1112, 1113, 1115 for text of Committee Reporst, see ¶ 3052

[¶ 2103] Code Sec. 1391. Designation procedure.

(a) In general. From among the areas nominated for designation under this section, the appropriate Secretaries may designate empowerment zones and enterprise communities.

(b) Number of designations.

(1) Enterprise communities. The appropriate Secretaries may designate in the aggregate 95 nominated areas as enterprise communities under this section, subject to the availability of eligible nominated areas. Of that number, not more than 65 may be designated in urban areas and not more than 30 may be designated in rural areas.

(2) Empowerment zones. The appropriate Secretaries may designate in the aggregate 9 nominated areas as empowerment zones under this section, subject to the availability of eligible nominated areas. Of that number, not more than 6 may be designated in urban areas and not more than 3 may be designated in rural areas. If 6 empowerment zones are designated in urban areas, no less than 1 shall be designated in an urban area the most populous city of which has a population of 500,000 or less and no less than 1 shall be a nominated area which includes areas in 2 States and which has a population of 50,000 or less. The Secretary of Housing and Urban Development shall designate empowerment zones located in urban areas in such a manner that the aggregate population of all such zones does not exceed 750,000.

(c) Period designations may be made. A designation may be made under this section only after 1993 and before 1996.

(d) Period for which designation is in effect.

(1) In general. Any designation under this section shall remain in effect during the period beginning on the date of the designation and ending on the earliest of—

(A) the close of the 10th calendar year beginning on or after such date of designation,

(B) the termination date designated by the State and local governments as provided for in their nomination, or

(C) the date the appropriate Secretary revokes the designation.

(2) Revocation of designation. The appropriate Secretary may revoke the designation under this section of an area if such Secretary determines that the local government or the State in which it is located—

(A) has modified the boundaries of the area, or

(B) is not complying substantially with, or fails to make progress in achieving the benchmarks set forth in, the strategic plan under subsection (f)(2).

(e) Limitations on designations. No area may be designated under subsection (a) unless—

(1) the area is nominated by 1 or more local governments and the State or States in which it is located for designation under this section,

(2) such State or States and the local governments have the authority—

(A) to nominate the area for designation under this section, and

(B) to provide the assurances described in paragraph (3),

[Footnote Code Sec. 1391] Code Sec. 1391 added by section 13301(a), P.L. 103-66.
Effective Date (Sec. 13303, P.L. 103-66) effective 8/10/93.

(3) such State or States and the local governments provide written assurances satisfactory to the appropriate Secretary that the strategic plan described in the application under subsection (f)(2) for such area will be implemented,

(4) the appropriate Secretary determines that any information furnished is reasonably accurate, and

(5) such State or States and local governments certify that no portion of the area nominated is already included in an empowerment zone or in an enterprise community or in an area otherwise nominated to be designated under this section.

(f) Application. No area may be designated under subsection (a) unless the application for such designation—

(1) demonstrates that the nominated area satisfies the eligibility criteria described in section 1392,

(2) includes a strategic plan for accomplishing the purposes of this subchapter that—

(A) describes the coordinated economic, human, community, and physical development plan and related activities proposed for the nominated area,

(B) describes the process by which the affected community is a full partner in the process of developing and implementing the plan and the extent to which local institutions and organizations have contributed to the planning process,

(C) identifies the amount of State, local, and private resources that will be available in the nominated area and the private/public partnerships to be used, which may include participation by, and cooperation with, universities, medical centers, and other private and public entities,

(D) identifies the funding requested under any Federal program in support of the proposed economic, human, community, and physical development and related activities,

(E) identifies baselines, methods, and benchmarks for measuring the success of carrying out the strategic plan, including the extent to which poor persons and families will be empowered to become economically self-sufficient, and

(F) does not include any action to assist any establishment in relocating from one area outside the nominated area to the nominated area, except that assistance for the expansion of an existing business entity through the establishment of a new branch, affiliate, or subsidiary is permitted if—

(i) the establishment of the new branch, affiliate, or subsidiary will not result in a decrease in employment in the area of original location or in any other area where the existing business entity conducts business operations, and

(ii) there is no reason to believe that the new branch, affiliate, or subsidiary is being established with the intention of closing down the operations of the existing business entity in the area of its original location or in any other area where the existing business entity conducts business operation, and

(3) includes such other information as may be required by the appropriate Secretary.

[For explanation, see ¶ 602, for text of Committee Report, see ¶ 3069]

[¶ 2104] Code Sec. 1392. Eligibility criteria.

(a) In general. A nominated area shall be eligible for designation under section 1391 only if it meets the following criteria:

(1) Population. The nominated area has a maximum population of—

(A) in the case of an urban area, the lesser of—

(i) 200,000, or

(ii) the greater of 50,000 or 10 percent of the population of the most populous city located within the nominated area, and

---

[Footnote Code Sec. 1392] Code Sec. 1392 added by section 13301(a), P.L. 103-66.
Effective Date (Sec. 13303, P.L. 103-66) effective 8/10/93.

(B) in the case of a rural area, 30,000.

(2) Distress. The nominated area is one of pervasive poverty, unemployment, and general distress.

(3) Size. The nominated area—

(A) does not exceed 20 square miles if an urban area or 1,000 square miles if a rural area,

(B) has a boundary which is continuous, or, except in the case of a rural area located in more than 1 State, consists of not more than 3 noncontiguous parcels,

(C)

(i) in the case of an urban area, is located entirely within no more than 2 contiguous States, and

(ii) in the case of a rural area, is located entirely within no more than 3 contiguous States, and

(D) does not include any portion of a central business district (as such term is used for purposes of the most recent Census of Retail Trade) unless the poverty rate for each population census tract in such district is not less than 35 percent (30 percent in the case of an enterprise community).

(4) Poverty Rate. The poverty rate—

(A) for each population census tract within the nominated area is not less than 20 percent,

(B) for at least 90 percent of the population census tracts within the nominated area is not less than 25 percent, and

(C) for at least 50 percent of the population census tracts within the nominated area is not less than 35 percent.

(b) Special rules relating to determination of poverty rate. For purposes of subsection (a)(4)—

(1) Treatment of census tracts with small populations.

(A) Tracts with no population. In the case of a population census tract with no population—

(i) such tract shall be treated as having a poverty rate which meets the requirements of subparagraphs (A) and (B) of subsection (a)(4), but

(ii) such tract shall be treated as having a zero poverty rate for purposes of applying subparagraph (C) thereof.

(B) Tracts with populations of less than 2,000. A population census tract with a population of less than 2,000 shall be treated as having a poverty rate which meets the requirements of subparagraphs (A) and (B) of subsection (a)(4) if more than 75 percent of such tract is zoned for commercial or industrial use.

(2) Discretion to adjust requirements for enterprise communities. In determining whether a nominated area is eligible for designation as an enterprise community, the appropriate Secretary may, where necessary to carry out the purposes of this subchapter, reduce by 5 percentage points one of the following thresholds for not more than 10 percent of the population census tracts (or, if fewer, 5 population census tracts) in the nominated area:

(A) The 20 percent threshold in subsection (a)(4)(A).

(B) The 25 percent threshold in subsection (a)(4)(B).

(C) The 35 percent threshold in subsection (a)(4)(C).

If the appropriate Secretary elects to reduce the threshold under subparagraph (C), such Secretary may (in lieu of applying the preceding sentence) reduce by 10 percentage points the threshold under subparagraph (C) for 3 population census tracts.

(3) Each noncontiguous area must satisfy poverty rate rule. A nominated area may not include a noncontiguous parcel unless such parcel separately meets (subject to paragraphs (1) and (2)) the criteria set forth in subsection (a)(4).

(4) Areas not within census tracts. In the case of an area which is not tracted for population census tracts, the equivalent county divisions (as defined by the Bureau of the Census for purposes of defining poverty areas) shall be used for purposes of determining poverty rates.

(c) Factors to consider. From among the nominated areas eligible for designation under section 1391 by the appropriate Secretary, such appropriate Secretary shall make designations of empowerment zones and enterprise communities on the basis of—

(1) the effectiveness of the strategic plan submitted pursuant to section 1391(f)(2) and the assurances made pursuant to section 1391(e)(3), and

(2) criteria specified by the appropriate Secretary.

[For explanation, see ¶ 602, for text of Committee Report, see ¶ 3069]

[¶ 2105] Code Sec. 1393. Definitions and special rules.

(a) In general. For purposes of this subchapter—

(1) Appropriate Secretary. The term "appropriate Secretary" means—

(A) the Secretary of Housing and Urban Development in the case of any nominated area which is located in an urban area, and

(B) the Secretary of Agriculture in the case of any nominated area which is located in a rural area.

(2) Rural area. The term "rural area" means any area which is—

(A) outside of a metropolitan statistical area (within the meaning of section 143(k)(2)(B)), or

(B) determined by the Secretary of Agriculture, after consultation with the Secretary of Commerce, to be a rural area.

(3) Urban area. The term "urban area" means an area which is not a rural area.

(4) Special rules for Indian reservations.

(A) In general. No empowerment zone or enterprise community may include any area within an Indian reservation.

(B) Indian reservation defined. The term "Indian reservation" has the meaning given such term by section 168(j)(6).

(5) Local government. The term "local government" means—

(A) any county, city, town, township, parish, village, or other general purpose political subdivision of a State, and

(B) any combination of political subdivisions described in subparagraph (A) recognized by the appropriate Secretary.

(6) Nominated area. The term "nominated area" means an area which is nominated by 1 or more local governments and the State or States in which it is located for designation under section 1391.

(7) Governments. If more than 1 State or local government seeks to nominate an area under this part, any reference to, or requirement of, this subchapter shall apply to all such governments.

(8) Special rule. An area shall be treated as nominated by a State and a local government if it is nominated by an economic development corporation chartered by the State.

(9) Use of census data. Population and poverty rate shall be determined by the most recent decennial census data available.

(b) Empowerment zone; enterprise community. For purposes of this title, the terms "empowerment zone" and "enterprise community" mean areas designated as such under section 1391.

[For explanation, see ¶ 602, for text of Committee Report, see ¶ 3069]

[Footnote Code Sec. 1393] Code Sec. 1393 added by section 13301(a), P.L. 103-66.
Effective Date (Sec. 13303, P.L. 103-66) effective 8/10/93.

[¶2106] **Code Sec. 1394. Tax-exempt enterprise zone facility bonds.**

(a) In general. For purposes of part IV of subchapter B of this chapter (relating to tax exemption requirements for State and local bonds), the term "exempt facility bond" includes any bond issued as part of an issue 95 percent or more of the net proceeds (as defined in section 150(a)(3)) of which are to be used to provide any enterprise zone facility.

(b) Enterprise zone facility. For purposes of this subsection—

(1) In general. The term "enterprise zone facility" means any qualified zone property the principal user of which is an enterprise zone business, and any land which is functionally related and subordinate to such property.

(2) Qualified zone property. The term "qualified zone property" has the meaning given such term by section 1397C; except that the references to empowerment zones shall be treated as including references to enterprise communities.

(3) Enterprise zone business. The term "enterprise zone business" has the meaning given to such term by section 1397B, except that—

(A) references to empowerment zones shall be treated as including references to enterprise communities, and

(B) such term includes any trades or businesses which would qualify as an enterprise zone business (determined after the modification of subparagraph (A)) if such trades or businesses were separately incorporated.

(c) Limitation on amount of bonds.

(1) In general. Subsection (a) shall not apply to any issue if the aggregate amount of outstanding enterprise zone facility bonds allocable to any person (taking into account such issue) exceeds—

(A) $3,000,000 with respect to any 1 empowerment zone or enterprise community, or

(B) $20,000,000 with respect to all empowerment zones and enterprise communities.

(2) Aggregate enterprise zone facility bond benefit. For purposes of subparagraph (A), the aggregate amount of outstanding enterprise zone facility bonds allocable to any person shall be determined under rules similar to the rules of section 144(a)(10), taking into account only bonds to which subsection (a) applies.

(d) Acquisition of land and existing property permitted. The requirements of sections 147(c)(1)(A) and 147(d) shall not apply to any bond described in subsection (a).

(e) Penalty for ceasing to meet requirements.

(1) Failures corrected. An issue which fails to meet 1 or more of the requirements of subsections (a) and (b) shall be treated as meeting such requirements if—

(A) the issuer and any principal user in good faith attempted to meet such requirements, and

(B) any failure to meet such requirements is corrected within a reasonable period after such failure is first discovered.

(2) Loss of deductions where facility ceases to be qualified. No deduction shall be allowed under this chapter for interest on any financing provided from any bond to which subsection (a) applies with respect to any facility to the extent such interest accrues during the period beginning on the first day of the calendar year which includes the date on which—

(i) substantially all of the facility with respect to which the financing was provided ceases to be used in an empowerment zone or enterprise community, or

(ii) the principal user of such facility ceases to be an enterprise zone business (as defined in subsection (b)).

(3) Exception if zone ceases. Paragraphs (1) and (2) shall not apply solely by reason of the termination or revocation of a designation as an empowerment zone or an enterprise community.

[Footnote Code Sec. 1394] Code Sec. 1394 added by section 13301(a), P.L. 103-66.
Effective Date (Sec. 13303, P.L. 103-66) effective 8/10/93.

(4) Exception for bankruptcy. Paragraphs (1) and (2) shall not apply to any cessation resulting from bankruptcy.

[For explanation, see ¶ 606, for Commitee Reports, see ¶ 3069.]

[¶ 2107] Code Sec. 1396. Empowerment zone employment credit.

(a) Amount of credit. For purposes of section 38, the amount of the empowerment zone employment credit determined under this section with respect to any employer for any taxable year is the applicable percentage of the qualified zone wages paid or incurred during the calendar year which ends with or within such taxable year.

(b) Applicable percentage. For purposes of this section, the term "applicable percentage" means the percentage determined in accordance with the following table:

In the case of wages paid or incurred during calendar year:	The applicable percentage is:
1994 through 2001	20
2002	15
2003	10
2004	5

(c) Qualified zone wages.

(1) In general. For purposes of this section, the term "qualified zone wages" means any wages paid or incurred by an employer for services performed by an employee while such employee is a qualified zone employee.

(2) Only first $15,000 of wages per year taken into account. With respect to each qualified zone employee, the amount of qualified zone wages which may be taken into account for a calendar year shall not exceed $15,000.

(3) Coordination with targeted jobs credit.

(A) In general. The term "qualified zone wages" shall not include wages taken into account in determining the credit under section 51.

(B) Coordination with paragraph (2). The $15,000 amount in paragraph (2) shall be reduced for any calendar year by the amount of wages paid or incurred during such year which are taken into account in determining the credit under section 51.

(d) Qualified zone employee. For purposes of this section—

(1) In general. Except as otherwise provided in this subsection, the term "qualified zone employee" means, with respect to any period, any employee of an employer if—

(A) substantially all of the services performed during such period by such employee for such employer are performed within an empowerment zone in a trade or business of the employer, and

(B) the principal place of abode of such employee while performing such services is within such empowerment zone.

(2) Certain individuals not eligible. The term "qualified zone employee" shall not include—

(A) any individual described in subparagraph (A), (B), or (C) of section 51(i)(1),

(B) any 5-percent owner (as defined in section 416(i)(1)(B)),

(C) any individual employed by the employer for less than 90 days,

(D) any individual employed by the employer at any facility described in section 144(c)(6)(B), and

(E) any individual employed by the employer in a trade or business the principal activity of which is farming (within the meaning of subparagraphs (A) or (B) of section 2032A(e)(5)), but only if, as of the close of the taxable year, the sum of—

[Footnote Code Sec. 1396] Code Sec. 1396 added by section 13301(a) of P.L. 103-66.
Effective Date (Sec. 13303 of P.L. 103-66) effective 8/10/93.

(i) the aggregate unadjusted bases (or, if greater, the fair market value) of the assets owned by the employer which are used in such a trade or business, and

(ii) the aggregate value of assets leased by the employer which are used in such a trade or business (as determined under regulations prescribed by the Secretary), exceeds $500,000.

(3) Special rules related to termination of employment.

(A) In general. Paragraph (2)(C) shall not apply to—

(i) a termination of employment of an individual who before the close of the period referred to in paragraph (2)(C) becomes disabled to perform the services of such employment unless such disability is removed before the close of such period and the taxpayer fails to offer reemployment to such individual, or

(ii) a termination of employment of an individual if it is determined under the applicable State unemployment compensation law that the termination was due to the misconduct of such individual.

(B) Changes in form of business. For purposes of paragraph (2)(C), the employment relationship between the taxpayer and an employee shall not be treated as terminated—

(i) by a transaction to which section 381(a) applies if the employee continues to be employed by the acquiring corporation, or

(ii) by reason of a mere change in the form of conducting the trade or business of the taxpayer if the employee continues to be employed in such trade or business and the taxpayer retains a substantial interest in such trade or business.

[For explanation, see ¶ 604, for text of Committee Report, see ¶ 3069]

[¶ 2108] **Code Sec. 1397. Other definitions and special rules.**

(a) Wages. For purposes of this subpart—

(1) In general. The term "wages" has the same meaning as when used in section 51.

(2) Certain training and educational benefits.

(A) In general. The following amounts shall be treated as wages paid to an employee:

(i) Any amount paid or incurred by an employer which is excludable from the gross income of an employee under section 127, but only to the extent paid or incurred to a person not related to the employer.

(ii) In the case of an employee who has not attained the age of 19, any amount paid or incurred by an employer for any youth training program operated by such employer in conjunction with local education officials.

(B) Related person. A person is related to any other person if the person bears a relationship to such other person specified in section 267(b) or 707(b)(1), or such person and such other person are engaged in trades or businesses under common control (within the meaning of subsections (a) and (b) of section 52). For purposes of the preceding sentence, in applying section 267(b) or 707(b)(1), "10 percent" shall be substituted for "50 percent".

(b) Controlled groups. For purposes of this subpart—

(1) all employers treated as a single employer under subsection (a) or (b) of section 52 shall be treated as a single employer for purposes of this subpart, and

(2) the credit (if any) determined under section 1396 with respect to each such employer shall be its proportionate share of the wages giving rise to such credit.

(c) Certain other rules made applicable. For purposes of this subpart, rules similar to the rules of section 51(k) and subsections (c), (d), and (e) of section 52 shall apply.

[For explanation, see ¶ 604 for Committee, see ¶ 3069

[Footnote Code Sec. 1397] Code Sec. 1397 added by section 13301(a), P.L. 103-66.
Effective Date (Sec. 13303, P.L. 103-66) effective 8/10/93.

[¶ 2109] **Code Sec. 1397A. Increase in expensing under section 179.**

(a) General rule. In the case of an enterprise zone business, for purposes of section 179—

(1) the limitation under section 179(b)(1) shall be increased by the lesser of—

(A) $20,000, or

(B) the cost of section 179 property which is qualified zone property placed in service during the taxable year, and

(2) the amount taken into account under section 179(b)(2) with respect to any section 179 property which is qualified zone property shall be 50 percent of the cost thereof.

(b) Recapture Rules similar to the rules under section 179(d)(10) shall apply with respect to any qualified zone property which ceases to be used in an empowerment zone by an enterprise zone business.

[For explanation, see ¶ 603, for text of Committee Report, see ¶ 3069]

[¶ 2110] **Code Sec. 1397B. Enterprise zone business defined.**

(a) In general. For purposes of this part, the term "enterprise zone business" means—

(1) any qualified business entity, and

(2) any qualified proprietorship.

(b) Qualified business entity. For purposes of this section, the term "qualified business entity" means, with respect to any taxable year, any corporation or partnership if for such year—

(1) every trade or business of such entity is the active conduct of a qualified business within an empowerment zone,

(2) at least 80 percent of the total gross income of such entity is derived from the active conduct of such business,

(3) substantially all of the use of the tangible property of such entity (whether owned or leased) is within an empowerment zone,

(4) substantially all of the intangible property of such entity is used in, and exclusively related to, the active conduct of any such business,

(5) substantially all of the services performed for such entity by its employees are performed in an empowerment zone,

(6) at least 35 percent of its employees are residents of an empowerment zone,

(7) less than 5 percent of the average of the aggregate unadjusted bases of the property of such entity is attributable to collectibles (as defined in section 408(m)(2)) other than collectibles that are held primarily for sale to customers in the ordinary course of such business, and

(8) less than 5 percent of the average of the aggregate unadjusted bases of the property of such entity is attributable to nonqualified financial property.

(c) Qualified proprietorship. For purposes of this section, the term "qualified proprietorship" means, with respect to any taxable year, any qualified business carried on by an individual as a proprietorship if for such year—

(1) at least 80 percent of the total gross income of such individual from such business is derived from the active conduct of such business in an empowerment zone,

(2) substantially all of the use of the tangible property of such individual in such business (whether owned or leased) is within an empowerment zone,

(3) substantially all of the intangible property of such business is used in, and exclusively related to, the active conduct of such business,

[Footnote Code Sec. 1397A] Code Sec. 1397A added by section 13301(a), P.L. 103-66.
Effective Date (Sec. 13303, P.L. 103-66) effective 8/10/93.
[Footnote Code Sec. 1397B] Code Sec. 1397B added by section 13301(a), P.L. 103-66.
Effective Date (Sec. 13303, P.L. 103-66) effective 8/10/93.

(4) substantially all of the services performed for such individual in such business by employees of such business are performed in an empowerment zone,

(5) at least 35 percent of such employees are residents of an empowerment zone,

(6) less than 5 percent of the average of the aggregate unadjusted bases of the property of such individual which is used in such business is attributable to collectibles (as defined in section 408(m)(2)) other than collectibles that are held primarily for sale to customers in the ordinary course of such business, and

(7) less than 5 percent of the average of the aggregate unadjusted bases of the property of such individual which is used in such business is attributable to nonqualified financial property.

For purposes of this subsection, the term "employee" includes the proprietor.

(d) Qualified business. For purposes of this section—

(1) In general. Except as otherwise provided in this subsection, the term "qualified business" means any trade or business.

(2) Rental of real property. The rental to others of real property located in an empowerment zone shall be treated as a qualified business if and only if—

(A) the property is not residential rental property (as defined in section 168(e)(2)), and

(B) at least 50 percent of the gross rental income from the real property is from enterprise zone businesses.

(3) Rental of tangible personal property. The rental to others of tangible personal property shall be treated as a qualified business if and only if substantially all of the rental of such property is by enterprise zone businesses or by residents of an empowerment zone.

(4) Treatment of business holding intangibles. The term "qualified business" shall not include any trade or business consisting predominantly of the development or holding of intangibles for sale or license.

(5) Certain businesses excluded. The term "qualified business" shall not include—

(A) any trade or business consisting of the operation of any facility described in section 144(c)(6)(B), and

(B) any trade or business the principal activity of which is farming (within the meaning of subparagraphs (A) or (B) of section 2032A(e)(5)), but only if, as of the close of the preceding taxable year, the sum of—

(i) the aggregate unadjusted bases (or, if greater, the fair market value) of the assets owned by the taxpayer which are used in such a trade or business, and

(ii) the aggregate value of assets leased by the taxpayer which are used in such a trade or business,

exceeds $500,000.

For purposes of subparagraph (B), rules similar to the rules of section 1397(b) shall apply.

(e) Nonqualified financial property. For purposes of this section, the term "nonqualified financial property" means debt, stock, partnership interests, options, futures contracts, forward contracts, warrants, notional principal contracts, annuities, and other similar property specified in regulations; except that such term shall not include—

(1) reasonable amounts of working capital held in cash, cash equivalents, or debt instruments with a term of 18 months or less, or

(2) debt instruments described in section 1221(4).

[For explanation, see ¶ 603, for text of Committee Report, see ¶ 3069]

[¶ 2111] Code Sec. 1397C. Qualified zone property defined

(a) General rule. For purposes of this part—

(1) In general. The term "qualified zone property" means any property to which section 168 applies (or would apply but for section 179) if—

(A) such property was acquired by the taxpayer by purchase (as defined in section 179(d)(2)) after the date on which the designation of the empowerment zone took effect,

(B) the original use of which in an empowerment zone commences with the taxpayer, and

(C) substantially all of the use of which is in an empowerment zone and is in the active conduct of a qualified business by the taxpayer in such zone.

(2) Special rule for substantial renovations. In the case of any property which is substantially renovated by the taxpayer, the requirements of subparagraphs (A) and (B) of paragraph (1) shall be treated as satisfied. For purposes of the preceding sentence, property shall be treated as substantially renovated by the taxpayer if, during any 24-month period beginning after the date on which the designation of the empowerment zone took effect, additions to basis with respect to such property in the hands of the taxpayer exceed the greater of (i) an amount equal to the adjusted basis at the beginning of such 24-month period in the hands of the taxpayer, or (ii) $5,000.

(b) Special rules for sale-leasebacks. For purposes of subsection (a)(1)(B), if property is sold and leased back by the taxpayer within 3 months after the date such property was originally placed in service, such property shall be treated as originally placed in service not earlier than the date on which such property is used under the leaseback.

[For explanation, see ¶ 603, for text of Committee Report, see ¶ 3069]

[¶ 2112] Code Sec. 1397D. Regulations.

The Secretary shall prescribe such regulations as may be necessary or appropriate to carry out the purposes of parts II and III, including—

(1) regulations limiting the benefit of parts II and III in circumstances where such benefits, in combination with benefits provided under other Federal programs, would result in an activity being 100 percent or more subsidized by the Federal Government,

(2) regulations preventing abuse of the provisions of parts II and III, and

(3) regulations dealing with inadvertent failures of entities to be enterprise zone businesses.

[For explanation, see ¶ 601, for text of Committee Report, see ¶ 3069]

[¶ 2113] Code Sec. 1402. Definitions.

* * * * * * * * * * * *

(b) Self-employment income. The term "self-employment income" means the net earnings from self-employment derived by an individual (other than a nonresident alien individual, except as provided by an agreement under section 233 of the Social Security Act) during any taxable year; except that such term shall not include—

[Footnote Code Sec. 1397C] Code Sec. 1397C was added by section 13301(a) of P.L. 103-66.
Effective Date (Sec. 13303 of P.L. 103-66) effective 8/10/93.
[Footnote Code Sec. 1397D] Code Sec. 1397D added by section 13301(a), P.L. 103-66.
Effective Date (Sec. 13303, P.L. 103-66) effective 8/10/93.

(1) [1]*in the case of the tax imposed by section 1401(a), that part of the net* earnings from self-employment which is in excess of (i) an amount equal to the [2]*contribution and benefit base (as determined under section 230 of the Social Security Act)* which is effective for the calendar year in which such taxable year begins, minus (ii) the amount of the wages paid to such individual during such taxable years; or

(2) the net earnings from self-employment, if such net earnings for the taxable year are less than $400.

For purposes of paragraph (1), the term "wages" (A) includes such remuneration paid to an employee for services included under an agreement entered into pursuant to the provisions of section 3121(1) (relating to coverage of citizens of the United States who are employees of foreign affiliates of American employers), as would be wages under section 3121(a) if such services constituted employment under section 3121(b), *and* (B) includes compensation which is subject to the tax imposed by section 3201 or 3211.[3] An individual who is not a citizen of the United States but who is a resident of the Commonwealth of Puerto Rico, the Virgin Islands, Guam, or American Samoa shall not, for purposes of this chapter be considered to be a nonresident alien individual. In the case of church employee income, the special rules of subsection (j)(2) shall apply for purposes of paragraph (2).

* * * * * * * * * * * *

[4]*(k) Repealed*

[¶ 2114] Code Sec. 1441. Withholding of tax on nonresident aliens.

* * * * * * * * * * * *

(c) Exceptions.

* * * * * * * * * * * *

(9) Interest income from certain portfolio debt investments. In the case of portfolio interest (within the meaning of 871(h)), no tax shall be required to be deducted and withheld from such interest unless the person required to deduct and withhold tax from such interest knows, or has reason to know, that such interest is not portfolio interest by reason of section [1]*871(h)(3) or (4).*

* * * * * * * * * * * *

[For explanation, see ¶ 1106, for Committee Reports, see ¶ 3056.]

[Footnote Code Sec. 1402] Matter in *italics* in Code Sec. 1402(b), (b)(1) and (k) added by sections 13207(b)(1)(A) through (C) and (b)(2) of P.L. 103-66 which struck out:

1. "that part of the net"
2. "applicable contribution base (as determined under subsection (k))"
3. "and (C) includes but only with respect to the tax imposed by section 1401(b), remuneration paid for medicare qualified government employment (as defined in section 3121(u)(3)) which is subject to the taxes imposed by sections 3101(b) and 3111(b)"
4. "(k) *Applicable contribution base.*

For purposes of this chapter—

"(1) *Old-age, survivors, and disability insurance.* For purposes of the tax imposed by section 1401(a), the applicable contribution base for any calendar year is the contribution and benefit base determined under section 230 of the Social Security Act for such calendar year.

"(2) *Hospital insurance.* For purposes of the tax imposed by section 1401(b), the applicable contribution base for any calendar year is the applicable contribution base determined under section 3121(x)(2) for such calendar year."

Effective Date (Secs. 13207(b)(1)(A) through (D) and (b)(2) of P.L. 103-66) effective for 1994 and later calendar yrs.

[Footnote Code Sec. 1441] Matter in *italics* in Code Sec. 1441(c)(9) added by section 13237(c)(4) of P.L. 103-66 which struck out:

1. "section 871(h)(3)"

Effective Date (Sec. 13237(d) of P.L. 103-66) effective for interest received after 12/31/93.

[¶ 2115] Code Sec. 1442. Withholding of tax on foreign corporations.

(a) General rule. In the case of foreign corporations subject to taxation under this subtitle, there shall be deducted and withheld at the source in the same manner and on the same items of income as is provided in section 1441 a tax equal to 30 percent thereof. For purposes of the preceding sentence, the references in section 1441(b) to sections 871(a)(1)(C) and (D) shall be treated as referring to sections 881(a)(3) and (4), the reference in section 1441(c)(1) to section 871(b)(2) shall be treated as referring to section 842 or section 882(a)(2), as the case may be, the reference in section 1441(c)(5) to section 871(a)(1)(D) shall be treated as referring to section 881(a)(4), the reference in section 1441(c)(8) to section 871(a)(1)(C) shall be treated as referring to section 881(a)(3), the references in section 1441(c)(9) to sections 871(h) and [1]*871(h)(3) or (4)* shall be treated as referring to sections 881(c) and [2]*881(c)(3) or (4)* , and the reference in section 1441(c)(10) to section 871(i)(2) shall be treated as referring to section 881(d).

* * * * * * * * * * * *

[For explanation, see ¶ 1106, for text of Committee Reports, see ¶ 3056.

[¶ 2116] Code Sec. 1445. Withholding of tax on dispositions of United States real property interests.

* * * * * * * * * * * *

(e) Special rules relating to distributions, etc., by corporations, partnerships, trusts, or estates.

(1) Certain domestic partnerships, trusts, and estates. In the case of any disposition of a United States real property interest as defined in section 897(c) (other than a disposition described in paragraph (4) or 5)) by a domestic partnership, domestic trust, or domestic estate, such partnership, the trustee of such trust, or the executor of such estate (as the case may be) shall be required to deduct and withhold under subsection (a) a tax equal to [1]*35 percent* (or, to the extent provided in regulations, 28 percent) of the gain realized to the extent such gain—

(A) is allocable to a foreign person who is a partner or beneficiary of such partnership, trust, or estate, or

(B) is allocable to a portion of the trust treated as owned by a foreign person under subpart E of part I of subchapter J.

(2) Certain distributions by foreign corporations. In the case of any distribution by a foreign corporation on which gain is recognized under subsection (d) or (e) of section 897, the foreign corporation shall deduct and withhold under subsection (a) a tax equal to [2]*35 percent* of the amount of gain recognized on such distribution under such subsection.

* * * * * * * * * * * *

[For explanation, see ¶ 301, for text of Committee Report, see ¶ 3043]

[Footnote Code Sec. 1442] Matter in *italics* in Code Sec. 1442(a) added by sections 13237(c)(5)(A) and (B) which struck out:
1. "871(h)(3)"
2. "881(c)(3)"

Effective Date (Secs. 13237(d) of P.L. 103-66) effective for interest received after 12/31/93.

[Footnote Code Sec. 1445] Matter in *italics* in Code Sec. 1445(e)(1) and (2) added by section 13221(c)(3) of P.L. 103-66 which struck out:
1. "34 percent"
2. "34 percent"

Effective Date (Sec. 13221(c)(3) of P.L. 103-66) effective 8/10/93.

[¶ 2117] Code Sec. 2001. Imposition and rate of tax.

* * * * * * * * * * * *

(c) Rate schedule.

(1) In general.

If the amount with respect to which the tentative tax to be computed is:	the tentative tax is:
Not over $10,000	18 percent of such amount.
Over $10,000 but not over $20,000	$1,800, plus 20 percent of the excess of such amount over $10,000.
Over $20,000 but not over $40,000	$3,800, plus 22 percent of the excess of such amount over $20,000.
Over $40,000 but not over $60,000	$8,200, plus 24 percent of the excess of such amount over $40,000.
Over $60,000 but not over $80,000	$13,000, plus 26 percent of the excess of such amount over $60,000.
Over $80,000 but not over $100,000	$18,200, plus 28 percent of the excess of such amount over $80,000.
Over $100,000 but not over $150,000	$23,800, plus 30 percent of the excess of such amount over $100,000.
Over $150,000 but not over $250,000	$38,800, plus 32 percent of the excess of such amount over $150,000.
Over $250,000 but not over $500,000	$70,800, plus 34 percent of the excess of such amount over $250,000.
Over $500,000 but not over $750,000	$155,800, plus 37 percent of the excess of such amount over $500,000.
Over $750,000 but not over $1,000,000	$248,300, plus 39 percent of the excess of such amount over $750,000.
Over $1,000,000 but not over $1,250,000	$345,800 plus 41 percent of the excess of such amount over $1,000,000.
Over $1,250,000 but not over $1,500,000	$448,300, plus 43 percent of the excess of such amount over $1,250,000.
Over $1,500,000 but not over $2,000,000	$555,800, plus 45 percent of the excess of such amount over $1,500,000.
Over $2,000,000 but not over $2,500,000	$780,800, plus 49 percent of the excess of such amount over $2,000,000.
[1]*Over $2,500,000 but not over $3,000,000*	$1,025,800, plus 53% of the excess over $2,500,000.
Over $3,000,000.	$1,290,800, plus 55% of the excess over $3,000,000.

2

[Footnote Code Sec. 2001] Matter in *italics* in Code Sec. 2001(c)(1) and (2) added by sections 13208(a), (b)(1) and (b)(2) of P.L. 103-66 which struck out:

1. "Over $2,500,000. . . . . $1,025,800, plus 50 percent of the excess over $2,500,000."
2. "(2) **Phase-in of 50 percent maximum rate.**

"(A) In General. In the case of decedents dying, and gifts made, before 1993, there shall be substituted for the last item in the schedule contained in paragraph (1) the items determined under this paragraph.

"(B) For 1982. In the case of decedents dying, and gifts made, in 1982, the substitution under this paragraph shall be as follows:

Over $2,500,000 but not over $3,000,000	$1,025,800, plus 53% of the excess over $2,500,000.
Over $3,000,000 but not over $3,500,000	$1,290,800, plus 57% of the excess over $3,000,000.
Over $3,500,000 but not over $4,000,000	$1,575,800, plus 61% of the excess over $3,500,000.
Over $4,000,000	$1,880,800, plus 65% of the excess over $4,000,000.

"(C) For 1983. In the case of decedents dying, and gifts made, in 1983, the substitution under this paragraph shall be as follows:

Over $2,500,000 but not over $3,000,000	$1,025,800, plus 53% of the excess over $2,500,000.
Over $3,000,000 but not over $3,500,000	$1,290,800, plus 57% of the excess over $3,000,000.
Over $3,500,000	$1,575,800, plus 60% of the excess over $3,500,000.

[3]*(2)* Phaseout of graduated rates and unified credit. The tentative tax determined under paragraph (1) shall be increased by an amount equal to 5 percent of so much of the amount (with respect to which the tentative tax is to be computed) as exceeds $10,000,000 but does not exceed $21,040,000. [4]

* * * * * * * * * * * * *

[For text of Committee Report, see ¶3035]

[¶2118] Code Sec. 2101. Tax imposed.

* * * * * * * * * * * * *

(b) Computation of tax. The tax imposed by this section shall be the amount equal to the excess (if any) of—

(1) a tentative tax computed under section 2001(c) on the sum of—

(A) the amount of the taxable estate, and

(B) the amount of the adjusted taxable gifts, over

(2) a tentative tax computed under section 2001(c) on the amount of the adjusted taxable gifts.

For purposes of the preceding sentence, there shall be appropriate adjustments in the application of [1]*section 2001(c)(2)* to reflect the difference between the amount of the credit provided under section 2102(c) and the amount of the credit provided under section 2010.

* * * * * * * * * * * * *

[¶2119] Code Sec. 2105. Property without the United States.

* * * * * * * * * * * * *

(b) Bank deposits and certain other debt obligations. For purposes of [1]*this subchapter, the following shall not be deemed property within the United States* —

(1) amounts described in section 871(i)(3), if any interest thereon would not be subject to tax by reason of section 871(i)(1) were such interest received by the decedent at the time of his death,

(2) deposits with a foreign branch of a domestic corporation or domestic partnership, if such branch is engaged in the commercial banking business, and

[2]***(3)*** *debt obligations, if, without regard to whether a statement meeting the requirements of section 871(h)(5) has been received, any interest thereon would be eligible for the exemption*

"(D) After 1983 and before 1993. In the case of decedents dying, and gifts made, after 1983 and before 1993 the substitution under this paragraph shall be as follows:

Over $2,500,000 but not over $3,000,000	$1,025,800, plus 53% of the excess over $2,500,000.
Over $3,000,000	$1,290,800, plus 55% of the excess over $3,000,000."

3. "(3)"
4. "($18,340,000 in the case of decedents dying, and gifts made, after 1992"

Effective Date (Sec. 13208(c) of P.L. 103-66) effective for decedents dying and gifts made after 12/31/92.

[Footnote Code Sec. 2101] Matter in *italics* in Code Sec. 2101(b) added by section 13208(b)(3) of P.L. 103-66 which struck out:

1. "section 2001(c)(3)"

Effective Date (Sec. 13208(c) of P.L. 103-66) effective in the case of decedents dying, and gifts made, after 12/31/92.

[Footnote Code Sec. 2105] Matter in *italics* in Code Sec. 2105(b) and (b)(3) added by sections 13237(b)(1) and (2) of p.L. 103-66 which struck out:

1. "this subchapter"
2. "(3) debt obligations, if, without regard to whether a statement meeting the requirements of section 871(h)(4) has been received, any interest thereon would be eligible for the exemption from tax under section 871(h)(1) were such interest received by the decedent at the time of his death,

shall not be deemed property within the United States."

Effective Date (Secs. 13237(d) of P.L. 103-66) effective for estates of decedents dying after 12/31/93.

from tax under section 871(h)(1) were such interest received by the decedent at the time of his death.

Notwithstanding the preceding sentence, if any portion of the interest on an obligation referred to in paragraph (3) would not be eligible for the exemption referred to in paragraph (3) by reason of section 871(h)(4) if the interest were received by the decedent at the time of his death, then an appropriate portion (as determined in a manner prescribed by the Secretary) of the value (as determined for purposes of this chapter) of such debt obligation shall be deemed property within the United States.

[For explanation, see ¶ 1106.]

[¶ 2120] Code Sec. 3121. Definitions.

(a) Wages. For purposes of this chapter, the term "wages" means all remuneration for employment, including the cash value of all remuneration (including benefits) paid in any medium other than cash; except that such term shall not include—

(1) *in the case of the taxes imposed by sections 3101(a) and 3111(a)* that part of the remuneration which, after remuneration (other than remuneration referred to in the succeeding paragraphs of this subsection) equal to the [1]*contribution and benefit base (as determined under section 230 of the Social Security Act)* with respect to employment has been paid to an individual by an employer during the calendar year with respect to which [2]*such contribution and benefit base* is effective, is paid to such individual by such employer during such calendar year. If an employer (hereinafter referred to as successor employer) during any calendar year acquires substantially all the property used in a trade or business of another employer (hereinafter referred to as a predecessor), or used in a separate unit of a trade or business of a predecessor, and immediately after the acquisition employs in his trade or business an individual who immediately prior to the acquisition was employed in the trade or business of such predecessor, then, for the purpose of determining whether the successor employer has paid remuneration (other than remuneration referred to in the succeeding paragraphs of this subsection) with respect to employment equal to the [3]*contribution and benefit base (as determined under section 230 of the Social Security Act)* to such individual during such calendar year, any remuneration (other than remuneration referred to in the succeeding paragraphs of this subsection) with respect to employment paid (or considered under this paragraph as having been paid) to such individual by such predecessor during such calendar year and prior to such acquisition shall be considered as having been paid by such successor employer;[4]

* * * * * * * * * * * * *

(x) Repealed.

[For text of Committee Report, see ¶ 3034]

[Footnote Code Sec. 3121] Matter in *italics* in Code Sec. 3121(a)(1) added by sections 13207(a)(1)(A)-(C) of P.L. 103-66 which struck out:

1. "applicable contribution base (as determined under subsection (x))"
2. "applicable contribution base (as determined under subsection (x))"
3. "such applicable contribution base"
4. "(x) **Applicable contribution base.**

For purposes of this chapter—

"(1) Old-age, survivors, and disability insurance. For purposes of the taxes imposed by sections 3101(a) and 3111(a), the applicable contribution base for any calendar year is the contribution and benefit base determined under section 230 of the Social Security Act for such calendar year.

"(2) Hospital insurance. For purposes of the taxes imposed by section 3101(b) and 3111(b), the applicable contribution base is—

"(A) $125,000 for calendar year 1991, and

"(B) for any calendar year after 1991, the applicable contribution base for the preceding year adjusted in the same manner as is used in adjusting the contribution and benefit base under section 230(b) of the Social Security Act."

Effective Date (Sec. 13207(e) of P.L. 103-66) effective for 1994 and later calendar yrs.

[¶2121] Code Sec. 3122. Federal service.

In the case of the taxes imposed by this chapter with respect to service performed in the employ of the United States or in the employ of any instrumentality which is wholly owned by the United States, including such service which is medicare qualified government employment (as defined in section 3121(u)(3)), including service, performed as a member of a uniformed service, to which the provisions of section 3121(m)(1) are applicable, and including service, performed as a volunteer or volunteer leader within the meaning of the Peace Corps Act, to which the provisions of section 3121(p) are applicable, the determination of the amount of remuneration for such service, and the return and payment of the taxes imposed by this chapter, shall be made by the head of the Federal agency or instrumentality having the control of such service, or by such agents as such head may designate. Nothing in this paragraph shall be construed to affect the Secretary's authority to determine under subsections (a) and (b) of section 3121 whether any such service constitutes employment, the periods of such employment, and whether remuneration paid for any such service constitutes wages. The person making such return may, for convenience of administration, make payments of the tax imposed under section 3111 with respect to such service without regard to the [1]*contribution and benefit base limitation* in section 3121(a)(1), and he shall not be required to obtain a refund of the tax paid under section 3111 on that part of the remuneration not included in wages by reason of section 3121(a)(1). Payments of the tax imposed under section 3111 with respect to service, performed by an individual as a member of a uniformed service, to which the provisions of section 3121(m)(1) are applicable, shall be made from appropriations available for the pay of members of such uniformed service. The provisions of this section shall be applicable in the case of service performed by a civilian employee, not compensated from funds appropriated by the Congress, in the Army and Air Force Exchange Service, Army and Air Force Motion Picture Service, Navy Exchanges, Marine Corps Exchanges, or other activities, conducted by an instrumentality of the United States subject to the jurisdiction of the Secretary of Defense, at installations of the Department of Defense for the comfort, pleasure, contentment, and mental and physical improvement of personnel of such Department; and for purposes of this section the Secretary of Defense shall be deemed to be the head of such instrumentality. The provisions of this section shall be applicable also in the case of service performed by a civilian employee, not compensated from funds appropriated by the Congress, in the Coast Guard Exchanges or other activities, conducted by an instrumentality of the United States subject to the jurisdiction of the Secretary of Transportation, at installations of the Coast Guard for the comfort, pleasure, contentment, and mental and physical improvement of personnel of the Coast Guard; and for purposes of this section the Secretary of Transportation shall be deemed to be the head of such instrumentality.

[¶2122] Code Sec. 3125. Returns in the case of governmental employees in States, Guam, American Samoa, and the District of Columbia.

(a) States. Except as otherwise provided in this section, in the case of the taxes imposed by sections 3101(b) and 3111(b) with respect to service performed in the employ of a State or any political subdivision thereof (or any instrumentality of any one or more of the foregoing which is wholly owned thereby), the return and payment of such taxes may be made by the head of the agency or instrumentality having the control of such service, or by such agents as such head may designate. The person making such return may, for convenience of administration, make

[Footnote Code Sec. 3122] Matter in *italics* in Code Sec. 3122 was added by section 13207(d)(4) of P.L. 103-66 which struck out:

1. "applicable contribution base limitation"

Effective Date (Sec. 13207(e) of P.L. 103-66) effective for 1994 and later calendar yrs.

payments of the tax imposed under section 3111 with respect to the service of such individuals without regard to the [1]*contribution and benefit base limitation* in section 3121(a)(1).

(b) Guam. The return and payment of the taxes imposed by this chapter on the income of individuals who are officers or employees of the Government of Guam or any political subdivision thereof or of any instrumentality of any one or more of the foregoing which is wholly owned thereby, and those imposed on such Government or political subdivision or instrumentality with respect to having such individuals in its employ, may be made by the Governor of Guam or by such agents as he may designate. The person making such return may, for convenience of administration, make payments of the tax imposed under section 3111 with respect to the service of such individuals without regard to the [2]*contribution and benefit base limitation* in section 3121(a)(1).

(c) American Samoa. The return and payment of the taxes imposed by this chapter on the income of individuals who are officers or employees of the Government of American Samoa or any political subdivision thereof or of any instrumentality of any one or more of the foregoing which is wholly owned thereby, and those imposed on such Government or political subdivision or instrumentality with respect to having such individuals in its employ, may be made by the Governor of American Samoa or by such agents as he may designate. The person making such return may, for convenience of administration, make payments of the tax imposed under section 3111 with respect to the service of such individuals without regard to the [3]*contribution and benefit base limitation* in section 3121(a)(1).

(d) District of Columbia. In the case of the taxes imposed by this chapter with respect to service performed in the employ of the District of Columbia or in the employ of any instrumentality which is wholly owned thereby, the return and payment of the taxes may be made by the Mayor of the District of Columbia or by such agents as he may designate. The person making such return may, for convenience of administration, make payments of the tax imposed by section 3111 with respect to such service without regard to the [4]*contribution and benefit base limitation* in section 3121(a)(1).

[¶ 2123] Code Sec. 3231. Definitions.

* * * * * * * * * * * * *

(e) Compensation. For purposes of this chapter—

* * * * * * * * * * * * *

(2) Application of contribution bases.

(A) Compensation in excess of applicable base excluded.

* * * * * * * * * * * * *

(iii) Hospital insurance taxes. Clause (i) shall not apply to—

(I) so much of the rate applicable under section 3201(a) or 3221(a) as does not exceed the rate of tax in effect under section 3101(b), and

(II) so much of the rate applicable under section 3211(a)(1) as does not exceed the rate of tax in effect under section 1401(b).

(B) Applicable base.

[Footnote Code Sec. 3125] Matter in *italics* in Code Sec. 3125 added by section 13207(d)(4) of P.L. 103-66 which struck out:

1. "applicable contribution base limitation"
2. "applicable contribution base limitation"
3. "applicable contribution base limitation"
4. "applicable contribution base limitation"

Effective Date (Sec. 13207(e) of P.L. 103-66) effective for 1994 and later calendar yrs.

[1]*(i) Tier 1 taxes. Except as provided in clause (ii), the term "applicable base" means for any calendar year the contribution and benefit base determined under section 230 of the Social Security Act for such calendar year.*

* * * * * * * * * * * *

[¶ 2124] Code Sec. 3301. Rate of tax.

There is hereby imposed on every employer (as defined in section 3306(a)) for each calendar year an excise tax, with respect to having individuals in his employ, equal to—

(1) 6.2 percent in the case of calendar years 1988 through [1]*1998* ; or

(2) 6.0 percent in the case of calendar year [2]*1999* and each calendar year thereafter;

of the total wages (as defined in section 3306(b)) paid by him during the calendar year with respect to employment (as defined in section 3306(c)).

[For explanation, see ¶ 123, for Committee Report, see ¶ 3083.]

[¶ 2125] Code Sec. 3507. Advance payment of earned income credit.

* * * * * * * * * * * *

(b) Earned income eligibility certificate. For purposes of this title, an earned income eligibility certificate is a statement furnished by an employee to the employer which—

(1) certifies that the employee will be eligible to receive the credit provided by section 32 for the taxable year,

(2) *certifies that the employee has 1 or more qualifying children (within the meaning of section 32(c)(3)) for such taxable year,*

[1]***(3)*** certifies that the employee does not have an earned income eligibility certificate in effect for the calendar year with respect to the payment of wages by another employer, and

[2]***(4)*** states whether or not the employee's spouse has an earned income eligibility certificate in effect.

For purposes of this section, a certificate shall be treated as being in effect with respect to a spouse if such a certificate will be in effect on the first status determination date following the date on which the employee furnishes the statement in question.

(c) Earned income advance amount.

* * * * * * * * * * * *

[Footnote Code Sec. 3231] Matter in *italics* in Code Sec. 3231(e)(2)(A)(iii) and (B)(i) added by section 13207(c)(1) and (2) of P.L. 103-66 which struck out:

1. "(i) Tier 1 taxes.

"(I) In general. Except as provided in subclause (II) of this clause and in clause (ii), the term 'applicable base' means for any calendar year the contribution and benefit base determined under section 230 of the Social Security Act for such calendar year.

"(II) Hospital insurance taxes. For purposes of applying so much of the rate applicable under section 3201(a) or 3221(a) (as the case may be) as does not exceed the rate of tax in effect under section 3101(b), and for purposes of applying so much of the rate of tax applicable under section 3211(a)(1) as does not exceed the rate of tax in effect under section 1401(b), the term 'applicable base' means for any calendar year the applicable contribution base determined under section 3121(x)(2) for such calendar year."

Effective Date (Secs. 13207(e) of P.L. 103-66) effective for 1994 and later calendar yrs.

[Footnote Code Sec. 3301] Matter in *italics* in Code Sec. 3301(a) and (2) added by sections 13751(1) and (2) of P.L. 103-66 which struck out:

1. "1996"
2. "1997"

Effective Date effective 8/10/93.

[Footnote Code Sec. 3507] Matter in *italics* in Code Sec. 3507(b)(2) through (4), (c)(2)(B)(i), (ii) and (f) added by sections 13131(d)(4) through (6) of P.L. 103-66 which struck out:

1. "(2)"
2. "(3)"

(2) Advance amount tables. The tables referred to in paragraph (1)(B)—

(A) shall be similar in form to the tables prescribed under section 3402 and, to the maximum extent feasible, shall be coordinated with such tables, and

(B) if the employee is not married, or if no earned income eligibility certificate is in effect with respect to the spouse of the employee, shall treat the credit provided by section 32 as if it were a credit—

[3]*(i) of not more than 60 percent of the credit percentage in effect under section 32(b)(1) for an eligible individual with 1 qualifying child and with earned income not in excess of the earned income amount in effect under section 32(b)(2) for such an eligible individual, which*

(ii) phases out at 60 percent of the phaseout percentage in effect under section 32(b)(1) for such an eligible individual between the phaseout amount in effect under section 32(b)(2) for such an eligible individual and the amount of earned income at which the credit under section 32(a) phases out for such an eligible individual, or

* * * * * * * * * * * *

(f) Internal Revenue Service notification. *The Internal Revenue Service shall take such steps as may be appropriate to ensure that taxpayers who have 1 or more qualifying children and who receive a refund of the credit under section 32 are aware of the availability of earned income advance amounts under this section.*

[For explanation, see ¶ 119 and ¶ 120, for text of Committee Report, see ¶ 3011]

[¶ 2126] Code Sec. 4001. [1] *Imposition of tax.*

(a) Imposition of tax. *There is hereby imposed on the 1st retail sale of any passenger vehicle a tax equal to 10 percent of the price for which so sold to the extent such price exceeds $30,000.*

(b) Passenger vehicle.

(1) In general. *For purposes of this subchapter, the term "passenger vehicle" means any 4-wheeled vehicle—*

(A) which is manufactured primarily for use on public streets, roads, and highways, and

(B) which is rated at 6,000 pounds unloaded gross vehicle weight or less.

---

3. "(i) of not more than the credit percentage under section 32(b)(1) (without regard to subparagraph (D) thereof) for an eligible individual with 1 qualifying child and with earned income not in excess of the amount of earned income taken into account under section 32(a)(1), which

"(ii) phases out between the amount of earned income at which the phaseout begins under section 32(b)(1)(B)(ii) and the amount of income at which the credit under section 32(a)(1) phases out for an eligible individual with 1 qualifying child, or"

Effective Date (Secs. 13131(e) of P.L. 103-66) effective for tax. yrs. begin. after 12/31/93.

[Footnote Code Sec. 4001] Matter in *italics* in Code Sec. 4001 added by section 13161(a) of P.L. 103-66 which struck out:

1. "Sec. 4001 Passenger vehicles.

"(a) Imposition of tax.

There is hereby imposed on the 1st retail sale of any passenger vehicle a tax equal to 10 percent of the price for which so sold to the extent such price exceeds $30,000.

"(b) Passenger vehicle.

"(1) In general. For purposes of subsection (a), the term 'passenger vehicle' means any 4-wheeled vehicle—

"(A) which is manufactured primarily for use on public streets, roads, and highways, and

"(B) which is rated at 6,000 pounds unloaded gross vehicle weight or less.

"(2) Special rules.

"(A) Trucks and vans. In the case of a truck or van, paragraph (1)(B) shall be applied by substituting 'gross vehicle weight' for 'unloaded gross vehicle weight'.

"(B) Limousines. In the case of a limousine, paragraph (1) shall be applied without regard to subparagraph (B) thereof.

"(c) Exceptions for taxicabs, etc.

The tax imposed by this section shall not apply to the sale of any passenger vehicle for use by the purchaser exclusively in the active conduct of a trade or business of transporting persons or property for compensation or hire."

Effective Date (Sec. 13161(c) of P.L. 103-66) effective 1/1/93, except that the provisions of section 4001(e) of the Internal Revenue Code of 1986 (as amended by subsection (a)) shall be effective 8/10/93.

(2) Special rules.

(A) Trucks and vans. In the case of a truck or van, paragraph (1)(B) shall be applied by substituting "gross vehicle weight" for "unloaded gross vehicle weight".

(B) Limousines. In the case of a limousine, paragraph (1) shall be applied without regard to subparagraph (B) thereof.

***(c) Exceptions for taxicabs, etc.** The tax imposed by this section shall not apply to the sale of any passenger vehicle for use by the purchaser exclusively in the active conduct of a trade or business of transporting persons or property for compensation or hire.*

***(d) Exemption for law enforcement uses, etc.** No tax shall be imposed by this section on the sale of any passenger vehicle—*

***(1)** to the Federal Government, or a State or local government, for use exclusively in police, fire-fighting, search and rescue, or other law enforcement or public safety activities, or in public works activities, or*

***(2)** to any person for use exclusively in providing emergency medical services.*

(e) Inflation adjustment.

***(1) In general.** If, for any calendar year, the excess (if any) of—*

(A) $30,000, increased by the cost-of-living adjustment for the calendar year, over

(B) the dollar amount in effect under subsection (a) for the calendar year.

is equal to or greater than $2,000, then the $30,000 amount in subsection (a) and section 4003(a) (as previously adjusted under this subsection) for any subsequent calendar year shall be increased by the amount of such excess rounded to the next lowest multiple of $2,000.

***(2) Cost-of-living adjustment.** For purposes of paragraph (1), the cost-of-living adjustment for any calendar year shall be the cost-of-living adjustment under section 1(f)(3) for such calendar year, determined by substituting "calendar year 1990" for "calendar year 1992" in subparagraph (B) thereof.*

***(f) Termination.** The tax imposed by this section shall not apply to any sale or use after December 31, 1999.*

[For explanation, see ¶ 1001 for text of Committee Report, see ¶ 3023

[¶ 2127] Code Sec. 4002. [1] *1st retail sale; uses, etc. treated as sales; determination of price.*

***(a) 1st retail sale.** For purposes of this subchapter, the term "1st retail sale" means the 1st sale, for a purpose other than resale, after manufacture, production, or importation.*

(b) Use treated as sale.

***(1) In general.** If any person uses a passenger vehicle (including any use after importation) before the 1st retail sale of such vehicle, then such person shall be liable for tax under this subchapter in the same manner as if such vehicle were sold at retail by him.*

***(2) Exemption for further manufacture.** Paragraph (1) shall not apply to use of a vehicle as material in the manufacture or production of, or as a component part of, another vehicle taxable under this subchapter to be manufactured or produced by him.*

[Footnote Code Sec. 4002] Matter in *italics* in Code Sec. 4002 added by section 13161(a) of P.L. 103-66, which struck out:

"4002 Boats.

"(a) Imposition of tax.

1. There is hereby imposed on the 1st retail sale of any boat a tax equal to 10 percent of the price for which so sold to the extent such price exceeds $100,000.

"(b) Exceptions.

The tax imposed by this section shall not apply to the sale of any boat for use by the purchaser exclusively in the active conduct of—

"(1) a trade or business of commercial fishing or transporting persons or property for compensation or hire, or

"(2) any other trade or business unless the boat is to be used predominantly in any activity which is of a type generally considered to constitute entertainment, amusement, or recreation."

Effective Date (Sec. 13162(c) of P.L. 103-66) effective 1/1/93, except that the provisions of section 4001(e) of hte Internal Revenue Code of 1986 (as amended by subsection (a)) shall be effective 8/10/93.

(3) ***Exemption for demonstration use.*** *Paragraph (1) shall not apply to any use of a passenger vehicle as a demonstrator.*

(4) ***Exception for use after importation of certain vehicles.*** *Paragraph (1) shall not apply to the use of a vehicle after importation if the user or importer establishes to the satisfaction of the Secretary that the 1st use of the vehicle occurred before January 1, 1991, outside the United States.*

(5) ***Computation of tax.*** *In the case of any person made liable for tax by paragraph (1), the tax shall be computed on the price at which similar vehicles are sold at retail in the ordinary course of trade, as determined by the Secretary.*

(c) ***Leases considered as sales.*** *For purposes of this subchapter—*

(1) ***In general.*** *Except as otherwise provided in this subsection, the lease of a vehicle (including any renewal or any extension of a lease or any subsequent lease of such vehicle) by any person shall be considered a sale of such vehicle at retail.*

(2) ***Special rules for long-term leases.***

(A) Tax not imposed on sale for leasing in a qualified lease. The sale of a passenger vehicle to a person engaged in a passenger vehicle leasing or rental trade or business for leasing by such person in a long-term lease shall not be treated as the 1st retail sale of such vehicle.

(B) Long-term lease. For purposes of subparagraph (A), the term "long-term lease" means any long-term lease (as defined in section 4052).

(C) Special rules. In the case of a long-term lease of a vehicle which is treated as the 1st retail sale of such vehicle—

(i) Determination of price. The tax under this subchapter shall be computed on the lowest price for which the vehicle is sold by retailers in the ordinary course of trade.

(ii) Payment of tax. Rules similar to the rules of section 4217(e)(2) shall apply.

(iii) No tax where exempt use by lessee. No tax shall be imposed on any lease payment under a long-term lease if the lessee's use of the vehicle under such lease is an exempt use (as defined in section 4003(b)) of such vehicle.

(d) ***Determination of price.***

(1) ***In general.*** *In determining price for purposes of this subchapter—*

(A) there shall be included any charge incident to placing the passenger vehicle in condition ready for use,

(B) there shall be excluded—

(i) the amount of the tax imposed by this subchapter,

(ii) if stated as a separate charge, the amount of any retail sales tax imposed by any State or political subdivision thereof or the District of Columbia, whether the liability for such tax is imposed on the vendor or vendee, and

(iii) the value of any component of such passenger vehicle if—

(I) such component is furnished by the 1st user of such passenger vehicle, and

(II) such component has been used before such furnishing, and

(C) the price shall be determined without regard to any trade-in.

(2) ***Other rules.*** *Rules similar to the rules of paragraphs (2) and (4) of section 4052(b) shall apply for purposes of this subchapter.*

[For explanation, see ¶ 1001, for text of Committee Report, see ¶ 3023]

[¶ 2128] Code Sec. 4003. [1] *Special rules.*

(a) ***Separate purchase of vehicle and parts and accessories therefor.*** *Under regulations prescribed by the Secretary—*

[1]**[Footnote Code Sec. 4003]** Matter in *italics* in Code Sec. 4003 added by section 13161(a) of P.L. 103-66 which strcuk out:

"4003 Aircraft.

"(a) Imposition of tax.

(1) ***In general.*** *Except as provided in paragraph (2), if—*

(A) the owner, lessee, or operator of any passenger vehicle installs (or causes to be installed) any part or accessory on such vehicle, and

(B) such installation is not later than the date 6 months after the date the vehicle was 1st placed in service,

then there is hereby imposed on such installation a tax equal to 10 percent of the price of such part or accessory and its installation.

(2) ***Limitation.*** *The tax imposed by paragraph (1) on the installation of any part or accessory shall not exceed 10 percent of the excess (if any) of—*

(A) the sum of—

(i) the price of such part or accessory and its installation,

(ii) the aggregate price of the parts and accessories (and their installation) installed before such part or accessory, plus

(iii) the price for which the passenger vehicle was sold, over

(B) $30,000.

(3) ***Exceptions.*** *Paragraph (1) shall not apply if—*

(A) the part or accessory installed is a replacement part or accessory,

(B) the part or accessory is installed to enable or assist an individual with a disability to operate the vehicle, or to enter or exit the vehicle, by compensating for the effect of such disability, or

(C) the aggregate price of the parts and accessories (and their installation) described in paragraph (1) with respect to the vehicle does not exceed $200 (or such other amount or amounts as the Secretary may by regulation prescribe).

The price of any part or accessory (and its installation) to which paragraph (1) does not apply by reason of this paragraph shall not be taken into account under paragraph (2)(A).

(4) ***Installers secondarily liable for tax.*** *The owners of the trade or business installing the parts or accessories shall be secondarily liable for the tax imposed by this subsection.*

(b) Imposition of tax on sales, etc., within 2 years of vehicles purchased tax-free.

(1) ***In general.*** *If—*

(A) no tax was imposed under this subchapter on the 1st retail sale of any passenger vehicle by reason of its exempt use, and

(B) within 2 years after the date of such 1st retail sale, such vehicle is resold by the purchaser or such purchaser makes a substantial nonexempt use of such vehicle,

---

[Footnote Code Sec. 4003 continued]

1. There is hereby imposed on the 1st retail sale of any aircraft a tax equal to 10 percent of the price for which so sold to the extent such price exceeds $250,000.

"(b) Aircraft.

For purposes of this section, the term 'aircraft' means any aircraft—

"(1) which is propelled by a motor, and

"(2) which is capable of carrying 1 or more individuals.

"(c) 80 percent general business use.

"(1) In general. The tax imposed by this section shall not apply to the sale of any aircraft if 80 percent of the use by the purchaser is in any trade or business.

"(2) Proof of business use. On the income tax return for each of the 1st 2 taxable years ending after the date an aircraft on which no tax was imposed by this section by reason of paragraph (1) was placed in service, the taxpayer filing such return shall demonstrate to the satisfaction of the Secretary that the use of such aircraft during each such year met the requirement of paragraph (1).

"(3) Imposition of luxury tax where failure of proof. If the requirement of paragraph (2) is not met for either of the taxable years referred to therein, the taxpayer filing such returns shall pay the tax which would (but for paragraph (1)) have been imposed on such aircraft plus interest determined under subchapter C of chapter 67 during the period beginning on the date such tax would otherwise have been imposed. If such taxpayer fails to pay the tax imposed pursuant to the preceding sentence, no deduction shall be allowed under section 168 for any taxable year with respect to the aircraft involved.

"(d) Other exceptions.

The tax imposed by this section shall not apply to the sale of any aircraft for use by the purchaser exclusively—

"(1) in the aerial application of fertilizers or other substances,

"(2) in the case of a helicopter, in a use described in paragraph (1) or (2) of section 4261(e),

"(3) in a trade or business of providing flight training, or

"(4) in a trade or business of transporting persons or property for compensation or hire."

Effective Date (Sec. 13161(c) of P.L. 103-66) effective 1/1/93.

then such sale or use of such vehicle by such purchaser shall be treated as the 1st retail sale of such vehicle for a price equal to its fair market value at the time of such sale or use.

(2) Exempt use. *For purposes of this subsection, the term "exempt use" means any use of a vehicle if the 1st retail sale of such vehicle is not taxable under this subchapter by reason of such use.*

(c) Parts and accessories sold with taxable passenger vehicle. *Parts and accessories sold on, in connection with, or with the sale of any passenger vehicle shall be treated as part of the vehicle.*

(d) Partial payments, etc. *In the case of a contract, sale, or arrangement described in paragraph (2), (3), or (4) of section 4216(c), rules similar to the rules of section 4217(e)(2) shall apply for purposes of this subchapter.*

[For explanation, see ¶ 1001, for text of Committee Report, see ¶ 3023]

[¶ 2129] Code Sec. 4004. Rules applicable to subpart A.

CAUTION. The amendments to Code Sec. 4004, following, are effective 1/1/91. Code Sec. 4004 is repealed effective 1/1/93.

(a) Exemption for law enforcement uses, etc. No tax shall be imposed under this subpart on the sale of any article—

(1) to the Federal Government, or a State or local government, for use exclusively in police, firefighting, search and rescue, or other law enforcement or public safety activities, or in public works activities, or

(2) to any person for use exclusively in providing emergency medical services.

(b) Separate purchase of article and parts and accessories therefor. Under regulations prescribed by the Secretary—

(1) In general. Except as provided in paragraph (2), if—

(A) the owner, lessee, or operator of any article taxable under this subpart (determined without regard to price) installs (or causes to be installed) any part or accessory on such article, and

(B) such installation is not later than the date 6 months after the date the article was 1st placed in service,

then there is hereby imposed on such installation a tax equal to 10 percent of the price of such part or accessory and its installation.

(2) Limitation. The tax imposed by paragraph (1) on the installation of any part or accessory shall not exceed 10 percent of the excess (if any) of—

(A) the sum of—

(i) the price of such part or accessory and its installation,

(ii) the aggregate price of the parts and accessories (and their installation) installed before such part or accessory, plus

(iii) the price for which the passenger vehicle, boat, or aircraft was sold, over

(B) $30,000 in the case of a passenger vehicle, $100,000 in the case of a boat, and $250,000 in the case of an aircraft.

(3) Exceptions. Paragraph (1) shall not apply if—

(A) the part or accessory installed is a replacement part or accessory,[1]

(B) the part or accessory is installed on a passenger vehicle to enable or assist an individual with a disability to operate the vehicle, or to enter or exit the vehicle, by compensating for the effect of such disability, or [2]

[Footnote Code Sec. 4004] Matter in *italics* in Code Sec. 4004(b)(3), (b)(3)(A), (B) and (C) added by sections 13162(a)(1) through (4) of P.L. 103-66 which struck out:

1. "or"
2. "(C)

Effective Date (Sec. 13162(b) of P.L. 103-66) effective 1/1/91.

Section 13162(c) of P.L. 103-66 provides:

[Footnote Code Sec. 4004 continued]

"(c) Period for filing claims. If refund or credit of any overpayment of tax resulting from the application of the amendments made by this section is prevented at any time before the close of the 1-year period beginning on the date of the enactment of this Act by the operation of any law or rule of law (including res judicata), refund or credit of such overpayment (to the extent attributable to such amendments) may, nevertheless, be made or allowed if claim therefor is filed before the close of such 1-year period."

Code Secs. 4006, 4007, 4011 and 4012 prior to the amendment of Subchapter A of chapter 31 read as follows:

"4006 Jewelry.

"(a) Imposition of tax.

There is hereby imposed on the 1st retail sale of any jewelry a tax equal to 10 percent of the price for which so sold to the extent such price exceeds $10,000.

"(b) Jewelry.

For purposes of subsection (a), the term 'jewelry' means all articles commonly or commercially known as jewelry, whether real or imitation, including watches.

"(c) Manufacture from customer's material.

If—

"(1) a person, in the course of a trade or business, produces jewelry from material furnished directly or indirectly by a customer, and

"(2) the jewelry is for the use of, and not for resale by, such customer,

the delivery of such jewelry to such customer shall be treated as the 1st retail sale of such jewelry for a price equal to its fair market value at the time of such delivery."

"4007 Furs.

"(a) Imposition of tax.

There is hereby imposed on the 1st retail sale of the following articles a tax equal to 10 percent of the price for which so sold to the extent such price exceeds $10,000:

"(1) Articles made of fur on the hide or pelt.

"(2) Articles of which such fur is a major component.

"(b) Manufacture from customer's material.

If—

"(1) a person, in the course of a trade or business, produces an article of the kind described in subsection (a) from fur on the hide or pelt furnished, directly or indirectly, by a customer, and

"(2) the article is for the use of, and not for resale by, such customer,

the delivery of such article to such customer shall be treated as the 1st retail sale of such article for a price equal to its fair market value at the time of such delivery."

"4011 Definitions and special rules.

"(a) 1st retail sale.

For purposes of this subchapter, the term '1st retail sale' means the 1st sale, for a purpose other than resale, after manufacture, production, or importation.

"(b) Use treated as sale.

"(1) In general. If any person uses an article taxable under this subchapter (including any use after importation) before the 1st retail sale of such article, then such person shall be liable for tax under this subchapter in the same manner as if such article were sold at retail by him.

"(2) Exemption for further manufacture. Paragraph (1) shall not apply to use of an article as material in the manufacture or production of, or as a component part of, another article taxable under this subchapter to be manufactured or produced by him.

"(3) Exemption for demonstration use of passenger vehicles. Paragraph (1) shall not apply to any use of a passenger vehicle as a demonstrator for a potential customer while the potential customer is in the vehicle.

"(4) Exception for use after importation of certain articles. Paragraph (1) shall not apply to the use of an article after importation if the user or importer establishes to the satisfaction of the Secretary that the 1st use of the article occurred before January 1, 1991, outside the United States.

"(5) Computation of tax. In the case of any person made liable for tax by paragraph (1), the tax shall be computed on the price at which similar articles are sold at retail in the ordinary course of trade, as determined by the Secretary.

"(c) Leases considered as sales.

For purposes of this subchapter—

"(1) In general. Except as otherwise provided in this subsection, the lease of an article (including any renewal or any extension of a lease or any subsequent lease of such article) by any person shall be considered a sale of such article at retail.

"(2) Special rules for certain leases of passenger vehicles, boats, and aircraft.

"(A) Tax not imposed on sale for leasing in a qualified lease. The sale of a passenger vehicle, boat, or aircraft to a person engaged in a leasing or rental trade or business of the article involved for leasing by such person in a qualified lease shall not be treated as the 1st retail sale of such article.

"(B) Qualified lease. For purposes of subparagraph (A), the term 'qualified lease' means—

"(i) any lease in the case of a boat or an aircraft, and

"(ii) any long-term lease (as defined in section 4052) in the case of any passenger vehicle.

"(C) Special rules. In the case of a qualified lease of an article which is treated as the 1st retail sale of such article—

"(i) Determination of price. The tax under this subchapter shall be computed on the lowest price for which the article is sold by retailers in the ordinary course of trade.

"(ii) Payment of tax. Rules similar to the rules of section 4217(e)(2) shall apply.

"(iii) No tax where exempt use by lessee. No tax shall be imposed on any lease payment under a qualified lease if the lessee's use of the article under such lease is an exempt use (as defined in section 4004(c)) of such article.

(C) the aggregate price of the parts and accessories (and their installation) described in paragraph (1) with respect to the taxable article does not exceed $200 (or such other amount or amounts as the Secretary may by regulation prescribe).

The price of any part or accessory (and its installation) to which paragraph (1) does not apply by reason of this paragraph shall not be taken into account under paragraph (2)(A).

(4) Installers secondarily liable for tax. The owners of the trade or business installing the parts or accessories shall be secondarily liable for the tax imposed by this subsection.

(c) Imposition of tax on sales, etc., within 2 years of articles purchased tax-free.

(1) In general. If—

(A) no tax was imposed under this subchapter on the 1st retail sale of any article by reason of its exempt use, and

(B) within 2 years after the date of such 1st retail sale, such article is resold by the purchaser or such purchaser makes a substantial non-exempt use of such article,

then such sale or use of such article by such purchaser shall be treated as the 1st retail sale of such article for a price equal to its fair market value at the time of such sale or use.

(2) Exempt use. For purposes of this subsection, the term "exempt use" means any use of an article if the 1st retail sale of such article is not taxable under this subchapter by reason of such use."

[For text of Committee Reports, see ¶ 3023]

[¶ 2130] Code Sec. 4041. Imposition of tax.

(a) Diesel fuel and special motor fuels.

[1](1) Tax on diesel fuel in certain cases.

(A) In general. There is hereby imposed a tax on any liquid other than gasoline (as defined in section 4083)—

[Footnote Code Sec. 4041 continued]

"(d) Determination of price.

"(1) In general. In determining price for purposes of this subchapter—

"(A) there shall be included any charge incident to placing the article in condition ready for use,

"(B) there shall be excluded—

"(i) the amount of the tax imposed by this subchapter,

"(ii) if stated as a separate charge, the amount of any retail sales tax imposed by any State or political subdivision thereof or the District of Columbia, whether the liability for such tax is imposed on the vendor or vendee, and

"(iii) the value of any component of such article if—

"(I) such component is furnished by the 1st user of such article, and

"(II) such component has been used before such furnishing, and

"(C) the price shall be determined without regard to any trade-in.

Subparagraph (B)(iii) shall not apply for purposes of the taxes imposed by sections 4006 and 4007.

"(2) Other rules. Rules similar to the rules of paragraphs (2) and (4) of section 4052(b) shall apply for purposes of this subchapter.

"(e) Parts and accessories sold with taxable article.

Parts and accessories sold on, in connection with, or with the sale of any article taxable under this subchapter shall be treated as part of the article.

"(f) Partial payments, etc.

In the case of a contract, sale, or arrangement described in paragraph (2), (3), or (4) of section 4216(c), rules similar to the rules of section 4217(e)(2) shall apply for purposes of this subchapter."

"4012 Termination. The taxes imposed by this subchapter shall not apply to any sale or use after December 31, 1999."

[Footnote Code Sec. 4041] Matter in *italics* in Code Sec. 4041(a)(1) and (2) added by sections 13163(d)(3) and (d)(4)(A) and (B), P.L. 103-66, which struck out:

1. "(1) Tax on diesel fuel where no tax imposed on fuel under section 4091.

"There is hereby imposed a tax on any liquid (other than any product taxable under section 4081)—

"(A) sold by any person to an owner, lessee, or other operator of a diesel-powered highway vehicle or diesel-powered boat for use as a fuel in such vehicle or boat, or

"(B) used by any person as a fuel in a diesel-powered highway vehicle or diesel-powered boat unless there was a taxable sale of such liquid under subparagraph (A).

"The rate of the tax imposed by this paragraph shall be the sum of the Highway Trust Fund financing rate and the diesel fuel deficit reduction rate in effect under section 4091 at the time of such sale or use.

"No tax shall be imposed by this paragraph on the sale or use of any liquid if there was a taxable sale of such liquid under section 4091."

(i) sold by any person to an owner, lessee, or other operator of a diesel-powered highway vehicle, a diesel-powered train, or a diesel-powered boat for use as a fuel in such vehicle, train, or boat, or

(ii) used by any person as a fuel in a diesel-powered highway vehicle, a diesel-powered train, or a diesel-powered boat unless there was a taxable sale of such fuel under clause (i).

(B) Exemption for previously taxed fuel. No tax shall be imposed by this paragraph on the sale or use of any liquid if tax was imposed on such liquid under section 4081 and the tax thereon was not credited or refunded.

(C) Rate of tax.

(i) In general. Except as otherwise provided in this subparagraph, the rate of the tax imposed by this paragraph shall be the rate of tax specified in section 4081(a)(2)(A) on diesel fuel which is in effect at the time of such sale or use.

(ii) Rate of tax on trains. In the case of any sale for use, or use, of diesel fuel in a train, the rate of tax imposed by this paragraph shall be—

(I) 6.8 cents per gallon after September 30, 1993, and before October 1, 1995,

(II) 5.55 cents per gallon after September 30, 1995, and before October 1, 1999, and

(III) 4.3 cents per gallon after September 30, 1999.

(iii) Rate of tax on certain buses.

(I) In general. Except as provided in subclause (II), in the case of fuel sold for use or used in a use described in section 6427(b)(1) (after the application of section 6427(b)(3)), the rate of tax imposed by this paragraph shall be 7.3 cents per gallon (4.3 cents per gallon after September 30, 1999).

(II) School bus and intracity transportation. No tax shall be imposed by this paragraph on any sale for use, or use, described in subparagraph (B) or (C) of section 6427(b)(2).

(D) Diesel fuel used in motorboats. In the case of any sale for use, or use, of fuel in a diesel-powered motorboat—

(i) effective during the period after September 30, 1999, and before January 1, 2000, the rate of tax imposed by this paragraph is 24.3 cents per gallon, and

(ii) the termination of the tax under subsection (d) shall not occur before January 1, 2000.

(2) Special motor fuels. There is hereby imposed a tax on benzol, benzene, naphtha, liquefied petroleum gas, casing head and natural gasoline, or any other liquid (other than kerosene, gas oil, or fuel oil, or any product taxable under section 4081) [2]—

(A) sold by any person to an owner, lessee, or other operator of a motor vehicle or motorboat for use as a fuel in such motor vehicle or motorboat, or

(B) used by any person as a fuel in a motor vehicle or motorboat unless there was a taxable sale of such liquid under subparagraph (A). [3]

The rate of the tax imposed by this paragraph shall be the rate of tax specified in section 4081(a)(2)(A) on gasoline which is in effect at the time of such sale or use.

(3) Compressed natural gas.

(A) In general. There is hereby imposed a tax on compressed natural gas—

(i) sold by any person to an owner, lessee, or other operator of a motor vehicle or motorboat for use as a fuel in such motor vehicle or motorboat, or

(ii) used by any person as a fuel in a motor vehicle or motorboat unless there was a taxable sale of such gas under clause (i).

[Footnote Code Sec. 4041 continued]

2. "or paragraph (1) of this subsection"

3. "The rate of the tax imposed by this paragraph shall be the sum of the Highway Trust Fund financing rate and the deficit reduction rate in effect under section 4081 at the time of such sale or use."

Effective Date (Sec. 13242(e), P.L. 103-66) effective 1/1/94.

Code Sec. 4041(a)(1) previously amended by sections 13163(a)(2)(A) and (B), P.L. 103-66.

Effective Date (Sec. 13163(d), P.L. 103-66) effective 1/1/94.

Matter in *italics* in Code Sec. 4041(a)(3) added by section 13241(e)(1), P.L. 103-66.

Effective Date (Sec. 13241(g), P.L. 103-66) effective 10/1/93.

The rate of the tax imposed by this paragraph shall be 48.54 cents per MCF (determined at standard temperature and pressure).

(B) Bus uses. No tax shall be imposed by this paragraph on any sale for use, or use, described in subparagraph (B) or (C) of section 6427(b)(2) (relating to school bus and intracity transportation).

(C) Administrative provisions. For purposes of applying this title with respect to the taxes imposed by this subsection, references to any liquid subject to tax under this subsection shall be treated as including references to compressed natural gas subject to tax under this paragraph, and references to gallons shall be treated as including references to MCF with respect to such gas.

(b) Exemption for off-highway business use; reduction in tax for qualified methanol and ethanol fuel.

(1) Exemption for off-highway business use.

(A) In general. No tax shall be imposed by subsection (a) or (d)(1) on liquids sold for use or used in an off-highway business use.

(B) Tax where other use. If a liquid on which no tax was imposed by reason of subparagraph (A) is used otherwise than in an off-highway business use, a tax shall be imposed by [4]*paragraph (1)(B), (2)(B), or (3)(A)(ii)* of subsection (a) (whichever is appropriate) and by the corresponding provision of subsection (d)(1)*(if any)*.

(C) Off-highway business use defined. For purposes of this subsection, the term "off-highway business use" has the meaning given to such term by section 6421(e)(2)*; except that such term shall not, for purposes of this subsection (a)(1), include use in a diesel-powered train*.

(2) Qualified methanol and ethanol fuel.

(A) In general. In the case of any qualified methanol or ethanol fuel—

(i) the [5]rate applicable under subsection (a)(2) shall be 5.4 cents per gallon less than the otherwise applicable rate (6 cents per gallon in the case of a mixture none of the alcohol in which consists of ethanol), and

* * * * * * * * * * * *

(c) Noncommercial aviation.

(1) Tax on nongasoline fuels where no tax imposed on fuel under section 4091. There is hereby imposed a tax [6]upon any liquid (other than any product taxable under section 4081)—

(A) sold by any person to an owner, lessee, or other operator of an aircraft, for use as a fuel in such aircraft in noncommercial aviation; or

(B) used by any person as a fuel in an aircraft in noncommercial aviation, unless there was a taxable sale of such liquid under this section.

[7]*The rate of the tax imposed by this paragraph shall be the rate of tax specified in section 4091(b)(1) which is in effect at the time of such sale or use.* No tax shall be imposed by this paragraph on the sale or use of any liquid if there was a taxable sale of such liquid under section 4091.

(2) Gasoline. There is hereby imposed a tax (at the rate specified in paragraph (3)) upon [8]*gasoline (as defined in section 4083)* —

[Footnote Code Sec. 4041 continued]

Matter in *italics* in Code Sec. 4041(b)(1)(B) added by section 13242(d)(5)(A)-(C), P.L. 103-66, which struck out:

4. "paragraph (1)(B) or (2)(B)"

5. "Highway Trust Fund financing"

Effective Date (Sec. 13242(e), P.L. 103-66) effective 1/1/94.

Matter in *italics* in Code Sec. 4041(c)(1) added by section 13241(b)(2)(B)(iii), P.L. 103-66, which struck out:

6. "of 17.5 cents a gallon"

Effective Date (Sec. 13241(g), P.L. 103-66) effective 10/1/93.

Matter in *italics* in Code Sec. 4041(c)(1) and (2) added by sections 13242(d)(6) and (7), P.L. 103-66, which struck out:

7. "The rate of the tax imposed by this paragraph shall be the sum of the Airport and Airway Trust Fund financing rate and the aviation fuel deficit reduction rate in effect under section 4091 at the time of such sale or use."

8. "any product taxable under section 4081"

Effective Date (Sec. 13242(e), P.L. 103-66) effective 1/1/94.

(A) sold by any person to an owner, lessee, or other operator of an aircraft, for use as a fuel in such aircraft in noncommercial aviation; or

(B) used by any person as a fuel in an aircraft in noncommercial aviation, unless there was a taxable sale of such product under subparagraph (A).

The tax imposed by this paragraph shall be in addition to any tax imposed under section 4081.

[9]***(3) Rate of tax.*** *The rate of tax imposed by paragraph (2) on any gasoline is 1 cent per gallon.*

* * * * * * * * * * * *

(5) Termination. The taxes imposed by paragraphs (1) and (2) shall apply during the period beginning on September 1, 1982, and ending on December 31, 1995.*The termination under the preceding sentence shall not apply to so much of the tax imposed by paragraph (1) as does not exceed 4.3 cents per gallon.*

(d) Additional taxes to fund leaking underground storage tank trust fund.

(1) Tax on sales and uses subject to tax under subsection (a). In addition to the taxes imposed by subsection (a), there is hereby imposed a tax of 0.1 cent a gallon on the sale or use of any liquid (other than liquefied petroleum gas) if tax is imposed by [10]*subsection (a)(1) or (2),* on such sale or use.

[11]*(2)* Liquids used in aviation. In addition to the taxes imposed by subsection (c), there is hereby imposed a tax of 0.1 cent a gallon on any liquid [12]*(other than gasoline (as defined in section 4083))* —

(A) sold by any person to an owner, lessee, or other operator of an aircraft for use as a fuel in such aircraft, or

(B) used by any person as a fuel in an aircraft unless there was a taxable sale of such liquid under subparagraph (A).

No tax shall be imposed by this paragraph on the sale or use of any liquid if there was a taxable sale of such liquid under section 4091.

[13]*(3)* Termination. The taxes imposed by this subsection shall not apply during any period during which the Leaking Underground Storage Tank Trust Fund financing rate under section 4081 does not apply. [14]

* * * * * * * * * * * *

(f) Exemption for farm use.

* * * * * * * * * * * *

[Footnote Code Sec. 4041 continued]

Matter in *italics* in Code Sec. 4041(c)(3) added by section 13241(b)(2)(A), P.L. 103-66, which struck out:

9. "(3) Rate of tax. The rate of tax imposed by paragraph (2) on any gasoline is the excess of 15 cents a gallon over the sum of the Highway Trust fund financing rate plus the deficit reduction rate at which tax was imposed on such gasoline under section 4081."

Effective Date (Sec. 13241(g), P.L. 103-66) effective 10/1/93.

Matter in *italics* in Code Sec. 4041(d)(1) added by section 13241(e)(2), P.L. 103-66, which struck out:

10. "subsection (a)"

Effective Date (Sec. 13241(g), P.L. 103-66) effective 10/1/93.

Matter in *italics* in Code Sec. 4041(d)(2) and (3) added by sections 13242(d)(9) and (10), P.L. 103-66, which struck out:

11. "(2) Tax on diesel fuel used in trains. There is hereby imposed a tax of 0.1 cent a gallon on any liquid (other than a product taxable under section 4081)—

"(A) sold by any person to an owner, lessee, or other operator of a diesel-powered train for use as a fuel in such train, or

"(B) used by any person as a fuel in a diesel-powered train unless there was a taxable sale of such liquid under subparagraph (A).

"No tax shall be imposed by this paragraph on the sale or use of any liquid if there was a taxable sale of such liquid under section 4091."

12. "(other than any product taxable under section 4081)"

13. "(3)"

14. "(4)"

Effective Date (Sec. 13242(e), P.L. 103-66) effective 1/1/94.

[15](3) **Repealed.**

(g) Other exemptions. Under regulations prescribed by the Secretary, no tax shall be imposed under this section—

(1) on any liquid sold for use or used as supplies for vessels or aircraft (within the meaning of section 4221(d)(3));

(2) with respect to the sale of any liquid for the exclusive use of any State, any political subdivision of a State, or the District of Columbia, or with respect to the use by any of the foregoing of any liquid as a fuel;

(3) upon the sale of any liquid for export, or for shipment to a possession of the United States, and in due course so exported or shipped; and

(4) with respect to the sale of any liquid to a nonprofit educational organization for its exclusive use, or with respect to the use by a nonprofit educational organization of any liquid as a fuel.

For purposes of paragraph (4), the term "nonprofit educational organization" means an educational organization described in section 170(b)(1)(A)(ii) which is exempt from income tax under section 501(a). The term also includes a school operated as an activity of an organization described in section 501(c)(3) which is exempt from income tax under section 501(a), if such school normally maintains a regular faculty and curriculum and normally has a regularly enrolled body of pupils or students in attendance at the place where its educational activities are regularly carried on. [16]

* * * * * * * * * * * *

(k) Fuels containing alcohol.

(1) In general. Under regulations prescribed by the Secretary, in the case of the sale or use of any liquid at least 10 percent of which consists of alcohol (as defined in section 4081(c)(3))—

(A) the [17]rates under paragraphs (1) and (2) of subsection (a) shall be the comparable rates under [18]*section 4081(c)* ,

(B) the rate of the tax imposed by subsection (c)(1) shall be the comparable rate under section [19]*4091(c)* , and

(C) no tax shall be imposed by subsection (c)(2).

* * * * * * * * * * * * *

(m) Certain alcohol fuels.

(1) In general. In the case of the sale or use of any partially exempt methanol or ethanol fuel—

[20]*(A) the rate of the tax imposed by subsection (a)(2) shall be—*

[Footnote Code Sec. 4041 continued]

Matter in *italics* in Code Sec. 4041(g) added by sections 13241(f)(1) and (2), P.L. 103-66, which struck out:

15. ""(3) Termination.

"Except with respect to the taxes imposed by subsection (d), paragraph (1) shall not apply on and after October 1, 1999."

16. "Except with respect to the taxes imposed by subsection (d), paragraphs (2) and (4) shall not apply on and after October 1, 1999."

Effective Date (Sec. 13241(g), P.L. 103-66) effective 10/1/93.

Matter in *italics* in Code Sec. 4041(k)(1)(A) and (B) added by sections 13242(d)(11)(A) and (B), and (d)(12), P.L. 103-66, which struck out:

17. "Highway Trust Fund financing"
18. "sections 4081(c) and 4091(c), as the case may be"
19. "4091(d)"

Effective Date (Sec. 13242(e), P.L. 103-66) effective 1/1/94.

Matter in *italics* in Code Sec. 4041(m)(1)(A) and (B) added by section 13242(d)(13) of P.L. 103-66, which struck out:

20. "(A) under subsection (a)(2)—

"(i) the Highway Trust Fund financing rate shall be 5.75 cents per gallon, and

"(ii) the deficit reduction rate shall be 5.55 cents per gallon.

"(B) the rate of the tax imposed by subsection (c)(1) shall be the comparable rate under section 4091(d)(1)."

Effective Date (Sec. 13242(e), P.L. 103-66) effective 1/1/94.

Code Sec. 4041(m)(1)(A) previously amended by section 13241(c), P.L. 103-66 which struck out:

"(A) under subsection (a)(2) the Highway Trust fund financing rate shall be 5.75 cents per gallon and the deficit reduction rate shall be 1.25 cents per gallon, and"

Effective Date (Sec. 13241(g), P.L. 103-66) effective 10/1/93.

(i) 11.3 cents per gallon after September 30, 1993, and before October 1, 1999, and
(ii) 4.3 cents per gallon after September 30, 1999, and
(B) the rate of the tax imposed by subsection (c)(1) shall be the comparable rate under section 4091(c)(1).

* * * * * * * * * * * * *

[For explanation, see ¶ 1002, ¶ 1005 and ¶ 1007, for text of Committee Report, see ¶ 3024, ¶ 3059 and ¶ 3060]

[¶ 2131] Code Sec. 4042. Tax on fuel used in commercial transportation on inland waterways.

* * * * * * * * * * * * *

(b) Amount of tax.

(1) In general. The rate of the tax imposed by subsection (a) is the sum of—

(A) the Inland Waterways Trust Fund financing rate, [1]

(B) the Leaking Underground Storage Tank Trust Fund financing rate [2], *and*

(C) the deficit reduction rate.

(2) Rates. For purposes of paragraph (1)—

* * * * * * * * * * * * *

(C) The deficit reduction rate is 4.3 cents per gallon.

[For explanation, see ¶ 1002, for text of Committee Report, see ¶ 3059]

[¶ 2132] Code Sec. 4081. [1] *Imposition of tax.*

(a) Tax imposed.

(1) Tax on removal, entry, or sale.

(A) In general. There is hereby imposed a tax at the rate specified in paragraph (2) on—

[Footnote Code Sec. 4042] Matter in *italics* in Code Sec. 4042(B)(1)(A)-(C) and (b)(2)(C) was added by sections 13241(d)(1)(A)-(C) and (d)(2) of P.L. 103-66, which struck out:
1. "and"
2. "."

Effective Date (Sec. 13241(g) of P.L. 103-66) effective 10/1/93.

[Footnote Code Sec. 4081] Matter in *italics* in Code Sec. 4081 added by section 13242(a) of P.L. 103-66 which struck out:

"Sec. 4081. Imposition of tax.
"(a) Tax imposed.
1. "(1) Tax on removal, entry, or sale.
"(A) In general. There is hereby imposed a tax at the rate specified in paragraph (2) on—
"(i) the removal of gasoline from any refinery,
"(ii) the removal of gasoline from any terminal,
"(iii) the entry into the United States of gasoline for consumption, use, or warehousing, and
"(iv) the sale of gasoline to any person who is not registered under section 4101 unless there was a prior taxable removal or entry of such gasoline under clause (i), (ii), or (iii).
"(B) Exception for bulk transfers to registered terminals. The tax imposed by this paragraph shall not apply to any removal or entry of gasoline transferred in bulk to a terminal if the person removing or entering the gasoline and the operator of such terminal are registered under section 4101.
"(2) Rates of tax.
"(A) In general. The rate of the tax imposed by this section is the sum of—
"(i) the Highway Trust Fund financing rate,
"(ii) the Leaking Underground Storage Tank Trust Fund financing rate, and
"(iii) the deficit reduction rate.
"(B) Rates. For purposes of subparagraph (A)—
"(i) the Highway Trust Fund financing rate is 11.5 cents a gallon,
"(ii) the Leaking Underground Storage Tank Trust Fund financing rate is 0.1 cent a gallon, and
"(iii) the deficit reduction rate is 6.8 cents per gallon.

[Footnote Code Sec. 4081 continued]
"(b) Treatment of removal or subsequent sale by blender or compounder.

"(1) In general. There is hereby imposed a tax at the rate specified in subsection (a) on gasoline removed or sold by the blender or compounder thereof.

"(2) Credit for tax previously paid. If—

"(A) tax is imposed on the removal or sale of gasoline by reason of paragraph (1), and

"(B) the blender or compounder establishes the amount of the tax paid with respect to such gasoline by reason of subsection (a),

the amount of the tax so paid shall be allowed as a credit against the tax imposed by reason of paragraph (1).

"(c) Gasoline mixed with alcohol at refinery, etc.

"(1) In general. Under regulations prescribed by the Secretary, subsection (a) shall be applied by multiplying the otherwise applicable rate by a fraction the numerator of which is 10 and the demoninator of which is—

"(A) 9 in the case of 10 percent gasohol,

"(B) 9.23 in the case of 7.7 percent gasohol, and

"(C) 9.43 in the case of 5.7 percent gasohol,

in the case of the removal or entry of any gasoline for use in producing gasohol at the time of such removal or entry. Subject to such terms and conditions as the Secretary may prescribe (including the application of section 4101), the treatment under the preceding sentence also shall apply to use in producing gasohol after the time of such removal or entry.

"(2) Later separation of gasoline from gasohol. If any person separates the gasoline from a mixture of gasoline and alcohol on which tax was imposed under subsection (a) at a Highway Trust Fund financing rate equivalent to an otherwise applicable rate by reason of this subsection (or with respect to which a credit or payment was allowed or made by reason of section 6427(f)(1)), such person shall be treated as the refiner of such gasoline. The amount of tax imposed on any sale of such gasoline by such person shall be reduced by the amount of tax imposed (and not credited or refunded) on any prior removal or sale of such fuel.

"(3) Alcohol defined. For purposes of this subsection, the term 'alcohol' includes methanol and ethanol but does not include alcohol produced from petroleum, natural gas, or coal (including peat). Such term does not include alcohol with a proof of less than 190 (determined without regard to any added denaturants).

"(4) Otherwise applicable rate. For purposes of this subsection—

"(A) In general. In the case of the Highway Trust Fund financing rate, the term 'otherwise applicable rate' means—

"(i) 6.1 cents a gallon for 10 percent gasohol,

"(ii) 7.342 cents a gallon for 7.7 percent gasohol, and

"(iii) 8.422 cents a gallon for 5.7 percent gasohol.

In the case of gasohol none of the alcohol in which consists of ethanol, clauses (i), (ii), and (iii) shall be applied by substituting '5.5 cents' for '6.1 cents', '6.88 cents' for '7.342 cents', and '8.08 cents' for '8.422 cents'.

"(B) 10 percent gasohol. The term '10 percent gasohol' means any mixture of gasoline with alcohol if at least 10 percent of such mixture is alcohol.

"(C) 7.7 percent gasohol. The term '7.7 percent gasohol' means any mixture of gasoline with alcohol if at least 7.7 percent, but not 10 percent or more, of such mixture is alcohol.

"(D) 5.7 percent gasohol. The term '5.7 percent gasohol' means any mixture of gasoline with alcohol if at least 5.7 percent, but not 7.7 percent or more, of such mixture is alcohol.

"(5) Termination. Paragraph (1) shall not apply to any removal or sale after September 30, 2000.

(d) Termination.

"(1) Highway trust fund financing rate.

On and after October 1, 1999, the Highway Trust Fund financing rate under subsection (a)(2) shall not apply.

"(2) Leaking underground storage tank trust fund financing rate. The Leaking Underground Storage Tank Trust Fund financing rate under subsection (a)(2) shall not apply after December 31, 1995.

"(3) Deficit reduction rate. On and after October 1, 1995, the deficit reduction rate under subsection (a)(2) shall not apply.

"(e) Refunds in certain cases.

Under regulations prescribed by the Secretary, if any person who paid the tax imposed by this section with respect to any gasoline establishes to the satisfaction of the Secretary that a prior tax was paid (and not credited or refunded) with respect to such gasoline, then an amount equal to the tax paid by such person shall be allowed as a refund (without interest) to such person in the same manner as if it were an overpayment of tax imposed by this section."

Effective Date (Sec. 13242(e) of P.L. 103-66) effective 1/1/94.

Section 13251(h) of P.L. 103-66 regarding floor stocks taxes provides:

"(h) Floor stocks taxes.

"(1) Imposition of tax. In the case of gasoline, diesel fuel, and aviation fuel on which tax was imposed under section 4081 or 4091 of the Internal Revenue Code of 1986 before October 1, 1993, and which is held on such date by any person, there is hereby imposed a floor stocks tax of 4.3 cents per gallon on such gasoline, diesel fuel, and aviation fuel.

"(2) Liability for tax and method of payment.

"(A) Liability for tax. A person holding gasoline, diesel fuel, or aviation fuel on October 1, 1993, to which the tax imposed by paragraph (1) applies shall be liable for such tax.

"(B) Method of payment. The tax imposed by paragraph (1) shall be paid in such manner as the Secretary shall prescribe.

"(C) Time for payment. The tax imposed by paragraph (1) shall be paid on or before November 30, 1993.

"(3) Definitions. For purposes of this subsection—

"(A) Held by a person. Gasoline, diesel fuel, and aviation fuel shall be considered as 'held by a person' if title thereto has passed to such person (whether or not delivery to the person has been made).

"(B) Gasoline. The term 'gasoline' has the meaning given such term by section 4082 of such Code.

"(C) Diesel fuel. The term 'diesel fuel' has the meaning given such term by section 4092 of such Code.

"(D) Aviation fuel. The term 'aviation fuel' has the meaning given such term by section 4092 of such Code.

(i) the removal of a taxable fuel from any refinery,

(ii) the removal of a taxable fuel from any terminal,

(iii) the entry into the United States of any taxable fuel for consumption, use, or warehousing, and

(iv) the sale of a taxable fuel to any person who is not registered under section 4101 unless there was a prior taxable removal or entry of such fuel under clause (i), (ii), or (iii).

(B) Exemption for bulk transfers to registered terminals or refineries. The tax imposed by this paragraph shall not apply to any removal or entry of a taxable fuel transferred in bulk to a terminal or refinery if the person removing or entering the taxable fuel and the operator of such terminal or refinery are registered under section 4101.

(2) Rates of tax.

(A) In general. The rate of the tax imposed by this section is—

(i) in the case of gasoline, 18.3 cents per gallon, and

(ii) in the case of diesel fuel, 24.3 cents per gallon.

(B) Leaking underground storage tank trust fund tax. The rates of tax specified in subparagraph (A) shall each be increased by 0.1 cent per gallon. The increase in tax under this subparagraph shall in this title be referred to as the Leaking Underground Storage Tank Trust Fund financing rate.

(b) Treatment of removal or subsequent sale by blender.

(1) In general. *There is hereby imposed a tax at the rate determined under subsection (a) on taxable fuel removed or sold by the blender thereof.*

(2) Credit for tax previously paid. *If—*

(A) tax is imposed on the removal or sale of a taxable fuel by reason of paragraph (1), and

(B) the blender establishes the amount of the tax paid with respect to such fuel by reason of subsection (a),

---

[Footnote Code Sec. 4081 continued]

"(E) Secretary. The term 'Secretary' means the Secretary of the Treasury or his delegate.

"(4) Exception for exempt uses. The tax imposed by paragraph (1) shall not apply to gasoline, diesel fuel, or aviation fuel held by any person exclusively for any use to the extent a credit or refund of the tax imposed by section 4081 or 4091 of such Code, as the case may be, is allowable for such use.

"(5) Exception for fuel held in vehicle tank. No tax shall be imposed by paragraph (1) on gasoline or diesel fuel held in the tax of a motor vehicle or motorboat.

"(6) Exception for certain amounts of fuel.

"(A) In general. No tax shall be imposed by paragraph (1)—

"(i) on gasoline held on October 1, 1993, by any person if the aggregate amount of gasoline held by such person on such date does not exceed 4,000 gallons, and

"(ii) on diesel fuel or aviation fuel held on October 1, 1993, by any person if the aggregate amount of diesel fuel or aviation fuel held by such person on such date does not exceed 2,000 gallons.

"The preceding sentence shall apply only if such person submits to the Secretary (at the time and in the manner required by the Secretary) such information as the Secretary shall require for purposes of this paragraph.

"(B) Exempt fuel. For purposes of subparagraph (A), there shall not be taken into account fuel held by any person which is exempt from the tax imposed by paragraph (1) by reason of paragraph (4) or (5).

"(C) Controlled groups. For purposes of this paragraph—

"(i) Corporations.

"(I) In general. All persons treated as a controlled group shall be treated as 1 person.

"(II) Controlled group. The term 'controlled group' has the meaning given to such term by subsection (a) of section 1563 of such Code; except that for such purposes the phrase 'more than 50 percent' shall be substituted for the phrase 'at least 80 percent' each place it appeals in such subsection.

"(ii) Nonincorporated persons under common control. Under regulations prescribed by the Secretary, principles similar to the principles of clause (i) shall apply to a group of persons under common control where 1 or more of such persons is not a corporation.

"(7) Other law applicable. All provisions of law, including penalties, applicable with respect to the taxes imposed by section 4081 of such Code in the case of gasoline and section 4091 of such Code in the case of diesel fuel and aviation fuel shall, insofar as applicable and not inconsistent with the provisions of this subsection, apply with respect to the floor stock taxes imposed by paragraph (1) to the same extent as if such taxes were imposed by such section 4081 or 4091."

Matter in *italics* in Code Sec. 4081(a)(2)(B)(iii) as amended by section 13242(a) of P.L. 103-66, before amendment by section 13242(a) of P.L. 103-66, struck out:

"(iii) the deficit reduction rate is 2.5 cents a gallon."

Effective Date (Sec. 13241(g) of P.L. 103-66) effective 10/1/93.

the amount of the tax so paid shall be allowed as a credit against the tax imposed by reason of paragraph (1).

(c) Taxable fuels mixed with alcohol. *Under regulations prescribed by the Secretary.*

(1) In general. *The rate of tax under subsection (a) shall be the alcohol mixture rate in the case of the removal or entry of any qualified alcohol mixture.*

(2) Tax prior to mixing.

(A) In general. In the case of the removal or entry of any taxable fuel for use in producing at the time of such removal or entry a qualified alcohol mixture, the rate of tax under subsection (a) shall be the applicable fraction of the alcohol mixture rate. Subject to such terms and conditions as the Secretary may prescribe (including the application of section 4101), the treatment under the preceding sentence also shall apply to use in producing a qualified alcohol mixture after the time of such removal or entry.

(B) Applicable fraction. For purposes of subparagraph (A), the applicable fraction is—

(i) in the case of a qualified alcohol mixture which contains gasoline, the fraction the numerator of which is 10 and the denominator of which is—

(I) 9 in the case of 10 percent gasohol,

(II) 9.23 in the case of 7.7 percent gasohol, and

(III) 9.43 in the case of 5.7 percent gasohol, and

(ii) in the case of a qualified alcohol mixture which does not contain gasoline, $^{10}/_{9}$.

(3) Alcohol; qualified alcohol mixture. *For purposes of this subsection—*

(A) Alcohol. The term "alcohol" includes methanol and ethanol but does not include alcohol produced from petroleum, natural gas, or coal (including peat). Such term does not include alcohol with a proof of less than 190 (determined without regard to any added denaturants).

(B) Qualified alcohol mixture. The term "qualified alcohol mixture" means—

(i) any mixture of gasoline with alcohol if at least 5.7 percent of such mixture is alcohol, and

(ii) any mixture of diesel fuel with alcohol if at least 10 percent of such mixture is alcohol.

(4) Alcohol mixture rates for gasoline mixtures. *For purposes of this subsection—*

(A) In general. The alcohol mixture rate for a qualified alcohol mixture which contains gasoline is the excess of the rate which would (but for this paragraph) be determined under subsection (a) over—

(i) 5.4 cents per gallon for 10 percent gasohol,

(ii) 4.158 cents per gallon for 7.7 percent gasohol, and

(iii) 3.078 cents per gallon for 5.7 percent gasohol.

In the case of mixture none of the alcohol in which consists of ethanol, clauses (i), (ii), and (iii) shall be applied by substituting "6 cents" for "5.4 cents", "4.62 cents" for "4.158 cents", and "3.42 cents" for "3.078 cents".

(B) 10 percent gasohol. The term "10 percent gasohol" means any mixture of gasoline with alcohol if at least 10 percent of such mixture is alcohol.

(C) 7.7 percent gasohol. The term "7.7 percent gasohol" means any mixture of gasoline with alcohol if at least 7.7 percent, but not 10 percent or more, of such mixture is alcohol.

(D) 5.7 percent gasohol. The term "5.7 percent gasohol" means any mixture of gasoline with alcohol if at least 5.7 percent, but not 7.7 percent or more, of such mixture is alcohol.

(5) Alcohol mixture rate for diesel fuel mixtures. *The alcohol mixture rate for a qualified alcohol mixture which does not contain gasoline is the excess of the rate which would (but for this paragraph) be determined under subsection (a) over 5.4 cents per gallon (6 cents per gallon in the case of a qualified alcohol mixture none of the alcohol in which consists of ethanol).*

(6) Limitation. *In no event shall any alcohol mixture rate determined under this subsection be less than 4.3 cents per gallon.*

(7) Later separation of fuel from qualified alcohol mixture. *If any person separates the taxable fuel from a qualified alcohol mixture on which tax was imposed under subsection (a) at a rate determined under paragraph (1) or (2) (or with respect to which a credit or payment* *was allowed or made by reason of section 6427(f)(1)), such person shall be treated as the refiner of such taxable fuel. The amount of tax imposed on any removal of such fuel by such person shall be reduced by the amount of tax imposed (and not credited or refunded) on any prior removal or entry of such fuel.*

(8) Termination. *Paragraphs (1) and (2) shall not apply to any removal, entry, or sale after September 30, 2000.*

(d) Termination.

(1) In general. *On and after October 1, 1999, each rate of tax specified in subsection (a)(2)(A) shall be 4.3 cents per gallon.*

(2) Leaking Underground Storage Tank Trust Fund financing rate. *The Leaking Underground Storage Tank Trust Fund financing rate under subsection (a)(2) shall not apply after December 31, 1995.*

(e) Refunds in certain cases. *Under regulations prescribed by the Secretary, if any person who paid the tax imposed by this section with respect to any taxable fuel establishes to the satisfaction of the Secretary that a prior tax was paid (and not credited or refunded) with respect to such taxable fuel, then an amount equal to the tax paid by such person shall be allowed as a refund (without interest) to such person in the same manner as if it were an overpayment of tax imposed by this section.*

[For explanation, see ¶ 1002 and ¶ 1005, for text of Committee Report, see ¶ 3060]

[¶ 2133] Code Sec. 4082. [1] *Exemptions for diesel fuel.*

(a) In general. *The tax imposed by section 4081 shall not apply to diesel fuel—*

(1) *which the Secretary determines is destined for a nontaxable use,*

(2) *which is indelibly dyed in accordance with regulations which the Secretary shall prescribe, and*

(3) *which meets such marking requirements (if any) as may be prescribed by the Secretary in regulations.*

Such regulations shall allow an individual choice of dye color approved by the Secretary or chosen from any list of approved dye colors that the Secretary may publish.

(b) Nontaxable use. *For purposes of this section, the term "nontaxable use" means—*

(1) *any use which is exempt from the tax imposed by section 4041(a)(1) other than by reason of a prior imposition of tax,*

(2) *any use in a train, and*

(3) *any use described in section 6427(b)(1) (after the application of section 6427(b)(3)).*

(c) Regulations. *The Secretary shall prescribe such regulations as may be necessary to carry out this section, including regulations requiring the conspicuous labeling of retail diesel fuel pumps and other delivery facilities to assure that persons are aware of which feel is available only for nontaxable uses.*

(d) Cross Reference. *For tax on train and certain bus uses of fuel purchased tax-free, see section 4041(a)(1).*

[For explanation, see ¶ 1005]

[Footnote Code Sec. 4082] Matter in *italics* in Code Sec. 4082 added by section 13242(a) of P.L. 103-66, which struck out:

"Sec. 4082 Definitions.

"(a) Gasoline.

1. For purposes of this subpart, the term 'gasoline' includes, to the extent prescribed in regulations—

"(1) gasoline blend stocks, and

"(2) products commonly used as additives in gasoline.

For purposes of paragraph (1), the term 'gasoline blend stocks' means any petroleum product component of gasoline.

"(b) Certain uses defined as removal.

If a refiner, importer, terminal operator, blender, or compounder uses (other than in the production of gasoline or special fuels referred to in section 4041) gasoline refined, imported, blended, or compounded by him, such use shall for the purposes of this chapter be considered a removal."

Effective Date (Sec. 13242(e) of P.L. 103-66) effective 1/1/94.

[¶ 2134] Code Sec. 4083. [1] *Definitions; special rule; administrative authority.*

(a) Taxable fuel. *For purposes of this subpart—*

(1) In general. *The term "taxable fuel" means—*

(A) gasoline, and

(B) diesel fuel.

(2) Gasoline. *The term "gasoline" includes, to the extent prescribed in regulations—*

(A) gasoline blend stocks, and

(B) products commonly used as additives in gasoline.

For purposes of subparagraph (A), the term "gasoline blend stock" means any petroleum product component of gasoline.

(3) Diesel fuel. *The term "diesel fuel" means any liquid (other than gasoline) which is suitable for use as a fuel in a diesel-powered highway vehicle, a diesel-powered train, or a diesel-powered boat.*

(b) Certain uses defined as removal. *If any person uses taxable fuel (other than in the production of gasoline, diesel fuel, or special fuels referred to in section 4041), such use shall for the purposes of this chapter be considered a removal.*

(c) Administrative authority.

(1) In general. *In addition to the authority otherwise granted by this title, the Secretary may in administering compliance with this subpart, section 4041, and penalties and other administrative provisions related thereto—*

(A) enter any place at which taxable fuel is produced or is stored (or may be stored) for purposes of—

(i) examining the equipment used to determine the amount or composition of such fuel and the equipment used to store such fuel, and

(ii) taking and removing samples of such fuel, and

(B) detain, for the purposes referred in subparagraph (A), any container which contains or may contain any taxable fuel.

(2) Inspection sites. *The Secretary may establish inspection sites for purposes of carrying out the Secretary's authority under paragraph (1)(B).*

(3) Penalty for refusal of entry. *The penalty provided by section 7342 shall apply to any refusal to admit entry or other refusal to permit an action by the Secretary authorized by paragraph (1), except that section 7342 shall be applied by substituting "$1,000" for "$500" for each refusal.*

[For explanation, see ¶ 1005 and ¶ '1007]

[¶ 2135] Code Sec. 4084. Cross references.

(1) For provisions to relieve farmers from excise tax in the case of gasoline used on the farm for farming purposes, see section 6420.

[Footnote Code Sec. 4083] Matter in *italics* if Code Sec. 4083 added by section 13242(a) of P.L. 103-66, which struck out:

"Sec. 4083 **Cross references.**

1. "(1) For provisions to relieve farmers from excise tax in the case of gasoline used on the farm for farming purposes, see section 6420.

"(2) For provisions to relieve purchasers of gasoline from excise tax in the case of gasoline used for certain nonhighway purposes, used by local transit systems, or sold for certain exempt purposes, see section 6421.

"(3) For provisions to relieve purchasers of gasoline from excise tax in the case of gasoline not used for taxable purposes, see section 6427."

Effective Date (Sec. 13242(e) of P.L. 103-66) effective 1/1/94.

[Footnote Code Sec. 4084] Code Sec. 4084 was added by section 13242(a).

Effective Date (Sec. 13242(e) of P.L. 103-66) effective 1/1/94.

(2) For provisions to relieve purchasers of gasoline from excise tax in the case of gasoline used for certain nonhighway purposes, used by local transit systems, or sold for certain exempt purposes, see section 6421.

(3) For provisions to relieve purchasers from excise tax in the case of taxable fuel not used for taxable purposes, see section 6427.

[¶ 2136] Code Sec. 4091. [1] *Imposition of tax.*

(a) Tax on sale.

(1) In general. *There is hereby imposed a tax on the sale of aviation fuel by the producer or the importer thereof or by any producer of aviation fuel.*

[Footnote Code Sec. 4091] Matter in *italics* in Code Sec. 4091 added by section 13242(a) of P.L. 103-66 which struck out:

"Sec. 4091. Imposition of tax.

"(a) In general.

1. There is hereby imposed a tax on the sale of any taxable fuel by the producer or the importer thereof or by any producer of a taxable fuel.

"(b) Rate of tax.

"(1) In general. The rate of the tax imposed by subsection (a) shall be the sum of—

"(A)

"(i) the Highway Trust Fund financing rate and the diesel fuel deficit reduction rate in the case of diesel fuel, and

"(ii) the Airport and Airway Trust Fund financing rate *and the aviation fuel deficit reduction rate* in the case of aviation fuel, and

"(B) the Leaking Underground Storage Tank Trust Fund financing rate in the case of any taxable fuel.

"(2) Highway Trust Fund financing rate. For purposes of paragraph (1), except as provided in subsection (c), the Highway Trust Fund financing rate is 17.5 cents per gallon.

"(3) Airport and Airway Trust Fund financing rate. For purposes of paragraph (1), except as provided in subsection (d), the Airport and Airway Trust Fund financing rate is 17.5 cents per gallon.

"(4) Diesel fuel deficit reduction rate. For purposes of paragraph (1), except as provided in subsection (c), the diesel fuel deficit reduction rate is *6.8 cents* per gallon.

"(5) Leaking Underground Storage Tank Trust fund financing rate. For purposes of paragraph (1), except as provided in subsection (c), the Leaking Underground Storage Tank Trust Fund financing rate is 0.1 cent per gallon.

"*(6) Aviation fuel deficit reduction rate.For purposes of paragraph (1), the aviation fuel deficit reduction rate is 4.3 cents per gallon.*

"*(7)* Termination of rates.

"(A) The Highway Trust Fund financing rate shall not apply on and after October 1, 1999.

"(B) The Airport and Airway Trust Fund financing rate shall not apply on and after January 1, 1996.

"(C) The Leaking Underground Storage Tank Trust Fund financing rate shall not apply during any period during which the Leaking Underground Storage Tank Trust Fund financing rate under section 4081 does not apply.

"(D) The diesel fuel deficit reduction rate shall not apply on and after October 1, 1995.

"(c) Reduced rate of tax for diesel fuel in alcohol mixture, etc.

Under regulations prescribed by the Secretary—

"(1) In general. The Highway Trust Fund financing rate shall be—

"(A) 12.1 cents per gallon in the case of the sale of any mixture of diesel fuel if—

"(i) at least 10 percent of such mixture consists of alcohol (as defined in section 4081(c)(3)), and

"(ii) the diesel fuel in such mixture was not taxed under subparagraph (B), and

"(B) 13.44 cents per gallon in the case of the sale of diesel fuel for use (at the time of such sale) in producing a mixture described in subparagraph (A).

In the case of a sale described in subparagraph (B), the Leaking Underground Storage Tank Trust Fund financing rate and the diesel fuel deficit reduction rate shall be 10/9th of the otherwise applicable such rates.

"(2) Later separation. If any person separates the diesel fuel from a mixture of the diesel fuel and alcohol on which tax was imposed under subsection (a) at a Highway Trust Fund financing rate equivalent to 12.1 cents a gallon by reason of this subsection (or with respect to which a credit or payment was allowed or made by reason of section 6427(f)(1)), such person shall be treated as the producer of such diesel fuel. The amount of tax imposed on any sale of such diesel fuel by such person shall be reduced by the amount of tax imposed (and not credited or refunded) on any prior sale of such fuel.

"(3) Termination. Paragraph (1) shall not apply to any sale after September 30, 2000.

"(d) Reduced rate of tax for aviation fuel in alcohol mixture, etc.

"(1) In general. The Airport and Airway Trust Fund financing rate shall be—

"(A) 4.1 cents per gallon in the case of the sale of any mixture of aviation fuel if—

"(i) at least 10 percent of such mixture consists of alcohol (as defined in section 4081(c)(3)), and

"(ii) the aviation fuel in such mixture was not taxed under subparagraph (B), and

"(B) 4.56 cents per gallon in the case of the sale of aviation fuel for use (at the time of such sale) in producing a mixture described in subparagraph (A).

[Footnote Code Sec. 4091 continued]

In the case of a sale described in subparagraph (B), the Leaking Underground Storage Tank Trust Fund financing rate shall be 1/9 cent per gallon.

"(2) Later separation. If any person separates the aviation fuel from a mixture of the aviation fuel and alcohol on which tax was imposed under subsection (a) at the Airport and Airway Trust Fund financing rate equivalent to 4.1 cents per gallon by reason of this subsection (or with respect to which a credit or payment was allowed or made by reason of section 6427(f)(1)), such person shall be treated as the producer of such aviation fuel. The amount of tax imposed on any sale of such aviation fuel by such person shall be reduced by the amount of tax imposed (and not credited or refunded) on any prior sale of such fuel.

"(3) Termination. Paragraph (1) shall not apply to any sale after September 30, 2000.

"(e) Lower rates of tax on alcohol mixtures not made from ethanol.

In the case of a mixture described in subsection (c)(1)(A)(i) or (d)(1)(A)(i) none of the alcohol in which is ethanol—

"(1) subsections (c)(1)(A) and (c)(2), and subsections (d)(1)(A) and (d)(2), shall each be applied by substituting rates which are 0.6 cents less than the rates contained therein, and

"(2) subsections (c)(1)(B) and (d)(1)(B) shall be applied by substituting rates which are 10/9 of the rates determined under paragraph (1)."

Effective Date (Sec. 13242(e) of P.L. 103-66) effective 1/1/94.

Section 13241(h) of P.L. 103-66, regarding floor stocks taxes provides:

"(h) Floor stocks taxes.—

"(1) Imposition of tax.—In the case of gasoline, diesel fuel, and aviation fuel on which tax was imposed under section 4081 or 4091 of the Internal Revenue Code of 1986 before October 1, 1993, and which is held on such date by any person, there is hereby imposed a floor stocks tax of 4.3 cents per gallon on such gasoline, diesel fuel, and aviation fuel.

"(2) Liability for tax and method of payment.—

"(A) Liability for tax.—A person holding gasoline, diesel fuel, or aviation fuel on October 1, 1993, to which the tax imposed by paragraph (1) applies shall be liable for such tax.

"(B) Method of payment.—The tax imposed by paragraph (1) shall be paid in such manner as the Secretary shall prescribe.

"(C) Time for payment.—The tax imposed by paragraph (1) shall be paid on or before November 30, 1993.

"(3) Definitions.—For purposes of this subsection—

"(A) Held by a person.—Gasoline, diesel fuel, and aviation fuel shall be considered as 'held by a person' if title thereto has passed to such person (whether or not delivery to the person has been made).

"(B) Gasoline.—The term 'gasoline' has the meaning given such term by section 4082 of such Code.

"(C) Diesel fuel.—The term 'diesel fuel' has the meaning given such term by section 4092 of such Code.

"(D) Aviation fuel.—The term 'aviation fuel' has the meaning given such term by section 4092 of such Code.

"(E) Secretary.—The term 'Secretary' means the Secretary of the Treasury or his delegate.

"(4) Exception for exempt uses.—The tax imposed by paragraph (1) shall not apply to gasoline, diesel fuel, or aviation fuel held by any person exclusively for any use to the extent a credit or refund of the tax imposed by section 4081 or 4091 of such Code, as the case may be, is allowable for such use.

"(5) Exception for fuel held in vehicle tank.—No tax shall be imposed by paragraph (1) on gasoline or diesel fuel held in the tax of a motor vehicle or motorboat.

"(6) Exception for certain amounts of fuel.—

"(A) In general.—No tax shall be imposed by paragraph (1)—

"(i) on gasoline held on October 1, 1993, by any person if the aggregate amount of gasoline held by such person on such date does not exceed 4,000 gallons, and

"(ii) on diesel fuel or aviation fuel held on October 1, 1993, by any person if the aggregate amount of diesel fuel or aviation fuel held by such person on such date does not exceed 2,000 gallons.

The preceding sentence shall apply only if such person submits to the Secretary (at the time and in the manner required by the Secretary) such information as the Secretary shall require for purposes of this paragraph.

"(B) Exempt fuel.—For purposes of subparagraph (A), there shall not be taken into account fuel held by any person which is exempt from the tax imposed by paragraph (1) by reason of paragraph (4) or (5).

"(C) Controlled groups.—For purposes of this paragraph—

"(i) Corporations.—

"(I) In general.—All persons treated as a controlled group shall be treated as 1 person.

"(II) Controlled group.—The term 'controlled group' has the meaning given to such term by subsection (a) of section 1563 of such Code; except that for such purposes the phrase 'more than 50 percent' shall be substituted for the phrase 'at least 80 percent' each place it appeals in such subsection.

"(ii) Nonincorporated persons under common control.—Under regulations prescribed by the Secretary, principles similar to the principles of clause (i) shall apply to a group of persons under common control where 1 or more of such persons is not a corporation.

"(7) Other law applicable.—All provisions of law, including penalties, applicable with respect to the taxes imposed by section 4081 of such Code in the case of gasoline and section 4091 of such Code in the case of diesel fuel and aviation fuel shall, insofar as applicable and not inconsistent with the provisions of this subsection, apply with respect to the floor stock taxes imposed by paragraph (1) to the same extent as if such taxes were imposed by such section 4081 or 4091."

Section 13243 of P.L. 103-66 regarding floor stocks tax provides:

"SEC. 13243. FLOOR STOCKS TAX.

"(a) In general.—There is hereby imposed a floor stocks tax on diesel fuel held by any person on January 1, 1994, if—

"(1) no tax was imposed on such fuel under section 4041(a) or 4091 of the Internal Revenue Code of 1986 as in effect on December 31, 1993, and

[Footnote Code Sec. 4091 continued]

"(2) tax would have been imposed by section 4081 of such Code, as amended by this Act, on any prior removal, entry, or sale of such fuel had such section 4081 applied to such fuel for periods before January 1, 1994.

"(b) Rate of tax.—The rate of the tax imposed by subsection (a) shall be the amount of tax which would be imposed under section 4081 of the Internal Revenue Code of 1986 if there were a taxable sale of such fuel on such date.

"(c) Liability and payment of tax.—

"(1) Liability for tax.—A person holding the diesel fuel on January 1, 1994, to which the tax imposed by this section applies shall be liable for such tax.

"(2) Method of payment.—The tax imposed by this section shall be paid in such manner as the Secretary shall prescribe.

"(3) Time for payment.—The tax imposed by this section shall be paid on or before July 31, 1994.

"(d) Definitions.—For purposes of this section—

"(1) Diesel fuel.—The term 'diesel fuel' has the meaning given such term by section 4083(a) of such Code.

"(2) Secretary.—The term 'Secretary' means the Secretary of the Treasury or his delegate.

"(e) Exceptions.—

"(1) Persons entitled to credit or refund.—The tax imposed by this section shall not apply to fuel held by any person exclusively for any use to the extent a credit or refund of the tax imposed by section 4081 is allowable for such use.

"(2) Compliance with dyeing required.—Paragraph (1) shall not apply to the holder of any fuel if the holder of such fuel fails to comply with any requirement imposed by the Secretary with respect to dyeing and marking such fuel.

"(f) Other laws applicable.—All provisions of law, including penalties, applicable with respect to the taxes imposed by section 4081 of such Code shall, insofar as applicable and not inconsistent with the provisions of this section, apply with respect to the floor stock taxes imposed by this section to the same extent as if such taxes were imposed by such section 4081.

Section 13254 of P.L. 103-66 regarding floor stocks taxes provides:

"Sec. 13245. Floor stocks tax on commercial aviation fuel held on October 1, 1995.

"(a) Imposition of tax.—In the case of commercial aviation fuel on which tax was imposed under section 4091 of the Internal Revenue Code of 1986 before October 1, 1995, and which is held on such date by any person, there is hereby imposed a floor stocks tax of 4.3 cents per gallon.

"(b) Liability for tax and method of payment.—

"(1) Liability for tax.—A person holding aviation fuel on October 1, 1995, to which the tax imposed by subsection (a) applies shall be liable for such tax.

"(2) Method of payment.—The tax imposed by subsection (a) shall be paid in such manner as the Secretary shall prescribe.

"(3) Time for payment.—The tax imposed by subsection (a) shall be paid on or before April 30, 1996.

"(c) Definitions.—For purposes of this subsection—

"(1) Held by a person.—Aviation fuel shall be considered as 'held by a person' if title thereto has passed to such person whether or not delivery to the person has been made).

"(2) Commercial aviation fuel.—The term 'commercial aviation fuel' means aviation fuel (as defined in section 4093 of such Code) which is held on October 1, 1995, for sale or use in commercial aviation (as defined in section 4092(b) of such Code).

"(3) Secretary.—The term 'Secretary' means the Secretary of the Treasury or his delegate.

"(d) Exception for exempt uses.—The tax imposed by subsection (a) shall not apply to aviation fuel held by any person exclusively for any use for which a credit or refund of the entire tax imposed by section 4091 of such Code is allowable for aviation fuel purchased after September 30, 1995, for such use.

"(e) Exception for certain amounts of fuel.—

"(1) In general.—No tax shall be imposed by subsection (a) on aviation fuel held on October 1, 1995, by any person if the aggregate amount of commercial aviation fuel held by such person on such date does not exceed 2,000 gallons. The preceding sentence shall apply only if such person submits to the Secretary (at the time and in the manner required by the Secretary) such information as the Secretary shall require for purposes of this paragraph.

"(2) Exempt fuel.—For purposes of paragraph (1), there shall not be taken into account fuel held by any person which is exempt from the tax imposed by subsection (a) by reason of subsection (d).

"(3) Controlled groups.—For purposes of this subsection—

"(A) Corporations.—

"(i) In general.—All persons treated as a controlled group shall be treated as 1 person.

"(ii) Controlled group.—The term 'controlled group' has the meaning given to such term by subsection (a) of section 1563 of such Code; except that for such purposes the phrase 'more than 50 percent' shall be substituted for the phrase 'at least 80 percent' each place it appears in such subsection.

"(B) Nonincorporated persons under common control.—Under regulations prescribed by the Secretary, principles similar to the principles of subparagraph (A) shall apply to a group of persons under common control where 1 or more of such persons is not a corporation.

"(f) Other law applicable.—All provisions of law, including penalties, applicable with respect to the taxes imposed by section 4091 of such Code shall, insofar as applicable and not inconsistent with the provisions of this section, apply with respect to the floor stock taxes imposed by subsection (a) to the same extent as if such taxes were imposed by such section 4091."

Matter in *italics* in Code Sec. 4091(b)(1)(A)(ii), (b)(4), (b)(6) and (7) before amended by section 13242(a) was added by section 13241(b)(1), (b)(2)(B)(i), and (b)(2)(B)(ii) which struck out '2.5 cents', '(6)'

Effective Date (Sec. 13241(g) of P.L. 103-66) effective 10/1/93.

(2) ***Use treated as sale.*** *For purposes of paragraph (1), if any producer uses aviation fuel (other than for a nontaxable use as defined in section 6427(l)(2)(B)) on which no tax has been imposed under such paragraph, then such use shall be considered a sale.*

(b) Rate of tax.

(1) ***In general.*** *The rate of the tax imposed by subsection (a) shall be 21.8 cents per gallon.*

(2) ***Leaking Underground Storage Tank Trust Fund tax.*** *The rate of tax specified in paragraph (1) shall be increased by 0.1 cent per gallon. The increase in tax under this paragraph shall in this title be referred to as the Leaking Underground Storage Tank Trust Fund financing rate.*

(3) ***Termination.***

(A) On and after January 1, 1996, the rate of tax specified in paragraph (1) shall be 4.3 cents per gallon.

(B) The Leaking Underground Storage Tank Trust Fund financing rate shall not apply during any period during which the Leaking Underground Storage Tank Trust Fund financing rate under section 4081 does not apply.

(c) Reduced rate of tax for aviation fuel in alcohol mixture, etc. *Under regulations prescribed by the Secretary.*

(1) ***In general.*** *The rate of tax under subsection (a) shall be reduced by 13.4 cents per gallon in the case of the sale of any mixture of aviation fuel if—*

(A) at least 10 percent of such mixture consists of alcohol (as defined in section 4081(c)(3)), and

(B) the aviation fuel in such mixture was not taxed under paragraph (2).

In the case of such a mixture none of the alcohol in which is ethanol, the preceding sentence shall be applied by substituting "14 cents" for "13.4 cents".

(2) ***Tax prior to mixing.*** *In the case of the sale of aviation fuel for use (at the time of such sale) in producing a mixture described in paragraph (1), the rate of tax under subsection (a) shall be 10/9 of the rate which would (but for this paragraph) have been applicable to such mixture had such mixture been created prior to such sale.*

(3) ***Later separation.*** *If any person separates the aviation fuel from a mixture of the aviation fuel and alcohol on which tax was imposed under subsection (a) at a rate determined under paragraph (1) or (2) (or with respect to which a credit or payment was allowed or made by reason of section 6427(f)(1)), such person shall be treated as the producer of such aviation fuel. The amount of tax imposed on any sale of such aviation fuel by such person shall be reduced by the amount of tax imposed (and not credited or refunded) on any prior sale of such fuel.*

(4) ***Limitation.*** *In no event shall any rate determined under paragraph (1) be less than 4.3 cents per gallon.*

(5) ***Termination.*** *Paragraphs (1) and (2) shall not apply to any sale after September 30, 2000.*

[For explanation, see ¶ 1002 and ¶ 1005, for text of Committee Report, see ¶ 3059]

[¶ 2137] **Code Sec. 4092.** [1] *Exemptions.*

(a) Nontaxable uses. *No tax shall be imposed by section 4091 on aviation fuel sold by a producer or importer for use by the purchaser in a nontaxable use (as defined in section 6427(1)(2)(B)).*

[Footnote Code Sec. 4092] Matter in *italics* in Code Sec. 4092 added by section 13242(a) of P.L. 103-66, which struck out:

"Sec. 4092 Definitions.

"(a) Taxable fuel.

1. For purposes of this subpart—

"(1) In general. The term 'taxable fuel' means—

"(A) diesel fuel, and

(b) No exemption from certain taxes on fuel used in commercial aviation. *In the case of fuel sold for use in commercial aviation (other than supplies for vessels or aircraft within the meaning of section 4221(d)(3)), subsection (a) shall not apply to so much of the tax imposed by section 4091 as is attributable to—*

(1) the Leaking Underground Storage Tank Trust Fund financing rate imposed by such section, and

(2) in the case of fuel sold after September 30, 1995, 4.3 cents per gallon of the rate specified in section 4091(b)(1).

For purposes of the preceding sentence, the term "commercial aviation" means any use of an aircraft other than in noncommercial aviation (as defined in section 4041(c)(4)).

(c) Sales to producer. *Under regulations prescribed by the Secretary, the tax imposed by section 4091 shall not apply to aviation fuel sold to a producer of such fuel.*

[For explanation, see ¶ 1005 for text of Committee, see ¶ 3024

[¶ 2138] **Code Sec. 4093.** [1] *Definitions.*

(a) Aviation fuel. *For purposes of this subpart, the term "aviation fuel" means any liquid (other than any product taxable under section 4081) which is suitable for use as a fuel in an aircraft.*

[Footnote Code Sec. 4093 continued]

"(B) aviation fuel.

"(2) Diesel fuel. The term 'diesel fuel' means any liquid (other than any product taxable under section 4081) which is suitable for use as a fuel in *a diesel-powered highway vehicle, a diesel-powered train, or diesel-powered boat.*

"(3) Aviation fuel. The term 'aviation fuel' means any liquid (other than any product taxable under section 4081) which is suitable for use as a fuel in an aircraft.

"(b) Producer.

For purposes of this subpart—

"(1) Certain persons treated as producers.

"(A) In general. The term 'producer' includes any person described in subparagraph (B) who elects to register under section 4101 with respect to the tax imposed by section 4091.

"(B) Persons described. A person is described in this subparagraph if such person is—

"(i) a refiner, compounder, blender, or wholesale distributor of a taxable fuel, or

"(ii) a dealer selling any taxable fuel exclusively to producers of such taxable fuel, or

"(iii) a retailer selling diesel fuel exclusively to purchasers as supplies for *vessels for use in an off-highway business use (as defined in section 6421(e)(2)(B)).*

To the extent provided in regulations, a retailer shall not be treated as not described in clause (iii) by reason of selling de minimis amounts of diesel fuel other than as supplies for *vessels for use in an off-highway business use (as defined in section 6421(e)(2)(B)).*

"(C) Tax-free purchasers treated as producers. Any person to whom any taxable fuel is sold tax-free under this subpart shall be treated as the producer of such fuel.

"(2) Wholesale distributor. For purposes of paragraph (1), the term 'wholesale distributor' includes any person who sells a taxable fuel to producers, retailers, or to users who purchase in bulk quantities and deliver into bulk storage tanks. Such term does not include any person who (excluding the term 'wholesale distributor' from paragraph (1)) is a producer or importer."

Effective Date (Sec. 13242(e) of P.L. 103-66) effective 1/1/94

Matter in *italics* in Code Sec. 4092(a)(2) and (b)(1) before amendment by section 13242(a) of P.L. 103-66, added by section 13163(a)(1) and (3) of P.L. 103-66 which struck out 'or a diesel-powered train' and 'commercial and noncommercial vessels'

Effective Date (Sec. 13163(d) of P.L. 103-66) effective 1/1/94.

[Footnote Code Sec. 4093] Matter in *italics* in Code Sec. 4093 added by section 13242(a) of P.L. 103-66 which struck out:

"Sec. 4093. Exemptions; special rule.

"(a) Heating oil.

1. The tax imposed by section 4091 shall not apply in the case of sales of any taxable fuel which the Secretary determines is destined for use as heating oil.

"(b) Sales to producer.

Under regulations prescribed by the Secretary, the tax imposed by section 4091 shall not apply in the case of sales of a taxable fuel to a producer of such fuel.

"(c) Exemption for nontaxable uses and bus uses.

"(1) In general. No tax shall be imposed by section 4091 on fuel sold by a producer or importer for use by the purchaser in a nontaxable use (as defined in section 6427(l)(2)) or a use described in section 6427(b)(1).

"(2) Exceptions.

(b) ***Producer.*** *For purposes of this subpart—*

(1) ***Certain persons treated as producers.***

(A) In general. The term "producer" includes any person described in subparagraph (B) and registered under section 4101 with respect to the tax imposed by section 4091.

(B) Persons described. A person is described in this subparagraph if such person is—

(i) a refiner, blender, or wholesale distributor of aviation fuel, or

[Footnote Code Sec. 4093 continued]

"(A) No exemption from certain taxes on fuel used in diesel-powered trains. In the case of fuel sold for use in a diesel-powered train, paragraph (1) shall not apply to so much of the tax imposed by section 4091 as is attributable to the Leaking Underground Storage Tank Trust Fund financing rate and the diesel fuel deficit reduction rate imposed under such section. The preceding sentence shall not apply in the case of fuel sold for exclusive use by a State or any political subdivision thereof.

" *(B) No exemption from Leaking Underground Storage Tank Trust Fund taxes on fuel used in commercial aviation. In the case of fuel sold for use in commercial aviation (other than supplies for vessels or aircraft within the meaning of section 4221(d)(3)), paragraph (1) also shall not apply to so much of the tax imposed by section 4091 as is attributable to the Leaking Underground Storage Tank Trust Fund financing rate imposed by such section. For purposes of the preceding sentence, the term "commercial aviation, means any use of an aircraft other than in noncommercial aviation (as defined in section 4041(c)(4)).*

"*(C) Certain bus uses. Paragraph (1) shall not apply to so much of the tax imposed by section 4091 as is not refundable by reason of the application of section 6427(b)(2)(A).*

"(3) Registration required. Except to the extent provided by the Secretary, paragraph (1) shall not apply to any sale unless—

"(A) both the seller and the purchaser are registered under section 4101, and

"(B) the purchaser's name, address, and registration number under such section are provided to the seller.

"(4) Information reporting.

"(A) Returns by producers and importers. Each producer or importer who makes a reduced-tax sale during the calendar year shall make a return (at such time and in such form as the Secretary may by regulations prescribe) showing with respect to each such sale—

"(i) the name, address, and registration number under section 4101 of the purchaser,

"(ii) the amount of fuel sold, and

"(iii) such other information as the Secretary may require.

"(B) Statements to purchasers. Every person required to make a return under subparagraph (A) shall furnish to each purchaser whose name is required to be set forth on such return a written statement showing the name and address of the person required to make such return, the registration number under section 4101 of such person, and the information required to be shown on the return with respect to such purchaser. The written statement required under the preceding sentence shall be furnished to the purchaser on or before January 31 of the year following the calendar year for which the return under subparagraph (A) is required to be made.

"(C) Returns by purchasers. Each person who uses during the calendar year fuel purchased in a reduced-tax sale shall make a return (at such time and in such form as the Secretary may by regulations prescribe) showing—

"(i) whether such use was a nontaxable use (as defined in section 6427(l)(2)) or a use described in section 6427(b)(1) and the amount of fuel so used,

"(ii) the date of the sale of the fuel so used,

"(iii) the name, address, and registration number under section 4101 of the seller, and

"(iv) such other information as the Secretary may require.

"(D) Reduced-tax sale. For purposes of this paragraph, the term 'reduced-tax sale' means any sale of taxable fuel on which the amount of tax otherwise required to be paid under section 4091 is reduced by reason of paragraph (1) (other than sales described in subsections (a) and (b) of this section).

"(d) Certain aviation fuel sales.

Under regulations prescribed by the Secretary, the Leaking Underground Storage Tank Trust Fund financing rate *and the aviation fuel deficit reduction rate* under section 4091 shall not apply to aviation fuel sold for use or used as supplies for vessels or aircraft (within the meaning of section 4221(d)(3)).

"(e) Cross references.

"(1) For imposition of tax where certain uses of diesel fuel or aviation fuel occur before imposition of tax by section 4091, see subsections (a)(1) and (c)(1) of section 4041.

"(2) For provisions allowing a credit or refund for fuel not used for certain taxable purposes, see section 6427."

Effective Date (Sec. 13242(e) of P.L. 103-66) effective 1/1/94.

Matter in *italics* in Code Sec. 4093(c)(2)(A), (B) and (d) before amended by section 13242(a) of P.L. 103-66 was added by sections 13241(f)(3) and (4) which struck out:

"(A) Certain Leaking Underground Storage Tank Trust Fund taxes. In the case of fuel sold for use in—

"(i) a diesel-powered train, and

"(ii) an aircraft,

paragraph (1) shall not apply to so much of the tax imposed by section 4091 as is attributable to the Leaking Underground Storage Tank Trust Fund financing rate imposed by such section.

"(B) Deficit reduction tax on fuel used in trains. In the case of fuel sold for use in a diesel-powered train, paragraph (1) also shall not apply to so much of the tax imposed by section 4091 as is attributable to the diesel fuel deficit reduction rate imposed by such section."

Effective Date (Sec. 13241(g) of P.L. 103-66) effective 10/1/93.

(ii) a dealer selling aviation fuel exclusively to producers of aviation fuel.

(C) Reduced rate purchasers treated as producers. Any person to whom aviation fuel is sold at a reduced rate under this subpart shall be treated as the producer of such fuel.

(2) Wholesale distributor. *For purposes of paragraph (1), the term "wholesale distributor" includes any person who sells aviation fuel to producers, retailers, or to users who purchase in bulk quantities and accept delivery into bulk storage tanks. Such term does not include any person who (excluding the term "wholesale distributor" from paragraph (1)) is a producer or importer.*

[For explanation, see ¶s 1002, 1005, 1014, 1015

[¶ 2139] Code Sec. 4101. Registration and bond.

(a) Registration. Every person required by the Secretary to register under this section with respect to the tax imposed by section [1]*4041(a)(1), 4081,* or 4091 shall register with the Secretary at such time, in such form and manner, and subject to such terms and conditions, as the Secretary may by regulations prescribe. A registration under this section may be used only in accordance with regulations prescribed under this section.

* * * * * * * * * * * * *

[For explanation, see ¶ 1005.]

[¶ 2140] Code Sec. 4102. Inspection of records by local officers.

Under regulations prescribed by the Secretary, records required to be kept with respect to taxes under this part shall be open to inspection by such officers of a State, or a political subdivision of any such State, as shall be charged with the enforcement or collection of any tax on [1]*any taxable fuel (as defined in section 4083)* .

[For explanation, see ¶ 1005]

[¶ 2141] Code Sec. 4103. Certain additional persons liable for tax where willful failure to pay.

In any case in which there is a willful failure to pay the tax imposed by section [1]*4041(a)(1), 4081,* or 4091, each person

(1) who is an officer, employee, or agent of the taxpayer who is under a duty to assure the payment of such tax and who willfully fails to perform such duty, or

(2) who willfully causes the taxpayer to fail to pay such tax,

shall be jointly and severally liable with the taxpayer for the tax to which such failure relates.

[For explanation, see ¶ 1005]

[Footnote Code Sec. 4101] Matter in *italics* in Code Sec. 4101(a) was added by section 13242(d)(1) of P.L. 103-66 which struck out:

1. "4081"

Effective Date (Sec. 13242(e) of P.L. 103-66) effective 1/1/94.

[Footnote Code Sec. 4102] Matter in *italics* in Code Sec. 4102 added by section 13242(d)(2) of P.L. 103-66 which struck out:

1. "gasoline"

Effective Date (Sec. 13242(e) of P.L. 103-66) effective 1/1/94.

[Footnote Code Sec. 4103] Matter in *italics* in Code Sec. 4103 added by section 13242(d)(1) of P.L. 103-66 which struck out:

1. "4081"

Effective Date (Sec. 13242(e) of P.L. 103-66) effective 1/1/94.

[¶2142] Code Sec. 4131. Imposition of tax.

* * * * * * * * * * * * *

[1]*(c) Application of section. The tax imposed by this section shall apply—*

(1) after December 31, 1987, and before January 1, 1993, and

(2) during periods after the date of the enactment of the Revenue Reconciliation Act of 1993.

[For explanation, see ¶1020, for text of Committee Report, see ¶3076]

[¶2143] Code Sec. 4221. Certain tax-free sales.

* * * * * * * * * * * * *

(c) Manufacturer relieved from liability in certain cases. In the case of any article sold free of tax under this section (other than a sale to which subsection (b) applies), and in the case

[Footnote Code Sec. 4131] Matter in *italics* in Code Sec. 4131(c) added by section 13421(a) of P.L. 103-66 which struck out:

1. "(c) Termination of tax if amounts collected exceed projected fund liability.

"(1) In general. If the Secretary estimates under paragraph (3) that the Vaccine Injury Compensation Trust Fund would not have a negative projected balance were the tax imposed by this section to terminate as of the close of any applicable date, no tax shall be imposed by this section after such date. "(2) Applicable date. For purposes of paragraph (1), the term 'applicable date' means—

"(A) the close of any calendar quarter ending on or after December 31, 1992, and

"(B) the 1st date on which petitions may not be filed under section 2111 and 2111(a) of the Public Health Service Act by reason of section 2134 of such Act and each date thereafter.

"(3) Estimates by Secretary.

"(A) In general. The Secretary shall estimate the projected balance of the Vaccine Injury Compensation Trust Fund as of—

"(i) the close of each calendar quarter ending on or after December 31, 1992, and

"(ii) such other times as are appropriate in the case of applicable dates described in paragraph (2)(B).

"(B) Determination of projected balance. In determining the projected balance of the Fund as of any date, the Secretary shall assume that—

"(i) the tax imposed by this section will not apply after such date, and

"(ii) there shall be paid from such Trust Fund all claims made or to be made against such Trust Fund—

"(I) with respect to vaccines administered before October 1, 1992, in the case of an applicable date described in paragraph (2)(A), or

"(II) with respect to petitions filed under section 2111 or section 2111(a) of the Public Health Service Act, in the case of an applicable date described in paragraph (2)(B)."

Effective Date effective 8/10/93.

Section 13421(c) of P.L. 103-66 regarding floor stocks tax provides:

"(c) Floor stocks tax.

"(1) Imposition of tax. On any taxable vaccine—

"(A) which was sold by the manufacturer, producer, or importer on or before the date of the enactment of this Act,

"(B) on which no tax was imposed by section 4131 of the Internal Revenue Code of 1986 (or, if such tax was imposed, was credited or refunded), and

"(C) which is held on such date by any person for sale or use,

there is hereby imposed a tax in the amount determined under section 4131(b) of such Code.

"(2) Liability for tax and method of payment.

"(A) Liability for tax. The person holding any taxable vaccine to which the tax imposed by paragraph (1) applies shall be liable for such tax.

"(B) Method of payment. The tax imposed by paragraph (1) shall be paid in such manner as the Secretary shall prescribe by regulations.

"(C) Time for payment. The tax imposed by paragraph (1) shall be paid on or before the last day of the 6th month beginning after the date of the enactment of this Act.

"(3) Definitions. For purposes of this subsection, terms used in this subsection which are also used in section 4131 of such Code shall have the respective meanings such terms have in such section.

"(4) Other laws applicable. All provisions of law, including penalties, applicable with respect to the taxes imposed by section 4131 of such Code shall, insofar as applicable and not inconsistent with the provisions of this subsection, apply to the floor stocks taxes imposed by paragraph (1), to the same extent as if such taxes were imposed by such section 4131."

of any article sold free of tax under section 4001(c), [1]*4001(d)*, or 4053(a)(6), if the manufacturer in good faith accepts a certification by the purchaser that the article will be used in accordance with the applicable provisions of law, no tax shall thereafter be imposed under this chapter in respect of such sale by such manufacturer.

[¶ 2144] Code Sec. 4222. Registration.

* * * * * * * * * * * * *

(d) Registration in the case of certain other exemptions. The provisions of this section may be extended to, and made applicable with respect to, the exemptions provided by sections 4001(c), [1]*4001(d)* , 4053(a)(6), 4064(b)(1)(C), 4101, and 4182(b), and the exemptions authorized under section 4293 in respect of the taxes imposed by this chapter, to the extent provided by regulations prescribed by the Secretary.

[¶ 2145] Code Sec. 4977. Tax on certain fringe benefits provided by an employer.

* * * * * * * * * * * * *

(c) Effect of election on section 132(a). If—

(1) an election under this section is in effect with respect to an employer for any calendar year, and

(2) at all times on or after January 1, 1984, and before the close of the calendar year involved, substantially all of the employees of the employer were entitled to employee discounts on goods or services provided by the employer in 1 line of business,

for purposes of paragraphs (1) and (2) of section 132(a) (but not for purposes of section [1]*132(i)(2)*), all employees of any line of business of the employer which was in existence on January 1, 1984, shall be treated as employees of the line of business referred to in paragraph (2).

[¶ 2146] Code Sec. 4980B. Failure to satisfy continuation coverage requirements of group health plans.

* * * * * * * * * * * * *

(f) Continuation coverage requirements of group health plans.

(1) In general. A group health plan meets the requirements of this subsection only if *the coverage of the costs of pediatric vaccines (as defined under section 2162 of the Public Health Service Act) is not reduced below the coverage provided by the plan as of May 1, 1993, and only if* each qualified beneficiary who would lose coverage under the plan as a result of a

[Footnote Code Sec. 4221] Matter in *italics* in Code Sec. 4221(c) added by section 13161(b)(1) of P.L. 103-66 which struck out:
1. "4002(b), 4003(c), 4004(a)"
Effective Date (Sec. 13161(c) of P.L. 103-66) effective 1/1/93.
[Footnote Code Sec. 4222] Matter in *italics* in Code Sec. 4222(d) added by section 13161(b)(2) which struck out:
1. "4002(b), 4003(c), 4004(a)"
Effective Date (Sec. 13161(c) of P.L. 103-66) effective 1/1/93.
[Footnote Code Sec. 4977] Matter in *italics* in Code Sec. 4977(c) added by section 13213(d)(3)(D) of P.L. 103-66, which struck out:
1. "section 132(g)(2)"
Effective Date (Sec. 13213(e) of P.L. 103-66) effective for reimbursements or other payments in respect of expenses incurred after 12/31/93.
[Footnote Code Sec. 4980B] Matter in *italics* in Code Sec. 4980B(f)(1) was added by section 13422(a)
Effective Date (Sec. 13422(b) of P.L. 103-66) effective for plan yrs. begin. after 8/10/93.

qualifying event is entitled to elect, within the election period, continuation coverage under the plan.

* * * * * * * * * * * * *

[For explanation, see ¶ 803, for Committee Reports, see ¶ 3076.]

[¶ 2147] Code Sec. 5000. Certain group health plans.

(a) Imposition of tax. There is hereby imposed on any employer*(including a self-employed person)* or employee organization that contributes to a nonconforming group health plan a tax equal to 25 percent of the employer's or employee organization's expenses incurred during the calendar year for each group health plan to which the employer *(including a self-employed person)* or employee organization contributes.

(b) Group health plan and large group health plan. For purposes of this section—

[1]*(1) **Group health plan.** The term "group health plan" means a plan (including a self-insured plan) of, or contributed to by, an employer (including a self-employed person) or employee organization to provide health care (directly or otherwise) to the employees, former employees, the employer, others associated or formerly associated with the employer in a business relationship, or their families.*

(2) Large group health plan. The term "large group health plan" means a plan of, or contributed to by, an employer or employee organization (including a self-insured plan) to provide health care (directly or otherwise) to the employees, former employees, the employer, others associated or formerly associated with the employer in a business relationship, or their families, that covers employees of at least one employer that normally employed at least 100 employees on a typical business day during the previous calendar year. *For purposes of the preceding sentence—*

(A) all employers treated as a single employer under subsection (a) or (b) of section 52 shall be treated as a single employer,

(B) all employees of the members of an affiliated service group (as defined in section 414(m)) shall be treated as employed by a single employer, and

(C) leased employees (as defined in section 414(n)(2)) shall be treated as employees of the person for whom they perform services to the extent they are so treated under section 414(n).

(c) Nonconforming group health plan. For purposes of this section, the term "nonconforming group health plan" means a group health plan or large group health plan that at any time during a calendar year does not comply with the requirements of subparagraphs (A) and (C) or subparagraph (B), respectively, [2]*of paragraph (1), or with the requirements of paragraph (2), of section 1862(b)* of the Social Security Act.

[For text of Committee Report, see ¶ 3082]

[Footnote Code Sec. 5000] Matter in *italics* in Code Sec. 5000(a) and (b)(1) added by sections 13561(e)(2)(A)(i) and (ii) of P.L. 103-66 which struck out:

1. "(1) Group health plan. The term 'group health plan' means any plan of, or contributed to by, an employer (including a self-insured plan) to provide health care (directly or otherwise) to the employer's employees, former employees, or the families of such employees or former employees."

Effective Date effective 8/10/93.

Matter in *italics* in Code Sec. 5000(b)(2) and (b)(2)(A)-(C) was added by section 13561(d)(2) of P.L. 103-66.

Effective Date (Sec. 13561(d)(3) of P.L. 103-66) effective 90 days after 8/10/93.

Matter in *italics* in Code Sec. 5000(c) added by section 13561(e)(2)(A)(iii) which struck out:

2. "of section 1862(b)(1)"

Effective Date effective 8/10/93.

[¶2148] Code Sec. 6033. Returns by exempt organizations.

* * * * * * * * * * * *

(e) Special rules relating to lobbying activities.

(1) Reporting requirements.

(A) In general. If this subsection applies to an organization for any taxable year, such organization—

(i) shall include on any return required to be filed under subsection (a) for such year information setting forth the total expenditures of the organization to which section 162(e)(1) applies and the total amount of the dues or other similar amounts paid to the organization to which such expenditures are allocable, and

(ii) except as provided in paragraphs (2)(A)(i) and (3), shall, at the time of assessment or payment of such dues or other similar amounts, provide notice to each person making such payment which contains a reasonable estimate of the portion of such dues or other similar amounts to which such expenditures are so allocable.

(B) Organizations to which subsection applies.

(i) In general. This subsection shall apply to any organization which is exempt from taxation under this subtitle other than an organization described in section 501(c)(3).

(ii) Special rule for in-house expenditures. This subsection shall not apply to the in-house expenditures (within the meaning of section 162(e)(5)(B)(ii)) of an organization for a taxable year if such expenditures do not exceed $2,000. In determining whether a taxpayer exceeds the $2,000 limit under this clause, there shall not be taken into account overhead costs otherwise allocable to activities described in subparagraphs (A) and (D) of section 162(e)(1).

(C) Allocation. For purposes of this paragraph—

(i) In general. Expenditures to which section 162(e)(1) applies shall be treated as paid out of dues or other similar amounts to the extent thereof.

(ii) Carryover of lobbying expenditures in excess of dues. If expenditures to which section 162(e)(1) applies exceed the dues or other similar amounts for any taxable year, such excess shall be treated as expenditures to which section 162(e)(1) applies which are paid or incurred by the organization during the following taxable year.

(2) Tax imposed where organization does not notify.

(A) In general. If an organization—

(i) elects not to provide the notices described in paragraph (1)(A) for any taxable year, or

(ii) fails to include in such notices the amount allocable to expenditures to which section 162(e)(1) applies (determined on the basis of actual amounts rather than the reasonable estimates under paragraph (1)(A)(ii)),

then there is hereby imposed on such organization for such taxable year a tax in an amount equal to the product of the highest rate of tax imposed by section 11 for the taxable year and the aggregate amount not included in such notices by reason of such election or failure.

(B) Waiver where future adjustments made. The Secretary may waive the tax imposed by subparagraph (A)(ii) for any taxable year if the organization agrees to adjust its estimates under paragraph (1)(A)(ii) for the following taxable year to correct any failures.

(C) Tax treated as income tax. For purposes of this title, the tax imposed by subparagraph (A) shall be treated in the same manner as a tax imposed by chapter 1 (relating to income taxes).

[Footnote Code Sec. 6033] Matter in *italics* in Code Sec. 6033(e) and (f) added by Sec. 13222(c) of P.L. 103-66, which struck out:

1. "(e)"

Effective Date (Sec. 13222(e) of P.L. 103-66) effective for amounts paid or incurred after 12/31/93.

*(3) **Exception where dues generally nondeductible.** Paragraph (1)(A) shall not apply to an organization which establishes to the satisfaction of the Secretary that substantially all of the dues or other similar amounts paid by persons to such organization are not deductible without regard to section 162(e).*

(f) Cross reference. For provisions relating to statements, etc., regarding exempt status of organizations, see section 6001. For reporting requirements as to certain liquidations, dissolutions, terminations, and contractions, see section 6043(b). For provisions relating to penalties for failure to file a return required by this section, see section 6652(c). For provisions relating to information required in connection with certain plans of deferred compensation, see section 6058. [For explanation, see ¶ 307, for Committee Reports, see ¶ 3044.]

[¶ 2149] Code Sec. 6050P. Returns relating to the cancellation of indebtedness by certain financial entities.

(a) In general. Any applicable financial entity which discharges (in whole or in part) the indebtedness of any person during any calendar year shall make a return (at such time and in such form as the Secretary may by regulations prescribe) setting forth—

(1) the name, address, and TIN of each person whose indebtedness was discharged during such calendar year,

(2) the date of the discharge and the amount of the indebtedness discharged, and

(3) such other information as the Secretary may prescribe.

(b) Exception. Subsection (a) shall not apply to any discharge of less than $600.

(c) Definitions and special rules. For purposes of this section—

(1) Applicable financial entity. The term "applicable financial entity" means—

(A) any financial institution described in section 581 or 591(a) and any credit union,

(B) the Federal Deposit Insurance Corporation, the Resolution Trust Corporation, and the National Credit Union Administration, and any other Federal executive agency (as defined in section 6050M), and any successor or subunit of any of the foregoing, and

(C) any other corporation which is a direct or indirect subsidiary of an entity referred to in subparagraph (A) but only if, by virtue of being affiliated with such entity, such other corporation is subject to supervision and examination by a Federal or State agency which regulates entities referred to in subparagraph (A).

(2) Governmental units. In the case of an entity described in paragraph (1)(B), any return under this section shall be made by the officer or employee appropriately designated for the purpose of making such return.

(d) Statements to be furnished to persons with respect to whom information is required to be furnished. Every applicable financial entity required to make a return under subsection (a) shall furnish to each person whose name is required to be set forth in such return a written statement showing—

(1) the name and address of the entity required to make such return, and

(2) the information required to be shown on the return with respect to such person.

The written statement required under the preceding sentence shall be furnished to the person on or before January 31 of the year following the calendar year for which the return under subsection (a) was made.

[For explanation, see ¶ 1204 for text of Committee Report, see ¶ 3063

[Footnote Code Sec. 6050P] Code Sec. 6050P was added by section 13252(a) of P.L. 103-66.

Effective Date (Sec. 13252(d) of P.L. 103-66) effective for discharges of indebtedness after 12/31/93, except as provided in Sec. 13252(d)(2) of this Act, which reads as follows:. "(2) Governmental entities. In the case of an entity referred to in section 6050P(c)(1)(B) of the Internal Revenue Code of 1986 (as added by this section), the amendments made by this section shall apply to discharges of indebtedness after the date of the enactment of this Act."

[¶ 2150] Code Sec. 6096. Designation by individuals.

(a) In general. Every individual (other than a nonresident alien) whose income tax liability for the taxable year is [1]*$3* or more may designate that [1]*$3* shall be paid over to the Presidential Election Campaign Fund in accordance with the provisions of section 9006(a). In the case of a joint return of husband and wife having an income tax liability of [2]*$6* or more, each spouse may designate that [1]*$3* shall be paid to the fund.

* * * * * * * * * * * * *

[For explanation, see ¶ 122]

[¶ 2151] Code Sec. 6103. Confidentiality and disclosure of returns and return information.

* * * * * * * * * * * * *

(d) Disclosure to State tax officials and State and local law enforcement agencies.

* * * * * * * * * * * * *

(4) Availability and use of death information.

(A) In general. No returns or return information may be disclosed under paragraph (1) to any agency, body, or commission of any State (or any legal representative thereof) during any period during which a contract meeting the requirements of subparagraph (B) is not in effect between such State and the Secretary of Health and Human Services.

(B) Contractual requirements. A contract meets the requirements of this subparagraph if—

(i) such contract requires the State to furnish the Secretary of Health and Human Services information concerning individuals with respect to whom death certificates (or equivalent documents maintained by the State or any subdivision thereof) have been officially filed with it, and

(ii) such contract does not include any restriction on the use of information obtained by such Secretary pursuant to such contract, except that such contract may provide that such information is only to be used by the Secretary (or any other Federal agency) for purposes of ensuring that Federal benefits or other payments are not erroneously paid to deceased individuals.

Any information obtained by the Secretary of Health and Human Services under such a contract shall be exempt from disclosure under section 552 of title 5, United States Code, and from the requirements of section 552a of such title 5.

(C) Special exception. The provisions of subparagraph (A) shall not apply to any State which on July 1, 1993, was not, pursuant to a contract, furnishing the Secretary of Health and Human Services information concerning individuals with respect to whom death certificates (or equivalent documents maintained by the State or any subdivision thereof) have been officially filed with it.

* * * * * * * * * * * * *

(l) Disclosure of returns and return information for purposes other than tax administration.

* * * * * * * * * * * * *

[Footnote Code Sec. 6096] Matter in *italics* in Code Sec. 6096(a) added by sections 13441(a)(1) and (2) of P.L. 103-66 which struck out:
1. "$1"
2. "$2"

Effective Date (Sec. 13441(b) of P.L. 103-66) effective for tax returns required to be filed after 12/31/93.

(7) Disclosure of return information to Federal, State, and local agencies administering certain programs under the Social Security Act, the Food Stamp Act of 1977 or Title 38, United States Code, ***or certain housing assistance programs*** **.**

(A) Return information from Social Security Administration. The Commissioner of Social Security shall, upon written request, disclose return information from returns with respect to net earnings from self-employment (as defined in section 1402), wages (as defined in section 3121(a) or 3401(a)), and payments of retirement income, which have been disclosed to the Social Security Administration as provided by paragraph (1) or (5) of this subsection, to any Federal, State, or local agency administering a program listed in subparagraph (D).

(B) Return information from Internal Revenue Service. The Secretary shall, upon written request, disclose current return information from returns with respect to unearned income from the Internal Revenue Service files to any Federal, State, or local agency administering a program listed in subparagraph (D).

(C) Restriction on disclosure. The Commissioner of Social Security and the Secretary shall disclose return information under subparagraphs (A) and (B) only for purposes of, and to the extent necessary in, determining eligibility for, or the correct amount of, benefits under a program listed in subparagraph (D).

(D) Programs to which rule applies. The programs to which this paragraph applies are:

(i) aid to families with dependent children provided under a State plan approved under part A of title IV of the Social Security Act;

(ii) medical assistance provided under a State plan approved under title XIX of the Social Security Act;

(iii) supplemental security income benefits provided under title XVI of the Social Security Act, and federally administered supplementary payments of the type described in section 1616(a) of such Act (including payments pursuant to an agreement entered into under section 212(a) of Public Law 93-66);

(iv) any benefits provided under a State plan approved under title I, X, XIV, or XVI of the Social Security Act (as those titles apply to Puerto Rico, Guam, and the Virgin Islands);

(v) unemployment compensation provided under a State law described in section 3304 of this title;

(vi) assistance provided under the Food Stamp Act of 1977;

(vii) State-administered supplementary payments of the type described in section 1616(a) of the Social Security Act (including payments pursuant to an agreement entered into under section 212(a) of Public Law 93-66); [1]

(viii) (I) any needs-based pension provided under chapter 15 of title 38, United States Code, or under any other law administered by the Secretary of Veterans Affairs;

(II) parents' dependency and indemnity compensation provided under section 1315 of title 38, United States Code;

(III) health-care services furnished under sections 1710(a)(1)(I), 1710(a)(2), 1710(b), and 1712(a)(2)(B) of such title; and

(IV) compensation paid under chapter 11 of title 38, United States Code, at the 100 percent rate based solely on unemployability and without regard to the fact that the disability or disabilities are not rated as 100 percent disabling under the rating schedule.

Only return information from returns with respect to net earnings from self-employment and wages may be disclosed under this paragraph for use with respect to any pro-

[Footnote Code Sec. 6103] Matter in *italics* in Code Sec. 6103(l)(7)(D)(vii) added by section 13403(a)(1) of P.L. 103-66 which struck out:
1. "and"
Effective Date (Sec. 13403(a)(1) of P.L. 103-66) effective 8/10/93.

gram described in clause (viii)(IV). Clause (viii) shall not apply after [2]*September 30, 1998* [3]*; and*

(ix) any housing assistance program administered by the Department of Housing and Urban Development that involves initial and periodic review of an applicant's or participant's income, except that return information may be disclosed under this clause only on written request by the Secretary of Housing and Urban Development and only for use by officers and employees of the Department of Housing and Urban Development with respect to applicants for and participants in such programs.
Clause (ix) shall not apply after September 30, 1998.

* * * * * * * * * * * * *

(12) Disclosure of certain taxpayer identity information for verification of employment status of medicare beneficiary and spouse of medicare beneficiary.

(A) Return information from Internal Revenue Service. The Secretary shall, upon written request from the Commissioner of Social Security, disclose to the Commissioner available filing status and taxpayer identity information from the individual master files of the Internal Revenue Service relating to whether any medicare beneficiary identified by the Commissioner was a married individual (as defined in section 7703) for any specified year after 1986, and, if so, the name of the spouse of such individual and such spouse's TIN.

(B) Return information from Social Security Administration. The Commissioner of Social Security shall, upon written request from the Administrator of the Health Care Financing Administration, disclose to the Administrator the following information:

(i) The name and TIN of each medicare beneficiary who is identified as having received wages (as defined in section 3401(a)), *above an amount (if any) specified by the Secretary of Health and Human Services,* from a qualified employer in a previous year.

(ii) For each medicare beneficiary who was identified as married under subparagraph (A) and whose spouse is identified as having received wages, *above an amount (if any) specified by the Secretary of Health and Human Services,* from a qualified employer in a previous year—

(I) the name and TIN of the medicare beneficiary, and

(II) the name and TIN of the spouse.

(iii) With respect to each such qualified employer, the name, address, and TIN of the employer and the number of individuals with respect to whom written statements were furnished under section 6051 by the employer with respect to such previous year.

(C) Disclosure by Health Care Financing Administration. With respect to the information disclosed under subparagraph (B), the Administrator of the Health Care Financing Administration may disclose—

(i) to the qualified employer referred to in such subparagraph the name and TIN of each individual identified under such subparagraph as having received wages from the employer (hereinafter in this subparagraph referred to as the "employee") for purposes of determining during what period such employee or the employee's spouse may be (or have been) covered under a group health plan of the employer and what benefits are or were covered under the plan (including the name, address, and identifying number of the plan),

(ii) to any group health plan which provides or provided coverage to such an employee or spouse, the name of such employee and the employee's spouse (if the spouse is a medicare beneficiary) and the name and address of the employer, and, for the purpose of presenting a claim to the plan—

[Footnote Code Sec. 6103 continued]

Matter in *italics* in Code Sec. 6103(l)(7)(D)(viii) added by section 13401(a) of P.L. 103-66 which struck out:

2. "September 30, 1997"

Effective Date (Sec. 13401(a) of P.L. 103-66) effective 8/10/93.

Matter in *italics* in Code Sec. 6103(l)(7)(D)(viii) added by section 13403(a)(2) of P.L. 103-66 which struck out:

3. "."

Effective Date (Sec. 13403(a)(2) of P.L. 103-66) effective 8/10/93.

(I) the TIN of such employee if benefits were paid under title XVIII of the Social Security Act with respect to the employee during a period in which the plan was a primary plan (as defined in section 1862(b)(2)(A) of the Social Security Act), and

(II) the TIN of such spouse if benefits were paid under such title with respect to the spouse during such period, and

(iii) to any agent of such Administrator the information referred to in subparagraph (B) for purposes of carrying out clauses (i) and (ii) on behalf of such Administrator.

(D) Special rules.

(i) Restrictions on disclosure. Information may be disclosed under this paragraph only for purposes of, and to the extent necessary in, determining the extent to which any medicare beneficiary is covered under any group health plan.

(ii) Timely response to requests. Any request made under subparagraph (A) or (B) shall be complied with as soon as possible but in no event later than 120 days after the date the request was made.

(E) Definitions. For purposes of this paragraph—

(i) Medicare beneficiary. The term "medicare beneficiary" means an individual entitled to benefits under part A, or enrolled under part B, of title XVIII of the Social Security Act, but does not include such an individual enrolled in part A under section 1818.

[4]*(ii) Group health plan. The term "group health plan" means any group health plan (as defined in section 5000(b)(1)).*

(iii) Qualified employer. The term "qualified employer" means, for a calendar year, an employer which has furnished written statements under section 6051 with respect to at least 20 individuals for wages paid in the year.

(F) Termination. Subparagraphs (A) and (B) shall not apply to—

(i) any request made after September 30, [5]*1998* , and

(ii) any request made before such date for information relating to—

(I) [6]*1997* or thereafter in the case of subparagraph (A), or

(II) [7]*1998* or thereafter in the case of subparagraph (B).

(13) Disclosure of return information to carry out income contingent repayment of student loans.

(A) In general. The Secretary may, upon written request from the Secretary of Education, disclose to officers and employees of the Department of Education return information with respect to a taxpayer who has received an applicable student loan and whose loan repayment amounts are based in whole or in part on the taxpayer's income. Such return information shall be limited to—

(i) taxpayer identity information with respect to such taxpayer,

(ii) the filing status of such taxpayer, and

(iii) the adjusted gross income of such taxpayer.

(B) Restriction on use of disclosed information. Return information disclosed under subparagraph (A) may be used by officers and employees of the Department of Education only for the purposes of, and to the extent necessary in, establishing the appropriate income contingent repayment amount for an applicable student loan.

(C) Applicable student loan. For purposes of this paragraph, the term "applicable student loan" means—

(i) any loan made under the program authorized under part D of title IV of the Higher Education Act of 1965, and

---

[Footnote Code Sec. 6103 continued]

Matter in *italics* in Code Sec. 6103(l)(12)(E)(ii), (F)(i) through (F)(ii)(II) added by sections 13561(a)(2)(C)(i) through (iii) and (e)(2)(B) of P.L. 103-66 which struck out:

4. "(ii) Group health plan. The term 'group health plan' means—
"(I) any group health plan (as defined in section 5000(b)(1)), and
"(II) any large group health plan (as defined in section 5000(b)(2))."
5. "1995"
6. "1994"
7. "1995"

Effective Date (Sec. 13561(a)(2)(C)(i) through (iii) and (e)(2)(B) of P.L. 103-66) effective 8/10/93.

(ii) any loan made under part B or E of title IV of the Higher Education Act of 1965 which is in default and has been assigned to the Department of Education.

(D) Termination. This paragraph shall not apply to any request made after September 30, 1998.

(m) Disclosure of taxpayer identity information.

* * * * * * * * * * * * *

[8]***(4) Individuals who owe an overpayment of Federal Pell Grants or who have defaulted on student loans administered by the Department of Education.***

(A) In general. Upon written request by the Secretary of Education, the Secretary may disclose the mailing address of any taxpayer—

(i) who owes an overpayment of a grant awarded to such taxpayer under subpart 1 of part A of title IV of the Higher Education Act of 1965, or

(ii) who has defaulted on a loan—

(I) made under part B, D, or E of title IV of the Higher Education Act of 1965, or

(II) made pursuant to section 3(a)(1) of the Migration and Refugee Assistance Act of 1962 to a student at an institution of higher education,

for use only by officers, employees, or agents of the Department of Education for purposes of locating such taxpayer for purposes of collecting such overpayment or loan.

(B) Disclosure to educational institutions, etc. Any mailing address disclosed under subparagraph (A)(i) may be disclosed by the Secretary of Education to—

(i) any lender, or any State or nonprofit guarantee agency, which is participating [9]*under part B or D* of title IV of the Higher Education Act of 1965, or

(ii) any educational institution with which the Secretary of Education has an agreement [10]*under subpart 1 of part A, or part D or E,* of title IV of such Act,

for use only by officers, employees, or agents of such lender, guarantee agency, or institution whose duties relate to the collection of student loans for purposes of locating individuals who have defaulted on student loans made under such loan programs for purposes of collecting such loans.

* * * * * * * * * * * * *

(p) Procedure and recordkeeping.

* * * * * * * * * * * * *

(3) Records of inspection and disclosure.

(A) System of recordkeeping. Except as otherwise provided by this paragraph, the Secretary shall maintain a permanent system of standardized records or accountings of all requests for inspection or disclosure of returns and return information (including the reasons for and dates of such requests) and of returns and return information inspected or disclosed under this section. Notwithstanding the provisions of section 552a(c) of title 5, United States Code, the Secretary shall not be required to maintain a record or accounting of requests for inspection or disclosure of returns and return information, or of returns and return information inspected or disclosed, under the authority of subsections (c), (e), (h)(1), (3)(A), or (4), (i)(4), (7)(A)(ii), or (8), (k)(1), (2), or (6), (l)(1), (4)(B), (5), (7), (8), (9), (10), [11]*(11), (12), or (13), (m)* , or (n). The records or accountings required to be maintained

[Footnote Code Sec. 6103 continued]

Matter in *italics* in Code Sec. 6103(m)(4), (m)(4)(B)(i) and (ii), (p)(3)(A), (p)(4) and (p)(4)(F)(ii) added by sections 13402(b)(1) through (3)(B)(ii) of P.L. 103-66 which struck out:

8. "(4) **Individuals who have defaulted on student loans administered by the Department of Education.**

"(A) In general. Upon written request by the Secretary of Education, the Secretary may disclose the mailing address of any taxpayer who has defaulted on a loan—

"(i) made under part B or E of title IV of the Higher Education Act of 1965, or

"(ii) made pursuant to section 3(a)(1) of the Migration and Refugee Assistance Act of 1962 to a student at an institution of higher education,

for use only by officers, employees, or agents of the Department of Education for purposes of locating such taxpayer for purposes of collecting such loan."

9. "under part B"

10. "under part E"

11. "(11), or (12), (m)"

under this paragraph shall be available for examination by the Joint Committee on Taxation or the Chief of Staff of such joint committee. Such record or accounting shall also be available for examination by such person or persons as may be, but only to the extent, authorized to make such examination under section 552a(c)(3) of title 5, United States Code.

(B) Report by the Secretary. The Secretary shall, within 90 days after the close of each calendar year, furnish to the Joint Committee on Taxation a report with respect to, or summary of, the records or accountings described in subparagraph (A) in such form and containing such information as such joint committee or the Chief of Staff of such joint committee may designate. Such report or summary shall not, however, include a record or accounting of any request by the President under subsection (g) for, or the disclosure in response to such request of, any return or return information with respect to any individual who, at the time of such request, was an officer or employee of the executive branch of the Federal Government. Such report or summary, or any part thereof, may be disclosed by such joint committee to such persons and for such purposes as the joint committee may, by record vote of a majority of the members of the joint committee, determine.

(C) Public report on disclosures. The Secretary shall, within 90 days after the close of each calendar year, furnish to the Joint Committee on Taxation for disclosure to the public a report with respect to the records or accountings described in subparagraph (A) which—

(i) provides with respect to each Federal agency, each agency, body, or commission described in subsection (d), (i)(3)(B)(i), or (l)(6), and the General Accounting Office the number of—

(I) requests for disclosure of returns and return information,

(II) instances in which returns and return information were disclosed pursuant to such requests or otherwise,

(III) taxpayers whose returns, or return information with respect to whom, were disclosed pursuant to such requests, and

(ii) describes the general purposes for which such requests were made,

(4) **Safeguards.** Any Federal agency described in subsection (h)(2), (h)(6), (i)(1), (2), (3), (5), or (8), (j)(1) or (2), (l)(1), (2), (3), (5), [12]*(10), (11), or (13),* or (o)(1), the General Accounting Office, or any agency, body, or commission described in subsection (d), (i)(3)(B)(i) or (8) or (l)(6), (7), (8), (9), or (12) shall, as a condition for receiving returns or return information—

(A) establish and maintain, to the satisfaction of the Secretary, a permanent system of standardized records with respect to any request, the reason for such request, and the date of such request made by or of it and any disclosure of return or return information made by or to it;

(B) establish and maintain, to the satisfaction of the Secretary, a secure area or place in which such returns or return information shall be stored;

(C) restrict, to the satisfaction of the Secretary, access to the returns or return information only to persons whose duties or responsibilities require access and to whom disclosure may be made under the provisions of this title;

(D) provide such other safeguards which the Secretary determines (and which he prescribes in regulations) to be necessary or appropriate to protect the confidentiality of the returns or return information;

(E) furnish a report to the Secretary, at such time and containing such information as the Secretary may prescribe, which describes the procedures established and utilized by such agency, body, or commission or the General Accounting Office for ensuring the confidentiality of returns and return information required by this paragraph; and

(F) upon completion of use of such returns or return information—

(i) in the case of an agency, body, or commission described in subsection (d), (i)(3)(B)(i), or (l)(6), (7), (8), or (9), return to the Secretary such returns or return information (along with any copies made therefrom) or make such returns or return informa-

[Footnote Code Sec. 6103 continued]

12. "(10), or (11),"

tion undisclosable in any manner and furnish a written report to the Secretary describing such manner,

(ii) in the case of an agency described in subsections (h)(2), (h)(6), (i)(1), (2), (3), (5), or (8), (j)(1) or (2), (l)(1), (2), (3), (5), (10), [13]*(11), (12), or (13),* or (o)(1), or the General Accounting Office, either—

(I) return to the Secretary such returns or return information (along with any copies made therefrom),

(II) otherwise make such returns or return information undisclosable, or

(III) to the extent not so returned or made undisclosable, ensure that the conditions of subparagraphs (A), (B), (C), (D), and (E) of this paragraph continue to be met with respect to such returns or return information, and

(iii) in the case of the Department of Health and Human Services for purposes of subsection (m)(6), destroy all such return information upon completion of its use in providing the notification for which the information was obtained, so as to make such information undisclosable;

except that the conditions of subparagraphs (A), (B), (C), (D), and (E) shall cease to apply with respect to any return or return information if, and to the extent that, such return or return information is disclosed in the course of any judicial or administrative proceeding and made a part of the public record thereof. If the Secretary determines that any such agency, body, or commission or the General Accounting Office has failed to, or does not, meet the requirements of this paragraph, he may, after any proceedings for review established under paragraph (7), take such actions as are necessary to ensure such requirements are met, including refusing to disclose returns or return information to such agency, body, or commission or the General Accounting Office until he determines that such requirements have been or will be met. In the case of any agency which receives any mailing address under paragraph (2), (4), (6), or (7) of subsection (m) and which discloses any such mailing address to any agent, or which receives any information under subsection (l)(12)(B) and which discloses any such information to any agent, this paragraph shall apply to such agency and each such agent (except that, in the case of an agent, any report to the Secretary or other action with respect to the Secretary shall be made or taken through such agency). For purposes of applying this paragraph in any case to which subsection (m)(6) applies, the term "return information" includes related blood donor records (as defined in section 1141(h)(2) of the Social Security Act).

* * * * * * * * * * * *

[For explanation, see ¶s 1206, 1207, 1208, 1209, 1210 for text of Committee Report, see ¶s 3072, 3073, 3074, 3081, 3082

[¶ 2152] Code Sec. 6115. Disclosure related to quid pro quo contributions.

(a) Disclosure requirement. If an organization described in section 170(c) (other than paragraph (1) thereof) receives a quid pro quo contribution in excess of $75, the organization shall, in connection with the solicitation or receipt of the contribution, provide a written statement which—

(1) informs the donor that the amount of the contribution that is deductible for Federal income tax purposes is limited to the excess of the amount of any money and the value of any property other than money contributed by the donor over the value of the goods or services provided by the organization, and

(2) provide the donor with a good faith estimate of the value of such goods or services.

[Footnote Code Sec. 6103 continued]
13. "(11), or (12),"
Effective Date (Secs. 13402(b)(1) through (3)(B)(ii) of P.L. 103-66) effective 8/10/93.
[Footnote Code Sec. 6115] Code Sec. 6115 was added by section 13173(a) of P.L. 103-66.
Effective Date (Sec. 13173(d) of P.L. 103-66) effective for quid pro quo contributions made on or after 1/1/94.

(b) Quid pro quo contribution. For purposes of this section, the term "quid pro quo contribution" means a payment made partly as a contribution and partly in consideration for goods or services provided to the payor by the donee organization. A quid pro quo contribution does not include any payment made to an organization, organized exclusively for religious purposes, in return for which the taxpayer receives solely an intangible religious benefit that generally is not sold in a commercial transaction outside the donative context.
[For explanation, see ¶ 1202, for text of Committee Report, see ¶ 3005]

[¶ 2153] [1]*Code Sec. 6116.* **Cross reference.** For inspection of records, returns, etc., concerning gasoline or lubricating oils, see section 4102.

[¶ 2154] **Code Sec. 6206. Special rules applicable to excessive claims under sections 6420, 6421, and 6427.**
Any portion of a payment made under section 6420, 6421, or 6427 which constitutes an excessive amount (as defined in section 6675(b)), and any civil penalty provided by section 6675, may be assessed and collected as if it were a tax imposed by section 4081 (with respect to payments under sections 6420 and 6421), or [1]*4041, 4081, or 4091* (with respect to payments under section 6427) and as if the person who made the claim were liable for such tax. The period for assessing any such portion, and for assessing any such penalty, shall be 3 years from the last day prescribed for the filing of the claim under section 6420, 6421, or 6427, as the case may be.

[¶ 2155] **Code Sec. 6302. Mode or time of collection.**

* * * * * * * * * * * * *

(f) Time for deposit of taxes on gasoline*and diesel fuel*.

(1) General rule. Notwithstanding section 518 of the Highway Revenue Act of 1982, any person whose liability for tax under section 4081 is payable with respect to semimonthly periods shall, not later than September 27, make deposits of such tax for the period beginning on September 16 and ending on September 22.

(2) Special rule where due date falls on Saturday, Sunday, or holiday. If, but for this paragraph, the due date under paragraph (1) would fall on a Saturday, Sunday, or holiday in the District of Columbia, such due date shall be deemed to be the immediately preceding day which is not a Saturday, Sunday, or such a holiday.

* * * * * * * * * * * * *

[Footnote Code Sec. 6116] Matter in *italics* in Code Sec. 6116 was added by section 13173(a) of P.L. 103-66, which struck out:
1. "6115"
Effective Date (Sec. 13173(d) of P.L. 103-66) effective for quid pro contributions made on or after 1/1/94.
[Footnote Code Sec. 6206] Matter in *italics* in Code Sec. 6206 added by section 13242(d)(14) of P.L. 103-66 which struck out:
1. "4041 or 4091"
Effective Date (Sec. 13242(e) of P.L. 103-66) effective 1/1/94.

[¶ 2156] Code Sec. 6412. Floor stocks refunds.

(a) In general.

(1) Tires and [1]*taxable fuel.* Where before October 1, 1999, any article subject to the tax imposed by section 4071 or 4081 has been sold by the manufacturer, producer, or importer and on such date is held by a dealer and has not been used and is intended for sale, there shall be credited or refunded (without interest) to the manufacturer, producer, or importer an amount equal to the difference between the tax paid by such manufacturer, producer, or importer on his sale of the article and the amount of tax made applicable to such article on and after October 1, 1999, if claim for such credit or refund is filed with the Secretary on or before March 31, 2000, based upon a request submitted to the manufacturer, producer, or importer before January 1, 2000, by the dealer who held the article in respect of which the credit or refund is claimed, and, on or before March 31, 2000, reimbursement has been made to such dealer by such manufacturer, producer, or importer for the tax reduction on such article or written consent has been obtained from such dealer to allowance of such credit or refund. No credit or refund shall be allowable under this paragraph with respect to [1]*taxable fuel* in retail stocks held at the place where intended to be sold at retail, nor with respect to [1]*taxable fuel* held for sale by a producer or importer of [1]*taxable fuel.*

* * * * * * * * * * * *

[¶ 2157] Code Sec. 6413. Special rules applicable to certain employment taxes.

* * * * * * * * * * * *

(c) Special refunds.

(1) In general. If by reason of an employee receiving wages from more than one employer during a calendar year the wages received by him during such year exceed the contribution and benefit base (as determined under section 230 of the Social Security Act) which is effective with respect to such year, the employee shall be entitled (subject to the provisions of section 31(b)) to a credit or refund of any amount of tax, with respect to such wages, imposed by [1]*section 3101(a) or section 3201(a) (to the extent of so much of the rate applicable under section 3201(a) as does not exceed the rate of tax in effect under section 3101(a))* , or by both such sections, and deducted from the employee's wages (whether or not paid to the Secretary), which exceeds the tax with respect to the amount of such wages received in such year which is equal to such contribution and benefit base. The term "wages" as used in this paragraph shall, for purposes of this paragraph, include "compensation" as defined in section 3231(e).

(2) Applicability in case of Federal and State employees, employees of certain foreign affiliates, and governmental employees in Guam, American Samoa, and the District of Columbia.

(A) Federal employees. In the case of remuneration received from the United States or a wholly-owned instrumentality thereof during any calendar year, each head of a Federal agency or instrumentality who makes a return pursuant to section 3122 and each agent, designated by the head of a Federal agency or instrumentality, who makes a return pursuant to such section shall, for purposes of this subsection, be deemed a separate employer, and the term "wages" includes for purposes of this subsection the amount, not to exceed an amount

[Footnote Code Sec. 6412] Matter in *italics* in Code Sec. 6412(a)(1) added by section 13242(d)(16) of P.L. 103-66, which struck out:
1. "gasoline"
Effective Date (Sec. 13242(e) of P.L. 103-66) effective 1/1/94.
[Footnote Code Sec. 6413] Matter in *italics* in Code Sec. 6413(c)(1), (c)(2)(B) and (C) and (c)(3) added by sections 13207(d)(1) through (3) of P.L. 103-66 which struck out:
1. "section 3101 or section 3201"

equal to the contribution and benefit base (as determined under section 230 of the Social Security Act) for any calendar year with respect to which such contribution and benefit base is effective, determined by each such head or agent as constituting wages paid to an employee.

(B) State employees. For purposes of this subsection, in the case of remuneration received during any calendar year, the term "wages" includes such remuneration for services covered by an agreement made pursuant to section 218 of the Social Security Act as would be wages if such services constituted employment; the term "employer" includes a State or any political subdivision thereof, or any instrumentality of any one or more of the foregoing; the term "tax" or "tax imposed by [2]*section 3101(a)* " includes, in the case of services covered by an agreement made pursuant to section 218 of the Social Security Act, an amount equivalent to the tax which would be imposed by [3]*section 3101(a)* , if such services constituted employment as defined in section 3121; and the provisions of this subsection shall apply whether or not any amount deducted from the employee's remuneration as a result of an agreement made pursuant to section 218 of the Social Security Act has been paid to the Secretary.

(C) Employees of certain foreign affiliates. For purposes of paragraph (1) of this subsection, the term "wages" includes such remuneration for services covered by an agreement made pursuant to section 3121(l) as would be wages if such services constituted employment; the term "employer" includes any American employer which has entered into an agreement pursuant to section 3121(l); the term "tax" or "tax imposed by [4]*section 3101(a)* ," includes, in the case of services covered by an agreement entered into pursuant to section 3121(l), an amount equivalent to the tax which would be imposed by [5]*section 3101(a)* , if such services constituted employment as defined in section 3121; and the provisions of paragraph (1) of this subsection shall apply whether or not any amount deducted from the employee's remuneration as a result of the agreement entered into pursuant to section 3121(l) has been paid to the Secretary.

* * * * * * * * * * * * *

[6]***(3) Repealed.***

* * * * * * * * * * * * *

[¶ 2158] Code Sec. 6416. Certain taxes on sales and services.

(a) Condition to allowance.

* * * * * * * * * * * * *

(4) Wholesale distributors to administer credits and refunds of gasoline tax.

(A) In general. For purposes of this subsection, a wholesale distributor who purchases any [1]*gasoline* on which tax imposed by section 4081 has been paid and who sells the [1]*gas-*

[Footnote Code Sec. 6413 continued]

2. "section 3101"
3. "section 3101"
4. "section 3101"
5. "section 3101"
6. "(3) **Separate application for hospital insurance taxes.** In applying this subsection with respect to—

"(A) the tax imposed by section 3101(b) (or any amount equivalent to such tax), and

"(B) so much of the tax imposed by section 3201 as is determined at a rate not greater than the rate in effect under section 3101(b),

the applicable contribution base determined under section 3121(x)(2) for any calendar year shall be substituted for 'contribution and benefit base (as determined under section 230 of the Social Security Act)' each place it appears."

Effective Date (Secs. 13207(e) of P.L. 103-66) effective for 1994 and later calendar yrs.

[Footnote Code Sec. 6416] Matter in *italics* in Code Sec. 6416(a)(4)(A)-(B) and (b)(2)-(3)(B) added by sections 13242(d)(17)(A)-(19)(B) of P.L. 103-66 which struck out:

1. "product"

Matter in *italics* in Code Sec. 6416(a)(4)(A)-(B) and (b)(2)-(3)(B) added by sections 13242(d)(17)(A)-(19)(B) of P.L. 103-66 which struck out:

oline to its ultimate purchaser shall be treated as the person (and the only person) who paid such tax.

(B) Wholesale distributor. For purposes of subparagraph (A), the term "wholesale distributor" has the meaning given such term by [2]*section 4093(b)(2)* (determined by substituting [3]*"any gasoline taxable under section 4081" for "aviation fuel" therein).*

(b) Special cases in which tax payments considered overpayments. Under regulations prescribed by the Secretary, credit or refund (without interest) shall be allowed or made in respect of the overpayments determined under the following paragraphs:

* * * * * * * * * * * *

(2) Specified uses and resales. The tax paid under chapter 32 (or under subsection (a) or (d) of section 4041 in respect of sales or under section 4051) in respect of any article shall be deemed to be an overpayment if such article was, by any person—

(A) exported;

(B) used or sold for use as supplies for vessels or aircraft;

(C) sold to a State or local government for the exclusive use of a State or local government;

(D) sold to a nonprofit educational organization for its exclusive use;

(E) in the case of any tire taxable under section 4071(a), sold to any person for use as described in section 4221(e)(3); or

(F) in the case of gasoline, used or sold for use in the production of special fuels referred to in section 4041.

Subparagraphs (C) and (D) shall not apply in the case of any tax paid under section 4064. In the case of the tax imposed by section 4131, subparagraphs (B), (C), and (D) shall not apply and subparagraph (A) shall apply only if the use of the exported vaccine meets such requirements as the Secretary may by regulations prescribe. This paragraph shall not apply in the case of*any tax imposed under section 4041(a)(1) or 4081 on diesel fuel and* any tax paid under section 4091 or 4121. In the case of the tax imposed by section 4131, subparagraphs (B), (C), and (D) shall not apply and subparagraph (A) shall apply only if the use of the exported vaccine meets such requirements as the Secretary may by regulations prescribe.

(3) Tax-paid articles used for further manufacture, etc. If the tax imposed by chapter 32 has been paid with respect to the sale of any article (other than coal taxable under section 4121) by the manufacturer, producer, or importer thereof and such article is sold to a subsequent manufacturer or producer before being used, such tax shall be deemed to be an overpayment by such subsequent manufacturer or producer if—

(A) in the case of any article other than [4]*any fuel taxable under section 4081 or 4091,* such article is used by the subsequent manufacturer or producer as material in the manufacture or production of, or as a component part of—

(i) another article taxable under chapter 32, or

(ii) an automobile bus chassis or an automobile bus body,

manufactured or produced by him; or

(B) in the case of [5]*any fuel taxable under section 4081 or 4091, such fuel* is used by the subsequent manufacturer or producer, for nonfuel purposes, as a material in the manufacture or production of any other article manufactured or produced by him.

[For text of Committee Report, see ¶ 3059]

[Footnote Code Sec. 6416 continued]

1. "product"
2. "section 4092(b)(2)"
3. "'a taxable fuel therein)."
4. "gasoline taxable under section 4081 and other than any fuel taxable under section 4091"
5. "gasoline taxable under section 4081 or any fuel taxable under section 4091, such gasoline or fuel"

Effective Date (Sec. 13242(e) of P.L. 103-66) effective 1/1/94.

[¶ 2159] **Code Sec. 6420. Gasoline used on farms.**

* * * * * * * * * * * * *

(c) Meaning of terms. For purposes of this section—

* * * * * * * * * * * * *

(5) Gasoline. The term "gasoline" has the meaning given to such term by [1]*section 4083(a)*.

* * * * * * * * * * * * *

[2]***(h) Repealed.***

* * * * * * * * * * * * *

[¶ 2160] **Code Sec. 6421. Gasoline used for certain nonhighway purposes, used by local transit systems, or sold for certain exempt purposes.**

* * * * * * * * * * * * *

(c) Exempt purposes. If gasoline is sold to any person for any purpose described in paragraph (2), (3), (4), or (5) of section 4221(a), the Secretary shall pay (without interest) to such person an amount equal to the product of the number of gallons of gasoline so sold multiplied by the rate at which tax was imposed on such gasoline by section 4081. *The preceding sentence shall apply notwithstanding paragraphs (2)(A) and (3) of subsection (f).*

* * * * * * * * * * * * *

(e) Definitions. For purposes of this section—

(1) Gasoline. The term "gasoline" has the meaning given to such term by [1]*section 4083(a).*

(2) Off-highway business use.

* * * * * * * * * * * * *

[2]*(B) Uses in boats.*

(i) In general. Except as otherwise provided in this subparagraph, the term "off-highway business use" does not include any use in a motorboat.

(ii) Fisheries and whaling. The term "off-highway business use" shall include any use in a vessel employed in the fisheries or in the whaling business.

(iii) Exception for diesel fuel. The term "off-highway business use" shall include the use of diesel fuel in a boat in the active conduct of—

(I) a trade or business of commercial fishing or transporting persons or property for compensation or hire, and

---

[Footnote Code Sec. 6420] Matter in *italics* in Code Sec. 6420(c)(5) added by section 13242(d)(20) which struck out:
1. "section 4082(b)"

Effective Date (Sec. 13242(e) of P.L. 103-66) effective 1/1/94.

Code Sec. 6420(h) was repealed by section 13241(f)(5) of P.L. 103-66, which struck out:
2. "(h) Termination. Except with respect to taxes imposed by section 4081 at the Leaking Underground Storage Tank Trust Fund financing rate, this section shall apply only with respect to gasoline purchased before October 1, 1999."

Effective Date (Sec. 13241(g) of P.L. 103-66)effective 10/1/93.

[Footnote Code Sec. 6421] Matter in *italics* in Code Sec. 6421(c) and (e)(1) added by section 13242(d)(20) and (22) of P.L. 103-66 which struck out:
1. "section 4082(b)"

Effective Date (Sec. 13242(e) of P.L. 103-66) effective 1/1/94.

Matter in *italics* in Code Sec. 6421(e)(2)(B) added by section 13163(b) of P.L. 103-66 which struck out:
2. "(B) Exception for use in motorboats. The term 'off-highway business use' does not include any use in a motorboat. The preceding sentence shall not apply to use in a vessel employed in the fisheries or in the whaling business."

Effective Date (Sec. 13163(d) of P.L. 103-66) effective 1/1/94.

(II) except as provided in clause (iv), any other trade or business.

(iv) Noncommercial boats. In the case of a boat used predominantly in any activity which is of a type generally considered to constitute entertainment, amusement, or recreation, clause (iii)(II) shall not apply to—

(I) the taxes under sections 4041(a)(1) and 4081 for the period after December 31, 1993, and before January 1, 2000, and

(II) so much of the tax under sections 4041(a)(1) and 4081 as does not exceed 4.3 cents per gallon for the period after December 31, 1999.

(f) Exempt sales; other payments or refunds available.

* * * * * * * * * * * * *

(2) Gasoline used in aviation. This section shall not apply in respect of gasoline which is used as a fuel in an aircraft—

(A) in noncommercial aviation (as defined in section 4041(c)(4)), or

(B) in aviation which is not noncommercial aviation (as so defined) with respect to the tax imposed by section 4081 at the Leaking Underground Storage Tank Trust Fund financing rate *and, in the case of fuel purchased after September 30, 1995, at so much of the rate specified in section 4081(a)(2)(A) as does not exceed 4.3 cents per gallon.*

[3]***(3) Gasoline used in trains.*** *In the case of gasoline used as a fuel in a train, this section shall not apply with respect to—*

(A) the Leaking Underground Storage Tank Trust Fund financing rate under section 4081, and

(B) so much of the rate specified in section 4081(a)(2)(A) as does not exceed—

(i) 6.8 cents per gallon after September 30, 1993, and before October 1, 1995,

(ii) 5.55 cents per gallon after September 30, 1995, and before October 1, 1999, and

(iii) 4.3 cents per gallon after September 30, 1999.

* * * * * * * * * * * * *

[4]***(i) Repealed.***

* * * * * * * * * * * * *

[For explanation, see ¶s 1007 and 1019, for text of Committee Reports, see ¶s 3024 and 3059]

[¶ 2161] Code Sec. 6427. Fuels not used for taxable purposes.

(a) Nontaxable uses. Except as provided in subsection (k), if tax has been imposed under [1]*paragraph (2) or (3) of section 4041(a) or section 4041(c)* on the sale of any fuel and the purchaser uses such fuel other than for the use for which sold, or resells such fuel, the Secretary shall pay (without interest) to him an amount equal to—

(1) the amount of tax imposed on the sale of the fuel to him, reduced by

(2) if he uses the fuel, the amount of tax which would have been imposed under section 4041 on such use if no tax under section 4041 had been imposed on the sale of the fuel.

Matter in *italics* in Code Sec. 6421(f)(2)(B) and (3) added by sections 13242(d)(23) and (24) of P.L. 103-66 which struck out:

3. "(3) Leaking underground storage tank trust fund tax and deficit reduction tax on gasoline used in trains.

"This section shall not apply with respect to the tax imposed by section 4081 at the Leaking Underground Storage Tank Trust Fund financing rate and at the deficit reduction rate on gasoline used as a fuel in a train."

Effective Date (Sec. 13242(e) of P.L. 103-66) effective 1/1/94.

Matter in *italics* in Code Sec. 6421(f)(3) and (i) added by section 13241(f)(6) and (7) of P.L. 103-66 which struck out

4. "(i) Effective date. Except with respect to taxes imposed by section 4081 at the Leaking Underground Storage Tank Trust Fund financing rate, this section shall apply only with respect to gasoline purchased before October 1, 1999."

Effective Date (Sec. 13241(g) of P.L. 103-66) effective 10/1/93.

[Footnote Code Sec. 6427] Matter in *italics* in Code Sec. 6427(a) and (b) added by sections 13242(d)(21) and (25)(A) and (B) P.L. 103-66 which struck out:

1. "sectio 4041(a) or (c)"

(b) Intercity, local, or school buses.

(1) Allowance. Except as otherwise provided in this subsection and subsection (k), [2]*if any fuel other than gasoline (as defined in section 4083(a))* on the sale of which tax was imposed by section 4041(a) or [3]*4081* is used in an automobile bus while engaged in—

(A) furnishing (for compensation) passenger land transportation available to the general public, or

(B) the transportation of students and employees of schools (as defined in the last sentence of section 4221(d)(7)(C)),

the Secretary shall pay (without interest) to the ultimate purchaser of such fuel an amount equal to the product of the number of gallons of such fuel so used multiplied by the rate at which tax was imposed on such fuel by section 4041(a) or [4]*4081* , as the case may be.

(2) [5]***Reduction* in refund in certain cases.**

(A) in general. Except as provided in subparagraphs (B) and (C), the rate of tax taken into account under paragraph (1) shall be [6]*7.4* cents per gallon less than the aggregate rate at which tax was imposed on such fuel by section 4041(a) or 4081, as the case may be.

* * * * * * * * * * * *

(c) Use for farming purposes. Except as provided in subsection (k), if any fuel on the sale of which tax was imposed under [7]*paragraph (2) or (3) of section 4041(a) or section 4041(c)* is used on a farm for farming purposes (within the meaning of section 6420(c)), the Secretary shall pay (without interest) to the purchaser an amount equal to the amount of the tax imposed on the sale of the fuel. For purposes of this subsection, if fuel is used on a farm by any person other than the owner, tenant, or operator of such farm, the rules of paragraph (4) of section 6420(c) shall be applied (except that "liquid taxable under section 4041" shall be substituted for "gasoline" each place it appears in such paragraph (4)).

* * * * * * * * * * * *

(f) Gasoline, diesel fuel, and aviation fuel used to produce certain alcohol fuels.

(1) In general. Except as provided in subsection (k), if any gasoline, diesel fuel, or aviation fuel on which tax was imposed by section 4081 or 4091 at the regular tax rate is used by any person in producing a mixture described in section 4081(c) [8]*or 4091(c)(1)(A)* (as the case may be) which is sold or used in such person's trade or business the Secretary shall pay (without interest) to such person an amount equal to the excess of the regular tax rate over the incentive tax rate with respect to such fuel.

[9]***(2) Definitions.*** *For purposes of paragraph (1)—*

(A) Regular tax rate. The term "regular tax rate" means—

[Footnote Code Sec. 6427 continued]

2. "if any fuel"
3. "4091"
4. "4091"

Effective Date (Secs. 13242(e) of P.L. 103-66) effective 1/1/94.

Matter in *italics* in Code Sec. 6427(b)(2) and (b)(2)(A) added by sections 13241(f)(8)(A) and (B) of P.L. 103-66 which struck out:

5. "3-cent reduction"
6. "3.1 cents"

Effective Date (Secs. 13241(g) of P.L. 103-66) effective 10/1/93.

Matter in *italics* in Code Sec. 6427(c), (f)(1) and (2), (h), (i)(1) through (5), (j)(1), (k)(2) and (l) added by sections 13242(c)(1), (2)(A)-(D), (d)(21), (d)(26)(A) and (B), (27), (28)(A) and (B), (28)(A) and (B), (29) and (31) of P.L. 103-66 which struck out:

7. "section 4041(a) or (c)"
8. ", 4091(c)(1)(A), or 4091(d)(1)(A)"
9. "(2) Definitions. For purposes of paragraph (1)—

"(A) Regular tax rate. The term 'regular tax rate' means—

"(i) in the case of gasoline, the aggregate rate of tax imposed by section 4081 determined without regard to subsection (c)(1) thereof,

"(ii) in the case of diesel fuel, the aggregate rate of tax imposed by section 4091 on such fuel determined without regard to subsection (c) thereof, and

"(iii) in the case of aviation fuel, the aggregate rate of tax imposed by section 4091 on such fuel determined without regard to subsection (d) thereof.

"(B) Incentive tax rate. The term 'incentive tax rate' means—

(i) in the case of gasoline or diesel fuel, the aggregate rate of tax imposed by section 4081 determined without regard to subsection (c) thereof, and

(ii) in the case of aviation fuel, the aggregate rate of tax imposed by section 4091 determined without regard to subsection (c) thereof.

* * * * * * * * * * * * *

(h) Gasoline blend stocks or additives not used for producing gasoline. *Except as provided in subsection (k), if any gasoline blend stock or additive (within the meaning of section* [10]*4083(a)(2)* is not used by any person to produce gasoline and such person establishes that the ultimate use of such gasoline blend stock or additive is not to produce gasoline, the Secretary shall pay (without interest) to such person an amount equal to the aggregate amount of the tax imposed on such person with respect to such gasoline blend stock or additive.

* * * * * * * * * * * * *

(i) Time for filing claims; period covered.

(1) General rule. Except as [11]*otherwise provided in this subsection,* not more than one claim may be filed under subsection (a), (b), (c), (d), (g), (h), (l) or (q) by any person with respect to fuel used (or a qualified diesel powered highway vehicle purchased) during his taxable year; and no claim shall be allowed under this paragraph with respect to fuel used (or a qualified diesel powered highway vehicle purchased) during any taxable year unless filed by the purchaser not later than the time prescribed by law for filing a claim for credit or refund of overpayment of income tax for such taxable year. For purposes of this paragraph, a person's taxable year shall be his taxable year for purposes of subtitle A.

* * * * * * * * * * * * *

(3) Special rule for [12]***alcohol mixture*** **credit.**

(A) In general. A claim may be filed under subsection (f) by any person with respect to [13]*gasoline or diesel fuel used to produce a qualified alcohol mixture (as defined in section 4081(c)(3))* for any period—

(i) for which $200 or more is payable under such subsection (f), and

(ii) which is not less than 1 week.

* * * * * * * * * * * * *

(C) Time for filing claim. No claim filed under this paragraph shall be allowed unless filed on or before the last day of the first quarter the earliest quarter included in the claim.

(4) Special rule for nontaxable uses of diesel fuel and aviation fuel taxed under section*4081* or 4091.

(A) In general. If at the close of any of the 1st 3 quarters of the taxable year of any person, at least $750 is payable under subsection (l) to such person with respect to fuel used during such quarter or any prior quarter during the taxable year (and for which no other claim has been filed), a claim may be filled under subsection (l) with respect to such fuel.

(B) Time for filing claim. No claim filed under this paragraph shall be allowed unless filed during the 1st quarter following the last quarter included in the claim.

(5) Special rule for vendor refunds.

(A) In general. A claim may be filed under subsection (l)(5) by any person with respect to fuel sold by such person for any period—

(i) for which $200 or more is payable under subsection (l)(5), and

(ii) which is not less than 1 week.

[Footnote Code Sec. 6427 continued]

"(i) in the case of gasoline, the aggregate rate of tax imposed by section 4081 with respect to fuel described in subsection (c)(1) thereof,

"(ii) in the case of diesel fuel, the aggregate rate of tax imposed by section 4091 with respect to fuel described in subsection (c)(1)(B) thereof, and

"(iii) in the case of aviation fuel, the aggregate rate of tax imposed by section 4091 with respect to fuel described in subsection (d)(1)(B) thereof."

10. "section 4082(b)"
11. "provided in paragraphs (2), (3), and (4)"
12. "gasohol"
13. "gasoline used to produce gasohol (as defined in section 4081(c)(1))"

Notwithstanding subsection (l)(1), paragraph (3)(B) shall apply to claims filed under the preceding sentence.

(B) Time for filing claim. No claim filed under this paragraph shall be allowed unless filed on or before the last day of the first quarter following the earliest quarter included in the claim.

(j) Applicable laws.

(1) In general. All provisions of law, including penalties, applicable in respect of the taxes imposed by [14]*sections 4041, 4081, and 4091* shall, insofar as applicable and not inconsistent with this section, apply in respect of the payments provided for in this section to the same extent as if such payments constituted refunds of overpayments of the tax so imposed.

* * * * * * * * * * * *

(k) Income tax credit in lieu of payment.

* * * * * * * * * * * *

(2) Exception. Paragraph (1) shall not apply to a payment of a claim filed under paragraph (2), (3), [15]*(4), or (5)* of subsection (i).

* * * * * * * * * * * *

[16]***(l) Nontaxable uses of diesel fuel and aviation fuel.***

(1) In general. *Except as otherwise provided in this subsection and in subsection (k), if—*

(A) any diesel fuel on which tax has been imposed by section 4041 or 4081, or

(B) any aviation fuel on which tax has been imposed by section 4091,

is used by any person in a nontaxable use, the Secretary shall pay (without interest) to the ultimate purchaser of such fuel an amount equal to the aggregate amount of tax imposed on such fuel under section 4041, 4081, or 4091, as the case may be.

(2) Nontaxable use. *For purposes of this subsection, the term "nontaxable use" means—*

(A) in the case of diesel fuel, any use which is exempt from the tax imposed by section 4041(a)(1) other than by reason of a prior imposition of tax, and

(B) in the case of aviation fuel, any use which is exempt from the tax imposed by section 4041(c)(1) other than by reason of a prior imposition of tax.

[Footnote Code Sec. 6427 continued]

14. "section 4041"

15. "or (4)"

16. "(l) Nontaxable uses of diesel fuel and aviation fuel taxed under section 4091.

"(1) In general. Except as provided in subsection (k) and in paragraphs (3) and (4) of this subsection, if any fuel on which tax has been imposed by section 4091 is used by any person in a nontaxable use, the Secretary shall pay (without interest) to the ultimate purchaser of such fuel an amount equal to the aggregate amount of tax imposed on such fuel under section 4091.

"(2) Nontaxable use. For purposes of this subsection, the term 'nontaxable use' means, with respect to any fuel, any use of such fuel if such use is exempt under section 4041 from the taxes imposed by subsections (a)(1) and (c)(1) of section 4041 (other than by reason of the imposition of tax on any sale thereof).

"(3) No refund of certain taxes on fuel used in diesel-powered trains. In the case of fuel used in a diesel-powered train, paragraph (1) shall not apply to so much of the tax imposed by section 4091 as is attributable to the Leaking underground Storage Tank Trust Fund financing rate and the diesel fuel deficit reduction rate imposed by such section. The preceding sentence shall not apply in the case of fuel sold for exclusive use by a State or any political subdivision thereof.

"(4) No refund of leaking underground storage tank trust fund taxes on fuel used in commercial aviation. In the case of fuel used in commercial aviation (as defined in section 4093(c)(2)(B)) (other than supplies for vessels or aircraft within the meaning of section 4221(d)(3)), paragraph (1) shall not apply to so much of the tax imposed by section 4091 as is attributable to the Leaking Underground Storage Tank Trust Fund financing rate imposed by such section."

Effective Date (Secs. 13242(e) of P.L. 103-66) effective 1/1/94.

Code Sec. 6427(l)(3) and (4) was previously amended by Sec. 13241(f)(9) of P.L. 103-66 which struck out:

"(3) No refund of Leaking Underground Storage Tank Trust Fund financing tax. Paragraph (1) shall not apply to so much of the tax imposed by section 4091 as is attributable to the Leaking Underground Storage Tank Trust Fund financing rate imposed by such section in the case of—

"(A) fuel used in a diesel-powered train, and

"(B) fuel used in any aircraft (except as supplies for vessels or aircraft within the meaning of section 4221(d)(3)).

"(4) No refund of deficit reduction tax on fuel used in trains. In the case of fuel used in a diesel-powered train, paragraph (1) also shall not apply to so much of the tax imposed by section 4091 as is attributable to the diesel fuel deficit reduction rate imposed by such section."

Effective Date (Sec. 13241(g) of P.L. 103-66) effective 10/1/93.

(3) ***Refund of certain taxes on fuel used in diesel-powered trains.*** *For purposes of this subsection, the term "nontaxable use" includes fuel used in a diesel-powered train. The preceding sentence shall not apply with respect to—*

(A) the Leaking Underground Storage Tank Trust Fund financing rate under sections 4041 and 4081, and

(B) so much of the rate specified in section 4081(a)(2)(A) as does not exceed—

(i) 6.8 cents per gallon after September 30, 1993, and before October 1, 1995,

(ii) 5.55 cents per gallon after September 30, 1995, and before October 1, 1999, and

(iii) 4.3 cents per gallon after September 30, 1999.

The preceding sentence shall not apply in the case of fuel sold for exclusive use by a State or any political subdivision thereof.

(4) ***No refund of certain taxes on fuel used in commercial aviation.*** *In the case of fuel used in commercial aviation (as defined in section 4092(b)) (other than supplies for vessels or aircraft within the meaning of section 4221(d)(3)), paragraph (1) shall not apply to so much of the tax imposed by section 4091 as is attributable to—*

(A) the Leaking Underground Storage Tank Trust Fund financing rate imposed by such section, and

(B) in the case of fuel purchased after September 30, 1995, as so much of the rate of tax specified in section 4091(b)(1) as does not exceed 4.3 cents per gallon.

(5) Registered vendors to administer claims for refund of diesel fuel sold to farmers and state and local governments.

(A) In general. Paragraph (1) shall not apply to diesel fuel used—

(i) on a farm for farming purposes (within the meaning of section 6420(c)), or

(ii) by a State or local government.

(B) Payment to ultimate, registered, vendor. The amount which would (but for subparagraph (A)) have been paid under paragraph (1) with respect to any fuel shall be paid to the ultimate vendor of such fuel, if such vendor—

(i) is registered under section 4101, and

(ii) meets the requirements of subparagraph (A), (B), or (D) of section 6416(a)(1).

[17]**(m) Repealed.**

* * * * * * * * * * * * *

[18]***(o) Repealed.***

* * * * * * * * * * * * *

[For explanation, see ¶s 1002, 1010, 1011, 1018 for text of Committee Report, see ¶ 3059

Code Sec. 6427(m) and (o) repealed by sections 13241(f)(9) and (10) of P.L. 103-66 which struck out:

17. "(m) Special rules with respect to noncommercial aviation.

For purposes of subsection (a), in the case of gasoline—

"(1) on which tax was imposed under section 4041(c)(2),

"(2) on which tax was not imposed under section 4081, and

"(3) which was not used as an off-highway business use (within the meaning of section 6421(e)(2)),

the amount of the payment under subsection (a) shall be an amount equal to the amount of gasoline used as described in subsection (a) or resold multiplied by the rate equal to the excess of the rate of tax imposed by section 4041(c)(2) over the rate of tax imposed by section 4081."

"(o) Termination of certain provisions. 18. Except with respect to taxes imposed by section 4041(d) and sections 4081 and 4091 at the Leaking Underground Storage Tank Trust Fund financing rate, subsections (a), (b), (c), (d), (g), (h), and (l) shall only apply with respect to fuels purchased before October 1, 1999."

Effective Date (Sec. 13241(g) of P.L. 103-66) effective 10/1/93.

[¶ 2162] Code Sec. 6611. Interest on overpayments.

* * * * * * * * * * * * *

[1]***(e) Disallowance of interest on certain overpayments.***

(1) Refunds within 45 days after return is filed. *If any overpayment of tax imposed by this title is refunded within 45 days after the last day prescribed for filing the return of such tax (determined without regard to any extension of time for filing the return) or, in the case of a return filed after such last date, is refunded within 45 days after the date the return is filed, no interest shall be allowed under subsection (a) on such overpayment.*

(2) Refunds after claim for credit or refund. *If—*

(A) the taxpayer files a claim for a credit or refund for any overpayment of tax imposed by this title, and

(B) such overpayment is refunded within 45 days after such claim is filed,

no interest shall be allowed on such overpayment from the date the claim is filed until the day the refund is made.

(3) IRS initiated adjustments. *If an adjustment initiated by the Secretary, results in a refund or credit of an overpayment, interest on such overpayment shall be computed by subtracting 45 days from the number of days interest would otherwise be allowed with respect to such overpayment.*

[For explanation, see ¶ 1205, for text on Committee Report, see ¶ 3066]

[¶ 2163] Code Sec. 6652. Failure to file certain information returns, registration statements, etc.

* * * * * * * * * * * * *

(k) Failure to make reports required under section 1202.
In the case of a failure to make a report required under section 1202(d)(1)(C) which contains the information required by such section on the date prescribed therefor (determined with regard to any extension of time for filing), there shall be paid (on notice and demand by the Secretary and in the same manner as tax) by the person failing to make such report, an amount equal to $50 for each report with respect to which there was such a failure. In the case of any failure due to negligence or intentional disregard, the preceding sentence shall be applied by substituting "$100" for "$50". In the case of a report covering periods in 2 or more years, the penalty determined under preceding provisions of this subsection shall be multiplied by the number of such years.

* * * * * * * * * * * * *

[Footnote Code Sec. 6611] Matter in *italics* in Code Sec. 6611(e) added by section 13271(a) of P.L. 103-66 which struck out:

1. "(e) **Income tax refund within 45 days after return is filed.**

If any overpayment of tax imposed by subtitle A is refunded within 45 days after the last date prescribed for filing the return of such tax (determined without regard to any extension of time for filing the return) or, in case the return is filed after such last date, is refunded within 45 days after the date the return is filed, no interest shall be allowed under subsection (a) on such overpayment."

Effective Date (Sec. 13271(b) of P.L. 103-66) effective as provided in Sec. 13271(b) of this Act, which reads as follows: "(b) Effective dates.

"(1) Paragraph (1) of section 6611(e) of the Internal Revenue Code of 1986 (as amended by subsection (a)) shall apply in the case of returns the due date for which (determined without regard to extensions) is on or after January 1, 1994.

"(2) Paragraph (2) of section 6611(e) of such Code (as so amended) shall apply in the case of claims for credit or refund of any overpayment filed on or after January 1, 1995, regardless of the taxable period to which such refund relates.

"(3) Paragraph (3) of section 6611(e) of such Code (as so amended) shall apply in the case of any refund paid on or after January 1, 1995, regardless of the taxable period to which such refund relates."

[Footnote Code Sec. 6652] Matter in *italics* was added by section 13113(c) of P.L. 103-66

Effective Date (Sec. 13113(e) of P.L. 103-66) effective for stock issued after 8/10/93.

[For explanation, see ¶703.]

[¶2164] Code Sec. 6654. Failure by individual to pay estimated income tax.

* * * * * * * * * * * * *

(d) Amount of required installments. For purposes of this section—

(1) Amount.

* * * * * * * * * * * * *

[1]*(C) Limitation on use of preceding year's tax.*

[Footnote Code Sec. 6654] Matter in *italics* in Code Sec. 6654(d)(1)(C), (j)(3)(A), and (l)(4) added by sections 13214(a), (b)(1) and (b)(2), P.L. 103-66, which struck out:

1. "(C) Limitation on use of preceding year's tax.

"(i) In general. In any case to which this subparagraph applies, clause (ii) of subparagraph (B) shall be applied as if it read as follows:

"(ii) the greater of—

"(I) 100 percent of the tax shown on the return of the individual for the preceding taxable year, or

"(II) 90 percent of the tax shown on the return for the current year, determined by taking into account the adjustments set forth in subparagraph (D)."

"(ii) Cases to which subparagraph applies. This subparagraph shall apply if—

"(I) the modified adjusted gross income for the current year exceeds the amount of the adjusted gross income shown on the return of the individual for the preceding taxable year by more than $40,000 ($20,000 in the case of a separate return for the current year by a married individual),

"(II) the adjusted gross income shown on the return for the current year exceeds $75,000 ($37,500 in the case of a married individual filing a separate return), and

"(III) the taxpayer has made a payment of estimated tax (determined without regard to subsection (g) and section 6402(b)) with respect to any of the preceding 3 taxable years (or a penalty has been previously assessed under this section for a failure to pay estimated tax with respect to any of such 3 preceding taxable years).

This subparagraph shall not apply to any taxable year beginning after December 31, 1996.

"(iii) May use preceding year's tax for first installment. This subparagraph shall not apply for purposes of determining the amount of the 1st required installment for any taxable year. Any reduction in an installment by reason of the preceding sentence shall be recaptured by increasing the amount of the 1st succeeding required installment (with respect to which the requirements of clause (iv) are not met) by the amount of such reduction.

"(iv) Annualization exception. This subparagraph shall not apply to any required installment if the individual establishes that the requirements of subclauses (I) and (II) of clause (ii) would not have been satisfied if such subclauses were applied on the basis of—

"(I) the annualized amount of the modified adjusted gross income for months in the current year ending before the due date for the installment determined by assuming that all items referred to in clause (i) of subparagraph (D) accrued ratably during the current year, and

"(II) the annualized amount of the adjusted gross income for months in the current year ending before the due date for the installment.

Any reduction in an installment under the preceding sentence shall be recaptured by increasing the amount of the 1st succeeding required installment (with respect to which the requirements of the preceding sentence are not met) by the amount of such reduction.

"(D) Modified adjusted gross income for current year. For purposes of this paragraph, the term "modified adjusted gross income" means the amount of the adjusted gross income shown on the return for the current year determined with the following modifications:

"(i) The qualified pass-thru items shown on the return for the preceding taxable year shall be treated as also shown on the return for the current year (and the actual qualified pass-thru items (if any) for the current year shall be disregarded).

"(ii) The amount of any gain from any involuntary conversion (within the meaning of section 1033) which is shown on the return for the current year shall be disregarded.

"(iii) The amount of any gain from the sale or exchange of a principal residence (within the meaning of section 1034) which is shown on the return for the current year shall be disregarded.

"(E) Qualified pass-thru item. For purposes of this paragraph—

"(i) In general. Except as otherwise provided in this subparagraph, the term "qualified pass-thru item" means any item of income, gain, loss, deduction, or credit attributable to an interest in a partnership or S corporation. Such term shall not include any gain or loss from the disposition of an interest in an entity referred to in the preceding sentence.

"(ii) 10-percent owners and general partners excluded. The term "qualified pass-thru item" shall not include, with respect to any year, any item attributable to—

"(I) an interest in an S corporation, if at any time during such year the individual was a 10-percent owner in such corporation, or

"(II) an interest in a partnership, if at any time during such year the individual was a 10-percent owner or general partner in such partnership.

(i) In general. If the adjusted gross income shown on the return of the individual for the preceding taxable year exceeds $150,000, clause (ii) of subparagraph (B) shall be applied by substituting "110 percent" for "100 percent".

(ii) Separate returns. In the case of a married individual (within the meaning of section 7703) who files a separate return for the taxable year for which the amount of the installment is being determined, clause (i) shall be applied by substituting "$75,000" for "$150,000".

(iii) Special rule. In the case of an estate or trust, adjusted gross income shall be determined as provided in section 67(e).

* * * * * * * * * * * * *

(j) Special rules for nonresident aliens. In the case of a nonresident alien described in section 6072(c):

* * * * * * * * * * * * *

(3) Amount of required installments.

(A) First required installment. In the case of the first required installment, subsection (d) shall be applied by substituting "50 percent" for "25 percent" in subsection (d)(1)(A) [2].

* * * * * * * * * * * * *

(l) Estates and trusts.

* * * * * * * * * * * * *

(4) Special rule for annualizations. In the case of any estate or trust to which this section applies, [3]*subsection (d)(2)(B)(i)* shall be applied by substituting "ending before the date 1 month before the due date for the installment" for "ending before the due date for the installment".

* * * * * * * * * * * * *

[For explanation, see ¶ 117, for text of Committee Report, see ¶ 3041]

[¶ 2165] Code Sec. 6655. Failure by corporation to pay estimated income tax.

* * * * * * * * * * * * *

(d) Amount of required installments. For purposes of this section—

(1) Amount.

* * * * * * * * * * * * *

(B) Required annual payment. Except as otherwise provided in this subsection, the term "required annual payment" means the lesser of—

"(iii) 10-percent owner. The term "10-percent owner" means—

"(I) in the case of an S corporation, an individual who owns 10 percent or more (by vote or value) of the stock in such corporation, and

"(II) in the case of a partnership, an individual who owns 10 percent or more of the capital interest (or the profits interest) in such partnership.

"(F) Other definitions and special rules. For purposes of this paragraph—

"(i) Current year. The term "current year" means the taxable year for which the amount of the installment is being determined.

"(ii) Special rule. If no return is filed for the current year, any reference in subparagraph (C) or (D) to an item shown on the return for the current year shall be treated as a reference to the actual amount of such item for such year.

"(iii) Marital status. Marital status shall be determined under section 7703."

2. "and subsection (d)(1)(C)(iii) shall not apply"

3. "paragraphs (1)(C)(iv) and (2)(B)(i) of subsection (d)"

Effective Date (Sec. 13214(c), P.L. 103-66) effective for tax. yrs. begin. after 12/31/93.

(i) [1]*100 percent* of the tax shown on the return for the taxable year (or, if no return is filed, [1] *100 percent* of the tax for such year), or

(ii) 100 percent of the tax shown on the return of the corporation for the preceding taxable year.

Clause (ii) shall not apply if the preceding taxable year was not a taxable year of 12 months, or the corporation did not file a return for such preceding taxable year showing a liability for tax.

(2) Large corporations required to pay [2]*100 percent* of current year tax.

* * * * * * * * * * * *

[3]**(3) Repealed.**

(e) Lower required installment where annualized income installment or adjusted seasonal installment is less than amount determined under Subsection (d).

* * * * * * * * * * * *

(2) Determination of annualized income installment.

(A) In general. In the case of any required installment, the annualized income installment is the excess (if any) of—

(i) an amount equal to the applicable percentage of the tax for the taxable year computed by placing on an annualized basis the taxable income, alternative minimum taxable income, and modified alternative minimum taxable income—

(I) for the first 3 months of the taxable year, in the case of the 1st required installment,

(II) for the first 3 months [4]of the taxable year, in the case of the 2nd required installment,

(III) for the first 6 months [5]of the taxable year in the case of the 3rd required installment, and

(IV) for the first 9 months [6]of the taxable year, in the case of the 4th required installment, over

(ii) the aggregate amount of any prior required installments for the taxable year.

(B) Special rules. For purposes of this paragraph—

(i) Annualization. The taxable income, alternative minimum taxable income, and modified alternative minimum taxable income shall be placed on an annualized basis under regulations prescribed by the Secretary.

(ii) Applicable percentage. [7]

[Footnote Code Sec. 6655] Matter in *italics* in Code Sec. 6655(d)(1)(B)(i), (d)(2), (d)(3), (e)(2)(A)(i)(II)-(IV), (e)(2)(B)(ii), (e)(2)(C), (e)(3)(A)(i), and (g)(3) added by sections 13225(a), (a)(2)(A)(i) and (ii), (a)(2)(B) and (C), (b)(1)(A)-(C), (b)(2) and (3) of P.L. 103-66, which struck out:

1. "91 percent"

Matter in *italics* in Code Sec. 6655(d)(1)(B)(i), (d)(2), (d)(3), (e)(2)(A)(i)(II)-(IV), (e)(2)(B)(ii), (e)(2)(C), (e)(3)(A)(i), and (g)(3) added by sections 13225(a), (a)(2)(A)(i) and (ii), (a)(2)(B) and (C), (b)(1)(A)-(C), (b)(2) and (3) of P.L. 103-66, which struck out:

1. "91 percent"
2. "91 percent"
3. "(3) **Temporary increase in amount of installment based on current year tax.** In the case of any taxable year beginning after June 30, 1992, and before 1997—

"(A) paragraph (l)(B)(i) and subsection (e)(3)(A)(i) shall be applied by substituting '97 percent' for '91 percent' each place it appears, and

"(B) the table contained in subsection (e)(2)(B)(ii) shall be applied by substituting '24.25', '48.50', '72.75', and '97' for '22.75', '45.50', '68.25', and '91.00', respectively."

4. "or for the first 5 months"
5. hbq;or for the first 8 months"
6. hbq;or for the first 11 months"
7.

"In the case of the following required installments:	The applicable percentage is:
1st	22.75
2nd	45.50

In the case of the following required installments:	*The applicable percentage is:*
1st	*25*
2nd	*50*
3rd	*75*
4th	*100*

(iii) Modified alternative minimum taxable income. The term "modified alternative minimum taxable income" has the meaning given to such term by section 59A(b).

(C) Election for different annualization periods.

(i) If the taxpayer makes an election under this clause—

(I) subclause (I) of subparagraph (A)(i) shall be applied by substituting "2 months" for "3 months",

(II) subclause (II) of subparagraph (A)(i) shall be applied by substituting "4 months" for "3 months",

(III) subclause (III) of subparagraph (A)(i) shall be applied by substituting "7 months" for "6 months", and

(IV) subclause (IV) of subparagraph (A)(i) shall be applied by substituting "10 months" for "9 months".

(ii) If the taxpayer makes an election under this clause—

(I) subclause (II) of subparagraph (A)(i) shall be applied by substituting "5 months" for "3 months",

(II) subclause (III) of subparagraph (A)(i) shall be applied by substituting "8 months" for "6 months", and

(III) subclause (IV) of subparagraph (A)(i) shall be applied by substituting "11 months" for "9 months".

(iii) An election under clause (i) or (ii) shall apply to the taxable year for which made and such an election shall be effective only if made on or before the date required for the payment of the first required installment for such taxable year.

(3) Determination of adjusted seasonal installment.

(A) In general. In the case of any required installment, the amount of the adjusted seasonal installment is the excess (if any) of—

(i) [8]*100 percent* of the amount determined under subparagraph (C), over

(ii) the aggregate amount of all prior required installments for the taxable year.

* * * * * * * * * * * * *

(g) Definitions and special rules.

* * * * * * * * * * * * *

(3) Certain tax-exempt organizations. For purposes of this section—

(A) Any organization subject to the tax imposed by section 511, and any private foundation, shall be treated as a corporation subject to tax under section 11.

(B) Any tax imposed by section 511, and any tax imposed by section 1 or 4940 on a private foundation, shall be treated as a tax imposed by section 11.

(C) Any reference to taxable income shall be treated as including a reference to unrelated business taxable income or net investment income (as the case may be).

In the case of any organization described in subparagraph (A), subsection (b)(2)(A) shall be applied by substituting "5th month" for "3rd month", [9]*and, except in the case of an elec-*

[Footnote Code Sec. 6655 continued]

3rd	68.25
4th	91.00"

8. "91 percent"
9. "and subsection (e)(2)(A)"

Effective Date (Sec. 13225(c) of P.L. 103-66) effective for tax. yrs. begin. after 12/31/93.

tion under subsection (e)(2)(C), subsection (e)(2)(A) shall be applied by substituting "2 months" for "3 months" and in clause (i)(I), by substituting "4 months" for "5 months" in clause (i)(II), by substituting "7 months" for "8 months" in clause (i)(III), and by substituting "10 months" for "11 months" in clause (i)(IV).

* * * * * * * * * * * * *

[For explanation, see ¶ 316, 317 and 318, for text of Committee Report, see ¶ 3047]

[¶ 2166] Code Sec. 6662. Imposition of accuracy-related penalty.

* * * * * * * * * * * * *

(d) Substantial understatement of income tax.

* * * * * * * * * * * * *

(2) Understatement.

* * * * * * * * * * * * *

(B) Reduction for understatement due to position of taxpayer or disclosed item. The amount of the understatement under subparagraph (A) shall be reduced by that portion of the understatement which is attributable to—

(i) the tax treatment of any item by the taxpayer if there is or was substantial authority for such treatment, or

[1]*(ii) any item if—*

(I) the relevant facts affecting the item's tax treatment are adequately disclosed in the return or in a statement attached to the return, and

(II) there is a reasonable basis for the tax treatment of such item by the taxpayer.

* * * * * * * * * * * * *

(e) Substantial valuation misstatement under chapter 1.

(1) In general. For purposes of this section, there is a substantial valuation misstatement under chapter 1 if—

(A) the value of any property (or the adjusted basis of any property) claimed on any return of tax imposed by chapter 1 is 200 percent or more of the amount determined to be the correct amount of such valuation or adjusted basis (as the case may be), or

(B)

(i) the price for any property or services (or for the use of property) claimed on any such return in connection with any transaction between persons described in section 482 is 200 percent or more (or 50 percent or less) of the amount determined under section 482 to be the correct amount of such price, or

[2]*(ii) the net section 482 transfer price adjustment for the taxable year exceeds the lesser of $5,000,000 or 10 percent of the taxpayer's gross receipts.*

(2) Limitation. No penalty shall be imposed by reason of subsection (b)(3) unless the portion of the underpayment for the taxable year attributable to substantial valuation misstatements under chapter 1 exceeds $5,000 ($10,000 in the case of a corporation other than an S corporation or a personal holding company (as defined in section 542)).

[Footnote Code Sec. 6662] Matter in *italics* in Code Sec. 6662(d)(2)(B)(ii) added by section 13251(a), P.L. 103-66, which struck out:

1. "(ii) any item with respect to which the relevant facts affecting the item's tax treatment are adequately disclosed in the return or in a statement attached to the return."

Effective Date (Sec. 13251(b), P.L. 103-66) effective for returns the due dates for which (determined without regard to extensions) are after 12/31/93.

Matter in *italics* in Code Sec. 6662(e)(1)(B)(ii), (e)(3)(B) and (D), and (h)(2)(A)(iii) added by sections 13236(a)-(d), P.L. 103-66, which struck out:

2. "(ii) the net section 482 transfer price adjustment for the taxable year exceeds $10,000,000."

(3) Net section 482 transfer price adjustment. For purposes of this subsection—

(A) In general. The term "net section 482 transfer price adjustment" means, with respect to any taxable year, the net increase in taxable income for the taxable year (determined without regard to any amount carried to such taxable year from another taxable year) resulting from adjustments under section 482 in the price for any property or services (or for the use of property).

[3]*(B) Certain adjustments excluded in determining threshold. For purposes of determining whether the threshold requirements of paragraph (1)(B)(ii) are met, the following shall be excluded:*

(i) Any portion of the net increase in taxable income referred to in subparagraph (A) which is attributable to any redetermination of a price if—

(I) it is established that the taxpayer determined such price in accordance with a specific pricing method set forth in the regulations prescribed under section 482 and that the taxpayer's use of such method was reasonable,

(II) the taxpayer has documentation (which was in existence as of the time of filing the return) which sets forth the determination of such price in accordance with such a method and which establishes that the use of such method was reasonable, and

(III) the taxpayer provides such documentation to the Secretary within 30 days of a request for such documentation.

(ii) Any portion of the net increase in taxable income referred to in subparagraph (A) which is attributable to a redetermination of price where such price was not determined in accordance with such a specific pricing method if—

(I) the taxpayer establishes that none of such pricing methods was likely to result in a price that would clearly reflect income, the taxpayer used another pricing method to determine such price and such other pricing method was likely to result in a price that would clearly reflect income,

(II) the taxpayer has documentation (which was in existence as of the time of filing the return) which sets forth the determination of such price in accordance with such other method and which establishes that the requirements of subclause (I) were satisfied, and

(III) the taxpayer provides such documentation to the Secretary within 30 days of request for such documentation.

(iii) Any portion of such net increase which is attributable to any transaction solely between foreign corporations unless, in the case of any such corporations, the treatment of such transaction affects the determination of income from sources within the United States or taxable income effectively connected with the conduct of a trade or business within the United States.

* * * * * * * * * * * * *

(D) Coordination with reasonable cause exception. For purposes of section 6664(c) the taxpayer shall not be treated as having reasonable cause for any portion of an underpayment attributable to a net section 482 transfer price adjustment unless such taxpayer meets the requirements of clause (i), (ii), or (iii) of subparagraph (B) with respect to such portion.

* * * * * * * * * * * * *

(h) Increase in penalty in case of gross valuation misstatements.

* * * * * * * * * * * * *

[Footnote Code Sec. 6662 continued]

3. "(B) Certain adjustments excluded in determining threshold. For purposes of determining whether the $10,000,000 threshold requirement of paragraph (1)(B)(ii) is met, there shall be excluded—

"(i) any portion of the net increase in taxable income referred to in subparagraph (A) which is attributable to any redetermination of a price if it is shown that there was a reasonable cause for the taxpayer's determination of such price and that the taxpayer acted in good faith with respect to such price, and

"(ii) any portion of such net increase which is attributable to any transaction solely between foreign corporations unless, in the case of any of such corporations, the treatment of such transaction affects the determination of income from sources within the United States or taxable income effectively connected with the conduct of a trade or business within the United States."

(2) Gross valuation misstatements. The term "gross valuation misstatements" means—

(A) any substantial valuation misstatement under chapter 1 as determined under subsection (e) by substituting—

(i) "400 percent" for "200 percent" each place it appears,

(ii) "25 percent" for "50 percent", and

[4]*(iii) in paragraph (1)(B)(ii)—*

(I) "$20,000,000" for "$5,000,000" and

(II) "20 percent" for "10 percent".

* * * * * * * * * * * *

[¶ 2167] Code Sec. 6714. Failure to meet disclosure requirements applicable to quid pro quo contributions.

(a) Imposition of penalty. If an organization fails to meet the disclosure requirement of section 6115 with respect to a quid pro quo contribution, such organization shall pay a penalty of $10 for each contribution in respect of which the organization fails to make the required disclosure, except that the total penalty imposed by this subsection with respect to a particular fundraising event or mailing shall not exceed $5,000.

(b) Reasonable cause exception. No penalty shall be imposed under this section with respect to any failure if it is shown that such failure is due to reasonable cause.

[For explanation, see ¶ 1009 and ¶ 1202, for text of Committee Report, see ¶ 3026]

[¶ 2168] Code Sec. 6714 [sic 6715]. Dyed fuel sold for use or used in taxable use.

(a) Imposition of penalty. If—

(1) any dyed fuel is sold or held for sale by any person for any use which such person knows or has reason to know is not a nontaxable use of such fuel,

(2) any dyed fuel held for use or used by any person for a use other than a nontaxable use and such person knew, or had reason to know, that such fuel was so dyed, or

(3) any person willfully alters, or attempts to alter, the strength or composition of any dye or marking done pursuant to section 4082 in any dyed fuel,

then, such person shall pay a penalty in addition to the tax (if any).

(b) Amount of penalty.

(1) In general. Except as provided in paragraph (2), the amount of the penalty under subsection (a) on each act shall be the greater of—

(A) $1,000, or

(B) $10 for each gallon of the dyed fuel involved.

(2) Multiple violations. In determining the penalty under subsection (a) on any person, paragraph (1) shall be applied by increasing the amount in paragraph (1)(A) by the product of such amount and the number of prior penalties (if any) imposed by this section on such person (or a related person or any predecessor of such person or related person).

(c) Definititons. For purposes of this section—

(1) Dyed fuel. The term "dyed fuel" means any dyed diesel fuel, whether or not the fuel was dyed pursuant to section 4082.

[Footnote Code Sec. 6662 continued]

4. "(iii) '$20,000,000' for '$10,000,000',"

Effective Date (Sec. 13236(e), P.L. 103-66) effective for tax. yrs. begin. after 12/31/93.

[Footnote Code Sec. 6714] Code Sec. 6714 was added by section 13173(b) of P.L. 103-66.

Effective Date (Sec. 13173(d) of P.L. 103-66) effective for quid pro quo contributions made on or after 1/1/94.

[Footnote Code Sec. 6714 [sic 6715]] Code Sec. 6714[sic 6715] was added by section 13242(c)(1) of P.L. 103-66.

Effective Date (Sec. 13242(e) of P.L. 103-66) effective 1/1/94.

(2) Nontaxable use. The term "nontaxable use" has the meaning given such term by section 4082(b).

(d) Joint and several liability of certain officers and employees. If a penalty is imposed under this section on any business entity, each officer, employee, or agent of such entity who willfully participated in any act giving rise to such penalty shall be jointly and severally liable with such entity for such penalty.

[For explanation, see ¶ 1009 and ¶ 1202, for text of Committee Report, see ¶ 3026]

[¶ 2169] Code Sec. 6724. Waiver; definitions and special rules.

* * * * * * * * * * * * *

(d) Definitions. For purposes of this part—

(1) Information return. The term "information return" means—

(A) any statement of the amount of payments to another person required by—

(i) section 6041(a) or (b) (relating to certain information at source),

(ii) section 6042(a)(1) (relating to payments of dividends),

(iii) section 6044(a)(1) (relating to payments of patronage dividends),

(iv) section 6049(a) (relating to payments of interest),

(v) section 6050A(a) (relating to reporting requirements of certain fishing boat operators),

(vi) section 6050N(a) (relating to payments of royalties), or

(vii) section 6051(d) (relating to information returns with respect to income tax withheld), and

(B) any return required by—

(i) section 6041A(a) or (b) (relating to returns of direct sellers),

(ii) section 6045(a) or (d) (relating to returns of brokers),

(iii) section 6050H(a) (relating to mortgage interest received in trade or business from individuals),

(iv) section 6050I(a) (relating to cash received in trade or business),

(v) section 6050J(a) (relating to foreclosures and abandonments of security),

(vi) section 6050K(a) (relating to exchanges of certain partnership interests),

(vii) section 6050L(a) (relating to returns relating to certain dispositions of donated property),

[1]*(viii) section 6050P (relating to returns relating to the cancellation of indebtedness by certain financial entities),*

(ix) section 6052(a) (relating to reporting payment of wages in the form of group [term] life insurance),

[2]*(x)* section 6053(c)(1) (relating to reporting with respect to certain tips),

[3]*(xi)* subsection (b) or (e) of section 1060 (relating to reporting requirements of transferors and transferees in certain asset acquisitions),

[4]*(xii)* subparagraph (A) or (C) of subsection (c)(4) of section 4093 (relating to information reporting with respect to tax on diesel and aviation fuels), or

[5]*(xiii)* section 4101(d) (relating to information reporting with respect to fuels taxes)

[6]*(xiv)* subparagraph (C) of section 338(h)(10) (relating to information required to be furnished to the Secretary in case of elective recognition of gain or loss).

[Footnote Code Sec. 6724] Matter in *italics* In Code Secs. 6724(d)(1)(B)(viii)-(xiv) and (d)(2)(P)-(T) added by sections 13252(b)(1) and (2) of P.L. 103-66, which struck out:

1. "(viii)"
2. "(ix)"
3. "(x)"
4. "(xi)"
5. "(xii)"
6. "(xiii)"

Such term also includes any form, statement, or schedule required to be filed with the Secretary with respect to any amount from which tax was required to be deducted and withheld under chapter 3 (or from which tax would be required to be so deducted and withheld but for an exemption under this title or any treaty obligation of the United States).

(2) Payee statement. The term "payee statement" means any statement required to be furnished under—

* * * * * * * * * * * *

[7]*(P) section 6050P(d) (relating to returns relating to the cancellation of indebtedness by certain financial entities),*

(Q) section 6051 (relating to receipts for employees),

[8]*(R)* section 6052(b) (relating to returns regarding payment of wages in the form of group-term life insurance),

[9]*(S)* section 6053(b) or (c) (relating to reports of tips), or

[10]*(T)* section 4093(c)(4)(B) (relating to certain purchasers of diesel and aviation fuels). Such term also includes any form, statement, or schedule required to be furnished to the recipient of any amount from which tax was required to be deducted and withheld under chapter 3 (or from which tax would be required to be so deducted and withheld but for an exemption under this title or any treaty obligation of the United States).

* * * * * * * * * * * *

[For explanation, see ¶ 1204]

[¶ 2170] Code Sec. 7652. Shipments to the United States.

* * * * * * * * * * * *

(f) Limitation on cover over of tax on distilled spirits. For purposes of this section, with respect to taxes imposed under section 5001 or this section on distilled spirits, the amount covered into the treasuries of Puerto Rico and the Virgin Islands shall not exceed the lesser of the rate of—

[1]*(1) $10.50 ($11.30 in the case of distilled spirits brought into the United States during the 5-year period beginning on October 1, 1993), or*

* * * * * * * * * * * *

[For Committee Report, see ¶ 3050.]

[Footnote Code Sec. 7652 continued]
7. "(P)"
8. "(Q)"
9. "(R)"
10. "(S)"

Effective Date (Sec. 13252(d) of P.L. 103-66) effective for discharges of indebtedness after 12/31/93, except as provided in Sec. 13252(d)(2) of this Act which reads as follows:

"(2) Governmental entities.—In the case of an entity referred to in section 6050P(c)(1)(B) of the Internal Revenue Code of 1986 (as added by this section [Sec. 13252(a) of P.L. 103-66]) the amendments made by this section shall apply to discharges of indebtedness after the date of enactment of this Act [8/10/93]."

[Footnote Code Sec. 7652] Matter in *italics* in Code Sec. 7652(f)(1) added by section 13227(e) of P.L. 103-66 which struck out:
1. "(1) $10.50, or"

Effective Date (Sec. 13227(f) of P.L. 103-66) effective 10/1/93

[¶ 2171] **Code Sec. 7701. Definitions.**

* * * * * * * * * * * *

(l) Regulations relating to conduit arrangements. *The Secretary may prescribe regulations recharacterizing any multiple-party financing transaction as a transaction directly among any 2 or more of such parties where the Secretary determines that such recharacterization is appropriate to prevent avoidance of any tax imposed by this title.*

[1]*(m)* Cross references.

(1) Other definitions. For other definitions, see the following sections of Title 1 of the United States Code:

(1) Singular as including plural, section 1.

(2) Plural as including singular, section 1.

(3) Masculine as including feminine, section 1.

(4) Officer, section 1.

(5) Oath as including affirmation, section 1.

(6) County as including parish, section 2.

(7) Vessel as including all means of water transportation, section 3.

(8) Vehicle as including all means of land transportation, section 4.

(9) Company or association as including successors and assigns, section 5.

(2) Effect of cross references. For effect of cross references in this title, see section 7806(a).

[For explanation, see ¶ 1109, for Committee Reports, see ¶ 3057.]

[¶ 2172] **Code Sec. 7871. Indian tribal governments treated as states for certain purposes.**

(a) General rule. An Indian tribal government shall be treated as a State—

* * * * * * * * * * * *

(6) for purposes of—

(A) section 105(e) (relating to accident and health plans), [1]

[2]*(B)* section 403(b)(1)(A)(ii) (relating to the taxation of contributions of certain employers for employee annuities), and

[3]*(C)* section 454(b)(2) (relating to discount obligations); and

* * * * * * * * * * * *

[Footnote Code Sec. 7701] Matter in *italics* in Code Sec. 7701(l) added by section 13238 of P.L. 103-66 which struck out:

1. "(l)"
"(m)"

Effective Date effective 8/10/93.

[Footnote Code Sec. 7871] Matter in *italics* in Code Sec. 7871(a)(6)(B) and (C) added by section 13222(d), P.L. 103-66, which struck out:

1. "(B) section 162(e) (relating to appearances, etc., with respect to legislation),"
2. "(C)"
3. "(D)"

Effective Date (Sec. 13222(e), P.L. 103-66) effective for amounts paid or incurred after 12/31/93.

[¶ 2173] Code Sec. 9502. Airport and airway trust fund.

* * * * * * * * * * * * *

(b) Transfer to airport and airway trust fund of amounts equivalent to certain taxes. There is hereby appropriated to the Airport and Airway Trust Fund—

(1) amounts equivalent to the taxes received in the Treasury after August 31, 1982, and before January 1, 1996, under subsections (c) and (e) of section 4041 (taxes on aviation fuel) and under sections 4261 and 4271 (taxes on transportation by air);

(2) amounts determined by the Secretary of the Treasury to be equivalent to the taxes received in the Treasury after August 31, 1982, and before January 1, 1996, under section 4081 [1]*(to the extent of 14 cents per gallon)* , with respect to gasoline used in aircraft;

* * * * * * * * * * * * *

(f) Definition of Airport and Airway Trust Fund financing rate. *For purposes of this section—*

(1) In general. *Except as otherwise provided in this subsection, the Airport and Airway Trust Fund financing rate is—*

(A) in the case of fuel used in an aircraft in noncommercial aviation (as defined in section 4041(c)(4)), 17.5 cents per gallon, and

(B) in the case of fuel used in an aircraft other than in noncommercial aviation (as so defined), zero.

(2) Alcohol fuels. *If the rate of tax on any fuel is determined under section 4091(c), the Airport and Airway Trust Fund financing rate is the excess (if any) of the rate of tax determined under section 4091(c) over 4.4 cents per gallon (10⁄9 of 4.4 cents per gallon in the case of a rate of tax determined under section 4091(c)(2)).*

(3) Termination. *Notwithstanding the preceding provisions of this subsection, the Airport and Airway Trust Fund financing rate is zero with respect to tax received after December 31, 1995.*

[¶ 2174] Code Sec. 9503. Highway trust fund.

* * * * * * * * * * * * *

(b) Transfer to highway trust fund of amounts equivalent to certain taxes.

(1) In general. There are hereby appropriated to the Highway Trust Fund amounts equivalent to the taxes received in the Treasury before October 1, 1999, under the following provisions—

* * * * * * * * * * * * *

(E) section 4081 (relating to tax on [1]*gasoline and diesel fuel), and*

[2]*(F)* section 4481 (relating to tax on use of certain vehicles).

* * * * * * * * * * * * *

[Footnote Code Sec. 9502] Matter in *italics* in Code Sec. 9502(b)(2) and (f) added by section 13242(d)(32) and (33) of P.L. 103-66, which struck out:

1. "(to the extent attributable to the Highway Trust Fund financing rate and the deficit reduction rate)"

Effective Date (Sec. 13242(e) of P.L. 103-66) effective 1/1/94.

[Footnote Code Sec. 9503] Matter in *italics* in Code Secs. 9503(b)(1)(E) and (f), (b)(4)(B), (b)(5), (c)(4)(D), (c)(5)(B), (c)(6)(D) and (e)(2) added by sections 13242(d)(34)(A) through (C), (35)(A) and (B), (36) through (39), and (40)(A) and (B), P.L. 103-66, which struck out:

1. "gasoline),"
2. "(F) section 4091 (relating to tax on diesel fuel), and"
   "(G)"

(4) Certain additional taxes not transferred to highway trust fund. For purposes of paragraph (1) and (2)—

(A) there shall not be taken into account the taxes imposed by section 4041(d), and

(B) there shall be taken into account the taxes imposed by sections 4041 [3] *and 4081* only to the extent attributable to the Highway Trust Fund financing [4]*rate.*

(5) General revenue deposits of certain taxes on alcohol mixtures. For purposes of this section, the amounts which would (but for this paragraph) be required to be appropriated under subparagraphs (A) [5] *and (E)* of paragraph (1) shall be reduced by—

(A) 0.6 cent per gallon in the case of taxes imposed on any mixture at least 10 percent of which is alcohol (as defined in section 4081(c)(3)) if any portion of such alcohol is ethanol, and

(B) 0.67 cent per gallon in the case of gasoline or diesel fuel used in producing a mixture described in subparagraph (A).

(c) Expenditures from highway trust fund.

* * * * * * * * * * * * *

(4) Transfers from the trust fund for motorboat fuel taxes.

* * * * * * * * * * * * *

(D) Motorboat fuel taxes. For purposes of this paragraph, the term "motorboat fuel taxes" means the taxes under section 4041(a)(2) with respect to special motor fuels used as fuel in motorboats and under section 4081 with respect to gasoline used as fuel in motorboats, but only to the extent such taxes are attributable to the Highway Trust Fund financing [6]*rate.*

* * * * * * * * * * * * *

(5) Transfers from the trust fund for small-engine fuel taxes.

* * * * * * * * * * * * *

(B) Small-engine fuel taxes. For purposes of this paragraph, the term "small-engine fuel taxes" means the taxes under section 4081 with respect to gasoline used as a fuel in the nonbusiness use of small-engine outdoor power equipment, but only to the extent such taxes are attributable to the Highway Trust Fund financing [7]*rate* .

(6) Transfers from trust fund of certain recreational fuel taxes, etc.

* * * * * * * * * * * * *

(D) Nonhighway recreational fuel taxes. For purposes of this paragraph, the term "nonhighway recreational fuel taxes" means taxes under section 4041 [8] *and 4081* (to the extent attributable to the Highway Trust Fund financing rate) with respect to—

(i) fuel used in vehicles on recreational trails or back country terrain (including vehicles registered for highway use when used on recreational trails, trail access roads not eligible for funding under title 23, United States Code, or back country terrain), and

(ii) fuel used in campstoves and other nonengine uses in outdoor recreational equipment.

Such term shall not include small-engine fuel taxes (as defined by paragraph (5)) and taxes which are credited or refunded.

* * * * * * * * * * * * *

(e) Establishment of mass transit account.

* * * * * * * * * * * * *

[Footnote Code Sec. 9503 continued]

3. ", 4081, and 4091"
4. "rates under such sections" Sec. 13242(d)(35)(B) amended Code Sec. 9503(b)(4)(C) which did not exist previously nor was it added by P.L. 103-66.
5. ", (E), and (F)"
6. "rates under such sections"
7. "rates under such sections"
8. ", 4081, and 4091"

(2) Transfers to mass transit account. The Secretary of the Treasury shall transfer to the Mass Transit Account the mass transit portion of the amounts appropriated to the Highway Trust Fund under subsection (b) which are attributable to taxes under sections 4041 [9] *and 4081* , imposed after March 31, 1983. For purposes of the preceding sentence, the term "mass transit portion" means an amount determined at the rate of [10]*2 cents* for each gallon with respect to which tax was imposed under section 4041 [11] *or 4081* .

* * * * * * * * * * * *

(f) Definition of Highway Trust Fund financing rate. *For purposes of this section—*

(1) In general. *Except as otherwise provided in this subsection, the Highway Trust Fund financing rate is—*

(A) in the case of gasoline and special motor fuels, 11.5 cents per gallon (14 cents per gallon after September 30, 1995), and

(B) in the case of diesel fuel, 17.5 cents per gallon (20 cents per gallon after September 30, 1995).

(2) Certain uses.

(A) Trains. In the case of fuel used in a train, the Highway Trust Fund financing rate is zero.

(B) Certain buses. In the case of diesel fuel used in a use described in section 6427(b)(1) (after the application of section 6427(b)(3)), the Highway Trust Fund financing rate is 3 cents per gallon.

(C) Certain boats. In the case of diesel fuel used in a boat described in clause (iv) of section 6421(e)(2)(B), the Highway Trust Fund financing rate is zero.

(D) Compressed natural gas. In the case of the tax imposed by section 4041(a)(3), the Highway Trust Fund financing rate is zero.

(E) Certain other nonhighway uses. In the case of gasoline and special motor fuels used as described in paragraph (4)(D), (5)(B), or (6)(D) of subsection (c), the Highway Trust Fund financing rate is 11.5 cents per gallon; and, in the case of diesel fuel used as described in subsection (c)(6)(D), the Highway Trust Fund financing rate is 17.5 cents per gallon.

(3) Alcohol fuels.

(A) In general. If the rate of tax on any fuel is determined under section 4041(b)(2)(A), 4041(k), or 4081(c), the Highway Trust Fund financing rate is the excess (if any) of the rate so determined over—

(i) 6.8 cents per gallon after September 30, 1993, and before October 1, 1999,

(ii) 4.3 cents per gallon after September 30, 1999.

In the case of a rate of tax determined under section 4081(c), the preceding sentence shall be applied by increasing the rates spsecified in clauses (i) and (ii) by 0.1 cent.

(B) Fuels used to produce mixtures. In the case of a rate of tax determined under section 4081(c)(2), subparagraph (A) shall be applied by substituting rates which are 1⁄9 of the rates otherwise applicable under clauses (i) and (ii) of subparagraph (A).

(C) Partially exempt methanol or ethanol fuel. In the case of a rate of tax determined under section 4041(m), the Highway Trust Fund financing rate is the excess (if any) of the rate so determined over—

(i) 5.55 cents per gallon after September 30, 1993, and before October 1, 1995, and

(ii) 4.3 cents per gallon after September 30, 1995.

[Footnote Code Sec. 9503 continued]

9. ", 4081, and 4091"

Effective Date (Secs. 13242(e) of P.L. 103-66) effective 1/1/94.

Matter in *italics* in Code Sec. 9503(e)(2) added by section 13244(a) of P.L. 103-66, which struck out:

10. "1.5 cents"

Effective Date (Sec. 13244(b) of P.L. 103-66) effective for amounts attributable to taxes imposed on or after 10/1/95.

Matter in *italics* in Code Secs. 9503(e)(2) and (f) added by sections 13242(d)(40)(B) and (41) of P.L. 103-66 which struck out:

11. ", 4081, or 4091"

Effective Date (Secs. 13242(e) of P.L. 103-66) effective 1/1/94.

*(4) **Termination.** Notwithstanding the preceding provisions of this subsection, the Highway Trust Fund financing rate is zero with respect to taxes received in the Treasury after June 30, 2000.*

[For text of Committee Report, see ¶ 3024 and ¶ 3059]

[¶ 2175] Code Sec. 9508. Leaking Underground Storage Tank Trust Fund.

* * * * * * * * * * * *

(b) Transfers to trust fund. There are hereby appropriated to the Leaking Underground Storage Tank Trust Fund amounts equivalent to—

(1) taxes received in the Treasury under section 4041(d) (relating to additional taxes on motor fuels),

(2) taxes received in the Treasury under section 4081 (relating to tax on gasoline *and diesel fuel*) to the extent attributable to the Leaking Underground Storage Tank Trust Fund financing rate under such section,

(3) taxes received in the Treasury under section 4091 (relating to tax on [1]aviation fuel) to the extent attributable to the Leaking Underground Storage Tank Trust Fund financing rate under such section,

* * * * * * * * * * * *

For purposes of this subsection, there shall not be taken into account the taxes imposed by sections 4041 and 4081 on diesel fuel sold for use or used as fuel in a diesel-powered boat.

[For text of Committee Report, see ¶ 3024]

[¶ 2176] Code Sec. 9510. Vaccine injury compensation trust fund.

* * * * * * * * * * * *

(c) Expenditures from trust fund.

(1) In general. Amounts in the Vaccine Injury Compensation Trust Fund shall be available, as provided in appropriation Acts, only for the payment of compensation under subtitle 2 of title XXI of the Public Health Service Act (as in effect on the date of the enactment of this section) for vaccine-related injury or death with respect to vaccines administered after September 30, 1988, [1]or for the payment of all expenses of administration (but not in excess of $6,000,000 for any fiscal year) incurred by the Federal Government in administering such subtitle.

* * * * * * * * * * * *

[For explanation, see ¶ 1020, for Committee Reports, see ¶ 3076.]

[Footnote Code Sec. 9508] Matter in *italics* in Code Sec. 9508(b)(2) and (3) added by sections 13242(d)(42)(A) and (B) of P.L. 103-66 which struck out:

1. "diesel fuel and"

Effective Date (Sec. 13242(e) of P.L. 103-66) effective 1/1/94.

Matter in *italics* in Code Sec. 9508(b) was added by section 13163(c)

Effective Date (Sec. 13163(d) of P.L. 103-66) effective 1/1/94.

1. Code Sec. 9508(b) was amended by section 13242(d)(42)(C) of P.L. 103-66 by substituting '4081' for '4091' in the material added by section 13163(c). This is an unworkable amendment.

Effective Date (Sec. 13242(e) of P.L. 103-66) effective 1/1/94.

[Footnote Code Sec. 9510] Matter in *italics* in Code Sec. 9510(c)(1) was added by section 13421(b) of P.L. 103-66 which struck out:

1. "and before October 1, 1992,"

Effective Date effective 8/10/93.

Act Sections Not Amending the Code

¶ 2500. Act Sections of P.L. 103-66 (Title XIII) or portions thereof that *do not amend* specific Code Sections are at ¶ 2501—2587. Sections of the Code as amended by P.L. 103-66 begin at ¶ 2001.

Title XIII—Revenue, Health Care, Human Resources, Income Security, Customs and Trade, Food Stamp Program, and Timber Sale Provisions Chapter 1—Revenue Provisions

Table of Contents

Chapter 1—Revenue Provisions

Subpart E—Tax Exempt Bonds

Part III—Expansion and Simplification of Earned Income Tax Credit

Part IV—Incentives for Investment in Real Estate

Subpart A—Extension of Qualified Mortgage Bonds and Low-Income Housing Credit

Subpart B—Passive Loss Rules

Subpart C—Provisions Relating to Real Estate Investments by Pension Funds

* * * * * * * * * * * *

[¶ 2501] **Sec. 13001. Short Title; etc.**

(a) Short title. —This chapter may be cited as the "Revenue Reconciliation Act of 1993".

(b) Amendment to 1986 Code. —Except as otherwise expressly provided, whenever in this chapter an amendment or repeal is expressed in terms of an amendment to, or repeal of, a section or other provision, the reference shall be considered to be made to a section or other provision of the Internal Revenue Code of 1986.

(c) Section 15 not to apply. —Except in the case of the amendments made by section 13221 (relating to corporate rate increase), no amendment made by this chapter shall be treated as a change in a rate of tax for purposes of section 15 of the Internal Revenue Code of 1986.

(d) Waiver of estimated tax penalties. —No addition to tax shall be made under section 6654 or 6655 of the Internal Revenue Code of 1986 for any period before April 16, 1994 (March 16, 1994, in the case of a corporation), with respect to any underpayment to the extent such underpayment was created or increased by any provision of this chapter.

(e) Table of contents. —

SUBPART C—PROVISIONS RELATING TO REAL ESTATE INVESTMENTS BY PENSION FUNDS

Sec. 13144. Real estate property acquired by a qualified organization.
Sec. 13145. Repeal of special treatment of publicly treated partnerships.
Sec. 13146. Title-holding companies permitted to receive small amounts of unrelated business taxable income.
Sec. 13147. Exclusion from unrelated business tax of gain from certain property.
Sec. 13148. Exclusion from unrelated business tax of certain fees and option premiums.
Sec. 13149. Treatment of pension fund investments in real estate investment trusts.

SUBPART D—DISCHARGE OF INDEBTEDNESS

Sec. 13150. Exclusion from gross income for income from discharge of qualified real property business indebtedness.

SUBPART E—INCREASE IN RECOVERY PERIOD FOR NONRESIDENTIAL REAL PROPERTY

Sec. 13151. Increase in recovery period for nonresidential real property.

PART V—LUXURY TAX

Sec. 13161. Repeal of luxury excise taxes other than on passenger vehicles.
Sec. 13162. Exemption from luxury excise tax for certain equipment installed on passenger vehicles for use by disabled individuals.
Sec. 13163. Tax on diesel fuel used in noncommercial boats.

PART VI—OTHER CHANGES

Sec. 13171. Alternative minimum tax treatment of contributions of appreciated property.
Sec. 13172. Substantiation requirement for deduction of certain charitable contributions.
Sec. 13173. Disclosure related to quid pro quo contributions.
Sec. 13174. Temporary extension of deduction for health insurance costs of self-employed individuals.

Subchapter B—Revenue Increases

PART I—PROVISIONS AFFECTING INDIVIDUALS

SUBPART A—RATE INCREASES

Sec. 13201. Increase in top marginal rate under section 1.
Sec. 13202. Surtax on high-income taxpayers.
Sec. 13203. Modifications to alternative minimum tax rates and exemption amounts.
Sec. 13204. Overall limitation on itemized deductions for high-income taxpayers made permanent.
Sec. 13205. Phaseout of personal exemption of high-income taxpayers made permanent.
Sec. 13206. Provisions to prevent conversion of ordinary income to capital gain.

SUBPART B—OTHER PROVISIONS

Sec. 13207. Repeal of limitation on amount of wages subject to health insurance employment tax.
Sec. 13208. Top estate and gift tax rates made permanent.
Sec. 13209. Reduction in deductible portion of business meals and entertainment.
Sec. 13210. Elimination of deduction for club membership fees.
Sec. 13211. Disallowance of deduction for certain employee remuneration in excess of $1,000,000.
Sec. 13212. Reduction in compensation taken into account in determining contributions and benefits under qualified retirement plans.
Sec. 13213. Modifications to deduction for moving expenses.
Sec. 13214. Simplification of individual estimated tax safe harbor based on last year's tax.
Sec. 13215. Social security and tier 1 railroad retirement benefits.

PART II—PROVISIONS AFFECTING BUSINESSES

Sec. 13221. Increase in top marginal rate under section 11.
Sec. 13222. Denial of deduction for lobbying expenses.
Sec. 13223. Mark to market accounting method for securities dealers.
Sec. 13224. Clarification of treatment of certain FSLIC financial assistance.
Sec. 13225. Modification of corporate estimated tax rules.
Sec. 13226. Modifications of discharge of indebtedness provisions.
Sec. 13227. Limitation on section 936 credit.
Sec. 13228. Modification to limitation on deduction for certain interest.

PART III—FOREIGN TAX PROVISIONS

SUBPART A—CURRENT TAXATION OF CERTAIN EARNINGS OF CONTROLLED FOREIGN CORPORATIONS

Sec. 13231. Earnings invested in excess passive assets.
Sec. 13232. Modification to taxation of investment in United States property.
Sec. 13233. Other modifications to subpart F.

SUBPART B—ALLOCATION OF RESEARCH AND EXPERIMENTAL EXPENDITURES

Sec. 13234. Allocation of research and experimental expenditures.

SUBPART C—OTHER PROVISION

Sec. 13235. Repeal of certain exceptions for working capital.
Sec. 13236. Modifications of accuracy-related penalty.
Sec. 13237. Denial of portfolio interest exemption for contingent interest.
Sec. 13238. Regulations dealing with conduit arrangements.
Sec. 13239. Treatment of export of certain softwood logs.

PART IV—TRANSPORTATION FUELS PROVISIONS

SUBPART A—TRANSPORTATION FUELS TAX

Sec. 13241. Transportation fuels tax.

SUBPART B—MODIFICATIONS TO TAX ON DIESEL FUEL

Sec. 13242. Modifications to tax on diesel fuel.
Sec. 13243. Floor stocks tax.

SUBPART C—OTHER PROVISIONS

Sec. 13244. Increased deposits into Mass Transit Account.
Sec. 13245. Floor stocks tax on aviation fuel held on October 1, 1995.

PART V—COMPLIANCE PROVISIONS

Sec. 13251. Modifications to substantial understatement penalty.
Sec. 13252. Returns relating to the cancellation of indebtedness by certain financial entities.

PART VI—TREATMENT OF INTANGIBLES

Sec. 13261. Amortization of goodwill and certain other intangibles.
Sec. 13262. Treatment of certain payments to retired or deceased partner.

PART VII—MISCELLANEOUS PROVISIONS

Sec. 13271. Disallowance of interest on certain overpayments of tax.
Sec. 13272. Denial of deduction relating to travel expenses.
Sec. 13273. Increase in withholding from supplemental wage payments.

Subchapter C—Empowerment Zones, Enterprise Communities, Rural Development Investment Areas, Etc.

PART I—EMPOWERMENT ZONES, ENTERPRISE COMMUNITIES, AND RURAL DEVELOPMENT INVESTMENT AREAS

Sec. 13301. Designation and treatment of empowerment zones, enterprise communities, and rural development investment areas.

Sec. 13302. Technical and conforming amendments.

Sec. 13303. Effective date.

PART II—CREDIT FOR CONTRIBUTIONS TO CERTAIN COMMUNITY DEVELOPMENT CORPORATIONS

Sec. 13311. Credit for contributions to certain community development corporations.

PART III—INVESTMENT IN INDIAN RESERVATIONS

Sec. 13321. Accelerated depreciation for property on Indian reservations.

Sec. 13322. Indian employment credit.

Subchapter D—Other Provisions

PART I—DISCLOSURE PROVISIONS

Sec. 13401. Disclosure of return information for administration of certain veterans programs.

Sec. 13402. Disclosure of return information to carry out income contingent repayment of student loans.

Sec. 13403. Use of return information for income verification under certain housing assistance programs.

PART II—PUBLIC DEBT LIMIT

Sec. 13411. Increase in public debt limit.

PART III—VACCINE PROVISIONS

Sec. 13421. Excise tax on certain vaccines made permanent.

Sec. 13422. Continuation coverage under group health plans of costs of pediatric vaccines.

PART IV—DISASTER RELIEF PROVISIONS

Sec. 13431. Modification of involuntary conversion rules for certain disaster-related conversions.

PART V—MISCELLANEOUS PROVISIONS

Sec. 13441. Increase in presidential election campaign check-off.

Sec. 13442. Special rule for hospital services.

Sec. 13443. Credit for portion of employer social security taxes paid with respect to employee cash tips.

Sec. 13444. Availability and use of death information.

[¶2502] Sec. 13101. Employer-provided educational assistance.

(a) Extension of exclusion. —

* * * * * * * * * * * * *

(2) Conforming amendment. —Paragraph (2) of section 103(a) of the Tax Extension Act of 1991 is hereby repealed.

* * * * * * * * * * * * *

(c) Effective dates. —

(1) Subsection (a). —The amendments made by subsection (a) shall apply to taxable years ending after June 30, 1992.

(2) Subsection (b). —The amendment made by subsection (b) shall apply to taxable years beginning after December 31, 1988.

[¶ 2503] Sec. 13102. Targeted jobs credit.

* * * * * * * * * * * * *

(b) Effective date. —The amendment made by subsection (a) shall apply to individuals who begin work for the employer after June 30, 1992.

[¶ 2504] Sec. 13111. Extension of research and clinical testing credits.

* * * * * * * * * * * * *

(c) Effective date. —The amendments made by this section shall apply to taxable years ending after June 30, 1992.

[¶ 2505] Sec. 13112. Modification of fixed base percentage for startup companies.

* * * * * * * * * * * * *

(c) Effective date. —The amendments made by this section shall apply to taxable years beginning after December 31, 1993.

[¶ 2506] Sec. 13113. 50-percent exclusion for gain from certain small business stock.

* * * * * * * * * * * * *

(d) Conforming amendments. —

* * * * * * * * * * * * *

(6) The table of sections for part I of subchapter P of chapter 1 is amended by adding after the item relating to section 1201 the following new item:

"Sec. 1202. 50-percent exclusion for gain from certain small business stock."

(e) Effective date. —The amendments made by this section shall apply to stock issued after the date of the enactment of this Act.

[¶ 2507] Sec. 13114. Rollover of gain from sale of publicly traded securities into specialized small business investment companies.

* * * * * * * * * * * * *

(c) clerical amendment. —The table of sections for part III of subchapter O of chapter 1 is amended by adding at the end the following new item: "Sec. 1044. Rollover of publicly traded securities gain into specialized small business investment companies."

(d) Effective date. —The amendments made by this section shall apply to sales on and after the date of the enactment of this Act, in taxable years ending on and after such date.

[¶ 2508] Sec. 13115. Modification to minimum tax depreciation rules.

* * * * * * * * * * * * *

(b) Effective dates.—

(1) In general. —Except as provided in paragraph (2), the amendments made by this section shall apply to property placed in service after December 31, 1993.

(2) Coordination with transitional rules. —The amendments made by this section shall not apply to any property to which paragraph (1) of section 56(a) of the Internal Revenue Code of 1986 does not apply by reason of subparagraph (C)(i) thereof.

[¶ 2509] Sec. 13116. Increase in expense treatment for small businesses.

* * * * * * * * * * * * *

(b) Effective date. —The amendment made by subsection (a) shall apply to taxable years beginning after December 31, 1992.

[¶ 2510] Sec. 13121. High-speed intercity rail facility bonds exempt from state volume cap.

* * * * * * * * * * * * *

(b) Effective date. —The amendment made by subsection (a) shall apply to bonds issued after December 31, 1993.

[¶2511] Sec. 13122. Permanent extension of qualified small issue bonds.

* * * * * * * * * * * *

(b) Effective date. —The amendment made by subsection (a) shall apply to bonds issued after June 30, 1992.

(c) Treatment under inducement regulations. —If the 1-year period specified in Treasury Regulation section 1.103-8(a)(5) (as in effect before July 1, 1993) or any successor regulation would (but for this subsection) expire after June 30, 1992, and before January 1, 1994, such period shall not expire before January 1, 1994.

[¶2512] Sec. 13131. Expansion and simplification of the income tax credit.

* * * * * * * * * * * *

(e) Effective date. —The amendments made by this section shall apply to taxable years beginning after December 31, 1993.

[¶2513] Sec. 13141. Permanent extension of qualified mortgage bonds.

* * * * * * * * * * * *

(f) Effective dates.—

(1) Bonds. —The amendment made by subsection (a) shall apply to bonds issued after June 30, 1992.

(2) Certificates. —The amendment made by subsection (b) shall apply to elections for periods after June 30, 1992.

(3) Subsections (c) and (e). —The amendments made by subsections (c) and (e) shall apply to qualified mortgage bonds issued and mortgage credit certificates provided on or after the date of enactment of this Act.

(4) Contract for deed agreements. —The amendments made by subsection (d) shall apply to loans originated and credit certificates provided after the date of the enactment of this Act.

[¶2514] Sec. 13142. Low-income housing credit.

(a) Permanent extension.—

* * * * * * * * * * * *

(2) Effective date. —The amendments made by paragraph (1) shall apply to periods ending after June 30, 1992.

(b) Modifications.—

* * * * * * * * * * * *

(6) Effective dates.—

(A) In general.—Except as provided in subparagraphs (B) and (C), the amendments made by this subsection shall apply to—

(i) determinations under section 42 of the Intern Revenue Code of 1986 with respect to housing credit dollar amounts allocated from State housing credit ceilings after June 30, 1992, or

(ii) buildings placed in service after June 30, 1992, to the extent paragraph (1) of section 42(h) of such Code does not apply to any building by reason paragraph (4) thereof, but only with respect to bonds issued after such date.

(B) Waiver authority and prohibited discrimination.—The amendments made by paragraphs (3) and (4) shall take effect on the date of the enactment of this Act.

(C) Home assistance. The amendment made by paragraph (2) shall apply to periods after the date of the enactment of this Act.

(c) Election to determine rent limitation based on number of bedrooms and deep rent skewing.—

(1) In the case of a building to which the amendments made by subsection (e)(1) or (n)(2) of section 7108 of the Revenue Reconciliation Act of 1989 did not apply, the taxpayer may elect to have such amendments apply to such building if the taxpayer has met the requirements of the procedures described in section 42(m)(1)(B)(iii) of the Internal Revenue Code of 1986.

(2) In the case of the amendment made by such subsection (e)(1), such election shall apply only with respect to tenants first occupying any unit in the building after the date of the election.

(3) In the case of the amendment made by such subsection (n)(2), such election shall apply only if rents of low-income tenants in such building do not increase as a result of such election.

(4) An election under this subsection may be made only during the 180 day period beginning on the date of the enactment of this Act and, once made, shall be irrevocable.

[¶ 2515] Sec. 13143. Application of passive loss rules to rental real estate activities.

* * * * * * * * * * * * *

(c) Effective date. —The amendments made by this section shall apply to taxable years beginning after December 31, 1993.

[¶ 2516] Sec. 13144. Real estate property acquired by a qualified organization.

* * * * * * * * * * * * *

(c) Effective dates.—

(1) In general. —The amendments made by this section shall apply to acquisitions on or after January 1, 1994.

(2) Small leases. —The provisions of section 514(c)(9)(G)(i) of the Internal Revenue Code of 1986 shall, in addition to any leases to which the provisions apply by reason of paragraph (1), apply to leases entered into on or after January 1, 1994.

[¶ 2517] Sec. 13145. Repeal of special treatment of publicly treated partnerships.

* * * * * * * * * * * * *

(b) Effective date. —The amendments made by subsection (a) shall apply to partnership years beginning on or after January 17, 1994.

[¶ 2518] Sec. 13146. Title-holding companies permitted to receive small amounts of unrelated business taxable income.

* * * * * * * * * * * * *

(c) Effective date. —The amendments made by this section shall apply to taxable years beginning on or after January 1, 1994.

[¶ 2519] Sec. 13147. Exclusion from unrelated business tax of gains from certain property.

* * * * * * * * * * * * *

(b) Effective date. —The amendment made by subsection (a) shall apply to property acquired on or after January 1, 1994.

[¶ 2520] Sec. 13148. Exclusion from unrelated business tax of certain fees and option premiums.

* * * * * * * * * * * * *

(c) Effective date. —The amendments made by this section shall apply to amounts received on or after January 1, 1994.

[¶ 2521] Sec. 13149. Treatment of pension fund investments in real estate investment trusts.

* * * * * * * * * * * * *

(b) Effective date. —The amendment made by this section shall apply to taxable years beginning after December 31, 1993.

[¶2522] Sec. 13150. Exclusion from gross income for income from discharge of qualified real property business indebtedness.

* * * * * * * * * * * * *

(d) Effective date. —The amendments made by this section shall apply to discharges after December 31, 1992, in taxable years ending after such date.

[¶2523] Sec. 13151. Increase in recovery period for nonresidential real property.

* * * * * * * * * * * * *

(b) Effective date.—

(1) In general. —Except as provided in paragraph (2), amendment made by subsection (a) shall apply to property placed in service by the taxpayer on or after May 13, 1993.

(2) Exception. —The amendments made by this section not apply to property placed in service by the taxpayer before January 1, 1994, if—

(A) the taxpayer or a qualified person entered into binding written contract to purchase or construct property before May 13, 1993, or

(B) the construction of such property was commenced or for the taxpayer or a qualified person before May 13, 1993.

For purposes of this paragraph, the term "qualified" means any person who transfers his rights in such a contract such property to the taxpayer but only if the property is placed in service by such person before such rights are transferred to the taxpayer.

[¶2524] Sec. 13161. Repeal of luxury excise taxes other than on vehicles.

(a) In general. —Subchapter A of chapter 31 (relating to retail excise taxes) is amended to read as follows:

"Subchapter A—Luxury Passenger Automobiles

"Sec. 4001. Imposition of tax.

"Sec. 4002. 1st retail sale; uses, etc. treated as sales; determination of price.

"Sec. 4003. Special rules."

* * * * * * * * * * * * *

(b) Technical amendments.—

* * * * * * * * * * * * *

(3) The table of subchapters for chapter 31 is amended striking the item relating to subchapter A and inserting the following: "Subchapter A. Luxury passenger vehicles."

(c) Effective date. —The amendments made by this section shall take effect on January 1, 1993, except that the provisions of section 4001(e) of the Internal Revenue Code of 1986 (as amended by subsection (a)) shall take effect on the date of the enactment of this Act.

[¶2525] Sec. 13162. Exemption from luxury excise tax for certain installed on passenger vehicles for use by disabled individuals.

* * * * * * * * * * * * *

(b) Effective date. —The amendments made by this section shall take effect as if included in the amendments made by section 11221(a) of the Omnibus Budget Reconciliation Act of 1990.

(c) Period for filing claims. —If refund or credit of any overpayment of tax resulting from the application of the amendments made by this section is prevented at any time before the close of the 1-year period beginning on the date of the enactment of this Act by the operation of any law or rule of law (including res judicata), refund or credit of such overpayment (to the extent attributable to such amendments) may, nevertheless, be made or allowed if claim therefor is filed before the close of such 1-year period.

[¶ 2526] Sec. 13163. Tax on diesel fuel used in noncommercial boats.

* * * * * * * * * * * * *

(d) Effective date. —The amendments made by this section shall take effect on January 1, 1994.

[¶ 2527] Sec. 13171. Alternative minimum tax treatment of contributions appreciated property.

* * * * * * * * * * * * *

(d) Effective date. —The amendments made by this section shall apply to contributions made after June 30, 1992, except that in the case of any contribution of capital gain property which is not tangible personal property, such amendments shall apply only if the contribution is made after December 31, 1992.

[¶ 2528] Sec. 13172. Substantiation requirement for deduction of charitable contributions.

* * * * * * * * * * * * *

(b) Effective date. —The provisions of this section shall apply to contributions made on or after January 1, 1994.

[¶ 2529] Sec. 13173. Disclosure related to quid pro quo contributions.

* * * * * * * * * * * * *

(c) Clerical amendments. —

(1) The table for subchapter B of chapter 61 is amended striking the item relating to section 6115 and inserting the following new items:

"Sec. 6115. Disclosure related to quid pro quo contributions.

"Sec. 6116. Cross reference."

(2) The table for part I of subchapter B of chapter 68 is amended by inserting after the item for section 6713 following new item:

"Sec. 6714. Failure to meet disclosure requirements applicable to quid pro quo contributions."

(d) Effective date. —The provisions of this section shall apply to quid pro quo contributions made on or after January 1, 1994.

[¶ 2530] Sec. 13174. Temporary extension of deduction for health costs of self-employed individuals.

(a) In general.—

* * * * * * * * * * * * *

(2) Conforming amendment. —Paragraph (2) of section 110(a) of the Tax Extension Act of 1991 is hereby repealed.

(3) Effective date. —The amendments made by subsection shall apply to taxable years ending after June 1992.

(b) Determination of eligibility for employer-sponsored health plan.—

* * * * * * * * * * * * *

(2) Effective date. —The amendment made by paragraph (shall apply to taxable years beginning after December 31, 1992.

[¶ 2531] Sec. 13201. Increase in top marginal rate under section 1.

* * * * * * * * * * * * *

(c) Effective date. —The amendments made by this section shall apply to taxable years beginning after December 31, 1992.

(d) Election to pay additional 1993 taxes in installments.—

(1) In general. —At the election of the taxpayer, additional 1993 taxes may be paid in 3 equal installments.

(2). Dates for paying installments. —In the case of any payable in installments by reason of paragraph (1)—

(A) the first installment shall be paid on or before due date for the taxpayer's taxable year beginning calendar year 1993,

(B) the second installment shall be paid on or the date 1 year after the date determined under (A), and

(C) the third installment shall be paid on or before date 2 years after the date determined under (A).

For purposes of the preceding sentence, the term "due" means the date prescribed for filing the taxpayer's determined without regard to extensions.

(3) Extension without interest. —For purposes of 6601 of the Internal Revenue Code of 1986, the date prescribed for the payment of any tax payable in installments paragraph (1) shall be determined with regard to the under paragraph (1).

(4) Additional 1993 taxes.—

(A) In general.—For purposes of this subsection, term "additional 1993 taxes" means the excess of —

(i) the taxpayer's net chapter 1 liability as on the taxpayer's return for the taxpayer's taxable beginning in calendar year 1993, over

(ii) the amount which would have been the net chapter 1 liability for such taxable year if liability had been determined using the rates would have been in effect under section 1 of Internal Revenue Code of 1986 for taxable beginning in calendar year 1993 but for the amendments made by this section and section 13202 and liability had otherwise been determined on the basis the amounts shown on the taxpayer's return.

(B) Net chapter 1 liability.—For purposes subparagraph (A), the term "net chapter 1 liability" means the liability for tax under chapter 1 of the Revenue Code of 1986 determined—

(i) after the application of any credit against tax other than the credits under sections 31 and 34, and

(ii) before crediting any payment of estimated for the taxable year.

(5) Acceleration of payments. —If the taxpayer does pay any Installment under this section on or before the date prescribed for its payment or if the Secretary of the or his delegate believes that the collection of any payable in installments under this section is in jeopardy, Secretary shall immediately terminate the extension under paragraph (1) and the whole of the unpaid tax shall be paid notice and demand from the Secretary.

(6) Election on return. —An election under paragraph (shall be made on the taxpayer's return for the taxpayer's taxable year beginning in calendar year 1993.

(7) Exception for estates and trusts. — shall not apply in the case of an estate or trust.

[¶ 2532] Sec. 13202. Surtax on high-income taxpayers.

* * * * * * * * * * * * * *

(c) Effective date. —The amendments made by this section shall apply to taxable years beginning after December 31, 1992.

[¶ 2533] Sec. 13203. Modifications to alternative minimum tax rates exemption amounts.

* * * * * * * * * * * * * *

(d) Effective date. —The amendments made by this section shall apply to taxable years beginning after December 31, 1992.

[¶ 2534] Sec. 13206. Provisions to prevent conversion of ordinary income capital gain.

(a) Interest embedded in financial transactions. —

* * * * * * * * * * * * * *

(2) Clerical amendment. —The table of sections for part of subchapter P of chapter 1 is amended by adding at the end thereof the following new item:

"Sec. 1258. Recharacterization of gain from certain financial transactions."

(3) Effective date. —The amendments made by this shall apply to conversion transactions entered into after 30, 1993.

(b) Repeal of certain exceptions to market discount rules.—

* * * * * * * * * * * * *

(3) Effective date. —The amendments made by this shall apply to obligations purchased (within the meaning of section 1272(d)(1) of the Internal Revenue Code of 1986) April 30, 1993.

(c) Treatment of stripped preferred stock.—

* * * * * * * * * * * * *

(3) Effective date. —The amendments made by subsection shall take effect on April 30, 1993.

(d) Treatment of capital gain under limitation on investment interest.—

* * * * * * * * * * * * *

(3) Effective date. —The amendments made by this shall apply to taxable years beginning after December 31, 1992.

(e) Treatment of certain appreciated inventory. —

* * * * * * * * * * * * *

(2) Effective date. —The amendment made by paragraph (shall apply to sales, exchanges, and distributions after April 30, 1993.

[¶ 2535] Sec. 13207. Repeal of limitation on amount of wages subject to health insurance employment tax.

* * * * * * * * * * * * *

(e) Effective date. —The amendments made by this section shall apply to 1994 and later calendar years.

[¶ 2536] Sec. 13208. Top estate and gift tax rates made permanent.

* * * * * * * * * * * * *

(c) Effective date. —The amendments made by this section shall apply in the case of decedents dying and gifts made after December 31, 1992.

[¶ 2537] Sec. 13209. Reduction in deductible portion of business meals entertainment.

* * * * * * * * * * * * *

(c) Effective date. —The amendments made by this section shall apply to taxable years beginning after December 31, 1993.

[¶ 2538] Sec. 13210. Elimination of deduction for club membership fees.

* * * * * * * * * * * * *

(c) Effective date. —The amendments made by this section shall apply to amounts paid or incurred after December 31, 1993.

[¶ 2539] Sec. 13211. Disallowance of deduction for certain remuneration in excess of $1,000,000.

* * * * * * * * * * * * *

(b) Effective date. —The amendment made by subsection (a) shall apply to amounts which would otherwise be deductible for taxable years beginning on or after January 1, 1994.

[¶ 2540] Sec. 13212. Reduction in compensation taken into account determining contributions and benefits under qualified retirement plans.

* * * * * * * * * * * * *

(d) Effective dates.—

(1) In general. —Except as provided in this the amendments made by this section shall apply to accruing in plan years beginning after December 31, 1993.

(2) Collectively bargained plans. —In the case of a maintained pursuant to 1 or more collective bargaining agreements between employee representatives and 1 or employers ratified before the date of the enactment of this Act, the amendments made by this section shall not apply contributions or benefits pursuant to such agreements for years beginning before the earlier of—

(A) the latest of—

(i) January 1, 1994

(ii) the date on which the last of such bargaining agreements terminates (without regard to extension, amendment, or modification of such on or after such date of enactment), or

(iii) in the case of a plan maintained pursuant collective bargaining under the Railway Labor Act, the date of execution of an extension or replacement of last of such collective bargaining agreements in effect on such date of enactment, or

(B) January 1, 1997.

(3) Transition rule for state and local plans. —

(A) In general.—In the case of an participant in a governmental plan (within the meaning section 414(d) of the Internal Revenue Code of 1986), dollar limitation under section 401(a)(17) of such Code not apply to the extent the amount of compensation which is allowed to be taken into account under the plan would reduced below the amount which was allowed to be taken account under the plan as in effect on July 1, 1993.

(B) Eligible participant.—For purposes subparagraph (A), an eligible participant is an who first became a participant in the plan during a plan beginning before the 1st plan year beginning after earlier of—

(i) the plan year in which the plan is amended reflect the amendments made by this section, or

(ii) December 31, 1995.

(C) Plan must be amended to incorporate limits.—paragraph shall not apply to any eligible participant of a plan unless the plan is amended so that the incorporates by reference the dollar limitation section 401(a)(17) of the Internal Revenue Code of effective with respect to noneligible participants for years beginning after December 31, 1995 (or earlier if plan amendment so provides).

[¶ 2541] Sec. 13213. Modifications to deduction for moving expenses.

* * * * * * * * * * * * *

(e) Effective date. —The amendments made by this section shall apply to expenses incurred after December 31, 1993; except that the amendments made by subsection (d) shall apply to reimbursements or other payments in respect of expenses incurred after such date.

[¶ 2542] Sec. 13214. Simplification of individual estimated tax safe based on last year's tax.

* * * * * * * * * * * * *

(c) Effective date. —The amendments made by this section shall apply to taxable years beginning after December 31, 1993.

[¶ 2543] Sec. 13215. Social Security and Tier 1 Railroad Retirement benefits.

* * * * * * * * * * * * *

(c) Transfers to the hospital insurance trust fund. —

(1) In general. —Paragraph (1) of section 121(e) of Social Security Amendments of 1983 (Public Law 92-21) is amended by—

(A) striking "There" and inserting: "(A) There";

(B) inserting "(i)" immediately following "equivalent to"; and

(C) striking the period and inserting the following: "less (ii) the amounts equivalent to the aggregate increase in tax liabilities under chapter 1 of the Internal Revenue Code of 1986 which is attributable to the amendments section 86 of such Code made by section 13215 of the Reconciliation Act of 1993.

'(B) There are hereby appropriated to the insurance trust fund amounts equal to the increase in liabilities described in subparagraph (A)(ii). Such appropriated amounts shall be transferred from the fund of the Treasury on the basis of estimates of such tax liabilities made by the Secretary of the Treasury. Transfers shall be made pursuant to a schedule made by the Secretary of the Treasury that takes into account estimated timing collection of such liabilities.'

(2) Definition. —Paragraph (3) of section 121(e) of Act is amended by redesignating subparagraph (B) as (C), and by inserting after subparagraph (A) the following subparagraph:
"(B) Hospital insurance trust fund.—The 'hospital insurance trust fund' means the fund pursuant to section 1817 of the Social Security Act.".

(3) Conforming amendment. —Paragraph (2) of section 121(of such Act is amended in the first sentence by striking "paragraph (1)" and inserting "paragraph (1)(A)".

(4) Technical amendments. —Paragraph (1)(A) of 121(e) of such Act, as redesignated and amended by (1), is amended by striking "1954" and inserting "1986".

(d) Effective date. —The amendments made by subsections (a) and (b) shall apply to taxable years beginning after December 31, 1993.

[¶ 2544] Sec. 13221. Increase in top marginal rate under section 11.

* * * * * * * * * * * * *

(d) Effective date. —The amendments made by this section shall pply to taxable years beginning on or after January 1, 1993; except hat the amendment made by subsection (c)(3) shall take effect on the ate of the enactment of this Act.

[¶ 2545] Sec. 13222. Denial of deduction for lobbying expenses.

* * * * * * * * * * * * *

(e) Effective date. —The amendments made by this section shall pply to amounts paid or incurred after December 31, 1993.

[¶ 2546] Sec. 13223. Mark to market accounting method for securities dealers.

* * * * * * * * * * * * *

(b) Conforming amendments.—

* * * * * * * * * * * * *

(2) The table of sections for subpart D of part II subchapter E of chapter 1 is amended by adding at the thereof the following new item:
"Sec. 475. Mark to market accounting method for dealers in securities."

(c) Effective date—

(1) In general. —The amendments made by this section apply to all taxable years ending on or after December 31, 1993.

(2) Change in method of accounting. — In the case of taxpayer required by this section to change its method of accounting for any taxable year—

(A) such change shall be treated as initiated by the taxpayer,

(B) such change shall be treated as made with consent of the Secretary, and

(C) except as provided in paragraph (3), the net of the adjustments required to be taken into account by the taxpayer under section 481 of the Internal Revenue Code 1986 shall be taken into account ratably over the year period beginning with the first taxable year on or after December 31, 1993.

(3) Special rule for floor specialists and market makers.—

(A) In general.—If—

(i) a taxpayer (or any predecessor) used the first-out (LIFO) method of accounting with respect any qualified securities for the 5-taxable year ending with its last taxable year ending before December 31, 1993, and

(ii) any portion of the net amount described paragraph (2)(C) is attributable to the use of method of accounting,

then paragraph (2)(C) shall be applied by taking such portion into account ratably over the 15-taxable year beginning with the first taxable year ending on or December 31, 1993.

(B) Qualified security.—For purposes of paragraph, the term "qualified security" means any security acquired—

(i) by a floor specialist (as defined in 1236(d)(2) of the Internal Revenue Code of 1986) connection with the specialist's duties as a on an exchange, but only if the security is one in which he specialist is registered with the exchange, or

(ii) by a taxpayer who is a market maker in connection with the taxpayer's duties as a market but only if—

(I) the security is included on the Association of Security Dealers Automated System,

(II) the taxpayer is registered as a maker in such security with the National of Security Dealers, and

(III) as of the last day of the taxable preceding the taxpayer's first taxable year on or after December 31, 1993, the taxpayer (or predecessor) has been actively and regularly as a market maker in such security for the period ending on such date (or, if shorter, the period beginning 61 days after the security listed in such quotation system and ending on date).

[¶ 2547] **Sec. 13224. Clarification of treatment of certain FSLIC assistance.**

(a) General rule. —For purposes of chapter 1 of the Internal Revenue Code of 1986—

(1) any FSLIC assistance with respect to any loss principal, capital, or similar amount upon the disposition any asset shall be taken into account as compensation for loss for purposes of section 165 of such Code, and

(2) any FSLIC assistance with respect to any debt shall taken into account for purposes of section 166, 585, or 593 such Code in determining whether such debt is worthless (or extent to which such debt is worthless) and in determining amount of any addition to a reserve for bad debts arising the worthlessness or partial worthlessness of such debts.

(b) FSLIC Assistance. —For purposes of this section, the term "FSLIC assistance" means any assistance (or right to assistance) with respect to a domestic building and loan association (as defined in section 7701(a)(19) of such Code without regard to subparagraph (C) thereof) under section 406(f) of the National Housing Act or section 21A of the Federal Home Loan Bank Act (or under any similar provision of law).

(c) Effective date.—

(1) In general. —Except as otherwise provided in subsection—

(A) The provisions of this section shall apply taxable years ending on or after March 4, 1991, but with respect to FSLIC assistance not credited before 4, 1991.

(B) If any FSLIC assistance not credited before March 1991, is with respect to a loss sustained or charge-off in a taxable year ending before March 4, 1991, for purposes determining the amount of any net operating loss carryover a taxable year ending on or after March 4, 1991, provisions of this section shall apply to such for purposes of determining the amount of the net loss for the taxable year in which such loss was or debt written off. Except as provided in the sentence, this section shall not apply to any assistance with respect to a loss sustained or charge-off in a taxable year ending before March 4, 1991.

(2) Exceptions. —The provisions of this section shall apply to any assistance to which the amendments made by section 1401(a)(3) of the Financial Institutions Reform, Recovery, Enforcement Act of 1989 apply.

[¶ 2548] Sec. 13225. Modification of corporate estimated tax rules.

* * * * * * * * * * * * *

(c) Effective date. —The amendments made by this section shall apply to taxable years beginning after December 31, 1993.

[¶ 2549] Sec. 13226. Modifications of discharge of indebtedness provisions.

(a) Repeal of stock for debt exception in determining income from discharge of indebtedness.—

* * * * * * * * * * * * *

(3) Effective date.—

(A) In general.—Except as otherwise provided in this paragraph, the amendments made by this subsection shall apply to stock transferred after December 31, 1994, in satisfaction of any indebtedness.

(B) Exception for title 11 cases. —The amendments satisfaction of any indebtedness if such transfer is in title 11 or similar case (as defined in section 368(a)(3)(A) of the Internal Revenue Code of 1986) which was filed on before December 31, 1993.

(b) Tax attributes subject to reduction.—

* * * * * * * * * * * * *

(4) Effective date. —The amendments made by subsection shall apply to discharges of indebtedness in taxable years beginning after December 31, 1993.

[¶ 2550] Sec. 13227. Limitation on section 936 credit.

* * * * * * * * * * * * *

(f) Effective date.— The amendments made by this section shall apply to taxable years beginning after December 31, 1993; except that the amendment made by subsection (e) shall take effect on October 1, 1993.

[¶ 2551] Sec. 13228. Modification to limitation on deduction for certain interest.

* * * * * * * * * * * * *

(d) Effective date. — The amendments made by this section shall apply to interest paid or accrued in taxable years beginning after December 31, 1993.

[¶ 2552] Sec. 13231. Earnings invested in excess passive assets.

* * * * * * * * * * * * *

(e) Effective date.— The amendments made by this section shall apply to taxable years of foreign corporations beginning after September 30, 1993, and to taxable years of United States shareholders in which or with which such taxable years of foreign corporations end.

[¶ 2553] Sec. 13232. Modification to taxation of investment in United States property.

* * * * * * * * * * * * *

(d) Effective date.— The amendments made by this section shall apply to taxable years of controlled foreign corporations beginning after September 30, 1993, and to taxable years of United States shareholders in which or with which such taxable years of controlled foreign corporations end.

[¶ 2554] Sec. 13233. Other modifications to subpart F.

(a) Same country exception not to apply to certain dividends.—

* * * * * * * * * * * * *

(2) Effective date.— The amendment made by paragraph (1) shall apply to taxable years of controlled foreign corporations beginning after September 30, 1993, and to taxable years of

United States shareholders in which or with which such taxable years of controlled foreign corporations end.

(b) Amendments to section 960(b).—

* * * * * * * * * * * * *

(2) Effective date.— The amendment made by paragraph (1) shall apply to taxable years beginning after September 30, 1993.

[¶ 2555] Sec. 13235. Repeal of certain exceptions for working capital.

* * * * * * * * * * * * *

(c) Effective date.— The amendments made by this section shall apply to taxable years beginning after December 31, 1992.

[¶ 2556] Sec. 13236. Modifications of accuracy-related penalty.

* * * * * * * * * * * * *

(e) Effective date.— The amendments made by this section shall apply to taxable years beginning after December 31, 1993.

[¶ 2557] Sec. 13237. Denial of portfolio interest exemption for contingent interest.

* * * * * * * * * * * * *

(d) Effective date.— The amendments made by this section shall apply to interest received after December 31, 1993; except that the amendments made by subsection (b) shall apply to the estates of decedents dying after December 31, 1993.

[¶ 2558] Sec. 13239. Treatment of export of certain softwood logs.

* * * * * * * * * * * * *

(e) Effective date.— The amendments made by this section shall apply to sales, exchanges, or other dispositions after the date of the enactment of this Act.

[¶ 2559] Sec. 13241. Transportation fuel tax.

* * * * * * * * * * * * *

(g) Effective date. —The amendments made by this section shall take effect on October 1, 1993.

(h) Floor stocks taxes. —

(1) Imposition of tax. —In the case of gasoline, diesel, fuel, and aviation fuel on which tax was imposed under section 4081 or 4091 of the Internal Revenue Code of 1986 before October 1, 1993, and which is held on such date by any person, there is hereby imposed a floor stocks tax of 4.3 cents per gallon on such gasoline, diesel fuel, and aviation fuel.

(2) Liability for tax and method of liability for tax and method of payment. —

(A) Liability for tax.—A person holding gasoline, diesel fuel, or aviation fuel on October 1, 1993, to which the tax imposed by paragraph (1) applies shall be liable for such tax.

(B) Method of payment.—The tax imposed by paragraph (1) shall be paid in such manner as the Secretary shall prescribe.

(C) Time for payment.—The tax imposed by paragraph (1) shall be paid on or before November 30, 1993.

(3) Definitions. —For purposes of this subsection—

(A) Held by a person.—Gasoline, diesel fuel, and aviation fuel shall be considered as "held by a person" if title thereto has passed to such person (whether or not delivery to the person has been made).

(B) Gasoline.—The term "gasoline" has the meaning given such term by section 4082 of such Code.

(C) Diesel fuel.—The term "diesel fuel" has the meaning given such term by section 4092 of such Code.

(D) Aviation fuel.—The term "aviation fuel" has the meaning given such term by section 4092 of such Code.

(E) Secretary.—The term "Secretary" means the Secretary of the Treasury or his delegate.

(4) Exemption for exempt uses. — The tax imposed by paragraph (1) shall not apply to gasoline, diesel fuel, or aviation fuel held by any person exclusively for any use to the extent a credit or refund of the tax imposed by section 4081 or 4091 of such Code, as the case may be, is allowable for such use.

(5) Exception for fuel held in vehicle tank. — No tax shall be imposed by paragraph (1) on gasoline or diesel fuel held in the tax of a motor vehicle or motorboat.

(6) Exception for certain amounts of fuel. —

(A) In general.— No tax shall be imposed by paragraph (1)—

(i) on gasoline held on October 1, 1993, by any person if the aggregate amount of gasoline held by such person on such date does not exceed 4,000 gallons, and

(ii) on diesel fuel or aviation fuel held on October 1, 1993, by any person if the aggregate amount of diesel fuel or aviation fuel held by such person on such date does not exceed 2,000 gallons. The preceding sentence shall apply only if such person submits to the Secretary (at the time and in the manner required by the Secretary) such information as the Secretary shall require for purposes of this paragraph.

(B) Exempt fuel.— For purposes of subparagraph (A), there shall not be taken into account fuel held by any person which is exempt from the tax imposed by paragraph (1) by reason of paragraph (4) or (5).

(C) Controlled groups.— For purposes of this paragraph—

(i) Corporations.—

(I) In general.— All persons treated as a controlled group shall be treated as 1 person.

(II) Controlled group.— The term "controlled group" has the meaning given to such term by subsection (a) of section 1563 of such Code; except that for such purposes the phrase "more than 50 percent" shall be substituted for the phrase "at least 80 percent" each place it appeals in such subsection.

(ii) nonincorporated persons under common control.— Under regulations prescribed by the Secretary, principles similar to the principles of clause (i) shall apply to a group of persons under common control where 1 or more of such persons is not a corporation.

(7) Other law applicable. — All provisions of law,including penalties, applicable with respect to the taxes imposed by section 4081 of such Code in the case of gasoline and section 4091 of such Code in the case of diesel fuel and aviation fuel shall, insofar as applicable and not inconsistent with the provisions of this subsection, apply with respect to the floor stock taxes imposed by paragraph (1) to the same extent as if such taxes were imposed by such section 4081 or 4091.

[¶ 2560] Sec. 13242. Modifications to tax on diesel fuel.

(a) In general. — Subparts A and B of part III of subchapter A of chapter 32 (relating to manufacturers excise taxes), as amended by subpart A, are amended to read as follows:

"Subpart A— Gasoline and Diesel Fuel

"Sec. 4081. Imposition of tax.
"Sec. 4082. Exemptions for diesel fuel.
"Sec. 4083. Definitions; special rule; administrative authority.
"Sec. 4084. Cross references.

* * * * * * * * * * * * *

"Subpart B—Aviation Fuel

"Sec. 4091. Imposition of tax.
"Sec. 4092. Exemptions.
"Sec. 4093. Definitions.

* * * * * * * * * * * * *

(b) Civil penalty For using reduced-rate fuel for taxable use, etc.—

* * * * * * * * * * * * *

(2) Clerical amendment. — The table of sections for such part I is amended by adding at the end thereof the following new item:

"Sec. 6714. Dyed fuel sold for use or used in taxable use, etc."

(d) Technical and Conforming Amendments. —

* * * * * * * * * * * * *

(43) The table of subparts for part III of subchapter A of chapter 32 is amended by striking the items relating to subparts A and B and inserting the following new items:

"Subpart A. Gasoline and diesel fuel.

"Subpart B. Aviation fuel."

(e) Effective date. —The amendments made by this section shall take effect on January 1, 1994.

[¶ 2561] Sec. 13243. Floor stocks tax.

(a) In general.—There is hereby imposed a floor stocks tax on diesel fuel held by any person on January 1, 1994, if—

(1) no tax was imposed on such fuel under section 4041(a) or 4091 of the Internal Revenue Code of 1986 as in effect on December 31, 1993, and

(2) tax would have been imposed by section 4081 of such Code, as amended by this Act, on any prior removal, entry, or sale of such fuel had such section 4081 applied to such fuel for periods before January 1, 1994.

(b) Rate of tax. —The rate of the tax imposed by subsection (a) shall be the amount of tax which would be imposed under section 4081 of the Internal Revenue Code of 1986 if there were a taxable sale of such fuel on such date.

(c) Liability and payment of tax. —

(1) Liability for tax. — A person holding the diesel fuel on January 1, 1994, to which the tax imposed by this section applies shall be liable for such tax.

(2) Method of payment. —The tax imposed by this section shall be paid in such manner as the Secretary shall prescribe.

(3) Time for payment. —The tax imposed by this section shall be paid on or before July 31, 1994.

(d) Definitions. —For purposes of this section—

(1) Diesel fuel. —The term "diesel fuel" has the meaning given such term by section 4083(a) of such Code.

(2) Secretary. —The term "Secretary" means the Secretary of the Treasury or his delegate.

(e) Exceptions.—

(1) Persons entitled to credit or refund. — The tax imposed by this section shall not apply to fuel held by any person exclusively for any use to the extent a credit or refund of the tax imposed by section 4081 is allowable for such use.

(2) Compliance with dyeing required. — Paragraph (1) shall not apply to the holder of any fuel if the holder of such fuel fails to comply with any requirement imposed by the Secretary with respect to dyeing and marking such fuel.

(f) Other laws applicable. —All provisions of law, including penalties, applicable with respect to the taxes imposed by section 4081 of such Code shall, insofar as applicable and not inconsistent with the provisions of this section, apply with respect to the floor stock taxes imposed by this section to the same extent as if such taxes were imposed by such section 4081.

[¶ 2562] Sec. 13244. Increased deposits into mass transit account.

* * * * * * * * * * * * *

(b) Effective date. —The amendment made by this section shall apply to amounts attributable to taxes imposed on or after October 1, 1995.

[¶ 2563] Sec. 13245. Floor stocks tax on commercial aviation fuel held on October 1, 1995.

(a) Imposition of tax.— In the case of commercial aviation fuel on which tax was imposed under section 4091 of the Internal Revenue Code of 1986 before October 1, 1995, and which is held on such date by any person, there is hereby imposed a floor stocks tax of 4.3 cents per gallon.

(b) Liability for tax and method of payment.—

(1) Liability for tax. — A person holding aviation fuel on October 1, 1995, to which the tax imposed by subsection (a) applies shall be liable for such tax.

(2) Method of payment. — The tax imposed by subsection (a) shall be paid in such manner as the Secretary shall prescribe.

(3) Time for payment. — The tax imposed by subsection (a) shall be paid on or before April 30, 1996.

(c) Definitions. — For purposes of this subsection—

(1) Held by a person. — Aviation fuel shall be considered as "held by a person" if title thereto has passed to such person (whether or not delivery to the person has been made).

(2) Commercial aviation fuel. — The term "commercial aviation fuel" means aviation fuel (as defined in section 4093 of such Code) which is held on October 1, 1995, for sale or use in commercial aviation (as defined in section 4092(b) of such Code).

(3) Secretary. — The term "Secretary" means the Secretary of the Treasury or his delegate.

(d) Exception for exempt uses. — The tax imposed by subsection (a) shall not apply to aviation fuel held by any person exclusively for any use for which a credit or refund of the entire tax imposed by section 4091 of such Code is allowable for aviation fuel purchased after September 30, 1995, for such use.

(e) Exception for certain amounts of fuel.—

(1) In general. — No tax shall be imposed by subsection (a) on aviation fuel held on October 1, 1995, by any person if the aggregate amount of commercial aviation fuel held by such person on such date does not exceed 2,000 gallons. The preceding sentence shall apply only if such person submits to the Secretary (at the time and in the manner required by the Secretary) such information as the Secretary shall require for purposes of this paragraph.

(2) Exempt fuel. — For purposes of paragraph (1), there shall not be taken into account fuel held by any person which is exempt from the tax imposed by subsection (a) by reason of subsection (d).

(3) Controlled groups. — For purposes of this subsection—

(A) Corporations.—

(i) In general.— All persons treated as a controlled group shall be treated as 1 person.

(ii) Controlled group.— The term "controlled group" has the meaning given to such term by subsection (a) of section 1563 of such Code; except that for such purposes the phrase "more than 50 percent" shall be substituted for the phrase "at least 80 percent" each place it appears in such subsection.

(B) Nonincorporated persons under common control.— Under regulations prescribed by the Secretary, principles similar to the principles of subparagraph (A) shall apply to a group of persons under common control where 1 or more of such persons is not a corporation.

(f) Other law applicable. — All provisions of law, including penalties, applicable with respect to the taxes imposed by section 4091 of such Code shall, insofar as applicable and not inconsistent with the provisions of this section, apply with respect to the floor stock taxes imposed by subsection (a) to the same extent as if such taxes were imposed by such section 4091.

[¶ 2564] Sec. 13251. Modifications to substantial understatement penalty.

* * * * * * * * * * * * *

(b) Effective date. —The amendment made by this section shall apply to returns the due dates for which (determined without regard to extensions) are after December 31, 1993.

[¶ 2565] Sec. 13252. Returns Relating to the Cancellation of Indebtedness by Certain Financial Entities.

* * * * * * * * * * * * *

(c) Clerical amendment. —The table of sections for subpart B of part III of subchapter A of chapter 61 is amended by adding at the end thereof the following new item:

"Sec. 6050P. Returns relating to the cancellation of indebtedness by certain financial entities."

(d) Effective date.—

(1) In general. —Except as provided in paragraph (2), the amendments made by this section shall apply to discharges of indebtedness after December 31, 1993.

(2) Governmental entities. —In the case of an entity referred to in section 6050P(c)(1)(B) of the Internal Revenue Code of 1986 (as added by this section), the amendments made by this section shall apply to discharges of indebtedness after the date of the enactment of this Act.

[¶ 2566] Sec. 13261. Amortization of goodwill and certain other intangibles.

* * * * * * * * * * * * *

(f) Technical and conforming amendments.—

* * * * * * * * * * * * *

(6) The table of sections for part VI of subchapter B of chapter 1 is amended by adding at the end thereof the following new item:

"Sec. 197. Amortization of goodwill and certain other intangibles".

(g) Effective date.—

(1) In general. — Except as otherwise provided in this subsection, the amendments made by this section shall apply with respect to property acquired after the date of the enactment of this Act.

(2) Election to have amendments apply to property acquired after July 25, 1991.—

(A) In general.— If an election under this paragraph applies to the taxpayer—

(i) the amendments made by this section shall apply to property acquired by the taxpayer after July 25, 1991,

(ii) subsection (c)(1)(A) of section 197 of the Internal Revenue Code of 1986 (as added by this section) (and so much of subsection (f)(9)(A) of such section 197 as precedes clause (i) thereof) shall be applied with respect to the taxpayer by treating July 25, 1991, as the date of the enactment of such section, and

(iii) in applying subsection (f)(9) of such section, with respect to any property acquired by the taxpayer on or before the date of the enactment of this Act, only holding or use on July 25, 1991, shall be taken into account.

(B) Election.— An election under this paragraph shall be made at such time and in such manner as the Secretary of the Treasury or his delegate may prescribe. Such an election by any taxpayer, once made—

(i) may be revoked only with the consent of the Secretary, and

(ii) shall apply to the taxpayer making such election and any other taxpayer under common control with the taxpayer (within the meaning of subparagraphs (A) and (B) of section 41(f)(1) of such Code) at any time after August 2, 1993, and on or before the date on which such election is made.

(3) Elective binding contract exception.—

(A) In general.— The amendments made by this section shall not apply to any acquisition of property by the taxpayer if—

(i) such acquisition is pursuant to a written binding contract in effect on the date of the enactment of this Act and at all times thereafter before such acquisition,

(ii) an election under paragraph (2) does not apply to the taxpayer, and

(iii) the taxpayer makes an election under this paragraph with respect to such contract.

(B) Election.—An election under this paragraph shall be made at such time and in such manner as the Secretary of the Treasury or his delegate shall prescribe. Such an election, once made—

(i) may be revoked only with the consent of the Secretary, and

(ii) shall apply to all property acquired pursuant to the contract with respect to which such election was made.

[¶ 2567] Sec. 13262. Treatment of certain payments to be retired or deceased partner.

* * * * * * * * * * * *

(c) Effective date.—

(1) In general. — The amendments made by this section shall apply in the case of partners retiring or dying on or after January 5, 1993.

(2) Binding contract exception. — The amendments made by this section shall not apply to any partner retiring on or after January 5, 1993, if a written contract to purchase such partner's interest in the partnership was binding on January 4,1993, and at times thereafter before such purchase.

[¶ 2568] Sec. 13271. Disallowance of Interest on Certain Overpayments of Tax.

* * * * * * * * * * * *

(b) Effective dDates.—

(1) Paragraph (1) of section 6611(e) of the Internal Revenue Code of 1986 (as amended by subsection (a)) shall apply in the case of returns the due date for which (determined without regard to extensions) is on or after January 1, 1994.

(2) Paragraph (2) of section 6611(e) of such Code (as so amended) shall apply in the case of claims for credit or refund of any overpayment filed on or after January 1, 1995, regardless of the taxable period to which such refund relates.

(3) Paragraph (3) of section 6611(e) of such Code (as so amended) shall apply in the case of any refund paid on or after January 1, 1995, regardless of the taxable period to which such refund relates.

[¶ 2569] Sec. 13272. Denial of deduction relating to travel expenses.

* * * * * * * * * * * *

(b) Effective date. —The amendment made by this section shall apply to amounts paid or incurred after December 31, 1993.

[¶ 2570] Sec. 13273. Increase in withholding from supplemental wage payments.
If an employee elects under Treasury Regulation 31.3402(g)-1 to determine the amount to be deducted and withheld from any supplemental wage payment by using a flat percentage rate, the rate to be used in determining the amount to be so deducted and withheld shall not be less than 28 percent. The preceding sentence shall apply to payments made after December 31, 1993.

[¶ 2571] Sec. 13301. Designations.

(a) In general.— Chapter 1 (relating to normal taxes and surtaxes) is amended by inserting after subchapter T the following new subchapter:

"Subchapter U— Designation and treatment of empowerment zones, enterprise communities, and rural development investment areas

"Part I. Designation.

"Part II. Tax-exempt facility bonds for empowerment zones and enterprise communities.

"Part III. Additional incentives for empowerment zones.

"Part IV. Regulations.

"Part I— Designation

"Sec. 1391. Designation procedure.
"Sec. 1392. Eligibility criteria.
"Sec. 1393. Definitions and special rules.

* * * * * * * * * * * * *

"Part II— Tax-Exempt Facility Bonds For Empowerment Zones And Enterprise Communities
"Sec. 1394. Tax-exempt enterprise zone facility bonds.

* * * * * * * * * * * * *

"Part III— Additional incentives for empowerment zones

"SUBPART A. Empowerment zone employment credit.

"SUBPART B. Additional expensing.

"SUBPART C. General provisions.

"Subpart A—Empowerment Zone Employment Credit
"Sec. 1396. Empowerment zone employment credit.
"Sec. 1397. Other definitions and special rules.

* * * * * * * * * * * * *

"Subpart B— Additional Expensing
"Sec. 1397A. Increase in expensing under section 179.

* * * * * * * * * * * * *

"Subpart C— General Provisions
"Sec. 1397B. Enterprise zone business defined.
"Sec. 1397C. Qualified zone property defined.

* * * * * * * * * * * * *

"Part IV— Regulations
"Sec. 1397D. Regulations.

* * * * * * * * * * * * *

(b) Clerical amendment. —The table of subchapters for chapter 1 is amended by inserting after the item relating to subchapter T the following new item:

"Subchapter U. Designation and treatment of empowerment zones, enterprise communities, and rural development investment areas."

[¶ 2572] Sec. 13303. Effective date.
The amendments made by this part shall take effect on the date of the enactment of this Act.

[¶ 2573] Sec. 13311. Credit for contributions to certain community development corporations.

(a) In general.— For purposes of section 38 of the Internal Revenue Code of 1986, the current year business credit shall include the credit determined under this section.

(b) **Determination of credit.**— The credit determined under this section for each taxable year in the credit period with respect to any qualified CDC contribution made by the taxpayer is an amount equal to 5 percent of such contribution.

(c) **Credit period.**— For purposes of this section, the credit period with respect to any qualified CDC contribution is the period of 10 taxable years beginning with the taxable year during which such contribution was made.

(d) **Qualified CDC contribution.**— For purposes of this section—

(1) **In general.**— The term "qualified CDC contribution" means any transfer of cash—

(A) which is made to a selected community development corporation during the 5-year period beginning on the datesuch corporation was selected for purposes of this section,

(B) the amount of which is available for use by such corporation for at least 10 years,

(C) which is to be used by such corporation for qualified low-income assistance within its operational area, and

(D) which is designated by such corporation for purposes of this section.

(2) **Limitations on amount designated.**— The aggregate amount of contributions to a selected community development corporation which may be designated by such corporation shall not exceed $2,000,000.

(e) **Selected community development corporations.**—

(1) **In general.**— For purposes of this section, the term "selected community development corporation" means any corporation—

(A) which is described in section 501(c)(3) of such Code and exempt from tax under section 501(a) of such Code,

(B) the principal purposes of which include promoting employment of, and business opportunities for, low-income individuals who are residents of the operational area, and

(C) which is selected by the Secretary of Housing and Urban Development for purposes of this section.

(2) **Only 20 corporations may be selected.**— The Secretary of Housing and Urban Development may select 20 corporations for purposes of this section, subject to the availability of eligible corporations. Such selections may be made only before July 1, 1994. At least 8 of the operational areas of the corporations selected must be rural areas (as defined by section 1393(a)(3) of such Code).

(3) **Operational areas must have certain characteristics.**— A corporation may be selected for purposes of this section only if its operational area meets the following criteria:

(A) The area meets the size requirements under section 1392(a)(3).

(B) The unemployment rate (as determined by the appropriate available data) is not less than the national unemployment rate.

(C) The median family income of residents of such area does not exceed 80 percent of the median gross income of residents of the jurisdiction of the local government which includes such area.

(f) **Qualified low-income assistance.**— For purposes of this section, the term "qualified low-income assistance" means assistance—

(1) which is designed to provide employment of, and business opportunities for, low-income individuals who are residents of the operational area of the community development corporation, and

(2) which is approved by the Secretary of Housing and Urban Development.

[¶ 2574] Sec. 13321. Accelerated depreciation for property on indian reservations.

* * * * * * * * * * * * *

(b) **Effective date.**— The amendment made by this section shall apply to property placed in service after December 31, 1993.

[¶ 2575] Sec. 13322. Indian employment credit.

* * * * * * * * * * * * *

(e) **Clerical amendment.**— The table of sections for subpart D of part IV of subchapter A of chapter 1 is amended by adding at the end thereof the following:

"Sec. 45A. Indian employment credit."

(f) Effective date.— The amendments made by this section shall apply to wages paid or incurred after December 31, 1993.

[¶ 2576] Sec. 13401. Disclosure of return information for administration of certain veterans programs.

(b) Effective date.— The amendment made by subsection (a) shall take effect on the date of the enactment of this Act.

[¶ 2577] Sec. 13402. Disclosure of return information to carry out income contingent repayment of student loans.

(c) Effective date.— The amendments made by this section shall take effect on the date of the enactment of this Act.

[¶ 2578] Sec. 13403. Use of return information for income verification under certain housing assistance programs.

(c) Effective date.— The amendments made by this section shall take effect on the date of the enactment of this Act.

[¶ 2579] Sec. 13411. Increase in public debt limit.

(a) General rule.— Subsection (b) of section 3101 of title 31, United States Code, is amended by striking out the dollar limitation contained in such subsection and inserting in lieu thereof "$4,900,000,000,000".

(b) Repeal of temporary increase.— Effective on and after the date of the enactment of this Act, section 1 of Public Law 103-12 is hereby repealed.

[¶ 2580] Sec. 13421. Excise tax on certain vaccines made permanent.

* * * * * * * * * * * * *

(c) Floor stocks tax.—

(1) Imposition of tax.— On any taxable vaccine—

(A) which was sold by the manufacturer, producer, or importer on or before the date of the enactment of this Act,

(B) on which no tax was imposed by section 4131 of the Internal Revenue Code of 1986 (or, if such tax was imposed, was credited or refunded), and

(C) which is held on such date by any person for sale or use,

there is hereby imposed a tax in the amount determined under section 4131(b) of such Code.

(2) Liability for tax and method of payment. —

(A) Liability for tax.—The person holding any taxable vaccine to which the tax imposed by paragraph (1) applies shall be liable for such tax.

(B) Method of payment.—The tax imposed by paragraph (1) shall be paid in such manner as the Secretary shall prescribe by regulations.

(C) Time for payment.—The tax imposed by paragraph (1) shall be paid on or before the last day of the 6th month beginning after the date of the enactment of this Act.

(3) Definitions.— For purposes of this subsection, terms used in this subsection which are also used in section 4131 of such Code shall have the respective meanings such terms have in such section.

(4) Other laws applicable.— All provisions of law, including penalties, applicable with respect to the taxes imposed by section 4131 of such Code shall, insofar as applicable and not inconsistent with the provisions of this subsection, apply to the floor stocks taxes imposed by paragraph (1), to the same extent as if such taxes were imposed by such section 4131.

[¶ 2581] Sec. 13422. Continuation coverage under group health plans of costs of pediatric vaccines.

* * * * * * * * * * * * *

(b) Effective date.— The amendment made by subsection (a) shall apply with respect to plan years beginning after the date of the enactment of this Act.

[¶ 2582] Sec. 13431. Modification of involuntary conversion rules for certain disaster-related conversions.

* * * * * * * * * * * *

(b) Effective date.— The amendment made by subsection (a) shall apply to property compulsorily or involuntarily converted as a result of disasters for which the determination referred to in section 1033(h)(2) of the Internal Revenue Code of 1986 (as added by this section) is made on or after September 1, 1991, and to taxable years ending on or after such date.

[¶ 2583] Sec. 13441. Increase in presidential election campaign fund check-off.

* * * * * * * * * * * *

(b) Effective date.— The amendments made by subsection (a) apply with respect to tax returns required to be filed after December 31, 1993.

[¶ 2584] Sec. 13442. Special rule for hospital services.

* * * * * * * * * * * *

(b) Effective date.— The provisions of this section shall apply to services provided after February 2, 1993, and on or before May 12, 1995.

[¶ 2585] Sec. 13443. Credit for portion of employer social security taxes paid with respect to employee cash tips.

(c) Clerical amendment.— The table of sections for subpart D of part IV of subchapter A of chapter 1 is amended by adding at the end the following new item:

(d) Effective date— The amendments made by this section shall apply with respect to taxes paid after December 31, 1993.

[¶ 2586] Sec. 13444. Availability and use of death information.

* * * * * * * * * * * *

(b) Effective date.—

(1) In general.— Except as provided in paragraph (2), the amendment made by subsection (a) shall take effect on the date one year after the date of the enactment of this Act.

(2) Special rule.— The amendment made by subsection (a) shall take effect on the date 2 years after the date of the enactment of this Act in the case of any State if it is established to the satisfaction of the Secretary of the Treasury that—

(A) under the law of such State as in effect on the date of the enactment of this Act, it is impossible for such State to enter into an agreement meeting the requirements of section 6103(d)(4)(B) of the Internal Revenue Code of 1986 (as added by subsection (a)), and

(B) it is likely that such State will enter into such an agreement during the extension period under this paragraph.

[¶ 2587] Sec. 13561. Medicare as secondary payer.

* * * * * * * * * * * *

(d) Application of aggregation rules.—

* * * * * * * * * * * *

(3) The amendments made by this subsection shall take effect 90 days after the date of enactment of this Act.

Next page is 651

Congressional Committee Reports Accompanying the Revenue Reconciliation Act of 1993

[¶3000]

This section reproduces all important parts of the official explanation of the Revenue Reconciliation Act of 1993 (Chapter 1 of Title XIII of the Omnibus Budget Reconciliation Act of 1993). The material comes from the House, Senate and Conference Committee Reports.

The Committee Reports are arranged in the order of the Act Sections of the Revenue Reconciliation Act of 1993.

[¶3001] Section 13101. Employer Provided Educational Assistance

(Code Sec. 127, 132)

[Senate Report]

Present Law

Prior to July 1, 1992, an employee's gross income and wages for income and employment tax purposes did not include amounts paid or incurred by the employer for educational assistance provided to the employee if such amounts were paid or incurred pursuant to an educational assistance program that met certain requirements (sec. 127). This exclusion, which expired with respect to amounts paid after June 30, 1992, was limited to $5,250 of educational assistance with respect to an individual during a calendar year. Education that did not qualify for the exclusion (e.g., because it exceeded the $5,250 limit) was excludable from income if and only if it qualified as a working condition fringe benefit (sec. 132). To be excluded as a working condition fringe, the cost of the education must have been a job-related deductible expense.

In the absence of the exclusion, for purposes of income and employment taxes, an employee generally is required to include in income and wages the value of educational assistance provided by the employer unless the cost of such assistance qualifies as a deductible job-related expense of the employee.

Reasons for Change

The exclusion from income for employer-provided educationalassistance programs has two intended purposes: (1) to increase the levels of education and training in the workforce and (2) to eliminate the potential complexity of determining whether education and training benefits provided by an employer constitute job-related expenses that are deductible by the employee as a working condition fringe benefit.

The committee believes that some of the benefits attributable to the exclusion for employer-provided educational assistance accrue to society at large by creating a better-educated workforce. Also, the committee believes that some individuals would underinvest in education if the Federal government did not subsidize the cost of their continuing education.

The committee believes it is appropriate to provide for a temporary extension of the exclusion to provide the opportunity for Congress to reevaluate the exclusion.

Explanation of Provision

The bill retroactively extends the exclusion for employer-provided educational assistance for 24 months (through June 30, 1994). In the case of a taxable year beginning in 1994, only amounts paid before July 1, 1994, by the employer for educational assistance for the employee can be taken into account in determining the amount excludable under section 127 for the taxable year.

The committee understands that the expiration of the exclusion and the retroactive extension creates a number of administrative problems for employers and employees because some employers and employees treated educational assistance provided between July 1, 1992, and December 31, 1992, as excludable from income, while some treated it as taxable income. If educational assistance provided during such period was treated as taxable, then the employee would be entitled to a refund of excess taxes paid. The committee intends that the Secretary will use his existing authority to the fullest extent possible to alleviate any administrative problems and to facilitate the recoupment of excess taxes paid in the simplest way possible.

The bill also clarifies the rule under which educational assistance that does not satisfy section 127 may be excluded from income if and only if it meets the requirements of a working condition fringe benefit.

Effective Date

The extension of the exclusion is effective for taxable years ending after June 30, 1992. The clarification to the working condition fringe benefit rule is effective for taxable years beginning after December 31, 1988.

[Conference Report]

Conference Agreement

The conference agreement follows the Senate amendment, except that the exclusion for employer-provided educational assistance is extended retroactively and through December 31, 1994.

The conferees intend that the Secretary will use his existing authority to the fullest extent possible to alleviate any administrative problems that may result from the expiration and retroactive extension of the exclusion and to facilitate in the simplest way possible the recoupment of excess taxes paid with respect to educational assistance provided in the last half of 1992.

Effective date

The conference agreement follows the Senate amendment.

[¶3002] Section 13102. Targeted Jobs Credit

(Code Sec. 51)

[House Explanation]

Present Law

Tax credit. The targeted jobs tax credit is available on an elective basis for hiring individuals from several targeted groups. The targeted groups consist of individuals who are either recipients of payments under means-tested transfer programs, economically disadvantaged, or disabled. The credit generally is equal to 40 percent of up to $6,000 of qualified first-year wages paid to a member of a targeted group. Thus, the maximum credit generally is $2,400 per individual. With respect to economically disadvantaged summer youth employees, however, the credit is equal to 40 percent of up to $3,000 of wages, for a maximum credit of $1,200. The credit expired for individuals who began work for an employer after June 30, 1992.

Certification of members of targeted groups. Generally, an individual is not treated as a member of a targeted group unless certain certification conditions are satisfied. On or before the day on which the individual begins work for the employer, the employer has to have received or have requested in writing from the designated local agency certification that the individual is a member of a targeted group. In the case of a certification of an economically disadvantaged youth participating in a cooperative education program, this requirement is satisfied if necessary certification is requested or received from the participating school on or before the day on which the individual begins work for the employer. The deadline for requesting certification of targeted group membership is extended until five days after the day the individual begins work for the employer, provided that, on or before the day the individual begins work, the individual has received a written preliminary determination of targeted group eligibility (a "voucher") from the designated local agency (or other agent or organization designated pursuant to a written agreement with the designated local agency). The "designated local agency" is the State employment security agency.

Authorization of appropriations. Present law authorized appropriations for administrative and publicity expenses relating to the credit through June 30, 1992. These monies were to be used by the Internal Revenue Service and the Department of Labor to inform employers of the credit program.

Reasons For Change

The committee believes that the targeted jobs tax credit provides a useful incentive for hiring disadvantaged individuals. Further, the committee believes that a permanent extension of the targeted jobs tax credit will provide greater certainty to employers as to the availability of the credit. In addition, the committee believes that the creation of a school-to-work program will help participants of the program acquire the skills necessary to compete in the changing workforce of America.

Explanation Of Provision

The bill permanently and retroactively extends the targeted jobs tax credit for individuals who begin work for the employer after June30, 1992. [1]In addition, the targeted jobs tax credit is expanded to include qualified participants in an approved school-to-work program beginning participation after December 31, 1993. A qualified participant in an approved school-to-work program is any individual aged 16 through 20 who is enrolled in an approved school-to-work program and certified to be making satisfactory progress toward completing the program. A program is considered to be an a proved school-to-work program only if it is a planned program of structured job training designed to integrate academic instruction and work-based learning and is approved by the Secretaries of Labor and Education. The total number of qualified participants in an approved school-to-work program is capped in each calendar year. The cap is as follows: 125,000 in 1994, 140,000 in 1995, 160,000 in 1996, 180,000 in 1997 and 200,000 in 1998 and each year thereafter. These amounts are to be allocated among the States in proportion to the number of eligible participants that are estimated to be served in approved school-to-work programs for that year. Such estimates will be published by the Secretaries of Labor and Education before the beginning of the year to which the allocation applies. Each State's allocation, in turn, will be allocated among its approved school-to-work programs in such manner as the Secretaries of Labor and Education prescribe. Because the approved school-to-work program is a work-study program, the credit would equal 40 percent of up to $3,000 of first-year wages, for a maximum credit of $1,200.

Effective Date

The extension of the targeted jobs tax credit is effective for individuals who begin work for the employer after June 30, 1992. The approved school-to-work program is effective for individuals beginning work for an employer after December 31, 1993.

[Conference Report]

Conference Agreement

Extension of credit. The conference agreement extends for 30 months the targeted jobs tax credit for individuals who begin work for the employer after June 30, 1992 and on or before December 31, 1994.

Approved school-to-work program. The conference agreement does not include the House bill provision.

Effective date. The extension of the targeted jobs tax credit is effective for individuals who begin work for the employer after June 30, 1992 and before December 31, 1994.

[¶3003] Sections 13111(a), 13112. Extension of Research Credit; Modification of Fixed Base Percentage for Startup Companies

(Code Sec. 41)

[House Explanation]

Present Law

The research and experimentation tax credit ("research tax credit") provides a credit equal to 20 percent of the amount by which a taxpayer's qualified research expenditures for a taxable year exceed its base amount for that year. The credit expired after June 30, 1992.

The base amount for the current year generally is computed by multiplying the taxpayer's "fixed-base percentage" by the average amount of the taxpayer's gross receipts for the four preceding years. If a taxpayer both incurred qualified research expenditures and had gross receipts during each of at least three years from 1984 through 1988, then its "fixed-base percentage" is the ratio that its total qualified research expenditures for the 19841988 period bears to its total gross receipts for that period (subject to a maximum ratio of .16). All other taxpayers (such as "start-up" firms)

[Footnote ¶3002] 1. See also description of targeted jobs tax credit for Empowerment Zones in Part III of the report on Title XIV.

are assigned a fixed-base percentage of .03.

In computing the credit, a taxpayer's base amount may not be less than 50 percent of its current-year qualified research expenditures.

Qualified research expenditures eligible for the credit consist of: (1) "in-house" expenses of the taxpayer for research wages and supplies used in research; (2) certain time-sharing costs or computer use in research; and (3) 65 percent of amounts paid by the taxpayer for contract research conducted on the taxpayer's behalf. The credit is not available for expenditures attributable to research that is conducted outside the United States. In addition, the credit is not available for research in the social sciences, arts, or humanities, nor is it available for research to the extent funded by any grant, contract, or otherwise by another person (or governmental entity).

The 20-percent research tax credit also applies to the excess of (1) 100 percent of corporate cash expenditures (including grants or contributions) paid for basic research conducted by universities (and certain scientific research organizations) over (2) the sum of (a) the greater of two fixed research floors plus (b) an amount reflecting any decrease in nonresearch giving to universities by the corporation as compared to such giving during a fixed-base period, as adjusted for inflation.

Deductions for expenditures allowed to a taxpayer under section 174 (or any other section) are reduced by an amount equal to 100 percent of the taxpayer's research tax credit determined for the taxable year. [2]

Reasons For Change

Technological development is an important component of economic growth. However, businesses may not find it profitable to invest in some research activities, because of the difficulty in capturing the full benefits from the research. (Costly technological advances made by one firm are often cheaply copied by its competitors.) A research tax credit can help to promote investment in research, so that research activities undertaken approach the optimal level for the overall economy. Therefore, in view of the long-term nature of many research projects, the committee believes that it is appropriate to permanently extend the research tax credit.

Explanation of Provision

The research tax credit (including the university basic research credit) is permanently extended.

The bill also adds a new rule regarding the determination of the fixed-base percentage of start-up companies. Under the provision, a taxpayer that did not have gross receipts in at least three years during the 1984-1988 period will be assigned a fixed base percentage of .03 for each of its first five taxable years after 1993 in which it incurs qualified research expenditures. The taxpayer's fixed-base percentage for its sixth through tenth taxable years after 1993 in which it incurred qualified research expenditures will be as follows: (1) for the taxpayer's sixth year, its fixed-base percentage will be one-sixth of its ratio of qualified research expenditures to gross receipts for its fourth and fifth years; (2) for its seventh year, its fixed-base percentage will be one-third of its ratio for its fifth and sixth years; (3) for its eighth year, its fixed-base percentage will be one-half of its ratio for its fifth through seventh years; (4) for its ninth year, its fixed-base percentage will be two-thirds of its ratio for its fifth through eighth years; and (5) for its tenth year, its fixed-base percentage will be five-sixths of its ratio for its fifth through ninth years. For subsequent taxable years, the taxpayer's fixed-base percentage will be its actual ratio of qualified research expenditures to gross receipts for five years selected by the taxpayer from its fifth through tenth taxable years.

In extending the research tax credit, the committee wishes to re-affirm Congressional intent that neither the enactment of the credit in 1981 nor the "targeting" modifications to the credit in 1986 affect the definition of "research or experimental expenditures" for purposes of section 174. Thus, the various new credit limitations enacted in the Tax Reform Act of 1986 apply in determining eligibility for the credit (in taxable years beginning after December 31, 1985), and do not determine eligibility of product development costs under section 174.

2. Taxpayers may alternatively elect to claim a reduced credit amount in lieu of reducing deductions otherwise allowed (sec.280C(c)(3))

Effective Date

The provision applies to expenditures paid or incurred after June 30, 1992.

[Conference Report]

Conference Agreement

Under the conference agreement, the research tax credit (including the university basic research credit) is extended for three years (i.e., for expenditures paid or incurred during the period July 1, 1992, through June 30, 1995.

The conference agreement also adds the rule contained in the House bill and the Senate amendment regarding the determination of the fixed-base of start-up firms in taxable years after the firm's start-up period. In addition, the conferees reiterate the intent expressed in the House bill committee report and the Senate amendment committee report that neither the enactment of the credit in 1981 nor the "targeting" modifications to the credit in 1986 affect the definition of "research or experimental expenditures" for purposes of section 174. Thus, the various new credit limitations enacted in the Tax Reform Act of 1986 apply in determining eligibility for the credit (in taxable years beginning after December 31, 1985), and do not determine eligibility of product development costs under section 174.

Effective date. The conference agreement applies to expenditures paid or incurred during the period July 1, 1992, through June 30, 1995.

[¶3004] Section 13111(b). Clinical Testing Credit

(Code Sec. 28)

[Conference Report]

Present Law

The orphan drug tax credit (sec. 28) provides a 50-percent nonrefundable tax credit for a taxpayer's qualified clinical testing expenses paid or incurred in the testing of certain drugs for rare diseases, generally referred to as "orphan drugs." Qualified testing expenses are costs incurred to test an orphan drug after the drug has been approved for human testing by the Food and Drug Administration (FDA) but before the drug has been approved for sale by the FDA. Present law defines a rare disease or condition as one that (1) affects less than 200,000 persons in the United States or (2) affects more than 200,000 persons, but there is no reasonable expectation that businesses could recoup the costs of developing a drug for such disease or condition from U.S. sales of the drug. These rare diseases and conditions include Huntington's disease, myoclonus, ALS (Lou Gehrig's disease), Tourette's syndrome, and Duchenne's dystrophy (a form of muscular dystrophy). [3]

The orphan drug tax credit expired after June 30, 1992.

House Bill

No provision.

Senate Amendment

No provision.

Conference Agreement

The conference agreement extends the orphan drug tax credit for 30 months (i.e., for qualified clinical testing expenses incurred during the period July 1, 1992, through December 31, 1994).

Effective date. —The provision is effective for qualified clinical testing expenses incurred during the period July 1, 1992, through December 31, 1994.

[¶3005] Section 13113. 50-Percent Exclusion for Gain from Certain Small Business Stock

[Footnote ¶3003 continued]

3. A taxpayer's otherwise allowable deduction for clinical testing expenses is reduced by the amount of any orphan drug tax credit allowed for the taxable year (sec. 280C(b)).

(Code Sec. 1202)

[House Explanation]

Present Law

Gain from the sale or exchange of stock held for more than one year generally is treated as long-term capital gain.

Net capital gain (i.e., long-term capital gain less short-term capital loss) of an individual is taxed at the same rates that apply to ordinary income, subject to a maximum rate of 28 percent.

Reasons for Change

The committee believes that targeted relief for investors who risk their funds in new ventures, small businesses, and specialized small business investment companies, will encourage investments in these enterprises. This should encourage the flow of capital to small businesses, many of which have difficulty attracting equity financing.

Explanation of Provision

In general

The provision generally permits a noncorporate taxpayer who holds qualified small business stock for more than 5 years to exclude 50 percent of any gain on the sale or exchange of the stock. The amount of gain eligible for the 50 percent exclusion is limited to the greater of (1) 10 times the taxpayer's basis in the stock or (2) $10 million gain from stock in that corporation.

Qualified small business stock

In order to qualify as small business stock, the following requirements must be met.

Eligible stock

The stock must be acquired by the taxpayer after December 31, 1992, at the original issuance (directly or through an underwriter) in exchange for money, other property (not including stock) or as compensation for services provided to the corporation (other than services performed as an underwriter of the stock).

In order to prevent evasion of the requirement that the stock be newly issued, the exclusion does not apply if the issuing corporation (1) purchases any stock from the stockholder (or a related person) within 2 years of the issuance of the stock or (2) redeems more than 5 percent (by value) of its own stock within 1 year of the issuance. For purposes of this anti-evasion rule, purchases by persons related to the issuing corporation are treated as purchases by the issuing corporation.

Qualified corporation

The corporation must be a qualified small business as of the date of issuance and during substantially all of the period that the taxpayer holds the stock.

A qualified small business is a subchapter C corporation other than: a DISC or former DISC, a corporation with respect to which an election under section 936 is in effect, a regulated investment company, a real estate investment trust, a real estate mortgage investment conduit, or a cooperative. The corporation also generally cannot own (i) real property the value of which exceeds 10 percent of its total assets or (ii) portfolio stock or securities the value of which exceeds 10 percent of its total assets in excess of liabilities.

Active business

At least 80 percent (by value) of the corporation's assets (including intangible assets) must be used by the corporation in the active conduct of a qualified trade or business. If in connection with any future trade or business, a corporation uses assets in certain startup activities, research and experimental activities or in-house research activities, the corporation is treated as using such assets in the active conduct of a qualified trade or business.

Assets that are held to meet reasonable working capital needs of the corporation, or are held for investment and are reasonably expected to be used within 2 years to finance future research and experimentation, are treated as used in the active conduct of a trade or business. In addition, certain rights to computer software are treated as assets used in the active conduct of a trade or business.

A qualified trade or business is any trade or business other than those involving the performance of services in the fields of health, law, engineering, architecture, accounting, actuarial science, performing arts, consulting, athletics, financial services, brokerage services, or any other trade or business where the principal asset of the trade or business is the reputation or skill of 1 or more of its employees. The term also excludes any banking, insurance, leasing, financing, investing, or similar business, any farming business (including the business of raising or harvesting trees), any business involving the production or extraction of products of a character for which percentage depletion is allowable, or any business of operating a hotel, motel, restaurant or similar business.

A corporation that is a specialized small business investment company ("SSBIC") is treated as meeting the active business test. An SSBIC is defined as any corporation (other than certain non-qualified corporations) that is licensed by the Small Business Administration under section 301(d) of the Small Business Act of 1958, as in effect on May 13, 1993.

Gross assets

As of the date of issuance, the excess of (1) the amount of cash and the aggregate adjusted bases of other property held by the corporation, over (2) the aggregate amount of indebtedness of the corporation that does not have an original maturity of more than one year (such as short-term payables), cannot exceed $50 million. For these purposes, amounts received in the issuance are taken into account.

If a corporation satisfies the gross assets test as of the date of issuance but subsequently exceeds the $50 million threshold, stock that otherwise constitutes qualified small business stock would not lose that characterization solely as a result of that subsequent event. If a corporation (or a predecessor corporation) exceeds the $50 million threshold at any time after December 31, 1992, the corporation can never again issue stock that would qualify for the exclusion.

Subsidiaries of issuing corporation

In the case of a corporation that owns at least 50 percent of the vote or value of a subsidiary, the parent corporation is deemed to own its ratable share of the subsidiary's assets, and to be liable for a ratable share of the subsidiary's indebtedness, for purposes of the "qualified corporation," "active business," and "gross assets" tests described above.

Pass-through entities

Gain from the disposition of qualified small business stock by a partnership, S corporation, regulated investment company or common trust fund that is taken into account by a partner, shareholder or participant (other than a C corporation) is eligible for the exclusion, provided that (1) all eligibility requirements with respect to qualified small business stock are met, (2) the stock was held by the entity for more than 5 years, and (3) the partner, shareholder or participant held its interest in the entity on the date the entity acquired the stock and at all times thereafter and before the disposition of the stock. In addition, a partner, shareholder, or participant cannot exclude gain received from an entity to the extent that the partner's, shareholder's, or participant's share in the entity's gain exceeded the partner's, shareholder's or participant's interest in the entity at the time the entity acquired the stock.

Certain tax-free and other transfers

If qualified small business stock is transferred by gift or at death, the transferee is treated as having acquired the stock in the same manner as the transferor, and as having held the stock during any continuous period immediately preceding the transfer during which it was held by the transferor. Qualified small business stock also may be distributed by a partnership to one or more of its partners, as long as (1) all eligibility requirements with respect to qualified small business stock are met, and (2) the partner held its interest in the partnership on the date the partnership acquired the stock and at all times thereafter and before the disposition of the stock. In addition, a partner cannot treat stock distributed by a partnership as qualified small business stock to the extent that the partner's share of the stock distributed by the partnership exceeded the partner's interest in the partnership at the time the partnership acquired the stock.

Transferees in other cases are not eligible for the exclusion. Thus, for example, if qualified small business stock is transferred to a partnership and the partnership disposes of the stock, any gain from the disposition will not be eligible for the exclusion.

In the case of certain incorporations and reorganizations where qualified small business stock is transferred for other stock, the transferor treats the stock received as qualified small business stock. The holding period of the original stock is added to that of the stock received. However, the amount of gain eligible for the exclusion is limited to the gain accrued as of the date of the incorporation or reorganization.

Special basis rules

If property (other than money or stock) is transferred to a corporation in exchange for its stock, the basis of the stock received is treated as not less than the fair market value of the property exchanged. Thus, only gains that accrue after the transfer are eligible for the exclusion.

Options, nonvested stock, and convertible instruments

Stock acquired by the taxpayer through the exercise of options or warrants, or through the conversion of convertible debt, is treated as acquired at original issue. The determination whether the gross assets test is met is made at the time of exercise or conversion, and the holding period of such stock is treated as beginning at that time.

In the case of convertible preferred stock, the gross assets determination is made at the time the convertible stock is issued, and the holding period of the convertible stock is added to that of the common stock acquired upon conversion.

Stock received in connection with the performance of services is treated as issued by the corporation and acquired by the taxpayer when included in the taxpayer's gross income in accordance with the rules of section 83.

Offsetting short positions

A taxpayer cannot exclude gain from the sale of qualified small business stock if the taxpayer (or a related person) held an offsetting short position with respect to that stock anytime before the 5-year holding period is satisfied. If the taxpayer (or a related person) acquires an offsetting short position with respect to qualified small business stock after the 5-year holding period is satisfied, the taxpayer must elect to treat the acquisition of the offsetting short position as a sale of the qualified small business stock in order to exclude any gain from that stock.

An offsetting short position is defined to be (1) a short sale of property substantially identical to the qualified small business stock (including writing a call option that the holder is more likely than not to exercise or selling the stock for future delivery) or (2) an option to sell substantially identical property at a fixed price.

Capital gains and investment interest

Any gain that is excluded from gross income under the provision is not taken into account in computing long-term capital gain or in applying the capital loss rules of sections 1211 and 1212. In addition, the taxable portion of the gain is taxed at a maximum rate of 28 percent.

The amount treated as investment income for purposes of the investment interest limitation does not include any gain that is excluded from gross income under the provision.

Minimum tax

One-half of any excluded gain is treated as a preference for purposes of the alternative minimum tax.

[Conference Report]

Conference Agreement

The conference agreement follows the House bill, with the following modifications:

In general

The agreement clarifies that the $10 million limitation on eligible gain is applied on a shareholder-by-shareholder basis. The conferees also wish to clarify that for purposes of the 10-times-basis limitation, basis is determined by valuing any contributed property at fair market value (at the date of contribution).

Qualified small business stock

Redemptions.

The agreement eliminates the rule in the House bill that treats purchases by persons related to an issuing corporation as purchases by the corporation for purposes of determining whether there has been a redemption. In lieu of this rule, a corporation is treated as purchasing an amount of its stock equal to the amount of its stock treated as redeemed under section 304(a).

Qualified corporation.

The agreement excludes from the definition of eligible corporation any corporation that has a direct or indirect subsidiary with respect to which an election under section 936 is in effect.

Active business.

The agreement clarifies that the active business requirement is met by a corporation with

80 percent of its assets used in the active conduct of one or more qualified trades or businesses.

Gross assets.

The conference agreement provides that the $50 million size limitation is based on the issuer's gross assets (i.e., the sum of the cash and the adjusted bases of other property held by the corporation) without subtracting the short-term indebtedness of the corporation. For purposes of this rule, the adjusted basis of property contributed to the corporation is determined as if the basis of the property immediately after the contribution were equal to its fair market value.

Subsidiaries of issuing corporation

The agreement provides that corporations that are part of a parent-subsidiary controlled group (using a more than 50% ownership test) are treated as a single corporation for purposes of the gross assets test. The conferees also wish to clarify that, for purposes of the active business requirement, a parent's ratable share of a subsidiary's assets (and activities) is based on the percentage of outstanding stock owned (by value).

Certain tax-free and other transfers

The conference agreement follows the House bill by limiting the gain that is eligible for exclusion on the sale of stock that was acquired through incorporation or reorganization where the stock acquired would not have been stock of a qualified small business (at the time acquired). The agreement, however, also provides that the limit will not apply to gain from stock that was acquired through incorporation or reorganization that would have been stock of a qualified small business.

Alternative minimum tax study

The conferees understand that the individual alternative minimum tax (AMT) may operate to disallow deductions that may be associated with the production of income, including section 212 expenses associated with income derived through partnerships. A provision was included in H.R. 11 last year to allow a certain amount of the distributive share of section 212 expenses of a partner in a partnership to be deductible for AMT purposes. Concern has been expressed that the present-law AMT treatment of section 212 expenses might create a disincentive for the long-term investments that Congress has intended to foster through the capital gains exclusion. Accordingly, the conferees urge that the Treasury Department study the question whether the present-law AMT treatment of section 212 expenses creates such a disincentive, and provide the House Committee on Ways and Means and the Senate Finance Committee with a report of such study by March 1, 1994. The study should include the Treasury Department's views and recommendations as to whether a statutory amendment is appropriate insofar as the AMT treatment of section 212 uses is concerned, along with a discussion of the merits and consequences of any such amendment.

Effective date

The conference agreement applies to stock issued after the date of enactment.

[¶3006] Section 13114. Rollover of Publicly Traded Securities Gain into Specialized Small Business Investment Companies

(Code Sec. 1044)

[House Explanation]

Present Law

In general, gain or loss is recognized on any sale, exchange or other disposition of property. The Internal Revenue Code contains provisions under which taxpayers may elect not to recognize gain realized on certain "like-kind" exchanges (sec. 1031), or for certain involuntary conversions (sec. 1033).

Reasons for Change

The committee believes that permitting gains to be deferred when the proceeds are reinvested in a specialized small business investment company ("SSBIC") is a worthwhile way to channel investment to these specialized small business companies that otherwise may have trouble attracting capital.

Explanation of Provision

The bill permits any corporation or individual to elect to roll over without payment of tax any capital gain realized upon the sale of publicly-traded securities where the corporation or individual uses the proceeds from the sale to purchase common stock or a partnership interest in an SSBIC within 60 days of the sale of the securities. To the extent the proceeds from the sale of the publicly-traded securities exceed the cost of the SSBIC common stock or partnership interest, gain will be recognized currently. The taxpayer's basis in the SSBIC common stock or partnership interest is reduced by the amount of any gain not recognized on the sale of the securities. [3]

Estates, trusts, S-corporations, and partnerships are not eligible to make this election to rollover gains. In addition, "publicly-traded securities" are defined as stock or debt traded on an established securities market. An SSBIC is defined as any partnership or corporation that is licensed by the Small Business Administration under section 301(d) of the small Business Investment Act of 1958, as in effect on May 13, 1993.

Effective Date

The provision is effective for sales of publicly-traded securities on or after the date of enactment.

[Conference Report]

Conference Agreement

The conference agreement follows the House bill.

[¶3007] Section 13115. Modification to Minimum Tax Depreciation Rules

(Code Sec. 56)

[Senate Explanation]

Present Law

A taxpayer is subject to an alternative minimum tax (AMT) to one extent that the taxpayer's tentative minimum tax exceeds the taxpayer's regular income tax liability. A taxpayer's tentative minimum tax generally equals 20 percent (24 percent in the case of an individual) of the taxpayer's alternative minimum taxable income in excess of an exemption amount. Alternative minimum taxable income (AMTI) is the taxpayer's taxable income increased by certain tax preferences and adjusted by determining the tax treatment of certain items in a manner which negates the deferral of income resulting from the regular tax treatment of those items.

One of the adjustments which is made to taxable income to arrive at AMTI relates to depreciation. For AMT purposes, depreciation on most personal property to which the modified Accelerated Cost Recovery System (MACRS) adopted in 1986 applies is calculated using the 150-percent declining balance method (switching to straight line in the year necessary to maximize the deduction) over the property's class life. The class lives of MACRS property generally are longer than the recovery periods allowed for regular tax purposes.

For taxable years beginning after 1989, the AMTI of a corporation is increased by an amount equal to 75 percent of the amount by which adjusted current earnings (ACE) of the corporation exceed AMTI (as determined before this adjustment). In general, ACE means AMTI with additional adjustments that generally follow the rules presently applicable to corporations in computing their earnings and profits. For purposes of ACE, depreciation is computed using the straight-line method over the class life of the property. Thus, a corporation generally must make two depreciation calculations for purposes of the AMT—once using the 150 percent declining balance method over the class life and again using the straight-line method over the class life. Taxpayers may elect to use either method for regular tax purposes. If a taxpayer uses the straight-line method for regular tax purposes, it must also use the straight-line method for AMT purposes.

Reasons for Change

The committee believes that the two depreciation calculations required by the corporate AMT is a source of considerable complexity.

[Footnote ¶3004 continued]

3. The amount of gain that an individual may elect to roll over under this provision for a taxable year is limited to the lesser of (1) $50,000 or (2) $500,000 reduced by the gain previously excluded under this provision. For corporations, these limits are $250,000 and $1,000,000.

In addition, the committee believes that requiring the AMTI of a corporation to be calculated, in part, by using the straight-line depreciation method contained in the ACE adjustment may present a disincentive to the investment in certain property.

Explanation of Provision

The depreciation component of the ACS adjustment is eliminated for property placed in service after December 31, 1993. Thus, corporations would compute AMT depreciation by using the rules generally applicable to individuals (i.e., the 150-percent declining balance method over the class life of the property for tangible personal property.)

Effective Date

The provision is effective for property placed in service after December 31, 1993.

[Conference Report]

Conference Agreement

The conference agreement follows the Senate amendment.

[¶3008] Section 13116. Increase in Expense Treatment for Small Businesses

(Code Sec. 179)

[Conference Report]

Present Law

In lieu of depreciation, a taxpayer with a sufficiently small amount of annual investment may elect to deduct up to $10,000 of the cost of qualifying property placed in service for the taxable year. In general, qualifying property is defined as depreciable tangible personal property that is purchased for use in the active conduct of a trade or business. The $10,000 amount is reduced (but not below zero) by the amount by which the cost of qualifying property placed in service during the taxable year exceeds $200,000. In addition, the amount eligible to be expensed for a taxable year may not exceed the taxable income of the taxpayer for the year that is derived from the active conduct of a trade or business (determined without regard to this provision). Any amount that is not allowed as a deduction because of the taxable income limitation may be carried forward to succeeding taxable years (subject to similar limitations).

Conference Agreement

The conference agreement increases the $10,000 amount allowed to be expensed under section 179 to $17,500 for property placed in service in taxable years beginning after December 31, 1992.

[¶3009] Section 13121. High-speed Intercity Rail Facility Bonds Exempt From State Volume Cap

(Code Sec. 146)

[House Explanation]

Present law

High-speed intercity rail facilities qualify for tax-exempt bond financing if trains operating on the facility are reasonably expected to carry passengers and their baggage at average speeds in excess of 150 miles per hour between stations. Such facilities need not be governmentally-owned, but the owner must irrevocably elect not to claim depreciation or any tax credit with respect to bond-financed property.

Twenty-five percent of each bond issue for high-speed intercity rail facilities must receive an allocation from a State private activity bond volume limitation. If facilities are located in two or more States, this requirement must be met on a State-by-State basis for the financing of facilities located in each State.

Reasons for change

The committee believes that bonds for high-speed rail facilities should not be subject to the State private activity bond volume limitations.

Explanation of provision

The bill exempts private activity bonds to provide high-speed rail facilities from State private activity bond volume limitations.

Effective date

The provision is effective for bonds issued after December 31, 1993.

Conference Agreement

The conference agreement follows the House bill, with a modification. Under the agreement, the requirement that 25 percent of each high-speed rail facility bond issue receive an allocation from a State private activity bond volume limitation would be repealed only if all the bond-financed property were governmentally owned. (Bonds issued for privately-owned property would remain subject to the current-law rules with respect to the 25-percent volume cap allocation requirement.)

Effective Date

The provision is effective for bonds issued after December 31, 1993.

[¶3010] Section 13122. Permanent Extension of Qualified Small Issue Bonds

(Code Sec. 144)

[House Explanation]

Present Law

In lieu of depreciation, a taxpayer with a sufficiently small amount of annual investment may elect to deduct up to $10,000 of the cost of qualifying property placed in service for the taxable year. In general, qualifying property is defined as depreciable tangible personal property that is purchased for use in the active conduct of a trade or business. The $10,000 amount is reduced (but not below zero) by the amount by which the cost of qualifying property placed in service during the taxable year exceeds $200,000. In addition, the amount eligible to be expensed for a taxable year may not exceed the taxable income of the taxpayer for the year that is derived from the active conduct of a trade or business (determined without regard to this provision). Any amount that is not allowed as a deduction because of the taxable income limitation may be carried forward to succeeding taxable years (subject to similar limitations).

Reasons for Change

The committee believes that increasing the amount allowed to be expensed will provide an incentive for small businesses to increase their investment in capital assets, thus promoting economic growth and increasing demand for productive assets.

Explanation of Provision

The $10,000 amount allowed to be expensed under section 179 is increased to $25,000.

Effective Date

The provision is effective for property placed in service in taxable years beginning after December 31, 1992.

[Conference Report]

Conference Agreement

The conference agreement follows the House bill with a modification with respect to qualified small-issue bonds that could not be issued within the regulatory one-year placed-in-service period due to the lapse of the program. Specifically, the conference agreement provides that the one-year placed-in-service period does not expire before January 1, 1994 for property with respect to which this one year period, under Treasury Regulation sec. 1.103-8(a)(5) or any successor regulation otherwise would expire after June 30, 1992, and before January 1, 1994. Because these bonds must be issued no later than December 31, 1993 and because carryforwards of qualified small-issue bonds are not allowed under the State private activity bond volume limitation rules, the applicable State volume limitation from which an allocation is required is that for calendar year 1993.

Effective Date

The extension is effective for bonds issued after June 30, 1992. The provision relating to Treasury regulation 1.103-8(a)(5) is effective on the date of enactment.

[¶3011] Section 13131. Expansion and Simplification of Earned Income Tax Credit

(Code Sec. 32, 162, 213, 3507)

[House Explanation]

Present Law

Eligible low-income workers can claim a refundable earned income tax credit (EITC) of up to 18.5 percent of the first $7,750 of earned income for 1993 (19.5 percent for taxpayers with more than one qualifying child). The maximum amount of credit for 1993 is $1,434 ($1,511 for taxpayers with more than one qualifying child).

This maximum credit is reduced by 13.21 percent of earned income (or adjusted gross income, if greater) in excess of $12,200 (13.93 percent for taxpayers with more than one qualifying child). The EITC is totally phased out for workers with earned income (or adjusted gross income, if greater) over $23,050. The maximum amount of earned income on which the EITC may be claimed, and the income threshold for the phaseout of the EITC, are indexed for inflation. Earned income consists of wages, salaries, other employee compensation, and net self-employment income. Present law provides that the credit rates for the EITC increase in 1994, as shown in the following table.

Year	One qualifying child		Two or more qualifying children	
	Credit rate	Phaseout rate	Credit rate	Phaseout rate
1993	18.5	13.21	19.5	13.93
1994 and after	23.0	16.43	25.0	17.86

The EITC can be received on an advance basis by a worker who elects to furnish a certificate of eligibility to his or her employer. For such a worker, the employer makes an advance payment of the credit at the time wages are paid.

A supplemental young child credit is available to taxpayers with qualifying children under the age of one year. This young child credit rate is 5 percent and the phase-out rate is 3.57 percent. It is computed on the same income base as the ordinary EITC. The maximum supplemental young child credit for 1993 is $388.

A supplemental health insurance credit is available to taxpayers who provide health insurance coverage for their qualifying children. This health insurance credit rate is 6 percent and the phase-out rate is 4.285 percent. It is computed on the same income base as the ordinary EITC, but the credit claimed cannot exceed the out-of-pocket cost of the health insurance coverage. In addition, the taxpayer is denied an itemized deduction for medical expenses of qualifying insurance coverage up to the amount of credit claimed. The maximum supplemental health insurance credit for 1993 is $465.

Reasons for Change

Providing a larger basic EITC to larger families recognizes the role the EITC can play in alleviating poverty. Moreover, this larger credit may provide work incentives and increase equity by reducing the tax burden for those workers with a lower ability to pay taxes. Further, the committee believes that extending the EITC to low-income working taxpayers without qualifying children will provide these taxpayers with an additional benefit for entering the labor force and reduce the burden of the individual income and payroll taxes on those with a lower ability to pay taxes. Finally, repeal of the supplemental young child and health insurance components of the EITC will ease compliance burdens for lower-income taxpayers while providing substantial simplification.

Explanation of Provision

For taxpayers with one qualifying child, the EITC will be increased to 26.60 percent of the first $7,750 of earned income in 1994. The maximum credit will be $2,062 which will be reduced by 16.16 percent of earned income (or adjusted gross income, if greater) in excess of $11,000. The credit will be completely phased out for taxpayers with earned income (or adjusted gross income, if greater) over $23,760. In 1995 and thereafter, the credit rate will increase to 34.37 percent. The maximum amount of earned income on which the credit could be claimed will be reduced to (an estimated) $6,170. Thus, the maximum credit in 1995 will be approximately $2,120 (which equals the maximum credit available in 1994, adjusted for projected inflation). The phase-out rate will remain the same as in 1994.

For taxpayers with two or more qualifying children, the EITC will be increased to 31.59 percent of the first $8,500 of earned income in 1994. The maximum credit will be $2,685 which will be reduced by 15.79 percent of earned income (or adjusted gross income, if greater) in excess of $11,000. Thus, in 1994, the credit will be completely phased out for taxpayers with earned income (or adjusted gross income, if greater) over $28,000. In 1995 and thereafter, the credit rate will increase to 39.66 percent. The maximum amount of earned income on which the credit could be claimed is expected to be approximately $8,730 in 1995 (which equals the 1994 level, adjusted for projected inflation). Thus, the maximum credit in 1995 is expected to be approximately $3,460. The phaseout rate for 1995 and thereafter will be 19.83 percent.

Under the bill, the EITC will also be extended to low-income workers who (1) do not have any qualifying children (including workers with children who are not qualifying children with respect to that worker); (2) are age 22 or older; and (3) who may not be claimed as a dependent on another taxpayer's return. For these taxpayers, the EITC will be 7.65 percent of the first $4,000 of earned income (for a maximum credit of $306 in 1994). The maximum credit will be reduced by 7.65 percent of earned income (or adjusted gross income, if greater) above $5,000. In 1994 the credit will be completely phased out for taxpayers with earned income (or adjusted gross income, if greater) over $9,000. This credit will not be available on an advance payment basis.

As under present law, all dollar thresholds for years after 1994 will be indexed for inflation.

The supplemental young child credit and the supplemental health insurance credit will be repealed.

The Committee understands that very few taxpayers utilize the advance payment option to receive the EITC ratably, rather than as a lump sum when the tax return is filed. The expansion of the EITC makes receipt of the EITC on an advance payment basis more important as a means to alleviate poverty throughout the year, as well as to provide a timely work incentive. Accordingly, the Committee encourages the Internal Revenue Service (IRS) to promote the advance payment option to eligible taxpayers. There are a number of strategies the IRS may pursue in this endeavor and the Committee expects the IRS to choose those strategies believed most effective. One possible strategy would be for the IRS to include notification of the advance payment option with refund checks sent to taxpayers who claim the EITC.

Effective Date

The provision is effective for taxable years beginning after December 31, 1993.

[Senate Explanation]

Explanation of Provision

For taxpayers with one qualifying child, the EITC will be increased to 26.0 percent of the first $7,750 of earned income in 1994. The maximum credit will be $2,015 which is reduced by 16.16 percent of earned income (or adjusted gross income, if greater) in excess of $11,000. The credit will be completely phased out for taxpayers with earned income (or adjusted gross income, if greater) over $23,470. In 1995 and thereafter, the credit rate will increase to 34.0 percent. The maximum amount of earned income on which the credit could be claimed will be (an estimated) $6,170 (this is a $6,000 base in 1994, adjusted for projected inflation). Thus, the maximum credit in 1995 will be approximately $2,098. The phase-out rate will remain the same as in 1994.

For taxpayers with two or more qualifying children, the EITC will be increased to 30.0 percent of the first $8,500 of earned income in 1994. The maximum credit will be $2,550 which is reduced by 15.94 percent of earned income (or adjusted gross income, if greater) in excess of $11,000. Thus, in 1994, the credit will be completely phased out for taxpayers with earned income (or adjusted gross income, if greater) over $27,000. The credit rate will increase over time and equal 34.0 percent in 1995 and 39.0 percent in 1996 and thereafter. The phase-out rate will be 18.06 percent in 1995 and 20.72 percent in 1996 and thereafter.

As under present law, all dollar thresholds for years after 1994 will be indexed for inflation.

The supplemental young child credit and the

supplemental health insurance credit will be repealed.

Effective Date

The provision is effective for taxable years beginning after December 31, 1993.

[Conference Report]

Conference Agreement

The conference agreement generally follows the House bill and the Senate amendment, with the following modifications.

For taxpayers with one qualifying child, the EITC is 26.3 percent of the first $7,750 of earned income in 1994. The maximum credit in 1994 is $2,038 and is reduced by 15.98 percent of earned income (or adjusted gross income, if greater) in excess of $11,000. For 1995 and thereafter, the credit rate increases to 34.0 percent. The maximum amount of earned income on which the credit could be claimed is (an estimated) $6,170 (this is a $6,000 base in 1994, adjusted for projected inflation). The phaseout rate for 1995 and thereafter is 15.98 percent.

For taxpayers with two or more qualifying children, the EITC is 30.0 percent of the first $8,425 of earned income in 1994. The maximum credit for 1994 is $2,527 and is reduced by 17.68 percent of earned income (or adjusted gross income, if greater) in excess of $11,000. The credit rate increases over time and equals 36.0 percent for 1995 and 40.0 percent for 1996 and thereafter. The phase-out rate is 20.22 percent for 1995 and 21.06 percent for 1996 and thereafter.

The EITC is extended to taxpayers with no qualifying children, as in the House bill, with a modification to the age requirement. Under the conference agreement, this credit for taxpayers with no qualifying children would only be available to taxpayers over age 25 and below age 65.

The Internal Revenue Service (IRS) is required to provide notice to taxpayers with qualifying children who receive a refund on account of the EITC that the credit may be available on an advance payment basis. To prevent taxpayers from incurring an unexpectedly large tax liability due to receipt of the EITC on an advance payment basis, the amount of advance payment allowable in a taxable year is limited to 60 percent of the maximum credit available to a taxpayer with one qualifying child. After providing these notices to taxpayers for two taxable years, the Secretary of Treasury is directed to study the effect of the notice program on utilization of the advance payment mechanism. Based on the results of this study, the Secretary may recommend modificationS to the notice program to the Committee on Ways and Means and the Committee on Finance.

Finally, the conferees are concerned that working homeless individuals may not claim the full amount of EITC to which they are entitled. The conferees urge the IRS to explore the use of outreach programs that target homeless individuals and that aim to educate these individuals of the availability of the EITC.

[¶3012] Section 13141. Permanent Extension of Qualified Mortgage Bonds

(Code Sec. 25, 143)

[House Explanation]

Present Law

Qualified mortgage bonds

Qualified mortgage bonds ("QMBs") are bonds the proceeds of which are used to finance the purchase, or qualifying rehabilitation or improvement, of single-family, owner-occupied residences located within the jurisdiction of the issuer of the bonds (sec. 143). Persons receiving QMB loans must satisfy a home purchase price, borrower income, first-time homebuyer, and other requirements. Part or all of the interest subsidy provided by QMBs is recaptured if the borrower experiences substantial increases in income and disposes of the subsidized residence within nine years after purchase.

Mortgage credit certificates

Qualified governmental units may elect to exchange QMB authority for authority to issue mortgage credit certificates ("MCCs") (sec. 25). MCCs entitle homebuyers to nonrefundable income tax credits for a specified percentage of interest paid on mortgage loans on their principal residences. Once issued, an MCC remains in effect as long as the loan remains outstanding and the residence being financed continues to be the certificate-recipient's principal residence. MCCs are subject to the same targeting requirements as QMBs.

Expiration

Authority to issue QMBs and to elect to trade in bond volume authority to issue MCCs expired after June 30, 1992.

Reasons for Change

committee believes that extending these programs permanently will provide greater planning certainty to States and local governments, thereby permitting these entities to assist first-time buyers more efficiently.

Explanation of Provision

The bill permanently extends the authority to issue QMBs and to elect to trade in private activity bond volume limit for authority to issue MCCs.

Effective Date

The extension of the QMB and MCC programs is effective after June 30, 1992.

[Conference Report]

Senate Amendment

The Senate amendment extends the authority to issue QMBs and to elect to trade in QMB authority for authority to issue MCCs for 24 months (through June 30, 1994).

Effective date. Same as the House bill.

Conference Agreement

The conference agreement follows the House bill with three modifications.

Treatment of certain housing affordability programs

The conference agreement provides that, in high housing cost areas, the fact that an issuer of QMBs or MCCs also provides certain mortgage loans or grants other than first mortgage loans or grants to homebuyers in conjunction with QMB or MCC financing will not preclude availability of the QMB- or MCC-assistance on the purchase of a residence. Qualifying subordinate mortgage loans or grants may not be financed directly or indirectly with tax-exempt private activity bonds. Also qualifying subordinate mortgage loans or grants either must be accompanied by a "resale price control restriction", (or in the case of loans must be, "shared appreciation loans"). Finally, the local government must retain its interest in the home's appreciation for a period at least as long as the Federal QMB and MCC recapture period. A resale price control restriction is defined as a deed restriction, right of repurchase, or similar mechanism which (1) requires the owner to sell the unit to a purchaser qualifying for QMB or MCC financing and (2) limits the resale price to an amount not exceeding the initial purchase price plus an indexed amount that is less than the full appreciation on the residence. A shared appreciation loan is defined as a below-market rate or deferred interest loan which entitles the governmental lender to a share of any appreciation in value (attributable to the portion of the residence financed with the shared appreciation loan) realized upon disposition of the residence as repayment for the subsidy provided by the loan. Any interest of a governmental unit in a QMB- or MCC-financed residence attributable to a qualifying subordinated mortgage loan will be disregarded for purposes of (1) the first-time homebuyer and owner-occupied residence requirements of the QMB and MCC programs; (2) the maximum purchase price limit for QMB-and MCC-financed residences; (3) the rules for determining who is the owner of a QMB-or MCC-financed residence; and (4) the rules for determining the effective rate of interest on QMB-financed loans. The terms of the subordinated mortgage loan or grant will be taken into account, however, for measuring the amount of the homeowner's gain, if any, under the QMB- and MCC-recapture restrictions. The conferees intend that the special rules for these housing affordability programs will not apply to any subordination loans or grant if the governmental unit's interest under the loan or grant is structured so as to realize an amount in excess of the pro rata portion of the appreciation on the residence financed with the subordinated mortgage loan or grant (e.g., by allocating to the governmental unit an amount of gain on disposition greater than the proportionate amount of the total subsidy to the homebuyer that is provided by the subordinated mortgage loan).

Treatment of certain contracts for deeds

The conference agreement also provides that, in the case of certain homebuyers whose family incomes do not exceed fifty percent of applicable median family income, ownership of land subject to certain contracts for deed does not violate the requirement that QMB-and

MCC-financed homebuyers be first-time homebuyers and that the financing provided be for new mortgages. Thus, QMB-financed loans may be made (and MCCs to be granted) to individuals who own and maintain their principal residence on land subject to these contracts for deed provided that the homebuyers satisfy (a) all otherwise applicable requirements of the QMB and MCC programs but for the contract for deed and (b) the special income limit. These loans may be used to repay the contract for deed and to finance a new residence on the land. Also, as under present law, these homebuyers will remain eligible for qualified home improvement loans to rehabilitate existing principal residences on the land held subject to the contracts for deed.

Treatment of certain two-family housing

The conference agreement expands a present-law exception to the requirement that all residences receiving qualified mortgage bond financing or MCCs be single family, owner-occupied housing to allow certain newly constructed two-family housing to qualify. Under the expanded exception, newly constructed two-family housing will be eligible for these subsidies if (a) the housing is located in a targeted area of economic distress (sec. 143(j)), (b) at least one of the two units is occupied as the principal residence of the mortgagor, and (c) the family income of the mortgagor is 140 percent or less of the applicable area median family income.[1]

Effective Date

The extension of the QMB and MCC programs is effective after June 30, 1992. The three modifications are effective for QMB and MCC-financing provided after the date of enactment.

[¶3013] Section 13142. Permanent Extension of Low-income Housing Credit

(Code Sec. 42)

[House Explanation]

Present Law

A tax credit is allowed in annual installments over 10 years for qualifying newly constructed or substantially rehabilitated low-income rental housing. For most qualifying housing, the credit has a present value of 70 percent of the qualified basis of the low-income housing units. For housing also receiving other Federal subsidies (e.g., tax-exempt bond financing) and for the acquisition cost (e.g., costs other than rehabilitation expenditures) of existing housing that is substantially rehabilitated, the credit has a present value of 30 percent of qualified costs. In qualified census tracts and difficult development areas, the 70-percent and 30-percent may be increased to 91-percent and 39-percent respectively.

The credit amount is based on the qualified basis of the housing units serving the low-income tenants. A residential rental project will qualify for the credit only if (1) 20 percent or more of the aggregate residential rental units in the project are occupied by individuals with 50 percent or less of area median income, or (2) 40 percent or more of the aggregate residential rental units in the project are occupied by individuals with 60 percent or less of area median income. These income figures are adjusted for family size. The low income set-aside is elected when the project is placed in service.

Maximum rents that may be charged families in units on which a credit is claimed depend on the number of bedrooms in the unit. The rent limitation is 30 percent of the qualifying income of a family deemed to have a size of 1.5 persons per bedroom (e.g., a two-bedroom unit has a rent limitation based on the qualifying income for a family of three).

To qualify for the credit, a building owner generally must receive a low-income housing credit allocation from the appropriate State credit authority. An exception is provided for property which is substantially financed with the proceeds of tax-exempt bonds subject to the State's private-activity bond volume limitation. The annual credit ceiling for each State is $1.25 per resident per year.

[Footnote ¶3006 continued]

[Footnote ¶3012] 1. The conferees intend, however, that the interest of a governmental unit will be disregarded under the recapture restriction if the governmental unit's interest is structured so as to capture any amount otherwise subject to Federal recapture e.g. by allocating to the governmental unit an amount of gain on disposition greater than the proportionate amount of the total subsidy to the homebuyer that is provided by the subordinated mortgage loan.

The low-income housing credit expired after June 30, 1992.

Reasons for Change

The committee believes the low income housing credit is a useful incentive for increasing the stock of affordable housing available to low-income individuals. Further, the committee believes that a permanent extension of the low-income housing credit will provide greater planning certainty needed for the efficient delivery of this Federal subsidy. Finally, the committee believes that building receiving assistance under the National Affordable Housing Act of 1990 should be eligible for the 70-percent credit as long as stricter income targeting requirements are satisfied.

Explanation of Provision

The bill permanently extends the low-income housing tax credit. [4]It also provides that a building shall not be treated as Federally subsidized solely by reason of assistance with respect to that building received under the National Affordable Housing Act of 1990 (as in effect on the date of enactment of this provision) if 40-percent or more of the aggregate residential rental units in the residential rental project receiving the assistance are occupied by individuals with 50-percent or less of area median income. These projects are eligible for the 70-percent and 30-percent credits but not for the 91-percent or 39-percent credits otherwise available in qualified census tracts and difficult development areas.

Effective Date

The provision generally is effective after June 30, 1992. The provision relating to Federal subsidies under the National Affordable Housing Act of 1990 is effective on the date of enactment.

[Senate Explanation]

Present Law

In general

A tax credit is allowed in annual installments over 10 years for qualifying newly constructed or substantially rehabilitated low-income residential rental housing. For most qualifying housing, the credit has a present value of 70 percent of the qualified basis of the low-income housing units. For housing also receiving other Federal subsidies (e.g., tax-exempt bond financing) and for the acquisition cost (e.g., costs other than rehabilitation expenditures) of existing housing that is substantially rehabilitated, the credit has a present value of 30 percent of qualified costs.

Full-time students

A housing unit generally is not eligible for the low-income housing tax credit if the tenants are full-time students who are not married individuals filing joint returns. Exceptions to this rule allow the credit to be claimed on housing units occupied by persons who are enrolled in certain job training programs or by students who are receiving Aid to Families with Dependent Children (AFDC) payments.

Deep-rent skewing

Generally, the credit amount is based on the qualified basis of the housing units serving low-income tenants. A residential rental project will qualify for the credit only if (1) 20 percent or more of the aggregate residential rental units in the project are occupied by individuals whose incomes do not exceed 50 percent of area median income, or (2) 40 percent or more of the aggregate residential rental units in the project are occupied by individuals whose incomes do not exceed 60 percent of area median income. These income figures are adjusted for family size. The low income set-aside is elected when the project is placed in service.

To qualify under the deep rent skewing exception from the general targeting requirements, at least 15 percent of the low-income units must be occupied by tenants whose incomes do not exceed 40 percent of area median income, the rents on such units must be restricted to 30 percent of the qualifying income limitation, and rents on the market rate units must be at least 200 percent of rents charged on comparable rent restricted units. For projects receiving allocations prior to 1990, rents on market rate units must be at least 300 percent of rents charged on comparable rent restricted units.

Maximum rent

The maximum rent that may be charged a family in a low-income housing tax credit knit depends on the number of bedrooms in that

4. See also description of low-income housing credit for Empowerment Zones in Part III of the report on Title XIV.

unit. Prior to 1990, maximum allowable rent was determined on the basis of the actual family size of the occupants.

Tenant occupancy

Under the general low-income tenant occupancy requirement, a residential rental project qualifies for the low-income housing tax credit only if at least: (1) 20 percent or more of the aggregate residential rental units in the project are occupied by individuals whose incomes do not exceed 50 percent of area median income or, (2) 40 percent or more of the aggregate residential rental units in the project are occupied by individuals whose incomes do not exceed 60 percent of area median income.

Income recertification

Generally, the owner of a low-income housing project must annually recertify tenant incomes to meet the low-income tenant occupancy requirements, regardless of whether the building is entirely occupied by low-income tenants.

Tenant protection

The low-income housing tax credit provisions in the Code do not include any specific provisions concerning the grounds far denial of admission to low-income housing projects, for termination of a tenancy, or for refusal to renew the lease of a tenant.

Developmental and operational costs

In general, housing credit agencies cannot allocate more low-income housing tax credits to a project than are necessary for the financial feasibility of the project and its viability as a qualified low-income housing project throughout the 10-year credit period. In making this determination, a housing credit agency must consider (1) the sources and uses of funds and the total financing of the project, (2) any proceeds expected to be generated by reason of tax benefits and (3) the percentage of the housing credit dollar amount to be used for project costs other than the costs of intermediaries.

Allocation between buyer and seller in month of disposition

The Code requires that the low-income housing tax credit be divided between a buyer and seller of a low-income housing tax credit project based upon the number of days during the year of disposition that the project was held by each. The Internal Revenue Service has issued guidance that requires a mid-month averaging convention.

The low-income housing tax credit expired after June 30, 1992.

Reasons for Change

The committee believes than the low-income housing tax credit is a useful incentive for increasing the stock of affordable housing available to low-income individuals. Further, the committee believes that a permanent extension of the low-income housing credit will provide greater planning certainty needed for the efficient delivery of this Federal subsidy without sacrificing necessary Congressional oversight of the program. Finally, the committee believes that the modifications to the credit will improve its operation.

Explanation of Provision

The bill permanently and retroactively extends the low-income housing tax credit. The bill also makes the following modifications:

Full-time students

The bill provides that a housing unit occupied entirely by full-time students may qualify for the credit if the full-time students are a single parent and his or her minor children and none of the tenants is a dependent of a third party. The bill also codifies the present-law exception regarding married students filing joint returns (which continues to apply to all buildings placed in service since original enactment of the low-income housing tax credit by the Tax Reform Act of 1986).

Deep-rent skewing

The bill allows an irrevocable election by the owner of a low-income building receiving a credit allocation before 1990 to satisfy the 200 percent rent restriction rather than the 300 percent rent restriction. The election is available only to taxpayers who enter into a compliance monitoring agreement with a housing credit agency. Further, the election applies only with respect to tenants first occupying any unit in the building after the date of the election, and must be made within 180 days after the date of enactment.

Maximum rent

The bill allows an irrevocable election by the owner of a low-income building placed in-service before 1990 to use either apartment size or family size in determining maximum allowable rent. The election is available only to taxpayers who enter into a compliance monitoring agreement with a housing credit agency. Further, the election applies only with respect to tenants first occupying any unit in the building after the date of the election, and must be made within 180 days after the date of enactment.

Tenant occupancy

The bill authorizes she Treasury Department to provide a waiver of penalties for de minimis errors in the application of low-income tenant occupancy requirement.

Income recertification

The bill authorizes the Treasury Department to grant a waiver from the annual recertification of tenant income for tenants in buildings that are occupied entirely by low-income tenants.

Tenant protection

The bill provides that an applicant may not be denied admission to a low-income housing tax credit project because the applicant holds a voucher or certificate of eligibility under Section 8 of the Housing Act of 1937.

Developmental and operational costs

The bill requires a housing credit agency to consider the reasonableness of the developmental and operational costs of a project as an additional factor in making its determination as to the proper amount of low-income housing tax credits to allocate to a project.

Reasons for a determination of unreasonableness might include, for example, costs not comparable to costs to develop or operate similar projects in the locality, inefficient development practices, building design of a nature above what is necessary to provide basic, safe housing for the intended population in the locality. The committee also intends that an allocating agency make a determination as to the appropriateness of amenities included in a project. Amenities, and the space attributable thereto, should be appropriate to the size and type of the resident population to be served.

Allocation between buyer and seller in month of disposition

The bill provides that the buyer and seller may agree to use either the exact number of days or the mid-month convention to determine the division of the credit in the month of disposition.

Effective Date

The extension of the low-income housing tax credit and the provisions relating to: (1) full-time students, and (2) developmental and operational costs are effective after June 30, 1992. The provisions relating to: (1) tenant occupancy, (2) income certification, (3) tenant protection, and (4) allocations between the buyer and seller are effective on the date of enactment. The elections relating to deep-rent skewing and maximum rent must be made within 180 days after the date of enactment.

[Conference Report]

Extension

The conference agreement follows the House bill and the Senate amendment.

Home funds

The conference agreement follows the House bill with a modification to the House bill requirement that 40 percent or more of the aggregate residential rental units in the residential rental project receiving the assistance are occupied by individuals with 50 percent or less of area median income. Specifically 40 percent would be reduced to 25 percent for entities described in Code section 142(d)(6), consistent with the income targeting rules currently applicable to such entities. The House bill requirement limiting this provision to the 70 percent and 30 percent credits but not for the 91 percent or 39 percent credits otherwise available in qualified census tracts and difficult development areas is retained.

Full-time students

The conference agreement follows the Senate amendment.

Deep-rent skewing

The conference agreement follows the Senate amendment with a modification. The modification provides that the irrevocable election would apply to both current and future tenants but would not allow rent increases on existing low-income tenants.

Maximum rent

The conference agreement follows the Senate amendment.

Income recertification

The conference agreement follows the Senate amendment with a modification. The conference agreement provides that third-party verification of a tenant's or prospect tenant's income from his combined assets is not necessary if (l) the combined assets do not exceed $5,000 and (2) the tenant or prospective tenant provides a signed, sworn statement to this effect to the building owner. Further the conferees do not intend to modify the treatment of individuals receiving section 8 assistance.

Tenant protection

The conference agreement follows the Senate amendment.

Development and operational costs

The conference agreement follows the Senate amendment with a clarification that the provision is not intended to create a national standard of reasonableness. The conferees intend for allocating agencies to set standards of reasonableness reflecting the applicable facts and circumstances including the location of the 'projects and the uses for which the projects are built.

Allocation between buyer and seller in month of dispositions

The conference agreement follows the Senate amendment.

Effective date

The extension of the low-income housing tax credit and the provision relating to: (1) full-time students, and (2) developmental and operational cost are effective after June 30, 1992. The provisions relating to: (1) tenant occupancy, (2) income recertification, (3) tenant protection, (4) allocations between the buyer and seller, and (5) HOME funds are effective on the date of enactment. The elections relating to maximum rent and deep-rent spewing must be made within 180 days after the date of enactment.

[¶3014] Section 13143. Application of Passive Loss Rules to Rental Real Estate Activities

(Code Sec. 469)

[House Explanation]

Present Law

The passive loss rules limit deductions and credits from passive trade or business activities. Deductions attributable to passive activities to the extent they exceed income from passive activities, generally may not be deducted against other income, such as wages, portfolio income, or business income that is not derived from a passive activity. Credits from passive activities may not reduce the taxpayer's tax liability, to the extent such credits exceed regular tax liability from passive activities. Deductions and credits that are suspended under these rules are carried forward and treated as deductions and credits from passive activities in the next year. The suspended losses from a passive activity are allowed in full when a taxpayer disposes of his entire interest in the passive activity to an unrelated person.

The passive loss rules apply to individuals, estates and trusts, closely held C corporations, and personal service corporations. A special rule permits closely held C corporations to apply passive activity losses and credits against active business income (or tax liability allocable thereto) but not against portfolio income.

Passive activities are defined to include trade or business activities in which the taxpayer does not materially participate. To materially participate in an activity, a taxpayer must be involved in the operations of the activity on a regular, continuous, and substantial basis. Except as provided in regulations, a taxpayer is treated as not materially participating in an activity held through a limited partnership interest. [5]

[Footnote ¶3013 continued]

5. Treas. Reg. section 1.469-5T(e) provides exceptions to this general rule for limited partnership interests in certain circumstances, including the circumstance where an individual taxpayer is both a general and a limited partner or where the taxpayer meets certain of the material participation tests (including the 500 hour test) applicable to persons other than limited partners.

Rental activities (including rental real estate activities) are also treated as passive activities, regardless of the level of taxpayer's participation. In general, rental activities cannot be treated as part of a larger activity that includes nonrental activities. A special rule permits the deduction of up to $25,000 of losses from rental real estate activities (even though they are considered passive), if the taxpayer actively participates in them. This $25,000 amount is allowed for taxpayers with adjusted gross incomes of $100,000 or less, and is phased out for taxpayers with adjusted gross incomes between $100,000 and $150,000. Active participation is a lesser standard of involvement than material participation. A taxpayer is treated as actively participating if, for example, he participates, in a significant and bona fide sense, in the making of management decisions or arranging for others to provide services (such as repairs). The active participation standard is not satisfied, however, if the taxpayer's interest is less than 10 percent (by value) of all interests in the activity. A taxpayer generally is deemed not to satisfy the active participation standard with respect to property he holds through a limited partnership interest.

If the taxpayer has suspended losses from a former passive activity (an activity that is not a passive activity for the current taxable year but was a passive activity for the taxable year in which the loss arose), the losses are offset against the income from such activity for the taxable year, and any excess after the offset continues to be treated as a loss from a passive activity.

Reasons for Change

The committee considers it unfair that a person who performs personal services in a real estate trade or business in which he materially participates may not offset losses from rental real estate activities against income from nonrental real estate activities or against other types of income such as portfolio investment income. The committee bill modifies the passive loss rule to alleviate this unfairness.

Explanation of Provision

The provision treats a taxpayer's rental real estate activities in which he materially participates as not subject to limitation under the passive loss rule if the taxpayer meets eligibility requirements relating to real property trades or businesses in which the taxpayer performs services. Whether a taxpayer materially participates in his rental real estate activities is determined as if each interest of the taxpayer in rental real estate is a separate activity, unless the taxpayer elects to treat all interests in rental real estate as one activity. The provision applies to individuals and closely held C corporations.

Real property trade or business means any real property development, redevelopment, construction, reconstruction, acquisition, conversion, rental, operation, management, leasing, or brokerage trade or business.

An individual taxpayer meets the eligibility requirements if more than half of the personal services the taxpayer performs in a trade or business are in real property trades or businesses in which he materially participates.

In the case of a joint return, it is intended that each spouse's personal services are taken into account separately. In determining material participation, however, the provision does not change the present-law rule (sec. 469(h)(5)) that the participation of the spouse of the taxpayer is taken into account. Thus, for example, a husband and wife filing a joint return meet the eligibility requirements of the provision if during the taxable year one spouse performs at least half of his or her business services in a real estate trade or business in which either spouse materially participates. The couple does not fail the eligibility requirements if less than half of their business services, taken together, are performed in real estate trades or businesses in which either of them materially participates, provided that more than half of one spouse's business services qualify.

Personal services performed as an employee are not treated as performed in a real estate trade or business unless the person performing services has more than a 5 percent ownership interest in the employer (within the meaning of sec. 416(i)(1)(B)).

A closely held C corporation meets the eligibility requirements if more than 50 percent of its gross receipts for the taxable year are derived from real property trades or businesses in which the corporation materially participates (within the meaning of sec. 469(h)(4)).

Material participation has the same meaning as under present law. Thus, as under present law, except as provided in regulations, no interest as a limited partner in a limited partnership is treated as an interest with respect to which the taxpayer materially participates. The election permitting a taxpayer to aggregate his rental real estate activities for purposes of determining whether such activities are treated as not passive under the provision is not intended to alter present law with respect to material participation through limited partnership interests.

Suspended losses from any rental real property activity that is treated as not passive by reason of the provision are treated as losses from a former passive activity. Thus, such suspended losses are limited to income from the activity, and are not allowed to offset other income. When the taxpayer disposes of his entire interest in the activity in a fully taxable transaction with an unrelated party, any remaining suspended losses allocable to the activity are allowed in full.

Modified adjusted gross income is determined without regard to any loss allowable by reason of this provision, for purposes of the present-law $25,000 allowance of losses and deduction-equivalent credits from certain rental activities.

Effective Date

The provision is effective with respect to taxable years beginning after December 31, 1993.

[Conference Report]

Senate Amendment

The senate amendment is the same as the House bill, except that an eligible taxpayer's net loss from rental real estate activities in which the taxpayer materially participates generally is allowed to offset income from real property trade or business activities. The loss allowed under the provision may not exceed the least of (1) the taxpayer's net loss for the taxable year from rental real estate activities in which the taxpayer materially participates, (2) the taxpayer's net loss for the taxable year from all rental real estate activities, (3) the taxpayer's net income for the taxable year from real property trade or business activities which are not passive activities, or (4) the taxpayer's taxable income for the taxable year (determined without regard to this provision). A similar rule applies with respect to passive activity credits. The Senate amendment does not apply to closely held C corporations.

Effective date

Same as the House bill.

Conference Agreement

The conference agreement follows the House bill, with a modification. Under the conference agreement, an individual taxpayer meets the eligibility requirements if (1) more than half of the personal services the taxpayer performs in trades or businesses during the taxable year are performed in real property trades or businesses in which the taxpayer materially participates, and (2) such taxpayer performs more than 750 hours of services during the taxable year in real property trades or businesses in which the taxpayer materially participates. In the case of a joint return, the eligibility requirements are met only if either spouse separately satisfies the requirements. Thus, one of the spouses separately must satisfy the requirement with respect to half of such spouse's personal services and the requirement with respect to 750 hours of services, without regard to services performed by the other spouse. In determining material participation, however, the conference agreement does not change the present-law rule that the participation of the spouse of the taxpayer is taken into account.

[¶3015] Section 13144. Real Estate Property Acquired by a Qualified Organization

(Code Sec. 514)

[House Explanation]

Present Law

In general, a qualified pension trust or an organization that is otherwise exempt from Federal income tax is taxed on income from a trade or business that is unrelated to the organization's exempt purposes (Unrelated Business Taxable Income or "UBTI") (sec. 511). Certain types of income, including rents, royalties, dividends, and interest are excluded from UBTI, except when such income is derived from "debt-financed property." Income from debt-financed property generally is treated as UBTI in proportion to the amount of debt financing (sec. 514(a)).

An exception to the rule treating income from debt-financed property as UBTI is available to pension trusts, educational institutions, and certain other exempt organizations (collectively referred to as "qualified organizations") that make debt-financed investments in real property (sec. 514(c)(9)(A)). Under this exception, income from investments in real property is not treated as income from debt-financed property. Mortgages are not considered real property for purposes of the exception.

The real property exception to the debt-financed property rules is available for investments in debt-financed property, only if the following six restrictions are satisfied: (1) the purchase price of the real property is a fixed amount determined as of the date of the acquisition (the "fixed price restriction"); (2) the amount of the indebtedness or any amount payable with respect to the indebtedness, or the time for making any payment of any such amount, is not dependent (in whole or in part) upon revenues, income, or profits derived from the property (the "participating loan restriction"); (3) the property is not leased by the qualified organization to the seller or to a person related to the seller (the "leaseback restriction"); (4) in the case of a pension trust, the seller or lessee of the property is not a disqualified person (the "disqualified person restriction"); (5) the seller or a person related to the seller (or a person related to the plan with respect to which a pension trust was formed) is not providing financing in connection with the acquisition of the property (the "seller-financing restriction"); and (6) if the investment in the property is held through a partnership, certain additional requirements are satisfied by the partnership (the "partnership restrictions") (sec. 524(c)(9)(B)(i) through (vi)).

Reasons for Change

The committee believes that modifications to the debt-financed income rules are desirable to permit qualified organizations to make debt-financed investments in real property on commercially reasonable terms in circumstances where the committee believes there is no potential for abuse.

Explanation of Provision

Relaxation of the leaseback and disqualified person restrictions

The provision relaxes the leaseback and disqualified person restrictions to permit a limited leaseback of debt-financed real property to the seller (or a person related to the seller) or to a disqualified person. [6] The exception applies only where (1) no more than 25 percent of the leasable floor space in a building (or complex of buildings) is leased back to the seller (or related party) or to the disqualified person, and (2) the lease is on commercially reasonable terms, independent of the sale and other transactions.

Relaxation of the seller-financing restriction

The provision relaxes the seller-financing restriction to permit seller financing on terms that are commercially reasonable independent of the sale and other transactions. The provision grants authority to the Treasury Department to issue regulations for the purpose of determining commercially reasonable financing terms.

The provision does not modify the present-law fixed price and participating loan restrictions. Thus, for example, income from real property acquired with seller-financing where the timing or amount of payment is based on revenue, income, or profits from the property generally will continue to be treated as income from debt-financed property, unless some other exception applies.

Relaxation of the fixed price and participating loan restriction for property acquired from financial institutions

The provision relaxes the fixed price and participating loan restrictions for certain sales of real property foreclosed upon by financial institutions. [7] The relaxation of these rules is limited to cases where: (1) a qualified organization acquires the property from a financial

[Footnote ¶3014 continued]

6. As under present law, a leaseback to a disqualified person is subject to the prohibited transaction rules set forth in section 4975.

7. For this purpose, financial institutions include financial institutions in conservatorship or receivership, certain affiliates of financial institutions, and government corporations that succeed to the rights and interests of a receiver or conservator.

institution that acquired the real property by foreclosure (or after an actual or imminent default), or was held by the selling financial institution at the time that it entered into conservatorship or receivership; (2) any gain recognized by the financial institution with respect to the property is ordinary income; (3) the stated principal amount of the seller financing does not exceed the financial institution's outstanding indebtedness (including accrued but unpaid interest) with respect to the property at the time of foreclosure or default; and (4) the present value of the maximum amount payable pursuant to any participation feature cannot exceed 30 percent of the total purchase price of the property (including contingent payments).

Effective Date

The provision is effective for acquisitions (and also for leases entered into) on or after January 1, 1994.

[Conference Report]

Senate Amendment

The Senate amendment is the same as the House bill.

Conference Agreement

The conference agreement follows the House bill and the Senate amendment.

[¶3016] Section 13145. Repeal of Special Treatment of Publicly Treated Partnerships

(Code Sec. 512)

[House Explanation]

Present Law

In general, the character of a partner's distributive share of partnership income is the same as if the income had been directly realized by the partner. Thus, whether a tax-exempt organization's share of income from a partnership (other than from a publicly-traded partnership) is treated as unrelated business income depends on the underlying character of the income (sec. 512(c)(1)).

By contrast, a tax-exempt organization's distributive share of gross income from a publicly-traded partnership (that is not otherwise treated as a corporation) automatically is treated as gross income derived from an unrelated trade or business (sec. 512(c)(2)(A)). The organization's share of the partnership deductions is allowed in computing the organization's UBTI (Sec. 512(c)(2)(B)).

Reasons for Change

The automatic UBTI rule effectively prevents pension funds and other tax-exempt organizations from investing in publicly-traded partnerships. The committee believes these investors could provide a valuable source of capital that should be available to publicly-traded partnerships.

Explanation of Provision

The provision repeals the rule that automatically treats income from publicly-traded partnerships as UBTI. Thus, under the provision, investments in publicly-traded partnerships are treated the same as investments in other partnerships for purposes of the UBTI rules.

Effective Date

The provision is effective for partnership years beginning on or after January 1, 1994.

[Conference Report]

Senate Amendment

The Senate amendment is the same as the House bill.

Conference Agreement

The conference agreement follows the House bill and the Senate amendment.

[¶3017] Section 13146. Title-holding Companies Permitted to Receive Small Amounts of Unrelated Business Taxable Income

(Code Sec. 501)

[House Explanation]

Present Law

Section 501(c)(2) provides tax-exempt status

to certain corporations or organized for the exclusive purpose of holding title to property and remitting any income from the property to one or more related tax-exempt organizations. Section 501(c)(25) provides tax-exempt status to certain corporations and trusts that are organized for the exclusive purposes of acquiring and holding title to real property, collecting income from such property, and remitting the income to no more than 35 shareholders or beneficiaries that are: (1) qualified pension, profit-sharing, or stock bonus plans (sec. 401(a)); (2) governmental pension plans (sec. 414(d)); (3) the United States, a State or political subdivision, or governmental agencies or instrumentalities; or (4) tax-exempt charitable, educational, religious, or other organizations described in section 501(c)(3). However, the IRS has taken the position that a title-holding company described in section 501(c)(2) or 501(c)(25) will lose its tax-exempt status if it generates any amount of certain types of UBTI. [8]

Reasons for Change

Typical investments of section 501(c)(2) and (c)(25) corporations include shopping centers, office buildings, and apartment buildings. These real estate investments typically generate rental income, which generally is not considered UBTI, but may also generate small amounts of income which could be treated as UBTI (e.g., money collected from laundry machines used by tenants, or from vending machines offered as a convenience to the patrons of a shopping center).

The committee believes that a section 501(c)(2) or (c)(25) organization should not lose its exemption merely because it receives small amounts of UBTI that are incidentally derived from the holding of real property.

Explanation of Provision

The provision permits a title-holding company that is exempt from tax under sections 501(c)(2) or 501(c)(25) to receive UBTI (that would otherwise disqualifY the company) up to 10 percent of its gross income for the taxable year, provided that the UBTI is incidentally derived from the holding of real property. For example, income generated from parking or operating vending machines located on real property owned by a title-holding company generally would qualify for the 10-percent de minimis rule, while income derived from an activity that is not incidental to the holding of real property (e.g., manufacturing) would not. In cases where unrelated income is incidentally derived from holding of real property, receipt by a title-holding company of such income (up to the 10-percent limit) will not jeopardize the title-holding company's tax-exempt status, but nonetheless, will be subject to tax as UBTI.

In addition, the provision provides that a section 501(c)(2) or 501(c)(25) title-holding company will not lose its tax-exempt status if UBTI that is incidentally derived from the holding of real property exceeds the 10-percent limitation, provided that the title-holding company establishes to the satisfaction of the Secretary of the Treasury that the receipt of UBTI in excess of the 10-percent limitation was inadvertent and reasonable steps are being taken to correct the circumstances giving rise to such excess UBTI.

Effective Date

The provision is effective for taxable years beginning on or after January 1, 1994.

[Conference Report]

Senate Amendment

The Senate amendment is the same as the House bill.

Conference Agreement

The conference agreement follows the House bill and the Senate amendment.

[¶3018] Section 13147. Exclusion from Unrelated Business Tax of Gains from Certain Property

(Code Sec. 512)

[House Explanation]

Present Law

In general, gains or losses from the sale, ex-

[Footnote ¶3015 continued]

8. IRS Notice 88-121, 1988-2 C.B. 457. See also Treas. Reg. sec. 1.501(c)(2)-1(a).

change or other disposition of property are excluded from UBTI (sec. 512(b)(5)). However, gains or losses from the sale, exchange or other disposition of property held primarily for sale to customers in the ordinary course of a trade or business are not excluded from UBTI (the "dealer UBTI rule") (sec. 512(b)(5)(B)).

Reasons for Change

Real property that is owned by troubled financial institutions often is sold in bundled packages. This enables the financial institution to dispose of the less desirable properties together with the more desirable properties. It also allows institutions with large portfolios of properties to pass on to purchasers some of the burden of an orderly liquidation of the properties.

The committee understands that the dealer UBTI rule effectively discourages pension funds and other tax-exempt organizations from investing in the properties bundled together by troubled financial institutions. The committee believes that these investors could provide a valuable source of capital for the purchase of these bundled properties.

Explanation of Provision

The provision provides an exception to the dealer UBTI rule by excluding gains and losses from the sale, exchange or other disposition of certain real property and mortgages acquired from financial institutions that are in conservatorship or receivership. Only real property and mortgages owned by a financial institution (or that was security for a loan held by the financial institution) at the time that the institution entered conservatorship or receivership are eligible for the exception.

The exclusion is limited to properties designated as disposal property within nine months of acquisition, and disposed of within two-and-a-half years of acquisition. The two-and-a-half year disposition period may be extended by the Secretary if an extension is necessary for the orderly liquidation of the property. No more than one-half by value of properties acquired in a single transaction may be designated as disposal property.

The exclusion is not available for properties that are improved or developed to the extent that the aggregate expenditures on development do not exceed 20 percent of the net selling price of the property.

Effective Date

The provision is effective for property acquired on or after January 1, 1994.

[Conference Report]

Senate Amendment

The Senate amendment is the same as the House bill.

Conference Agreement

The conference agreement follows the House bill and the Senate amendment.

[¶ 3019] Section 13148. Exclusion from Unrelated Business Tax of Certain Fees and Option Premiums

(Code Sec. 512)

[House Explanation]

Present Law

Income from a trade or business that is unrelated to an exempt organization's purpose generally is UBTI. Passive income such as dividends, interest, royalties, and gains or losses from the sale, exchange or other disposition of property generally is excluded from UBTI (sec. 512(b)). In addition, gains on the lapse or termination of options on securities are explicitly exempted from UBTI (sec. 512(b)(5)).

Present law is unclear on whether premiums from unexercised options on real estate and loan commitment fees are UBTI.

Reasons for Change

The committee believes that gains and losses from options should be treated consistently for purposes of the UBTI. In addition, the committee believes that taxing loan commitment fees and premiums from unexercised options on real estate is inconsistent with the generally tax-free treatment of income from investment activities accorded to exempt organizations.

Explanation of Provision

The provision expands the current exception for gains on the lapse or termination of options on securities to gains or losses from such options (without regard to whether they are written by the organization), from options on real property, and from the forfeiture of good-faith deposits (that are consistent with established business practice) for the purchase, sale or lease of real property.

In addition, the provision excludes loan commitment fees from UBTI. For purposes of this provision, loan commitment fees are non-refundable charges made by a lender to reserve a sum of money with fixed terms for a specified period of time. These charges are to compensate the lender for the risk inherent in committing to make the loan (e.g., for the lender's exposure to interest rate changes and for potential lost opportunities).

Effective Date

The provision is effective for premiums or loan commitment fees that are received on or after January 1, 1994.

[Conference Report]

Senate Amendment

The Senate amendment is the same as the House bill.

Conference Agreement

The conference agreement follows the House bill and the Senate amendment.

[¶ 3020] Section 13149. Treatment of Pension Fund Investments in Real Estate Investment Trusts

(Code Sec. 856)

[House Explanation]

Present Law

A real estate investment trust ("REIT") is not taxed on income distributed to shareholders. A corporation does not qualify as a REIT if at any time during the last half of its taxable year more than 50 percent in value of its outstanding stock is owned, directly or indirectly, by five or fewer individuals ("the five or fewer rule"). A domestic pension trust is treated as a single individual for purposes of this rule.

Dividends paid by a REIT are not UBTI, [9] unless the stock in the REIT is debt-financed. Depending on its character, income earned by a partnership may be UBTI (Sec. 512(c)). Special rules treat debt-financed income earned by a partnership as UBTI (sec. 514(c)(9)(B)(vi)).

Reasons for Change

The committee believes that relaxation of the five or fewer rule is appropriate to encourage pension fund investment in REITs. Such investment, however, may permit circumvention of the UBIT. Accordingly, in certain circumstances, UBIT is imposed on a pension trustholding shares in a REIT if direct ownership of the REIT assets by the pension trust would have resulted in UBIT.

Explanation of Provision

Qualification as a REIT

The bill provides that a pension trust generally is not treated as a single individual for purposes of the five-or-fewer rule. Rather, the bill treats beneficiaries of the pension trust as holding stock in the REIT in proportion to their actuarial interests in the trust. This rule does not apply if disqualified persons, within the meaning of section 4975(e)(2) (other than by reason of subparagraphs (B) and (I)), together own five percent or more of the value of the REIT stock and the REIT has earnings and profits attributable to a period during which it did not qualifY as a REIT. [10]

In addition, the bill provides that a REIT cannot be a personal holding company and, therefore, is not subject to the personal holding company tax on its undistributed income.

Unrelated business taxable income

Under the bill, certain pension trusts owning more than 10 percent of a REIT must treat a percentage of dividends from the REIT as

[Footnote ¶ 3017 continued]

9. See Rev. Rul. 66-151, 1966-1 C.B. 151.

10. Moreover, as under present law, any investment by a pension trust must be in accordance with the fiduciary rules of the Employee Retirement Security Act ("ERISA") and the prohibited transaction rules of the Code and ERISA.

UBTI. This percentage is the gross income derived from an unrelated trade or business (determined as if the REIT were a pension trust) divided by the gross income of the REIT for the year in which the dividends are paid. Dividends are not treated as UBTI, however, unless this percentage is at least five percent.

The UBTI rule applies only if the REIT qualifies as a REIT by reason of the above modification of the five or fewer rule. Moreover, the UBTI rule applies only if (1) one pension trust owns more than 25 percent of the value of the REIT, or (2) a group of pension trusts individually holding more than 10 percent of the value of the REIT collectively own more than 50 percent of the value of the REIT.

Effective Date

The provision applies to taxable years beginning on or after January 1, 1994.

[Conference Report]

Senate Amendment

The Senate amendment is the same as the House bill.

Conference Agreement

The conference agreement follows the House bill and the Senate amendment.

[¶3021] Section 13150. Exclusion from Gross Income for Income from Discharge of Qualified Real Property Business Indebtedness

(Code Sec. 108, 703, 1017)

[House Explanation]

Present Law

The discharge of indebtedness generally gives rise to gross income to the debtor taxpayer. Present law provides exceptions to this general rule. Among the exceptions are rules providing that income from the discharge of indebtedness of the taxpayer is excluded from income if the discharge occurs in a title 11 case, the discharge occurs when the taxpayer is insolvent, or in the case of certain farm indebtedness. The amount excluded from income under these exceptions is applied to reduce tax attributes of the taxpayer.

Present law also provides that if the debt of a purchaser of property to the seller of such property which arose out of the purchase of such property is reduced, and the reduction would otherwise be treated as income to the purchaser from the discharge of indebtedness, the the reduction is treated as a purchase price adjustment (sec. 108(e)(5)). This rule applies only if the reduction does not occur in a title 11 case or when the purchaser is insolvent.

Prior law provided an elective exception for the discharge of qualified business indebtedness, defined as indebtedness incurred or assumed by an individual in connection with property used in his trade or business. The excludable amount was limited to the basis of the taxpayer's depreciable property and the excludable amount was applied to reduce the basis of depreciable property of the taxpayer. The taxpayer could elect to treat inventory as depreciable property for this purpose. If the amount of discharge income exceed the basis of depreciable property, the excess was included in gross income for the year of the discharge. This exception was repealed by the Tax Reform Act of 1986.

Reasons for Change

The committee understands that real property has declined in value in some areas of the nation, in some cases to such a degree that the property can no longer support the debt with which it is encumbered. The committee believes that where an individual has discharge of indebtedness that results from a decline in value of business real property securing that indebtedness, it is appropriate to provide for deferral, rather than current inclusion, of the resulting income. Generally, that deferral should not extend beyond the period that the taxpayer owns the property.

Explanation of Provision

The bill provides an election to taxpayers other than C corporations to exclude from gross income certain income from discharge of qualified real property business indebtedness. The amount so excluded cannot exceed the basis of certain depreciable real property of the taxpayer and is treated as a reduction in the basis of that property.

Qualified real property business indebtedness is indebtedness that (1) is incurred or assumed in connection with real property used in a trade or business, (2) is secured by that real property, and (3) with respect to which the taxpayer has made an election under this provision. Indebtedness incurred or assumed on or after January 1, 1993 is not qualified real property business indebtedness unless it is either (1) debt incurred to refinance qualified real property business debt incurred or assumed before that date (but only to the extent the amount of such debt does not exceed the amount of debt being refinanced) or (2) qualified acquisition indebtedness. Qualified real property business indebtedness does not include qualified farm indebtedness.

Qualified acquisition indebtedness is debt incurred to acquire, construct or substantially improve real property that is secured by such debt, and debt resulting from the refinancing of qualified acquisition debt, to the extent the amount of such debt does not exceed the amount of debt being refinanced.

The amount excluded under the provision with respect to the discharge of any qualified real property business indebtedness may not exceed the the excess of (1) the outstanding principal amount of such debt (immediately before the discharge), over (2) the fair market value (immediately before the discharge) of the business real property which is security for the debt. For this purpose, the fair market value of the property is reduced by the outstanding principal amount of any other qualified real property indebtedness secured by the property immediate before the discharge.

For example, assume that on July 1, 1993, Individual J owns a building worth $150,000, used in his trade or business, that is subject to a first mortgage securing a debt of J's of $110,000 and second mortgage securing a second debt of J's of $90,000. J is neither a bankrupt nor insolvent and neither debt is qualified farm indebtedness. J agrees with his second mortgagee to reduce the second mortgage debt to $30,000, resulting in discharge of indebtedness income in the amount of $60,000. Under the provision, assuming that J has sufficient basis in business real property to absorb the reduction (see below), J can elect to exclude $50,000 of that discharge from gross income. This is because the principal amount of the discharged debt immediately before the discharge (i.e., $90,000) exceeds the fair market value of the property securing it (i.e., $150,000 of free and clear value less $110,000 of other qualified business real property debt or $40,000) by $50,000. The remaining $10,000 of discharge is included in gross income.

The amount excluded under the provision may not exceed the aggregate adjusted bases (determined as of the first day of the next taxable year or, if earlier, the date of disposition) of depreciable real property held by the taxpayer immediately before the discharge, determined after any reductions under subsections (b) and (g) of section 108. Depreciable real property acquired in contemplation of the discharge is treated as not held by the taxpayer immediately before the discharge.

The amount of debt discharge excluded under the provision is applied, using the rules of section 1017 (as modified by the provision), to reduce the basis of business real property held by the taxpayer at the beginning of the taxable year following the taxable year in which the discharge occurs. The election under sec. 1017(b)(3) to treat inventory as qualified property does not apply. If the taxpayer disposes of real property (in the transaction that gave rise to the discharge or otherwise) prior to the first day of the next taxable year, then the reduction in basis of such property is made as of the time immediately before the disposition.

In the case of discharge of indebtedness of a partnership, the determination of whether debt is qualified real property indebtedness (and the application of the fair market value limitation) is made at the partnership level. For example, if partnership debt is discharged, the determination of whether the debt was incurred or assumed in connection with real property used in a trade or business is made by reference to the trade or business of the partnership and real property owned by the partnership. The election to apply the provision is made at the partner level, however, on a partner by partner basis. An interest of a partner in a partnership that owns depreciable real property is treated as depreciable real property to the extent of the partner's proportionate interest in the depreciable real property held by the partnership. The partnership's basis in depreciable real property with respect to such partner is correspondingly reduced.

The deemed distribution (under Code section 752) arising from the reduction in a partner's share of partnership liabilities attributable to the discharge of partnership debt is treated as follows. The allocation of an amount of debt discharge income to a partner results in that partner's basis in the partnership being increased by such amount (sec. 705). The reduction in a partner's share of partnership liabilities caused by the debt discharge also results in a deemed distribution (under sec. 752) which in turn results in a reduction (under sec. 733) of the partner's basis in his partnership interest. This section 733 basis reduction is separate from any reduction in basis of the partner's interest under the provision, i.e., the basis reduction that occurs as a result of treating the partnership interest as depreciable real property to the extent of the partner's proportionate interest in the depreciable real property held by the partnership (provided the partnership makes a corresponding reduction in the basis of depreciable partnership real property with respect to that partner).

In this provision to income from the discharge of indebtedness of an S corporation, the election is made by the S corporation (sec. 1363(c)), and the exclusion and basis reduction are both made at the S corporation level (sec. 108(d)(7)). The shareholders' basis in their stock is not adjusted by the amount of debt discharge income that is excluded at the corporate level. As a result of these rules, if an amount is excluded from the income of an S corporation under this provision, the income flowing through to the shareholders will be reduced (compared to what the shareholders' income would have been without the exclusion). Where the reduced basis in the corporation's depreciable property later results in additional income (or a smaller loss) to the corporation because of reduced depreciation or additional gain (or smaller loss) on disposition of the property, the additional income (or smaller loss) will flow through to the shareholders at that time, and will then result in a larger increase (or smaller reduction) in the shareholder's basis than if this provision had not previously applied. Thus, the provision simply defers income to the shareholders.

If depreciable real property, the basis of which was reduced under this provision, is disposed of, then for purposes of determining the amount of recapture under section 1250: (1) any such basis reduction is treated as a deduction allowed for depreciation, and (2) the determination of what would have been the depreciation adjustment under the straight line method is made as if there had been no such reduction. Thus, the amount of the basis reduction that is recaptured as ordinary income is reduced over the time the taxpayer continues to hold the property, as the taxpayer forgoes depreciation deductions due to the basis reduction.

Effective Date

The provision is effective with respect to discharges after December 31, 1992 in taxable years ending after that date.

[Conference Report]

Senate Amendment

No provision.

Conference Agreement

The conference agreement follows the House bill.

[¶3022] Section 13151. Increase in Recovery Period for Nonresidential Real Property

(Code Sec. 168)

[House Explanation]

Present Law

A taxpayer is allowed to recover, through annual depreciation allowances, the cost or other basis of nonresidential real property (other than land) that is used in a trade or business or that is held for the production of rental income. For regular tax purposes, the amount of the depreciation deduction allowed with respect to nonresidential real property for any taxable year generally is determined by using the straigt-line method and a recovery period of 31.5 years. For alternative minimum tax purposes, the amount of the depreciation deduction allowed with respect to nonresidential real property for any taxable year is determined by using the straight-line method and a recovery period of 40 years.

Reasons for Change

The committee believes that the recovery period for nonresidential real property under present law results in depreciation allowances that are larger than the actual decline in value of the property. In order to more accurately measure the economic income derived from the use of nonresidential real property in a trade or business or an investment activity, the recovery period for the depreciation of such property should be increased.

Explanation of Provision

The bill requires the depreciation deduction allowed with respect to nonresidential real property for regular tax purposes to be determined by using a recovery period of 39 years. The bill does not change the depreciation deduction allowed with respect to nonresidential real property for alternative minimum tax purposes.

Effective Date

The bill generally applies to property placed in service on or after February 25, 1993. The provision does not apply to property that a taxpayer places in service before January 1, 1994, if (1) the taxpayer or a qualified person entered into a binding written contract to purchase or construct the property before February 25, 1993, or (2) construction of the property was commenced by or for the taxpayer or a qualified person before February 25, 1993. A qualified person for this purpose is any person who transfers rights in such a contract or such property to the taxpayer, but only if the property is not placed in service by such person before such rights are transferred to the taxpayer.

[Conference Report]

Senate Amendment

The Senate amendment is the same as the House bill, except that the recovery period is 38 years.

Effective date. Same as the House bill.

Conference Agreement

The conference agreement follows the House bill, with a modification to the effective date.

Effective date. Under the conference agreement, the provision generally applies to property placed in service on or after May 13, 1993. The provision does not apply to property that a taxpayer places in service before January 1, 1994, if (1) the taxpayer or a qualified person entered into a binding written contract to purchase or construct the property before May 13, 1993, or (2) construction of the property was commenced by or for the taxpayer or a qualified person before May 13, 1993. A qualified person for this purpose is any person who transfers rights in such a contract or such property to the taxpayer, but only if the property is not placed in service by such person before such rights are transferred to the taxpayer. The conferees wish to clarify that the provision does not change the recovery period of any property to which the ACRS amendments made by section 201 of the Tax Reform Act of 1986 do not apply.

[¶ 3023] Sections 13161, 13162. Repeal of Luxury Excuse Taxes Other Than on Passenger Vehicles; Exemption from Luxury Excise Tax for Certain Equipment Installed on Passenger Vehicles for Use by Disabled Individuals

(Code Sec. 4001, 4002, 4003, 4004, 4005, 4006, 4007, 4008, 4009, 4010, 4011, 4012)

[House Explanation]

Present Law

Present law imposes a 10-percent excise tax on the portion of the retail price of the following items that exceeds the thresholds specified: automobiles above $30,000; boats above $100,000; aircraft above $250,000; jewelry above $10,000; and furs above $10,000. The tax also applies to subsequent purchases of component parts and accessories occurring within six months of the date the automobile, boat, or aircraft is placed in service.

The tax generally applies only to the first retail sale after manufacture, production or importation of items subject to the tax. It does not apply to subsequent sales of these items. The taxes on automobiles, boats, and aircraft generally do not apply to items used in trade or business.

The tax applies to sales before January 1, 2000.

Reasons for Change

During the recent recession, the boat, aircraft, jewelry, and fur industries have suffered job losses and increased unemployment. The committee believes that it is appropriate to eliminate the burden these taxes impose in the interests of fostering economic recovery in those and related industries.

The committee recognizes that in the absence of indexation of the threshold above which the tax on automobiles applies, even modest inflation will subject more automobiles to the luxury tax than were subject to the tax when it was first enacted.

The committee further believes that it is unfair and inappropriate to treat as luxury purchases those accessories or modifications which must be purchased by an individual with a disability to enable him or her to operate or to enter or exit a vehicle.

The committee further believes it is more appropriate to tax demonstrator cars when they are sold instead of when a dealer begins to use them as them as a demonstrator.

Explanation of Provision

Repeal of luxury tax on boats, aircraft, jewelry, and fur

The bill repeals the luxury excise tax imposed on boats, aircraft, jewelry, and furs.

Indexing of tax on automobiles

The bill modifies the luxury excise tax on automobiles to provide that the $30,000 threshold is indexed annually for inflation occurring after 1991. Consequently, the applicable threshold for 1993 will be $30,000 increased by the 1992 inflation rate.

Exemption for certain equipment installed on passenger vehicles for use by disabled individuals

The bill provides that the luxury excise tax does not apply to a part or accessory installed on a passenger vehicle to enable or assist an individual with a disability to operate the vehicle, or to enter or exit the vehicle, in order to compensate for the effect of the disability. This exception does not apply to accessories commonly available from the manufacturer or dealer, such as power steering, power door locks, power seats, or power windows.

Exemption for demonstrator vehicles

The bill exempts passenger vehicle dealers from paying the luxury tax on vehicles used as demonstrators for potential customers. Under the provision, the tax, if any, is to be assessed and paid on the sales price of the vehicle when the vehicle is sold.

Effective Date

The repeal of the luxury excise taxes on boats, aircraft, jewelry, and furs is effective for sales on or after January 1, 1993. The indexation of the threshold applicable to passenger vehicles is effective for sales on or after January 1, 1993. The provision relating to the purchase of accessories or modifications by disabled persons is effective for purchases after December 31, 1990. The provision relating to the use before sale of demonstrator vehicles is effective for vehicles used after December 31, 1992.

Persons entitled to a refund may request it from the seller from whom the taxed item was purchased. The seller then obtains the refund as provided under present-law Code section 6416.

[Conference Report]

Senate Amendment

The Senate amendment is the same as the House bill.

Conference Agreement

The conference agreement follows the House bill and the Senate amendment except for the indexation of the threshold applicable to passenger vehicles. The conference agreement provides that indexation will occur in increments of $2,000. The threshold for any year will be computed by increasing $30,000 by the cumulative inflation since 1990 with the result rounded down to the nearest increment of $2,000. In addition, the conference agreement modifies the effective date to provide that indexation of the threshold applicable to passenger vehicles is effective for sales on or after the date of enactment. The applicable threshold for purchases in 1993, on or after the date of enactment, will be $30,000 increased by the 1991 and 1992 inflation rates (8.49 percent), or $32,547, which when rounded down to the nearest $2,000 is a threshold of $32,000.

[¶ 3024] Section 13163. Tax on Diesel Fuel Used in Noncommercial Boats

(Code Sec. 4041, 4092, 6421, 9503, 9508)

[Senate Explanation]

Present Law

Federal excise taxes generally are imposed on gasoline and special motor fuels used in highway transportation and by certain off-highway recreational trail vehicles and by motorboats (14 cents per gallon). A Federal excise tax also is imposed on diesel fuel (20 cents per gallon) used in highway transportation. Diesel fuel used in trains is taxed at 2.5 cents per gallon.

The revenues from these taxes, minus the 2.5 cents per gallon General Fund rate are deposited in the Highway Trust Fund (through September 30, 1999), the National Recreational Trails Trust Fund (through September 30, 1997), or the Aquatic Resources Trust Fund (through September 30, 1997). Revenues from the remaining 2.5 cents per gallon are retained in the General Fund through September 30, 1995, after which time the 2.5-cents-per-gallon portion of the taxes (including the tax on diesel fuel used in trains) is scheduled to expire. [2]

An additional 0.1-cent-per-gallon tax applies to these fuels to finance the Leaking Underground Storage Trust Fund, generally through December 31, 1995.

Diesel fuel used in motorboats is not currently taxed.

Reasons for Change

The bill eliminates the discrepancy between gasoline used by motorboats (which is taxable) and diesel fuel used by similar boats (which is not taxable).

Explanation of Provision

The bill extends the current 20.1-cents-per-gallon diesel fuel excise taxes to diesel fuel used by noncommercial motorboats. [3] Fuel used by boats for commercial fishing, transportation for compensation or hire, or for business use other than predominantly for entertainment, amusement, or recreation, remains exempt.

The tax is collected at the same point in the distribution chain as the highway diesel fuel tax. [4]

The revenues from the 20.1-cents-per-gallon tax on diesel fuel used by motorboats will be retained in the General Fund.

The 20.1-cents-per-gallon diesel fuel excise tax applies to use of diesel fuel in noncommercial motorboats between January 1, 1994, and December 31, 1999.

Effective Date

The provision is effective after December 31, 1993, and before January 1, 2000.

[Conference Report]

The conference agreement follows the Senate amendment with the modification that the revenues from the 20.1-cents-per-gallon tax will be retained in the General Fund. In addition, separate provisions of the conference agreement establish a transportation fuels tax and modify the point of collection for diesel fuel tax. [6] Diesel fuel used by noncommercial motorboats also is subject to the 4.3-cents-per gallon transportation fuels tax, also beginning on January 1, 1994. The tax on diesel fuel used by noncommercial motorboats will be collected at the same point as the tax on highway diesel fuels.

[Footnote ¶ 3020 continued]

2. A separate committee provision extends the 2.5-cents-per-gallon rate through September 30, 1999, and transfers applicable highway-related revenues to the Highway Trust Fund for the extended period. (See section 8244 of the bill, Item II.D.2., below.)

3. A separate committee provision imposes a 4.3-cents-per-gallon transportation fuels tax effective October 1, 1993. Diesel fuel used by noncommercial motorboats also is subject to the transportation fuels tax beginning at that time. (See section 8241 of the bill, Item II.D.1, below.)

4. A separate provision of the bill modifies the point of collection for highway diesel fuel. (See section 8242 of the bill, Item II.D.1., below).

6. See section 13241 and sections 13242 and 13243 of the conference agreement, Items II.D.2. and II.D.3. below.

[¶ 3025] Section 13171. Alternative Minimum Tax Treatment of Contributions of Appreciated Property

(Code Sec. 56, 57)

[House Explanation]

Present Law

Donations of appreciated property

In computing taxable income, a taxpayer who itemizes deductions generally is allowed to deduct the fair market value of property contributed to a charitable organization.[12] However, in the case of a charitable contribution of inventory or other ordinary-income property, short-term capital gain property, or certain gifts to private foundations, the amount of the deduction is limited to the taxpayer's basis in the property.[13] In the case of a charitable contribution of tangible personal property, a taxpayer's deduction is limited to the adjusted basis in such property if the use by the recipient charitable organization is unrelated to the organization's tax-exempt purpose (sec. 170(e)(1)(B)(i)).

For purposes of computing alternative minimum taxable income (AMTI), the deduction for charitable contributions of capital gain property (real, personal, or intangible) is disallowed to the extent that the fair market value of the property exceeds its adjusted basis (sec. 57(a)(6)). However, in the case of a contribution made in a taxable year beginning in 1991 or made before July 1, 1992, in a taxable year beginning in 1992, this rule does not apply to contributions of tangible personal property.

For taxable years beginning after 1989, the AMTI of a corporation is increased by 75 percent of the amount by which adjusted current earnings (ACE) exceeds AMTI (calculated before this adjustment). ACE generally is computed pursuant to the rules that a corporation uses to determine its earnings and profits (sec. 56(g)).

Valuation procedures

Present law and current IRS practice do not provide for a procedure by which a taxpayer may seek determination of the IRS' position with respect to the value of property prior to the taxpayer donating the property to a charitable organization. However, if a taxpayer claims a charitable contribution deduction for a noncash gift in excess of $5,000 per item or group of similar items (other than certain publicly traded securities), the taxpayer must attach to his income tax return a separate form (Form 8283), which provides specific information on the donated property and which is signed by a qualified appraiser.[14]

Reasons for Change

The committee believes that the temporary AMT exception for contributions of appreciated property induced additional charitable giving. Thus, by permanently extending this rule and expanding it to apply to all appreciated property gifts, taxpayers will be allowed the same charitable contribution deduction for both regular tax and AMT purposes. This will provide an additional incentive for taxpayers to make charitable contributions of appreciated property.

In addition, to reduce uncertainty and disputes arising from charitable contributions of property, the committee believes that the Treasury Department should develop a proposed procedure under which the Secretary's position as to the value of tangible personal property can be ascertained for Federal income tax purposes prior to the donation of such property to a charity.

Explanation of Provisions

Permanent AMT relief for donated appreciated property

The bill eliminates the treatment of contri-

[Footnote ¶ 3024 continued]

12. The amount of the deduction allowable for a taxable year with respect to a charitable contribution may be reduced depending on the type of property contributed, the type of charitable organization to which the property is contributed, and the income of the taxpayer (secs. 170(b) and 170(e)).

13. Section 170(e)(3) provides an augmented deduction for certain corporate contributions of inventory property for the care of the ill, the needy, or infants.

14. The Form 8283 must be attached to the income tax return (Form 1040) in all cases where total noncash contributions exceed $500, but the Form 8283 need not be signed by a qualified appraiser unless the $5,000 threshold per item or group of similar items is exceeded. In the case of donated art for which a deduction of $20,000 or more is claimed, a complete copy of the signed appraisal must be attached to the Form 8283.

butions of appreciated property (real, personal, and intangible) as a tax preference for AMT purposes. In addition, the bill provides that no adjustment related to the earnings and profits effects of any charitable contribution shall be made in computing the ACE component of the corporate AMT.

Thus, the difference between the fair market value of donated appreciated property and the adjusted basis of such property is not treated as a tax preference item for alternative minimum tax (AMT) purposes. If a taxpayer makes a gift to charity of property (other than inventory or other ordinary income property, short-term capital gain property, or certain gifts to private foundations) that is real property, intangible property, or tangible personal property the use of which is related to the donee's tax-exempt purpose, the taxpayer is allowed to claim a deduction for both regular tax and AMT purposes in the amount of the property's fair market value (subject to present-law percentage limitations). [15]

Treasury report on advance valuation procedure

Not later than one year after the date of enactment of the bill, the Secretary of the Treasury is required to submit a report to the House Committee on Ways and Means and the Senate Committee on Finance, reporting on the development of a procedure under which a taxpayer could elect to seek an agreement with the Secretary as to the value of tangible personal property prior to the donation of such property to a qualifying charitable organization (provided that time limits for donation and any other conditions contained in the agreement are satisfied). The report should address the setting of possible threshold amounts for claimed value (and the payment of fees by a taxpayer) in order for a taxpayer to seek agreement under the procedure, possible limitations on applying procedure only to items with significant artistic or cultural value, and recommendations for legislative action needed to implement the procedure.

Effective Date

The provision governing the AMT treatment of gifts of appreciated property is effective for contributions of tangible personal property made after June 30, 1992, and contributions of other property made after December 31, 1992.

The Treasury Department must report to Congress not later than one year after enactment on the development of an advance valuation procedure.

[Conference Report]

Senate Amendment

Permanent AMT relief for donated appreciated property

The Senate amendment is the same as the House bill.

Treasury report on advance valuation procedure

No provision.

Conference Agreement

Permanent AMT relief for donated appreciated property

The conference agreement follows the House bill and the Senate amendment. [20]

Treasury report on advance valuation procedure

The conference agreement follows the Senate amendment, but the conferees intend that the Secretary of the Treasury will report to Congress on the development of an advance valuation procedure as contemplated under the House bill statutory provision.

[¶ 3026] Sections 13172, 13173. Substantiation and Disclosure of Charitable Contributions

[Footnote ¶ 3025 continued]

15. Contributions of inventory or other ordinary income property, short-term capital gain property, and certain gifts to private foundations continue to be governed by present-law rules.

20. The provision is effective for contributions of tangible personal property made after June 30, 1992, and of other property made after December 31, 1992. Thus, the conferees wish to clarify that the relief provided by the provision does not apply to any carryover from a contribution made prior to the applicable effective date (see Rev. Rul. 90-111, 1990-2 C.B. 30).

(Code Sec. 170, 6115, 6714)

[Senate Explanation]

Present Law

An individual taxpayer who itemizes deductions must separately state (on Schedule A to the Form 1040) the aggregate amount of charitable contributions made by cash or check and the aggregate amount made by donated property other than cash or check.

A taxpayer is not required to provide specific information on his or her return regarding a claimed charitable contribution made by cash or check; nor in such a case is a donee organization required to file an information return with the IRS, regardless of the amount of cash or check involved. However, taxpayers must provide certain information (on Form 8283) if the amount of the claimed deduction for all noncash contributions exceeds $500. [1]

A payment to a charity (regardless of whether it is termed a "contribution") in exchange for which the payor receives an economic benefit is not deductible under section 170, except to the extent that the taxpayer can demonstrate that the payment exceeds the fair market value of the benefit received from the charity. [2]

The Code does not require a tax-exempt organization that is eligible to receive tax-deductible contributions to state explicitly, in its solicitations for support from members or the general public, whether an amount paid to the organization is deductible as a charitable contribution or whether all or part of the payment constitutes consideration for goods or services furnished to the payor. [3] In contrast, tax-exempt organizations that are NOT eligible to receive tax-deductible contributions are required to state expressly in certain fund-raising solicitations that contributions or gifts to the organization are not deductible as charitable contributions for Federal income tax purposes (sec. 6113). [4] A penalty is imposed on such organizations for failure to comply with the section 6113 disclosure requirement, unless reasonable cause is shown (sec. 6710).

Tax-exempt organizations generally are required to file an annual information return (Form 990) with the IRS. However, churches (and their affiliated organizations), as well as tax-exempt organizations (other than private foundations) that normally have gross receipts in each taxable year of not more than $25,000, are not required to file the Form 990. [5] If a charity is required to file a Form 990, then it must report, among other items, the names and addresses of all persons who contributed, bequeathed, or devised $5,000 or more (in cash or other property) during the taxable year. [6]

Reasons for Change

Difficult problems of tax administration arise with respect to fundraising techniques in

[Footnote ¶ 3025 continued]

[Footnote ¶ 3026] 1. If the claimed deduction for a noncash gift exceeds $5,000 per item or group of similar items (other than certain publicly traded securities), a qualified appraiser must sign the Form 8283, and an authorized representative of the donee charity also must sign the Form 8283, acknowledging receipt of the gift and providing certain other information. In certain situations, information reporting by the donee charity is required if it subsequently disposes of donated property (sec. 6050L).

2. See, e.g., Rev. Rul. 67-246, 1967-2 C.B. 104. Under current IRS practice, certain small items and token benefits (e.g., key chains and bumper stickers) that have insubstantial value are disregarded, such that the full amount of the contribution is deductible. Rev. Proc. 90-12, 1990-1 C.B. 471, provides that tokens or benefits given to the donor in connection with a contribution will be considered to have insubstantial value if (1) the payment occurs in the context of a fundraising campaign in which the charity informs patrons how much of their payment is a deductible contribution, AND (2) EITHER (a) the fair market value of all the benefits received in connection with the payment is not more than two percent of the payment, or $50, WHICHEVER IS LESS, OR (b) the payment made by the patron is $25 or more (adjusted for inflation) and the only benefits received in connection with the payment are token items (e.g., key chains or mugs) that bear the organization's name or logo and that (in the aggregate) are within the limits for "low-cost items" under section 513(h)(2). See also Rev. Proc. 92-49, 1992-26 IRB 18 (amplifying Rev. Proc. 90-12, by allowing charities to distribute certain low-cost items to contributors without affecting the deductibility of the contribution).

3. However, Schedule A to the Form 1040 (and the accompanying instructions) inform taxpayers that if they made a contribution to a charity and received a benefit in return, the value of that benefit must be subtracted in calculating the charitable contribution deduction.

4. However, the disclosure requirement of section 6113 does not apply to an organization the gross receipts of which in each taxable year are normally not more than $100,000, nor does the disclosure requirement apply to any solicitation made by letter or telephone call if such letter or call is not part of a coordinated fundraising campaign soliciting more than 10 persons during the calendar year (sec. 6113(b)(2)(A) and (c)(2)).

5. See section 6033(a)(2) and Rev. Proc. 83-23, 1983-1 C.B. 687.

6. See section 6033(b)(5) and Treas. Reg. sec. 1.6033-2(a)(2)(ii)(f). The names and addresses of substantial contributors to a public charity must be reported to the IRS but are not subject to public inspection (sec. 6104(e)(1)(C)).

which an organization that is eligible to receive tax deductible contributions provides goods or services in consideration for payments from donors. Organizations that engage in such fundraising practices often do not inform their donors that all or a portion of the amount paid by the donor may not be deductible as a charitable contribution. Consequently, the committee believes that there will be increased compliance with present-law rules governing charitable contribution deductions if a taxpayer who claims a separate charitable contribution of $250 or more is required to obtain substantiation from the donee indicating the amount of the contribution and whether any goods, service, or privilege was received by the donor in exchange for making the contribution. In addition, the committee believes it is appropriate that when a charity receives a quid pro quo contribution in excess of $75 (i.e., a payment exceeding $75 made partly as a gift and partly in consideration for a benefit furnished to the payor), the charity should inform the donor that the deduction under section 170 is limited to the amount by which the payment exceeds the value of the goods or service furnished by the charity, and should provide a good faith estimate of the value of such goods or service.

Explanation of Provisions

The bill contains the following two provisions that require substantiation and disclosure relating to certain charitable contributions:

Substantiation requirement

Section 170 is amended to provide that no deduction is allowed under that section for any contribution of $250 or more [7] unless the taxpayer has written substantiation from the donee organization of the contribution (including a good faith estimate of the value of any good or service that has been provided to the donor in exchange for making the gift to the donee). [8]

This provision does not impose an information reporting requirement upon charities; rather, it places the responsibility upon taxpayers who claim an itemized deduction for a contribution of $250 or more to request (and maintain in their records) substantiation from the charity of their contribution (and any good or service received in exchange). [9] Taxpayers may not rely solely on a canceled check as substantiation for a donation of $250 or more.

Under the provision, the substantiation must be obtained by the taxpayer prior to filing his or her return for the taxable year in which the contribution was made (or if earlier, the due date, including extensions, for filing such return). [10] Substantiation is not required if the donee organization files a return with the IRS (in accordance with Treasury regulations) reporting information sufficient to substantiate the amount of the deductible contribution.

The provision explicitly provides that, if in return for making a contribution of $250 or more to a religious organization, a donor receives in return solely an intangible religious benefit that generally is not sold in commercial transactions outside the donative context (e.g., admission to a religious ceremony [11]), then such a religious benefit may be disre-

[Footnote ¶3026 continued]

7. Separate payments generally will be treated as separate contributions and will not be aggregated for the purposes of applying the $250 threshold. In cases of contributions paid by withholding from wages, the deduction from each paycheck will be treated as a separate payment. However, it is expected that the Treasury Department will issue anti-abuse rules to prevent avoidance of the substantiation requirement by a contributor simply writing multiple checks on the same date.

8. If the donee organization provided no goods or services to the taxpayer in consideration of the taxpayer's contribution, the written substantiation is required to include a statement to that effect. The substantiation need NOT contain the taxpayer's social security number or taxpayer identification number (TIN).

9. In the case where a taxpayer makes a noncash contribution claimed by the taxpayer to be worth $250 or more, the taxpayer is required to obtain from the charity a receipt that describes the donated property (and indicates whether any good or service was given to the taxpayer in exchange), but the provision specifically provides that the charity is not required to value the property it receives from the taxpayer.

10. The provision requires that the written acknowledgment provide information sufficient to substantiate the amount of the deductible contribution, but the acknowledgment need not take any particular form. Thus, for example, acknowledgments may be made by letter, postcard, or computer-generated forms. Further, a donee organization may prepare a separate acknowledgment for each contribution, or may provide donors with periodic (e.g., annual) acknowledgments that set forth the required information for each contribution of $250 or more made by the donor during the period. It is intended that a charitable organization that knowingly provides a false written substantiation to a donor may be subject to the penalties provided for by section 6701 for aiding and abetting an understatement of tax liability.

11. This exception does not apply, for example, to tuition for education leading to a recognized degree, travel services, or consumer goods. However, it is intended that de minimis tangible benefits furnished to contributors that are incidental to a religious ceremony (such as wine) generally may be disregarded.

garded for purposes of the substantiation requirement.

Information disclosure for quid pro quo contributions

A charitable organization that receives a quid pro quo contribution in excess of $75 (meaning a payment exceeding $75 "made partly as a contribution and partly in consideration for goods or services provided to the payor by the donee organization") is required, in connection with the solicitation or receipt of such a contribution, to provide a written statement to the donor that (1) informs the donor that the amount of the contribution that is deductible for Federal income tax purposes is limited to the excess of the amount of any money (and the value of any property other than money) contributed by the donor over the value of the goods or services provided by the organization, and (2) provides the donor with a good faith estimate of the value of goods or services furnished to the donor by the organization. [12]

The disclosure requirement applies to all quid pro quo contributions where the donor makes payment of more than $75. [13] Thus, for example, if a charity receives a $100 contribution from a donor, in exchange for which the donor receives a dinner valued at $40, then the charity must inform the donor in writing that only $60 is deductible as a charitable contribution. However, the provision does not apply if only de minimis, token goods or services are given to a donor (see Rev. procs. 90-12 and 92-49, discussed above). In addition, as with the substantiation provision (described above), the provision does not apply to a contribution, in return for which the contributor receives solely an intangible religious benefit that generally is not sold in a commercial context outside the donative context. [14] Furthermore, the provision does not apply to transactions that have no donative element (e.g., sales of goods by a museum gift shop that are not, in part, donations).

The provision also provides that penalties ($10 per contribution, but capped at $5,000 per particular fundraising event or mailing) may be imposed upon charities that fail to make the required disclosure, unless the failure was due to reasonable cause. The penalties will apply if an organization either fails to make any disclosure in connection with a quid pro quo contribution or makes a disclosure that is incomplete or inaccurate (e.g., an estimate not determined in good faith of the value of goods or services furnished to the donor).

Effective Date

The provisions are effective for contributions made after December 31, 1993. [15]

[Conference Report]

Senate Amendment

The Senate amendment contains the following two provisions that require substantiation and disclosure relating to certain charitable contributions:

Substantiation requirement

Section 170 is amended to provide that no deduction is allowed under that section far a separate contribution of $250 or more [9]unless the taxpayer has written substantiation from the donee organization of the contribution (including a good faith estimate of the value of any good or service that has been provided to the donor in exchange for making the gift to

[Footnote ¶ 3026 continued]

12. The committee intends that the disclosure be made in a manner that is reasonably likely to come to the attention of the donor. For example, a disclosure of the required information in small print set forth within a larger document might not meet the requirement.

13. For purposes of the $75 threshold, separate payments made at different times of the year with respect to separate fundraising events generally will not be aggregated. However, to prevent avoidance of the quid pro quo disclosure requirement by a contributor simply writing multiple checks on the same date, contributions that are part of a single transaction will be aggregated for purposes of the $75 threshold.

14. No inference is intended, however, whether or not any payment outside the scope of the quid pro quo disclosure proposal or substantiation proposal is deductible (in full or in part) under the present-law requirements of section 170.

15. The committee intends that, following enactment of the bill, the Secretary of the Treasury will expeditiously issue a notice or other announcement providing guidance with respect to the substantiation and disclosure provisions. In this regard, it is expected that such Treasury guidance will urge charities to assist taxpayers in meeting the substantiation requirement.

9. Separate payments generally will be treated as separate contributions and will not be aggregated for the purposes of applying the $250 threshold. In cases of contributions paid by withholding from wages, the deduction from each paycheck will be treated as a separate payment. However, the Senate committee explanation states that it is expected that the Secretary of the Treasury will issue anti-abuse rules to prevent avoidance of the substantiation requirement by writing multiple checks on the same date.

the donee).[10]

This provision does not impose an information reporting requirement upon charities; rather, it places the responsibility upon taxpayers who claim an itemized deduction for a contribution of $250 or more to request (and maintain in their records) substantiation from the charity of their contribution (and any good or service received in exchange).[11] Taxpayers may not rely solely on a canceled check as substantiation for a donation of $250 or more.

Under the provision, a taxpayer must obtain substantiation prior to filing his or her return for the taxable year in which the contribution was made (or if earlier, the due date, including extensions, for filing such return).[12] Substantiation is not required if the donee organization files a return with the IRS (in accordance with Treasury regulations) reporting information sufficient to substantiate the amount of the deductible contribution.[13]

The provision explicitly provides that, if in return for making a contribution of $250 or more to a religious organization, a donor receives in return solely an intangible religious benefit that generally is not sold in commercial transactions outside the donative context (e.g., admission to a religious ceremony[14]), then such a religious benefit may be disregarded for purposes of the substantiation requirement.

Information disclosure for quid pro quo contributions

A charitable organization that receives a quid pro quo contribution in excess of $75 (meaning a payment exceeding $75 "made partly as a contribution and partly in consideration for goods or services provided to the payor by the donee organization") is required, in connection with the solicitation or receipt of such a contribution, to provide a written statement to the donor that (1) informs the donor that the amount of the contribution that is deductible for Federal income tax purposes is limited to the excess of the amount of any money (and the value of any property other than money) contributed by the donor over the value of the goods or services provided by the organization, and (2) provides the donor with a good faith estimate of the value of goods or services furnished to the donor by the organization.[15]

The disclosure requirement applies to all and pro quo contributions where the donor makes a payment of more than $75.[16]Thus, for example, if a charity receives a $100 contribution from a donor, in exchange for which the donor receives a dinner valued at $40, then the charity must inform the donor in writing that only $60 is deductible as a charitable contribution. However, the provision does not apply if only de minimis, token goods or services are given to a donor (see Rev. Procs. 90-

[Footnote ¶ 3026 continued]

10. If the donee organization provided no goods or services to the taxpayer in consideration of the taxpayer's contribution, the written substantiation is required to include a statement to that effect. The substantiation need NOT contain the taxpayer's social security number or taxpayer identification number (TIN).

11. In the case where a taxpayer makes a noncash contribution claimed by the taxpayer to be worth $250 or more, the taxpayer is required to obtain from the charity a receipt that describes the donated property (and indicates whether any good or service was given to the taxpayer in exchange), but the provision specifically provides that the charity is not required to value the property it receives from the taxpayer.

12. The provision requires that the written acknowledgment provide information sufficient to substantiate the amount of the deductible contribution, but the acknowledgment need not take any particular form. Thus, for example, acknowledgments may be made by letter, postcard, or computer-generated forms. Further, a donee organization may prepare a separate acknowledgment for each contribution, or may provide donors with periodic (e.g., annual) acknowledgments that set forth the required information for each contribution of $250 or more made by the donor during the period. The Senate committee explanation states that is intended that a charitable organization that knowingly provides a false written substantiation to a donor may be subject to the penalties provided for by section 6701 for aiding and abetting an understatement of tax liability.

13. In addition, the Senate amendment provides that the Secretary of the Treasury shall issue regulations as may be necessary to carry out the purposes of the substantiation provision, including regulations that may provide that some or all of the requirements of the provision do not apply in appropriate cases.

14. This exception does not apply, for example, to tuition for education leading to a recognized degree, travel services, or consumer goods. However, the Senate committee explanation states that it is intended that de minimis tangible benefits furnished to contributors that are incidental to a religious ceremony (such as wine) generally may be disregarded.

15. The Senate committee explanation states that it is intended that the disclosure be made in a manner that is reasonably likely to come to the attention of the donor. For example, a disclosure of the required information in small print set forth within a larger document might not meet the requirement.

16. For purposes of the $75 threshold, separate payments made at different times of the year with respect to separate fundraising events generally will not be aggregated. However, the conferees intend that the Secretary will issue anti-abuse rules to prevent avoidance of the quid pro quo disclosure requirement by writing multiple checks for the same transaction.

12 and 92-49, discussed above). In addition, as with the substantiation provision (described above), the provision does not apply to a contribution in return for which the contributor receives solely an intangible religious benefit that generally is not sold in a commercial transaction outside the donative context. [17] Furthermore, the provision does not apply to transactions that have no donative element (e.g., sales of goods by a museum gift shop that are not, in part, donations).

The provision also provides that penalties ($10 per contribution, but capped at $5,000 per particular fundraising event or mailing) may be imposed upon charities that fail to make the required disclosure, unless the failure was due to reasonable cause. The penalties will apply if an organization either fails to make any disclosure in connection with a quid pro quo contribution or makes a disclosure that is incomplete or inaccurate (e.g., an estimate not determined in good faith of the value of goods or services furnished to the donor).

Effective date

The provisions are effective for contributions made after December 31, 1993. [18]The Senate committee explanation states that it is intended that the disclosure be made in a manner that is reasonably likely to come to the attention of the donor. For example, a disclosure of the required information in small print set forth within a larger document might not meet the requirement.

Conference Agreement

The conference agreement follows the Senate amendment.

However, with respect to the substantiation provision, the conference agreement clarifies that in cases where, in consideration (in whole or in part) for a contribution of $250 or more, a religious organization furnishes to the contributor solely an intangible religious benefit generally not sold in a commercial transaction outside the donative context, the written substantiation must contain a statement to the effect that an intangible religious benefit was so furnished, but the substantiation need not further describe, nor provide a valuation for, such benefit. [19]

In addition, the conferees intend that the authority granted to the Secretary of the Treasury to issue regulations providing that some or all of the requirements of the substantiation provision do not apply in appropriate cases shall be exercised to clarify the treatment of contributions made through payroll deductions.

[¶ 3027] Section 13174. Temporary Extension of Deduction for Health insurance Costs of Self-employed Individuals

(Code Sec. 162)

[House Explanation]

Present Law

Under present law, an incorporated business can generally deduct, as an employee compensation expense, the full cost of any health insurance coverage provided for its employees (including owners serving as employees) and its employees' spouses and dependents. Self-employed individuals can fully deduct the cost of health insurance for employees as employee compensation, but can deduct the cost of health insurance coverage for the individual and this or her dependents to the extent that the cost of the coverage, together with other allowable medical expenses, exceeds 7.5 percent of adjusted gross income. Other individuals (e.g., employees who are not covered by an employer-sponsored plan) who purchase health insurance can deduct the cost of the insurance only to the extent that it, together with their other medical expenses, exceeds 7.5 per-

17. The Senate committee explanation states that no inference is intended, however, regarding the full or partial deductibility of any payment outside the scope of the quid pro quo disclosure provision or substantiation provision under the present-law requirements of section 170.

18. The Senate committee explanation states that it is intended that, following enactment of the bill, the Secretary of the Treasury will expeditiously issue a notice or other announcement providing guidance with respect to the substantiation and disclosure provisions. In this regard, it is expected that such Treasury guidance will urge charities to assist taxpayers in meeting the substantiation requirement.

19. As under the Senate amendment, charities are not required to make any disclosure under the quid pro quo disclosure provision when no benefit OTHER THAN an intangible religious benefit is furnished to the donor.

cent of adjusted gross income.

For coverage prior to July 1, 1992, a self-employed individual was allowed to deduct as a business expense up to 25 percent of the amount paid for health insurance coverage for the taxpayer, the taxpayer's spouse, and the taxpayer's dependents. Only amounts paid prior to July 1, 1992, for coverage before that date were eligible for the deduction. The deduction was not allowed if the self-employed individual or his or her spouse was eligible for employer-paid health benefits.

Reasons for Change

The 25-percent deduction for health insurance costs of self-employed individuals was added by the Tax Reform Act of 1986 to reduce the disparity between the tax treatment of owners of incorporated and unincorporated businesses. The provision was originally enacted on a temporary basis and has been extended several times since enactment.

The committee believes it is appropriate to extend the 25-percent deduction retroactively and to extend it prospectively again on a temporary basis. The provision is not extended for a longer period at this time because it is expected that the deduction will be addressed as part of forthcoming comprehensive health care legislation.

Explanation of Provision

The 25-percent deduction is extended retroactively from July 1, 1992, through December 31, 1993. In addition, the bill provides that the determination of whether a self-employed individual or his or her spouse are eligible for employer-paid health benefits is made on a monthly basis.

Effective Date

The provision is effective for taxable years ending after June 30, 1992.

[Conference Report]

Senate Amendment

The Senate amendment is the same as the House bill.

Conference Agreement

The conference agreement follows the House bill and the Senate amendment.

[¶3028] Section 13201. Increase in Top Marginal Rate under Section 1

(Code Sec. 1)

[House Explanation]

Present Law

Regular tax rates

For 1993, the individual income tax rates are as follows --

If taxable income is:	Then income tax equals:
Single individuals	
$0-$22,100	15 percent of taxable income.
$22,100-$53,500	$3,315.00 plus 28% of the amount over $22,100.
Over $53,500	$12,107.00 plus 31% of the amount over $53,500.
Heads of household	
$0-$29,600	15 percent of taxable income.
$29,600-$76,400	$4,440.00 plus 28% of the amount over $29,600.
Over $76,400	$17,544.00 plus 31% of the amount over $76,400.
Married individuals filing joint returns	
$0-$36,900	15 percent of taxable income.
$36,900-$89,150	$5,535 plus 28% of the amount over $36,900.
Over $89,150	$20,165 plus 31% of the amount over $89,150.
Married individuals filing separate returns	
$0-$18,450	15 percent of taxable income.
$18,450-$44,575	$2,767.50 plus 28% of the amount over $18,450.
Over $44,575	$10,082.50 plus 31% of the amount over $44,575.
Estates and trusts	
$0-$3,750	15 percent of taxable income.
$3,750-$11,250	$562.50 plus 28% of the amount over $3,750.
Over $11,250	$2,662.50 plus 31% of the amount over $11,250.

The individual income tax brackets are indexed each year for inflation.

Reasons For Change

To raise revenue to reduce the Federal deficit, to improve tax equity, and to make the individual income tax system more progressive, the committee believes that a higher marginal tax rate should be imposed on taxpayers with a greater ability to pay taxes. Additionally, the progressivity of the individual income tax system would be enhanced by creating a two-tier alternative minimum tax schedule for individual taxpayers and by permanently extending the existing limitation on itemized deductions and the phaseout of personal exemptions for higher-income taxpayers.

Explanation Of Provision

New marginal tax rates

The bill imposes a net 36-percent marginal tax rate on taxable income in excess of the following thresholds: !TA Filing status Applicable Threshold Married individuals filing joint returns $140,000 Heads of households $127,500 Unmarried individuals $115,000 Married individuals filing separate returns $ 70,000 Estates and trusts $ 5,500 !EN

For estates and trusts, the 15-percent rate will apply to income up to $1,500, the 28-percent rate will apply to income between $1,500 and $3,500, and the 31-percent rate will apply to income between $3,500 and $5,500. Under this modified tax rate schedule for estates and trusts, the benefits of the rates below the 39.6-percent surtax-included rate (described below) for 1993 will approximate the benefits of the 15- and 28-percent rates for 1993 under present law.

As under present law, the tax rate bracket thresholds are indexed for inflation. However, indexing of thresholds for the 36-percent rate will apply to taxable years beginning after December 31, 1994.

Effective Date

The provision is effective for taxable years beginning after December 31, 1992. Withholding tables for 1993 will not be revised to reflect the changes in tax rates.

[Conference Report]

The conference agreement follows the House bill.

In addition, the conference agreement contains a provision permitting individual taxpayers to elect to pay their additional 1993 taxes that are attributable to the rate increases contained in the conference agreement in three annual installments. The first installment must be paid on or before the due date for the individual's taxable year that begins in calendar year 1993; the second installment must be paid on or before the date one year after that date; and the third installment must be paid on or before the date two years after that date. The election must be made on the tax return for the individual's taxable year that begins in 1993 (which, in general, is due on April 15, 1994).

The amount eligible for this installment payment election is the excess of the individual's net liability nder chapter 1 of the Code as shown on the individual's tax return over the amount that would have been the individual's net liability but for the amendments made by the conference report that alter the individual tax rates (i.e., the 36 percent and 39.6 percent marginal tax rates). These amounts are computed after the application of any credit (except for credit for wage withholding and the credit for special fuel uses) and before crediting any payment of estimated tax. Amounts required to be shown on the return but not actually shown on the return are ineligible for this installment payment election.

The Secretary shall immediately terminate this installment payment election, and the whole amount of the unpaid tax shall be paid immediately upon notice and demand from the Secretary, if either (1) the taxpayer does not pay any installment on or before the required date, or (2) the Secretary believes that the collection of any amount under this installment payment election is in jeopardy.

Because this installment payment election applies only to amounts actually shown on the individual's tax return, those amounts are considered to be assessed. Consequently, the 10-year statute of limitations is applicable to collection after assessment (sec. 6502) is applicable to these installment payments.

[¶ 3029] Section 13202. Surtax on High-Volume Taxpayers

(Code Sec. 1)

[House Explanation]

Reasons For Change

To raise revenue to reduce the Federal deficit, to improve tax equity, and to make the individual income tax system more progressive, the committee believes that a higher marginal tax rate should be imposed on taxpayers with a greater ability to pay taxes. Additionally, the progressivity of the individual income tax system would be enhanced by creating a two-tier alternative minimum tax schedule for individual taxpayers and by permanently extending the existing limitation on itemized deductions and the phaseout of personal exemptions for higher-income taxpayers.

Explanation of Provision

Surtax on higher-income taxpayers

The bill provides a 10-percent surtax on individuals with taxable income in excess of $250,000 and on estates and trusts with taxable income in excess of $7,500. For married taxpayers filing separate returns, the threshold amount for the surtax will be $125,000. The surtax will be computed by applying a 39.6-percent rate to taxable income in excess of the applicable threshold. Under this method of computation, unlike a simple 10-percent increase in tax liability, capital gains income will not be subject to tax at a rate in excess of the current 28-percent maximum rate. The thresholds for the surtax will be indexed for inflation in the same manner as other individual income tax rate thresholds for taxable years beginning after December 31, 1994.

Effective Date

The provision is effective for taxable years beginning after December 31, 1992. Withholding tables for 1993 will not be revised to reflect the changes in tax rates.

Conference Report

The conference agreement follows the House bill.

In addition, the conference agreement contains a provision permitting individual taxpayers to elect to pay their additional 1993 taxes that are attributable to the rate increases contained in the conference agreement in three annual installments. The first installment must be paid on or before the due date for the individual's taxable year that begins in calendar year 1993; the second installment must be paid on or before the date one year after that date; and the third installment must be paid on or before the date two years after that date. The election must be made on the tax return for the individual's taxable year that begins in 1993 (which, in general, is due on April 15, 1994).

The amount eligible for this installment payment election is the excess of the individual's net liability under chapter 1 of the Code as shown on the individual's tax return over the amount that would have been the individual's net liability but for the amendments made by the conference report that alter the individual tax rates (i.e., the 36 percent and 39.6 percent marginal tax rates). These amounts are computed after the application of any credit (except the credit for wage withholding and the credit for special fuel uses) and before crediting any payment of estimated tax. Amounts required to be shown on the return but not actually shown on the return are ineligible for this installment payment election.

The Secretary shall immediately terminate this installment payment election, and the whole amount of the unpaid tax shall be paid immediately upon notice and demand from the Secretary, if either (1) the taxpayer does not pay any installment on or before the required date, or (2) the Secretary believes that the collection of any amount under this installment payment election is in jeopardy.

Because this installment payment election applies only to amounts actually shown on the individual's tax return, those amounts are considered to be assessed. Consequently, the 10-year statute of limitations applicable to collection after assessment (sec. 6502) is applicable to these installment payments.

[¶ 3030] Section 13203. Modification to Alternative Minimum Tax Rates and Exemption Amounts

(Code Sec. 55)

[House Explanation]

Present Law

Alternative minimum tax

An individual taxpayer is subject to an alternative minimum tax (AMT) to the extent that the taxpayer's tentative minimum tax exceeds the taxpayer's regular tax liability. A taxpayer's tentative minimum tax generally equals 24 percent of alternative minimum taxable income (AMTI) in excess of an exemption amount. The exemption amount is $40,000 for married taxpayers filing joint returns, $30,000 for unmarried taxpayers filing as single or head of household, and $20,000 for married taxpayers filing separate returns, estates, and trusts. The exemption amount is phased out for taxpayers with AMTI above specified thresholds. These thresholds are: $150,000 for married taxpayers filing joint returns, $112,500 for unmarried taxpayers filing as single or head of household, and $75,000 for married taxpayers filing separate returns, estates, and trusts. The exemption is completely phased out for individuals with AMTI above $310,000 (married taxpayers filing joint returns) or $232,500 (unmarried taxpayers filing as single or head of household).

Reasons For Change

To raise revenue to reduce the Federal deficit, to improve tax equity, and to make the individual income tax system more progressive, the committee believes that a higher marginal tax rate should be imposed on taxpayers with a greater ability to pay taxes. Additionally, the progressivity of the individual income tax system would be enhanced by creating a two-tier alternative minimum tax schedule for individual taxpayers and by permanently extending the existing limitation on itemized deductions and the phaseout of personal exemptions for higher-income taxpayers.

Explanation Of Provision

Alternative minimum tax

The bill provides a two-tiered graduated rate schedule for the AMT for taxpayers other than corporations. A 26-percent rate will apply to the first $175,000 of a taxpayer's AMTI in excess of the exemption amount, and a 28-percent rate will apply to AMTI more than $175,000 above the exemption amount. For married individuals filing separate returns, the 28-percent rate will apply to AMTI more than $87,500 above the exemption amount. The bill will increase the exemption amount to $45,000 for married individuals filing joint returns, to $33,750 for unmarried individuals, and to $22,500 for married individuals filing separate returns, estates, and trusts.

Effective Date

The provision is effective for taxable years beginning after December 31, 1992. Withholding tables for 1993 will not be revised to reflect the changes in tax rates.

[Conference Report]

Conference Agreement

The conference agreement follows the House bill.

[¶ 3031] Section 13204. Overall Limitation on Itemized Deductions for High-Income Taxpayers Made Permanent

(Code Sec. 68)

[House Explanation]

Present Law

Itemized deduction limitation

Under present law, individuals who do not elect the standard deduction may claim itemized deductions (subject to certain limitations) for certain expenses incurred during the taxable year. Among these deductible expenses are unreimbursed medical expenses, unreimbursed casualty and theft losses, charitable contributions qualified residence interest, State and local income and property taxes, unreimbursed employee business expenses, and certain other miscellaneous expenses.

Certain itemized deductions are allowed only to the extent that the amount exceeds a specified percentage of the taxpayer's adjusted gross income (AGI). Unreimbursed medical expenses for care of the taxpayer and the taxpayer's spouse and dependents are deductible only to the extent that the total of these expenses exceeds 7.5 percent of the taxpayer's AGI. Nonbusiness, unreimbursed casualty or theft losses are deductible only to the extent that the amount of loss arising from each casualty or theft exceeds $100 and only to the extent that the net amount of casualty and theft losses exceeds 10 percent of the taxpayer's AGI. Unreimbursed employee business expenses and certain other miscellaneous expenses are deductible only to the extent that the total of these expenses exceeds 2 percent of the taxpayer's AGI.

The total amount of otherwise allowable itemized deductions (other than medical expenses, casualty and theft losses, and investment interest) is reduced by 3 percent of the amount of the taxpayer's AGI in excess of $108,450 in 1993 (indexed for inflation). Under this provision, otherwise allowable itemized deductions may not be reduced by more than 80 percent. In computing the reduction of total itemized deductions, all present-law limitations applicable to such deductions are first applied and then the otherwise allowable total amount of deductions is reduced in accordance with this provision.

The reduction of otherwise allowable itemized deductions does not apply to taxable years beginning after December 31, 1995.

Explanation Of Provision

Itemized deduction limitation and phaseout of personal exemptions

The bill makes permanent the provisions that limit itemized deductions and phase out personal exemptions.

[Conference Report]

Conference Agreement

The conference agreement follows the House bill.

[¶3032] Section 13205. Phaseout of Personal Exemption of High Income Taxpayers Made Permanent

(Code Sec. 151)

[House Explanation]

Present Law

Personal exemption phaseout

Present law permits a personal exemption deduction from gross income for an individual, the individual's spouse, and each dependent. For 1993, the amount of this deduction is $2,350 for each exemption claimed. This exemption amount is adjusted for inflation. The deduction for personal exemptions is phased out for taxpayers with AGI above a threshold amount (indexed for inflation) which is based on filing status. For 1993, the threshold amounts are $162,700 for married taxpayers filing joint returns, $81,350 for married taxpayers filing separate returns, $135,600 for unmarried taxpayers filing as head of household, and $108,450 for unmarried taxpayers filing as single.

The total amount of exemptions that may be claimed by a taxpayer is reduced by 2 percent for each $2,500 (or portion thereof) by which the taxpayer's AGI exceeds the applicable threshold (the phaseout rate is 2 percent for each $1,250 for married taxpayers filing separate returns). Thus, the personal exemptions claimed are phased out over a $122,500 range (which is not indexed for inflation), beginning at tile applicable threshold.

This provision does not apply to taxable years beginning after December 31, 1996.

Reasons For Change

To raise revenue to reduce the Federal deficit, to improve tax equity, and to make the individual income tax system more progressive, the committee believes that a higher marginal tax rate should be imposed on taxpayers with a greater ability to pay taxes. Additionally, the progressivity of the individual income tax system would be enhanced by creating a two-tier alternative minimum tax schedule for individual taxpayers and by permanently extending the existing limitation on itemized deductions and the phaseout of personal exemptions for higher-income taxpayers.

Itemized deduction limitation and phaseout of personal exemptions

The bill makes permanent the provisions that limit itemized deductions and phase out personal exemptions.

Conference Report

Conference Agreement

The conference agreement follows the House bill.

[¶ 3033] Section 13206. Provisions to Prevent Conversion of Ordinary Income to Capital Gains

(Code Sec. 305, 1258, 1276, 1277, 1278)

[House Explanation]

Present Law

Generally, a market discount bond is a bond that is acquired for a price that is less than the principal amount of the bond. [19] Market discount generally arises when the value of a debt obligation declines after issuance (typically, because of an increase in prevailing interest rates or a decline in the credit-worthiness of the borrower).

Gain on the disposition of a market discount bond generally must be recognized as ordinary income to the extent of the market discount that has accrued. This ordinary income rule, however, does not apply to tax-exempt obligations or to market discount bonds issued on or before July 18, 1984. Under current law, income attributable to accrued market discount on tax-exempt bonds is not tax-exempt but is taxable as capital gain if the bond is held as a capital asset.

Reasons for Change

The committee is concerned about taxpayers being able to purchase market discount bonds as a means of converting returns on investments that are in the nature of interest on debt to capital gains. The committee therefore believes that the market discount rule should apply to tax-exempt bonds and to all taxable bonds, regardless of whether they were issued after July 18, 1984.

Explanation of Provision

The bill extends the ordinary income rule to tax-exempt obligations and to market discount bonds issued on or before July 18, 1984. Thus, gain on the disposition of a tax-exempt obligation or any other market discount bond that is acquired for a price that is less than the principal amount of the bond generally will be treated as ordinary income (instead of capital gain) to the extent of accrued market discount.

Effective Date

The provision is effective for bonds purchased after April 30, 1993. Thus, current owners of tax-exempt bonds and other market discount bonds issued on or before July 18, 1984, will not be required to treat accrued market discount as ordinary income, if they acquired their bonds before May 1, 1993.

Accrual of income by holders of stripped preferred stock

Present Law

In general, if a bond is issued at a price approximately equal to its redemption price at maturity, the expected return to the holder of the bond is in the form of periodic interest payments. In the case of original issue discount ("OID") bonds, however, the issue price is below the redemption price, and the holder receives part or all of his expected return in the form of price appreciation. The difference between the issue price and the redemption price is the OID, and a portion of the OID is required to be accrued and included in the income of the holder annually. Similarly, for certain preferred stock that is issued at a discount from its redemption price, a portion of the redemption premium must be included in income annually.

A stripped bond (i.e., a bond issued with interest coupons some of which are subsequently "stripped" so that the ownership of the bond is separated from the ownership of the interest coupons) generally is treated as a bond issued with OID equal to (1) the stated redemption price of the bond at maturity minus (2) the amount paid for the stripped bond.

If preferred stock is stripped of some of its dividend rights, however, the stripped stock is not subject to the rules that apply to stripped

[Footnote ¶ 3026 continued]

19. Or, in the case of a bond issued with original issue discount (OIC), a price that is less than the amount of hte issue price plus accrued OID.

bonds or to the rules that apply to bonds and certain preferred stock issued at a discount.

Reasons For Change

The committee believes that the purchaser of stripped preferred stock may, in effect, be purchasing at a discount the right to a fixed amount payable at a future date. The committee is concerned that taxpayers may purchase stripped preferred stock as a means of converting ordinary income to capital gains. Therefore, under these circumstances, the committee believes that the rules that apply to stripped bonds provide the appropriate tax treatment.

Explanation of Provision

The bill treats the purchaser of stripped preferred stock (and a person who strips preferred stock and disposes of the stripped dividend rights) in generally the same way that the purchaser of a stripped bond would be treated under the OID rules. Thus, stripped stock is treated like a bond issued with OID equal to (1) the stated redemption price of the stock minus (2) the amount paid for the stock. The discount accrued under the provision is treated as ordinary income and not as interest or dividends.

Stripped preferred stock is defined as any preferred stock where the ownership of the stock has been separated from the right to receive any dividend that has not yet become payable. The provision applies to stock that is limited and preferred as to dividends, does not participate in corporate growth to any significant extent, and has a fixed redemption price.

No inference is intended as to as to the treatment of stripped preferred stock for tax purposes with respect to any issues not directly addressed by this legislation, including the availability of the dividends received deduction to a holder of dividends stripped from preferred stock, the allocation of basis by the creator of stripped preferred stock, or the proper characterization of a purported sale of stripped dividend rights.

Effective Date

The bill is effective for stripped stock that is purchased after April 30, 1993.

d. Treatment Of Net Capital Gains As Investment Income

Present Law

In the case of a taxpayer other than a corporation, deductions for interest on indebtedness that is allocable to property held for investment ("investment interest") are limited to the taxpayer's net investment income for the taxable year. Disallowed investment interest is carried forward to the next taxable year. Investment income includes gross income (other than gain on disposition) from property held for investment and any net gain attributable to the disposition of property held for investment.

Investment interest that is allowable is deductible against income taxable at ordinary income rates. The net capital gain (i.e., net long-term capital gain less net short-term capital loss) of a noncorporate taxpayer is taxed at a maximum rate of 28 percent.

Prior to 1986, when a significant rate differential existed between long-term capital gains and ordinary income, long-term capital gains were not included in investment income for purposes of computing the investment interest limitation.

Reasons for Change

The committee believes it is inappropriate for a taxpayer who recognizes long term capital gain taxable at favorable rate to be able to use that gain to deduct otherwise non-deductible investment interest against ordinary income. Because the bill increases the rate differential between ordinary income and the net capital gains rate, the possibility of such inappropriate rate arbitrage is increased. The committee believes that the opportunities for this type of rate conversion should be reduced.

Explanation of Provision

The bill generally excludes net capital gain attributable to the disposition of property held for investment from investment income for purposes of computing the investment interest limitation. A taxpayer, however, can elect to include so much of his net capital gain in investment income as the taxpayer chooses if he also reduces the amount of net capital gain eligible for the 28-percent maximum capital gains rate by the same amount.

Effective Date

The provision is effective for taxable years beginning after December 31, 1992.

e. Definition of "substantially appreciated" inventory

Present Law

Under present law, amounts received by a partner in exchange for his interest in a partnership are treated as ordinary income to the extent they are attributable to substantially appreciated inventory of the partnership. In addition, distributions by a partnership in which a partner receives substantially appreciated inventory in exchange for his interest in certain other partnership property (or receives certain other property in exchange for substantially appreciated inventory) are treated as a taxable sale or exchange of property, rather than as a nontaxable distribution.

For these purposes, inventory is treated as substantially appreciated if the value of the partnership's inventory exceeds both 120 percent of its adjusted basis and 10 percent of the value of all partnership property (other than money).

Reasons for Change

The committee believes that the 10-percent exception creates opportunities for avoidance of the appreciated inventory rule through the manipulation of the partnership's gross assets. The committee also believes that disregarding inventory that is acquired principally to avoid the appreciated inventory rule is necessary to prevent circumvention of the rule.

Explanation of Provision

The bill eliminates the requirement that the partnership's inventory exceed 10 percent of the value of all partnership property in order to be substantially appreciated. Thus, if the partnership's inventory is worth more than 120 percent of its adjusted basis, the inventory is treated as substantially appreciated. In addition, any inventory property acquired with a principal purpose to reduce the appreciation to less than 120 percent in order to avoid ordinary income treatment will be disregarded in applying the 120-percent test.

Effective Date

The provision applies to sales, exchanges, and distributions after April 30, 1993.

[Senate Explanation]

Present Law

a. Recharacterization of capital gain as ordinary income for certain financial transactions

Under present law, the maximum rate of individual income tax on ordinary income is 31 percent. Interest from a loan generally is treated as ordinary income.

Gain or loss from the sale or exchange of a capital asset generally is treated as capital gain or loss. Net capital gain (i.e., net long-term capital gain less net short-term capital loss) of an individual is subject to a maximum tax rate of 28 percent. Capital losses are deductible only to the extent of capital gains for the year plus, in the case of noncorporate taxpayers, ordinary income of up to $3,000.

Reasons for Change

The committee is aware that taxpayers are able to enter into transactions the economic substance of which is indistinguishable from loans in terms of the return anticipated and the risks borne by the taxpayer. However, because of their form, these transactions may permit taxpayers to take the position for tax purposes that their return is capital gain rather than ordinary income. The committee is concerned that, because of the increased differential between the rates of tax on ordinary income and capital gain that results from this bill, taxpayers may enter into such transactions for purposes of avoiding the intended higher rates on ordinary income. In addition, the committee is concerned that these transactions can be used to circumvent the capital loss limitation rules. Accordingly, the committee believes that providing rules that would treat gain from such transactions as ordinary income is appropriate.

Explanation of Provision

Under the provision, capital gain from the disposition or other termination of any position that was part of a "conversion transaction" will be recharacterized as ordinary income, [1] with certain limitations discussed below. No inference is intended as to when income from a conversion transaction is properly treated as capital gain under present law.

[Footnote ¶ 3033 continued]

[Footnote ¶ 3033] 1. The provision is not intended to change the treatment of gain from the sale of property for purposes such as the unrelated business income tax for tax-exempt organizations and the gross income requirement for regulated investment companies.

A conversion transaction is a transaction, generally consisting of two or more positions taken with regard to the same or similar property, where substantially all of the taxpayer's return is attributable to the time value of the taxpayer's net investment in the transaction. In a conversion transaction, the taxpayer is in the economic position of a lender — he has an expectation of a return from the transaction which in substance is in the nature of interest and he undertakes no significant risks other than those typical of a lender.

A transaction, however, is not a conversion transaction subject to the provision unless it also satisfies one of the following four criteria: (1) the transaction consists of the acquisition of property by the taxpayer and a substantially contemporaneous agreement to sell the same or substantially identical property in the future; (2) the transaction is a straddle, within the meaning of section 1092 [2] ;(3) the transaction is one that was marketed or sold to the taxpayer on the basis that it would have the economic characteristics of a loan but the interest-like return would be taxed as capital gain; or (4) the transaction is described as a conversion transaction in regulations to be promulgated on a prospective basis by the Secretary of the Treasury.

In addition, transactions (which may include positions other than options or section 1256 contracts) of options dealers and commodities traders in the normal course of their trade or business of dealing in options or trading section 1256 contracts, respectively, generally will not be considered conversion transactions. The term "options dealer" generally means any person registered with an appropriate national securities exchange as a market maker or specialist in listed options. The term "commodities trader" generally means any person who is a member of a domestic board of trade which is designated as a contract market by the Commodity Futures Trading Commission. Commodities traders also, to the extent permitted by Treasury regulations, include persons entitled to trade as a member (e.g., persons who are registered with a board of trade as users of memberships or who are eligible for member rates for the clearing of trades on the board of trade). Special rules limit the availability of the options dealer and commodities trader exception for limited partners or limited entrepreneurs in an entity that is an options dealer or a commodities trader.

Under the provision, gain realized by a taxpayer from disposition or other termination of a position that was part of a conversion transaction that would otherwise be treated as capital gain will be treated as ordinary income (but not as interest) for all purposes of the Internal Revenue Code. The amount of gain so recharacterized will not exceed the amount of interest that would have accrued on the taxpayer's net investment for the relevant period at a yield equal to 120% of the "applicable rate". This limit is subject to appropriate reduction to reflect prior inclusion of ordinary income items from the conversion transaction or the capitalization of interest on acquisition indebtedness under section 263(g). The "applicable rate" is the applicable Federal rate under section 1274(d) at the time the taxpayer enters into the conversion transaction (if the conversion transaction has a definite term) or the Federal short term rate determined under section 6621(b) (if the conversion transaction has an indefinite term).

For example, assume that X purchases stock for $100 on January 1, 1994, and on that same day agrees to sell it to Y on January 1, 1996 for $115. Assume that the applicable rate is 5%. [3] On January 1, 1996, X delivers the stock to Y in exchange for $115 in satisfaction of their agreement. Assume that, under current law, X would have recognized a capital gain of $15. Under the provision, $12.36 of that amount would be recharacterized as ordinary income (i.e., 120% of 5% compounded for two years, applied to an investment of $100).

In determining a taxpayer's net investment in a conversion transaction, the source of the taxpayer's funds generally will not be taken into account. Assume in the above example that X borrowed $90 of the purchase price of the stock from a bank and was required under section 263(g) to capitalize $10 of interest on that debt into the cost of the stock. Then X's net investment in the transaction will still be $100, even though X's basis is $110 to reflect the capitalized $10 of interest. However, of

[Footnote ¶3033 continued]

2. Except that stock also is treated as personal property in defining a straddle for purposes of the conversion transcation provision.

3. For simplicity, the applicable rate is assumed to be compounded on an annual basis.

the gain of $5, only $2.36 will be recharacterized as ordinary income under the provision. This is because the limitation amount of $12.36 will be reduced by the $10 of capitalized interest.

A special rule is included for situations in which the taxpayer has a built-in loss with respect to a position that becomes part of a conversion transaction. Assume that, prior to January 1, 1994, X had purchased the stock in the previous example for $150, and had used that stock as part of a conversion transaction entered into on January 1, 1994, when the stock's value had declined to $100. Under these facts, the stock would be valued at $100 for purposes of this provision, and the results would be the same as in the example, except that X also would recognize the $50 built-in loss when the asset was delivered to Y. The character of that $50 loss would not be affected by this provision.

Amounts that a taxpayer may be committed to provide in the future generally will not be treated as an investment until such time as such amounts are committed to the transaction and unavailable to the taxpayer to invest in other ways. For example, assume that on January 1, 1994, X enters into a long futures contract committing X to purchase a certain quantity of gold on March 1 for $1,000. Also on January 1, 1994, X enters into a short futures contract to sell the same quantity of gold on April 1 for $1,006. Under these contracts, X is not required to make any investment at the time they are entered into, but is required to make a "margin" deposit (which may or may not bear interest), as securlty for his obligations thereunder. Suppose X terminates both contracts on February 1 for a net profit of $2. No part of that $2 is subject to recharacterization under this provision, since X has no investment in the transaction on which the $2 could be considered to be an interest equivalent return.

A taxpayer's net investment in a conversion transaction generally will be the aggregate amount invested by the taxpayer in the conversion transaction less any amount received by the taxpayer as consideration for entering into any position held as part of the conversion transaction, such as when the taxpayer is the grantor of an option. For example, suppose that on January 1, 1994, X acquires non-publicly-traded common stock for $100 and, on the same day grants Y a call option on the same stock for $106, exercisable any time prior to February 1, 1995. Y pays X a premium of $10 for the call option. At the time X grants Y the call option, there is no substantial certainty that Y will exercise the option. Under these facts, X's net investment in the transaction comprised of the stock purchase and the granting of the option would be $90 (i.e., the $100 paid for the stock minus the $10 received for granting the option). X's return on that investment will be $16 if Y exercises the call option (the excess of $106 of sales proceeds over the net investment of $90). However, if Y does not exercise the option, X's return will be the difference between $90 and the value of the stock on February 1, 1995. The transaction consisting of the stock purchase and the grant of the option is one in which X takes on a risk not typical of a lender and is not a conversion transaction.

Effective Date

The provision is effective for conversion transactions entered into after April 30, 1993.

Conference Report

a. Recharacterization of cpiatal gain as ordinary income for certain financial transactions

Senate Amendment

The Senate amendment is the same as the House bill, except that the amendment clarifies that property or positions may be part of a conversion transaction, and that transactions of options dealers and commodities traders in the normal course of their trade or business of dealing in options or section 1256 contracts, respectively, generally will not be considered to be conversion transactions.

Conference Agreement

The conference agreement follows the Senate amendment, with a clarification of the determination of the "applicable rate," a clarification of the conferees' intent with respect to transactions entered into by options dealers and commodities traders, and a modification to the definition of commodities trader.

First, the conferees clarify that the Secretary has the authority (under sec. 1274(d)(1)(D)) to provide for the use of an applicable rate lower than the applicable Federal rate in appropriate cases. Second, the conferees clarify that transactions (including transactions involving positions other than options or section 1256 contracts) of options dealers and commodities traders in the normal course of their trade or business of dealing in options or trading section 1256 contracts, respectively, will not be considered conversion transactions, except as provided in the special rules noted below.

Third, under the agreement, the term "commodities trader" includes any person who is a member of a domestic board of trade (including a member having member trading privileges only with respect to a portion of the contracts available for trading on the board of trade) which is designated as a contract market by the Commodity Futures Trading Commission. "Commodities trader" also, except as otherwise provided by Treasury regulations, includes a person entitled to trade as a member, such as a lessee of a membership or an entity that is (or is affiliated with) a beneficial owner of a membership if such entity is eligible for any preferential rates available to members with respect to transaction fees or margins imposed by the board of trade or for the clearing of trades on the board of trade. Other persons eligible for such member rates also will be treated as "commodities traders" for purposes of the exception; however, the Secretary may promulgate regulations that prevent unwarranted expansion of the exception, by excluding from the definition of "commodities trader" a person who acquires some attributes of board of trade membership for the principal purpose of qualifying for the "commodities trader" exception or whose margins or fees are substantially more than the margins or fees associated with owned or leased memberships.

Special rules limit the availability of the options dealer and commodities trader exception for limited partners or limited entrepreneurs in an entity that is an options dealer or a commodities trader.

b. Repeal of certain exceptions to the market discount rules

Senate Amendment

The Senate amendment is the same as the House bill.

Conference Agreement

The conference agreement follows the House bill and the Senate amendment, with a technical amendment of the definition of revised issue price in Code section 1278(a)(4) to account for the accrual of tax-exempt original issue discount.

c. Accrual of income by holders of stripped preferred stock

Senate Amendment

The Senate amendment is the same as the House bill.

Conference Agreement

The conference agreement follows the House bill and the Senate amendment.

d. Treatment of net capital gains as investment income

Senate Amendment

The Senate amendment is the same as the House bill.

Conference Agreement

The conference agreement follows the House bill and the Senate amendment.

e. Definition of "substantially appreciated" inventory

Senate Amendment

The Senate amendment is the same as the House bill.

Conference Agreement

The conference agreement follows the House bill and the Senate amendment.

[¶ 3034] Section 13207. Repeal of Limitation on Amount of Wages Subject to Health Insurance Employment Tax

(Code Sec. 3121)

[House Explanation]

Present Law

As part of the Federal Insurance Contributions Act (FICA), a tax is imposed on employees and employers up to a maximum amount of employee wages. The tax is comprised of two parts: old-age, survivor, and disability insurance (OASDI) and Medicare hospital insurance (HI). For wages paid in 1993 to covered employees the HI tax rate is 1.45 percent on both the employer and the employee on the first $135,000 of wages and the OASDI tax rate is 6.2 percent on both the employer and the employee on the first $57,600 of wages.

Under the Self-Employment Contributions Act of 1954 (SECA), a tax is imposed on an individual's self-employment income. The self-employment tax rate is the same as the total rate for employers and employees (i.e., 2.9 percent for HI and 12.40 percent for OASDI). For 1993, the HI tax is applied to the first $135,000 of self-employment income and the OASDI tax is applied to the first $57,600 self-employment income. In general, the tax is reduced to the extent that the individual had wages for which employment taxes were withheld during the year.

The cap on wages and self-employment income subject to FICA and SECA taxes is indexed to changes in the average wages in the economy.

Reasons For Change

The committee believes that eliminating the cap on wages and self-employment income subject to the HI tax will increase the progressivity of the tax system. In addition, the increased revenues will provide necessary funding for the Hospital Insurance Trust Fund and will enhance its long-term solvency.

Explanation Of Provision

The bill repeals the dollar limit on wages and self-employment income subject to HI taxes.

Effective Date

The provision is effective for wages and income received after December 31, 1993.

[Senate Explanation]

Reasons for Change

The committee believes that eliminating the cap on wages and self-employment income subject to the HI tax will increase the progressivity of the tax system. In addition, the increased revenues will provide necessary funding for the Hospital Insurance Trust Fund and will enhance its long-term solvency.

Explanation of Provision

The bill repeals the dollar limit on wages and self-employment income subject to HI taxes.

Effective Date

The provision is effective for wages and income received after December 31, 1993.

[Conference Report]

House Bill

The bill repeals the dollar limit on wages and self-employment income subject to HI taxes.

Effective date.. —The provision is effective for wages and income received after December 31, 1993.

Senate Amendment

The Senate amendment is the same as the House bill. The legislative history to the Senate amendment expresses the concern of the Senate that HI taxes paid by high-income workers under the provision would bear little relation to Medicare benefits such workers could expect to receive, and that this may make the HI program look more like welfare than social insurance. It is suggested that it may be appropriate to revisit the issue in the context of health care reform or Medicare financing improvements.

Effective date.. —The Senate amendment is the same as the House bill.

Conference Agreement

The conference agreement follows the House bill and the Senate amendment.

[¶ 3035] Section 13208. Top Estate and Gift Tax Rates Made Permanent

(Code Sec. 2001)

[House Explanation]

Present Law

A Federal gift tax is imposed on transfers by gift during life and a Federal estate tax is imposed on transfers at death. The Federal estate and gift taxes are unified, so that a single graduated rate schedule is applied to an individual's cumulative gifts and bequests. For decedents dying (or gifts made) after 1992, the estate and gift tax rates begin at 18 percent on the first $10,000 of taxable transfers and reach a maximum of 50 percent on taxable transfers over $2.5 million. Previously, for the nine-year period beginning after 1983 and ending before 1993, two additional brackets applied at the top of the rate schedule: a rate of 53 percent on taxable transfers exceeding $2.5 million and below $3 million, and a maximum marginal tax rate of 55 percent on taxable transfers exceeding $3 million. The generation-skipping transfer tax is computed by reference to the maximum Federal estate tax rate (sec. 2641).

In order to phase out the benefit of the graduated brackets and unified credit, the estate and gift tax is increased by five percent on cumulative taxable transfers between $10 million and $18,340,000, for decedents dying and gifts made after 1992. (Prior to 1993, this phase out of the graduated rates and unified credit applied to cumulative taxable transfers between $10 million and $21,040,000.

Reasons For Change

To raise revenue to address the Federal deficit, to improve tax equity, and to make the tax system more progressive, the committee believes that the top two estate and gift tax rates which expired at the end of 1992 should be reinstated.

Explanation Of Provision

The bill provides that, for taxable transfers over $2.5 million but not over $3 million, the estate and gift tax rate is 53 percent. For taxable transfers over $3 million, the estate and gift tax rate is 55 percent. The phase out of the graduated rates and unified credit applies with respect to cumulative taxable transfers between $10 million and $21,040,000. Also, since the generation-skipping transfer tax is computed by reference to the maximum Federal estate tax rate, the rate of tax on generation-skipping transfers under the bill is 55 percent.

Effective Date

The provision is effective for decedents dying, gifts made, and generation skipping transfers occurring after December 31, 1992.

[Conference Report]

Senate Amendment

The Senate amendment is the same as the House bill.

Conference Agreement. The conference agreement follows the House bill and the Senate amendment.

[¶ 3036] Section 13209. Reduction in Deductible Portion of Business Meals and Entertainment

(Code Sec. 274)

[House Explanation]

Present Law

In general, a taxpayer is permitted a deduction for all ordinary and necessary expenses paid or incurred during the taxable year in carrying on any trade or business and, in the case of an individual, for the production of income. No deduction generally is allowed for personal, living, or family expenses.

Meal and entertainment expenses incurred for business or investment reasons are deductible if certain legal and substantiation requirements are met. The amount of the deduction generally is limited to 80 percent of the expense that meets these requirements. No deduction is allowed, however, for meal or beverage expenses that are lavish or extravagant under the circumstances.

Reasons For Change

Generally, some portion of business meal and entertainment expenses represent personal consumption (even if the expenses serve a legitimate business purpose). The committee believes that denial of some part of the deduction is appropriate as a proxy for income inclusion of the consumption element of the meal or entertainment. The committee believes that increasing the portion of such expenses for which a deduction is denied is appropriate in the context of deficit-reduction legislation.

Explanation Of Provision

The bill reduces the deductible portion of otherwise allowable business meals and entertainment expenses from 80 percent to 50 percent.

Effective Date

The provision is effective for taxable years beginning after December 31, 1993.

[Conference Report]

Conference Agreement

The conference agreement follows the House bill.

[¶ 3037] Section 13210. Elimination of Deduction for Club Membership Fees

(Code Sec. 274)

[Senate Explanation]

Present Law

No deduction is permitted for club dues unless the taxpayer establishes that his or her use of the club was primarily for the furtherance of the taxpayer's trade or business and the specific expense was directly related to the active conduct of that trade or business (Code Sec. 274(a)). No deduction is permitted for an initiation or similar fee that is payable only upon joining a club if the useful life of the fee extends over more than one year. Such initial fees are nondeductible capital expenditures.[1]

Reasons For Change

Under present law, taxpayers can obtain a tax deduction for dues for a club (such as a country club) with respect to which some element of personal pleasure and enjoyment is present. The committee believes that it is inappropriate to permit a deduction for such expenditures. Denying a deduction for club dues also simplifies present law, in that a strict nondeductibility rule is easier to comply with than the present-law rule requiring an assessment of the primary purpose of the use of the club.

Explanation of Provision

Under the bill, no deduction is permitted for club dues. This rule applies to all types of clubs, including business, social, athletic, luncheon, and sporting clubs. Specific business expenses (e.g., meals) incurred at a club are deductible only to the extent they otherwise satisfy the standards for deductibility.

Effective Date

The provision is effective for taxable years beginning after December 31, 1993.

[Conference Report]

The conference agreement follows the Senate amendment.

[¶ 3038] Section 13211. Disallowance of Deduction for Certain Employee Remuneration in Excess of $1,000,000

(Code Sec. 162)

[Senate Explanation]

Present Law

The gross income of an employee includes any compensation received for services rendered. An employer is allowed a corresponding deduction for reasonable salaries and other compensation. Whether compensation is reasonable is determined on a case-by-case basis. However, the reasonableness standard has been used primarily to limit payments by closely-held companies where nondeductible dividends bay be disguised as deductible compensation.

Reasons for Change

Recently, the amount of compensation received by corporate executives has been the subject of scrutiny and criticism. The committee believes that excessive compensation will be reduced if the deduction for compensation (other than performance-based compensation) paid to the top executives of publicly held corporations is limited to $1 million per year.

Explanation of Provision

In general

Under the bill, for purposes of the regular

[Footnote ¶ 3033 continued]

[Footnote ¶ 3037] 1. Kenneth D. Smith, 24 T CM 899 (1965).

income tax and the alternative minimum tax, the otherwise allowable deduction for compensation paid or accrued with respect to a covered employee of a publicly held corporation is to be limited to no more than $1 million per year. [1]

Definition of publicly held corporation

For this purpose, a corporation is treated as publicly held if the corporation has a class of common equity securities that is required to be registered under section 12 of the Securities Exchange Act of 1934. In general, the Securities Exchange Act requires a corporation to register its common equity securities under section 12 if (1) the securities are listed on a national securities exchange or (2) the corporation has $5 million or more of assets and 500 or more holders of such securities. A corporation is not considered publicly held under the bill if registration of its equity securities is voluntary. Such a voluntary registration might occur, for example, if a corporation that otherwise is not required to register its equity securities does so in order to take advantage of other procedures with regard to public offerings of debt securities.

Covered employees

Covered employees are defined by reference to the Securities and Exchange Commission (SEC) rules governIng disclosure of executive compensation. Thus, with respect to a taxable year, a person is a covered employee if (1) the employee is the chief executive officer of the corporation (or an individual acting in such capacity) as of the close of the taxable year or (2) the employee's total compensation is required to be reported for the taxable year under the Securities Exchange Act of 1934 because the employee is one of the four highest compensated officers for the taxable year (other than the chief executive officer). If disclosure is required with respect to fewer than four executives (other than the chief executive officer) under the SEC rules, then only those for whom disclosure is required are covered employees.

Compensation subject to the deduction limitation

In general

Unless specifically excluded, the deduction limitation applies to all remuneration for services, including cash and the cash value of all remuneration (including benefits) paid in a medium other than cash. If an individual is a covered employee for a taxable year, the deduction limitation applies to all compensation not explicitly excluded from the deduction limitation, regardless of whether the compensation is for services as a covered employee and regardless of when the compensation was earned. The $1 million cap is reduced by excess parachute payments (as defined in sec. 280G) that are not deductible by the corporation.

The deduction limitation applies when the deduction would otherwise be taken. Thus, for example, in the case of a nonqualified stock option, the deduction is normally taken in the year the option is exercised, even though the option was granted with respect to services performed in a prior year. [2]

Certain types of compensation are not subject to the deduction limit and are not taken into account in determining whether other compensation exceeds $1 million. The following types of compensation are not taken into account: (1) remuneration payable on a commission basis; (2) remuneration payable solely on account of the attainment of one or more performance goals if certain outside director and shareholder approval requirements are met; (3) payments to a tax-qualified retirement plan (including salary reduction contributions), (4) amounts that are excludable from the executive's gross income (such as employer-provided health benefits and miscellaneous fringe benefits (sec. 132)), and (5) any remuneration payable under a written binding contract which was in effect on February 17, 1993, and all times thereafter before such remuneration was paid and which was not modified thereafter in any material respect before such remuneration was paid.

[Footnote ¶3038 continued]

[Footnote ¶3038] 1. The provision does not modify the present-law requirement that, in order to be deductible, compensation must be reasonable. Thus, as under present law, in under certain circumstances compensation less than $1 million may not be deductible.

2. Of course, if the executive is no longer a covered employee at the time the options are exercised, then the deduction limitation would not apply.

Commissions

In order to qualify for the exception for compensation paid in the form of commissions, the commission must be payable solely on account of income generated directly by the individual performance of the executive receiving such compensation. Thus, for example, compensation that equals a percentage of sales made by the executive qualifies for the exception. Remuneration does not fail to be attributable directly to the executive merely because the executive utilizes support services, such as secretarial or research services, in generating the income. However, compensation is paid on account of broader performance standards, such as income produced by a business unit of the corporation, the compensation would not qualify for the exception because it is not paid with regard to income that is directly attributable to the individual executive.

Other performance-based compensation

Compensation qualifies for the exception for performance-based compensation only if (1) it is paid solely on account of the attainment of one or more performance goals, (2) the performance goals are established by a compensation committee consisting solely of two or more outside directors, (3) the material terms under which the compensation is to be paid, including the performance goals, are disclosed to and approved by the shareholders in a separate vote prior to payment, and (4) prior to payment, the compensation committee certifies that the performance goals and any other material terms were in fact satisfied.

Compensation is not treated as paid solely on account of the attainment of one or more performance goals unless it is paid pursuant to a preestablished objective formula or standard that precludes discretion. In general, this means that a third party with knowledge of the relevant performance results could calculate the amount to be paid. It is intended that what constitutes a performance goal be broadly defined, and include, for example, any performance standard that is applied to the individual executive, a business unit (e.g., a division or a line of business), or the corporation as a whole. Performance standards could include, for example, increases in stock price, market share, sales, or earnings per share.

Compensation does not qualify for the performance-based exception if the executive has a right to receive the compensation notwithstanding the failure of (1) the compensation committee to certify attainment of the performance goal or (2) the shareholders to approve the compensation.

Stock options or other stock appreciation rights generally are treated as meeting the exception for performance-based compensation, provided that the requirements for outside director and shareholder approval are met (without the need for certification that the performance standards have been met), because the amount of compensation attributable to the options or other rights received by the executive would be based on an increase in the corporation's stock price. This does not apply, however, to stock-based compensation that is dependent on factors other than corporate performance. For example, if a stock option is granted to an executive with an exercise price that is less than the current fair market value of the stock at the time of grant, then the executive would have the right to receive compensation on the exercise of the option even if the stock price decreases or stays the same. Thus, stock options that are granted with an exercise price that is less than the fair market value of the stock at the time of grant do not meet the requirements for performance-based compensation. Similarly, if the executive is otherwise protected from decreases in the value of the stock (such as through automatic repricing), the compensation is not performance-based.

In contrast to options or other stock appreciation rights, grants of restricted stock are not inherently performance-based because the executive may receive compensation even if the stock price decreases or stays the same. Thus, a grant of restricted stock is treated like cash compensation and does not satisfy the definition of performance-based compensation unless the grant or vesting of the restricted stock is based upon the attainment of a performance goal and otherwise satisfies the standards for performance-based compensation under the bill.

For purposes of the exception for performance-based compensation, a director is considered an outside director if he or she is not a current employee of the corporation (or related entities), is not a former employee of the corporation (or related entities) who is receiving compensation for prior services (other than benefits under a tax-qualified pension plan), was not an officer of the corporation (or related entities) at any time, and is not currently receiving compensation for personal services in any capacity (e.g., for services as a consultant) other than as a director.

In order to meet the shareholder approval requirement, the material terms under which the compensation is to be paid must be disclosed. In developing standards as to whether disclosure is adequate, it is intended that the Secretary take into consideration the SEC rules regarding disclosure.

The shareholder approval requirement is met if, after disclosure of material terms, the compensation is approved in a separate vote by a majority of shares voting in the separate vote.

In the case of compensation paid pursuant to a plan (including a stock option plan), the shareholder approval requirement generally is satisfied if the shareholders approve the specific terms of the plan and the class of executives to which it applies and the amount of compensation payable under the plan is not subject to discretion. Further shareholder approval of payments under the plan is not required after the plan has been approved. Of course, if there are material changes to the plan, shareholder approval would have to be obtained again in order for the exception to apply to payments under the modified plan.

Under present law, in the case of a privately held company that becomes publicly held, the prospectus is subject to the rules similar to those applicable to publicly held companies. Thus, if there has been disclosure that would satisfy the rules described above, persons who buy stock in the publicly held company will be aware of existing compensation arrangements. No further shareholder approval is required of compensation arrangements existing prior to the time the company became public unless there is a material modification of such arrangements.

Compensation payable under a written binding contract

Remuneration payable under a written binding contact which was in effect on February 17, 1993, and at all times thereafter before such remuneration was paid is not subject to the deduction limitation. Compensation paid pursuant to a plan qualifies for this exception provided that the right to participate in the plan is part of a written binding contract with the covered employee in effect on February 17, 1993. For example, suppose a covered employee was hired by XYZ Corporation on January 17, 1993, and one of the terms of the written employment contract is that the executive is eligible to participate in the "XYZ Corporation Executive Deferred Compensation Plan" in accordance with the terms of the plan. Assume further that the terms of the plan provide for participation after 6 months of employment, amounts payable under the plan are not subject to discretion, and the corporation does not have the right to amend materially the plan or terminate the plan. Provided that the other conditions of the binding contract exception are met (e.g., the plan itself is in writing), payments under the plan are grandfathered, even though the employee was not actually a participant in the plan on February 17, 1993.

The fact that a plan was in existence on February 17, 1993, is not by itself sufficient to qualify the plan for the exception for binding written contracts.

The exception for remuneration paid pursuant to a binding written contract ceases to apply to amounts paid after there has been a material modification to the terms of the contract. The exception does not apply to new contracts entered into or renewed after February 17, 1993. For purposes of this rule, any contract that is entered into on or before February 17, 1993, and that is renewed after such date is treated as a new contract entered into on the day the renewal takes effect. A contract that is terminable or cancelable unconditionally at will by either party to the contract without the consent of the other, or by both parties to the contract, is treated as a new contract entered into on the date any such termination or cancellation, if made, would be effective. However, a contract is not treated as so terminable or cancelable if it can be terminated or cancelled only by terminating the employment relationship of the covered employee.

Effective Date

The provision applies to compensation that is otherwise deductible by the corporation in a taxable year beginning on or after January 1, 1994.

Conference Report

Conference Agreement

In general

The conference agreement follows the Senate amendment, with certain modifications and clarifications.

Under the conference agreement, for purposes of the regular income tax and the alternative minimum tax, the otherwise allowable deduction for compensation paid or accrued with respect to a covered employee of a publicly held corporation is limited to no more than $1 million per year. [44]

Definition of publicly held corporation

For purposes of this provision, a corporation is treated as publicly held if the corporation has a class of common equity securities that is required to be registered under section 12 of the Securities Exchange Act of 1934. In general, the Securities Exchange Act requires a corporation to register its common equity securities under section 12 if (1) the securities are listed on a national securities exchange or (2) the corporation has $5 million or more of assets and 500 or more holders of such securities. A corporation is not considered publicly held under the provision if registration of its equity securities is voluntary. Such a voluntary registration might occur, for example, if a corporation that otherwise is not required to register its equity securities does so in order to take advantage of other procedures with regard to public offerings of debt securities.

Covered employees

Covered employees are defined by reference to the Securities and Exchange Commission (SEC) rules governing disclosure of executive compensation. Thus, with respect to a taxable year, a person is a covered employee if (1) the employee is the chief executive officer of the corporation (or an individual acting in such capacity) as of the close of the taxable year or (2) the employee's total compensation is required to be reported for the taxable year under the Securities Exchange Act of 1934 because the employee is one of the four highest compensated officers for the taxable year (other than the chief executive officer). If disclosure is required with respect to fewer than four executives (other than the chief executive officer) under the SEC rules, then only those for whom disclosure is required are covered employees.

Compensation subject to the deduction limitation

In general

Unless specifically excluded, the deduction limitation applies to all remuneration for services, including cash and the cash value of all remuneration (including benefits) paid in a medium other than cash. If an individual is a covered employee for a taxable year, the deduction limitation applies to all compensation not explicitly excluded from the deduction limitation, regardless of whether the compensation is for services as a covered employee and regardless of when the compensation was earned. The $1 million cap is reduced by excess parachute payments (as defined in sec. 280G) that are not deductible by the corporation.

The deduction limitation applies when the deduction would otherwise be taken. Thus, for example, in the case of a nonqualified stock option, the deduction is normally taken in the year the option is exercised, even though the option was granted with respect to services performed in a prior year. [45]

Certain types of compensation are not subject to the deduction limit and are not taken into account in determining whether other compensation exceeds $1 million. The following types of compensation are not taken into account: (1) remuneration payable on a commission basis; (2) remuneration payable solely on account of the attainment of one or more performance goals if certain outside director and shareholder approval requirements are met; (3) payments to a tax-qualified retirement plan (including salary reduction contributions); (4) amounts that are excludable from the executive's gross income (such as employer provided health benefits and miscellaneous fringe benefits (sec. 132)); and (5) any remuneration payable under a written binding contract which was in effect on February 17, 1993, and

[Footnote ¶ 3038 continued]

44. The provision does not modify the present-law requirement that, in order to be deductible, compensation must be reasonable. Thus, as under present law, in certain circumstances compensation less than $1 million may not be deductible.

45. Of course, if the executive is no longer a covered employee at the time the options are exercised, then the deduction limitation would not apply.

all times thereafter before such remuneration was paid and which was not modified thereafter in any material respect before such remuneration was paid.

Commissions

In order to qualify for the exception for compensation paid in the form of commissions, the commission must be payable solely on account of income generated directly by the individual performance of the executive receiving such compensation. Thus, for example, compensation that equals a percentage of sales made by the executive qualifies for the exception. Remuneration does not fail to be attributable directly to the executive merely because the executive utilizes support services, such as secretarial or research services, in generating the income. However, if compensation is paid on account of broader performance standards, such as income produced by a business unit of the corporation, the compensation would not qualify for the exception because it is not paid with regard to income that is directly attributable to the individual executive.

Other performance-based compensation

In general. Compensation qualifies for the exception for performance-based compensation only if (1) it is paid solely on account of the attainment of one or more performance goals, (2) the performance goals are established by a compensation committee consisting solely of two or more outside directors, (3) the material terms under which the compensation is to be paid, including the performance goals, are disclosed to and approved by the shareholders in a separate vote prior to payment, and (4) prior to payment, the compensation committee certifies that the performance goals and any other material terms were in fact satisfied.

Definition of performance-based compensation. Compensation (other than stock options or other stock appreciation rights) is not treated as paid solely on account of the attainment of one or more performance goals unless the compensation is paid to the particular executive pursuant to a preestablished objective performance formula or standard that precludes discretion. [46] In general, this means that a third party with knowledge of the relevant performance results could calculate the amount to be paid to the executive. It is intended that what constitutes a performance goal be broadly defined, and include, for example, any objective performance standard that is applied to the individual executive, a business unit (e.g., a division or a line of business), or the corporation as a whole. Performance standards could include, for example, increases in stock price, market share, sales, or earnings per share. Stock options or other stock appreciation rights generally are treated as meeting the exception for performance-based compensation, provided that the requirements for outside director and shareholder approval are met (without the need for certification that the performance standards have been met), because the amount of compensation attributable to the options or other rights received by the executive would be based solely on an increase in the corporation's stock price. In the case of stock options, it is intended that the directors may retain discretion as to the exact number of options that are granted to an executive, provided that the maximum number of options that the individual executive may receive during a specified period is predetermined. Stock-based compensation is not treated as performance-based if it is dependent on factors other than corporate performance. For example, if a stock option is granted to an executive with an exercise price that is less than the current fair market value of the stock at the time of grant, then the executive would have the right to receive compensation on the exercise of the option even if the stock price decreases or stays the same. Thus, stock options that are granted with an exercise price that is less than the fair market value of the stock at the time of grant do not meet the requirements for performance-based compensation. Similarly, if the executive is otherwise protected from decreases in the value of the stock (such as through automatic repricing), the compensation is not performance-based. In contrast to options or other stock appreciation rights, grants of restricted stock are not inherently performance-based because the executive may receive compensation even if the stock price decreases or stays the same. Thus, a grant of restricted stock is treated like cash compensation and does not satisfy the definition of performance-based compensation un-

[Footnote ¶3038 continued]

46. Discretion does not exist merely because the outside directors have the authority to interpret a compensation plan, agreement, or contract in accordance with its terms.

less the grant or vesting of the restricted stock is based upon the attainment of a performance goal and otherwise satisfies the standards for performance-based compensation under the bill. Compensation does not qualify for the performance-based exception if the executive has a right to receive the compensation notwithstanding the failure of (1) the compensation committee to certify attainment of the performance goal (or goals) or (2) the shareholders to approve the compensation.

Definition Of Outside Directors. For purposes of the exception for performance-based compensation, a director is considered an outside director if he or she is not a current employee of the corporation (or related entities), is not a former employee of the corporation (or related entities) who is receiving compensation for prior services (other than benefits under a tax-qualified pension plan), was not an officer of the corporation (or related entities) at any time, and is not currently receiving compensation for personal services in any capacity (e.g., for services as a consultant) other than as a director.

Shareholder approval and adequate disclosure In order to meet the shareholder approval requirement, the material terms under which the compensation is to be paid must be disclosed and, after disclosure of such terms, the compensation must be approved by a majority of shares voting in a separate vote. In the case of performance-based compensation paid pursuant to a plan (other than a stock option plan), the shareholder approval requirement generally is satisfied if the shareholders approve the specific terms of the plan, including the class of executives to which it applies. In the case of a stock option plan, the shareholders generally must approve the specific terms of the plan, the class of executives to which it applies, the option price (or formula under which the price is determined), and the maximum number of shares subject to option that can be awarded under the plan to any executive. Further shareholder approval of payments under a plan or grants of options is not required after the plan has been approved. Of course, if there are material changes to the plan, shareholder approval would have to be obtained again in order for the exception to apply to payments under the modified plan. It is intended that not all the details of a plan (or agreement) need be disclosed in all cases. In developing standards as to whether disclosure of the terms of a plan or agreement is adequate, the Secretary should take into account the SEC rules regarding disclosure. To the extent consistent with those rules, however, disclosure should be as specific as possible. It is expected that shareholders will, at a minimum, be made aware of the general performance goals on which the executive's compensation is based and the maximum amount that could be paid to the executive if such performance goals were met. For example, it would not be adequate if the shareholders were merely informed that an executive would be awarded $x "if the executive meets certain performance goals established by the compensation committee." Under present law, in the case of a privately held company that becomes publicly held, the prospectus is subject to the rules similar to those applicable to publicly held companies. Thus, if there has been disclosure that would satisfy the rules described above, persons who buy stock in the publicly held company will be aware of existing compensation arrangements. No further shareholder approval is required of compensation arrangements existing prior to the time the company became public unless there is a material modification of such arrangements. It is intended that similar rules apply in the case of other business transactions.

Compensation payable under a written binding contract Remuneration payable under a written binding contract which was in effect on February 17, 1993, and at all times thereafter before such remuneration was paid is not subject to the deduction limitation. Compensation paid pursuant to a plan qualifies for this exception provided that the right to participate in the plan is part of a written binding contract with the covered employee in effect on February 17, 1993. For example, suppose a covered employee was hired by XYZ Corporation on January 17, 1993, and one of the terms of the written employment contract is that the executive is eligible to participate in the "XYZ Corporation Executive Deferred Compensation Plan" in accordance with the terms of the plan. Assume further that the terms of the plan provide for participation after 6 months of employment, amounts payable under the plan are not subject to discretion, and the corporation does not have the right to amend materially the plan or terminate the plan (except on a prospective basis before any services are performed with respect to the applicable period for which such compensation is to be paid). Provided that the other conditions of the binding contract exception are met (e.g., the plan itself is in writing), payments under the plan are grandfathered, even though the employee was not actually a participant in the plan on February 17, 1993. [47] The fact that a plan was in existence on February 17, 1993, is not by itself sufficient to qualify the plan for the exception for binding written contracts. The exception for remuneration paid pursuant to a binding written contract ceases to apply to amounts paid after there has been a material modification to the terms of the contract. The exception does not apply to new contracts entered into or renewed after February 17, 1993. For purposes of this rule, any contract that is entered into on or before February 17, 1993, and that is renewed after such date is treated as a new contract entered into on the day the renewal takes effect. A contract that is terminable or cancelable unconditionally at will by either party to the contract without the consent of the other, or by both parties to the contract, is treated as a new contract entered into on the date any such termination or cancellation, if made, would be effective. However, a contract is not treated as so terminable or cancelable if it can be terminated or cancelled only by terminating the employment relationship of the covered employee.

Effective Date

The conference agreement follows the Senate amendment.

[¶3039] Section 13212. Reduction in Compensation Taken Into Account in Determining Contributions and Benefits Under Qualified Retirement Plans

(Code Sec. 401, 404, 408, 505)

[Senate Explanation]

Present Law

Under present law, the amount of a participant's compensation that can be taken into account under a tax-qualified pension plan is limited (sec. 401(a)(17)). The limit applies for determining the amount of the employer's deduction for contributions to the plan as well as for determining the amount of the participant's benefits. The limit on includible compensation is $235,840 for 1993, and is adjusted annually for inflation. The limit in effect at the beginning of a plan year applies for the entire plan year. The indexed limit in effect for a plan year does not apply to any prior plan years.

Reasons For Change

The limit on compensation taken into account under a qualified pension plan serves as a useful backstop to the nondiscrimination requirements applicable to qualified plans. By limiting the compensation taken into account under a plan, an employer is deemed to be providing greater benefits as a percentage of pay to an employee with compensation in excess of the cap than would be the case if all of the employee's compensation were taken into account. As a result, under the nondiscrimination rules rank-and-file employees be entitled to benefits that are a larger percentage of their pay.

The committee believes that the goal of reducing the extent to which employers discriminate in the provision of pension benefits in favor of highly compensated employees can be better served by reducing further the compensation taken into account under qualified plans.

The committee is aware that in some cases State constitutions preclude benefit formulas from being reduced. Accordingly, the committee believes it is appropriate to provide a limited transition rule for existing employees of governmental organizations. However, the committee also believes that State and local governments should be encouraged to conform their tax-qualified pension plans to Federal requirements and so, as a condition of the transition relief, requires the Federal compensation limit to be incorporated into the plan by reference.

The committee believes it is appropriate to provide a delayed effective date in the case of collectively bargained plans.

[Footnote ¶3038 continued]

47. Of course, as discussed below in the text, the grandfather ceases to apply if the plan is materially amended.

Explanation of Provision

Under the bill, the limit on compensation taken into account under a qualified plan (sec. 401(a)(17)) is reduced to $150,000. This limit is indexed for cost-of-living adjustments in increments of $10,000. Corresponding changes are also made to other provisions (secs. 404(l), 408(k)(3)(C), (6)(D)(ii), and (8), and 505(b)(7)) that take into account the section 401(a)(17) limit.

Effective Date

The provision is generally effective for benefits accruing in plan years beginning after December 31, 1993. Special transition rules apply in the case of governmental plans and plans maintained pursuant to a collective bargaining agreement.

In the case of an eligible participant in a plan maintained by a State or local government, the limit on compensation taken into account is the greater of the limit under the proposal and the compensation allowed to be taken into account under the plan as in effect on July 1, 1993. For purposes of this rule, an eligible participant is an individual who first became a participant in the plan during a plan year beginning before the first plan year beginning after the earlier of: (1) the plan year in which the plan is amended to reflect the proposal, or (2) December 31, 1995. This special rule does not apply unless the plan is amended to incorporate the dollar limit in effect under section 401(a)(17) by reference, effective with respect to persons other than eligible participants for benefits accruing in plan years beginning after December 31, 1995 (or earlier if the plan amendment so provides).

In the case of a plan maintained pursuant to one or more collective bargaining agreements ratified before the date of enactment, the provision does not apply to contributions or benefits accruing under such agreements in plan years beginning before the earlier of (1) the latest of (a) January 1, 1994, (b) the date on which the last of such collective bargaining agreements terminates (without regard to any extension or modification on or after the date of enactment), or (c) in the case of a plan maintained pursuant to collective bargaining under the Railway Labor Act, the date of execution of an extension or replacement of the last of such collect bargaining agreements in effect on the date of enactment, or (2) January 1, 1997.

Conference Report

Conference Agreement

The conference agreement follows the Senate amendment.

[¶ 3040] Section 13213. Modification to Deduction for Certain Moving Expenses

(Code Sec. 217)

[House Explanation]

Present Law

An employee or self-employed individual may claim a deduction from gross income for certain expenses incurred as a result of moving to a new residence in connection with beginning work at a new location (sec. 217) if the taxpayer's new job is at least 35 miles further from his former residence than was his former job (or at least 35 miles from his former residence, if he has no former place of work). The deduction is not subject to the floor that generally limits a taxpayer's allowable miscellaneous itemized deductions to those amounts that exceed 2 percent of his adjusted gross income. Any amount received directly or indirectly by such individual as a reimbursement of moving expenses must be included in the taxpayer's gross income as compensation (sec. 82). The taxpayer may offset this income by deducting the moving expenses that would otherwise qualify as deductible items under section 217.

Deductible moving expenses are the expenses of transporting the taxpayer and members of his household, as well as his household goods and personal effects, from the old residence to the new residence; the cost of meals and lodging enroute; the expenses for premove househunting trips; temporary living expenses for up to 30 days in the general location of the new job; and certain expenses related to either the sale or settlement of a lease on the old residence or the purchase of or the acquisition of a lease on a new residence in the general location of the new job.

The moving expense deduction is subject to a number of limitations. A maximum of $1,500 can be deducted for pre-move househunting and temporary living expenses in the general location of the new job. A maximum of $3,000 (reduced by any deduction claimed for househunting or temporary living expenses) can be deducted for certain qualified expenses for the sale or purchase of a residence or settlement or acquisition of a lease. If both a husband and wife begin new jobs in the same general location, the move is treated as a single commencement of work. If a husband and wife file separate returns, the maximum deductible amounts available to each are one-half the amounts otherwise allowed.

Reasons For Change

The committee believes that the cost of meals incurred during a move are nondeductible personal expenses since the taxpayer would have eaten these meals at either location. In addition, the committee believes that the appropriate tax treatment for costs incurred for selling and buying a home is (1) a reduction in the amount realized upon the sale of the home and (2) an increase in the basis of the home purchased. Also, the committee believes that disallowing the moving expense deduction for the costs of settling old leases and acquiring new leases restores some fairness to the tax system since these expenses are nondeductible personal expenses for most taxpayers.

Explanation Of Provision

The provision excludes from the definition of moving expenses: (1) the costs of meals consumed while traveling and while living in temporary quarters near the new workplace, and (2) the costs of selling (or settling an unexpired lease on) the old residence and buying (or acquiring a lease on) the new residence.

Effective Date

The provision is effective for expenses incurred after December 31, 1993.

[Senate Explanation]

Reasons For Change

The committee believes that no deduction is justified for certain expenses that do not directly relate to the cost of moving. Such expenses include those related to: (1) sale of the old residence, (2) settlement of a lease on the old residence, (3) acquisition of a lease on or purchase of a new residence in the general location of the new job. [1] Also, the committee believes that it is unfair to provide a deduction for such expenses under sec. 217 to some taxpayers while denying it to others.

Further, the committee believes that the expense of meals in this context are primarily a personal living expense rather than an expense incurred for business purposes and should be afforded similar tax treatment to other personal expenses, namely nondeductibility.

Explanation of Provision

The provision excludes from the definition of moving expenses: (1) the costs of selling (or settling an unexpired lease on) the old residence and buying (or acquiring a lease on) the new residence, and (2) the costs of meals consumed while traveling and while living in temporary quarters near the new workplace. In addition, an overall $10,000 cap is imposed on allowable moving expenses.

Conference Report

In general

The conference agreement follows the House bill with the following modifications: (1) the cost of pre-move househunting trips is excluded from the definition of moving expenses; (2) the cost of temporary living expenses for up to 30 days in the general location of the new job is excluded from the definition of moving expenses; (3) the mileage limit is increased from 35 miles to 50 miles; (4) moving expenses not paid or reimbursed by the taxpayer's employer are allowable as a deduction in calculating adjusted gross income; and (5) moving expenses paid or reimbursed by the taxpayer's employer are excludable from gross income.

Definition of moving expenses

Under the conference agreement, moving expenses are defined as the reasonable costs of (1) moving household goods and personal ef-

[Footnote ¶3038 continued]

[Footnote ¶3040] 1. These amounts may generally be capitalized into the basis of the underlying asset.

fects from the former residence to the new residence and (2) traveling (including lodging during the period of travel) from the former residence to the new place of residence. Moving expenses do not include any expenses for meals.

Employer-paid moving expenses

Moving expenses are excludable from gross income and wages for income and employment tax purposes to the extent paid for by the taxpayer's employer (whether directly or through reimbursement). Moving expenses are not excludable if the taxpayer actually deducted the expenses in a prior taxable year. The conferees intend that the employer treat moving expenses as excludable unless it has actual knowledge that the employee deducted the expenses in a prior year. The employer has no obligation to determine whether the individual deducted the expenses.

The conferees intend that rules similar to the rules relating to accountable plans under section 62(c) will apply to reimbursed expenses.

Moving expenses not paid for by the employer

Moving expenses are deductible in computing adjusted gross income to the extent not paid for by the taxpayer's employer (whether directly or through reimbursement). Allowing such a deduction will treat taxpayers whose expenses are not paid for by their employer in a comparable manner to taxpayers whose moving expenses are paid for by their employer.

Effective date

The conference agreement follows the House bill and the Senate amendment.

[¶3041] Section 13214. Simplification of Individual Estimated Tax Safe Harbor Based on Last Year's Tax

(Code Sec. 6654)

[House Explanation]

Present Law

Under present law, an individual taxpayer generally is subject to an addition to tax for any underpayment of estimated tax. An individual generally does not have an underpayment of estimated tax if he or she makes timely estimated tax payments at least equal to: (1) 100 percent of the tax shown on the return of the individual for the preceding year (the "100 percent of last year's liability safe harbor") or (2) 90 percent of the tax shown on the return for the current year. Income tax withholding from wages is considered to be a payment of estimated taxes. For estimated tax purposes, some trusts and estates are treated as individuals.

In addition, for taxable years beginning after 1991 and before 1997, a special rule provides the 100 percent of last year's liability safe harbor generally is not available to a taxpayer that (1) has a modified adjusted gross income (AGI) in the current year that exceeds the taxpayer's AGI in the preceding year by more than $40,000 ($20,000 in the case of a separate return by a married individual) and (2) has a modified AGI in excess of $75,000 in the current year ($37,500 in the case of a separate return by a married individual)

Reasons For Change

The committee believes that the application of the special rule that denies the use of the 100 percent of last year's liability safe harbor is unduly cumbersome. In order to simplify the calculation of estimated taxes for individuals, the special rule is replaced with a new, permanent safe harbor that applies to individuals with a preceding year AGI above a certain threshold.

Explanation Of Provision

The special rule that denies the use of the 100 percent of last year's liability safe harbor is repealed for taxable years beginning after 1993. However, the 100 percent of last year's liability safe harbor is modified to be a 110 percent of last year's liability safe harbor for any individual with an AGI of more than $150,000 as shown on the return for the preceding taxable year. For this purpose, the AGI of a trust or an estate is determined pursuant to rules similar to those in Code section 67(e).

For taxable years beginning after 1993, the bill does not change the availability of (1) the

100 percent of last year's liability safe harbor for an individual with a preceding year AGI of $150,000 or less, or (2) the present-law rule that allows any individual to base estimated tax payments on 90 percent of the tax shown on the return for the current year.

Effective Date

The provision is effective for estimated tax payments applicable to taxable years beginning after December 31, 1993.

[Conference Report]

Senate Amendment

The Senate amendment is the same as the House bill.

Conference Agreement

The conference agreement follows the House bill and the Senate amendment.

[¶3042] Section 13215. Social Security and Tier 1 Railroad Retirement Benefits

(Code Sec. 86)

[Senate Explanation]

Present Law

Under present law, a portion of Social Security and Railroad Retirement Tier 1 benefits are includible in gross income for taxpayers whose provisional incomes exceed a threshold amount. For purposes of this computation, a taxpayer's provisional income includes modified adjusted gross income (adjusted gross income plus tax-exempt interest plus certain foreign source income) plus one-half of the taxpayer's Social Security or Railroad Retirement Tier 1 benefit. The threshold amount is $32,000 for married taxpayers filing joint returns, $25,000 for unmarried taxpayers, and $0 for married taxpayers filing separate returns. A taxpayer is required to include in gross income the lesser of: (1) 50 percent of the taxpayer's Social Security or Railroad Retirement Tier 1 benefit, or (2) 50 percent of the excess of the taxpayer's provisional income over the applicable threshold amount.

Proceeds from the income taxation of these benefits are credited quarterly to the Old-Age and Survivors Insurance Trust Fund, the Disability Insurance Trust Fund, or the Social Security Equivalent Benefit Account (of the Railroad Retirement system), as appropriate.

Reasons For Change

The committee desires to more closely conform the income tax treatment of Social Security benefits and private pension benefits by increasing the maximum amount of Social Security benefits included in gross income for certain higher-income beneficiaries. Reducing the exclusion for Social Security benefits for these beneficiaries will enhance both the horizontal and vertical equity of the individual income tax system by treating all income in a more similar manner. To limit the effect of this provision to taxpayers with a greater ability to pay taxes, the present-law income thresholds are maintained. In addition, the committee believes that revenues attributable to the increased portion of Social Security benefits included in gross income should be retained in the General Fund.

Explanation Of Provision

The bill provides that, for taxpayers with provisional incomes above the applicable thresholds, a taxpayer's gross income includes the lesser of: (1) 85 percent of the taxpayer's Social Security or Railroad Retirement Tier 1 benefit, or (2) 85 percent of the excess of the taxpayer's provisional income over the applicable present-law threshold amounts. A taxpayer's provisional income for purposes of this computation (modified adjusted gross income plus one-half of the taxpayer's Social Security or Railroad Retirement Tier 1 benefit) will be calculated the same as under present law.

Proceeds from the income taxation of Social Security and Railroad Retirement Tier 1 benefits attributable to the increased portion of benefits included in gross income will be retained in the (1) 85 percent of the taxpayer's Social Security benefit of (2) the sum of: (a) the smaller of (i) the amount included under present law; or (ii) $3,500 (for unmarried taxpayers) or $4,000 (for married taxpayers filing joint returns), [1] plus, (b) 85 percent of the excess of the taxpayer's provisional income over the applicable new threshold amounts.

For married taxpayers filing separate returns, gross income will include the lesser of 85 percent of the taxpayer's Social Security benefit or 85 percent of the taxpayer's provisional income.

For purposes of this computation, a taxpayer's provisional income (modified adjusted gross income plus one-half of the taxpayer's Social Security or Railroad Retirement Tier 1 benefit) is calculated the same as under present law.

Revenues from the income taxation of Social Security and Railroad Retirement Tier 1 benefits attributable to the increased portion of benefits included in gross income will be transferred to the Medicare Hospital Insurance (HI) Trust Fund.

Effective Date

The provision is effective for taxable years beginning after December 31, 1993.

[Conference Report]

The conference agreement follows the Senate amendment, except that present law applies to taxpayers with provisional income below $34,000 for unmarried individuals and $44,000 for married individuals filing joint returns. The conference agreement does not change the present-law election permitting a taxpayer to treat a lump-sum payment of benefits as received in the year to which benefits are attributable. Taxpayers electing this treatment compute the amount of benefits includible in gross income using the inclusion formula that applies to the taxable year to which the benefits are attributable. For example, if in 1994, a taxpayer receives a lump-sum payment of benefits that includes benefits attributable to 1992 and 1993, the amount of benefits attributable to 1992 and 1993 that is includible in gross income is determined using the present-law inclusion formula. The amount of benefits attributable to 1994 that is includible in gross income is computed using the inclusion formula in the conference agreement.

Effective date. The conference agreement follows the House bill and the Senate amendment.

[¶3043] Section 13221. Increase in Top Marginal Rate Under Section 11

(Code Sec. 11(b), 852(b)(3), 1201, 1445(e))

[House Explanation]

Explanation of Provision

The bill provides a new 35-percent marginal tax rate on corporate taxable income in excess of $10 million. The maximum rate of tax on corporate net capital gains is also 35 percent.

A corporation with taxable income in excess of $15 million is required to increase its tax liability by the lesser of 3 percent of the excess or $100,000. This increase in tax recaptures the benefits of the 34-percent rate in a manner analogous to the recapture of the benefits of the 15- and 25-percent rates.

Effective Date

The 35-percent marginal rate is effective for taxable years beginning on or after January 1, 1993. Under existing law provisions regarding changes in tax rates during a taxpayer's taxable year (section 15 of the Code), a fiscal year corporation is required to use a "blended rate" for its fiscal year that includes January 1, 1993. Accordingly, the corporation's tax liability will be a weighted average of the tax resulting from applying the existing corporate rate schedule and the tax resulting from applying the changes described above, weighted by the number of days before and after January 1, 1993. Penalties for the underpayment of estimated taxes, however, are waived for underpayments of 1993 taxes attributable to the changes in tax rates.

[Conference Report]

Senate Amendment

The Senate amendment is the same as the House bill.

Conference Agreement

The conference agreement follows the

[Footnote ¶3042] 1. These figures equal 50 percent of the difference between the present law threholds for 50 percent Social Security benefit inclusion and the proposed new thresholds for 85 percent Social Security benefit inclusion.

House bill and the Senate amendment.

Some taxpayers may be subject to the increased corporate tax rates with respect to a taxable year that has already ended. Those taxpayers may have filed an application for an extension of the time for filing their corporate income tax returns pursuant to section 6081. For such a filing to be valid, the taxpayer must remit "the amount of the properly estimated unpaid tax liability" (Treas. Reg. sec. 1.6081-3). The conferees intend that the IRS apply this provision by computing that amount by reference to the law in effect on the date the application for the extension was filed.

[¶3044] Section 13222. Denial of Deduction for Lobbying Expenses

(Code Sec. 162(e), 170(f), 6033)

[House Explanation]

Explanation of Provision

Under the bill, taxpayers may not deduct certain lobbying expenses under section 162. For purposes of this disallowance rule, lobbying expenses are defined as any amount paid or incurred in connection with any attempt to influence legislation through communication with any member or employee a legislative body, or with any government official or employee who may participate in the formulation of legislation. [31]

The disallowance rule applies to attempts to influence legislation through communications with the executive branch as well as the legislative branch of the Federal, or any State or local, government. [32] An exception to the general disallowance rule is provided to permit taxpayers to deduct expenditures for providing technical advice or assistance to a governmental body or to a committee or other subdivision thereof in response to a specific written request by such governmental entity. [33] (However, the bill does not provide exceptions similar to the other exceptions of present-law section 4911(d)(2), such as the exception for nonpartisan analysis.)

The present-law disallowance of business deductions for expenses of grass roots lobbying and participation in political campaigns remains in effect under the bill. [34] Present-law rules which prevent charities from engaging in a substantial amount of lobbying also remain in effect.

The bill provides for a flow-through rule to disallow a deduction for a portion of the membership dues (or similar amounts) [35] paid to an organization which engages in political or lobbying activities. Under the bill, the disallowed portion of such payments will be the portion allocable to political or lobbying expenditures incurred by the organization. [36] As under present law, trade associations and similar organi-

31. The committee intends that the Secretary of the Treasury will provide guidance for distinguishing (1) attempts to influence legislation, from (2) mere monitoring of legislative activities where there is no attempt to influence the formulation or enactment of legislation. In cases where an individual or organization monitors legislation and subsequently attempts to influence the formulation or enactment of the same (or similar) legislation, it is intended that the costs of the monitoring activities generally will be treated as a nondeductible lobbying expense.

32. For purposes of the provision, the term "legislation" has the same meaning as under section 4911(e)(2), which, in turn, defines "legislation" as including "action with respect to Acts, bills, governing body, or by the public in a referendum, initiative, constitutional amendment, or similar procedure." Treasury regulations provide that "legislation" for purposes of section 4911(e)(2) includes action by legislative bodies but does not include action by "executive, judicial, or administrative bodies" (Treas. Reg. sec. 56.4911-2(d)(3)). Treasury regulations further provide that "administrative bodies" includes school boards, housing authorities, sewer and water districts, zoning boards, and other similar Federal State, or local special purpose bodies, whether elective or appointive (Treas. Reg. sec. 56.4911-2(d)(4)). Thus, communications with, and attempts to influence, members of a local zoning board (acting in their capacity as members of that board, regardless of whether or not such members are elected to their position) will not be affected by the provision.

33. In order for this exception to apply, the written request must be made in the name of the governmental body (not an individual member or employee thereof) and must be specifically directed to the particular taxpayer that incurs what otherwise would be disallowed lobbying expenses. Responding to a general notice to the public to submit comments on proposed legislation would not satisfy the requirements of this exception.

34. In addition, the present-law rule disallowing a deduction for lobbying of foreign governments would remain in effect.

35. Amounts that are similar to dues include voluntary payments made by members and special assessments imposed by the recipient organization to conduct lobbying activities. This is similar to the treatment of special assessments for grassroots lobbying or campaign expenses under present-law Treasury Regulation section 1.162-20(c)(3).

36. For this purpose, lobbying expenditures incurred by an organization will be allocated first to dues paid to the organization, and any excess amount of lobbying expenditures will be carried forward and allocated to dues paid to the organization in the following year.

zations will not lose their tax-exempt status under the bill merely because they conduct lobbying activities. Trade associations and similar organizations are required to report to their members (and the IRS) the portion of membership dues (or similar payments) allocable to lobbying activities. However, the Secretary of the Treasury is granted authority to provide by regulation that this reporting requirement generally applicable to organizations will not apply where unnecessary to effectuate the purposes of the provision (e.g., where an organization incurs insubstantial lobbying expenses, or where the disallowed portion of such expenditures will not materially affect the tax liability of dues-paying members).

Organizations will be subject to penalties for failing to meet the reporting requirements of the provision. In addition to the normal reporting penalties (generally, $50 for each failure to report to the IRS or organization member), a special penalty applies if an organization materially underreports its lobbying expenses to its members (meaning the aggregate amount of nondeductible dues reported to members is less than 75 percent of the correct amount). This special penalty is equal to the amount of lobbying or political expenses not reported multiplied by the highest corporate tax rate (to approximate the amount of tax which would have been paid by the organization's members had they been notified of the disallowed amounts).

Effective Date

The provision is effective for amounts paid or incurred after December 31, 1993.

[Conference Report]

The conference agreement includes a lobbying expense disallowance rule that contains elements from both the House bill and the Senate amendment.

General rule

Under the conference agreement, no deduction is allowed under section 162 for any amount paid or incurred in connection with (1) influencing Federal or State legislation or (2) any communication with certain covered Federal executive branch officials in an attempt to influence the official actions or positions of such officials.

The present-law rules disallowing business deductions for expenses of grass roots lobbying and participation in political campaigns will remain in effect. Similarly, the conferees intend that the present-law rule disallowing a deduction for lobbying of foreign governments will remain in effect.

Scope of general rule

The conference agreement applies to attempts to influence Federal or State legislation (as defined in present-law section 4911(e)(2)) through communication with a member or employee of Congress or a State legislative body, or with any other government official or employee who may participate in the formulation of legislation. [8] In addition, the conference agreement disallows a deduction for costs incurred in connection with any direct communication with a "covered executive branch official" in an attempt to influence the official actions or positions of such official. [9] For this purpose, the term "covered executive branch official" means the following Federal officials: (1) the president; (2) the Vice President; (3) an individual serving in a position in level I of the Executive Schedule (e.g., a Cabinet member) [10] or any other individual designated by the President as having Cabinet-level status; (4) any immediate deputy of an individual listed in (3) above; (5) the two most senior-level officers of each agency within the Exec-

[Footnote ¶ 3044 continued]

8. Thus, if a taxpayer communicates with any executive branch official or employee (regardless of rank) in an attempt to influence the official's or employee's participation in the Federal or State legislative process, then costs incurred in connection with the communication are nondeductible. Under present-law section 4911 regulations, "legislation" does not include actions of Federal or State administrative or special purpose bodies, whether elective or appointive (Treas. Reg. sec. 56.4911-2(d)(4)).

9. The conferees intend that direct communications include all written and oral communications with covered executive branch officials. A communication will be considered to be a direct communication with a covered executive branch official if such official is the intended primary recipient of the communication, regardless of whether the communication is formally addressed to the official.

10. See 5 U.S. Code sec. 5312.

utive Office of the President; [11] and (6) any other officer or employee of the White House Office of the Executive Office of the President.

The conference agreement does not apply to attempts to influence legislative actions of a "local council or similar governing body." [12] The conferees intend that any legislative body of a political subdivision of a State (e.g., a county or city council) be considered to be a "local council or similar governing body." Thus, attempts to influence the actions of such local bodies are not affected by the conference agreement and remain subject to present-law rules. [13]

De minimis rule

The conference agreement provides a de minimis rule that exempts certain in-house lobbying expenditures from the general disallowance rule if a taxpayer's total amount of such expenditures for a taxable year does not exceed $2,000 (computed without taking into account general overhead costs otherwise allocable to lobbying). For purposes of this rule, "in-house expenditures" means expenditures for lobbying (e.g., labor and materials costs) other than (1) payments to a person engaged in the trade or business of lobbying to conduct lobbying for the taxpayer (e.g., a payment to hire a professional lobbyist), and (2) dues or other similar payments that are allocable to lobbying (e.g., association dues).

Thus, so long as a taxpayer's in-house lobbying expenditures do not exceed $2,000, such expenditures (including allocable overhead) may be disregarded and are not subject to the disallowance rule. However, payments made by a taxpayer to third-party lobbyists and dues payments allocable to lobbying are subject to the disallowance rules of the conference agreement, regardless of whether or not the taxpayer's in-house expenses are exempted under the de minimis rule. [14] In addition, the de minimis rule contained in the conference agreement does not apply to expenses incurred for political activity, grass-roots lobbying, or foreign lobbying, which continue to be disallowed in their entirety under present-law ruled.

Activities in support of lobbying

The conference agreement provides that any amount paid or incurred for research for, or preparation, planning, or coordination of, any lobbying activity subject to the general disallowance rule described above will be treated as paid or incurred in connection with such lobbying activity.

The conferees intend that the Secretary of the Treasury will provide guidance for distinguishing costs incurred in connection with (1) attempts to influence legislation from (2) mere monitoring of legislative activities where there is no attempt to influence the formulation or enactment of legislation. In cases where a taxpayer (or tax-exempt organization) monitors legislation and subsequently attempts to influence the formulation or enactment of the same (or similar) legislation, the conferees intend the costs of the monitoring activities generally will be treated as incurred "in connection with" nondeductible lobbying activity. [15]

In determining the expenses incurred in connection with any direct communication with a covered executive branch official in an attempt to influence the official actions or positions of such official, only the costs attributable to the direct communication itself are nondeductible under the conference agreement.

[Footnote ¶3044 continued]

11. In the case of councils or other agencies within the Executive Office of the president with respect to which the president, Vice president or one or more Cabinet members serve as ranking members, the covered officers include the two most senior administrative officers (other than the ranking members) of the council or agency.

12. The conference agreement provides that, for purposes of the section 162 lobbying rules, a tribal government of an Indian reservation will be treated as a "local council or similar governing body." Thus, lobbying with respect to such tribal governments continues to be governed by present-law rules.

13. Under present law, at the local government level, lobbying expenses are deductible only if incurred in direct connection with communications to government officials (or an organization of which the taxpayer is a member) with respect to local legislation of direct interest to the taxpayer (and to the organization). Expenditures for grass roots lobbying with respect to local legislation or for participation in local elections are not deductible.

14. The conference agreement includes a de minimis rule primarily to provide administrative convenience to taxpayers. Therefore, if, during a taxable year, a taxpayer incurs in-house expenditures in excess of $2,000, then the full amount of its lobbying expenses must be determined and such amount (including the first $2,000 of in-house expenditures) is subject to the disallowance rule.

15. In addition, the conferees intend that the Secretary of the Treasury will permit taxpayers to adopt reasonable methods for allocating expenses to lobbying (and related research and other background) activities in order to reduce taxpayer recordkeeping responsibilities.

Thus, for example, if a taxpayer works for an extended period to influence the actions of non-covered executive branch officials and, at the end of the project, a covered executive branch official approves the final decision through a separate communication with the taxpayer (e.g., a briefing or review of the matter), only the direct costs of the communication with the covered official would be disallowed (and not the costs of the work product from the earlier period). In contrast, if a taxpayer conducts research and analysis with a view toward directly communicating with a covered executive branch official, the costs of such research and analysis would be disallowed as attributable to the direct communication with the covered official.

Exceptions

The conference agreement does not include any of the statutory exceptions to the general disallowance rule that are contained in the House bill or Senate amendment. However, the conferees wish to clarify that (consistent with pre-1962 interpretations) any communication compelled by subpoena, or otherwise compelled by Federal or State law, does not constitute an "attempt to influence" legislation or an official's actions and, therefore, is not subject to the general disallowance rule.

Association dues

The conference agreement provides a flow-through rule to disallow a deduction for a portion of the membership dues (or similar payments [16]) paid to a tax-exempt organization (other than a charitable organization) which engages in political or lobbying activities. Trade associations and similar organizations generally are required under the conference agreement to provide annual information disclosure (but not Form 1099 information reporting) to members estimating the portion of their dues allocable to lobbying. However, such disclosure is not required for an organization that (1) incurs only de minimis amounts of in-house lobbying expenditures; (2) elects to pay a proxy tax on its lobbying expenditures incurred during the taxable year; or (3) establishes pursuant to Treasury regulation (or other procedure) that substantially all of its dues monies are paid by members not entitled fro deduct such dues in computing their taxable income.

De minimis rule

Under the conference agreement, in-house lobbying expenses of $2,000 or less incurred by a tax-exempt organization during a taxable year are exempt from the general disallowance rule. This de minimis rule for tax-exempt organizations operates in the same manner as the de minimis rule for taxable businesses (described above). That is, in determining whether the $2,000 de minimis exception applies, an organization is required to take into account any direct in-house expenses incurred for lobbying activities (i.e., labor and materials costs), but may disregard indirect expenses (i.e., a portion of general overhead) otherwise allocable to lobbying. Amounts paid to outside lobbyists (or as dues to another organization that lobbies) do not qualify for the de minimis exception.

Information disclosure

Tax-exempt organizations that engage in more than a de minimis amount of in-house lobbying (or make payments to third-party lobbyists or other associations that lobby) generally are required to meet certain disclosure requirements. First, the organization must disclose on its annual tax return both the total amount of its lobbying and political expenditures (as defined by the provisions of the conference agreement), and the total amount of dues (or similar payments) allocable to such expenditures. For this purpose, an organization's lobbying expenditures for the taxable year are allocated to the dues received during the taxable year. Any excess amount of lobbying expenditures is carried forward and allocated to dues received in the following taxable year.

An organization also is required to provide notice to each person paying dues (or similar payments) at the time of assessment or payment of such dues (or similar payments) of the portion of dues that the organization reasonably estimates will be allocable to the organization' s lobbying expenditures during the year and that is, therefore, not deductible by the member. This estimate must be provided at the

[Footnote ¶3044 continued]

16. Payments that are similar to dues include voluntary payments made by members and special assessments imposed by the recipient organization to conduct lobbying activities. This is comparable to the treatment of special assessments for grass roots lobbying or campaign expenses under present-law Treasury Regulation section 1.162-20(c)(3).

time of assessment or payment of such dues and be reasonably calculated to provide organization members with adequate notice of the nondeductible amount. [17] If an organization's actual lobbying and political expenditures for a taxable year exceed the estimated allocable amount of such expenditures (either because of higher-than-anticipated lobbying expenses or lower-than-projected dues receipts), then the organization is required to pay a proxy tax on the excess amount or may seek permission to adjust the following year's notice of estimated expenditures, as described below.

Proxy tax

As an alternative to the disclosure requirements described above, an organization may elect to pay a proxy tax on the total amount of its lobbying expenditures (up to the amount of dues and other similar payments received by the organization) during the taxable year. If, for the current taxable year, an organization does not provide its members with reasonable notice of anticipated lobbying expenditures allocable to dues, then the organization is subject to the proxy tax on its aggregate lobbying expenditures for such year. Similarly, as stated above, an organization is required to pay a proxy tax on the amount by which its actual lobbying and political expenditures for a taxable year exceed the estimated allocable amount of such expenditures. [18]

If the amount of lobbying expenditures exceeds the amount of dues and other similar payments for the taxable year, the proxy tax is imposed on an amount equal to the dues and similar payments; any excess lobbying expenditures are carried forward to the next taxable year. [19] The proxy tax rate is equal to the highest corporate rate in effect for the taxable year. If an organization elects to pay the proxy tax rather than to provide any information disclosure to members, no portion of any dues or other payments made by members of the organization will be deemed non-deductible as the result of the organization's lobbying activities.

Waiver

If an organization establishes to the satisfaction of the Secretary of the Treasury (pursuant to regulation or other procedure) that substantially all of the dues monies it receives are paid by members who (even if lobbying were not involved) are not entitled to deduct their dues payments, then the organization is not subject to the disclosure requirements or the proxy tax. The conferees intend that the waiver be available to any organization that receives 90 percent or more of its total dues (and similar payments) from persons not entitled to deduct such payments. [20] The conference agreement contemplates that waivers will be provided pursuant to Treasury Department regulation or other Treasury Department procedure.

Penalties

Any organization that underreports the total amount of its lobbying expenses in any taxable year is required to pay the proxy tax (at the highest corporate tax rate) on any undisclosed or underreported amount. This tax may be imposed regardless of whether the organization has elected disclosure of lobbying expenses to its members or payment of the proxy tax for the taxable year. In such cases, the conferees intend that the proxy tax be imposed in addition to interest charges and any

[Footnote ¶3044 continued]

17. The conferees intend that such notice be provided in a conspicuous and easily recognizable format. See section 6113 and the regulations issued thereunder for guidance regarding the appropriate format of the disclosure statement.

18. In this case, the conference agreement grants the Secretary of the Treasury authority to waive the proxy tax otherwise imposed if an organization agrees to adjust its notice of estimated lobbying expenditures provided to members in the following year. Further, the conferees intend that the Secretary will prescribe regulations governing the treatment of organizations that incur actual lobbying expenditures below the estimated amount.

19. For example, if during a taxable year, an organization receives $100,000 in dues, spends $150,000 on lobbying and elects to pay the proxy tax (rather than provide flow-through disclosure to members), the proxy tax for that year would be imposed on $100,000 of lobbying expenditures. The remaining $50,000 of lobbying expenditures would be carried forward to the subsequent year, during which the organization could comply with the disclosure requirements outlined above or elect to pay the proxy tax with respect to such amount, as well as any additional lobbying expenditures incurred during that subsequent year.

20. Examples of such organizations include organizations that receive 90 percent or more of their dues monies from members that are tax-exempt charities or who are individuals not entitled to deduct the dues payments in determining taxable income because the payments are not ordinary and necessary business expenses. Another example would be a union that establishes to the satisfaction of the Secretary that 90 percent or more of its dues monies are paid by individuals who do not deduct such dues because of the operation of the two-percent floor on miscellaneous itemized deductions (sec. 67).

other penalties which may apply.[21]

Charities

Under the conference agreement, charitable organizations described in section 501(c)(3) are not subject to the disclosure requirements (or proxy tax option) imposed on other tax-exempt organizations. However, the conference agreement does contain an anti-avoidance rule designed to prevent donors from using charities as a conduit to conduct lobbying activities, the costs of which would be nondeductible if conducted directly by the donor.

Therefore, the conference agreement provides that no deduction will be allowed under sections 170 or 162 for amounts contributed to a charity that conducts lobbying activities, if (1) the charity's lobbying activities regard matters of direct financial interest to the donor's trade or business and (2) a principal purpose of the contribution is to avoid the general disallowance rule that would apply if the contributor directly had conducted such lobbying activities [22]

The conferees intend that the determination regarding a principal purpose of the contribution for purposes of this rule be based on the facts and circumstances surrounding the contribution, including the existence of any formal or informal instructions relating to the charity's use of the contribution for lobbying efforts (including nonpartisan analysis), the temporal nexus between the making of the contribution and conduct of the lobbying activities, and any historical pattern of contributions by the donor to the charity.

Anti-cascading rule

The conference agreement contains a special provision to prevent a "cascading" of the lobbying disallowance rule. The purpose of the provision is to ensure that, when multiple parties are involved, the general lobbying disallowance rule results in the denial of a deduction at only one level. Thus, the conference agreement provides that, in the case of a taxpayer engaged in the trade or business of lobbying activities or a taxpayer who is an employee and receives employer reimbursements for lobbying expenses, the disallowance rule does not apply to expenditures of the taxpayer in conducting such activities directly on behalf of a client or employer. Instead, the lobbying payments made by the client (or employer) to the lobbyist (or employee) are nondeductible under the general disallowance rule.

The anti-cascading rule applies where there is a direct, one-on-one relationship between the taxpayer and the entity conducting the lobbying activity, such as a client or employee relationship. Thus, the conferees intend that the anti-cascading rule will not apply to dues or other payments to taxable membership organizations which act to further the interests of their members rather than the interests of any one particular member. Such organizations are themselves subject to the general disallowance rule based on the amount of their lobbying expenditures, and dues payments to such organizations are not affected by the conference agreement.

Effective date

The conference agreement is effective for amounts paid or incurred after December 31, 1993.

[¶ 3045] Section 13223. Mark-to-Market Accounting Method for Dealers in Securities

(Code Sec. 475)

[House Explanation]

Present Law

A taxpayer that is a dealer in securities is required for Federal income tax purposes to maintain an inventory of securities held for

[Footnote ¶ 3044 continued]

21. See, e.g., section 6652(c)(1)(A)(ii).

22. The conference agreement does not alter present-law rules under sections 501(c)(3) and 4911 regarding the impact of lobbying on a charity's tax-exempt status. Thus, even if a contributor is subject to the anti-avoidance rule in a particular case because its payment to a charity is made with a principal purpose of funding "lobbying" as defined under section 162, the charity's tax-exempt status will not be jeopardized if its activity qualifies as non-partisan analysis or does not constitute "substantial lobbying" under the present-law section 501(c)(3) or section 4911 standards.

sale to customers. A dealer in securities is allowed for Federal income tax purposes to determine (or value) the inventory of securities held for sale based on: (1) the cost of the securities; (2) the lower of the cost or market (LCM) value of the securities; or (3) the market value of the securities.

If the inventory of securities is determined based on cost, unrealized gains and losses with respect to the securities are not taken into account for Federal income tax purposes. If the inventory of securities is determined based on the LCM value, unrealized losses (but not unrealized gains) with respect to the securities are taken into account for Federal income tax purposes. If the inventory of securities is determined based on market value, both unrealized gains and losses with respect to the securities are taken into account for Federal income tax purposes.

Under the so-called 'wash sale rule,' losses on the sale of securities are not allowed if the taxpayer acquires substantially identical securities within 30 days of the loss transaction. The wash sale rule does not apply to security dealers. Thus, a securities dealer that determines its inventory based on the cost of its securities may recognize losses on those securities that have built-in losses by selling the securities at year end, even if identical securities are acquired immediately to replenish the dealer's inventory.

Explanation of Provision

In general

The bill provides two general rules (the 'mark-to-market rules') that apply to certain securities that are held by a dealer in securities. First, any such security that is inventory in the hands of the dealer is required to be included in inventory at its fair market value. Second, any such security that is not inventory in the hands of the dealer and that is held as of the close of an taxable year is treated as sold by the dealer for its fair market vale on the last business day of the taxable year and any gain or loss is required to be taken into account by the dealer in determining gross income for that taxable year. [37]

If gain or loss is taken into account with respect to a security by reason of the second mark-to-market rule, then the amount of gain or loss subsequently realized as a result of a sale, exchange, or other disposition of the security, or as a result of the application of the mark-to-market rules, is to be appropriately adjusted to reflect such gain or loss. In addition, the bill authorizes the Treasury Department to promulgate regulations that provide for the application of the second mark-to-market rule at times other than the close of a taxable year or the last business day of a taxable year.

The mark-to-market rules do not apply for purposes of determining the holding period of any security. In addition, the mark-to-market rules do not apply in determining whether gain or loss is recognized by any other taxpayer that may be a party to a contract with a dealer in securities.

Character of gain or loss

Any gain or loss taken into account under the provision (or any gain or loss recognized with respect to a security that would be subject to the provision if held at the end of the year) generally is treated as ordinary gain or loss. This character rule does not apply to any gain or loss allocable to any period during which the security (1) is a hedge of a position, right to income, or a liability that is not subject to a mark-to-market rule under the provision, or (2) is held by the taxpayer other than in its capacity as a dealer in securities. In addition, the character rule does not apply to any security that is improperly identified (as described in detail below) by the taxpayer.

No inference is intended as to the character of any gain or loss recognized in taxable years prior to the enactment of this provision or any gain or loss recognized with respect to any property to which this character rule does not apply.

Definitions

A dealer in securities is defined as any taxpayer that either (1) regularly purchases securities from, or sells securities to, customers in the ordinary course of a trade or business, or (2) regularly offers to enter into, assume, offset, assign, or otherwise terminate positions in

[Footnote ¶ 3044 continued]

37. For purpose of this provision, a security is treated as sold to a person that is not related to the dealer even if the security is itself a contact between the dealer and a related person. Thus, for example, sections 267 and 707(b) of the Code are not to apply to any less that is required to be taken into account under this provision.

securities with customers in the ordinary course of a trade or business.

A security is defined as: (1) any share of stock in a corporation; (2) any partnership or beneficial ownership interest in a widely-held or publicly-traded partnership or trust; (3) any note, bond, debenture, or other evidence of indebtedness; (4) any interest rate, current, or equity notional principal contract (but not any other notional principal contract such as a notional principal contract that is based on the price of oil, wheat, or other commodity); and (5) any evidence of an interest in, or any derivative financial instrument in, any currency or in a security described in (1) through (4) above, including any option, forward contract, short position, or any similar financial instrument in such a security or currency.

In addition, a security is defined to include any position if: (1) the position is not a security described in the preceding paragraph; (2) the position is a hedge with respect to a security described in the receding paragraph; and (3) before the close of the day on which the position was acquired or entered into (or such other time as the Treasury Department may specify in regulations), the position is clearly identified in the dealer's records as a hedge with respect to a security described in the preceding paragraph.

A security, however, is not to include a contract to which section 1256(a) of the Code applies, unless such contract is a hedge of a security to which the provision applies. The special character rule of the bill (rather than the special character rule of section 1256(a)) will any such contract that is a hedge of a security to which the bill applies.

A hedge is defined as any position that reduces the dealer's risk of interest rate or price changes or currency fluctuations, including any position that is reasonably expected to become a hedge within 60 days after the acquisition of the position.

Exceptions to the mark-to-market rules

Notwithstanding the definition of security, the mark-to-market rules generally do not apply to: (1) any security that is held for investment; [38] (2) any evidence of indebtedness that is acquired (including originated) by a dealer in the ordinary course of its trade or business, but only if the evidence of indebtedness is not held for sale; (3) any security which is a hedge with respect to a security that is not subject to the mark-to-market rules (i.e., any security that is a hedge with respect to (a) a security held for investment, or (b) an evidence of indebtedness described in (2); and (4) any security which is a hedge with respect to position, right to income is not a security in the hands of the taxpayer. [39] Whether or not a security or evidence of indebtedness is required to be marked-to-market under the applicable financial accounting rules is not dispositive for purposes of determining whether such security or evidence of indebtedness is treated as held for investment or as not held for sale under the provision.

To the extent provided in regulations to be promulgated by the Treasury Department, the exceptions to the mark-to-market rules for certain hedges do not apply to any security that is held by a taxpayer in its capacity as a dealer in securities. Thus, regulations may provide that the exceptions to the mark-to-market rules for certain hedges do not apply to securities that are entered into with customers in the ordinary course of a trade or business. In addition, a dealer may not treat a security that is identified as a hedge or as an investment as also held in its capacity as dealer. Thus, securities identified as qualifying for one of the exceptions to the mark-to-market rules may not be accounted for using the LCM or other inventory method of accounting.

In addition, the exceptions to the mark-to-market rules do not apply unless, before the close of the day on which the security (including any evidence of indebtedness) is acquired, originated, or entered into (or such other time as the Treasury Department may specify in regulations), [40] the security is clearly identified in the dealer's records as being described in

[Footnote ¶ 3045 continued]

38. To the extent provided in regulations to be promulgated by the Treasury Department, the exception to the mark-to-market rules for a security that is held for investment is not to apply to any notional principal contract or any derivative financial instrument that is held by a dealer in such securities.

39. For purposes of the mark-to-market rules, debt issued by a taxpayer is not a security in the hands of such taxpayer.

40. It is anticipated that the Treasury regulations will permit a dealer that originates evidences of indebtedness in the ordinary course of a trade or business to identify such evidences of indebtedness as not held for sale based on the accounting practices of the dealer but in no event later than the date that is 30 days after the date that any such evidence of indebted-

one of the exceptions listed above. [41]

It is anticipated that the identification rules with respect to hedges will be applied in such a manner as to minimize the imposition of additional accounting burdens on dealers in securities. For example, it is understood that certain dealers in securities use accounting systems which treat certain transactions entered into between separate business units as if such transactions were entered into with unrelated third parties. It is anticipated that for purposes of the mark-to-market rules, such an accounting system generally will provide an adequate identification of hedges with third parties.

In addition to clearly identifying a security as qualifying for one of the exceptions to the mark-to-market rules listed above, a dealer must continue to hold the security in a capacity that qualifies the security for one of the exceptions listed above. If at any time after the close of the day on which the security was acquired, originated, or entered into (or such other time as the Treasury Department may specify in regulations), the security is not held in a capacity that qualifies the security for one of the exceptions listed above, then the mark-to-market rules are to apply to any changes in value of such security that occur after the security no longer qualifies for an exception. [42]

Improper identification

The bill provides that if (1) a dealer identifies a security as qualifying for an exception to the mark-to-market rules but the security does not qualify for that exception, or (2) a dealer fails to identify a position that is not a security as a hedge of a security but the position is a hedge of a security, then the mark-to-market rules are to apply to any such security or position, except that loss is to be recognized under the mark-to-market rules prior to the disposition of the security or position only to the extent of gain previously recognized under the mark-to-market rules (and not previously taken into account under this provision) with respect to the security or position.

Other rules

The bill provides that the uniform cost capitalization rules of section 263A of the Code and the rules of section 263(g) of the Code that require the capitalization of certain interest and carrying charges in the case of straddles do not apply to any security to which the mark-to-market rules apply because the fair market value of a security should include the costs that the dealer would otherwise capitalize.

In addition, a security subject to the provision is not to be treated as sold and reacquired for purposes of section 1091 of the Code. Section 1092 of the Code will apply to any loss recognized under the mark-to-market rules (but will have no effect if all the offsetting positions that make up the straddle are subject to the mark-to-market rules).

[Footnote ¶3045 continued]

ness is originated. Further, it is anticipated that the Treasury regulations will permit a dealer that enters into commitments to acquire mortgages to identify such commitments as being held for investment if the dealer acquires the mortgages and holds the mortgages as investments. It is anticipated that this identification of commitments to acquire mortgages will occur within a reasonable period after the acquisition of the mortgages but in no event later than the date that is 30 days after the date that the mortgages are acquired.

41. A security is to be treated as clearly identified in a dealer's records as being described in one of the exceptions listed above if all of securities of the taxpayer that are not so described are clearly identified in the dealer's records as not being described in such exception.

42. Any gain or loss that is attributable to the period that the security was not subject to the mark-to-market rules generally is to be taken into account at the lime that the security is actually sold (rather than treated as sold by reason of the mark-to-market rules). Conversely, different rules apply to a security that originally is held by the taxpayer in a capacity that subjects the security to the mark-to-market rules, but later becomes otherwise eligible for an exception from the mark-to-market rules. For example, assume that a security to which the mark-to-market rules apply is hedged (and thus the hedge is subject to the mark-to-market rules) and the security (but not the hedge) is sold before year end. In such case, the 'naked' hedge generally will be subject to the mark-to-market rules at the year end. However, the Treasury Department has authority to issue regulations that would allow the taxpayer to identify, on the date the security is sold, the 'naked' hedge as a security to which one of the exceptions to the mark-to-market rules (assuming the 'naked' hedge otherwise qualifies for the exception). In making this identification, it is anticipated that the taxpayer would be required to apply the mark-to-market rules to the 'naked' hedge as of the date of the sale of the security, take any resulting gain or loss into account for the taxable year of sale, and treat the 'naked' hedge as a security to which the exceptions to the mark-to-market rules apply. Whether or not the taxpayer is allowed under regulations to make the identification described above (and whether or not the taxpayer makes the identification), any gain or loss attributable to the period after the date of sale of the security will not be subject to special character rule of the bill if the hedge is not held by the taxpayer in its capacity as a dealer during such period. Thus, if the 'naked' hedge is a capital asset in the hands of the taxpayer, any gain or loss recognized with respect to the 'naked' hedge that is attributable to the period after the date of sale of the security will be capital gain or loss.

Furthermore, the bill provides that (1) the mark-to-market rules do not apply to any section 988 transaction (generally, a foreign currency transaction) that is part of a section 988 hedging transaction, and (2) the determination of whether a transaction is a section 988 transaction is to be made without regard to whether the transaction would otherwise be marked-to-market under the bill.

For purposes of the provision, fair market value generally is determined by valuing each security on an individual security basis. Thus, if a taxpayer holds a large block of securities of the same type, the securities should be valued without taking any blockage discount into account. It is expected that the Treasury Department will authorize the use of appropriate valuation methods that will alleviate unnecessary compliance burdens of taxpayers under the bill.

The bill also authorizes the Treasury Department to promulgate regulations which provide for the treatment of a hedge that reduce a dealer's risk of interest rate or price changes or currency fluctuations with respect to securities that are subject to the mark-to-market rules as well as with respect to securities, positions, rights to income, or liabilities that are not subject to the mark-to-market rules. It is anticipated that the Treasury regulations may allow taxpayers to treat any such hedge as not subject to the mark-to-market rules provided that such treatment is consistently followed from year to year.

Finally, the bill authorizes the Treasury Department to promulgate such regulations as may be necessary or appropriate to carry out the provisions of the bill, including rules to prevent the use of year-end transfers, related persons, or other arrangements to avoid the provisions of the bill. Such authority includes coordinating the mark-to-market rules with the original issue discount rules.

Other hedging transactions

The bill provides that any gain or loss with respect to hedges that are subject to the mark-to-market rules of the bill will be treated as ordinary gain or loss.

The committee understands that hedging transactions are also important to the management of risks by businesses that are not subject to these mark-to-market rules. Hedging transactions are part of a sound business strategy in fields as diverse as farming, banking, manufacturing and energy production.

The committee also understands that there has been increased uncertainty concerning the tax treatment of hedging transactions following a decision by the Supreme Court in 1988, Arkansas Best Corp. v. Commissioner, 485 U.S. 212 (1988). That decision held that a taxpayer could not claim an ordinary loss from the sale of subsidiary stock that purportedly had been acquired for the purpose of preserving the business reputation of the taxpayer. The committee believes that decision has created significant uncertainty for taxpayers engaging in legitimate business hedging transactions.

The level of uncertainty regarding the tax treatment of hedging transactions is a matter of great concern to the committee for it is the consumer who pays for the lack of good risk management and for market uncertainty. The committee believes this is a significant issue. To the extent a solution may require coordination between the executive and legislative branches, the committee urges the Administration, in the strongest terms, to advise the committee, within 90 days of the enactment of this Act, how best to proceed.

Effective Date

In general

The provision applies to taxable years ending on or after December 31, 1993. A taxpayer that is required to change its method of accounting to comply with the requirements of the provision is treated as having initiated the change in method of accounting and as having received the consent of the Treasury Department to make such change. The net amount of the section 481(a) adjustment is to be taken into account ratably over a 5-taxable year period beginning with the first taxable year ending on or after December 31, 1993.

The principles of section 8.03(1) and (2) of Rev. Proc. 92-20, 1992-12 I.R.B. 10, are to apply to the section 481(a) adjustment. It is anticipated that section 8.03(1) of Rev. Proc. 92-20 will be applied by taking into account all securities of a dealer that are subject to the mark-to-market rules (including those securities that are not inventory in the hands of the dealer). In addition, it is anticipated that net operating losses will be allowed to offset the section 481(a) adjustment, tax credit carryforwards will be allowed to offset any tax attributable to the section 481(a) adjustment, and, for purposes of determining liability for estimated taxes, the section 481(a) adjustment will be taken into account ratably throughout the taxable year in question.

In determining the amount of the section 481(a) adjustment for taxable years beginning before the date of enactment of the mark-to-market rules, the identification requirements are to be applied in a reasonable manner. It is anticipated that any security that was identified as being held for investment under section 1236(a) of the Code as of the last day of the taxable year preceding the taxable year of change is to be treated as held for investment for purposes of the mark-to-market rules. It is also anticipated that any other security that was held as of the last day of the taxable year preceding the taxable year of change is to be treated as properly identified if the dealer's records as of such date support such identification. [43]

Special rule for certain floor specialists and market makers

To the extent that a portion of the section 481(a) adjustment of a taxpayer is attributable to the use of the LIFO inventory method of accounting for any qualified security, such portion of the adjustment is taken into account ratably over the shorter of (1) a 20-taxable year period or (2) the number of years the taxpayer (or any predecessor) had utilized the LIFO inventory method for that security, beginning with the first taxable year ending on or after December 31, 1993. In no event may the period be less than 5 years. For this purpose, 'qualified security' means any security acquired (1) by a floor specialist (as defined in section 1236(d)(2)) in connection with the specialist's duties as a specialist on an exchange, but only if the security is one in which the specialist is registered with the exchange or (2) by a taxpayer who is a market maker in connection with the taxpayer's duties as market maker, but only if (a) the security is included on the National Association of Security Dealers Automated Quotation System, (b) the taxpayer is registered as a market maker in such security with the National Association of Security Dealers, and (c) as of the last day of the taxable year preceding the taxpayer's first taxable year ending on or after December 31, 1993, the taxpayer (or a predecessor of the taxpayer) has been actively engaged as a market maker in such security for a 2-year period ending on such date (or, if shorter, the period beginning 61 days after the security was listed in such quotation system and ending on such date.) The portion of the section 481(a) adjustment that is attributable to the use of the LIFO inventory method of accounting for any qualified security is determined under the rules described in section 312(n)(4) (without regard to the effective date of such section). In addition, the portion of the section 481(a) adjustment that is attributable to the use of the LIFO inventory method of accounting for qualified securities may not exceed the taxpayer's overall section 481(a) adjustment that is attributable to the use of the LIFO inventory method of accounting for any qualified security is determined under the rules described in section 312(n)(4) (without regard to the effective date of such section). In addition, the portion of the section 481(a) adjustment that is attributable to the use of the LIFO inventory method of accounting for qualified securities may not exceed the taxpayer's overall section 481(a) adjustment for all securities under the proposal.

[Senate Explanation]

Effective Date

In general

The provision applies to taxable years ending on or after December 31, 1993. A taxpayer that is required to change its method of accounting to comply with the requirements of the provision is treated as having initiated the change in method of accounting and as having received the consent of the Treasury Department to make such change. The net amount of the section 481(a) adjustment is to be taken into account ratably over a 5-taxable year period beginning, with the first taxable year ending on or after December 31, 1993.

The principles of section 8.03(1) and (2) of Rev. Proc. 92-20, 1992-12 I.R.B. 10, are to

[Footnote ¶ 3045 continued]

43. In addition, it is anticipated that in order for any security that is held on the date of enactment of the mark-to-market rules to qualify for one of the exceptions to the mark-to-market rules, the security must be identified as being described in one of the exceptions within a reasonable period after the date of enactment but in no event later than the date that is 30 days after the date of enactment.

apply to the section 481(a) adjustment. It is anticipated that section 8.03(1) of Rev. Proc. 92-20 will be applied by taking into account all securities of a dealer that are subject to the mark-to-market rules (including those securities that are not inventory in the hands of the dealer). In addition, it is anticipated that net operating losses will be allowed to offset the section 481(a) adjustment, tax credit carryforwards will be allowed to offset any tax attributable to the section 481(a) adjustment, and, for purposes of determining liability for estimated taxes, the section 481(a) adjustment will be taken into account ratably throughout the taxable year in question.

In determining the amount of the section 481(a) adjustment for taxable years beginning before the date of enactment of the mark-to-market rules, the identification requirements are to be applied in a reasonable manner. It is anticipated that any security that was identified as being held for investment under section 1236(a) of the Code as of the last day of the taxable year preceding the taxable year of change is to be treated as held for investment for purposes of the mark-to-market rules. It is also anticipated that any other security that was held as of the last day of the taxable year preceding the taxable year of change is to be treated as properly identified if the dealer's records as of such date support such identification.[7]

Special rule for certain floor specialists and market makers

To the extent that a portion of the section 481(a) adjustment of a taxpayer is attributable to the use of the LIFO inventory method of accounting for at least five taxable years for any qualified security, such portion of the adjustment is taken into account ratably over a 15-taxable year period, beginning with the first taxable year ending on or after December 31, 1993. For this purpose, 'qualified security' means any security acquired (1) by a floor specialist (as defined in section 1236(d)(2)) in connection with the specialist's duties as a specialist on an exchange, but only if the security is one in which the specialist is registered with the exchange or (2) by a taxpayer who is a market maker in connection with the taxpayer's duties as market maker, but only if (a) the security is included on the National Association of Security Dealers Automated Quotation System, (b) the taxpayer is registered as a market maker in such security with the National Association of Security Dealers, and (c) as of the last day of the taxable year preceding the taxpayer's first taxable year ending on or after December 31, 1993, the taxpayer (or a predecessor of the taxpayer) has been actively engaged as a market maker in such security for a 2-year period ending on such date (or, if shorter, the period beginning 61 days after the security was listed in such quotation system and ending on such date). The portion of the section 481(a) adjustment that is attributable to the use of the LIFO inventory method of accounting for any qualified security is determined under the rules described in section 312(n)(4) (without regard to the effective date of such section). In addition, the portion of the section 481(a) adjustment that is eligible to be taken into account over the 15-year period may not exceed the taxpayer's overall section 481(a) adjustment for all securities under the proposal.

[Conference Report]

Senate Amendment

In general

Except as provided below, the Senate amendment generally is the same as the House bill.

Exceptions to the mark-to-market rules

Under the Senate amendment, the mark-to-market rules generally do not apply to: (1) any security that is held for investment; (2) any security that is a hedge with respect to a security that is not subject to the mark-to-market rules (i.e., any security that is a hedge with respect to a security held for investment); or (3) any security which is a hedge with respect to a position, right to income, or a liability that is not a security in the hands of the taxpayer. Under the Senate amendment, securities held for investment include debt instruments acquired (including originated) by the taxpayer in the ordinary course of a trade or business of the

[Footnote ¶ 3045 continued]

7. In addition, it is anticipated that in order for any security that is held on the date of enactment of the mark-to-market rules to qualify for one of the exceptions to the mark-to-market rules, the security must be identified as being described in one of the exceptions within a reasonable period after the date of enactment but in no event later than the date that is 30 days after the date of enactment.

taxpayer and not held for sale.

Effective date

The effective date of the Senate amendment generally is the same as that of the House bill.

However, under the Senate amendment, to the extent that a portion of the section 481 (a) adjustment of a floor specialist or a market maker is attributable to the use of the LIFO inventory method of accounting for any qualified security, such portion of the adjustment generally is taken into account ratably over a 15-taxable year period if the taxpayer (or any predecessor) had utilized the LIFO inventory method for that security for at least 5 years.

Conference Agreement

The conference agreement generally follows the House bill, with the following modifications:

Exceptions to the mark-to-market rules

The exceptions to the mark-to-market rules do not apply unless, before the close of the day on which the security (including any evidence of indebtedness) is acquired, originated, or entered into (or such other time as the Treasury Department may specify in regulations), the security is clearly identified in the dealer's records as being described in one of the exceptions listed above. The conferees anticipate that the Treasury regulations will permit a financial institution that is treated as a dealer under the provision and that originates evidences of indebtedness in the ordinary course of a trade or business to identify such evidences of indebtedness as held for investment based on the accounting practices of the institution, but in no event later than the date that is 30 days after the date that any such evidence of indebtedness is originated. Where appropriate, Treasury regulations may provide similar identification rules for similar debt that is acquired, rather than originated, by a financial institution. Further, it is anticipated that the Treasury regulations will permit a dealer that enters into commitments to acquire mortgages to identify such commitments as being held for investment if the dealer acquires the mortgages and holds the mortgages as investments. It is anticipated that this identification of commitments to acquire mortgages will occur within an appropriate period after the acquisition of the mortgages, but in no event later than the date that is 30 days after the date that the mortgages are acquired.

Further, the conferees anticipate that the identification rules with respect to hedges will be applied in such a manner as to minimize the imposition of additional accounting burdens on dealers in securities. For example, it is understood that certain taxpayers engage in risk management strategies known as 'global hedging.' Under global hedging, the positions of one business unit of the taxpayer may be counter-balanced by positions of another separate business unit; any remaining net risk of the enterprise may then be hedged by entering into positions with unrelated third parties. The conferees understand that taxpayers engaging in global hedging often use accounting systems that clearly identify and treat the transactions entered into between the separate business units as if such transactions were entered into with unrelated third parties. The conferees anticipate that, subject to Treasury regulations, such an accounting system generally will provide adequate evidence for purposes of determining whether, and to what extent, a hedge with a third party is (1) a hedge of a security that is subject to the mark-to-market rules or (2) a hedge of a position, right to income, or a liability that is not subject to a mark-to-market rule, for purposes of applying the mark-to-market rules and the special character rule to a hedge with a third party.

Regulatory authority

The provision grants authority to the Treasury Department to promulgate regulations as may be necessary or appropriate to carry out the provisions of the bill. Such authority includes the authority to promulgate such regulations to prevent the use of year-end transfers, related persons, or other arrangements to take unintended advantage of the provisions of the bill. For instance, assume that an individual who is not subject to the mark-to-market rules contributes a security that has a built-in loss in the hands of the individual to a partnership that is subject to the mark-to-market rules. Consistent with rules that govern the treatment of a security that ceases to qualify for one of the exceptions to the mark-to-market rules in the hands of a single taxpayer, the Treasury regulations may provide that any loss that arose prior to the contribution to the partnership may not be taken into account by the partnership under the mark-to-market rules and that the suspended loss may be taken into account when the security is sold. Conversely, assume that prior to year end, a partnership that is subject to the mark-to-market rules distributes a security with a built-in gain to a partner that is not subject to such rules. Consistent with the authority to apply the mark-to-market rules at times other than at the end of a taxable year, the Treasury regulations may provide that the mark-to-market rules are to apply to the partnership with respect to such security as of the date of distribution.

Valuation of securities

The conference agreement does not provide any explicit rules mandating valuation methods that are required to be used for purposes of applying the mark-to-market rules. However, the conferees expect that the Treasury Department will authorize the use of valuation methods that will alleviate unnecessary compliance burdens for taxpayers and clearly reflect income for Federal income tax purposes.

Other hedging transactions

The conference agreement generally provides that any gain or loss with respect to hedges that are subject to the mark-to-market rules of the bill will be treated as ordinary gain or loss. The conferees understand that hedging transactions are also important to the management of risks by businesses that are not subject to these mark-to-market rules. Hedging transactions are part of a sound business strategy in fields as diverse as farming, banking, manufacturing and energy production. However, the conferees understand that there may be a level of uncertainty regarding the tax treatment of such hedging transactions following a decision by the United States Supreme Court in 1988, Arkansas Best Corp. v. Commissioner, 485 U.S. 212 (1988). Despite subsequent litigation, (e.g., Federal National Mortgage Association V. Commissioner, 100 T.C. No. 36 (June 17, 1993)), the scope of the United States Supreme Court decision, and its effect on hedging transactions, may be unclear in some instances. The conferees believe that this is a significant issue. To the extent a solution to this issue may require coordination between the executive and legislative branches, the conferees urge the Administration, in the strongest terms, to advise the House Ways and Means and the Senate Finance Committees, within 90 days of the enactment of this Act, how best to proceed.

Effective date

The conference agreement adopts the effective date contained in the Senate amendment.

[¶3046] Section 13224. Clarification of Treatment of Certain FSLIC Financial Assistance.

(Code Sec. 165, 166, 585, 593)

[House Explanation]

Present Law and Background

A taxpayer may claim a deduction for a loss on the sale or other disposition of property only to the extent that the taxpayer's adjusted basis for the property exceeds the amount realized on the disposition and the loss is not compensated for by insurance or otherwise (sec. 165 of the Code). In the case of a taxpayer on the specific charge-off method of accounting for bad debts, a deduction is allowable for the debt only to the extent that the debt becomes worthless and the taxpayer does not have a reasonable prospect of being reimbursed for the loss. If the taxpayer accounts for bad debts on the reserve method, the worthless portion of a debt is charged against the taxpayer's reserve for bad debts, potentially increasing the taxpayer's deduction for an addition to this reserve.

A special statutory tax rule, enacted in 1981, excluded from a thrift institution's income financial assistance received from the Federal Savings and Loan Insurance Corporation (FSLIC) [44], and prohibited a reduction in the tax basis of the thrift institution's assets on

[Footnote ¶3045 continued]

44. Until it was abolished by the Financial Institutions Reform, Recovery and Enforcement Act of 1989 (FIRREA), FSLIC insured the deposits of its member savings and loan associations and was responsible for insolvent member institutions. FIRREA abolished FSLIC and established the FSLIC Resolution Fund (FRF) to assume all of the assets and liabilities of FSLIc (other than those expressly assumed or transferred to the Resolution Trust Corporation (RTC)). FRF is administered by the Federal Deposit Insurance Corporation (FDIC). The term "FSLIC" is used hereafter to refer to FSLIC and any successor to FSLIC.

account of the receipt of the assistance. Under the Technical and Miscellaneous Revenue Act of 1988 (TAMRA), taxpayers generally were required to reduce certain tax attributes by one-half the amount of financial assistance received from the FSLIC pursuant to certain acquisitions of financially troubled thrift institutions occurring after December 31, 1988. These special rules were repealed by FIRREA, but still apply to transactions that occurred before May 10, 1989.

Prior to the enactment of FIRREA, the FSLIC entered into a number of assistance agreements in which it agreed to provide loss protection to acquirers of troubled thrift institutions by compensating them for the difference between the book value and sales proceeds of "covered assets." "Covered assets" typically are assets that were classified as nonperforming or troubled at the time of the assisted transaction but could include other assets as well. Many of these covered assets are also subject to yield maintenance guarantees, under which the FSLIC guaranteed the acquirer a minimum return or yield on the value of the assets. The assistance agreements also generally grant the FSLIC the right to purchase covered assets. In addition, many of the assistance agreements permit the FSLIC to order assisted institutions to write down the value of covered assets on their books to fair market value in exchange for a payment in the amount of the write-down.

Under most assistance agreements, one or more Special Reserve Accounts are established and maintained to account for the amount of FSLIC assistance owed by the FSLIC to the acquired entity. The assistance agreements generally specify the precise circumstances under which amounts with respect to covered assets are debited to an account. Under the assistance agreements, these debit entries generally are made subject to prior FSLIC direction or approval. When amounts are so debited, the FSLIC generally becomes obligated to pay the debited balance in the account to the acquirer at such times and subject to such offsets as are specified in the assistance agreement.

In September 1990, the Resolution Trust Corporation (RTC), in accordance with the requirements of FIRREA, issued a report to Congress and the Oversight Board of the RTC on certain FSLIC-assisted transactions (the "1988/89 FSLIC transactions"). The report recommended further study of the covered loss and other tax issues relating to these transactions. A March 4, 1991 Treasury Department report ("Treasury report") on tax issues relating to the 1988/89 FSLIC transactions concluded that deductions should not be allowed for losses that are reimbursed with exempt FSLIC assistance. The Treasury report states that the Treasury view is expected to be challenged in the courts and recommended that Congress enact clarifying legislation disallowing these deductions.[45]

Reasons for Change

Allowing tax deductions for losses on covered assets that are compensated for by FSLIC assistance gives thrift institutions a perverse incentive to minimize the value of these assets when sold. The FSLIC, and not the institution, bears the economic burden corresponding to any reduction in value because it is required to reimburse the thrift institution for the loss. However, the tax benefit to the thrift institution and its affiliates increases as tax losses are enhanced. The thrift institution, therefore, has an incentive to minimize the value of covered assets in order to maximize its claimed tax loss and the attendant tax savings.

It is desirable to clarify, as of the date of the Treasury Report, that FSLIC assistance with respect to certain losses is taken into account as compensation for purposes of the loss and bad debt deduction provisions of the Code.

Explanation of Provision

General rule

Any FSLIC assistance with respect to any loss of principal, capital, or similar amount upon the disposition of an asset shall be taken into account as compensation for such loss for purposes of section 165 of the Code. Any FSLIC assistance with respect to any debt shall be taken into account for purposes of determining whether such debt is worthless (or the extent to which such debt is worthless) and in determining the amount of any addition to a reserve for bad debts. For this purpose, FSLIC assistance means any assistance or

[Footnote ¶3046 continued]

45. Department of the Treasury, Report on Tax Issues Relating to the 1988/89 Federal Savings and Loan Insurance Corporation Assisted Transactions, March, 1991 at pp. 16-17.

right to assistance with respect to a domestic building and loan association (as defined in section 7701(a)(19) of the Code without regard to subparagraph (C) thereof) under section 406(f) of the National Housing Act or section 21A of the Federal Home Loan Bank Act (or under any similar provision of law).[46]

Thus, if a taxpayer disposes of an asset entitled to FSLIC assistance, no deduction is allowed under section 165 of the Code for a loss (if any) on the disposition of the asset to the extent the assistance agreement contemplates a right to receive FSLIC assistance with respect to the loss. Similarly, if a loan held by a taxpayer constitutes an asset entitled to FSLIC assistance, the thrift institution shall not charge off any amount of the loan covered by the assistance agreement against the bad debt reserve and no charge-off will be taken into account in computing an addition to the reserve under the experience method, to the extent the assistance agreement contemplates a right to receive FSLIC assistance on a write-down of such asset under the agreement or on a disposition. The institution also shall not be allowed to deduct such amount of the loan under the specific charge-off method.[47]

It is intended that the right to FSLIC assistance for purposes of this provision is to be determined by reference to the gross amount of FSLIC assistance that is contemplated by the assistance agreement with respect to the sale or other disposition, or write-down, without taking into account any offsets that might reduce the net amount FSLIC is obligated to pay under the agreement. For example, under an assistance agreement an institution's right to be reimbursed for a loss on the disposition or write-down of an asset may be reflected as a debit to a Special Reserve Account, while certain other items that will reduce the ultimate amount of assistance to be paid may be reflected as credits to the account. In such a case, the gross amount of FSLIC assistance contemplated by the agreement is the amount represented by the debit, without regard to any offset.

Financial assistance to which the FIRREA amendments apply

The provision does not apply to any financial assistance to which the amendments made by section 1401(a)(3) of FIRREA apply.

No inference

No inference is intended as to prior law or as to the treatment of any item to which this provision does not apply.

Effective Date

In general

The provision applies to financial assistance credited on or after March 4, 1991, with respect to (1) assets disposed of and charge-offs made in taxable years ending on or after March 4, 1991; and (2) assets disposed of and charge-offs made in taxable years ending before March 4, 1991, but only for purposes of determining the amount of any net operating loss carryover to a taxable year ending on or after March 4, 1991.

For this purpose, financial assistance generally is considered to be credited when the taxpayer makes an approved debit entry to a Special Reserve Account required to be maintained under the assistance agreement to reflect the asset disposition or write-down. An amount will also be considered to be credited prior to March 4, 1991 if the asset was sold, with prior FSLIC approval, before that date.

An amount is not deemed to be credited for purposes of the provision merely because the FSLIC has approved a management or business plan or similar plan with respect to an asset or group of assets, or has otherwise generally approved a value with respect to an asset.

As an example of the application of the effective date of the provision, assume that a thrift institution is subject to a FSLIC assistance agreement that, through the use of a Special Reserve Account, operates to compensate the institution for the difference between the book and fair market values of certain covered assets upon their disposition or write-down. Further assume that on February 1, 1991 the thrift institution wrote down a cov-

[Footnote ¶ 3046 continued]

46. FSLIC assistance for purposes of the provision does not include "net worth assistance". "Net worth assistance" is generally computed at the time of an acquisition, without targeting loss coverage to ultimate dispositions or write-downs with respect to particular assets.

47. It is expected that, for purposes of the adjusted current earnings adjustment of the corporate alternative minimum tax, there will not be any net positive adjustment to the extent that FSLIC assistance is taken into account as compensation for a loss or in determining worthlessness and there is, therefore, no deductible loss or bad debt charge-off.

ered asset that has a book value and tax basis of $100 to $60, the asset's fair market value. With FSLIC approval, the institution debited the Special Reserve Account prior to March 4, 1991, to reflect the write-down of $40, and properly submitted to the FSLIC a summary of the account that reflected that debit, along with other debits for the quarter ended March 31, 1991. The provision would not apply to a loss claimed by the thrift institution with respect to the write-down of the covered asset on February 1, 1991. The same result would apply if the institution had sold the asset for $60 on February 1 with prior FSLIC approval. In the sale case, the provision would not apply even if there were no debit to the Special Reserve Account prior to March 4, 1991, so long as the FSLIC approved the amount of the reimbursable loss for purposes of providing assistance under the agreement.

Application to certain net operating losses

The provision applies to the determination of any net operating loss [48] carried into a taxable year ending on or after March 4, 1991, to the extent that the net operating loss is attributable to a loss or charge-off for which the taxpayer had a right to FSLIC assistance which had not been credited before March 4, 1991.

For example, assume a calendar year thrift institution is a party to a FSLIC assistance agreement that compensates the institution for the amount that covered loans are written down or charged off pursuant to the agreement. The agreement provides that the institution must receive the prior approval of the FSLIC to write down a loan for purposes of this compensation. Further assume that the institution uses the experience method to account for bad debts for tax purposes, and that in 1990 it charged off $100 with respect to a covered loan. Assume that this charge-off initially reduced the taxpayer's bad debt reserve balance by $100 and allowed the taxpayer to increase its addition to its reserve by $100 to bring the reserve to an appropriate balance. The taxpayer deducted this amount and utilized $20 for the year ended in 1990 (i.e., the last taxable year of the taxpayer ending before March 4, 1991). This produced a net operating loss of $80 for the remainder. The net operating loss is carried forward to 1991 (a taxable year of the taxpayer ending on or after March 4, 1991). Assume that the taxpayer did not debit the Special Reserve Account prior to March 4, 1991. The net operating loss carried to 1991 would be redetermined taking into account the provision. Applying the provision to 1990 would result in disallowing the charge-off of the $100 loan against the experience method reserve, in effect disallowing the $100 addition to the reserve. In such case, the taxpayer would continue to owe no tax for 1990, but the $80 net operating loss would be disallowed. However, the taxpayer's tax liability for 1990 would not be redetermined under the provision.

As a further example, assume that the net operating loss described in the example directly above were carried back to, and absorbed in, an earlier year ending prior to March 4, 1991 (rather than being carried forward). In that case, the provision would not apply to reduce the net operating loss carryback.

Estimated taxes

Finally, in accordance with the general estimated tax penalty provisions of the bill, no addition to tax is to be made under section 6654 or 6655 of the Code for any period before March 16, 1994 in the case of a corporation (April 16, 1994 in the case of an individual). However, in providing this relief, no inference is intended as to prior law, the effect of the provision on prior law, or the treatment of any item to which this provision does not apply.

[Conference Report]

Senate Amendment

The Senate amendment is the same as the House bill.

Conference Agreement

The conference agreement is the same as the House bill and the Senate amendment.

As stated in both the House and Senate committee reports, It is expected that for purposes of the adjusted current earnings adjustment of the corporate alternative minimum tax, there will not be any net positive adjustment to the extent that FSLIC assistance is taken into account as compensation for a loss

[Footnote ¶3046 continued]

48. For purposes of determining any alternative minimum tax net operating loss carryover to periods ending on or after March 4, 1991, it is expected that the principles described in the preceding footnote will apply.

or in determining worthlessness and there is, therefore, no deductible loss or bad debt charge off. The conferees wish to clarify that this result is expected to apply to all taxpayers, including those who received IRS determinations regarding the treatment of FSLIC assistance for earnings and profits purposes in the form of a ruling or closing agreement. The conferees also wish to clarify that, for all taxpayers, Treasury is expected to treat such FSLIC assistance for other earnings and profits purposes in a manner that is consistent with the purposes of this provision.

[¶3047] Section 13225. Modification of Corporate Estimated Tax Rules

(Code Sec. 6655)

[House Explanation]

Present Law

A corporation is subject to an addition to tax for any underpayment of estimated tax. For taxable years beginning after June 30, 1992, and before 1997, a corporation does not have an underpayment of estimated tax if it makes four equal timely estimated tax payments that total at least 97 percent of the tax liability shown on its return for the current taxable year. A corporation may estimate its current year tax liability prior to year-end by annualizing its income through the period ending with either the month or the quarter ending prior to the estimated tax payment due date. For taxable years beginning after 1996, the 97-percent requirement becomes a 91-percent requirement.

A corporation that is not a "large corporation" generally may avoid the addition to tax if it makes four timely estimated tax payments each equal to at least 25 percent of the tax liability shown on its return for the preceding taxable year. A large corporation may also use this rule with respect to its estimated tax payment for the first quarter of its current taxable year. A large corporation is one that had taxable income of $1 million or more for any of the three preceding taxable years.

Explanation of Provision

In general

For taxable years beginning after December 31, 1993, a corporation that does not use the 100 percent of last year's liability safe harbor for its estimated tax payments is required to base its estimated tax payments on 100 percent (rather than 97 percent or 91 percent) of the tax shown on its return for the current year, whether such tax is determined on an actual or annualized basis.

The bill does not change the present-law availability of the 100 percent of last year's liability safe harbor for large or small corporations.

Annualization periods

In addition, the bill modifies the rules relating to income annualization for corporate estimated tax purposes. In general, the bill (1) adds a new, third set of periods over which corporations may elect to annualize income and (2) requires corporations to annually elect which of the three periods they will use to annualize income for the year.

Specifically, under the bill, annualized income is to be determined based on the corporation's income for the first 3 months of the taxable year (in the case of the first and second estimated tax installments); the first 6 months of the taxable year (in the case of the third estimated tax installment); and the first 9 months of the taxable year (in the case of the fourth estimated tax installment). Alternatively, a corporation may elect to determine its annualized income based on the corporation's income for either: (1) the first 2 months of the taxable year (in the case of the first estimated tax installment); the first 4 months of the taxable year (in the case of the second estimated tax installment); the first 7 months of the taxable year (in the case of the third estimated tax installment); and the first 10 months of the taxable year (in the case of the fourth estimated tax installment); or (2) the first 3 months of the taxable year (in the case of the first estimated tax installment); the first 5 months of the taxable year (in the case of the second estimated tax installment); the first 8 months of the taxable year (in the case of the third estimated tax installment); and the first 11 months of the taxable year (in the case of the fourth estimated tax installment). An election to use either of the annualized income patterns described in (1) or (2) above must be made on or before the due date of the first estimated tax installment for the taxable year for which the election is to apply, in a manner prescribed by the Secretary of the Treasury.

Effective Date

The provision is effective for taxable years beginning after December 31, 1993.

[Conference Report]

Senate Amendment

The Senate amendment is the same as the House bill.

Conference Agreement

The conference agreement follows the House bill and the Senate amendment.

[¶ 3048] Section 13226(a). Repeal the Stock-for-Debt Exception to Cancellation of Indebtedness Income

(Code Sec. 108)

[Senate Explanation]

Present Law

Gross income generally includes cancellation of indebtedness (COD) income. Taxpayers in title 11 cases and insolvent taxpayers, however, generally exclude COD income from gross income but reduce tax attributes by the amount of COD income. The amount of COD income that an insolvent taxpayer excludes cannot exceed the amount by which the taxpayer is insolvent.

The amount of COD income generally is the difference between the adjusted issue price of the debt being cancelled and the amount of cash and the value of any property used to satisfy the debt. Thus, for purposes of determining the amount of COD income of a debtor corporation that transfers stock to a creditor in satisfaction of its indebtedness, the corporation generally is treated as realizing COD income equal to the excess of the adjusted issue price of the debt over the fair market value of the stock. However, if the debtor corporation is in a title 11 case or is insolvent, the excess of the debt discharged over the fair market value of the transferred stock generally does not constitute COD income (the "stock-for-debt exception"). [1] Thus, a corporate debtor that qualifies for the stock-for-debt exception is not required to reduce its tax attributes as a result of the debt discharge. The stock-for-debt exception does not apply to the issuance of certain preferred stock, nominal or token shares of stock, or stock to unsecured creditors on a relatively disproportionate basis. In the case of an insolvent debtor not in a title 11 case, the exception applies only to the extent the debtor is insolvent.

Reasons for Change

The committee believes that the present-law stock-for-debt exception distorts the proper measurement of economic income. In addition, because the stock-for-debt exception results in the forgiveness of tax related to COD income without a corresponding reduction in tax attributes, a corporation emerging from bankruptcy may enjoy a significant tax advantage not enjoyed by either a comparable solvent firm that restructures its debt outside bankruptcy or a start-up company. Finally, the ancillary rules surrounding the eligibility for, and the mechanics of, the stock-for debt exception are complex and cumbersome.

Explanation of Provision

The provision repeals the stock-for-debt exception. Thus, regardless of whether a debtor corporation is insolvent or in bankruptcy, the transfer of its stock in satisfaction of its indebtedness is treated as if the corporation satisfied the indebtedness with an amount of money equal to the fair market value of the stock that had been transferred. Under the provision, a bankrupt or insolvent corporation may exclude from income all or a portion of the COD income created by the transfer of its stock in satisfaction of indebtedness by reduc-

[Footnote ¶ 3046 continued]

[Footnote ¶ 3048] 1. In addition, if the debtor corporation issues both stock and other consideration to a creditor in satisfaction of indebtedness, the non-stock consideration is generally treated as satisfying an amount of debt equal to the value of such consideration, with the stock being considered as satisfying the remainder. Thus, if such transaction qualifies for the stock-for-debt exception, the entire amount of COD income realized by the debtor corporation in the transaction generally is excluded from gross income.

ing tax attributes.

Effective Date

The provision is effective for stock transferred in satisfaction of any indebtedness after June 17, 1993, unless (1) the transfer is in a title 11 or similar case filed on or before June 17, 1993; (2) the transfer occurs on or before December 31, 1993, and the transfer is pursuant to a binding contract in effect on June 17, 1993; or (3) the transfer occurs on or before December 31, 1993, and the taxpayer had filed with the SEC on or before June 17, 1993, a registration statement which proposed a stock-for-debt exchange with respect to such indebtedness, and which discussed the possible application of the stock-for-debt exception to such exchange.

[Conference Report]

The conference agreement follows the Senate amendment with the following modifications.

The conference agreement provides authority to the Treasury Department to promulgate such regulations as are necessary to coordinate the present-law rules regarding the acquisition by a corporation of its debt from a shareholder as a contribution to capital (sec. 108 (e)(6)) with the repeal of the stock-for-debt exception.

In addition, the conferees clarify that no inference is intended with the enactment of this provision as to the treatment of any cancellation of the indebtedness of any entity that is not a corporation in exchange for an ownership or equity interest in such entity.

Effective Date

The provision is effective for stock transferred after December 31, 1994, in satisfaction of any indebtedness, unless the transfer is in a title 11 or similar case that was filed on or before December 31, 1993.

[¶3049] Section 13226(b). Amendments to Attribute Reduction Rules for Debt Cancellation Income

(Code Sec. 108(b))

[Senate Explanation]

Present Law

The discharge of indebtedness generally gives rise to gross income to the debtor taxpayer. Present law provides exceptions to this general rule. Among the exceptions are rules providing that income from the discharge of indebtedness of the taxpayer is excluded from income if the discharge occurs in a title 11 case, the discharge occurs when the taxpayer is insolvent, or in the case of certain farm indebtedness (sec. 108(a)(1)). The amount excluded from income under these exceptions is applied to reduce tax attributes of the taxpayer. The tax attributes reduced (in order) are (1) net operating losses and carryovers, (2) general business credit carryovers, (3) net capital losses and capital loss carryovers, (4) the basis of certain property of the taxpayer, and (5) foreign tax credit carryovers (sec. 108(b)). The amount of the reduction is generally one dollar for each dollar excluded, except that the reduction in the case of credits is 33-1/3 cents for each dollar excluded.

Under present law, the passive loss rules limit deductions and credits from passive trade or business activities (sec. 469) Deductions attributable to passive activities, to the extent they exceed income from passive activities, generally may not be deducted against other income, such as wages, portfolio income, or business income that is not derived from a passive activity. A similar rule applies with respect to credits from passive activities. Deductions and credits suspended under these rules are carried forward to the next taxable year, and suspended losses are allowed in full when the taxpayer disposes of his entire interest in the passive activity to an unrelated person. Passive losses and credits are not tax attributes that are reduced under the rule relating to exclusion of discharge of indebtedness income.

Present law generally allows a minimum tax credit against a taxpayer's regular tax for the taxable year, for taxpayers who paid alternative minimum tax in a prior year (sec. 53). The minimum tax credit generally is the excess of (1) the sum of the minimum tax imposed for all prior taxable years following 1986, over (2) the amount allowed as a minimum tax credit for those prior taxable years. For purposes of determining this excess, in the case of a taxpayer other than a corporation, the minimum tax imposed does not include the minimum tax attributable to exclusion preferences (i.e., adjustments and items of tax preference in sec. 56(b)(1) and sec. 57(a)(1), (5) and (6)), and is determined without regard to sec. 59(a)(2) (relating to the alternative minimum tax foreign tax credit). The minimum tax credit cannot exceed the taxpayer's regular tax liability for the taxable year (reduced by certain credits allowable and reduced by the taxpayer's tentative minimum tax for the taxable year). Minimum tax credits are not tax attributes that are reduced under the rule relating to exclusion of discharge of indebtedness income.

Reasons for Change

Reduction of tax attributes in lieu of current inclusion of certain discharge of indebtedness income provides deferral rather than permanent exclusion of such discharge of indebtedness income. The committee understands that the rationale for providing deferral of discharge of indebtedness income if the taxpayer is insolvent, bankrupt, or in the case of certain farm debt is to provide that a debtor coming out of bankruptcy (or an insolvent debtor outside bankruptcy) is not burdened with an immediate tax liability. The present-law rules were intended to carry out Congressional intent of deferring, but eventually collecting within a reasonable period, tax on ordinary income realized from debt discharge. [1] The committee believes that adding passive losses and credits and minimum tax credits to the attributes that are reduced in this circumstance is fully consistent with the purpose and operation of this deferral mechanism.

Explanation of Provision

The bill adds to the attributes that are reduced in the case of a discharge of indebtedness of the taxpayer that is excludable from income under section 108(a)(1). The attributes added are (1) minimum tax credits as of the beginning of the taxable year immediately after the taxable year of the discharge (following general business credit carryovers (present-law sec. 108(b)(2)(B))), and (2) passive activity loss and credit carryovers from the taxable year of the discharge (following basis of property (present-law sec. 108(b)(2)(D))). The amount of the reduction is generally one dollar for each dollar excluded, except that the reduction in the case of credits is 33-1/3 cents for each dollar excluded.

Effective Date

The provision is effective for taxable years beginning after December 31, 1993.

[Conference Agreement]

The conference agreement follows the Senate amendment.

[¶ 3050] Section 13227. Limitation on Section 936 Credit.

(Code Sec. 56, 936, 7652)

[Senate Explanation]

Present Law

Section 936 credit

Certain domestic corporations with business operations in the U.S. possessions [1] may elect the use of the section 936 credit which generally eliminates the U.S. tax on certain income related to their operations in the possessions. [2] Income exempt from U.S. tax under this provision falls into two broad categories: active business income, which in order to be exempt must be income treated as foreign source income derived from the active conduct of a trade or business within a U.S. possession or from the sale or exchange of substantially all of the assets that were used in such a trade or business; and investment income, which in order to be exempt must be derived from certain investments in the possessions or in certain Caribbean Basin countries. The investment income exempted under the provision is known

[Footnote ¶ 3049] 1. Bankruptcy Tax Act of 1980, Report of the Committee on Ways and Means of the House of Reps. (Rpt. No. 96-833, 96th Cong., 2d Sess.) 9; Report of the Senate Committee on Finance (Rpt. No. 96-1035, 96th Cong., 2d Sess.) 10.

[Footnote ¶ 3050] 1. Possessions to which special tax rules presently apply include Puerto Rico, Guam, American Samoa, the Commonwealth of the Northern Mariana Islands, and the U.S. Virgin Islands.

2. In contrast to the foreign tax credit, the possessions tax credit is a "tax sparing" credit. That is, the credit is granted whether or not the electing corporation pays income tax to the possession.

as "qualified possession source investment income" (QPSII). For these and other purposes, income derived within a possession is encompassed within the term "foreign source income."

In order to qualify for the section 936 credit, a domestic corporation must satisfy two requirements. Under one requirement, the corporation must be treated as having derived at least 75 percent of its gross income from the active conduct of a trade or business within a possession over a three-year period. Under the other requirement, the corporation must be treated as having derived at least 80 percent of its gross income from sources within a possession during that same three-year period.

Three alternative rules are provided that relate to allocating income from intangible property between a domestic corporation that elects the section 936 credit (a "possession corporation") and its U.S. shareholders. The general rule prohibits the possession corporation from being allocated any return on intangible property. A possession corporation can instead elect to subject itself to one of two other allocation rules, if it satisfies certain conditions.

One such rule is referred to as the "cost sharing method." Use of this method requires the possession corporation to pay to the appropriate members of its affiliated group of corporations (including foreign affiliates) an amount which represents its current share of the costs of the research and development expenses of the group. The Code determines that share to be the greater of (1) the total amount of the group's research and development expenses concerning the possession corporation's product area, multiplied by 110 percent of the proportion of the corporation's product area sales as compared to total product area sales of the group; or (2) the amount of the royalty payment or inclusion that would be required under sections 367(d) and 482 with respect to intangible assets which the corporation is treated as owning under the cost sharing method, were the corporation a foreign corporation (whether or not the intangible assets actually are transferred to the corporation). By making this cost sharing payment, the possession corporation becomes entitled to include in its income a return from certain intangibles, primarily manufacturing intangibles, associated with the products it manufactures in the possessions.

The alternative elective rule is referred to as the "profit split" method. This method generally permits allocation to the possession corporation of 50 percent of the affiliated group of U.S. corporations' combined taxable income derived from sales of products which are manufactured in a possession. [3]

Dividends paid by a possession corporation to a U.S. shareholder may qualify for the deduction for dividends received from a domestic corporation (sec. 243). In cases where at least 80 percent of the stock of the possession corporation is owned by a single domestic corporation, the possession corporation's possession source income generally may be distributed without the parent corporation incurring any resulting regular U.S. income tax.

Taxes paid or accrued by a possession corporation to foreign countries or possessions on income which is taken into account in determining the section 936 credit are neither deductible nor allowable for purposes of determining the foreign tax credit.

A possession corporation's income, the tax on which is allowed to be offset by the section 936 credit, is not included in the alternative minimum taxable income (AMTI) of the possession corporation. Thus, a possession corporation generally is exempt not only from the regular income tax but also from the alternative minimum tax (AMT). Moreover, dividends received by a U.S. corporation from a possession corporation generally do not constitute AMTI of the recipient corporation since, as described above, they may be offset by the dividends received deduction.

For purposes of determining a U.S. corporation's adjustment to AMTI based on adjusted current earnings (ACE), a deduction is allowed for certain dividends received. Specifically, a deduction is available (to the extent allowed under section 243 or 245) for any dividend that qualifies for the 100-percent deductions for dividends received for regular tax purposes, or that is received from a 20-percent owned corporation (as defined in section 243(c)(2)), but only to the extent that the divi-

[Footnote ¶ 3050 continued]

3. A special allocation of research and development expenses as required by section 936(h)(5)(C)(ii)(II) can cause the proportion of the combined taxable income which is allocable to the possession corporation to be less than 50 percent.

dend is attributable to income of the paying corporation which is subject to U.S. income tax DETERMINED AFTER THE APPLICATION OF SECTION 936. A dividend received by a U.S. corporation from its wholly-owned possession corporation subsidiary generally does not qualify for the dividends received deduction, and thus increases the ACE of the recipient, because the income of the possession corporation typically is not taxed by the United States due to the section 936 credit.

For purposes of computing the foreign tax credit, the Code provides that dividends received from a possession corporation are characterized as foreign source income. Unless an exception applies, dividends are subject to the separate foreign tax credit limitation for passive income. In computing the AMT foreign tax credit, 75 percent of any withholding or income tax paid to a possession with respect to dividends received from a possession corporation generally is treated as a creditable tax. [4] Moreover, for such computation, taxes paid to a possession by a possession corporation are deemed to be such a withholding tax for this purpose to the extent they would be treated as taxes paid by the recipient of the dividend under rules similar to the rules of the indirect foreign tax credit (secs. 78 and 902) if the possession corporation were a foreign corporation.

Cover over of excise taxes

U.S. excise taxes generally do not apply within the possessions, including Puerto Rico and the U.S. Virgin Islands. Articles that are manufactured in the possessions and brought into the United States for use or consumption are taxed on entry into the United States in the same manner as if the articles were imported from a foreign country. Thus, general excise tax principles tax these articles at the same rate that applies to domestically produced like articles.

In the case of excise taxes on certain articles brought into the United States from Puerto Rico and the Virgin Islands, and in the case of the distilled spirits excise tax on rum, a portion of the revenues is transferred ("covered over") to the treasuries of Puerto Rico and the Virgin Islands. This revenue cover over is significantly limited, both as to the taxes included and as to activities (e.g., manufacturing value added) that must occur in the possession from which the article comes as a condition of payment.

For example, revenues equal to $10.50 (less an administrative fee) per proof gallon of the $13.50 per proof gallon excise tax on rum imported from any foreign country is covered over to Puerto Rico and the Virgin Islands. On the other hand, cover over of tobacco excise tax revenues to Puerto Rico is limited to products where significant manufacturing value is added in the possession from which the product enters the United States, and no cover over is allowed for taxes on distilled spirits other than rum. Further, no cover over is permitted for many other excise taxes, e.g., the fuels excise taxes currently included in the Code.

Reasons for Change

The committee recognizes the importance of the possession tax credit to the possessions generally, and to Puerto Rico in particular. Although the section 936 tax credit was enacted to foster economic development in the U.S. possessions, studies have indicated that a disproportionate share of the tax benefits attributable to section 936 is realized by certain industries that create relatively few jobs in the possessions. [5] These industries tend to be those for which a large portion of taxable income is derived from the use of intangible assets (e.g., exploitation of patents, tradenames, or secret formulas). The committee is concerned, moreover, that a disproportionate share of the cost that all U.S. taxpayers bear in order to provide the section 936 credit may have inured to the benefit of the stockholders of the possession corporations, as compared to the U.S. citizens residing in the possessions. The committee is concerned, however, that some reductions in the tax benefits available to section 936 companies that have been proposed might have detrimental effects on the possessions and might influence the outcome of the

[Footnote ¶3050 continued]

4. The amount of tax allowable for purposes of the credit is limited to 75 percent of possessions tax paid in order to correspond to the portion of a dividend from a possession corporation that would be included in the recipient shareholder's AMTI as a result of the ACE adjustment.

5. See, for example, Pharmaceutical Industry -- Tax Benefits of Operating in Puerto Rico, United States General Accounting Office Briefing Report, to the Chairman, Special Committee on Aging, U.S. Senate, GAO/GGD-92-72-BR, Appendix I, Tables I.1 and I.2, pp. 12-14.

scheduled plebiscite relating to the political status of Puerto Rico.

To address these concerns without causing economic dislocation in the possessions, the committee believes that a targeted approach is to limit the tax benefit available to a possession corporation based on a measure of the possession-based economic activity attributable to the corporation in the possession (e.g., a measurement based on the corporation's employment of persons and investment in business property in the possessions). The committee anticipates that under the economic-activity-based limit established by the bill, the section 936 credits of possession corporations will continue to be substantial, and in many cases, will not be reduced relative to present law. However, in recognition of those cases where a substantial reduction in possession corporations' section 936 credits might result under this limit (for example, in the case of a possession corporation that reports high levels of profit in relation to its levels of employment and investment in the possessions), the committee believes it appropriate to allow taxpayers the option to utilize an alternative credit limitation equal to a stated percentage of the credit allowable under present law.

The committee is concerned that the changes made by the bill may result in a temporary reduction in tax receipts by the governments of the possessions. In recognition of this possibility, the committee believes it appropriate to allow certain possession corporations to include a portion of income taxes paid to a possession in the economic-activity credit limitation base. Similarly, the committee believes it appropriate to provide a temporary increase in the level of cover over to the governments of Puerto Rico and the Virgin Islands of rum excise taxes.

The committee also recognizes the importance to certain Caribbean countries and to the financial structure of Puerto Rico of the QPSII funds that currently are held on deposit by possession corporations. As of year-end 1986, the Treasury Department reported that possession corporations held approximately $15 billion in Puerto Rican financial assets. [6] The committee is concerned that reliance on an economic-activity-based limit on the portion of section 936 credit attributable to QPSII might not provide sufficient incentive to prevent taxpayers with possession corporation subsidiaries from liquidating their financial investments in Puerto Rico. Thus, the bill places no limitation on the effective U.S. tax exemption for QPSII.

Explanation of Provision

Section 936 credit

In general, the bill provides that the section 936 credit allowed to a possession corporation for a taxable year against U.S. tax on its active business income (i.e., income derived from the active conduct of a possession-based business, or from the sale of assets used in such a business) is determined as under present law, but is subject to either of two alternative limitations. One alternative limitation is based on factors that reflect the corporation's economic activity in the possessions (the "economic-activity limitation"), and the other limitation is based on a statutorily defined percentage of the section 936 credit that would be allowable under present-law rules (the "percentage limitation").

The option of which alternative limitation to apply is left to the taxpayer. In order to utilize the percentage limitation, however, a corporation must elect use of that limitation for its first taxable year beginning after 1993 for which it claims a section 936 credit. Once a possession corporation elects to use the percentage limitation, it must continue to compute its section 936 credit under that limitation for all subsequent taxable years unless the election is revoked.

The bill includes a consistency rule that requires all affiliated possession corporations to utilize the same alternative limitation. If, for example, a possession corporation that uses the percentage limitation becomes a member of an affiliated group that contains a second possession corporation that uses the economic-activity limitation, then the first corporation will be deemed to have revoked its election to use the percentage limitation. The determination whether a possession corporation is part of an affiliated group generally is made by reference to the consolidated return rules, except that stock owned by attribution under the rules of section 1563 is treated as owned directly, and the exclusions from the definition of "includible corporation" listed in section

[Footnote ¶ 3050 continued]

6. The Operation and Effect of the Possessions Corporation System of Taxation -- Sixth Report, March 1989, p. 3.

1504(b) are disregarded. The bill also grants authority to the Treasury Secretary to develop rules that would treat 2 or more possession corporations as members of the same affiliated group to prevent avoidance of the consistency rule through deconsolidation or other means.

The bill does not limit the present-law section 936 credit against U.S. tax on QPSII.

Economic-activity limitation

In general

Under the economic activity limitation, the credit allowed to a possession corporation for a taxable year against U.S. tax on its business income may not exceed the sum of the following three components: (1) 95 percent of qualified compensation; (2) an applicable percentage of depreciation deductions claimed for regular tax purposes by the corporation for the taxable year with respect to qualified tangible property -- i.e., tangible property located in a possession and used there by the corporation in the active conduct of its trade or business; and (3) if the corporation does not elect the profit-split method for computing its income, a portion of the possession income taxes it incurs during the taxable year. In order to compute the U.S. tax liability (if any) on the active business income of a possession corporation under the economic-activity limitation, the sum of the three components listed above is subtracted from an amount of pre-credit U.S. tax that would be owed if taxable income of the possession corporation were grossed up by qualified possession compensation and depreciation on qualified tangible property.

Compensation

For purposes of the economic-activity limitation, qualified compensation generally is the sum of (1) the aggregate amount of the possession corporation's qualified possession wages for the taxable year, and (2) its allocable employee fringe benefit expenses for the taxable year. The bill defines "qualified possession wages" as wages paid or incurred by the possession corporation during the taxable year to any employee for services performed in a possession, but only if the services are performed while the principal place of employment of the employee is within that possession. For example, wages paid for services performed in Puerto Rico by a full-time employee of the possession corporation who resides in Puerto Rico generally would be qualified possession wages. On the other hand, wages paid by the same company to a U.S.-based employee who provides only temporary services in Puerto Rico would not meet the standard for inclusion in the wage base for determining the possession corporation's active business credit limitation.

For this purpose, the term wages refers to the Federal Unemployment Tax Act (FUTA) definition of wages, and the cumulative amount of wages for each employee that are taken into account for a taxable year in computing the credit limitation may not exceed 85 percent of the maximum earnings subject to tax under the OASDI portion of Social Security (currently $57,600). The bill specifies that the Treasury Secretary will provide rules for making appropriate adjustments to this limit in the cases of part-time employees and of employees whose principal place of employment is not within a possession for the entire year. In addition, the bill does not include in qualified possession wages amounts paid to employees who are assigned by the employer to perform services for another person, unless the principal trade or business of the employer (and any related possession corporations) is to make employees available for temporary periods to other persons in return for compensation.

Allocable employee fringe benefit expenses are equal to the aggregate amount allowable to the possession corporation as a deduction for the taxable year of the fringe benefits listed below, multiplied by a fraction the numerator of which is the aggregate amount of the corporation's qualified possession wages (as defined above) for the year and the denominator of which is the aggregate amount of the wages it pays or incurs during that year. In no event, however, may the corporation's allocable employee fringe benefit expenses for a taxable year exceed 15 percent of the aggregate amount of its qualified possession wages for that year.

Fringe benefit expenses that are taken into account for purposes of determining the credit limitation are (1) employer contributions under a stock bonus, pension, profit-sharing, or annuity plan, (2) employer-provided coverage under any accident or health plan for employees, and (3) the cost of life or disability insurance provided to employees. Fringe benefit expenses do not include any amount that is treated as wages.

Depreciation

Depreciation deductions taken into account in determining the economic-activity limitation are as follows. With respect to short-life qualified tangible property (i.e., qualified tangible property to which section 168 applies and which is 3-year or 5-year property as classified under section 168(e)), 50 percent of the depreciation deductions allowable to the possession corporation for the taxable year are taken into account. With respect to medium-life qualified tangible property (i.e., qualified tangible property to which section 168 applies and which is classified as 7-year or 10-year property under section 168(e)), 75 percent of such deductions are taken into account. With respect to long-life qualified tangible property (i.e., all other qualified tangible property to which section 168 applies), 100 percent of such deductions are taken into account.

Possession income tax

As a general rule for possession corporations that do not elect the profit-split method, taxes paid or accrued to a possession with respect to taxable income which is taken into account in computing the section 936 credit are factored into the credit-limitation base. However, possession income taxes paid in excess of a 9-percent effective rate of tax are not included for purposes of determining the limitation. Moreover, only the portion of taxes satisfying the effective-rate requirement that are allocable (on a pro-rata basis taking all possession income taxes into account) to nonsheltered income are so included. The portion of possession income taxes allocated to nonsheltered income is determined by computing the ratio of two hypothetical U.S. tax amounts that are computed under the assumption that no credit or deduction is allowed for possession income taxes, and then multiplying that ratio by the taxable income of the corporation, computed under the assumption that no credit or deduction is allowed for possession income taxes, and that all other deductions are allowed as under present law.

The numerator of the ratio described above is the U.S. tax liability of the possession corporation that would arise under the bill by virtue of the economic-activity limitation determined without regard to any credit or deduction for possession income taxes. The denominator of the ratio is the U.S. tax liability of the possession corporation that would be imposed on the income of the corporation (such income being computed under the rules that apply under current section 936) without regard to any credit or deduction for possession income taxes.

A possession corporation that utilizes the profit-split method for allocating any income from intangible property for the taxable year is not permitted to include any taxes in its credit-limitation base. Such a corporation, however, is allowed a deduction for a portion of its possession income taxes paid or accrued during that taxable year. The deductible portion of possession income taxes is the portion that is allocable (on a pro-rata basis) to the corporation's taxable income (computed before taking into account any deduction for such taxes), the U.S. tax on which is not offset by the section 936 credit as a result of the bill's limitation.

Denial of double benefit

For purposes of computing the pre-section 936 credit U.S. income tax liability of a possession corporation that utilizes the economic-activity limitation, the bill requires the corporation to compute taxable income by reducing its otherwise deductible amounts of compensation and depreciation by the amounts that are included in its credit-limitation base.

Election to treat affiliated corporations as one corporation

For purposes of computing the economic-activity limitation, the bill allows an affiliated group of corporations (generally as defined in sec. 1504, but treating possession corporations and foreign corporations as includible corporations) to elect to treat all affiliated possession corporations as one corporation. For a group so electing, the available consolidated credit amount is to be allocated among the possession corporations of the group under rules prescribed by the Treasury Secretary. Any election to consolidate applies to the taxable year for which made and to all succeeding taxable years unless revoked with the consent of the Treasury Secretary.

Example

To illustrate the operation of the economic-activity limitation, consider a U.S. corporation that has elected the application of section 936.

Assume that the corporation has neither elected to use the percentage limitation nor to use the profit-split method for computing its income. Further assume that the corporation pays cash wages of $18, of which $15 are qualified possession wages, and the corporation makes pension, accident, health and life insurance payments of $3 with respect to its employees for the taxable year. Assume also that the corporation is entitled to $5 in depreciation deductions for short-life qualified tangible property and $2 for long-life qualified tangible property and that it pays $6 in possession income taxes.

Assume that the corporation has $100 of taxable income for the year, computed in accordance with the present-law rules for determining the taxable income of a possession corporation (that is, taking into account compensation and depreciation deductions otherwise allowed by the Code, but no deduction for possession income taxes). Assume that this $100 is comprised of $90 of active business income, $5 of QPSII, and $5 of other taxable income, if it claims compensation and depreciation deductions otherwise allowed by the Code, but no deduction for possession income taxes. But for the limitation imposed by the bill, the corporation's section 936 credit would be $33.25 (35% of $95), and it would have U.S. tax liability equal $1.75 (($100 x 35%) - $33.25).

Under the bill, the section 936 credit on U.S. tax attributable to QPSII remains at $1.75 (35% of $5). However, the remaining $31.50 of the otherwise allowable credit is subject to the economic-activity limitation.

As stated above, of the $18 of wages, $15 are qualified possession wages (i.e., they are below 85% of the applicable limit and are paid for services performed in a possession to employees whose principal place of employment is in the possession). Therefore, $2.50 in fringe benefit expenses (i.e., 15/18 of $3) potentially are includible in the credit-limitation base. However, allocable fringe benefit expenses are limited to 15% of qualified possession wages, which in this case equals $2.25 (15% of $15). The total of qualified possession wages and allocable employee fringe benefit expenses therefore is $17.25, and the compensation component of the credit-limitation base thus is $16.39 (95% of $17.25).

The depreciation component of the credit-limitation base is $4.50 -- i.e., the sum of (1) 50% of the $5 depreciation on the short-life property, and (2) 100% of the $2 depreciation on the long-life property.

The sum of the depreciation and compensation components of the credit-limitation base therefore is $20.89.

The $6 of possession income taxes paid by the corporation represents a 6-percent effective rate of possession tax. Thus, none of these taxes are disqualified from inclusion in the credit-limitation base as a result of the 9-percent-effective-tax-rate provision of the bill. However, only the portion of the $6 that is allocated to nonsheltered income is includible in the credit-limitation base. This portion is determined by comparing the increase in tax attributable to the compensation and depreciation components of the credit limitation (as well as the associated denial of deductibility) to the tax that the corporation would pay in the absence of the section 936 credit and the deductibility denial provision.

The increase in tax attributable to the compensation and depreciation components of the credit limitation and the associated denial of deductibility is determined as follows. Without the limitation, the corporation's U.S. tax liability would be $1.75 as computed above. With the limitation and the denial of deductions (not considering the possession income tax component of the credit limitation), the corporation's U.S. tax liability would be calculated in the following manner. The corporation's taxable income would be $100, plus qualified compensation ($17.25) and depreciation ($7.00), yielding $124.25. The U.S. tax would be 35% of this amount, or $43.49. That amount would be reduced by (1) the active-business section 936 credit ($20.89) and (2) the QPSII credit ($1.75). Therefore, net U.S. tax liability would be $20.85. Thus, the limitation results in an increase in the corporation's U.S. tax liability of $19.10. This $19.10 must be compared to the U.S. tax which the corporation would pay in the absence of the credit and the deductibility denial provision. That tax would be $35 (35% of $100). The amount of possession income taxes which can be included in the credit limitation thus is $3.27 ((19.10/35) x $6).

The total limitation on the active-business credit is $24.16 (i.e., compensation ($16.39) plus depreciation ($4.50) plus possession income taxes ($3.27)). In addition, the corporation can also claim a full credit of $1.75 against its U.S. tax on QPSII. Therefore, the corporation's total section 936 credit for the year may not exceed $25.91. After applying that credit, the corporation's net U.S. tax liability is $17.58 ($43.49 - $25.91).

Percentage limitation

Under the percentage limitation, the section 936 credit allowed to a possession corporation against U.S. tax on business income for a taxable year is limited to an applicable percentage (40 percent once fully phased in) of the credit that would be allowable under present-law rules. Under a transition rule that provides a 5-year phase in, the applicable percentage is as follows:

Taxable years beginning in:	Applicable percentage
1994	60%
1995	55%
1996	50%
1997	45%
1998 and thereafter	40%

Thus, for example, if a possession corporation's section 936 credit on business income for a taxable year beginning after 1997, as computed under present law would be $1,000,000, the bill limits the allowable credit for that year to $400,000.

A taxpayer that utilizes the percentage limitation is permitted a deduction for a portion of its possession income taxes paid or accrued during the taxable year. The portion of the taxes so deductible is the portion that is allocable (on a pro-rata basis) to the corporation's taxable income (computed before taking into account any deduction for possession tax), the U.S. tax on which is not offset by the section 936 credit as a result of the limitation.

To illustrate the operation of this rule, assume that for a taxable year beginning after 1997, a possession corporation that has elected the use of the percentage limitation has active business income from its possession-based operations of $900,000 and QPSII of $100,000, yielding pre-credit U.S. tax amounts of $315,000 and $35,000, respectively. Further assume that the corporation incurs possession taxes in the amount of $50,000 for that year. The corporation's section 936 credit for the year would be limited to $161,000 (i.e., a full credit against tax on QPSII and a 40-percent credit against tax on active business income). In this case, $27,0045 [sic] ($50,000 x (189,000/350,000)) of possession tax may be deducted by the possession corporation, thereby reducing its taxable income to $973,000. Thus, its pre-section 936 credit U.S. tax liability is $340,550, and its post-credit U.S. tax liability is $179,550.

Foreign tax credit limitation for dividends from possession corporations

The bill also creates a new separate foreign tax credit limitation category for purposes of computing the AMT foreign tax credit. The new category includes the portion of dividends received from a possession corporation for which the dividends received deduction is disallowed, and thus is included in alternative minimum taxable income.

Excise tax cover over

The bill also temporarily increases the cover over of rum excise taxes to Puerto Rico and the Virgin Islands from $10.50 per proof gallon to $11.30 per proof gallon. This increased cover over rate applies for excise taxes imposed in 1994 through 1998. This temporary increase in cover over applies only to excise taxes on rum. Further, it is not the committee's intent in increasing the rum excise tax cover over amount that this action be cited as precedent for any future cover over of either other present excise taxes or taxes that may be enacted as part of this bill or future legislation.

Effective Date

The provision is effective for taxable years beginning after December 31, 1993.

[Conference Report]

The conference agreement follows the Senate amendment with modifications and clarifications described below.

First, the conference agreement does not include the provision requiring a reduction of 2.5 percent of a taxpayer's otherwise allowable section 936 credit.

Second, the conference agreement provides that the economic-activity limitation base includes 60 percent of qualified compensation, 15 percent of depreciation deductions for short-life qualified tangible property, 40 percent of depreciation deductions for medium-life qualified tangible property, and 65 percent of depreciation deductions for long-life qualified tangible property. The conference agreement further provides that there is no disallowance of deductions for compensation or deprecation amounts which are included in the credit-limitation base.

Third, the conference agreement provides that the temporary increase in the cover over of rum excise taxes to Puerto Rico and the Virgin Islands applies in the case of distilled spirits brought into the United States during the five-year period beginning on October 1, 1993.

In addition, the conferees intend that the Secretary take into account the significant nature of the modifications made by the conference agreement to the operation of the section 936 credit in cases where a possession corporation either seeks to change its method of allocating income from intangible property or to revoke its election to use the section 936 credit.

[¶3051] Section 13228. Enhance Earnings Stripping Rules

(Code Sec. 163(j))

[House Explanation]

* * * *

Present Law

Interest deductions in general

Interest expenses of a U.S. corporate taxpayer are generally deductible, whether or not the interest is paid to a related party and whether or not the interest income is subject to U.S. taxation in the hands of the recipient. For example, interest income may be exempt from U.S. tax if the recipient generally is exempt under Code section 401 or section 501. As another example, the income may be exempt from U.S. tax if the recipient is a foreign person and either the Code imposes no tax or a treaty eliminates the U.S. tax that otherwise would apply under the Code .

Interest paid to certain related persons

In certain cases where interest is paid by a corporation to a related person, and no U.S. tax is imposed on the recipient's interest income, the so-called "earnings stripping rules" in the Code provide for denial of interest deductions by the debtor to the extent that the corporation's net interest expense exceeds 50 percent of its adjusted taxable income (sec. 163(j)). The disallowance cannot exceed the amount of tax-exempt interest paid to related persons; such interest is known as "disqualified interest." The disallowance does not apply to interest on debt with a fixed term that was issued on or before July 10, 1989, or that was issued after that date pursuant to certain written binding contracts in effect on that date.

For this purpose, a taxpayer's adjusted taxable income generally is its taxable income computed without regard to net interest expense, net operating loss carryovers, or any deduction allowable for depreciation, amortization, or depletion, and computed with such other adjustments as are provided by regulations. An interest recipient is considered to be related to the debtor if the recipient and debtor would be treated as related under the rules of section 267(b) or would be subject to the controlled partnership rules of section 707(b)(1).

A corporation's interest deductions for a taxable year are not limited under the earnings stripping provision unless the ratio of debt to equity of the corporation as of the close of the taxable year (or on such other days during the taxable year as regulations may prescribe) exceeds 1.5 to 1. The ratio of debt to equity means the ratio that the total indebtedness of the corporation bears to the sum of its money and all other assets, reduced (but not below zero) by such total indebtedness, taking into account such adjustments as the Secretary may prescribe in regulations. For this purpose, the amount taken into account with respect to any asset is that asset's adjusted basis for purposes of determining gain.

Any amount of interest disallowed under the earnings stripping provision is permitted to be carried forward as disqualified interest to a subsequent taxable year. In addition, a taxpayer is permitted to carry forward any excess limitation from its three most recent taxable years. The term excess limitation means the excess (if any) of 50 percent of the debtor's adjusted taxable income over its net interest expense. The excess limitation carried forward reduces the disallowance that would otherwise occur in the year to which the excess is carried.

If a treaty between the United States and any foreign country reduces, but does not eliminate, the 30-percent U.S. tax prescribed by the Code with respect to interest that the taxpayer pays to a related person, the interest is subject to disallowance in the same proportion that the treaty's rate reduction (from the 30-percent statutory rate) bears to 30 percent.

The question of whether a payment to a pass-through entity (such as a partnership, regulated investment company, or real estate investment trust) is treated as a payment to a person related to the debtor generally is determined at the entity level. However, if interest paid to a pass-through entity is treated as paid to a related person, the question of whether the recipient is tax-exempt is determined at the partner (or other beneficial owner) level.

In the case of corporations that form part of a U.S. affiliated group (whether or not such corporations file a consolidated return), the earnings stripping limitation generally applies on a group basis.

Interest paid to an unrelated person on debt guaranteed by a related person

The Treasury is authorized to provide such regulations as may be appropriate to prevent the avoidance of the purposes of the earnings stripping rules, including regulations that disallow deductions for interest paid to unrelated creditors in certain cases: for example, certain cases involving guarantees of the debt by parties related to the debtor, and cases involving so-called "back-to-back loans." The legislative history accompanying the bill enacting the provision, however, indicates an intent that regulations generally not subject third-party interest to disallowance whenever a guarantee is given in the ordinary course. [55] The legislative history further indicates an expectation that any regulations applying the earnings stripping rules to third-party debt guaranteed by a person related to the debtor would not apply to debt outstanding prior to notice of the rule (to the extent that the regulations depart from positions the Service and Treasury might properly take under analogous principles of law that would recharacterize guaranteed debt as equity).

To date, Treasury has promulgated no proposed or final regulations that interpret the application of the earnings stripping rules to third-party debt that is guaranteed by a person related to the debtor.

Reasons for Change

Guarantees and the erosion of the U.S. tax base

Where a group of related corporations earns income that is at least in part subject to U.S. tax, the committee believes that it is important to preserve for U.S. taxing jurisdiction an appropriate share of the net income of the group. The committee is aware of provisions in the Code that are designed specifically with this purpose in mind. The committee considers the earnings stripping provision to be so designed.

The operative effect of the earnings stripping provision is to deny deductions for interest expenses deemed to be excessive under the criteria of the provision. Where the deductions

[Footnote ¶ 3050 continued]

55. The conference report on the Omnibus Budget Reconciliation Act of 1989, which added the earnings stripping rules to the Code, includes the following language: "Some have argued that the House report's discussion of parent-guaranteed debt would potentially have made ordinary third-party financing transactions subject to the disallowance rule, in view of the common practice of having parents guarantee the debt of their subsidiaries in order to reduce the cost of third-party borrowings. The conferees intend to clarify that the provision is not to be interpreted generally to subject third-party interest to disallowance under the rule whenever such a guarantee is given in the ordinary course. On the other hand, the conferees do not intend to preclude Treasury from disallowing interest on a guaranteed third-party debt, in appropriate circumstances where the use of guaranteed third-party debt is a device for avoiding the operation of the earnings stripping rules, just as Treasury is not precluded from disallowing interest on a back-to-back loan." House Rept. No. 101-386, 101st Cong., 1st Sess. 567 (1989). The conference report reference to back-to-back loans echoes language in the House Report on the 1989 Act: "Under current law, back-to-back loans that have no substance are collapsed. See Rev. Rul. 84-152, 1984-2 C.B. 381, Rev. Rul. 84-153, 1984-2 C.B. 383, and Rev. Rul. 87-89, 1987-2 C.B. 195. The bill directs the Secretary to issue such regulations as may be appropriate to prevent the avoidance of the purposes of the bill. The committee intends that such regulations will treat back-to-back loans through third parties (whether related or unrelated), as well as similar arrangements, like direct loans to related parties." House Rept. No. 101-247, 101st Cong., 1st Sess. 1246 (1989).

are for interest paid to tax-exempt related parties, net income is shifted from the payor to the related party. The committee, like the Congress in 1989, is aware that the earnings stripping provision can be fully effective only to the extent that taxpayers are unable to circumvent its effect through the device of borrowing on the credit of persons whose assets are outside of U.S. taxing jurisdiction. The same "excess" interest deductions, and the same resultant "shifting" of net income out of U.S. taxing jurisdiction, is obtainable through borrowing by U.S. corporations on such credit.

A U.S. corporation can borrow on such credit by borrowing from an unrelated party and having the debt guaranteed by a related party that is exempt from U.S. tax. Although the interest on guaranteed debt is paid to an unrelated lender, the debt serves as a substitute for a direct related party loan to the extent that money is fungible. An affiliated group requires funding for all of its activities and assets, and has flexibility as to the source and use of its funds. Even money borrowed for a specific purpose frees up funds for other purposes.

Had the U.S. corporation borrowed from the related tax-exempt person and the related tax-exempt person been funded in part by loans from unrelated persons an in part by equity, the earnings stripping provision by its terms might have applied. However, absent the future issuance of regulations, that provision generally does not now apply to interest paid on a guaranteed loan from the unrelated person to the U.S. corporation. Yet the two alternative funding methods are similar.

For example, assume that a foreign corporation with no U.S. operations owns all the stock of a U.S. corporation that conducts a U.S. business. Assume that, aside from its stock in the U.S. subsidiary, the foreign parent has foreign operating assets that substantially exceed the operating assets of the U.S. corporation. Assume that creditors are willing to lend to the group, and due to various types of guarantees that will be provided by the parent, the parties are indifferent (aside from tax considerations) as to the identity of the corporation that is legally considered to be the primary obligor on any single obligation.

If the primary obligor on all the loans is the parent corporation, and the parent lends to the U.S. subsidiary, then the earnings stripping rules will be implicated if the related party interest is exempt from gross basis tax and the amount of debt and interest incurred by the subsidiary is excessive under those rules. However, because all parties are indifferent as to which corporation is the primary obligor on any loan, the transactions can be structured so that the same excessive level of debt and interest is owed directly by the U.S. subsidiary to the unrelated creditors, and the earnings stripping rules will not be implicated.

The committee is concerned about the extent to which the amount of U.S. tax paid with respect to the U.S. operations of the group depends on whether, on the one hand, the creditors all lend to the parent which in turn lends to the subsidiary, or on the other hand, the creditors lend to the subsidiary. In either case, the loans from the unrelated creditors may be viewed as supporting the income-producing activities of the group as a whole. However, in each case the financing could be structured so that an excessive amount of interest deductions may be claimed against the only income of the group that is subject to U.S. tax -- namely, the amount earned by the U.S. subsidiary -- unless in each case a provision, such the earnings stripping provision, applies so as to prevent an inappropriate U.S. deduction of expenses of earning income outside U.S. taxing jurisdiction. [56]

How should the law treat guarantees?

When a U.S. corporation borrows on the credit of a tax-exempt person, it is the committee's view that, beyond some threshold, the interest on such a loan is properly considered to be an expense of holding the assets and generating the income of the tax-exempt person. The committee notes that other provisions of present law limit the deductions that may

[Footnote ¶3051 continued]

56. Even in the absence of such a corrective provision, the same base erosion could not occur if both corporations, and their assets and income, were solely domestic and fully subject to U.S. tax. In that case, to the extent interest deductions offset income of the U.S. subsidiary, the deductions become unavailable to offset income of the U.S. parent that is subject to U.S. tax. If on the other hand one of the domestic corporations has income that is not subject to U.S. tax, such a corrective provision is necessary to prevent base erosion. Present law provides one. A U.S. affiliated group with foreign and domestic income that chooses the benefits of the foreign tax credit, for example, is required to compute the foreign tax credit limitation by allocating and apportioning interest expense as if the group were single corporation (sec. 864(e)).

be taken for expenses, including interest, in analogous circumstances. These provisions adopt approaches to the limitation of deductions that differ from the one applied under the earnings stripping rules. [57]

For reasons of administrability, certainty, and consistency with existing tax treaties, Congress enacted section 163(j), and thereby chose to address the erosion of the U.S. tax base through interest deductions, in the case of a U.S. corporation owned by persons exempt from U.S. tax, by limiting related party interest deductions based on an approximation of the cash flow of the corporation and on the debt-to-equity ratio of the corporation. Because the committee is not willing to abandon that approach in favor of either a less objective model or a fundamental departure from accepted practice, the committee believes that this approach generally should be preserved. The committee also now believes, however, that whatever objective standards apply to related party loans should also apply to unrelated party loans guaranteed by related persons that are exempt from U.S. tax. To the extent that lenders and borrowers are indifferent (aside from tax considerations) between the two financing methods, the committee believes that the tax law should treat the two methods with similar indifference. The committee sees little purpose in applying two different tax treatments to the two cases, if taxpayers can elect between them with little economic consequence other than tax savings.

Treatment of guaranteed loans from U.S. lenders

As discussed above, the committee believes that the purpose of the earnings stripping rules is to preserve for U.S. taxing jurisdiction an appropriate share of the net income of a group of related companies. Whether the unrelated party to whom the group member pays interest is or is not a net basis U.S. taxpayer is not relevant to the measurement of the group's U.S.-taxable income, in the committee's view. [58] Such treatment is consistent with the application of section 163(j) under present law to a related party loan in cases where the tax-exempt lender borrows from a U.S. taxpayer, which is an appropriate result, in the committee's view. [59]

The committee also notes other factors that may be taken into account in considering the justification for applying the provision to guaranteed loans from U.S. lenders. The committee is concerned hat taxpayers not avoid the purposes of the provision through the use of conduit arrangements, including transactions in which the "conduit" is a U.S. taxpayer. Certain types of guarantees can be used to achieve results similar to those achieved with back-to-back loans. As a practical matter, it can be difficult for the IRS to identify and combat conduit arrangements on a case-by-case basis. Applying section 163(j) to all guaranteed debt avoids this difficulty.

[Footnote ¶ 3051 continued]

57. For example, assume that a foreign corporation with substantial foreign operations conducts a U.S. business in branch form. Assume further that the branch borrows money from a U.S. lender. Under regulations, the interest on this loan (extended to the single corporation that engages in worldwide operations) is not necessarily deductible in the United States. Rather, the foreign corporation may claim a deduction for interest based on that portion of its worldwide debt that corresponds to a ratio of its U.S. assets to its worldwide assets (Treas. Reg. sec. 1.882-5). Similarly, where a U.S. corporation with foreign income borrows on the strength of its worldwide assets and income, and a portion of its net income that is from foreign sources is effectively exempt from U.S. tax due to foreign tax credits, some of the interest expense must be treated as reducing the foreign-source portion of net income. Such treatment increases the portion of total net income that is ineligible for shelter from U.S. tax via the foreign tax credit (Treas. Reg. sec. 1.861-9T). The Code and the regulations contain rules to ensure that the same economic result follows where the assets and liabilities of such an enterprise are split up into multiple domestic corporations (sec. 864(e); Treas. Reg. sec. 1.861-11T).

58. In other circumstances, the committee believes it appropriate that under present provisions of the Code, a deduction is denied for interest expenses that are considered to be incurred in the production of tax exempt income, in order to ensure an appropriate measurement of the net income that is not exempt from tax; and the committee further believes it to be appropriate that under those Code provisions it is immaterial that the interest is paid to an unrelated U.S. taxpayer. See Treas. Reg. sec. 1.882-5; Code sec. 265(a) (a taxpayer is denied interest deductions on indebtedness incurred or continued to purchase or carry tax-exempt municipal bonds, regardless of the fact that the taxpayer may pay that interest to another domestic taxpayer.

59. That is, a loan made by a U.S. lender will be subject to U.S. tax on a net basis whether the loan is made to the foreign or the U.S. borrower. By contrast, a guaranteed loan from an unrelated foreign lender to a U.S. corporation, the interest payments on which are subject to gross basis U.S. tax, differs significantly from a loan by the foreign lender to the foreign parent which then loans to the U.S. subsidiary. In the second case the interest payments received by the unrelated lender are NOT subject to U.S. tax. Thus, it may be argued that it is appropriate to view the gross basis tax imposed in the first case as additional U.S. tax incurred by reason of the guaranteed loan, which in turn serves as an adequate substitute for interest deduction disallowance to the U.S. borrower.

In addition, it may be noted that a typical U.S.-taxpaying financial intermediary that might engage in (guaranteed) lending differs from other types of taxpayers in the extent to which it is itself leveraged with debt. Because of this leverage, the "spread" that generally represents a bank's net taxable income from a loan is small relative to the interest deduction that can be claimed by the debtor. The bank's depositors, in turn may include domestic or foreign tax-exempt entities. The combined U.S. net basis tax paid by the financial intermediary and its depositors on a fixed amount of interest income may thus be substantially less than the tax saved by the taxable borrower by reason of an equal amount of interest deductions. Were that combined U.S. net basis tax to be relevant to the operation of the bill, it would be very difficult to ascertain the appropriate disallowance of interest deductions.

Taking into account the high degree to which financial intermediaries are leveraged with debt under the guarantee rules is consistent with the treatment of financial intermediaries under present law earnings stripping rules. Such leverage is taken into account under present law in that disallowance is based on the excessiveness of NET interest expenses of a taxpayer which generally has the effect of insulating financial intermediaries themselves from exposure to interest disallowance.

Explanation of Provision

In general

Interest may be treated as disqualified interest under the earnings stripping rules without regard to whether it is interest on a fixed-term obligation issue before, on, or after July 10, 1989. In addition, interest paid on a loan from an unrelated party generally as treated as disqualified interest if no gross-basis U.S. income tax is imposed on the interest, a related person guaranteed the loan, and the related person is either exempt from U.S. Federal income tax or is a foreign person. Thus, deductions may be disallowed for interest described above to the extent that the other conditions for disallowance under the earnings stripping rules apply.

Interest on guaranteed debt

Taxes imposed on the interest

In order for the interest paid or accrued to an unrelated person to be disqualified due to a guarantee, there must be no gross basis U.S. income tax imposed on the interest. A "gross basis tax" is a U.S. income tax that is imposed without regard to deductions. For example, the 30 percent statutory tax on interest paid to a foreign person under Code section 871(a) or 881(a) is a "gross basis tax" for this purpose. If a treaty reduces the statutory gross basis tax without eliminating it, a ratable portion of this interest would be treated as having had no gross basis tax imposed on it. For example, if the treaty-reduced rate were 15 percent, then, as under present law in the case of a payment to a related person, half of the interest would be treated as subject to the full 30 percent gross basis tax, and the other half would be treated as subject to no gross basis tax.

Interest may be disqualified, however, whether or not it is subject to net basis U.S. income tax. (A "net basis tax" is simply a U.S. income tax that is not a gross basis tax.) For example, interest paid to a U.S. bank and reported as gross income may be treated as disqualified interest if the loan is guaranteed.

Taxes imposed on the guarantor

In order for the interest paid or accrued to an unrelated person to be disqualified due to a guarantee, the guarantor must be an organization exempt from income taxation or a foreign person, and the guarantor must not be described in either of two exceptions: one that applies where the debtor owns a controlling interest in the guarantor, and another that applies to cases, identified by regulation, where the interest on the indebtedness would have been subject to net basis tax if the interest had been paid to the guarantor.

For purposes of the controlled guarantor exception, a controlling interest in a corporation means direct or indirect ownership of at least 80 percent of the total voting power, and 80 percent of the value, of all classes of the corporation's stock. A controlling interest in any other entity means direct or indirect ownership of at least 80 percent of the profit and capital interests in the entity.

With respect to the other exception regarding cases where net basis tax hypothetically would have been imposed, the committee anticipates that the Secretary would exercise its authority to treat a foreign guarantor like a taxable U.S. person where the foreign person conducts a trade or business within the United States, and the Treasury is satisfied that income on a hypothetical loan by the foreign person to the debtor, similar to the third-party guaranteed loan, would have been effectively connected with the conduct of that U.S. trade or business, and taxed in the United States for that reason, after the application of any relevant treaty. The committee is concerned, however, that the hypothetical nature of such a test, if not designed properly, might tempt taxpayers to take aggressive reporting positions. Therefore, the committee intends that the Secretary have broad discretion to limit the scope of the exception to cases where the Secretary is fully satisfied that taxpayers are prevented from engaging in tax avoidance schemes, such as establishing an insubstantial U.S. trade or business for the purpose of qualifying for the exception.

Definition of guarantee

Except as provided in regulations, a guarantee is defined to include any arrangement under which a person directly or indirectly assures, on a conditional or unconditional basis, the payment of another's obligation. The committee intends that the term be interpreted broadly enough to encompass any form of credit support. This includes a commitment to make a capital contribution to the debtor or otherwise maintain its financial viability. It includes an arrangement reflected in a "comfort letter," regardless whether the arrangement gives rise to a legally enforceable obligation. If a guarantee is contingent upon the occurrence of an event, the provision would apply as if the event had occurred.

Relationship to treaties

The committee understands that the impact of this provision may fall heavily on foreign-based multinational enterprises. However, the provision generally applies to guarantees provided by all tax-exempt U.S. persons and tax-exempt foreign persons. The committee does not believe that the impact of the provision on foreign-owned entities conflicts with U.S. tax treaties.

The provision does not, for example, distinguish between payments to U.S. residents on the one hand and payments to residents of other countries, on the other. In either case, deductions can be denied or not depending on the presence or absence of a disqualifying guarantee. Furthermore, the earnings stripping rules deny deductions only in cases believed to satisfy an objective standard of "thin capitalization." As set out more fully in the conference report accompanying the 1989 Act, disallowance in such cases may be consistent with treaties regardless of whether the disallowance applies only to thinly capitalized foreign-owned companies. [60] Moreover, the committee believes that the provision does not inappropriately subject similarly situated persons to dissimilar treatment. Some U.S. tax provisions under current law affect only foreign-owned U.S. businesses, but these provisions are designed solely to provide comparable treatment for these and other U.S. taxpayers in areas where the fact of foreign ownership interferes with the effective operation of domestic tax rules. In short, the committee believes that different but comparable tax treatment that reflects the different circumstances of foreign-owned and domestic-owned businesses does not necessarily constitute discrimination against foreign-owned U.S. businesses.

Effective Date

The provision applies to any interest paid or accrued in taxable years beginning after December 31, 1993.

[Conference Report]

The conference agreement follows the House bill.

[¶ 3052] Sections 13231--13233. Current Taxation of Earnings of Controlled Foreign Corporations

(Code Sec. 951, 954, 956, 956A, 959, 960, 1293, 1296, 1297)

[Senate Explanation]

[Footnote ¶ 3051 continued]

60. H.R. Rep. No. 101-386, 101st Cong., 1st Sess. 569-70 (1989).

Present Law

In general

U.S. persons generally are taxed currently by the United States on their worldwide income. U.S. tax on foreign source income may be reduced by credits for foreign income taxes paid by the U.S. person. Foreign income earned by a foreign corporation, the stock of which is owned in whole or in part by U.S. persons, generally is not taxed by the United States until the foreign corporation repatriates those earnings by payment of a dividend to its U.S. stockholders. If a foreign corporation pays a dividend to a domestic corporation that owns 10 percent or more of the voting stock of the foreign corporation, the domestic corporation may receive credits for foreign income taxes paid by the foreign corporation. This is sometimes known as the "indirect" foreign tax credit.

The Code sets forth several regimes providing exceptions to the general rule that defers U.S. tax on foreign income earned through foreign corporations. One such regime applies only to certain substantial U.S. shareholders in U.S.-controlled foreign corporations. Other regimes apply to other U.S. persons owning stock in predominantly "passive" foreign corporations. Still other regimes are primarily applicable to U.S. persons owning stock in domestic corporations, but also can be applied to U.S. persons owning stock in foreign corporations.

Controlled foreign corporations

General provisions. Under the controlled foreign corporation rules of subpart F (secs. 951-964), a controlled foreign corporation is defined generally as any foreign corporation if U.S. persons own more than 50 percent of the corporation's stock, taking into account only so-called "U.S. shareholders": namely, those U.S. persons that own (directly, indirectly or by attribution) at least 10 percent of its voting stock (sec. 957). A "U.S. shareholder," so defined, may be taxed currently by the United States on its proportionate share of the controlled foreign corporation's "subpart F income." The U.S. shareholder may claim an indirect foreign tax credit for its proportionate share of the foreign income taxes paid by the controlled foreign corporation on the subpart F income (sec. 960). Subpart F income typically is foreign income that is relatively movable from one taxing jurisdiction to another and that is subject to low rates of foreign tax relative to the U.S. rate. Subpart F income consists of foreign base company income, insurance income, and certain income relating to international boycotts and other violations of public policy. Excluded from the definition of subpart F income, among other things, are certain dividends and interest received from a related corporation organized and operated in the same foreign country as the recipient.

Investment of earnings in U.S. property. In addition to taxation of subpart F income and taxation of actual repatriations of earnings not already taxed as subpart F income, a U.S. shareholder may also be subject to U.S. taxation on the controlled foreign corporation's current or accumulated earnings (other than earnings that were previously taxed to the U.S. shareholders as subpart F income), at the time of any increase for the year in the amount of those earnings invested by the controlled foreign corporation in certain U.S. property (as defined in section 956). Thus, for example, assume that a controlled foreign corporation has an active foreign manufacturing business. It earns no subpart F income and has no U.S. property. It has $100 of accumulated earnings, all of which are invested in the foreign business. Assume that in the current year the foreign corporation disposes of $50 worth of foreign business assets and places the proceeds in a U.S. real estate investment or lends them to its U.S. shareholders. In either case, the U.S. shareholders are rehired to include $50 in gross income for the current year.

Receipt of previously taxed earnings and profits. Earnings and profits of a controlled foreign corporation that have been included in the income of U.S. shareholders before actual repatriation are not included again in the shareholders' gross income when such earnings are in fact distributed to the U.S. shareholders (sec. 959(a)). Earnings actually distributed are treated as comprising first amounts that were previously taxed as investments in U.S. property under section 956 (sec. 959(c)(1)), next amounts that were previously taxed as subpart F income under section 951(a)(1)(A) (sec. 959(c)(2)), and last amounts of other earnings (sec. 959(c)(3)). A U.S. shareholder is permitted to increase its foreign tax credit limitation in the year of the distribution of previously taxed earnings and profits (sec. 960(b)). The increase equals the excess of the amount by which its foreign tax credit limitation for the year of the income inclusion was increased as a result of that inclusion, over the amount of foreign taxes which were allowable as a credit in that year and which would not have been so allowable but for the income inclusion. The increase in the foreign tax credit limitation may not, however, exceed the amount of the foreign taxes actually paid with respect to the distribution of previously taxed earnings and profits. All such determinations are made separately for each controlled foreign corporation, for each taxable year, and for each foreign tax credit limitation category.

Passive foreign investment companies

Definitions. If any foreign corporation (including a controlled foreign corporation) is a so-called "passive foreign investment company" (PFIC), U.S. persons (including 10-percent "U.S. shareholders") that own stock in the PFIC may be subject to one of two other sets of operating rules that eliminate or reduce the benefits of deferral (secs. 1291-1297). A PFIC generally is defined as any foreign corporation if (1) 75 percent or more of its gross income for the taxable year consists of passive income, or (2) 50 percent or more of its assets consist of passive assets, defined as assets that produce, or are held for the production of, passive income (sec. 1296(a)). Assets generally are measured by their fair market value; however, a foreign corporation may elect (on a permanent basis) to have its assets measured by their adjusted bases. Passive income does not include any income derived in the active conduct of a banking business by an institution licensed to do business as a bank in the United States, or, to the extent provided in regulations, by any other corporation (sec. 1296(b)(2)(A)). According to IRS Notice 89-81, 1989-2 C.B. 399, forthcoming Treasury regulations will provide that income effectively connected with the active conduct of a U.S. trade or business pursuant to a license to do business as a bank in the United States, as well as income derived in bona fide banking activities (as defined in Notice 89-81) conducted abroad by a U.S. licensed bank, will be treated as income other than passive income. In addition, a foreign corporation that is not licensed to do business as a bank in the United States, but that qualifies as an active foreign bank (or "qualified affiliate") under conditions set forth in Notice 89-81, will be permitted to treat its income derived in the performance of bona fide banking activities as not passive income.

Look-through rules. In determining whether foreign corporations that own subsidiaries are PFICs, look-through treatment is provided in certain cases (sec. 1296(c)). Under this look-through rule, a foreign corporation that owns, directly or indirectly, at least 25 percent of the value of the stock of another corporation is treated as owning a proportionate part of the other corporation's assets and income. Thus, amounts such as interest and dividends received from foreign or domestic subsidiaries are eliminated from the shareholder's income in applying the income test, and the stock or debt investment is eliminated from the shareholder's assets in applying the asset test. In addition to the look-through rule applicable to 25-percent-owned subsidiaries, interest, dividends, rents, and royalties received from related persons that are not subject to section 1296(c) look-through treatment are excepted from treatment as passive income to the extent that, under regulations prescribed by the Secretary, those amounts are allocable to income of the payor that is not passive income (sec. 1296(b)(2)(C)).[1] As a corollary, the characterization of the assets that generate the income will follow the characterization of the income so that, for example, a loan to a related person will be treated as a passive asset only if the interest on the loan is treated as passive income.

Tax treatment of PFICs. Under the tax rules applicable at the election of a U.S. person owning PFIC stock, the U.S. person includes currently in gross income its share of the PFIC's total earnings, with a separate election to defer payment of tax, subject to an interest charge, on income not currently received. As under the controlled foreign corporation rules, the distribution of earnings and profits that were previously included in the income of an electing shareholder under these rules is not treated as a dividend to the shareholder (sec. 1293(c)). A nonelecting U.S. person owning

[Footnote ¶ 3051 continued]

[Footnote ¶ 3052] 1. A related person is defined by reference to the related person definition applicable for purposes of the controlled foreign corporation rules (that is, sec. 954(d)(3)).

PFIC stock pays no current tax on the PFIC's undistributed income. However, when realizing income earned through ownership of PFIC stock (such as certain amounts distributed by the PFIC or capital gains from selling PFIC stock), the nonelecting U.S. person may pay an additional interest charge. This interest charge is related to the value of delaying income realization, and therefore delaying tax, by investing indirectly in assets through a foreign corporation.

Accumulated earnings tax

In addition to the corporate income tax, the Code also imposes a tax, at the rate of 28 percent, on the accumulated taxable income of any corporation (with certain exceptions) formed or availed of for the purpose of avoiding income tax with respect to its shareholders (or the shareholders of any other corporation), by permitting its earnings and profits to accumulate instead of being distributed (secs. 531, 532(a)). The specified tax-avoidance purpose generally is determined by the fact that the earnings and profits of the corporation are allowed to accumulate beyond the reasonable needs of the business (sec. 533). The accumulated earnings tax acts as an approximation of the tax that would have been incurred by the shareholders on dividends actually distributed by the corporation. The accumulated earnings tax does not apply to certain specified types of corporations, including PFICs (sec. 532(b)) The accumulated earnings tax does apply, by its terms, to most other foreign corporations including controlled foreign corporations. However, foreign earnings and profits of foreign corporations generally are not subject to the accumulated earnings tax (see Treas. reg. sec. 1.532-1(c)).

Reasons for Change

Inclusions based on excess passive assets

The committee is aware that the deferral of U.S. tax on income of U.S. persons earned through foreign corporations may tend to favor foreign investment over U.S. investment, and can provide an incentive to engage in certain tax-haven activities. The committee understands that prior enactments that permit deferral of U.S. tax on most types of active business income derived through controlled foreign corporations have been justified as enhancing the competitiveness of U.S.-owned business operations abroad. In fact, Congress referred to such concerns in rejecting the President's proposal to eliminate all deferral in the Revenue Act of 1962. [2] The committee believes, however, that deferral of U.S. tax on accumulated active business profits is not necessary to maintain the competitiveness of business activities conducted by controlled foreign corporations where such accumulated profits are held in the form of excessive accumulations of passive assets. The controlled foreign corporation rules impose current U.S. tax on certain passive income earned by a controlled foreign corporation. The PFIC rules restrict the benefits of deferral in the case of foreign corporations that allow undistributed earnings and profits to accumulate in passive investments to such an extent that the amount of the corporation's passive assets equals or exceeds the amount of its active business assets. The committee believes that neither of these regimes sufficiently restricts the benefits of deferral in the case of controlled foreign corporations that accumulate excessive quantities of earnings and profits, without reinvesting them in active business assets, and without subjecting them to U.S. income taxation (with proper allowance for foreign tax credits) in the hands of the U.S. shareholders. The committee understands that, although the accumulated earnings tax nominally applies to controlled foreign corporations, its application to foreign corporations (including controlled foreign corporations) is limited. Moreover, the accumulated earnings tax of present law employs a subjective analysis to determine the reasonable business needs for accumulating earnings in the form of passive assets. The committee believes it appropriate to impose on controlled foreign corporations a new type of limitation on accumulating deferred earnings that turns on objective rather than subjective criteria. The committee is concerned that some limitations on accumulating deferred earnings that have been proposed might have had inappropriate application to earnings accumulated by controlled foreign corporations in past years. The committee believes that a better approach is to impose a new limitation on deferral that applies to amounts earned in future years.

[Footnote ¶ 3051 continued]

2. "Testimony in hearings before [the House Committee on Ways and Means]suggested . . . that to impose the U.S. tax currently on the U.S. shareholders of American-owned businesses operating abroad would place such firms at a disadvantage with other firms located in the same areas not subject to U.S. tax." H.R. Rep. No. 1447, 87th Cong., 2d Sess. 57-58 (1962).

Modification of section 956

The committee has carefully considered how best to structure the bill's provisions as to income inclusions of earnings invested in excess passive assets. The committee believes that the provisions of present law applicable to income inclusions of earnings invested in U.S. property under section 956 could be improved, and that those provisions of present law are, in some ways, conceptually parallel to the bill's excess passive assets provisions. The committee believes that the bill's structure and operating rules for the excess passive assets provisions are also appropriate for inclusions of earnings invested in U.S. property, and, accordingly, modifies the latter provisions in the bill.

Measurement of assets under the PFIC rules

The committee understands that many foreign corporations that are subject to the PFIC rules hold assets (such as tangible or intangible business assets) the fair market value of which is difficult to determine. This difficulty is faced primarily by those PFICs that are also controlled foreign corporations, rather than those PFICs that are foreign-controlled investment funds (which tend to hold marketable assets). The committee is aware that the process of determining the fair market value of such foreign assets is a source of complexity and administrative burden for taxpayers, and is an enforcement problem for the Internal Revenue Service. The committee believes that measurement by adjusted basis is well established in the case of controlled foreign corporations' investments of earnings in U.S. property, and is highly appropriate to the task of measuring the earnings of a controlled foreign corporation that are invested in excess passive assets. The committee is not persuaded that a different method should apply for purposes of measuring assets when testing a controlled foreign corporation for its status as a PFIC. The committee recognizes, however, that when a controlled foreign corporation incurs research and experimental expenditures, the practical effect may be to enhance the corporation's ability to generate active business income over an extended period; yet because such expenditures are commonly deductible under section 174, these types of expenditures may affect the corporation's adjusted tax basis in its assets differently than expenditures to generate active business income over an extended period that take the form of investment in TANGIBLE assets. Therefore the committee believes that certain adjustments to tax basis should be made to take account of this difference. In addition, the committee believes that in certain cases it is also appropriate to make adjustments that take into account either tangible OR intangible assets that are used by the corporation in its active business, but are not owned by the company.

Foreign securities brokers and dealers

When the PFIC rules were enacted in 1986, Congress believed that foreign corporations conducting an active business as dealers in stocks, securities and derivative financial products generally would be excluded from qualification as PFICs under both the asset and income tests. Specifically, Congress expected that foreign securities dealers would not qualify as PFICs under the asset test, because more than 50 percent of their assets would consist of inventory securities and other assets that produce income treated as not passive under the dealer exception of section 954(c). Congress also expected that foreign securities dealers would not qualify as PFICs under the gross income test, inasmuch as a substantial portion of their gross income would be commission income (not passive) from underwriting issues of stocks and securities. [3] The committee is informed, however, that foreign securities dealers do not always earn sufficient gross income in the form of underwriting commissions to avoid qualification as PFICs under the gross income test. For example, securities dealers may earn substantial amounts of interest and dividend income from securities held as inventory for sale to customers. Securities dealers may also earn substantial amounts of interest income from transactions incidental to the business of dealing in securities, such as margin loans and reverse repurchase transactions. The committee is further informed that inventory securities held by a foreign corporate securities dealer may not represent more than 50 percent of the corporation's assets. As a result, a foreign securities dealer may qualify as a PFIC under the asset test. In most cases, moreover, the committee is

[Footnote ¶ 3051 continued]

3. H.R. Rep. No. 99-841, 99th Cong., 2d Sess. II-644 (1986) (Conference Report to accompany H.R. 3838, the Tax Reform Act of 1986).

informed that inventory securities represent less than 75 percent of the assets of a foreign securities dealer, so that most foreign securities dealers would be considered to hold excess passive assets under the bill. In contrast, existing provisions of the Code and IRS Notice 89-81 ensure that income and assets attributable to bona fide banking activities conducted by a foreign bank or a qualified affiliate are not treated as passive income and assets, if certain conditions are satisfied. The committee is informed, however, that there is considerable overlap between the activities designated as bona fide banking activities under Notice 89-81 and the activities conducted by foreign securities dealers. For example, foreign securities dealers may regularly arrange and engage in foreign exchange transactions, enter into interest rate and currency swaps and other hedging transactions, and underwrite issues of stock, debt obligations and other securities. Each of these activities is designated in Notice 89-81 as a bona fide banking activity. The committee believes that it is appropriate to provide an exception, similar to that provided under section 1296(b)(2)(A), for income earned by foreign securities brokers and dealers in an active securities business. The committee believes that the availability of this exception should be restricted to U.S. shareholders of controlled foreign corporations in order to ensure that the exception cannot be used by U.S. portfolio investors to avoid the PFIC rules.

Effect on foreign tax credit limitation of distributions of previously taxed earnings

The provisions that permit an indirect foreign tax credit to be claimed in the event of a distribution of previously taxed earnings are particularly difficult to administer. This difficulty arises because taxpayers must determine the amount of excess foreign tax credit limitation associated with a distribution of previously taxed earnings on a separate category by separate category basis, on a foreign corporation by foreign corporation basis, as well as on a year by year basis. Additional complexities arise because taxpayers are required as a result of distributions to trace earnings and profits up tiers of foreign corporations. The bill simplifies present law by requiring taxpayers to establish excess limitation accounts only on a separate category by separate category basis; the taxpayer will not be required to track earnings on a controlled foreign corporation by controlled foreign corporation or a year by year basis. In addition, the Tax Reform Act of 1986 revised the indirect foreign tax credit by providing for a multi-year "pooling" mechanism. This mechanism was designed to ameliorate the problems associated with timing mismatches of earnings and profits and foreign tax payments by placing all post-1986 earnings and profits and foreign tax payments in respective pools, and by providing for averaging of these respective amounts for purposes of claiming the indirect credit. The committee believes that the rules of section 960(b) that apply for purposes of determining adjustments to the foreign tax credit limitation should also employ the multi-year pooling concept. In addition, the committee believes it is appropriate to substitute the multi-year pooling concept for the current annual accounting rules that apply to investments of earnings in U.S. property; therefore, the bill adopts a pooling approach in its operating rules for income inclusions based on excess passive assets and income inclusions based on investments in U.S. property.

Explanation of Provision

In general

The bill limits the availability of deferral of U.S. tax on certain earnings of controlled foreign corporations. As explained in detail below, the bill generally requires current inclusions in the income of U.S. shareholders of a controlled foreign corporation to the extent of the corporation's accumulated earnings invested in excess passive assets. The bill also conforms the treatment of earnings of controlled foreign corporations invested in U.S. property to the new rules for earnings invested in excess passive assets, and makes related modifications to other rules applicable to controlled foreign corporations and PFICs.

Inclusions based on excess passive assets

Amount included. The bill adds new section 956A to the Code, which measures the amount of retained earnings of a controlled foreign corporation that is potentially subject to inclusion in the income of a U.S. shareholder of the foreign corporation as a result of the foreign corporation's investment in "excess passive assets." The amount determined under section 956A with respect to a U.S. shareholder of a controlled foreign corporation is the lesser of two amounts. The first amount is the excess (if any) of the U.S. shareholder's pro rata share of the controlled foreign corporation's "excess passive assets," over that portion of the retained earnings of the foreign corporation that is treated as having been previously included in the income of the U.S. shareholder on account of excess passive assets. [4] The second amount, defined as the "applicable earnings" of the controlled foreign corporation, is the U.S. shareholder's pro rata share of the controlled foreign corporation's total current earnings and profits (but not reduced by a deficit in accumulated earnings and profits) and earnings and profits to the extent accumulated in taxable years beginning after September 30, 1993, [5] reduced by the portion of such post-1993 retained earnings of the foreign corporation that was previously included in the income of the U.S. shareholder on account of either investments in U.S. property or investments in excess passive assets. Under this definition, a controlled foreign corporation can never have a deficit in applicable earnings. The income inclusion for a U.S. shareholder of the controlled foreign corporation is the amount determined as above under new section 956A; less retained earnings of the controlled foreign corporation that are treated as having been previously taxed to the U.S. shareholder as subpart F income of the controlled foreign corporation under section 951(a)(1)(A), to the extent that such previously taxed earnings were accumulated in taxable years beginning after September 30, 1993 (new sec. 951(a)(1)(C)). (See the discussion of the bill's rules for the treatment of previously taxed income under "Coordination and ordering provisions," below.)

Excess passive assets. "Excess passive assets" are defined as the excess (if any) for the taxable year of the average amount of passive assets held by the controlled foreign corporation as of the close of each quarter of its taxable year, over 25 percent of the average amount of total assets held by the controlled foreign corporation as of the close of each quarter of its taxable year. For this purpose, an asset is measured generally by its adjusted basis as determined for purposes of computing earnings and profits. [6] The bill provides a special rule to take into account research and experimental expenditures, and to take into account assets leased or licensed to the foreign corporation, in computing adjusted basis (see description below of certain modifications to the PFIC rules). The committee intends that the measurement of assets as of the close of each quarter of the taxable year shall disregard short-term loans or other temporary arrangements with regard to the corporations's assets, where one of the principal purposes of such an arrangement was to avoid taking passive assets into account for purposes of this provision. Passive assets are defined generally as under the PFIC rules, i.e., assets held by the controlled foreign corporation that produce passive income (as defined in sec. 1296(b)) or that are held for the production of passive income. The PFIC look-through rules applicable to 25-percent-owned subsidiaries and certain payments received from related persons apply for this purpose. The bill modifies certain definitions of assets and income for purposes of the PFIC rules (see description below of certain modifications of the PFIC rules). These modifications are also applicable for purposes of determining excess passive assets under section 956A.

Coordination and ordering provisions. Passive assets for purposes of the excess passive assets provisions do not include any assets that are treated as U.S. property for purposes of section 956. The bill provides that actual distributions during the taxable year and their effects on the determination of earnings and

[Footnote ¶ 3051 continued]

4. Under the previously taxed income rules of section 959, retained earnings of the foreign corporation that are treated as having been previously included in the income of the U.S. shareholder include retained earnings that were previously included in the income of another U.S. person that is a proven predecessor in interest to the U.S. shareholder. In addition, as discussed below under "Coordination and ordering provisions," under the bill's rules for the treatment of previously taxed income, the amount of earnings treated as having been previously included in the income of the shareholder on account of excess passive assets (i.e., the amount of earnings described in section 959(c)(1)(B)) includes not only earnings that actually resulted in an inclusion of income under section 951(a)(1)(C), but also earnings that would have resulted in such an inclusion but for being attributable to earnings that had been previously taxed as subpart F income under section 951(a)(1)(A).

5. Earnings and profits generally are computed in the foreign corporation's functional currency, in accordance with the rules of sections 986 and 964. Earnings and profits with respect to pre-1987 taxable years are initially computed in U.S. dollars in accordance with the rules of Treas. reg. sec. 1.964-1, and are then translated into the foreign corporation's functional currency at the "spot" rate that prevailed on the first day of the foreign corporation's first taxable year beginning after December 31, 1986, as provided in IRS Notice 88-70, 1988-2 C.B. 369.

6. Unlike the PFIC rules of present law, the bill offers no option to measure assets by fair market value.

profits, previously taxed amounts, or any other item are taken into account prior to the determination of amounts under section 956 that are subject to income inclusion under section 951(a)(1)(B), and amounts under section 956A that are subject to income inclusion under section 951(a)(1)(C). [7] The bill further provides that all amounts of assets, earnings included in income, previously taxed amounts, and any other item determined for purposes of the excess passive assets provisions are to be determined after the application of section 956 (and income inclusions thereunder) for the taxable year. Previous income inclusions under section 956A are treated similarly to previous income inclusions under section 956 for purposes of the ordering rules applicable to the different categories of previously taxed income under section 959(c). Thus, when the controlled foreign corporation makes an actual distribution of its earnings to its shareholders, the earnings distributed are treated as first attributable to the retained earnings that were required in prior years to be included in income as investments in excess passive assets under section 956A (amounts of earnings described in sec. 959(c)(1)(B)), together with the retained earnings that were required in prior years to be included in income as investments in U.S. property under section 956 (amounts of earnings described in sec. 959(c)(1)(A)). The attribution between the two categories is made on a pro rata basis. As under present law, distributed earnings are treated as next attributable to the retained earnings that were required in prior years to be included in income as subpart F income under section 951(a)(1)(A) (amounts of earnings described in sec. 959(c)(2)), and last attributable to other earnings and profits (amounts of earnings described in sec. 959(c)(3)). As under present law, distributions of earnings described in section 959(c)(2) are treated as attributable to more recent years first. The same present-law rule also applies to earnings described in section 959(c)(3). Amounts that would be included in income as investments in U.S. property under section 956 are treated as first attributable to the retained earnings that were required to be included in income as subpart F income under section 951(a)(1)(A) (amounts of earnings described in sec. 959(c)(2)), and then attributable to other earnings and profits. Amounts that would be included in income as investments in excess passive assets under section 956A are treated as first attributable to the retained earnings that were required to be included in income as subpart F income under section 951(a)(1)(A) (amounts of earnings described in sec. 959(c)(2)) to the extent that such earnings were accumulated in taxable years beginning after September 30, 1993, then attributable to earnings and profits that were not required to be included in income as subpart F income (amounts of earnings described in sec. 959(c)(3)). As under present law in the case of investments in U.S. property, to the extent that an amount would be included in income as either an investment in U.S. property or an investment in excess passive assets, but for being attributable to earnings that had been previously taxed as subpart F income under section 951(a)(1)(A), that amount of earnings is converted from an amount treated as previously taxed under section 951(a)(1)(A) (amounts of earnings described in sec. 959(c)(2)), to an amount treated as previously taxed under subparagraph (B) or (C) of section 951(a)(1) (amounts of earnings described in subparagraph (A) or (B) of sec. 959(c)(1)), as the case may be. Therefore, for example, the amount of earnings treated as having been previously included in the income of the shareholder on account of excess passive assets (i.e. the amount of earnings described in section 959(c)(1)(B)) includes not only earnings that actually resulted in an inclusion of income under section 951(a)(1)(C), but also earnings that would have resulted in such an inclusion but for being attributable to earnings that had been previously taxed as subpart F income under section 951(a)(1)(A).

Example. The above rules are illustrated by the following multi-year example: [8]

Year 1. Assume that a U.S. corporation owns all the stock of a controlled foreign corporation, which is not (and has never been) a PFIC. The foreign corporation holds an average of 100 of assets, of which 35 are passive, and no U.S. property. Further assume that the foreign corporation has accumulated earnings and profits of 25 at the close of year 1, none of which is subpart F income or has otherwise

[Footnote ¶ 3051 continued]

7. As under current law, actual distributions are taken into account after the application of section 951(a)(1)(A).

8. This example assumes that all years at issue begin after the effective date of the bill, i.e., after September 30, 1993.

previously been included in the income of a U.S. shareholder under subpart F, and 15 of which was earned in taxable years beginning after September 30, 1993. Under the bill, the foreign corporation is treated as having excess passive assets of 10. The amount determined under section 956A is also 10: that is, the lesser of the 10 of excess passive assets or the 15 of post-1993 accumulated earnings. Therefore, for year 1, 10 is included in the U.S. corporation's income as earnings invested in excess passive assets under section 951(a)(1)(C). Also, 10 of the foreign corporation's earnings is treated as previously taxed and described in subsection (c)(1)(B) of section 959 (as income previously taxed under section 951(a)(1)(C)), attributable to taxable years beginning after September 30, 1993. The controlled foreign corporation's accumulated earnings of 25 are unchanged by the inclusion in income under section 951(a)(1)(C).

Year 2. Next assume that in year 2, the controlled foreign corporation still has average total assets of 100, but now 40 (rather than 35) of these assets are passive. Also assume that the foreign corporation earns 5 of subpart F interest income in year 2, and makes no actual distributions of earnings and profits. (For simplicity, assume for this purpose that the new earnings have been taken into account in arriving at the figure of 100 for average assets.) As a result, the foreign corporation holds accumulated earnings and profits of 30 at the close of year 2, 20 of which was earned in taxable years beginning after September 30, 1993. The interest income of 5 is included in the U.S. corporation's income as subpart F income under sec. 951(a)(1)(A). Under the bill, before computing whether there is an additional income inclusion on account of excess passive assets, the 5 of subpart F earnings is treated as previously taxed and described in subsection (c)(2) of section 959 (as income previously taxed under section 951(a)(1)(A)), attributable to taxable years beginning after September 30, 1993. The year 2 amount determined under section 956A is 5. It is the lesser of two amounts. The first amount is 5, or the difference between the 15 of excess passive assets in year 2 and the 10 of previous inclusions of earnings invested in excess passive assets. The second amount is 10, or the difference between the 20 of post-1993 accumulated earnings and the 10 of previous inclusions of excess passive assets. The amount included in the U.S. corporation's year 2 income on account of its (increased) investment in excess passive assets, however, is zero. This results from the 5 of subpart F income under section 951(a)(1)(A) that the foreign corporation earned in year 2, and the ordering rules of section 959 as modified by the bill. Under the bill, there is no excess of the amount determined under section 956A (5, as noted above) over the amount of the foreign corporation's retained earnings that have been included in the U.S. corporation's income under section 951(a)(1)(A), attributable to taxable years beginning after September 30, 1993 (also 5). The bill also provides, in this case, that the earnings in the amount of 5 that would have been included in income under section 951(a)(1)(C) but for the previously taxed subpart F income are to be treated as described in section 959(c)(1)(B) (i.e., as earnings previously taxed as investments in excess passive assets) rather than in section 959(c)(2) (i.e., as earnings previously taxed as subpart F income under section 951(a)(1)(A)). Therefore, at the end of year 2, 15 is the total amount of earnings (10 from year 1 plus 5 from year 2) treated as described in section 959(c)(1), and the accumulated earnings of 30 are unaffected by the income inclusions.

Year 3. Assume that, as in year 2, the foreign corporation has an average of 40 of passive assets and 100 of total assets. Assume further that the foreign corporation earns another 5 of subpart F interest income, earns 10 of other income, and makes an actual distribution of 20 to the U.S. corporation. (Again, for simplicity, assume that the new earnings and the distribution have been taken into account in arriving at the figure of 100 for total assets.) The foreign corporation thus holds accumulated earnings and profits of 45 at year end, before taking the current-year distribution into account, of which 35 are attributable to taxable years beginning after September 30, 1993. As in year 2, the year 3 subpart F interest income of 5 is included in the U.S. corporation's income (under sec. 981(a)(1)(A)). Also as in year 2, under the bill, before computing whether there is in income inclusion for year 3 on account of excess passive assets, the subpart F earnings of 5 are treated as previously taxed and described in section 959(c)(2) (as income previously taxed under section 951(a)(1)(A)), attributable to taxable years beginning after September 30, 1993. The bill provides that the actual distribution of 20 is accounted for next. The distribution of earnings is treated as attributable first to the cumulative earnings described in section 959(c)(1) (15, in this case all described in section 959(c)(1)(B), and all attributable to taxable years beginning after September 30, 1993), and next to the cumulative earnings described in section 959(c)(2) (5, in this case all from year 3, all attributable to taxable years beginning after September 30, 1993). Thus, the distribution of 20 is treated as fully attributable to previously taxed earnings, and, after the distribution, no portion of the foreign corporation's retained earnings is treated as previously taxed income described by subsection (c)(1) or (c)(2) of section 959. Next, if the foreign corporation had invested any of its earnings in U.S. property under section 956, the amount of the income inclusion under section 951(a)(1)(B) would be determined. In this case, there is none. Last, the income inclusion (if any) under section 956A is determined. The amount determined under section 956A is 15. This is the lesser of 15 (the amount of excess passive assets, unreduced because no portion of the foreign corporation's retained earnings is treated as previously taxed under section 951(a)(1)(C)), and 15 (the amount of post-1993 accumulated earnings, unreduced because no portion of the foreign corporation's retained earnings is treated as previously taxed under subparagraph (B) or (C) of section 951(a)(1)). The amount included in the U.S. corporation's income for year 3 under section 951(a)(1)(C) is the 15 determined under section 956A, again unreduced because no portion of the foreign corporation's retained earnings is treated as previously taxed under section 951(a)(1)(A). The U.S. corporation has a total income inclusion under subpart F of 20 for year 3: 5 under section 951(a)(1)(A) plus 15 under section 951(a)(1)(C). As of the end of year 3, the taxpayer treats 15 of earnings as described in section 959(c)(1)(B) (i.e., as earnings previously taxed as investments in excess passive assets), and has accumulated earnings of 25, of which 15 are attributable to taxable years beginning after September 30, 1993.

Special rules for decontrolled foreign corporations. Proper adjustments are to be made to the measurement of assets and earnings in the case of any foreign corporation that ceases to be U.S.-controlled during the taxable year. The determination of the pro rata share held in such a corporation by any U.S. shareholder is to be made on the basis of stock ownership on the last day during the taxable year on which the foreign corporation is a controlled foreign corporation. The determination of excess passive assets for such a taxable year is made by taking into account only those quarters of the taxable year that end prior to such day, and averaging only over such reduced number of quarters. The determination of current earnings and profits for such a taxable year is made by taking into account only a pro rata portion of the corporation's current earnings and profits for that entire year, based on the part of that year during which the foreign corporation is a controlled foreign corporation.

Aggregation and antiabuse rules. The bill provides an aggregation rule applicable to any chain of controlled foreign corporations that are connected through stock ownership, where more than 50 percent, by vote or value, of the stock of each member of the chain (other than the top-tier controlled foreign corporation) is owned, directly or indirectly, by one or more other controlled foreign corporations that are members of the chain ("CFC chain"). Under this rule, the amount of excess passive assets for the CFC chain would be determined on the basis of the sum of the assets of each controlled foreign corporation in the CFC chain and the sum of the passive assets of each controlled foreign corporation in the CFC chain. The total applicable earnings for the CFC chain would be determined as the sum of the applicable earnings of each controlled foreign corporation in the CFC chain. [9] Each controlled foreign corporation in the CFC chain would be treated as holding its pro rata share of the excess passive assets of the CFC chain, on the basis of that controlled foreign corporation's percentage share of the total applicable earnings of the CFC chain. The bill provides regulatory authority under which the Treasury is instructed to prescribe such regulations as may be necessary to carry out the purposes of the excess passive assets provisions, and to

[Footnote ¶ 3051 continued]

9. Inasmuch as the amount of a controlled foreign corporation's applicable earnings can never be less than zero, a corporation with no current earnings and an accumulated deficit is not taken into account in determining the sum of the applicable earnings of all controlled foreign corporations in the CFC chain.

prevent their avoidance. Within this authority, the committee intends that the Treasury prescribe regulations under which the earnings and assets of two or more controlled foreign corporations that are related but are not part of the same CFC chain may be treated as if they were part of the same CFC chain, if one of the principal purposes for separately organizing, acquiring, or maintaining such multiple corporations is to avoid an inclusion under the excess passive assets provision. In making the determination as to purpose, the committee expects that the regulations may take into account various presumptions, including (but not limited to) those set forth in temporary Treas. reg. sec. 1.954-1T(b)(4).

Modification of section 956

The bill treats earnings invested by a controlled foreign corporation in U.S. property under revised rules that parallel those that govern the treatment of excess passive assets, as described above. Under the revised rules, the amount determined under section 956 with respect to a U.S. shareholder of a controlled foreign corporation is the lesser of two amounts. The first amount is the excess (if any) of the U.S. shareholder's pro rata share of the U.S. property of the controlled foreign corporation, over that portion of the retained earnings of the foreign corporation that is treated as having been previously included in the income of the U.S. shareholder on account of earnings invested in U.S. property. [10] The second amount is the U.S. shareholder's pro rata share of the controlled foreign corporation's current and accumulated earnings and profits (but not reduced by a deficit in accumulated earnings and profits), reduced by the portion of the retained earnings of the foreign corporation that was previously included in the income of the U.S. shareholder on account of either investments in U.S. property or investments in excess passive assets. The income inclusion for a U.S. shareholder of the controlled foreign corporation is the amount determined as above under section 956, less retained earnings of the controlled foreign corporation that are treated as having been previously taxed to the U.S. shareholder as subpart F income of the controlled foreign corporation under section 951(a)(1)(A) (see sec. 951(a)(1)(B), as modified by the bill). (See the discussion of the bill's rules for the treatment of previously taxed income under "Coordination and ordering provisions," above.) As noted above, the bill provides that actual distributions during the taxable year and their effects on the determination of earnings and profits, previously taxed amounts, or any other item, are taken into account prior to the determination of amounts under section 956 that are subject to income inclusion under section 951(a)(1)(B), and amounts under section 956A that are subject to income inclusion under section 951(a)(1)(C). The controlled foreign corporation's U.S. property is measured as the average of the adjusted basis (as determined for purposes of calculating earnings and profits) of such property held (directly or indirectly) by the controlled foreign corporation as of the close of each quarter of its taxable year, less any liability to which the property is subject (as under present law). The committee intends that the measurement of assets as of the close of each quarter of the taxable year shall disregard short-term loans or other temporary arrangements with regard to the corporations's assets, where one of the principal purposes of such an arrangement was to avoid taking assets into account for purposes of this provision. Examples of what the IRS views as such arrangements are discussed in Rev. Rul. 89-73 (1989-1 C.B. 258), interpreting present law. The bill is not intended to change the measurement of U.S. property that may apply, for example, in the case of certain short-term obligations, as provided in IRS Notice 88-108 (1988-2 C.B. 445), interpreting present law. Obligations subject to the special treatment of IRS Notice 88-108 are those that are collected within 30 days of their issuance, but the exclusion of such short-term obligations does not apply if the controlled

[Footnote ¶3051 continued]

10. As noted above, under the previously taxed income rules of section 959, retained earnings of the foreign corporation that are treated as having been previously included in the income of the U.S. shareholder include retained earnings that were previously included in the income of another U.S. person that is a proven predecessor in interest to the U.S. shareholder. In addition, as discussed above under "Coordination and ordering provisions," under the bill's rules for the treatment of previously taxed income, the amount of earnings treated as having been previously included in the income of the shareholder on account of investments of earnings in U.S. property (i.e., the amount of earnings described in section 959(c)(1)(A)) includes not only earnings that actually resulted in an inclusion of income under section 951(a)(1)(B), but also earnings that would have resulted in such an inclusion but for being attributable to earnings that had been previously taxed as subpart F income under section 951(a)(1)(A).

foreign corporation holds obligations that would constitute U.S. property if held by the controlled foreign corporation on the date of measurement (determined without regard to this 30-day rule) for aggregate periods totalling at least 60 days in the taxable year, without regard to whether any such obligations are held on the date of measurement.

Same-country dividend rule

The bill limits the application of the same-country exception to the determination of subpart F income in the case of certain dividends received by controlled foreign corporations. Amounts distributed with respect to stock owned by the controlled foreign corporation do not qualify for the same-country exception to the extent that the distributed earnings and profits were accumulated by the distributing corporation during periods when the controlled foreign corporation did not hold the stock. The bill's limitation applies, and thus the same-country exception does not apply, even in cases where the controlled foreign corporation receiving the distribution did not exist at the time the distributed earnings and profits were accumulated, but the stock of the distributing corporation was held by the shareholders of the receiving corporation at such time. The committee intends that no inference be drawn from the bill as to the proper interpretation of temporary Treas. reg. sec. 1.954-2T(b)(3)(iii) (which also imposes limitations on the same-country exception from the treatment of dividends as subpart F income).

Effect on foreign-tax credit limitation of distributions of previously taxed earnings

Under the bill, receipt of a distribution of previously taxed income by a U.S. shareholder of one or more controlled foreign corporations increases the U.S. shareholder's foreign tax credit limitation to the extent of the aggregate amount in a single "excess limitation account" maintained by that U.S. shareholder for each of its separate foreign tax credit limitation categories. That account reflects the cumulative amount by which the U.S. shareholder's foreign tax credit limitation had been increased on account of subpart F income inclusions (in excess of the foreign taxes allowed as a credit on account of such inclusions) in taxable years beginning after September 30, 1993, less the total amount by which the account was used to increase the U.S. shareholder's foreign tax credit limitation upon prior distributions of previously taxed earnings and profits. The treatment described in the paragraph above applies to a taxpayer that (1) chose to have the benefits of the foreign tax credit for a taxable year beginning after September 30, 1993, in which that taxpayer had an inclusion of subpart F income (if there were creditable foreign taxes paid or accrued for that year); (2) chooses to have the benefits of the foreign tax credit for any taxable year in which earnings that were so included are actually distributed and treated as previously taxed; and (3) pays, is deemed to pay, or accrues creditable foreign taxes for the year in which the distribution is received. The committee intends that any distribution in a taxable year beginning after September 30, 1993, be treated as comprising earnings attributable to taxable years beginning after September 30, 1993, to the extent of such earnings, then earnings attributable to taxable years beginning prior to October 1, 1993. The committee anticipates that Treasury regulations will provide guidance as to the application of these provisions in the case of taxpayers that choose to have the benefits of the foreign tax credit in some but not all years. In the case of a foreign tax credit carryback to a taxable year beginning after September 30, 1993, the increase in the excess limitation account resulting from subpart F income inclusions for that taxable year is reduced by the amount of foreign taxes allowed as a credit by reason of the carryback, if such foreign taxes would not have been allowed as a credit for that year but for the subpart F income inclusions for that year.

Modification of certain PFIC rules in the case of U.S. shareholders of controlled foreign corporations

Measurement of assets. The bill modifies the present-law rules for applying the PFIC asset test in the case of U.S. shareholders of controlled foreign corporations. In testing a controlled foreign corporation for PFIC status with respect to its "U.S. shareholders," under the bill, assets generally are measured by adjusted basis as determined for purposes of calculating earnings and profits, with no option to use fair market value. Adjusted basis for this purpose is modified to take into account certain research and experimental expenditures and certain payments for the use of intangible property that is licensed to the controlled foreign corporation. First, the aggregate adjusted basis of the total assets of the controlled foreign corporation is increased by the total amount of research and development expenditures made by the controlled foreign corporation, for qualified research or experimental expenditures (as defined for purposes of Code section 174 and the Treasury regulations thereunder), taking into account payments and expenditures (including cost-sharing payments) made in the current taxable year and the two most recent preceding taxable years. In addition, the aggregate adjusted basis of the total assets of the controlled foreign corporation is increased by the amount of three times the total payments made during the taxable year to unrelated persons and related U.S. persons for the use of intangible property with respect to which the controlled foreign corporation is a licensee, and which the controlled foreign corporation uses in the active conduct of its trade or business. Payments made to related foreign persons are not taken into account. For purposes of this rule, intangible property is defined as under section 936(h)(3)(B) of the Code.

Treatment of certain securities dealers. The bill excludes from the definition of passive income under the PFIC rules income derived in the active conduct of a securities business by certain corporations registered in the United States as brokers or dealers in securities, and, to the extent provided in Treasury regulations, income so derived by any other corporation engaged in the active conduct of a trade or business as a broker or dealer in securities. As with the asset-valuation rule above, this exclusion applies only to a controlled foreign corporation, and only for purposes of the treatment of its U.S. shareholders. The bill provides that similar rules apply in determining whether the income of a related person is passive (whether or not the related person is a corporation), solely for purposes of classifying amounts paid to a controlled foreign corporation as passive or not pursuant to the PFIC related-person rule (sec. 1298(b)(2)(C)). [11] The committee anticipates that Treasury regulations will provide guidance as to what constitutes the active conduct of a trade or business as a broker or dealer in securities. The committee further anticipates that such regulations will provide that income derived from the performance of bona fide securities-related activities in the course of the active conduct of such a business generally will be treated as income other than passive income. The committee intends that, in practice, the effect of this provision shall be only to mitigate the effect of the PFIC rules and the excess passive assets rules on a company insofar as it is actively engaged in the business of providing the services of a financial intermediary to unrelated parties, rather than used as a vehicle for investment in stock, securities, or other financial products on behalf of its shareholders or other related parties. There are other instances in the Code and regulations where it is necessary to draw similar distinctions, and the Treasury is invited to consider whether any tests employed in those provisions are suitable in light of the purposes of this provision. For example, the controlled foreign corporation rules may require a determination as to whether a foreign corporation is a regular dealer (within the meaning of section 954(c)(1)(B)) in stocks, securities, or derivative financial products during its taxable year. As another example, the PFIC rules exempt a foreign corporation, to the extent provided in regulations, from passive characterization of its income from the active conduct of a banking business. Guidance has been issued under that provision analogous to the guidance that might be issued under this provision of the bill. As a third example, guidance has been issued under the foreign tax credit limitation regulations for identifying financial services entities. As in the cases of the PFIC bank rules and the foreign tax credit limitation rules on financial services entities, the committee believes that the Treasury could consider a variety of activities that may indicate the existence of an active securities business. [12] In addition, in appropriate circumstances, the

[Footnote ¶ 3051 continued]

11. For example, in the case of U.S. shareholders of a controlled foreign corporation that is engaged in the active conduct of a trade or business as a broker or dealer in securities, and that receives interest, dividents, rent, or royalties from a related person (which may or may not be a corporation), the determination of the amount of such income that is allocable to income of the related person other than passive income is made by applying the exception for certain income of securities brokers and dealers to the income of the related person, whether or not the related person is a coporation, solely for purposes of applying the PFIC income test to income earned by the controlled foreign corporation through the related person.

12. Such activities might include: (a) purchasing or selling inventory securities such as stock, debt obligations, commodity futures or other securities or derivative financial products (including notional principal contracts) from or to unrelated persons, arranging such purchases or sales on behalf of unrelated persons who are customers in the course of a business as a

Treasury might consider it relevant that a foreign corporation is or is not registered or authorized in the country in which it conducts its principal securities broker or dealer operations to conduct the bona fide securities activities that it performs in that country, and is subject to the appropriate securities regulatory authorities of that jurisdiction. [13] The foregoing list of possible approaches and factors to take into account is not intended to be exclusive of other approaches or factors not mentioned. Nor is it intended to suggest that the presence of any of the factors mentioned above, of the passing or failing of any test existing under present law, must be used by Treasury to determine the outcome of the question whether a foreign corporation is engaged in the active conduct of a trade or business as a broker or dealer in securities. The committee does not intend to limit the Treasury's discretion to fashion rules suitable to the purposes of the provision. The committee does intend, however, that Treasury clarify the issue of what income qualifies as derived in the active conduct of a trade or business as a broker or dealer in securities, by issuing guidance in time for taxpayers to file returns reporting subpart F income inclusions on account of excess passive assets. As under the exceptions for active banking and insurance income of Code section 1296(b)(2), the committee intends that the Secretary's regulatory authority under the bill be exercised so as to apply the PFIC provisions to any income derived by persons engaged in bona fide securities-related activities where necessary to prevent individuals from earning what is essentially tax-deferred portfolio investment income through a foreign corporation. Also, as under section 1296(b)(2), the committee intends that income derived by persons engaged in bona fide securities-related activities that are basically widely-held incorporated investment vehicles will be treated as passive for purposes of the

[Footnote ¶ 3051 continued]

securities broker, and holding stock, debt obligations and other securities as inventory for sale to such customers; (b) arranging notional principal contracts and other hedging transactions for, or entering into such transactions or any other derivative financial products with, unrelated persons who are customers; (c) arranging foreign exchange transactions for, or engaging in foreign exchange transactions with, unrelated persons who are customers; (d) underwriting issues of stocks, debt obligations or other securities under best-efforts or firm-commitment agreements with unrelated persons; (e) purchasing, selling, discounting, or negotiating on a regular basis for unrelated persons notes, drafts, checks, bills of exchange, acceptances or other evidences of indebtedness; (f) lending inventory stocks or securities to unrelated persons; (g) engaging in hedging activities directly related to bona fide securities activities described in items (a) through (f) of this list; (h) servicing mortgages; (i) investment banking activities; (j) providing financial or investment advisory services, investment management services, fiduciary services, trust services, or custodial services to unrelated persons; (k) providing margin or other financing for unrelated persons who are customers, secured by securities or money market instruments, including repurchase agreements, or financing in connection with any of the bona fide securities activities described in items (a) through (j) of this list; (l) disposing of any property (whether tangible or intangible, personal or real) that was used or acquired in the active conduct of the securities business, but only to the extent that the property was held in connection with a bona fide securities activity; and (m) any other activity that the Secretary may determine to be a bona fide securities activity that is commonly conducted by active foreign securities dealers in the ordinary course of their securities business.

13. One approach that the Treasury may wish to consider in drafting regulations under this provision would be to treat a controlled foreign corporation as an active foreign securities broker or dealer for a taxable year if it satisfies a securities-related activity test, a gross income test and a licensing requirement. To satisfy the securities-related activity test, the foreign corporation could be required to qualify as (i) a "regular dealer" in stocks, securities and derivative financial products within the meaning of section 954(c) and the regulations thereunder, (ii) a "qualified affiliate" or (iii) to the extent provided in the regulations, a qualified foreign securities broker. Under the gross income test of the regulations, the foreign corporation could be required to derive at least 60 percent of its total gross income for the taxable year from bona fide securities-related activities. The PFIC look-through rules of sections 1296(b)(2)(C) and 1296(c) would not apply for purposes of this test. Under the licensing requirement of the regulations, a controlled foreign corporation (other than a qualified affiliate) that is not registered as a securities broker or dealer under the Securities Exchange Act of 1934 could be required to be licensed or authorized in the country in which it conducts its principal securities dealer operations (or, in the case of a qualified foreign securities broker, its principal securities broker operations) to conduct the bona fide securities-related activities that it performs in that country. These activities would be required to be subject to the appropriate securities regulatory authorities of that country. A "qualified affiliate" could be defined as a foreign corporation that regularly performs in the ordinary course of its trade or business at least one bona fide securities-related activity, and that is also a member of an affiliated group that (1) derives 50 percent or more of its total gross income for the year from bona fide securities-related activities, and (2) includes a corporation that either actively conducts business in the United States as a registered securities broker or dealer or qualifies as a "regular dealer" in stock, securities and derivative financial products under section 954(c) and the regulations thereunder or (to the extent provided in regulations) as a qualified foreign securities broker. The regulations could also require that the gross income of the registered securities broker or dealer, "regular dealer" or qualified foreign securities broker represent at least 20 percent of the total gross income of the affiliated group for the year. It might be necessary for Treasury regulations to modify the definition of affiliated group provided in section 1504 in order to carry out the purposes of this provision, such as to accommodate the inclusion of foreign corporations and the ownership of stock by U.S. shareholders that are U.S. partnerships.

PFIC definition. Under existing law, any allocation of passive income earned by, or passive assets held by, a foreign corporation to stock held by particular shareholders of the corporation (e.g., to foreign shareholders that are not subject to the PFIC provisions) is not respected for purposes of the application of the PFIC provisions to that foreign corporation and its shareholders. Accordingly, in the case of a controlled foreign corporation that is eligible for the securities exception, the committee intends that any allocation of particular items of income or assets to stock held by particular shareholders of the foreign corporation not be respected for purposes of the application of the PFIC and excess passive asset provisions to that foreign corporation and its shareholders.

Treatment of certain income inclusions as distributions. Under the bill, inclusions of income on account of investments of earnings of a controlled foreign corporation in U.S. property, or ownership of excess passive assets, are treated as distributions for purposes of computing the interest charge on excess distributions to the U.S. shareholders of PFICs that are controlled foreign corporations. Accordingly, such inclusions of income are subject to treatment as excess distributions under section 1291(b) of the PFIC rules. Such inclusions of income are taken into account as amounts received with respect to the PFIC stock (e.g., in prior years) in the determination of whether or not there is an excess distribution for the taxable year.

Treatment of certain leased assets for PFIC purposes

The bill treats certain leased property as assets held by the foreign corporation for purposes of the PFIC asset test. This rule applies to tangible personal property with respect to which the foreign corporation is the lessee under a lease with a term of at least 12 months. Under the bill, the measure of leased property for purposes of applying the asset test is the unamortized portion of the present value of the payments under the lease. The committee intends that regulations provide guidance for determining the unamortized portion of the present value of the payments. Present value is to be determined, under regulations, as of the beginning of the lease term, and, except as provided in regulations, by using a discount rate equal to the applicable Federal rate determined under the rules applicable to original discount instruments (sec. 1274(d)), substituting under those rules the term of the lease for the term of the debt instrument. In applying those rules, options to renew or extend the lease are not to be taken into account. Also, the special rule to be applied under section 1274(d)(2) in the case of a sale or exchange is disregarded. Property leased by a corporation is not taken into account in testing for PFIC status under the asset test either if the lessor is a related person (as that term is defined under the foreign base company rules) with respect to the lessee, or if a principal purpose of leasing the property was to avoid the PFIC provisions.

Effective Date

The provision generally is effective for taxable years of foreign corporations beginning after September 30, 1993, and for taxable years of domestic shareholders in which or with which such taxable years end. The provision modifying the rules for increasing the foreign tax credit limitation upon distributions of previously taxed income is effective for actual distributions of earnings that are included under subpart F in taxable years of U.S. shareholders beginning after September 30, 1993. In the case of any distributions of earnings that were included under subpart F in taxable years of U.S. shareholders beginning prior to October 1, 1993, the rules of present law will continue to apply.

[Conference Report]

Conference Agreement

The conference agreement follows the Senate amendment, with certain modifications.

Inclusions based on excess passive assets

Aggregation rule. The conference agreement clarifies the Senate amendment's aggregation rule for the determination of excess passive assets of related controlled foreign corporations. The aggregation rule in the conference agreement applies to a "CFC group" of controlled foreign corporations, clarifying that the group can include one or more chains of related controlled foreign corporations, linked by common ownership by a top-tier controlled foreign corporation. As is true for a "CFC chain" under the Senate amendment, the CFC group under the conference agreement determines the amount of excess passive assets for the group by treating all group members as a single corporation, and then apportions such aggregate excess passive assets among the members of the group on a pro rata basis in accordance with each member's percentage share of the total applicable earnings of the CFC group. The conferees wish to clarify that under the conference agreement, as is typically the case where a group of corporations is treated as a single corporation for tax purposes, intercompany stock and obligations generally are disregarded in the determination of excess passive assets. For example, stock owned by one member of the group in another member of the group is disregarded, as are intercompany loans, other intercompany receivables, and intercompany licenses. As another example, assume that one member of the group provides goods or services to an unrelated customer, thereby acquiring a trade or service receivable. Assume further that the group member then factors the receivable to another member of the group, and the second member later receives the payment from the customer, which gives rise to income for the second member which is treated as passive interest income. During the period when the receivable is held by the second group member, the basis of the receivable in the hands of group, for purposes of applying the conference agreement to the group, would reflect the cost incurred by the second member to acquire the receivable in the factoring transaction with the first member. The conferees intend that the characterization of the receivable as a passive or nonpassive asset for purposes of determining excess passive assets depend on the activities by which the group as a whole derived the receivable. If the receivable properly would be viewed as a nonpassive asset based on those activities (without regard to which member of the group carried out the activities), the conferees anticipate that interest incidentally received by the second group member generally would not cause the receivable to be characterized as a passive asset (see, e.g., Notice 88-22, 1988-1 C.B. 489). Inasmuch as stock owned by one member of the group in another member of the group would be disregarded, the look-through rule of section 1296(c) does not apply within a CFC group. However, the look-through rule of section 3296(c) does apply in the case of stock owned by one or more members of the CFC group in a foreign corporation that is not a member of the CFC group. For example, if one member of the CFC group owns 20 percent of the stock of another controlled foreign corporation that is not a member of the CFC group, and a second member of the CFC group owns 10 percent of the stock of such non-member controlled foreign corporation, the CFC group would be treated as owning 30 percent of the assets of the non-member controlled foreign corporation under the look-through rule of section 3296(c). For purposes of the conference agreement's aggregation rule and look-through rule, all amounts of assets and earnings must be converted into units of a single currency, ordinarily the U.S. dollar. The conferees anticipate that Treasury will provide guidance as to the translation method appropriate to such conversion. The conferees anticipate that Treasury will authorize the use of the spot rate on the date of measurement for such purpose. In addition, the conferees anticipate that Treasury may authorize an alternative method, under which the U.S. shareholders of a controlled foreign corporation would be permitted to determine the adjusted basis of the assets of the controlled foreign corporation using the historical cost in U.S. dollars of the foreign currency-denominated assets, in cases where the Secretary is satisfied that such historical costs can be established in a reasonably administrable fashion consistent with the purposes of the provision. Until guidance is issued by the Secretary, the conferees intend that taxpayers be permitted to convert asset costs to a single currency using any reasonable method (which may be, for example, a spot-rate conversion method or a historical dollar-cost method), so long as the method is consistently applied to all controlled foreign corporations (whether or not members of a CFC group) in all taxable years.

Treatment of certain previously taxed PFIC inclusions. The House bill and the Senate amendment provide rules for avoiding the double taxation of income in the case of subpart F inclusions under section 951(a)(1)(A) from controlled foreign corporations with excess passive assets. The conference agreement adds a similar coordination rule for controlled foreign corporations that are also PFICs, and that are subject to current inclusion of income under section 1293. Under the conference agreement, any inclusion of income under section 1293 to a U.S. shareholder of a controlled foreign corporation that is also a PFIC is treated as an inclusion of income under section 951(a)(1)(A) for purposes of the rules of subpart F pertaining to previously taxed income.

Modification of certain PFIC rules

Treatment of certain banking and securities income. Present law provides regulatory authority to the Treasury to except from the definition of passive income certain income derived in the active conduct of a banking business. The House bill and the Senate amendment provide similar authority, in the case of U.S. shareholders of a PFIC that is also a controlled foreign corporation, with respect to certain income derived in the active conduct of a securities business. The conferees are informed that there is a significant commonality between the business activities that may be conducted by a controlled foreign corporation in the course of a banking business and the business activities that may be conducted by a controlled foreign corporation in the course of a securities business. The conferees intend to clarify that these grants of regulatory authority are sufficiently broad to encompass, in appropriate circumstances, the income derived by a single controlled foreign corporation in the active conduct of a business that consists in part of banking activities and in part of securities activities.

Study on treatment of certain financing and credit services businesses. The conference agreement provides that certain income derived in the conduct of a banking or insurance business, or, in the case of U.S. shareholders of a controlled foreign corporation, a securities business, may be excluded from the definition of passive income for purposes of the PFIC rules and the excess passive assets rules. These rules, however, do not apply to income derived in the conduct of financing and credit services businesses. The conferees intend that the Treasury Department study the tax treatment of income derived in the conduct of financing and credit services businesses, and provide the House Committee on Ways and Means and the Senate Committee on Finance with a report of such study by March 1, 1994. The study should include the Treasury's views and recommendations as to whether the PFIC rules and the excess passive assets rules should be amended insofar as they relate to the treatment of such income, along with a discussion of the merits and consequences of any such amendment. In addition, the study should address any special considerations that might pertain in this regard with respect to a foreign corporation that is not a controlled foreign corporation, and discuss the extent to which appropriate anti-abuse rules would be sufficient to address special concerns that might arise in this context.

Special rule for certain intangible property. The Senate amendment provides a special rule for determining the basis of assets in the case of certain research and experimental expenditures and certain payments for the use of intangible property that is licensed to the controlled foreign corporation. Payments made to related foreign persons are not taken into account. The conference agreement clarifies that all research and experimental expenditures that are taken into account for purposes of this special rule are net of any reimbursements (such as cost-sharing payments, to the extent they represent such expenditures) received by the controlled foreign corporation with respect to such expenditures. In addition, the conference agreement clarifies that payments made by a controlled foreign corporation for the use of intangible property are disregarded if one principal purpose of licensing the intangible property was to avoid the PFIC rules or the excess passive assets provisions. For example, assume a domestic corporation licensed intangible property through a controlled foreign corporation to an unrelated person, rather than directly to the unrelated person, and one principal purpose for licensing the property indirectly was to increase the measurement of the controlled foreign corporation's active assets. In such a case, the payment made by the controlled foreign corporation to its domestic parent with respect to the intangible property would not be taken into account. As another example, assume a controlled foreign corporation licensed intangible property to its domestic parent and the U.S. parent relicensed all or a portion of the intangible property rights to a second controlled foreign corporation, and one principal purpose for licensing the property indirectly was to increase the measurement of the second controlled foreign corporation's active assets. In such a case, the payment made by the second controlled foreign corporation to its domestic parent with respect to the intangible property would not be taken into account.

Study on treatment of certain marketing expenditures. The conference agreement increases the adjusted basis of the assets of a controlled foreign corporation by reference to expenditures deductible under section 174. When a controlled foreign corporation incurs research and experimental expenditures, the practical effect may be to enhance the corporation's ability to generate active business income over an extended period; yet inasmuch as such expenditures are commonly deductible under section 174, these types of expenditures may affect the corporation's adjusted basis in its assets differently than expenditures to generate active business income over an extended period that take the form of a purchase of tangible or intangible assets. The conference agreement provides for adjustments to the adjusted basis of the assets of the controlled foreign corporation to take account of this difference. Taxpayers have argued that the practical effect of marketing expenditures that are properly deductible under section 162 as ordinary and necessary business expenses may also be to enhance the corporation's ability to generate active business income over an extended period. The conferees intend that the Treasury Department study the question whether similar basis adjustments should be made for such expenses, and provide the House Committee on Ways and Means and the Senate Committee on Finance with a report of such study by March 1, 1994. The study should include the Treasury's views and recommendations as to whether the excess passive assets rules should be amended insofar as they relate to the treatment of such expenses, along with a discussion of the merits and consequences of any such amendment.

Modifications to section 956

Special rule for U.S. property acquired before foreign corporation is U.S. controlled. The conference agreement includes a provision that clarifies the application of section 956 of the Code, as modified by the bill, in the case of U.S. property acquired by a foreign corporation before the foreign corporation becomes a controlled foreign corporation. Under the conference agreement, the measure of U.S. property held by a controlled foreign corporation for any taxable year generally does not include any specific items of U.S. property that were acquired by the foreign corporation before the first day on which the foreign corporation was treated as a controlled foreign corporation. The aggregate amount of U.S. property so excluded with respect to a controlled foreign corporation for any taxable year, however, cannot exceed the applicable earnings of the controlled foreign corporation to the extent that they were accumulated in periods prior to the first day on which the foreign corporation was treated as a controlled foreign corporation. [76] The conferees note that applicable earnings are reduced, under the conference agreement, both by actual distributions and by income inclusions of excess passive assets or U.S. property. The conference agreement also provides regulatory authority under which the Treasury is instructed to prescribe such regulations as may be necessary to carry out the purposes of section 956, and to prevent their avoidance. Within this authority, the conferees anticipate that the Treasury may prescribe regulations that, for example, would prevent taxpayers from taking advantage of the differences between the excess passive assets rules and the rules of section 956.

Study on investments in U.S. property. The conferees understand that a controlled foreign corporation is not treated as holding U.S. property under section 956 if it invests in an obligation of an unrelated U.S. corporation. A similar rule, however, is not applicable to an investment in an obligation of an unrelated U.S. person other than a corporation. The conferees intend that the Treasury Department study the tax treatment of investments by controlled foreign corporations in obligations of U.S. persons other than corporations, and provide the House Committee on Ways and Means and the Senate Committee on Finance with a report of such study by December 31, 1993. The study should include the Treasury's views and recommendations as to whether the rules of section 956 should be amended insofar as they relate to the treatment of investments by controlled foreign corporations in the obligations of unrelated U.S. persons other than corporations, along with a discussion of the merits and consequences of any such

[Footnote ¶3051 continued]

76. Under the present-law ordering rules for the attribution of actual distributions or income inclusions to years of earnings, earnings from more recent years are treated as distributed or included before earnings from earlier years. Thus, the pre-acquisition earnings, which operate as a limit to the exclusion of certain U.S. property acquired before the foreign corporation became a controlled foreign corporation, will not be treated as distributed or included until actual distributions or income inclusions from the controlled foreign corporation carry out all more recent earnings.

amendment.

Other modifications to the subpart F rules

The House bill and the Senate amendment limit the availability of the same-country exception applicable to the determination of subpart F income in the case of certain dividends received by controlled foreign corporations. Under the conference agreement, amounts distributed with respect to stock owned by the controlled foreign corporation do not qualify for the same-country exception to the extent that the distributed earnings and profits were accumulated by the distributing corporation during periods when the controlled foreign corporation did not hold the stock either directly or indirectly through a chain of one or more subsidiaries, each of which qualifies as a same-country corporation. For example, the same-country exception is available under the conference agreement in the case of a chain of three wholly owned same-country subsidiaries, where the middle-tier subsidiary is liquidated prior to the payment of a dividend from the lowest tier subsidiary to the highest tier subsidiary, and the dividend comprises earnings of the lowest tier subsidiary that were accumulated solely during periods when it was (indirectly) owned by the highest tier subsidiary.

[¶3053] Section 13234. Allocation of Research and Experimental Expenditures.

(Code Sec. 864)

[Senate Explanation]

Present Law

Foreign tax credit and source rules

Under the Code, each item of income is assigned either a U.S. source or a foreign source. The foreign tax credit for foreign taxes paid on foreign source income is limited to the amount of U.S. tax otherwise payable on foreign source income. The foreign tax credit is not available against U.S. tax on U.S. source income. (This is known as the foreign tax credit limitation.) A shift in the source of income from foreign to U.S. may increase net U.S. tax for some taxpayers by reducing the foreign tax credit limitation.

In determining foreign source taxable income for purposes of computing the foreign tax credit limitation, and for other tax purposes, taxpayers are required to allocate and apportion expenses between foreign source income and U.S. source income (Code secs. 861-864). A shift in the allocation and apportionment of expenses from U.S. source to foreign source gross income decreases foreign source taxable income, and may increase U.S. tax by reducing the foreign tax credit limitation.

Research and experimental expense allocation regulation

Treasury regulation section 1.861-8 (promulgated in 1977) sets forth detailed rules for allocating and apportioning several categories of expenses, including deductible research and experimental expenditures ("research expense"). The regulation provides that research expense is ordinarily considered definitely related to all gross income reasonably connected with one or more of 32 product categories based on two-digit classifications of the Standard Industrial Classification ("SIC") system. Research expense is not traced solely to the income generated by the particular product which benefitted from the research activity. Instead, it is associated with all the income within the SIC product group in which the product is classified.

The Treasury regulation contemplates that taxpayers will sometimes undertake research solely to meet legal requirements imposed by a particular governmental entity with respect to improvement or marketing of specific products or processes. In some cases, such research cannot reasonably be expected to generate income (beyond de minimis amounts) outside that governmental entity's jurisdiction. If so, the deductions allowable for the associated research expense are allocated solely to gross income from the geographic source that includes that jurisdiction.

After research expense incurred to meet legal requirements is allocated under the above rule, any remaining research expense generally is apportioned to foreign source income based on the ratio of total foreign source sales receipts in the SIC product group with which the expense is identified to the total worldwide sales receipts in that product group (the "sales" or "gross receipts" method). In computing this fraction, sales by a party controlled or uncontrolled by the taxpayer may be taken into account if the party can reasonably be expected to benefit from the research expense. However, the regulation provides that a taxpayer using the sales method may first apportion at least 30 percent of research expense remaining after allocation to meet legal requirements exclusively to income from the geographic source where over half of the taxpayer's research and development is performed.

Thus, for example, a taxpayer that performs more than 50 percent of its research and development in the United States may automatically apportion at least 30 percent of its remaining research expense to U.S. source income. A taxpayer can choose to apportion to the geographic source where more than 50 percent of its research and development is performed a percentage of research expense significantly greater than 30 percent if the taxpayer establishes that the higher percentage is warranted because the research and development is reasonably expected to have a very limited or long-delayed application outside that geographic source.

Alternatively, subject to certain limitations, a taxpayer may elect to apportion its research expense remaining after any allocation to meet legal requirements under one of two optional gross income methods. Under these optional methods, a taxpayer generally apportions its research expense on the basis of relative amounts of gross income from U.S. and foreign sources. If a taxpayer makes an automatic place-of-performance apportionment, the taxpayer may not use either optional gross income method.

The basic limitation on the use of the optional gross income methods is that the respective portions of a taxpayer's research expense apportioned to U.S. and foreign source income using these methods can not be less than 50 percent of the respective portions that would be apportioned to each income grouping using sales method (including the place-of-performance apportionment).

If this 50-percent limitation is satisfied with respect to both income groupings, the taxpayer may apportion the amount of its research expense that remains after allocation under the legal requirements test ratably on the basis of foreign and U.S. gross income. If the 50-percent limitation is not satisfied with respect to one of the income groupings, then the taxpayer must apportion to that income grouping 50 percent of the amount of its research expense which would have been apportioned to that income grouping under the sales/place-of-performance method. A taxpayer electing an optional gross income method may be able then to reduce the amount of its research expense apportioned to foreign source income to as little as one-half of the amount that would be apportioned to foreign source income under the sales method.

For example, consider a taxpayer with $110 of U.S.-performed research expense and equal U.S. and foreign sales. Assume that $10 of the research expense is to meet U.S. legal requirements and is allocated to U.S. source income. Of the remaining $100, 30 percent ($30) is exclusively apportioned to U.S. source income under the automatic place-of-performance rule and the remaining $70 is divided evenly between U.S. and foreign source income, using the sales method. Thus, under this method $35 would be allocated to foreign source income and $75 would be allocated to U.S. source income. Under the optional gross income methods, the $35 of research expense allocated to foreign sources can be reduced as much as 50 percent, to $17.50. This can occur, for example, if the foreign sales were made by a foreign subsidiary that did not repatriate earnings to the U.S. corporation, and thus a disproportionately high fraction of the U.S. corporation's income is from U.S. sources.

Statutory allocation of research and experimental expense

The Economic Recovery Tax Act of 1981 (ERTA) provided that, for a taxpayer's first two taxable years beginning within two years after the date of its enactment (August 13, 1981), all research and experimental expenditures (within the meaning of sec. 174) paid or incurred in those years for research activities conducted in the United States were to be allocated or apportioned to income from sources within the United States (sec. 223 of ERTA).

This two-year moratorium on the research expense allocation regulation was effectively extended for two additional years by the Tax Reform Act of 1984 (the "1984 Act"). Under section 126 of the 1984 Act, for taxable years beginning generally after August 13, 1983, and on or before August 1, 1985, all of a taxpayer's research and experimental expenditures (within the meaning of sec. 174) attributable to research activities conducted in the United States were to be allocated to income from sources within the United States.

One reason Congress cited for enacting the original two-year moratorium was that some foreign countries do not allow deductions under their tax laws for expenses of research activities conducted in the United States. Taxpayers argued that this disallowance caused U.S.-based research to be disadvantaged. First, U.S.-based research expense is deemed to be allocated to income from a foreign country which may not recognize that such amount is deductible. The allocation of this U.S.-based research expense to foreign source income had the effect of reducing the foreign tax credit of U.S. taxpayers. Because those taxpayers could take their deductions if the research occurred in the foreign country, taxpayers argued that there was an incentive to shift their research expenditures to those foreign countries whose laws disallow tax deductions for research activities conducted in the United States but allow tax deductions for research undertaken locally.

Accordingly, Congress concluded that the Treasury Department should study the impact of the allocation of research expense under the 1977 regulation on U.S.-based research activities and on the availability of the foreign tax credit. Pending the outcome of the study, Congress concluded that research expense should be charged to the cost of generating U.S. source income, regardless of whether the research was a direct or indirect cost of producing foreign source income.

On the ground that a reduction in research and development might adversely affect the competitive position of the United States, the 1983 Treasury report recommended the two-year extension of the moratorium that was ultimately enacted by Congress in 1984. The extension was intended to allow Congress to consider further the results of the Treasury study.

The Consolidated Omnibus Budget Reconciliation Act of 1985 (the "1985 Act") extended the moratorium on the application of the research expense allocation regulation generally for one additional taxable year beginning after August 1, 1985, and on or before August 1, 1986.

The Tax Reform Act of 1986 (the "1986 Act") permitted the moratorium on application of the research expense allocation regulation to expire. However, for taxable years beginning after August 1, 1986, and on or before August 1, 1987, application of the regulation was liberalized by the 1986 Act in three respects, which were intended by Congress to provide an additional tax incentive to conduct research in the United States while Congress analyzed whether any additional permanent incentive was necessary.

The first liberalization under the 1986 Act was that for the specified one-year period, 50 percent of all remaining amounts allowable as a deduction for qualified research and experimental expenditures (that is, research and experimental expenditures within the meaning of section 174 that are attributable to activities conducted in the United States) after allocation of legally required research expense could be apportioned to U.S. source income. The 1986 Act thus had the effect of increasing the automatic place-of-performance apportionment percentage for U.S.-based research expense from 30 percent to 50 percent.

The 1986 Act further provided that, for the specified one-year period, the portion of those amounts allowable as a deduction for qualified research and experimental expenditures that remained after any legal requirements allocation and the 50 percent automatic place-of-performance apportionment were apportioned either on the basis of sales or gross income. Thus, the 1986 Act's second effective liberalization of the regulation was to allow the automatic place-of-performance apportionment temporarily to taxpayers who elected to apportion research expense using the optional gross income method, rather than only to taxpayers that used the standard sales method of apportionment.

Third, the 1986 Act had the effect of temporarily suspending the regulatory rule that prohibits taxpayers from using the optional gross income method to reduce allocation of research expense to foreign source income by more than 50 percent of the amount that would be allocated to foreign source income under the sales method.

The temporary modifications made by the

1986 Act to the research allocation regulation applied for purposes of computing taxable income from U.S. sources and taxable income from sources outside the United States. The modifications applied only to the allocation of expenditures for research and experimental activities conducted in the United States, and only for the purposes of geographic sourcing of income; the modifications did not apply for other purposes such as the computation of combined taxable income of a FSC (or DISC) and its related supplier. Also, the modifications did not apply to any expenditure for the acquisition or improvement of land, or for the acquisition or improvement of depreciable or depletable property to be used in connection with research or experimentation.

The Technical and Miscellaneous Revenue Act of l988 (the "1988 Act") further modified, again on a temporary basis, the rules for sourcing research expense. These modifications were effective only for the first four months of a taxpayer's first taxable year beginning after August 1, 1987 (treating all applicable expenditures in that taxable year as if they were incurred ratably over the year). Generally, for the remainder of a taxpayer's first taxable year beginning after August 1, 1987, (and for subsequent taxable years), the research expense allocation regulation was applicable. Under the 1988 Act, the treatment of research expense incurred to meet certain legal requirements was unchanged. After applying the legal requirements rule, however, the 1988 Act modifications provided that 64 percent of the remaining U.S.-based research expense was allocated to U.S. source income and 64 percent of the remaining foreign-based research expense was allocated to foreign source income. Following that allocation, the remaining research expense was allocated and apportioned either on the basis of sales or gross income. However, if the gross income method of apportionment was utilized, the amount apportioned to foreign source income could be no less than 30 percent of the amount that would have been apportioned to foreign source income had the sales method been used.

The Omnibus Budget Reconciliation Act of 1989 (the "1989 Act") extended, again on a temporary basis, the rules for sourcing research expenditures that were contained in the 1988 Act. The 1989 Act also codified these rules in section 864(f) of the Internal Revenue Code. As codified in 1989, these rules were effective only for the first nine months of a taxpayer's first taxable year beginning after August 1, 1989, and before August 2, 1990 (treating all applicable expenditures in that taxable year as if they were incurred ratably over the year). Under the 1989 Act, for the remainder of a taxpayer's first taxable year beginning after August 1, 1989, and before August 2, 1990 (and for subsequent taxable years), the research expense allocation regulation was to apply.

The Omnibus Budget Reconciliation Act of 1990 (the "1990 Act") further extended the statutory allocation rules that were codified in the 1989 Act. Under the 1990 Act, the rules of section 864(f) applied to the taxpayer's first two taxable years beginning after August 1, 1989, and on or before August 1, 1991.

The most recent statutory extension of the rules of section 864(f) was included in the Tax Extension Act of 1991, which was applicable generally for the first six months of the first taxable year beginning after August 1, 1991. For this purpose total research expenses for the year were deemed to be incurred evenly throughout the year. For expenses deemed paid or incurred during the remainder of the year, the research expense allocation regulation applied.

On June 24, 1992, it was announced that the Treasury Department and the IRS had undertaken a review of the research expense allocation regulation, and that in light of this review, the IRS temporarily would not require that taxpayers apply the regulation (Rev. Proc. 92-56, 1992-28 I.R.B. 7, amplified by Rev. Proc. 92-69, 1992-36 I.R.B. 18). According to these Revenue Procedures, taxpayers would not be required to apply the regulation with respect to research expenses incurred during what would ordinarily be an 18-month transition period -- that is, the last six months of the taxpayer's first taxable year beginning after August 1, 1991 and the immediately succeeding taxable year -- provided that such expense was allocated and apportioned in accordance with a method based on the temporary statutory provision, described above, applicable generally through the first six months of the first taxable year beginning after August 1, 1991. The Revenue Procedures stated that this transition method was not intended to suggest any views about the proper allocation and apportionment of research expense, and that it was intended solely to provide taxpayers with transition relief and to minimize audit controversy and facilitate business planning during the conduct of the regulatory review.

Reasons for Change

In the 12 years since the first temporary moratorium on the 1977 regulation was enacted, Congress, the Treasury Department, and representatives of affected industries have intensely scrutinized the effects of the research expense allocation rules on research activities. /1/[1] That scrutiny has not resulted in an unambiguous recommendation regarding the appropriateness of allocating U.S.-based research expense to U.S. source income under either the 1977 regulation, the complete moratorium, or the partial moratoria of the 1986 and subsequent Acts. On the one hand, there are those who argue that the moratorium and the partial moratoria had a beneficial effect on U.S. research activity and on U.S. competitiveness in world-wide markets. On the other hand, there are those whose studies prompt them to conclude otherwise. Furthermore, the tax costs of both the total and the partial moratoria have been significant, and the tax benefits they have bestowed are distributed somewhat arbitrarily among taxpayers. At the same time, these taxpayers have faced a prolonged period of uncertainty as to the research expense allocation rules that will apply in the coming years, making it more difficult for them to predict the after-tax costs of the research in which they generally must engage, if at all, over extended future periods.

The committee continues to believe that settling the rules for allocation of research expense would enhance the research activities of U.S. companies. However, the committee has chosen not to settle the rules permanently at this time. In the interim, the committee is persuaded that it is appropriate to continue to apply the substantive rules temporarily applicable under section 864(f) for another year.

Explanation of Provision

The bill temporarily extends the research allocation rules set forth in Code section 864(f), except that the portion of research expense automatically allocated and apportioned to income sourced in the place of performance of the research is 50 percent, rather than 64 percent. Thus, for research expense other than amounts incurred to meet certain legal requirements, and thus allocable to one geographical source, 50 percent of U.S.-incurred research expense is allocated and apportioned to U.S. source income, and 50 percent of foreign-incurred research expense is allocated and apportioned to foreign source income. The remaining research expense is allocated and apportioned either on the basis of sales or gross income, but subject to the condition that if income-based apportionment is used, the amount apportioned to foreign source income can be no less than 30 percent of the amount that would have been apportioned to foreign source income had the sales method been used.

The bill provides regulatory authority for the implementation of certain adjustments regarding section 936 companies. In addition, the bill authorizes the Treasury to prescribe such regulations as may be appropriate to carry out the purposes of this provision, including regulations relating to the determination of whether research activities are conducted inside or outside the United States and making such adjustments as may be appropriate in the case of cost sharing arrangements and contract research.

Effective Date

The provision applies to the first taxable year (beginning before August 1, 1994) that commences immediately following the taxpayer's last taxable year to which Rev. Proc. 92-56 applies, or would have applied had the taxpayer been in existence and elected the benefits of that Revenue Procedure.

[Conference Report]

Present Law

In order that the foreign tax credit will offset only the U.s. tax on the taxpayer's foreign source taxable income, a limitation formula is prescribed in the Code. To compute the limitations, it is necessary to divide the taxable income of a U.S. person into U.S. source taxable income, foreign source taxable income in

[Footnote ¶3052 continued]

[Footnote ¶3053] 1. See, e.g., Interaction Between U.S. Tax Policy and Domestic Research and Development: Hearing on S.58 and S.716 Before the Subcomm. on Taxation and Debt Management of the Senate Comm. on Finance, 100th Cong., 1st Sess. (1987).

each applicable separate limitation category, and foreign source taxable income in the general foreign tax credit limitation category.

Foreign source taxable income in any limitation category equals foreign source gross income in that category less the expenses, losses and other deductions properly apportioned or allocated to that income. A Treasury regulation issued in 1977 describes methods for allocating expenses between U.S. and foreign source income, including rules for the allocation of research expenses. Since 1981, however, the research expense allocation regulation has been subject to a series of statutory temporary suspensions and modifications. The most recent temporary statutory provision (set forth in Code section 864(f)) was applicable generally for the first six months of the first taxable year beginning after August 1, 1991. For this purpose, total research expenses for the year were deemed to be incurred evenly throughout the year.

For expenses deemed paid or incurred during the first six months of the year referred to above (other than amounts incurred to meet certain legal requirements, and thus allocable to one geographical source), 64 percent of U.S.-incurred research expenses were allocated to U.S. source income, and 64 percent of foreign-incurred research expenses were allocated to foreign source income. The remainder of research expenses were allocated and apportioned either on the basis of sales or gross income, but subject to the condition that if income-based apportionment was used, the amount apportioned to foreign source income could have been no less than 30 percent of the amount that would have been apportioned to foreign source income had the sales method been used.

The Treasury has announced that during what would ordinarily be an 18-month period following the six-month period referred to above -- that is, the last six months of the taxpayer's first taxable year beginning after August 1, 1991 and the immediately succeeding taxable year -- taxpayers may continue to allocate research expenses in accordance with the method set forth in Code section 864(f). In granting the transitional period, Treasury stated that the transitional method was not intended to suggest any particular views about the proper allocation and apportionment of research expenses. Rather, Treasury stated, the transition method was intended solely to provide taxpayers with transitional relief and to minimize audit controversy and facilitate business planning during the conduct of the regulatory review.

House Bill

The House bill makes permanent the research allocation rules of Code section 864(f), except that the portion of research expense automatically allocated and apportioned to income sourced in the place of performance of the research is 50 percent, rather than 64 percent. Thus, for research expense other than amounts incurred to meet certain legal requirements, and thus allocable to one geographical source, 50 percent of U.S.-incurred research expense is allocated and apportioned to U.S. source income, and 50 percent of foreign-incurred research expense is allocated and apportioned to foreign source income. The remaining research expense is allocated and apportioned either on the basis of sales or gross income, but subject to the condition that if income-based apportionment is used, the amount apportioned to foreign source income can be no less than 30 percent of the amount that would have been apportioned to foreign source income had the sales method been used.

The House bill provides regulatory authority for the implementation of certain adjustments regarding section 936 companies. In addition, the bill authorizes the Treasury to prescribe such regulations as may be appropriate to carry out the purposes of this provision, including regulations relating to the determination of whether research activities are conducted inside or outside the United States and making such adjustments as may be appropriate in the case of cost sharing arrangements and contract research.

Effective date

The House bill provision applies to taxable years ending after date of enactment, except that it does not apply to any taxable year to which Rev. Proc. 92-56 applies, or would have applied had the taxpayer elected the benefits of that Revenue Procedure.

Senate Amendment

The Senate amendment temporarily adopts for one year the provisions (including those providing regulatory authority) adopted permanently in the House bill. The Senate amendment applies to the first taxable year (beginning on or before August 1, 1994) following the taxpayer's last taxable year to which Rev. Proc. 92-56 applies, or would have applied had the taxpayer elected the benefits of that Revenue Procedure.

Conference Agreement

The conference agreement follows the Senate amendment.

[¶3054] Section 13235. Repeal of Certain Exceptions for Working Capital

(Code Sec. 904, 907, 954)

[House Explanation]

Present Law

Foreign tax credit separate limitations

Foreign tax credit limitations are computed separately for certain categories of foreign source income, including passive income, high withholding tax interest, financial services income, shipping income, dividends from each noncontrolled section 902 corporation, certain distributions from DISCs and FSCs, certain types of income earned by a FSC, and all other (i.e., "overall basket" or "general basket") income. Passive income generally includes income which is of a kind which would be foreign personal holding company income as defined under Code section 954(c) (e.g., interest and dividends) and typically is not subject to high levels of foreign tax. The separate limitation for passive income generally prevents the crosscrediting of high foreign taxes on income which falls in the general basket against the residual U.S. tax on passive income.

The separate foreign tax credit limitation for passive income was enacted in 1986 an replaced the prior law separate foreign tax credit limitation for passive interest income. [74] Prior law excluded from the passive interest separate limitation category interest derived from any transaction which is directly related to the active conduct by the taxpayer of a trade or business in a foreign country. Regulations under prior law expressly treated certain types of interest from working capital as interest derived from a transaction which is directly related to the active conduct of a trade or business. [75]No such general working capital exception exists under the passive income definition as established in 1986. As a result of the interaction of the Code and pre-1987 Treasury regulations, however, the working capital exception has been retained for the oil and gas and shipping industries. [76]

Special limitation on credits for foreign extraction taxes and taxes on foreign oil related income

In addition to the foreign tax credit limitations that apply to all foreign tax credits, a special limitation is placed on foreign income taxes on foreign oil and gas extraction income (FOGEI). Under this special limitation,

74. P.L. 99-514, sec. 1201(a) (1986).

75. Former Treas. Reg. sec. 1.904-4(b)

76. Section 904(d)(2)(A)(iii)(IV) provides that the separate foreign tax credit limitation for passive income does not include foreign oil and gas extraction income as defined in section 907(c). Regulations promulgated under section 907 include in the definition of foreign oil and gas extraction income certain interest earned on working capital (i.e., interest on bank deposits or on any other temporary investment which is not in excess of funds reasonably necessary to meet the taxpayer's working capital requirements and specifically anticipated business needs) that is related to activities with respect to which the taxpayer derives foreign oil and gas extraction income (Treas. Reg. sec. 1.907(c)-1(f)(3)). Treasury Reg. sec. 1.907(c)-1(f)(3) also includes certain interest on working capital within the definition of foreign oil related income if the working capital is required for the taxpayer's business operations which generate foreign oil related income. Section 954(b)(8) provides that income which is foreign base company oil related income (defined under sec. 954(g) to include foreign oil related income) is NOT considered foreign personal holding company income. Only interest that is of a kind which would be foreign personal holding company income is passive for foreign tax credit limitation purposes (sec. 904(d)(A)). Like interest on working capital related to foreign oil and gas extraction income, therefore, interest on working capital related to foreign oil related income is excluded from the separate foreign tax credit limitation for passive income. Similarly, income which is treated as foreign base company shipping income under section 954(f) is NOT considered foreign personal holding company income (sec. 954(b)(6)), and interest income on working capital associated with a taxpayer's foreign base company-shipping operations is treated as foreign base company shipping income under regulations (Treas. Reg. secs. 1.954-6(e)(2)(ii) and 1.955A-2(b)(2)(i)). Moreover, the statutory foreign tax credit separate limitation provisions provide a special overlap rule under which income described in any other separate limitation category (in this case, the separate limitation for shipping income) is not considered passive income (secs. 904(d)(2)(A)(iii)(I) and 904(d)(2)(D)).

amounts claimed as taxes paid on FOGEI of a U.S. corporation qualify as creditable taxes (if they otherwise so qualify) only to the extent they do not exceed the product of the highest marginal U.S. tax rate on corporations (presently 34 percent) multiplied by such extraction income. Foreign taxes paid in excess of that amount on such income are, in general, neither creditable nor deductible (unless a credit carryover provision applies).

A similar special limitation may apply to foreign taxes paid on foreign oil related income (FORI) in certain cases where that type of income is subjected to a materially greater level of tax by a foreign jurisdiction than non oil and gas income generally would be. Under this limitation, a portion of the foreign taxes on FORI may be deductible, but not creditable.

As previously described, regulations issued prior to 1986 and still effective define FOGEI and FORI to include interest on working capital related to extraction or oil related activities, as the case may be. [77] Thus, under current regulations, FOGEI and FORI include what generally would be considered as passive income for foreign tax credit limitation purposes.

Reasons For Change

The committee understands that for taxpayers not engaged in oil and gas or shipping operations, present law treats interest income on working capital as subject to the separate foreign tax credit limitation for passive income. For the reasons stated in connection with the adoption of the separate foreign tax credit limitation for passive income in 1986, the committee believes that this is appropriate. [78] The committee also believes that the foreign tax credit rules should operate fairly and uniformly to all taxpayers. Thus, the committee believes it is appropriate to conform the rules that apply to the treatment of passive income earned by taxpayers with oil and gas and shipping operations with the rules that apply to similar income earned by other taxpayers.

Similarly, as a general principle, the statutory FOGEI and FORI rules of section 907 are intended to prevent the crediting of high foreign taxes on FOGEI and FORI against the residual U.S. tax on other types of lower-taxed foreign source income. However, for example, if a taxpayer has both high-taxed FOGEI, and also FOGEI which bears little or no foreign income tax, such as interest income on working capital, the current rules permit high FOGEI taxes to be credited against the residual U.S. tax on that interest income. The committee believes that this result is inappropriate.

Explanation Of Provision

In general

The bill prevents the cross-crediting of foreign taxes on FOGEI, FORI, and shipping income by placing certain passive income related to oil and gas and shipping operations in the passive category for foreign tax credit limitation purposes. In addition, the bill excludes certain passive income related to foreign oil and gas extraction or other foreign oil related activities from the computation of the FOGEI and FORI foreign tax credit limitations.

Foreign tax credit separate limitations

With respect to the separate foreign tax credit limitation for passive income, the bill eliminates the present-law exclusion of FOGEI from the definition of passive income. Thus, if a taxpayer has gross income that falls within the definition of passive income under section 904, and also satisfies the definition of FOGEI under section 907, the income would be treated as passive income in determining the taxpayer's foreign tax credit.

In addition, the bill amends the present-law rule applicable to income which by definition qualifies both as foreign personal holding company income under section 954(c) and as foreign base company oil related income under section 954(g). The bill provides that such income is to be treated as foreign personal holding company income. As such, the income generally would be passive income for foreign tax credit purposes.

Likewise, the bill specifies that dividend or interest income that by definition qualifies as both foreign personal holding company in-

[Footnote ¶ 3054 continued]

77. Treas. Reg. sec. 1.907(c)-1(f)(3). The current version of this regulation, adopted in 1991 (see T.D. 8338), was preceded by Treas. Reg. sec. 1.907(c)-1A(e)(3) (see T.D. 7961; T.D. 8160).

78. See, e.g., Staff of the Joint Committee on Taxation, 100th Cong., 1st Sess., General Explanation of the Tax Reform Act of 1986, at 863 (1987).

come and foreign base company shipping income is to be treated as foreign personal holding company income. Thus, for foreign tax credit purposes, the income would fall in the passive basket rather than in the separate basket for shipping income.

Special FOGEI and FORI limitations

The bill provides that the term "foreign oil and gas extraction income" does not include any dividend or interest income which is passive income as defined for foreign tax credit limitation purposes. Since, as discussed above, the bill treats gross interest income on working capital related to foreign oil and gas extraction activities, for example, as passive income, such income is not considered FOGEI for purposes of computing the special limitation for foreign taxes paid on FOGEI.

In addition, the bill specifies that the term "foreign oil related income" does not include any dividend or interest income which is passive income as defined under the foreign tax credit provisions. As a result, for example, gross interest income on working capital related to activities which generate foreign oil related income would not be treated as FORI for purposes of computing the special limitation for foreign taxes paid on FORI.

Effective Date

The provision applies to income earned in taxable years beginning after December 31, 1992.

[Conference Report]

Present Law

Foreign tax credit separate limitations

Foreign tax credit limitations are computed separately for certain categories of foreign source income, including passive income, high withholding tax interest, financial services income, shipping income, dividends from each noncontrolled section 902 corporation, certain distributions from DISCs and FSCs, certain types of income earned by a FSC, and all other (i.e., "overall basket" or "general basket") income. Passive income generally includes income which is of a kind which would be foreign personal holding company income as defined under Code section 954(c) (e.g., interest and dividends) and typically is not subject to high levels of foreign tax. The separate limitation for passive income generally prevents the cross-crediting of high foreign taxes on income which falls in the general basket against the residual U.S. tax on passive income.

The separate foreign tax credit limitation for passive income was enacted in 1986 and replaced the prior law separate foreign tax credit limitation for passive interest income. [1] Prior law excluded from the passive interest separate limitation category interest derived from any transaction which is directly related to the active conduct by the taxpayer of a trade or business in a foreign country. Regulations under prior law expressly treated certain types of interest on working capital as interest derived from a transaction which is directly related to the active conduct of a trade or business. [2] No such general working capital exception exists under the passive income definition as established in 1986. As a result of the interaction of the Code and Treasury regulations originally developed prior to 1987, however, the working capital exception has been retained for the oil and gas and shipping industries.

Special limitations on credits for foreign extraction taxes and taxes on foreign oil related income

In addition to the foreign tax credit limitations that apply to all creditable foreign taxes, a special limitation is placed on foreign income taxes on foreign oil and gas extraction income (FOGEI). Under this special limitation, amounts claimed as taxes paid on FOGEI of a U.S. corporation qualify as creditable taxes (if they otherwise so qualify) only to the extent they do not exceed the product of the highest marginal U.S. tax rate on corporations (presently 34 percent) multiplied by such extraction income. Foreign taxes paid in excess of that amount on such income are, in general, neither creditable nor deductible (unless a credit carryover provision applies).

A similar special limitation may apply to foreign taxes paid on foreign oil related income (FORI) in certain cases where that type of income is subjected to a materially greater level of tax by a foreign jurisdiction than non

[Footnote ¶ 3054 continued]
[Footnote ¶ 3054] 1. P.L. 99-514, sec. 1201(a) (1986).
2. Former Treas. Reg. sec. 1.904-4(b).

oil and gas income generally would be. Under this limitation, a portion of the foreign taxes on FORI may be deductible, but not creditable.

As previously described, regulations issued prior to 1986 and still effective define FOGEI and FORI to include interest on working capital related to extraction or oil related activities, as the case may be. Thus, under current regulations, FOGEI and FORI include what generally would be considered as passive income for foreign tax credit limitation purposes.

House Bill

In general

The House bill prevents the cross-crediting of foreign taxes on FOGEI, FORI, and shipping income by placing certain passive income related to oil and gas and shipping operations in the passive category for foreign tax credit limitation purposes. In addition, the House bill excludes certain passive income related to foreign oil and gas extraction or other foreign oil related activities from the computation of the FOGEI and FORI foreign tax credit limitations.

Foreign tax credit separate limitations

With respect to the separate foreign tax credit limitation for passive income, the House bill eliminates the present-law exclusion of FOGEI from the definition of passive income. Thus, if a taxpayer has gross income that falls within the definition of passive income under section 904, and also satisfies the definition of FOGEI under section 907, the income would be treated as passive income in determining the taxpayer's foreign tax credit.

In addition, the House bill amends the present-law rule applicable to income which by definition qualifies both as foreign personal holding company income under section 954 (c) and as foreign base company oil related income under section 954 (g). The House bill provides that such income is to be treated as foreign personal holding company income. As such, the income generally would be passive income for foreign tax credit purposes.

Likewise, the House bill specifies that dividend or interest income that by definition qualifies as both foreign personal holding company income and foreign base company shipping income is to be treated as foreign personal holding company income. Thus, for foreign tax credit purposes, the income would fall in the passive basket rather than in the separate basket for shipping income.

Special FOGEI and FORI limitations

The House bill provides that the term "foreign oil and gas extraction income" does not include any dividend or interest income which is passive income as defined for foreign tax credit limitation purposes. Since, as discussed above, the House bill treats gross interest income on working capital related to foreign oil and gas extraction activities, for example, as passive income, such income is not considered FOGEI for purposes of computing the special limitation for foreign taxes paid on FOGEI.

In addition, the House bill specifies that the term "foreign oil related income" does not include any dividend or interest income which is passive income as defined under the foreign tax credit provisions. As a result, for example, gross interest income on working capital related to activities which generate foreign oil related income would not be treated as FORI for purposes of computing the special limitation for foreign taxes paid on FORI.

Effective date

The provision applies to income earned in taxable years beginning after December 31, 1992.

Senate Amendment

The Senate amendment is the same as the House bill.

Conference Agreement

The conference agreement is the same as the House bill and Senate amendment with clarifications.

The conference agreement clarifies that for purposes of applying section 954(f), dividends and interest received from a foreign corporation in respect of which taxes are deemed paid under section 902 are classified as foreign base company shipping income (as under present law) to the extent attributable to foreign base company shipping income. Similarly, the conferees intend that dividends and interest received from a foreign corporation in respect of which taxes are deemed paid under section 902 are classified as FOGEI or FORI, respectively, to the extent attributable to FOGEI or FORI.

The conferees also wish to clarify the treatment (under sec. 954(b)(6)(B)) of a post-effective date corporate distribution of income earned by the payor in a pre-effective date year. The determination whether such pre-effective date income was shipping income for this purpose will be made under the laws defining shipping income in effect for the year in which the income was earned.

[¶3055] Section 13236. Modifications of Accuracy Related Penalty.

(Code Sec. 6662)

[House Explanation]

Present Law

Penalties for valuation misstatements

Valuation questions are frequently central to disputes between taxpayers and the IRS. Certain types of valuation misstatements are subject to penalty. A "substantial" valuation misstatement may result in a penalty of 20 percent of the underpayment of tax attributable to the misstatement (sec. 6662(a) and (b)(2)). The penalty for a "gross" valuation misstatement is 40 percent of the tax underpayment (sec. 6662(h)).

As in the case of accuracy-related penalties generally under section 6662, no valuation misstatement penalty is imposed if it is shown that there was reasonable cause for the underpayment of tax and that the taxpayer acted in good faith (see sec. 6664(c)). No valuation misstatement penalty is imposed if the portion of the underpayment for the taxable year attributable to substantial valuation misstatements does not exceed $5,000 ($10,000 in the case of a corporation other than an S corporation or a personal holding company).

The term "substantial valuation misstatement" includes three types of misstatement (sec. 6662(e)). It includes claiming on a tax return that the value of any property is 200 percent or more of the amount determined to be correct. The term "gross valuation misstatement" refers to three similar, but more extreme, forms of misstatement (sec. 6662(h)). It includes claiming on a tax return that the value of any property is 400 percent or more of the amount determined to be correct.

Misstatement penalties and section 482 adjustments

The two other types of substantial valuation misstatement and gross valuation misstatement are defined by provisions enacted in the Omnibus Budget Reconciliation Act of 1990 (the "1990 Act"). These provisions address certain cases involving transactions between persons under common ownership or control, as those terms are used in section 482. The IRS Commissioner has the authority in such cases to distribute, apportion, or allocate income, deductions, credits, or allowances between or among such persons where the Commissioner determines it to be necessary in order to prevent evasion of taxes or clearly to reflect income.

Under the 1990 Act, a substantial valuation misstatement includes claiming a price for any property or services (or use of property), in connection with any transaction between persons described in section 482, that is 200 percent or more (or 50 percent or less) of the amount determined under section 482 to be the correct amount of the price. [79] In addition, under the 1990 Act there is a substantial valuation misstatement if the net section 482 transfer price adjustment for the taxable year exceeds $10 million. [80] The net section 482 transfer price adjustment is the net increase in taxable income for a taxable year resulting from adjustments under section 482 in the price for any property or services (or use of property).

Certain increases in taxable income resulting from section 482 adjustments are disregarded in determining whether a taxpayer's net section 482 transfer price adjustment exceeds the $10 million or $20 million thresholds. A net increase in taxable income attributable to a price redetermination is disregarded, for example, if it is shown that there was a reasonable cause for the taxpayer's determina-

[Footnote ¶3054 continued]

79. The analogous "gross valuation misstatement" is defined in the same terms, except for replacing "200" with "400" and replacing "50 percent" with "25 Percent."

80. The analogous "gross valuation misstatement" involves a net section 482 transfer price adjustment of $20 million.

tion of the price, and that the taxpayer acted in good faith with respect to the price (sec. 6662(e)(3)(B)(i)). [81]

Regulations under sections 482, 6662, and 6664: Final, temporary, and proposed

Current penalty regulations

There are no temporary or final regulations specifically addressed to the 1990 Act valuation misstatement penalties relating to section 482 adjustments. There is a final regulation under the reasonable cause/good faith exception that applies generally to all valuation misstatement penalties and other accuracy-related penalties under Code section 6662 (Treas. Reg. sec. 1.6664-4). Under this regulation, the determination of whether a taxpayer acted with reasonable cause and in good faith is made on a case-by-case basis, taking into account all pertinent facts and circumstances. The most important factor in making the determination is the extent of the taxpayer's effort to assess its proper tax liability. Circumstances that may or may not indicate reasonable cause and good faith are described in the regulation.

Proposed penalty regulations on net section 482 transfer price adjustments

In January 1993 the Treasury Department published a proposed regulation specifically addressed to the 1990 Act valuation misstatement penalty provisions (58 Fed. Reg. 5304 (Jan. 21, 1993)). The proposed regulation would provide exclusive rules for determining the circumstances in which reasonable cause and good faith would and would not reduce or eliminate penalties that would otherwise apply to net section 482 transfer price adjustments in excess of $10 million or $20 million. [82]

By contrast, the preamble indicates that a valuation misstatement involving a related party transfer price 200 percent or more (or 50 percent or less) of the amount determined under section 482 to be the correct price is subject to the general reasonable cause/good faith regulations under section 6664(c). In addition, according to the preamble, if such a valuation misstatement satisfies the reasonable cause and good faith exclusion provisions under proposed sec. 1.6662-5(j)(5), then the taxpayer will be considered to have acted with reasonable cause and good faith for purposes of the general rules. By its terms, the proposed regulation would apply to taxable years beginning after April 21, 1993.

Under the proposed regulation, there are two elements to the reasonable cause and good faith exclusion from the definition of a net section 482 transfer price adjustment. '[83] Both elements must be satisfied by the taxpayer to prevent imposition of the penalty.

The proposed regulations state that the first element is a reasonable effort by the taxpayer to accurately determine its proper tax liability. This determination must be made no later than the time the return is filed for the tax year, and documentation must be contemporaneous with that determination. The documentation must include an analysis indicating that the result was an arm's length result within the meaning of the regulations promulgated under section 482. It is presumed that the taxpayer did not make a reasonable effort to accurately determine its proper tax liability if it possesses contemporaneous documentation of how a transfer price was determined, but does not provide the documentation to the IRS within 30 days of an IRS request.

The second element of the reasonable cause and good faith exclusion is whether the taxpayer reasonably believed that its transfer pricing methodology produced an arm's length result. The proposed regulation states that the determination of whether the taxpayer has such a reasonable belief is made in light of the experience and knowledge of the taxpayer. Various factors are discussed that may be taken into account in making that determination.

Section 482 regulations

Final regulations under section 482 are in

[Footnote ¶ 3055 continued]

81. In addition, any portion of the net increase in taxable income attributable to a transaction solely between foreign corporations is disregarded (unless the treatment of that transaction affects the determination of any such foreign corporation's income from sources within the United States or taxable income effectively connected with the conduct of a trade or business in the United States).

82. These exclusive rules are contained in proposed Reg. sec. 1.6662-5(j)(5). According to the preamble to the proposed regulation, a net section 482 transfer price adjustment for which the rules of sec. 1.6662-5(j)(5) are NOT satisfied will also NOT satisfy the general reasonable cause and good faith exception under section 6664(c). 58 Fed. Reg. at 5305.

'83. Prop. Reg. sec. 1.6662-5(j)(5), 58 Fed. Reg. at 5308.

force, and have not been amended since 1988. In January 1993, however, the Treasury Department promulgated temporary regulations under section 482, generally effective for taxable years beginning after April 21, 1993. These temporal regulations amend aspects of the existing final section 482 regulations.

The temporary regulations would, for example, revise the circumstances under which taxpayers may use a method NOT specified in these regulations, in order to establish the arm's length consideration for a "controlled transaction" -- a transaction between members of a commonly controlled group of taxpayers -- involving the transfer of tangible or intangible property. (Any method NOT specified in the section 482 regulations has popularly been referred to in the past as a "fourth method," in light of the fact that many cases involve transactions for which the final regulations specify only three methods.)

Under the temporary section 482 regulations, a taxpayer may use such an unspecified method only if three conditions are satisfied (Treas. Reg. secs. 1.482-3T(e)(2) and 1.482-1T(d)(2)). First, the taxpayer must disclose the use of the method by attaching an appropriate disclosure statement to the timely filed U.S. income tax return for the taxable year of the controlled transaction. Second, the taxpayer must prepare contemporaneous supporting documentation setting forth (a) the specific analysis adopted, (b) an analysis of why the method used provides the most accurate measure of an arm's length price, and (c) the data supporting its application. Third, within 30 days of a written request, the taxpayer must furnish this documentation to the IRS district director.

Reasons for Change

The committee is aware that section 482 disputes between taxpayers and the IRS continue to impose significant administrative burdens on the parties; and the committee continues to be concerned about the amount of revenue that is potentially lost by the Treasury due to difficulties in exercising the Secretary's authority to adjust income under section 482.

The committee is concerned, for example, about any case where a taxpayer uses related party transfer prices or other arrangements with no apparent consideration as to whether the taxable income reported, and the tax paid, conforms with the standards made applicable by section 482. The committee believes that the threat of penalties for substantial and gross valuation misstatements, as amended in 1990, might discourage such behavior, so long as the conditions under which the penalties may be imposed are sufficiently broad and well-defined.

The committee believes that current law is deficient in this respect, however. According to the Administration, the IRS has not attempted to apply the transfer pricing related penalties since their enactment in 1990. [84] Moreover, the minimum amount of net section 482 transfer price adjustment necessary before a penalty can apply is too great in the committee's view. In addition, the committee questions the usefulness of the debate that ensues upon audit as the IRS examiner seeks to determine a reasonable intercompany price and the taxpayer and its representatives attempt to create post hoc arguments to justify a tax return position that was taken with little or no regard whether it could be justified under section 482 standards. The committee is instead inclined to agree with the view, expressed in the past, that administration of and compliance with, section 482 will be improved by encouraging taxpayers "to document the methodology used in establishing intercompany transfer prices prior to filing the tax return" and to provide such documentation within a reasonable time after request. [85] The committee does not believe that a section 482 adjustment that exceeds the threshold generally should escape the penalty unless the taxpayer can show that the return position was arrived at after bestowing a reasonable amount of attention to the issue.

Explanation of Provision

In general

The provision creates new thresholds based on gross receipts for imposing the substantial valuation and gross valuation misstatement penalties in the case of a net section 482

[Footnote ¶3055 continued]

84. Department of the Treasury, Summary of the Administration's Revenue Proposals 55 (February 1993).

85. Notice 88-123 ("A Study of Intercompany Pricing under Section 482 of the Code"), 1988-2 C.B. 458, 462; Tax Underpayments by U.S. Subsidiaries of Foreign Companies: Hearings Before the Subcomm. on Oversght of the House Comm. on Ways and Means, 101st Cong., 2d Sess. 124, 125 (1990) (testimony of Edward Romoff, IRS).

transfer price adjustment. It also lowers the fixed dollar threshold for imposing the substantial valuation misstatement penalty in the case of a net section 482 transfer price adjustment. Finally, the provision replaces the statutory reasonable cause/good faith exception to the definition of the term "net section 482 transfer price adjustment" with a more objective exception that can be met by taxpayers that attend to potential section 482 issues at the time they file their tax returns. Taxpayers that do not meet the standard may not escape the penalties attached to a net section 482 transfer price adjustment by recourse to the general reasonable cause/good faith exception from the accuracy and fraud-related penalties.

Penalty thresholds

The threshold amount of net section 482 transfer price adjustment that generally triggers a substantial valuation misstatement penalty is lowered from $10,000,000 to $5,000,000. In addition, the term substantial valuation misstatement is expanded to include a case where the net section 482 transfer price adjustment for the taxable year exceeds 10 percent of the taxpayer's gross receipts. Under the bill the term gross valuation misstatement includes a case where the net section 482 transfer price adjustment exceeds 20 percent of gross receipts.

Definition of a net section 482 transfer price adjustment

In measuring the amount of a taxpayer's net section 482 transfer price adjustment, a net increase in taxable income attributable to a section 482 adjustment is to be disregarded only if the taxpayer satisfies one of two sets of statutory requirements. One such penalty "safe harbor" applies where the taxpayer determined a transfer price using a method specified in regulations; the other penalty safe harbor applies where the method used was not specified in the regulations. Satisfying the conditions for such a safe harbor does not affect the Commissioner's authority to make a section 482 adjustment.

Use of a specified method

The taxpayer meets the first set of requirements if it establishes that each of three criteria were met.

First, the taxpayer must establish that the price it used was determined under a pricing method specified in the section 482 regulations. For example, in a year governed by the temporary regulations under section 482 published in January 1993, a controlled transfer of tangible property could be subject to one of four "specified methods": the comparable uncontrolled price method, the resale price method, the cost plus method or the comparable profits method (Treas. Reg. sec. 1.482-3T(a)(1)-(4)). Any other method would not be a "specified" method for purposes of this penalty provision. The committee is aware that there are various other types of transactions, such as the performance of services which are an integral part of the business activity of the renderer, as described in Treas. Reg. sec. 1.482-2A(b)(7), that generally are not the subject of any pricing methods specified in the present section 482 regulations. In these cases, the Committee understands that it will not be possible for the taxpayer to avoid the penalty by establishing that it had met the criteria for using the safe harbor applicable to prices determined under a specified method, unless such regulations are subsequently revised to incorporate specific pricing methods.

Second, the taxpayer must establish that it applied the specified method reasonably. In order for the application of the method to have been reasonable, the committee intends that any procedural or other requirements imposed under the regulations must have been observed. For example, if adjustments required under a particular method were not made, the application of that method would not be reasonable. In addition, if more than one method is potentially applicable, the committee intends that in order to be applied reasonably, the method applied must be chosen under appropriate criteria (currently, the so-called "best method rule" set forth in Treas. Reg. sec. 1.482-1T(b)(2)).

Third, the taxpayer must establish that it had documentation, in existence as of the time of filing its original return, setting forth the reasonable determination of the price as described above. Upon an IRS request for the documentation, the taxpayer is required to provide it to the IRS within 30 days.

Use of an unspecified method

A taxpayer that did not apply a specified method in accordance with the above criteria may nevertheless have its net increase in taxable income attributable to a section 482 adjustment disregarded in determining the amount of its net section 482 transfer price adjustment. In order to do so, the taxpayer must meet each of three criteria.

First, the taxpayer must establish that none of the methods specified in the section 482 regulations was likely to result in a price that would clearly reflect income. With respect to those various types of transactions, such as the performance of services which are an integral part of the business activity of the renderer, as described in Treas. Reg. sec. 1.482-2A(b)(7), that generally are not the subject of any pricing methods specified in the section 482 regulations, it will be unnecessary to establish that no specified method would be likely to lead to a clear reflection of income; rather, it will be necessary to establish that no specified methods potentially apply.

Second, the taxpayer must establish that it used another method that WAS likely to result in a price that would clearly reflect income. Third, the taxpayer must establish that it had documentation, in existence as of the time of filing its original return, setting forth the determination of the price, establishing that the specified methods were not likely to result in a price that would clearly reflect income, and establishing that the method used was likely to result in a price that would clearly reflect income. Upon an IRS request for the documentation, the taxpayer is required to provide it within 30 days.

In establishing that no specified method was likely to result in a clear reflection of income, and that an unspecified method was likely to so result, the committee anticipates that it will be necessary for the taxpayer to set forth good and sufficient reasons why it reached these conclusions. For example, one reason that a particular specified method would not be likely to result in a clear reflection of income might be the unavailability of data relating to comparable uncontrolled transactions that would be necessary in order to apply that method. One reason that a particular unspecified method would be likely to result in a clear reflection of income might be that it properly took into account the significant factors which unrelated parties engaged in transactions at arm's length would have considered, and accorded appropriate weight to such factors.

Another reason that might be relevant in some cases would be the prior development by the IRS and the taxpayer, after a thorough review of the factors that account for a clear reflection of income under the particular circumstances that pertain to a particular taxpayer, of a particular agreed unspecified method. Such a method may be embodied, for example, in an advance pricing agreement. If the taxpayer's documentation establishes the prior agreement of the IRS, establishes that the taxpayer applied the agreed method reasonably and consistently with its prior application, and establishes that the facts and circumstances surrounding the use of the method have not materially changed since the time of the agreement, the committee anticipates that, for purposes of applying the penalty, the taxpayer generally will be treated as having established adequate justification for failure to use a specified method and its use instead of the unspecified method.

Rules applicable to uses of either a specified or unspecified method

In the case of a valuation misstatement due to a net section 482 transfer price adjustment, no penalty would be excused for reasonable cause and good faith unless the above requirements are met.

The committee intends that the application of any method would not be considered reasonable if the taxpayer became aware prior to filing its tax return that such application more likely than not did not result in a clear reflection of income.

Since the transfer pricing method that the taxpayer selects is to be applied prior to filing the tax return for the current taxable year, in some cases it only will be possible to apply such method based on data from a preceding year or years. Sole reliance on such data is acceptable (solely for purposes of section 6662(e)) unless more current reliable data becomes available prior to filing the tax return.

Effective Date

The provision is effective for taxable years beginning after December 31, 1993.

[Conference Report]

Senate Amendment

The Senate amendment is the same as the House bill.

Conference Agreement

The conference agreement follows the House bill and the Senate amendment. The conferees note that under the agreement, a taxpayer that does not apply a pricing method specified in the section 482 regulations may nevertheless have its net increase in taxable income attributable to a section 482 adjustment disregarded in determining the amount of its net section 482 transfer price adjustment, but in order to do so the taxpayer must establish (among other things) that none of the methods specified in the section 482 regulations was likely to result in a price that would clearly reflect income. With respect to those various types of transactions that generally are not the subject of any pricing methods specified in the section 482 regulations, the conferees wish to clarify that to meet the above requirement, it will be necessary simply to establish that the transaction is of a type for which no methods are specified in the section 482 regulations.

[¶ 3056] Section 13237. Denial of Portfolio Interest Exemption for Contingent Interest

(Code Sec. 871, 881, 1441, 1442, 2105)

[House Explanation]

Present Law

Deductibility of interest

As a general rule, a deduction is allowed for all interest paid or accrued on indebtedness. Whether a financial instrument is treated as debt for Federal income tax purposes depends on the facts of the particular case. Under existing law, an instrument may qualify as debt even if it provides the holder with significant equity participation rights. For example, the IRS has rule that in certain cases, contingent interest paid on a shared appreciation mortgage loan used to finance the purchase of a personal residence may be deductible by a cash basis payor. [86] As another example, contingent interest based on a share of the borrower's profits has been determined to be deductible in certain cases./87/ [87]

Interest received by foreign persons

The Code provides that U.S. source interest income earned by a nonresident alien individual or a foreign corporation that is not effectively connected with the conduct of a U.S. trade or business generally is subject to a gross-basis 30-percent withholding tax. A significant statutory exemption from that tax applies to so-called "portfolio interest" received by foreign persons.

Portfolio interest generally is defined as any U.S. source interest (including original issue discount) that is not effectively connected with the conduct of a trade or business and (1) is paid on an obligation that satisfies certain registration requirements or specified exceptions thereto, and (2) is not received by a 10-percent owner of the issuer of the obligation, taking into account shares owned by attribution. [88]

Foreign investment in U.S. real property -- shared appreciation debt

A foreign person's gain on the disposition of a U.S. real property interest (USRPI) is treated as income that is effectively connected with the conduct of a U.S. trade or business, and thus is subject to net-basis tax at ordinary U.S. income tax rates pursuant to the Foreign Investment in Real Property Tax Act of 1980 (FIRPTA). USRPIs include interests (other than solely as a creditor) in (1) real property, and (2) domestic corporations that are U.S. real property holding corporations (USRPHCs).

Whether a financial instrument is considered debt under any provisions of the Code is not determinative of whether it constitutes an "interest solely as a creditor" for purposes of FIRPTA. Regulations provide that an interest in real property other than an interest solely as

[Footnote ¶ 3055 continued]

86. Rev. Rul. 83-51, 1983-1 C.B. 48.

87. See, e.g., Dorzback v. Collison, 195 F.2d 69 (3d Cir.1952).

88. Certain additional exceptions to this general rule apply only in the case of a corporate recipient of interest. In such a case, the term portfolio interest generally excludes (1) interest received by a bank on a loan extended in the ordinary course of its business (except in the case of interest paid on an obligation of the United States), and (2) interest received by a controlled foreign corporation from a related person.

a creditor includes any right to share in the appreciation in the value of, or in the gross or net proceeds or profits generated by, the real property. Similarly, an interest in an entity (such as a USRPHC) other than an interest solely as a creditor includes any right to share in the appreciation in the value of an interest in, or the assets of, the entity, or a right to share in the gross or net proceeds or profits derived by, the entity.

Regulations further provide that amounts otherwise treated for tax purposes as principal and interest payments on debt obligations of all kinds (including obligations that are interests other than solely as a creditor) do not give rise to gain or loss that is subject to U.S. tax under FIRPTA. [89] Thus, a foreign owner of a note that pays interest contingent on appreciation in U.S. real property incurs U.S. income tax if he disposes of the note, but may not incur U.S. income tax if he holds the note and receives interest payments under its terms.

Reasons For Change

The committee is concerned that the complete exemption from U.S. tax granted by the portfolio interest rules may give foreign investors a strong incentive to structure their U.S. investments which provide equity participation rights so that the returns therefrom will be characterized as interest income as opposed to other, taxable forms of income. The committee believes that such structuring of investments results in a significant erosion of the U.S. tax base, and that in such cases, allowance of the tax exemption is not appropriate. For example, the committee believes that the tax exemption should not apply in cases where a debt instrument held by a foreign investor pays interest that is contingent on profits generated from the disposition of U.S. real property held by the borrower.

Congress enacted the tax exemption for portfolio interest earned by foreign persons in 1984. [90]The exemption was enacted because Congress believed it important that U.S. businesses have direct access to the Eurobond market as a source of capital. In addition, Congress did not want withholding taxes on interest paid on portfolio debt or the necessity for U.S. borrowers to create uneconomic corporate structures in order to make the interest exempt from U.S. tax to impair borrowers' ability to utilize that market. [91] The committee believes that the limits placed on the scope of the portfolio interest exemption by the bill do not depart from the original purposes of the exemption.

Explanation Of Provision

The bill makes the portfolio interest exemption inapplicable to certain contingent interest income received by foreign persons. In the case of an instrument on which a foreign holder earns both contingent and non-contingent interest, denial of the portfolio interest exemption applies only to the portion of the interest which is contingent interest.

Under the bill, contingent interest includes interest determined by reference to any of the following attributes of the debtor or any related person: receipts, sales, or other cash flow; income or profits; or changes in the value of property. [92] Thus, for example, the receipt by a foreign person of interest that is computed as a percentage of the borrower's profits would not be entitled to the tax exemption for portfolio interest. The bill does not treat interest as contingent merely because its payment can be impaired by a default on the debt obligation by the borrower.

In addition, contingent interest includes interest determined by reference to any dividend, partnership distribution, or similar payment made by the debtor or a related person. For example, interest is contingent under the bill where its receipt by the foreign investor is contingent upon the payment of a dividend to the shareholders of the corporate borrower.

The bill provides a number of exceptions to the general definition of contingent interest as

[Footnote ¶ 3056 continued]

89. Treas. Reg. sec. 1.897-1(h). FIRPTA applies in the case of a "disposition" of a USRPI. Treasury Reg. sec. 1.897-1(h) generally defines a disposition as a transaction that gives rise to gain under section 1001 of the Code. Section 1001 does not apply to interest received on indebtedness.

90. Sec. 127 of P.L. 98-369.

91. Staff of the Joint Committee on Taxation, General Explanation of the Revenue Provisions of the Deficit Reduction Act of 1984, (JCS-41-84), December 31,1984,pp.391-392.

92. For purposes of determining whether interest is contingent interest under the bill, the term related person means any person who is related to the borrower under Code section 267(b) or 707(b)(1). In addition, a related person, for this purpose, includes a party to an arrangement undertaken for a purpose of avoiding the application of this provision of the bill.

detailed above. Under one such exception, interest is not considered contingent solely because the timing of the interest or any related principal payment is subject to a contingency. For example, assume that a debt obligation accrues fixed interest at a competitive market rate. If in any period prior to the instrument's maturity date the debtor has insufficient cash to make an interest payment, the debt agreement allows the borrower to defer the payment, but does not eliminate the borrower's liability for the deferred amount (or for interest that accrues on that amount). In this case, the interest is not considered contingent interest under the bill.

As another example,. assume a debt obligation that is a regular interest in a Real Estate Mortgage Interest Conduit (REMIC) pays fixed interest at a competitive market rate. However, the period during which the debt obligation is to remain outstanding depends on the extent to which the qualified mortgages held by the REMIC are prepaid (and on other contingencies related to the income earned or expenses incurred by the REMIC). The interest received from the REMIC would not, because of this feature, be treated as contingent interest.

Portfolio interest treatment is not denied under the bill solely because the interest is paid with respect to nonrecourse or limited recourse indebtedness. For example, this exception would apply where a corporation issues a limited recourse debt instrument that pays fixed interest at a competitive market rate and is secured by trade receivables of the corporation.

Interest also is not denied portfolio treatment under the bill if all or substantially all of it is determined by reference to certain other amounts of interest that is NOT described as contingent above (or by reference to the principal amount of indebtedness on which such other interest is paid). An example of what is intended to be covered by this exception is a regular interest in a REMIC which pays annual amounts of interest equal to a percentage of the interest earned by the REMIC on qualified mortgages, where the interest earned by the REMIC is not considered contingent interest under the rules of the provision.

In determining whether all or substantially all of an amount of interest payable on a debt obligation is computed by reference to another amount of interest that is not contingent interest, other factors that affect the amount of interest payable on the debt obligation, but which are not contingencies as contemplated by the bill, are not taken into account. For example, assume a regular interest in a REMIC pays annual amounts of interest equal to the interest received by the REMIC on qualified mortgages in excess of an established threshold -- the outstanding principal amounts on the qualified mortgages multiplied by a variable rate based on LIBOR [93] that is subject to a cap. Under the bill, the fact that the amount of interest paid by the REMIC varies inversely with LIBOR does not cause the interest to be treated as contingent interest.

Another of the bill's exceptions provides that interest is not denied portfolio treatment solely because the debtor or a related person enters into a hedging transaction to reduce the risk of interest rate or currency fluctuations with respect to such interest. Interest also is not denied portfolio treatment under the bill if it is determined by reference to changes in the value of (or any index of the value of) actively traded property other than a USRPI. For this purpose, the term "property" includes stock, and the term "actively traded" has the meaning given to that term under section 1092(d) of the Code. In general, portfolio treatment also is not denied if the interest is determined by reference to the yield (or any index of the yield) on such actively traded property. However, this exception for interest contingent on the yield of actively traded property does not apply if the property is a debt instrument that itself pays contingent interest as described above, or the actively traded property is stock or other property that represents a beneficial interest in the debtor or a related person.

By adding this set of exceptions, the committee intends to clarify that, for example, portfolio treatment is not denied in the case of a debt instrument that pays interest in an amount determined by reference to the value of a commodities index merely because the debtor hedges its interest rate risk on the debt by acquiring an offsetting position in com-

[Footnote ¶ 3056 continued]
93. The London Inter-Bank Offered Rate.

modities which produces a cash flow that correlates with the interest payments. As another example, portfolio treatment is not denied in the case of a debt instrument that pays interest in an amount determined by reference to the value of a stock market index merely due to the fact that an affiliate of the debtor holds stock which is publicly traded on that market.

The committee intends that the exceptions to the provision not be utilized by taxpayers to inappropriately avoid its application. For example, assume a corporation issues a nonrecourse debt obligation that accrues interest at a rate significantly in excess of the market rate. Pursuant to the provisions of that instrument, if in any period prior to the date of maturity of the obligation the debtor has insufficient cash flow to pay the interest, the obligation to pay the interest is deferred, but not eliminated. However, at the time of issuance of the obligation, the debtor and creditor reasonably expect that a significant portion of the accrued interest will be deferred, and ultimately will never be paid. In such a case, the committee intends that the exceptions to the application of the provision for nonrecourse indebtedness and for the timing of principal or interest payments should not apply. Thus, the interest received on the obligation would not qualify for portfolio treatment.

The bill provides that application of the provision may be extended to any type of continent interest not specifically described in the bill, if identified by the Treasury Secretary in regulations. The Secretary is granted authority under the bill to issue such regulations to supplement the statutory description of contingent interest in order to address cases where a denial of the portfolio interest exemption is necessary or appropriate to prevent avoidance of U.S. income tax. The bill additionally provides that the Secretary may by regulation exempt any type of interest from denial, under the bill, of portfolio treatment.

The committee intends that the provision not override existing treaties that reduce or eliminate U.S. withholding tax on interest paid to foreign persons.

Effective Date

The provision applies to interest received after December 31, 1993. It does not apply, however, to any interest paid or accrued with respect to any indebtedness with a fixed term that was issued on or before April 7, 1993, or was issued after such date pursuant to a written binding contract in effect on such date and at all times thereafter before such indebtedness was issued.

[Conference Report]

Present Law

Estate tax treatment of portfolio obligations

As a general rule, estate tax on the transfer of the taxable estate of every decedent nonresident who was not a citizen of the United States. For this purpose, the value of the gross estate of such a decedent that is subject to tax is that part of his or her gross estate which at the time of death (or as provided in section 2104(b) is situated in the United States. Certain types of property are specifically excluded by statute from a nonresident decedent's gross estate. One type of property granted such an exclusion is a debt obligation if any interest thereon would be eligible for the exemption from income tax for portfolio interest where such interest received by the decedent at the time of his or her death, determined without regard to whether a statement has been received that the beneficial owner of the obligation is not a United States person.

Senate Amendment

The Senate amendment is the same as the House bill.

Conference Agreement

The conference agreement follows the House bill and the Senate amendment with one clarification. In addition, the conference agreement provides specific rules for the estate tax treatment of contingent interest obligations.

The conferees wish to clarify the treatment under the provision of a debt instrument with a minimum non-contingent interest rate. For example, assume that the interest rate on a debt instrument is stated as the greater of either of two amounts--6% of the principal amount of 10% of gross profits. In such a case, only the gross-profits-based interest is contingent interest. The conferees wish to clarify that with respect to such an instrument, only the excess of the contingent amount, if any, only the minimum fixed interest amount is disqualified from portfolio interest treatment.

The conference agreement provides that, for purposes of determining the gross estate of a nonresident noncitizen decedent subject to the estate tax, a special rule applies to debt instruments that provide for both contingent and noncontingent interest. Under the conference agreement, an appropriate portion of the value of such an instrument, as determined in a manner prescribed by the Secretary of the Treasury, is treated as property within the United States and, thus, is included in the decedent's gross estate. Until rules are issued that provide guidance as to the proper method for determining the appropriate portion of such an instrument that is treated as situated in the United States, the conferees intend that taxpayers be permitted to use any reasonable method for making such determination.

The estate tax provision is effective for decedents dying after December 31, 1993. The provision does not apply to any obligation with a fixed term that was issued on or before April 7, 1993, or was issued after such date pursuant to a written binding contract in effect on such date and at all times thereafter before it was issued.

[¶3057] Section 13238. Regulations Dealing with Conduit Arrangements

(Code Sec. 7701)

[House Explanation]

Present Law

The tax treatment of a transaction may depend on the identity of the parties to the transaction. For example, a loan by a controlled foreign corporation to a related U.S. borrower is treated as an investment in U.S. property under Code section 956, and as such, may result in an inclusion of income to U.S. shareholders of the foreign corporation. On the other hand, an income inclusion to the U.S. shareholders of the foreign corporation would not have resulted had the loan been made by the same foreign corporation to an unrelated foreign borrower.

Under the Code, payments of interest by U.S. persons to related foreign persons may be subject to 30-percent gross-basis withholding tax. On the other hand, no such tax applies to payments by U.S. persons to unrelated foreign persons of so-called portfolio interest. Under treaties, payments of interest by U.S. persons to related foreign persons who are resident in the treaty country may be subject to little or no U.S. gross-basis tax. By contrast, if the related recipient of interest is resident in a country with respect to which no U.S. income tax treaty is in force, the 30-percent gross basis tax would be imposed.

Courts have stated that the incidence of taxation depends upon the substance of a transaction as a whole. /94/[94] In certain cases, courts have recharacterized transactions in order to impose tax consistent with this principle. For example, where three parties have engaged in a chain of transactions, the courts have at times ignored the "middle" party as a mere "conduit," and imposed tax as if a single transaction had been carried out between the parties at the ends of the chain.

In Aiken Industries, Inc. v. Commissioner, /95/[95] the Tax Court recharacterized an interest payment by a U.S. person on its note held by a related treaty-country resident, which in turn had a precisely matching obligation to a related non-treaty-country resident, as a payment directly by the U.S. person to the non-treaty-country resident. The transaction in its recharacterized form resulted in a loss of the treaty protection that would otherwise have applied on the payment of interest by the U.S. person to the treaty-country resident, and thus subjected the interest payment to 30-percent U.S. tax.

The IRS has taken the position that it will apply a similar result in cases where the back-to-back related party debt obligations are less closely matched than those in Aiken Industries, so long as the intermediary entity does not obtain complete dominion and control over the interest payments. [96] The IRS has taken an analogous position where an unrelated financial intermediary is interposed between the

[Footnote ¶3056 continued]

94. See, e.g., Commissioner v. Court Holding Co., 324 U.S. 331 (1945).

95. 56 T.C. 925 (1971), acq. on another issue, 1972-2 C.B. 1.

96. Rev. Rul. 84-152, 1984-2 C.B. 381; Rev. Rul. 84-153, 1984-2 C.B. 383.

two related parties as lender to one and borrower from the other, as long as the intermediary would not have made or maintained the loan on the same terms without the corresponding borrowing. [97] In a recent technical advice memorandum, the IRS has taken the position that interest payments by a U.S. company to a related, treaty-protected financial intermediary may be treated as payments by the U.S. company directly to the foreign parent of the financial intermediary even though the matching payments from the intermediary to the parent are not interest payments, but rather are dividends. /98/[98]

Reasons For Change

The committee is concerned that taxpayers may be inappropriately avoiding U.S. tax by intricately structuring financial transactions which utilize multiple entities, where one or more of those entities serve as a conduit. The committee believes that the above cited IRS rulings appropriately ignore conduit entities and properly recharacterize the transactions described therein. However, the committee does not intend that the Secretary be bound, in developing regulations, by the standards on which those rulings are based, if the Secretary deems it necessary or appropriate to adopt other standards in order to properly recharacterize a financing transaction. In legislating in this area, it is not the intent of the committee to cast a negative inference on positions taken by the IRS under present law.

By granting regulatory authority to provide detailed rules in this complicated area, the committee seeks to bolster the Treasury's ability to prevent unwarranted avoidance of tax through multiple-party financial engineering, as well as to provide a mechanism for issuing additional guidance to taxpayers entering into financial transactions.

Explanation of Provision

The bill authorizes the Treasury Secretary to promulgate regulations that set forth rules for recharacterizing any multiple-party financing transaction as a transaction directly among any two or more of such parties where the Secretary determines that such recharacterization is appropriate to prevent avoidance of any tax imposed by the Internal Revenue Code.

The committee intends that the provision apply not solely to back-to-back loan transactions, but also to other financing transactions. For example, it would be within the proper scope of the provision for the Secretary to issue regulations dealing with multiple-party transactions involving debt guarantees or equity investments.

Effective Date

The provision is effective on date of enactment.

[Conference Report]

Present Law

The tax treatment of a transaction may depend on the identity of the parties to the transaction. For example, a loan by a controlled foreign corporation to a related U.S. borrower is treated as an investment in U.S. property under Code section 956, and as such, may result in an inclusion of income to U.S. shareholders of the foreign corporation. On the other hand, an income inclusion to the U.S. shareholders of the foreign corporation would not have resulted had the loan been made by the same foreign corporation to an unrelated foreign borrower.

Under the Code, payments of interest by U.S. persons to related foreign persons may be subject to 30-percent gross-basis withholding tax. On the other hand, no such tax applies to payments by U.S. persons to unrelated foreign persons of so-called portfolio interest. Under treaties, payments of interest by U.S. persons to related foreign persons who are resident in the treaty country may be subject to little or no U.S. gross-basis tax. By contrast, if the related recipient of interest is resident in a country with respect to which no U.S. income tax treaty is in force, the 30-percent gross-basis tax would be imposed.

Courts have stated that the incidence of taxation depends upon the substance of a transaction as a whole. /1/[1] In certain cases, courts have recharacterized transactions in order to impose tax consistent with this principle. For example, where three parties have engaged in a chain of transactions, the courts have at

[Footnote ¶ 3057 continued]

97. Sev. Rul. 87-89, 1987-2 C.B. 195.

98. Tech. Adv. Mem. 9133004 (May 3, 1991).

[Footnote ¶ 3057] 1. See, e.g., Commissioner v. Court Holding Co., 324 U.S. 331 (1945)

times ignored the "middle" party as a mere "conduit," and imposed tax as if a single transaction had been carried out between the parties at the ends of the chain.

In Aiken Industries. Inc. v. Commissioner, /2/[2] the Tax Court recharacterized an interest payment by a U.S. person on its note held by a related treaty-country resident, which in turn had a precisely matching obligation to a related non-treaty-country resident, as a payment directly by the U.S. person to the non-treaty-country resident. The transaction in its recharacterized form resulted in a loss of the treaty protection that would otherwise have applied on the payment of interest by the U.S. person to the treaty-country resident, and thus caused the interest payment to give rise to 30-percent U.S. tax.

The IRS has taken the position that it will apply a similar result in cases where the back-to-back related party debt obligations are less closely matched than those in Aiken Industries, so long as the intermediary entity does not obtain complete dominion and control over the interest payments. /3/[3] The IRS has taken an analogous position where an unrelated financial intermediary is interposed between the two related parties as lender to one and borrower from the other, as long as the intermediary would not have made or maintained the loan on the same terms without the corresponding borrowing. /4/[4] In a recent technical advice memorandum, the IRS has taken the position that interest payments by a U.S. company to a related, treaty-protected financial intermediary may be treated as payments by the U.S. company directly to the foreign parent of the financial intermediary even though the matching payments from the intermediary to the parent are not interest payments, but rather are dividends. /5/[5]

House Bill

The House bill authorizes the Treasury Secretary to promulgate regulations that set forth rules for recharacterizing any multiple-party financing transaction as a transaction directly among any two or more of such parties where the Secretary determines that such recharacterization is appropriate to prevent avoidance of any tax imposed by the Internal Revenue Code.

It is intended that the provision apply not solely to back-to-back loan transactions, but also to other financing transactions. For example, it would be within the proper scope of the provision for the Secretary to issue regulations dealing with multiple-party transactions involving debt guarantees or equity investments.

Effective date. The provision is effective on date of enactment.

[Senate Amendment]

The Senate amendment is the same as the House bill.

Conference Agreement

The conference agreement follows the House bill and the Senate amendment.

[¶3058] Section 13239. Treatment of Export of Certain Softwood Logs

(Code Sec. 865, 927, 954, 993)

[Senate Explanation]

Present Law

Rules for sourcing income

Subject to significant exceptions, income from the sale of personal property generally is sourced on the basis of the residence of the seller. One set of exceptions apply to sales of inventory property. Income derived from the purchase of inventory property within the United States and its sale outside the United States constitutes foreign source income. Similarly, income derived from the purchase of inventory property outside the United States and its sale within the United States constitutes domestic source income. Income attributable to the marketing of inventory property by U.S. residents in other cases may also have its source determined to be the place of sale. For this purpose, the place of sale generally is the place where title to the property passes to the purchaser (the "title passage" rule).

[Footnote ¶3057 continued]

2. 56 T.C. 925 (1971), acq. on another issue, 1972-2 C.B. 1.
3. Rev. Rul. 84-152, 1984-2 C.B. 381; Rev. Rul. 84-153, 1984-2 C.B. 383.
4. Rev. Rul. 87-89, 1987-2 C.B. 195.
5. Tech. Adv. Mem. 9133004 (May 3, 1991).

Income derived from the production of property in the United States and its sale elsewhere is treated as having a divided source. When a U.S. producer sells part of its output to wholly independent distributors or other selling concerns in such a way as to establish fairly the independent factory or production price unaffected by considerations of tax liability, the division of the income between foreign and domestic source must be based on that independent price (Treas. Reg. sec. 1.863-3(b)(2), Example (1); Phillips Petroleum Co. v. Commissioner, 97 T.C. 30 (1991); Notice 89-10, 1989-1 C.B. 631). Under the independent factory price (IFP) method the portion of income attributable to production activity is determined by reference to the IFP and is sourced in the country of production (the United States in the case of a U.S. exporter). The balance of taxable income is attributed to sales activity and is presumed to arise outside the country of production (the United States). When the IFP method cannot be used, Treasury regulations permit the source of 50 percent of export income to be based on the location of the property held or used in the production or sale of the property exported (generally the United States) and the source of the other 50 percent to be determined under the title passage rule.

Income earned by foreign corporations

The United States exerts jurisdiction to tax all income, whether derived in the United States or elsewhere, of U.S. citizens, residents, and corporations. By contrast, the United States taxes nonresident aliens and foreign corporations only on income with a sufficient nexus to the United States. In the case of income earned by a U.S.-owned foreign corporation, generally no U.S. tax is imposed until that income is distributed to the U.S. shareholders as a dividend.

When a U.S.-controlled foreign corporation earns so-called "subpart F income," the United States generally taxes the corporation's 10-percent U.S. shareholders currently on their pro-rata share of that income regardless of whether the income is actually distributed currently to the shareholders. Included among the types of income deemed distributed (generally referred to as "subpart F income") is foreign base company sales income.

Certain subpart F income derived by a controlled foreign corporation that is an export trade corporation (ETC) from certain export activities is exempt from current taxation. Under this exemption, the subpart F income of an ETC is reduced by certain amounts that constitute export trade income (as defined in section 971). No foreign corporation may qualify as an ETC unless it has so qualified generally since 1971.

Foreign sales corporations

A portion of the income of an eligible foreign sales corporation (FSC) that is generated from export property is exempt from Federal income tax. If the income earned by the FSC is determined under special administrative pricing rules, then the exempt foreign trade income generally is 15/23 of the foreign trade income the FSC derives from the transaction. In addition, a domestic corporation is allowed a 100-percent dividends-received deduction for dividends distributed from the FSC out of earnings attributable to certain foreign trade income. Thus, there generally is no corporate level tax imposed on a portion of the income from exports of a FSC.

Foreign trade income is defined as the gross income of a FSC attributable to foreign trading gross receipts. Foreign trade income includes both the profits earned by the FSC itself from exports and commissions earned by the FSC from products exported by others and services related thereto. In general, the term foreign trading gross receipts means the gross receipts of a FSC which are attributable to the export of certain goods and services. Foreign trading gross receipts are the gross receipts of the FSC that are attributable to the following types of transactions: the sale of export property, the lease or rental of export property, services related and subsidiary to the sale or lease of export property, engineering and architectural services, and export management services.

Export property, for purposes of the FSC rules, is defined as property that is (1) manufactured, produced, grown, or extracted in the United States by a person other than a FSC, (2) held primarily for sale, lease, or rental, in the ordinary conduct of a trade or business by, or to, a FSC, for direct use, consumption, or disposition outside the United States, and (3) not more than 50 percent of the fair market value of which is attributable to articles imported into the United States.

Domestic International Sales Corporations

Prior law provided for a system of tax deferral for corporations known as Domestic International Sales Corporations, or "DISCs," and their shareholders. Under this system, the profits of a DISC were not taxed to the DISC but were taxed to the shareholders of the DISC when distributed or deemed distributed to them. Each year, a DISC was deemed to have distributed a portion of its income, thereby subjecting that income to current taxation in its shareholders' hands. Federal income tax could generally be deferred on the remaining portion of the DISC's taxable income until the income was actually distributed to the shareholders.

Under current law, a DISC is permitted to continue to defer income attributable to $10 million or less of qualified export receipts. However, unlike the prior-law DISC rules, an interest charge is imposed on the shareholders of the DISC. The amount of the interest is based on the tax otherwise due on the deferred income computed as if the income were distributed. Taxable income of the DISC attributable to qualified export receipts that exceed $10 million is deemed distributed to the DISC's shareholders.

To qualify for DISC treatment, at least 95 percent of a domestic corporation's gross receipts must consist of qualified export receipts. In general, qualified export receipts are receipts, including commission receipts, derived from the sale or lease for use outside the United States of export property, or from the furnishing of services related or subsidiary to the sale or lease of export property. Export property must be manufactured, produced, grown, or extracted in the United States.

Reasons for Change

The committee believes that the justification for any tax benefit should be based on the amount of desired behavior induced by the benefit. In this instance, the committee believes that taxpayers are bearing the cost of a tax benefit that may be inducing little, if any, desired behavior, and may if anything be having an undesirable effect on the nation's economic well-being. In particular, the committee is concerned about features of the Code that may tend to accelerate the removal of old-growth forests, and the committee understands that the export of raw logs may in effect cause American milling jobs to themselves be exported overseas.

Explanation of Provision

The provision amends certain provisions of the Code as they apply to activities that generated income from unprocessed timber which is a softwood. For this purpose, the term "unprocessed timber" means any log, cant, or similar form of timber.

The provision excludes from the definition of "export property" for purposes of the FSC rules any unprocessed timber which is a softwood. Similarly, the provision excludes from the definition of "export property" for purposes of the DISC rules any unprocessed timber which is a softwood.

The provision also amends the sales source rules as they apply to inventory property. In this case, the bill provides that any income from the sale of any unprocessed timber which is a softwood and which was cut from an area located in the United States would be domestic source income.

Finally, the provision treats as subpart F foreign base company sales income any income derived by a controlled foreign corporation in connection with the sale of any unprocessed timber which is a softwood and was cut from an area located in the United States. In addition, the provision treats as subpart F foreign base company sales income any income derived by a controlled foreign corporation from the milling of any such timber outside the United States. Any income treated as subpart F income under the proposal that is earned by an export trade corporation would not be subject to reduction by the export trade income of the corporation.

Effective Date

The provision is effective for transactions occurring after date of enactment of the proposal.

[Conference Report]

Conference Agreement

The conference agreement follows the Senate amendment.

[¶3059] Section 13241. Transportation Fuels Tax

(Code Sec. 4041, 4042, 4081, 4091, 6416, 6421, 6427, 9502, 9503)

[Senate Explanation]

Present Law

Several separate Federal excise taxes are imposed on specified transportation fuels. Taxable fuels include motor fuels (gasoline, diesel fuel and special motor fuels [1]) used for highway transportation; gasoline used in motorboats; diesel fuel used in trains; fuels used in inland waterways transportation; and, aviation fuel (gasoline and jet fuel) used in most aviation.

In general, gasoline and special motor fuels used in highway vehicles and motorboats are taxed at a total rate of 14.1 cents per gallon; highway diesel fuel is taxed at a total rate of 20.1 cents per gallon; noncommercial aviation gasoline is taxed at a total rate of 15.1 cents per gallon; noncommercial aviation jet fuel is taxed at a total rate of 17.6 cents per gallon; commercial aviation fuels are taxed at a total rate of 0.1 cent per gallon; railroad diesel fuel is taxed at a total rate of 2.6 cents per gallon; and inland waterways fuels are taxed at a total rate of 17.1 cents per gallon in 1993 (increasing to 19.1 cents per gallon in 1994 and 20.1 cents per gallon in 1995 and thereafter).

Revenues from most of these excise taxes are deposited in various trust funds to finance specific Federal public works and environmental programs. The set of fuels subject to each tax generally reflects the purposes of the trust fund to which the revenues are dedicated. The above rates also include a general deficit reduction tax (in effect through September 30, 1995 [2]) imposed on highway motor fuels, motorboat gasoline and special motor fuels, and train diesel fuel. Revenues from this deficit reduction tax are retained in the General Fund of the Treasury.

One of the dedicated excise taxes is a 0.1 cent per gallon tax (0.05 cent per gallon for qualified ethanol and methanol fuels) imposed on all of the fuels listed above, except liquefied petroleum gas. This tax, in effect through 1995, is deposited into the Leaking Underground Storage Tank ("LUST") Trust Fund, which is used to fund cleanup costs associated with leaking underground storage tanks containing petroleum products.

Certain fuel uses are exempt from the LUST excise tax. Exempt uses include No. 2 residual fuel oil [3] used as heating oil; gasoline and diesel fuel used on farms for farming purposes; off-highway business uses of fuel (for example, fuel used to operate pumps, generators, compressors, forklift trucks, or bulldozers, or fuel used in vessels used by fisheries or whaling businesses); fuels used by State and local governments; fuels used by nonprofit educational organizations; exported fuels, including fuels used in international aviation and international shipping; and fuel for military ships and aircraft.

The gasoline excise tax (including the LUST rate on gasoline) is imposed when the fuel leaves terminal storage facilities (i.e., at the terminal rack). The diesel fuel excise tax is imposed on the wholesale sale of that fuel.

Reasons for Change

The committee believes that deficit reduction is critical to the nation's economic wellbeing and that responsible actions must be taken to address growing annual budget deficits and the increasing balance of federal government debt. It is the committee's view that the revenues raised by a broad-based transportation fuels excise tax will make an important contribution toward reducing the deficit.

The committee also believes that a transportation fuels tax should further other important objectives. The committee understands that in 1992, approximately two-thirds of domestic consumption of petroleum was for transportation uses. [4] By providing an incentive to reduce motor fuel consumption, this tax should tend to improve environmental problems that result from the transport, storage and burning of petroleum products to power motor vehicles, vessels, and aircraft. In addition, reduced

[Footnote ¶3057 continued]

[Footnote ¶3059] 1. Special motor fuels include benzol, benzene, naphtha, liquefied petroleum gas, casing head and natural gasoline, and any other liquid (other than kerosene, gas oil, fuel, or gasoline) sold for use in motor vehicles or motorboats.

2. See Item II.D.3., below, for the extension and transfer of the deficit reduction tax rate.

3. No. 2 residual fuel oil can be used either as diesel fuel or as home heating oil.

4. In 1992, the United States consumed approximately 33,000 quadrillion Btu of petroleum-based energy. Transportation accounted for approximately 22,000 quadrillion Btu. See, U.S. Department of Energy, Energy Information Agency, Monthly Energy Review, May 1993.

consumption of petroleum products should decrease U.S. reliance on imported oil.

Explanation of Provision

In general

The bill imposes an additional, permanent, deficit reduction excise tax of 4.3 cents per gallon on all transportation fuels currently subject to the LUST excise tax (i.e., highway, rail, aviation, and inland waterway fuels), on liquefied petroleum gases currently taxable as special motor fuels, and on diesel fuel used in noncommercial motorboats. [5] Ethanol, methanol and their ether derivatives are fully taxable at the 4.3-cent rate. The committee recognizes, however, that the impact of the transportation tax on ethanol, methanol, and their derivative ethers, as well as on other alternative fuels, requires further analysis, and the committee intends that these matters be addressed in the conference on this legislation.

The new deficit reduction tax is to be collected in the same manner as the existing excise taxes on these fuels (although, as described in Item II.D.2., below, a separate provision in the bill changes the point of collection for the present-law diesel fuel excise tax).

Fuel uses that are exempt from the current LUST excise tax will be exempt from the new tax.

Disposition of revenues

Revenues from the new transportation fuels excise tax will be retained in the General Fund of the Treasury.

Effective Date

The transportation fuels tax provisions are effective on October 1, 1993. Floor stocks taxes are imposed on taxable products held for sale or for use (other than in an exempt use) as a fuel beyond the applicable product's tax collection point on October 1, 1993.

Conference Report

The conference agreement follows the Senate amendment, with the following modifications.

The tax base is expanded to include compressed natural gas (CNG) used in highway motor vehicles or motorboats, and jet fuel used in noncommercial aviation. In addition, gasoline and jet fuel used in commercial aviation is subject to the 4.3 cent-per-gallon rate beginning on October 1, 1995 (with appropriate floor stocks taxes being imposed on that date).

CNG used in highway vehicles or motorboats is taxed at a rate of 48.54 cents per mcf (thousand cubic feet) at standard temperature and pressure. The tax is collected on the retail sale or use of CNG under the same provisions as the special motor fuels tax currently is collected.

Revenues from the new 4.3-cents-per-gallon tax (48.54 cents per mcf on compressed natural gas) are retained in the General Fund of the Treasury.

Effective date. The provision is effective on October 1, 1993, with appropriate floor stocks taxes being imposed on that date.

[¶3060] Sections 13242 and 13243. Modification of Diesel Fuel Tax Collection

(Code Sec. 4041, 4081, 4091)

[Senate Explanation]

Present Law

Diesel fuel tax collection

Excise taxes totalling 20.1 cents per gallon generally are imposed on the sale of highway diesel fuel by a producer or importer. A reduced rate of 3.1 cents per gallon applies to sales of diesel fuel for use in certain intercity buses. A rate of 2.6 cents per gallon applies to sales of diesel fuel for use in trains.

Diesel fuel may be sold without the payment of tax in the following cases: (1) sales of heating oil, (2) sales to other producers, and (3) sales for nontaxable uses including (a) use other than as fuel in a diesel-powered highway vehicle or diesel-powered train (such as use in any boat), (b) use in off-highway business use,

[Footnote ¶3059 continued]

5. A separate provision in the bill (described in Item I.E.2.) extends the current 20.1-cents-per-gallon diesel fuel excise tax (including the LUST rate) to diesel fuel used by noncommercial motorboats.

(c) use on a farm for farming purposes, (d) exclusive use by a State or local government, (e) export, (f) exclusive use by a nonprofit educational organization, (g) use by certain aircraft museums, and (h) use in certain qualified local buses. A sale may be made without the payment of tax only if certain prescribed conditions are satisfied, which may include registration by the buyer and seller and certification of exempt use by the buyer to the seller.

The producer making a taxable sale generally is liable for the tax. The term producer generally includes refiners, compounders, blenders, wholesale distributors of diesel fuel and dealers selling any diesel fuel exclusively to producers of diesel fuel. Producers must be registered with the Treasury Department to purchase without payment of tax and, as a condition of registration, may be required to post a bond. Thus, in general, most diesel fuel tax is collected at the wholesale distributor level.

Exempt and reduced-rate users who buy diesel fuel after tax has been paid on the fuel may file a claim for credit or refund. These users must, however, keep business records that will enable the Treasury Department to verify the amount claimed.

Gasoline tax collection

Taxes totalling 14.1 cents a gallon generally are imposed on (1) the removal of gasoline from any refinery, (2) the removal of gasoline from any terminal, (3) the entry of gasoline into the United States, and (4) the sale to any unregistered person unless there was a prior taxable removal or entry of the gasoline under (1), (2), or (3) above. The tax, however, does not apply to any entry or removal of gasoline transferred in bulk to a terminal if all the persons involved (including the terminal operator) are registered. Thus, tax generally is imposed when gasoline is removed by truck from a terminal (this is called removal at the "terminal rack"). Taxpayers who use gasoline for an exempt use, such as for farming or for off-highway business use, are eligible to claim a credit or refund of the excise tax included in the price of the gasoline.

Under Treasury Department regulations, the person liable for the tax imposed on gasoline removed from a terminal rack is the "position holder," which, in general, is the person that holds the inventory position to gasoline as reflected on the records of the terminal operator (i.e., has a contract with the terminal operator for the use of storage facilities and terminaling services at a terminal). In addition, the terminal operator may be jointly and severally liable for the tax if the position holder is not registered with Treasury. As a condition of registration, terminal operators, position holders, and other persons involved in bulk transfers of gasoline, may be required to post a bond in such sum as the Treasury determines.

Reasons for Change

Recent reports have suggested that there may be substantial levels of diesel fuel tax evasion. In particular, at a hearing in 1992 on shortfalls in Highway Trust Fund collections, the Department of Transportation estimated that the level of diesel fuel tax evasion is between 15 and 25 percent of total gallons consumed. [1] Advancing the collection point of the diesel fuel taxes reduces the number of times the fuel changes ownership prior to tax, and reduces the number of taxpayers. As a result, the diesel fuel taxes should be easier to collect and payments of tax should be easier to monitor.

In addition, the committee intends to minimize the additional burden that may be imposed on exempt users of diesel fuel as a result of the collection point change. Thus, the committee intends that the collection point change be accomplished in a manner that would preserve the present exemptions from the diesel fuel tax and the ability of exempt users to buy diesel fuel (including heating oil) without payment of tax.

Explanation of Provision

Point of collection

The bill provides that the full 20.1 cents per gallon diesel fuel excise tax will be imposed on removal from a terminal (i.e., at the terminal rack) under generally the same rules as the

[Footnote ¶ 3059 continued]

[Footnote ¶ 3060] 1. Statement of Eugene R. McCormick, Federal Highway Administration, Department of Transportation, Hearing on Shortfall in Highway Trust Fund Collections, Subcommittee on Investigations and Oversight of the House Committee on Public Works and Transportation (May 5, 1992).

gasoline tax currently is collected.[2] Thus, tax generally will be imposed when diesel fuel is removed by truck from a registered terminal. However, unlike the gasoline tax, removal of diesel fuel that is destined for an exempt use will not be taxed as the fuel is removed from the terminal if the dyeing requirements described below are satisfied. Any diesel fuel that is destined for an exempt use that is not dyed (as required below) will be subject to tax on removal.[3]

Thus, for example, removal of diesel fuel that is destined for use as heating oil or for off-highway farming purposes will not be taxed as the fuel is removed from the terminal if the dyeing requirements are satisfied. In addition, removal of diesel fuel that is destined for use by certain intercity buses and by trains will not be taxed as the fuel is removed from the terminal if the dyeing requirements are satisfied. The special tax rates of 3.1 cents per gallon for diesel fuel used by intercity buses and of 2.6 cents per gallon for diesel fuel used by trains (other than certain State and local governmentally owned and operated trains) will continue to be imposed on the sale of the fuels at the time that the fuel is sold to these reduced-rate users.

As stated above, in order to permit diesel fuel to be removed from a terminal without payment of tax, the bill requires the fuel to be indelibly dyed in accordance with regulations to be prescribed by the Treasury Department. The committee expects the Treasury Department to coordinate the dyeing that will be required for purposes of the highway diesel tax with the dyeing that will be required for purposes of the Clean Air Act. For fuel that is not dyed under the Clean Air Act, the color of the dye may be chosen by the person who is dyeing the fuel but the color must be approved by the Treasury Department or selected from a list of approved colors (in order to distinguish diesel fuel that has been removed without payment of tax from that which has been removed with payment of tax). The committee expects that one color that will be approved for purposes of dyeing for the highway diesel tax is the color that is used for purposes of dyeing for the Clean Air Act.

The Treasury Department is expected to enforce the dyeing requirement vigorously and to check regularly to ensure that terminal operators maintain removal systems that prevent undyed fuel from being removed without payment of tax, that any fuel that is removed without payment of tax is dyed, and that dyes are maintained in a secure location.

As under present law, most exempt or reduced-rate users that use tax-paid undyed diesel fuel are permitted a refund if the user establishes that a prior tax was paid with respect to the fuel and that the fuel has been used for an exempt or reduced-rate use. Thus, for example, an intercity bus company that qualified for the 3.1-cents-per-gallon reduced rate could apply for a refund of 17 cents per gallon if it could show it purchased undyed fuel (which had been subject to the full 20.1-cents-per-gallon tax) rather than dyed fuel.

However, similar to the present law for certain gasoline vendors, only registered ultimate vendors (in lieu of the farmer or State or local government) will be permitted to apply for excise tax refunds or credits for any sales of undyed (tax-paid) diesel fuel for use on a farm for a farming purposes or by a State or local government. Vendors will be able to file an expedited claim for refund of these taxes for any period for which the claim is $200 or more and the period is not less than one week. If the Treasury Department does not pay a proper claim for refund filed under these procedures within 20 days, the Treasury Department will pay interest on the refund.

Administrative provisions

As under present law, the Treasury Department is permitted to require appropriate registration of persons necessary to implement the diesel fuel tax, including diesel fuel refiners and dye manufacturers. The Treasury Department also is authorized to require position

[Footnote ¶ 3060 continued]

2. The 4.3 cents-per-gallon deficit reduction rate that is included in this bill also will be collected on removal of diesel fuel from a terminal. All rates described below will be increased by the new deficit reduction rate, unless a specific exemption is provided.

3. The tax imposed by this bill (sec. 8163) on diesel fuel that is used by noncommercial motorboats will be collected at the terminal rack. Diesel fuel that is used by commercial motorboats (which will be an exempt use) will not be taxed as the fuel is removed from the terminal if the dyeing requirements are met. If a tax is imposed on the removal of diesel fuel that is subsequently used as supplies for vessels (within the meaning of sec. 4221(d)(3)), the wholesale distributor of the fuel may apply for the refund (see sec. 6416(b) (2)).

holders, terminal operators, and other appropriate persons to keep records and to report the quantity of dyed and undyed fuel that is removed from a terminal or refinery.

As under the present law gasoline tax rules, the Treasury Department is permitted to prescribe rules and administrative procedures for determining the liability for payment of tax. These regulations are expected to provide that a terminal operator will be jointly and severally liable for any unpaid tax if a position holder is not registered with the Treasury Department. In addition, the terminal operator may be held jointly and severally liable for any unpaid tax if the terminal operator failed to keep any required records or to make any required reports on the removal of dyed and undyed diesel fuel.

In addition, a new penalty is to be imposed on any person who sold dyed fuel to a person whom it knew or had reason to know would use the fuel for a taxable use, or any person who knew or had reason to know that it used dyed fuel for a taxable use. This new penalty is the greater of $1,000 or twice the otherwise applicable tax on the diesel fuel so used. The Treasury Department also is authorized to require the conspicuous labeling of retail diesel fuel pumps (and other delivery facilities) to assure that persons are aware of which fuel is available for nontaxable uses.

Effective Date

The provision applies to diesel fuel removed from terminals after December 31, 1993. A floor stocks tax is imposed on diesel fuel held for sale or in bulk quantities for taxable use on January 1, 1994; the tax applies only to diesel fuel held beyond the terminal rack on January 1, 1994, and the amount of tax is reduced by any tax previously imposed on the fuel under section 4041 or 4091. The Treasury Department further is authorized to require dyeing of bulk quantities of diesel fuel held beyond the terminal rack for nontaxable uses on that date.

[Conference Report]

Conference Agreement

The conference agreement follows the Senate amendment, except that marking is permitted (as provided by regulations) for fuel that is destined for an exempt use. In addition, the conference agreement clarifies that Treasury has authority to physically inspect terminals, dyes and dyeing equipment and storage facilities, and downstream storage facilities; to stop, detain and inspect vehicles, and to establish vehicle inspection sites. The conference agreement provides a $1,000 penalty on facility owners who refuse to permit the Treasury to perform its inspection duties.

The agreement also modifies the penalty for persons who improperly sell or use dyed fuel to be the greater of $1,000 or $10 for each gallon of dyed fuel involved in the violation. For repeated violations, the penalty is multiplied of prior penalties that has been imposed under this provision. Any officer, employee, or agent who willfully participated in any act giving rise to the above penalties will be jointly and severally liable with any business entity that is liable for the penalty. Dyed fuel means any fuel that is dyed, regardless of whether or not the fuel was dyed to administer compliance with the diesel fuel tax provisions.

Effective date. The conference agreement follows the Senate amendment.

[¶ 3062] Section 13251. Modifications To Substantial Understatement Penalty

(Code Sec. 66621)

[Senate Explanation]

Present Law

A 20-percent penalty is imposed on any portion of an underpayment of tax that is attributable either to a substantial understatement of income tax on a return, or to negligence or disregard of rules or regulations (sec. 6662).

For this purpose, an understatement [2] is considered substantial if it exceeds the greater of

[Footnote ¶ 3060 continued]

2. An "understatement" of income tax is the excess of the tax required to be shown on the return over the tax imposed which is shown on the return (reduced by any rebates of tax).

10 percent of the tax required to be shown on the year's return or $5,000 ($10,000 for corporations other than S corporations and personal holding companies). In determining whether an understatement is substantial, the amount of the understatement is reduced by any portion attributable to an item if (1) the treatment of the item on the return is or was supported by substantial authority, or (2) facts relevant to the tax treatment of the item were adequately disclosed on the tax return (or a statement attached to the return), provided that the treatment of the disclosed item was not "frivolous" (Treas. Reg. sec. 1.6662-4). Special rules apply to tax shelters.

The term "negligence" includes any failure to make a reasonable attempt to comply with the internal revenue laws, a failure to exercise ordinary and reasonable care in the preparation of a tax return, and a failure to keep adequate books and records or to substantiate items properly (Treas. Reg. sec. 1.6662-3(b)(1)). The term "disregard" includes any careless, reckless, or intentional disregard of rules or regulations (sec. 6662(c)). The penalty for negligence or disregard of rules or regulations does not apply where the position taken is adequately disclosed, the position is not "frivolous", and the taxpayer has adequate books and records and has substantiated items properly (Treas. Reg. sec. 1.6662-3(c)). [3]

A $250 penalty with respect to a return or claim for refund of income tax may be imposed on the preparer if any understatement of tax liability on the return or claim for refund resulted from a position that did not have a realistic possibility of being sustained on its merits and the preparer knew or reasonably should have known of the position (sec. 6694(a)). The penalty is $1,000 per return or claim for refund if the understatement is due to any reckless or intentional disregard of rules or regulations (sec. 6694(b)). These penalties may be avoided where the position taken on the return or claim for refund is adequately disclosed and is not "frivolous" (Treas. Reg. secs. 1.6694-2(c), 1.6694-3(c)(2)). [4]

A "frivolous" position with respect to an item for purposes of all of these penalty provisions is one that is "patently improper" (Treas. Reg. sec. 1.6662-3(b)(3), 1.6662-4(e)(2)(i), 1.6694-2(c)(2), 1.6694-3(c)(2)).

Reasons For Change

The committee believes that the "frivolous" standard does not sufficiently discourage taxpayers and preparers from taking unreasonable return positions. Accordingly, to encourage compliance, the committee believes that a tougher standard should be imposed.

Explanation Of Provision

Under the bill, the "reasonable basis" standard replaces the "not frivolous" standard for purposes of the accuracy-related and income tax return preparer penalties. The committee intends that "reasonable basis" be a relatively high standard of tax reporting, that is, significantly higher than "not patently improper." This standard is not satisfied by a return position that is merely arguable or that is merely a colorable claim.

Under the bill, a taxpayer can avoid a substantial understatement penalty by adequately disclosing a return position only if the position has at least a reasonable basis. Similarly, a taxpayer can avoid the penalty that applies to disregarding rules or regulations by adequately disclosing a return position only if the position has at least a reasonable basis. The disclosure exception is no longer relevant with respect to the penalty for negligence, because a taxpayer generally is not considered to have been negligent with respect to a return position, regardless of whether it was disclosed, if the position has a reasonable basis. Also, a preparer can avoid a penalty by adequately disclosing a return position only if the position has at least a reasonable basis.

The bill also eliminates the reasonable cause and good faith exception for fraud, because fraud is inconsistent with reasonable cause and good faith.

Effective Date

The provision applies to tax returns due (without regard to extensions) after December 31, 1993.

[Footnote ¶3062 continued]

3. In the case of a position contrary to a regulation, the position taken must also represent a good faith challenge to the validity of the regulation.

4. In the case of a position contrary to a regulation, the position taken must also represent a good faith challenge to the validity of the regulation.

[Conference Report]

The conference agreement follows the Senate amendment. The conferees intend that "reasonable basis" be a relatively high stndard of tax reporting, that is, significantly higher than "not patently improper." This standard is not satisfied by a return position that is merely arguable or that is merely a colorable claim.

[¶ 3063] Section 13252. Returns Relating to the Cancellation of Indebtedness by Certain Financial Entities

(Code Sec. 6050P)

[Senate Explanation]

Explanation of Provision

The bill requires "applicable financial entities" to file information returns with the IRS regarding any discharge of indebtedness (within the meaning of sec. 61(a)(12)) [8] of $600 or more. Such information returns are retired regardless of whether the debtor is subject to tax on the discharged debt. For example, Congress does not expect reporting financial institutions and agencies to determine whether the debtor qualifies for an exclusion under section 108.

The information return must set forth the name, address and taxpayer identification number of the person whose debt was discharged, the amount of debt discharged, and the date on which the debt was discharged. [9] The information return must be filed in the manner and at the time specified by the IRS. The same information also must be provided to the person whose debt is discharged by January 31 of the year following the discharge.

For purposes of the bill, "applicable financial entities" include: (1) the FDIC, the RTC, the National Credit Union Administration, and any successor or subunit of any of them; [10] (2) any financial institution (described in secs. 581 or 591(a)); (3) any credit union; and (4) any subsidiary of an entity described in (2) or (3) which, by virtue of being affiliated with such entity, is subject to supervision and examination by a Federal or State agency regulating such entities. Other Federal agencies required to report under the current Treasury Department guidelines are also subject to this provision, so that all Federal agencies are subject to uniform rules.

Under the bill, the penalties for failure to file correct information reports with the IRS, and to furnish statements to taxpayers, are similar to those imposed with respect to a failure to provide other information returns. For example, the penalty for failure to furnish statements to taxpayers is generally $50 per failure, subject to a maximum of $100,000 for any calendar year. [11] These penalties are not applicable if the failure is due to reasonable cause and not to willful neglect.

[Conference Report]

Senate Amendment

The Senate amendment is the same as the House bill with a technical modification clarifying that other Federal agencies (which are required to report under the current Treasury Department guidelines> are also subject to this provision, so that all Federal agencies are subject to uniform rules.

Conference Agreement

The conference agreement follows the Senate amendment, except that non-governmental entities are only required to report under the provision with respect to discharges of indebtedness after December 31, 1993. Accordingly, governmental entities are required to report under the provision with respect to discharges of indebtedness after the date of enactment. The conferees do not intend that this provision alter the present law determination of when a discharge of indebtedness occurs under section 61(a)(12).

[Footnote ¶ 3062 continued]

8. This provision is not intended to alter the present law determination of when a discharge of indebtedness occurs under section 61(a)(12).

9. The date of discharge is required to facilitate the use of such information returns with respect to fiscal year taxpayers.

10. With respect to these entities, any return required by the bill shall be made by the officer or employee appropriately designated to make these returns.

11. In the case of intentional disregard of the filing requirements, the penalty is not less than $100 per failure and the $100,000 annual limitation does not apply.

[¶3064] Section 13261. Amortization of Goodwill and Certain Other Intangibles

(Code Sec. 197, 167)

[House Explanation]

Present Law

In determining taxable income for Federal income tax purposes, a taxpayer is allowed depreciation or amortization deductions for the cost or other basis of intangible property that is used in a trade or business or held for the production of income if the property has a limited useful life that may be determined with reasonable accuracy. Treas. Reg. sec. 1.167(a)-(3). These Treasury Regulations also state that no depreciation deductions are allowed with respect to goodwill.

The U.S. Supreme Court recently held that a taxpayer able to prove that a particular asset can be valued, and that the asset has a limited useful life which can be ascertained with reasonable accuracy, may depreciate the value over the useful life regardless of how much the asset appears to reflect the expectancy of continued patronage. However, the Supreme Court also characterized the taxpayer's burden of proof as "substantial" and stated that it "often will prove too great to bear." Newark Morning Ledger Co. v. United States, ___ U.S. ___, 61 U.S.L.W. 4313 at 4320, 4319 (April 20, 1993).

Reasons For Change

The Federal income tax treatment of the costs of acquiring intangible assets is a source of considerable controversy between taxpayers and the Internal Revenue Service. Disputes arise concerning (1) whether an amortizable intangible asset exists; (2) in the case of an acquisition of a trade or business, the portion of the purchase price that is allocable to an amortizable intangible asset; and (3) the proper method and period for recovering the cost of an amortizable intangible asset. These types of disputes can be expected to continue to arise, even after the decision of the U.S. Supreme Court in Newark Morning Ledger Co. v. United States, supra.

It is believed that much of the controversy that arises under present law with respect to acquired intangible assets could be eliminated by specifying a single method and period for recovering the cost of most acquired intangible assets and by treating acquired goodwill and going concern value as amortizable intangible assets. It is also believed that there is no need at this time to change the Federal income tax treatment of self-created intangible assets, such as goodwill that is created through advertising and other similar expenditures.

Accordingly, the bill requires the cost of most acquired intangible assets, including goodwill and going concern value, to be amortized ratably over a 14-year period [15-year period. Ed.]. It is recognized that the useful lives of certain acquired intangible assets to which the bill applies may be shorter than 14 years, while the useful lives of other acquired intangible assets to which the bill applies may be longer than 14 years [15 years. Ed.].

Explanation Of Provision

In general

The bill allows an amortization deduction with respect to the capitalized costs of certain intangible property (defined as a section 197 intangible) that is acquired by a taxpayer and that is held by the taxpayer in connection with the conduct of a trade or business or an activity engaged in for the production of income. The amount of the deduction is determined by amortizing the adjusted basis (for purposes of determining gain) of the intangible ratably over a 14-year period [15-year period. Ed.] that begins with the month that the intangible is acquired. [126]No other depreciation or amortization deduction is allowed with respect to a section 197 intangible that is acquired by a taxpayer.

In general, the bill applies to a section 197 intangible acquired by a taxpayer regardless of whether it is acquired as part of a trade or business. In addition, the bill generally applies to a section 197 intangible that is treated as acquired under section 338 of the Code. The bill generally does not apply to a section 197

[Footnote ¶3063 continued]

126. In the case of a short taxable year, the amortization deduction is to be based on the number of months in such taxable year.

intangible that is created by the taxpayer if the intangible is not created in connection with a transaction (or series of related transactions) that involves the acquisition of a trade or business or a substantial portion thereof.

Except in the case of amounts paid or incurred under certain covenants not to compete (or under certain other arrangements that have substantially the same effect as covenants not to compete) and certain amounts paid or incurred on account of the transfer of a franchise, trademark, or trade name, the bill generally does not apply to any amount that is otherwise currently deductible (i.e., not capitalized) under present law.

No inference is intended as to whether a depreciation or amortization deduction is allowed under present law with respect to any intangible property that is either included in, or excluded from, the definition of a section 197 intangible. In addition, no inference is intended as to whether an asset is to be considered tangible or intangible property for any other purpose of the Internal Revenue Code.

Definition of section 197 intangible

In general. The term "section 197 intangible" is defined as any property that is included in any one or more of the following categories: (1) goodwill and going concern value; (2) certain specified types of intangible property that generally relate to workforce, information base, know-how, customers, suppliers, or other similar items; (3) any license, permit, or other right granted by a governmental unit or an agency or instrumentality thereof. (4) any covenant not to compete (or other arrangement to the extent that the arrangement has substantially the same effect as a covenant not to compete) entered into in connection with the direct or indirect acquisition of an interest in a trade or business (or a substantial portion thereof); and (5) any franchise, trademark, or trade name. Certain types of property, however, are specifically excluded from the definition of the term "section 197 intangible." The term "section 197 intangible" does not include: (1) any interest in a corporation, partnership, trust, or estate; (2) any interest under an existing futures contract, foreign currency contract, notional principal contract, interest rate swap, or other similar financial contract; (3) any interest in land; (4) certain computer software; (5) certain interests in films, sound recordings, video tapes, books, or other similar property; (6) certain rights to receive tangible property or services; (7) certain interests in patents or copyrights; (8) any interest under an existing lease of tangible property; (9) any interest under an existing indebtedness (except for the deposit base and similar items of a financial institution); (10) a franchise to engage in any professional sport, and any item acquired in connection with such a franchise; and (11) certain transaction costs. In addition, the Treasury Department is authorized to issue regulations that exclude certain rights of fixed duration or amount from the definition of a section 197 intangible.

Goodwill and going concern value. For purposes of the bill, goodwill is the value of a trade or business that is attributable to the expectancy of continued customer patronage, whether due to the name of a trade or business, the reputation of a trade or business, or any other factor. In addition, for purposes of the bill, going concern value is the additional element of value of a trade or business that attaches to property by reason of its existence as an integral part of a going concern. Going concern value includes the value that is attributable to the ability of a trade or business to continue to function and generate income without interruption notwithstanding a change in ownership. Going concern value also includes the value that is attributable to the use or availability of an acquired trade or business (for example, the net earnings that otherwise would not be received during any period were the acquired trade or business not available or operational).

>Workforce, information base, know-how, customer-base intangibles, supplier-based intangibles and other similar items

Workforce. The term "section 197 intangible" includes workforce in place (which is sometimes referred to as agency force or assembled workforce), the composition of a workforce (for example, the experience, education, or training of a workforce), the terms and conditions of employment whether contractual or otherwise, and any other value placed on employees or any of their attributes. Thus, for example, the portion (if any) of the purchase price of an acquired trade or business that is attributable to the existence of a highly-skilled workforce is to be amortized over the 14-year period [15-year period. Ed.] specified in the bill. As a further example, the cost of acquiring an existing employment contract (or contracts) or a relationship with employees or consultants (including but not limited to any "key employee" contract or relationship) as part of the acquisition of a trade or business is to be amortized over the 14-year period [15-year period. Ed.] specified in the bill.

Information base. The term "section 197 intangible" includes business books and records, operating systems, and any other information base including lists or other information with respect to current or prospective customers (regardless of the method of recording such information). Thus, for example, the portion (if any) of the purchase price of an acquired trade or business that is attributable to the intangible value of technical manuals, training manuals or programs, data files, and accounting or inventory control systems is to be amortized over the 14-year period [15-year period. Ed.] specified in the bill. As a further example, the cost of acquiring customer lists, subscription lists, insurance expirations, [127] patient or client files, or lists of newspaper, magazine, radio or television advertisers is to be amortized over the 14-year period [15-year period. Ed.] specified in the bill.

Know-how. The term "section 197 intangible" includes any patent, copyright, formula, process, design, pattern, know-how, format, or other similar item. For this purpose, the term "section 197 intangible" is to include package designs, computer software, and any interest in a film, sound recording, video tape, book, or other similar property, except as specifically provided otherwise in the bill. [128]

Customer-based intangibles. The term "section 197 intangible" includes any customer-based intangible, which is defined as the composition of market, market share, and any other value resulting from the future provision of goods or services pursuant to relationships with customers (contractual or otherwise) in the ordinary course of business. Thus, for example, the portion (if any) of the purchase price of an acquired trade or business that is attributable to the existence of customer base, circulation base, undeveloped market or market growth, insurance in force, mortgage servicing contracts, investment management contracts, or other relationships with customers that involve the future provision of goods or services, is to be amortized over the 14-year period [15-year period. Ed.] specified in the bill. On the other hand, the portion (if any) of the purchase price of an acquired trade or business that is attributable to accounts receivable or other similar rights to income for those goods or services that have been provided to customers prior to the acquisition of a trade or business is not to be taken into account under the bill. [129] In addition, the bill specifically provides that the term "customer-based intangible" includes the deposit base and any similar asset of a financial institution. Thus, for example, the portion (if any) of the purchase price of an acquired financial institution that is attributable to the checking accounts, savings accounts, escrow accounts and other similar items of the financial institution is to be amortized over the 14-year period [15-year period. Ed.] specified in the bill.

Supplier-based intangibles. The term "section 197 intangible" includes any supplier-based intangible, which is defined as the value resulting from the future acquisition of goods or services pursuant to relationships (contractual or otherwise) in the ordinary course of business with suppliers of goods or services to be used or sold by the taxpayer. Thus, for example, the portion (if any) of the purchase price of an acquired trade or business that is attributable to the existence of a favorable relationship with persons that provide distribution services (for example, favorable shelf or display space at a retail outlet), the existence of a favorable credit rating, or the existence of favorable supply contracts, is to be amortized over the 14-year period [15-year period. Ed.]

[Footnote ¶3064 continued]

127. Insurance expirations are records that are maintained by insurance agents with respect to insurance customers. These records generally include information relating to the type of insurance, the amount of insurance, and the expiration of the insurance.

128. See below for a description of the exceptions for certain patents, certain computer software, and certain interests in films, sound recordings, video tapes, books, or other similar property.

129. As under present law, the portion of the purchase price of an acquired trade or business that is attributable to accounts receivable is to be allocated among such receivables and is to be taken into account as payment is received under each receivable or at the time that a receivable becomes worthless.

specified in the bill. [130]

Other similar items. The term "section 197 intangible" also includes any other intangible property that is similar to workforce, information base, know-how, customer-based intangibles, or supplier-based intangibles.

Licenses, permits, and other rights granted by governmental units. The term "section 197 intangible" also includes any license, permit, or other right granted by a governmental unit or any agency or instrumentality thereof (even if the right is granted for an indefinite period or the right is reasonably expected to be renewed for an indefinite period.) [131] Thus, for example, the capitalized cost of acquiring from any person a liquor license, a taxi-cab medallion (or license), an airport landing or takeoff right (which is sometimes referred to as a slot), a regulated airline route, or a television or radio broadcasting license is to be amortized over the 14-year period [15-year period. Ed.] specified in the bill. For purposes of the bill, the issuance or renewal of a license, permit, or other right granted by a governmental unit or an agency or instrumentality thereof is to be considered an acquisition of such license, permit, or other right.

Covenants not to compete and other similar arrangements. The term "section 197 intangible" also includes any covenant not to compete (or other arrangement to the extent that the arrangement has substantially the same effect as a covenant not to compete; hereafter "other similar arrangement") entered into in connection with the direct or indirect acquisition of an interest in a trade or business (or a substantial portion thereof). For this purpose, an interest in a trade or business includes not only the assets of a trade or business, but also stock in a corporation that is engaged in a trade or business or an interest in a partnership that is engage d in a trade or business. Any amount that is paid or incurred under a covenant not to compete (or other similar arrangement) entered into in connection with the direct or indirect acquisition of an interest in a trade or business (or a substantial portion thereof) is chargeable to capital account and is to be amortized ratably over the 14-year period [15-year period. Ed.] specified in the bill. In addition, any amount that is paid or incurred under a covenant not to compete (or other similar arrangement) after the taxable year in which the covenant (or other similar arrangement) was entered into is to be amortized ratably over the remaining months in the 14-year amortization period [15-year amortization period. Ed.] that applies to the covenant (or other similar arrangement) as of the beginning of the month that the amount is paid or incurred. For purposes of this provision, an arrangement that requires the former owner of an interest in a trade or business to continue to perform services (or to provide property or the use of property) that benefit the trade or business is considered to have substantially the same effect as a covenant not to compete to the extent that the amount paid to the former owner under the arrangement exceeds the amount that represents reasonable compensation for the services actually rendered (or for the property or use of property actually provided) by the former owner. As under present law, to the extent that the amount paid or incurred under a covenant not to compete (or other similar arrangement) represents additional consideration for the acquisition of stock in a corporation, such amount is not to be taken into account under this provision but, instead, is to be included as part of the acquirer's basis in the stock

Franchises, trademarks, and trade names. The term "section 197 intangible" also includes any franchise, trademark, or trade name. For this purpose, the term "franchise" is defined, as under present law, to include any agreement that provides one of the parties to the agreement the right to distribute, sell, or provide goods, services, or facilities, within a specified area. [132]In addition, as provided under present law, the renewal a franchise, trademark, or trade name is to be treated as an acquisition of such franchise, trademark, or trade name. [133]

[Footnote ¶ 3064 continued]

130. See below, however, for a description of the exception for certain rights to receive tangible property or services from another person.

131. A right granted by a governmental unit or an agency or instrumentality thereof that constitutes an interest in land or an interest under a lease of tangible property is excluded from the definition of a section 197 intangible. See below for a description of the exceptions for interests in land and for interests under leases of tangible property.

132. Section 1253(b)(1) of the Code.

133. Only the costs incurred in connection with the renewal, however, are to be amortized over the 14-year period that begins with the month that the franchise, trademark, or trade name is renewed. Any costs incurred in connection with the issu-

The bill continues the present-law treatment of certain contingent amounts that are paid or incurred on account of the transfer of a franchise, trademark, or trade name. Under these rules, a deduction is allowed for amounts that are contingent on the productivity, use, or disposition of a franchise, trademark, or trade name only if (1) the contingent amounts are paid as part of a series of payments that are payable at least annually throughout the term of the transfer agreement, and (2) the payments are substantially equal in amount or payable under a fixed formula.[134] Any other amount, whether fixed or contingent, that is paid or incurred on account of the transfer of a franchise, trademark, or trade name is chargeable to capital account and is to be amortized ratably over the 14-year period [15-year period. Ed.] specified in the bill.

Exceptions to the definition of a section 197 intangible

In general. The bill contains several exceptions to the definition of the term "section 197 intangible." Several of the exceptions contained in the bill apply only if the intangible property is not acquired in a transaction (or series of related transactions) that involves the acquisition of assets which constitute a trade or business or a substantial portion of a trade or business. It is anticipated that the Treasury Department will exercise its regulatory authority to require any intangible property that would otherwise be excluded from the definition of the term "section 197 intangible" to be taken into account under the bill under circumstances where the acquisition of the intangible property is, in and of itself, the acquisition of an asset which constitutes a trade or business or a substantial portion of a trade or business. The determination of whether acquired assets constitute a substantial portion of a trade or business is to be based on all of the facts and circumstances, including the nature and the amount (of the assets acquired as well as the nature and amount of the assets retained by transferor. It is not intended, however, that the value of the assets acquired relative to the value of the assets retained by the transferor is determinative of whether the acquired assets constitute a substantial portion of a trade or business. For purposes of the bill, a group of assets is to constitute a trade or business if the use of such assets would constitute a trade or business for purposes of section 1060 of the Code (i.e., if the assets are of such a character that goodwill or going concern value could under any circumstances attach to the assets). In addition, the acquisition of a franchise, trademark or trade name is to constitute the acquisition of a trade or business or a substantial portion of a trade or business. In determining whether a taxpayer has acquired an intangible asset in a transaction (or series of related transactions) that involves the acquisition of assets that constitute a trade or business or a substantial portion of a trade or business, only those assets acquired in a transaction (or a series of related transactions) by a taxpayer (and persons related to the taxpayer) from the same person (and any related person) are to be taken into account. In addition, any employee relationships that continue (or covenants not to compete that are entered into) as part of the transfer of assets are to be taken into account in determining whether the transferred assets constitute a trade or business or a substantial portion of a trade or business.

Interests in a corporation, partnership, trust, or estate. The term 'section 197 intangible" does not include any interest in a corporation, partnership, trust, or estate. Thus, for example, the bill does not apply to the cost of acquiring stock, partnership interests, or interests in a trust or estate, whether or not such interests are regularly traded on an established market.[135]

Interests under certain financial contracts. The term "section 197 intangible" does not include any interest under an existing futures contract, foreign currency contract, notional principal contract, interest rate swap, or other similar financial contract, whether or not such interest is regularly traded on an established market. Any interest under a mortgage servicing contract, credit card servicing contract or other contract to service indebtedness issued by another person, and any interest under an as-

[Footnote ¶3064 continued]

ance (or an earlier renewal) of a franchise, trademark, or trade name are to continue to be taken into account over the remaining portion of the amortization period that began at the time of such issuance (or earlier renewal).

134. Section 1253(d)(1) of the Code.

135. A temporal interest in property, outright or in trust, may not be used to convert a section 197 intangible into property that is amortizable more rapidly than ratably over the 14-year period specified in the bill.

sumption reinsurance contract [136] is not excluded from the definition of the term "section 197 intangible" by reason of the exception for interests under certain financial contracts.

Interests in land. The term "section 197 intangible" does not include any interest in land. Thus, the cost of acquiring an interest in land is to be taken into account under present law rather than under the bill. For this purpose, an interest in land includes a fee interest, life estate, remainder, easement, mineral rights, timber rights, grazing rights, riparian rights, air rights, zoning variances and any other similar rights with respect to land. An interest in land is not to include an airport landing or takeoff right, a regulated airline route, or a franchise to provide cable television services. The costs of acquiring licenses, permits, and other rights relating to improvements to land, such as building construction or use permits, are to be taken into account in the same manner as the underlying improvement in accordance with present law.

Certain computer software. The term "section 197 intangible" does not include computer software (whether acquired as part of a trade or business or otherwise) that (1) is readily available for purchase by the general public; (2) is subject to a non-exclusive license; and (3) has not been substantially modified. In addition, the term "section 197 intangible" does not include computer software which is not acquired in a transaction (or a series of related transactions) that involves the acquisition of assets which constitute a trade or business or a substantial portion of a trade or business. For purposes of the bill, the term "computer software" is defined as any program (i.e., any sequence of machine-readable code) that is designed to cause a computer to perform a desired function. The term "computer software" includes any incidental and ancillary rights with respect to computer software that (1) are necessary to effect the legal acquisition of the title to, and the ownership of, the computer software, and (2) are used only in connection with the computer software. The term "computer software" does not include any data base or similar item (other than a data base or item that is in the public domain and that is incidental to the software [137] regardless of the form in which it is maintained or stored. If a depreciation deduction is allowed with respect to any computer software that is not a section 197 intangible, the amount of the deduction is to be determined by amortizing the adjusted basis of the computer software ratably over a 36-month period that begins with the month that the computer software is placed in service. For this purpose, the cost of any computer software that is taken into account as part of the cost of computer hardware or other tangible property under present law is to continue to be taken into account in such manner under the bill. In addition, the cost of any computer software that is currently deductible (*i.e.,* not capitalized) under present law is to continue to be taken into account in such manner under the bill.

Certain interests in films, sound recordings, video tapes, books, or other similar property. The term "section 197 intangible" does not include any interest (including an interest as a licensee) in a film, sound recording, video tape, book, or other similar property (including the right to broadcast or transmit a live event) if the interest is not acquired in a transaction (or a series of related transactions) that involves the acquisition of assets which constitute a trade or business or a substantial portion of a trade or business.

Certain rights to receive tangible property or services. The term "section 197 intangible" does not include any right to receive tangible property or services under a contract (or any right to receive tangible property or services granted by a governmental unit or an agency or instrumentality thereof) if the right is not acquired in a transaction (or a series of related transactions) that involves the acquisition of assets which constitute a trade or business or a substantial portion of a trade or business. If a depreciation deduction is allowed with respect to a right to receive tangible property or services that is not a section 197 intangible, the amount of the deduction is to be determined in accordance with regulations to be promulgated by the Treasury Department. It is anticipated that the regulations may provide that in the case of an amortizable right to receive tangible property or services in substantially equal amounts over a fixed period that is not renew-

[Footnote ¶3064 continued]

136. See below for a description of the treatment of assumption reinsurance contracts.

137. For example, a data base would not include a dictionary feature used to spell-check a word processing program.

able, the cost of acquiring the right will be taken into account ratably over such fixed period. It is also anticipated that the regulations may provide that in the case of a right to receive a fixed amount of tangible property or services over an unspecified period, the cost of acquiring such right will be taken into account under a method that allows a deduction based on the amount of tangible property or services received during a taxable year compared to the total amount of tangible property or services to be received. For example, assume that a taxpayer acquires from another person a favorable contract right of such person to receive a specified amount of raw materials each month for the next three years (which is the remaining life of the contract) and that the right to receive such raw materials is not acquired as part of the acquisition of assets that constitute a trade or business or a substantial portion thereof (i.e., such contract right is not a section 197 intangible). It is anticipated that the taxpayer may be required to amortize the cost of acquiring the contract right ratably over the three-year remaining life of the contract. Alternatively, if the favorable contract right is to receive a specified amount of raw materials during an unspecified period, it is anticipated that the taxpayer may be required to amortize the cost of acquiring the contract right by multiplying such cost by a fraction, the numerator of which is the amount of raw materials received under the contract during any taxable year and the denominator of which is the total amount of raw materials to be received under the contract. It is also anticipated that the regulations may require a taxpayer under appropriate circumstances to amortize the cost of acquiring a renewable right to receive tangible property or services over a period that includes all renewal options exercisable by the taxpayer at less than fair market value.

Certain interests in patents or copyrights. The term "section 197 intangible" does not include any interest in a patent or copyright which is not acquired in a transaction (or a series of related transactions) that involves the acquisition of assets which constitute a trade or business or a substantial portion of a trade or business. If a depreciation deduction is allowed with respect to an interest in a patent or copyright and the interest is not a section 197 intangible then the amount of the deduction is to be determined in accordance with regulations to be promulgated by the Treasury Department. It is expected that the regulations may provide that if the purchase price of a patent is payable on an annual basis as a fixed percentage of the revenue derived from the use of the patent, then the amount of the depreciation deduction allowed for any taxable year with respect to the patent equals the amount of the royalty paid or incurred during such year. [138]

Interests under leases of tangible property. The term "section 197 intangible" does not include any interest as a lessor or lessee under an existing lease of tangible property (whether real or personal). [139] The cost of acquiring an interest as a lessor under a lease of tangible property where the interest as lessor is acquired in connection with the acquisition of the tangible property is to be taken into account as part of the cost of the tangible property. For example, if a taxpayer acquires a shopping center that is leased to tenants operating retail stores, the portion (if any) of the purchase price of the shopping center that is attributable to the favorable attributes of the leases is to be taken into account as a part of the basis of the shopping center and is to be taken into account in determining the depreciation deduction allowed with respect to the shopping center. The cost of acquiring an interest as a lessee under an existing lease of tangible property is to be taken into account under present law (see section 178 of the Code and Treas. Reg. sec. 1.162-11(a)) rather than under the provisions of the bill. [140] In the case of any interest as a lessee under a lease of tangible property that is acquired with any other intangible property (either in the same transaction or series of related transactions), however, the portion of the total purchase price that is allocable to the interest as a lessee is not to exceed the excess of (1) the present value of the fair market value rent for the use of the tangible property for the term of

[Footnote ¶ 3064 continued]

138. See *Associated Patentees, Inc.*, 4. T.C. 979 (1945); and Rev. Rul. 67-136, 1967-1 C.B. 58.

139. The bill provides that a sublease is to be treated in the same manner as a lease of the underlying property. Thus, the term "section 197 intangible" does not include any interest as a sublessor or sublessee of intangible property.

140. The lease of a gate at an airport for the purpose of loading and unloading passengers and cargo is a lease of tangible property for this purpose. It is anticipated that such treatment will serve as guidance to the Internal Revenue Service and taxpayers in resolving existing disputes.

the lease, [141] over (2) the present value of the rent reasonably expected to be paid for the use of the tangible property for the term of the lease.

Interests under indebtedness. The term "section 197 intangible" does not include any interest (whether as a creditor or debtor) under any indebtedness that was in existence on the date that the interest was acquired. [142] Thus, for example, the value of assuming an existing indebtedness with a below-market interest rate is to be taken into account under present law rather than under the bill. In addition, the premium paid for acquiring the right to receive an above-market rate of interest under a debt instrument may be taken into account under section 171 of the Code, which generally allows the amount of the premium to be amortized on a yield-to-maturity basis over the remaining term of the debt instrument. This exception for interests under existing indebtedness does not apply to the deposit base and other similar items of a financial institution.

Professional sports franchises. The term "section 197 intangible" does not include a franchise to engage in professional baseball, basketball, football, or other professional sport, and any item acquired in connection with such a franchise. Consequently, the cost of acquiring a professional sports franchise and related assets (including any goodwill, going concern value, or other section 197 intangibles) is to be allocated among the assets acquired as provided under present law (see, for example, section 1056 of the Code) and is to be taken into account under the provisions of present law.

Certain transaction costs. The term section 197 intangible does not include the amount of any fees for professional services, and any transaction costs, incurred by parties to a transaction with respect to which any portion of the gain or loss is not recognized under part III of subchapter C. This provision addresses a concern that some taxpayers might attempt to contend that the 14-year amortization provided by the provision applies to any such amounts that may be required to be capitalized under present law but that do not relate to any asset with a readily identifiable useful life. [143] The exception is provided solely to clarify that section 197 is not to be construed to provide 14-year amortization [15-year amortization. Ed.] for any such amounts. No inference is intended that such amounts would (but for this provision) be properly characterized as amounts eligible for such 14-year amortization [15-year amortization. Ed.] nor is any inference intended that any amounts not specified in this provision should be so characterized. In addition, no inference is intended regarding the proper treatment of professional fees or transaction costs in other circumstances under present law.

Regulatory authority regarding rights of fixed term or duration. The bill authorizes the Treasury Department to issue regulations that exclude a right received under a contract, or granted by a governmental unit or an agency or instrumentality thereof, from the definition of a section 197 intangible if (l) the right is not acquired in a transaction (or a series of related transactions) that involves the acquisition of assets which constitute a trade or business (or a substantial portion thereof) and (2) the right either (A) has a fixed duration of less than 14 years [15 years. Ed.] or (B) is fixed as to amount [144] and the cost is properly recoverable (without regard to this provision) under a method similar to the unit of production method. Generally, it is anticipated that the mere fact that a taxpayer will have the opportunity to renew a contract or other right on the same terms as are available to others, in a competitive auction or similar process that is

[Footnote ¶ 3064 continued]

141. In no event is the present value of the fair market value rent for the use of the tangible property for the term of the lease to exceed the fair market value of the tangible property as of the date of acquisition. The present value of such rent is presumed to be less than the value of the tangible property if the duration of the lease is less than the economic useful life of the property.

142. For purposes of this exception, the term "interest under any existing indebtedness" is to include mortgage servicing rights to the extent that the rights are stripped coupons under section 1286 of the Code. See Rev. Rul. 91-46, 1991-34 I.R.B. 5 (August 26, 1991).

143. See, e.g., INDOPCO, Inc. v. Commissioner, 112 S. Ct. 1039 (1992).

144. For example, an emission allowance granted a public utility under Title IV of the Clean Air Act Amendments of 1990 is a right that is limited in amount within the meaning of this provision, because each allowance grants a right to a fixed amount of emissions. It is expected that the Treasury Department will provide guidance regarding the interaction of section 461 with these provisions. No inference is intended that would require the Treasury Department to disturb the result in Rev. Proc. 92-91, 1992-46 I.R.B. 32.

designed to reflect fair market value and in which the taxpayer is not contractually advantaged, will not be taken into account in determining the duration of such right or whether it is for a fixed amount. However, the fact that competitive bidding occurs at the time of renewal and that there are or may be modifications in price (or in terms or requirements relating to the right that increase the cost to the bidder) shall not be within the scope of the preceding sentence unless the bidding also actually produces a fair market value price comparable to the price that would obtain if the rights were purchased immediately after renewal from a person (other than the person granting the renewal) in an arm's length transaction. Furthermore, it is expected that, as under present law, the Treasury Department will take into account all the facts and circumstances, including any facts indicating an actual practice of renewals or expectancy of renewals. For example, assume Company A enters into a license with Company B to use certain know-how developed by B. In addition, assume that the license is for five years, that the license cannot be renewed by A except on terms that are fully available to A's competitors and that the price paid by A will reflect the arm's length price that a third party would pay A for the license immediately after renewal. Finally, assume that the license does not constitute a substantial portion of a trade or business and is not entered into as part of a transaction (or series of related transactions) that constitute the acquisition of a trade or business or substantial portion thereof. It is anticipated that in these circumstances the regulations will provide that the license is not a section 197 intangible because it is of fixed duration. The regulations may also prescribe rules governing the extent to which renewal options and similar items will be taken into account for the purpose of determining whether rights are fixed in duration or amount. It is also anticipated that such regulations may pre-scribe the appropriate method of amortizing the capitalized costs of rights which are excluded by such regulations from the definition of a section 197 intangible.

Exception for certain self-created intangibles

The bill generally does not apply to any section 197 intangible that is created by the taxpayer if the section 197 intangible is not created in connection with a transaction (or a series of related transactions) that involves the acquisition of assets which constitute a trade or business or a substantial portion thereof. For purposes of this exception, a section 197 intangible that is owned by a taxpayer is to be considered created by the taxpayer if the intangible is produced for the taxpayer by another person under a contract with the taxpayer that is entered into prior to the production of the intangible. For example, a technological process or other know-how that is developed specifically for a taxpayer under an arrangement with another person pursuant to which the taxpayer retains all rights to the process or know-how is to be considered created by the taxpayer. The exception for "self-created" intangibles does not apply to the entering into (or renewal of) a contract for the use of a section 197 intangible. Thus, for example, the exception does not apply to the capitalized costs incurred by a licensee in connection with the entering into (or renewal of) a contract for the use of know-how or other section 197 intangible. These capitalized costs are to be amortized over the 14-year period [15-year period. Ed.] specified in the bill. In addition, the exception for "self-created" intangibles does not apply to: (1) any license, permit, or other right that is granted by a governmental unit or an agency or instrumentality thereof; (2) any covenant not to compete (or other similar arrangement) entered into in connection with the direct or indirect acquisition of an interest in a trade or business (or a substantial portion thereof); and (3) any franchise, trademark, or trade name. Thus, for example, the capitalized costs incurred in connection with the development or registration of a trademark or trade name are to be amortized over the 14-year period [15-year period. Ed.] specified in the bill.

Special rules

Determination of adjusted basis. The adjusted basis of a section 197 intangible that is acquired from another person generally is to be determined under the principles of present law that apply to tangible property that is acquired from another person. Thus, for example, if a portion of the cost of acquiring an amortizable section 197 intangible is contingent, the adjusted basis of the section 197 intangible is to be increased as of the beginning of the month that the contingent amount is paid or incurred. This additional amount is to be amortized ratably over the remaining months in the 14-year amortization period [15-year amortization period. Ed.] that applies to the intangible as of the beginning of the month that the contingent amount is paid or incurred.

Treatment of certain dispositions of amortizable section 197 intangibles. Special rules apply if a taxpayer disposes of a section 197 intangible that was acquired in a transaction or series of related transactions and, after the disposition, [145] the taxpayer retains other section 197 intangibles that were acquired in such transaction or series or related transactions. [146] First, no loss is to be recognized by reason of such a disposition. Second, the adjusted bases of the retained section 197 intangibles that were acquired in connection with such transaction or series of related transactions are to be increased by the amount of any loss that is not recognized. The adjusted basis of and such retained section 197 intangible is increased by the product of (1) the amount of the loss that is not recognized solely by reason of this provision, and (2) a fraction, the numerator of which is the adjusted basis of the intangible as of the date of the disposition and the denominator of which is the total adjusted bases of all such retained section 197 intangibles as of the date of the disposition. For purposes of these rules, all persons treated as a single taxpayer under section 41(f)(1) of the Code are treated as a single taxpayer. Thus, for example, a loss is not to be recognized by a corporation upon the disposition of a section 197 intangible if after the disposition a member of the same controlled group as the corporation retains other section 197 intangibles that were acquired in the same transaction (or a series of related transactions) as the section 197 intangible that was disposed of. It is anticipated that the Treasury Department will provide rules for taking into account the amount of any loss that is not recognized due to this rule (for example, by allowing the corporation that disposed of the section 197 intangible to amortize the loss over the remaining portion of the 14-year amortization period [15-year amortization period. Ed.]).

Treatment of certain nonrecognition transactions. If any section 197 intangible is acquired in a transaction to which section 332, 351, 361, 721, 731, 1031, or 1033 of the Code applies (or any transaction between members of the same affiliated group during any taxable year for which a consolidated return is filed), [147] the transferee is to be treated as the transferor for purposes of applying this provision with respect to the amount of the adjusted basis of the transferee that does not exceed the adjusted basis of the transferor. For example, assume that an individual owns an amortizable section 197 intangible that has been amortized under section 197 for 4 full years and has a remaining unamortized basis of $300,000. In addition, assume that the individual exchanges the asset and $100,000 for a like-kind amortizable section 197 intangible in a transaction to which section 1031 applies. Under the bill, $300,000 of the basis of the acquired amortizable section 197 intangible is to be amortized over the 10 years remaining in the original 14-year amortization period [15-year amortization period. Ed.] for the transferred asset and the other $100,000 of basis is to be amortized over the 14-year period [15-year period. Ed.] specified in the bill. [148]

Treatment of certain partnership transactions. Generally, consistent with the rules described above for certain nonrecognition transactions, a transaction in which a taxpayer acquires an interest in an intangible held through a partnership (either before or after the transaction)

[Footnote ¶3064 continued]

145. For this purpose, the abandonment of a section 197 intangible or any other event that renders a section 197 intangible worthless is to be considered a disposition of a section 197 intangible.

146. These special rules do not apply to a section 197 intangible that is separately acquired (i.e., a section 197 intangible that is acquired other than in a transaction or a series of related transactions that involve the acquisition of other section 197 intangibles). Consequently, a loss may be recognized upon the disposition of a separately acquired section 197 intangible. In no event, however, is the termination or worthlessness of a portion of a section 197 intangible to be considered the disposition of a separately acquired section 197 intangible. For example, the termination of one or more customers from an acquired customer list or the worthlessness of some information from an acquired data base is not to be considered the disposition of a separately acquired section 197 intangible.

147. The termination of a partnership under section 708(b)(1)(B) of the Code is a transaction to which this rule applies. In such a case, the bill applies only to the extent that the adjusted basis of the section 197 intangibles before the termination exceeds the adjusted basis of the section 197 intangibles after the termination. (See the example below in the discussion of "Treatment of certain partnership transactions.")

148. No inference is intended whether any asset treated as a section 197 intangible under the bill is eligible for like kind exchange treatment.

will be treated as an acquisition to which the bill applies only if, and to the extent that, the acquiring taxpayer obtains, as a result of the transaction, an increased basis for such intangible. [149] For example, assume that A, B and C each contribute $700 for equal shares in partnership P, which on January 1, 1994, acquires as its sole asset an amortizable section 197 intangible for $2,100. Assume that on January 1, 1998, (1) the sole asset of P is the intangible acquired in 1994, (2) the intangible has an unamortized basis of $1,500 and A, B, and C each have a basis of $500 in their partnership interests, and (3) D (who is not related to A, B, or C) acquires A's interest in P for $800. Under the bill, if there is no section 754 election in effect for 1998, there will be no change in the basis or amortization of the intangible and D will merely step into the shoes of A with respect to the intangible. D's share of the basis in the intangible will be $500, which will be amortized over the 10 years remaining in the amortization period for the intangible. On the other hand, if a section 754 election is in effect for 1998, then D will be treated as having an $800 basis for its share of P's intangible. Under section 197, D's share of income and loss will be determined as if P owns two intangible assets. D will be treated as having a basis of $500 in one asset, which will continue to be amortized over the 10 remaining years of the original 14-year life [15-year life. Ed.] With respect to the other asset, D will be treated as having a basis of $300 (the amount of step-up obtained by D under section 743 as a result of the section 754 election) which will be amortized over a 14-year period [15-year period. Ed.] starting with January of 1998. B and C will each continue to share equally in a $1,000 basis in the intangible and amortize that amount over the remaining 10-year life. As an additional example, assume the same facts as described above, except that D acquires both A's and B's interests in P for $1,600. Under section 708, the transaction is treated as if P is liquidated immediately after the transfer, with C and D each receiving their pro rata share of P's assets which they then immediately contribute to a new partnership. The distributions in liquidation are governed by section 731. Under the bill, C's interest in the intangible will be treated as having a $500 basis, with a remaining amortization period of 10 years. D will be treated as having an interest in two assets: one with a basis of $1,000 and a remaining amortization period of 10 years, and the other with a basis of $600 and a new amortization period of 14 years [15 years. Ed.]. As discussed more fully below, the bill also changes the treatment of payments made in liquidation of the interest of a deceased or retired partner in exchange for goodwill. Except in the case of payments made on the retirement or death of a general partner of a partnership for which capital is not a material income-producing factor, such payments will not be treated as a distribution of partnership income. Under the bill, however, if the partnership makes an election under section 754, section 734 will generally provide the partnership the benefit of a stepped-up basis for the retiring or deceased partner's share of partnership goodwill and an amortization deduction for the increase in basis under section 197. For example, using the facts from the preceding examples, assume that on January 1, 1998, A retires from the partnership in exchange for a payment from the partnership of $800, all of which is in exchange for A's interest in the intangible asset owned by P. Under the bill, if there is a section 754 election in effect for 1998, P will be treated as having two amortizable section 197 intangibles: one with a basis of $1,500 and a remaining life of 10 years, and the other with a basis of $300 and a new life of 14 years [15 years. Ed.].

Treatment of certain reinsurance transactions. The bill applies to any insurance contract that is acquired from another person through an assumption reinsurance transaction (but not through an indemnity reinsurance transaction). [150] The amount taken into account as the adjusted basis of such a section 197 intangible, however, is to equal the excess of (1) the amount paid or incurred by the acquirer/reinsurer under the assumption reinsur-

[Footnote ¶ 3064 continued]

149. This discussion is subject to the application of the anti-churning rules which are discussed below.

150. An assumption reinsurance transaction is an arrangement whereby one insurance company (the reinsurer) becomes soley liable to policyholders on contracts transferred by another insurance company (the ceding company). In addition, for purposes of the bill, an assumption reinsurance transaction is to include any acquisition of an insurance contract that is treated as occurring by reason of an election under section 338 of the Code.

ance transaction,[151] over (2) the amount of the specified policy acquisition expenses (as determined under section 848 of the Code) that is attributable to premiums received under the assumption reinsurance transaction. The amount of the specified policy acquisition expenses of an insurance company that is attributable to premiums received under an assumption reinsurance transaction is to be amortized over the period specified in section 848 of the Code.

Treatment of amortizable section 197 intangible as depreciable property. For purposes of chapter 1 of the Internal Revenue Code, an amortizable section 197 intangible is to be treated as property of a character which is subject to the allowance for depreciation provided in section 167. Thus, for example, an amortizable section 197 intangible is not a capital asset for purposes of section 1221 of the Code, but an amortizable section 197 intangible held for more than one year generally qualifies as property used in a trade or business for purposes of section 1231 of the Code. As further examples, an amortizable section 197 intangible is to constitute section 1245 property, and section 1239 of the Code is to apply to any gain recognized upon the sale or exchange of an amortizable section 197 intangible, directly or indirectly, between related persons.

Treatment of certain amounts that are properly taken into account in determining the cost of property that is not a section 197 intangible. The bill does not apply to any amount that is properly taken into account under present law in determining the cost of property that is not a section 197 intangible. Thus, for example, no portion of the cost of acquiring real property that is held for the production of rental income (for example, an office building, apartment building or shopping center) is to be taken into account under the bill (i.e., no goodwill, going concern value or any other section 197 intangible is to arise in connection with the acquisition of such real property). Instead, the entire cost of acquiring such real property is to be included in the basis of the real property and is to be recovered under the principles of present law applicable to such property.

Modification of purchase price allocation and reporting rules for certain asset acquisitions. Sections 338(b)(5) and 1060 of the Code authorize the Treasury Department to promulgate regulations that provide for the allocation of purchase price among assets in the case of certain asset acquisitions. Under regulations that have been promulgated pursuant to this authority, the purchase price of an acquired trade or business must be allocated among the assets of the trade or business using the "residual method." Under the residual method specified in the Treasury regulations, all assets of an acquired trade or business are divided into the following classes: (1) Class I assets, which generally include cash and cash equivalents; (2) Class II assets, which generally include certificates of deposit, U.S. government securities, readily marketable stock or securities, and foreign currency; (3) Class III assets, which generally include all assets other than those included in Class I, II, or IV (generally all furniture, fixtures, land, buildings, equipment, other tangible property, accounts receivable, covenants not to compete, and other amortizable intangible assets); and (4) Class IV assets, which include intangible assets in the nature of goodwill or going concern value. The purchase price of an acquired trade or business (as first reduced by the amount of the assets included in Class I) is allocated to the assets included in Class II and Class III based on the value of the assets included in each class. To the extent that the purchase price (as reduced by the amount of the assets in Class I) exceeds the value of the assets included in Class II and Class III, the excess is allocable to assets included in Class IV. It is expected that the present Treasury regulations which provide for the allocation of purchase price in the case of certain asset acquisitions will be amended to reflect the fact that the bill allows an amortization deduction with respect to intangible assets in the nature of goodwill and going concern value. It is anticipated that the residual method specified in the regulations will be modified to treat all amortizable section 197 intangibles as Class IV assets and that this modification will apply to any acquisition of property to which the bill applies. Section 1060 also authorizes the Treasury Department to require the transferor and trans-

[Footnote ¶ 3064 continued]

151. The amount paid or incurred by the acquirer/reinsurer under an assumption reinsurance transaction is to be determined under the principles of present law. (See Treas. Reg. sec. 1.817-4(d)(2).)

feree in certain asset acquisitions to furnish information to the Treasury Department concerning the amount of any purchase price that is allocable to goodwill or going concern value. The bill provides that the information furnished to the Treasury Department with respect to certain asset acquisitions is to specify the amount of purchase price that is allocable to amortizable section 197 intangibles rather than the amount of purchase price that is allocable to goodwill or going concern value. In addition, it is anticipated that the Treasury Department will exercise its existing regulatory authority to require taxpayers to furnish such additional information as may be necessary or appropriate to carry out the provisions of the bill, including the amount of purchase price that is allocable to intangible assets that are not amortizable section 197 intangibles.[152]

General regulatory authority. The Treasury Department is authorized to prescribe such regulations as may be appropriate to carry out the purposes of the bill including such regulations as may be appropriate to prevent avoidance of the purposes of the bill through related persons or otherwise. It is anticipated that the Treasury Department will exercise its regulatory authority where appropriate to clarify the types of intangible property that constitute section 197 intangibles.

Study

The Treasury Department is directed to conduct a continuing study of the implementation and effects of the bill, including effects on merger and acquisition activities (including hostile takeovers and leveraged buyouts). It is expected that the study will address effects of the legislation on the pricing of acquisitions and on the reported values of different types of intangibles (including goodwill). The Treasury Department is to report the initial results of such study as expeditiously as possible and no later than December 31, 1994. The Treasury Department is to provide additional reports annually thereafter.

Report regarding backlog of pending cases

The purpose of the provision is to simplify the law regarding the amortization of intangibles. The severe backlog of cases in audit and litigation is a matter of great concern, and any principles established in such cases will no longer have precedential value due to the provision. Therefore, the Internal Revenue Service is urged in the strongest possible terms to expedite the settlement of cases under present law. In considering settlements and establishing procedures for handling existing controversies in an expedient and balanced manner, the Internal Revenue Service is strongly encouraged to take into account the principles of the bill so as to produce consistent results for similarly situated taxpayers. However, no inference is intended that any deduction should be allowed in these cases for assets that are not amortizable under present law. The Treasury Department is required to report annually to the House Ways and Means Committee and the Senate Finance Committee, regarding the volume of pending disputes in audit and litigation involving the amortization of intangibles and the progress made in resolving such disputes. It is expected that the report will also address the effects of the provision on the volume and nature of disputes regarding the amortization of intangibles. The first such report is to be made no later than December 31, 1994.

Effective Date

In general

The provision generally applies to property acquired after the date of enactment of the bill. As more fully described below, however, a taxpayer may elect to apply the bill to all property acquired after July 25, 1991. In addition, a taxpayer that does not make this election may elect to apply present law (rather than the provisions of the bill) to property that is acquired after the date of enactment of the bill pursuant to a binding written contract in effect on the date of enactment of the bill and at all times thereafter until the property is acquired. Finally, special "anti-churning" rules may apply to prevent taxpayers from converting existing goodwill, going concern value, or any other section 197 intangible for which a depreciation or amortization deduction would not have been allowable under present law into amortizable property to which the bill applies.

Election to apply bill to property acquired

[Footnote ¶3064 continued]

152. There is no intention to codify any aspect of the existing regulations under section 1060 or other provisions. Furthermore, it is expected that the Treasury Department will review the operation of the regulations under sections 1060 and 338 in light of new section 197.

after July 25, 1991

A taxpayer may elect to apply the bill to all property acquired by the taxpayer after July 25, 1991. If a taxpayer makes this election, the bill also applies to all property acquired after July 25, 1991, by any taxpayer that is under common control with the electing taxpayer (within the meaning of subparagraphs (A) and (B) of section 41(f)(1)) of the Code) at any time during the period that began on November 22, 1991, and that ends on the date that the election is made. [153] The election is to be made at such time and in such manner as may be specified by the Treasury Department, [154] and the election may be revoked only with the consent of the Treasury Department.

Elective binding contract exception

A taxpayer may also elect to apply present law (rather than the provisions of the bill) to property that is acquired after the date of enactment of the bill if the property is acquired pursuant to a binding written contract that was in effect on the date of enactment of the bill and at all times thereafter until the property is acquired. This election may not be made by any taxpayer that is subject to either of the elections described above that apply the provisions of the bill to property acquired before the date of enactment of the bill. The election is to be made at such time and in such manner as may be specified by the Treasury Department,[155] and the election may be revoked only with the consent of the Treasury Department.

Anti-churning rules

Special rules are provided by the bill to prevent taxpayers from converting existing goodwill, going concern value, or any other section 197 intangible for which a depreciation or amortization deduction would not have been allowable under present law into amortizable property to which the bill applies. Under these "anti-churning" rules, goodwill, going concern value, or any other section 197 intangible for which a depreciation or amortization deduction would not be allowable but for the provisions of the bill [156] may not be amortized as an amortizable section 197 intangible if: (1) the section 197 intangible is acquired by a taxpayer after the date of enactment of the bill; and (2) either (a) the taxpayer or a related person held or used the intangible at any time during the period that begins on July 25, 1991, and that ends on the date of enactment of the bill; (b) the taxpayer acquired the intangible from a person that held such intangible at any time during the period that begins on July 25, 1991, and that ends on the date of enactment of the bill and, as part of the transaction, the user of the intangible does not change; or (c) the taxpayer grants the right to use the intangible to a person (or a person related to such person) that held or used the intangible at any time during the period that begins on July 25, 1991, and that ends on the date of enactment of the bill. The anti-churning rules, however, do not apply to the acquisition of any intangible by a taxpayer if the basis of the intangible in the hands of the taxpayer is determined under section 1014(a) (relating to property acquired from a decedent). For purposes of the anti-churning rules, a person is related to another person if: (1) the person bears a relationship to that person which would be specified in section 267(b)(1) or 707(b)(1) of the Code if those sections were amended by substituting 20 percent for 50 percent; or (2) the persons are engaged in trades or businesses under common control (within the meaning of subparagraphs (A) and (B) of section 41(f)(1) of the Code). A person is treated as related to another person if such relationship exists immediately before or immediately after the acquisition of the intangible involved. In addition, in determining whether the anti-churning rules apply with respect to any increase in the basis of partnership property under section 732, 734, or 743 of the Code, the determinations are to

[Footnote ¶ 3064 continued]

153. However, with certain exceptions, an amortization deduction is not to be allowed under the bill for goodwill, going concern value, or any other section 197 intangible for which a depreciation or amortization deduction would not be allowable but for the provisions of the bill if: (1) the section 197 intangible is acquired after July 25, 1991; and (2) either (a) the taxpayer or a related person held or used the intangible on July 25, 1991; (b) the taxpayer acquired the intangible from a person that held such intangible on July 25, 1991, and, as part of the transaction, the user of the intangible does not change; or (c) the taxpayer grants the right to use the intangible to a person (or a person related to such person) that held or used the intangible on July 25, 1991. See below for a more detailed description of these "anti-churning" rules.

154. It is anticipated that the Treasury Department will require the election to be made on the timely filed Federal income tax return of the taxpayer for the taxable year that includes the date of enactment of the bill.

155. It is anticipated that the Treasury Department will require the election to be made on the timely filed Federal income tax return of the taxpayer for the taxable year that includes the date of enactment of the bill.

156. Amounts that are properly deductible pursuant to section 1253 under present law are to be treated for purposes of the anti-churning provision as amounts for which depreciation or amortization is allowable under present law.

be made at the partner level and each partner is to be treated as having owned or used the partner's proportionate share of the partnership property. Thus, for example, the anti-churning rules do not apply to any increase in the basis of partnership property that occurs upon the acquisition of an interest in a partnership that has made a section 754 election if the person acquiring the partnership interest is not related to the person selling the partnership interest.[157] These "anti-churning" rules are not to apply to any section 197 intangible that is acquired from a person with less than a 50-percent relationship to the acquirer to the extent that: (1) the seller recognizes gain on the transaction with respect to such intangible; and (2) the seller agrees, notwithstanding any other provision of the Code, to pay a tax on such gain which, when added to any other Federal income tax imposed on such gain, equals the product of such gain and the highest rate of tax imposed by section 1 or 11 of the Code, whichever is applicable. The seller is treated as satisfying the second requirement if the excess of (1) the total tax liability for the year of the transaction over (2) what its tax liability for such year would have been had the sale of the intangible (but not the remainder of the transaction) been excluded from the computation equals or exceeds the product of the gain on that asset times the relevant maximum rate. The bill also contains a general anti-abuse rule that applies to any section 197 intangible that is acquired by a taxpayer from another person. Under this rule, a section 197 intangible may not be amortized under the provisions of the bill if the taxpayer acquired the intangible in a transaction one of the principal purposes of which is to (1) avoid the requirement that the intangible be acquired after the date of enactment of the bill or (2) avoid any of their anti-churning rules described above that are applicable to goodwill, going concern value, or any other section 197 intangible for which a depreciation or amortization deduction would not be allowable but for the provisions of the bill. Finally, the special rules described above that apply in the case of a transactions described in section 332, 351, 361, 721, 731, 1031, or 1033 of the Code also apply for purposes of the effective date. Consequently, if the transferor of any section 197 property is not allowed an amortization deduction with respect to such property under this provision, then the transferee is not allowed an amortization deduction under this provision to the extent of the adjusted basis of the transferee that does not exceed the adjusted basis of the transferor. In addition, this provision is to apply to any subsequent transfers of any such property in a transaction described in section 332, 351, 361, 721, 731, 1031, or 1033.

Conference Report

Senate Amendment

The Senate Amendment is the same as the House bill with the following modifications: The amount of deduction with respect to any amortizable section 197 intangible is determined by amortizing 75 percent of the adjusted basis of the intangible over 14 years. The remaining 25 percent of adjusted basis is not amortizable. Purchased mortgage servicing rights not acquired with a trade or business or substantial portion thereof are excluded from the definition of a section 197 intangible. Any depreciation deduction allowable with respect to such excluded rights must be taken over 9 years (108 months) on a straight-line basis. In addition to the provisions of the House bill regarding computer software, special allocation and amortization rules apply to acquisitions of certain businesses that have made certain computer software expenditures. Fifty percent of the amortizable portion of "amortizable section 197 intangibles" (i.e., 50 percent of 75 percent of the basis of such assets) is amortized on a straight-line basis over 5 years. The remaining 50 percent of 75 percent is amortized over 14 years under the general rule of the provision. The Senate amendment does not contain any requirement of reports from the Treasury department.

[Footnote ¶3064 continued]

157. In addition to these rules, it is anticipated that rules similar to the anti-churning rules under section 168 of the Code will apply in determining whether persons are related. (See Prop. Treas. Reg. 1.168-4 (February 16, 1984).) For example, it is anticipated that a corporation, partnership, or trust that owned or used property at any time during the period that begins on July 25, 1991, and that ends on the date of enactment of the bill and that is no longer in existence will be considered to be in existence for purposes of determining whether the taxpayer that acquired the property is related to such corporation, partnership, or trust. As a further example, it is anticipated that in the case of a transaction to which section 338 of the Code applies, the corporation that is treated as selling its assets will not to be considered related to the corporation that is treated as purchasing the assets if at least 80 percent of the stock of the corporation that is treated as selling its assets is acquired by purchase after July 25, 1991.

Conference Agreement

The conference agreement follows the House bill, deleting the statutory requirements of reports from the Treasury Department and with the following additional modifications:

Period of amortization

The straight line amortization period for an amortizable section 197 intangible is 15 years rather than 14 years.

Treasury regulatory authority regarding rights of fixed duration or amount

As a conforming amendment to the change in amortization period, under the conference agreement the Treasury regulatory authority regarding rights of fixed duration or amount applies to rights that have a fixed duration of less than 15 years (rather than 14 years).

Purchased mortgage servicing rights

The conference agreement follows the Senate bill in excluding purchased mortgage servicing rights (not acquired in connection with the acquisition of a trade or business or substantial portion thereof) from the definition of a section 197 intangible. Any depreciation deduction allowable with respect to such excluded rights must be computed on a straight line basis over a period of 9 years (108 months). [33]

Technical correction regarding losses on covenants not to compete

The conference agreement contains a technical correction conforming the statute to both the House and Senate committee reports regarding the amortization of covenants not to compete. The correction provides that a covenant not to compete (or other arrangement to the extent such arrangement has substantially the same effect as a covenant not to compete) shall not be considered to have been disposed of or to have become worthless until the disposition or worthlessness of all interests in the trade or business or substantial portion thereof that was directly or indirectly acquired in connection with such covenant (or other arrangement). Thus, for example, in the case of an indirect acquisition of a trade or business (e.g., through the acquisition of stock that is not treated as an asset acquisition), it is clarified that a covenant not to compete (or other arrangement) entered into in connection with the indirect acquisition cannot be written off faster than on a straight-line basis over 15 years (even if the covenant or other arrangement expires or otherwise becomes worthless) unless all the trades or businesses indirectly acquired (e.g., acquired through such stock interest) are also disposed of or become worthless.

Modification of related party rule for purposes of the July 25, 1991 election

The conference agreement modifies the rules regarding the effect of an election on certain related parties, in order to reflect the passage of time since the election was originally proposed (H. Res. 292, introduced November 22, 1991). The conference agreement provides that an election by a taxpayer affects all property acquired by that taxpayer since July 25, 1991, and also affects all property acquired since that date by parties that are related to the taxpayer at any time between August 2, 1993 (rather than November 22, 1991) and the date of the election. Consistent with the operation of the consolidated return rules, for this purpose it is intended that any property acquired after July 25, 1991 by an entity that is a member of an affiliated group filing a consolidated return at the time of such acquisition is treated as property acquired by the taxpayer group filing such return for purposes of any election by that taxpayer group. An election by an affiliated group filing a consolidated return would not force an election to be made by an acquirer of a former group member, even if such acquirer would normally continue the treatment of such former group member's assets (e.g., an acquirer in a transaction that does not affect the inside basis of the assets of the former group member). Similarly, a failure by the former group to make an election would not affect the ability of the former group member, or a new acquirer that is related to such member on the date of the election, to make an election that would affect the post-July 25, 1991 intangible asset acquisitions of that former group member (including such intangible asset acquisitions made while it was a member of the former group). [34] The conferees expect

[Footnote ¶ 3064 continued]

33. Consistent with both the House and Senate bills, purchased mortgage servicing rights are not depreciable to the extent that the rights are stripped coupons under section 1286 of the Code. To the extent that the rights are stripped coupons under section 1286 of the Code, they will not be amortized on a straight line basis over 108 months. See Rev. Rul. 91-46, 1991-2 C.B. 358.

34. For example, assume the following facts. Corporation P is the parent of an affiliated group filing a consolidated return that includes subsidiary S. The P group files its consolidated return on the basis of the calendar year. S acquires certain in-

that the Treasury Department will provide rules regarding appropriate adjustments, if any, to be made where property acquired after July 25, 1991 has been transferred from one related party group to another in a transaction that would not involve a change in asset basis and one or both groups independently make a July 25, 1991 election that would affect the amortization of such property.[35]

Reports regarding backlog of pending cases and implementation and effects of the bill

The conferees reiterate the intended purpose of the provision, as stated in both the House and Senate reports, to simplify the law regarding the amortization of intangibles. The severe backlog of cases in audit and litigation is a matter of great concern to the conferees; and any principles established in such cases will no longer have precedential value due to the provision contained in the conference agreement. Therefore, the conferees urge the Internal Revenue Service in the strongest possible terms to expedite the settlement of cases under present law. In considering settlements and establishing procedures for handling existing controversies in an expedited and balanced manner, the conferees strongly encourage the Internal Revenue Service to take into account the principles of the bill so as to produce consistent results for similarly situated taxpayers. However, no inference is intended that any deduction should be allowed in these cases for assets that are not amortizable under present law. The conferees intend that the Treasury Department report annually to the House Ways and Means Committee and the Senate Finance Committee regarding the volume of pending disputes in audit and litigation involving the amortization of intangibles and the progress made in resolving disputes. It is intended that the report also address the effects of the provision on the volume and nature of disputes regarding the amortization of intangibles. It is intended that the first such report shall be made no later than December 3l, 1994. The conferees also intend that the Treasury Department conduct a continuing study of the implementation and effects of the bill, including effects on merger and acquisition activities including hostile takeovers and leveraged buyouts). It is expected that the study will address effects of the legislation on the pricing of acquisitions and on the reported values of different types of intangibles (including goodwill). It is intended that the Treasury Department will report the initial results of such study as expeditiously as possible and no later than December 31, l994. The Treasury Department is expected to provide additional reports annually thereafter.

[¶3065] Section 13262. Treatment of Certain Payments to Retired or Deceased Partner

(Code Sec. 736)

[House Explanation]

Present Law

Payments for purchase of goodwill and accounts receivable

A current deduction generally is not allowed for a capital expenditure (i.e., an expenditure that yields benefits beyond the current taxable year). The cost of goodwill acquired in connection with the assets of a going concern normally is a capital expenditure, as is the cost of acquiring accounts receivable. The cost of acquiring goodwill is recovered only when the goodwill is disposed of, while at the cost of acquiring accounts receivable is taken into account only when the receivable is disposed of

[Footnote ¶3064 continued]

tangible assets on August 1, 1991. The stock of S is sold to corporation X on December 31, 1992, in a transaction in which S's adjusted basis in its assets is not changed. Corporation X is also the parent of an affiliated group filing a consolidated return that now includes S. S remains in the X group. Under the conference agreement, if the X group makes the July 25, 1991 election, such election does not require the P group also to make the election. If the P group makes the July 25, 1991 election, the election will affect the amortization deductions allowed on the P group's 1991 and 1992 consolidated returns with respect to the assets acquired by S on August 1, 1991. Such election does not require the X group also to make the election.

35. For example, such rules would apply if a corporation that is a member of an affiliated group filing a consolidated return acquires property after July 25, 1991 and then, before August 2, 1993 becomes a member of another group in a transaction that does not affect the basis of that corporation's assets. In such a case, the first group could make the election for periods when the corporation was included in that group's consolidated return. In addition, the second group could make the election because the corporation was related to the second group on August 2, 1993.

or becomes worthless.

Payments made in liquidation of partnership interest

The tax treatment of a payment made in liquidation of the interest of a retiring or deceased partner depends upon whether the payment is made in exchange for the partner's interest in partnership property. A liquidating payment made in exchange for such property is treated as a distribution by the partnership (sec. 736(b)). Such distribution generally results in gain to the retiring partner only to the extent that the cash distributed exceeds such partner's adjusted basis in the partnership interest.

A liquidating payment not made in exchange for the partner's interest in partnership property receives either of two possible treatments. If the amount of the payment is determined without reference to partnership income, it is treated as a guaranteed payment and is generally deductible (sec. 736(a)(2)). If the amount of payment is determined by reference to partnership income, the payment is treated as a distributive share of partnership income, thereby reducing the distributive shares of other partners (which is equivalent to a deduction) (sec. 736(a)(2)).

A special rule treats amounts paid for goodwill of the partnership (except to the extent provided in the partnership agreement) and unrealized receivables as not made in exchange for an interest in partnership property (sec. 736(b)(2)(B)). Thus, such amounts may be deductible. Unrealized receivables include unbilled amounts, accounts receivable, depreciation recapture, market discount, and certain other items (sec. 751(c)).

Sale or exchange of a partnership interest

The sale or exchange of a partnership interest results in capital gain or loss to the transferor partner, except to the extent that ordinary income or loss is recognized with respect to the partner's share of the partnership's unrealized receivables and substantially appreciated inventory items (sec. 741). It is often unclear whether a payment by a partnership to a retiring partner is made in sale or exchange of, or in liquidation of, a partnership interest.

Reasons For Change

In general

By treating a payment for unstated goodwill and unrealized receivables as a guaranteed payment or distributive share, present law in effect permits a deduction for an amount that would otherwise constitute a capital expenditure. This treatment does not measure partnership income properly. It also threatens to erode the rule requiring capitalization of such payments generally. Under present law, a prospective buyer of a business may structure the transaction so as to currently deduct such an amount by first entering into a partnership with the seller and then liquidating the seller's partnership interest.

Section 736 was intended to simplify the taxation of payments in liquidation. Instead, it has created confusion as to whether a particular payment is a payment in liquidation or is made pursuant to a sale of the partnership interest to the continuing partners. The proposal reduces this confusion by eliminating a primary difference between sales and liquidations.

The special treatment of goodwill was apparently predicated on the assumption that the adverse positions of the taxpayers will result in a stated price equal to the true value of the goodwill. That assumption is false. If the value of the preferential rate (if any) and the income deflection are not equal, the stated goodwill and total retirement payments will likely be set so as to maximize the combined tax savings for both retiring and continuing partners.

It is recognized, however, that general partners in service partnerships do not ordinarily value goodwill in liquidating partners. Accordingly, such partners may continue to receive the special rule of present law.

Unrealized receivables

When originally enacted, the term "unrealized receivables" was limited to unbilled amounts and accounts receivable. The tax deferral resulting from immediate deduction of amounts paid for these items is relatively short because payment is usually received in the near future. Such deferral is considerably longer, however, with respect to the deduction of other items now included in the expanded definition of unrealized receivables, such as depreciation recapture on business assets, which are slow to give rise to ordinary income.

Explanation Of Provision

In general

The bill generally repeals the special treatment of liquidation payments made for goodwill and unrealized receivables. Thus, such payments would be treated as made in exchange for the partner's interest in partnership property, and not as a distributive share or guaranteed payment that could give rise to a deduction or its equivalent. The bill does not change present law with respect to payments made to a general partner in a partnership in which capital is not a material income-producing factor. The determination of whether capital is a material income-producing factor would be made under principles of present and prior law. /158/[158] For purposes of this provision, capital is not a material income-producing factor where substantially all the gross income of the business consists of fees, commissions, or other compensation for personal services performed by an individual. The practice of his or her profession by a doctor, dentist, lawyer, architect, or accountant will not, as such, be treated as a trade or business in which capital is a material income-producing factor even though the practitioner may have a substantial capital investment in professional equipment or in the physical plant constituting the office from which such individual conducts his or her practice so long as such capital investment is merely incidental to such professional practice. In addition, the bill does not affect the deductibility of compensation paid to a retiring partner for past services.

Unrealized receivables

The bill also repeals the special treatment of payments made for unrealized receivables (other than unbilled amounts and accounts receivable) for all partners. Such amounts would be treated as made in exchange for the partner's interest in partnership property. Thus, for example, a payment for depreciation recapture would be treated as made in exchange for an interest in partnership property, and not as a distributive share or guaranteed payment that could give rise to a deduction or its equivalent.

Effective Date

The provision generally applies to partners retiring or dying on or after January 5, 1993. The provision does not apply to any partner who retires on or after January 5, 1993, if a written contract to purchase the partner's interest in the partnership was binding on January 4, 1993 and at all times thereafter until such purchase. For this purpose, a written contract is to be considered binding only if the contract specifies the amount to be paid for the partnership interest and the timing of any such payments.

Conference Agreement

* * * *

The conference agreement is the same as the House bill. * * * *

[¶ 3066] Section 13271. Disallowance of Interest on Certain Overpayments of Tax

(Code Sec. 6611)

[House Explanation]

Present Law

No interest is paid by the Government on a refund arising from an original income tax return if the refund is issued by the 45th day after the later of the due date for the return (determined without regard to any extensions) or the date the return is filed (sec. 6611(e)).

There is no parallel rule for refunds of taxes other than income taxes (i.e., employment, excise, and estate and gift taxes), for refunds of any type of tax arising from amended returns, or for claims for refunds of any type of tax.

If a taxpayer files a timely original return with respect to any type of tax and later files an amended return claiming a refund, and if the IRS determines that the tax payer is due a refund on the basis of the amended return, the IRS will pay the refund with interest computed from the due date of the original return.

[Footnote ¶ 3064 continued]

158. E.g., sections 401(c)(2) and 911(d) of the Code and old section 1348(b)(1)(A) of the Code.

Reasons For Change

The committee believes that it is inappropriate for the payment of interest on tax refunds to be determined by the type of tax involved; all types of taxes should be treated similarly. The committee further believes that it is appropriate to alter the interest rules to provide a 45-day processing period with respect to amended returns, claims for refund and IRS-initiated adjustments.

Explanation Of Provision

No interest is to be paid by the Government on a refund arising from any type of original tax return if the refund is issued by the 45th day after the later of the due date for the return (determined without regard to any extensions) or the date the return is filed.

A parallel rule applies to amended returns and claims for refunds: if the refund is issued by the 45th day after the date the amended return or claim for refund is filed, no interest is to be paid by the Government for that period of up to 45 days (interest would continue to be paid for the period from the due date of the return to the date the amended return or claim for refund is filed). If the IRS does not issue the refund by the 45th day after the date the amended return or claim for refund is filed, interest would be paid (as under present law) for the period from the due date of the original return to the date the IRS pays the refund.

A parallel rule also applies to IRS-initiated adjustments (whether due to computational adjustments or audit adjustments). With respect to these adjustments, the IRS is to pay interest for 45 fewer days than it otherwise would.

Effective Date

The extension of the 45-day processing rule is effective for returns required to be filed (without regard to extensions) on or after January 1, 1994. The amended return rule is effective for amended returns and claims for refunds filed on or after January 1, 1995 (regardless of the taxable period to which they relate). The rule relating to IRS-initiated adjustments applies to refunds paid on or after January 1, 1995 (regardless of the taxable period to which they relate).

[Conference Report]

Conference Agreement

The conference agreement follows the House bill and the Senate amendment.

[¶3067] Section 13272. Denial of Deduction Relating to Travel Expenses

(Code Sec. 274)

[House Explanation]

Present Law

In general, a taxpayer is permitted a deduction for all ordinary and necessary expenses paid or incurred during the taxable year (1) in carrying on any trade or business and (2) in the case of an individual, for the production of income. Such deductible expenses may include reasonable travel expenses paid or incurred while away from home, such as transportation costs and the cost of meals and lodging.

In the case of ordinary and necessary business expenses, if a taxpayer travels to a destination and while at that destination engages in both business and personal activities, travel expenses to and from such destination are deductible only if the trip is related primarily to the taxpayer's trade or business. If the trip is primarily personal in nature, expenses while at the destination that are properly allocable to the taxpayer's trade or business are deductible even though the traveling expenses to and from the destination are not deductible (Treas. Reg. sec. 1.162-2(b)(1)).

Under Treasury regulations, if the taxpayer's spouse accompanies the taxpayer on a business trip, expenses attributable to the spouse's travel are not deductible unless it is adequately shown that the spouse's presence on the trip has a bona fide business purpose (Treas. reg. sec. 1.162-2(c)). The performance of some incidental service by spouse does not cause the expenses to qualify as deductible business expenses. Under the Treasury regulations, the same rules apply to any other members of the taxpayer's family who accompany the taxpayer on such a trip.

Reasons For Change

The committee believes that no deduction should be allowed for travel expenses paid or incurred with respect to a spouse, dependent, or other individual accompanying a person on business travel unless such expenses are legitimate business expenses of the taxpayer claiming the deduction. The committee believes that merely accompanying or being related to the traveling employee does not convert otherwise nondeductible personal expenses to deductible business expenses.

Explanation Of Provision

The bill denies a deduction for travel expenses paid or incurred with respect to a spouse, dependent, or other individual accompanying a person on business travel, unless (1) the spouse, dependent, or other individual accompanying the person is a bona fide employee of the person paying or using the expenses, (2) the travel of the spouse, dependent, or other individual is for a bona fide business purpose, and (3) the expenses of the spouse, dependent, or other individual would otherwise be deductible. No inference is intended as to the deductibility of these expenses under present law. The denial of the deduction does not apply to expenses that would otherwise qualify as deductible moving expenses.

Effective Date

The provision is effective for amounts paid or incurred after December 31, 1993.

[Conference Report]

Senate Amendment

The Senate amendment is the same as the House bill.

Conference Agreement

The conference agreement follows the House bill and the Senate amendment.

[¶3068] Section 13273. Increase in Withholding from Supplemental Wage Payments

(Code Sec. 3402(g))

[House Explanation]

Present Law

Under Treasury regulations, withholding on supplemental wage payments (such as bonuses, commissions, and overtime pay) that are not paid concurrently with wages (or that are paid concurrently with wages, but are separately stated) for a payroll period may be done at a rate of 20 percent (at the employer's election) (Treas. Reg. sec. 31.3402(g)-1). [172]

Reasons for Change

The committee believes that it is appropriate to raise the withholding rate on supplemental wage payments so that withholding more closely approximates the ultimate tax liability with respect to these payments.

Explanation Of Provision

The bill increases the applicable withholding rate on supplemental wage payments to 28 percent.

Effective Date

The provision is effective for payments made after December 31, 1993.

[Conference Report]

Senate Amendment

The Senate amendment is the same as the House bill.

Conference Agreement

The conference agreement follows the House bill and the Senate amendment.

[¶3069] Sections 13301--13303. Empowerment Zones and Enterprise Communities, etc

[Footnote ¶3065 continued]

172. If the employer chooses not to use the 20-percent method, withholding may be computed by aggregating the supplemental payments with regular wages paid within the same calendar year for the last preceding payroll period or the current payroll period. The employer would then use withholding tables to determine the total tax on this aggregate amount. The amount to be withheld for the supplemental wages is the total tax less any amount already withheld for regular wages included in the aggregate amount.

(Code Sec. 1391-1397D)

[House Explanation]

Present Law

The Internal Revenue Code does not contain general rules that target specific geographic areas for special Federal income tax treatment. Within certain Code sections, however, there are definitions of targeted areas for limited purposes (e.g., low-income housing credit and qualified mortgage bond provisions target certain economically distressed areas). In addition, present law provides favorable Federal income tax treatment for certain U.S. corporations that operate in Puerto Rico, the U.S. Virgin Islands, or a possession of the United States to encourage the conduct of trades or businesses within these areas.

Reasons for Change

The committee believes that special consideration should be given to the problems of distressed urban and rural areas. Revitalization of economically distressed areas through expanded business and employment opportunities, especially for residents of those distressed areas, should help alleviate both economic and social problems, including distress resulting from narcotics and crime. The committee believes that Federal tax incentives could play a rule in revitalizing distressed areas. The committee also believes that Federal tax incentives for distressed areas should be provided in conjunction with State and local programs.

Explanation of Provisions

Designation of eligible areas

In general. A total of 10 empowerment zones and 100 enterprise communities will be designated (subject to availability of eligible areas) during 1994 and 1995. Empowerment zones and enterprise communities will be designated from areas nominated by State and local governments or a governing body of an Indian reservation. Empowerment zones will be eligible for additional tax incentives beyond those provided in the areas designated as enterprise communities. The Secretary of Housing and Urban Development (HUD) will designate in eligible urban areas six empowerment zones and 65 enterprise communities. (The six empowerment zones located in urban areas will include at least one zone in an urban area the most populous city of which has a population of 500,000 or less.) The Secretary of Agriculture will designate in eligible rural areas [174] three empowerment zones and 30 enterprise communities. In addition, the Secretary of the Interior will designate in eligible Indian reservation areas one empowerment zone and five enterprise communities. [175] Nominated areas located in Indian reservations also will be eligible for designation (provided the bill's criteria are met) as rural areas. All designations will be made in consultation with an Enterprise Board (to be established in the future), which will include officials from various Federal agencies. The designations will be made prior to January 1, 1996. Designations of areas as empowerment zones or enterprise communities generally will remain in effect for 10 years. An area's designation could be revoked if the local government(s) or State(s) modifies the boundaries of the designated area or does not comply with its agreed-upon strategic plan for the area (described below). [176]

Eligibility criteria for zones. The eligibility criteria for urban areas, rural areas, and Indian reservations generally are the same (except as noted below). To be eligible for designation, a nominated area is required to possess ALL of the following characteristics:

Resident population. An eligible urban area is subject to a maximum population of the lesser of (1) 200,000, or (2) the greater of 50,000 or 10 percent of the population of the most populous city within the nominated area. (In addition, the Secretary of HUD is required to designate empowerment zones located in urban areas in such a manner that the AGGREGATE population of such zones does not exceed 750,000.) Rural areas are subject to a maxi-

[Footnote ¶ 3068 continued]

. An area will be treated as nominated by a State or local government if it is nominated by such other entity as may be specified by an Enterprise Board (to be established in the future).

174. For purposes of the bill, a "rural area" means any area which is (1) outside a metropolitan statistical area as defined by the Secretary of Commerce, or (2) determined by the Secretary of Agriculture to be a rural area. For purposes of the bill, the term "urban area" means an area which is not a rural area.

175. Under the bill, the term "Indian reservation" means a reservation as defined in (1) section 3(d) of the Indian Financing Act of 1974 (25 U.S.C. 1452(d)), or (2) section 4(10) of the Indian Child Welfare Act of 1978 (25 U.S.C. 1903(10)).

176. An area's designation may be revoked only after a hearing on the record at which officials of the State and local governments are given an opportunity to participate.

mum population of 30,000. Indian reservations are not subject to a population limit.

General condition. An eligible area must have a condition of pervasive poverty, unemployment, and general economic distress (which may include distress from a high incidence of crime and narcotics use).

Area. The nominated area must either (1) have a continuous boundary, or (2) except in the case of a rural area located in more than one State, consist of not more than three noncontiguous parcels. Urban areas must be located entirely within no more than two contiguous States, and rural areas must be located entirely within no more than three contiguous States.

Size. The nominated area must not exceed (1) 20 square miles for urban areas, or (2) 1,000 square miles for rural areas and Indian reservations.

Poverty. Each of the census tracts within a nominated area must have a poverty rate of at least 20 percent; [177] at least 90 percent of the area's census tracts must each have a poverty rate of at least 25 percent; and at least 50 percent of the area's census tracts must each have a poverty rate of at least 35 percent. [178] For purposes of these measurements, unpopulated census tracts and census tracts with limited populations and 75 percent or more zoned for commercial or industrial use will be treated as satisfying the bill's 20-percent and 25-percent poverty rate criteria. With respect to empowerment zones, each census tract located in a central business district (as such term is used for purposes of the most recent Census of Retail Trade) must have a poverty rate of at least 35 percent. With respect to enterprise communities, each census tract located in a central business district must have a poverty rate of at least 30 percent. [179] If the nominated area consists of noncontiguous parcels, each parcel must separately satisfy the above poverty criteria.

Strategic plan. A strategic plan must be submitted by the nominating body for purposes of accomplishing the goals of this legislation.

Contents of strategic plan. In order for a nominated area to be eligible for designation the local government(s) and State(s) in which the area is located [180] are required to provide a strategic plan that: (1) describes the coordinated economic, human, community, and physical development plan and related activities proposed for the nominated area; (2) describes the proce ss by which the affected community is a full partner in the process of developing and implementing the plan and the extent to which local institutions and organizations have contributed to the planning process; (3) identifies the amount of State, local, and private resources that will be available in the nominated area and the private/public partnerships to be used, which may include participation by, and cooperation with, universities, medical centers, and other private and public entities; (4) identifies the funding requested under any Federal program in support of the proposed economic, human, community, and physical development and related activities; (5) identifies baselines, methods, and benchmarks for measuring the success of carrying out the strategic plan, including the extent to which poor persons and families will be empowered to become economically self-sufficient, and (6) generally does not include any action to assist any establishment in relocating from an area outside the nominated area to the nominated area. [181]

[Footnote ¶ 3068 continued]

177. The poverty rate is to be determined by the 1990 census or subsequent census dates. If areas are not tracted as population census tracts, the equivalent county divisions as defined by the Bureau of the Census for purposes of defining poverty areas would be treated as population census tracts.

178. With respect to an area nominated to be an empowerment zone, the appropriate Secretary may reduce one of these poverty criteria by five percentage points for not more than 10 percent of the population census tracts (up to a maximum of five population census tracts) in the nominated area. With respect to an area nominated to be an enterprise community, the appropriate Secretary may reduce one of the poverty criteria as described in the preceding sentence or, as an alternative, may reduce the 35-percent poverty threshold by ten percentage points (i.e., to 25 percent) for up to three population census tracts.

179. The appropriate Secretary has no discretion to reduce the 35-percent poverty rate threshold for tracts located in a central business district that is part of an empowerment zone or to reduce the 30-percent poverty rate threshold for tracts located in a central business district that is part of an enterprise community.

180. In the case of an Indian reservation, the reservation governing body is deemed to be both the State and local governments with respect to such area.

181. The bill provides that the required strategic plan may not include any action to assist any business in relocating from one area outside the nominated area to the nominated area, except that assistance for the expansion of an existing business

Selection process and criteria. From among the eligible areas, designations of empowerment zones and enterprise communities will be made on the basis of (1) the effectiveness of the strategic plan for a nominated area and the assurances that such plan will be implemented and (2) criteria specified by the Enterprise Board.

Tax incentives for empowerment zones

Employer wage credit. A 25-percent credit against income tax liability is available to all employers for the first $20,000 of qualified wages paid to each employee who (1) is a zone resident (i.e., his or her principal place of abode is within the zone [182], and (2) performs substantially all employment services within the zone in a trade or business of the employer. The maximum credit per qualified employee is $5,000 per year. Wages paid to a qualified employee continue to be eligible for the credit if the employee earns more than $20,000, although only the first $20,000 of wages will be eligible for the credit. [183] The wage credit is available with respect to a qualified employee, regardless of the number of other employees who work for the employer or whether the employer meets the definition of an "enterprise zone business" (which applies for the investment tax incentives described below). [184] The credit will be phased out beginning in 2001. The credit rate will be reduced to 20 percent in 2001, 15 percent in 2002, 10 percent in 2003, and five percent in 2004. The credit will not be available after December 31, 2004. Qualified wages include the first $20,000 of "wages," defined to include (1) salary and wages as generally defined for FUTA purposes, and (2) certain training and educational expenses paid on behalf of a qualified employee, provided that (a) the expenses are paid to an unrelated third party and are excludable from gross income of the employee under section 127 (which is retroactively and permanently extended under another provision of the bill), or (b) in the case of an employee under age 19, the expenses are incurred by the employer in operating a youth training program in conjunction with local education officials. The credit is allowed with respect to full-time and part-time employees. However, the employee must be employed by the employer for a minimum period of at least 90 days. Wages are not eligible for the credit if paid to certain relatives of the employer or, if the employer is a corporation or partnership, certain relatives of a person who owns more than 50 percent of the business. In addition, wages are not eligible for the credit if paid to a person who owns more than five percent of the stock (or capital or profits interests) of the employer. [185] An employer's deduction otherwise allowed for wages paid is reduced by the amount of credit claimed for that taxable year. Wages are not be taken into account for purposes of the empowerment zone employment credit if taken into account in determining the employer's targeted jobs tax credit (TJTC). The credit is allowable to offset up to 25 percent of alternative minimum tax liability.

Definition of "enterprise zone business". The investment tax incentives for empowerment zones described below (but not the labor incentives described above) are available only with respect to trade or business activities that satisfy the criteria for an "enterprise zone business." Under the proposal, an "enterprise zone business" is defined as a corporation or partnership (or proprietorship) if for the taxa-

[Footnote ¶ 3068 continued]
entity through establishment of a new branch, affiliate, or subsidiary is permitted if (1) the establishment of the new branch, affiliate, or subsidiary will not result in a decrease in employment in the area of original location or in any other area where the existing business entity conducts business operations, and (2) there is no reason to believe that the new branch, affiliate, or subsidiary is being established with the intention of closing down the operations of the existing business entity in the area of its original location or in any other area where the existing business entity conducts business operations.

182. The committee intends that employers will undertake reasonable measures to verify an employee's residence within the zone, so that the employer will be able to substantiate any wage credit claimed under the bill.

183. To prevent avoidance of the $20,000 limit, all employers of a controlled group of corporations (or partnerships or proprietorships under common control) would be treated as a single employer.

184. Employers would be required to take reasonable steps to notify all qualified zone employees of the availability to eligible individuals of receiving advance payments of the earned income tax credit (EITC).

185. The wage credit is not available with respect to any individual employed at any facility described in present-law section 144(c)(6)(B) (i.e., a private or commercial golf course, country club, massage parlor, hot tub facility, suntan facility, racetrack or other facility used for gambling, or any store the principal business of which is the sale of alcoholic beverages for consumption off premises). In addition, the wage credit is not available with respect to any individual employed by a trade or business the principal activity of which is farming (within the meaning of subparagraphs (A) and (B) of section 2032A(e)(5)), but only if, as of the close of the preceding taxable year, the sum of the aggregate unadjusted bases (or, if greater, the fair market value) of assets of the farm exceed $500,000.

ble year: (1) the sole trade or business of the corporation or partnership is the active conduct of a qualified business within an empowerment zone; [189] (2) at least 80 percent of the total gross income is derived from the active conduct of a "qualified business" within a zone; (3) substantially all of the use of its tangible property occurs within a zone; (4) substantially all of its intangible property is used in, and exclusively related to, the active conduct of such business; (5) substantially all of the services performed by employees are performed within a zone; (6) at least 35 percent of the employees are residents of the zone [190]; and (7) no more than five percent of the average of the aggregate unadjusted bases of the property owned by the business is attributable to (a) certain financial property, or (b) collectibles not held primarily for sale to customers in the ordinary course of an active trade or business. A "qualified business" is defined as any trade or business other than a trade or business that consists predominantly of the development or holding of intangibles for sale or license. [191] In addition, the leasing of real property that is located within the empowerment zone to others is treated as a qualified business only if (1) the leased property is not residential property, and (2) at least 50 percent of the gross rental income from the real property is from enterprise zone businesses. The rental of tangible personal property to others is not a qualified business unless substantially all of the rental of such property is by enterprise zone businesses or by residents of an empowerment zone. Activities of legally separate (even if related) parties would not be aggregated for purposes of determining whether an entity qualifies as an enterprise zone business.

Increased section 179 expensing. The expensing allowance for certain depreciable business property provided under section 179 is increased to $75,000 for qualified zone property of an enterprise zone businesses (as defined above). In addition, the types of property eligible for section 179 expensing are expanded to include buildings used in enterprise zone businesses. "Qualified zone property" is defined as depreciable tangible property (including buildings), provided that: (1) such property was acquired by the taxpayer (but not from a related party) after the zone designation took effect; (2) the original use of the property in the zone commences with the taxpayer [192]; and (3) substantially all of the use of the property is in the zone in the active conduct of a trade or business by the taxpayer in the zone. In the case of property which is substantially renovated by the taxpayer, however, such property need not be acquired by the taxpayer after zone designation or originally used by the taxpayer within the zone if during any 24-month period after zone designation the additions to the taxpayer's basis in such property exceed 100 percent of the taxpayer's basis in such property at the beginning of the period or $5,000 (whichever is greater). [193] As under present law, the section 179 expensing allowance is phased out for certain taxpayers with investment in qualified property during the taxable year above a specified threshold. However, under the bill, the present-law phase-out range is applied by decreasing the amount of the cost of qualified zone property that is deductible under section 179 by one-half of the amount by which the cost of qualified zone property (other than real estate) and other section 179 property exceeds $200,000. Thus, the section 179 deduction applicable to qualified zone property is completely phased-out when the cost of qualified zone property (other than real estate) and other section 179 property

[Footnote ¶3068 continued]

189. This requirement does not apply to a business carried on by an individual as a proprietorship.

190. For this purpose, the term "employee" includes a self-employed individual (within the meaning of section 401(c)(1)). The Committee intends that the Secretary of the Treasury will prescribe regulations to determine the appropriate treatment of part-time employees for purposes of calculating whether 35 percent of the employees are residents of the empowerment zone.

191. However, the bill specifically provides that a "qualified business" does not include (1) any trade or business consisting of the operation of any facility described in present-law section 144(c)(6)(B) (i.e., a private or commercial golf course, country club, massage parlor, hot tub facility, suntan facility, racetrack or other facility used for gambling, or any store the principal business of which is the sale of alcoholic beverages for consumption off premises, or (2) any trade or business the principal activity of which is farming (within the meaning of subparagraphs (A) or (B) of section 2032A(e)(5)), but only if, as of the close of the preceding taxable year, the sum of the aggregate unadjusted bases (or, if greater, the fair market value) of assets of the farm exceed $500,000.

192. Thus, used property may constitute qualified zone property so long as it has not previously been used within the empowerment zone.

193. Qualified zone property does not include any property to which the alternative depreciation system under section 168(g) applies, determined (1) without regard to section 168(g)(7), and (2) after application of section 280F(b).

placed in service during the taxable year reaches $350,000. For example, assume that a taxpayer places $270,000 of qualified zone property (none of which is real estate) in service during the taxable year and that the taxpayer does not place any property in service outside the zone. Under the bill, the taxpayer will be allowed to claim a section 179 deduction of $40,000 ($75,000 section 179 amount less $35,000 (one-half of the difference between $270,000 and $200,000)). As under present-law section 179, all component members of a controlled group are treated as one taxpayer for purposes of the expensing allowance and application of the phaseout range (sec. 179(d)(6)). Also, as under present law, the $75,000 expensing allowance is to apply at both the partnership (and S corporation) and partner (and shareholder) levels. The increased expensing allowance would apply for purposes of the alternative minimum tax (i.e., it is not treated as an adjustment for purposes of the alternative minimum tax). The section 179 expensing deduction will be recaptured if the property is not used predominantly in a enterprise zone business (under rules similar to present-law section 179(d)(10)).

Tax-exempt financing

In general. The bill creates a new category of exempt facility private activity bonds, qualified enterprise zone facility bonds for use in empowerment zones. Generally qualified enterprise zone facility bonds are bonds 95 percent or more of the net proceeds of which is used to finance qualified zone property (as generally defined under the bill) for a qualified enterprise zone business (as generally defined under the bill) and land located in the empowerment zone which is functionally related and subordinate to the qualified zone property. These bonds may only be issued while a zone designation is in effect.

Special rules on issue size and use to finance certain facilities. The aggregate face amount of all outstanding qualified enterprise zone bonds per qualified enterprise zone business may not exceed $3 million for each zone. In addition total outstanding qualified enterprise zone bond financing for each qualified enterprise zone business may not exceed $20 million for all zones. For purposes of these determinations, the aggregate amount of outstanding enterprise zone facility bonds allocable to any business shall be determined under rules similar to rules contained in section 144(a)(10). As with other exempt facility bonds, these bonds may be issued only to finance identified facilities. The committee does not intend, however that the $3 million per enterprise zone business requirement will limit issuance of a single issue of bonds (in excess of $3 million) for more than one identified facility, provided that the $3 million limit is satisfied with respect to each zone business. However the committee realizes that ease of marketing these exempt facility bonds like other exempt facility bonds may require common marketing of separate issues of bonds for discrete facilities if such issues are simultaneous or proximate in time. The bill exempts qualified enterprise zone facility bonds from the general restrictions on financing the acquisition of existing property (sec. 147(d)). Additionally, these bonds are exempted from the general restriction on financing land (or an interest therein) with 25 percent or more of the net proceeds of a bond issue (sec. 147(c)(1)(A)). Unless otherwise noted, all tax-exempt bond rules relating to exempt facility bonds shall apply to qualified enterprise zone facility bonds.

Penalty for failure to continue as zone business or to use bond-financed property in the zone business. The bill extends change-in-use rules to qualified enterprise zone facility bonds. Accordingly, interest on all bond-financed loans to a business that no longer qualifies as an enterprise zone business, or on loans to finance property that ceases to be used by the business in the enterprise zone, becomes nondeductible, effective from the first day of the taxable year in which the disqualification or cessation of use occurs. This penalty is waived if: (1) the issuer and principal user in good faith attempted to meet these requirements and (2) any failure to meet such requirements is corrected within a reasonable period after such failure is first discovered. This penalty does not apply solely by reason of the termination or revocation of a designation as an empowerment zone. The good faith rule described above also applies to certain other requirements of qualified enterprise zone facility bonds.

Partial exemption from State volume limitations. Under the bill, only 25 percent of the amount of qualified enterprise zone facility bonds is subject to the State private activity volume cap, provided that enterprise zone residents possess more than a 50-percent ownership interest in the principal user of the bond-proceeds. If the resident ownership requirement is not satisfied, then 50 percent of the qualified enterprise zone facility bonds (rather than 25 percent) is subject to the State private activity volume cap.

Exception from bank pro rata interest deduction disallowance. The bill exempts financial institutions to the extent that they have invested in qualified enterprise zone facility bonds from the general rule denying them a ratable portion of their otherwise allowable interest expense deductions (sec. 265(b)).

Tax incentives available in both empowerment zones and enterprise communities

Tax-exempt financing. Under the bill, the tax-exempt financing benefits described above are available (with one modification) to otherwise qualifying businesses that are located in enterprise communities. The one modification to the tax-exempt financing benefits is that 50 percent (rather than 25 percent) of the amount of the enterprise zone facility bonds is subject to the State private activity volume cap, regardless of whether enterprise zone residents possess more than a 50 percent ownership interest in the principal user of the bond-proceeds.

Effective Date

Empowerment zone and enterprise community designations will be made only during calendar years 1994 and 1995. The tax incentives will be available during the period that the designation remains in effect, which generally will be a period of 10 years.

[Conference Explanation]

III. Empowerment Zones and Enterprise Communities

1.Tax benefits for empowerment zones and enterprise communities

Senate Amendment

. No provision. (However, section 15001 of the Senate amendment states that it is the sense of the Senate that Congress should adopt Federal enterprise zone legislation.)

Conference Agreement

The conference agreement generally follows the House bill in providing certain tax benefits for areas designated as empowerment zones and enterprise communities. However, the conference agreement makes certain modifications regarding the designation of areas as zones or communities as well as the extent and nature of tax incentives available in such areas. [23]

Designation of eligible areas

In general. The conference agreement follows the House bill, except that Indian reservations are not eligible for designation as empowerment zones or enterprise communities. The conference agreement provides separate tax incentives for businesses operating in Indian reservations in sections 13411 and 13412. Thus, under the conference agreement, nine empowerment zones and 95 enterprise communities will be designated (subject to availability of eligible areas) during 1994 and 1995. Six empowerment zones and 65 enterprise communities will be located in eligible urban areas [24] and three empowerment zones and 30 enterprise communities will be located in rural areas. [25]

Eligibility criteria for zones. The conference agreement follows the House bill, except that, with respect to an area nominated to be an empowerment zone, the conference agreement does not allow the appropriate Secretary (the Secretary of HUD with respect to urban areas and the Secretary of Agriculture with respect to rural areas) discretion to reduce the applica-

[Footnote ¶ 3068 continued]

23. The conference agreement does not include section 15001 of the Senate amendment (the sense of the Senate resolution).

24. The conference agreement provides that, if six urban empowerment zones are designated, not less than one urban empowerment zone must be designated in an area the most populous city of which has a population of 500,000 or less, and not less than one urban empowerment zone shall be a nominated area (1) with a population of 50,000 or less, and (2) which includes areas located in two States.

25. The conference agreement does not provide for the creation of an Enterprise Board which, under the House bill, was to participate in the designation of eligible areas as empowerment zones and enterprise communities. In addition, the conference agreement does not provide a procedure for the revocation of an area's designation as an eligible zone or community. However, the conferees intend that (i) the Secretary will promulgate rules regarding both the selection and revocation processes and (ii) a designation will be revoked only after a hearing on the record involving officials of the State and local governments. The conferees further intend that, if an area's zone or community designation is revoked, the relevant Secretary shall not designate another area as a zone or community in lieu thereof.

ble poverty criteria in a nominated area. [26] In addition, as under the House bill, no area may be designated as an empowerment zone or enterprise community unless the nominating State and local governments provide written assurances that their strategic plan will be implemented. [27] "General distress" may be indicated by factors such as high crime rates, high vacancy rates, or designation of an area as a disaster area or high intensity drug trafficking area ("HIDTA") under the Anti-Drug Abuse Act of 1988; job loss (including manufacturing job loss); and economic distress due to closures of military bases or restrictions on timber harvesting. In addition, consideration should be given to communities along the U.S. border in which population has increased significantly, without a corresponding expansion of basic infrastructure, and in which a significant portion of the area's population reside in substandard housing.

Tax incentives for empowerment zones

The conference agreement provides the following tax incentives for areas designated as empowerment zones:

Employer wage credit. A 20-percent credit against income tax liability is available to all employers for the first $15,000 of qualified wages paid to each employee who (1) is a zone resident (i.e., his or her principal place of abode is within the zone [28]), and (2) performs substantially all employment services within the zone in a trade or business of the employer. The maximum credit per qualified employee is $3,000 per year. Wages paid to a qualified employee continue to be eligible for the credit if the employee earns more than $15,000, although only the first $15,000 of wages will be eligible for the credit. [29] The wage credit is available with respect to a qualified employee, regardless of the number of other employees who work for the employer or whether the employer meets the definition of an "enterprise zone business" (which applied for the increased section 179 expensing and the tax-exempt financing provisions described below). [30] The credit will be phased out beginning in 2002. The credit rate will be reduced to 15 percent in 2002, 10 percent in 2003, and five percent in 2004. The credit will not be available after December 31, 2004. Qualified wages include the first $15,000 of "wages," defined to include (1) salary and wages as generally defined for FUTA purposes, and (2) certain training and educational expenses paid on behalf of a qualified employee, provided that (a) the expenses are paid to an unrelated third party and are excludable from gross income of the employee under section 127 (which is retroactively and permanently extended under another provision of the bill), or (b) in the case of an employee under age 19, the expenses are incurred by the employer in operating a youth training program in conjunction with local education officials. The credit is allowed with respect to full-time and part-time employees. However, the employee must be employed by the employer for a minimum period of at least 90 days. Wages are not eligible for the credit if paid to certain relatives of the employer or, if the employer is a corporation or partnership, certain relatives of a person who owns more than 50 percent of the business. In addition, wages are not eligible for the credit if paid to a person who owns more than five percent of the stock (or capital or profits interests) of the employer. [31] An employer's deduction otherwise allowed for wages paid is reduced by the amount of credit

[Footnote ¶ 3068 continued]

26. With respect to an area nominated to be an enterprise community, the appropriate Secretary may reduce one of the poverty criteria by five percentage points for not more than 10 percent of the population census tracts (up to a maximum of five alternative, may reduce the 35-percent poverty threshold by 10 percentage points (i.e., to 25 percent) for up to three population census tracts.

27. The conferees intend that, in the case of an urban empowerment zone located in two States, the nominating States and local governments shall provide written assurances satisfactory to the Secretary of HUD that the incentives afforded the zone on the account of the designation will be distributed equitably between the two States.

28. The conferees intend that employers will undertake reasonable measures to verify an employee's residence within the zone, so that the employer will be able to substantiate a wage credit claimed under the conference agreement.

29. To prevent avoidance of the $15,000 limit, all employers of a controlled group of corporations (or partnerships or proprietorships under common control) will be treated as a single employer.

30. The conferees intend that employers take reasonable steps to notify all qualified zone employees of the availability to eligible individuals of advance payments of the earned income tax credit (EITC).

31. The wage credit is not available with respect to any individual employed at any facility described in present-law section 144(c)(6)(B) (i.e., a private or commercial golf course, country club, massage parlor, hot tub facility, suntan facility, racetrack or other facility used for gambling, or any store the principal business of which is the sale of alcoholic beverages for consumption off premises). In addition, the wage credit is not available with respect to any individual employed by a trade or business the principal activity of which is farming (within the meaning of subparagraphs (A) and (B) of section

claimed for that taxable year. Wages are not be taken into account for purposes of the empowerment zone employment credit if taken into account in determining the employer's targeted jobs tax credit (TJTC). The credit is allowable to offset up to 25 percent of alternative minimum tax liability.

Increased section 179 expensing. For an enterprise zone business, the expensing allowance for certain depreciable business property provided under section 179 is increased by the lesser of: (1) $20,000 or (2) the cost of section 179 property that is "qualified zone property" (as defined in the House bill) and that is placed in service during the taxable year. As under present law, the types of property eligible for section 179 expensing under this provision do not include buildings. As under present law, the section 179 expensing allowance is phased out for certain taxpayers with investment in qualified property during the taxable year above a specified threshold. However, under the conference agreement, the present-law phase-out range is applied by taking into account only one-half of the cost of qualified zone property that is section 179 property. In applying the section 179 phaseout, the cost of section 179 property that is not qualified zone property is not reduced. In general, all other provisions of present-law section 179 apply to the increased expensing for enterprise zone businesses. Thus, all component members of a controlled group are treated as one taxpayer for purposes of the expensing allowance and the application of the phaseout range (sec. 179(d)(6)). The limitations apply at both the partnership (and S corporation) and partner (and shareholder) levels. The increased expensing allowance is allowed for purposes of the alternative minimum tax (i.e., it is not treated as an adjustment for purposes of the alternative minimum tax). The section 179 expensing deduction will be recaptured if the property is not used predominantly in a enterprise zone business (under rules similar to present-law section 179(d)(10)).

Definition of "enterprise zone business". The conference agreement follows the House bill.

Tax-exempt facility bonds available for both empowerment zones and enterprise communities

In general. The conference agreement creates a new category of exempt facility private activity bonds -- qualified enterprise zone facility bonds -- for use in empowerment zones and enterprise communities. These bonds are fully subject to the State private activity bond volume limitations. Generally, qualified enterprise zone facility bonds are bonds 95 percent or more of the net proceeds of which are used to finance: (1) qualified zone property the principal user of which is a qualified enterprise zone business, and (2) functionally related and subordinate land located in the empowerment zone or enterprise community. Qualified zone property for these purposes is generally defined as under the House bill, except that it also includes property which would qualify as qualified zone property but for the fact that it is located in an enterprise community rather than in an empowerment zone. For these purposes, the term "enterprise zone business" has the same meaning generally given to it under the House bill, but also includes a business located in a zone or community which would qualify as an enterprise zone business if it were separately incorporated. [32] These bonds may only be issued while an empowerment zone or enterprise community designation is in effect.

Special rules on issue size and use to finance certain facilities. The aggregate face amount of all outstanding qualified enterprise zone bonds per qualified enterprise zone business may not exceed $3 million for each zone or community. In addition, total outstanding qualified enterprise zone bond financing for each principal user of these bonds may not exceed $20 million for all zones and communities. For purposes of these determinations, the aggregate amount of outstanding enterprise zone facility bonds allocable to any business shall be determined under rules similar to rules contained in section 144(a)(10). As with other exempt facility bonds, these bonds may be issued only to finance identified facilities. However, the $3 million-per-enterprise zone busi-

[Footnote ¶ 3068 continued]

2032A(e)(5)), but only if, as of the close of the preceding taxable year, the sum of the aggregate unadjusted bases (or, if greater, the fair market value) of assets of the farm exceed $500,000.

32. For example, an establishment which is part of a national chain could qualify as an enterprise zone business for purposes of the tax-exempt financing incentive, provided that such establishment would satisfy the definition of an enterprise zone business if it were separately incorporated.

ness requirement should not limit issuance of a single issue of bonds (in excess of $3 million) for more than one identified facility, provided that the $3 million limit is satisfied with respect to each zone business. The conferees recognize that it may be necessary to permit common marketing of separate issues of bonds for discrete facilities (if such issues are simultaneous or proximate in time) to enable qualified enterprise zone facility bonds to be marketed in a manner comparable to other exempt facility bonds. The conference agreement exempts qualified enterprise zone facility bonds from the general restrictions on financing the acquisition of existing property (sec. 147(d)). Additionally, these bonds are exempted from the general restriction on financing land (or an interest therein) with 25 percent or more of the net proceeds of a bond issue (sec. 147(c)(1)(A)). Unless otherwise noted, all other tax-exempt bond rules relating to exempt facility bonds (including the restrictions on bank deductibility of interest allocable to tax-exempt bonds) apply to qualified enterprise zone facility bonds.

Penalty for failure to continue as zone business or to use bond-financed property in the zone business. The conference agreement extends change-in-use rules to qualified enterprise zone facility bonds. Accordingly, interest on all bond-financed loans to a business that no longer qualifies as an enterprise zone business, or on loans to finance property that ceases to be used by the business in the empowerment zone or enterprise community, becomes nondeductible, effective from the first day of the taxable year in which the disqualification or cessation of use occurs. This penalty is waived if: (1) the issuer and principal user in good faith attempted to meet these requirements and (2) any failure to meet such requirements is corrected within a reasonable period after such failure is first discovered. This penalty does not apply solely by reason of the termination or revocation of a designation as an empowerment zone or enterprise community. The good faith rule described above also applies to certain other requirements of qualified enterprise zone facility bonds.

Effective date

The conference agreement follows the House bill.

[¶3070] Section 13311. Credit for Contributions to Certain Community Development Corporations

(Code Sec. 38)

[House Explanation]

Present Law

There are no tax credits available for contributions to community development corporations (CDC).

Reasons for Change

The committee believes that special consideration should be given to the problems of distressed urban and rural areas. Revitalization of economically distressed areas through expanded business and employment opportunities, especially for residents of those distressed areas, should help alleviate both economic and social problems. The committee believes it is important to encourage participation of the private sector in these revitalization efforts.

Explanation of Provision

Under the provision, a taxpayer will receive a credit for qualified cash contributions made to certain community development corporations (CDCs). If a taxpayer makes a qualified contribution, the credit may be claimed by the taxpayer for each taxable year during a 10-year period beginning with the taxable year during which the contribution was made. The credit that may be claimed for each year is equal to five percent of the amount of the contribution to the CDC. Thus, during the 10-year credit period, the taxpayer may claim aggregate credit amounts totalling 50 percent of the contribution.

For purposes of this provision, a qualified contribution is defined as any transfer of cash that meets the following requirements: (1) it is made to one of up to 10 CDCs selected by the Secretary of HUD, provided that the contribution is made during the five-year period after the CDC is so selected by the Secretary of HUD; (2) the amount is available for use by the CDC for at least 10 years; [196] (3) the contribution is to be used by the CDC to provide qualified low-income assistance '[197] within its operational area; and (4) the CDC designates the contribution as eligible for the credit. The aggregate amount of contributions which may be designated by a selected CDC as eligible for the credit may not exceed $4 million.

Prior to July 1, 1994, the Secretary of HUD may select up to 10 CDCs as eligible to participate in the program (subject to the availability of eligible CDCs). [198] To be selected, a CDC must have the following characteristics: (1) it must be a tax-exempt charity described in section 501(c)(3) of the Code; (2) its principal purposes must include promoting employment and business opportunities for individuals who are residents of its operational area; and (3) its operational area must (a) meet the geographic limitations that would apply if the area were designated as an empowerment zone or enterprise community, (b) have an unemployment rate that is not less than the national average, and (c) have a median family income which does not exceed 80 percent of the median family income of residents within the jurisdiction of the local government.

The credit is subject to the general business credit limitations of section 38 and, therefore, may not be used to reduce tentative minimum tax.

Effective Date

The provision is effective on the date of enactment.

[Conference Explanation]

Conference Agreement

The conference agreement follows the House bill, except that the aggregate amount of contributions which may be designated by a selected CDC as eligible for the credit may not exceed $2 million, and the Secretary of HUD may select up to 20 CDCs as eligible to participate in the program. [72] In addition, the conferees intend that, in selecting CDCs, the Secretary of HUD shall give priority to corporations with a demonstrated record of performance in administering community development programs which target at least 75 percent of the jobs emanating from their investment funds to low income or unemployed individuals.

[¶ 3071] Section 13321. Accelerated Depreciation for Property on Indian Reservations

(Code Sec. 168)

[Conference Report]

Present Law

The Internal Revenue Code does not contain general rules that target specific geographic areas for special Federal income tax treatment. Within certain Code sections, however, there are definitions of targeted areas for limited purposes (e.g., low-income housing credit and qualified mortgage bond provisions target certain economically distressed areas). In addition, present law provides favorable Federal income tax treatment for certain U.S. corporations that operate in Puerto Rico, the U.S. Virgin Islands, or a possession of the United Stated to encourage the conduct of trades or businesses within these areas.

House Bill

No provision.

[Footnote ¶ 3069 continued]

196. The contribution of the CDC must be available for use by the CDC for up to a 10-year period, but need not meet the requirements of a "contribution or gift" for purposes of section 170. In other words, a contribution eligible for the credit under the bill may be made in the form of a 10-year loan (or other long-term investment), the principal of which is to be returned to the taxpayer after the 10-year period. However, in the case of a donation of cash made by a taxpayer to an eligible CDC, the taxpayer would be allowed to claim a charitable contribution deduction (subject to the present-law rules under section 170) and, in addition, could claim the credit under the bill's provisions.

'197. The bill defines "qualified low-income assistance" as assistance (1) which is designed to provide employment and business opportunities to individuals who are residents of the operational area of the CDC, and (2) which is approved by the Secretary of HUD.

198. At least four of the selected CDCs must operate in rural areas.

72. Under the conference agreement, at least eight of the selected CDCs must operate in rural areas.

Senate Amendment

In general

Under the Senate amendment, businesses located on Indian reservations [1] generally are allowed a credit against income tax liability for certain investments (the "Indian reservation credit") and a credit against income tax liability for certain wages and health insurance costs (the "Indian employment credit").

Indian reservation credit

A credit against income tax liability is allowed for investments in certain property located or used within an Indian reservation which has a level of unemployment that greatly exceeds the national average. In general, the amount of the credit allowed a taxpayer for any taxable year equals the sum of: (1) 10 percent of the qualified investment in "reservation personal property" placed in service by the taxpayer during the taxable year; and (2) 15 percent of the qualified investment in "new reservation construction property" and "reservation infrastructure investment" placed in service by the taxpayer during the taxable year.

The full amount of the credit is allowed only if the Indian unemployment rate [2] on the applicable Indian reservation exceeds 300 percent of the national average unemployment rate at any time during the calendar year in which the property is placed in service or during either of the immediately preceding two calendar years. [3] If the Indian unemployment rate on the applicable Indian reservation exceeds 150 percent but does not exceed 300 percent of the national average unemployment rate at any time during the relevant calendar years, then only one-half of the otherwise allowable credit may be claimed (i.e., the credit rates are 7.5 percent and 5 percent). If the Indian unemployment rate on the applicable Indian reservation does not exceed 150 percent of the national average unemployment rate at any time during the relevant calendar years, then no credit is allowed.

For purposes of the credit, "reservation personal property" is defined as property: (1) for which a depreciation deduction is allowable under section 168 of the Code; (2) which is not nonresidential real property, residential rental property, or any other real property with a class life of more than 12.5 years; (3) which is used by the taxpayer predominantly in the active conduct of a trade or business within an Indian reservation; and (4) which is not used or located outside the Indian reservation on any regular basis.

In addition, "new reservation construction property" is defined as property: (1) which is nonresidential real property, residential rental property, or any other real property with a class life of more than 12.5 years for which a depreciation deduction is allowable under section 168 of the Code; (2) which is located in an Indian reservation; (3) which is used by the taxpayer predominantly in the active conduct of a trade or business within an Indian reservation; [4] and (4) which is originally placed in service by the taxpayer.

Further, "reservation infrastructure investment" is defined as property: (1) for which a depreciation deduction is allowable under section 168 of the Code (whether real or personal property); (2) which benefits the tribal infrastructure; (3) which is available to the general public; and (4) which is placed in service in connection with the taxpayer's active conduct of a trade or business within an Indian reservation. The term "reservation infrastructure investment" is to include otherwise qualifying property that is used or located outside an In-

[Footnote ¶3071 continued]

[Footnote ¶3071] 1. For purposes of the Indian employment and investment incentives, the term "Indian reservation" means a reservation as defined in (1) section 3(d) of the Indian Financing Act of 1974 (25 U.S.C. 1452(d)), as in effect on the date of enactment of the provision, or (2) section 4(10) of the Indian Child Welfare Act of 1978 (25 U.S.C. 1903(10)), as in effect on the date of enactment of the provision.

2. The Indian unemployment rate is to be based on the number of Indians unemployed and able to work and is to be certified by the Secretary of the Interior.

3. A special rule applies to qualifying property that has (or is a component of a project that has) an estimated construction period of more than two years or a cost of more than $1 million. With respect to such property, the relevant unemployment rate is the rate during the calendar year in which the taxpayer enters into a binding agreement to make a qualified investment (or, if earlier, the first calendar year in which the taxpayer has expended at least 10 percent of the qualified investment) or during the immediately preceding calendar year.

4. The active conduct of a trade or business for purposes of the Indian reservation credit includes the rental to others of real property located in an Indian reservation. In addition, the credit for new reservation construction property is allowed with respect to otherwise qualifying property that is used to furnish lodging.

dian reservation only if the purpose of the property is to connect to existing tribal infrastructure in the reservation (including, but not limited to, roads, power lines, water systems, railroad spurs, and communications facilities).

Notwithstanding the above definitions, property will not qualify for the Indian reservation credit if the property is acquired (directly or indirectly) by the taxpayer from a person who is related to the taxpayer (within the meaning of section 465(b) (3) (C) of the Code). In addition, property will not qualify for the credit if the property (or any portion thereof) is placed in service for purposes of conducting or housing certain gaming activities. [5] Finally, property will not qualify for the Indian reservation credit if the energy credit or the rehabilitation credit is allowed with respect to the property.

In the case of reservation personal property and new reservation construction property, the qualified investment for purposes of determining the amount of the credit is the taxpayer's basis in the property. In the case of reservation infrastructure investment, the qualified investment for purposes of determining the amount of the credit is the amount expended by the taxpayer for the acquisition or construction of the property. The at-risk rules of section 49 of the Code also apply in determining the amount of the qualified investment for purposes of the Indian reservation credit.

The basis of new reservation construction property is reduced by the full amount of the credit allowed with respect to the property. The basis of reservation personal property and reservation infrastructure investment is reduced by only 50 percent of the credit allowed with respect to the property. The Indian reservation credit is recaptured (i.e., the amount of tax due is increased) if, before the end of the applicable recovery period with respect to the property, the property is disposed of by the taxpayer, or, in the case of reservation personal property, is removed from the Indian reservation, converted, or otherwise ceases to be reservation personal property with respect to the taxpayer.

Effective date

Under the Senate amendment, the Indian reservation credit applies to property placed in service after December 31, 1993.

Conference Agreement

The conference agreement provides the following tax incentives for Indian reservations. [6]

Accelerated Depreciation

With respect to certain property used in connection with the conduct of a trade or business within an Indian reservation, depreciation deductions for purposes of section 168 will be determined using the following recovery periods:

3-year property	2 years
5-year property	3 years
7-year property	4 years
10-year property	6 years
15-year property	9 years
20-year property	12 years
Nonresidential real property	22 years

"Qualified Indian reservation property" eligible for accelerated depreciation includes property which is (1) used by the taxpayer predominantly in the active conduct of a trade or business within an Indian reservation [7] (2) not used or located outside the reservation on a regular basis, (3) not acquired (directly or indirectly) by the taxpayer from a person who is related to the taxpayer (within the meaning of section 465(b)(43)(C)), and (4) described in the recovery-period table above. [8] In addition, property is not "qualified Indian reservation property" if it is placed in service for pur-

[Footnote ¶3071 continued]

5. The limitation applies to class I, II, or III gaming as defined in section 4 of the Indian Regulatory Act (25 U.S.C. 2703), as in effect on the date of enactment of the provision.

6. As under the Senate amendment, the term "Indian reservation" means a reservation as defined in (1) section 3(d) of the Indian Financing Act of 1974 (25 U.S.C. 1452(d)), as in effect on the date of enactment of this provision, or (2) section 4(10) of the Indian Child Welfare Act of 1978 (25 U.S.C. 1903(10)), as in effect on the date of enactment of this provision.

7. The conference agreement treats the rental of real property located within a reservation as an active trade or business.

8. In addition, the conference agreement provides that accelerated depreciation is not available for any property to which the alternative depreciation system under section 168(g) applies (determined without regard to subsection 168(g) (7) and after application of section 280F(b)).

poses of conducting gaming activities. [9]

The conference agreement includes a special rule for "qualified infrastructure property" which may be eligible for the accelerated depreciation even if located outside an Indian reservation, provided that the purpose of such property is to connect with qualified infrastructure property located within the reservation (e.g., roads, power lines, water systems, railroad spurs, and communications facilities). For this purpose, "qualified infrastructure property" must be property that is (1) allowed a depreciation deduction under section 168, (2) benefits the tribal infrastructure, (3) available to the general public, and (4) placed in service in connection with the taxpayer's active conduct of a trade or business within a reservation.

The depreciation deduction allowed for regular tax purposes is also allowed for purposes of the alternative minimum tax.

Effective Date

The accelerated depreciation for Indian reservations is available with respect to property placed in service on or after January 1, 1994, and before December 31, 2003.

[¶ 3071A] Section 13322. Indian Employment Credit

(Code Sec. 45A)

[Conference Report]

Present Law

The Internal Revenue Code does not contain general rules that target specific geographic areas for special Federal income tax treatment. Within certain Code sections, however, there are definitions of targeted areas for limited purposes (e.g., low-income housing credit and qualified mortgage bond provisions target certain economically distressed areas). In addition, present law provides favorable Federal income tax treatment for certain U.S. corporations that operate in Puerto Rico, the U.S. Virgin Islands, or a possession of the United Stated to encourage the conduct of trades or businesses within these areas.

House Bill

No provision.

Senate Amendment

In general

Under the Senate amendment, businesses located on Indian reservations [1] generally are allowed a credit against income tax liability for certain investments (the "Indian reservation credit") and a credit against income tax liability for certain wages and health insurance costs (the "Indian employment credit").

Indian employment credit

A credit against income tax liability is also allowed to employers for certain wages and health insurance costs paid or incurred by the employer with respect to certain employees. In general, the amount of the credit allowed an employer for any taxable year equals 10 percent [2] of the sum of (1) the wages paid or incurred by the employer for services performed by an employee while the employee is a qualified employee ("qualified wages"); [3] and (2) the amount paid or incurred by the employer for health insurance (other than health insurance provided pursuant to a salary reduction arrangement) to the extent that such amount is attributable to coverage provided to an employee while the employee is a qualified employee ("qualified employee health insurance costs").

[Footnote ¶ 3071A continued]

9. For this purpose, gaming activities include class I, II, or III gaming, as defined in section 4 of the Indian Regulatory Act (25 U.S.C. sec. 2703), as in effect on the date of enactment of this provision.

[Footnote ¶ 3071A] 1. For purposes of the Indian employment and investment incentives, the term "Indian reservation" means a reservation as defined in (1) section 3(d) of the Indian Financing Act of 1974 (25 U.S.C. 1452(d)), as in effect on the date of enactment of the provision, or (2) section 4(10) of the Indian Child Welfare Act of 1978 (25 U.S.C. 1903(10)), as in effect on the date of enactment of the provision.

2. If, for the entire taxable year of the employer, at least 85 percent of the employees of the employer are enrolled members of an Indian tribe or spouses of enrolled members of an Indian tribe, then the amount of the credit for such taxable year is to be determined by using a 30-percent rate rather than the 10-percent rate.

3. Wages are not eligible for the credit if attributable to services rendered by an employee during the first year he or she begins work for the employer if any portion of such wages is taken into account in determining the targeted jobs tax credit (TJTC) under present-law section 51.

The credit is available to an employer, however, only to the extent its qualified wages and health insurance costs during the current year exceed such wages and costs incurred by the employer during 1993. Specifically, the amount of the credit allowed an employer for any taxable year is limited to an amount equal to the credit rate multiplied by the excess (if any) of (1) the sum of the qualified wages and qualified health insurance costs paid or incurred by the employer during the taxable year with respect to employees whose wages (which are paid or incurred by the employer) for such taxable year do not exceed the amount determined at an annual rate of $30,000 (as adjusted for inflation for years beginning after 1993), over (2) the sum of the qualified wages and qualified health insurance costs paid or incurred by the employer (or any predecessor) during the 1993 calendar year with respect to employees whose wages (which are paid or incurred by the employer or any predecessor) for such taxable year do not exceed the amount determined at an annual rate of $30,000. [4] For purposes of this limitation, all employees of a controlled group of corporations (or partnerships or proprietorships under common control) are treated as employed by a single employer.

In general, an individual is a qualified employee of an employer for any period only if: (1) the individual is an enrolled member of an Indian tribe or the spouse of an enrolled member of an Indian tribe; [5] (2) substantially all of the services performed during such period by the employee for such employer are performed within an Indian reservation; (3) the principal place of abode of the employee while performing such services is on or near the Indian reservation within which the services are performed; and (4) the employee began work for such employer on or after January 1, 1994.

An employee may be treated as a qualified employee for a maximum period of seven years after the day on which the employee first begins work for the employer. In addition, an employee will not be treated as a qualified employee for any taxable year of the employer if the total amount of wages paid or incurred by the employer with respect to such employee during such taxable year (whether or not for services rendered within the Indian reservation) exceeds an amount determined at an annual rate of $30,000 (as adjusted for inflation for years beginning after 1993). Further, an employee will be treated as a qualified employee for a taxable year of the employer only if more than 50 percent of the wages paid or incurred by the employer to such employee during such taxable year are for services performed in a trade or business of the employer.

Qualified employees do not include certain relatives or dependents of the employer (described under present-law section 51(i)(1)) or, if the employer is a corporation, certain relatives of a person who owns more than 50 percent of the corporation. In addition, any person who owns more than five percent of the stock of the employer (or if the employer is not a corporation, more than five percent of the capital or profits interests in the employer) cannot be a qualified employee. Finally, a qualified employee does not include any individual if the services performed by the individual for the employer involve certain gaming activities or are performed in a building housing such gaming activities. [6]

The Indian employment credit is allowed with respect to full-time and part-time employees. However, if an employee is terminated less than one year after the date of initial employment, the amount of credits previously claimed by the employer with respect to that employee generally is recaptured (unless the employee voluntarily leaves, becomes disabled, or is fired due to misconduct).

An employer's deduction otherwise allowed for wages is reduced by the amount of the

[Footnote ¶ 3071A continued]

4. In the case of a short taxable year, the qualified wages and the qualified health insurance costs paid or incurred by the employer are to be annualized and the limitation for such taxable year is to equal the otherwise applicable limitation determined using such annualized amounts multiplied by a fraction, the numerator of which is the number of days in the taxable year and the denominator of which is 365.

5. For this purpose, an Indian tribe is defined as any Indian tribe, band, nation, pueblo, or other organized group or community, including any Alaska Native village, or regional or village corporation, as defined in, or established pursuant to, the Alaska Native Claims Settlement Act (43 U.S.C. 1601 et. seq.), as in effect on the date of enactment of the provision, which is recognized as eligible for the special programs and services provided by the United States to Indians because of their status as Indians.

6. The limitation applies to class I, II, or III gaming as defined in section 4 of the Indian Regulatory Act (25 U.S.C. 2703), as in effect on the date of enactment of the provision.

credit claimed for the taxable year. The Senate amendment also provides that the employment credit is not refundable. Finally, the Indian employment credit is subject to the general business credit limitations of section 38, [7] and, therefore, the credit may not be used to reduce tentative minimum tax.

Effective date

Under the Senate amendment, the Indian employment credit applies to wages paid or incurred after December 31, 1993.

Conference Agreement

The conference agreement provides the following tax incentives for Indian reservations. [8]

Indian employment credit

The conference agreement follows the Senate amendment, except that (1) a single-rate 20-percent credit applies (rather than the two-tiered 10-percent and 30-percent credit rates of the Senate amendment); and (2) the credit is available only for the first $20,000 of qualified wages and qualified employee health insurance costs paid to each qualified employee.

As under the Senate amendment, a tribal member or spouse is a qualified employee only if he or she works on a reservation (and lives on or near that reservation) and is paid wages that do not exceed $30,000 annually. [9] The credit is an incremental credit, such that an employer's current-year qualified wages and qualified employee health insurance costs (up to $20,000 per employee) are eligible for the credit only to the extent that the sum of such costs exceeds the sum of comparable costs paid during 1993 to employees whose wages did not exceed $30,000.

Effective date

The wage credit is available for wages paid or incurred on or after January 1, 1994, in a taxable year that begins before December 31, 2003.

[¶ 3072] Section 13401. Disclosure of Return Information for Administration of Certain Veterans Programs

(Code Sec. 6103)

[House Explanation]

Present Law

The Internal Revenue Code prohibits disclosure of tax returns and return information, except to the extent specifically authorized by the Internal Revenue Code (sec. 6103). Unauthorized disclosure is a felony punishable by a fine not exceeding $5,000 or imprisonment of not more than five years, or both (sec. 7213). An action for civil damages also may be brought for unauthorized disclosure (sec. 7431).

Among the disclosures permitted under the Code is disclosure to the Department of Veterans Affairs ("DVA") of self-employment tax information and certain tax information supplied to the Internal Revenue Service and Social Security Administration by third parties. Disclosure is permitted to assist DVA in determining eligibility for, and establishing correct benefit amounts under, certain of its needs-based pension and other programs (sec. 6103(l)(7)(D)(viii)). The income tax returns filed by the veterans themselves are not disclosed to DVA.

The DVA is required to comply with the safeguards currently contained in the Code and in section 1137(c) of the Social Security Act (governing the use of disclosed tax information). These safeguards include independent verification of tax data, notification to the individual concerned, and the opportunity to contest agency findings based on such information.

7. No portion of the unused business credit for any taxable year that is attributable to the Indian employment credit may be carried back to a taxable year ending before the date of enactment of the provision.

8. As under the Senate amendment, the term "Indian reservation" means a reservation as defined in (1) section 3(d) of the Indian Financing Act of 1974 (25 U.S.C. 1452(d)), as in effect on the date of enactment of this provision, or (2) section 4(10) of the Indian Child Welfare Act of 1978 (25 U.S.C. 1903(10)), as in effect on the date of enactment of this provision.

9. The $30,000 amount for determining qualified employees is adjusted for inflation beginning after 1994.

The DVA disclosure provision is scheduled to expire after September 30, 1997.

Reasons for Change

The committee believes that it is appropriate to extend the authority to disclose tax information to DVA for an additional year to provide sufficient time to assess the impact of such disclosure on taxpayers' voluntary compliance with the tax laws.

Explanation of Provision

The bill extends the authority to disclose tax information to the DVA for one year, through September 30, 1998.

Effective Date

The provision applies after September 30, 1997.

[Conference Report]

The conference agreement follows the House bill and section 7901 of the Senate amendment.

[¶3073] Section 13402. Disclosure of Return Information to Carry Out Income Contingent Repayment of Student Loans

(Code Sec. 6103)

[House Explanation]

Present Law

The Internal Revenue Code prohibits disclosure of tax returns and return information except to the extent specifically authorized by the Code (sec. 6103). Unauthorized disclosure is a felony punishable by a fine not exceeding $5,000 or imprisonment of not more than five years, or both (sec. 7213). An action for civil damages also may be brought for unauthorized disclosure (sec. 7431). No tax information may be furnished by the Internal Revenue Service (IRS) to another agency unless the other agency establishes procedures satisfactory to the IRS for safeguarding the tax information it receives (sec. 6103(p)).

The IRS may disclose to the Department of Education the mailing address of taxpayers who have defaulted on certain student loans. The Department of Education may in turn make this information available to its agents and to the holders of such loans (and their agents) for the purpose of locating the taxpayers and collecting the loan.

Reasons for Change

The committee believes that the Department of Education should be provided with access to tax return information to assist it carrying out modifications of the Federal student loan program. One component of those modifications will permit students to elect to repay their loans on an income-contingent basis: the amount of each loan payment would be proportional to the former student's income.

The committee, however, is also concerned about the increasing number of requests for disclosure of confidential tax information for nontax purposes and the effect of such disclosure on voluntary taxpayer compliance. Accordingly, only the Department of Education and its employees have been given access to the tax return information necessary to implement income-contingent repayment and the access has been granted only temporarily. The committee also believes that any plan to involve further the IRS in loan collection should be thoroughly studied before implementing legislation is proposed.

Explanation of Provision

The bill gives the Department of Education access to certain tax return information in order to implement this direct student loan program. The only information the Department of Education is permitted to obtain is the name, address, taxpayer identification number, filing status, and adjusted gross income of the former student. Disclosure of this information may be made only to Department of Education employees and may only be used by these employees in establishing the appropriate income-contingent repayment amount for an applicable student loan. Applicable student loans are loans under the new direct student loan program and other student loans that are in default and have been assigned to the Department of Education. The Department of Education and its employees would be subject to the restrictions on unauthorized disclosure in present law. The committee anticipates that information will be provided by means of low-cost computer exchanges of information.

The bill also permits the Department of Education to obtain the mailing address of any taxpayer who owes an overpayment (i.e., has received more than the proper amount) on a Federal Pell Grant or who has defaulted on certain additional student loans administered by the Department of Education.

The bill requires the Treasury Department, in consultation with the Department of Education, to conduct a study of the feasibility of student loan repayment through wage withholding or other means involving the Internal Revenue Service. The study is to include an examination of (1) whether the IRS could conduct such a system of student loan repayment within its current resources and without impairing its ability to collect tax revenues, (2) the impact of increased disclosure of tax information on voluntary compliance with the tax laws, (3) the effect of such a system of student loan repayment on collections and repayment of such loans, and (4) the ability of the IRS to service student loans. The study must be submitted to the Congress within six months of the date of enactment. If the Treasury Department finds that the IRS's current resources are inadequate to permit the IRS to increase its involvement in student loan collection, then it should identify the amount of additional resources or appropriations needed.

The authority to disclose tax information to the Department of Education for purposes of establishing the direct student loan program expires on September 30, 1998.

The authority to permit the Department of Education to obtain the mailing address of any taxpayer who owes an overpayment on a Federal Pell Grant or who has defaulted on certain additional student loans administered by the Department of Education is permanent.

Effective Date

The provision is effective on the date of enactment.

[Conference Report]

Access to certain tax return information to implement direct student loan program

With respect to this provision, the conference agreement follows section 14402 of the House bill and section 7902 of the Senate amendment.

Access to mailing addresses of taxpayers owing overpayments of Pell Grants

With respect to this provision, the conference agreement follows section 14402 of the House bill and section 7902 of the Senate amendment.

Evaluation of student loan repayment through wage withholding

With respect to this provision, the conference agreement does not include the provisions in sections 4032, 4033, or 14402 of the House bill or sections 12011 or 12055 of the Senate amendment.

The conferees direct the Treasury Department, in consultation with the Department of Education, to conduct a study of the feasibility of implementing a system for the repayment of Federal student loans through wage withholding or other means involving the IRS. Such study should include an examination of: (1) whether the IRS could implement such a system of student loan repayment with its current resources and without adversely affecting its ability to collect tax revenues, (2) the cumulative impact of increased disclosure of tax information and increased IRS involvement in nontax collection activities on voluntary compliance with the tax laws, (3) the ability of the IRS to enforce collection of student loans using an alternate system of dispute resolution, penalties, and collection devices, (4) the effect of separating loan collection from other loan servicing functions, and (5) the anticipated effect on the management of Federal student loan collections and on borrower repayment of such loans. If the study concludes that IRS collection is feasible, the Treasury Department and the Department of Education should develop a plan to implement such a collection system. The feasibility study and any plan that is developed, together with any legislative recommendations that the Secretaries may deem advisable, should be submitted to the Congress within six months of the date of enactment.

Effective date

The provisions in the conference agreement are effective on the date of enactment.

[¶ 3074] Section 13403. Use of Return Information for Income Verification

Under Certain Housing Assistance Programs

(Code Sec. 6103)

[Senate Explanation]

Present Law

The Internal Revenue Code prohibits disclosure of tax returns and return information, except to the extent specifically authorized by the Internal Revenue Code (sec. 6103). Unauthorized disclosure is a felony punishable by a fine not exceeding $5,000 or imprisonment of not more than five years, or both (sec. 7213). An action for civil damages also may be brought for unauthorized disclosure (sec. 7431). No tax information may be furnished by the IRS to another agency unless the other agency establishes procedures satisfactory to the IRS for safeguarding the tax information it receives (sec. 6103(p)).

Reasons for Change

The committee believes that the Department of Housing and Urban Development (HUD) should be provided with access to certain items of tax information to assist HUD in determining eligibility for, and establishing correct benefit levels under, certain HUD programs.

The committee, however, is also concerned about the increasing number of requests for disclosure of confidential tax information for nontax purposes and the effect of such disclosure on voluntary taxpayer compliance. Accordingly, HUD's access to tax information has been granted only temporarily to provide the Treasury Department sufficient time to conduct a study on the effectiveness of such disclosure and HUD's compliance with safeguards contained in the Code.

Explanation of Provision

The bill permits disclosure of certain tax information with respect to applicants for, and participants in, certain HUD programs. Such disclosure may be made only to HUD employees and is to be used solely in verifying the taxpayer's eligibility for (or correct amount of benefits under) those HUD programs. The committee anticipates that information will be provided by means of low cost computer exchanges of information. The bill extends the current law restrictions on unauthorized disclosure to HUD and its employees. HUD employees may not redisclose tax information to State or local housing agencies, public housing authorities, or any other third party. However, they may inform such parties of the fact that a discrepancy exists between the information provided by the applicant (or participant) and information provided by other sources.

Effective Date

The provision is effective on the date of enactment. The authority to disclose tax information to HUD under the bill expires after September 30, 1998.

[Conference Report]

The conference agreement follows section 7903 of the Senate amendment. The conferees anticipate that information will be provided to HUD by means of low-cost computer exchanges of information. The conferees intend that the Treasury Department, in consultation with HUD, shall conduct a study to determine (1) whether the tax return information disclosed to HUD is being used effectively, (2) whether HUD is complying with the Code's safeguards against unauthorized disclosure of the information, and (3) the impact on the privacy rights of applicants and participants in HUD housing programs. The study shall be submitted to the tax-writing committees before January 1, 1998.

[¶ 3076] Section 13421 and 13422. Excise Tax on Certain Vaccines Made Permanent; Continuation Coverage Under Group Health Plans of Costs of Pediatric Vaccines

(Code Sec. 4131, 4980B(f), 9510)

[House Explanation]

Present Law

The Vaccine Injury Compensation Trust Fund ("Vaccine Trust Fund") provides a source of revenue to compensate individuals who are injured (or die) as a result of the administration of certain vaccines: diphtheria, pertussis, and tetanus ("DPT"); diphtheria and tetanus ("DT"); measles, mumps, and rubella ("MMR"); and polio. The Vaccine Trust Fund provides the funding source for the National Vaccine Injury Compensation Program ("Program"), which provides a substitute, Federal "no-fault" insurance system for the State-law tort and private liability insurance systems otherwise applicable to vaccine manufacturers.

Under the Program, all persons who were immunized with a covered vaccine after the effective date of the Program, October 1, 1988, are prohibited from commencing a civil action in State court for vaccine-related damages unless they first file a petition with the United States Claims Court, where such petitions are assigned to a special master and governed by streamlined procedural rules designed to expedite the proceedings. [200] In these cases, the Federal Government is the respondent party in the proceedings, and the claimant generally must show only that certain medical conditions (or death) followed the administration of a covered vaccine and that the first onset of symptoms occurred within a prescribed time period. [201] Compensation under the Program generally is limited to actual and projected unreimbursed medical, rehabilitative, and custodial expenses, lost earnings, pain and suffering (or, in the event of death, a recovery for the estate) up to $250,000, and reasonable attorney's fees. [202] Only if the final settlement under the Program is rejected may the claimant proceed with a civil tort action in the appropriate State court, where recovery generally will be governed by State tort law principles [203], subject to certain limitations and specifications imposed by the National Childhood Vaccine Injury Act of 1986. [204]

The Vaccine Trust Fund is funded by a manufacturer's excise tax on DPT, DT, MMR, and polio vaccines (and any other vaccines used to prevent these diseases). Prior to the expiration of the vaccine excise tax, the excise tax per dose was $4.56 for DPT, $0.06 for DT, $4.44 for MMR, and $0.29 for polio vaccines.

The vaccine excise tax expired after December 31, 1992. Amounts in the Vaccine Trust Fund are available for the payment of compensation under the Program with respect to vaccines administered after September 30, 1988, and before October 1, 1992.

Reasons For Change

To enhance compliance with the nation's childhood immunization efforts, the committee believes it is appropriate to extend permanently the vaccine excise taxes and the authority for compensation to be paid from the Vaccine Trust Fund for certain damages resulting from the administration of vaccines. In addition, the committee believes it is appropriate that the Secretary of the Treasury, in consultation with the Secretary of Health and Human Services, study the administration of the National Vaccine Injury Compensation Program and Vaccine Trust Fund to determine whether additional vaccines should be included in the Program or other modifications (such as adjustments to the excise tax rates) are warranted. The committee also believes it is ap-

[Footnote ¶ 3071A continued]

200. Persons who received vaccines before the Program's effective date of October 1, 1988 ("retrospective cases") also may be eligible for compensation under the Program if they had not yet received compensation and elected to file a petition with the United States Claims Court on or before January 31, 1991. Under the program, awards in retrospective cases are somewhat limited compared to "prospective cases" (i.e., those where the vaccine was administered on or after October 1, 1988). Awards in retrospective cases are not paid out of the Vaccine Trust Fund but are paid out of funds specially authorized by Congress. See 42 U.S.C. sec. 300aa-15(i), (j) (appropriating $80 million for fiscal year 1989 and for each subsequent year).

201. Compensation may not be awarded, however, if there is a preponderance of the evidence that the claimant's condition or death resulted from factors unrelated to the vaccine in question.

202. 42 U.S.C. sec. 300aa-15. The committee wishes to clarify its understanding that amounts received by a claimant from the Vaccine Trust Fund constitute damages received on account of personal injuries or sickness for purposes of the exlusion from gross income provided by the general rules of section 104(a)(2).

203. In most State proceedings, significant issues arise whether injuries suffered by an individual after immunization were, in fact, caused by the vaccine administered and whether the manufacturer was at fault in either the manufacturer or marketing of the vaccine.

204. Title III, P.L. 99-660. This Act preempts State tort law to a limited extent by imposing limits on recovery from vaccine manufacturers. Among the limitations are a prohibition on compensation if the injury or death resulted from side effects that were unavoidable; a presumption that manufacturers are not negligent in manufacturing or marketing vaccines if they complied, in all material respects, with Federal Food and Drug Administration requirements; and limits on punitive damage awards.

propriate to facilitate the financing of the childhood immunization program through the establishment of a new trust fund.

Explanation Of Provisions

Permanent extension of excise tax and Program funding

The bill permanently extends the excise taxes imposed on certain vaccines. Authorization for compensation to be paid from the Vaccine Trust Fund under the National Vaccine Injury Compensation Program for certain damages resulting from vaccines administered after September 30, 1988, also is permanently extended. [205]

Study

The Secretary of the Treasury, in consultation with the Secretary of Health and Human Services, is directed to conduct a study of: (1) the estimated amount that will be paid from the Vaccine Trust Fund with respect to vaccines administered after September 30, 1988; (2) the rates of vaccine-related injury or death with respect to various types of vaccines; (3) new vaccines and immunization practices being developed or used for which amounts may be paid from the Vaccine Trust Fund; (4) whether additional vaccines should be included in the National Vaccine Injury Compensation Program; and (5) the appropriate treatment of vaccines produced by State governmental entities. Not later than one year after the date of enactment, the Secretary of the Treasury must submit a report detailing his findings to the House Committee on Ways and Means and the Senate Committee on Finance.

Childhood immunization program trust fund

The bill establishes a new Childhood Immunization Trust Fund ("Childhood Trust Fund") in the Internal Revenue Code. Monies in the Childhood Trust Fund are to be available, subject to appropriations Acts, for the childhood immunization entitlement program (under part A of subtitle 3 of title XXI of the Public Health Service Act), adopted by the Committee on Energy and Commerce as part of its reconciliation recommendations.

Maintenance-of-effort requirement in childhood immunization program

The bill makes the failure of health plans that provide coverage for the cost of pediatric vaccines as of May 1, 1993, to continue to provide that coverage subject to the excise tax penalty (under sec. 4980B(f)) applicable to plans that fail to provide COBRA continuation coverage.

Effective Date

The extension of coverage under the National Vaccine Injury Compensation Program is effective for vaccines administered on or after October 1, 1992. The extension of the vaccine excise taxes is effective on the date of enactment, with a floor stocks tax imposed on vaccines purchased after December 31, 1992, that are being held for sale or use on the date of enactment.

The maintenance-of-effort requirement applies to plans years beginning after the date of enactment.

[Conference Report]

Senate Amendment

Permanent extension of excise tax and Program funding

The Senate amendment is the same as the House bill.

Study

No provision.

Childhood immunization program trust fund

No provision for a childhood immunization program trust fund.

Maintenance-of-effort requirement for pediatric vaccine health care coverage

No tax provision.

Conference Agreement

Permanent extension of excise tax and Program funding.

The conference agreement follows the House bill and the Senate amendment.

[Footnote ¶ 3076 continued]

205. The committee intends that the Secretary of the Treasury expeditiously (within 60 days of enactment) adopts rules for purposes of Code section 4221 for determining the conditions under which exported vaccines to be administered to individuals not eligible for compensation under the program are not subject to tax.

Study

The conference agreement follows the Senate amendment, but the conferees intend that the Secretary of the Treasury will conduct a study of the Vaccine Trust Fund and related matters as contemplated by the statutory provision contained in the House bill, including a report to the House Committee on Ways and Means and the Senate Committee on Finance within one year after the date of enactment.

Childhood immunization program trust fund

The conference agreement does not include the House bill provision for a childhood immunization program trust fund.

Maintenance-of-effort requirement for pediatric vaccine health care coverage

The conference agreement follows the House bill.

[¶ 3077] Section 13431. Modification of Involuntary Conversion Rules for Certain Disaster Related Conversions

(Code Sec. 1033)

[Conference Report]

Present Law

Under present law, no gain is recognized by the taxpayer if property is involuntarily converted into property similar or related in service or use. If property is involuntarily converted into money or property not similar or related in service or use to the converted property, then gain generally is recognized. If during the applicable period, however, the taxpayer replaces the converted property with property similar or related in service or use to the converted property, the taxpayer may elect to recognize gain only to the extent that the amount realized upon such conversion exceeds the cost of the replacement property. The applicable period begins with the date of the disposition of the converted property (or the earliest date of the threat or imminence of requisition or condemnation of the converted property, whichever is earlier) and generally ends two years after the close of the first taxable year in which any part of the gain upon conversion is realized.

House Bill

No provision.

Senate Amendment

No provision.

Conference Agreement

The conference agreement contains provisions applicable to taxpayers whose principal residence [1] (or any of its contents) is involuntarily converted as a result of a Presidentially declared disaster. In such cases, no gain is recognized by reason of the receipt of insurance proceeds for unscheduled personal property that was part of the contents of such residence. In the case of any other insurance proceeds for such residence or its contents, the proceeds may be treated as a common pool of funds. If such pool of funds is used to purchase any property similar or related in service or use to the converted residence (or its contents), the taxpayer may elect to recognize gain only to the extent that the amount of the pool of funds exceeds the cost of the replacement property.

In addition, the conference agreement extends the ending of the applicable period for the replacement of property involuntarily converted as a result of a Presidentially declared disaster to four years after the close of the first taxable year in which any part of the gain upon conversion is realized.

The conference agreement applies to residences located in areas subject to a disaster that resulted in a subsequent determination by the President that assistance by the Federal Government was warranted under the Disaster Relief and Emergency Assistance Act.

Effective date. The provisions are effective for property involuntarily converted as a result of disasters for which a Presidential declaration is made on or after September 1, 1991, and to taxable years ending on or after such date.

[Footnote ¶ 3076 continued]

[Footnote ¶ 3077] 1. Principal residence is defined as under section 1034, except that renters receiving insurance proceeds as a result of the involuntary conversion of their property in a rented residence also qualify for relief under this provision to the extent the rented residence would constitute their principal residence if they owned it.

[¶3078] Section 13441. Increase in Presidential Election Campaign Fund Check-Off

(Code Sec. 6096)

[Senate Explanation]

Present Law

The Presidential Election Campaign Fund ("Fund") provides for public financing of a portion of qualified Presidential election campaign expenditures, and certain qualified convention costs (sec. 9001 et seq.). The Fund is financed through the voluntary designation by individual taxpayers on tax returns of $1 of tax liability, which is commonly known as the Presidential election campaign checkoff. The Treasury Department accumulates revenues in the Fund over a four-year period, and then disburses funds to eligible candidates for President, Vice President, and conventions during the presidential election year.

Reasons for Change

The Federal Election Commission is projecting a shortfall in the Presidential Election Campaign Fund for the 1996 election cycle. The committee consequently believes it is appropriate to increase the amount of the checkoff, which has not been increased since it was enacted in 1966.

Explanation of Provision

The bill increases amount of the checkoff from $1 to $3.

Effective Date

The provision is effective for tax returns required to be filed after December 31, 1993.

Conference Report

The conference agreement follows the Senate amendment.

[¶3079] Section 13442. Special Rule for Hospital Services

(Code Sec. 162)

[Conference Report]

Present Law

Under present law, employers can generally deduct the full cost of health coverage provided to participants under a group health plan. Under New York state law, commercial insurers of inpatient hospital services, group health plans, health maintenance organizations, and Blue Cross and Blue Shield corporations are required to reimburse hospitals for inpatient hospital services at various rates set by the state of New York. In February of 1993, a Federal district court invalidated a number of New York statutes imposing inpatient hospital-rate surcharges on the ground that they were preempted by the Employee Retirement Income Security Act of 1974 (ERISA), but ordered insurers of inpatient hospital services to comply with New York's rate-setting statutes pending a final determination of the case.

House Bill

No provision. (However, section 4203 of the House bill would have temporarily waived ERISA preemption as applied to the New York surcharges and certain other New York statutes.)

Senate Amendment

No provision.

Conference Agreement

In general, the conference agreement disallows employer deductions for any amounts paid or incurred in connection with a group health plan (including amounts reimbursed through a voluntary employees' beneficiary association (VEBA)) if the plan fails to reimburse hospitals for inpatient services provided in the state of New York at the same rate that licensed commercial insurers are required to reimburse hospitals for inpatient services for individuals not covered by a group health plan. For purposes of this provision, a licensed commercial insurer is a commercial insurer licensed to do business in the state of New York and authorized to write accident and health insurance, and whose policies provide inpatient hospital coverage on an expense incurred basis. Blue Cross and Blue Shield is not a licensed commercial insurer for this purpose.

If a group health plan provides inpatient hospital services through a health maintenance organization (HMO), the conference agreement disallows employer deductions in connection with the plan if the plan fails to reimburse hospitals for inpatient services at the same rate (without regard to exempt individuals) that HMOs are required to reimburse hospitals for individuals not covered by a group health plan.

If a group health plan provides coverage for inpatient hospital services through a Blue Cross and Blue Shield corporation, the conference agreement disallows employer deductions in connection with the plan if the plan fails to reimburse hospitals for inpatient services at the same rate that such corporations are required to reimburse hospitals for individuals not covered by a group health plan.

The deduction disallowance does not apply to any group health plan which is not required under the laws of the state of New York (determined without regard to this provision or other provisions of Federal law) to reimburse for hospital services at the rates described above. Thus, self-insured plans are not subject to the deduction disallowance with respect to the 11 percent surcharge imposed on commercial insurers through March 31, 1993. Similarly, the deduction disallowance does not apply to self-insured plans that do not provide for reimbursement directly to hospitals on an expense incurred basis. The deduction denial also does not apply to payments by self-insured plans exempt from New York's all-payer reimbursement system because of agreements in effect on May 1, 1985.

No inference is intended as to whether any provision of the New York all-payer hospital reimbursement system is preempted by ERISA.

Effective date. The provision is effective with respect to inpatient hospital services provided to participants after February 2, 1993, and on or before May 12, 1995.

[¶3080] Section 13443. Credit for Portion of Employer Social Security Taxes Paid with Respect to Employee Cash Tips

(Code Sec. 45B)

[Conference Report]

Present Law

Under present law, all employee tip income is treated as employer-provided wages for purposes of the Federal Unemployment Tax Act (FUTA) and the Federal Insurance Contributions Act (FICA). For purposes of the minimum wage provisions of the Fair Labor Standards Act (FLSA), reported tips are treated as employer-provided wages to the extent they do not exceed one-half of such minimum wage.

House Bill

No provision.

Senate Amendment

No provision.

Conference Agreement

The conference agreement provides a business tax credit for food or beverage establishments in an amount equal to the employer's FICA tax obligation (7.65 percent) attributable to reported tips with respect to the food or beverage establishment in excess of those treated as wages for purposes of satisfying the minimum wage provisions of the FLSA. A food or beverage establishment is any trade or business (or portion thereof) which provides food or beverages for consumption on the premises and with respect to which the tipping of employees serving food or beverages by customers is customary. No credit is allowed with respect to FICA taxes paid on tips that are not received in connection with the provision of food or beverages on the premises of the establishment. It is intended that the rules under section 6053(c)(4) apply [1] in determining whether the tips are received with respect to a trade or business (or portion thereof) which provides food or beverages and with respect to which the tipping of employees serving food or beverages by customers is customary.

To prevent double dipping, no deduction is allowed for any amount taken into account in

[Footnote ¶3080] 1. Section 6053(c)(4) is to be applied without regard to the number of employees.

determining the credit. The conference agreement prohibits carryback of unused FICA credits to a taxable year ending before the date of enactment.

Effective date. The provision is effective for taxes paid after December 31, 1993.

[¶3081] Section 13444. Availability and Use of Death Information

(Code Sec. 6103)

[Conference Report]

Present Law

The Secretary of Health and Human Services is authorized to enter into voluntary contracts with the States for the purpose of obtaining death certificate and other related information. In addition, the Secretary is authorized to redisclose this information to other Federal, State, and local agencies for certain specified purposes, subject to such safeguards as the Secretary determines are necessary to prevent any unauthorized redisclosure. However, because these contracts with the States are entirely voluntary, the States are able, at their discretion, to include contract provisions preventing the Secretary from redisclosing this information to other Federal, State, and local agencies.

House Bill

The House bill prohibits a State from using an individual's Social Security account number in the administration of any driver's license or motor vehicle registration law where the State has not entered into a contract to provide death certificate and related information to the Secretary, or where the State is a party to a contract with the Secretary which includes any restrictions on the use of the death information provided to the Secretary by the State, except to the extent that such use may be restricted under section 205(r)(6) of the Social Security Act.

In addition, the House bill requires the Secretary of Health and Human Services to conduct a study of possible improvements in the current methods of gathering and reporting death information by Federal, State, and local governments that would result in more efficient and expeditious handling of such information. The House bill also requires the Secretary to submit a written report by June 1, 1994, to the Committee on Ways and Means and the Committee on Finance setting forth the results of this study, together with such administrative and legislative recommendations as the Secretary considers appropriate.

Effective date. The House bill is effective one year afterthe date of enactment.

Senate Amendment

No provision.

Conference Agreement

The conference agreement follows the House bill, with modifications. The conference agreement prohibits the disclosure of Federal tax returns or return information to any agency, body or commission of any State in connection with the administration of State tax laws where the State has not entered into a contract to provide death certificate and related information to the Secretary, or where the State is a party to a contract with the Secretary that includes any restrictions on the use of the death information provided to the Secretary by the State, except that such contract may provide that such information is only to be used for purposes of ensuring that Federal benefits or other payments are not erroneously paid to deceased individuals. The conference agreement does not apply to any State that, on July 1, 1993, was not furnishing by contract any death certificate or related information to the Secretary of Health and Human Services. The conference agreement does not include the provision in the House bill prohibiting a State from using Social Security account numbers for certain purposes.

Effective date. The conference agreement is effective one year after the date of enactment, except that it is effective two years after the date of enactment with respect to a State if it is established to the satisfaction of the Secretary of the Treasury that it is legally impossible under existing State law for such a contract to be signed. The conferees intend that the authority of the Secretary of the Treasury to grant an extension of the effective date insure that those States that have not yet entered into a contract with the Federal Government allowing for government-wide dissemination of death information have up to two years to resolve, through their State legislatures, any legal impediments to the timely signing of such a contract.

[¶3082] Section 13561. Medicare as a Secondary Payer

(Code Sec. 5000, 6103)

[Conference Report]

Present Law

(a) Extension of Transfer of Data.—OBRA 89 authorized the establishment of a database to identify working beneficiaries and their spouses to improve identification of cases in which Medicare is secondary to other third party payers. The data match links Internal Revenue Service (IRS) tax records with data from the Social Security Administration (SSA) and the Health Care Financing Administration (HCFA). OBRA 90 extended through September 30, 1995 the requirements established in OBRA 90 pertaining to identification of secondary payer situations.

(b) Extension of Medicare Secondary Payer for Disabled Beneficiaries.—Medicare is secondary payer to certain group health plans, offered by employers of 100 or more, covering disabled beneficiaries. The authority for this provision expires September 30, 1995.

(c) Extension of 18-Month Rule for ESRD Beneficiaries.—Medicare is secondary payer to certain employer group health plans covering beneficiaries with end stage renal disease (ESRD) beneficiaries during the first 18 months of a beneficiary's entitlement to Medicare on the basis of ESRD. The authority for this provision expires September 30, 1995.

(d) Medicare Secondary Payer Reforms.—

(1) Improved Identification and Enforcement of Medicare Secondary Payer Situations.—The Department of HHS identifies Medicare secondary payer cases in the following ways: beneficiary questionnaires; provider identification of third party coverage when services are provided; Medicare contractor screening and data collection and exchange; and data transfers with other Federal and State agencies including the Internal Revenue Service and the Social Security Administration.

The Secretary is authorized to develop standards, criteria, procedures and reporting requirements to evaluate the performance of organizations facilitating Medicare payments to providers of services. Primary payers are required to make payments for any item or service for which Medicare is secondary payer when they receive notice that payments are due. The Secretary is authorized to charge interest on late recoveries under the Medicare Secondary Payer program.

(2) Application to Members of Religious Orders.—Medicare secondary payer provisions do not apply to certain members of religious orders for items and services furnished on or after October 1, 1989.

(3)Uniform Rules for Size of Employer.—Under current law, different rules apply to employer size and type of eligibility for Medicare. For the working aged, secondary payer rules apply to employers with 20 or more employees. For the disabled, secondary payer rules apply to employers with 100 or more employees. For beneficiaries with end stage renal disease, secondary payer rules apply to all employers, regardless of the number of employees.

(4) Permanent Application to Disabled Active Individuals.—Under current law, Medicare is secondary payer to a large group health plan providing benefits to a disabled active individual, which is defined as an individual who (1) is eligible for Medicare on the basis of disability; and (2) continues to be treated as an employee by an employer, in the basis of commonly accepted indicators of employee status, even though the individual is not currently working. This provision expires October 1, 1995.

House Bill

(a) Extension of Transfer of Data.—W&M: The authorization for requirements pertaining to the IRS/SSA/HCFA data match would be extended through September 30, 1998.

E&C: The requirement for employers to respond to carriers would be extended through September 30, 1998.

(b) Extension of Medicare Secondary Payer for Disabled Beneficiaries.—W&M: The Medicare secondary payer requirements for disabled beneficiaries would be extended for three additional years through September 30, 1998.

E&C: Similar to W&M provision. (p>(c) Extension of 18-Month Rule for ESRD Beneficiaries.—W&M: The Medicare secondary payer requirements for beneficiaries with end stage renal disease (ESRD) would be extended for three additional years through September 30, 1998.

E&C: Similar to W&M provision.

(c) Medicare Secondary Payer Reforms.—

(1) Improved Identification and Enforcement of Medicare Secondary Payer Situations.—W&M: The Administrator of HCFA would be required to mail questionnaires to individuals, before such individuals become entitled to benefits under Part A or enroll in Part B, to determine whether the individual is covered under a primary plan. In addition, the provision would clarify that payments would not be denied for covered services solely on the grounds that a beneficiary's questionnaire fails to note the existence of other health plan coverage.

Providers and suppliers would be required to complete information on claim forms regarding potential coverage under other plans.

Civil monetary penalties would be established for an entity that knowingly, willfully and repeatedly fails to complete a claim form with accurate information.

Contractors would be required to submit a report to the Secretary annually regarding steps taken to recover mistaken payments. The Secretary would be required to evaluate the performance of contractors in identifying cases in which Medicare is secondary payer.

The provision would clarify the Secretary's authority to charge interest if payment is not received within 60 days after notice is given.

The definition of a non complying plan would be clarified to include a plan that refuses to refund amounts to HCFA demanded through the Medicare secondary payer provisions.

E&C: Similar provisions.

(2) Application to Members of Religious Orders.—W&M: The provision, effective as if included in OBRA 89 would clarify that the Medicare secondary payer provisions do not apply to secondary payer situations identified after October 1, 1989 for services provided prior to such date to members of religious orders who are considered "deemed employees" because of an election of Social Security coverage.

E&C: Identical Provision.

(3) Uniform Rules for Size of Employer.—W&M: For purposes of determining the application of Medicare secondary payer provisions to employer gorup health plans, aggregation rules as defined in the Internal Revenue Code would be used to determine size of employer.

E&C: The provision would expand the Medicare secondary payer provisions to apply to employers with 20 or more employees. Employers, multiemployers, or multiple employer group health plans of 20 or more would be required to comply with secondary payer rules for all Medicare beneficiaries.

(4) Permanent Application to Disabled Active Individuals.—W&M: No provision.

E&C: The provision for the disabled would be modified to tie directly to employment status consistent with the provision that applies to aged beneficiaries. The provision would be made permanent.

Senate Amendment

(a) Extension of Transfer of Data.—Similar to W&M provision.

(b) Extension of Medicare Secondary Payer for Disabled Beneficiaries.—Identical to S&M provision.

(c) Extension of 18-Month Rule for ESRD Beneficiaries.—The provision would extend the requirement that Medicare be secondary payer to specified group health plans for beneficiaries who are entitled to Medicare solely on the basis of end state renal disease for 24 months until September 30, 1998. This would apply with respect to items and services furnished after the third calendar month beginning after enactment.

(d) Medicare Secondary Payer Reform.—

(1) Improved Identification and Enforcement of Medicare Secondary Payer Situations.—No provision.

(2) Application to Members of Religious Orders.—The conference agreement includes the Senate amendment.

(3) Uniform Rules for Size of Employer.—

The conference agreement includes the Senate amendment to clarify employer aggregation rules, with an amendment to maintain current law thresholds applied to employers with respect to disabled and ESRD beneficiaries.

(4) Permanent Application to Disabled Active Individuals.—The conference agreement includes the House provision clarifying the definition of active employee for disabled beneficiaries to conform with the definition for working aged beneficiaries. A disabled beneficiary would be considered an active employee if covered under an employer plan by virtue of the individual's current employment status.

[¶3083] Section 13751. Extension of Current Federal Unemployment Rate.

(Code Sec. 3301)

[House Explanation]

Present Law

The Federal unemployment tax of 0.8 percent is paid by employers on the first $7,000 paid annually to each employee. Of the 0.8 percent tax rate, 0.6 percentage point is permanent and 0.2 percentage point is scheduled to expire at the end of 1996.

Explanation of Provision

The 0.2 percent surtax would be extended for 2 years through 1998.

Effective Date

Date of enactment.

[Conference Report]

The conference agreement follows the House bill.

Next page is 901

¶ 4000. Table of Code sections affected by '93 Act

The principal Code Sections added or amended by the Revenue Reconciliation Act of 1993 changes covered in this Analysis are listed in the first column. The paragraphs of this Analysis at which they are discussed are in the second column.

Code Sec.	Analysis ¶
1(a)	101, 102
1(b)	101, 102
1(c)	101, 102
1(d)	101, 102
1(e)	902
1(f)	101, 902
1(h)	109
11(b)	301
25(h)	721
28(e)	719
32(b)	119
32(c)	120
32(i)	119
38(b)	315, 604, 609
38(c)	605
39(b)	315
39(d)	604, 609
41(c)	716
41(h)	715
42(g)	708, 709
42(h)	710
42(i)	707, 711
42(m)	706
42(o)	705
45A(a) (new)	607
45A(b)	609
45A(c)	609
45A(d)	609
45A(e)	609
45A(f)	609
45B (new)	315
45B(a)	315
45B(b)	315
45B(c)	315
45B(d)	315
51(c)	717
51(i)	718
53(d)	703
55(b)	114
55(d)	114
56(g)	309, 321, 1118
57(a)	115, 703
62(a)	201
68	203
86(a)	106
86(c)	106
108(a)	503
108(b)	312
108(c)	503
108(d)	503
108(e)	311
127(d)	802
132(a)	201
132(g)	201
132(i)	802
143(a)	721
143(d)	723
143(i)	723
143(k)	722, 723, 724
144(a)	720
146(g)	725
151(d)	204
162(e)	307
162(l)	119, 202
162(m)	308
162(n)	320
163(d)	109
163(j)	1107
163(m)	308
167(c)	423
167(e)	111
167(f)	410, 412, 414, 417, 422
168(c)	502
168(j)	610
170(f)	307, 1201
172(b)	703
172(d)	703
179(b)	701
196(c)	604, 609
197 (new)	401
197(a)	402, 433
197(b)	402
197(c)	402, 427
197(d)	402, 404, 406, 407, 408, 409, 413, 415, 416, 418, 419, 420, 424
197(e)	409, 410, 411, 412, 414, 417, 420, 422, 423, 424, 425
197(f)	418, 419, 420, 421, 423, 429, 431, 433, 435
197(g)	433
2001(c)	901
217(b)	201
217(c)	201
274(a)	305
274(e)	305
274(m)	306
274(n)	304
280C(a)	604, 609
305(e)	111
381(c)	607
401(a)	801
404(l)	801
408(k)	801
453A(c)	116, 310
469(c)	501
469(i)	501
475 (new)	314
475(a)	314
475(b)	314
475(c)	314
475(d)	314
475(e)	314
501(c)	509
505(b)	801
512(b)	505, 507
514(c)	504, 508
531	302
541	303
642(c)	703
642(f)	433
643(a)	703
691(c)	703
703(b)	503

¶ 4100. Retroactive tax benefits and restrictions

¶ 4200. Effective dates by '93 Act section

Here is a list of the principal effective dates arranged according to the sections of the Act. (Variations of date for minor parts of particular sections are not given).

Sec.	*Subject and Paragraph*	*Principal Effective Date*
	EDUCATION AND INVESTMENT INCENTIVES	
13101	Employer-provided educational assistance (¶ 802)	Tax years ending after June 30, '92. Tax years beginning after Dec. 31, '88.
13102	Targeted jobs credit (¶ 717)	For individuals who begin work for the employer after June 30, '92.
13111	Extension of research and clinical testing credits (¶s 715, 719)	Tax years ending after June 30, '92.
13112	Modification of fixed base precentage for startup companies (¶ 716)	Tax years beginning after Dec. 31, '93.
13113	50-percent exclusion for gain from certain small business stock (¶s 702, 703, 726)	For stock issued after Aug. 10, '93.
13114	Rollover of gain from sale of publicly traded securities into specialized small business investment companies (¶ 704)	For sales on and after Aug. 10, '93, in tax years ending on and after Aug. 10, '93.
13115	Modification to minimum tax depreciation rules (¶ 309)	Generally for property placed in service after Dec. 31, '93.
13116	Increase in expense treatment for small businesses (¶ 701)	Tax years beginning after Dec. 31, '92.
13121	High-speed intercity rail facility bonds exempt from state volume cap (¶ 725)	For bonds issued after Dec. 31, '93.
13122	Permanent extension of qualified small issue bonds (¶ 720)	For bonds issued after June 30, '92.
	EARNED INCOME TAX CREDIT	
13131	Expansion and simplification of earned income tax credit (¶s 119, 120)	Tax years beginning after Dec. 31, '93.
	REAL ESTATE INVESTMENT	
13141	Permanent extension of qualified mortgage bonds (¶s 721, 722, 723, 724)	For bonds issued after June 30, '92. For elections for periods after June 30, '92. For qualified mortgage bonds issued and mortgage certificates provided on or after Aug. 10, '93. For loans originated and credit certificates provided after Aug. 10, '93.

Sec.	*Subject and Paragraph*	*Principal Effective Date*
13142	Low-income housing credit (¶s 705-714)	For periods ending after June 30, '92. For housing credit dollar amounts (determined under Code Sec. 42) allocated from state housing credit ceilings after June 30, '92 or buildings placed in service after June 30, '92 to the extent the state ceiling limits do not apply to any building because the buildings are financed by tax-exempt bonds. Aug. 10, '93. Periods after Aug. 10, '93.
13143	Application of passive loss rules to rental real estate activities (¶ 501)	For taxable years beginning after Dec. 31, '93.
13144	Real estate property acquired by a qualified organization (¶ 504)	For acquisitions on or after Jan. 1, '94. For leases entered into on or after Jan. 1, '94.
13145	Repeal of special treatment of publicly treated partnerships (¶ 508)	For partnership years beginning on or after Jan. 1, '94.
13146	Title-holding companies permitted to receive small amounts of unrelated business taxable income (¶ 509)	Tax years beginning on or after Jan. 1, '94.
13147	Exclusion from unrelated business tax of gains from certain property (¶ 507)	For property acquired on or after Jan. 1, '94.
13148	Exclusion from unrelated business tax or certain fees and option premiums (¶ 505)	For amounts received on or after Jan. 1, '94.
13149	Treatment of pension fund investments in real estate investment trusts (¶ 506)	Tax years beginning after Dec. 31, '93.
13150	Exclusion from gross income for income from discharge of qualified real property business indebtedness (¶ 503)	For discharges after Dec. 31, '92, in tax years ending after Dec. 31, '92.
13151	Increase in recovery period for nonresidential real property (¶ 502)	Generally for property placed in service by the taxpayer on or after May 13, '93.
	LUXURY TAX	
13161	Repeal of luxury excise taxes other than on passenger vehicles (¶ 1000)	Jan. 1, '93, for repeal of the boat, aircraft, jewelry and fur taxes. Aug. 10, '93 for indexing for inflation of $30,000 threshold amount. Jan. 1, '93 for expansion of demonstrator vehicle use exemption.

Sec.	*Subject and Paragraph*	*Principal Effective Date*
13162	Exemption from luxury excise tax for certain equipment installed on passenger vehicles for use by disabled individuals (¶ 1000)	For purchases after Dec. 31, '90.
13163	Tax on diesel fuel used in noncommercial boats (¶ 1007)	Jan. 1, '94.
	OTHER TAXES	
13171	Alternative minimum tax treatment of contributions of appreciated property (¶s 115, 124, 309A)	Contributions of capital gain property that isn't tangible personal property made after Dec. 31, '92. Contributions of all other capital gain property made after June 30, '92.
13172	Substantiation requirement for deduction of certain charitable contributions (¶ 1201)	For contributions made on or after Jan. 1, '94.
13173	Disclosure related to quid pro quo contributions (¶ 1202)	For quid pro quo contributions made on or after Jan. 1, 94.
13174	Temporary extension of deduction for health insurance costs of self-employed individuals (¶ 202)	Tax years ending after June 30, '92. Tax years beginning after Dec. 31, '92.
	INCOME TAX RATE INCREASES	
13201	Increase in top marginal rate under Code Sec. 1 (¶s 101, 102, 103, 116, 302, 303, 310, 902)	Tax years beginning after Dec. 31, '92.
	TAX INCREASES FOR INDIVIDUALS	
13202	Surtax on high-income taxpayers (¶ 902)	Tax years beginning after Dec. 31, '92.
13203	Modifications to alternative minimum tax rates and exemption amounts (¶ 114)	Tax years beginning after Dec. 31, '92.
13204	Overall limitation on itemized deductions for high-income taxpayers made permanent (¶ 203)	Aug. 10, '93.
13205	Phaseout of personal exemption of high-income taxpayers made permanent (¶ 204)	Aug. 10, '93.
13206	Provisions to prevent conversion of ordinary income to capital gain (¶s 109, 110, 111, 112, 113)	For conversion transactions entered into after Apr. 30, '93. For obligations purchased (within the meaning of Code Sec. 1272(d)(1)) after Apr. 30, '93. Apr. 30, '93. Tax years beginning after Dec. 31, '92. For sales, exchanges, and distributions after Apr. 30, '93.

Sec.	*Subject and Paragraph*	*Principal Effective Date*
13207	Repeal of limitation on amount of wages subject to health insurance employment tax (¶s 107, 108)	'94 and later calendar years.
	ESTATE AND GIFT TAX RATE INCREASE	
13208	Top estate and gift tax rates made permanent (¶ 901)	For decedents dying and gifts made after Dec. 31, '92.
	DEDUCTION LIMITATIONS AND OTHER REVENUE RAISERS	
13209	Reduction in deductible portion of business meals and entertainment (¶ 304)	Tax years beginning after Dec. 31, '93.
13210	Elimination of deduction for club membership fees (¶ 305)	For amounts paid or incurred after Dec. 31, '93.
13211	Disallowance of deduction for certain employee remuneration in excess of $1,000,000 (¶ 308)	For amounts which would otherwise be deductible for tax years beginning on or after Jan. 1, '94.
13212	Reduction in compensation taken into account in determining contributions and benefits under qualified retirement plans (¶ 801)	Generally effective for benefits accruing in plan years beginning after Dec. 31, '93.
13213	Modifications to deduction for moving expenses (¶ 201)	For expenses incurred after Dec. 31, '93, except that the exclusion of employer reimbursements applies to reimbursements or other payments for expenses incurred after Dec. 31, '93.
13214	Simplification of individual estimated tax safe harbor based on last year's tax (¶ 117)	Tax years beginning after Dec. 31, '93.
13215	Social Security and Tier 1 Railroad Retirement benefits (¶ 106)	Tax years beginning after Dec. 31, '93.
	BUSINESS PROVISIONS	
13221	Increase in top marginal rate under Code Sec. 11 (¶ 301)	Generally for tax years beginning on or after Jan. 1, '93.
13222	Denial of deduction for lobbying expenses (¶ 307)	For amounts paid or incurred after Dec. 31, '93.
13223	Mark to market accounting method for securities dealers (¶ 314)	All tax years ending on or after Dec. 31, '93.
13224	Clarification of treatment of certain FSLIC financial assistance (¶ 319)	Generally for tax years ending on or after Mar. 4, '91, but only for FSLIC assistance not credited before Mar. 4, '91.
13225	Modification of corporate estimated tax rules (¶s 316, 317, 318)	Tax years beginning after Dec. 31, '93.

Sec.	*Subject and Paragraph*	*Principal Effective Date*
13226	Modifications of discharge of indebtedness provisions (¶s 311, 312)	For stock transferred after Dec. 31, '94 in satisfaction of any indebtedness, except if such transfer is in a title 11 or similar case (as defined in Code Sec. 368(a)(3)(A)) which was filed on or before Dec. 31, '93. For discharges of indebtedness in tax years beginning after Dec. 31, '93.
13227	Limitation on Code Sec. 936 credit (¶s 1116, 1117, 1118)	For tax years beginning after Dec. 31, '93.
13228	Modification to limitation on deduction for certain interest (¶ 1109)	For interest paid or accrued in tax years beginning after Dec. 31, '93.
	FOREIGN TAX PROVISIONS	
13231	Earnings invested in excess passive assets (¶s 1110-1115)	For tax years of foreign corporations beginning Sept. 30, '93, and for tax years of US shareholders in which or with which such tax years of foreign corporations end.
13232	Modification to taxation of investment in United States property (¶ 1101)	For tax years of controlled foreign corporations beginning after Sept. 30, '93, and for tax years of US shareholders in which or with which such tax years of controlled foreign corporations end.
13233	Other modifications to Subpart F (¶s 1102, 1108)	For tax years of controlled foreign corporations beginning after Sept. 30, '93, and for tax years of US shareholders in which or with which such tax years of controlled foreign corporations end. Tax years beginning after Sept. 30, '93.
13234	Allocation of research and experimental expenditures (¶ 1103)	For taxpayer's first tax year beginning on or before Aug. 1, '94 and following taxpayer's last tax year to which Rev Proc 92-56 applies.
13235	Repeal of certain exceptions for working capital (¶ 1104)	Tax years beginning after Dec. 31, '92.
13236	Modifications of accuracy-related penalty (¶ 1105)	Tax years beginning after Dec. 31, '93.
13237	Denial of portfolio interest exemption for contingent interest (¶ 1106)	Generally for interest received after Dec. 31, '93. For estates of decedent's dying after Dec. 31, '93.
13238	Regulations dealing with conduit arrangements (¶ 1109)	Aug. 10, '93.
13239	Treatment of export of certain softwood logs (¶ 1119)	For sales, exchanges, or other dispositions after Aug. 10, '93.
	TRANSPORTATION FUELS PROVISIONS	
13241	Transportation fuels tax (¶s 1002, 1003, 1012-1019)	Oct. 1,'93.
13242	Modifications to tax on diesel fuel (¶s 1005, 1008, 1009, 1010, 1011)	Generally Jan. 1, '94.

Sec.	*Subject and Paragraph*	*Principal Effective Date*
13243	Floor stocks tax (¶ 1006)	For diesel fuel held on Jan. 1, '94 which meets certain conditions.
13245	Floor stocks tax on commercial aviation fuel held on October 1, 1995 (¶ 1004)	For aviation fuel held on Oct. 1, '95.
	COMPLIANCE PROVISIONS	
13251	Modifications to substantial understatement penalty (¶ 1203)	For returns the due dates for which (determined without regard to extensions) are after Dec. 31, '93.
13252	Returns relating to the cancellation of indebtedness by certain financial entitites (¶ 1204)	Generally for discharges of indebtedness after Dec. 31, '93, except for certain governmental entities after Aug. 10, '93.
	INTANGIBLES	
13261	Amortization of goodwill and certain other intangibles (¶s 401-437)	Generally for property acquired after Aug. 10, '93.
13262	Treatment of certain payments to retired or deceased partner (¶ 313)	Generally for partners retiring or dying on or after Jan. 5, '93.
	OVERPAYMENTS, REFUNDS AND TRAVEL EXPENSE DEDUCTION	
13271	Disallowance of interest on certain overpayments of tax (¶ 1205)	For returns the due date for which (determined without extensions) is on or after Jan. 1, '94. For claims for credit or refund of any overpayment filed on or after Jan. 1, '95, regardless of the tax period to which such refund relates. For any refund paid on or after Jan. 1, '95, regardless of the tax period to which such refund relates.
13272	Denial of deduction relating to travel expenses (¶ 306)	For amounts paid or incurred after Dec. 31, '93.
13273	Increase in withholding from supplemental wage payments (¶ 118)	Payments made after Dec. 31, '93.
	EMPOWERMENT ZONES AND ENTERPRISE COMMUNITIES	
13301	Designation and treatment of empowerment zones, enterprise communities, and rural development investment areas (¶s 601, 602, 603, 604, 606)	Aug. 10, '93.
13302	Technical and conforming amendments (¶s 605, 607, 718)	Aug. 10, '93.
	COMMUNITY DEVELOPMENT CORPORATIONS CREDIT	
13311	Credit for contributions to certain community development corporations (¶ 608)	Aug. 10, '93.

Sec.	Subject and Paragraph	Principal Effective Date
	INDIAN RESERVATIONS INVESTMENT	
13321	Accelerated depreciation for property on Indian reservations (¶ 610)	For property placed in service after Dec. 31, '93.
13322	Indian employment credit (¶ 609)	For wages paid or incurred after Dec. 31, '93.
	DISCLOSURE PROVISIONS	
13401	Disclosure of return information for administration of certain veterans programs (¶ 1210)	Aug. 10, '93.
13402	Disclosure of return information to carry out income contingent repayment of student loans (¶ 1208)	Aug. 10, '93.
13403	Use of return information for income verification under certain housing assistance programs (¶ 1209)	Aug. 10, '93.
	VACCINE PROVISIONS	
13421	Excise tax on certain vaccines made permanent (¶ 1020)	Aug. 11, '93.
13422	Continuation coverage under group health plans of costs of pediatric vaccines (¶ 803)	For plan years beginning after Aug. 10, '93.
	DISASTER RELIEF	
13431	Modification of involuntary conversion rules for certain disaster-related conversions (¶ 121)	For property compulsorily or involuntarily converted by presidentially declared disasters determined on or after Sept. 1, '91 and to tax years ending on or after Sept. 1, '91.
	MISCELLANEOUS PROVISIONS	
13441	Increase in presidential election campaign fund check-off (¶ 122)	For tax returns required to be filed after Dec. 31, '93.
13442	Special rule for hospital services (¶ 320)	For services provided after Feb. 2, '93, and on or before May 12, '95.
13443	Credit for portion of employer Social Security taxes paid with respect to employee cash tips (¶ 315)	For taxes paid after Dec. 31, '93.
13444	Availability and use of death information (¶ 1207)	Generally Aug. 10, '94.
13561	Medicare as secondary payer (¶s 321, 1206)	Aug. 10, '93, except that the aggregation rules are effective 90 days after Aug. 10, '93.
13751	Extension of current federal unemployment rate (¶ 123)	Aug. 10, '93

¶ 4300. FTC 2d ¶s affected by '93 Act

The Federal Tax Coordinator 2d paragraphs affected by the Revenue Reconciliation Act of 1993 changes covered in this Analysis are listed in the first column. The second column lists the paragraph in this Analysis where the new provision is discussed.

FTC 2d ¶	Analysis ¶
A-1100	101
A-1104 *et seq.*	105
A-2701	201
A-2704	203
A-3502	101, 204
A-4201 *et seq.*	119
A-4202	119
A-4205	119
A-4208	119
A-4212	119
A-6030 *et seq.*	108
A-8101	114
A-8101.1	114
A-8101.5	114
A-8106	309, 502
A-8115	115
A-8130.2	1118
A-8130.4	309
A-8135.1	703
B-2016	435
B-3900 *et seq.*	110
B-3914 *et seq.*	313
B-3921	110
B-3922	110
B-4026	430
B-4027	432
B-4102	313
B-4104	313
B-4106	313
C-1003	902
C-1006	904
C-2222	433
C-2301	703
C-7002	902
C-7005	904
C-7301	703
D-1003	301
D-1004	301
D-1005	301
D-2200 *et seq.*	111
D-2601	302
D-3202	303
D-4414	801
D-6901 *et seq.*	505
D-6905	505, 507
D-6909	508
D-7141	504
D-7141 *et seq.*	504
D-7142	504
D-7143	504
D-7144	504
D-7145	504
D-7146	504
E-3504 *et seq.*	319
E-3506	319
E-5102	421
E-6155	301
E-6510	506
E-6511	506
F-3600	430
F-3601	430
G-2250 *et seq.*	314
G-2657	435
G-5021	314
G-6317	116, 310
G-6934	314
H-2064	802
H-3603	427
H-4723	118
H-4765	315
H-4769 *et seq.*	107
H-4780	123
H-4786	123
H-4786.1	123
H-6965 *et seq.*	801
H-10009	801
I-3000 *et seq.*	121
I-4305	113
I-4359.3	113
I-5250	420
I-5261	420
I-6017	301
J-1431	106
J-3060	112
J-3151 *et seq.*	606
J-3152 *et seq.*	606
J-3175 *et seq.*	721
J-3204 *et seq.*	721
J-3208	720
J-3232	725
J-3249 *et seq.*	606
J-3251	720
J-3252 *et seq.*	606
J-3520	113
J-3604	112
J-3657	112
J-3742	113
J-3907	111
J-3950 *et seq.*	112
J-3951	112
J-3952	112
J-3955	112
J-3960	112
J-7301	311
J-7307	311
J-7404	312
K-3900 *et seq.*	1201
K-3936	1201
K-3960	1201
K-5315	109
K-5317	109
K-5340 *et seq.*	112
K-5343	112
K-5363	1107
K-5610	424
L-1612	410
L-1701	306
L-1739	306
L-2100 *et seq.*	304
L-2105	306
L-2126	305
L-2136	304
L-2155	305
L-2301	427

FTC 2d ¶	Analysis ¶
L-2400 *et seq.*	307
L-2601	427
L-3510	202
L-3511	202
L-3616	201
L-3623 *et seq.*	201
L-3637	201
L-4901	423
L-5157	405
L-5602	425
L-7681.1	111, 424
L-7711	424
L-7712	423
L-7750	404
L-7750 *et seq.*	401
L-7755	405
L-7756	406
L-7759	418
L-7761	401
L-7763	408
L-7765	414
L-7772	412
L-7776	416, 419, 420
L-7811	502
L-7930	502
L-7960 *et seq.*	603, 701
L-7967	603
L-7985	603
L-8230 *et seq.*	435
L-9904	411
L-15100 *et seq.*	604
L-15200	315
L-15202 *et seq.*	605
L-15209 *et seq.*	315, 604
L-15212	604
L-15300 *et seq.*	715
L-15311	715, 716
L-15312	715
L-15600	719
L-15703	703
L-15705	710
L-15706	714
L-15811	707
L-16012	706
L-16016	713
L-17800 *et seq.*	717
L-17806	604

FTC 2d ¶	Analysis ¶
L-17816	718
M-1905	121
M-4118	501
M-4600	501
M-4900	501
M-5003	501
M-5004	501
M-5100	501
M-5110	501
O-1500	1116
O-1514	1116
O-1673	1119
O-1781	1119
O-1782	1119
O-1783	1119
O-1785	1119
O-2001	1112, 1115
O-2022	1111
O-2663	1108
O-2721 *et seq.*	1104
O-2784	1101
O-2787	1101
O-2836	1111
O-4082	1104, 1118
O-4209	1102
O-4295	1104
O-4302	1104
O-10923	1118
O-11021 *et seq.*	1103
O-11026	1103
O-11761	301
P-1309	420
P-1400	402
P-1401	430
P-1419	430
Q-8004	901
Q-8008	901
R-7008	901
R-7009	901
R-9566	901
S-2506	1001
S-3236	315
S-5200	104
S-5203	117
S-5203.1	117
S-5203.1 *et seq.*	117

FTC 2d ¶	Analysis ¶
S-5203.8	117
S-5300 *et seq.*	903
S-5301	117
S-5301 *et seq.*	117
S-5404	316
S-5415	317
S-5422	318
S-5604	317
S-5702	103
S-5704	122
S-5705	122
S-6324	1207
S-6348	1208
S-6353	1209, 1210
S-6354	1206
S-6405	1209
S-6500 *et seq.*	1209
T-8003	113
V-2107	1203
V-2167	1203
V-2201	1105
V-2203	1105
V-2207	1105
V-3305	1209
W-1800 *et seq.*	1002
W-1801	1005
W-1803 *et seq.*	1005
W-1827	1017
W-1828 *et seq.*	1005
W-1829	1016
W-1836	1019
W-1860 *et seq.*	1002, 1007
W-1861	1007
W-1867 *et seq.*	1002, 1005
W-1868 *et seq.*	1005
W-1888 *et seq.*	1005
W-1890	1015
W-1901	1002
W-1914 *et seq.*	1005
W-1916	1018
W-1950 *et seq.*	1020
W-1953 *et seq.*	1020
W-4500 *et seq.*	1001
W-4504	1001
W-4511	1001
W-4511 *et seq.*	1001
W-4700 *et seq.*	1002

FTC 2d ¶	Analysis ¶
W-4702	1002
W-4702 *et seq.*	1005, 1007
W-4730	1002
W-4731	1012
W-4734	1013
W-4736	1013
W-4748	1002
W-4800 *et seq.*	1002

¶ 4400. TG ¶s affected by '93 Act

The Tax Guide paragraphs affected by the Revenue Reconciliation Act of 1993 changes covered in this Analysis are listed in the first column. The second column lists the paragraph in this Analysis where the new provision is discussed.

TG ¶	Analysis ¶
501	101
504	301
505	902
510	901
511	901
1004	101, 204
1063	105
1072	201
1074	203
1203	721
1240 *et seq.*	119
1242	119
1243	119
1244	119
1301 *et seq.*	108
1351	114
1352	114
1353	114
1355	309, 502
1363	115
1381	309, 1118
1385	703
1406	104, 117, 903
1411	117
1449	103
1462	122
1584	432
1643	435
1690 *et seq.*	110
1691 *et seq.*	313
1694	110
1695	110
1704	313
1705	313
1707	313
1743	117
1786	433
1789	703
2162	302
2171	303
2375	430
2388	430
2490	316
2493	317, 318
2497	317
2697 *et seq.*	314
2820	314
2904	116
2904	310
3130	427
3165	201
3222	802
3516	118
3579.62	315
3579.99	107
3579.120	123
3579.180	123
3579.181	123
3681	801
4101	435
4155	113
4232 *et seq.*	121
4413	301
4532	420
4644	402
4668	420
5063	112
5069	112
5074	113
5096	112
5097	112
5098	112
5099	112
5139	111
5265	312
5269	311
5276	311
5291	112
5296 *et seq.*	606
5300 *et seq.*	606
5301	720
5303	721
5305	606, 720
5316	106
5418	424
5439	502
5490 *et seq.*	603, 701
5493	603
5498	603
5581	111
5593	401, 404
5595	401, 408, 412, 419
5700 *et seq.*	604
5701	315
5703	605
5706	315, 604
5708	604
5800 *et seq.*	717
5806	718
5809	604
5830 *et seq.*	715
5838	715, 716
5860	705
5861	710
5863	707
5866	705
5890	719
6145	427
6178	202
6250	427
6285 *et seq.*	307
6327	201
6330 *et seq.*	201
6411	423
6626	121
6660	501
6665	501
6681	501
6683	501
6742	306
6773	306
6830 *et seq.*	304
6833	304
6865	305
7120	112
7189	1107
7197	109
7199	109
7230	424
7390 *et seq.*	1201
7396	1201
7796	319

TG ¶	Analysis ¶
7847	301
7856	506
8005	505
8006	505, 507
8009	508
8019	504
8138	1116
8141	1116
8163	1119
8247	1108
8264	1101
8298	1118
8312	1103
8321	1112, 1115
8353	314
8394	301
8437	1104, 1118
8960	901
9000 *et seq.*	1001
9001	1001
9008	1001
9008 *et seq.*	1001
9052 *et seq.*	1002
9053	1002, 1005, 1007
9053 *et seq.*	1007
9057	1012, 1013
9062	1002
9101	1005
9101 *et seq.*	1002
9101.1	1005
9105	1005
9107	1017, 1019
9108 *et seq.*	1002
9113	1005, 1007
9113 *et seq.*	1002
9114 *et seq.*	1005
9118	1007
9119	1002
9123	1005, 1015
9125	1005
9134	1020
9134 *et seq.*	1020
9261	1001
9333	315
9638	113
9678	1209
9766	1203
9770	1105
9774	1203

¶ 4500. USTR ¶s affected by '93 Act

The United States Tax Reporter paragraphs affected by the Revenue Reconciliation Act of 1993 changes covered in this Analysis are listed in the first column. The second column lists the paragraph in this Analysis where the new provision is discussed.

USTR ¶	Analysis ¶
14.08	902
114.01	301
114.02	301
140.8	101
154 *et seq.*	105, 904
254	721
284	719
324 *et seq.*	119
324.01	119
384 *et seq.*	604
384.02	605
384.04	604
394.02	604
414 *et seq.*	715
414.01	715, 716, 720
424.03	706
424.04	707
514	604, 717, 718
554.01	114
564.01	309
564.03	1118
574	115
684.02	203
824	201
864.04	106
1034	112
1084.02	312
1084.04	311
1235.01(10)	420
1274	802
1424 *et seq.*	606
1434	721
1464.01	725
1474.01	606
1504.01	606
1514	101, 204
1622.11	423
1624.010	425
1624.060	305
1624.114	306
1624.119	306
1624.355	427
1624.403	202
1634.058	1107
1674.001(6)	411
1674.006	424
1674.013	401, 404
1674.025	412
1674.033	410
1674.117	424
1675.014(5)	414
1675.014(85)	401
1675.015(25)	418
1675.016(15)	408
1675.018(10)	419
1675.018(25)	420
1675.022(65)	406, 416
1675.023	423
1684.02	502
1684.03	502
1688.408	435
1704.401	1201
1704.50	1201
1714 *et seq.*	424
1744	427
1794 *et seq.*	701
2174	201
2174.01	201
2635.18(50)	427
2674	435
2714.04	113
2744.01	304, 305
2744.03	305
3384	430
3384.09	430
4014.18	801
4044	801
453A4	116
4694	501
4694.03	501
4694.06	501
4694.40 *et seq.*	501
4964.60	501
5054.01	801
5124	505, 507, 508
5144	504
5934.01	319
5934.36	319
6414.07	902
6424.06	433
7364.01	313
7364.02	313
7364.03	313
7514.01	110
7514.02	110, 313
7544	432
7554	430
8484	421
8524.02	301
8564.01	506
8614.29	1103
8974	114
9044.01	1104
9074.03	1104
9214.14	1119
9314.06	1116
9544.02	1108
9544.04	1104
9564.01	1101
9594 *et seq.*	1111
9934.01	1119
10,334 *et seq.*	121
10,564	420
10,604	402, 405, 430, 630
10,924	113
12,215.55(25)	405
12,534.01	420
12,714	112
12,714.01	112
12,714.04	113
12,764.01	112
12,764.02	112
12,914.01	1112, 1115
12,914.04	1111
14,024	108
14,454	301
34,024.13	118

Next page is 951.

Index

References are to paragraph numbers

References are to paragraph numbers

References are to paragraph numbers

References are to paragraph numbers

References are to paragraph numbers

References are to paragraph numbers

References are to paragraph numbers

References are to paragraph numbers

References are to paragraph numbers

G

References are to paragraph numbers

References are to paragraph numbers

References are to paragraph numbers

References are to paragraph numbers

References are to paragraph numbers

References are to paragraph numbers

References are to paragraph numbers

References are to paragraph numbers

References are to paragraph numbers